HERITAGE
AFRICAN AMERICAN READINGS FOR WRITING

Joyce M. Jarrett
Hampton University

Doreatha Drummond Mbalia
University of Wisconsin at Milwaukee

Margaret Giles Lee
Hampton University

PRENTICE HALL   Upper Saddle River, New Jersey 07458

Library of Congress Cataloging-in-Publication Data

Heritage, African American readings for writing / [selected by] Joyce
M. Jarrett, Doreatha Drummond Mbalia, Margaret Giles Lee,
     p.   cm.
     Includes bibliographical references and index.
     ISBN 0-13-291303-8 (pbk.)
     1. Readers—Afro-Americans.   2. Afro-Americans—Civilization—
Problems, exercises, etc.   3. English language—Readers.
4. College readers.   I. Jarrett, Joyce M.   II. Mbalia, Doreatha D.
III. Lee, Margaret Giles.
     PE1127.B55H47   1997
808′.0427′08996073—dc20   96-2955
                                                     CIP

TO AFRICAN AMERICAN WRITERS
who through their artistic endeavors
committed themselves
to preserving the heritage
of people of African descent

Editorial/Production Supervision
    and Interior Design: **Joan E. Foley**
Editorial Director: **Charlyce Jones Owen**
Acquisitions Editor: **Maggie Barbieri**
Editorial Assistant: **Joan Polk**
Marketing Manager: **Gina Sluss**
Interior and Cover Art: **Maria Piper**
Prepress and Manufacturing Buyer: **Mary Ann Gloriande**

For permission to use copyrighted material, grateful
acknowledgment is made to the copyright holders on
pages 469–474, which are hereby made part of this copyright page.

This book was set in 10/12 ITC Bookman Light by Digitype,
and was printed and bound by Courier Companies, Inc.
The cover was printed by Phoenix Color Corp.

© 1997 by Prentice-Hall, Inc.
Simon & Schuster/A Viacom Company
Upper Saddle River, New Jersey 07458

Printed in the United States of America
10   9   8   7   6   5   4

ISBN 0-13-291303-8

Prentice-Hall International (UK) Limited, *London*
Prentice-Hall of Australia Pty., Limited, *Sydney*
Prentice-Hall Canada Inc., *Toronto*
Prentice-Hall Hispanoamericana, S.A., *Mexico*
Prentice-Hall of India Private Limited, *New Delhi*
Prentice-Hall of Japan, Inc., *Tokyo*
Simon & Schuster Asia Pte. Ltd., *Singapore*
Editora Prentice-Hall do Brasil, Ltda., *Rio de Janeiro*

Contents

Rhetorical Contents

Description

Illustration

Process

Comparison and Contrast

Classification

Definition

Cause and Effect

Preface

Heritage, a collection of fiction, poetry, drama, and nonfiction by and about African Americans, is a writing text, designed to appeal to writers who are interested in African American culture and the extent to which it touches every facet of American society. To emphasize that African American culture is not monolithic, we have chosen a wide range of subjects that reflect its diversity. Believing that thought-provoking writing is often the result of an inspired beginning, we have selected readings less for their use as models and more for their potential to spark the mind or touch the soul of the reader.

Our text, unlike other ethnic, multi-cultural anthologies used in writing classes, provides students with more than inviting selections; it is also an excellent writing guide. The integration of reading and writing is woven throughout. Having included nearly one hundred engaging selections, each followed by probing questions and stimulating writing assignments, we hope not only to illustrate the beauty and power of the canon, but also to motivate students, particularly through their written discourse, to discover the individual, yet universal significance of the literature.

Unlike the more generic writing texts, ours focuses on the quality of writing rather than on just form. *Heritage* has been designed to help students write more substantively, not by presenting superficial topics, but by allowing students to use provocative readings as a springboard for exploring meaningful issues and for developing their own voice. Even though there is a separate writing review section, writing is shifted from its often intimidating prominence to a means through which writers discover more about themselves and society. Readings have been chosen with writers in mind, with consideration given to interest level, vocabulary, length, readability, as well as to intrinsic literary value.

ORGANIZATION

This text is divided into two parts. Part I, "Planning Writing," provides users with a succinct but clear writing guide. In this section readers are given a writing inventory to help them understand their own writing habits and preferences.

Writing as a process is presented from an unstructured and structured approach, showing writing in various stages from paragraph to essay. Prewriting, drafting, revising/editing, and organizational strategies are also reviewed.

Part II consists of the actual readings. Each selection is introduced with a biographical sketch of the author and definitions of potentially difficult terms. At the end of the selection, the reader will find discussion questions and writing suggestions. Professional and student works represent all genres, with subjects spanning gender, generational, and philosophical lines. Thematically organized, readings range from such subjects as *Slavery*, *Family*, and *Civil Rights*, to those on *Reading/Writing/Education*, *Arts/Sciences/Media* and *Intraracial Prejudice* and *Interracial Prejudice*. At the end of Part II, are five supplemental readings that are more in-depth and challenging.

In addition to the two major divisions, the text provides other helpful sections: a glossary of literary and writing terms, a suggested bibliography for those wishing to explore a subject more fully, and a video list for readers and instructors to supplement text selections.

An *Instructor's Manual* contains answers to discussion questions.

ACKNOWLEDGMENTS

We wish to thank the following individuals: Maggie Barbieri, Prentice Hall English editor and Joan Foley, project manager, for their guidance and encouragement throughout the completion of this text; our students, with whom we worked and through whom we were inspired for permitting us to use their compositions; and the following reviewers for their sound advice: William Chapman, Prairie View A&M University; Dennis Gabriel, Cuyahoga Community College; and Brian Reed, Bethune-Cookman College.

Joyce M. Jarrett
Doreatha Drummond Mbalia
Margaret Giles Lee

1

Planning Writing

Writing is a form of communication, and to communicate effectively, you, like all writers, must continuously work on sharpening your skills. You probably spend more time than you would like trying to write more effectively and more easily. There is, however, only one sure secret to successful writing: your willingness to work hard at it. Accepting the following facts should help you approach writing more positively, which, in turn, will likely help you communicate your ideas more effectively.

1. Writing requires both effort and discipline. Although you may jot down your thoughts fairly quickly at first, you must later work at making your writing clear and interesting to your reader.
2. There is no set procedure (recipe) that, if followed, will lead to acceptable writing. Often an individual writing task will dictate a particular approach. Not only is there no single method, you will find that even the steps you develop in responding to a particular task will need to be revisited. After completing your draft, you may find it necessary to revise the thesis or the outline. Don't worry. Going back to revise is normal. Writing is recursive, which means that even though you may complete one stage of writing, you may return to it. It is not unusual to go back and forth until the job is done.
3. Papers with correct form and without grammatical errors may not necessarily prove to be worthwhile reading. Clear purpose, focus, and interesting content are what will define your paper's worth, not its form or grammatical correctness.

Before you can become an effective writer, you must clarify your own views on writing. Answering the following questions will help you learn more about your attitudes toward writing so you can choose the approach that works best for you. Check all responses that apply.

Writing Inventory

1. Generally, which word or words best describe(s) your attitude about writing?
   a. exciting
   b. enjoyable
   c. a chore
   d. _____

2. What types of writing do you like best?
   a. letter writing
   b. diary writing
   c. essay writing
   d. research writing
   e. _____

3. When do you do your best writing?
   a. morning
   b. afternoon
   c. evening
   d. late night
   e. _____

4. Where do you prefer to write?
   a. the library
   b. your own room
   c. _____

5. What kind of atmosphere do you prefer for writing?
   a. totally quiet and in the library
   b. alone and quiet
   c. alone with music
   d. in a room with others
   e. _____

6. What happens when you begin writing?
   a. thoughts flow freely
   b. thoughts come and go
   c. thoughts come too slowly
   d. _____

Interpretation of Inventory

1. The way you feel about writing will affect how you approach the task. If you enjoy writing, you will find your job easier; if you think writing is a chore, writing will be more difficult. Just re-

member that it takes longer to do things you don't like. Plan accordingly.

2. You have probably already discovered the pleasure of developing the types of writing you enjoy. If one of your assignments requires a type of writing that you enjoy less or are less familiar with, you should allow additional time.

3. Learn those times of the day or night when you are at your best. Schedule particularly demanding writing tasks when your energy level is highest.

4. Choose a place where you are most productive. Try to establish a particular location that will become your all-business-no-fun-and-games place. Retreat to such a place, especially for demanding assignments.

5. Just as it is important for you to know the right work location, you must also know the ideal atmosphere you need to get your work done. You may even discover that music helps you work better. However, if you are someone who usually works best in silence, seek it, even if it means changing your location.

6. If your thoughts come and go when you are drafting, allow adequate time for those unproductive periods. Allow even *more* time if you often find writing painstaking. Even if writing comes easily, you must still be cautious. Allow enough time so that if your writing does not flow freely, you are not thrown into panic, because writing lapses are normal. Usually, they last only a short while, and sometimes they are important parts of the writing process, since they can give you the much needed opportunity to mull over an idea.

SELECTING A TOPIC

Writing, after all, begins with ideas. Understanding both your own views about writing and your approach to writing tasks will help you in planning how to present your ideas in your paper. There are several strategies that will help you first to explore your ideas and then to narrow them down so you can select a topic which can adequately be discussed in your paper. Freewriting, brainstorming, and asking questions are techniques that can help you select an essay topic.

Freewriting is the process of writing down your thoughts in a continuous flow, free of worry about grammar, spelling, or structure. The purpose of freewriting is to force you to begin the writing process. The procedure is simple: (1) Think of a particular topic and write it at the top of your paper. (2) For a set period, write as much as you can about that subject. (3) Don't give in to writing blocks—

write until the designated time is up, even if that means writing, "I can't think of anything else to say—let's see. . . . "

Freewriting can be unfocused or focused. With unfocused freewriting, you simply write whatever comes to mind. With focused freewriting, on the other hand, you focus on a particular topic and write about it continuously. Focused freewriting works particularly well in helping you discover how much you know about a chosen topic.

Note the following examples.

Unfocused Freewriting

I am glad the semester is nearly over. I have learned a lot, but this term was really demanding. Mr. Jones told our African American history class that we could select our own topic for the final paper. That's a real challenge. Though I have not selected the topic, I do know that I need to begin working on it now. I can't afford not to put my best effort into this project. Darn, it seems as if I am faced with one challenge after another.

Focused Freewriting

Challenges

It's scary being a first-generation college student. I feel so much family pressure to make good. My parents have worked so hard to get me to college. I wonder—I forgot what I was going to say . . . Well, I don't think that they mean to make me feel this way. What else do I want to say about challenges? I know, I need to remind myself that I'm up to the challenge of college because I *am*!

Brainstorming, unlike freewriting, is the process of listing and grouping words and phrases as quickly as they come to you. Once you have listed them, you may want to put related ideas together by grouping them.

A brainstorming example follows:

challenges

do well in calculus and French
organize my time
know as much as I can about my heritage
get carburetor rebuilt
submit my final paper by Nov. 30
complete my house chores on time
read the Sunday *Times* to Aunt Bebe

Grouping, like brainstorming, also involves listing ideas. However, unlike brainstorming, grouping is the process of arranging related ideas together so you can better determine the extent to which your ideas are related. Notice how the previous items that appeared under brainstorming have been grouped.

personal challenges	**school challenges**	**home challenges**
1. organize time	1. do well in calculus & French	1. complete chores on time
2. learn more about heritage	2. submit paper by Nov. 30	2. read to Aunt Bebe
3. get carburetor rebuilt		

Asking questions can also help you narrow a topic. Become a reporter: Begin by asking the journalists' questions—who, when, what, why, where, and how. Then jot down every question you can think of about your topic. This strategy is particularly good in helping you see how complex the topic can be.

challenges

1. What makes tasks challenging?
2. Why do I feel pressured to succeed just because I'm a first-generation college student?
3. How can I better organize my time?
4. Where can I learn more about my heritage?
5. What can I do to learn more about it?
6. When will I be up to the financial challenge of getting my carburetor rebuilt?
7. Who can I get to repair my carburetor cheaply?

CONSIDERING YOUR PURPOSE AND UNDERSTANDING YOUR AUDIENCE

Two other important steps in the writing process are considering your purpose and understanding your audience. In considering your purpose, you must decide whether you are communicating with the reader or if you are writing to inform, to persuade, or to express yourself. Once you have established your purpose, consider your audience. Doing so will guide you in gathering information on your topic and deciding how you will present it. Although an instructor will, of course, read your paper, you should always try to write for a real audience. Ask yourself who else would be interested in or would need to know about the information in your paper. Additionally, ask yourself the following questions: (1) Is my audience a specialized group with interests in a given field, for example, doctors, teachers, police officers, or is it a general audience? and (2) What type of tone (your attitude toward the subject) should I use with my audience? Will I be excited, angry, happy, and so on?

DEVELOPING THE THESIS

You probably remember being told by your writing instructors that in order to write a strong essay, you must start with a thesis. But what exactly does that mean? Simply put, a thesis should be a single, specific idea on which you base your entire essay. Although the thesis is often found in the beginning of your essay, it can appear anywhere in your paper, or can even be implied. The thesis must be narrow enough to be discussed thoroughly in your essay.

Note the following example:

General Thesis

African American youth should have a better understanding of their heritage.

The preceding example is too broad; it does not guide the writer or reader in a specific direction. It would be possible to write a book on such a general idea. Reading the sample sentence we are left to wonder—What does "understanding heritage" mean? What specific areas are crucial in our understanding of heritage? Why is awareness of heritage by youth so important?

Specific Thesis

African American youth must know the contributions their ancestors have made to civilization before they can better appreciate their heritage.

Notice that with the specific thesis the essay will address the relationship of the awareness of cultural contributions to one's appreciation of heritage, rather than discussing heritage in general. The writer using the specific thesis has a clear direction for the essay.

SUPPORTING THE THESIS

Once you have a specific thesis, you will need to support it with details to make your point understood. Think of your audience. What type of example(s) does your audience need in order to understand and appreciate the points you are making? There are several ways through which you can develop details. The approach you take will depend on how much or how little you know about your subject. Consider the following tips:

1. Freewrite, brainstorm, ask questions.
2. Read as much as you can about the subject.
3. Talk informally with others to get ideas.
4. Talk informally with professionals who have specific information on the topic. (This will help you clarify information you are discovering.)

Using examples is effective in explaining your subject. Abstract topics—such as pride, fear, anger—are best understood through the use of concrete examples.

ORGANIZATIONAL STRATEGIES

Once you have narrowed your thesis and thought about specific ways of supporting it, decide on the overall organizational strategy you will use in your paper. In other words, decide what approach you will take to get your point across.

Think of the following organizational strategies as structures that will give you options in how you present your ideas. Let your thesis guide you in selecting what method(s) will work best in the development of your paper. While an essay will usually have a dominant organization, that organization is often complemented by others. You will discover in considering these strategies that they work together. Don't be reluctant to use as many of them as you need in order to make your paper clear and easy to follow. You will want to consider the following organizational strategies:

1. Illustration—Using a series of examples to support a given point. These examples are usually presented in some type of logical order, for example, from least important to most or from most important to least.

If you were considering illustration as the organizational strategy for the previous sample thesis on African American youths and their appreciation of heritage, you would give examples to illustrate how youths' knowledge of specific contributions heighten their appreciation of heritage.

2. Description and Narration—Using vivid details and/or a story to make a point. In using these strategies (which are often used together) you can paint pictures with your carefully chosen words. Don't be reluctant to use description freely. Generally, the more details you provide, the clearer your writing will be. In using narration, you must be careful not to let the story dominate. Remember, the story only reinforces your main point. An advantage of using storytelling is that readers are often drawn to stories. In the story only details relevant to the main idea should be included.

If you use description and narration to develop the sample thesis, you would recount a descriptive story showing how someone's knowledge of cultural contributions increased his or her appreciation of heritage.

3. Process—Writing to tell the reader how to do something or to explain how something has been done. In this type of organization the procedure is as important as the end result.

If you were organizing the sample thesis in this way, you would focus on explaining how youth might learn more about contributions of their ancestors, perhaps even showing specifically how such awareness leads to greater appreciation of heritage.

4. Comparison and Contrast—Pointing out the similarities and/or differences between two subjects. In using this type of organization, you must use common elements in comparing or contrasting subjects.

If you use comparison and contrast to develop the sample thesis, you might decide to contrast the cultural unawareness of one group to the cultural awareness of another in order to show how one leads to greater appreciation of heritage.

5. Classification—Placing something into discrete and separate categories. The greatest challenge in using this type of organization

is making sure that each of the categories is distinct so each group is clearly distinguishable from the other.

If you use this form of organization in developing the sample thesis, you may decide to focus on youth with different types of attitudes about heritage. For example, you could show how various attitudes about heritage lead to a greater or lesser appreciation of it.

6. Cause and Effect—Examining the reasons for a certain condition or event (causes) or evaluating the results that a certain condition or event has had on something or someone else (effects).

If you were to use this form of organization in developing the sample thesis, you could look at what has caused many African American youth not to have more appreciation for heritage. Another approach could focus on the effect of increased appreciation of heritage on today's African American youth.

7. Definition—Relying on meaning to explain a word, phrase, or action. There are three basic ways of giving the definition of a word: (1) giving a synonym, (2) giving a formal (dictionary-type) definition, and (3) giving an extended definition (giving several examples of what a word means).

If you choose to use definition in developing the sample thesis, you may want to define *heritage* before exploring how one develops a greater appreciation of it. After defining the word, you might also use illustration or some other type of organizational strategies in making your point.

8. Persuasion—Attempting to persuade your reader to accept (or at least to consider) your point of view. This type of organization is nearly always used with other types of strategies, because much of what we write is written to persuade. In convincing others, you may choose to give illustrations, compare and contrast, clarify terms, tell a story. Let your thesis guide you in selecting what methods will work best in the development of the paper.

If you use persuasion in developing the sample thesis, you should be able to convince your reader that learning about cultural contributions will increase appreciation of heritage among African American youth.

OTHER ORGANIZATIONAL TIPS

Once you have your thesis and have selected the overall structure for your paper, you must *organize ideas* in such a way that the reader can effortlessly understand your thoughts and can readily see how those thoughts relate to one another and to the thesis. A formal outline may not always be necessary, but some type of plan is helpful in enabling you to order primary points and to determine ideas you want to place first, second, and so on. Your essay must also have *coherence*, a logical order in which ideas are arranged. This type of ordering helps the reader better understand how information is related.

Organizing your paper in this way will help you maintain essay *unity*, including only those points that are relevant to the thesis. To decide if information is relevant, ask yourself if the details you have included expand the reader's understanding of the subject. If additional details don't add to the subject, leave them out. More is not necessarily better.

Not only is good organization helpful to the reader, but a guiding plan will also keep you focused as you write your paper. You are less likely to distract your reader by taking unnecessary detours or by circling an issue when you really need to forge ahead.

2

Writing the First Draft

Once you have developed a specific thesis and have organized your ideas in a general plan, you are ready to write the first draft. Although some of us can remember when we had to conform to the same writing pattern, most of us now know that writing methods can be as varied as nature. In fact, if we had just consulted with the professional writers, the ones who write for a living (novelists, poets, journalists), these experts would have straightened us out a long time ago.

Toni Morrison, the Nobel Prize winning novelist, once said that she "wrote" while washing the dishes! Of course, Morrison used the word *write* to describe that mental process of thinking about ideas which occur whenever we are assigned a piece of writing or whenever we decide we are going to write. With so many obligations that demand our time and attention, the time spent "sitting" to write may not be sufficient. We may have to "stand" to write or "walk" to write or "drive" to write. Once we have mentally composed our ideas, then we can physically write them on a sheet of paper or type them on the computer when it is convenient for us to do so. What is important is that writers—whether beginning writers or professional writers—choose the approach that works best for them.

Even when you have chosen the method you think is best suited for you, there are times when your thoughts will not flow freely. Sometimes you may find yourself staring at the blank page or the computer screen. As you prepare to write the first draft of your essay, you may find it helpful to do one of the following:

1. Review your organizing plan.
2. Go back to look at your brainstorming list or your freewriting.
3. Freewrite or brainstorm again, if necessary.
4. Write an entry in your diary or journal.
5. Write a letter to a friend or a relative.
6. Take a walk or do a chore.

DRAFTING TIPS

Once you begin writing, the following drafting tips may prove help-ful:

1. Use different pages for each main point of your plan. Using one page for each of the main points allows you to write about parts of your essay out of sequence. It also leaves you room to add ideas as you go along.
2. Write your thesis and the part of the plan you are working on at the top of each sheet of paper. This procedure will help you stay focused on your thesis statement and thus help you avoid getting off your topic.
3. Double-space if you are typing or skip every other line if you are writing. Double-spacing or skipping lines is helpful to writers who want to come back and add ideas. Some writers, however, simply choose to leave wide margins.
4. Try not to interrupt the flow of your ideas by worrying about paragraph development, unity and coherence, or grammar, spelling, and mechanics. The main concern you should have in composing the draft is recording your ideas. Often, when writers stop to check spelling or grammar, the flow of ideas is inter-rupted. Instead of interrupting the writing process, why not circle or underline the word or words you want to check? After you've completed your draft (or during a writing break), you can check for these concerns.

BEGINNINGS AND ENDINGS

Sometimes a writer may know only the thesis statement of the essay before writing the first draft. For some students, the way the paper begins and ends is a decision that is made only after the body of the paper is written. Other students prefer to begin writing their drafts by starting at the beginning. Whatever your choice, remember that the beginning of the essay (the introduction) and the ending of the essay (the conclusion) are just as important as any other part of the essay.

Give both the introduction and the conclusion considerable thought. Don't forget that first and last impressions are important. Think of your reader (audience), for example, your instructor, the admissions officer of a graduate or law school, or a prospective employer. The introduction to your essay may give the reader an immediately favorable or unfavorable opinion of you that can last throughout the essay, if indeed he or she chooses to complete it after reading the introduction.

You may find these questions helpful in planning your introduction and conclusion: What is my writing purpose? Who is my audience?

Ways of Beginning Your Essay

In considering ways of introducing your subject, think about the kind of general information that would most likely help the reader clearly see what your thesis statement will be about. You must also compose an introduction that blends in with your thesis. Ask yourself the following question: What is the most effective way of introducing my subject to my reader?

The following ways of beginning your essay may prove helpful to you:

1. Tell a short story (anecdote). An anecdote may help set the tone for your essay.
2. Present an interesting piece of data. An interesting statistic, for example, that may be unknown to your readers, helps prepare them for the discussion in the body of your essay.
3. Use a direct quotation. A direct quotation from an authoritative source helps convince the reader of your point of view.
4. Define a term. A definition of a term that is important to your discussion will help the reader better understand your essay.
5. Offer the pros or cons of an argument. An introduction that begins with a point of view that is the opposite of your own gives the reader a sense of fair play.

Ways of Ending Your Essay

The conclusion to your paper is just as important as your introduction, perhaps even more so, since it gives the reader a final impression of your subject. It is similar to eating a bowl of butter pecan ice cream: After a scrumptious feast, a bad nut in your last spoonful leaves an unpleasant taste in your mouth.

Consider the following ways of ending your paper:

1. Make a prediction. If you have written an essay about the high content of lead found in the drinking water in the inner cities of the United States, you may want to make a prediction concerning equality in relation to health.

2. Ask a question. If you have discussed racial or gender discrimination, you may want to end your essay by asking whether or not freedom exists in a society that discriminates against a segment of its population.

3. Call for action. If you are writing a letter to an editor of a newspaper about some issue you feel has gone unaddressed in your community, a call for action is an appropriate conclusion.

4. Make recommendations. If you have pointed out problems such as trespassing and robberies that exist in your community, you may want to make recommendations for solving them.

5. Summarize main points. If you are writing a long essay, such as a research paper, your reader may need to be reminded of the main points of your discussion.

THE FIRST DRAFT

A plan and a draft of the sample thesis statement presented in "Planning Your Paper" follow. These examples may prove helpful in showing you how informal a plan can be as well as how unfinished a first draft may look.

Essay Plan

Thesis Statement:	African American youths must know the contributions their ancestors have made to civilization in order to better appreciate their heritage.

Point 1:	—Problems caused by not knowing contributions
	low self-esteem
	    eyes
	    hair
	    nose
	crime
	drugs

Point 2:	—Contributions made to civilization before the fifteenth century (before the slave trade) first people first language

	father of medicine
	pyramids
	University of Timbuktu
Point 3:	—Contributions made to civilization after the fifteenth century
	labor of African Americans
	inventors
	slave heroes and heroines
	political activists
Point 4:	—Upliftment caused by knowing contributions

(Notice that in this first draft the introduction is incomplete and the conclusion is omitted; it also includes grammar, punctuation, and spelling errors.)

To Know One's History Is to Know and Appreciate Oneself

1   African American youths must know the contributions their ancestors have made to civilization in order to better appreciate their heritage.

2   The problems caused by not knowing these contributions are numerous. The most serious perhaps being lack of self-esteem. African American youth are wearing blue and green contact lenses because they have been taught that blue and green eyes are prettier than brown eyes. Some youths are lightning their skin color. Others are pressing, gerri curling and finger waving their hair because they have been taught that the quality of their hair is inferior to that of white Americans. Plastic surgery is performed on noses that are thought to be too big (wide?). Plastic surgery can be expensive. In addition, the murders committed by African American youth against each other may also be a sign of low self-esteem. If you don't think much of yourself, your looks or your accomplishments, how can you respect the lives of others who look just like you?

3   African American youth can take pride in the fact that African people was the first people on earth. They contributed the first and second languages to humankind: the Nubian language of Meroe and the hieroglyphs of Egypt. The father of medicine, Imhotep, was born in Africa around 2980 B.C., the pyramids were designed and built by Africans. The famous University of Timbucktu was founded in West Africa during the Ghana-Mali-Songhai dynasty. Scholars from all over the world came to study at

this University. Before the slave trade, African people made tools such as the plow, axe, and hoe, and manufactured cloth and leather goods. An agricultural people, Africans' primary principal was working for the benefit of the group, and giving everyone, weather old, young, male, or female, an equal chance to grow in society.

4   During the slave trade, Africans continued to make impressive contributions, though many did not receive credit for them. After the Civil War, Lewis Latimer invented the first electric light with a carbon filament; Garrett Morgan invented the gas mask and the automatic traffic light; and George Washington Carver invented over three hundred products from the peanut. Moreover, the political activism of Marcus Garvey, Ida B. Wells, Malcolm X, and Martin Luther King, Jr. made it possible for African Americans to survive in the U.S. with a measure of dignity. Such slave heroes as Frederick Douglass, Harriet Tubman, David Walker, Sojourner Truth, and Nat Turner risked their own lives to free their people.

3

Revising and Editing

Revising and editing are perhaps the most important steps in the writing process, for it is in these steps that your draft is transformed from a crude, unsophisticated, and perhaps illogical and undeveloped early attempt at expression to a more refined and polished draft that represents the best that you, the writer, can produce at the time. Revising and editing are interdependent processes that involve careful review and analysis of the draft, with the writer often going back and forth within the essay in order to improve its overall quality.

It is said that "writing is revision." Revision is the act of "seeing again" or "re-envisioning" the essay, that is, looking at it with the goal of improving the organization and development of the essay. This procedure includes reexamining the purpose and audience, changing the thesis if necessary, rearranging sentences and paragraphs for unity and coherence, and reassessing the quantity and quality of supporting details.

After making necessary revisions to the draft, you are ready to begin cleaning up the essay by editing—making grammatical, punctuation, spelling, mechanical, and word choice improvements. Editing provides a finishing touch to the essay.

PRACTICAL GUIDES FOR REVISING AND EDITING

Here are some practical guides you may find helpful as you go through the revising and editing processes.

1. Give yourself enough time to write your essay, to put it aside (for at least a day), and to review it thoroughly before submitting it. Sufficient time allows you to come back to the essay with a fresh perspective.
2. Make sure your point is developed sufficiently. You may need to write additional drafts to carry out the purpose of the essay.
3. Read the essay aloud. Reading aloud helps you hear possible problem areas.
4. Ask someone, perhaps a friend, to read the essay. A second reader can give you another perspective on the essay. Also, having someone read the essay aloud to you can accomplish the same goal.
5. Pay special attention to problem areas that your instructor or others have pointed out in previous essays. Doing so helps you be more alert to your specific writing weaknesses.
6. Concentrate first on the larger elements—thesis, purpose, audience, arrangement of ideas, and supporting details. These elements should be your first concern because they represent the core of the writing and serve to carry out your intentions for the essay.
7. Examine later the grammar, punctuation, spelling, mechanics, and style of the essay. Making corrections and changes in these elements is the final step toward polishing the essay.

REVISING AND EDITING GUIDE

When reviewing your essay in preparation for revising and editing it, consider the following five aspects in writing:

Revision

Organization: I have examined the following:
                 Purpose
                 Audience
                 Introduction
                 Thesis sentence
                 Relevance of ideas
                 Logical order of ideas
                 Use of transitions
                 Conclusion

Development: I have included the following:
              Enough details to support the main idea
              Specific details to support the main idea

Editing

Grammar: I have reviewed the essay for the following:
             Fragments
             Comma splices
             Fused sentences
             Subject-verb agreement
             Pronoun-antecedent agreement
             Pronoun usage
             Verb form
             Verb tense
             Adjective or adverb usage

Mechanics: I have reviewed the essay for the following:
             Punctuation: comma, semicolon, colon, apostrophe
             Spelling
             Capitalization

Style: I have reviewed the essay for the following:
             Appropriate tone and language
             Correct word choices
             Effective sentence types, variety, and length
             Wordiness

REVISING AND EDITING EXAMPLE

The following revised and rewritten drafts illustrate the revising and editing process of the essay on the importance of African American youth developing greater appreciation of themselves through studying their heritage. You may want to review the first draft of this essay, which appears at the end of Chapter 2.

Revision Comments

After careful review of the first draft, the student determined that the following revisions were necessary:

Refocusing the thesis statement: The original thesis sentence was, "African American youths must know the contributions their ancestors have made to civilization in order to better appreciate *their heritage.*" After reconsidering this thesis in relation to the content of the essay, as well as to its title, the student decided to replace the words *their heritage* with the word *themselves* to have the thesis state, "African American youths must know the contributions their ancestors have made to civilization in order to better appreciate *themselves.*"

Insufficient Details: The beginning of the essay (the introduction) needs more details to provide background information for the thesis and to make clear the purpose of the essay. A short story about the writer's own observations regarding the portrayal of African Americans may accomplish this.

Lack of Unity: In the second paragraph, the sentence "Plastic surgery can be expensive" is not directly related to the main idea of the essay. Therefore, it should be omitted.

Lack of Coherence: In the fourth paragraph, the sentence about the slave heroes Douglass, Tubman, and so on, is out of logical order. It should be placed before the "Civil War" sentence, since these heroes worked to abolish slavery before the Civil War ended slavery.

Lack of Ending: The essay needs an ending (a conclusion) to leave the reader with a final thought about the main idea of the essay. A call for action or prediction may accomplish this.

Editing Comments

After careful review of the draft, the student also determined that the following editing changes were necessary.

Misspelled Words: In the second paragraph, the word *lightning* should be lightening, and the word *gerri* should be spelled *jheri.* In the third paragraph, the word *Timbucktu* should be spelled *Timbuktu.*

Fragment: In the second paragraph, the second group of words, "The most serious perhaps being lack of self-esteem" is a fragment. It should be connected to the first sentence by replacing the period with a comma: "The problems caused by not knowing these contributions are numerous, the most serious perhaps being lack of self-esteem."

Subject-Verb Agreement Error: In the third paragraph, the first sentence should read "African American youth can take pride in the fact that African people *were* the first people on earth."

Comma Splice: In the third paragraph, the comma that separates the "The father of medicine" sentence from the "the pyramids" sentence should be replaced with a period to form two separate sentences: "The father of medicine, Imhotep, was born in Africa around 2980 B.C. The pyramids were . . . "

Word Choice Errors: In the last sentence in the third paragraph, the word *principal* should be replaced with the word *principle;* in this same sentence, the word *weather* should be replaced with the word *whether.*

REVISED AND EDITED DRAFT

The following draft illustrates the student's revising and editing notes based on the preceding revising and editing comments.

To Know One's History is to Know and
Appreciate Oneself

1   African American youths must know the contri-   *Refocus thesis—change "their heritage" to "themselves"*

Add background info.—story about my experiences
butions their ancestors have made to civilization in order to better appreciate their heritage.

2   The problems caused by not knowing these contributions are numerous. The most serious perhaps

being lack of self-esteem. African American

youths are wearing blue and green contact lenses

because they have been taught that blue and green

eyes are prettier than brown eyes. Some youths

lightening
are lightning their skin color. Others are press-
jheri
ing, gerri curling and finger waving their hair

because they have been taught that the quality of

their hair is inferior to that of white

Americans. Plastic surgery is performed on noses

that are thought to be too big (wide?). ~~Plastic~~
(irrelevant)
~~surgery can be expensive.~~ In addition, the mur-

ders committed by African American youths against

each other may also be a sign of low self-esteem.

If you don't think much of yourself, your looks,
or your accomplishments, how can you respect the
lives of others who look just like you?

3   African American youths can take pride in the
fact that African people **were** ~~was~~ the first people on
earth. They contributed the first and second languages to humankind: the Nubian language of Meroe
and the hieroglyphs of Egypt. The father of medicine, Imhotep, was born in Africa around 2980
B.C. **T**he pyramids were designed and built by
Africans. The famous University of **Timbuktu** ~~Timbucktu~~ was
founded in West Africa during the Ghana-Mali-
Songhai dynasty. Scholars from all over the
world came to study at this University. Before
the slave trade, African people made tools such
as the plow, axe, and hoe, and manufactured
cloth and leather goods. An agricultural people,
Africans' primary **principle** ~~principal~~ was to work for the
benefit of the group, and giving everyone,
whether ~~weather~~ old, young, male, or female, an equal
chance to grow in society.

4   During the slave trade, Africans continued to
make impressive contributions, though many did
not receive credit for them. After the Civil
War, Lewis Latimer invented the first electric
light with a carbon filament; Garrett Morgan
invented the gas mask and the automatic traffic
light; and George Washington Carver invented
over three hundred products from the peanut.

Moreover, the political activism of Marcus
Garvey, Ida B. Wells, Malcolm X, and Martin
Luther King, Jr.⌄made it possible for African
Americans to survive in the U.S. with a measure
of dignity. [Such slave heroes as Frederick
Douglass, Harriet Tubman, David Walker,
Sojourner Truth, and Nat Turner risked their own
lives to free their people.

Place before "Civil War" sentence

Add a conclusion, perhaps a summary or prediction

SECOND (REWRITTEN) DRAFT

The following is the student's second draft, written to include the preceding revising and editing changes.

To Know One's History Is to Know and Appreciate Oneself

1   I wonder what percentage of African American youths perceives a positive image of themselves. In public school, for example, I can remember that in February, "Black History Month," our teachers devoted some time to discussing Martin Luther King, Jr., and Harriet Tubman. But that was about the extent of African American history that we received. Until I got to college, the overwhelming message I received from television commercials to news broadcasts was that African Americans, youths in particular, were either imitators of white society or criminals. Once I discovered the many positive ways in which people of African descent have influenced the world, I felt an indescribable pride in myself and for my people. Therefore, I have come to the firm conclusion that African American youths must know the contributions their ancestors have made to civilization in order to better appreciate themselves.

2   The problems caused by not knowing these contributions are numerous, the most serious perhaps being lack

of self-esteem. African American youths are wearing blue and green contact lenses because they have been taught that blue and green eyes are prettier than brown eyes. Some youths are lightening their skin color. Others are pressing, jheri curling, and finger waving their hair because they have been taught that the quality of their hair is inferior to that of white Americans. Plastic surgery is performed on noses that are thought to be too wide. In addition, the murders committed by African American youths against each other may also be a sign of low self-esteem. If you don't think much of yourself, your looks, or your accomplishments, how can you respect the lives of others who look just like you?

3   African American youths can take pride in the fact that African people were the first people on earth. They contributed the first and second languages to humankind: the Nubian language of Meroe and the hieroglyphs of Egypt. The father of medicine, Imhotep, was born in Africa around 2980 B.C. The pyramids were designed and built by Africans. The famous University of Timbuktu was founded in West Africa during the Ghana-Mali-Songhai dynasty. Scholars from all over the world came to study at this university. Before the slave trade, African people made tools such as the plow, axe, and hoe, and manufactured cloth and leather goods. An agricultural people, Africans' primary principle was to work for the benefit of the group, and giving everyone, whether old, young, male, or female, an equal chance to grow in society.

4   During the slave trade, Africans continued to make impressive contributions, though many did not receive credit for them. Such slave heroes as Frederick Douglass, Harriet Tubman, David Walker, Sojourner Truth, and Nat Turner risked their own lives to free their people. After the Civil War, Lewis Latimer invented the first electric light with a carbon filament; Garrett Morgan invented the gas mask and the automatic traffic light; and George Washington Carver invented over three hundred products from the peanut. Moreover, the political activism of Marcus Garvey, Ida B. Wells, Malcolm X, and Martin Luther King, Jr., made it possible for African Americans to survive in the U.S. with a measure of dignity.

5   The impact that this information has had on my life is absolutely amazing. I see myself as the offspring of a race of giants who were not just capable of surviving under extreme pressure, but were also capable of making great strides in spite of overwhelming odds. Other African American youth cannot help but to be uplifted as I was, once they know about the contributions of our ancestors.

4

Slavery

HOW BUCK WON HIS FREEDOM

Anonymous

African American folktales, often remembered for their humor and/or cleverness, played an important role in cultural history. These anonymous crafty tales, passed on from person to person and from one generation to the next, helped slaves in the United States preserve their humanity in oppression. The following folktale demonstrates the extent to which slaves had to resort to trickery to "right" the wrongs of an unjust system.

Buck was the shrewdest slave on the big Washington planta- 1
tion. He could steal things almost in front of his master's eyes
without being detected. Finally, after having had his chickens
and pigs stolen until he was sick, Master Henry Washington
called Buck to him one day and said, "Buck, how do you manage to steal without getting caught?"

"Dat's easy, Massa," replied Buck, "dat's easy. Ah kin steal 2
yo' clo'es right tonight, wid you aguardin' 'em."

"No, no," said the master, "you may be a slick thief, but you 3
can't do that. I will make a proposition with you: If you steal my

suit of clothes tonight, I will give you your freedom, and if you fail to steal them, then you will stop stealing my chickens."

"Aw right, Massa, aw right," Buck agreed. "Dat's uh go." 4

That night about nine o'clock the master called his wife 5
into the bedroom, got his Sunday suit of clothes, laid it out on the table, and told his wife about the proposition he had made with Buck. He got on one side of the table and had his wife get on the other side, and they waited. Pretty soon, through a window that was open, the master heard the mules and the horses in the stable lot running as if someone were after them.

"Here wife," said he, "you take this gun and keep an eye on 6
this suit. I am going to see what's the matter with those animals."

Buck, who had been out to the horse lot and started the 7
stampede to attract the master's attention, now approached the open window. He was a good mimic, and in tones that sounded like his master's he called out, "Ol' lady, ol' lady, ol' lady, you better hand me that suit. That damn thief might steal it while I'm gone."

The master's wife, thinking that it was her husband ask- 8
ing for his suit, took it from the table and handed it out the window to Buck. This is how Buck won his freedom.

Discussion Questions

1. How did Buck win his freedom?
2. What does this tale reveal about the lives of slaves?
3. To what extent does Buck's use of language reveal that he wears a mask in front of his master?
4. What does the folktale tell you about Buck?
5. How does this tale serve as evidence that the creativity of African Americans was not destroyed in slavery?
6. Although this folktale relies primarily on narration in recounting the story, what other method of organization is used?
7. What is the lesson of the folktale?

Writing Assignments

1. Write a short tale using a younger person as your audience, and teach him or her a lesson.
2. Write an essay describing a time when you or someone you know outsmarted someone else.
3. Write an essay describing the process by which you finally achieved a goal that you had hoped to achieve for some time.

BURY ME IN A FREE LAND

Frances Ellen Watkins Harper

Born free in Baltimore, Frances Ellen Watkins Harper (1825–1911) is one of the best known antislavery poets of the antebellum period. Her notable works include a short story, "The Two Offers" (1859); her narrative Moses, A Story of the Nile *(1870); a very popular volume of poetry,* Poems on Miscellaneous Subjects *(1874), from which the following selection is taken; and a novel* Iola LeRoy *(1892). The following poem reflects the extent to which slaves must have longed for "free land," even in death.*

Vocabulary

galling   (stanza 5)   irritating

> Make me a grave where'er you will,   1
> In a lowly plain, or a lofty hill;
> Make it among earth's humblest graves,
> But not in a land where men are slaves.
>
> I could not rest if around my grave   2
> I heard the steps of a trembling slave;
> His shadow above my silent tomb
> Would make it a place of fearful gloom.
>
> I could not rest if I heard the tread   3
> Of a coffle gang[1] to the shambles led,
> And the mother's shriek of wild despair
> Rise like a curse on the trembling air.
>
> I could not sleep if I saw the lash   4
> Drinking her blood at each fearful gash,
> And I saw her babes torn from her breast,
> Like trembling doves from their parent nest.
>
> I'd shudder and start if I heard the bay   5
> Of bloodhounds seizing their human prey,
> And I heard the captive plead in vain
> As they bound afresh his galling chain.

[1]coffle gang   (stanza 3)   A train of slaves fastened together.

If I saw young girls from their mothers' arms 6
Bartered and sold for their youthful charms,
My eye would flash with a mournful flame,
My death-paled cheek grow red with shame.

I would sleep, dear friends, where bloated might 7
Can rob no man of his dearest right;
My rest shall be calm in any grave
Where none can call his brother a slave.

I ask no monument, proud and high, 8
To arrest the gaze of the passers-by;
All that my yearning spirit craves,
Is bury me not in a land of slaves.

Discussion Questions

1. Why does the writer want to be buried in a free land?
2. According to the poem, what kind of injustices did slaves suffer?
3. What are some of the reasons the speaker gives for not wishing to be buried in a land where "men" were slaves?
4. In the sixth stanza, why were girls "bartered and sold"?
5. What is the tone of the poem?
6. What does the title of the poem tell you about the speaker?
7. In what way does description help the poet make her point?
8. Study the structure of the poem. How has the poet chosen to organize her ideas? Is that organization effective? Why or why not?

Writing Assignments

1. The institution of slavery glaringly revealed one people's inhumanity to another. Write an essay in which you provide a current example of such inhumanity.
2. Write an essay about some societal problems that you do not believe will be corrected in your lifetime. Explain why you feel as you do.
3. Write an essay focusing on the negative effects that some inconsiderate act has had on you or someone you know.

THE SLAVE MISTRESS

Linda Brent

Born Harriet Ann Jacobs, the author (1813–1897) lived in a slave state for twenty-seven years. Upon arriving in Philadelphia, she was encouraged to publish Incidents in the Life of a Slave Girl *(1860), a sketch of her life, and she did so under the name of Linda Brent. She wrote not "to attract attention" to herself, but to show the people of the free states the "deep and dark and foul . . . abominations" of slavery. The following selection from* Incidents *describes a condition of slavery peculiar to the slave woman.*

Vocabulary

malevolence	(paragraph 2)	hostility
vigilance	(paragraph 2)	attention
asylum	(paragraph 2)	institution
buoyant	(paragraph 2)	happy
vile	(paragraph 3)	hateful

I would ten thousand times rather that my children should be the half-starved paupers of Ireland than to be the most pampered among the slaves of America. I would rather drudge out my life on a cotton plantation, till the grave opened to give me rest, than to live with an unprincipled master and a jealous mistress. The felon's home in a penitentiary is preferable. He may repent, and turn from the error of his ways, and so find peace; but it is not so with a favorite slave. She is not allowed to have any pride of character. It is deemed a crime in her to wish to be virtuous. 1

Mrs. Flint possessed the key to her husband's character before I was born. She might have used this knowledge to counsel and to screen the young and the innocent among her slaves; but for them she had no sympathy. They were the objects of her constant suspicion and malevolence. She watched her husband with unceasing vigilance; but he was well practised in means to evade it. What he could not find opportunity to say in words he manifested in signs. He invented more than were ever thought of in a deaf and dumb asylum. I let them pass, as if I did not understand what he meant; and many were 2 the curses and threats bestowed on me for my stupidity. One day he caught me teaching myself to write. He frowned, as if he was not well pleased; but I suppose he came to the conclusion that such an accomplishment might help to advance his favorite scheme. Before long, notes were often slipped into my hand. I would return them, saying, "I can't read them, sir." "Can't you?" he replied; "then I must read them to you." He always finished the reading by asking, "Do you understand?" Sometimes he would complain of the heat of the tea room, and order his supper to be placed on a small table in the piazza. He would seat himself there with a well-satisfied smile, and tell me to stand by and brush away the flies. He would eat very slowly, pausing between mouthfuls. These intervals were employed in describing the happiness I was so foolishly throwing away, and in threatening me with the penalty that finally awaited my stubborn disobedience. He boasted much of the forbearance he had exercised towards me, and reminded me that there was a limit to his patience. When I succeeded in avoiding opportunities for him to talk to me at home, I was ordered to come to his office, to do some errand. When there, I was obliged to stand and listen to such language as he saw fit to address to me. Sometimes I so openly expressed my contempt for him that he would become violently enraged, and I wondered why he did not strike me. Circumstanced as he was, he probably thought it was better policy to be forbearing. But the state of things grew worse and worse daily. In desperation I told him that I must and would apply to my grandmother for protection. He threatened me with death, and worse than death, if I made any complaint to her. Strange to say, I did not despair. I was naturally of a buoyant disposition, and always I had a hope of somehow getting out of his clutches. Like many a poor, simple slave before me, I trusted that some threads of joy would yet be woven into my dark destiny.

I had entered my sixteenth year, and every day it became more apparent that my presence was intolerable to Mrs. Flint. Angry words frequently passed between her and her husband. He had never punished me himself, and he would not allow any body else to punish me. In that respect, she was never satisfied; but, in her angry moods, no terms were too vile for her to bestow upon me. Yet I, whom she detested so bitterly, had far more pity for her than he had, whose duty it was to make her life happy. I never wronged her, or wished to wrong her; and one word of kindness from her would have brought me to her feet.

Discussion Questions

1. What kind of experiences does Linda have with Mr. Flint? With Mrs. Flint?
2. How does Mr. Flint harass Linda?
3. What life does Linda see as preferable to her life as a slave?
4. The narrator says that a favorite slave is not allowed to have any pride of character. What do you think she means?
5. Why is Mrs. Flint jealous of Linda?
6. Specifically, what is Linda's dilemma? What does her response to her situation tell you about her?
7. What details in particular make Linda Brent's narrative believable?
8. What is the theme of the story?

Writing Assignments

1. Write an essay discussing a problem that women confront today in the workplace.
2. In an essay describe a time when you had to use trickery in addressing a problem rather than dealing with it directly.
3. Write an essay focusing on the idea of "powerlessness."

HOW A SLAVE WAS MADE A MAN

Frederick Douglass

An ex-slave, Frederick Douglass (1817–1895) fled North at an early age and became a powerful orator and writer who provided leadership and guidance in fighting the institution of slavery. He is said to have been influential in President Lincoln's "Great Emancipation" efforts as well as a force in the passage of the Fourteenth and Fifteenth Amendments. Douglass published three accounts of his slave struggles: The Narrative of the Life of Frederick Douglass *(1845), from which the following selection is taken;* My Bondage and My Freedom *(1855); and* The Life and Times of Frederick Douglass *(1881). In the selection that follows you can see the courage Douglass exhibited even in slavery.*

Vocabulary

languished	(1)	faded
shrouded	(3)	veiled
moorings	(4)	docks
turbid	(4)	unclean
goaded	(5)	angered
sundry	(7)	various
quailed	(7)	snapped

If at any one time of my life more than another, I was made to drink the bitterest dregs of slavery, that time was during the first six months of my stay with Mr. Covey. We were worked in all weathers. It was never too hot or too cold; it could never rain, blow, hail, or snow, too hard for us to work in the field. Work, work, work, was scarcely more the order of the day than of the night. The longest days were too short for him, and the shortest nights too long for him. I was somewhat unmanageable when I first went there, but a few months of this discipline tamed me. Mr. Covey succeeded in breaking me. I was broken in body, soul, and spirit. My natural elasticity was crushed, my intellect languished, the disposition to read departed, the cheerful spark that lingered about my eye died; the dark night of slavery closed in upon me; and behold a man transformed into a brute!

1

Sunday was my only leisure time. I spent this in a sort of   2
beast-like stupor, between sleep and wake, under some large
tree. At times I would rise up, a flash of energetic freedom
would dart through my soul, accompanied with a faint beam of
hope, that flickered for a moment, and then vanished. I sank
down again, mourning over my wretched condition. I was
sometimes prompted to take my life, and that of Covey, but was
prevented by a combination of hope and fear. My sufferings on
this plantation seem now like a dream rather than a stern reality.

Our house stood within a few rods of the Chesapeake Bay,   3
whose broad bosom was ever white with sails from every quarter of the habitable globe. Those beautiful vessels, robed in
purest white, so delightful to the eye of freemen, were to me so
many shrouded ghosts, to terrify and torment me with
thoughts of my wretched condition. I have often, in the deep
stillness of a summer's Sabbath, stood all alone upon the lofty
banks of that noble bay, and traced, with saddened heart and
tearful eye, the countless number of sails moving off to the
mighty ocean. The sight of these always affected me powerfully.
My thoughts would compel utterance; and there, with no audience but the Almighty, I would pour out my soul's complaint,
in my rude way, with an apostrophe to the moving multitude of
ships:—

"You are loosed from your moorings and are free; I am fast   4
in my chains, and am a slave! You move merrily before the gentle gale, and I sadly before the bloody whip! You are freedom's
swift-winged angels, that fly round the world; I am confined in
bands of iron! O that I were free! O, that I were on one of your
gallant decks, and under your protecting wing! Alas! betwixt
me and you, the turbid waters roll. Go on, go on. O that I could
also go! Could I but swim! If I could fly! O, why was I born a
man, of whom to make a brute! The glad ship is gone; she
hides in the dim distance. I am left in the hottest hell of unending slavery. O God, save me! God, deliver me! Let me be free! Is
there any God? Why am I a slave? I will run away. I will not
stand it. Get caught, or get clear, I'll try it. I had as well die
with ague as the fever. I have only one life to lose. I had as well
be killed running as die standing. Only think of it; one hundred
miles straight north, and I am free! Try it? Yes! God helping me,
I will. It cannot be that I shall live and die a slave. I will take to
the water. This very bay shall yet bear me into freedom. The
steamboats steered in a north-east course from North Point. I

will do the same; and when I get to the head of the bay, I will turn my canoe adrift, and walk straight through Delaware into Pennsylvania. When I get there, I shall not be required to have a pass; I can travel without being disturbed. Let but the first opportunity offer, and, come what will, I am off. Meanwhile, I will try to bear up under the yoke. I am not the only slave in the world. Why should I fret? I can bear as much as any of them. Besides, I am but a boy, and all boys are bound to some one. It may be that my misery in slavery will only increase my happiness when I get free. There is a better day coming."

Thus I used to think, and thus I used to speak to myself;   5 goaded almost to madness at one moment, and at the next reconciling myself to my wretched lot.

I have already intimated that my condition was much   6 worse, during the first six months of my stay at Mr. Covey's, than in the last six. The circumstances leading to the change in Mr. Covey's course toward me form an epoch in my humble history. You have seen how a man was made a slave; you shall see how a slave was made a man. On one of the hottest days of the month of August, 1833, Bill Smith, William Hughes, a slave named Eli, and myself, were engaged in fanning wheat.[1] Hughes was clearing the fanned wheat from before the fan. Eli was turning, Smith was feeding, and I was carrying wheat to the fan. The work was simple, requiring strength rather than intellect; yet, to one entirely unused to such work, it came very hard. About three o'clock of that day, I broke down; my strength failed me; I was seized with a violent aching of the head, attended with extreme dizziness; I trembled in every limb. Finding what was coming, I nerved myself up, feeling it would never do to stop work. I stood as long as I could stagger to the hopper with grain. When I could stand no longer, I fell, and felt as if held down by an immense weight. The fan of course stopped; every one had his own work to do; and no one could do the work of the other, and have his own go on at the same time.

Mr. Covey was at the house, about one hundred yards   7 from the treading-yard where we were fanning. On hearing the fan stop, he left immediately, and came to the spot where we were. He hastily inquired what the matter was. Bill answered that I was sick, and there was no one to bring wheat to the fan.

[1]fanning wheat (6)   Driving away the outer covering of grain by means of air current.

I had by this time crawled away under the side of the post and rail-fence by which the yard was enclosed, hoping to find relief by getting out of the sun. He then asked where I was. He was told by one of the hands. He came to the spot, and, after looking at me awhile, asked me what was the matter. I told him as well as I could, for I scarce had strength to speak. He then gave me a savage kick in the side, and told me to get up. I tried to do so, but fell back in the attempt. He gave me another kick, and again told me to rise. I again tried, and succeeded in gaining my feet; but, stooping to get the tub with which I was feeding the fan, I again staggered and fell. While down in this situation, Mr. Covey took up the hickory slat with which Hughes had been striking off the half-bushel measure, and with it gave me a heavy blow upon the head, making a large wound, and the blood ran freely; and with this again told me to get up. I made no effort to comply, having now made up my mind to let him do his worst. In a short time after receiving this blow, my head grew better. Mr. Covey had now left me to my fate. At this moment I resolved, for the first time, to go to my master, enter a complaint and ask his protection. In order to do this, I must that afternoon walk seven miles; and this, under the circumstances, was truly a severe undertaking. I was exceedingly feeble; made so as much by the kicks and blows which I received, as by the severe fit of sickness to which I had been subjected. I, however, watched my chance, while Covey was looking in an opposite direction, and started for St. Michael's. I succeeded in getting a considerable distance on my way to the woods, when Covey discovered me, and called after me to come back, threatening what he would do if I did not come. I disregarded both his calls and his threats, and made my way to the woods as fast as my feeble state would allow; and thinking I might be overhauled by him if I kept the road, I walked through the woods, keeping far enough from the road to avoid detection, and near enough to prevent losing my way. I had not gone far before my little strength again failed me. I could go no farther. I fell down, and lay for a considerable time. The blood was yet oozing from the wound on my head. For a time I thought I should bleed to death; and think now that I should have done so, but that the blood so matted my hair as to stop the wound. After lying there about three quarters of an hour, I nerved myself up again, and started on my way, through bogs and briers, barefooted and bareheaded, tearing my feet sometimes at nearly every step; and after a journey of about seven miles, occupying some five hours to perform it, I arrived at master's store. I then presented an appearance enough to affect any but a heart of iron. From the crown of my head to my feet, I was covered with blood. My hair was all clotted with dust and blood; my shirt was stiff with blood. My legs and feet were torn in sundry places with briers and thorns, and were also covered with blood. I suppose I looked like a man who had escaped a den of wild beasts, and barely escaped them. In this state I appeared before my master, humbly entreating him to interpose his authority for my protection. I told him all the circumstances as well as I could, and it seemed, as I spoke, at times to affect him. He would then walk the floor, and seek to justify Covey by saying he expected I deserved it. He asked me what I wanted. I told him, to let me get a new home; that as sure as I lived with Mr. Covey again, I should live with but to die with him; that Covey would surely kill me; he was in a fair way for it. Master Thomas ridiculed the idea that there was any danger of Mr. Covey's killing me, and said that he knew Mr. Covey; that he was a good man, and that he could not think of taking me from him; that, should he do so, he would lose the whole year's wages; that I belonged to Mr. Covey for one year, and that I must go back to him, come what might; and that I must not trouble him with any more stories, or that he would himself *get hold of me.* After threatening me thus, he gave me a very large dose of salts, telling me that I might remain in St. Michael's that night, (it being quite late,) but that I must be off back to Mr. Covey's early in the morning; and that if I did not, he would *get hold of me,* which meant that he would whip me. I remained all night, and according to his orders, I started off to Covey's in the morning, (Saturday morning,) wearied in body and broken in spirit. I got no supper that night, or breakfast that morning. I reached Covey's about nine o'clock; and just as I was getting over the fence that divided Mrs. Kemp's fields from ours, out ran Covey with his cowskin, to give me another whipping. Before he could reach me, I succeeded in getting to the cornfield; and as the corn was very high, it afforded me the means of hiding. He seemed very angry, and searched for me a long time. My behavior was altogether unaccountable. He finally gave up the chase, thinking, I suppose, that I must come home for something to eat; he would give himself no further trouble in looking for me. I spent that day mostly in the woods, having the alternative before me,—to go home and be whipped to death, or stay in the woods and be starved to death. That night, I fell in with Sandy Jenkins, a slave with whom I was somewhat acquainted. Sandy had a free wife who lived about four miles from Mr. Covey's; and it being Saturday, he was on his way to see her. I told him my circumstances, and he very kindly invited me to go home with him. I went home with him, and talked this whole matter over, and got his advice as to what course it was best for me to pursue. I found Sandy an old adviser. He told me, with great solemnity, I must go back to Covey; but that before I went, I must go with him into another part of the woods, where there was a certain *root*, which, if I would take some of it with me, carrying it *always on my right side,* would render it impossible for Mr. Covey, or any other white man, to whip me. He said he had carried it for years; and since he had done so, he had never received a blow, and never expected to while he carried it. I at first rejected the idea, that the simple carrying of a root in my pocket would have any such effect as he had said, and was not disposed to take it; but Sandy impressed the necessity with much earnestness, telling me it could do no harm, if it did no good. To please him, I at length took the root, and, according to his direction, carried it upon my right side. This was Sunday morning. I immediately started for home; and upon entering the yard gate, out came Mr. Covey on his way to meeting. He spoke to me very kindly, bade me drive the pigs from a lot near by, and passed on towards the church. Now, this singular conduct of Mr. Covey really made me begin to think that there was something in the *root* which Sandy had given me; and had it been on any other day than Sunday, I could have attributed the conduct to no other cause than the influence of that root; and as it was, I was half inclined to think the *root* to be something more than I at first had taken it to be. All went well till Monday morning. On this morning, the virtue of the *root* was fully tested. Long before daylight, I was called to go and rub, curry, and feed, the horses. I obeyed, and was glad to obey. But whilst thus engaged, whilst in the act of throwing down some blades from the loft, Mr. Covey entered the stable with a long rope; and just as I was half out of the loft, he caught hold of my legs, and was about tying me. As soon as I found what he was up to, I gave a sudden spring, and as I did so, he holding to my legs, I was brought sprawling on the stable floor. Mr. Covey seemed now to think he had me, and could do what he pleased; but at this moment—from whence came the spirit I don't know—I resolved to fight; and, suiting my action to the resolution, I seized Covey hard by the throat; and as I did so, I rose. He held on to me, and I to him. My resistance was so entirely unexpected, that Covey seemed taken all aback. He trembled like a leaf. This gave me assurance, and I held him uneasy, causing the blood to run where I touched him with the ends of my fingers. Mr. Covey soon called out to Hughes for help. Hughes came, and, while Covey held me, attempted to tie my right hand. While he was in the act of doing so, I watched my chance, and gave him a heavy kick close under the ribs. This kick fairly sickened Hughes, so that he left me in the hands of Mr. Covey. This kick had the effect of not only weakening Hughes, but Covey also. When he saw Hughes bending over with pain, his courage quailed. He asked me if I meant to persist in my resistance. I told him I did, come what might; that he had used me like a brute for six months, and that I was determined to be used so no longer. With that, he strove to drag me to a stick that was lying just out of the stable door. He meant to knock me down. But just as he was leaning over to get the stick, I seized him with both hands by his collar, and brought him by a sudden snatch to the ground. By this time, Bill came. Covey called upon him for assistance. Bill wanted to know what he could do. Covey said, "Take hold of him, take hold of him!" Bill said his master hired him out to work, and not to help to whip me; so he left Covey and myself to fight our own battle out. We were at it for nearly two hours. Covey at length let me go, puffing and blowing at a great rate, saying that if I had not resisted, he would not have whipped me half so much. The truth was, that he had not whipped me at all. I considered him as getting entirely the worst end of the bargain; for he had drawn no blood from me, but I had from him. The whole six months afterwards, that I spent with Mr. Covey, he never laid the weight of his finger upon me in anger. He would occasionally say, he didn't want to get hold of me again. "No," thought I, "you need not; for you will come off worse than you did before."

This battle with Mr. Covey was the turning-point in my career as a slave. It rekindled the few expiring embers of freedom, and revived within me a sense of my own manhood. It recalled the departed self-confidence, and inspired me again with a determination to be free. The gratification afforded by the triumph was a full compensation for whatever else might follow, even death itself. He only can understand the deep satisfaction which I experienced, who has himself repelled by force the bloody arm of slavery. I felt as I never felt before. It was a glorious resurrection, from the tomb of slavery, to the heaven of freedom. My long-crushed spirit rose, cowardice departed, bold defiance took its place; and I now resolved that, however long I might remain a slave in form, the day had passed forever when I could be a slave in fact. I did not hesitate to let it be known of me, that the white man who expected to succeed in whipping, must also succeed in killing me.

From this time I was never again what might be called   9
fairly whipped, though I remained a slave four years afterwards. I had several fights, but was never whipped.

Discussion Questions

1. Douglass states, "You have seen how a man was made a slave. You shall see how a slave was made a man." How is a man made into a slave? How is a slave made into a man?
2. Why did Mr. Covey kick Douglass when Covey was told of Douglass's illness?
3. How did Douglass's first six months with Covey differ from his last?
4. Why did Douglass's master send him back to Covey?
5. How was Douglass's battle with Covey a turning point in his life as a slave?
6. How does Douglass's use of cause and effect help you better understand the dilemma that Douglass faced?
7. For what audience has Douglass written his narrative?

Writing Assignments

1. Write an essay describing a time when you resisted someone or something that threatened you.
2. In an essay contrast the way you were before some significant event occurred in your life and the way you were after that event.
3. Write an essay recalling an event that has changed your life.

Student Essay:
FRUITS OF LABOR, FRUITS OF SORROW, FRUITS OF LOVE

Hakimah Alim Gregory

Vocabulary

chattel   (3)   personal, moveable property
succession (3)   sequence

One of the most effective methods that the white slave master
employed to transform an African woman into a slave was to
destroy her family unit. In doing so, the slave master destroyed
the African woman's most sacred source of value and livelihood, thus effectively weakening her resistance.

The African mother learned soon after her arrival in America that neither her body nor the bodies of her children, present and unborn, belonged to her. She learned that the life and
death of African women and children were at the mercy of the
slave trader. He had two evil methods of securing the obedience
of the slaves. There was the breaking-in process, which was
used by the slave traders to break the slaves' spirits by molding
the captives into accepting their lowly position. This was often
achieved by forcing the slaves to either endure or watch grave
acts of cruelty that were committed against themselves or fellow slaves. One cruel ritual involved tying a naked pregnant
African woman to a tree. A slave trader then plunged a knife
into her belly, cut it, and ripped her unborn child from her
womb. As the victim struggled with death, the fetus was held
before the faces of the horrified audience and eventually
thrown onto the ground.

During slavery, Africans were not classified as human, but
treated as chattel by the slave owner. This made it easier for
him to use the African as he would a piece of machinery, to be
used, sold, and discarded at his will. Therefore, while the
African woman was defined in terms of her breeding capacity,
the concept of motherhood and the care for her children were
minimized. The master's primary interest in the slave woman
was the potential increase in wealth that each new African
birth represented. It was not uncommon for slave women to be
forced to conceive up to ten children, each in dangerously rapid

1

2

3

succession. Profit from these births would be gained by either selling the child, once he or she reached a certain age, or by integrating the child into the owner's labor force. Because the slave master's desire to profit preceded any respectful, humane responsibility, many marriages, when they were allowed to occur at all, were done for purposes of breeding and were not recognized or protected by law. Many times, however, the slave master did not bother to mate Africans to bear children. Instead, he and his white hired help impregnated African slave women themselves. Throughout the era of slavery, the African woman was raped and sexually exploited more than any other woman in history.

Physically, the African woman was continually subjected to   4 brutal labor throughout her pregnancy and childbirth. After her child was born, the new mother was given little, if any, time to recover. The mother often returned to the fields with a child as young as two weeks fastened to her back and placed underneath a nearby tree. She used the few periods granted for break to nurse her child, giving up her only opportunity to relieve herself or refresh herself with a drink of water. Once the child was past nursing age, the mother had to leave the child with an "Auntie," usually an older African woman no longer considered profitable in the fields, who was appointed to care for the young children while their parents labored from "can't see in the morning to can't see at night." Although the house slave sometimes found her physical conditions better than those of the field slave, she was always forced to put the care of the master's household and children before the care of her own.

The conditions under which the African woman was forced   5 to maintain a family called for her to make sacrifices without any guarantee of results. Despite the great odds, the African mother often extended herself in any way possible to make the survival of her children probable and their living conditions just a bit more bearable. The African mother suffered through infant mortality and forced abortions to produce children for the survival of her family in the United States.

Discussion Questions

1. What was the "breaking-in" process?
2. What was the slave master's primary interest in the slave woman?
3. Why were marriages allowed between slaves?

4. How was the slave woman treated during her pregnancy and after childbirth?

5. Who was the "Auntie" on the slave plantation?

6. What rhetorical strategy (or strategies) has the writer used to develop her essay?

7. Does the writer give sufficient details to support her thesis? Support your answer.

Writing Assignments

1. Write an essay in which you discuss racist methods used to discriminate against an oppressed race or culture.

2. Write an essay in which you discuss sacrifices made by your mother or grandmother in an attempt to protect your family.

5

African American Women

THE SKY IS GRAY

Ernest J. Gaines

Ernest J. Gaines (1933–   ) was born in Oscar, Louisiana. He received his B.A. degree in 1957 from San Francisco State College and then studied fiction writing at Stanford University. Among his works of fiction are The Autobiography of Miss Jane Pittman *(1971) and "A Gathering of Old Men" (1983). Much of his fiction, including the following selection taken from* Bloodline *(1968), examines the struggle of African Americans to survive in poor rural areas of Louisiana.*

"Fasten that coat, let's go," Mama says.   1

"You don't have to leave," the lady says.   2

Mama don't answer the lady, and we right out in the cold   3
again. I'm warm right now—my hands, my ears, my feet—but I
know this ain't go'n last too long. It done sleet so much now
you got ice everywhere you look.

We cross the railroad tracks, and soon's we do, I get cold.   4
That wind goes through this little old coat like it ain't even
there. I got on a shirt and a sweater under the coat, but that

wind don't pay them no mind. I look up and I can see we got a long way to go. I wonder if we go'n make it 'fore I get too cold.

We cross over to walk on the sidewalk. They got just one 5 sidewalk back here, and it's over there.

After we go just a little piece, I smell bread cooking. I look, 6 then I see a baker shop. When we get closer, I can smell it more better. I shut my eyes and make 'tend I'm eating. But I keep them shut too long and I butt up 'gainst a telephone post. Mama grabs me and see if I'm hurt. I ain't bleeding or nothing and she turns me loose.

I can feel I'm getting colder and colder, and I look up to 7 see how far we still got to go. Uptown is 'way up yonder. A half mile more, I reckon. I try to think of something. They say think and you won't get cold. I think of that poem, "Annabel Lee." I ain't been to school in so long—this bad weather—I reckon they done passed "Annabel Lee" by now. But passed it or not, I'm sure Miss Walker go'n make me recite it when I get there. That woman don't never forget nothing. I ain't never seen nobody like that in my life.

I'm still getting cold, "Annabel Lee" or no "Annabel Lee," 8 I'm still getting cold. But I can see we getting closer. We getting there gradually.

Soon 's we turn the corner, I see a little old white lady up 9 in front of us. She's the only lady on the street. She's all in black and she's got a long black rag over her head.

"Stop," she says. 10

Me and Mama stop and look at her. She must be crazy to 11 be out in all this bad weather. Ain't got but a few other people out there, and all of them's men.

"Y'all done ate?" she says. 12

"Just finish," Mama says. 13

"Y'all must be cold then?" she says. 14

"We headed for the dentist," Mama says. "We'll warm up 15 when we get there."

"What dentist?" the old lady says. "Mr. Bassett?" 16

"Yes, ma'am," Mama says. 17

"Come on in," the old lady says. "I'll telephone him and tell 18 him y'all coming."

Me and Mama follow the old lady in the store. It's a little 19 bitty store, and it don't have much in there. The old lady takes off her head rag and folds it up.

"Helena?" somebody calls from the back. 20

"Yes, Alnest?" the old lady says. 21

"Did you see them?" 22

"They're here. Standing beside me."   23

"Good. Now you can stay inside."   24

The old lady looks at Mama. Mama's waiting to hear what   25
she brought us in here for. I'm waiting for that, too.

"I saw y'all each time you went by," she says. "I came out   26
to catch you, but you were gone."

"We went back of town," Mama says.   27

"Did you eat?"   28

"Yes, ma'am."   29

The old lady looks at Mama a long time, like she's thinking   30
Mama might be just saying that. Mama looks right back at her.
The old lady looks at me to see what I have to say. I don't say
nothing. I sure ain't going 'gainst my mama.

"There's food in the kitchen," she says to Mama. "I've been   31
keeping it warm."

Mama turns right round and starts for the door.   32

"Just a minute," the old lady says. Mama stops. "The boy'll   33
have to work for it. It isn't free."

"We don't take no handout," Mama says.   34

"I'm not handing out anything," the old lady says. "I need   35
my garbage moved to the front. Ernest has a bad cold and can't
go out there."

"James'll move it for you," Mama says.   36

"Not unless you eat," the old lady says. "I'm old, but I have   37
my pride, too, you know."

Mama can see she ain't go'n beat this old lady down, so   38
she just shakes her head.

"All right," the old lady says. "Come into the kitchen."   39

She leads the way with that rag in her hand. The kitchen   40
is a little bitty little old thing, too. The table and the stove just
'bout fill it up. They got a little room to the side. Somebody in
there laying 'cross the bed—cause I can see one of his feet.
Must be the person she was talking to: Ernest or Alnest—
something like that.

"Sit down," the old lady says to Mama. "Not you," she says   41
to me. "You have to move the cans."

"Helena?" the man says in the other room.   42

"Yes, Alnest?" the old lady says.   43

"Are you going out there again?"   44

"I must show the boy where the garbage is, Alnest," the   45
old lady says.

"Keep that shawl over your head," the old man says.   46

"You don't have to remind me. Alnest. Come, boy," the old   47
lady says.

We go out in the yard. Little old back yard ain't no bigger   48
than the store or the kitchen. But it can sleet here just like it
can sleet in any big back yard. And 'fore you know it, I'm trembling.

"There," the old lady says, pointing to the cans. I pick up   49
one of the cans and set it right back down. The can's so light,
I'm go'n see what's inside of it.

"Here," the old lady says. "Leave that can alone."   50

I look back at her standing there in the door. She's got   51
that black rag wrapped round her shoulders, and she's pointing one of her little old fingers at me.

"Pick it up and carry it to the front," she says. I go by her   52
with the can, and she's looking at me all the time. I'm sure the
can's empty. I'm sure she could've carried it herself—maybe
both of them at the same time. "Set it on the sidewalk by the
door and come back for the other one," she says.

I go and come back, and Mama looks at me when I pass   53
her. I get the other can and take it to the front. It don't feel a bit
heavier than that first one. I tell myself I ain't go'n be nobody's
fool, and I'm go'n look inside this can to see just what I been
hauling. First, I look up the street, then down the street. Nobody coming. Then I look over my shoulder toward the door.
That little old lady done slipped up there quiet 's mouse, watching me again. Look like she knowed what I was go'n do.

"Ehh, Lord," she says. "Children, children. Come in here,   54
boy, and go wash your hands."

I follow her in the kitchen. She points toward the bath-   55
room, and I go in there and wash up. Little bitty old bathroom,
but it's clean, clean. I don't use any of her towels; I wipe my
hands on my pants legs.

When I come back in the kitchen, the old lady done dished   56
up the food. Rice, gravy, meat—and she even got some lettuce
and tomato in a saucer. She even got a glass of milk and a
piece of cake there, too. It looks so good, I almost start eating
'fore I say my blessing.

"Helena?" the old man says.   57
"Yes, Alnest?"   58
"Are they eating?"   59
"Yes," she says.   60
"Good," he says. "Now you'll stay inside."   61

The old lady goes in there where he is and I can hear them 62
talking. I look at Mama. She's eating slow like she's thinking. I
wonder what's the matter now. I reckon she's thinking 'bout
home.

The old lady comes back in the kitchen. 63

"I talked to Dr. Bassett's nurse," she says. "Dr. Bassett will 64
take you as soon as you get there."

"Thank you, ma'am," Mama says. 65

"Perfectly all right," the old lady says. "Which one is it?" 66

Mama nods toward me. The old lady looks at me real sad. 67
I look sad, too.

"You're not afraid, are you?" she says. 68

"No, ma'am," I say. 69

"That's a good boy," the old lady says. "Nothing to be 70
afraid of. Dr. Bassett will not hurt you."

When me and Mama get through eating, we thank the old 71
lady again.

"Helena, are they leaving?" the old man says. 72

"Yes, Alnest." 73

"Tell them I say good-bye." 74

"They can hear you, Alnest." 75

"Good-bye both mother and son," the old man says. "And 76
may God be with you."

Me and Mama tell the old man good-bye, and we follow the 77
old lady in the front room. Mama opens the door to go out, but
she stops and comes back in the store.

"You sell salt meat?" she says. 78

"Yes." 79

"Give me two bits worth." 80

"That isn't very much salt meat," the old lady says. 81

"That's all I have," Mama says. 82

The old lady goes back of the counter and cuts a big piece 83
off the chunk. Then she wraps it up and puts it in a paper
bag.

"Two bits," she says. 84

"That looks like awful lot of meat for a quarter," Mama 85
says.

"Two bits," the old lady says. "I've been selling salt meat 86
behind this counter twenty-five years. I think I know what I'm
doing."

"You got a scale there," Mama says. 87

"What?" the old lady says. 88

"Weigh it," Mama says. 89

"What?" the old lady says. "Are you telling me how to run   90
my business?

"Thanks very much for the food," Mama says.   91

"Just a minute," the old lady says.   92

"James," Mama says to me. I move toward the door.   93

"Just one minute, I said," the old lady says.   94

Me and Mama stop again and look at her. The old lady takes   95
the meat out of the bag and unwraps it and cuts 'bout half of it
off. Then she wraps it up again and juggs it back in the bag and
gives the bag to Mama. Mama lays the quarter on the counter.

"Your kindness will never be forgotten," she says. "James,"   96
she says to me.

We go out, and the old lady comes to the door to look at   97
us. After we go a little piece I look back, and she's still there
watching us.

The sleet's coming down heavy, heavy now, and I turn up   98
my coat collar to keep my neck warm. My mama tells me turn
it right back down.

"You not a bum," she says. "You a man."   99

Discussion Questions

1. What type of mother is Octavia?
2. Do you think that James understands his mother's intentions? What indications is the reader given to suggest that James understands his mother's actions?
3. In what ways does the mother try to prepare her son for life?
4. Do you think that Octavia should have taken the larger portion of meat? Why or why not?
5. What do you think is the meaning of the title?
6. Why do you think that Gaines chooses to have young James narrate the story?
7. What is the author's purpose in creating a mother whose voice is heard only on rare, necessary occasions?

Writing Assignments

1. Write an essay about an incident when a person seemed to have had too little or too much pride.
2. Write an essay about someone who has tried to set an example for you.
3. Write an essay discussing someone you know who sacrifices her or his own needs or wishes on behalf of others.

I AM A BLACK WOMAN

Mari Evans

Born in Toledo, Ohio, Mari Evans wrote and printed her first story in the fourth grade in a school newspaper and has been writing ever since. She has taught African American literature at several universities since 1969. Evans is most widely known for her poetry, which reflects her concern for African Americans. She once said, ". . . when I write, I write according to the title of poet Margaret Walker's classic: 'for my people'." The following poem reflects Evans's commitment. It is taken from her book of poetry, I Am a Black Woman *(1970).*

Vocabulary

arpeggio	(1)	musical chords played in rapid succession
canebrake	(2)	a dense growth of cane plants
assailed	(3)	assaulted, attacked with violent blows, verbally attacked
impervious	(3)	not open to, incapable of being penetrated or affected

I am a black woman   1
the music of my song
some sweet arpeggio of tears
is written in a minor key
and I
can be heard humming in the night
Can be heard
              humming
in the night

I saw my mate leap screaming to the sea   2
and I/with these hands/cupped the lifebreath
from my issue in the canebrake
I lost Nat's swinging body in a rain of tears
and heard my son scream all the way from Anzio[1]

[1]Anzio   (2)   A town and port on the western coast of Italy; the site of a World War II beachhead (January 1944).

for Peace he never knew. . . . I
learned Da Nang[2] and Pork Chop Hill[3]
in anguish
Now my nostrils know the gas
and these trigger tire/d fingers
seek the softness in my warrior's beard

I   3
am a black woman
tall as a cypress
strong
beyond all definition still
defying place
and time
and circumstance
  assailed
    impervious
      indestructible
Look
  on me and be
renewed

Discussion Questions

1. Specifically, how would you characterize the speaker in the poem?
2. Who does the "I" represent in the poem?
3. How does the poem help us understand African American history?
4. What is the significance of the last line?
5. Why do you think the poet omits punctuation marks and shifts words to the right of the page?
6. What image of the black woman do you visualize from the poet's use of descriptive words and phrases?
7. Why do you think Evans chooses to begin her stanzas with the same sentence pattern: the personal pronoun plus the verb?

[2]Da Nang (2)   Site of one of the battles during the Vietnam War.
[3]Pork Chop Hill (2)   Site of a major battle during the Korean War.

Writing Assignments

1. Write an essay describing a woman who influences or has influenced your life.
2. Write an essay describing something you do to forget your pain.
3. In an essay, discuss the various ways African American women have been depicted on television shows.

THOSE "SUPER STRONG" BLACK WOMEN

Tansey Thomas

The following excerpt was written as a letter to an editor of a newspaper in 1974. It describes some of the myths of the African American woman.

Vocabulary

hypertension (6) high blood pressure
abject (7) disgusting, wretched
jibes (11) agrees with (informal English)

To the Editor:

1   The past three years have been very significant for black women, both nationally and on the campus.

2   On campus, the women are prouder, surer of themselves, friendlier and more hopeful. Oh, there are still the notes of despair, but watch their actions and you will find determination to get where they want to be, which is born of hope.

3   Needless to say, we are far from being out of the woods. We still have the problems of racism and poverty, but I would like to attack some of the myths about black women.

4   1. The myth of the nagging, castrating black woman. Most studies show that black women complain much less than their white counterparts although black women suffer much more deprivation.

5   2. The myth of the strong super women. It seems apparent that many people regard a black woman like a black cat—she has nine lives and therefore you can treat her any kind of way and she will survive. Toss her off a 10 story building and she will land on her feet every time. She needs no help. This flies in the face of the facts of the high mortality rate of black women, at some ages twice the rate of white women; the high maternal death rate; the fact that a black woman is eight times more likely to get raped than a white woman.

6   Seventeen times more black women suffer from hypertension than white women. The person most fearful for her personal safety in this country is the black woman. Yet, she needs nothing?

3. The myth of the free black woman. There is this ridicu-   7
lous myth that black women have always been so much freer
than black men; you know, so much less oppressed. This is believed by many black women, also. They are free to be raped,
free to be murdered, free to be insulted, free to live in abject
poverty, free to be prostitutes. In other words, free for the worst
this society has to offer. How else can you explain the fact that
we are at the bottom of the social and economic heap? Being
defenseless and vulnerable has been mistaken for freedom.

I would like to see some role reversals, or at least, in some   8
of the rhetoric.

Like black men should stand by their women; black men   9
should be more understanding and supportive of their women.

I would like to see some conferences by black men on the   10
needs of black women and children. And don't say "let's deal
with black people" because it has been noted that black "people" usually means black men.

Yes, these past three years have been very significant for   11
black women, especially the younger ones. There have been increased interest in and opportunities for them, token though
they may be. This jibes with the recent report of a tremendous
decrease in the birth rate among low-income black women during the 60s. It also marks a move of a large segment of low-
income black women from the domestic job market to clerical
and sales jobs during the 60s. The hopes of black women are
even higher for the 70s. Right on!

Discussion Questions

1. What are some of the myths about black women that Thomas
   cites? Can you think of others?
2. What are the role reversals that Thomas wants to see in U.S. society?
3. According to Thomas, how were the 1960s different from the
   1970s for black women?
4. Have conditions changed for African American women today? Offer evidence to support your answer.
5. What is the tone of this letter?
6. Do you think the letter is persuasive? Why or why not?
7. What is Thomas's purpose in using comparison and contrast in
   the letter?
8. Is the author's numbering of the myths in this letter effective or
   ineffective? Explain your answer.

Writing Assignments

1. Write an essay in which you attack myths of some ethnic group or some occupation, for example, white males, lawyers, doctors, the disabled.
2. In an essay, describe a race or group of people other than your own that you feel has been misunderstood. Explain why you feel this way.
3. Write an essay in which you discuss another group (to which you do not belong) that is perceived as strong (or a group that is perceived as weak).

SLAVERY AND WOMANHOOD

Angela Y. Davis

Angela Yvonne Davis (1944–   ) was born in Birmingham, Alabama. On August 18, 1970, Davis, professor of philosophy at the University of California-Los Angeles, was placed on the Federal Bureau of Investigation's ten-most-wanted list for owning guns used to commit a crime. Cries of "Free Angela" were heard throughout the world, and eventually she was found innocent of all charges. Since that time, Angela Davis has written and published numerous works, including Women, Race and Class *(1983), from which the following selection on the abuse of slave women is taken.*

Vocabulary

chattel	(1)	an item of movable personal property
ideology	(1)	a body of ideas that influences a person or a group
anomalies	(1)	irregular or abnormal things
diametrical	(2)	exactly opposite; contrary
expediency	(4)	self interests
appraised	(5)	considered, valued
exaltation	(5)	praise or honor
coercion	(7)	the use of force
exploitation	(8)	selfish of unethical use
orthodox	(8)	following established traditions or beliefs

The slave system defined Black people as *chattel.* Since women, no less than men, were viewed as profitable labor-units, they might as well have been genderless as far as the slaveholders were concerned. In the words of one scholar, "the slave woman was first a full-time worker for her owner, and only incidentally a wife, mother and homemaker." Judged by the evolving nineteenth-century ideology of femininity, which emphasized women's roles as nurturing mothers and gentle companions and housekeepers for their husbands, Black women were practically anomalies. 1

Though Black women enjoyed few of the dubious benefits of the ideology of womanhood, it is sometimes assumed that the typical female slave was a houseservant—either a cook, maid, or mammy for the children in the "big house." Uncle Tom 2 and Sambo have always found faithful companions in Aunt Jemima and the Black Mammy—stereotypes which presume to capture the essence of the Black woman's role during slavery. As is so often the case, the reality is actually the diametrical opposite of the myth. Like the majority of slave men, slave women, for the most part, were field workers. While a significant proportion of border-state slaves may have been house-servants, slaves in the Deep South—the real home of the slaveocracy—were predominantly agricultural workers. Around the middle of the nineteenth century, seven out of eight slaves, men and women alike, were field workers.

3   Just as the boys were sent to the fields when they came of age, so too were the girls assigned to work the soil, pick the cotton, cut the cane, harvest the tobacco. An old woman interviewed during the 1930s described her childhood initiation to field work on an Alabama cotton plantation:

> We had old ragged huts made out of poles and some of the cracks chinked up with mud and moss and some of them wasn't. We didn't have no good beds, just scaffolds nailed up to the wall out of poles and the old ragged bedding throwed on them. That sure was hard sleeping, but even that felt good to our weary bones after them long hard days' work in the field. I 'tended to the children when I was a little gal and tried to clean house just like Old Miss tells me to. Then as soon as I was ten years old, Old Master, he say, "Git this here nigger to that cotton patch."

Jenny Proctor's experience was typical. For most girls and women, as for most boys and men, it was hard labor in the fields from sunup to sundown. Where work was concerned, strength and productivity under the threat of the whip outweighed considerations of sex. In this sense, the oppression of women was identical to the oppression of men.

4   But women suffered in different ways as well, for they were victims of sexual abuse and other barbarous mistreatment that could only be inflicted on women. Expediency governed the slaveholders' posture toward female slaves: when it was profitable to exploit them as if they were men, they were regarded, in effect, as genderless, but when they could be exploited, punished and repressed in ways suited only for women, they were locked into their exclusively female roles.

5   When the abolition of the international slave trade began to threaten the expansion of the young cotton-growing industry, the slaveholding class was forced to rely on natural reproduction as the surest method of replenishing and increasing

the domestic slave population. Thus a premium was placed on the slave woman's reproductive capacity. During the decades preceding the Civil War, Black women came to be increasingly appraised for their fertility (or for the lack of it): she who was potentially the mother of ten, twelve, fourteen or more became a coveted treasure indeed. This did not mean, however, that as mothers, Black women enjoyed a more respected status than they enjoyed as workers. Ideological exaltation of motherhood— as popular as it was during the nineteenth century—did not extend to slaves. In fact, in the eyes of the slaveholders, slave women were not mothers at all; they were simply instruments guaranteeing the growth of the slave labor force. They were "breeders"—animals, whose monetary value could be precisely calculated in terms of their ability to multiply their numbers.

Since slave women were classified as "breeders" as op-   6 posed to "mothers," their infant children could be sold away from them like calves from cows. One year after the importation of Africans was halted, a South Carolina court ruled that female slaves had no legal claims whatever on their children. Consequently, according to this ruling, children could be sold away from their mothers at any age because "the young of slaves . . . stand on the same footing as other animals."

As females, slave women were inherently vulnerable to all   7 forms of sexual coercion. If the most violent punishments of men consisted of floggings and mutilations, women were flogged and mutilated, as well as raped. Rape, in fact, was an uncamoflaged expression of the slaveholder's economic mastery and the overseer's control over Black women as workers.

The special abuses inflicted on women thus facilitated the   8 ruthless economic exploitation of their labor. The demands of this exploitation caused slaveowners to cast aside their orthodox sexist attitudes except for purposes of repression. If Black women were hardly "women" in the accepted sense, the slave system also discouraged male supremacy in Black men. Because husbands and wives, fathers and daughters were equally subjected to the slavemasters' absolute authority, the promotion of male supremacy among the slaves might have prompted a dangerous rupture in the chain of command. Moreover, since Black women as workers could not be treated as the "weaker sex" or the "housewife," Black men could not be candidates for the figure of "family head" and certainly not for "family provider." After all, men, women and children alike were all "providers" for the slaveholding class.

In the cotton, tobacco, corn and sugar-cane fields, women 9
worked alongside their men. In the words of an ex-slave:

> The bell rings at four o'clock in the morning and they have half
> an hour to get ready. Men and women start together, and the
> breeders must work as steadily as the men and perform the
> same work as the men.

Most slaveowners established systems of calculating their slaves'
yield in terms of the average rates of productivity they demanded.
Children, thus, were frequently rated as quarter hands. Women,
it was generally assumed, were full hands—unless they had been
expressly assigned to be "breeders" or "sucklers," in which case
they sometimes ranked as less than full hands.

Slaveowners naturally sought to ensure that their "breed- 10
ers" would bear children as often as biologically possible. But
they never went so far as to exempt pregnant women and
mothers with infant children from work in the fields. While
many mothers were forced to leave their infants lying on the
ground near the area where they worked, some refused to leave
them unattended and tried to work at the normal pace with
their babies on their backs. An ex-slave described such a case
on the plantation where he lived:

> One young woman did not, like the others, leave her child at the
> end of the row, but had contrived a sort of rude knapsack, made
> of a piece of coarse linen cloth, in which she fastened her child,
> which was very young, upon her back; and in this way carried it
> all day, and performed her task at the hoe with the other people.

On other plantations, the women left their infants in the care of
small children or older slaves who were not able to perform
hard labor in the fields. Unable to nurse their infants regularly,
they endured the pain caused by their swollen breasts. In one
of the most popular slave narratives of the period, Moses
Grandy related the miserable predicament of slave mothers:

> On the estate I am speaking of, those women who had sucking
> children suffered much from their breasts becoming full of milk,
> the infants being left at home. They therefore could not keep up
> with the other hands: I have seen the overseer beat them with raw
> hide, so that the blood and milk flew mingled from their breasts.

Pregnant women were not only compelled to do the normal 11
agricultural work, they could also expect the floggings workers
normally received if they failed to fulfill their day's quota or if
they "impudently" protested their treatment.

> A woman who gives offense in the field, and is large in a family way, is compelled to lie down over a hole made to receive her corpulency, and is flogged with the whip or beat with a paddle, which has holes in it; at every stroke comes a blister. One of my sisters was so severely punished in this way, that labor was brought on, and the child was born in the field. This very overseer, Mr. Brooks, killed in this manner a girl named Mary. Her father and mother were in the field at that time.

On those plantations and farms where pregnant women were dealt with more leniently, it was seldom on humanitarian grounds. It was simply that slaveholders appreciated the value of a slave child born alive in the same way that they appreciated the value of a newborn calf or colt.

When timid attempts at industrialization were made in the   12
pre-Civil War South, slave labor complemented—and frequently competed with—free labor. Slaveowning industrialists used men, women and children alike, and when planters and farmers hired out their slaves, they found women and children in as great demand as men.

Discussion Questions

1. Describe the lifestyle of the typical slave woman.
2. Why was the slave mother not allowed to be a mother to her children?
3. What was the slave woman's relationship to her husband?
4. What evidence does Davis give to support her argument that men and women were equal in slavery?
5. What were problems peculiar to the slave woman and not to the slave man?
6. How effective is Davis's use of illustration and persuasion in this essay?
7. What is the thesis of Davis's essay? Is it implied or written?

Writing Assignments

1. Write an essay comparing the role of today's woman to the role of the slave woman.
2. Using evidence from the essay, argue that gender did not protect the woman from the horrors of slavery.
3. Write an essay describing the kind of problems women face today.

Student Essay:
ISLAM AND AFRICAN AMERICAN WOMEN

Vernell Munadi

Vocabulary

regimen (3)   habit

The African American woman suffers from a double oppression. First, because some African American males lack the ability or interest in fulfilling their duties as husbands and fathers, many African American women are forced to assume the responsibilities of mother, father, homemaker, and breadwinner. Secondly, because of her acceptance of the Western lifestyle, the African American woman has also been oppressed both mentally and physically, keeping her at the lowest levels of society. She is often looked upon as a sex object or an ignorant person who receives welfare. Therefore, through the practice of the universal religion of Islam, the African woman is saved from this double oppression and elevated to her rightful place in society.

Islam is the fastest growing religious community in North America, particularly among African Americans. Many women in this country are realizing the realities of gender oppression and wearing their hijab[1] as a symbol of liberation. While many outside of the Islamic faith may feel that Muslim women are oppressed, Muslim women feel that Islam encourages intellectualism and education of women. Many of these women would argue that if they were as oppressed as their critics suggest, then why are there so many Western-educated women being attracted to Islam?

It is evident that the African American community of the United States is in trouble because of the fundamental breakdown of the basic family unit and the African American male-female relationship. Some attribute the trouble to African American men, some of whom have no code of ethics to control their behavior and no fear of punishment for their actions. Islam gives the man and the woman a specific purpose and disciplines them both by charging them with five daily prayers, dietary restrictions

1

2

3

---

[1]hijab   (2)   The veil; the Islamic woman's adherence to acceptable dress: covering everything except her face and hands.

(no pork, a scientifically proven killer), forbiddance of alcohol and other drugs, and a regimen of personal hygiene.

The goal of Islam in terms of the woman, through protec-   4
tion and financial maintenance, is to elevate her by allowing her to fulfill her role as the center of the community. From the time she is a girl, she lives in the house of her father who provides for her. If her father is deceased, then her uncle or older brother takes on this responsibility.

When a women is married, she moves into her husband's   5
home and from that point, she becomes sole manager of that house; it belongs to her. She runs it the way she sees fit because it is where she will raise her children. If her husband can afford it, she is also entitled to a housekeeper, especially when housecleaning becomes so burdensome that it interferes with the time spent with her children and husband.

A Muslim woman is totally liberated from the preoccupa-   6
tion of food, clothing, and shelter. Her husband is responsible for providing them. In the event that he becomes unemployed, he cannot ask his wife to work, since working is not her responsibility. However, if she does decide to help him temporarily, it must be her decision and it is a charity to him because she is temporarily relieving him of his responsibility. Even if she decides not to work, there is relief available from the Islamic community. If a wife wishes to work and her working does not interfere with the rearing of her children or with managing the household and her husband agrees to it, she may work.

In Islam, it is the woman who is placed in the midst of the   7
children, to educate them, to train them, and to nurture them. It is the children in any society who carry the society's traditions into the future. In controlling the development of the children, it is the Muslim woman who quietly, but firmly controls the Islamic community because "the hand that rocks the cradle, rules the world." As an Islamic woman, I only wish that more African American women would come to see the benefits of this religion.

Discussion Questions

1. What are the roles of the African American male and female in the Muslim family?
2. In what way can the beliefs of the Islamic faith strengthen the husband-wife relationship?

3. How does the author argue against the notion of Islam as a religion that oppresses women?

4. What does Islam offer the African American male?

5. Under what condition is the Islamic woman permitted to work?

6. To what extent do you feel that the author's use of comparison and contrast in her essay is an effective organizational strategy?

7. "Therefore" is used to introduce the last sentence of the first paragraph. What other transition(s) could be used? Explain your substitution.

Writing Assignments

1. Write an essay discussing major challenges of male-female relationships today.

2. Write an essay in which you discuss the husband-wife relationship as dictated by some other religion.

6

African American Men

A FLING ON THE TRACK

Bill Cosby

William H. Cosby, Jr. (1937–) was born in Germantown, Pennsylvania. He earned a B.A. degree from Temple University and both the M.A. and the Ed.D. degrees from the University of Massachusetts. He was the first African American co-star of a television dramatic series, I Spy, *and was the star and producer of the popular 1980s sitcom,* The Cosby Show. *Winner of eight Grammy and four Emmy awards, and the NAACP Image Award, Cosby is the author of* The Wit and Wisdom of Fat Albert *(1973),* Bill Cosby's Personal Guide to Power Tennis *(1986), and* Love and Marriage *(1989), from which this essay is taken. Here Cosby recounts his adolescent breakup with a girlfriend.*

Vocabulary

sentimentalist (3)   one who has or shows emotions
token   (17)   reminder

During my last year of high school, I fell in love so hard   1
with a girl that it made my love for Sarah McKinney seem like a
stupid infatuation with a teacher. Charlene Gibson was the

Real Thing and she would be Mrs. Charlene Cosby, serving me hot dogs and watching me drive to the hoop and giving me the full-court press for the rest of my life.

In tribute to our great love, I was moved to give Charlene   2 something to wear. A Temple T-shirt didn't seem quite right and neither did my Truman button. What Charlene needed was a piece of jewelry; and I was able to find the perfect one, an elegant pin, in my mother's dresser drawer.

Ten days after I made this grand presentation, Charlene   3 dumped me; but, sentimentalist that she was, she kept the pin. When I confessed my dark deed to my mother, she didn't throw a brick at me, she merely wanted to have the pin back, a request that I felt was not unreasonable since I had stolen it. Moreover, retrieving the pin was important to *me,* but for a romantic notion: I wanted to punish Charlene. Paying back the person with whom you have recently been in love is one of life's most precious moments.

"I want that pin back," I said to Charlene on the phone.   4

"I can't do that," she replied.   5

"Why not?"   6

"You *lost* it?"   7

"That's what I just said."   8

"How could you *lose* it?"   9

"Easy. First I had it, then I didn't."   10

And so, I went to her house, where her mother said she   11 wasn't home. Nervously I told her mother why I needed the pin returned and she understood without saying I had done anything wrong. Of course, she didn't have the world's sharpest judgment because she still thought I was a wonderful person. In fact, *all* the mothers of the girls who rejected me thought I was a wonderful person; I would have made a fine father to those girls.

"Mrs. Gibson," I said, "Charlene told me she lost the pin.   12 I'm not saying I don't believe her, but I don't."

"Just one minute, William," she said, and she turned and   13 went upstairs. Moments later, she returned with the pin. And then I went home and waited for the satisfaction of Charlene calling me to say:

How dare you go to my house and ask my mother for that   14 *pin!*

But no call from her came.   15

Probably because she's ashamed of lying to me, I told my-   16 self; *but maybe because she truly likes me and wants to keep the pin for that reason.*

I was convincing myself that Charlene wanted to have an   17
elegant token of me and that now I should call *her* to rekindle
this wondrous love-hate relationship, for Charlene and I had
been meant for each other: she was a liar and I was a thief.
Two such people, who had been so deeply in love, should have
had a chance to keep torturing each other. We once had kissed
for almost three hours, inhaling each other and talking about
how many children we should have. True, she was the kind of
girl who might be having children by other men too, but there
was still a softness about her I liked, a softness that matched
the one in my head. We had been too close for our relationship
to end with her dumping me. We had to get back together so I
could dump *her.*

Discussion Questions

1. Why did Cosby want to "punish" Charlene?
2. What do you think Cosby means by his statement that "I would
have made a wonderful father to those girls"?
3. Do you believe that Cosby was still in love with Charlene after
their breakup? Explain your answer.
4. What is the tone of this essay?
5. What are some characteristics of narration that are particularly
effective in this story?
6. Why do you think Cosby chose to give his story this title?

Writing Assignments

1. Write an essay about a time when you fell in or out of love.
2. Write an essay about a time when you or someone you know got
revenge for a hurtful act.
3. Write an essay about a time when you or someone you know was
the target of revenge.

BLACKS IN VIETNAM

Robert Mullen

*Robert W. Mullen (1937–   ) is professor of speech at North-
ern Kentucky University. He earned his B.S. and M.S. degrees from Emerson College and his Ph.D. from Ohio State
University. He is the author of* Blacks in America's Wars
(1973), from which this excerpt is taken; Rhetorical Strategies of Black America *(1980); and* Blacks and Vietnam
*(1981). In this excerpt, Mullen describes the impact of the
Vietnam War on the African Americans who participated in
it.*

Vocabulary

defoliate	(2)	to cause the leaves to fall off, especially by the use of a chemical spray or dust
cynicism	(4)	an attitude of questioning the sincerity of someone's motives or actions
rationales	(4)	justifications
succinct	(4)	brief, concise
disaffection	(5)	withdrawal of affection or loyalty
ameliorate	(23)	improve

The Vietnam War, probably more than any other single   1
event in decades, demonstrated to Black Americans that the
reason for their lack of material progress was not so much this
society's lack of financial and material resources to improve
housing, education, and job opportunities as its lack of willingness to *commit* the resources to those uses.

The government's prosecution of the war at the cost of   2
tens of billions of dollars a year, and its willingness to ultimately invest the manpower of several million GIs to carry it
out, showed that the resources were indeed available. But it
also showed that the government was willing to mobilize these
resources to kill National Liberation Front fighters in Vietnam,
to bomb the countryside of North and South Vietnam, to burn
villages, defoliate crops and forests, to take many innocent
lives, and to create millions of refugees, while it was not willing
to mobilize those resources to replace slum housing or improve
ghetto education.

By 1969, according to the [previously cited] *Newsweek*   3
poll, Blacks were already persuaded by a margin of seven to
one that "Vietnam is directly pinching the homefront war on
poverty."

In a very basic sense, the massive opposition of Afro-   4
Americans to U.S. policy in Vietnam reflected the growth of
cynicism about American society. Old rationales no longer were
taken as good coin. Earlier feelings that if Blacks could only
prove themselves American society would open up to them
were replaced by a feeling that American society was not closed
to them out of misunderstanding but through conscious policy.
Perhaps the most succinct expression of the cynicism about
the United States was contained in the comment of one Afro-
American who was heavily involved in the civil rights struggle
in Mississippi. "Our criticism of Vietnam policy," he said, "does
not come from what we know of Vietnam, but from what we
know of America."

The widespread opposition of Afro-Americans to the Viet-   5
nam War and their unwillingness to accept manifestations of
racism in the armed forces resulted in much disaffection
among Black GIs. As a 1971 NAACP report stated, "an uncomfortable number of young Black servicemen are disenchanted,
alienated and have lost faith in the capacity and the will of the
armed forces to deal honestly with their problems."

This lack of faith in the capacity and willingness of the   6
armed forces to change the prevailing racism led GIs to feel
that they themselves must protest against racism and act
against it. The common oppression of Blacks forged a tremendous bond between them in Vietnam. As one Black GI put it:
"In Vietnam, whenever you saw a brother and gave him the
power sign he gave it right back."

There was little feeling among the troops that their own   7
demands for equality should be subordinated to the war effort.
This was especially true since most GIs, Black and white, did
not feel that the war had anything to do with their interests. As
Aaron Cross, a young Black GI observed: "I didn't want to go to
Vietnam. I didn't think I had anything to fight for. I don't think
anyone knew why I was over there. . . . I often wondered what
they would have told my parents if I had been killed. That I
died for my country?"

The new spirit of the Black GIs often threw their white offi-   8
cers into a panic. Officers in Vietnam began to develop a para-
noic fear of giving direct orders to Afro-American GIs for fear of

getting "fragged." The number of actual cases of "fragging," throwing a fragmentation grenade into an officer's tent, was probably exaggerated. But enough cases did take place to keep many officers on edge. And the practice was not restricted to Black GIs. White GIs in Vietnam, who were also affected by antiwar sentiment at home and by a realization that the war had nothing to do with their interests, also engaged in the practice.

But much more significant than fragging was the develop- 9 ment of organized groups resisting racism and opposing the war in the armed forces. These groups probably reached their high point in 1970 in Germany. General Michael S. Davison, the commander of the Seventh Army, acknowledged that in that year "Black dissident organizations could turn out 1500 soldiers for a demonstration." It is estimated that there were twenty such organizations in ten cities in Germany. These groups held rallies and protest marches and published underground newspapers. Some of their activities were coordinated with German radical student groups, like the July 4, 1970, rally at the University of Heidelberg attended by over 1000 GIs, most of them Black.

Perhaps the action by Black GIs in Germany that most 10 embarrassed the army was a petition signed by over 100 Black GIs from the Berlin area, 60 from Frankfurt, and 56 from Darmstad addressed to Soviet and East German authorities asking them, as parties with some say over the international administration of West Berlin, to act against the discrimination against Black GIs in West Berlin by the American and West German authorities.

Organized activity, however, was not restricted to Ger- 11 many. In the United States there were also numerous demonstrations, rallies, and groups formed by Black and white GIs. One of the earliest of such occurrences was the case of the Fort Hood 43. In August 1968, at the time of the Chicago Democratic National Convention, units at Fort Hood, Texas, were put on alert for possible use in Chicago for "riot control" duty. Several hundred Black GIs gathered to protest this assignment, and forty-three were arrested and court martialed.

In early 1969, Black GIs at Fort Jackson, South Car- 12 olina, organized an antiwar group called GIs United Against the War in Vietnam. It was organized by a Black GI, Joe Miles, a member of the Young Socialist Alliance and Socialist Workers Party. Miles began GIs United by playing tape recordings of Malcolm X's speeches in his barracks. GIs United later expanded its membership to white antiwar GIs as well as Blacks, Puerto Ricans, and Chicanos. From January to May 1969 GIs United was able to hold regular meetings of fifty or more GIs on base. In May, the army arrested eight of the leaders of the group and placed them in the stockade. Due to a national defense campaign, however, the Army was unable to successfully court-martial the GIs, and charges against them were dropped.

At Fort McClellan, Alabama, on November 15, 1971, seventy-one Black GIs and sixty-eight Black WACs were arrested after a series of demonstrations and mass meetings on post opposing racial discrimination. Most eventually had the charges against them dropped or were discharged from the armed forces. 13

But it was in the navy that some of the most dramatic incidents involving Blacks took place. The navy has had the smallest percentage of Blacks of any of the services, with only 6.9 percent of the enlisted men, 4 percent of the noncommissioned officers, and 0.9 percent of the officers being Afro-Americans. 14

Two of the largest incidents in the navy took place in the same week in October 1972 on the aircraft carriers *Kitty Hawk* and *Constellation.* On the *Kitty Hawk,* fights between Black and white seamen lasted for fifteen hours and resulted in the hospitalization of forty whites and six Blacks. 15

Four days later, racial turmoil resulted in the cancellation of a training exercise on the *Constellation* and forced the ship to return to port. Upon arriving in port, 122 Black sailors and 8 white sailors staged a dockside sitdown, raised clenched fist salutes, and refused to reboard the vessel. 16

Within the month of these two incidents, clashes were reported between Blacks and whites aboard the assault ship *USS Sumpter* and a battle took place on the *USS Hassayampa* in the Philippines. Major battles on Midway Island and in Norfolk, Virginia, took place a month later. 17

In all these incidents, 196 men, almost all Black, were arrested. Of these, 147 received "non-judicial punishment," and 15 had charges dropped or were found not guilty. 18

These clashes were the result of the Black sailors' unwillingness to accept racist insults, and their protest against the discrimination in assignments and promotions in the Navy. 19

In conclusion, history indicates that white America gener-   20
ally restricted Black participation in the armed forces until
emergency situations forced the use of Black manpower. But,
at the same time, the Black American traditionally viewed his
military record as proof of his loyalty and as a claim to full citizenship. Seeking participation in America's wars, he held the
hope that his sacrifices would bring the reward of increased
rights to America's biggest minority. It was this optimism that
had been one of the major factors behind his loyalty from the
Revolutionary War to Korea.

But even as early as 1766, some Blacks counseled that it   21
was inconsistent for them to fight for American independence
while the country adhered to the tenets of slavery. In later wars
this sentiment was expressed in terms of an unwillingness to
forget that the real enemy was at home in America.

At the end of the war, Black veterans returned to their in-   22
ferior status in American society, either as slaves or as separate and unequal citizens, the recipients of inferior education,
the worst jobs, and white violence, North and South.

During the course of the Vietnam War, the majority of   23
Afro-Americans and most Afro-American political groups opposed the war, seeing it as a waste of Black youth, a waste of
resources that could be better used to ameliorate the conditions of America's poor, and often a racist war against a colored
people struggling for self-determination.

For the first time, the great majority of Blacks, inside and   24
outside the military, were unwilling to defer their demands until the end of the war. They felt they did not have to *prove* their
right to citizenship through military service, but rather that
they should not be forced to fight and possibly die for a society
unwilling to grant them full civil and human rights.

Discussion Questions

1. Why did some black Americans oppose the Vietnam War?
2. What was the purpose of the black GIs' and sailors' protests and demonstrations during the war?
3. Why did some black GIs feel that "the real enemy was at home in America"?
4. Why have blacks traditionally sought participation in America's wars?

5. To what conditions did black American veterans return after the war?
6. How does Mullen use illustration to show that black Americans who participated in the war formed a "tremendous bond"?
7. For what audience do you think this excerpt is written? Explain your answer.

Writing Assignments

1. Write an essay that describes a current problem that you feel would justify protest or demonstration.
2. Interview someone you know who participated in a war, and write an essay illustrating that person's experiences.
3. Write an essay discussing one of the following terms: "cynicism," "discrimination," "hatred," "deceit," "loyalty," or a similar term of your choice.

BLACK MEN AND PUBLIC SPACE

Brent Staples

Brent Staples (1951–) received his Ph.D. degree in psychology from the University of Chicago. He has written for several magazines and newspapers, including the Chicago Sun-Times, and The New York Times where he writes about politics and culture for the editorial board. His works include "Parallel Time" (1994). This essay, originally entitled "Just Walk on By: A Black Man Ponders His Power to Alter Public Space," was first published in Ms. magazine in September 1986. In this excerpt, Staples describes his feelings about how people, especially white women, react when they encounter him on the street late at night.

Vocabulary

uninflammatory	(1)	not causing excitement or anger
unwieldy	(2)	hard to manage, troublesome
quarry	(2)	anything being hunted or pursued
wayfarers	(2)	persons who travel on foot
errant	(2)	wandering
taut	(4)	tense
berth	(7)	distance, space
skittish	(7)	nervous, frightened
congenial	(7)	friendly
constitutionals	(8)	walks for health

My first victim was a woman—white, well dressed, probably in her early twenties. I came upon her late one evening on a deserted street in Hyde Park, a relatively affluent neighborhood in an otherwise mean, impoverished section of Chicago. As I swung onto the avenue behind her, there seemed to be a discreet, uninflammatory distance between us. Not so. She cast back a worried glance. To her, the youngish black man—a broad six feet two inches with a beard and billowing hair, both hands shoved into the pockets of a bulky military jacket—seemed menacingly close. After a few more quick glimpses, she picked up her pace and was soon running in earnest. Within seconds she disappeared into a cross street.

That was more than a decade ago. I was twenty-two years old, a graduate student newly arrived at the University of

1

2

Chicago. It was in the echo of that terrified woman's footfalls that I first began to know the unwieldy inheritance I'd come into—the ability to alter public space in ugly ways. It was clear that she thought herself the quarry of a mugger, a rapist, or worse. Suffering a bout of insomnia, however, I was stalking sleep, not defenseless wayfarers. As a softy who is scarcely able to take a knife to a raw chicken—let alone hold it to a person's throat—I was surprised, embarrassed, and dismayed all at once. Her flight made me feel like an accomplice in tyranny. It also made it clear that I was indistinguishable from the muggers who occasionally seeped into the area from the surrounding ghetto. That first encounter, and those that followed, signified that a vast, unnerving gulf lay between nighttime pedestrians—particularly women—and me. And I soon gathered that being perceived as dangerous is a hazard in itself. I only needed to turn a corner into a dicey situation, or crowd some frightened, armed person in a foyer somewhere, or make an errant move after being pulled over by a policeman. Where fear and weapons meet—and they often do in urban America—there is always the possibility of death.

In that first year, my first away from my hometown, I was 3 to become thoroughly familiar with the language of fear. At dark, shadowy intersections in Chicago, I could cross in front of a car stopped at a traffic light and elicit the *thunk, thunk, thunk, thunk* of the driver—black, white, male, or female—hammering down the door locks. On less traveled streets after dark, I grew accustomed to but never comfortable with people who crossed to the other side of the street rather than pass me. Then there were the standard unpleasantries with police, doormen, bouncers, cab drivers, and others whose business it is to screen out troublesome individuals *before* there is any nastiness.

I moved to New York nearly two years ago and I have re- 4 mained an avid night walker. In central Manhattan, the near-constant crowd cover minimizes tense one-on-one street encounters. Elsewhere—visiting friends in SoHo,[1] where sidewalks are narrow and tightly spaced buildings shut out the sky—things can get very taut indeed. . . . "

The fearsomeness mistakenly attributed to me in public 5 places often has a perilous flavor. The most frightening of these

[1] Soho   (4)   A district of lower Manhattan.

confusions occurred in the late 1970s and early 1980s when I worked as a journalist in Chicago. One day, rushing into the office of a magazine I was writing for with a deadline story in hand, I was mistaken for a burglar. The office manager called security and, with an ad hoc posse, pursued me through the labyrinthine halls, nearly to my editor's door. I had no way of proving who I was. I could only move briskly toward the company of someone who knew me.

Another time I was on assignment for a local paper and   6
killing time before an interview. I entered a jewelry store on the city's affluent Near North Side. The proprietor excused herself and returned with an enormous red Doberman pinscher straining at the end of a leash. She stood, the dog extended toward me, silent to my questions, her eyes bulging nearly out of her head. I took a cursory look around, nodded, and bade her good night. Relatively speaking, however, I never fared as badly as another black male journalist. He went to nearby Waukegan, Illinois, a couple of summers ago to work on a story about a murderer who was born there. Mistaking the reporter for the killer, police hauled him from his car at gunpoint and but for his press credentials would probably have tried to book him. Such episodes are not uncommon. Black men trade tales like this all the time. . . .

I began to take precautions to make myself less threaten-   7
ing. I move about with care, particularly late in the evening. I give a wide berth to nervous people on subway platforms during the wee hours, particularly when I have exchanged business clothes for jeans. If I happen to be entering a building behind some people who appear skittish, I may walk by, letting them clear the lobby before I return, so as not to seem to be following them. I have been calm and extremely congenial on those rare occasions when I've been pulled over by the police.

And on late-evening constitutionals along streets less trav-   8
eled by, I employ what has proved to be an excellent tension-reducing measure: I whistle melodies from Beethoven and Vivaldi and the more popular classical composers. Even steely New Yorkers hunching toward nighttime destinations seem to relax, and occasionally they even join in the tune. Virtually everybody seems to sense that a mugger wouldn't be warbling bright, sunny selections from Vivaldi's *Four Seasons.* It is my equivalent of the cowbell that hikers wear when they know they are in bear country.

Discussion Questions

1. What is the main idea of Staples's essay?
2. What examples does Staples use to support his main idea?
3. What is the tone of the essay?
4. Why are black men generally seen as "criminals" in U.S. society?
5. How does Staples feel about his "power to alter public space"?
6. What precautions does Staples take to make himself "less threatening"?
7. How effective is Staples's use of description? Explain your answer.
8. How did Staples choose to begin his essay? What are some other options?

Writing Assignments

1. Write an essay about a time when you or someone you know felt threatened in a particular situation.
2. Write an essay about a time when you or someone you know was misunderstood or mistreated in a particular situation because of preconceived ideas about you or that person.
3. Write an essay that illustrates a stereotypical perception held by some people about a particular segment of society, for example, the elderly or women.

RESPECT ON THE STREETS

Elijah Anderson

Elijah Anderson is the Charles and William Day Professor of Social Sciences at the University of Pennsylvania. A sociologist, Anderson studies urban society, specifically life in the inner cities. He is the author of A Place on the Corner *(1978),* Streetwise: Race, Class and Change in the Urban Community *(1990), and* "The Code of the Streets" *(1994), which first appeared in the* Atlantic Monthly *and from which this excerpt is taken. Here Anderson describes the desperate search for respect by African American young men in poor inner-city communities.*

Vocabulary

deter	(2)	prevent, discourage
tatters	(3)	pieces, shreds
intricately	(3)	bound up with
circumscribed	(3)	limited
prerogatives	(4)	rights, privileges
ruthlessness	(4)	cruelty
existential	(4)	based on experience
implicit	(5)	implied, understood
incomprehensible	(6)	unable to be understood
demeanor	(6)	behavior
alluring	(6)	tempting, fascinating
internalized	(8)	taken inside oneself
imminent	(8)	about to occur
compunctions	(8)	feelings of guilt
quid pro quo	(8)	equal exchange
deferential	(8)	courteous, respectful

Among young people, whose sense of self-esteem is particularly   1
vulnerable, there is an especially heightened concern with being disrespected. Many inner-city young men in particular
crave respect to such a degree that they will risk their lives to
attain and maintain it.

The issue of respect is thus closely tied to whether a per-   2
son has an inclination to be violent, even as a victim. In the
wider society people may not feel required to retaliate physically after an attack, even though they are aware that they

have been degraded or taken advantage of. They may feel a great need to defend themselves *during* an attack, or to behave in such a way as to deter aggression (middle-class people certainly can and do become victims of street-oriented youths), but they are much more likely than street-oriented people to feel that they can walk away from a possible altercation with their self-esteem intact. Some people may even have the strength of character to flee, without any thought that their self-respect or esteem will be diminished.

In impoverished inner-city black communities, however,   3
particularly among young males and perhaps increasingly among females, such flight would be extremely difficult. To run away would likely leave one's self-esteem in tatters. Hence people often feel constrained not only to stand up and at least attempt to resist during an assault but also to "pay back"—to seek revenge—after a successful assault on their person. This may include going to get a weapon or even getting relatives involved. Their very identity and self-respect, their honor, is often intricately tied up with the way they perform on the streets during and after such encounters. This outlook reflects the circumscribed opportunities of the inner-city poor. Generally people outside the ghetto have other ways of gaining status and regard, and thus do not feel so dependent on such physical displays.

By Trial of Manhood

On the street, among males these concerns about things and   4
identity have come to be expressed in the concept of "manhood." Manhood in the inner city means taking the prerogatives of men with respect to strangers, other men, and women—being distinguished as a man. It implies physicality and a certain ruthlessness. Regard and respect are associated with this concept in large part because of its practical application: if others have little or no regard for a person's manhood, his very life and those of his loved ones could be in jeopardy. But there is a chicken-and-egg aspect to this situation: one's physical safety is more likely to be jeopardized in public *because* manhood is associated with respect. In other words, an existential link has been created between the idea of manhood and one's self-esteem, so that it has become hard to say which is primary. For many inner-city youths, manhood and respect are flip sides of the same coin; physical and psychological well-

being are inseparable, and both require a sense of control, of being in charge.

The operating assumption is that a man, especially a real 5
man, knows what other men know—the code of the streets. And if one is not a real man, one is somehow diminished as a person, and there are certain valued things one simply does not deserve. There is thus believed to be a certain justice to the code, since it is considered that everyone has the opportunity to know it. Implicit in this is that everybody is held responsible for being familiar with the code. If the victim of a mugging, for example, does not know the code and so responds "wrong," the perpetrator may feel justified even in killing him and may feel no remorse. He may think, "Too bad, but it's his fault. He should have known better."

So when a person ventures outside, he must adopt the 6
code—a kind of shield, really—to prevent others from "messing with" him. In these circumstances it is easy for people to think they are being tried or tested by others even when this is not the case. For it is sensed that something extremely valuable is at stake in every interaction, and people are encouraged to rise to the occasion, particularly with strangers. For people who are unfamiliar with the code—generally people who live outside the inner city—the concern with respect in the most ordinary inter-actions can be frightening and incomprehensible. But for those who are invested in the code, the clear object of their demeanor is to discourage strangers from even thinking about testing their manhood. And the sense of power that attends the ability to deter others can be alluring even to those who know the code without being heavily invested in it—the decent inner-city youths. Thus a boy who has been leading a basically decent life can, in trying circumstances, suddenly resort to deadly force.

Central to the issue of manhood is the widespread belief 7
that one of the most effective ways of gaining respect is to man-ifest "nerve." Nerve is shown when one takes another person's possessions (the more valuable the better), "messes with" someone's woman, throws the first punch, "gets in someone's face," or pulls a trigger. Its proper display helps on the spot to check others who would violate one's person and also helps to build a reputation that works to prevent future challenges. But since such a show of nerve is a forceful expression of disrespect toward the person on the receiving end, the victim may be greatly offended and seek to retaliate with equal or greater force. A display of nerve, therefore, can easily provoke a life-

threatening response, and the background knowledge of that possibility has often been incorporated into the concept of nerve.

True nerve exposes a lack of fear of dying. Many feel that it is acceptable to risk dying over the principle of respect. In fact, among the hard-core street-oriented, the clear risk of violent death may be preferable to being "dissed" by another. The youths who have internalized this attitude and convincingly display it in their public bearing are among the most threatening people of all, for it is commonly assumed that they fear no man. As the people of the community say, "They are the baddest dudes on the street." They often lead an existential life that may acquire meaning only when they are faced with the possibility of imminent death. Not to be afraid to die is by implication to have few compunctions about taking another's life. Not to be afraid to die is the quid pro quo of being able to take somebody else's life—for the right reasons, if the situation demands it. When others believe this is one's position, it gives one a real sense of power on the streets. Such credibility is what many inner-city youths strive to achieve, whether they are decent or street-oriented, both because of its practical defensive value and because of the positive way it makes them feel about themselves. The difference between the decent and the street-oriented youth is often that the decent youth makes a conscious decision to appear tough and manly; in another setting—with teachers, say, or at his part-time job—he can be polite and differential. The street-oriented youth, on the other hand, has made the concept of manhood a part of his very identity; he has difficulty manipulating it—it often controls him.

8

Discussion Questions

1. According to Anderson, why do many inner-city young men crave respect to such a great degree?
2. What is the relationship between self-respect and violence in the inner city?
3. What does the concept of "manhood" mean in the inner city?
4. According to Anderson, what is considered "true nerve" among hard-core inner-city youth?
5. What is the difference between the "decent and the street-oriented youth"?

6. How does Anderson use definition to develop this excerpt?

7. What is the thesis of this excerpt?

Writing Assignments

1. Write an essay that discusses your concept of one of the following: respect, honor, self-esteem, nerve, manhood (or womanhood).

2. Write an essay in which you describe the "code" of your neighborhood or community.

3. Write an essay in which you or someone you know was affected by violence of some kind.

Student Essay:
ARE BLACK MALES BECOMING
AN ENDANGERED SPECIES?

Dwayne Griffin

Vocabulary

verge   (1)   edge
imminent (5)   immediate

To say today that a specific group of people is on the verge   1
of extinction is something some might find unbelievable. However, it is true. The black male, since his arrival in the Americas, has been through years of oppression—slavery, racism,
and stereotypes. Today, black men are a group at risk. Steps
must be taken to reverse this plague that has our black men on
the verge of extinction.

One of, if not the most, detrimental causes of turmoil is a   2
short life expectancy. The most disturbing fact of the black
male's life expectancy is that it is shorter than any other race
or sex. The young black male, according to numerous news reports, has a much higher death rate than a white youth, primarily because the greatest causes of death among black
youths are homicide, drug abuse, suicide, and accidents
whereas accidents and cardiovascular disease are the primary
causes of death among white youth.

Another factor affecting the existence of the black male is
physical health and illnesses. Many members of the black community, especially men, receive inadequate health-care services. This problem has long been a contributing factor to the
short life span of black males. Even today with improved health
services, black men still have a higher rate of cancer compared
to any other group in the United States. Reports indicate that
the most prevalent form of cancer found in black males—lung
cancer—is one of the most difficult forms of cancer to cure and
the easiest to prevent.

However, today the stereotype associating black males   3
with crime and violence has sadly become a reality. Just last
week my friend, who is a sociology major, gave me a shocking
statistic: "Even though Black men account for only about 7

percent of the population, they make up half the population of males in local, state, and federal jails and penitentiaries." Crime in the black community and among black males is at an all-time high. Black males account for the majority of Americans killed in crime-related incidents each year. Blacks for the most part aren't just killing members of other races but, in fact, are killing one another. Black-on-black crime is on the rise as are drug and gang-related homicides. There is no end in sight.

Alcohol and drug abuse are also threats to the black 4 man's health. Alcohol abuse is a more serious problem for black men than it is for white men, white women, and black women. The consequences of alcohol abuse, which affects both the personal and social lives of black men, include substantial increases in the rates of homicides, arrests, accidents, assaults, and physical illnesses. The alcohol problems among black men are further compounded by obstacles that make treatment of the disease difficult. These obstacles include few alcohol treatment centers in black communities, lack of drug and alcohol education, and the lack of funding for treatment.

The most publicized danger to the black male's existence 5 is that of unemployment. This is the issue concerning black males on which the media focus. Unemployment is so widespread among black males that they are twice as likely to be jobless as their white counterparts. Since it may contribute to crime and violence or to health-related problems, unemployment poses the most imminent and devastating threat to the black man and his family.

The black male is in grave danger. Answers must be found 6 to address the many conditions that threaten not only his survival, but the survival of the African American family.

Discussion Questions

1. According to Griffin, what are major threats to the African American male?

2. The author has his own ranking of these problems. Which do you feel is the greatest threat? Support your answer.

3. Why does the author consider black males an endangered species?

4. What are some of the greatest causes of death among black youth?

5. What are health concerns that affect black men?

6. To what extent does the author's use of illustration increase the essay's credibility?
7. Why do you think the author chose to use a question as his title? Would a statement have been a better choice? Why or why not?

Writing Assignments

1. Write an essay responding to the following sentence: _____ is becoming an endangered species.
2. Write an essay in which you disprove some misconception regarding the African American male.

7

Childhood • Adolescence Growing Up

GORILLA, MY LOVE

Toni Cade Bambara

Born Toni Cade, Bambara (1939–95), who grew up in New York City, attended Queens College and City College of New York. She edited two short story anthologies before publishing two collections of her own: Gorilla, My Love *(1972) and* The Sea Birds Are Still Alive *(1977). The Salt Eaters (1980), a remarkable first novel, was acclaimed in the* New Yorker *as "a book full of marvels." In the following selection, the title story of her 1972 collection, Bambara shows us a young girl's struggle with disappointment.*

That was the year Hunca Bubba changed his name. Not a   1
change up, but a change back, since Jefferson Winston Vale
was the name in the first place. Which was news to me cause
he'd been my Hunca Bubba my whole lifetime, since I couldn't
manage Uncle to save my life. So far as I was concerned it was
a change completely to somethin soundin very geographical
weatherlike to me, like somethin you'd find in a almanac. Or
somethin you'd run across when you sittin in the navigator
seat with a wet thumb on the map crinkly in your lap, watchin

the roads and signs so when Granddaddy Vale say "Which way, Scout," you got sense enough to say take the next exit or take a left or whatever it is. Not that Scout's my name. Just the name Granddaddy call whoever sittin in the navigator seat. Which is usually me cause I don't feature sittin in the back with the pecans. Now, you figure pecans all right to be sittin with. If you thinks so, that's your business. But they dusty sometime and make you cough. And they got a way of slidin around and dippin down sudden, like maybe a rat in the buckets. So if you scary like me, you sleep with the lights on and blame it on Baby Jason and, so as not to waste good electric, you study the maps. And that's how come I'm in the navigator seat most times and get to be called Scout.

So Hunca Bubba in the back with the pecans and Baby   2
Jason, and he in love. And we got to hear all this stuff about this woman he in love with and all. Which really ain't enough to keep the mind alive, though Baby Jason got no better sense than to give his undivided attention and keep grabbin at the photograph which is just a picture of some skinny woman in a countrified dress with her hand shot up to her face like she shame fore cameras. But there's a movie house in the background which I ax about. Cause I am a movie freak from way back, even though it do get me in trouble sometime.

Like when me and Big Brood and Baby Jason was on our   3
own last Easter and couldn't go to the Dorset cause we'd seen all the Three Stooges they was. And the RKO Hamilton was closed readying up for the Easter Pageant that night. And the West End, the Regun and the Sunset was too far, less we had grownups with us which we didn't. So we walk up Amsterdam Avenue to the Washington and *Gorilla, My Love* playin, they say, which suit me just fine, though the "my love" part kinda drag Big Brood some. As for Baby Jason, shoot, like Granddaddy say, he'd follow me into the fiery furnace if I say come on. So we go in and get three bags of Havmore potato chips which not only are the best potato chips but the best bags for blowin up and bustin real loud so the matron come trottin down the aisle with her chunky self, flashin that flashlight dead in your eye so you can give her some lip, and if she answer back and you already finish seein the show anyway, why then you just turn the place out. Which I love to do, no lie. With Baby Jason kickin at the seat in front, egging me on, and Big Brood mumblin bout what fiercesome things we goin do. Which means me. Like when the big boys come up on us talkin

bout Lemme a nickel. It's me that hide the money. Or when the bad boys in the park take Big Brood's Spaudeen[1] way from him. It's me that jump on they back and fight awhile. And it's me that turns out the show if the matron get too salty.

So the movie come on and right away it's this churchy   4
music and clearly not about no gorilla. Bout Jesus. And I am ready to kill, not cause I got anything gainst Jesus. Just that when you fixed to watch a gorilla picture you don't wanna get messed around with Sunday School stuff. So I am mad. Besides, we see this raggedy old brown film *King of Kings* every year and enough's enough. Grownups figure they can treat you just anyhow. Which burns me up. There I am, my feet up and my Havmore potato chips really salty and crispy and two jawbreakers in my lap and the money safe in my shoe from the big boys, and here comes this Jesus stuff. So we all go wild. Yellin, booin, stompin and carryin on. Really to wake the man in the booth up there who musta went to sleep and put on the wrong reels. But no, cause he holler down to shut up and then he turn the sound up so we really gotta holler like crazy to even hear ourselves good. And the matron ropes off the children section and flashes her light all over the place and we yell some more and some kids slip under the rope and run up and down the aisle just to show it take more than some dusty ole velvet rope to tie us down. And I'm flingin the kid in front of me's popcorn. And Baby Jason kickin seats. And it's really somethin. Then here come the big and bad matron, the one they let out in case of emergency. And she totin that flashlight like she gonna use it on somebody. This here the colored matron Brandy and her friends call Thunderbuns. She do not play. She do not smile. So we shut up and watch the simple ass picture.

Which is not so simple as it is stupid. Cause I realize that   5
just about anybody in my family is better than this god they always talkin about. My daddy wouldn't stand for nobody treatin any of us that way. My mama specially. And I can just see it now, Big Brood up there on the cross talking bout Forgive them Daddy cause they don't know what they doin. And my Mama say Get on down from there you big fool, whatcha think this is, playtime? And my Daddy yellin to Granddaddy to get him a ladder cause Big Brood actin the fool, his mother side of the family showin up.

---

[1]Spaudeen (3)   Probably from "Spaulding," the sporting goods company, makers of rubber balls.

And my mama and her sister Daisy jumpin on them Romans beatin them with they pocketbooks. And Hunca Bubba tellin them folks on they knees they better get out the way and go get some help or they goin to get trampled on. And Granddaddy Vale sayin Leave the boy alone, if that's what he wants to do with his life we ain't got nothin to say about it. Then Aunt Daisy givin him a taste of that pocketbook, fussin bout what a damn fool old man Granddaddy is. Then everybody jumpin in his chest like the time Uncle Clayton went in the army and come back with only one leg and Granddaddy say somethin stupid about that's life. And by this time Big Brood off the cross and in the park playin handball or skully or somethin. And the family in the kitchen throwin dishes at each other, screamin bout if you hadn't done this I wouldn't had to do that. And me in the parlor trying to do my arithmetic yellin Shut it off.

Which is what I was yellin all by myself which make me a sittin target for Thunderbuns. But when I yell We want our money back, that gets everybody in chorus. And the movie windin up with this heavenly cloud music and the smart-ass up there in his hole in the wall turns up the sound again to drown us out. Then there comes Bugs Bunny which we already seen so we know we been had. No gorilla my nuthin. And Big Brood say Awwww sheeet, we goin to see the manager and get our money back. And I know from this we business. So I brush the potato chips out of my hair, which is where Baby Jason like to put em, and I march myself up the aisle to deal with the manager who is a crook in the first place for lying out there sayin *Gorilla, My Love* playin. And I never did like the man cause he oily and pasty at the same time like the bad guy in the serial, the one that got a hideout behind a push-button bookcase and play "Moonlight Sonata" with gloves on. I knock on the door and I am furious. And I am alone, too. Cause Big Brood suddenly got to go so bad even though my mama told us bout goin in them nasty bathrooms. And I hear him sigh like he disgusted when he get to the door and see only a little kid there. And now I'm really furious cause I get so tired grownups messin over kids just cause they little and can't take em to court. What is it, he say to me like I lost my mittens or wet on myself or am somebody's retarded child. When in reality I am the smartest kid P.S. 186 ever had in its whole lifetime and you can ax anybody. Even them teachers that don't like me cause I won't sing them Southern songs or back off when they tell me my questions are out of order. And cause my Mama come up

6

there in a minute when them teachers start playin the dozens behind colored folks. She stalk in with her hat pulled down bad and that Persian lamb coat draped back over one hip on account of she got her fist planted there so she can talk that talk which gets us all hypnotized, and teacher be comin undone cause she know this could be her job and her behind cause Mama got pull with the Board and bad by her own self anyhow.

So I kick the door open wider and just walk right by him and sit down and tell the man about himself and that I want my money back and that goes for Baby Jason and Big Brood too. And he still trying to shuffle me out the door even though I'm sitting which shows him for the fool he is. Just like them teachers do fore they realize Mama like a stone on that spot and ain't backin up. So he ain't gettin up off the money. So I was forced to leave, takin the matches from under his ashtray, and set a fire under the candy stand, which closed the raggedy ole Washington down for a week. My Daddy had the suspect it was me cause Big Brood got a big mouth. But I explained right quick what the whole thing was about and I figured it was even-steven. Cause if you say Gorilla, My Love, you suppose to mean it. Just like when you say you goin to give me a party on my birthday, you gotta mean it. And if you say me and Baby Jason can go South pecan haulin with Granddaddy Vale, you better not be comin up with no stuff about the weather look uncertain or did you mop the bathroom or any other trickified business. I mean even gangsters in the movies say My word is my bond. So don't nobody get away with nothin far as I'm concerned. So Daddy put his belt back on. Cause that's the way I was raised. Like my Mama say in one of them situations when I won't back down, Okay Badbird, you right. Your point is well-taken. Not that Badbird my name, just what she say when she tired arguin and know I'm right. And Aunt Jo, who is the hardest head in the family and worse even than Aunt Daisy, she say, You absolutely right Miss Muffin, which also ain't my real name but the name she gave me one time when I got some medicine shot in my behind and wouldn't get up off her pillows for nothin. And even Granddaddy Vale—who got no memory to speak of, so sometime you can just plain lie to him, if you want to be like that—he say, Well if that's what I said, then that's it. But this name business was different they said. It wasn't like Hunca Bubba had gone back on his word or anything. Just that he was thinkin bout gettin married and was usin his real name now. Which ain't the way I saw it at all.

7

So there I am in the navigator seat. And I turn to him and   8
just plain ole ax him. I mean I come right on out with it. No
sense goin all around that barn the old folks talk about. And
like my mama say, Hazel—which is my real name and what she
remembers to call me when she bein serious—when you got
somethin on your mind, speak up and let the chips fall where
they may. And if anybody don't like it, tell em to come see your
mama. And Daddy look up from the paper and say, You hear
your mama good, Hazel. And tell em to come see me first. Like
that. That's how I was raised.

So I turn clear round in the navigator seat and say, "Look   9
here, Hunca Bubba or Jefferson Windsong Vale or whatever
your name is, you gonna marry this girl?"

"Sure am," he say, all grins.   10

And I say, "Member that time you was baby-sittin me   11
when we lived at four-o-nine and there was this big snow and
Mama and Daddy got held up in the country so you had to stay
for two days?"

And he say, "Sure do."   12

"Well. You remember how you told me I was the cutest   13
thing that ever walked the earth?"

"Oh, you were real cute when you were little," he say,   14
which is suppose to be funny. I am not laughin.

"Well. You remember what you said?"   15

And Granddaddy Vale squintin over the wheel and axin   16
Which way, Scout. But Scout is busy and don't care if we all
get lost for days.

"Watcha mean, Peaches?"   17

"My name is Hazel. And what I mean is you said you were   18
going to marry *me* when I grew up. You were going to wait.
That's what I mean, my dear Uncle Jefferson." And he don't say
nuthin. Just look at me real strange like he never saw me before in life. Like he lost in some weird town in the middle of
night and looking for directions and there's no one to ask. Like
it was me that messed up the maps and turned the road posts
round. "Well, you said it, didn't you?" And Baby Jason lookin
back and forth like we playin ping-pong. Only I ain't playin. I'm
hurtin and I can hear that I am screamin. And Granddaddy
Vale mumblin how we never gonna get to where we goin if I
don't turn around and take my navigator job serious.

"Well, for cryin out loud, Hazel, you just a little girl. And I   19
was just teasin."

" 'And I was just teasin,' " I say back just how he said it   20
so he can hear what a terrible thing it is. Then I don't say
nuthin. And he don't say nuthin. And Baby Jason don't say
nuthin nohow. Then Granddaddy Vale speak up. "Look here,
Precious, it was Hunca Bubba what told you them things. This
here, Jefferson Winston Vale." And Hunca Bubba say, "That's
right. That was somebody else. I'm a new somebody."

"You a lyin dawg," I say, when I meant to say treacherous   21
dog, but just couldn't get hold of the word. It slipped away from
me. And I'm crying and crumplin down in the seat and just
don't care. And Granddaddy say to hush and steps on the gas.
And I'm losin my bearins and don't even know where to look on
the map cause I can't see for cryin. And Baby Jason cryin too.
Cause he is my blood brother and understands that we must
stick together or be forever lost, what with grownups playin
change-up and turnin you round every which way so bad. And
don't even say they sorry.

Discussion Questions

1. How would you characterize the narrator?
2. Why is the narrator upset with Hunca Bubba?
3. How is the narrator's movie problem similar to her problem with Hunca Bubba?
4. Are you surprised by the narrator's reaction at the end of the story? Explain your answer.
5. Why does Bambara entitle her story "Gorilla, My Love"?
6. To what extent is Bambara's use of description an effective means of organization for her story?
7. What is the theme of the story?

Writing Assignments

1. Write an essay about a time when you felt betrayed by an adult.
2. Write an essay about a time when what you were promised was not what you received.
3. In an essay, describe an incident when a minor occurrence opened up a wound and caused you to overreact.

ALICE

Paulette Childress White

Paulette Childress White (1948–   ), the mother of five sons, was born and continues to live in Detroit. White has used that city as the setting of her poetry and short stories. She wrote Love Poems to a Black Junkie *(1975) and* The Water-melon Dress: Portrait of a Woman: Poems and Illustrations *(1984). In 1977, White published in* Essence *magazine her first short story, "Alice," which appears here. Notice that the story, which shows how perceptions change as one grows, is like a long poem with its rhythms and movement.*

Vocabulary

bellowing   (5)   shouting

Alice. Drunk Alice. Alice of the streets. Of the party. Of the   1
house of dark places. From whom without knowing I hid love
all my life behind remembrances of her house where I went
with Momma in the daytime to borrow things, and we found
her lounging in the front yard on a dirty plastic lawn chair
drinking warm beer from the can in a little brown bag where
the flies buzzed in and out of the always-open door of the
house as we followed her into the cool, dim rank-smelling
rooms for what it was we'd come. And I fought frowns as my
feet caught on the sticky gray wooden floor but looked up to
smile back at her smile as she gave the dollar or the sugar or
the coffee to Momma who never seemed to notice the floor or
the smell or Alice.

Alice, tall like a man, with soft wooly hair spread out in   2
tangles like a feathered hat and her face oily and her legs ashy,
whose beauty I never quite believed because she valued it so
little but was real. Real like wild flowers and uncut grass, real
like the knotty sky-reach of a dead tree. Beauty of warm brown
eyes in a round dark face and of teeth somehow always white
and clean and of lips moist and open, out of which rolled the
voice and the laughter, deep and breathless, rolling out the
strong and secret beauty of her soul.

Alice of the streets. Gentle walking on long legs. Close-   3
kneed. Careful. Stopping sometimes at our house on her way to

unknown places and other people. She came wearing loose, flowered dresses and she sat in our chairs rubbing the too-big knees that sometimes hurt, and we gathered, Momma, my sisters and I, to hear the beautiful bad-woman talk and feel the rolling laughter, always sure that she left more than she came for. I accepted the tender touch of her hands on my hair or my face or my arms like favors I never returned. I clung to the sounds of her words and the light of her smiles like stolen fruit.

Alice, mother in a house of dark places. Of boys who   4
fought each other and ran cursing through the wild back rooms where I did not go alone but sometimes with Alice when she caught them up and knuckled their heads and made them cry or hugged them close to her saying funny things to tease them into laughter. And of the oldest son, named for his father, who sat twisted into a wheelchair by sunny windows in the front where she stayed with him for hours giving him her love, filling him with her laughter and he sat there—his words strained, difficult but soft and warm like the sun from the windows.

Alice of the party. When there was not one elsewhere she   5
could make one of the evenings when her husband was not storming the dim rooms in drunken fits or lying somewhere in darkness filling the house with angry grunts and snores before the days he would go to work. He sat near her drinking beer with what company was there—was always sure to come— greedy for Alice and her husband, who leaned into and out of each other, talking hard and laughing loud and telling lies and being real. And there were rare and wondrously wicked times when I was caught there with Daddy who was one of the greedy ones and could not leave until the joy-shouting, table-slapping arguments about God and Negroes, the jumping up and down, the bellowing "what about the time" talks, the boasting and reeling of people drunk with beer and laughter and the ache of each other was over and the last ones sat talking sad and low, sick with themselves and too much beer. I watched Alice growing tired and ill and thought about the boys who had eaten dinners of cake and soda pop from the corner store, and I struggled to despise her for it against the memory of how, smiling they'd crept off to their rooms and slept in peace. And later at home I, too, slept strangely safe and happy, hugging the feel of that sweet fury in her house and in Alice of the party.

Alice, who grew older as I grew up but stayed the same   6
while I grew beyond her, away from her. So far away that once,

on a clear early morning in the spring, when I was eighteen and smart and clean on my way to work downtown in the high-up office of my government job, with eyes that would not see I cut off her smile and the sound of her voice calling my name. When she surprised me on a clear spring morning, on her way somewhere or from somewhere in the streets and I could not see her beauty, only the limp flowered dress and the tangled hair and the face puffy from too much drinking and no sleep, I cut off her smile. I let my eyes slide away to say without speaking that I had grown beyond her. Alice, who had no place to grow in but was deep in the soil that fed me.

It was eight years before I saw Alice again and in those 7 eight years Alice had buried her husband and one of her boys and lost the oldest son to the county hospital where she traveled for miles to take him the sun and her smiles. And she had become a grandmother and a member of the church and cleaned out her house and closed the doors. And in those eight years I had married and become the mother of sons and did not always keep my floors clean or my hair combed or my legs oiled and I learned to like the taste of beer and how to talk bad-woman talk. In those eight years life had led me to the secret laughter.

Alice, when I saw her again, was in black, after the funeral 8 of my brother, sitting alone in an upstairs bedroom of my mother's house, her face dusted with brown powder and her gray-streaked hair brushed back into a neat ball and her wrinkled hands rubbing the tight-stockinged, tumor-filled knees and her eyes quiet and sober when she looked at me where I stood at the top of the stairs. I had run upstairs to be away from the smell of food and the crowd of comforters come to help bury our dead when I found Alice sitting alone in black and was afraid to smile remembering how I'd cut off her smile when I thought I had grown beyond her and was afraid to speak because there was too much I wanted to say.

Then Alice smiled her same smile and spoke my name in 9 her same voice and rising slowly from the tumored knees said, "Come on in and sit with me." And for the very first time I did.

Discussion Questions

1. How does the narrator's childhood image of Alice change from her adult image of Alice?
2. The narrator presents several descriptive snapshots of Alice. What are her positive and negative characteristics?

3. The author uses many similes (comparisons using *like* or *as*). What are two similes that you think are particularly effective? Explain your answer.

4. How does the narrator grow "beyond and away from" Alice?

5. Why does the narrator say that Alice was "deep in the soil that fed" her?

6. Why does the narrator at the end of the story say that she sat with Alice for the first time?

7. What is a cause-and-effect relationship illustrated in this story?

8. White begins many paragraphs with fragments. Why do you think the author uses the fragments rather than complete sentences? What is your assessment of her stylistic choice?

Writing Assignments

1. Write an essay in which you describe how your childhood perceptions of someone changed once you became an adult.

2. Write an essay in which you describe something that you do less well as an adult than you did as a child.

3. Write an essay about someone who has had an indirect, but substantial influence on your life.

LIVING JIM CROW

Richard Wright

Born in Natchez, Mississippi, and educated in the Chicago public school system, Richard Wright (1908–1960) is probably best known for his well-received novel Native Son *(1940). Wright wrote three other novels, a book of short stories, and four nonfiction works. In the following selection from* Black Boy *(1945), an autobiographical work, Wright recounts some of his humiliating experiences through which he gained his Jim Crow education.*

Vocabulary

cinders	(1)	hot coals
appalling	(2)	disgusting
barrage	(2)	attack
fortifications	(2)	barriers
profusely	(2)	freely
delirious	(7)	mentally wandering, confused
chamois	(61)	cotton cloth

I

My first lesson in how to live as a Negro came when I was quite small. We were living in Arkansas. Our house stood behind the railroad tracks. Its skimpy yard was paved with black cinders. Nothing green ever grew in that yard. The only touch of green we could see was far away, beyond the tracks, over where the white folks lived. But cinders were good enough for me and I never missed the green growing things. And anyhow cinders were fine weapons. You could always have a nice hot war with huge black cinders. All you had to do was crouch behind the brick pillars of a house with your hands full of gritty ammunition. And the first woolly black head you saw pop out from behind another row of pillars was your target. You tried your very best to knock it off. It was great fun.

I never fully realized the appalling disadvantages of a cinder environment till one day the gang to which I belonged found itself engaged in a war with the white boys who lived beyond the tracks. As usual we laid down our cinder barrage,

1

2

thinking that this would wipe the white boys out. But they replied with a steady bombardment of broken bottles. We doubled our cinder barrage, but they hid behind trees, hedges, and the sloping embankments of their lawns. Having no such fortifications, we retreated to the brick pillars of our homes. During the retreat a broken milk bottle caught me behind the ear, opening a deep gash which bled profusely. The sight of blood pouring over my face completely demoralized our ranks. My fellow-combatants left me standing paralyzed in the center of the yard, and scurried for their homes. A kind neighbor saw me and rushed me to a doctor, who took three stitches in my neck.

I sat brooding on my front steps, nursing my wound and waiting for my mother to come from work. I felt that a grave injustice had been done me. It was all right to throw cinders. The greatest harm a cinder could do was leave a bruise. But broken bottles were dangerous; they left you cut, bleeding, and helpless. 3

When night fell, my mother came from the white folks' kitchen. I raced down the street to meet her. I could just feel in my bones that she would understand. I knew she would tell me exactly what to do next time. I grabbed her hand and babbled out the whole story. She examined my wound, then slapped me. 4

"How come yuh didn't hide?" she asked me. "How come yuh awways fightin'?" 5

I was outraged, and bawled. Between sobs I told her that I didn't have any trees or hedges to hide behind. There wasn't a thing I could have used as a trench. And you couldn't throw very far when you were hiding behind the brick pillars of a house. She grabbed a barrel stave, dragged me home, stripped me naked, and beat me till I had a fever of one hundred and two. She would smack my rump with the stave, and, while the skin was still smarting, impart to me gems of Jim Crow[1] wisdom. I was never to throw cinders any more. I was never to fight any more wars. I was never, never, under any conditions, to fight *white* folks again. And they were absolutely right in clouting me with the broken milk bottle. Didn't I know she was working hard every day in the hot kitchens of the white folks to make money to take care of me? When was I ever going to learn to be a good boy? She couldn't be bothered with my fights. She 6

[1]Jim Crow (6)   Systematic practice of segregating, suppressing, and discriminating against African Americans.

finished by telling me that I ought to be thankful to God as long as I lived that they didn't kill me.

All that night I was delirious and could not sleep. Each   7
time I closed my eyes I saw monstrous white faces suspended from the ceiling, leering at me.

From that time on, the charm of my cinder yard was gone.   8
The green trees, the trimmed hedges, the cropped lawns grew very meaningful, became a symbol. Even today when I think of white folks, the hard, sharp outlines of white houses surrounded by trees, lawns, and hedges are present somewhere in the background of my mind. Through the years they grew into an over-reaching symbol of fear.

It was a long time before I came in close contact with   9
white folks again. We moved from Arkansas to Mississippi. Here we had the good fortune not to live behind the railroad tracks, or close to white neighborhoods. We lived in the very heart of the local Black Belt. There were black churches and black preachers; there were black schools and black teachers; black groceries and black clerks. In fact, everything was so solidly black that for a long time I did not even think of white folks, save in remote and vague terms. But this could not last forever. As one grows older one eats more. One's clothing costs more. When I finished grammar school I had to go to work. My mother could no longer feed and clothe me on her cooking job.

There is but one place where a black boy who knows no   10
trade can get a job, and that's where the houses and faces are white, where the trees, lawns, and hedges are green. My first job was with an optical company in Jackson, Mississippi. The morning I applied I stood straight and neat before the boss, answering all his questions with sharp yessirs and nosirs. I was very careful to pronounce my *sirs* distinctly, in order that he might know that I was polite, that I knew where I was, and that I knew he was a *white* man. I wanted that job badly.

He looked me over as though he were examining a prize   11
poodle. He questioned me closely about my schooling, being particularly insistent about how much mathematics I had had. He seemed very pleased when I told him I had had two years of algebra.

"Boy, how would you like to try to learn something around   12
here?" he asked me.

"I'd like it fine, sir," I said, happy. I had visions of "working   13
my way up." Even Negroes have those visions.

"All right," he said. "Come on." 14

I followed him to the small factory. 15

"Pease," he said to a white man of about thirty-five, "this is 16
Richard. He's going to work for us."

Pease looked at me and nodded. 17

I was then taken to a white boy of about seventeen. 18

"Morrie, this is Richard, who's going to work for us." 19

"Whut yuh sayin' there, boy!" Morrie boomed at me. 20

"Fine!" I answered. 21

The boss instructed these two to help me, teach me, give 22
me jobs to do, and let me learn what I could in my spare time.

My wages were five dollars a week. 23

I worked hard, trying to please. For the first month I got 24
along O.K. Both Pease and Morrie seemed to like me. But one
thing was missing. And I kept thinking about it. I was not
learning anything and nobody was volunteering to help me.
Thinking they had forgotten that I was to learn something
about the mechanics of grinding lenses, I asked Morrie one day
to tell me about the work. He grew red.

"Whut yuh tryin' t' do, nigger, git smart?" he asked. 25

"Naw; I ain't tryin' t' git smart," I said. 26

"Well, don't, if yuh know whut's good for yuh!" 27

I was puzzled. Maybe he just doesn't want to help me, I 28
thought. I went to Pease.

"Say, are yuh crazy, you black bastard?" Pease asked me, 29
his gray eyes growing hard.

I spoke out, reminding him that the boss had said I was to 30
be given a chance to learn something.

"Nigger, you think you're *white*, don't you?" 31

"Naw, sir!" 32

"Well, you're acting mighty like it!" 33

"But, Mr. Pease, the boss said . . . " 34

Pease shook his fist in my face. 35

"This is a *white* man's work around here, and you better 36
watch yourself!"

From then on they changed toward me. They said good- 37
morning no more. When I was just a bit slow in performing
some duty, I was called a lazy black son-of-a-bitch.

Once I thought of reporting all this to the boss. But the 38
mere idea of what would happen to me if Pease and Morrie
should learn that I had "snitched" stopped me. And after all,
the boss was a white man too. What was the use?

The climax came at noon one summer day. Pease called 39

me to his work-bench. To get to him I had to go between two
narrow benches and stand with my back to a wall.

"Yes, sir," I said.   40

"Richard, I want to ask you something," Pease began   41
pleasantly, not looking up from his work.

"Yes, sir," I said again.   42

Morrie came over, blocking the narrow passage between   43
the benches. He folded his arms, staring at me solemnly.

I looked from one to the other, sensing that something was   44
coming.

"Yes, sir," I said for the third time.   45

Pease looked up and spoke very slowly.   46

"Richard, *Mr.* Morrie here tells me you call me *Pease*."   ·   47

I stiffened. A void seemed to open up in me. I knew this   48
was the show-down.

He meant that I had failed to call him *Mr.* Pease. I looked   49
at Morrie. He was gripping a steel bar in his hands. I opened
my mouth to speak, to protest, to assure Pease that I had never
called him simply *Pease,* and that I had never had any intentions of doing so, when Morrie grabbed me by the collar, ram-
ming my head against the wall.

"Now, be careful, nigger!" snarled Morrie, baring his teeth.   50
"I heard yuh call 'im *Pease!* 'N' if yuh say yuh didn't, yuh're
callin' me a *lie,* see?" He waved the steel bar threateningly.

If I had said: No, sir, Mr. Pease, I never called you *Pease,* I   51
would have been automatically calling Morrie a liar. And if I
had said: Yes, sir Mr. Pease, I called you *Pease,* I would have
been pleading guilty to having uttered the worst insult that a
Negro can utter to a southern white man. I stood hesitating,
trying to frame a neutral reply.

"Richard, I asked you a question!" said Pease. Anger was   52
creeping into his voice.

"I don't remember calling you *Pease,* Mr. Pease," I said   53
cautiously. "And if I did, I sure didn't mean . . . "

"You black son-of-a-bitch! You called me *Pease,* then!" he   54
spat, slapping me till I bent sideways over a bench. Morrie was
on top of me, demanding:

"Didn't yuh call 'im *Pease?* If yuh say yuh didn't, I'll rip yo'   55
gut string loose with this bar, yuh black granny dodger! Yuh
can't call a white man a lie 'n' git erway with it, you black son-
of-a-bitch!"

I wilted. I begged them not to bother me. I knew what they   56
wanted. They wanted me to leave.

"I'll leave," I promised. "I'll leave right *now.*"   57

They gave me a minute to get out of the factory. I was warned not to show up again, or tell the boss. 58

I went. 59

When I told the folks at home what had happened, they called me a fool. They told me that I must never again attempt to exceed my boundaries. When you are working for white folks, they said, you got to "stay in your place" if you want to keep working. 60

II

My Jim Crow education continued on my next job, which was portering in a clothing store. One morning, while polishing brass out front, the boss and his twenty-year-old son got out of their car and half dragged and half kicked a Negro woman into the store. A policeman standing at the corner looked on, twirling his nightstick. I watched out of the corner of my eye, never slackening the strokes of my chamois upon the brass. After a few minutes, I heard shrill screams coming from the rear of the store. Later the woman stumbled out, bleeding, crying, and holding her stomach. When she reached the end of the block, the policeman grabbed her and accused her of being drunk. Silently, I watched him throw her into a patrol wagon. 61

When I went to the rear of the store, the boss and his son were washing their hands at the sink. They were chuckling. The floor was bloody and strewn with wisps of hair and clothing. No doubt I must have appeared pretty shocked, for the boss slapped me reassuringly on the back. 62

"Boy, that's what we do to niggers when they don't want to pay their bills," he said, laughing. 63

His son looked at me and grinned. 64

"Here, hava cigarette," he said. 65

Not knowing what to do, I took it. He lit his and held the match for me. This was a gesture of kindness, indicating that even if they had beaten the poor old woman, they would not beat me if I knew enough to keep my mouth shut. 66

"Yes, sir," I said, and asked no questions. 67

After they had gone, I sat on the edge of a packing box and stared at the bloody floor till the cigarette went out. 68

That day at noon, while eating in a hamburger joint, I told my fellow Negro porters what had happened. No one seemed surprised. One fellow, after swallowing a huge bite, turned to me and asked: 69

"Huh! Is tha' all they did t' her?" 70

"Yeah. Wasn't tha' enough?" I asked.   71

"Shucks! Man, she's a lucky bitch!" he said, burying his   72
lips deep into a juicy hamburger. "Hell, it's a wonder they didn't
lay her when they got through."

III

I was learning fast, but not quite fast enough. One day, while I   73
was delivering packages in the suburbs, my bicycle tire was
punctured. I walked along the hot, dusty road, sweating and
leading my bicycle by the handle-bars.

A car slowed at my side.   74

"What's the matter boy?" a white man called.   75

I told him my bicycle was broken and I was walking back   76
to town.

"That's too bad," he said. "Hop on the running board."   77

He stopped the car. I clutched hard at my bicycle with one   78
hand and clung to the side of the car with the other.

"All set?"   79

"Yes, sir," I answered. The car started.   80

It was full of young white men. They were drinking. I   81
watched the flask pass from mouth to mouth.

"Wanna drink, boy?" one asked.   82

I laughed as the wind whipped my face. Instinctively obey-   83
ing the freshly planted precepts of my mother, I said:

"Oh, no!"   84

The words were hardly out of my mouth before I felt some-   85
thing hard and cold smash me between the eyes. It was an
empty whisky bottle. I saw stars, and fell backwards from the
speeding car into the dust of the road, my feet becoming entangled in the steel spokes of my bicycle. The white men piled out
and stood over me.

"Nigger, ain't yuh learned no better sense'n tha' yet?"   86
asked the man who hit me. "Ain' yuh learned t' say *sir* t' a
white man yet?"

Dazed, I pulled to my feet. My elbows and legs were bleed-   87
ing. Fists doubled, the white man advanced, kicking my bicycle
out of the way.

"Aw, leave the bastard alone. He's got enough," said one.   88

They stood looking at me. I rubbed my shins, trying to   89
stop the flow of blood. No doubt they felt a sort of contemptuous pity, for one asked:

"Yuh wanna ride t' town now, nigger? Yuh reckon yuh   90
know enough t' ride now?"

"I wanna walk," I said, simply. 91

Maybe it sounded funny. They laughed. 92

"Well, walk, yuh black son-of-a-bitch!" 93

When they left they comforted me with: 94

"Nigger, yuh sho better be damn glad it wuz us yuh talked 95
t' tha' way. Yuh're a lucky bastard, 'cause if yuh'd said tha' t'
somebody else, yuh might've been a dead nigger now."

Discussion Questions

1. What is the significance of the title?
2. Why does Pease and Morrie's behavior change toward the narrator? In what way does the question they ask the narrator in paragraph 50 reflect their behavioral change?
3. What does "stay in your place" mean in the context of the story?
4. Why do the store boss and son invite the narrator to have a cigarette with them after the woman leaves?
5. Why do the young white men offer the narrator a ride the first time?
6. What lessons did Wright learn from his Jim Crow education?
7. Why is the author's use of process important to our understanding of Wright's Jim Crow education?
8. Why do you think Wright chose to divide this essay into three parts?

Writing Assignments

1. Write an essay that describes lessons about life you learned while growing up.
2. Write an essay recounting an incident that you considered a no-win situation.
3. Write an essay in which you discuss some lesson that must be experienced rather than taught.

MARGUERITE'S GRADUATION

Maya Angelou

*Author, poet, playwright, political activist, singer, profes-
sional stage and screen performer, the talented Maya Angelou (1928–) was born Marguerite Johnson in St. Louis,
Missouri. Angelou is best known for her autobiographical
books, which include the following:* I Know Why the Caged
Bird Sings *(1969),* Gather Together in My Name *(1974),*
Singin' and Swingin' and Gettin' Merry Like Christmas
(1976), The Heart of a Woman *(1982), and* Maya Angelou
Boxed *(1994). The following selection from* I Know Why the
Caged Bird Sings *recounts Angelou's bitter disappointment
at her graduation.*

Vocabulary

reprieve	(2)	delayed punishment
presentiment	(12)	indication, hunch
dais	(13)	platform, stage
piqued	(13)	aroused
bootblack	(23)	one who shines shoes
penance	(23)	compensation for an offense
constrained	(24)	held back, restricted
decasyllabic	(26)	having ten syllables
farcical	(27)	laughable, ridiculous
presumptuous	(27)	bold, overconfident
abomination	(29)	anything disgusting
perfunctory	(31)	thoughtless, automatic
palpable	(32)	real, visible
elocution	(36)	style or manner of speaking
auctioned	(44)	sold to the highest bidder

Amazingly the great day finally dawned and I was out of bed 1
before I knew it. I threw open the back door to see it more
clearly, but Momma said, "Sister, come away from that door
and put your robe on."

I hoped the memory of that morning would never leave 2
me. Sunlight was itself young, and the day had none of the insistence maturity would bring it in a few hours. In my robe and
barefoot in the backyard, under cover of going to see about my
new beans, I gave myself up to the gentle warmth and thanked

God that no matter what evil I had done in my life He had allowed me to live to see this day. Somewhere in my fatalism I had expected to die, accidentally, and never have the chance to walk up the stairs in the auditorium and gracefully receive my hard-earned diploma. Out of God's merciful bosom I had won reprieve.

Bailey[1] came out in his robe and gave me a box wrapped 3
in Christmas paper. He said he had saved his money for months to pay for it. It felt like a box of chocolates, but I knew Bailey wouldn't save money to buy candy when we had all we could want under our noses.

He was as proud of the gift as I. It was a soft-leather- 4
bound copy of a collection of poems by Edgar Allan Poe, or, as Bailey and I called him, "Eap." I turned to "Annabel Lee" and we walked up and down the garden rows, the cool dirt between our toes, reciting the beautifully sad lines.

Momma made a Sunday breakfast although it was only 5
Friday. After we finished the blessing, I opened my eyes to find the watch on my plate. It was a dream of a day. Everything went smoothly and to my credit, I didn't have to be reminded or scolded for anything. Near evening I was too jittery to attend to chores, so Bailey volunteered to do all before his bath.

Days before, we had made a sign for the Store, and as we 6
turned out the lights Momma hung the cardboard over the doorknob. It read clearly: CLOSED. GRADUATION.

My dress fitted perfectly and everyone said that I looked 7
like a sunbeam in it. On the hill, going toward the school, Bailey walked behind with Uncle Willie, who muttered, "Go on, Ju." He wanted him to walk ahead with us because it embarrassed him to have to walk so slowly. Bailey said he'd let the ladies walk together, and the men would bring up the rear. We all laughed nicely.

Little children dashed by out of the dark like fireflies. 8
Their crepe-paper dresses and butterfly wings were not made for running and we heard more than one rip, dryly, and the regretful "uh uh" that followed.

The school blazed without gaiety. The windows seemed 9
cold and unfriendly from the lower hill. A sense of ill-fated timing crept over me, and if Momma hadn't reached for my hand I would have drifted back to Bailey and Uncle Willie, and possi-

---

[1]Bailey (3)   The author's brother.

bly beyond. She made a few slow jokes about my feet getting cold, and tugged me along to the now-strange building.

Around the front steps, assurance came back. There were   10
my fellow "greats," the graduating class. Hair brushed back, legs oiled, new dresses and pressed pleats, fresh pocket hand-kerchiefs and little handbags, all homesewn. Oh, we were up to snuff, all right. I joined my comrades and didn't even see my family go in to find seats in the crowded auditorium.

The school band struck up a march and all classes filed in   11
as had been rehearsed. We stood in front of our seats, as as-signed, and on a signal from the choir director, we sat. No sooner had this been accomplished than the band started to play the national anthem. We rose again and sang the song, af-ter which we recited the pledge of allegiance. We remained standing for a brief minute before the choir director and the principal signaled to us, rather desperately I thought, to take our seats. The command was so unusual that our carefully re-hearsed and smooth-running machine was thrown off. For a full minute we fumbled for our chairs and bumped into each other awkwardly. Habits change or solidify under pressure, so in our state of nervous tension we had been ready to follow our usual assembly pattern: the American national anthem, then the pledge of allegiance, then the song every Black person I knew called the Negro National Anthem. All done in the same key, with the same passion and most often standing on the same foot.

Finding my seat at last, I was overcome with a presenti-   12
ment of worse things to come. Something unrehearsed, un-planned, was going to happen, and we were going to be made to look bad. I distinctly remember being explicit in the choice of pronoun. It was "we," the graduating class, the unit, that con-cerned me then.

The principal welcomed "parents and friends" and asked   13
the Baptist minister to lead us in prayer. His invocation was brief and punchy, and for a second I thought we were getting on the high road to right action. When the principal came back to the dais, however, his voice had changed. Sounds always af-fected me profoundly and the principal's voice was one of my favorites. During the assembly it melted and lowed weakly into the audience. It had not been in my plan to listen to him, but my curiosity was piqued and I straightened up to give him my attention.

He was talking about Booker T. Washington, our "late   14
great leader," who said we can be as close as the fingers on the
hand, etc. . . . Then he said a few vague things about friendship and the friendship of kindly people to those less fortunate
than themselves. With that his voice nearly faded, thin, away.
Like a river diminishing to a stream and then to a trickle. But
he cleared his throat and said, "Our speaker tonight, who is
also our friend, came from Texarkana to deliver the commencement address, but due to the irregularity of the train schedule,
he's going to, as they say, 'speak and run.' " He said that we
understood and wanted the man to know that we were most
grateful for the time he was able to give us and then something
about how we were willing always to adjust to another's program, and without more ado—"I give you Mr. Edward Donleavy."

Not one but two white men came through the door off-   15
stage. The shorter one walked to the speaker's platform, and
the tall one moved to the center seat and sat down. But that
was our principal's seat, and already occupied. The dislodged
gentleman bounced around for a long breath or two before the
Baptist minister gave him his chair, then with more dignity
than the situation deserved, the minister walked off the stage.

Donleavy looked at the audience once (on reflection, I'm   16
sure that he wanted only to reassure himself that we were really there), adjusted his glasses and began to read from a sheaf
of papers.

He was glad "to be here and to see the work going on just   17
as it was in the other schools."

At the first "Amen" from the audience I willed the offender   18
to immediate death by choking on the word. But Amens and
Yes, sir's began to fall around the room like rain through a
ragged umbrella.

He told us of the wonderful changes we children in   19
Stamps[2] had in store. The Central School (naturally, the white
school was Central) had already been granted improvements
that would be in use in the fall. A well-known artist was coming
from Little Rock to teach art to them. They were going to have
the newest microscopes and chemistry equipment for their laboratory. Mr. Donleavy didn't leave us long in the dark over who

---

[2]Stamps (19)   Town in Arkansas.

made these improvements available to Central High. Nor were we to be ignored in the general betterment scheme he had in mind.

He said that he had pointed out to people at a very high   20
level that one of the first-line football tacklers at Arkansas Agricultural and Mechanical College had graduated from good old Lafayette County Training School. Here fewer Amen's were heard. Those few that did break through lay dully in the air with the heaviness of habit.

He went on to praise us. He went on to say how he had   21
bragged that "one of the best basketball players at Fisk sank his first ball right here at Lafayette County Training School."

The white kids were going to have a chance to become   22
Galileos and Madame Curies and Edisons and Gauguins, and our boys (the girls weren't even in on it) would try to be Jesse Owenses and Joe Louises.

Owens and the Brown Bomber were great heroes in our   23
world, but what school official in the white-goddom[3] of Little Rock had the right to decide that those two men must be our only heroes? Who decided that for Henry Reed to become a scientist he had to work like George Washington Carver, as a bootblack, to buy a lousy microscope? Bailey was obviously always going to be too small to be an athlete, so which concrete angel glued to what country seat had decided that if my brother wanted to become a lawyer he had to first pay penance for his skin by picking cotton and hoeing corn and studying correspondence books at night for twenty years?

The man's dead words fell like bricks around the audito-   24
rium and too many settled in my belly. Constrained by hard-learning manners I couldn't look behind me, but to my left and right the proud graduating class of 1940 had dropped their heads. Every girl in my row had found something new to do with her handkerchief. Some folded the tiny squares into love knots, some into triangles, but most were wadding them, then pressing them flat on their yellow laps.

On the dais, the ancient tragedy was being replayed. Pro-   25
fessor Parsons sat, a sculptor's reject, rigid. His large, heavy body seemed devoid of will or willingness, and his eyes said he was no longer with us. The other teachers examined the flag (which was draped stage right) or their notes, or the windows which opened on our now-famous playing diamond.

[3]white-goddom   (23)   Top white policy makers.

Graduation, the hush-hush magic time of frills and gifts   26
and congratulations and diplomas, was finished for me before
my name was called. The accomplishment was nothing. The
meticulous maps, drawn in three colors of ink, learning and
spelling decasyllabic words, memorizing the whole of *The Rape
of Lucrece*[4]—it was for nothing. Donleavy had exposed us.

We were maids and farmers, handymen and washer-   27
women, and anything higher that we aspired to was farcical
and presumptuous.

Then I wished that Gabriel Prosser and Nat Turner[5] had   28
killed all whitefolks in their beds and that Abraham Lincoln
had been assassinated before the signing of the Emancipation
Proclamation, and that Harriet Tubman[6] had been killed by
that blow on her head and Christopher Columbus had drowned
in the *Santa Maria.*

It was awful to be a Negro and have no control over my   29
life. It was brutal to be young and already trained to sit quietly
and listen to charges brought against my color with no chance
of defense. We should all be dead. I thought I should like to see
us all dead, one on top of the other. A pyramid of flesh with the
whitefolks on the bottom, as the broad base, then the Indians
with their silly tomahawks and teepees and wigwams and
treaties, the Negroes with their mops and recipes and cotton
sacks and spirituals sticking out of their mouths. The Dutch
children should all stumble in their wooden shoes and break
their necks. The French should choke to death on the
Louisiana Purchase (1803) while silkworms ate all the Chinese
with their stupid pigtails. As a species, we were an abomina-
tion. All of us.

Donleavy was running for election, and assured our par-   30
ents that if he won we could count on having the only colored
paved playing field in that part of Arkansas. Also—he never
looked up to acknowledge the grunts of acceptance—also, we
were bound to get some new equipment for the home economics building and the workshop.

He finished, and since there was no need to give any more   31
than the most perfunctory thank-you's, he nodded to the men
on the stage, and the tall white man who was never introduced

[4]*The Rape of Lucrece* (26)   Long narrative poem by William Shakespeare.
[5]Gabriel Prosser and Nat Turner (28)   Leaders of slave rebellion in the
early 1800s in Virginia.
[6]Harriet Tubman (28)   Popular Underground Railroad leader who led over
three hundred slaves to freedom.

joined him at the door. They left with the attitude that now they were off to something really important. (The graduation ceremonies at Lafayette County Training School had been a mere preliminary.)

The ugliness they left was palpable. An uninvited guest   32
who wouldn't leave. The choir was summoned and sang a modern arrangement of "Onward, Christian Soldiers," with new words pertaining to graduates seeking their place in the world. But it didn't work. Elouise, the daughter of the Baptist minister, recited "Invictus"[7] and I could have cried at the impertinence of "I am the master of my fate, I am the captain of my soul."

My name had lost its ring of familiarity and I had to be   33
nudged to go and receive my diploma. All my preparations had fled. I neither marched up to the stage like a conquering Amazon, nor did I look in the audience for Bailey's nod of approval. Marguerite Johnson, I heard the name again, my honors were read, there were noises in the audience of appreciation, and I took my place on the stage as rehearsed.

I thought about colors I hated: ecru, puce, lavender, beige   34
and black.

There was shuffling and rustling around me, then Henry   35
Reed was giving his valedictory address, "To Be or Not to Be." Hadn't he heard the whitefolks? We couldn't *be*, so the question was a waste of time. Henry's voice came out clear and strong. I feared to look at him. Hadn't he got the message? There was no "nobler in the mind" for Negroes because the world didn't think we had minds, and they let us know it. "Outrageous fortune"? Now, that was a joke. When the ceremony was over I had to tell Henry Reed some things. That is, if I still cared, Not "rub," Henry, "erase." "Ah, there's the erase." Us.

Henry had been a good student in elocution. His voice rose   36
on tides of promise and fell on waves of warnings. The English teacher had helped him to create a sermon winging through Hamlet's soliloquy. To be a man, a doer, a builder, a leader, or to be a tool, an unfunny joke, a crusher of funky toadstools. I marveled that Henry could go through with the speech as if we had a choice.

I had been listening and silently rebutting each sentence   37
with my eyes closed; then there was a hush, which in an audience warns that something unplanned is happening. I looked

---

[7]"Invictus" (32)   Poem by William Ernest Henley.

up and saw Henry Reed, the conservative, the proper, the A student, turn his back to the audience and turn to us (the proud graduating class of 1940) and sing, nearly speaking,

> "Lift ev'ry voice and sing
> Till earth and heaven ring
> Ring with the harmonies of Liberty . . . "

It was the poem written by James Weldon Johnson. It was the music composed by J. Rosamond Johnson. It was the Negro National Anthem. Out of habit we were singing it.

Our mothers and fathers stood in the dark hall and joined   38
the hymn of encouragement. A kindergarten teacher led the small children onto the stage and the buttercups and daisies and bunny rabbits marked time and tried to follow:

> "Stony the road we trod
> Bitter the chastening rod
> Felt in the days when hope, unborn, had died.
> Yet with a steady beat
> Have not our weary feet
> Come to the place for which our fathers sighed?"

Each child I knew had learned that song with his ABC's   39
and along with "Jesus Loves Me This I Know." But I personally had never heard it before. Never heard the words, despite the thousands of times I had sung them. Never thought they had anything to do with me.

On the other hand, the words of Patrick Henry had made   40
such an impression on me that I had been able to stretch myself tall and trembling and say, "I know not what course others may take, but as for me, give me liberty or give me death."

And now I heard, really for the first time: 41

> "We have come over a way that with tears
> has been watered,
> We have come, treading our path through
> the blood of the slaughtered."

While echoes of the song shivered in the air, Henry Reed   42
bowed his head, said "Thank you," and returned to his place in the line. The tears that slipped down many faces were not wiped away in shame.

We were on top again. As always, again. We survived. The   43
depths had been icy and dark, but now a bright sun spoke to
our souls. I was no longer simply a member of the proud graduating class of 1940; I was a proud member of the wonderful,
beautiful Negro race.

Oh, Black known and unknown poets, how often have   44
your auctioned pains sustained us? Who will compute the
lonely nights made less lonely by your songs, or the empty pots
made less tragic by your tales?

If we were a people much given to revealing secrets, we   45
might raise monuments and sacrifice to the memories of our
poets, but slavery cured us of that weakness. It may be
enough, however, to have it said that we survive in exact relationship to the dedication of our poets (include preachers, musicians and blues singers).

Discussion Questions

1. How is Marguerite different at the end of the graduation speech
   than she is at the beginning of the ceremony?
2. To what extent does Mr. Donleavy's "promised gift" reflect his
   racist views?
3. How does Mr. Donleavy's speech spoil the hopes and dreams of
   the graduates and their families?
4. How appropriate to the occasion is Henry Reed's valedictory address?
5. Why does the singing of "Lift Every Voice and Sing" renew the
   graduates' hopes and lift their spirits?
6. What does Marguerite mean when she says that she had never
   heard the song even though she had sung it a thousand times?
7. Angelou uses many rhetorical strategies—narration, comparison-
   contrast, cause and effect, and description—to make her point.
   How does each contribute to the reader's understanding and appreciation of the story?
8. What do you think is a major theme of the story?

Writing Assignments

1. Write an essay in which you contrast a mood of anticipation that
   you have experienced with a later one of disappointment.
2. Write an essay describing something memorable about your
   graduation.
3. Write an essay about a time when something or someone caused
   you to feel better about something that had previously depressed
   you.

Student Essay:
STONE CITY

Jerome Mason

Vocabulary

forged	(4)	walked slowly, but steadily
synchronized	(6)	harmonized, blended

Being successful can mean different things to different people. 1
To some people it can mean getting a great job, or accumulating a large sum of money; to others it can mean achieving some
other goal that a person feels is important. In my life, I have
had as many successes as failures, some big and some small.
The most important things that I have accomplished are very
personal things that give meaning to my life, such as being admitted to the University of Wisconsin-Milwaukee (UWM). It
meant more to me than just being able to further my educational horizons; it was a fulfillment of a childhood dream.

Most of my childhood was spent living in a house on the 2
east side of Milwaukee, a little over a mile away from the university in a section of town now called Riverwest. The area has
lots of parks and trails alongside the Milwaukee River. When I
was about nine, I used to go to those nearby parks with my
older brother and his friends when they would let me go with
them. We would hike up and down the trails as if we were on
an expedition into the wild of some far-off country. Mostly, we
would end up down by the river catching frogs or turtles or
whatever we could find. We would always stay on the west side
of the Locust Street Bridge because our mother would not allow
us to go on the other side by ourselves. Of course, I often
crossed the bridge in the family car, but I had never gone over
it on foot.

Then one morning on the way to school, my buddy sug- 3
gested that we go to the other side of the bridge. I had never
skipped school, but the idea of going on an adventure sounded
much more exciting than school. We took an alternate route to
school so that none of the other kids would see us as we set
out to see just what lay ahead on the other side of that bridge.

We forged across the long bridge, which, at the time, 4
seemed like the link to another world. It felt as if we were ex-

ploring strange new territories, discovering a new land unknown to the rest of the world. In a childlike way, we were doing just that. Just on the other side of the bridge was a long concrete trail close to the river. We wandered down the trail for a while and then decided to climb up the riverbank to see what was at the top.

When we reached the peak, not too far off in the distance,   5 we spotted three huge stone buildings towering over the tops of the neighboring houses. There was no question that this was the direction in which we wanted to head. To keep a low profile, we stuck to the back streets and alleys as much as possible. When we reached the street where the huge buildings stood, we came upon an awesome sight: a large isolated community, which seemed to us to be a stone city. We had to investigate and find out more about this mysterious place. We explored a couple of the buildings and saw people in large classrooms that looked like movie theaters. The doors to all the buildings were open, so we just roamed around, going from building to building.

One of the buildings was more like a shopping mall with-   6 out the department stores; it had lots of restaurants and offices, and there was even a recreation room and a bowling alley in the basement. This is the building where we found lots of people "hanging out." They seemed to be coming from every direction. Some were studying big books, and others were eating and talking. The motion of the people appeared almost chaotic, yet synchronized. Everything they were doing seemed to be important, exciting; they just seemed to be enjoying themselves as if they were at a carnival or something. I was feeding on the intensity of it all. I felt like there was an electric current flowing through my veins. It was as if I was in the place where the people ran the world. This was living!

No one said anything to us, and we figured that we were   7 safe, since we were far from anybody who would recognize us. We were wrong. Someone had recognized us. A student teacher who had recently completed his field placement in our classroom came over and asked us why we were not in school. We were caught! The adventure was over. We told him the truth in hopes that he wouldn't take us back to school to be punished.

He didn't take us back to the school, but he told us that   8 he was going to telephone later to see if we had made it without him. On the way back, I was worried about facing the consequences, but I was also glad we had found out what a university was like. I had become enlightened. I had discovered a whole other world on the far side of that bridge that I never even knew existed.

This experience greatly influenced me. After my adventure, 9 I became fascinated with the university. Every chance I could get to go over there, I took. I found out that the university offered summer youth programs, which I attended every year after that while I was in grade school. Being involved in these activities was important to me because it made me feel connected to the university. In my mind, UWM was the place to be if you wanted to be more than just average; it was the place to be if you wanted to be great.

In the community where I grew up, there wasn't a strong 10 emphasis on education at the college level. I didn't know of any professional people in my neighborhood outside of my teachers at school who had careers that required a college degree. Sadly, as time passed, I began to feel that it was unrealistic for me to think that I would ever be able to have a chance to do something like go to college. I started to feel as though college, careers, and things like that were only for privileged, well-to-do white people. They were not for a fairly average, everyday young black male like me. Therefore, I started losing interest in school and had lost interest completely by the time I was midway through high school. I stopped thinking about ever going to college; it seemed way beyond my reach.

I eventually dropped out of high school and ended up go- 11 ing to an alternative school where I received my general equivalency diploma (G.E.D.). By the time I had turned eighteen, all of my childhood dreams of going to college one day and becoming successful had completely faded.

When I entered the work force, I had no direction, nor did 12 I have any idea of what kind of work I wanted to do. I just took whatever jobs were offered to me, even though not one of those jobs seemed to satisfy or replace the feeling of being connected to something important, like that feeling I had as a child visiting the great stone city.

After several years of going through life's ups and downs, I 13 decided that it was time for me to pursue what was really important to me. It was time to fulfill my life's dreams. At twenty-five, I enrolled in the human services program at the Milwaukee Area Technical College. When I completed my studies there, I transferred to the social welfare program at the University of Wisconsin-Milwaukee. When I was accepted at the university, it was like a dream come true. Although I do plan to graduate and go on to do other things, I have already achieved personal success. To me, being successful is achieving your own personal dreams, whatever they may be.

Discussion Questions

1. Why were the writer's descriptions of the stone city particularly effective? To what extent did the author's first time experience affect his description of it?
2. What were the circumstances that led the author to UWM for the first time?
3. What fascinated the author about the university?
4. Some people reading this story would say that skipping school may have saved the narrator's life. Would you agree with such an assessment? Why or why not?
5. Why did the author's hopes of attending the university fade as he grew older and entered high school?
6. What do you learn about the narrator as a result of the decisions that he made?
7. What predominant rhetorical strategies does the writer use in developing his essay?
8. What type of beginning does Mason use to introduce his essay?

Writing Assignments

1. Write an essay in which you show how the decisions that some of us make reveal much about the kind of people we are.
2. Write an essay discussing a fulfilled (or unfulfilled) childhood dream.

8

Family

MOTHER TO SON

Langston Hughes

Langston Hughes (1902–1967) was born in Joplin, Missouri. As an undergraduate, he attended both Columbia University and Lincoln University. In 1921, he published in the Crisis *his famous poem, "The Negro Speaks of Rivers." He published his first book of poetry,* The Weary Blues, *in 1926 and his second volume,* Fine Clothes to the Jew, *in 1927. In the 1940s, he created the memorable Jesse B. Semple, a humorous character who speaks straightforwardly about the African American experience. The following selection, from Langston Hughes's* Selected Poems *(1926), offers sound advice to youth in any generation: Life is a constant struggle.*

> Well, son, I'll tell you:
> Life for me ain't been no crystal stair.
> It's had tacks in it,
> And splinters,
> And boards torn up,   5
> And places with no carpet on the floor—
> Bare.

But all the time
I'se been a-climbin' on,
And reachin' landin's,   10
And turnin' corners,
And sometimes goin' in the dark
Where there ain't been no light.
So boy, don't you turn back.
Don't you set down on the steps   15
'Cause you finds it's kinder hard.
Don't you fall now—
For I'se still goin', honey.
I'se still climbin',
And life for me ain't been no crystal stair.   20

Discussion Questions

1. Other than thc obvious relationship between mother and son, what other relationship(s) does the poem suggest?
2. Why do you think the author uses a colon in the first line?
3. How do the images of crystal stairs and torn-up stairs symbolize one's struggle in life?
4. What is the mother's advice to the son?
5. How is the mother a role model for her son?
6. How does the mother feel about facing obstacles?
7. How does Hughes use comparison and contrast in the poem?
8. Do you think the author's use of dialect is effective? Why or why not?

Writing Assignments

1. In an essay, write about an image, such as a river or a tree, that helps describe your life.
2. In an essay, discuss some useful advice you once received from your mother or from some other elder.
3. In an essay, describe a time when you decided not to follow the advice of one of your parents. Also discuss the consequences of your decision.

SUCH A PARADISE THAT I LIVED

Jamaica Kincaid

Jamaica Kincaid (1949–   ) was born in St. John's, Antigua, to a Carib-Indian mother from Dominica. In 1966, she came to the United States to complete her education and decided to stay. She has written for such magazines as Ms., *the* New Yorker, Rolling Stone, *and* Paris Review. *Her works include* At the Bottom of the River *(1983) and her most recent novel is* Lucy *(1991). The following excerpt, taken from her second book* Annie John *(1985), is a semi-autobiographical account of the warm and loving relationship that exists among a young girl, her mother, and her father.*

Vocabulary

chemise (1) a loose-fitting dress

1

From time to time, my mother would fix on a certain place in our house and give it a good cleaning. If I was at home when she happened to do this, I was at her side, as usual. When she did this with the trunk, it was a tremendous pleasure, for after she had removed all the things from the trunk, and aired them out, and changed the camphor balls,[1] and then refolded the things and put them back in their places in the trunk, as she held each thing in her hand she would tell me a story about myself. Sometimes I knew the story first hand, for I could remember the incident quite well; sometimes what she told me had happened when I was too young to know anything; and sometimes it happened before I was even born. Whichever way, I knew exactly what she would say, for I had heard it so many times before, but I never got tired of it. For instance, the flowers on the chemise, the first garment I wore after being born, were not put on correctly, and that is because when my mother was embroidering them I kicked so much that her hand was unsteady. My mother said that usually when I kicked around in her stomach and she told me to stop I would, but on that day I paid no attention at all. When she told me this story, she

[1] camphor balls (1) Crystalline balls used to keep away insects.

would smile at me and say, "You see, even then you were hard to manage." It pleased me to think that, before she could see my face, my mother spoke to me in the same way she did now. On and on my mother would go. No small part of my life was so unimportant that she hadn't made a note of it, and now she would tell it to me over and over again. I would sit next to her and she would show me the very dress I wore on the day I bit another child my age with whom I was playing. "Your biting phase," she called it. Or the day she warned me not to play around the coal pot, because I liked to sing to myself and dance around the fire. Two seconds later, I fell into the hot coals, burning my elbows. My mother cried when she saw that it wasn't serious, and now, as she told me about it, she would kiss the little black patches of scars on my elbows.

As she told me the stories, I sometimes sat at her side,   2
leaning against her, or I would crouch on my knees behind her back and lean over her shoulder. As I did this, I would occasionally sniff at her neck, or behind her ears, or at her hair. She smelled sometimes of lemons, sometimes of sage, sometimes of roses, sometimes of bay leaf. At times I would no longer hear what it was she was saying; I just liked to look at her mouth as it opened and closed over words, or as she laughed. How terrible it must be for all the people who had no one to love them so and no one whom they loved so, I thought. My father, for instance. When he was a little boy, his parents, after kissing him goodbye and leaving him with his grandmother, boarded a boat and sailed to South America. He never saw them again, though they wrote to him and sent him presents—packages of clothes on his birthday and at Christmas. He then grew to love his grandmother, and she loved him, for she took care of him and worked hard at keeping him well fed and clothed. From the beginning, they slept in the same bed, and as he became a young man they continued to do so. When he was no longer in school and had started working, every night, after he and his grandmother had eaten their dinner, my father would go off to visit his friends. He would then return home at around midnight and fall asleep next to his grandmother. In the morning, his grandmother would awake at half past five or so, a half hour before my father, and prepare his bath and breakfast and make everything proper and ready for him, so that at seven o'clock sharp he stepped out the door off to work. One morning, though, he overslept, because his grandmother didn't wake him up. When he awoke, she was still lying next to

him. When he tried to wake her, he couldn't. She had died lying next to him sometime during the night. Even though he was overcome with grief, he built her coffin and made sure she had a nice funeral. He never slept in that bed again, and shortly afterward he moved out of that house. He was eighteen years old then.

When my father first told me this story, I threw myself at him at the end of it, and we both started to cry—he just a little, I quite a lot. It was a Sunday afternoon; he and my mother and I had gone for a walk in the botanical gardens. My mother had wandered off to look at some strange kind of thistle, and we could see her as she bent over the bushes to get a closer look and reach out to touch the leaves of the plant. When she returned to us and saw that we had both been crying, she started to get quite worked up, but my father quickly told her what had happened and she laughed at us and called us her little fools. But then she took me in her arms and kissed me, and she said that I needn't worry about such a thing as her sailing off or dying and leaving me all alone in the world. But if ever after that I saw my father sitting alone with a faraway look on his face, I was filled with pity for him. He had been alone in the world all that time, what with his mother sailing off on a boat with his father and his never seeing her again, and then his grandmother dying while lying next to him in the middle of the night. It was more than anyone should have to bear. I loved him so and wished that I had a mother to give him, for, no matter how much my own mother loved him, it could never be the same.

When my mother got through with the trunk, and I had heard again and again just what I had been like and who had said what to me at what point in my life, I was given my tea—a cup of cocoa and a buttered bun. My father by then would return home from work, and he was given his tea. As my mother went around preparing our supper, picking up clothes from the stone heap, or taking clothes off the clothesline, I would sit in a corner of our yard and watch her. She never stood still. Her powerful legs carried her from one part of the yard to the other, and in and out of the house. Sometimes she might call out to me to go and get some thyme or basil or some other herb for her, for she grew all her herbs in little pots that she kept in a corner of our little garden. Sometimes when I gave her the herbs, she might stoop down and kiss me on my lips and then on my neck. It was in such a paradise that I lived.

Discussion Questions

1. How does cleaning become a time of bonding for Annie and her mother?
2. What kind of relationship exists among Annie, her mother, and her father?
3. How does the story of Annie's paternal great-grandmother relate to the rest of the story?
4. Why does Annie admire her mother?
5. What strategy (or strategies) does Kincaid use to convince her readers that she lived in a paradise as a young child?
6. How effective is Kincaid's placement of her thesis as the last sentence in the essay?

Writing Assignments

1. Write an essay about a special time in your childhood.
2. In an essay, recount a special bonding time between you and someone you love.
3. Write an essay about a memorable object that belongs to you or your family.

THOSE WINTER SUNDAYS

Robert Hayden

Born in Detroit, Michigan, Robert Hayden (1913–1980) attended Wayne State University as an undergraduate and received his M.A. from the University of Michigan. He taught English at Fisk University and at the University of Michigan. Hayden published the following books of poetry: Heart-Shape in the Dust (1940), A Ballad of Remembrance (1962), Selected Poems (1966), and Words in the Mourning Time (1971). Some of his most memorable poems are those concerning slavery that appear in the 1966 volume: "Runagate Runagate," "Middle Passage," and "Frederick Douglass." The following selection, first published in Angels and Accents: New and Selected Poems (1975), recounts an African American youth's recollection of his harsh, but loving childhood environment.

Vocabulary

chronic (9) occurring frequently, continuing for long periods of time

austere (14) strict or harsh

Sundays too my father got up early
and put his clothes on in the blueblack cold,
then with cracked hands that ached
from labor in the weekday weather made
banked fires blaze. No one ever thanked him.   5
I'd wake and hear the cold splintering, breaking.
When the rooms were warm, he'd call,
and slowly I would rise and dress,
fearing the chronic angers of that house,
Speaking indifferently to him,   10
who had driven out the cold
and polished my good shoes as well.
What did I know, what did I know
of love's austere and lonely offices?

Discussion Questions

1. What is the relationship between the speaker of the poem (the persona) and his father?

2. What kind of man is the persona's father?

3. What is the meaning of the line, "speaking indifferently to him"?

4. What is the meaning of the speaker's statement, "I would rise and dress, fearing the chronic angers of that house"?

5. What does the speaker realize now that he did not realize as a young child?

6. How is illustration used effectively to show the father's love is one that is demonstrated, not stated?

7. How effective is Hayden's use of a question to end his poem?

Writing Assignments

1. Often, appreciation for others' good deeds on your behalf comes well after the deeds are done. Write an essay discussing this idea.

2. Think of a pleasant time in your past and write an essay describing it.

3. In an essay, discuss the feelings you have (or once had) about an idol or role model.

INTEGRATED HOUSING: AN EXPLODED DREAM?

Lorraine Hansberry

*Born in Chicago, Illinois, Lorraine Hansberry (1930–1965)
became interested in the theatre while still in high school.
She studied stage design and drama from 1948 to 1950 at
the University of Wisconsin. Her first play,* A Raisin in the
Sun, *from which the following selection is taken, won the
New York Drama Critics' Circle Award for best play of
1959. She was the first African American playwright to win
this award. In 1973, the play was revived as a musical and
won a Tony Award. Her other play,* The Sign in Sidney
Brustein's Window, *was produced in 1965. Hansberry died
of cancer at the young age of 34. "Integrated Housing: An
Exploded Dream?" concerns the Younger family's joyous
anticipation of moving to a better neighborhood, but this joy
is dampened by the news that the "better neighborhood"
does not want "Negroes" living there.*

Vocabulary

exuberant	(5)	joyous
burlesque	(67)	comic theatrical entertainment
pantomime	(86)	communication by means of facial and body gestures

Act II, Scene 3

TIME *Saturday, moving day, one week later.*

Before the curtain rises, RUTH's *voice, a strident, dramatic church
alto, cuts through the silence.*

*It is, in the darkness, a triumphant surge, a penetrating state-
ment of expectation: "Oh, Lord, I don't feel no ways tired! Children,
oh, glory hallelujah!"*

As the curtain rises we see that RUTH *is alone in the living room,
finishing up the family's packing. It is moving day. She is nailing
crates and tying cartons.* BENEATHA *enters, carrying a guitar case, and
watches her exuberant sister-in-law.*

RUTH HEY!
BENEATHA (*Putting away the case*) Hi.

RUTH (*Pointing at a package*) Honey—look in that package there and see what I found on sale this morning at the South Center. (RUTH *gets up and moves to the package and draws out some curtains*) Lookahere—hand-turned hems!

BENEATHA   How do you know the window size out there?

RUTH (*Who hadn't thought of that*) Oh—Well, they bound to fit   5
something in the whole house. Anyhow, they was too good a bargain to pass up. (RUTH *slaps her head, suddenly remembering something*) Oh, Bennie—I meant to put a special note on that carton over there. That's your mama's good china and she wants 'em to be very careful with it.

BENEATHA   I'll do it.

(BENEATHA *finds a piece of paper and starts to draw large letters on it*)

RUTH   You know what I'm going to do soon as I get in that new house?

BENEATHA   What?

RUTH   Honey—I'm going to run me a tub of water up to here . . . (*With her fingers practically up to her nostrils*) And I'm going to get in it—and I am going to sit . . . and sit . . . and sit in that hot water and the first person who knocks to tell *me* to hurry up and come out—

BENEATHA   Gets shot at sunrise.   10

RUTH (*Laughing happily*) You said it, sister! (*Noticing how large* BENEATHA *is absent-mindedly making the note*) Honey, they ain't going to read that from no airplane.

BENEATHA (*Laughing herself*) I guess I always think things have more emphasis if they are big, somehow.

RUTH (*Looking up at her and smiling*) You and your brother seem to have that as a philosophy of life. Lord, that man—done changed so 'round here. You know—you know what we did last night? Me and Walter Lee?

BENEATHA   What?

RUTH (*Smiling to herself*) We went to the movies. (*Looking at*   15
BENEATHA *to see if she understands*) We went to the movies. You know the last time me and Walter went to the movies together?

BENEATHA   No.

RUTH   Me neither. That's how long it been. (*Smiling again*) But we went last night. The picture wasn't much good, but that didn't seem to matter. We went—and we held hands.

BENEATHA   Oh, Lord!

RUTH   We held hands—and you know what?   20

BENEATHA   What?

RUTH When we come out of the show it was late and dark and all the stores and things was closed up . . . and it was kind of chilly and there wasn't many people on the streets . . . and we was still holding hands, me and Walter.

BENEATHA You're killing me.

(WALTER *enters with a large package. His happiness is deep in him; he cannot keep still with his new-found exuberance. He is singing and wiggling and snapping his fingers. He puts his package in a corner and puts a phonographic record, which he has brought in with him, on the record player. As the music comes up he dances over to* RUTH *and tries to get her to dance with him. She gives in at last to his raunchiness and in a fit of giggling allows herself to be drawn into his mood and together they deliberately burlesque an old social dance of their youth)*

BENEATHA (*Regarding them a long time as they dance, then drawing in her breath for a deeply exaggerated comment which she does not particularly mean*) Talk about—olddddddddddd-fashionedddddddd—Negroes!

WALTER (*Stopping momentarily*) What kind of Negroes?

(*He says this in fun. He is not angry with her today, nor with anyone. He starts to dance with his wife again*)

BENEATHA Old-fashioned.   25

WALTER (*As he dances with* RUTH) You know, when these *New Negroes* have their convention—(*Pointing at his sister*)—that is going to be the chairman of the Committee on Unending Agitation. (*He goes on dancing, then stops*) Race, race, race! . . . Girl, I do believe you are the first person in the history of the entire human race to successfully brainwash yourself. (BE-NEATHA *breaks up and he goes on dancing. He stops again, enjoying his tease*) Damn, even the N double A C P takes a holiday sometimes! (BENEATHA *and* RUTH *laugh. He dances with* RUTH *some more and starts to laugh and stops and pantomimes someone over an operating table*) I can just see that chick someday looking down at some poor cat on an operating table before she starts to slice him, saying . . . (*Pulling his sleeves back maliciously*) "By the way what are your views on civil rights down there? . . ."

He laughs at her again and starts to dance happily. The bell sounds)

BENEATHA Sticks and stones may break my bones but . . . words will never hurt me!

(BENEATHA *goes to the door and opens it as* WALTER *and* RUTH *go on with the clowning.* BENEATHA *is somewhat surprised to see a quiet-looking middle-aged white man in a business suit holding his hat and a briefcase in his hand and consulting a small piece of paper)*

MAN   Uh—how do you do, miss. I am looking for a Mrs.—(*He looks at the slip of paper*) Mrs. Lena Younger?

BENEATHA   (*Smoothing her hair with slight embarrassment*) Oh—yes, that's my mother. Excuse me. (*She closes the door and turns to quiet the other two*) Ruth! Brother! Somebody's here. (*Then she opens the door. The man casts a curious quick glance at all of them*) Uh—come in please.

MAN   (*Coming in*) Thank you.   30

BENEATHA   My mother isn't here just now. Is it business?

MAN   Yes . . . well, of a sort.

WALTER   (*Freely, the Man of the House*) Have a seat. I'm Mrs. Younger's son. I look after most of her business matters.

(RUTH *and* BENEATHA *exchange amused glances*)

MAN   (*Regarding* WALTER, *and sitting*) Well—My name is Karl Lindner . . .

WALTER   (*Stretching out his hand*) Walter Younger. This is my   35
wife—(RUTH *nods politely*)—and my sister.

LINDNER   How do you do.

WALTER   (*Amiably, as he sits himself easily on a chair, leaning with interest forward on his knees and looking expectantly into the newcomer's face*) What can we do for you, Mr. Lindner!

LINDNER   (*Some minor shuffling of the hat and briefcase on his knees*) Well—I am a representative of the Clybourne Park Improvement Association—

WALTER   (*Pointing*) Why don't you sit your things on the floor?

LINDNER   Oh—yes. Thank you. (*He slides the briefcase and hat*   40
under the chair) And as I was saying—I am from the Clybourne Park Improvement Association and we have had it brought to our attention at the last meeting that you people—or at least your mother—has bought a piece of residential property at— (*He digs for the slip of paper again*)—four o six Clybourne Street . . .

WALTER   That's right. Care for something to drink? Ruth, get Mr. Lindner a beer.

LINDNER   (*Upset for some reason*) Oh—no, really. I mean thank you very much, but no thank you.

RUTH   (*Innocently*) Some coffee?

LINDNER   Thank you, nothing at all.

(BENEATHA *is watching the man carefully*)

LINDNER   Well, I don't know how much you folks know about   45
our organization. (*He is a gentle man; thoughtful and somewhat
labored in his manner*) It is one of these community organizations set up to look after—oh, you know, things like block up-
keep and special projects and we also have what we call our
New Neighbors Orientation Committee . . .
BENEATHA   (*Drily*) Yes—and what do they do?
LINDNER   (*Turning a little to her and then returning the main
force to* WALTER) Well—it's what you might call a sort of welcoming committee, I guess. I mean they, we, I'm the chairman of
the committee—go around and see the new people who move
into the neighborhood and sort of give them the lowdown on
the way we do things out in Clybourne Park.
BENEATHA   (*With appreciation of the two meanings, which escape* RUTH *and* WALTER) Un-huh.
LINDNER   And we also have the category of what the association
calls—(*He looks elsewhere*)—uh—special community prob-
lems . . .
BENEATHA   Yes—and what are some of those?   50
WALTER   Girl, let the man talk.
LINDNER   (*With understated relief*) Thank you. I would sort of
like to explain this thing in my own way. I mean I want to ex-
plain to you in a certain way.
WALTER   Go ahead.
LINDNER   Yes. Well, I'm going to try to get right to the point. I'm
sure we'll all appreciate that in the long run.
BENEATHA   Yes.   55
WALTER   Be still now!
LINDNER   Well—
RUTH   (*Still innocently*) Would you like another chair—you don't
look comfortable.
LINDNER   (*More frustrated than annoyed*) No, thank you very
much. Please. Well—to get right to the point I—(*A great breath,
and he is off at last*) I am sure you people must be aware of
some of the incidents which have happened in various parts of
the city when colored people have moved into certain areas—
(BENEATHA *exhales heavily and starts tossing a piece of fruit up
and down in the air*) Well—because we have what I think is going to be a unique type of organization in American community
life—not only do we deplore that kind of thing—but we are trying to do something about it. (BENEATHA *stops tossing and turns
with a new and quizzical interest to the man*) We feel—(*Gaining

confidence in his mission because of the interest in the faces of the people he is talking to)—we feel that most of the trouble in this world, when you come right down to it—(*He hits his knee for emphasis*)—most of the trouble exists because people just don't sit down and talk to each other.

RUTH (*Nodding as she might in church, pleased with the remark*) You can say that again, mister.   60

LINDNER (*More encouraged by such affirmation*) That we don't try hard enough in this world to understand the other fellow's problem. The other guy's point of view.

RUTH Now that's right.

(BENEATHA *and* WALTER *merely watch and listen with genuine interest*)

LINDNER Yes—that's the way we feel out in Clybourne Park. And that's why I was elected to come here this afternoon and talk to you people. Friendly like, you know, the way people should talk to each other and see if we couldn't find some way to work this thing out. As I say, the whole business is a matter of *caring* about the other fellow. Anybody can see that you are a nice family of folks, hard working and honest I'm sure. (BE-NEATHA *frowns slightly, quizzically, her head tilted regarding him*) Today everybody knows what it means to be on the outside of *something*. And of course, there is always somebody who is out to take the advantage of people who don't always understand.

WALTER What do you mean?

LINDNER Well—you see our community is made up of people   65
who've worked hard as the dickens for years to build up that little community. They're not rich and fancy people; just hard-working, honest people who don't really have much but those little homes and a dream of the kind of community they want to raise their children in. Now, I don't say we are perfect and there is a lot wrong in some of the things they want. But you've got to admit that a man, right or wrong, has the right to want to have the neighborhood he lives in a certain kind of way. And at the moment the overwhelming majority of our people out there feel that people get along better, take more of a common interest in the life of the community, when they share a common background. I want you to believe me when I tell you that race prejudice simply doesn't enter into it. It is a matter of the people of Clybourne Park believing, rightly or wrongly, as I say, that for the happiness of all concerned that our Negro families are happier when they live in their own communities.

BENEATHA *(With a grand and bitter gesture)* This, friends, is the Welcoming Committee!

WALTER *(Dumfounded, looking at* LINDNER*)* Is this what you came marching all the way over here to tell us?

LINDNER Well, now we've been having a fine conversation. I hope you'll hear me all the way through.

WALTER *(Tightly)* Go ahead, man.

LINDNER You see—in the face of all things I have said, we are   70 prepared to make your family a very generous offer . . .

BENEATHA Thirty pieces and not a coin less!

WALTER Yeah?

LINDNER *(Putting on his glasses and drawing a form out of the briefcase)* Our association is prepared, through the collective effort of our people, to buy the house from you at a financial gain to your family.

RUTH Lord have mercy, ain't this the living gall!

WALTER All right, you through?   75

LINDNER Well, I want to give you the exact terms of the financial arrangement—

WALTER We don't want to hear no exact terms of no arrangements. I want to know if you got any more to tell us 'bout getting together?

LINDNER *(Taking off his glasses)* Well—I don't suppose that you feel . . .

WALTER Never mind how I feel—you got any more to say 'bout how people ought to sit down and talk to each other? . . . Get out of my house, man.

(He turns his back and walks to the door)

LINDNER *(Looking around at the hostile faces and reaching and*   80 *assembling his hat and briefcase)* Well—I don't understand why you people are reacting this way. What do you think you are going to gain by moving into a neighborhood where you just aren't wanted and where some elements—well—people can get awful worked up when they feel that their whole way of life and everything they've ever worked for is threatened.

WALTER Get out.

LINDNER *(At the door, holding a small card)* Well—I'm sorry it went like this.

WALTER Get out.

LINDNER *(Almost sadly regarding* WALTER*)* You just can't force people to change their hearts, son.

(He turns and puts his card on a table and exits. WALTER *pushes*

the door to with stinging hatred, and stands looking at it. RUTH *just sits and* BENEATHA *just stands. They say nothing.*

. . . .

[*Later* WALTER's *friend* BOBO *visits and brings disturbing news.*] 85
RUTH   Why don't you answer the door, man?
WALTER   (*Suddenly bounding across the floor to her*) 'Cause sometimes it hard to let the future begin! (*Stooping down in her face*)
I got wings! You got Wings!
All God's children got wings!
(*He crosses to the door and throws it open. Standing there is a very slight little man in a not too prosperous business suit and with haunted frightened eyes and a hat pulled down tightly, brim up, around his forehead.* WALTER *leans deep in the man's face, still in his jubilance*)
When I get to heaven gonna put on my wings,
Gonna fly all over God's heaven . . .
(*The little man just stares at him*)
Heaven—
(*Suddenly he stops and looks past the little man into the empty hallway*) Where's Willy, man?
BOBO   He ain't with me.
WALTER   (*Not disturbed*) Oh—come on in. You know my wife.
BOBO   (*Dumbly, taking off his hat*) Yes—h'you, Miss Ruth.
RUTH   (*Quietly, a mood apart from her husband already, seeing* 90
BOBO) Hello, Bobo.
WALTER   You right on time today . . . Right on time. That's the way! (*He slaps* BOBO *on his back*) Sit down . . . lemme hear.
(RUTH *stands stiffly and quietly in back of them, as though somehow she senses death, her eyes fixed on her husband*)
BOBO   (*His frightened eyes on the floor, his hat in his hands*) Could I please get a drink of water, before I tell you about it, Walter Lee?
(WALTER *does not take his eyes off the man.* RUTH *goes blindly to the tap and gets a glass of water and brings it to* BOBO)
WALTER   There ain't nothing wrong, is there?
BOBO   Lemme tell you—
WALTER   Man—didn't nothing go wrong? 95
BOBO   Lemme tell you—Walter Lee. (*Looking at* RUTH *and talking to her more than to* WALTER) You know how it was. I got to tell you how it was. I mean first I got to tell you how it was all the way . . . I mean about the money I put in, Walter Lee . . .

WALTER (*With taut agitation now*) What about the money you put in?

BOBO Well—it wasn't much as we told you—me and Willy—(*He stops*) I'm sorry, Walter. I got a bad feeling about it. I got a real bad feeling about it . . .

WALTER Man, what you telling me about all this for? . . . Tell me what happened in Springfield . . .

BOBO Springfield. 100

RUTH (*Like a dead woman*) What was supposed to happen in Springfield?

BOBO (*To her*) This deal that me and Walter went into with Willy—Me and Willy was going to go down to Springfield and spread some money 'round so's we wouldn't have to wait so long for the liquor license . . . That's what we were going to do. Everybody said that was the way you had to do, understand, Miss Ruth?

WALTER Man—what happened down there?

BOBO (*A pitiful man, near tears*) I'm trying to tell you, Walter.

WALTER (*Screaming at him suddenly*) THEN TELL ME, GOD- 105 DAMMIT . . . WHAT'S THE MATTER WITH YOU?

BOBO Man . . . I didn't go to no Springfield, yesterday.

WALTER (*Halted, life hanging in the moment*) Why not?

BOBO (*The long way, the hard way to tell*) 'Cause I didn't have no reasons to . . .

WALTER Man, what are you talking about!

BOBO I'm talking about the fact that when I got to the train 110 station yesterday morning—eight o'clock like we planned . . . Man—*Willy didn't never show up.*

WALTER Why . . . where was he . . . where is he?

BOBO That's what I'm trying to tell you . . . I don't know . . . I waited six hours . . . (*Breaking into tears*) That was all the extra money I had in the world . . . (*Looking up at* WALTER *with the tears running down his face*) Man, Willy is gone.

WALTER Gone, what you mean Willy is gone? Gone where? You mean he went by himself. You mean he went off to Springfield by himself—to take care of getting the license—(*Turns and looks anxiously at* RUTH) You mean maybe he didn't want too many people in on the business down there? (*Looks to* RUTH *again, as before*) You know Willy got his own ways. (*Looks back to* BOBO) Maybe you was late yesterday and he just went on down there without you. Maybe—maybe—he's been callin' you at home tryin' to tell you what happened or something. Maybe—maybe—he just got sick. He's somewhere—he's got to be somewhere. We just got to find him—me and you got to find him. (*Grabs* BOBO *senselessly by the collar and starts to shake him*) We got to!

BOBO (*In sudden angry, frightened agony*) What's the matter with you, Walter! *When a cat take off with your money he don't leave you no maps!*

WALTER (*Turning madly, as though he is looking for* WILLY *in the very room*) Willy! . . . Willy . . . don't do it . . . Please don't do it . . . Man, not with that money . . . Man, please not with that money . . . Oh, God . . . Don't let it be true . . . (*He is wandering around, crying out for* WILLY *and looking for him or perhaps for help from God*) Man . . . I trusted you . . . Man, I put my life in your hands . . . (*He starts to crumble down on the floor as* RUTH *just covers her face in horror,* MAMA *opens the door and comes into the room, with* BENEATHA *behind her*) Man . . . (*He starts to pound the floor with his fists, sobbing wildly*) *That money is made out of my father's flesh . . .* 115

BOBO (*Standing over him helplessly*) I'm sorry, Walter . . . (*Only* WALTER's *sobs reply.* BOBO *puts on his hat*) I had my life staked on this deal, too . . .

(*He exits*)

MAMA (*To* WALTER) Son—(*She goes to him, bends down to him, talks to his bent head*) Son . . . Is it gone? Son, I gave you sixty-five hundred dollars. Is it gone? All of it? Beneatha's money too?

WALTER (*Lifting his head slowly*) Mama . . . I never . . . went to the bank at all . . .

MAMA (*Not wanting to believe him*) You mean . . . your sister's school money . . . you used that too . . . Walter?

WALTER Yessss! . . . All of it . . . It's all gone . . . 120

(*There is total silence,* RUTH *stands with her face covered with her hands;* BENEATHA *leans forlornly against a wall, fingering a piece of red ribbon from the mother's gift.* MAMA *stops and looks at her son without recognition and then, quite without thinking about it, starts to beat him senselessly in the face.* BENEATHA *goes to them and stops it*)

BENEATHA Mama!

(MAMA *stops and looks at both of her children and rises slowly and wanders vaguely, aimlessly away from them*)

MAMA I seen . . . him . . . night after night . . . come in . . . and look at that rug . . . and then look at me . . . the red showing in his eyes . . . the veins moving in his head . . . I seen him grow thin and old before he was forty . . . working

and working and working like somebody's old horse . . .
killing himself . . . and you—you give it all away in a day . . .
BENEATHA Mama—
MAMA Oh, God . . . (*She looks up at Him*) Look down here—
and show me the strength.
BENEATHA Mama—
MAMA (*Folding over*) Strength . . .
BENEATHA (*Plaintively*) Mama . . .   125
MAMA Strength!

CURTAIN

Discussion Questions

1. What is the mood of the Younger family before Mr. Lindner's visit?
   Use specific examples from the play to support your answer.
2. What is the Clybourne Park Improvement Association?
3. What proposal does Mr. Lindner have for the Younger family?
4. What are the two strategies Mr. Lindner uses to persuade the
   Younger family not to move?
5. How do Ruth, Walter, and Beneatha react to Mr. Lindner's offer?
6. What bad news does Bobo give Walter Lee?
7. To develop her theme, Hansberry uses many rhetorical strategies, including illustration, comparison and contrast, and cause
   and effect. How can you argue that cause and effect is the dominant strategy?
8. How would a poem or short story about the Younger family differ
   from this play?

Writing Assignments

1. Write an essay describing a time when you had planned for
   something and, at the last minute, your plans were ruined.
2. Write an essay describing the differences between two neighborhoods in your city.
3. In an essay, recount an incident when some type of discrimination prevented you from realizing your dream.

Student Essay:
THE POSITIVE ENVIRONMENT IN BLACK FEMALE-HEADED FAMILIES

Camille Gray

In recent years, there has been a substantial increase in the number of families headed by single black females. This increase can be attributed to social factors such as divorce, separation, a shortage of eligible black men to marry, and an increase in the number of single women with children. Much negative attention, mostly from the media, has been given to families headed by black females. The negative images displayed on television and in newspapers and magazines tend to concentrate on poor black families who are either receiving some form of assistance from a federal or state agency or who are living well below the U.S. poverty level. All too often these negative images dominate how the black female-headed family is viewed. However, what the media fails to acknowledge are the positive aspects of black female-headed households.

The current trend of females heading families in the black community can be looked at as a method of adaptability and survival for black families in the United States. In many cases, this survival strategy has had positive results. For example, contrary to popular belief, the majority of black female-headed families offer nurturing and supportive environments for the children who are in them. Evidence shows that even though a male is not present in the home, children can be and are socialized to function effectively in mainstream American society.

Natural support systems help make the black female-headed family environment one that is nurturing and supportive. A natural support system can be both inside and outside of the household. The functions of this support system include, but are not limited to, the socialization of the children, providing care for younger children, disciplining children, and teaching age and sex roles to children. This natural support system consists of, but is not limited to, close and distant relatives, extended family, and close friends. This type of arrangement is beneficial to both the mother and the children for several reasons. For the child, the support system often provides role models who provide guidance in areas such as education and religion. For the mother, this arrangement often provides much needed child care so that she can secure gainful employment to provide for her family.

Another important positive aspect of child-rearing prac-   4
tices within the context of the black female-headed household is the bonding between the mother and the children. This bonding is crucial because it has a tremendous impact on a child's behavior inside and outside of the home. Despite the claim made by some studies that there is a relationship between the number of parents in the household, parent-child bonding, and juvenile delinquency, children who are raised by hard-working black mothers are often well behaved, close to and protective of their mothers, and very responsible. For example, many children of eight and up fulfill responsibilities around the house that help the family function smoothly. Usually, the responsibilities are assigned according to a child's age and ability, not according to his or her gender.

Too often, black female-headed households are negatively   5
portrayed. However, instead of stereotyping these types of families and the mothers who run them, the media should commend black females who head households by working hard and raising disciplined and responsible children.

Discussion Questions

1. How are black female-headed families portrayed in the media?
2. In many of these families, what is the relationship between the mother and her children?
3. How do the children function in these families?
4. What is a "natural support system"?
5. How does the author think the media should portray black female-headed families?
6. How does Gray use both illustration and persuasion to support her thesis?
7. What type of ending does the author choose? What other ways could Gray have ended her essay?

Writing Assignments

1. Write an essay describing the type of family you grew up in.
2. In an essay, discuss whether or not you think there should be one type of family that serves as the model family for us all.

9

Male-Female Relationships

LIKE A WINDING SHEET

Ann Petry

Ann Petry (1911–   ), novelist and short story writer, was born in Old Saybrook, Connecticut. She is the author of a novella, In Darkness and Confusion *(1949); a children's book,* The Drugstore Cat *(1949); and three novels,* The Street *(1946),* Country Place *(1947), and* The Narrows *(1953). Most of her works contrast the city and the small town. "Like a Winding Sheet," (1945), one of her best known short stories, is about a man's struggle to control his rage.*

Vocabulary

enmeshed   (85)   entangled

He had planned to get up before Mae did and surprise her by   1
fixing breakfast. Instead he went back to sleep and she got out
of bed so quietly he didn't know she wasn't there beside him
until he woke up and heard the queer soft gurgle of water running out of the sink in the bathroom.

He knew he ought to get up but instead he put his arms 2
across his forehead to shut the afternoon sunlight out of his
eyes, pulled his legs up close to his body, testing them to see if
the ache was still in them.

Mae had finished in the bathroom. He could tell because 3
she never closed the door when she was in there and now the
sweet smell of talcum powder was drifting down the hall and
into the bedroom. Then he heard her coming down the hall.

"Hi, babe," she said affectionately. 4

"Hum," he grunted, and moved his arms away from his 5
head, opened one eye.

"It's a nice morning." 6

"Yeah," he rolled over and the sheet twisted around him, 7
outlining his thighs, his chest. "You mean afternoon, don't ya?"

Mae looked at the twisted sheet and giggled. 8

"Looks like a winding sheet," she said. "A shroud—." 9
Laughter tangled with her words and she had to pause for a
moment before she could continue. "You look like a huckleberry—in a winding sheet—"

"That's no way to talk. Early in the day like this," he 10
protested.

He looked at his arms silhouetted against the white of the 11
sheets. They were inky black by contrast and he had to smile
in spite of himself and he lay there smiling and savouring the
sweet sound of Mae's giggling.

"Early?" She pointed a finger at the alarm clock on the 12
table near the bed, and giggled again. "It's almost four o'clock.
And if you don't spring up out of there you're going to be late
again."

"What do you mean 'again'?" 13

"Twice last week. Three times the week before. And once 14
the week before and—"

"I can't get used to sleeping in the day time," he said fret- 15
fully. He pushed his legs out from under the covers experimen-
tally. Some of the ache had gone out of them but they weren't
really rested yet. "It's too light for good sleeping. And all that
standing beats the hell out of my legs."

"After two years you oughtta be used to it," Mae said. 16

He watched her as she fixed her hair, powdered her face, 17
slipping into a pair of blue denim overalls. She moved quickly
and yet she didn't seem to hurry.

"You look like you'd had plenty of sleep," he said lazily. He 18
had to get up but he kept putting the moment off, not wanting

to move, yet he didn't dare let his legs go completely limp because if he did he'd go back to sleep. It was getting later and later but the thought of putting his weight on his legs kept him lying there.

When he finally got up he had to hurry and he gulped his 19
breakfast so fast that he wondered if his stomach could possibly use food thrown at it at such a rate of speed. He was still wondering about it as he and Mae were putting their coats on in the hall.

Mae paused to look at the calendar. "It's the thirteenth," 20
she said. Then a faint excitement in her voice. "Why it's Friday the thirteenth." She had one arm in her coat sleeve and she held it there while she stared at the calendar. "I oughtta stay home," she said. "I shouldn't go otta the house."

"Aw don't be a fool," he said. "To-day's payday. And pay- 21
day is a good luck day everywhere, any way you look at it." And as she stood hesitating he said, "Aw, come on."

And he was late for work again because they spent fifteen 22
minutes arguing before he could convince her she ought to go to work just the same. He had to talk persuasively, urging her gently and it took time. But he couldn't bring himself to talk to her roughly or threaten to strike her like a lot of men might have done. He wasn't made that way.

So when he reached the plant he was late and he had to 23
wait to punch the time clock because the day shift workers were streaming out in long lines, in groups and bunches that impeded his progress.

Even now just starting his work-day his legs ached. He 24
had to force himself to struggle past the out-going workers, punch the time clock, and get the little cart he pushed around all night because he kept toying with the idea of going home and getting back in bed.

He pushed the cart out on the concrete floor, thinking that 25
if this was his plant he'd make a lot of changes in it. There were too many standing up jobs for one thing. He'd figure out some way most of 'em could be done sitting down and he'd put a lot more benches around. And this job he had—this job that forced him to walk ten hours a night, pushing this little cart, well, he'd turn it into a sitting down job. One of those little trucks they used around railroad stations would be good for a job like this. Guys sat on a seat and the thing moved easily, taking up little room and turning in hardly any space at all, like on a dime.

He pushed the cart near the foreman. He never could re- 26
member to refer to her as the forelady even in his mind. It was
funny to have a woman for a boss in a plant like this one.

She was sore about something. He could tell by the way 27
her face was red and her eyes were half shut until they were
slits. Probably been out late and didn't get enough sleep. He
avoided looking at her and hurried a little, head down, as he
passed her though he couldn't resist stealing a glance at her
out of the corner of his eyes. He saw the edge of the light colored slacks she wore and the tip end of a big tan shoe.

"Hey, Johnson!" the woman said. 28

The machines had started full blast. The whirr and the 29
grinding made the building shake, made it impossible to hear
conversations. The men and women at the machines talked to
each other but looking at them from just a little distance away
they appeared to be simply moving their lips because you
couldn't hear what they were saying. Yet the woman's voice cut
across the machine sounds—harsh, angry.

He turned his head slowly. "Good Evenin', Mrs. Scott," he 30
said and waited.

"You're late again." 31

"That's right. My legs were bothering me." 32

The woman's face grew redder, angrier looking. "Half this 33
shift comes in late," she said. "And you're the worst one of all.
You're always late. Whatsa matter with ya?"

"It's my legs," he said. "Somehow they don't ever get 34
rested. I don't seem to get used to sleeping days. And I just
can't get started."

"Excuses. You guys always got excuses," her anger grew 35
and spread. "Every guy comes in here late always has an excuse. His wife's sick or his grandmother died or somebody in
the family had to go to the hospital," she paused, drew a deep
breath. "And the niggers are the worse. I don't care what's
wrong with your legs. You get in here on time. I'm sick of you
niggers—"

"You got the right to get mad," he interrupted softly. "You 36
got the right to cuss me four ways to Sunday but I ain't letting
nobody call me a nigger."

He stepped closer to her. His fists were doubled. His lips 37
were drawn back in a thin narrow line. A vein in his forehead
stood out swollen, thick.

And the woman backed away from him, not hurriedly but 38
slowly—two, three steps back.

"Aw, forget it," she said. "I didn't mean nothing by it. It   39
slipped out. It was a accident." The red of her face deepened
until the small blood vessels in her cheeks were purple. "Go on
and get to work," she urged. And she took three more slow
backward steps.

He stood motionless for a moment and then turned away   40
from the red lipstick on her mouth that made him remember
that the foreman was a woman. And he couldn't bring himself
to hit a woman. He felt a curious tingling in his fingers and he
looked down at his hands. They were clenched tight, hard,
ready to smash some of those small purple veins in her face.

He pushed the cart ahead of him, walking slowly. When he   41
turned his head, she was staring in his direction, mopping her
forehead with a dark blue handkerchief. Their eyes met and
then they both looked away.

He didn't glance in her direction again but moved past the   42
long work benches, carefully collecting the finished parts, going
slowly and steadily up and down, back and forth the length of
the building and as he walked he forced himself to swallow his
anger, get rid of it.

And he succeeded so that he was able to think about what   43
had happened without getting upset about it. An hour went by
but the tension stayed in his hands. They were clenched and
knotted on the handles of the cart as though ready to aim a
blow.

And he thought he should have hit her anyway, smacked   44
her hard in the face, felt the soft flesh of her face give under the
hardness of his hands. He tried to make his hands relax by offering them a description of what it would have been like to
strike her because he had the queer feeling that his hands were
not exactly a part of him any more—they had developed a separate life of their own over which he had no control. So he dwelt
on the pleasure his hands would have felt—both of them cracking at her, first one and then the other. If he had done that his
hands would have felt good now—relaxed, rested.

And he decided that even if he'd lost his job for it he   45
should have let her have it and it would have been a long time,
maybe the rest of her life before she called anybody else a nigger.

The only trouble was he couldn't hit a woman. A woman   46
couldn't hit back the same way a man did. But it would have
been a deeply satisfying thing to have cracked her narrow lips
wide open with just one blow, beautifully timed and with all his

weight in back of it. That way he would have gotten rid of all the energy and tension his anger had created in him. He kept remembering how his heart had started pumping blood so fast he had felt it tingle even in the tips of his fingers.

With the approach of night, fatigue nibbled at him. The corner of his mouth dropped, the frown between his eyes deepened, his shoulders sagged; but his hands stayed tight and tense. As the hours dragged by he noticed that the women workers had started to snap and snarl at each other. He couldn't hear what they said because of the sound of machines but he could see the quick lip movements that sent words tumbling from the sides of their mouths. They gestured irritably with their hands and scowled as their mouths moved.   47

Their violent jerky motions told him that it was getting close on to quitting time but somehow he felt that the night still stretched ahead of him, composed of endless hours of steady walking on his aching legs. When the whistle finally blew he went on pushing the cart, unable to believe that it had sounded. The whirring of the machines died away to a murmur and he knew then that he'd really heard the whistle. He stood still for a moment filled with a relief that made him sigh.   48

Then he moved briskly, putting the cart in the store room, hurrying to take his place in the line forming before the paymaster. That was another thing he'd change, he thought. He'd have the pay envelopes handed to the people right at their benches so there wouldn't be ten or fifteen minutes lost waiting for the pay. He always got home about fifteen minutes late on payday. They did it better in the plant where Mae worked, brought the money right to them at their benches.   49

- He stuck his pay envelope in his pants' pocket and followed the line of workers heading for the subway in a slow moving stream. He glanced up at the sky. It was a nice night, the sky looked packed full to running over with stars. And he thought if he and Mae would go right to bed when they got home from work they'd catch a few hours of darkness for sleeping. But they never did. They fooled around—cooking and eating and listening to the radio and he always stayed in a big chair in the living room and went almost but not quite to sleep and when they finally got to bed it was five or six in the morning and daylight was already seeping around the edges of the sky.   50

He walked slowly, putting off the moment when he would have to plunge into the crowd hurrying toward the subway. It   51

was a long ride to Harlem and to-night the thought of it appalled him. He paused outside an all-night restaurant to kill
time, so that some of the first rush of workers would be gone
when he reached the subway.

The lights in the restaurant were brilliant, enticing. There   52
was life and motion inside. And as he looked through the window he thought that everything within range of his eyes
gleamed—the long imitation marble counter, the tall stools, the
white porcelain topped tables and especially the big metal coffee urn right near the window. Steam issued from its top and a
gas flame flickered under it—a lively, dancing, blue flame.

A lot of the workers from his shift—men and women—were   53
lining up near the coffee urn. He watched them walk to the
porcelain topped tables carrying steaming cups of coffee and he
saw that just the smell of the coffee lessened the fatigue lines
in their faces. After the first sip their faces softened, they
smiled, they began to talk and laugh.

On a sudden impulse he shoved the door open and joined   54
the line in front of the coffee urn. The line moved slowly. And as
he stood there the smell of the coffee, the sound of the laughter
and of the voices, helped dull the sharp ache in his legs.

He didn't pay any attention to the girl who was serving the   55
coffee at the urn. He kept looking at the cups in the hands of
the men who had been ahead of him. Each time a man stepped
out of the line with one of the thick white cups the fragrant
steam got in his nostrils. He saw that they walked carefully so
as not to spill a single drop. There was a froth of bubbles at the
top of each cup and he thought about how he would let the
bubbles break against his lips before he actually took a big
deep swallow.

Then it was his turn. "A cup of coffee," he said, just as he   56
had heard the others say.

The girl looked past him, put her hands up to her head   57
and gently lifted her hair away from the back of her neck, tossing her head back a little. "No more coffee for awhile," she said.

He wasn't certain he'd heard her correctly and he said,   58
"What?" blankly.

"No more coffee for awhile," she repeated.   59

There was silence behind him and then uneasy movement.   60
He thought someone would say something, ask why or protest,
but there was only silence and then a faint shuffling sound as
though the men standing behind him had simultaneously
shifted their weight from one foot to the other.

He looked at her without saying anything. He felt his hands 61
begin to tingle and the tingling went all the way down to his finger tips so that he glanced down at them. They were clenched
tight, hard, into fists. Then he looked at the girl again. What he
wanted to do was hit her so hard that the scarlet lipstick on her
mouth would smear and spread over her nose, her chin, out toward her cheeks, so hard that she would never toss her head
again and refuse a man a cup of coffee because he was black.

He estimated the distance across the counter and reached 62
forward, balancing his weight on the balls of his feet, ready to
let the blow go. And then his hands fell back down to his sides
because he forced himself to lower them, to unclench them and
make them dangle loose. The effort took his breath away because his hands fought against him. But he couldn't hit her.
He couldn't even now bring himself to hit a woman, not even
this one, who had refused him a cup of coffee with a toss of her
head. He kept seeing the gesture with which she had lifted the
length of her blond hair from the back of her neck as expressive of her contempt for him.

When he went out the door he didn't look back. If he had 63
he would have seen the flickering blue flame under the shiny
coffee urn being extinguished. The line of men who had stood
behind him lingered a moment to watch the people drinking
coffee at the tables and then they left just as he had without
having had the coffee they wanted so badly. The girl behind the
counter poured water in the urn and swabbed it out and as she
waited for the water to run out she lifted her hair gently from
the back of her neck and tossed her head before she began
making a fresh lot of coffee.

But he walked away without a backward look, his head 64
down, his hands in his pockets, raging at himself and whatever
it was inside of him that had forced him to stand quiet and still
when he wanted to strike out.

The subway was crowded and he had to stand. He tried 65
grasping an overhead strap and his hands were too tense to
grip it. So he moved near the train door and stood there swaying back and forth with the rocking of the train. The roar of the
train beat inside his head, making it ache and throb, and the
pain in his legs clawed up into his groin so that he seemed to
be bursting with pain and he told himself that it was due to all
that anger-born energy that had piled up in him and not been
used and so it had spread through him like a poison—from his
feet and legs all the way up to his head.

Mae was in the house before he was. He knew she was   66
home before he put the key in the door of the apartment. The
radio was going. She had it tuned up loud and she was singing
along with it.

"Hello, Babe," she called out as soon as he opened the   67
door.

He tried to say "hello" and it came out half a grunt and   68
half sigh.

"You sure sound cheerful," she said.   69

She was in the bedroom and he went and leaned against   70
the door jamb. The denim overalls she wore to work were carefully draped over the back of a chair by the bed. She was
standing in front of the dresser, tying the sash of a yellow
housecoat around her waist and chewing gum vigorously as
she admired her reflection in the mirror over the dresser.

"Whatsa matter?" she said. "You get bawled out by the   71
boss or somep'n?"

"Just tired," he said slowly. "For God's sake do you have to   72
crack that gum like that?"

"You don't have to lissen to me," she said complacently.   73
She patted a curl in place near the side of her head and then
lifted her hair away from the back of her neck, ducking her
head forward and then back.

He winced away from the gesture. "What you got to be al-   74
ways fooling with your hair for?" he protested.

"Say, what's the matter with you, anyway?" she turned   75
away from the mirror to face him, put her hands on her hips.
"You ain't been in the house two minutes and you're picking on
me."

He didn't answer her because her eyes were angry and he   76
didn't want to quarrel with her. They'd been married too long
and got along too well and so he walked all the way into the
room and sat down in the chair by the bed and stretched his
legs out in front of him, putting his weight on the heels of his
shoes, leaning way back in the chair, not saying anything.

"Lissen," she said sharply. "I've got to wear those overalls   77
again tomorrow. You're going to get them all wrinkled up leaning against them like that."

He didn't move. He was too tired and his legs were throb-   78
bing now that he had sat down. Besides the overalls were already wrinkled and dirty, he thought. They couldn't help but
be for she'd worn them all week. He leaned further back in the
chair.

"Come on, get up," she ordered. 79

"Oh, what the hell," he said wearily and got up from the 80
chair. "I'd just as soon live in a subway. There'd be just as
much place to sit down."

He saw that her sense of humor was struggling with her 81
anger. But her sense of humor won because she giggled.

"Aw, come on and eat," she said. There was a coaxing note 82
in her voice. "You're nothing but a old hungry nigger trying to
act tough and—" she paused to giggle and then continued,
"You—"

He had always found her giggling pleasant and deliber- 83
ately said things that might amuse her and then waited, listening for the delicate sound to emerge from her throat. This time
he didn't even hear the giggle. He didn't let her finish what she
was saying. She was standing close to him and that funny tingling started in his finger tips, went fast up his arms and sent
his fist shooting straight for her face.

There was the smacking sound of soft flesh being struck 84
by a hard object and it wasn't until she screamed that he realized he had hit her in the mouth—so hard that the dark red
lipstick had blurred and spread over her full lips, reaching up
toward the tip of her nose, down toward her chin, out toward
her cheeks.

The knowledge that he had struck her seeped through him 85
slowly and he was appalled but he couldn't drag his hands
away from her face. He kept striking her and he thought with
horror that something inside him was holding him, binding
him to this act, wrapping and twisting about him so that he
had to continue it. He had lost all control over his hands. And
he groped for a phrase, a word, something to describe what
this thing was like that was happening to him and he thought
it was like being enmeshed in a winding sheet—that was it—
like a winding sheet. And even as the thought formed in his
mind his hands reached for her face again and yet again.

Discussion Questions

1. What type of person does Johnson appear to be at the beginning
   of the story?
2. What is the relationship between Johnson and Mrs. Scott, the
   forelady?
3. Why does Johnson refrain from hitting the two white women
   even though he wants to do so very much?

4. Why does Johnson beat his wife? Why is he unable to stop beating her once he starts? Does this behavior surprise you? Why or why not?
5. Is there evidence to suggest that Johnson's behavior is out of character? Why or why not?
6. What is the significance of the story's title?
7. How does Petry use comparison and contrast in this story?
8. What are some of the transitions that help the reader move smoothly through the story?

Writing Assignments

1. Write an essay describing the consequences of your (or someone else's) uncontrolled anger.
2. Write an essay describing a time when you or someone you know did something completely out of character. Discuss what you feel caused such an action.
3. Write an essay discussing anger, stress, frustration, abuse, or violence.

A SUMMER TRAGEDY

Arna Bontemps

Arna Wendell Bontemps (1902–1973), one of the leading figures of the Harlem Renaissance and the first African American historical novelist, was born in Alexandria, Louisiana. His works include a romantic novel, God Sends Sunday *(1931), which he and Countee Cullen adapted for Broadway in 1946 as "Saint Louis Woman";* Black Thunder *(1936) with Langston Hughes;* The Poetry of the Negro: 1746–1946 *(1949);* Book of Negro Folklore *(1958); a collection of poetry,* Personals *(1963); and a book of stories and essays,* The Old South *(1973). In this short story, "A Summer Tragedy," a couple works together to find a solution to their problems.*

Vocabulary

obstinate	(1)	difficult to manage
gnarled	(5)	twisted
negligible	(5)	barely existing, having little value
semblance	(8)	likeness
stupor	(25)	daze
fodder	(72)	straw and hay used as food for horses and cattle
anguish	(105)	great mental or physical pain
cavernous	(106)	hollow

Old Jeff Patton, the black share farmer, fumbled with his bow   1
tie. His fingers trembled and the high, stiff collar pinched his throat. A fellow loses his hand for such vanities after thirty or forty years of simple life. Once a year, or maybe twice if there's a wedding among his kinfolks, he may spruce up; but generally fancy clothes do nothing but adorn the wall of the big room and feed the moths. That had been Jeff Patton's experience. He had not worn his stiff-bosomed shirt more than a dozen times in all his married life. His swallow-tailed coat[1] lay on the bed beside him, freshly brushed and pressed, but it was as full of holes as the overalls in which he worked on weekdays. The

---

[1] swallow-tailed coat   (1)   A man's full-dress coat that tapers down in two long tails in the back.

moths had used it badly. Jeff twisted his mouth into a hideous toothless grimace as he contended with the obstinate bow. He stamped his good foot and decided to give up the struggle.

"Jennie," he called.   2

"What's that, Jeff?" His wife's shrunken voice came out of   3
the adjoining room like an echo. It was hardly bigger than a whisper.

"I reckon you'll have to he'p me wid this heah bow tie,   4
baby," he said meekly. "Dog if I can hitch it up."

Her answer was not strong enough to reach him, but   5
presently the old woman came to the door, feeling her way with a stick. She had a wasted, dead-leaf appearance. Her body, as scrawny and gnarled as a string bean, seemed less than nothing in the ocean of frayed and faded petticoats that surrounded her. These hung an inch or two above the tops of her heavy unlaced shoes and showed little grotesque piles where the stockings had fallen down from her negligible legs.

"You oughta could do a heap mo' wid a thing like that'n   6
me—beingst as you got yo' good sight."

"Looks like I oughta could," he admitted. "But my fingers   7
is gone democrat on me. I get all mixed up in the looking glass an' can't tell wicha way to twist the devilish thing."

Jennie sat on the side of the bed, and old Jeff Patton got   8
down on one knee while she tied the bow knot. It was a slow and painful ordeal for each of them in this position. Jeff's bones cracked, his knee ached, and it was only after a half dozen attempts that Jennie worked a semblance of a bow into the tie.

"I got to dress maself now," the old woman whispered.   9
"These is ma old shoes an' stockings, and I ain't so much as unwrapped ma dress."

"Well, don't worry 'bout me no mo', baby," Jeff said. "That   10
'bout finishes me. All I gotta do now is slip on that old coat 'n ves' an' I'll be fixed to leave."

Jennie disappeared again through the dim passage into   11
the shed room. Being blind was no handicap to her in that black hole. Jeff heard the cane placed against the wall beside the door and knew that his wife was on easy ground. He put on his coat, took a battered top hat from the bed post, and hobbled to the front door. He was ready to travel. As soon as Jennie could get on her Sunday shoes and her old black silk dress, they would start.

Outside the tiny log house, the day was warm and mellow 12
with sunshine. A host of wasps were humming with busy excitement in the trunk of a dead sycamore. Gray squirrels were
searching through the grass for hickory nuts, and blue jays were
in the trees hopping from branch to branch. Pine woods
stretched away to the left like a black sea. Among them were
scattered scores of log houses like Jeff's, houses of black share
farmers.[2] Cows and pigs wandered freely among the trees. There
was no danger of loss. Each farmer knew his own stock and
knew his neighbor's as well as he knew his neighbor's children.

Down the slope to the right were the cultivated acres on 13
which the colored folks worked. They extended to the river,
more than two miles away, and they were today green with the
unmade cotton crop. A tiny thread of a road, which passed directly in front of Jeff's place, ran through these green fields like
a pencil mark.

Jeff, standing outside the door, with his absurd hat in his 14
left hand, surveyed the wide scene tenderly. He had been forty-
five years on these acres. He loved them with the unexplained
affection that others have for the countries to which they belong.

The sun was hot on his head, his collar still pinched his 15
throat, and the Sunday clothes were intolerably hot. Jeff transferred the hat to his right hand and began fanning with it. Suddenly the whisper that was Jennie's voice came out of the shed
room.

"You can bring the car round front whilst you's waitin'," it 16
said feebly. There was a tired pause; then it added, "I'll soon be
fixed to go."

"A'right, baby," Jeff answered. "I'll get it in a minute." 17

But he didn't move. A thought struck him that made his 18
mouth fall open. The mention of the car brought to his mind,
with new intensity, the trip he and Jennie were about to take.
Fear came into his eyes; excitement took his breath. Lord, Jesus!

"Jeff. . . . O Jeff," the old woman's whisper called. 19

He awakened with a jolt. "Hunh, baby?" 20

"What you doin'?" 21

"Nuthin. Jes studyin'. I jes been turnin' things round 'n 22
round in ma mind."

---

[2] share farmers (12)   Farmers who work the land for a share of the crop.

"You could be gettin' the car," she said.   23

"Oh yes, right away, baby."   24

He started round to the shed, limping heavily on his bad   25
leg. There were three frizzly chickens in the yard. All his other
chickens had been killed or stolen recently. But the frizzly
chickens had been saved somehow. That was fortunate indeed,
for these curious creatures had a way of devouring "poison"
from the yard and in that way protecting against conjure and
black luck and spells. But even the frizzly chickens seemed
now to be in a stupor. Jeff thought they had some ailment; he
expected all three of them to die shortly.

The shed in which the old T-model Ford stood was only a   26
grass roof held up by four corner poles. It had been built by
tremulous hands at a time when the little rattletrap car had
been regarded as a peculiar treasure. And miraculously, despite wind and downpour, it still stood.

Jeff adjusted the crank and put his weight upon it. The   27
engine came to life with a sputter and bang that rattled the old
car from radiator to tail light. Jeff hopped into the seat and put
his foot on the accelerator. The sputtering and banging increased. The rattling became more violent. That was good. It
was good banging, good sputtering and rattling, and it meant
that the aged car was still in running condition. She could be
depended on for this trip.

Again Jeff's thought halted as if paralyzed. The suggestion   28
of the trip fell into the machinery of his mind like a wrench. He
felt dazed and weak. He swung the car out into the yard, made
a half turn, and drove around to the front door. When he took
his hands off the wheel, he noticed that he was trembling violently. He cut off the motor and climbed to the ground to wait
for Jennie.

A few minutes later she was at the window, her voice rat-   29
tling against the pane like a broken shutter.

"I'm ready, Jeff."   30

He did not answer, but limped into the house and took her   31
by the arm. He led her slowly through the big room, down the
step, and across the yard.

"You reckon I'd oughta lock the do'?" he asked softly.   32

They stopped and Jennie weighed the question. Finally   33
she shook her head.

"Ne' mind the do'," she said. "I don't see no cause to lock   34
up things."

"You right," Jeff agreed. "No cause to lock up."   35

Jeff opened the door and helped his wife into the car. A   36
quick shudder passed over him. Jesus! Again he trembled.

"How come you shaking so?" Jennie whispered.   37

"I don't know," he said.   38

"You mus' be scairt, Jeff."   39

"No, baby, I ain't scairt."   40

He slammed the door after her and went around to crank   41
up again. The motor started easily. Jeff wished that it had not
been so responsive. He would have liked a few more minutes in
which to turn things around in his head. As it was, with Jennie
chiding him about being afraid, he had to keep going. He
swung the car into the little pencilmark road and started off toward the river, driving very slowly, very cautiously.

Chugging across the green countryside, the small battered   42
Ford seemed tiny indeed. Jeff felt a familiar excitement, a thrill,
as they came down the first slope to the immense levels on
which the cotton was growing. He could not help reflecting that
the crops were good. He knew what that meant, too; he had
made forty-five of them with his own hands. It was true that he
had worn out nearly a dozen mules, but that was the fault of
old man Stevenson, the owner of the land. Major Stevenson
had the odd notion that one mule was all a share farmer
needed to work a thirty-acre plot. It was an expensive notion,
the way it killed mules from overwork, but the old man held to
it. Jeff thought it killed a good many share farmers as well as
mules, but he had no sympathy for them. He had always been
strong, and he had been taught to have no patience with weakness in men. Women or children might be tolerated if they were
puny, but a weak man was a curse. Of course, his own children—

Jeff's thought halted there. He and Jennie never men-   43
tioned their dead children any more. And naturally, he did not
wish to dwell upon them in his mind. Before he knew it, some
remark would slip out of his mouth and that would make Jennie feel blue. Perhaps she would cry. A woman like Jennie
could not easily throw off the grief that comes from losing five
grown children within two years. Even Jeff was still staggered
by the blow. His memory had not been much good recently. He
frequently talked to himself. And, although he had kept it a secret, he knew that his courage had left him. He was terrified by
the least unfamiliar sound at night. He was reluctant to venture far from home in the daytime. And that habit of trembling
when he felt fearful was now far beyond his control. Sometimes

he became afraid and trembled without knowing what had
frightened him. The feeling would just come over him like a
chill.

The car rattled slowly over the dusty road. Jennie sat erect   44
and silent with a little absurd hat pinned to her hair. Her useless eyes seemed very large, very white in their deep sockets.
Suddenly Jeff heard her voice, and he inclined his head to
catch the words.

"Is we passed Delia Moore's house yet?" she asked.   45
"Not yet," he said.   46
"You must be drivin' mighty slow, Jeff."   47
"We just as well take our time, baby."   48
There was a pause. A little puff of steam was coming out   49
of the radiator of the car. Heat wavered above the hood. Delia
Moore's house was nearly half a mile away. After a moment
Jennie spoke again.

"You ain't really scairt, is you, Jeff?"   50
"Nah, baby, I ain't scairt."   51
"You know how we agreed—we gotta keep on goin'."   52
Jewels of perspiration appeared on Jeff's forehead. His   53
eyes rounded, blinked, became fixed on the road.

"I don't know," he said with a shiver. "I reckon it's the only   54
thing to do."

"Hm."   55

A flock of guinea fowls, pecking in the road, were scattered   56
by the passing car. Some of them took to their wings; others
hid under bushes. A blue jay, swaying on a leafy twig, was annoying a roadside squirrel. Jeff held an even speed till he came
near Delia's place. Then he slowed down noticeably.

Delia's house was really no house at all, but an aban-   57
doned store building converted into a dwelling. It sat near a
crossroads, beneath a single black cedar tree. There Delia, a
cattish old creature of Jennie's age, lived alone. She had been
there more years than anybody could remember, and long ago
had won the disfavor of such women as Jennie. For in her
young days Delia had been gayer, yellower, and saucier than
seemed proper in those parts. Her ways with menfolks had
been dark and suspicious. And the fact that she had had as
many husbands as children did not help her reputation.

"Yonder's old Delia," Jeff said as they passed.   58
"What she doin'?"   59
"Jes sittin' in the do'," he said.   60
"She see us?"   61
"Hm," Jeff said. "Musta did."   62

That relieved Jennie. It strengthened her to know that her   63
old enemy had seen her pass in her best clothes. That would
give the old she-devil something to chew her gums and fret
about. Jennie thought. Wouldn't she have a fit if she didn't find
out? Old evil Delia! This would be just the thing for her. It
would pay her back for being so evil. It would also pay her,
Jennie thought, for the way she used to grin at Jeff—long ago,
when her teeth were good.

The road became smooth and red, and Jeff could tell by   64
the smell of the air that they were nearing the river. He could
see the rise where the road turned and ran along parallel to the
stream. The car chugged on monotonously. After a long silent
spell, Jennie leaned against Jeff and spoke.

"How many bale o' cotton you think we got standin'?" she   65
said.

Jeff wrinkled his forehead as he calculated.   66
" 'Bout twenty-five, I reckon."   67
"How many you make las' year?"   68
"Twenty-eight," he said. "How come you ask that?"   69
"I's jes thinkin'," Jennie said quietly.   70
"It don't make a speck o' difference though," Jeff reflected.   71
"If we get much or if we get little, we still gonna be in debt to
old man Stevenson when he gets through counting up agin us.
It's took us a long time to learn that."

Jennie was not listening to these words. She had fallen   72
into a trance-like meditation. Her lips twitched. She chewed
her gums and rubbed her gnarled hands nervously. Suddenly,
she leaned forward, buried her face in the nervous hands, and
burst into tears. She cried aloud in a dry, cracked voice that
suggested the rattle of fodder on dead stalks. She cried aloud
like a child, for she had never learned to suppress a genuine
sob. Her slight old frame shook heavily and seemed hardly able
to sustain such violent grief.

"What's the matter, baby?" Jeff asked awkwardly.   73
"Why you cryin' like all that?"   74
"I's jes thinkin'," she said.   75
"So you the one what's scairt now, hunh?"   76
"I ain't scairt, Jeff. I's jes thinkin' 'bout leavin' eve'thing   77
like this—eve'thing we been used to. It's right sad-like."

Jeff did not answer, and presently Jennie buried her face   78
again and cried.

The sun was almost overhead. It beat down furiously on   79
the dusty wagon-path road, on the parched roadside grass and
the tiny battered car. Jeff's hands, gripping the wheel, became

wet with perspiration; his forehead sparkled. Jeff's lips parted. His mouth shaped a hideous grimace. His face suggested the face of a man being burned. But the torture passed and his expression softened again.

"You mustn't cry, baby," he said to his wife. "We gotta be   80
strong. We can't break down."

Jennie waited a few seconds, then said, "You reckon we   81
oughta do it, Jeff? You reckon we oughta go 'head an' do it, really?"

Jeff's voice choked; his eyes blurred. He was terrified to   82
hear Jennie say the thing that had been in his mind all morning. She had egged him on when he had wanted more than anything in the world to wait, to reconsider, to think things over a little longer. Now she was getting cold feet. Actually, there was no need of thinking the question through again. It would only end in making the same painful decision once more. Jeff knew that. There was no need of fooling around longer.

"We jes as well to do like we planned," he said. "They ain't   83
nothin' else for us now—it's the bes' thing."

Jeff thought of the handicaps, the near impossibility, of   84
making another crop with his leg bothering him more and more each week. Then there was always the chance that he would have another stroke, like the one that had made him lame. Another one might kill him. The least it could do would be to leave him helpless. Jeff gasped—Lord, Jesus! He could not bear to think of being helpless, like a baby, on Jennie's hands. Frail, blind Jennie.

The little pounding motor of the car worked harder and   85
harder. The puff of steam from the cracked radiator became larger. Jeff realized that they were climbing a little rise. A moment later the road turned abruptly, and he looked down upon the face of the river.

"Jeff."   86
"Hunh?"   87
"Is that the water I hear?"   88
"Hm. Tha's it."   89
"Well, which way you goin' now?"   90
"Down this-a way," he said. "The road runs 'long 'side o'   91
the water a lil piece."

She waited a while calmly. Then said she, "Drive faster."   92
"A'right, baby," Jeff said.   93
The water roared in the bed of the river. It was fifty or sixty   94
feet below the level of the road. Between the road and the water

there was a long smooth slope, sharply inclined. The slope was dry, the clay hardened by prolonged summer heat. The water below, roaring in a narrow channel, was noisy and wild.

"Jeff." 95

"Hunh?" 96

"How far you goin'?" 97

"Jes a lil piece down the road." 98

"You ain't scairt, is you, Jeff?" 99

"Nah, baby," he said trembling. "I ain't scairt." 100

"Remember how we planned it, Jeff. We gotta do it like we said. Brave-like." 101

"Hm." 102

Jeff's brain darkened. Things suddenly seemed unreal, like figures in a dream. Thoughts swam in his mind foolishly, hysterically, like little blind fish in a pool within a dense cave. They rushed again. Jeff soon because dizzy. He shuddered violently and turned to his wife. 103

"Jennie, I can't do it. I can't." His voice broke pitifully. 104

She did not appear to be listening. All the grief had gone from her face. She sat erect, her unseeing eyes wide open, strained and frightful. Her glossy black skin had become dull. She seemed as thin, as sharp and bony, as a starved bird. Now, having suffered and endured the sadness of tearing herself away from beloved things, she showed no anguish. She was absorbed with her own thoughts, and she didn't even hear Jeff's voice shouting in her ear. 105

Jeff said nothing more. For an instant there was light in his cavernous brain. The great chamber was, for less than a second, peopled by characters he knew and loved. They were simple, healthy creatures, and they behaved in a manner that he could understand. They had quality. But since he had already taken leave of them long ago, the remembrance did not break his heart again. Young Jeff Patton was among them, the Jeff Patton of fifty years ago who went down to New Orleans with a crowd of country boys to the Mardi Gras doings. The gay young crowd, boys with candy-striped shirts and rouged brown girls in noisy silks, was like a picture in his head. Yet it did not make him sad. On that very trip Slim Burns had killed Joe Beasley—the crowd had been broken up. Since then Jeff Patton's world had been the Greenbriar Plantation. If there had been other Mardi Gras carnivals, he had not heard of them. Since then there had been no time; the years had fallen on him like waves. Now he was old, worn out. Another paralytic stroke 106 (like the one he had already suffered) would put him on his back for keeps. In that condition, with a frail blind woman to look after him, he would be worse off than if he were dead.

Suddenly Jeff's hands became steady. He actually felt   107 brave. He slowed down the motor of the car and carefully pulled off the road. Below, the water of the stream boomed, a soft thunder in the deep channel. Jeff ran the car onto the clay slope, pointed it directly toward the stream and put his foot heavily on the accelerator. The little car leaped furiously down the steep incline toward the water. The movement was nearly as swift and direct as a fall. The two old black folks, sitting quietly side by side, showed no excitement. In another instant the car hit the water and dropped immediately out of sight.

A little later it lodged in the mud of a shallow place. One   108 wheel of the crushed and upturned little Ford became visible above the rushing water.

Discussion Questions

1. How does Bontemps convey the idea that the Pattons are about to go on an important trip?
2. What images of poverty does Bontemps present in the story?
3. What kind of relationship exists between Jeff and Jennie?
4. What physical and economic factors influence Jeff and Jennie's decision to take their journey? Is their decision a well-thought-out one? Support your answer.
5. What are the couple's feelings as they approach the river, especially in paragraph 106?
6. Do you believe that Jeff and Jennie take the courageous or the cowardly way to solve their problems? Explain your answer.
7. How effective is Bontemps's use of description in developing this story? Explain your answer.
8. How does the opening paragraph set the tone for the story?

Writing Assignments

1. Write an essay describing your feelings as you prepared to do something you anticipated with great joy or great fear.
2. Write an essay relating a time when economic or physical conditions forced you to do something drastic.
3. Write an essay in which you agree or disagree with the following statement: "There is no such thing as a hopeless situation."

JUST DON'T NEVER GIVE UP ON LOVE

Sonia Sanchez

Sonia Sanchez (1934–   ) was born in Birmingham, Alabama. An activist, poet, playwright, editor, and teacher, she is the author of several works, including her first book of poetry, Homecoming *(1969),* It's a New Day *(1971),* A Blues Book for Blue Black Magical Women *(1973),* I've Been a Woman: New and Selected Poems *(1981), and* homegirls and hand grenades *(1984). In this selection, a young woman describes an unexpected encounter with an old woman in the park.*

Vocabulary

ruminating	(1)	meditating
impropriety	(6)	improper action or behavior
spunk	(13)	courage
buddah	(14)	evil, disgusting woman
crocheted keloids	(14)	raised scars having the appearance of being knitted with one hooked needle
confessionals	(15)	secrets
anticlimactic	(25)	declining in disappointing contrast to a previous rise

Feeling tired that day, I came to the park with the children. I saw her as I rounded the corner, sitting old as stale beer on the bench, ruminating on some uneventful past. And I thought, "Hell, No rap from the roots today. I need the present. On this day. This Monday. This July day buckling me under her summer wings, I need more than old words for my body to squeeze into." 1

I sat down at the far end of the bench, draping my legs over the edge, baring my back to time and time unwell spent. I screamed to the children to watch those curves threatening their youth as they rode their ten-speed bikes against midwestern rhythms. 2

I opened my book and began to write. They were coming again, those words insistent as his hands had been pounding inside me, demanding their time and place. I relaxed as my hands moved across the paper like one possessed. 3

I wasn't sure just what it was I heard. At first I thought it 4
was one of the boys calling me so I kept on writing. They knew
the routine by now. Emergencies demanded a presence. A facial confrontation. No long-distance screams across trees and
space and other children's screams. But the sound pierced the
pages and I looked around, and there she was inching her
bamboo-creased body toward my back, coughing a beaded sentence off her tongue.

"Guess you think I ain't never loved, huh girl? Hee. Hee. 5
Guess that what you be thinking, huh?"

I turned. Startled by her closeness and impropriety, I stut- 6
tered, "I, I, I, Whhhaat dooooo you mean?"

"Hee. Hee. Guess you think I been old like this fo'ever, 7
huh?" She leaned toward me, "Huh? I was so pretty that mens
brought me breakfast in bed. Wouldn't let me hardly do no
hard work at all."

"That's nice, ma'am. I'm glad to hear that." I returned to 8
my book. I didn't want to hear about some ancient love that
she carried inside her. I had to finish a review for the journal. I
was already late. I hoped she would get the hint and just sit
still. I looked at her out of the corner of my eyes. She quit and I
continued my work.

"He could barely keep hisself in changing clothes. But he 9
was pretty. My first husband looked like the sun. I used to say
his name over and over again till it hung from my ears like dia-
monds. Has you ever loved a pretty man, girl?"

I raised my eyes, determined to keep a distance from this 10
woman disturbing my day.

"No ma'am. But I've seen many a pretty man. I don't like 11
them though cuz they keep their love up high in a linen closet
and I'm too short to reach it."

Her skin shook with laughter. 12

"Girl you gots some spunk about you after all. C'mon over 13
here next to me. I wants to see yo' eyes up close. You looks so
uneven sittin over there."

Did she say uneven? Did this old buddah splintering 14
death say uneven? Couldn't she see that I had one eye shorter
than the other; that my breath was painted on porcelain; that
one breast crocheted keloids under this white blouse?

I moved toward her though. I scooped up the years that 15
had stripped me to the waist and moved toward her. And she
called to me to come out, come out wherever you are young
woman, playing hide and go seek with scarecrow men. I gathered myself up at the gateway of her confessionals.

"Do you know what it mean to love a pretty man girl?" She   16
crooned in my ear. "You always running behind a man like that
girl while he cradles his privates. Ain't no joy in a pretty yellow
man, cuz he always out pleasurin' and givin' pleasure."

I nodded my head as her words sailed in my ears. Here   17
was the pulse of a woman whose black ass shook the world
once.

She continued. "A woman crying all the time is pitiful. Piti-   18
ful I says. I wuz pitiful sitting by the window every night like a
cow in the fields chewin' on cud. I wanted to cry out, but not
even God hisself could hear me. I tried to cry out till my mouth
wuz split open at the throat. I 'spoze there is a time all womens
has to visit the slaughter house. My visit lasted five years."

Touching her hands, I felt the summer splintering in   19
prayer; touching her hands, I felt my bones migrating in red
noise. I asked, "When did you see the butterflies again?"

Her eyes wandered like quicksand over my face. Then she   20
smiled, "Girl don't you know yet that you don't never give up on
love? Don't you know you has in you the pulse of winds? The
noise of dragon flies?" Her eyes squinted close and she said,
"One of them mornings he woke up callin' me and I wuz gone. I
wuz gone running with the moon over my shoulders. I looked
no which way at all. I had inside me 'nough knives and spoons
to cut/scoop out the night. I wuz a tremblin' as I met the
mornin'."

She stirred in her eighty-four-year-old memory. She   21
stirred up her body as she talked. "They's men and mens.
Some good. Some bad. Some breathing death. Some breathing
life. William wuz my beginnin'. I come to that man spittin'
metal and he just pick me up and fold me inside him. I wuz
christen' with his love."

She began to hum. I didn't recognize the song; it was a   22
prayer. I leaned back and listened to her voice rustling like silk.
I heard cathedrals and sonnets; I heard tents and revivals and
a black woman spilling black juice among her ruins.

"We all gotta salute death one time or 'nother girl. Death   23
be waitin' outdoors trying to get inside. William died at his job.
Death just turned 'round and snatched him right off the
street."

Her humming became the only sound in the park. Her   24
voice moved across the bench like a mutilated child. And I
cried. For myself. For this woman talkin' about love. For all the
women who have ever stretched their bodies out anticipating
civilization and finding ruins.

The crashing of the bikes was anticlimactic. I jumped up,   25
rushed toward the accident. Man. little man. Where you bicy-
cling to so very fast? Man. Second little man. Take it slow. It all
passes so fast any how.

As I walked the boys and their bikes toward the bench, I   26
smiled at this old woman waiting for our return.

"I want you to meet a great lady, boys."   27

"Is she a writer, too, ma?"   28

"No honey. She's a lady who has lived life instead of writ-   29
ing about it."

"After we say hello can we ride a little while longer?   30
Please!"

"Ok. But watch your manners now and your bones after-   31
wards."

"These are my sons, ma'am."   32

"How you do sons? I'm Mrs. Rosalie Johnson. Glad to   33
meet you."

The boys shook her hand and listened for a minute to her   34
words. Then they rode off, spinning their wheels on a city neutral with pain.

As I stood watching them race the morning, Mrs. Johnson   35
got up.

"Don't go," I cried. "You didn't finish your story."   36

"We'll talk by-and-by. I comes out here almost everyday. I   37
sits here on the same bench everyday. I'll probably die sittin'
here one day. As good a place as any I 'magine."

"May I hug you, ma'am? You've helped me so much today.   38
You've given me strength to keep on looking."

"No. Don't never go looking for love girl. Just wait. It'll   39
come. Like the rain fallin' from the heaven, it'll come. Just
don't never give up on love."

We hugged; then she walked her eighty-four-year-old walk   40
down the street. A black woman. Echoing gold. Carrying cou-
plets from the sky to crease the ground.

Discussion Questions

1. What is the narrator's first impression of the old woman? Why
   does that impression change?
2. How would you characterize the woman? How does she differ
   from the narrator?
3. What is the old woman's philosophy of love? How have her experiences with men during her youth helped develop her philosophy?

4. Why does the narrator want to introduce the woman to her sons?

5. What is the significance of the essay's title?

6. How does Sanchez's use of description help the reader characterize the narrator?

7. Why do you think Sanchez chose to use a double negative in her title?

Writing Assignments

1. Write an essay that illustrates one of the following statements:

   a. Experience is the best teacher.

   b. One can never judge a book by its cover.

2. Write an essay in which you describe a time when you were given helpful or interesting advice from an older person.

3. Write an essay about someone who unexpectedly made a difference in your life.

TEA CAKE AND JANIE

Zora Neale Hurston

*Zora Neale Hurston (1907–1960) was born in Eatonville,
Florida, and is the author of three novels:* Jonah's Gourd
Vine *(1934),* Their Eyes Were Watching God *(1937), from
which this excerpt is taken, and* Seraph on the Suwanee
(1948). Her works also include her autobiography, Dust
Tracks on the Road *(1943), and several volumes of folklore.
This story describes the newfound love between Tea Cake
and Janie, despite disapproval from their friends and
townspeople.*

Vocabulary

step off	(26)	get married
flommuck	(29)	flop, failure
kerflommuck	(37)	announcement, important issue
stand up wid	(39)	marry

"Pheoby," Sam Watson said one night as he got in the bed, "Ah   1
b'lieve yo' buddy is all tied up with dat Tea Cake shonough.
Didn't b'lieve it at first."

"Aw she don't mean nothin' by it. Ah think she's sort of   2
stuck on dat undertaker up at Sanford."

"It's somebody 'cause she looks mighty good dese days.   3
New dresses and her hair combed a different way nearly every
day. You got to have something to comb hair over. When you
see uh woman doin' so much rakin' in her head, she's combin'
at some man or 'nother."

" 'Course she kin do as she please, but dat's uh good   4
chance she got up at Sanford. De man's wife died and he got
uh lovely place tuh take her to—already furnished. Better'n her
house Joe left her."

"You better sense her intuh things then 'cause Tea Cake   5
can't do nothing' but help her spend whut she got. Ah reckon
dat's whut he's after. Throwin' away whut Joe Starks worked
hard tuh git tuh gether."

"Dat's de way it looks. Still and all, she's her own woman.   6
She oughta know by now whut she wants tuh do."

"De men wuz talkin' 'bout it in de grove tuhday and givin'   7 her and Tea Cake both de devil. Dey figger he's spendin' on her now in order tuh make her spend on him later."

"Umph! Umph! Umph!"   8

"Oh dey got it all figgered out. Maybe it ain't as bad as   9
they say, but they talk it and make it sound real bad on her part."

"Dat's jealousy and malice. Some uh dem very mens wants   10
tuh do whut dey claim deys skeered Tea Cake is doin'."

"De Pastor claim Tea Cake don't 'low her tuh come tuh   11
church only once in awhile 'cause he want dat change tuh buy gas wid. Just draggin' de woman away from church. But anyhow, she's yo' bosom friend, so you better go see 'bout her. Drop uh lil hint here and dere and if Tea Cake is tryin' tuh rob her she kin see and know. Ah laks de woman and Ah sho would hate tuh see her come up like Mrs. Tyler."

"Ah mah God, naw! Reckon Ah better step over dere to-   12
morrow and have some chat wid Janie. She jus' ain't thinkin' whut she doin', dat's all."

The next morning Pheoby picked her way over to Janie's   13
house like a hen to a neighbor's garden. Stopped and talked a little with everyone she met, turned aside momentarily to pause at a porch or two—going straight by walking crooked. So her firm intention looked like an accident and she didn't have to give her opinion to folks along the way.

Janie acted glad to see her and after a while Pheoby   14
broached her with, "Janie, everybody's talkin' 'bout how dat Tea Cake is draggin' you round tuh places you ain't used tuh. Baseball games and huntin' and fishin'. He don't know you'se useter uh more high time crowd than dat. You always did class off."

"Jody classed me off. Ah didn't. Naw, Pheoby, Tea Cake   15
ain't draggin' me off nowhere Ah don't want tuh go. Ah always did want tuh git round uh whole heap, but Jody wouldn't 'low me tuh. When Ah wasn't in de store he wanted me tuh jes sit wid folded hands and sit dere. And Ah'd sit dere wid de walls creepin' up on me and squeezin' all de life outa me. Pheoby, dese educated women got uh heap of things to sit down and consider. Somebody done tole 'em what to set down for. Nobody ain't told poor me, so sittin' still worries me. Ah wants tuh utilize mahself all over."

"But, Janie, Tea Cake, whilst he ain't no jail-bird, he ain't   16
got uh dime tuh cry. Ain't you skeered he's jes after yo' money—him bein' younger than you?"

"He ain't never ast de first penny from me yet, and if he   17
love property he ain't no different from all de rest of us. All dese
ole men dat's settin' round me is after de same thing. They's
three mo' widder women in town, how come dey don't break
dey neck after dem? 'Cause dey ain't got nothin', dat's why."

"Folks seen you out in colors and dey thinks you ain't   18
payin' de right amount uh respect tuh yo' dead husband."

"Ah ain't grievin' so why do Ah hafta mourn? Tea Cake   19
love me in blue, so Ah wears it. Jody ain't never in his life
picked out no color for me. De world picked out black and
white for mournin', Joe didn't. So Ah wasn't wearin' it for him.
Ah was wearin' it for de rest of y'all."

"But anyhow, watch yo'self, Janie, and don't be took ad-   20
vantage of. You know how dese young men is wid older women.
Most of de time dey's after whut dey kin git, then dey's gone lak
uh turkey through de corn."

"Tea Cake don't talk dat way. He's aimin' tuh make hisself   21
permanent wid me. We done made up our mind tuh marry."

"Janie, you'se yo' own woman, and Ah hope you know   22
whut you doin'. Ah sho hope you ain't lak uh possum—de older
you gits, de less sense yuh got. Ah'd feel uh whole heap better
'bout yuh if you wuz marryin' dat man up dere in Sanford. He
got somethin' tuh put long side uh whut you got and dat make
it more better. He's endurable."

"Still and all Ah'd ruther be wid Tea Cake."   23

"Well, if yo' mind is already made up, 'tain't nothin' no-   24
body kin do. But you'se takin' uh awful chance."

"No mo' than Ah took befo' and no mo' than anybody else   25
takes when dey gits married. It always changes folks, and
sometimes it brings out dirt and meanness dat even de person
didn't know they had in 'em theyselves. You know dat. Maybe
Tea Cake might turn out lak dat. Maybe not. Anyhow Ah'm
ready and willin' tuh try 'im."

"Well, when you aim tuh step off?"   26

"Dat we don't know. De store is got tuh be sold and then   27
we'se goin' off somewhere tuh git married."

"How come you sellin' out de store?"   28

" 'Cause Tea Cake ain't no Jody Starks, and if he tried tuh   29
be, it would be uh complete flommuck. But de minute Ah marries 'im everybody is gointuh be makin' comparisons. So us is
goin' off somewhere and start all over in Tea Cake's way. Dis
ain't no business proposition, and no race after property and ti-

tles. Dis is uh love game. Ah done lived Grandma's way, now Ah means tuh live mine."

"What you mean by dat, Janie?" 30

"She was borned in slavery time when folks, dat is black 31 folks, didn't sit down anytime dey felt lak it. So sittin' on porches lak de white madam looked lak uh mighty fine thing tuh her. Dat's whut she wanted for me—don't keer whut it cost. Git up on uh high chair and sit dere. She didn't have time tuh think whut tuh do after you got up on de stool uh do nothin'. De object wuz tuh git dere. So Ah got up on de high stool lak she told me, but Pheoby, Ah done nearly languished tuh death up dere. Ah felt like de world wuz cryin' extry and Ah ain't read de common news yet."

"Maybe so, Janie. Still and all Ah'd love tuh experience it 32 for just one year. It look lak heben tuh me from where Ah'm at."

"Ah reckon so." 33

"But anyhow, Janie, you be keerful 'bout dis sellin' out 34 and goin' off wid strange men. Look whut happened tuh Annie Tyler. Took whut little she had and went off tuh Tampa wid dat boy dey call Who Flung. It's somethin' tuh think about."

"It sho is. Still Ah ain't Mis' Tyler and Tea Cake ain't no 35 Who Flung, and he ain't no stranger tuh me. We'se just as good as married already. But Ah ain't puttin' it in de street. Ah'm tellin' you."

"Ah just lak uh chicken. Chicken drink water, but he don't 36 peepee."

"Oh, Ah know you don't talk. We ain't shame faced. We 37 jus' ain't ready tuh make no big kerflommuck as yet."

"You doin' right not tuh talk it, but Janie, you'se takin' uh 38 mighty big chance."

" 'Tain't so big uh chance as it seem lak, Pheoby. Ah'm 39 older than Tea Cake, yes. But he done showed me where it's de thought dat makes de difference in ages. If people thinks de same they can make it all right. So in the beginnin' new thoughts had tuh be thought and new words said. After Ah got used tuh dat, we gits 'long jus' fine. He done taught me de maiden language all over. Wait till you see de new blue satin Tea Cake done picked out for me tuh stand up wid him in. High heel slippers, necklace, earrings, *everything* he wants tuh see me in. Some of dese mornin's and it won't be long, you gointuh wake up callin' me and Ah'll be gone."

Discussion Questions

1. Why do the townspeople disapprove of the relationship between Janie and Tea Cake?
2. How does Tea Cake differ from Joe Starks?
3. What is the relationship between Tea Cake and Janie?
4. What does Janie mean when she says she has lived "Grandma's way"? What kind of life did her grandmother want for Janie?
5. How do females' attitudes toward love and marriage today compare with those of Janie and Pheoby?
6. How does Hurston use illustration to show the love that Tea Cake and Janie have for one another?
7. Do you think that Hurston's use of black dialect and folk expressions adds to or takes away from the story? Why or why not?

Writing Assignments

1. Write an essay discussing today's views on older women-younger men relationships.
2. Write an essay describing how you get along better with an older person than with someone your own age.
3. Write an essay by completing the following statement: "I wish I had the courage to _____."

Student Essay:
POSITIVE AFFIRMATIONS AMONG AFRICAN AMERICAN MEN AND WOMEN

Jason Orr

Vocabulary

perennial	(1)	annual
insurmountable	(2)	not capable of being resolved
affirmations	(5)	positive truths

As I travel the country each summer to attend my annual family reunion, a pattern is beginning to emerge. After all the children are fed and all the prizes are given out, without fail the women of the family migrate to one corner of the park and commence to have their perennial discussion of—well, you may have guessed by now—black men. I'm sure you've seen the scene. It is the same one depicted in the novel by Terry McMillan, *Waiting to Exhale*.[1] In these conversations one million and one excuses are given why black women might stray from black men. I will give you three why they should not. 1

The first reason why black women should not seek out relationships in other races is really elementary. The fact is that there are basic cultural differences that make it difficult and sometimes even impossible for other races, especially European Americans, to relate to black people. To some extent, these differences are understandable. However, there are many rituals that are sacred to the black community and should be kept that way. Take, for instance, African American cuisine. I have not tasted any cooking that can rival the cooking of black folk, and yet outsiders frown when talking of chitterlings, cornbread, and collard greens. Another example is the African American parties and gatherings. Have you seen an outsider at a party "thrown" by blacks? It is not a sight that is pleasing to the eye. The manner in which African Americans worship God in the Baptist church is clearly different from the way white Baptists worship God. Finally, black music has a style all its own, even though today there are many white musicians who attempt to 2

[1] *Waiting to Exhale* (1)   A well-received 1992 novel by Terry McMillan that focuses on difficulties in African American male-female relationships.

imitate this style. In the end, it all comes down to the fact that there are insurmountable differences that separate black culture from others.

Another reason black women should date and marry   3
within their race is one that has to do with the future. I have seen too many products of interracial marriages grow up with identity problems. There are too many problems that face the black community already without having to worry about a person of another race raising a black child. When interracial couples have children, they are repeating the cycle of the confused black child that asks, "Mommy, am I white or black?" There is only one person that can raise a black boy or girl and that is a black man or woman.

The most important reason why black women should date   4
within their race is that there are far too many strong black men to choose from. Being a student at a predominantly black college, I stand among the top male prospects in the world. Please, do not get me wrong. College helps, but it does not make a man's education. There are lessons to be learned in the street, home, and church that will never be taught in the classroom by a professor holding the highest degree. Too many times I hear women categorizing black men: too poor, too ugly, too conceited, too humble, too dark, gay, straight, divorced, addicted to drugs. Yet, there is one category that is the largest and the most overlooked: the positive, strong, well-rounded black man.

The black man is someone to be cherished. Therefore,   5
what should be emphasized at family reunions and at the roundtable conferences that occur so frequently among black women is the positive affirmations of the black male. If not, the black community will keep turning, but it will definitely be for the worst.

Discussion Questions

1. What is Orr's principal complaint?
2. What three reasons does he give to support his argument? How valid are these reasons?
3. What do you perceive as the strength and weakness of his argument? Explain your response.
4. What kind of rituals does the author consider sacred to the black community?
5. According to the author, who can best raise a black child?

6. Does the author offer sufficient evidence to make his argument a convincing one?

7. How effective is the conclusion? Explain your answer.

Writing Assignments

1. Write an essay stating your own reasons why people should (should not) date outside of their race or culture.

2. Write an essay describing the rituals or cultural practices within your ethnic or religious group.

10

Civil Rights

WORKING FOR SNCC

David Rubel

*David Rubel is a writer and journalist whose work has ap-
peared in such publications as the* Washington Post *and
the* Boston Globe. *After graduating from Columbia University, he worked as a correspondent for the Pacific News
Service and later became a mathematics textbook editor.
Currently he is a children's book editor in New York City. In
the following selection taken from* Fannie Lou Hamer: From
Sharecropping to Politics *(1990), Rubel describes how
Hamer and fellow Student Nonviolent Coordinating Committee (SNCC) worker Robert Moses sought to win voting
rights for blacks in Ruleville, Mississippi, in the early
1960s.*

The Student Nonviolent Coordinating Committee (SNCC) wasn't   1
like most other civil rights organizations. Because it followed a
legal strategy, the National Association for the Advancement of
Colored People (NAACP) rarely sent people into small, backwater towns like Ruleville. But SNCC came to Ruleville because
SNCC went everywhere in the rural South.

Led by young staff members and volunteers, SNCC favored forceful, direct action. Grass-roots organizing was its specialty. 2

In its first few years of experience. SNCC had focused its attention on the sit-ins and the other mass demonstrations. But by the summer of 1961, some SNCC staff members, particularly Robert Moses, wanted to shift SNCC resources to voter-registration drives. 3

Moses admitted that the sit-ins had achieved some real gains. But he pointed out that the freedom to eat at a Woolworth's lunch counter was not the same as freedom from police brutality or the right to obtain a fair trial. 4

To win these civil rights in Mississippi, Moses argued, African Americans would have to influence the sheriffs and judges of Mississippi. And the only sure way to do that, he knew, was to register and vote. The system had to be changed at its roots. 5

In August 1961, SNCC decided to pursue both sit-ins and registration drives. Moses was picked to lead the registration effort. 6

Moses was the perfect man for this difficult job. He was already well known within the movement as a tireless and capable worker. And he was also a born leader. With large, tranquil eyes hidden behind thick, plastic-framed glasses, he spoke with a calm voice and chose his words slowly and carefully. 7

Perhaps Moses' style came from the time he spent as a mathematics teacher, but wherever it came from, it inspired and reassured the people with whom he worked. "He could walk into a place where a lynch mob had just left and make up a bed and prepare to go to sleep, as if the situation was normal," one SNCC worker said. 8

Moses set up SNCC field offices all over the state of Mississippi because the only way he saw to register African Americans to vote was to go out into the fields and talk to those who weren't registered. 9

Many of the unregistered African Americans would need help, of course. Like Fannie Lou Hamer herself, many didn't even know they could vote. Others would need help with the forms. Almost all of them would need help to pass the tricky literacy test.[1] 10

---

[1] literacy test (10)   A test to prove that people wishing to vote could read and write.

But, as Moses knew, all of this could be taught. What   11
would be more difficult to provide would be the courage each
new registrant needed to challenge Mississippi's system of
white domination. All their lives, the poor blacks of Mississippi
had lived in fear of whites. All their lives, they had been told
that whites were superior. Fannie Lou Hamer had never believed it, but she was one of the exceptions.

Most of Hamer's neighbors found it very difficult to forget   12
what the whites had taught them, particularly when so many
violent whites were happy to remind them of these lessons.

Fannie Lou Hamer returned to Ruleville that winter of   13
1962 as a field secretary for SNCC. She immediately started organizing a local poverty program. This included asking the federal government for food and clothing for the needy families of
Ruleville. She also began the work of organizing the townspeople politically. This was her most important task. In the fields
by day and in the churches by night, Hamer talked to people
about the movement and about their right to vote.

In addition to all this, Hamer even found time to cook for   14
all the SNCC workers who regularly came to town.

Fannie Lou Hamer soon became one of SNCC's most effec-   15
tive fundraisers. She often traveled north to speak to white audiences about the desperation of black Mississippians and their
desire for change. "I'm sick and tired of being sick and tired,"
Hamer would tell them.

So far there had been no repeat of the September 10   16
shootings, but the harassment continued. One morning before
daylight, two policemen came into the Hamers' bedroom with
their guns drawn. They pretended to conduct a search, but
they had no warrant. Their real purpose was to scare the
Hamers.

Another time, the Hamers received a water bill for $9,000,   17
when they didn't even have running water. Nevertheless, Pap
was arrested over this bill.

These years were very difficult ones for the Hamers,   18
though it must have helped to know that they had the movement behind them. Fannie Lou's $10-a-week SNCC salary
barely allowed the family to get by, but friends and neighbors
helped out when they could.

Still, it was difficult to keep going. After all, most SNCC   19
volunteers were much younger and much better educated than
Fannie Lou Hamer was. They also didn't have families to support. But what Fannie Lou Hamer lacked in those areas, she
more than made up for in courage and determination.

January 10, 1963, was a Thursday. It was also the day   20
that Fannie Lou Hamer, on her third try, became one of the
first of Sunflower County's 30,000 African Americans to register to vote. She had been studying sections of the Mississippi
state constitution, hoping to get one on the test that she could
interpret. She did get one, and she passed.

When election day came that fall, however, Hamer was still   21
denied her right to vote because she couldn't afford the money
to pay the Mississippi poll tax.[2]

Discussion Questions

1. Why do you think the author begins this essay by making a distinction between SNCC and the other civil rights organizations?
2. Why did Robert Moses want to shift emphasis from mass demonstrations to voter-registration drives?
3. What characteristics made Moses a "born leader"?
4. What leadership traits did Fannie Lou Hamer have?
5. What are some of the many obstacles that prevented black Mississippians from voting?
6. To what extent does the author's use of cause and effect enhance
   your understanding of the civil rights struggles that Hamer and
   Moses faced?
7. Why do you think the author chose to add paragraph 21 rather
   than ending the essay with paragraph 20? What does that final
   paragraph tell us about Hamer in particular and the civil rights
   movement in general?

Writing Assignments

1. Write an essay about an extraordinary person you know.
2. Write an essay about an organization, community, or individual
   that you feel has misused power. Try to also explain why this
   misuse of power occurred.
3. Write an essay in which you explore the meaning of "power."

[2] poll tax (21)   An unlawful tax that blacks were required to pay in order
to vote.

EMMETT TILL IS DEAD

Anne Moody

*Anne Moody (1940–   ) was born in Wilkinson County,
Mississippi, a rural poverty area. After receiving a bachelor's degree from Tougaloo College, Moody became active in
the Civil Rights Movement and carried her activities north to
Cornell University. In the following excerpt from her autobiographical novel, Coming of Age in Mississippi (1968),
Moody reflects on how her racial consciousness was raised
as a result of the murder of Emmett Till.*

Not only did I enter high school with a new name, but also with   1
a completely new insight into the life of Negroes in Mississippi. I
was now working for one of the meanest white women in town,
and a week before school started Emmett Till[1] was killed.

Up until his death, I had heard of Negroes found floating   2
in a river or dead somewhere with their bodies riddled with bullets. But I didn't know the mystery behind these killings then. I
remember once when I was only seven I heard Mama and one
of my aunts talking about some Negro who had been beaten to
death. "Just like them low-down skunks killed him they will do
the same to us," Mama had said. When I asked her who killed
the man and why, she said, "An Evil Spirit killed him. You gotta
to be a good girl or it will kill you too." So since I was seven, I
had lived in fear for that "Evil Spirit." It took me eight years to
learn what that spirit was.

I was coming from school the evening I heard about Em-   3
mett Till's death. There was a whole group of us, girls and
boys, walking down the road headed home. A group of about
six high school boys were walking a few paces ahead of me and
several other girls. We were laughing and talking about something that had happened in school that day. However, the six
boys in front of us weren't talking very loud. Usually they kept
up so much noise. But today they were just walking and talking among themselves. All of a sudden they began to shout at
each other.

[1] Emmett Till (1)   A black youth who was murdered in Mississippi for his
"forward" behavior toward a white woman. The white men, tried for killing Till, were
acquitted by an all-white jury.

"Man, what in the hell do you mean?" 4

"What I mean is these goddamned white folks is gonna 5
start some shit here, you just watch!"

"That boy wasn't but fourteen years old and they killed 6
him. Now what kin a fourteen-year-old boy do with a white
woman? What if he did whistle at her, he might have thought
the whore was pretty."

"Look at all these white men here that's fucking over our 7
women. Everybody knows it too and what's done about that?
Look how many white babies we got walking around in our
neighborhoods. Their mamas ain't white either. That boy was
from Chicago, shit, everybody fuck everybody up there. He
probably didn't even think of the bitch as white."

What they were saying shocked me. I knew all of those 8
boys and I had never heard them talk like that. We walked on
behind them for a while listening. Questions about who was
killed, where, and why started running through my mind. I
walked up to one of the boys.

"Eddie, what boy was killed?" 9

"Moody, where've you been?" he asked me. "Everybody 10
talking about that fourteen-year-old boy who was killed in
Greenwood by some white men. You don't know nothing that's
going on besides what's in them books of yours, huh?"

Standing there before the rest of the girls, I felt so stupid. 11
It was then that I realized I really didn't know what was going
on all around me. It wasn't that I was dumb. It was just that
ever since I was nine, I'd had to work after school and do my
lessons on lunch hour. I never had time to learn anything, to
hang around with people my own age. And you never were told
anything by adults.

That evening when I stopped off at the house on my way 12
to Mrs Burke's, Mama was singing. Any other day she would
have been yelling at Adline and Junior them to take off their
school clothes. I wondered if she knew about Emmett Till. The
way she was singing she had something on her mind and it
wasn't pleasant either.

> I got a shoe, you got a shoe,
> All of God's chillun got shoes;
> When I get to hebben, I'm gonna put on my shoes,
> And gonna tromp all over God's hebben.
> When I get to hebben I'm gonna put on my shoes,
> And gonna walk all over God's hebben.

Mamma was dishing up beans like she didn't know any-   13
one was home. Adline, Junior, and James had just thrown
their books down and sat themselves at the table. I didn't usually eat before I went to work. But I wanted to ask Mama about
Emmett Till. So I ate and thought of some way of asking her.

"These beans are some good, Mama," I said, trying to   14
sense her mood.

"Why is you eating anyway? You gonna be late for work.   15
You know how Miss Burke is," she said to me.

"I don't have much to do this evening. I kin get it done be-   16
fore I leave work," I said.

The conversation stopped after that. Then Mama started   17
humming that song again.

> When I get to hebben, I'm gonna put on my shoes,
> And gonna tromp all over God's hebben.

She put a plate on the floor for Jennie Ann and Jerry.

"Jennie Ann! You and Jerry sit down here and eat and   18
don't put beans all over the floor."

Ralph, the baby, started crying, and she went in the bed-   19
room to give him his bottle. I got up and followed her.

"Mama, did you hear about that fourteen-year-old Negro   20
boy who was killed a little over a week ago by some white
men?" I asked her.

"Where did you hear that?" she said angrily.   21

"Boy, everybody really thinks I am dumb or deaf or some-   22
thing. I heard Eddie them talking about it this evening coming
from school."

"Eddie them better watch how they go around here talk-   23
ing. These white folks git a hold of it they gonna be in trouble,"
she said.

"What are they gonna be in trouble about, Mama? People   24
got a right to talk, ain't they?"

"You go on to work before you is late. And don't you let on   25
like you know nothing about that boy being killed before Miss
Burke them. Just do your work like you don't know nothing,"
she said. "That boy's a lot better off in heaven than he is here,"
she continued and then started singing again.

On my way to Mrs Burke's that evening, Mama's words   26
kept running through my mind. "Just do your work like you
don't know nothing." "Why is Mama acting so scared?" I
thought. "And what if Mrs Burke knew we knew? Why must I

pretend I don't know? Why are these people killing Negroes? What did Emmett Till do besides whistle at that woman?"

By the time I got to work, I had worked my nerves up some. I was shaking as I walked up on the porch. "Do your work like you don't know nothing." But once I got inside, I couldn't have acted normal if Mrs Burke were paying me to be myself.   27

I was so nervous, I spent most of the evening avoiding them, going about the house dusting and sweeping. Everything went along fairly well until dinner was served.   28

"Don, Wayne, and Mama, y'all come on to dinner. Essie, you can wash up the pots and dishes in the sink now. Then after dinner you won't have as many," Mrs Burke called to me.   29

If I had the power to mysteriously disappear at that moment, I would have. They used the breakfast table in the kitchen for most of their meals. The dining room was only used for Sunday dinner or when they had company. I wished they had company tonight so they could eat in the dining room while I was at the kitchen sink.   30

"I forgot the bread," Mrs Burke said when they were all seated. "Essie, will you cut it and put it on the table for me?"   31

I took the cornbread, cut it in squares, and put it on a small round dish. Just as I was about to set it on the table, Wayne yelled at the cat. I dropped the plate and the bread went all over the floor.   32

"Never mind, Essie," Mrs Burke said angrily as she got up and got some white bread from the breadbox.   33

I didn't say anything. I picked up the cornbread from around the table and went back to the dishes. As soon as I got to the sink, I dropped a saucer on the floor and broke it. Didn't anyone say a word until I had picked up the pieces.   34

"Essie, I bought some new cleanser today. It's setting on the bathroom shelf. See if it will remove the stains in the tub," Mrs Burke said.   35

I went to the bathroom to clean the tub. By the time I got through with it, it was snow white. I spent a whole hour scrubbing it. I had removed the stains in no time but I kept scrubbing until they finished dinner.   36

When they had finished and gone into the living room as usual to watch TV, Mrs Burke called me to eat. I took a clean plate out of the cabinet and sat down. Just as I was putting the first forkful of food in my mouth, Mrs Burke entered the kitchen.   37

"Essie, did you hear about that fourteen-year-old boy who 38
was killed in Greenwood?" she asked me, sitting down in one of
the chairs opposite me.

"No, I didn't hear that," I answered, almost choking on the 39
food.

"Do you know why he was killed?" she asked and I didn't 40
answer.

"He was killed because he got out of his place with a white 41
woman. A boy from Mississippi would have known better than
that. This boy was from Chicago. Negroes up North have no respect for people. They think they can get away with anything.
He just came to Mississippi and put a whole lot of notions in
the boys' heads here and stirred up a lot of trouble," she said
passionately.

"How old are you, Essie?" she asked me after a pause. 42

"Fourteen. I will soon be fifteen though," I said. 43

"See, that boy was just fourteen too. It's a shame he had 44
to die so soon." She was so red in the face, she looked as if she
was on fire.

When she left the kitchen I sat there with my mouth open 45
and my food untouched. I couldn't have eaten now if I were
starving. "Just do your work like you don't know nothing" ran
through my mind again and I began washing the dishes.

I went home shaking like a leaf on a tree. For the first time 46
out of all her trying, Mrs Burke had made me feel like rotten
garbage. Many times she had tried to instill fear within me and
subdue me and had given up. But when she talked about Emmett Till there was something in her voice that sent chills and
fear all over me.

Before Emmett Till's murder, I had known the fear of 47
hunger, hell, and the Devil. But now there was a new fear
known to me—the fear of being killed just because I was black.
This was the worst of my fears. I knew once I got food, the fear
of starving to death would leave. I also was told that if I were a
good girl, I wouldn't have to fear the Devil or hell. But I didn't
know what one had to do or not do as a Negro not to be killed.
Probably just being a Negro period was enough, I thought.

A few days later, I went to work and Mrs Burke had about 48
eight women over for tea. They were all sitting around in the
living room when I got there. She told me she was having a
"guild meeting," and asked me to help her serve the cookies
and tea.

After helping her, I started cleaning the house. I always swept the hallway and porch first. As I was sweeping the hall, I could hear them talking. When I heard the word "nigger," I stopped and listened. Mrs Burke must have sensed this, because she suddenly came to the door. 49

"Essie, finish the hall and clean the bathroom," she said hesitantly. "Then you can go for today. I am not making dinner tonight." Then she went back in the living room with the rest of the ladies. 50

Before she interrupted my listening, I had picked up the words "NAACP" and "that organization". Because they were talking about niggers, I knew NAACP had something to do with Negroes. All that night I kept wondering what could that NAACP mean? 51

Later when I was sitting in the kitchen at home doing my lessons, I decided to ask Mama. It was about twelve-thirty. Everyone was in bed but me. When Mama came in to put some milk in Ralph's bottle, I said, "Mama, what do NAACP mean?" 52

"Where did you git that from?" she asked me, spilling milk all over the floor. 53

"Mrs Burke had a meeting tonight—" 54

"What kind of meeting?" she asked, cutting me off. 55

"I don't know. She had some women over—she said it was a guild meeting," I said. 56

"A guild meeting," she repeated. 57

"Yes, they were talking about Negroes and I heard some woman say 'that NAACP' and another 'that organization,' meaning the same thing." 58

"What else did they say?" she asked me. 59

"That's all I heard. Mrs Burke must have thought I was listening, so she told me to clean the bathroom and leave." 60

"Don't you ever mention that word around Mrs Burke or no other white person, you heah! Finish your lesson and cut that light out and go to bed," Mama said angrily and left the kitchen. 61

"With a Mama like that you'll never learn anything," I thought as I got into bed. All night long I thought about Emmett Till and the NAACP. I even got up to look up NAACP in my little concise dictionary. But I didn't find it. 62

The next day at school, I decided to ask my homeroom teacher Mrs Rice the meaning of NAACP. When the bell sounded for lunch, I remained in my seat as the other students left the room. 63

"Are you going to spend your lunch hour studying again   64
today, Moody?" Mrs Rice asked me.

"Can I ask you a question, Mrs Rice?" I asked her.   65

"You *may* ask me a question, yes, but I don't know if you 66
can or not," she said.

"What does the word NAACP mean?" I asked.   67

"Why do you want to know?"   68

"The lady I worked for had a meeting and I overheard the   69
word mentioned."

"What else did you hear?"   70

"Nothing. I didn't know what NAACP meant, that's all." I   71
felt like I was on the witness stand or something.

"Well, next time your boss has another meeting you listen   72
more carefully. NAACP is a Negro organization that was established a long time ago to help Negroes gain a few basic rights,"
she said.

"What's it gotta do with the Emmett Till murder?" I asked. 73

"They are trying to get a conviction in Emmett Till's case. 74
You see the NAACP is trying to do a lot for the Negroes and get
the right to vote for Negroes in the South. I shouldn't be telling
you all this. And don't you dare breathe a word of what I said.
It could cost me my job if word got out I was teaching my students such. I gotta go to lunch and you should go outside too
because it's nice and sunny out today," she said leaving the
room. "We'll talk more when I have time."

About a week later, Mrs Rice had me over for Sunday din-   75
ner, and I spent about five hours with her. Within that time, I
digested a good meal and accumulated a whole new pool of
knowledge about Negroes being butchered and slaughtered by
whites in the South. After Mrs Rice had told me all this, I felt
like the lowest animal on earth. At least when other animals
(hogs, cows, etc.) were killed by man, they were used as food.
But when man was butchered or killed by man, in the case of
Negroes by whites, they were left lying on a road or found floating in a river or something.

Mrs Rice got to be something like a mother to me. She told   76
me anything I wanted to know. And made me promise that I
would keep all this information she was passing on to me to
myself. She said she couldn't, rather didn't want to, talk about
these things to other teachers, that they would tell Mr Willis
and she would be fired. At the end of that year she was fired. I
never found out why. I haven't seen her since then.

Discussion Questions

1. Why was Emmett Till murdered?
2. Why does Moody's mother tell her to "do your work like you don't know nothing"?
3. How does Moody feel after hearing the news of Till's murder?
4. Why do you think Mrs. Rice is fired?
5. Why do Mrs. Burke and the other ladies in the guild talk about the NAACP?
6. In what way does the mother's desire to protect her daughter result in her hurting her?
7. To what extent does Moody's use of comparison and contrast help us understand the racial conditions in the story?
8. What is the theme of the story?

Writing Assignments

1. Write an essay illustrating a coming-of-age experience that you have had.
2. Write an essay in which you describe an event that devastated your group or community. What was your personal response?
3. Write an essay in which you recount a time when you or someone you know was encouraged to keep quiet, when speaking up should have been the thing to do.

HOWARD UNIVERSITY: A RUDE AWAKENING

Cleveland Sellers

Cleveland Sellers, Jr. (1944–   ), was born in Denmark, South Carolina. A political activist himself, he met Stokely Carmichael (Kwame Toure) while a student at Howard University. In 1965, Sellers was elected program secretary of SNCC (Student Nonviolent Coordinating Committee). He was arrested for his participation in the Orangeburg Massacre and was later released on bail so he could attend college. In the following excerpt from River of No Return *(1973), his memoirs of the civil rights movement, Sellers reveals his disappointment regarding the apathy of many college students.*

Vocabulary

expendable	(3)	unnecessary
exasperation	(9)	frustration
flamboyant	(14)	showy, flashy
bombast	(14)	egotism, airs
kooks	(19)	oddballs, weirdos
affiliate	(20)	ally, partner

Howard University was a big disappointment. I arrived on campus in September, 1962. Filled with the unbounded enthusiasm peculiar to seventeen-year-olds, I expected to see everyone, students, instructors and administrators, passionately involved in the movement. I was eager to participate in emotion-packed mass meetings, tense strategy sessions and frequent demonstrations. Unfortunately, I didn't find any of these things.

When I attempted to discuss the movement with the guys in my dormitory, they would grunt and change the subject. They were much more interested in cars, fraternities, clothes, parties and girls. They loved to sit in bull sessions for hours discussing them. They also spent a lot of time talking about the high-paying jobs they intended to get after graduating. By the end of my first semester, I felt like an outcast. I tried to discuss my feelings and interests with my instructors—I needed help from someone who understood what I was going through—but

1

2

they were harder to talk to than my classmates. Their primary concerns seemed to be their cars, their homes, their professional associations and their salaries.

The administrators were no different. They were remote men who never seemed to have enough time really to hear what students were saying. They related to us as if we were cogs in a giant machine: those cogs which did not conform to the machine's program were expendable. 3

There was a great deal of interest among almost everyone on campus in *the Howard image,* which was designed to create the impression that there were no substantial differences between Howard's students and those at elite white colleges. Students went to absurd lengths to conform to *the image.* The guys wore suits, jackets and ties everywhere—including football games and breakfasts. The girls wore stockings and heels. Many of them refused to date men whose clothes did not fit *the image.* 4

I refused to conform. I had always been a very casual dresser and saw no reason to change. I liked to wear blue jeans, sweat shirts, army jackets and sneakers. Although I did not relish the outsider-outcast role that was accorded me because of my clothes, I was determined not to change. 5

"I have the right to dress in any way I please!" I snapped at my roommate one night when he attempted to scold me for wearing blue jeans to a big dance. 6

"But, Cleve," he responded, "you'll never get/a girlfriend. No girl's gonna be caught dead with you if you keep dressing like a refugee from World War I." 7

My roommate was in love with Howard. He was having a ball. He couldn't understand why I had so much trouble adjusting. 8

"Fuck it, man," he said to me one night in exasperation after I asked him if he didn't feel some responsibility to try to improve racial conditions. 9

"Don't confront me with that Martin Luther King shit. Everybody's gotta go for himself and I'm going for me. If niggas down South don't like the way they're being treated, they oughtta leave. I'm not going to join no picket lines and get the shit beat outta me by them crazy-ass Ku Klux-ers! 10

"I'm interested in four things," he added. "A degree, a good job, a good woman and a good living. That's all. You and Martin Luther King can take care of the demonstrating and protesting. I have *no* use for them!" 11

My roommate was typical. Although few stated their feel-   12
ings so bluntly, most of Howard's students shared his attitude.

I met my first real friend near mid-semester. He was a tall,   13
lanky junior with sparkling eyes and an infectious smile. Although he was from New York, we had many things in common, the most important being our intense interest in the
movement. We both had a burning passion to do something
about the plight of blacks. His name was Stokely Carmichael.

From the day we met, I considered Stokely a special   14
friend, a special person. Although he was flamboyant and extremely cocky, there was something about his manner that attracted people. Everyone on campus knew him. Few of his ad-
mirers ever got close enough to him to see what I saw: an
extremely sensitive person who generally disguised his sensitivity with bombast.

Stokely, who had worked in Mississippi for SNCC the pre-   15
vious summer, belonged to a campus organization called the
Nonviolent Action Group (NAG). It was just what I had been
looking for. I joined immediately.

NAG was organized in 1960, soon after the first sit-ins in   16
Greensboro. Some of its initial demonstrations attracted as
many as two hundred participants. One demonstration conducted during the summer of 1960 attracted five congressmen.

During its first year, NAG's members succeeded in deseg-   17
regating about twenty-five facilities, including lunch counters,
restaurants, a movie theater and Washington, D.C.'s only
amusement park. At least one hundred persons were arrested
in connection with demonstrations conducted by NAG.

The organization's name symbolized the determination of   18
its members to "nag" the conscience of Washington. The name
also reflected the theme of passive-aggressive protest that characterized that stage of the civil rights movement.

By the time I joined NAG in the winter of 1962, most of   19
Howard's students had lost interest in it. Picket lines and
demonstrations were not considered glamorous activities anymore. The twenty-five to thirty students who belonged to the
organization were considered "kooks."

NAG was a "Friends of SNCC" affiliate. This meant that   20
those of us who belonged to it were unofficial members of
SNCC. As members of NAG, we could attend some SNCC meetings and vote in some SNCC elections. There were scores of
other Friends of SNCC groups on other campuses, especially in
the North. Most of these organizations devoted their energies to

fund-raising projects; few were actively involved in campus or community politics.

NAG was different. Although we sponsored dances and 21 benefits for SNCC, that was not our primary task. Our primary task was demonstrating. We had a lot of good people, most of whom were Howard students—Courtland Cox, Murial Tillenez, Stokely, Stanley Wise, William (Bill) Mahoney, Ed Brown (Rap's brother) and Phil Hutchins.

Whenever black people in the city of Washington needed 22 pickets, they would get in touch with NAG. It didn't matter to us if it was cold outside. If we thought we could help black people, we didn't mind demonstrating.

We frequently picketed various government departments. 23 We weren't afraid of any of them. At different times the second semester, we picketed the Justice Department, Congress and the White House.

By the end of my second semester at Howard, I went on 24 campus only to eat, sleep, attend classes and participate in periodic NAG rallies. I spent the rest of my time demonstrating and getting to know the people who lived in the huge black ghetto surrounding the campus. Unlike our classmates, the people in the community had a great deal of respect for those of us who belonged to NAG. We were great heroes to the young kids.

Discussion Questions

1. What is the "movement" to which Sellers refers in the first paragraph?
2. Why was Sellers disappointed in the students at Howard University?
3. What was the primary purpose of the NAG and SNCC organizations?
4. What were some of the contributions NAG made to the civil rights movement?
5. What type of person is Sellers? Cite specific details in the essay to support your answer.
6. Why were many of Howard's students apathetic to the "movement"?
7. What types of rhetorical organization does Sellers use in his essay?
8. What do you think is the purpose of paragraph 1?

Writing Assignments

1. Write an essay in which you discuss how an event or a place was a disappointment to you.
2. Sellers describes several activities that Howard students found interesting in 1962. Write an essay describing what many university students find interesting today.
3. Write an essay describing your university's image.

I HAVE A DREAM

Martin Luther King, Jr.

A clergyman and civil rights leader, Martin Luther King, Jr. (1929–1968), was born in Atlanta, Georgia, and was educated at Morehouse College, Crozer Theological Seminary, and Boston University. As a nonviolent advocate, Dr. King encouraged others to resist segregation. He led a boycott of blacks against the city's segregated bus system in Montgomery, Alabama (1955–1956), and in 1963 he organized a massive march on Washington during which time he delivered his famous "I Have a Dream" speech, which appears here. Among his best known works are Stride Toward Freedom *(1958), a history of the Montgomery bus boycott, and "Letter from Birmingham Jail" (1964). Although he was the 1964 Nobel Peace Prize recipient, Dr. King met a violent death. On April 4, 1968, he was assassinated in Memphis, Tennessee, while in the city to support striking sanitation workers.*

Vocabulary

manacles	(2)	chains
unalienable	(4)	that which cannot be given or taken away
inextricably	(12)	hopelessly tangled
redemptive	(16)	freeing
interposition	(22)	act of coming between parties in a dispute
nullification	(22)	act of refusing to recognize or enforce a law
prodigious	(27)	enormous, gigantic

Five score years ago, a great American, in whose symbolic shadow we stand today, signed the Emancipation Proclamation. This momentous decree came as a great beacon of light of hope to millions of Negro slaves who had been seared in the flames of withering injustice. It came as a joyous daybreak to end the long night of their captivity.   1

But one hundred years later, the Negro still is not free. One hundred years later, the life of the Negro is still sadly crippled by the manacles of segregation and the chains of discrimination.   2

One hundred years later, the Negro lives on a lonely island of poverty in the midst of a vast ocean of material prosperity.   3

One hundred years later, the Negro is still languished in the corners of American society and finds himself an exile in his own land. So we have come here today to dramatize a shameful condition.

In a sense we have come to our nation's capital to cash a   4
check. When the architects of our republic wrote the magnificent words of the Constitution and the Declaration of Independence, they were signing a promissory note to which every American was to fall heir. This note was a promise that all men, yes, black men as well as white men, would be granted the unalienable rights of life, liberty, and the pursuit of happiness.

It is obvious today that America has defaulted on this   5
promissory note insofar as her citizens of color are concerned. Instead of honoring this sacred obligation, America has given the Negro people a bad check; which has come back marked "insufficient funds."

But we refuse to believe that the bank of justice is bank-   6
rupt. We refuse to believe that there are insufficient funds in the great vaults of opportunity of this nation. So we have come to cash this check—a check that will give us upon demand the riches of freedom and the security of justice.

We have also come to this hallowed spot to remind Amer-   7
ica of the fierce urgency of now. This is no time to engage in the luxury of cooling off or to take the tranquilizing drug of gradualism. Now is the time to make real the promises of democracy. Now is the time to rise from the dark and desolate valley of segregation to the sunlit path of racial justice. Now is time to lift our nation from the quick sands of racial injustice and to the solid rock of brotherhood. Now is the time to make justice a reality for all of God's children.

It would be fatal for the nation to overlook the urgency of   8
the movement and to underestimate the determination of the Negro. This sweltering summer of the Negro's legitimate discontent will not pass until there is an invigorating autumn of freedom and equality. Nineteen sixty-three is not an end but a beginning. Those who hope that the Negro needed to blow off steam and will now be content will have a rude awakening if the nation returns to business as usual.

There will be neither rest nor tranquility in America until   9
the Negro is granted his citizenship rights. The whirlwinds of revolt will continue to shake the foundations of our nation until the bright day of justice emerges.

But there is something that I must say to my people who   10
stand on the warm threshold which leads into the palace of
justice. In the process of gaining our rightful place we must not
be guilty of wrongful deeds.

Let us not seek to satisfy our thirst for freedom by drink-   11
ing from the cup of bitterness and hatred. We must forever
conduct our struggle on the high plane of dignity and discipline. We must not allow our creative protest to degenerate into
physical violence. Again and again we must rise to the majestic
heights of meeting physical force with soul force.

The marvelous new militancy which has engulfed the Ne-   12
gro community must not lead us to a distrust of all white people, for many of our white brothers, as evidenced by their presence here today, have come to realize that their destiny is tied
up with our destiny and they have come to realize that their
freedom is inextricably bound to our freedom. This offense we
share, mounted to storm the battlements of injustice, must be
carried forth by a bi-racial army. We cannot walk alone.

And as we walk, we must make the pledge that we shall   13
always march ahead. We cannot turn back. There are those
who are asking the devotees of civil rights, "When will you be
satisfied?" We can never be satisfied as long as the Negro is the
victim of the unspeakable horrors of police brutality.

We can never be satisfied as long as our bodies, heavy   14
with fatigue of travel, cannot gain lodging in the motels of the
highways and the hotels of the cities. We cannot be satisfied as
long as the Negro's basic mobility is from a smaller ghetto to a
larger one.

We can never be satisfied as long as our children are   15
stripped of their selfhood and robbed of their dignity by signs
stating "for whites only." We cannot be satisfied as long as a
Negro in Mississippi cannot vote and a Negro in New York believes he has nothing for which to vote. No, we are not satisfied,
and we will not be satisfied until justice rolls down like waters
and righteousness like a mighty stream.

I am not unmindful that some of you have come here out   16
of excessive trials and tribulation. Some of you have come fresh
from narrow jail cells. Some of you have come from areas
where your quest for freedom left you battered by the storms of
persecution and staggered by the winds of police brutality. You
have been the veterans of creative suffering. Continue to work
with the faith that unearned suffering is redemptive.

Go back to Mississippi; go back to Alabama; go back to   17
South Carolina; go back to Georgia; go back to Louisiana; go
back to the slums and ghettoes of the Northern cities, knowing
that somehow this situation can, and will, be changed. Let us
not wallow in the valley of despair.

So I say to you, my friends, that even though we must face   18
the difficulties of today and tomorrow, I still have a dream. It is
a dream deeply rooted in the American dream that one day this
nation will rise up and live out the true meaning of its creed—
we hold these truths to be self-evident, that all men are created
equal.

I have a dream that one day on the red hills of Georgia,   19
sons of former slaves and sons of former slave-owners will be
able to sit down together at the table of brotherhood.

I have a dream that one day, even the state of Mississippi,   20
a state sweltering with the heat of injustice, sweltering with the
heat of oppression, will be transformed into an oasis of freedom
and justice.

I have a dream my four little children will one day live in a   21
nation where they will not be judged by the color of their skin
but by content of their character. I have a dream today!

I have a dream that one day, down in Alabama, with its vi-   22
cious racists, with its governor having his lips dripping with the
words of interposition and nullification, that one day, right
there in Alabama, little black boys and black girls will be able
to join hands with little white boys and white girls as sisters
and brothers. I have a dream today!

I have a dream that one day every valley shall be exalted,   23
every hill and mountain shall be made low, the rough places
shall be made plain, and the crooked places shall be made
straight and the glory of the Lord will be revealed and all flesh
shall see it together.

This is our hope. This is the faith that I go back to the   24
South with.

With this faith we will be able to bear out of the mountain   25
of despair a stone of hope. With this faith we will be able to
transform the jangling discords of our nation into a beautiful
symphony of brotherhood.

With this faith we will be able to work together, to pray to-   26
gether, to struggle together, to go to jail together, to stand up
for freedom together, knowing that we will be free one day. This
will be the day when all of God's children will be able to sing
with new meaning "my country 'tis of thee; sweet land of lib-

erty; of thee I sing; land where my fathers died, land of the pilgrim's pride; from every mountain side, let freedom ring." And if America is to be a great nation, this must become true.

So let freedom ring from the prodigious hilltops of New Hampshire. 27

Let freedom ring from the mighty mountains of New York. 28

Let freedom ring from the heightening Alleghenies of Pennsylvania. 29

Let freedom ring from the snow-capped Rockies of Colorado. 30

Let freedom ring from the curvaceous slopes of California. 31

But not only that. 32

Let freedom ring from Stone Mountain of Georgia. 33

Let freedom ring from Lookout Mountain of Tennessee. 34

Let freedom ring from every hill and molehill of Mississippi, from every mountainside, let freedom ring. 35

And when we allow freedom to ring, when we let it ring from every village and hamlet, from every state and city, we will be able to speed up that day when all of God's children—black men and white men, Jews and Gentiles, Catholics and Protestants—will be able to join hands and to sing in the words of the old Negro spiritual, "Free at last, free at last; thank God Almighty, we are free at last." 36

Discussion Questions

1. What is King's dream?
2. What examples does King offer to support his argument that there was no democracy in the 1960s for blacks in the United States?
3. What do you think King means by his statement, "We have come to the nation's capital to cash a check"?
4. King relies on his skillful use of descriptive language, such as the example in question 3, to make his points clear. What are some other examples?
5. To what extent does King's repetition of phrases such as "One hundred years later," "Now is the time," "I have a dream" enhance the effectiveness of his speech?
6. To what extent, if any, has King's dream become a reality for African Americans today?
7. To what extent does King's use of illustration and description help strengthen his argument?

8. What in the speech indicates that King has an understanding of his audience?

Writing Assignments

1. In an essay argue whether or not King's dream of an America where "all men are created equal" has become a reality.
2. Write an essay describing one of your dreams.
3. Write an essay in which you describe a society free of one of today's ills: AIDS, drugs, sexism.

Student Essay:
THE CRIMINAL JUSTICE SYSTEM AND POOR BLACKS

Marshall Mercy

Vocabulary

disproportionate (4)   mismatched

The black man's place within American society has been well   1
defined since he was forced to come here. His place within
white society is either to work hard for the white man, which
does not benefit him but does benefit his oppressor, or to be
caged in like an animal because he is believed not to be fit to
live within a "democratic society."

Prominent sociologists have proven that the criminal jus-   2
tice system is more unfairly applied to lower income people
than to higher income people. Sociologists also offer evidence
that the majority of people who are arrested, convicted, and
punished are black males. Black males are more likely to go to
prison or to have a record by the age of twenty-six than any
other ethnic group. Although blacks are the minority, only 12%
of the population of the United States, they are the majority
within the prison system. Blacks are the least likely to be
paroled and the most likely to receive capital punishment.
Blacks on death row are more likely to be executed than their
white counterparts who commit the same crimes.

It seems that ever since the black man was stolen from his   3
home, forced to work on the hot plantation fields in the South,
forced to be poor and at the very mercy of the white man, he
has been denied the privileges guaranteed to others. In the
1800s the black male was discriminated against because he
was not allowed to testify against whites, but was allowed to
testify against other blacks. In the 1960s, through the struggle
for civil rights, blacks were again discriminated against when
they were thrown in jail for marching and protesting the mistreatment they received. In the 1990s, blacks in general and
black males in particular are still suffering at the hands of the
dominant society—white males.

From police brutality, highlighted by the Rodney King   4
case, to the disproportionate numbers of blacks on death row,

the black male is subjected to prejudices on the basis of race and class. As a result, he has been forced to be always in the pursuit of equality, liberty, and justice.

Discussion Questions

1. What principal arguments does Mercy give to support her statement that the criminal justice system is less "just" toward blacks?
2. To what extent is the author's use of logical persuasion effective?
3. Why does Mercy place quotation marks around "democratic society"?
4. How does the author show the history of discrimination blacks have suffered in the United States?
5. From reading the essay, what do you know about the author?
6. Mercy chooses illustration as one of her dominant rhetorical strategies. Are her examples sufficient to support his thesis?

Writing Assignments

1. Write an essay describing your ideas of a fair criminal justice system of the future.
2. Write an essay discussing the weakness and/or strength of the U.S. criminal justice system.

11

Freedom • Equality
Unity • Protest

FREEDOM

Joyce M. Jarrett

Teacher, writer, poet, Joyce M. Jarrett (1951–   ) was born in Meridian, Mississippi. A first-generation college student, Jarrett graduated from Tennessee State University and Vanderbilt University. Currently, she is associate professor of English at Hampton University. She is a co-author of Pathways: A Text for Developing Writers *(1990) and* Heritage: African American Readings for Writing *(1996). All of her creative works have grown out of her African American experience. In the selection here, which was first published in* Between Worlds *(1986), Jarrett reflects on one of her struggles during the civil rights movement.*

Vocabulary

hordes	(2)	groups or crowds
irate	(3)	angry
denigrating	(3)	insulting and belittling
constraints	(10)	restrictions
overt	(10)	obvious, apparent
futile	(10)	useless

"Born free, as free as the wind blows, as free as the grass grows, born free to follow your heart." (Don Black)

My first illusion of freedom came in 1966, many years fol-   1
lowing the Supreme Court's decision on school desegregation.
Of course, to a fifteen-year-old girl, isolated, caged like a rodent
in the poverty-stricken plains of the Magnolia State,[1] Brown
vs. the Board of Education had no meaning. Though many
must have thought that my decision to attend the all-white city
high school that fall, along with 49 other blacks, was made in
protest or had evolved from a sense of commitment for the betterment of my people, nothing could have been further from the
truth. Like a rat finding a new passageway, I was propelled to
my new liberty more out of curiosity than out of a sense of mission.

On the first day of school, I was escorted by hordes of na-   2
tional guardsmen. Like a funeral procession, the steady stream
of official-looking cars followed me to the campus. Some patrol-
men were parked near campus gates, while others, with guns
strapped to their sides, stood near building entrances. Though
many of my escorts had given me smiles of support, still I was
not prepared for what I encountered upon entering *my* new
school.

There, I had to break through lines of irate white protes-   3
tors, spraying obscenities at me while carrying their denigrat-
ing signs: "KKK Forever," read one; "Back to Africa," said another. And as I dashed toward the school door, blinded with
fear, I nearly collided with another sign that screamed, "Nigger
Go Home."

Once inside the fortress, I was ushered by school adminis-   4
trators and plain-clothes police to and from my respective
classes. The anger and fear that I had felt outside of those walls
were numbed by the surprisingly uneventful classroom experiences—until I went to geometry, my last scheduled class for
that day.

As I sauntered into the classroom and took a seat, there   5
was a flurry of activity. When everyone had settled, I sat in the
center of the class, surrounded by empty desks—on each side,
and in front and back.

"We have a nigger in the class," someone shouted.   6

---

[1] Magnolia State   (1)   Mississippi.

"Let's get quiet and make the best of it," Mr. Moore smugly 7
replied. Then he proceeded with the course orientation.

Near the end of the class, I mustered up enough courage 8
to ask a question, so, nervously, I raised my hand. Keeping
silent, Mr. Moore stared, and stared, and stared at me until my
arm grew heavy and began to tremble. My heart sank, and my
picture of freedom shattered in infinite pieces as he said, "I see
that there are no questions. Class dismissed."

I have always blamed myself for that crushing moment. 9
Why did I allow myself to be overlooked? Why did I not feel
free? That painful, dehumanizing incident within itself did not
provide any answers, though it signaled the beginning of my
search. And finally, through years of disappointments, I discovered the truth—the truth that had evaded me during those
high school years.

Freedom is not a gift, but a right. Officials did not, could 10
not, award "freedom." It had to be something that I wanted,
craved, demanded. The Supreme Court had liberated me of
many external restrictions, but I had failed to liberate myself.
In some instances internal constraints can be more binding
than the overt ones. It is impossible to enslave one who has liberated oneself and futile to pry off the external chains of an internally bound person. Only when there is emancipation of
both body and soul are any of us truly *free* to follow our hearts.

Discussion Questions

1. In the first paragraph, what is the curiosity to which the narrator
   refers?
2. Why were National Guardsmen needed to escort Jarrett to the
   school?
3. How did Mr. Moore demonstrate his racism?
4. Why does the narrator blame herself for the incident in Mr.
   Moore's class? Would you have blamed yourself had you been in
   the narrator's place?
5. To what extent does the narrator's attitude change after the incident?
6. What does the narrator mean when she says, "It is impossible to
   enslave one who has liberated oneself and futile to pry off the external chains of an internally bound person"?
7. The predominant organization of the essay is definition. To what
   extent does the writer use other strategies—illustration, cause

and effect, comparison and contrast—to help the reader understand her definition of "freedom"?

8. In what way, if any, would the essay change had the writer used her concluding paragraph as her opening paragraph? Explain your answer.

Writing Assignments

1. Write an essay describing an incident that caused you to develop a mature awakening.
2. Write an essay in which you define one of the following terms: freedom, racism, discrimination, commitment, struggle.
3. Write an essay about something you did (good or bad) for the wrong reason.

WE WEAR THE MASK

Paul Laurence Dunbar

*Paul Laurence Dunbar (1872–1906) was the first nationally
known African American poet. He published six volumes of
poetry, four novels, and four volumes of short stories. Despite his national reputation, however, Dunbar faced a
dilemma as a poet: His publishers wanted him to write poetry portraying African Americans who were always happy
and content. His best and most serious poetry detailing the
struggles of his people was discouraged. Dunbar solved the
dilemma of being forced to write about happy African Americans content with living conditions in the United States by
using dialect. He wrote his most serious poetry, including
the following selection, in standard English. Published in
The Complete Poems (1913), "We Wear the Mask" is a
poem whose subject is one that has been explored since
slavery: African Americans must hide their true feelings in
racist America.*

Vocabulary

guile	(1)	fraud, dishonesty
myriad	(1)	countless
subtleties	(1)	those things or ideas that are not obvious
vile	(3)	foul, evil

We wear the mask that grins and lies,   1
It hides our cheeks and shades our eyes,—
This debt we pay to human guile;
With torn and bleeding hearts we smile,
And mouth with myriad subtleties.

Why should the world be overwise,   2
In counting all our tears and sighs?
Nay, let them only see us, while
   We wear the mask.

We smile, but, O great Christ, our cries   3
To thee from tortured souls arise
We sing, but oh the clay is vile
Beneath our feet, and long the mile;
But let the world dream otherwise,
   We wear the mask!

Discussion Questions

1. How would you describe the mask?
2. Why does the "we" in the poem wear the mask?
3. What lies behind the mask?
4. What or who is the "world" referred to in the second stanza?
5. Is there a solution offered in the poem to the problem of mask wearing? Explain your answer.
6. How does Dunbar combine the strategies of comparison and contrast and description to explain the title of the poem?
7. How does the exclamation point at the end of the last line affect the ending of the poem?

Writing Assignments

1. Write an essay illustrating an individual or a group in our society that wears a mask.
2. Write an essay describing an incident in which you were forced to wear a mask.
3. In an essay, recount the horror you found in some incident.

IF WE MUST DIE

Claude McKay

*Born in Jamaica, British West Indies, Claude McKay
(1889–1948) was a well-known poet in both Jamaica and
the United States. He came to the United States in 1912 and
studied at Tuskegee Institute and Kansas State College. After deciding on a literary career, McKay moved to Harlem,
New York, and contributed greatly to the literary period
known as the Harlem Renaissance. In the United States, he
published two collections of poetry,* Spring in New Hampshire and Other Poems *(1920) and* Harlem Shadows *(1922).
He also published four novels:* Home to Harlem *(1928),*
Banjo *(1929),* Gingertown *(1932), and* Banana Bottom
*(1933). "If We Must Die," first published in 1919 in the mag-
azine* The Liberator, *is a poem written in reaction to the race
riots that occurred throughout major cities in the United
States during the "bloody" summer of 1919. Its message of
defiance in the face of overwhelming odds has made this
work the theme poem of the Harlem Renaissance.*

If we must die, let it not be like hogs   1
Hunted and penned in an inglorious spot,
While round us bark the mad and hungry dogs,
Making their mock at our accursed lot.

If we must die, O let us nobly die,   2
So that our precious blood may not be shed
In vain; then even the monsters we defy
Shall be constrained to honor us though dead!

O kinsmen! we must meet the common foe!   3
Though far outnumbered let us show us brave,
And for their thousand blows deal one
    deathblow!

What though before us lies the open grave?   4
Like men we'll face the murderous, cowardly
    pack,
Pressed to the wall, dying, but fighting back!

Discussion Questions

1. Who is the "we" in the poem? Who is the "monster"?
2. Why does the persona (speaker) think that if "we" fight back, the "monster" will honor us?
3. How significant is it that the image of "we" changes from one of hogs to men? Explain your answer.
4. How does the poem deal with death?
5. What is the tone of the poem?
6. How does McKay use persuasion as a means of convincing his audience to accept his message?
7. What is the significance of using a subordinate clause as the title of the poem?

Writing Assignments

1. In an essay, recount an instance when you acted defiantly against overwhelming odds.
2. Write an essay that explains a principle you feel is worth dying for.
3. Write an essay in which you explore the term *honor.*

THE RAP ON FREDERICK DOUGLASS

Roger Guenveur Smith

Roger Guenveur Smith is an actor and the creator of "Frederick Douglass Now," a one-man multimedia show. First published in the New York Times, *February 19, 1990, just five days after Douglass's birthday, the following rap was extracted from the one-man show.*

If there is no struggle there is no progress
That was the rap of Brother Frederick Douglass
From 1818 to 1895
Frederick Douglass is still alive
No jive: 5
In 1985 he was alive
In 1986 we threw him in the mix
In 1987 he was looking down from heaven
In 1988 he said:
Mash down Aparthate   10
Smash down Aparthate
Mash down Smash down Bash down Aparthate.
In '89 he was right on time
Now check it out while I bust this rhyme:
They love Black music but they hate Black people.   15
They love this rhythm
They love this rhyme
But when it comes to the struggle they don't have the time
They love Michael Jackson on MTV
They love Eddie Murphy and Mr. T.   20
They love Bill Cosby and Bob Marley
And some say to me "I love Spike Lee"
But they don't give a damn if we are free
They don't know a thing about our History
This History?   25
Yes.
It was a long a long a long a long a long long journey
And you don't stop
Everybody's rapping about money and sex
But nobody's rapping about Malcolm X: 30
El Hajj Malik was very unique
He came to I and I right off the street
But they shot him down in the Audubon Ballroom
Now they're just rapping and doing the wild thing on his
    tomb.   35

Boom boom boom boom
They shot him down
Boom boom
Shot him down because he wore the crown
Malcolm X?   40
He never played the clown
Now I'm not saying that we can't have no fun
That's not my idea of Revolution
But please don't forget about Paul Robeson:[1]
Big Paul   45
He was the king of them all y'all
All-American at playing ball
But that wasn't all y'all
He was Phi Beta Kappa, Shakespearean rapper
Big Paul stood tall y'all   50
Yes he was born in the USA
But in his heyday they took his passport away
Why?
Because they didn't like what he had to say:
"Here I stand, an African American   55
Son of a slave from cradle to the grave."
Are you now or have you ever been
aware of him?
Understood why they were scared of him?
This History?   60
Yes.
It was a long a long a long a long a long long journey
And you don't stop
Until the break of a new dawn
Like Marvin Gaye say: "Let's get it on"   65
You've got to be strong in this Babylon[2]
Because you'll never know yourself until you're back
    against the wall
Until you're Black
And you're under attack
Young and gifted and under attack   70
We must fight back
How we gonna do that?
We must learn to read and learn to write
And organize ourselves to fight
Fight for what?

---

[1] Paul Robeson (43)   An African American activist, actor, and singer popular from the 1920s through the 1940s.
[2] Babylon (65)   Any city or place of great luxury and corruption, often used to refer to the United States.

For our life   75
(That's the death)
Frederick Douglass will never run out of breath:
If there is not struggle there is not progress
Yes.

                                                                    80

Discussion Questions

1. What is the meaning of the word *Aparthate*?
2. In what ways does Smith urge African Americans to fight for their lives?
3. What does the speaker mean when he says that Frederick Douglass is still alive?
4. What does the speaker want the reader to realize about Douglass, Malcolm, and Robeson?
5. What examples does Smith use to support his choice of illustration as a rhetorical strategy?
6. How can you argue that the line, "If there is no struggle there is no progress," is the main idea of "The Rap on Frederick Douglass"?

Writing Assignments

1. Write a rap expressing your views on an issue.
2. Write an essay urging the importance of knowing one's history.
3. Think of an historical figure, and write an essay showing the extent to which that figure continues to influence today's society.

STUDENT ESSAY:
AFFIRMATIVE ACTION: THE CONTROVERSIAL TOPIC

James Mitchener

Vocabulary

blatant	(2)	completely obvious
equilibrium	(2)	a state of intellectual or emotional balance
quotas	(3)	proportional parts or shares

At the heart of the affirmative action issue is whether or not an attempt to ensure equal treatment for all racial and ethnic groups does not in fact result in reverse discrimination. By giving minorities advantages, some white males feel they are put at a disadvantage, which on the surface is an arguable point.

In assessing the need for affirmative action, one must try to think of another solution to blatant acts of discrimination. If there are solutions better than the one we have in affirmative action, most of us are unaware of them. One journalist made a interesting comparison concerning this very issue. He said, "Reverse racism is a correct description of affirmative action only if one considers the cancer racism to be morally and medically indistinguishable from the therapy we apply to it. A cancer is an invasion of the body's equilibrium, and so is chemotherapy; but we do not decline to fight the disease because the medicine we employ is also disruptive of normal functioning." In essence, regardless of how disruptive affirmative action may be, it is the only remedy to the problem of discrimination.

Another issue surrounding affirmative action is that some believe quotas take away from the quality of organizations. Some say that quality is lost when a person's race is more important than a person's talent. While this statement may be true, the painful truth is that talented minorities, who often are just as, if not more qualified than whites, must be given a chance to prove themselves. Such a chance is important, especially since many employers seem still to believe that white males are superior. Affirmative action is necessary because of this predominant idea.

I am sure that affirmative action will remain a very controversial topic for years to come. Until better solutions are found to combat discrimination, Americans must endure affirmative action because for now it is the only sure way to break the race barrier.

Discussion Questions

1. Why is affirmative action a controversial topic?
2. What is the author's assessment of the effectiveness of affirmative action?
3. Why does Mitchener compare affirmative action to chemotherapy?
4. Why does the author argue the necessity of quotas?
5. How could Mitchener have used extended definition as an effective strategy to support his thesis statement?
6. How effective is the author's ending? Explain your answer.

Writing Assignments

1. In an essay, describe another remedy that may be regarded as problematic or disruptive, but necessary.
2. Write an essay in which you present opposing views to the Mitchener essay.

12

Arts • Sciences • Media

SHINING LIGHT OF A POET AND PIONEER

Earl Caldwell

Earl Caldwell (1941–   ) is a columnist with the New York Daily News. *Born in Clearfield, Pennsylvania, he attended the University of Buffalo. Caldwell has been a reporter for several newspapers: the* Clearfield Progress, *the* Intelligencer Journal *(Lancaster, Pennsylvania), the* Democrat and Chronicle *(Rochester, New York), the* Washington Star, *the* New York Post, *and the* New York Times. *He has the distinction of being the only reporter in Memphis with Dr. Martin Luther King, Jr., when King was assassinated in 1968. His account of the murder was headlined in newspapers across the country and abroad. The following article, which appeared in* The Amsterdam News *(1993), is a tribute to the life and career of African American journalist Robert C. Maynard.*

Vocabulary

piqued	(7)	aroused, exited
ombudsman	(9)	one who investigates citizens' complaints
formidable	(11)	awesome, powerful
lexicon	(12)	vocabulary
demystification	(13)	making less difficult to understand

"And yet do I marvel at this curious thing: To make a poet black,   1
and bid him sing!" (From "Yet Do I Marvel" by Countee Cullen.)

For the journalist Robert C. Maynard, the words of the   2
poet Countee Cullen made a perfect fit. More than anything
else, Bob Maynard was a newspaperman. He fell in love with
the craft as a kid growing up in the tough neighborhoods of the
Bedford-Stuyvesant section of Brooklyn. And in his life, which
spanned 56 years, that never changed, it never did.

In the world that he loved, Maynard did it all. He rose to   3
the top as a writer, reporter and editor. Eventually, he broke
through to become the first African-American to own and publish a major daily newspaper.

So large were his accomplishments that when he died two   4
days ago, his peers looked at the whole of what he had
achieved and they gave him the kind of acclaim rarely given in
the newspaper industry.

Bob Maynard made himself special. Much of the time,   5
what a newspaperman accomplishes gets measured almost entirely by the words he puts on paper. Maynard passed that
test—but for him that was just a starting place. He also possessed what Countee Cullen called "this curious thing."

He had a voice. It was a voice that was deep and rich and   6
full, and he coupled that with the enormous command he had
of the language. The combination of the two brought life to
Cullen's words: *"To make a poet black, and bid him sing."*

Maynard came of age in a newspaper industry that virtu-   7
ally held out a sign: "For white males only." That merely piqued
his determination. It only made him ready for battle. And he
did that. The New York City of his youth was a town filled with
newspapers, yet he couldn't get a start on any of the dailies. No
problem. He went out of town. After some breakthrough experience on some black weeklies, he wound up in southeastern
Pennsylvania in the town of York. When he was finished there,
he was managing editor and on the recommended list for a Nie-
man fellowship at Harvard.

He came away from that experience with so much going   8
for him that the door was opened. Editors at the Washington
Post—a newspaper with credentials that say "top of the line"—
beckoned him.

At the Post, Maynard did it all. There was nothing he   9
couldn't cover. He started on the streets working riots, and he
wound up at the White House covering former President Lyndon Johnson. Maynard wasn't finished. He showed a mind so
sharp that he was made an editorial writer, which meant he

was chosen to speak for the paper. Later, he was the readers' advocate as the newspaper's ombudsman.

All those experiences positioned Maynard for the work   10
that was to change the industry. He set out to train young jour-nalists, those who had been locked out because they were not white. He could have made some noise as a rabble-rouser. But that was not his way, not his style.

And Bob Maynard *had* style. It was in his voice; it was in   11
his body language, and yes, it was in his soul. Together, it amounted to a formidable array of skills.

He stated the goal: "We want to remove from the lexicon of   12
American journalism the words, 'We can't find any qualified mi-norities.'"

Just to train young people to get them into newsrooms   13
was a major task. But for Maynard, that was only part of the job. He believed everybody, regardless of race or sex, had to know why it was important. So he brought a whole different language to the mission. These were his words: portrayal, di-versity, demystification.

He was brilliant—spellbinding, too—in describing the   14
damage that the media was inflicting in their portrayals of those who were not white.

He was eloquent in arguing the case for diversity in the   15
newsroom—in detailing the ways diversity makes America bet-ter and stronger.

He demystified that which had been complicated, and he   16
did it in a way that brought the publishers' association to em-brace his "Year 2000 strategy" for a complete desegregation of the news business.

As it happened, Maynard didn't get all the years he should   17
have had. So he will be buried this morning in Oakland, Calif., where he owned and published the daily paper until his health gave out. But for him, you say this: *My, how he used the time he had.*

Discussion Questions

1. How did Maynard open doors that had been closed to him as a journalist?
2. According to Caldwell, what was Maynard's primary goal as a journalist? How did he accomplish this goal?
3. What was Maynard's journalistic philosophy? How did this phi-losophy relate to his "Year 2000 strategy"?

4. How does Caldwell describe Maynard's "style"?

5. How does Caldwell use illustration to portray Maynard as both a poet and a pioneer?

6. Why is Caldwell's use of a famous quotation particularly effective in introducing his article?

Writing Assignments

1. Write an essay about someone considered a pioneer in his or her field.

2. Write an essay describing your particular style of doing something that may be different from others' style of doing it.

3. People confront problems differently. Write an essay showing two different approaches to the same problem.

CROSSOVER DREAMS AND RACIAL REALITIES

William Barlow

William Barlow (1943–   ) is associate professor of radio, television, and film at Howard University in Washington, D.C. He is the author of "Looking Up at Down": The Emergence of Blues Culture *(1989) and co-author of* Split Image: African Americans in the Mass Media *(1990), from which the following excerpt is taken. This excerpt describes the role and the dilemma of African American radio stations.*

Vocabulary

advocacy	(1)	actively supporting
lucrative	(1)	profitable
formidable	(2)	difficult to overcome
demographic	(2)	related to size and distribution of people
emulate	(3)	imitate

By the end of the 1980s, black radio in the United States had reached a new plateau. For the first time in its history there were both network and chain operations controlled by African American broadcasters. Furthermore, there now existed a bona fide national advocacy organization, the National Black Media Coalition, capable of coordinating on a national level the ongoing struggles against discrimination in radio employment and ownership. Consequently, the number of black-owned commercial broadcasting outlets has recently been increasing at its fastest rate ever. Moreover, it continued to be lucrative for advertisers to target the urban black consumer. Education and income levels for African Americans in the urban markets rose considerably in the 1970s, and the trend carried over into and lasted through the 1980s. In addition, research on black listeners during this period indicated that there were more of them as a group, and that they listened to more radio than their white counterparts. Ninety-seven percent of all African Americans listen to radio each week, and they listen to an average of thirty hours per week, 20 percent more than white listeners. This should give African American broadcasters a competitive edge in the urban markets with large black populations. Indeed, it appears that black commercial radio might be able to

1

terminate, or at least minimize, its historical dependency on white broadcasters.

However, there still exist a number of structural factors 2
that are formidable obstacles to the goal of African American independence and self-sufficiency in radio broadcasting. For example, recent demographic patterns in the growing black middle-class population reveal a move to the suburbs, like that of the white middle class before them. The result is a significant fragmentation of the black urban audience, an event that has affected recent programming decisions. Fearing the loss of their most affluent listeners, even the leading black-controlled stations in the large urban markets have adopted crossover urban contemporary or urban adult formats. Some radio industry observers have heralded this as a breakthrough opening up the possibility of a new era of multiethnic commercial formats. But careful scrutiny of the airways reveals that, while the urban and adult contemporary formats have succeeded in allowing white artists greater access to black-controlled stations, African American artists have not gained corresponding exposure on white rock stations, except for crossover superstars like Michael Jackson and Prince. Urban contemporary and its spin-offs allow black broadcasters to anticipate the new demographic realities of the urban market, and in so doing to profit from these changes by converting them into higher ratings. However, this change also tends to undercut African American musicians and their music by narrowing their access to black radio outlets; moreover, those replaced by white crossover acts are invariably those with the least exposure in the first place. As has been the case so often in the past, the structure of the radio industry, its way of doing business, presents African Americans seeking an independent broadcast voice with a conflict of interest. The price of success all too often requires that the specific communication needs of the entire black community be forsaken.

On the other front, the upsurge in public radio in the 3
1970s and 1980s has opened up new terrain for African American broadcasters. They have responded by establishing over fifty college- and community-based public outlets. While some of the black college stations try to emulate successful commercial stations in their markets, most are engaged in promoting new African American musical talent, preserving African American musical traditions, and providing news and information for the local black populations within reach of their signals. In

general, the black public stations, in league with the more progressive black commercial outlets, are on the cutting edge of the movement to establish and maintain a self-sufficient African American presence on the radio airways. The white-controlled radio industry has been forced to open its doors to black employment and even ownership, no matter how reluctantly. Further, the negative images and stereotypes that characterized the portrayal of African Americans in the earlier years of broadcasting have all but vanished from radio's airways. These are important advances in the overall African American struggle to achieve racial equality and cultural self-determination. While black stations still only make up less than 2 percent of the total number of radio outlets broadcasting in the U.S.A. today, they are a crucial 2 percent, strategically located in all of the major black population centers in the country. Although they broadcast to local audiences, collectively they can also be quite effective in mobilizing black people on a national level for political campaigns like Jesse Jackson's bids for the presidency, or the more successful effort to have Martin Luther King, Jr.'s birthday declared a national holiday, or the ongoing campaign in the U.S.A. to end apartheid in South Africa. Black radio has played a vital role in furthering causes of this nature and no doubt will continue to do so in the future.

Discussion Questions

1. What accounts for the growth in the number of black-owned commercial broadcasting outlets by the end of the 1980s?
2. Why do you think African Americans listen to radio 20 percent more each week than whites?
3. How has the move to the suburbs, by the growing African American population, affected the African American broadcasting industry?
4. How have African American musicians been affected by not gaining corresponding exposure on white radio stations? How has this lack of exposure affected African American radio stations? What has been the effect on the African American community?
5. What seems to be the primary benefit of African American radio stations in major black population centers in the United States?
6. What is the meaning of the essay's title?
7. What is the cause-and-effect relationship described by Barlow?

8. The beginning and ending paragraphs of this essay are both considerably long. What effect, if any, does their length have on the
quality of the essay?

Writing Assignments

1. Write an essay describing the kind of music played most often on
your college radio station or on one of your favorite local stations.
Why do you think this kind of music is played more often than
other kinds?

2. Write a letter persuading your favorite radio station to omit or include a certain type of music or to provide a service that it currently does not provide.

3. Write an essay evaluating the effectiveness of a medium (other
than radio) in shaping the image of African Americans.

TV'S BLACK WORLD

Henry Louis Gates, Jr.

*Henry Louis Gates, Jr. (1950–   ), leading literary critic
and Harvard professor of English, has written extensively
on issues of African American culture and race relations. He
has also edited several collections of African American literature. His* The Signifying Monkey: A Theory of African
American Literary Criticism *(1989) won an American Book
Award. The following excerpt, taken from "TV's Black World
Turns—But Stays Unreal," which first appeared in the* New
York Times *in 1989, gives a historical perspective on
African American television shows and the myths that have
been associated with them.*

Vocabulary

genre	(5)	kind, type
metaphorical	(7)	comparable, similar
purveyed	(8)	provided, offered
questing	(10)	searching, seeking
feisty	(10)	touchy, excitable
benevolent	(10	kind, helpful
paternalism	(10)	father-child relationship
motif	(11)	theme
fetish	(13)	object of excessive attention
subliminal	(13)	subconscious
sass	(16)	daring, recklessness
protocol	(20)	ceremonial courtesies
palatable	(21)	agreeable
militates	(21)	works (against)

In 1933, Sterling Brown, the great black poet and critic, di- 1
vided the full range of black character types in American literature into seven categories: the contented slave; the wretched freeman; the comic Negro; the brute Negro; the tragic mulatto; the
local color Negro, and the exotic primitive. It was only one small
step to associate our public negative image in the American mind
with the public negative social roles that we were assigned and to
which we were largely confined. "If only they could be exposed to
the *best* of the race," the sentiment went, "then they would see
that we were normal human beings and treat us better." . . .

What lies behind these sorts of arguments is a belief that   2
social policies affecting black Americans were largely determined by our popular images in the media. But the success of
The Cosby Show has put the lie to that myth: *Cosby* exposes
more white Americans than ever before to the most nobly idealized blacks in the history of entertainment, yet social and economic conditions for the average black American have not been
bleaker in a very long time.

To make matters worse, *Cosby* is also one of the most   3
popular shows in apartheid South Africa, underscoring the
fact that the relationship between how whites treat us and their
exposure to "the best" in us is far from straightforward. (One
can hear the Afrikaaner speaking to his black servants: "When
you people are like Cliff and Clair, *then* we will abandon
apartheid.")

There are probably as many reasons to like *The Cosby*   4
Show as there are devoted viewers—and there are millions of
them. I happen to like it because my daughters (ages nine and
seven) like it, and I enjoy watching them watch themselves in
the depictions of middle-class black kids, worrying about
school, sibling rivalries, and family tradition. But I also like
Cosby because its very success has forced us to rethink completely the relation between black social progress and the images of blacks that American society fabricates, projects, and
digests.

But the *Cosby* vision of upper-middle-class blacks and   5
their families is comparatively recent. And while it may have
constituted the dominant image of blacks for the last five years,
it is a direct reaction against the lower-class ghetto comedies of
the 70s, such as *Sanford and Son* (1972–77), *Good Times*
(1974–79), *That's My Mama* (1974–75), and *What's Happening!!* (1976–79). The latter three were single-mother-dominated
sitcoms. Although *Good Times* began with a nuclear family,
John Amos—who had succeeded marvelously in transforming
the genre of the black maternal household—was soon killed off,
enabling the show to conform to the stereotype of a fatherless
black family.

Even *The Jeffersons* (1975–85) conforms to this mold.   6
George and Louise began their TV existence as Archie Bunker's
working-class neighbors, saved their pennies, then "moved on
up," as the theme song says, to Manhattan's East Side. *The Jeffersons* also served as a bridge between sitcoms depicting the
ghetto and those portraying the new black upper class.

In fact, in the history of black images on television, char-   7
acter types have distinct pasts and, as is also the case with
white shows, series seem both to lead to other series and to
spring from metaphorical ancestors.

Pure Street in a Brooks Brothers Suit

Let's track the evolution of the *Cosby* type on television. While   8
social engineering is easier on the little screen than in the big
city, Sterling Brown's list of black stereotypes in American literature proves quite serviceable as a guide to the images TV has
purveyed for the last two decades. Were we writing a new sitcom using these character types, our cast might look like this—
contented slave: Andy, Fred Sanford, J. J. *(Good Times)*;
wretched freeman: George Jefferson; comic Negro: Flip Wilson;
brute Negro: Mr. T *(The A-Team)*, Hawk *(Spenser: for Hire)*;
tragic mulatto: *Julia,* Elvin *(Cosby)*, Whitley *(A Different World)*;
local color Negro: Meschach Taylor *(Designing Women)*; exotic
primitive: Link *(Mod Squad* 1968–73); most black characters
on MTV. If we add the category of Noble Negro (Cliff Huxtable,
Benson), our list might be complete.

We can start with George Jefferson, who we might think of   9
as a Kingfish *(Amos 'n' Andy)* or as a Fred Sanford *(Sanford and
Son)* who has finally made it. Jefferson epitomized Richard
Nixon's version of black capitalism, bootstrap variety, and all of
its terrifying consequences. Jefferson was anything but a man
of culture; unlike the *Cosby* living room, his East Side apartment had no painting by Jacob Lawrence or Charles White, Ro-
mare Bearden or Varnette Honeywood.[1] Despite his new-found
wealth, Jefferson was pure street, draped in a Brooks Brothers
suit. You did not want to live next to a George Jefferson, and
you most certainly did not want your daughter to marry one.

The Jeffersons was part of a larger trend in television in   10
the depiction of black men. We might think of this as their domestication, in direct reaction to the questing, macho images of
black males shown in the 60s news clips of the civil rights
movement, the Black Panthers, and the black power movement. While Jefferson (short, feisty, racist, rich, vulgar) repre-

[1] Jacob Lawrence   (9)   African American painters.
    Charles White
    Romare Bearden
    Varnette Honeywood

sents one kind of domestication, a more curious kind was the cultural dwarfism represented by *Diff'rent Strokes* (1978–86) and *Webster* (1983–87), in which small black "boys" (arrested adolescents who were much older than the characters they played) were adopted by tall, successful white males. These establishment figures represented the myth of the benevolent paternalism of the white upper class, an American myth as old as the abolitionist movement.

Indeed, one central motif of nineteenth-century American art is a sculpted tall white male (often Lincoln) towering above a crouched or kneeling adult or adolescent slave, in the act of setting them free. *Webster* and *Diff'rent Strokes* depict black orphans who are rescued from blackness and poverty; adopted, and raised just like any other upper-middle-class white kid, prep schools and all. These shows can be thought of as TV's fantasy of Lyndon Johnson's "Great Society" and the war on poverty rolled into one.   11

The formula was not as successful with a female character. An attempt to use the same format with a black woman, Shirley Hemphill (*One in a Million,* 1980) lasted only six months. *The White Shadow* (1978–1981) was a variation of this paternal motif, in which wild and unruly ghetto kids were tamed with a basketball.   12

These small black men signaled to the larger American audience that the very idea of the black male could be, and had been, successfully domesticated. Mr. T—whose 1983–87 *A-Team* run paralleled that of *Webster*—might appear to be an exception. We are forced to wonder, however, why such an important feature of his costume—and favorite fetish—was those dazzling gold chains, surely a subliminal suggestion of bondage.   13

This process of paternal domestication, in effect, made Cliff Huxtable's character a logical next step. In fact, I think of the evolution of the Huxtable character, generationally, in this way: imagine if George Jefferson owned the tenement building in which Florida and her family from *Good Times* lived. After John Amos dies, Jefferson evicts them for nonpayment of rent. Florida, destitute and distraught, tries to kill George. The state puts her children up for adoption.   14

They are adopted by Mr. Drummond *(Diff'rent Strokes)* and graduate from Dalton, Exeter, and Howard. Gary Coleman's grandson becomes an obstetrician, marries a lovely lawyer   15 named Clair, and they move to Brooklyn Heights. And there you have it: the transformation of the character type of the black male on television.

And while Clair Huxtable is a refreshingly positive depic-   16
tion of an intelligent, successful black woman, she is clearly a descendant of *Julia* (1968–71), though a Julia with sensuality and sass. The extent of typecasting of black women as mammy figures, descended from the great Hollywood "Mammy" of *Gone with the Wind,* is astonishing; Beulah, Mama in *Amos 'n' Andy,* Geraldine *(Flip Wilson,* 1970–75), Florida, Nel in *Gimme a Break* (1981–88), Louise *(The Jeffersons);* Eloise *(That's My Mama,* 1974–75).

Is TV Depicting a Different World?

And what is the measure of the Huxtables' nobility? One of the   17
reasons *Cosby* and its spin-off, *A Different World,* are so popular is that the black characters in them have finally become, in most respects just like white people.

While I applaud *Cosby's* success at depicting (at long last)   18
the everyday concerns of black people (love, sex, ambition, generational conflicts, work and leisure) far beyond reflex responses to white racism, the question remains: has TV managed to depict a truly "different world"? As Mark Crispin Miller puts it, "By insisting that blacks and whites are entirely alike, television denies the cultural barriers that slavery necessarily created; barriers that have hardened over years and years, and that still exist"—barriers that produced different cultures, distinct worlds.

And while *Cosby* is remarkably successful at introducing   19
most Americans to traditional black cultural values, customs, and norms, it has not succeeded at introducing America to a truly different world. The show that came closest—that presented the fullest range of black character types—was the 1987–88 series *Frank's Place,* starring Tim Reid and his wife Daphne Maxwell Reid and set in a Creole restaurant in New Orleans.

Unfortunately, Mr. Reid apparently has learned his lesson: 20
his new series, *Snoops,* in which his wife also stars, is a black detective series suggestive of *The Thin Man.* The couple is thoroughly middle class: he is a professor of criminology at Georgetown; she is head of protocol at the State Department, "Drugs

and murder and psychotic people," Mr. Reid said in a recent interview. "I think we've seen enough of that in real life."

But it is also important to remember that the early 70s   21
ghetto sitcoms—(*Good Times* and *Sanford*) were no more realistic than *Cosby* is. In fact, their success made the idea of ghetto life palatable for most Americans, robbing it of its reality as a place of exile, a place of rage, and frustration, and death. And perhaps with *Cosby*'s success and the realization that the very structure of the sitcom (in which every character is a type) militates against its use as an agent of social change, blacks will stop looking to TV for our social liberation. As a popular song in the early 70s put it, "The revolution will not be televised."

Discussion Questions

1. What is Gates's dissatisfaction with the portrayal of blacks on television?
2. According to Gates, what have been the negative consequences of *The Cosby Show* in terms of its presentation of black images? What positive contributions of the show does Gates cite?
3. How does Gates prove incorrect the belief that social policies affecting blacks were largely determined by popular black images in the media?
4. Why was it necessary in the 1960s and 1970s to present an image of "domesticated" black men on television?
5. What is the "myth of the benevolent paternalism" of the white upper class?
6. What is the "process of paternal domestication" to which Gates refers? How does this process relate to the evolution of the character of Cliff Huxtable?
7. What is the thesis of this excerpt?
8. How does Gates use illustration effectively to develop his thesis?

Writing Assignments

1. Write an essay that analyzes the character types on current African American television shows.
2. Write an essay describing how other ethnic groups are depicted on television or in the movies.
3. Write an essay about a particular stereotype that society holds about your ethnic group or culture.

THE SLAVE INVENTOR

Portia James

Portia P. James wrote The Real McCoy: African-American Invention and Innovation, 1619–1930 *(1989) for the Smithsonian Institution's exhibit on African American inventors. In this excerpt from Chapter 3, James discusses the dilemma of the slave inventor.*

Vocabulary

query	(2)	question, inquiry
affidavit	(6)	a written statement or oath
supererogation	(6)	act done beyond what is required
surplussage	(6)	quantity in excess of what is needed
culling	(10)	picking out

Although few written accounts fully identify slaves by name, reports of slaves inventing new devices and machines persisted. The slave inventor found himself in an unlikely position that must have strained the assumptions of slavery to the utmost. Nothing illustrates the slave inventor's dilemma more clearly than the story of "Ned," a slave mechanic in Pike County, Mississippi, and the manner in which the U.S. Patent Office, handled the question of patenting the cotton scraper he invented. Ned's situation provoked the federal government to draft legislation that specifically addressed the legal status of slave inventors. 1

Oscar J. E. Stuart, a prominent white planter and the proud owner of Ned, wrote to Secretary of the Interior Jacob Thompson on August 25, 1857, with a query about Ned and his valuable invention. Ned had constructed a new and innovative cotton scraper that local planters heralded as "a great labor-saving machine." With the assistance of one man and two horses it could, Stuart asserted, do the work of four men, four horses, two single scrapers, and two ploughs. Stuart wrote Thompson to request letters patent for himself as owner of Ned and therefore as owner of Ned's invention. 2

Ordinarily Stuart would have addressed his request to the U.S. Patent Office, but the commissioner of patents, Joseph Holt, was a northerner. Realizing that in the minds of those 3 uninitiated in the assumptions of slavery it might be problematic for one man to receive the patent for another's invention, Stuart appealed to Secretary Thompson as "a Mississippian, and southern man."

Although Stuart admitted that the concept for the invention came entirely from Ned, he reminded Thompson that in the tradition of southern law "the master is the owner of the fruits of the labor of the slave both intilectual [sic], and manual." Stuart went on to express his concern that there might be a question whether the patent should be awarded to the "servile race" rather than to the "political race," that is, to Ned as opposed to himself. Stuart concluded rather ironically that if this view were to prevail, "the value of the slave to his master is excluded, and the equal protection and benefit of government to all citizens . . . is subverted."

Such a request should not have been surprising given the numbers of first-rate slave craftsmen and the reports of their inventions, but the appearance of Stuart's letter in the secretary's office seemed to cause a certain amount of confusion. Secretary Thompson replied to Stuart that the question was a new one and would have to be forwarded to Attorney General Jeremiah Black for an opinion.

Meanwhile, Stuart wrote a letter to the commissioner of patents. Interestingly enough, he had Ned sign an "affidavit" stating that he had invented the machine and was indeed the slave of Stuart. The implications of the affidavit must have made Stuart extremely uncomfortable, for he explained: "The affidavit of the Negro I regarded as a matter of supererogation, mere surplussage, neither strengthening or diminishing whatever merits there might be in my application.". . .

The decision not to allow either slaves or their owners to receive patents for slave inventions meant that such inventions could not enjoy any legal protection, or, more important, any formal recognition. The attorney general's opinion stood until the end of the Civil War and the passage of the Thirteenth and Fourteenth Amendments.

After this historic exchange of letters about his invention, Ned disappeared from history, and nothing is known of what became of him. Ironically enough, in 1860 O. J. E. Stuart and his family went into the full-time business of manufacturing and marketing Ned's Double Cotton Scraper. Their advertising broadside includes this enthusiastic testimony: "I am glad to know that your implement is the invention of a Negro slave—

thus giving the lie to the abolition cry that slavery dwarfs the mind of the Negro. When did a free Negro ever invent anything?" After the end of the Civil War O. J. E. Stuart left Mississippi, because, it is said, of the "excesses" of Reconstruction. . . .

Largely because of the inability to identify slaves and the   9 inventions they created, there has been speculation about the unacknowledged contributions of slaves to particular inventions. Two of the most persistent and widespread rumors are the stories that Eli Whitney's idea for the cotton gin came from slaves working on the plantation of General Nathaniel Greene and that Cyrus McCormick's harvester was primarily inspired by his slave assistant, Joe Anderson. While Anderson himself is not recorded as claiming any significant role in the conceptualization of the reaper, he worked closely with McCormick during its construction. Anderson does say that he served as "blower and striker" for the blacksmith who made the harvesters.

Another factor to keep in mind is the process of invention   10 itself. Even though all applications for patents must meet a test of originality, most if not all inventions are based on previous discoveries of materials, formulas, principles, techniques, and mechanisms. In most cases a patented invention is merely an improvement on a current device or technique. Eli Whitney, for example, has been charged with borrowing the idea for the cotton gin from a simple comblike device that slaves used to clean the cotton. Whitney is said to have merely enlarged upon the idea of the comb to create the cotton gin, which works very much like an oversized comb culling the seeds and debris from the cotton. Whitney may have borrowed the idea, which though valuable was still incomplete. He may have used the principle behind the slaves' device and applied it to the broader problem—how to clean vast quantities of cotton. But this is the very essence of invention. In this sense, the process of invention can be seen as a kind of pyramid, with each new invention resting on a number of previous discoveries.

Discussion Questions

1. Before the passage of the Confederacy Patent Act of 1861, why could inventions by slaves not be patented? Why were most slaves not given credit for their inventions even after the act?
2. How did Ned's slavemaster, Stuart, justify his request to obtain a patent for Ned's invention?

3. To what extent did the unjust system of slavery have an ironic effect on Stuart's request for a patent?

4. How are most if not all inventions based on previous discoveries?

5. What is the thesis of this essay? Does the last paragraph of the essay strengthen or weaken the thesis? Explain your answer.

6. How is cause and effect used to show the problem of the slave inventor?

Writing Assignments

1. Write an essay illustrating how you, someone you know, or someone you have heard or read about has not been given credit for his or her contributions.

2. Write an essay describing other dilemmas that slaves experienced.

3. "One cannot enslave another without enslaving oneself." Write an essay in which you agree or disagree with this statement.

Student Essay:
THE EUGENICS STERILIZATION MOVEMENT

Karie Wermeling

Vocabulary

capitalist	(2)	pertaining to an economic system encouraging private ownership
encompassing	(2)	surrounding
impoverished	(3)	poor
recipients	(5)	receivers
mandates	(6)	laws
ideology	(6)	body of ideas or beliefs
diligence	(7)	attentive care

Eugenics is the movement devoted to improving the human species by controlling heredity. Sterilization is a procedure that makes one incapable of reproduction. When we couple the two terms, *eugenics* and *sterilization,* we define a movement devoted to improving the human species in an effort to control heredity by making one incapable of reproducing. The eugenics sterilization movement has a long history within the United States, of forcing the African American woman to become sterile.

In America, the eugenics sterilization movement was popular during the nineteenth century because it offered sound, justifiable reasoning to the Anglo-Saxon Protestant communities for controlling and/or ridding the United States of the African American race. Charles Darwin stated that God created all living beings with either a favorable variation or an unfavorable variation. However, he did not define what either of these was. Francis Galton, another prominent natural scientist like Charles Darwin, and many others in the Caucasian community took it upon themselves to do the defining. They characterized low intelligence and poor class status as unfavorable variations. The white capitalist society, to justify its enslavement of a whole race of people, labeled the African American as an individual of extreme low intelligence—one incapable of obtaining and sustaining knowledge. Racists, including those within the science fields, began to promote the idea that African Americans have a smaller brain and encompassing skull. In 1840, Dr. Samuel Morton set out to prove this true. White racists, especially those who were slaveholders, used Morton's study to support their belief that African Americans were inferior in intelligence. And because they were "proved" to be intellectually inferior, they were seen as unfavorably varied.

African Americans were also labeled unfavorable beings because of their poor class status. At the time the eugenics sterilization movement was developing, legalized slavery flourished in the South. Black individuals were the ones who served the white community with their entire energy, yet received nothing in return. They were left impoverished. Because of this poverty, African Americans were the poorest of persons residing in the United States. Having such a characteristic, as well as being deemed people of low intelligence, the black race was defined as a race of people who were unfavorably varied. Francis Galton and his colleagues offered testimony before Congress, made political speeches, and wrote numerous books and articles that promoted the concept of white superiority and the need for race purity. These eugenic-minded scientists also promoted the idea that the lower races, African Americans being the lowest, would bring about the destruction of the white race.

Therefore, the two characteristics, low intelligence and poor class status, became a racial factor in the eugenics sterilization movement. Racists were then justified in choosing the black race as the target for imposed sterilization policies.

Early in the history of the eugenics sterilization movement, the need to sterilize those with undesirable variations was widely accepted. Also, it was widely believed that African Americans should be the majority targeted as the recipients of sterilization. However, it was never the intention to sterilize each and every black individual. Those in favor of sterilization knew it was only necessary to sterilize one gender of a given race in order to control or exterminate it. That gender, of course, was the female.

Therefore, the African American female was specifically, forcefully targeted by sterilization mandates. There are two main reasons why this selection was made. First, the black female was regarded as the ultimate inferior being in American society. The white, male-dominated capitalist society defined any woman, white or black, as inferior. But if a woman was also an African American, she was regarded as a human being lower in status than all others—in body, mind, and soul. The flourishing ideology was that if one was going to sterilize a group, one should sterilize the group that resides at the bottom of the social ladder. So, in light of this, those who were sterilizing the black woman felt they were doing no wrong. Society felt justified because it believed, thanks to the proof offered by Francis Galton and other natural scientists, that inferior beings

deserved and required inferior treatment so the remaining society could reach a state of perfection and prosper forever.

    The second reason for choosing the African American fe-   7
male for sterilization was that she was seen as a sexual delinquent. Her only concern in life was to satisfy her endless desire
for sexual intercourse. This notion of being unintelligent and
oversexed rendered the black woman as one incapable of utilizing birth control methods, methods that require intelligence
and diligence. Because the American society believed the black
female could not effectively control her sexual desires and/or
pregnancies, it felt it had a right and a duty to regulate them
for her. Infertility would allow her to maintain her sexually active life while society rested assured knowing that no undesirable offspring would result.

    The design of the eugenics sterilization movement was   8
complete. The white race understood what needed to be done,
sterilization, in order to combat population and social problem
growth. They also understood who should be the victims of
forced sterilization: the African American woman. The design of
the movement was regarded as perfect. And the widespread acceptance of the movement within nineteenth-century America
caused it to be powerfully enforced.

Discussion Questions

1. Specifically, what was the eugenics sterilization movement?
2. How does Wermeling view scientists such as Francis Galton? Why do you think she perceives Galton and his colleagues as she does?
3. Why was the eugenics sterilization movement popular in the nineteenth century?
4. How did white racists support their beliefs that African Americans were inferior?
5. Why was the African American female selected for sterilization?
6. How important is Wermeling's use of definition to the reader's understanding of the topic? Explain your answer.
7. What transitions are particularly effective in helping the author achieve unity among paragraphs?

Writing Assignments

1. Write an essay in which you discuss the effect(s) that racial or sexist practices have on targeted people.
2. Write an essay justifying some action that may be (or may seem to be) unfair to others.

13

Religion • Church

SALVATION

Langston Hughes

Langston Hughes (1902–1967) was born in Joplin, Missouri. As an undergraduate, he attended both Columbia University and Lincoln University. In 1921, he published in the Crisis *his famous poem, "The Negro Speaks of Rivers." Later, he published his first book of poetry,* The Weary Blues, *in 1926 and his second volume,* Fine Clothes to the Jew, *in 1927. In the 1940s he created the memorable Jesse B. Semple, a humorous character who speaks straightforwardly about the African American experience. In the following selection from his autobiography,* The Big Sea *(1940), Hughes recounts a religious service at which he felt pressured to acknowledge a false salvation.*

Vocabulary

dire	(3)	terrible, frightful
rounder's son	(6)	son of a prodigal (or good-for-nothing) father
knickerbockered	(11)	gathered or banded just below the knee

I was saved from sin when I was going on thirteen. But not re-   1
ally saved. It happened like this. There was a big revival at my
Auntie Reed's church. Every night for weeks there had been
much preaching, singing, praying, and shouting, and some
very hardened sinners had been brought to Christ, and the
membership of the church had grown by leaps and bounds.
Then just before the revival ended, they held a special meeting
for children, "to bring the young lambs to the fold." My aunt
spoke of it for days ahead. That night I was escorted to the
front row and placed on the mourners' bench with all the other
young sinners, who had not yet been brought to Jesus.

My aunt told me that when you were saved you saw a   2
light, and something happened to you inside! And Jesus came
into your life! And God was with you from then on! She said
you could see and hear and feel Jesus in your soul. I believed
her. I had heard a great many old people say the same thing
and it seemed to me they ought to know. So I sat there calmly
in the hot, crowded church, waiting for Jesus to come to me.

The preacher preached a wonderful rhythmical sermon, all   3
moans and shouts and lonely cries and dire pictures of hell,
and then he sang a song about the ninety and nine safe in the
fold, but one little lamb was left out in the cold. Then he said:
"Won't you come? Won't you come to Jesus? Young lambs,
won't you come?" And he held out his arms to all us young sinners there on the mourners' bench. And the little girls cried.
And some of them jumped up and went to Jesus right away.
But most of us just sat there.

A great many old people came and knelt around us and   4
prayed, old women with jet-black faces and braided hair, old
men with work-gnarled hands. And the church sang a song
about the lower lights are burning, some poor sinners to be
saved. And the whole building rocked with prayer and song.

Still I kept waiting to *see* Jesus.   5

Finally all the young people had gone to the altar and were   6
saved, but one boy and me. He was a rounder's son named
Westley. Westley and I were surrounded by sisters and deacons
praying. It was very hot in the church, and getting late now. Finally Westley said to me in a whisper: "God damn! I'm tired o'
sitting here. Let's get up and be saved." So he got up and was
saved.

Then I was left all alone on the mourners' bench. My aunt   7
came and knelt at my knees and cried, while prayers and songs

swirled all around me in the little church. The whole congregation prayed for me alone, in a mighty wail of moans and voices. And I kept waiting serenely for Jesus, waiting, waiting—but he didn't come. I wanted to see him, but nothing happened to me. Nothing! I wanted something to happen to me, but nothing happened.

I heard the songs and the minister saying: "Why don't you come? My dear child, why don't you come to Jesus? Jesus is waiting for you. He wants you. Why don't you come? Sister Reed, what is this child's name?"   8

"Langston," my aunt sobbed.   9

"Langston, why don't you come? Why don't you come and   10
be saved? Oh, Lamb of God! Why don't you come?"

Now it was really getting late. I began to be ashamed of   11
myself, holding everything up so long. I began to wonder what God thought about Westley, who certainly hadn't seen Jesus either, but who was now sitting proudly on the platform, swinging his knickerbockered legs and grinning down at me, surrounded by deacons and old women on their knees praying. God had not struck Westley dead for taking his name in vain or for lying in the temple. So I decided that maybe to save further trouble, I'd better lie, too, and say that Jesus had come, and get up and be saved.

So I got up.   12

Suddenly the whole room broke into a sea of shouting, as   13
they saw me rise. Waves of rejoicing swept the place. Women leaped in the air. My aunt threw her arms around me. The minister took me by the hand and led me to the platform.

When things quieted down, in a hushed silence, punctu-   14
ated by a few ecstatic "Amens," all the new young lambs were blessed in the name of God. Then joyous singing filled the room.

That night, for the last time in my life but one—for I was   15
a big boy twelve years old—I cried. I cried, in bed alone, and couldn't stop. I buried my head under the quilts, but my aunt heard me. She woke up and told my uncle I was crying because the Holy Ghost had come into my life, and because I had seen Jesus. But I was really crying because I couldn't bear to tell her that I had lied, that I had deceived everybody in the church, that I hadn't seen Jesus, and that now I didn't believe there was a Jesus any more, since he didn't come to help me.

Discussion Questions

1. What is the purpose of the "mourner's bench"?
2. In what way does Hughes's aunt unknowingly create his conflict?
3. Why does Westley decide to "get saved"?
4. Hughes confronts two disappointments that evening at the revival. What are they?
5. What is praiseworthy about Hughes's reluctance to go up to the altar and about his crying in bed?
6. In what way does Hughes's use of description enhance the reader's ability to see and feel the mounting pressure felt by both the narrator as well as members of the congregation?
7. How do the first two sentences of the story prepare the reader for the plot and theme?

Writing Assignments

1. In an essay describe a time when you were pressured to do something you did not want to do, and then regretted your action.
2. Write an essay in which you argue against conforming to someone else's habits, beliefs, or behavior.
3. Sometimes peer pressure can be positive. Write an essay illustrating this point.

THE CREATION

James Weldon Johnson

Poet, lyricist, fiction writer, government official, James Weldon Johnson (1871–1938) was born in Jacksonville, Florida. He received his B.A. degree from Atlanta University, attended Columbia University, and was admitted to the Florida bar in 1897. He served as U.S. consul to Venezuela and Nicaragua and as a prominent member of the NAACP. Primarily known for his poetry, he wrote God's Trombones: Seven Negro Sermons in Verse *(1927) from which the poem here is taken. He wrote a novel,* The Autobiography of an Ex-Colored Man *(1912), and in collaboration with his brother, composer J. Rosamond Johnson, he wrote the lyrics to several songs, the most popular of which is "Lift Every Voice and Sing," often referred to as the Negro national anthem. In "The Creation" Johnson retells the biblical story in verse.*

Vocabulary

cypress (2) an evergreen tree that grows in swampy areas

And God stepped out on space, 1
And he looked around and said:
I'm lonely—
I'll make me a world.

And far as the eye of God could see 2
Darkness covered everything.
Blacker than a hundred midnights
Down in a cypress swamp.

Then God smiled, 3
And the light broke,
And the darkness rolled up on one side,
And the light stood shining on the other,
And God said: That's good!

Then God reached out and took the light in His hands, 4
And God rolled the light around in His hands
Until He made the sun;
And He set that sun a-blazing in the heavens.

And the light that was left from making the sun
God gathered it up in a shining ball
And flung it against the darkness,
Spangling the night with the moon and stars.
Then down between
The darkness and the light
He hurled the world;
And God said: That's good!

Then God himself stepped down—   5
And the sun was on His right hand,
And the moon was on His left;
The stars were clustered about His head,
And the earth was under His feet.
And God walked, and where He trod
His footsteps hollowed the valleys out
And bulged the mountains up.

Then He stopped and looked and saw   6
That the earth was hot and barren.
So God stepped over to the edge of the world
And He spat out the seven seas—
He batted His eyes, and the lightnings flashed—
He clapped His hands, and the thunders rolled—
And the waters above the earth came down,
The cooling waters came down.

Then the green grass sprouted,   7
And the little red flowers blossomed,
The pine tree pointed his finger to the sky,
And the oak spread out his arms,
The lakes cuddled down in the hollows of the ground,
And the rivers ran down to the sea;
And God smiled again,
And the rainbow appeared,
And curled itself around His shoulder.
Then God raised His arm and He waved His hand
Over the sea and over the land,
And He said: Bring forth! Bring forth!
And quicker than God could drop His hand,
Fishes and fowls
And beasts and birds
Swam the rivers and the seas,
Roamed the forests and the woods,
And split the air with their wings.
And God said: That's good!

Then God walked around, 8
And God looked around
On all that He had made.
He looked at His sun,
and He looked at His moon,
And He looked at His little stars;
He looked on His world
With all its living things,
And God said: I'm lonely still.

Then God sat down— 9
On the side of a hill where He could think;
By a deep, wide river He sat down;
With His head in His hands,
God thought and thought,
Till He thought: I'll make me a man!

Up from the bed of the river 10
God scooped the clay;
And by the bank of the river
He kneeled Him down;
And there the great God Almighty
Who lit the sun and fixed it in the sky,
Who flung the stars to the most far corner of the night,
Who rounded the earth in the middle of His hand;
This Great God,
Like a mammy bending over her baby,
Kneeled down in the dust
Toiling over a lump of clay
Till He shaped it in His own image;

Then into it He blew the breath of life, 11
And man became a living soul.
Amen. Amen.

Discussion Questions

1. In what way does Johnson use darkness and light to suggest positive and negative images? To what extent do these images affect African Americans today?
2. What image of the woman is conveyed by the use of the pronouns *His* and *He?* And what image is conveyed by the creation of *man?*
3. How does the account of creation found in Genesis, Chapter 1, differ from Johnson's?

4. How does the use of descriptive phrases such as "spat out the seven seas" and "hollowed the valleys out" help the reader see the process of creation?
5. What do you think is Johnson's purpose in this poem?

Writing Assignments

1. Describe a process you used in creating _____.
   Use as many strong action verbs as you can in describing this process.
2. "The Creation" gives us one of several theories regarding the beginning of our world. Write an essay in which you explore other theories.
3. Write an essay in which you speculate about the origin of something.

THE DYNAMIC TENSION IN THE BLACK CHURCH

Michael A. Battle, Sr.

Michael A. Battle (1950–   ), currently the chaplain at Hampton University, is a noted preacher, professor, lecturer, and author. He is a graduate of Trinity College, Hartford, Connecticut, Duke University Divinity School, and Howard University. Battle has authored and/or edited several books and articles, including Voices of Experience *(1985). In the following excerpt taken from his 1994 book,* The African-American Church at Work, *Battle discusses the challenges of today's black church.*

Vocabulary

transformation	(1)	change
prophetic	(2)	foretelling
repentant	(2)	regretful
existential	(4)	current
pietistic	(4)	hypocritical
proclamation	(5)	announcement
imperative	(5)	urgent
status quo	(7)	the existing condition or state of affairs

The Black Church is often misunderstood by those who are critical of her commitment to preach a gospel which sees social change as an inseparable part of the Gospel of Jesus Christ. There are some within the Black Church who suggest that the Church should be concerned exclusively with the condition of the soul, as if the soul of man exists in a vacuum separated from the rest of that which makes humans human. These voices of narrow view say that we should avoid and abandon the call to social transformation. The response of the Black Church is a response which correctly finds support in the ministry of Jesus. 1

Jesus stood on the cutting edge of social transformation as a prophetic voice meeting people at the point of their need. His was a voice which called for the least to become the focus of attention, and for the greatest to become providers of service to others. Jesus stood at the crossroad between the despised and rejected on one hand, and the chosen and privileged on the other hand, and declared that each has equal access to the 2

promises of God. Where injustice was the daily practice of
the law, Jesus called for an advanced understanding of the
spirit of the law. The call to social transformation is inseparable from the message of the Christ who overthrew the money
changers in the temple, ate with sinners, paid attention to beggars, heard the cries of the wounded, and was moved by the
presence of a sick woman who, in a crowd, reached out to
touch him. Social transformation was a part of the ministry of
the Christ who found room in his heart and among his peers
for a repentant tax collector, a Roman soldier's child, and for
the rich Zacchees.[1] It is a gross error of interpretation to suggest that Jesus appealed only to the poor. His appeal was an
universal appeal. "Whosoever will, let him come." This includes
the rich and the powerful, for they are needed if social transformation is to occur.

    In light of her commitment to social transformation, it is   3
not difficult to understand why much of the leadership in the
Black community has come from the Black Church. Our
Churches have been the greatest training ground for leadership
skills because, in our churches, we have been afforded opportunity to assume responsibility in an environment which provides nurture.

    Allan Boesak, in his book entitled *The Finger of God,*   4
states that it is the unenviable task of preachers to wrestle
honestly with the Word of God to experience its critical power,
for themselves and for the people they preach to—but always
within the situation and the experience of their people, so that
the preaching will be understandable and relevant. It is preaching that addresses their deepest existential problems, preaching that speaks to the whole of their existence, for Blacks, this
means that the preacher must address not merely their 'being'
in the world, but their 'being Black' in the world. Relevant
preaching can not be a kind of preaching that is a pietistic pie-
in-the-sky-when-you-die theology that passes for the gospel
truth.

    While holding on to the undeniable truth of the assured   5
hope for eternal life, the Black church has always seen the concerns of this earthly life to be of such tremendous importance
that they are not to be ignored in a blind pursuit of heaven.
Thus Black theology has always addressed the situation in life

---

[1] Zacchees   (2)   (Also known as Zaccheus) was a chief among the
                                   Publicans.

where Black people have been. In slavery, Black Theology, through the music of the spirituals, wrestled with the tension between sociology and theology. Listen carefully to the spirituals and you will discover what Wyatt Tee Walker,[2] in his analysis of the song tradition of Black People, describes as the political and religious message of the spirituals. *Go Down Moses* was a song which celebrated the hope of liberation from slavery as well as celebrated the theological hope of eternal life; *Swing Low Sweet Chariot* was as much about the underground railroad as it was about the life of the prophet Elijah. When Black folk sang "I got shoes, you got shoes, all God's children got shoes, when I get to heaven I'm gonna put on my shoes and shout all over God's heaven;" they were making a bold proclamation about the equality of man and about the temporary nature of man's authority over man. It is imperative to recognize the genius of our forefathers, who in the singing of the spirituals heard Jesus say, when I was captive you worked for my liberation. They also heard Him say, "I have come to set the captives free." . . .

Our neighborhoods will not be renewed if those who "make   6
it" continue to abandon them. Our businesses will not progress unless we support them; our children will not escape the threat of another generation lost unless we lead them. Our communities will not overcome the invasion of drugs unless we learn ourselves and teach our children the reality that drugs are destructive. The Black Church must stand in the gap with a relevant message and with relevant programs. Where families are disjointed, let the church become the extended family; when there are no places for youth to become involved in constructive activities, let the churches work together with each other and with the cities to provide places of refuge; where there is an absence of self-confidence, let the churches preach the message of a Christ who sees in the least of us value and goodness.

The Black Church must never be content to allow for the   7
preservation of the status quo. She must continue to be an agent of social transformation. When Blacks were not permitted to worship in freedom, the Black Church became the haven. When Blacks were not allowed access to educational opportunity, the Black Church started schools. When death benefits were not provided for black families through the non-black

[2] Wyatt Tee Walker   (5)   Prominent African American minister.

insurance companies, the Black Church started its own companies. When Blacks could not get loans in the financial institutions, the Black Church started credit unions. We must revive that self-help mentality. We must nurture the dynamic tension in the Black Church.

Discussion Questions

1. According to Battle, why do some people have a misconception regarding the mission of the "Black Church"?
2. How does Battle support his argument that "the call to social transformation" is inseparable from God's message?
3. For what particular audience is the essay intended? Support your answer.
4. What do you think Battle means when he says the church must nurture "dynamic tension"? What do you think is his definition of "tension"?
5. How does Battle's use of comparison and contrast strengthen his argument?
6. The introduction is an excellent beginning for the essay. Why is it particularly effective?

Writing Assignments

1. Write an essay in which you attempt to clarify a subject that has also been misunderstood.
2. Write an essay in which you explore those times when positive tension has been necessary.
3. Write an essay about a positive or negative condition concerning your church, school, local government, or community.

THE STUMBLING BLOCK

Paul Laurence Dunbar

Paul Laurence Dunbar (1872–1906) was a nationally known African American poet. He published six volumes of poetry. After making a name for himself as a poet, Dunbar remained a productive artist as he experimented with other genres. Between 1898 and 1904 he wrote four novels, four volumes of short stories, several dramatic sketches, lyrics for musical compositions, and even two plays for a friend, though neither play was actually published. In the short story here, from The Best Short Stories of Paul Laurence Dunbar *(1938), the main character is perceived by those around her as having a "stumblin' block" that threatens her salvation.*

Vocabulary

unflecked	(1)	unspotted
abashed	(3)	embarrassing
devoirs	(6)	respect, courtesy
rude	(6)	rural, unrefined
prostrated	(6)	kneeled down in adoration
torrent	(8)	overflow
exhortations	(9)	prayers
taper	(10)	something that gives off a feeble light
palate	(10)	sense of taste
irreverence	(11)	lack of respect or love
proselyte	(11)	a new religious convert
rogue	(12)	rascal, villain
skeptic	(12)	doubter
fervor	(12)	devotion, enthusiasm
asunder	(12)	apart

It was winter. The gray old mansion of Mr. Robert Selfridge, of Fayette County, Kentucky, was wrapped in its usual mantle of winter somberness, and the ample plantation stretching in every direction thereabout was one level plain of unflecked whiteness. At a distance from the house the cabins of the Negroes stretched away in a long, broken black line that stood out in bold relief against the extreme whiteness of their surroundings. 1

About the center of the line, as dark and uninviting as the   2
rest, with its wide chimney of scrap limestone turning clouds of
dense smoke into the air, stood a cabin.

There was nothing in its appearance to distinguish it from   3
the other huts clustered about. The logs that formed its sides
were just as seamy, the timbers of the roof had just the same
abashed, brow-beaten look; and the keenest eye could not have
detected the slightest shade of difference between its front and
the bare, unwhitewashed fronts of its scores of fellows. Indeed,
it would not have been mentioned at all, but for the fact that
within its confines lived and thrived the heroine of this story.

Of all the girls of the Selfridge estate, black, brown, or yel- 4
low, Anner 'Lizer was, without dispute, conceded to be the
belle. Her black eyes were like glowing coals in their sparkling
brightness; her teeth were like twin rows of shining ivories; her
brown skin was as smooth and soft as silk, and the full lips
that enclosed her gay and flexile tongue were tempting enough
to make the heart of any dusky swain throb and his mouth water.

Was it any wonder, then, that Sam Merritt—strapping, big   5
Sam, than whom there was not a more popular man on the
place—should pay devoted court to her?

Do not gather from this that it was Sam alone who paid   6
his *devoirs* to this brown beauty. Oh, no! Anner 'Lizer was the
"bright particular star" of that plantation, and the most desired
of all blessings by the young men thereabout. But Sam, with
his smooth but fearless ways, Sam with his lightsome foot, so
airy in the dance, Sam, handsome Sam, was the all-preferred.
If there was a dance to go to, a corn-husking to attend, a social
at the rude little log church, Sam was always the lucky man
who was alert and *able* to possess himself of Anner 'Lizer's
"comp'ny." And so, naturally, people began to connect their
names, and the rumor went forth, as rumors will, that the two
were engaged; and, as far as engagements went among the
slaves in those days, I suppose it was true. Sam had never exactly prostrated himself at his sweetheart's feet and openly declared his passion; nor had she modestly snickered behind her
fan and murmured Yes in the approved fashion of the present.
But he had looked his feelings, and she had looked hers, while
numerous little attentions bestowed on each other, too subtle
to be detailed, and the attraction which kept them constantly
together, were earnests of their intentions more weighty than
words could give. And so, let me say, without further explana-

tion, that Sam and Anner 'Lizer were engaged. But when did the course of true love ever run smooth?

There was never a time but there were some rocks in its 7 channel around which the little stream had to glide or over which it had to bound and bubble; and thus it was with the loves of our young friends. But in this case the crystal stream seemed destined neither to bound over nor glide by the obstacle in its path, but rather to let its merry course be checked thereby.

It may, at first, seem a strange thing to say, but it was 8 nevertheless true, that the whole sweep and torrent of the trouble had rise in the great religious revival that was being enthusiastically carried on at the little Baptist meeting-house. Interest, or perhaps, more correctly speaking, excitement ran high, and regularly as night came round, all the hands on the neighboring plantations flocked to the scene of their devotions.

There was no more regular attendant at these meetings, 9 nor more deeply interested listener to the pastor's inflammatory exhortations, than Anner 'Lizer. The weirdness of the scene and the touch of mysticism in the services—though, of course, she did not analyze it thus—reached her emotional nature and stirred her being to its depths. Night after night found her in her pew, the third bench from the rude pulpit, her large eyes, dilated to their fullest capacity, following the minister through every motion, seeming at times in their steadiness to look him through and beyond to the regions he was describing—the harp-ringing heaven of bliss or the fire-filled home of the damned.

Now Sam, on the other hand, could not be induced to at- 10 tend these meetings; and when his fellow-servants were at the little church praying, singing, and shouting, he was to be found sitting in one corner of his cabin, picking his banjo, or scouring the woods, carrying ax and taper, and, with a dog trotting at his heels, hunting for that venison of the Negro palate—'coon.

Of course this utter irreverence on the part of her lover 11 shocked Anner 'Lizer; but she had not entered far enough into the regions of the ecstasy to be a proselyte; so she let Sam go his way, albeit with reluctance, while she went to church unattended. But she thought of Sam; and many a time when she secretly prayed to get religion she added a prayer that she might retain Sam.

He, the rogue, was an unconscious but pronounced skep- 12 tic; and day by day, as Anner 'Lizer became more and more possessed by religious fervor, the breach between them widened; still widening gradually until the one span that connected the two hearts was suddenly snapped asunder on the night when Anner 'Lizer went to the mourners' bench. . . .

Night came, and with it the usual services. Anner 'Lizer   13
was one of the earliest of the congregation to arrive, and she went immediately to the mourners' bench. In the language of the congregation, "Eldah Johnson sholy did preach a powahful sermon" that night. More sinners were convicted and brought to their knees, and, as before, these recruits were converted and Anner 'Lizer left. What was the matter?

That was the question which everyone asked, but there   14
were none found who could answer it. The circumstance was all the more astounding from the fact that this unsuccessful mourner had not been a very wicked girl. Indeed, it was to have been expected that she might shake her sins from her shoulders as she would discard a mantle, and step over on the Lord's side. But it was not so.

But when a third night came and passed with the same   15
result, it became the talk of three plantations. To be sure, cases were not lacking where people had "mourned" a week, two weeks, or even a month; but they were woeful sinners and those were times of less spiritual interest; but under circumstances so favorable as were now presented, that one could long refrain from "gittin' religion" was the wonder of all. So, after the third night, everybody wondered and talked, and not a few began to lean to Phiny's explanation, that "de ole snek in de grass had been a-goin' on doin' all her dev'ment on de sly, so's *people* wouldn't know it; but de *Lawd* he did, an' he payin' her up fu' it now."

Sam Merritt alone did not talk, and seemed perfectly indif-   16
ferent to all that was said. When he was in Phiny's company and she rallied him about the actions of his "gal," he remained silent.

On the fourth night of Anner 'Lizer's mourning, the con-   17
gregation gathered as usual at the church. For the first half-hour all went on as usual, and the fact that Anner 'Lizer was absent caused no remark, for everyone thought she would come in later. But time passed and she did not come, "Eldah Johnsing's" flock became agitated. Of course there were other mourners, but the one particular one was absent; hence the dissatisfaction. Every head in the house was turned toward the door, whenever it was opened by some late comer; and around

flew the whisper, "I wunner ef she's quit mou'nin'; you aint' heerd of her gittin' 'ligion, have you?" No one had.

Meanwhile the object of their solicitude was praying just the same, but in a far different place. Grasping, as she was, at everything that seemed to give her promise of relief, somehow Uncle Eben's words had had a deep effect upon her. So, when night fell and her work was over, she had gone up into the woods to pray. She had prayed long without success, and now she was crying aloud from the very fullness of her heart, "O Lawd, sen' de light—sen' de light!" Suddenly, as if in answer to her prayer, a light appeared before her some distance away. 18

The sudden attainment of one's desires often shocks one; so with our mourner. For a moment her heart stood still and the thought came to her to flee, but her mind flashed back over the words of one of the hymns she had heard down at church, "Let us walk in de light," and she knew that before she walked in the light she must walk toward it. So she rose and started in the direction of the light. How it flickered and flared, disappeared and reappeared, rose and fell, even as her spirits, as she stumbled and groped her way over fallen logs and through briers! Her limbs were bruised and her dress torn by the thorns. But she heeded it not; she had fixed her eye—physical and spiritual—on the light before her. It drew her with an irresistible fascination. Suddenly she stopped. An idea had occurred to her. Maybe this light was a Jack-o'-lantern! For a moment she hesitated, then promptly turned her pocket wrong side out, murmuring, "De Lawd'll tek keer o' me." On she started; but lo! the light had disappeared! What! had the turning of the pocket indeed worked so potent a charm? 19

But no! it reappeared as she got beyond the intervention of a brush pile which had obscured it. The light grew brighter as she grew fainter; but she clasped her hands and raised her eyes in unwavering faith, for she found that the beacon did not recede, but glowed with a steady and stationary flame. 20

As she drew near, the sound of sharp strokes came to her ears, and she wondered. Then, as she slipped into the narrow circle of light, she saw that it was made by a taper which was set on a log. The strokes came from a man who was chopping down a tree in which a 'coon seemed to have taken refuge. It needed no second glance at the stalwart shoulders to tell her that the man was—Sam. Her step attracted his attention, and he turned. 21

"Sam!" 22

"Anner 'Lizer!" 23

And then they both stood still, too amazed to speak. Fi-   24
nally she walked across to where he was standing, and said:
"Sam, I didn't come out heah to fin' you, but de Lawd has
'p'inted it so, 'ca'se he knowed I orter speak to you." Sam
leaned hopelessly on his ax; he thought she was going to ex-
hort him.

Anner 'Lizer went on: "Sam, you's my stumblin' block in   25
de highroad to salvation. I's been tryin' to git 'ligion fu' fo'
nights, an' I cain't do it jes' on you' 'count. I prays an' I prays,
an' jes as I's a'mos' got it, jes as I begin to heah de cha'iot
wheels a-rollin', yo' face comes right in 'tween an' drives it all
away. Tell me now, Sam, so's to put me out of my 'spense, does
you want to ma'y me, er is you goin' to ma'y Phiny? I jes' wants
you to tell me, not dat I keers pussonally, but so's my min' kin
be at res' spi'tu'lly, an' I kin git 'ligion. Jes' say yes er no; I
wants to be settled one way er t' other."

"Anner 'Lizer," said Sam, reproachfully, "you know I wants   26
to ma'y you jes' ez soon ez Mas' Rob'll let me."

"Dere now," said Anner 'Lizer, "bless de Lawd!" And some-   27
how Sam had dropped the ax and was holding her in his arms.

It boots not whether the 'coon was caught that night or   28
not, but it is a fact that Anner 'Lizer set the whole place afire by
getting religion at home early the next morning. And the same
night the minister announced that "de Lawd had foun' out de
sistah's stumblin' block an' removed it f'om de path."

Discussion Questions

1. Why do Anner 'Lizer and Sam Merritt grow apart?
2. How significant is it that the only person on the plantation who doesn't talk about Anner 'Lizer's inability to "get religion" is Sam?
3. What is Anner 'Lizer's stumblin' block?
4. Why do you think Anner 'Lizer does not respond to the cries of the church members? To what extent is it significant that she "gets religion" at home and not at church?
5. How would you describe the church's method of taking in new members?
6. To what extent does the author's use of cause and effect help the reader better understand Anner 'Lizer's conversion?
7. What is the setting of the story? To what extent do you feel the story is influenced by the setting?

Writing Assignments

1. Write an essay describing a time when you had a stumbling block.
2. Write an essay describing a time when you were pressed to do something you were not committed to doing.
3. Write an essay supporting your view on this statement: "We spend too much of our time living out others' expectations."

Student Essay:
THE TRADITION OF IFA

Karl Nichols

Vocabulary

paganism	(1)	beliefs or practices of those who have little or no religion
heathenism	(1)	beliefs of uncivilized or irreligious people
animism	(1)	the act of attributing conscious life to nature
repository	(2)	a storage place, room, or container
divination	(2)	the art or practice of foreseeing or foretelling future events
arbiter	(3)	someone who decides a disputed issue
natal	(3)	relating to or present at one's birth
derivative	(5)	something obtained or received from a specific source
deification	(6)	the act of making a god or of worshipping an object

Before the advent of Christianity and Islam, the continent of   1
Africa possessed a multitude of religions that evolved and were
honored by many Africans. Many of these African religions
were commonly labeled as "traditional religions" and were
wrongfully referred to by the West as paganism, heathenism,
and even animism. However, today the ancient African religion
of IFA is one of many systems that has survived and spread
from the continent of Africa to areas in Cuba, Trinidad, Brazil,
Haiti, and America. By properly understanding the origin of
IFA, the purpose of orisha and ancestor worship and divination, African Americans may better appreciate traditional
African religions.

The philosophy of IFA originated with the Yoruba peoples   2
of West Africa in Nigeria. IFA mythology relates that the creation of humankind arose in the sacred city of Ile Ife just outside of Lagos (Nigeria). According to many anthropologists, the
Yoruba created a highly sophisticated city-state empire that
was comparable to ancient Athens. The Yoruba regard IFA as
the repository of their beliefs and moral values. In fact, the IFA
divination system and various poetic chants are used to vali-
date important aspects of the Yoruba culture. Thus, IFA divination is performed during all important rites of passages: nam-

ing ceremonies, marriages, funerals, and installations of kings. The Yoruba consider IFA the voice of the divinities and the wisdom of the ancestors. One of the central beliefs of IFA is that only two events in our lives are predetermined: the day we are born and the day we are supposed to die. Everything else can be forecast and changed by performing ancestor worship and divination and by worshiping the orisha.

The idea of ancestor and orisha worship pertains to communicating with higher energies of nature and with dead blood relatives. The orisha are energies or deities that represent aspects of nature. Osun represents sweet waters, love, money, and conception. Shango (a warrior) represents thunder and lightning, strategy; Esu (messenger of Oludumare) is owner of roads and opportunities, and of spiritual energy; Yemonja/Olukun (provider of wealth) represents the ocean and mother; Obatala (arbiter of justice) represents the head, clarity; Oya (female warrior) represents the marketplace, tornadoes, and change of fortune; Ogun (owner of metals) represents the fierce warrior, honor, and integrity. These various orishas make up the universal body of God, which then constitutes the natal personalities of humans. IFA teaches that each of us has a single orisha energy from the universe that is dominant within all of us. This dominant energy is called our guardian orisha. For instance, if someone were suffering from too much pressure from work, he or she would find it helpful to tap into the energy of Obatala, orisha of the head, justice, coolness, and clear thinking.

In IFA, ancestor worship is a formalized structure for the living to connect with the wisdom and knowledge of dead blood relatives. The energy of deceased relatives is connected to the family by the world's population. Ritual offerings and prayers to deceased blood relatives are an integral part of everyday life. Unlike the Jewish and Christian traditions, IFA sees life as a continuum that enables one to actually communicate with departed family members. Ancestor worship is said to be the connection with the past and the road map to a better future.

Another basic belief of IFA is the use of divination to forecast life events. Through information obtained through divination, a person is able to know something about the future and the outcomes of all of his or her undertakings. The IFA system of divination is based on 16 basic and 256 derivative figures obtained either by the manipulation of sixteen palm nuts, or by the toss of a chain of eight half seed shells. Each Odu contains

600 ese, or poems of IFA and range from short to long passages that rely on proverbs, stories, and allegories to pinpoint correct counsel for inquiring minds. Most of the poems in each Odu contain stories related to the character or theme in the Odu concerned. Some believe that IFA is the means through which Yoruba culture informs and regenerates itself and preserves all that is considered good and memorable in that society. IFA divination is practiced by the Yoruba and Benin Edo of Nigeria; the Fon of Dahomey; the Ewe, of Tog; and the Santeria of Cuba and Brazil.

IFA religion, which carries a strong tradition of culture   6
and spiritual conduct, is widely practiced all over the globe. Without a doubt the most powerful indication of the African American's rich African ancestry lies in spirituality. If religions are truly a deification of one's culture, African Americans should seek refuge in the black gods of the orisha.

Discussion Questions

1. What are the basic beliefs of IFA?
2. Why do you think this religion has been referred to as "paganistic" by those in Western culture?
3. Are there some IFA beliefs that may be present in African American culture today? Support your answer.
4. What does the author mean when he says each of us has a "guardian orisha"?
5. Why does the author say that African Americans should "seek refuge" in IFA?
6. Should Nichols have used the strategy of definition more extensively in this essay? Explain your answer.
7. What is the purpose of the last sentence in the essay?

Writing Assignments

1. Write an essay in which you show how your religion or personal beliefs reflect your culture.
2. In an essay, describe a religious or cultural ceremony celebrated by your family.

14

Heritage • Identity

TO KNOW ONE'S HISTORY IS TO KNOW ONESELF

John Henrik Clarke

One of the most important historians of Africa and African Americans, John Henrik Clarke (1915–   ) was born in Union Springs, Alabama. He studied at New York University, the New School for Social Research, the University of Ibadan (Nigeria), and the University of Ghana. He also has served as a writer for both the Pittsburgh Courier *and the* Ghana Evening News *(Accra, Ghana). Clarke has always urged African Americans to study their African heritage. In the summer of 1993, Clarke spoke before an audience of hundreds of African educators from throughout the world, teaching them the importance of placing Africa at the center of their lives. He has written and edited many books; one of his most recent publications is* Africans Away from Home *(1988). The following excerpt from "A Search for Identity" (1970) documents Clarke's belief that if African Americans do not know their history, they do not know themselves.*

During my first year in high school I was doing chores and, be-   1
cause the new high school did not even have a cloak room, I

had to hold the books and papers of a guest lecturer. The speaker had a copy of a book called *The New Negro*. Fortunately I turned to an essay written by a Puerto Rican of African descent with a German-sounding name. It was called "The Negro Digs Up His Past," by Arthur A. Schomburg.[1] I knew then that I came from a people with a history older even than that of Europe. It was a most profound and overwhelming feeling—this great discovery that my people did have a place in history and that, indeed, their history is older than that of their oppressors.

The essay, "The Negro Digs Up His Past," was my intro-   2
duction to the ancient history of the black people. Years later when I came to New York, I started to search for Arthur A. Schomburg. Finally, one day I went to the 135th Street library and asked a short-tempered clerk to give me a letter to Arthur A. Schomburg. In an abrupt manner she said, "You will have to walk up three flights." I did so, and there I saw Arthur Schomburg taking charge of the office containing the Schomburg collection of books relating to African people the world over, while the other staff members were out to lunch. I told him impatiently that I wanted to know the history of my people, and I wanted to know it right now and in the quickest possible way. His patience more than matched my impatience. He said, "Sit down, son. What you are calling African history and Negro history is nothing but the missing pages of world history. You will have to know general history to understand these specific aspects of history." He continued patiently, "You have to study your oppressor. That's where your history got lost." Then I began to think that at last I will find out how an entire people—my people—disappeared from the respected commentary of human history.

It took time for me to learn that there is no easy way to   3
study history. (There is, in fact, no easy way to study anything.) It is necessary to understand all the components of history in order to recognize its totality. It is similar to knowing where the tributaries of a river are in order to understand the nature of what made the river so big. Mr. Schomburg, therefore, told me to study general history. He said repeatedly, "Study the history of your oppressor."

---

[1] Arthur A. Schomburg. "The Negro Digs Up His Past," in *The New Negro*, ed. Alain Locke (New York: Albert and Charles Boni, 1925), pp. 231–37.

I began to study the general history of Europe, and I dis- 4
covered that the first rise of Europe—the Greco-Roman period—was a period when Europe "borrowed" very heavily from
Africa. This early civilization depended for its very existence on
what was taken from African civilization. At that time I studied
Europe more than I studied Africa because I was following Mr.
Schomburg's advice, and I found out how and why the slave
trade started.

When I returned to Mr. Schomburg, I was ready to start a 5
systematic study of the history of Africa. It was he who is really
responsible for what I am and what value I have for the field of
African history and the history of black people the world over.

I grew up in Harlem during the depression, having come 6
to New York at the age of seventeen. I was a young depression
radical—always studying, always reading; taking advantage of
the fact that in New York City I could go into a public library
and take out books, read them, bring them back, get some
more, and even renew them after six weeks if I hadn't finished
them. It was a joyous experience to be exposed to books. Actually, I went through a period of adjustment because my illegitimate borrowing of books from the Jim Crow library of Columbus, Georgia, had not prepared me to walk freely out of a
library with a book without feeling like a thief. It took several
years before I felt that I had every right to go there.

During my period of growing up in Harlem, many black 7
teachers were begging for black students, but they did not have
to beg me. Men like Willis N. Huggins, Charles C. Serfait, and
Mr. Schomburg literally trained me not only to study African
history and black people the world over but to teach this history.

My Teaching

All the training I received from my teachers was really set in 8
motion by my great grandmother's telling me the stories of my
family and my early attempts to search first for my identity as a
person, then for the definition of my family, and finally for the
role of my people in the whole flow of human history.

One thing that I learned very early was that knowing his- 9
tory and teaching it are two different things, and the first does
not necessarily prepare one for the second. At first I was an exceptionally poor teacher because I crowded too many of my

facts together and they were poorly organized. I was nervous, overanxious, and impatient with my students. I began my teaching career in community centers in Harlem. However, I learned that before I could become an effective teacher, I had to gain better control of myself as a human being. I had to acquire patience with young people who giggled when they were told about African kings. I had to understand that these young people had been so brainwashed by our society that they could see themselves only as depressed beings. I had to realize that they had in many ways adjusted to their oppression and that I needed considerable patience, many teaching skills, and great love for them in order to change their attitudes. I had to learn to be a more patient and understanding human being. I had to take command of myself and understand why I was blaming people for not knowing what I knew, and blaming students for not being so well versed in history. In effect, I was saying to them, "How dare you not know this?"

After learning what I would have to do with myself and my subject matter in order to make it more understandable to people with no prior knowledge, I began to become an effective teacher. I learned that teaching history requires not only patience and love but also the ability to make history interesting to the students. I learned that the good teacher is partly an entertainer, and if he loses the attention of his class, he has lost his lesson. A good teacher, like a good entertainer, first must hold his audience's attention. Then he can teach his lesson. 10

I taught African history in community centers in the Harlem neighborhood for over twenty years before I had any regular school assignment. My first regular assignment was as director of the Heritage Teaching Program at Haryou-Act, an antipoverty agency in Harlem. Here I had the opportunity after school to train young black persons in how to approach history and how to use history as an instrument of personal liberation. I taught them that taking away a people's history is a way to enslave them. I taught them that history is a two-edged sword to be used for oppression or liberation. The major point that I tried, sometimes successfully, to get across to them is that history is supposed to make one self-assured but not arrogant. It is not supposed to give one any privileges over other people, but it should make one see oneself in a new way in relation to other people. 11

After five years in the Haryou-Act project, I accepted my 12 first regular assignment at the college at which I still teach. I serve also as visiting professor at another university and as an instructor in black heritage during the summer program conducted for teachers by the history department of a third major university. I also travel to the extent that my classes will permit, training teachers how to teach about black heritage. The black power explosion and the black studies explosion have pushed men like me to the forefront in developing approaches to creative and well-documented black curricula. Forced to be in the center of this arena, I have had to take another inventory of myself and my responsibilities. I have found young black students eager for this history and have found many of them having doubts about whether they really had a history in spite of the fact that they had demanded it. I have had to learn patience all over again with young people on another level.

On the college level I have encountered another kind of 13 young black student—much older than those who giggled—the kind who does not believe in himself, does not believe in history, and who consequently is in revolt. This student says in effect, "Man, you're turning me on. You know that we didn't rule ancient Egypt." I have had to learn patience all over again as I learned to teach on a level where students come from a variety of cultural backgrounds.

In all my teaching, I have used as my guide the following 14 definition of heritage, and I would like to conclude with it.

> Heritage, in essence, is the means by which people have used their talents to create a history that gives them memories they can respect and that they can use to command the respect of other people. The ultimate purpose of heritage and heritage teaching is to use people's talents to develop awareness and pride in themselves so that they themselves can achieve good relationships with other people.

Discussion Questions

1. How did Arthur Schomburg motivate Clarke to learn about African American history?
2. How did Clarke discover that he came from a people whose history was older than that of Europe?
3. How does Clarke describe a people with a history?
4. According to Clarke, what is the ultimate purpose of heritage?
5. How has Clarke's learning about his history influenced his teaching?

6. How does Clarke use cause and effect to explain the significance of the title?
7. What do you think is Clarke's purpose for narrating his personal experiences both as a high school student and as a teacher?

Writing Assignments

1. In an essay, describe your introduction to your heritage.
2. Write an essay about some interesting person in your family's history.
3. Write an essay responding to the following statement: "Those who forget their history are destined to repeat it."

KUNTA KINTE IS BORN

Alex Haley

When he was fifty-four years old, Alex Haley (1920–1992) published his monumental book, Roots: The Saga of an American Family *(1976). Chronicling Haley's descent from the African named Kunta Kinte, this work (and the subsequent television miniseries) had a tremendous influence, especially on African Americans. It taught them to be proud of their heritage and to enthusiastically seek their roots. Haley was also the co-writer of* The Autobiography of Malcolm X. *According to Haley, this work "represents the best I could put on paper of what Malcolm said about his own life from his own mouth." The following selection, from Chapter 1 of* Roots, *documents the rich African culture in which Kunta Kinte is born.*

Vocabulary

presaged	(1)	warned of in advance, predicted
pestles	(2)	instruments used to pound, grind, or mash
couscous	(2)	African dish of steamed, crushed grain
mortars	(2)	bowls made of hard material in which substances are crushed with pestles
pungent	(3)	sharp, penetrating
calabash	(4)	a tropical tree; the fruit of this tree
sheathed	(4)	enclosed
savanna	(4)	a flat, treeless grassland of tropical regions

Early in the spring of 1750, in the village of Juffure, four days   1
upriver from the coast of The Gambia, West Africa, a manchild
was born to Omoro and Binta Kinte. Forcing forth from Binta's
strong young body, he was as black as she was, flecked and
slippery with Binta's blood, and he was bawling. The two wrinkled midwives, old Nyo Boto and the baby's Grandmother
Yaisa, saw that it was a boy and laughed with joy. According to
the forefathers, a boy firstborn, presaged the special blessings
of Allah not only upon the parents but also upon the parents'
families; and there was the prideful knowledge that the name of
Kinte would thus be both distinguished and perpetuated.

It was the hour before the first crowing of the cocks, and   2
along with Nyo Boto and Grandma Yaisa's clatterings, the first

sound the child heard was the muted, rhythmic *bomp-a-bomp-
a-bomp* of wooden pestles as the other women of the village
pounded couscous grain in their mortars, preparing the traditional breakfast of porridge that was cooked in earthen pots
over a fire built among three rocks.

The thin blue smoke went curling up, pungent and pleas- 3
ant, over the small dusty village of round mud huts as the
nasal wailing of Kajali Demba, the village alimamo, began, calling men to the first of the five daily prayers that had been offered up to Allah for as long as anyone living could remember.
Hastening from their beds of bamboo cane and cured hides
into their rough cotton tunics, the men of the village filed
briskly to the praying place, where the alimamo led the worship: *"Allahu Akbar! Ashadu an lailahailala!"* (God is great! I
bear witness that there is only one God!) It was after this, as
the men were returning toward their home compounds for
breakfast, that Omoro rushed among them, beaming and excited, to tell them of his firstborn son. Congratulating him, all
of the men echoed the omens of good fortune.

Each man, back in his own hut, accepted a calabash of 4
porridge from his wife. Returning to their kitchens in the rear
of the compound, the wives fed next their children, and finally
themselves. When they had finished eating, the men took up
their short, bent-handled hoes, whose wooden blades had been
sheathed with metal by the village blacksmith, and set off for
their day's work of preparing the land for farming of the
groundnuts and the couscous and cotton that were the primary men's crops, as rice was that of the women, in this hot,
lush savanna country of The Gambia.

By ancient custom, for the next seven days, there was but 5
a single task with which Omoro would seriously occupy himself: the selection of a name for his firstborn son. It would have
to be a name rich with history and with promise, for the people
of his tribe—the Mandinkas—believed that a child would develop seven of the characteristics of whomever or whatever he
was named for.

On behalf of himself and Binta, during this week of think- 6
ing, Omoro visited every household in Juffure, and invited each
family to the naming ceremony of the newborn child, traditionally on the eighth day of his life. On that day, like his father
and his father's father, this new son would become a member
of the tribe.

When the eighth day arrived, the villagers gathered in the 7 early morning before the hut of Omoro and Binta. On their heads, the women of both families brought calabash containers of ceremonial sour milk and sweet munko cakes of pounded rice and honey. Karamo Silla, the jaliba of the village, was there with his tan-tang drums; and the alimamo, and the arafang, Brima Cesay, who would some day be the child's teacher; and also Omoro's two brothers, Janneh and Saloum, who had journeyed from far away to attend the ceremony when the drumtalk news of their nephew's birth had reached them.

As Binta proudly held her new infant, a small patch of his   8
first hair was shaved off, as was always done on this day, and all of the women exclaimed at how well formed the baby was. Then they quieted as the jaliba began to beat his drums. The alimamo said a prayer over the calabashes of sour milk and munko cakes, and as he prayed, each guest touched a calabash brim with his or her right hand, as a gesture of respect for the food. Then the alimamo turned to pray over the infant, entreating Allah to grant him long life, success in bringing credit and pride and many children to his family, to his village, to his tribe—and, finally, the strength and the spirit to deserve and to bring honor to the name he was about to receive.

Omoro then walked out before all of the assembled people   9
of the village. Moving to his wife's side, he lifted up the infant and, as all watched, whispered three times into his son's ear the name he had chosen for him. It was the first time the name had ever been spoken as this child's name, for Omoro's people felt that each human being should be the first to know who he was.

The tan-tang drum resounded again; and now Omoro   10
whispered the name into the ear of Binta, and Binta smiled with pride and pleasure. Then Omoro whispered the name to the arafang, who stood before the villagers.

"The first child of Omoro and Binta Kinte is named   11
Kunta!" cried Brima Cesay.

As everyone knew, it was the middle name of the child's   12
late grandfather, Kairaba Kunta Kinte, who had come from his native Mauretania into The Gambia, where he had saved the people of Juffure from a famine, married Grandma Yaisa, and then served Juffure honorably till his death as the village's holy man.

One by one, the arafang recited the names of the Maure-   13
tanian forefathers of whom the baby's grandfather, old Kairaba Kinte, had often told. The names, which were great and many,

went back more than two hundred rains. Then the jaliba pounded on his tan-tang and all of the people exclaimed their admiration and respect at such a distinguished lineage.

Out under the moon and the stars, alone with his son that eighth night, Omoro completed the naming ritual. Carrying little Kunta in his strong arms, he walked to the edge of the village, lifted his baby up with his face to the heavens, and said softly, *"Fend kiling dorong leh warrata ka iteh tee."* (Behold—the only thing greater than yourself.)   14

Discussion Questions

1. How was the news of the newborn infant communicated to other villages?
2. Why was selecting a meaningful historical name for one's son important to the Mandinka people?
3. Kunta Kinte was born into the Mandinka nation, rich in African tradition. What are some of the traditions that Haley records?
4. What does the story tell you about the role of the male in the Mandinka family?
5. What is the role of the women in the Juffure village?
6. What do you think were the jobs of the jaliba, the aragang, and the alimamo in the village?
7. What process is involved in naming a child?
8. How effective would it have been for Haley to begin his story with the last paragraph?

Writing Assignments

1. Write an essay in which you describe a ritual or ceremony that is a part of your family tradition or heritage.
2. Write an essay discussing a particular tradition of someone else's culture that you find interesting.
3. Write an essay describing any significant event of your birth, such as any special celebrations that took place or how you were named.

TO THOSE OF MY SISTERS
WHO KEPT THEIR NATURALS

NEVER TO LOOK A HOT COMB IN THE TEETH.

Gwendolyn Brooks

Gwendolyn Brooks (1917–   ) is still on the lecture circuit, conducting creative writing workshops at colleges and universities throughout the United States. Perhaps what is most remarkable about this African American poet is not her ability to learn and to grow from younger poets such as Haki R. Madhubuti (don l. lee), but her untiring, selfless efforts to spark young people to write creatively. Since the publication of her A Street in Bronzeville *(1945), Ms. Brooks has published many volumes of poetry, including* Annie Allen *(1949),* Riot *(1969),* Becomings *(1975),* Primer for Blacks *(1980), and* Blacks *(1987). In all of her volumes, she offers snapshot descriptions of poor, frustrated, or troubled African Americans, living in urban areas in the North. In 1950, she became the first African American to receive the Pulitzer Prize for poetry. In 1994, she received the National Book Lifetime Achievement Award. Currently, she directs the Gwendolyn Brooks Center for Black Literature and Creative Writing in Chicago. The following selection celebrates those "sisters" who have proudly kept their hair in its natural state.*

Sisters!   1
I love you.
Because you love you.
Because you are erect.
Because you are also bent.   5
In season, stern, kind.
Crisp, soft—in season.
And you withhold.
And you extend.
And you Step out.   10
And you go back.
And you extend again.
Your eyes, loud-soft, with crying and
    with smiles,

are older than a million years.
And they are young.   15
You reach, in season.
You subside, in season.
And ALL
below the richrough righttime of your hair.
                                                         20
You have not bought Blondine[1].
You have not hailed the hot-comb recently.
You never worshiped Marilyn Monroe.
You say: Farrah's hair[2] is hers.
You have not wanted to be white.
Nor have you testified to adoration of that   25
        state
with the advertisement of imitation
(*never* successful because the hot-comb is laughing too.)

Discussion Questions

1. What do the words *sisters* and *naturals* mean in the title?
2. What is the meaning of the subtitle?
3. Why does the persona (speaker) love sisters?
4. What is the significance of the references to "Blondine," Marilyn Monroe, and Farrah?
5. How does Brooks describe the "natural" woman?
6. What reason does Brooks offer for some women wanting to change their natural hair?
7. How does Brooks use cause and effect to convey her message?
8. At the beginning of the poem, how effective is Brooks's strategy of separating the main clause, "I love you," from the three subordinate clauses that follow it?

Writing Assignments

1. Write an essay celebrating some aspect of your culture or heritage.
2. Write an essay dedicated to someone or some group that has stood up for its convictions.
3. In an essay, discuss some seemingly insignificant habit or behavior that you have, or that someone else has, which actually suggests more than it does at first glance.

[1] Blondine (21)   Blond hair dye.
[2] Farrah's hair (24)   Straight blond hair like that of the actress, Farrah Fawcett.

MY BLACKNESS IS THE BEAUTY OF THIS LAND

Lance Jeffers

Lance Jeffers (1919–1985) was born in Nebraska and raised by his grandparents. He received his B. A. in English and his M. A. in English education at Columbia University. He taught at Howard University and North Carolina State University. Although he wrote short stories and a novel, Jeffers is most noted for his poetry. His books of poetry include When I Know the Power of My Black Hand *(1974),* O Africa, Where I Baked My Bread *(1977), and* Grandsire *(1979). The following selection is the title poem of Jeffers's first book of poetry,* My Blackness Is the Beauty of This Land *(1970). Strength, pride, and defiance in the face of oppression are the poem's subject.*

Vocabulary

drawling	(5)	natural speaking, characterized by lengthening or adding vowels as in a southern drawl
thrall	(8)	enslaved
gouging	(26)	deceiving
derision	(28)	ridicule; the act of making fun of someone or something

My blackness is the beauty of this land,   1
my blackness,
tender and strong, wounded and wise,
my blackness:
I, drawling black grandmother, smile muscular and sweet,   5
unstraightened white hair soon to grow in earth,
work-thickened hand thoughtful and gentle on
    grandson's head,
my heart is bloody-razored by a million memories' thrall:

    remembering the crook-necked cracker who spat
        on my naked body,   10
    remembering the splintering of my son's spirit
        because he remembered to be proud
    remembering the tragic eyes in my daughter's
        dark face when she learned her color's meaning.

and my own dark rage a rusty knife with teeth to gnaw   15
    my bowels,

my agony ripped loose by anguished shouts in Sunday's
    humble church,
my agony rainbowed to ecstasy when my feet oversoared
    Montgomery's slime,   20

ah, this hurt, this hate, this ecstasy before I die,
and all my love a strong cathedral!
My blackness is the beauty of this land!

Lay this against my whiteness, this land!
Lay me, young Brutus[1] stamping hard on the cat's tail,   25
gutting the Indian, gouging the nigger.
booting Little Rock's Minniejean Brown[2] in the buttocks
    and boast, my sharp white teeth derision-bared as I the
    conqueror crush!
Skyscraper-I, white hands burying God's human clouds
    beneath the dust!   30
Skyscraper-I, slim blond young Empire
    thrusting up my loveless bayonet to rape the sky,
then shrink all my long body with filth and in the gutter lie
as lie I will to perfume this armpit garbage,

While I here standing black beside   35
wrench tears from which the lies would suck the salt
to make me more American than America . . .
But yet my love and yet my hate shall civilize this land,
this land's salvation.

Discussion Questions

1. What is the meaning of the title?

2. What images of black are described in the poem?

3. Describe the image of white as it is used in the poem.

4. Historically, how have whites related to other racial or ethnic groups?

5. Why does Jeffers write that the black person is more "American than America"?

6. What is the meaning of the last two lines of the poem?

7. How does Jeffers's use of comparison and contrast help the reader to "see" the United States from the point of view of black people?

[1] Brutus (25)   Roman political and military leader who participated in the assassination of Julius Caesar.

[2] Minniejean Brown (27)   One of the "Little Rock Nine," students chosen in 1957 to desegregate the local high school in Little Rock, Arkansas.

8. Why do you think the poet chose to begin some of his lines with uppercase letters and some with lowercase letters?

Writing Assignments

1. Write an essay about what you perceive as the beauty of _____.

2. Write an essay describing the beauty and/or ugliness of America.

3. Write an essay responding to the following statement: "I see my _____ when I look at _____."

Student Essay:
KWANZAA: AN AFRICAN AMERICAN HOLIDAY

William Weir

As I grew into adulthood, I began to realize that for a religious   1
holiday, Christmas seemed to be nothing more than a commercial circus with little reference to its intended religious significance. Therefore, I was quite happy to find out about Kwanzaa,
an African American holiday that is celebrated around Christmas.

In 1966, Maulana Karenga, a scholar and professor, es-   2
tablished Kwanzaa for African Americans to better understand
their history and culture. Developed from the African tradition
of celebrating the harvest season, Kwanzaa is the only original
African American holiday and is ranked by some African Americans as important as Christmas, Easter, and Hanukkah are to
mainstream society.

Kwanzaa is divided into seven days beginning on Decem-   3
ber 26 and ending on January 1. Varying combinations of the
three red, one black, and three green candles are lit on each of
the seven days. Each candle represents the seven principles of
Kwanzaa, which are called the *Nguzo Saba,* the Swahili word
for principles. Each day begins with the greeting *Habari gani?,*
in Swahili, meaning, "What's new?" or "What's happening?" The
response given is the principle of the day. The seven principles
are as follows: *umoja* (unity), *kujichagulia* (self-determination),
ujima (collective work and responsibility), *ujamaa* (cooperative
economics), *nia* (purpose), *kuumba* (creativity), and *imani*
(faith). After lighting the candles, family, friends, and community discuss the principle of the day as it relates to the African
American experience.

A few other symbols are used in the celebration. The red,   4
black, and green flag, originally developed by Marcus Garvey
and his organization—the Universal Negro Improvement Association (UNIA)—is displayed in a prominent place. The color red
stands for the blood that African Americans shed throughout
their ordeal in the Western world; the black symbolizes the people; the green represents the motherland, Africa. Other symbols include the unity cup; the *kinara* (the candle holder); the
Kwanzaa mat; the *muhindi* (the corn representing the children

and their value to the life cycle of people of African descent); and the *zuwadi* (gifts given to children on January 1). These gifts should be educational, represent heritage, and/or be handcrafted.

Kwanzaa is not a religious holiday; it is a holiday during which African Americans celebrate their heritage. Therefore, even if you celebrate Christmas, you may still find it rewarding to celebrate Kwanzaa. 5

Discussion Questions

1. What is the author's view of Christmas?
2. What is Kwanzaa?
3. How is Kwanzaa celebrated?
4. What are some of the Kwanzaa symbols?
5. Why does the author say Kwanzaa can be celebrated by African Americans who celebrate Christmas?
6. Why do you think Weir chooses to use comparison and contrast in this essay?
7. How effective is the beginning and the ending of the essay?

Writing Assignments

1. In an essay, discuss a cultural tradition celebrated in your family.
2. Write an essay discussing a holiday that you think is negatively or positively observed.

15

Reading • Writing Education

DISCOVERING THE WRITER IN ME

Terry McMillan

Terry McMillan (1951–   ) was born in Port Huron, Michigan, graduated from the University of California at Berkeley, and briefly studied screenwriting at Columbia University. Her works include Mama *(1987);* Disappearing Acts *(1989);* Breaking Ice: An Anthology of Contemporary African-American Fiction *(1990); and* Waiting to Exhale *(1992), which appeared on the* New York Times *best-seller list for fourteen weeks and was made into a movie in 1995; and* How Stella Got Her Groove Back *(1996). In this excerpt from the introduction to* Breaking Ice, *McMillan describes how she discovered her abilities as a writer.*

Vocabulary

eccentric	(1)	odd, unconventional
horde	(2)	crowd
warrant	(5)	justify
provocative	(5)	exciting
verbose	(9)	wordy
vignettes	(11)	sketches, pictures
inherent	(12)	inborn, natural
philanthropy	(12)	love of humankind

As a child, I didn't know that African-American people wrote   1
books. I grew up in a small town in northern Michigan, where
the only books I came across were the Bible and required reading for school. I did not read for pleasure, and it wasn't until I
was sixteen when I got a job shelving books at the public library that I got lost in a book. It was a biography of Louisa May
Alcott. I was excited because I had not really read about poor
white folks before; her father was so eccentric and idealistic
that at the time I just thought he was crazy. I related to Louisa
because she had to help support her family at a young age,
which was what I was doing at the library.

Then one day I went to put a book away, and saw James   2
Baldwin's face staring up at me. "Who in the world is this?" I
wondered. I remember feeling embarrassed and did not read
his book because I was too afraid. I couldn't imagine that he'd
have anything better or different to say than Thomas Mann,
Henry Thoreau, Ralph Waldo Emerson, Nathaniel Hawthorne,
Ernest Hemingway, William Faulkner, etc. and a horde of other
mostly white male writers that I'd been introduced to in Literature 101 in high school. I mean, not only had there not been
any African-American authors included in any of those textbooks, but I'd never been given a clue that if we did have anything important to say that somebody would actually publish
it. Needless to say, I was not just naïve, but had not yet acquired an ounce of black pride. I never once questioned why
there were no representative works by us in any of those textbooks. After all, I had never heard of any African-American
writers, and no one I knew hardly read *any* books.

And then things changed.   3

It wasn't until after Malcolm X had been assassinated that   4
I found out who he was. I know I should be embarrassed about
this, but I'm not. I read Alex Haley's biography of him and it literally changed my life. First and foremost, I realized that there
was no reason to be ashamed of being black, that it was ridiculous. That we had a history, and much to be proud of. I began
to notice how we had actually been treated as less than human; began to see our strength as a people whereas I'd only
been made aware of our inferiorities. I started thinking about
my role in the world and not just on my street. I started *thinking.* Thinking about things I'd never thought about before, and
the thinking turned into questions. But I had more questions
than answers.

So I went to college. When I looked through the catalog   5
and saw a class called Afro-American Literature, I signed up

and couldn't wait for the first day of class. Did *we* really have enough writers to warrant an entire class? I remember the text-book was called *Dark Symphony: Negro Literature in America* because I still have it. I couldn't believe the rush I felt over and over once I discovered Countee Cullen, Langston Hughes, Ann Petry, Zora Neale Hurston, Ralph Ellison, Jean Toomer, Richard Wright, and rediscovered and read James Baldwin, to name just a few. I'm surprised I didn't need glasses by the end of the semester. My world opened up. I accumulated and gained a totally new insight about, and perception of, our lives as "black" people, as if I had been an outsider and was finally let in. To discover that our lives held as much significance and importance as our white counterparts was more than gratify-ing, it was exhilarating. Not only had we lived diverse, interest-ing, provocative, and relentless lives, but during, through, and as a result of all these painful experiences, some folks had taken the time to write it down.

Not once, throughout my entire four years as an under-   6
graduate did it occur to me that I might one day *be* a writer. I mean, these folks had genuine knowledge and insight. They also had a fascination with the truth. They had something to write about. Their work was bold, not flamboyant. They learned how to exploit the language so that readers would be affected by what they said and how they said it. And they had talent.

I never considered myself to be in possession of many of   7
the above, and yet when I was twenty years old, the first man I fell in love with broke my heart. I was so devastated and felt so helpless that my reaction manifested itself in a poem. I did not sit down and say, "I'm going to write a poem about this." It was more like magic. I didn't even know I was writing a poem until I had written it. Afterward, I felt lighter, as if something had hap-pened to lessen the pain. And when I read this "thing" I was shocked because I didn't know where the words came from. I was scared, to say the least, about what I had just experienced, because I didn't understand what had happened.

For the next few days, I read that poem over and over in   8
disbelief because *I* had written it. One day, a colleague saw it lying on the kitchen table and read it. I was embarrassed and shocked when he said he liked it, then went on to tell me that he had just started a black literary magazine at the college and he wanted to publish it. Publish it? He was serious and it found its way onto a typeset page.

Seeing my name in print excited me. And from that point   9
on, if a leaf moved on a tree, I wrote a poem about it. If a crack
in the sidewalk glistened, surely there was a poem in that.
Some of these verbose things actually got published in various
campus newspapers that were obviously desperate to fill up
space. I did not call myself a poet; I told people I wrote poems.

Years passed.   10

Those poems started turning into sentences and I started   11
getting nervous. What the hell did I think I was doing? Writing
these little go-nowhere vignettes. All these beginnings. And who
did I think I was, trying to tell a story? And who cared? Even
though I had no idea what I was doing, all I knew was that I
was beginning to realize that a lot of things mattered to me,
things disturbed me, things that I couldn't change. Writing became an outlet for my dissatisfactions, distaste, and my way of
trying to make sense of what I saw happening around me. It
was my way of trying to fix what I thought was broken. It later
became the only way to explore personally what I didn't understand. The problem, however, was that I was writing more
about ideas than people. Everything was so "large," and eventually I had to find a common denominator. I ended up asking
myself what I really cared about: it was people, and particularly
African-American people.

The whole idea of taking myself seriously as a writer was   12
terrifying. I didn't know any writers. Didn't know how you knew
if you "had" it or not. Didn't know if I was or would ever be
good enough. I didn't know how you went about the business
of writing, and besides, I sincerely wanted to make a decent living. (I had read the horror stories of how so few writers were
able to live off of their writing alone, many having lived like bohemians.[1]) At first, I thought being a social worker was the
right thing to do, since I was bent on saving the world (I was an
idealistic twenty-two years old), but when I found I couldn't do
it that way, I had to figure out another way to make an impact
on folks. A positive impact. I ended up majoring in journalism
because writing was "easy" for me, but it didn't take long for
me to learn that I did not like answering the "who, what, when,
where, and why" of anything. I then—upon the urging of my
mother and friends who had graduated and gotten "normal"
jobs—decided to try something that would still allow me to

---

[1] bohemians (12)   Persons with artistic or literary interests who disregard
conventional standards of behavior.

"express myself" but was relatively safer, though still risky: I went to film school. Of course what was inherent in my quest to find my "spot" in the world was this whole notion of affecting people on some grand scale. Malcolm and Martin caused me to think like this. Writing for me, as it's turned out, is philanthropy. It didn't take years for me to realize the impact that other writers' work had had on me, and if I was going to write, I did not want to write inconsequential, mediocre stories that didn't conjure up or arouse much in a reader. So I had to start by exciting myself and paying special attention to what I cared about, what mattered to me.

    Film school didn't work out. Besides, I never could stop   13 writing, which ultimately forced me to stop fighting it. It took even longer to realize that writing was not something you aspired to be, it was something you did because you had to.

Discussion Questions

1. Why did McMillan feel embarrassed and afraid when she saw James Baldwin's picture on a book?

2. How did McMillan discover African American writers on a large scale?

3. When did McMillan first discover she might be a writer? What purpose did writing serve for her?

4. Of what significance was McMillan's discovery that "writing was not something that you aspired to be, it was something you did because you had to"?

5. How does McMillan use narration to trace her growth as a writer?

6. Why is the first sentence of the essay an effective one?

Writing Assignments

1. McMillan uses words such as "scared," "embarrassed," "shocked," "nervous," and "terrifying" to describe her early writing experiences. Write an essay in which you describe your early writing experiences.

2. Write an essay describing the impact on you of a particular reading, for example, a poem, a book, or an essay.

3. Write an essay in which you respond to the following: "Writing for me is _____."

SEND YOUR CHILDREN TO THE LIBRARIES

Arthur Ashe

Arthur Ashe (1943–1993), born in Richmond, Virginia, was a graduate of UCLA and the world's leading African American professional tennis player. Ranked twice as the number-one player in the world, he was captain of the U.S. Davis Cup team in 1981. After suffering a heart attack in 1979, he retired from competitive play and began writing articles for newspapers and magazines. His books include Portrait in Motion *(1976);* Mastering Your Tennis Strokes *(1978); and his autobiographies,* Off the Court *(1981) and* Days of Grace: A Memoir *(1993). He is also editor of* A Hard Road to Glory: A History of the African-American Athlete *(1988). In this article (1977), originally published in the* New York Times, *Ashe emphasizes the importance of education for African American children.*

Vocabulary

pretentious	(2)	showy
dubious	(3)	doubtful
emulate	(4)	imitate
lure	(4)	attraction
viable	(9)	practical

Since my sophomore year at University of California, Los Angeles, I have become convinced that we blacks spend too much time on the playing fields and too little time in the libraries. 1

Please don't think of this attitude as being pretentious just because I am a black, single professional athlete. 2

I don't have children, but I can make observations. I strongly believe the black culture expends too much time, energy and effort raising, praising and teasing our black children as to the dubious glories of professional sport. 3

All children need models to emulate—parents, relatives or friends. But when the child starts school, the influence of the parent is shared by teachers and classmates, by the lure of books, movies, ministers and newspapers, but most of all by television. 4

Which televised events have the greatest number of viewers?—Sports—The Olympics, Super Bowl, Masters, World 5

Series, pro basketball playoffs, Forest Hills. ABC-TV even has
sports on Monday night prime time from April to December.

So your child gets a massive dose of O.J. Simpson, Ka-   6
reem Abdul-Jabbar, Muhammad Ali, Reggie Jackson, Dr. J.
and Lee Elder and other pro athletes. And it is only natural
that your child will dream of being a pro athlete himself.

But consider these facts: For the major professional sports   7
of hockey, football, basketball, baseball, golf, tennis and boxing, there are roughly only 3,170 major league positions available (attributing 200 positions to golf, 200 to tennis and 100 to
boxing). And the annual turnover is small.

We blacks are a subculture of about 28 million. Of the   8
$13\frac{1}{2}$ million men, 5 to 6 million are under 20 years of age, so
your son has less than one chance in 1,000 of becoming a pro.
Less than one in a thousand. Would you bet your son's future
on something with odds of 999 to 1 against you? I wouldn't.

Unless a child is exceptionally gifted, you should know by   9
the time he enters high school whether he has a future as an
athlete. But what is more important is what happens if he
doesn't graduate or doesn't land a college scholarship and
doesn't have a viable alternative job career. Our high school
dropout rate is several times the national average, which contributes to our unemployment rate of roughly twice the national average.

And how do you fight the figures in the newspapers every   10
day. Ali has earned more than $30 million boxing, O.J. just
signed for 2\frac{1}{2}$ million, Dr. J. for almost $3 million, Reggie
Jackson for $2.8 million, Nate Archibald for $400,000 a year.
All that money, recognition, attention, free cars, girls, jobs in
the offseason—no wonder there is Pop Warner football, Little
League baseball, National Junior Tennis League tennis, hockey
practice at 5 A.M. and pickup basketball games in any center
city at any hour.

There must be some way to assure that the 999 who   11
try but don't make it to pro sports don't wind up on the street
corners or in the unemployment lines. Unfortunately, our most
widely recognized role models are athletes and entertainers—
"runnin'" and "jumpin'" and "singin'" and "dancin.'" While
we are 60 percent of the National Basketball Association,
we are less than 4 percent of the doctors and lawyers. While
we are about 35 percent of major league baseball we are less
than 2 percent of the engineers. While we are about 40 percent of the National Football League, we are less than 11 per-

cent of construction workers such as carpenters and bricklayers.

Our greatest heroes of the century have been athletes— 12
Jack Johnson, Joe Louis and Muhammad Ali. Racial and economic discrimination forced us to channel our energies into athletics and entertainment. These were the two ways out of the ghetto, the ways to get that Cadillac, those alligator shoes, that cashmere sport coat.

Somehow, parents must instill a desire for learning along- 13
side the desire to be Walt Frazier. Why not start by sending black professional athletes into high schools to explain the facts of life.

I have often addressed high school audiences and my 14
message is always the same. For every hour you spend on the athletic field, spend two in the library. Even if you make it as a pro athlete, your career will be over by the time you are 35. So you will need that diploma.

Have these pro athletes explain what happens if you break 15
a leg, get a sore arm, have one bad year or don't make the cut for five or six tournaments. Explain to them the star system, wherein for every O.J. earning millions there are six or seven others making $15,000 or $20,000 or $30,000 a year.

But don't just have Walt Frazier or O.J. or Abdul-Jabbar ad- 16
dress your class. Invite a benchwarmer or a guy who didn't make it. Ask him if he sleeps every night. Ask him whether he was graduated. Ask him what he would do if he became disabled tomorrow. Ask him where his old high school athletic buddies are.

We have been on the same roads—sports and entertain- 17
ment—too long. We need to pull over, fill up at the library and speed away to Congress and the Supreme Court, the unions and the business world. We need more Barbara Jordans, Andrew Youngs, union card-holders, Nikki Giovannis and Earl Graveses. Don't worry: we will still be able to sing and dance and run and jump better than anybody else.

I'll never forget how proud my grandmother was when I 18
graduated from U.C.L.A. in 1966. Never mind the Davis Cup in 1968, 1969 and 1970. Never mind the Wimbledon title, Forest Hills, etc. To this day, she still doesn't know what those names mean.

What mattered to her was that of her more than 30 chil- 19
dren and grandchildren, I was the first to be graduated from college, and a famous college at that. Somehow, that made up for all those floors she scrubbed all those years.

Discussion Questions

1. Someone not reading this essay closely might mistakenly think that Ashe is discouraging young blacks from aspiring to be professional athletes. What is he really arguing?
2. What reasons does Ashe give to explain why blacks have historically entered the fields of athletics and entertainment?
3. What are the chances of a black child becoming a professional athlete? Does Ashe's use of statistics strengthen or weaken his argument?
4. What does Ashe propose as a means of giving students a realistic view of the world of professional sports?
5. Who is the audience for this essay?
6. Does it surprise you that as a professional athlete Ashe would take the position he does in this essay? Explain your answer.
7. How does Ashe use illustration to develop his argument?
8. How effective is the concluding paragraph of this essay? Explain your answer.

Writing Assignments

1. Ashe uses many examples of African American role models. Select one of these examples, or one of your own, and write an essay discussing his or her accomplishments.
2. Write an essay discussing your proposed career and the kind of education required for it.
3. Sometimes the glamour of a job may blind one to its many demands. Write an essay discussing a career that has been glamorized and some of the challenges associated with it.

MY SELF-EDUCATION

Malcolm X

*Born Malcolm Little in Omaha, Nebraska, Malcolm X
(1925–1965) was one of the most powerful and controversial African American leaders during the 1960s. While serving seven years in prison for burglary, he joined the Nation
of Islam, headed by Elijah Muhammad, and later became
the national spokesperson for the organization. Following a
holy pilgrimage to Mecca in 1964, he took the name of El
Hajj Malik El-Shabazz and separated himself from the Nation of Islam. At the time of his assassination, he had
formed his own group, The Organization of Afro-American
Unity. In this excerpt from his* Autobiography *(1965), co-au-
thored with Alex Haley, Malcolm X describes his self-education.*

Vocabulary

articulate	(2)	clearly spoken
emulate	(4)	imitate
riffling	(6)	shuffling
burrowing	(9)	digging a hole in the ground
engrossing	(16)	occupying one's complete attention
feigned	(18)	pretended
digressing	(27)	getting off the subject

It was because of my letters that I happened to stumble
upon starting to acquire some kind of homemade education. 1

I became increasingly frustrated at not being able to express what I wanted to convey in letters that I wrote, especially
those to Mr. Elijah Muhammad.[1] In the street, I had been the
most articulate hustler out there—I had commanded attention
when I said something. But now, trying to write simple English,
I not only wasn't articulate, I wasn't even functional. How
would I sound writing in slang, the way I would *say* it, something such as, "Look, daddy, let me pull your coat about a cat,
Elijah Muhammad—" 2

---

[1] Elijah Muhammad   (2)   Leader of the Nation of Islam, 1935–1975.

Many who today hear me somewhere in person, or on tele- 3
vision, or those who read something I've said, will think I went
to school far beyond the eighth grade. This impression is due
entirely to my prison studies.

It had really begun back in the Charlestown Prison, when 4
Bimbi[2] first made me feel envy of his stock of knowledge.
Bimbi had always taken charge of any conversations he was in,
and I had tried to emulate him. But every book I picked up had
few sentences which didn't contain anywhere from one to
nearly all of the words that might as well have been in Chinese.
When I just skipped those words, of course, I really ended up
with little idea of what the book said. So I had come to the Norfolk Prison Colony still going through only book-reading motions. Pretty soon, I would have quit even these motions, unless
I had received the motivation that I did.

I saw that the best thing I could do was get hold of a dic- 5
tionary—to study, to learn some words. I was lucky enough to
reason also that I should try to improve my penmanship. It was
sad. I couldn't even write in a straight line. It was both ideas
together that moved me to request a dictionary along with some
tablets and pencils from the Norfolk Prison Colony school.

I spent two days just riffling uncertainly through the dic- 6
tionary's pages. I'd never realized so many words existed! I did-
n't know *which* words I needed to learn. Finally, just to start
some kind of action, I began copying.

In my slow, painstaking, ragged handwriting, I copied into 7
my tablet everything printed on that first page, down to the
punctuation marks.

I believe it took me a day. Then, aloud, I read back, to my- 8
self, everything I'd written on the tablet. Over and over, aloud,
to myself, I read my own handwriting.

I woke up the next morning, thinking about those words— 9
immensely proud to realize that not only had I written so much
at one time, but I'd written words that I never knew were in the
world. Moreover, with a little effort, I also could remember what
many of these words meant. I reviewed the words whose meanings I didn't remember. Funny thing, from the dictionary first
page right now, that "aardvark" springs to my mind. The dictionary had a picture of it, a long-tailed, long-eared, burrowing

---

[2] Bimbi (4) A fellow inmate whose encyclopedic learning and verbal facility greatly impressed Malcolm X.

African mammal, which lives off termites caught by sticking
out its tongue as an anteater does for ants.

I was so fascinated that I went on—I copied the diction- 10
ary's next page. And the same experience came when I studied
that. With every succeeding page, I also learned of people and
places and events from history. Actually the dictionary is like a
miniature encyclopedia. Finally the dictionary's A section had
filled a whole tablet—and I went on into the B's. That was the
way I started copying what eventually became the entire dictionary. It went a lot faster after so much practice helped me to
pick up handwriting speed. Between what I wrote in my tablet,
and writing letters, during the rest of my time in prison I would
guess I wrote a million words.

I suppose it was inevitable that as my word-base broad- 11
ened, I could for the first time pick up a book and read and
now begin to understand what the book was saying. Anyone
who has read a great deal can imagine the new world that
opened. Let me tell you something: from then until I left that
prison, in every free moment I had, if I was not reading in the
library, I was reading on my bunk. You couldn't have gotten me
out of books with a wedge. Between Mr. Muhammad's teachings, my correspondence, my visitors, . . . and my reading of
books, months passed without my even thinking about being
imprisoned. In fact, up to then, I never had been so truly free
in my life.

The Norfolk Prison Colony's library was in the school 12
building. A variety of classes was taught there by instructors
who came from such places as Harvard and Boston universities. The weekly debates between inmate teams were also held
in the school building. You would be astonished to know how
worked up convict debaters and audiences would get over subjects like "Should Babies Be Fed Milk?"

Available on the prison library's shelves were books on 13
just about every general subject. Much of the big private collection that Parkhurst[3] had willed to the prison was still in crates
and boxes in the back of the library—thousands of old books.
Some of them looked ancient: covers faded, old-time parch-
ment-looking binding. Parkhurst . . . seemed to have been
principally interested in history and religion. He had the money

[3] Parkhurst (13)   Charles Henry Parkhurst (1842–1933); U.S. clergyman,
reformer, and president of the Society for the Prevention of Crime.

and the special interest to have a lot of books that you wouldn't have in a general circulation. Any college library would have been lucky to get that collection.

As you can imagine, especially in a prison where there was   14
heavy emphasis on rehabilitation, an inmate was smiled upon if he demonstrated an unusually intense interest in books. There was a sizable number of well-read inmates, especially the popular debaters. Some were said by many to be practically walking encyclopedias. They were almost celebrities. No university would ask any student to devour literature as I did when this new world opened to me, of being able to read and *understand.*

I read more in my room than in the library itself. An in-   15
mate who was known to read a lot could check out more than the permitted maximum number of books. I preferred reading in the total isolation of my own room.

When I had progressed to really serious reading, every   16
night at about ten P.M. I would be outraged with the "lights out." It always seemed to catch me right in the middle of something engrossing.

Fortunately, right outside my door was a corridor light   17
that cast a glow into my room. The glow was enough to read by, once my eyes adjusted to it. So when "lights out" came, I would sit on the floor where I could continue reading in that glow.

At one-hour intervals the night guards paced past every   18
room. Each time I heard the approaching footsteps, I jumped into bed and feigned sleep. And as soon as the guard passed, I got back out of bed onto the floor area of that light-glow, where I would read for another fifty-eight minutes—until the guard approached again. That went on until three or four every morning. Three or four hours of sleep a night was enough for me. Often in the years in the streets I had slept less than that.

The teachings of Mr. Muhammad stressed how history   19
had been "whitened"—when white men had written history books, the black man simply had been left out. Mr. Muhammad couldn't have said anything that would have struck me much harder. I had never forgotten how when my class, me and all of those whites, had studied seventh-grade United States history back in Mason, the history of the Negro had been covered in one paragraph, and the teacher had gotten a big laugh with his joke, "Negroes' feet are so big that when they walk, they leave a hole in the ground."

This is one reason why Mr. Muhammad's teachings spread   20
so swiftly all over the United States, among *all* Negroes,
whether or not they became followers of Mr. Muhammad. The
teachings ring true—to every Negro. You can hardly show me a
black adult in America—or a white one, for that matter—who
knows from the history books anything like the truth about the
black man's role. In my own case, once I heard of the "glorious
history of the black man," I took special pains to hunt in the library for books that would inform me on details about black
history.

I can remember accurately the very first set of books that   21
really impressed me. I have since bought that set of books and
I have it at home for my children to read as they grow up. It's
called *Wonders of the World.* It's full of pictures of archeological
finds, statues that depict, usually, non-European people.

I found books like Will Durant's[4] *Story of Civilization.* I   22
read H.G. Wells'[5] *Outline of History. Souls of Black Folk* by
W.E.B. Du Bois[6] gave me a glimpse into the black people's history before they came to this country. Carter G. Woodson's[7]
Negro History opened my eyes about black empires before the
black slave was brought to the United States, and the early Negro struggles for freedom.

J.A. Rogers'[8] three volumes of *Sex and Race* told about   23
race-mixing before Christ's time; and Aesop being a black man
who told fables; about Egypt's Pharaohs; about the great Coptic
Christian Empires;[9] about Ethiopia, the earth's oldest continuous black civilization, as China is the oldest continuous civilization. . . .

I have often reflected upon the new vistas that reading   24
opened to me. I knew right there in prison that reading had
changed forever the course of my life. As I see it today, the ability to read awoke inside me some long dormant craving to be
mentally alive. I certainly wasn't seeking any degree, the way a

[4] Will Durant   (22)   U.S. author and historian (1885–1981).
[5] H.G. Wells   (22)   English novelist and historian (1866–1946).
[6] W.E.B. Du Bois   (22)   William Edward Burghardt Du Bois, distinguished
black scholar, author, and activist (1868–1963). Du Bois was the first director of the
NAACP and was an important figure in the Harlem Renaissance; his best-known
book is *Souls of Black Folk.*
[7] Carter G. Woodson (22)   distinguished African American historian
(1875–1950); considered the father of black history.
[8] J.A. Rogers   (23)   African American historian and journalist (1883–1965).
[9] Coptic Christian Empire   (23)   Territory of the Coptic Church, a native
Egyptian Christian church that maintains some of its African religious practices.

college confers a status symbol upon its students. My home-made education gave me, with every additional book that I read, a little bit more sensitivity to the deafness, dumbness, and blindness that was afflicting the black race in America. Not long ago, an English writer telephoned me from London, asking questions. One was, "What's your alma mater?" I told him, "Books." You will never catch me with a free fifteen minutes in which I'm not studying something I feel might be able to help the black man.

Yesterday I spoke in London, and both ways on the plane across the Atlantic I was studying a document about how the United Nations proposes to insure the human rights of the oppressed minorities of the world. The American black man is the world's most shameful case of minority oppression. What makes the black man think of himself as only an internal United States issue is just a catch-phrase, two words, "civil rights." How is the black man going to get "civil rights" before first he wins his *human* rights? If the American black man will start thinking about his *human* rights, and then start thinking of himself as part of one of the world's great peoples, he will see he has a case for the United Nations.   25

I can't think of a better case! Four hundred years of black blood and sweat invested here in America, and the white man still has the black man begging for what every immigrant fresh off the ship can take for granted the minute he walks down the gangplank.   26

But I'm digressing. I told the Englishman that my alma mater was books, a good library. Every time I catch a plane, I have with me a book that I want to read—and that's a lot of books these days. If I weren't out here every day battling the white man, I could spend the rest of my life reading, just satisfying my curiosity—because you can hardly mention anything I'm not curious about. I don't think anybody ever got more out of going to prison than I did. In fact, prison enabled me to study far more intensively than I would have if my life had gone differently and I had attended some college. I imagine that one of the biggest troubles with colleges is there are too many distractions, too much panty-raiding, fraternities, and boola-boola and all of that. Where else but in a prison could I have attacked my ignorance by being able to study intensely sometimes as much as fifteen hours a day?   27

Discussion Questions

1. What inspired Malcolm X to educate himself in prison?
2. What did he learn from his vast reading? What effect did it have on him?
3. How did copying the dictionary contribute to Malcolm X's education?
4. What examples does Malcolm X give to support his statement that history had been "whitened"?
5. Why does Malcolm X say that "I don't think anybody got more out of going to prison than I did"?
6. What is the tone of this excerpt?
7. How does Malcolm X use process to trace his self-education?
8. What is the purpose of this excerpt?

Writing Assignments

1. Write an essay explaining how knowledge gained from something you have recently read enlightened you on some issue.
2. Based on what you learned in your American history class, write an essay in which you agree or disagree with Malcolm X's statement that the "glorious history of the black man was omitted from history books."
3. Think of an activity other than reading that you feel has empowered you. Write an essay explaining why you feel empowered by this particular activity.

WHO I AM AND HOW I WRITE

Mari Evans

Poet Mari Evans was born in Toledo, Ohio, and studied at the University of Toledo. She has worked as a television producer-director and currently is a college professor. Her books of poetry include I Am a Black Woman *(1970),* Where Is All the Music? *(1968),* Nightstar: Poems From 1973–1978 *(1982), and* Black Women Writers (1950–1980): A Critical Evaluation *(1983), from which this excerpt is taken. Evans's works are noted for their powerful emphases on the beauty of blackness. In the following selection, Evans describes her father's influence on her development as a writer.*

Vocabulary

vulnerability	(2)	openness to criticism or attack
indomitable	(2)	not easily discouraged
inscribing	(3)	impressing deeply
caprice	(3)	impulse
aesthetically	(6)	with sensitivity to art and beauty
imbued	(6)	filled
pathos	(6)	quality to arouse emotions
diaspora	(7)	scattering of people outside their homeland
ergo	(11)	therefore
blatantly	(12)	with obvious offensiveness
remanded	(12)	sent back
internment	(12)	confinement or impoundment, especially during a war

. . . I cannot imagine a writer who is not continually reaching, who contains no discontent that what he is producing is not more than it is. . . .

Who I am is central to how I write and what I write; and I am the continuation of my father's passage. I have written for as long as I have been aware of writing as a way of setting down feelings and the stuff of imaginings. 1

No single living entity really influenced my life as did my father, who died two Septembers ago. An oak of a man, his five 2 feet eight loomed taller than Kilimanjaro.[1] He lived as if he were poured from iron, and loved his family with a vulnerability that was touching. Indomitable, to the point that one could not have spent a lifetime in his presence without absorbing something beautiful and strong and special.

He saved my first printed story, a fourth-grade effort accepted by the school paper, and carefully noted on it the date, our home address, and his own proud comment. By this action inscribing on an impressionable Black youngster both the importance of the printed word and the accessibility of "reward" for even a slight effort, given the right circumstances. For I knew from what ease and caprice the story had come.

Years later, I moved from university journalism to a by-lined column in a Black-owned weekly and, in time, worked variously as an industrial editor, as a research associate with responsibility for preparing curriculum materials, and as director of publications for the corporate management of a Job Corps installation.

I have always written, it seems. I have not, however, always been organized in my approach. Now, I find I am much more productive when I set aside a specific time and uncompromisingly accept that as commitment. The ideal, for me, is to be able to write for long periods of time on an eight-hour-a-day basis. That is, to begin to write—not to prepare to write, around eight-thirty, stop for lunch, resume writing around twelve-thirty and stop for the day around four-thirty when I begin to feel both fulfilled and exhausted by the effort. For most Black writers that kind of leisure is an unaccustomed luxury. I enjoyed it exactly once, for a two-week period. In that two weeks I came face to face with myself as a writer and liked what I saw of my productive potential. . . .

I originally wrote poems because certain things occurred to me in phrases that I didn't want to lose. The captured phrase is a joyous way to approach the molding and shaping of a poem. More often now, however, because my conscious direction is different, I choose the subject first, then set about the task of creating a work that will please me aesthetically and that will treat the subject with integrity. A work that is imbued with the urgency, the tenderness, the pathos, needed to transmit to readers my sense of why they should involve themselves with what it is I have to say.

[1] Kilimanjaro (2) The highest mountain in Africa.

I have no favorite themes nor concerns except the overall   7
concern that Black life be experienced throughout the diaspora
on the highest, most rewarding, most productive levels. Hardly
chauvinistic, for when that is possible for our Black family/na-
tion it will be true and possible for all people.

My primary goal is to command the reader's attention. I   8
understand I have to make the most of the first few seconds his
or her eye touches my material. Therefore, for me, the poem is
structure and style as well as theme and content; I require
something of my poems visually as well as rhetorically. I work
as hard at how the poem "looks" as at crafting; indeed, for me
the two are synonymous.

I revise endlessly, and am not reluctant to consider a   9
poem "in process" even after it has appeared in print. I am not
often completely pleased with any single piece, therefore, I remember with great pleasure those rare "given" poems. "If There
Be Sorrow" was such a piece, and there were others, but I remember "Sorrow" because that was the first time I experienced
the exquisite joy of having a poem emerge complete, without
my conscious intervention.

The title poem for my second volume, *I Am a Black*   10
Woman, on the other hand, required between fifteen and twenty
revisions before I felt comfortable that it could stand alone.

My attempt is to be as explicit as possible while maintain-   11
ing the integrity of the aesthetic; consequently, I work so hard
for clarity that I suspect I sometimes run the risk of being, as
Ray Durem put it, "not sufficiently obscure." Since the Black
creative artist is not required to wait on inspiration nor to rely
on imagination—for Black life is drama, brutal and compelling—
one inescapable reality is that the more explicitly Black writers
speak their truths the more difficult it is for them to publish. My
writing is pulsed by my understanding of contemporary realities:
I am Afrikan first, then woman, then writer, but I have never had
a manuscript rejected because I am a woman: I have been rejected more times than I can number because the content of a
manuscript was, to the industry-oriented reader, more "Black"
ergo "discomforting" than could be accommodated.

Nevertheless, given the crisis nature of the Black position   12
at a time of escalating state-imposed repression and containment, in a country that has a history of blatantly genocidal
acts committed against three nonwhite nations (Native Americans, the Japanese of Hiroshima/Nagasaki, the inhabitants of
Vietnam), a country that has perfected the systematic destruc-

tion of a people, their land, foliage, and food supply; a country that at the stroke of a presidential pen not only revoked the rights and privileges of citizenship for 110,000 American citizens (identifiable, since they were nonwhite) for what they "could" do, but summarily remanded those citizens to American internment camps, I understand that Black writers have a responsibility to use the language in the manner it is and always has been used by non-Black writers and by the state itself: as a political force.

I think of myself as a political writer inasmuch as I am deliberately attempting the delivery of political concepts and premises through the medium of the Black aesthetic, seeing the various art forms as vehicles.   13

As a Black writer embracing that responsibility, approaching my Black family/nation from within a commonality of experience, I try for a poetic language that says, "This is *who* we are, where we have been, *where* we are. This, is where we must go. And *this,* is what we must do."   14

Discussion Questions

1. How did Evans's father influence her development as a writer?
2. What is Evans's approach to writing poems?
3. Evans implies that revision is an important part of the writing process. What does this idea reveal about the art of writing?
4. According to Evans, why is it more difficult for black writers to publish their works than it is for nonblack writers?
5. According to Evans, what is the responsibility of black writers?
6. How would you characterize Evans?
7. Evans uses a variety of rhetorical strategies in developing her essay. Identify as many strategies as you can. How is each used in the essay?
8. How does the opening quotation set the tone for the essay?

Writing Assignments

1. Write an essay in which you agree or disagree with the following statement: African American writers have a responsibility to use their writing to help other African Americans.
2. Write an essay discussing your views on writing or your writing habits.
3. Write an essay explaining how someone (a writer, a teacher, a parent, a friend, etc.) has influenced your writing development.

Student Essay:
PUBLIC SCHOOLS FOR AFRICAN AMERICAN MALES: ARE THEY NECESSARY?

Byron T. Thompson

Vocabulary

disproportionately	(2)	unequally
detrimental	(2)	causing damage or harm

America has a new endangered species: the African American 1
male. Usually, the term *endangered species* is used to refer to
animals that have their existence continually threatened. But
now, America has created a human endangered species. Statistics, research studies, and common knowledge serve as proof
that black males are one of the most threatened species on
earth.

America's public schools surface as the single largest con- 2
tributor of the many divisions of institutional racism that have
led black males to their current endangered state. The mistakes begin in elementary school, which is probably the most
critical period in the black male child's development. First of
all, teachers generally are white females who often do not understand black boys. Studies show that these teachers unjusti-
fiably and disproportionately place black children, especially
boys, in "special" classes. This unfair treatment is detrimental
to their future education.

Contrary to popular belief, black boys do have positive at- 3
titudes about school. One survey showed that nearly all black
boys expected to graduate, but almost half felt that their teachers did not set high enough standards for them.* The majority
of them felt that they should be pushed harder. Another survey, conducted by the same group of people who surveyed the
black boys, showed that six out of ten teachers believed that
black boys would not go to college.* In essence, black boys
have their academic potential substantially doubted before they
even set foot in the classroom.

* Garibaldi, Antoine M. "Educating and Motivating African-American Males to
Succeed." *Journal of Negro Education* 61 (1993):129–131.

It should be obvious that a change is needed in America's   4
public school systems. One option that has become a reality is
the development of public schools that are specifically designed
with the needs of black males in mind. But there is considerable opposition to the formation of such schools from both
African Americans and Caucasians. Parents, teachers, and administrators are among the opposition. Citing various reasons,
many feel that it is a step backward toward segregation, an improper discriminatory use of public funds, and simply the
wrong answer to the problem.

Milwaukee's African American immersion schools[1] serve   5
as an example that refutes those opposing viewpoints. Founded
in 1991 after years of research and study, the Martin Luther
King Jr. Elementary School was opened in Milwaukee, Wisconsin, on a goal-oriented, developmental concept. It is open to all
students, but is specifically designed for black boys and promotes African American heritage. Besides having an open enrollment policy, this school was transformed from a school that
already had a greater than 90 percent black enrollment; therefore, it does not promote segregation, nor is it discriminatory.

The school's concept is to instill a notion of inclusion   6
through more accurate portrayals of black people in order to
eliminate feelings of exclusion that black youth currently face.
The common practice in today's schools is to eliminate or
strongly distort images that deal with African Americans. Other
than to mention the deeds of Dr. Martin Luther King, George
Washington Carver, and Harriet Tubman, there is virtually no
reference in texts or by teachers to the magnitude in which
African Americans contributed to the building and prosperity of
this country. When teachers discuss Jim Crow laws,[2] slavery,
and the like, the evils that were associated with them are not
adequately covered, nor are the negative effects that they had
on blacks. In short, blacks are portrayed as intruders to this
country, whereas the correct interpretation would be to tell
how Africans brought to America were intruded upon. An increase in self-esteem is certain to occur when the learning environment changes from one which promotes false images that
produce negativity to one which promotes true images that encourage positivity.

[1] African American immersion schools   (5)   Schools for African Americans
that include African American history and culture as part of their curricula.
[2] Jim Crow Laws   (6)   Legal and systematic practice of segregating, suppressing, and discriminating against African Americans.

Not only will schools for African American males change   7
attitudes, but also will help black males socially and academically. Since the goals of the African American immersion
schools focus on the development of social skills, communication, problem solving, and critical thinking (areas not often
stressed in regular public schools), a tremendous impact on
the boys will result because they will be receiving vital lessons
that would not be taught to them otherwise. Also included
within this curriculum is the promotion of true self-identity of
both males and females, since often their everyday environment is one that instills within them attitudes and beliefs that
will not enable them to properly function in society.

With so much potential for improvement, it must be con-   8
cluded that schools for African American males are necessary.
The long-term effects will benefit all of society. The number of
black male high school graduates will produce more black male
college graduates who will become productive members of society.

Discussion Questions

1. What reasons does Thompson give to support his view that
   African American males are an "endangered species"?
2. What happens in an African American immersion school that
   does not occur in a regular school?
3. What is the basis of Thompson's argument that the African
   American immersion schools are not a form of reverse discrimination? Do you agree or disagree with this argument?
4. How does Thompson argue that schools for African American
   males will benefit all of society?
5. What is the tone of this essay?
6. How does Thompson use comparison and contrast to develop his
   argument?
7. Thompson chose to predict outcomes in his conclusion. What
   other type of effective ending could he have chosen?

Writing Assignments

1. Write an essay in which you discuss the strengths or weaknesses
   of a public school education.
2. Write an essay describing improvements you would make in your
   former school(s) if you were principal.
3. Write an essay in which you discuss some things you wish you
   had learned earlier in school.

16

Political Philosophies

BOOKER T. AND W.E.B.

Dudley Randall

Poet, editor, and founder of Broadside Press, Dudley Randall (1914–   ) was influential in helping publish the poetry of artists such as Haki R. Madhubuti (don l. lee), Sonia Sanchez, Nikki Giovanni, and Etheridge Knight. In addition to editing and co-editing volumes of poems, he wrote "Poem Counterpoem" (1966) with Margaret Danner and "Cities Burning" (1970). In his well-known poetic dialogue between Booker T. Washington and W.E.B. DuBois, which follows, Randall reflects the historical philosophical controversy between the two political leaders.

Vocabulary

cheek	(1)	arrogance
grouse	(3)	informal word for "complain"
avail	(4)	to be of use

"It seems to me," said Booker T.,   1
"It shows a mighty lot of cheek
To study chemistry and Greek
When Mister Charlie[1] needs a hand
To hoe the cotton on his land,
And when Miss Ann[2] looks for a cook,
Why stick your nose inside a book?"

"I don't agree," said W. E. B.   2
"If I should have the drive to seek
Knowledge of chemistry or Greek,
I'll do it. Charles and Miss can look
Another place for hand or cook.
Some men rejoice in skill of hand,
And some in cultivating land,
But there are others who maintain
The right to cultivate the brain."

"It seems to me," said Booker T.,   3
"That all you folks have missed the boat
Who shout about the right to vote,
And spend vain days and sleepless nights
In uproar over civil rights.
Just keep your mouths shut, do not grouse,
But work, and save, and buy a house."

"I don't agree," said W. E. B.   4
"For what can property avail
If dignity and justice fail?
Unless you help to make the laws,
They'll steal your house with trumped-up clause.
A rope's as tight, a fire as hot,
No matter how much cash you've got.
Speak soft, and try your little plan,
But as for me, I'll be a man."

"It seems to me," said Booker T.—   5

"I don't agree,"   6
Said W. E. B.

[1] Mister Charlie and [2]Miss Ann (1)   Terms used to symbolize the slave
master and his wife; have been broadened to mean any white male or female authority figure.

Discussion Questions

1. Why does Randall choose to omit the last names in the title?
2. What are the two political philosophies presented in the poem? Discuss each one.
3. What do you think accounts for the differences in the men's philosophies?
4. Do you think that the poet communicates a strong preference for one of the views. What is his preference? Support your answer.
5. What rhetorical strategies are used to help the reader highlight the difference between Washington and Dubois?
6. What do the last three lines say about the argument?

Writing Assignments

1. Write an essay in which you support either Booker T. or W.E.B.'s philosophy.
2. Write an essay in which you contrast two views or strategies on abolishing racism.
3. Write an essay in which you contrast the views of a controversial issue, for example, health-care reform or prayer in public schools.

ATLANTA EXPOSITION ADDRESS

Booker T. Washington

Booker T. Washington (1856–1915) was born to a white slave-holding father and a black slave mother in Franklin County, Virginia. He was educated at Hampton Institute (now Hampton University) and went on to become founder and president of Tuskegee Institute, which emphasized the value of vocational education as a stepping-stone to economic empowerment for its students. Washington wrote twelve books. The most important of these are his autobiography Up from Slavery *(1901),* The Future of the American Negro *(1899), and* Life of Frederick Douglass *(1907). A controversial high point in Washington's career was his address to the Atlanta Cotton States and International Exposition in 1895. In that speech, excerpted here, he accepts social and legal segregation while promising racial cooperation.*

Vocabulary

injunction	(3)	command, order
gewgaws	(4)	knickknacks, trinkets
folly	(6)	nonsense
ostracized	(6)	shut out, ignored

Mr. President and Gentlemen of the Board of Directors and Citizens: One-third of the population of the South is of the Negro race. No enterprise seeking the material, civil, or moral welfare of this section can disregard this element of our population and reach the highest success. I but convey to you, Mr. President and Directors, the sentiment of the masses of my race when I say that in no way have the value and manhood of the American Negro been more fittingly and generously recognized than by the managers of this magnificent Exposition at every stage of its progress. It is a recognition that will do more to cement the friendship of the two races than any occurrence since the dawn of freedom.   1

Not only this, but the opportunity here afforded will awaken among us a new era of industrial progress. Ignorant and inexperienced, it is not strange that in the first years of our new life we began at the top instead of at the bottom; that a   2 seat in Congress or the State Legislature was more sought than real estate or industrial skill; that the political convention or stump speaking had more attractions than starting a dairy farm or truck garden.

A ship lost at sea for many days suddenly sighted a 3 friendly vessel. From the mast of the unfortunate vessel was seen a signal, "Water, water; we die of thirst!" The answer from the friendly vessel at once came back: "Cast down your bucket where you are." A second time the signal, "Water, water; send us water!" ran up from the distressed vessel, and was answered: "Cast down your bucket where you are." The captain of the distressed vessel, at last heeding the injunction, cast down his bucket, and it came up full of fresh, sparkling water from the mouth of the Amazon River. To those of my race who depend upon bettering their condition in a foreign land, or who underestimate the importance of cultivating friendly relations with the Southern white man, who is his next door neighbor, I would say: "Cast down your bucket where you are"—cast it down in making friends in every manly way of the people of all races by whom we are surrounded.

Cast it down in agriculture, mechanics, in commerce, in 4 domestic service, and in the professions. And in this connection it is well to bear in mind that whatever other sins the South may be called to bear, when it comes to business, pure and simple, it is in the South that the Negro is given a man's chance in the commercial world, and in nothing is this Exposition more eloquent than in emphasizing this chance. Our greatest danger is, that in the great leap from slavery to freedom we may overlook the fact that the masses of us are to live by the productions of our hands, and fail to keep in mind that we shall prosper in proportion as we learn to dignify and glorify common labor, and put brains and skill into the common occupations of life; shall prosper in proportion as we learn to draw the line between the superficial and the substantial, the ornamental gewgaws of life and the useful. No race can prosper till it learns that there is as much dignity in tilling a field as in writing a poem. It is at the bottom of life we must begin, and not at the top. Nor should we permit our grievances to overshadow our opportunities.

To those of the white race who look to the incoming of 5 those of foreign birth and strange tongue and habits for the prosperity of the South, were I permitted I would repeat what I say to my own race, "Cast down your bucket where you are."

Cast it down among the 8,000,000 Negroes whose habits you know, whose fidelity and love you have tested in days when to have proved treacherous meant the ruin of your firesides. Cast down your bucket among these people who have, without strikes and labor wars, tilled your fields, cleared your forests, builded your railroads and cities, and brought forth treasures from the bowels of the earth, and helped make possible this magnificent representation of the progress of the South. Casting down your bucket among my people, helping and encouraging them as you are doing on these grounds, and, with education of head, hand and heart, you will find that they will buy your surplus land, make blossom the waste places in your fields, and run your factories. While doing this, you can be sure in the future, as in the past, that you and your families will be surrounded by the most patient, faithful, law-abiding, and unresentful people that the world has seen. As we have proved our loyalty to you in the past, in nursing your children, watching by the sick bed of your mothers and fathers, and often following them with tear-dimmed eyes to their graves, so in the future, in our humble way, we shall stand by you with a devotion that no foreigner can approach, ready to lay down our lives, if need be, in defense of yours, interlacing our industrial, commercial, civil, and religious life with yours in a way that shall make the interests of both races one. In all things that are purely social we can be as separate as the fingers, yet one as the hand in all things essential to mutual progress. . . .

The wisest among my race understand that the agitation   6
of questions of social equality is the extremest folly, and that progress in the enjoyment of all the privileges that will come to us must be the result of severe and constant struggle rather than of artificial forcing. No race that has anything to contribute to the markets of the world is long in any degree ostracized. It is important and right that all privileges of the law be ours, but it is vastly more important that we be prepared for the exercise of those privileges. The opportunity to earn a dollar in a factory just now is worth infinitely more than the opportunity to spend a dollar in an opera house.

In conclusion, may I repeat that nothing in thirty years   7
has given us more hope and encouragement, and drawn us so near to you of the white race, as this opportunity offered by the Exposition; and here bending, as it were, over the altar that represents the results of the struggles of your race and mine, both starting practically empty-handed three decades ago, I

pledge that, in your effort to work out the great and intricate problem which God has laid at the doors of the South, you shall have at all times the patient, sympathetic help of my race; only let this be constantly in mind that, while from representations in these buildings of the products of field, of forest, of mine, of factory, letters, and art, much good will come, yet far above and beyond material benefits will be the higher good, that let us pray God will come, in a blotting out of sectional differences and racial animosities and suspicions, in a determination to administer absolute justice, in a willing obedience among all classes to the mandates of law. This, coupled with our material prosperity, will bring into our beloved South a new heaven and a new earth.

Discussion Questions

1. In this address Washington presents his economic and social plan for southern blacks and whites. What is his message to each?
2. What does Washington mean in his "Cast-down-your-buckets-where-you-are" passage?
3. What does Washington mean when he says, "No race can prosper till it learns that there is as much dignity in tilling a field as in writing a poem"?
4. What image of African Americans does Washington present to "those of the white race"? Give examples. What is your response to that image?
5. What rhetorical strategies other than persuasion does Washington use?
6. What is the thesis of Washington's speech?

Writing Assignments

1. Write an essay in which you recount a situation when you or someone you know protested. Explain why the protest was memorable.
2. Using Washington's speech as a model, write your own speech to be addressed to _____ proposing _____.
3. Write an essay in which you or someone you know used one approach to solving a problem, but should have used another approach. Explain your response.

GARVEY SPEAKS AT MADISON SQUARE GARDEN

Marcus Garvey

Born in St. Ann's Bay, Jamaica, Marcus Garvey (1887–1940), perhaps more than any other leader, has had a far-reaching effect on African Americans as a result of his inspiring a revolution in black consciousness. He organized the Universal Negro Improvement Association (UNIA), aimed at uniting people of African descent throughout the world to establish "a country and government absolutely their own." Of all political organizations, the UNIA, still in existence today, has the record for having the largest worldwide membership of people of African descent. Finding color discrimination among Jamaicans a problem, Garvey moved his political base to the United States. Later, after a questionable prison conviction, he was deported but continued to carry his message throughout the world. He established a UNIA newspaper, The Negro World, *in 1918, and collections of his writings and speeches,* Philosophy and Opinions of Marcus Garvey, *were published in 1923 and 1926. In the following speech delivered at Madison Square Garden (1924), Garvey reflects much of the UNIA philosophy.*

Vocabulary

succored	(5)	supported
imperialism	(5)	economic or political domination of one nation over another
rancor	(10)	bitterness, grudge
encumbered	(11)	hindered

No Exclusive Right to the World

Let no black man feel that he has the exclusive right to the world, and other men none, and let no white man feel that way, either. The world is the property of all mankind, and each and every group is entitled to a portion. The black man now wants his, and in terms uncompromising he is asking for it.   1

The Universal Negro Improvement Association represents the hopes and aspirations of the awakened Negro. Our desire is for a place in the world; not to disturb the tranquillity of other men, but to lay down our burden and rest our weary backs and   2 feet by the banks of the Niger, and sing our songs and chant our hymns to the God of Ethiopia. Yes, we want rest from the toil of centuries, rest of political freedom, rest of economic and industrial liberty, rest to be socially free and unmolested, rest from lynching and burning, rest from discrimination of all kinds.

Out of slavery we have come with our tears and sorrows, and we now lay them at the feet of American white civilization. We cry to the considerate white people for help, because in their midst we can scarce help ourselves. We are strangers in a strange land. We cannot sing, we cannot play on our harps, for our hearts are sad. We are sad because of the tears of our mothers and the cry of our fathers. Have you not heard the plaintive wail? It is your father and my father burning at stake; but, thank God, there is a larger humanity growing among the good and considerate white people of this country, and they are going to help. They will help us to recover our souls.

As children of captivity we look forward to a new day and a new, yet ever old, land of our fathers, the land of refuge, the land of the Prophets, the land of the Saints, and the land of God's crowning glory. We shall gather together our children, our treasures and our loved ones, and, as the children of Israel, by the command of God, faced the promised land, so in time we shall also stretch forth our hands and bless our country.

Good and dear America that has succored us for three hundred years knows our story. We have watered her vegetation with our tears for two hundred and fifty years. We have built her cities and laid the foundations of her imperialism with the mortar of our blood and bones for three centuries, and now we cry to her for help. Help us, America, as we helped you. We helped you in the Revolutionary War. We helped you in the Civil War, and, although Lincoln helped us, the price is not half paid. We helped you in the Spanish-American War. We died nobly and courageously in Mexico, and did we not leave behind us on the stained battlefields of France and Flanders[1] our rich blood to mark the poppies' bloom, and to bring back to you the glory of the flag that never touched the dust? We have no regrets in service to America for three hundred years, but we pray that America will help us for another fifty years until we have solved the troublesome problem that now confronts us. We know and realize that two ambitious and competitive races

3

4

5

---

[1] Flanders   (5)   Refers to U.S. involvement in bitter and bloody trench warfare during World War I.

cannot live permanently side by side, without friction and trouble, and that is why the white race wants a white America and the black race wants and demands a black Africa.

Let white America help us for fifty years honestly, as we   6
have helped her for three hundred years, and before the expiration of many decades there shall be no more race problem. Help us to gradually go home, America. Help us as you have helped the Jews. Help us as you have helped the Irish. Help us as you have helped the Poles, Russians, Germans and Armenians.

The Universal Negro Improvement Association proposes a   7
friendly co-operation with all honest movements seeking intelligently to solve the race problem. We are not seeking social equality; we do not seek intermarriage, nor do we hanker after the impossible. We want the right to have a country of our own, and there foster and reestablish a culture and civilization exclusively ours. Don't say it can't be done. The Pilgrims and colonists did it for America, and the new Negro, with sympathetic help, can do it for Africa.

Back to Africa

The thoughtful and industrious of our race want to go back   8
to Africa, because we realize it will be our only hope of permanent existence. We cannot all go in a day or year, ten or twenty years. It will take time under the rule of modern economics, to entirely or largely depopulate a country of a people, who have been its residents for centuries, but we feel that, with proper help for fifty years, the problem can be solved. We do not want all the Negroes in Africa. Some are no good here, and naturally will be no good there. The no-good Negro will naturally die in fifty years. The Negro who is wrangling about and fighting for social equality will naturally pass away in fifty years, and yield his place to the progressive Negro who wants a society and country of his own.

Negroes are divided into two groups, the industrious and adventurous, and the lazy and dependent. The industrious and   9
adventurous believe that whatsoever others have done it can do. The Universal Negro Improvement Association belongs to this group, and so you find us working, six million strong, to the goal of an independent nationality. Who will not help? Only the mean and despicable "who never to himself hath said, this is my own, my native land." Africa is the legitimate, moral and righteous home of all Negroes, and now, that the time is coming for all to assemble under their own vine and fig tree, we feel it our duty to arouse every Negro to a consciousness of himself.

White and black will learn to respect each other when they   10
cease to be active competitors in the same countries for the same
things in politics and society. Let them have countries of their
own, wherein to aspire and climb without rancor. The races can
be friendly and helpful to each other, but the laws of nature separate us to the extent of each and every one developing by itself.

We want an atmosphere all our own. We would like to gov-   11
ern and rule ourselves and not be encumbered and restrained.
We feel now just as the white race would feel if they were governed and ruled by the Chinese. If we live in our own districts,
let us rule and govern those districts. If we have a majority in
our communities, let us run those communities. We form a majority in Africa and we should naturally govern ourselves there.
No man can govern another's house as well as himself. Let us
have fair play. Let us have justice. This is the appeal we make
to white America.

Discussion Questions

1. What is the objective of the UNIA?
2. According to Garvey, what are some of the contributions that
   African Americans have made to the United States?
3. What is one of the reasons Garvey gives for reclaiming Africa for
   all people of African descent?
4. Why does Garvey say that the thoughtful and industrious Negro
   wants to return to Africa?
5. Why does Garvey think that white and black people should rule
   their own separate countries?
6. Why does Garvey appeal to the "considerate white people" for
   help with his plan?
7. To what extent does Garvey's use of classification help him clarify his point?
8. In paragraph 5, Garvey poses a series of questions. To what extent are these questions effective?

Writing Assignments

1. Based on what you know about African Americans in the United
   States, write an essay arguing for or against their returning to
   Africa.
2. Write an essay discussing the success or lack of success of integration in your neighborhood or school.
3. Write an essay discussing the different types of racial, ethnic, or
   social groups that exist in your school or community.

BECOMING A REPUBLICAN

Tony Brown

Tony Brown (1933–   ) was born in Charleston, West Virginia, and received his B.A. and M.S.W. degrees from Wayne State University. Currently, Brown is a very successful media personality. He is talk show host of Tony Brown's Journal, *a syndicated newspaper columnist, a film director, and a television and film producer. He is also a commentator for the National Public Radio program* All Things Considered. *In 1977, he founded Tony Brown Productions. A registered Republican, Brown wrote the following article, which appeared in the* Wall Street Journal *(August 1991). In it, he attempts to explain why he became a Republican.*

Vocabulary

fascism	(3)	a type of dictatorship
totalitarian	(3)	systematic, absolute control
demagoguery	(4)	power gained by appealing to people's emotions or prejudices
tacit	(4)	not spoken; understood from actions
polarization	(5)	two conflicting and contrasting views
insidious	(5)	harmful yet subtle
enclaves	(6)	distinct territorial, cultural, or social units

"A veteran black TV personality and longtime battler of   1
racism is dropping a bombshell on his fans by ceremoniously
joining the Republican Party," columnist Mary Papenfuss wrote
in the *New York Post* last week after my announcement on July
8 that I was ceasing to be a political independent and was joining the party that was organized in 1854 to oppose the expansion of slavery.

Blacks responded after the end of slavery by voting for the   2
party of the man who signed the Emancipation Proclamation,
Abraham Lincoln. Blacks affiliated with the Republican Party,
such as the remarkable Frederick Douglass, a former slave and
an abolitionist who insisted that "power concedes nothing without a demand," emerged as national heroes. Republicans in
Congress were the architects of Reconstruction, a 10-year pe-

riod of unprecedented political power for black people. They initiated the 13th Amendment, which outlawed slavery, the 14th Amendment, which guaranteed blacks citizenship, and the 15th Amendment, which extended the right to vote to former slaves, as well as the Civil Rights Act of 1866.

Independent Thinking

Ironically, it is the right of a black to be a member of the Republican Party that is being openly questioned in 1991. And unfortunately, the First Amendment's guarantee of free speech has not been taken seriously by some black intellectuals and leaders. Many of them perpetuate an intellectual fascism and foster a totalitarian environment in which any independent thinking black who breaks lock-step with their often self-serving Democratic worldview is severely condemned, and even ostracized.

How did blacks move from the party that gave them civil and political rights to a previously all-white Democratic Party with a history of racist demagoguery, support for slavery and Jim Crow, and tacit approval of lynching? The movement began during the Depression, when the social programs of Franklin Roosevelt severed the close ties that blacks had felt in the Republicans. But many blacks remained loyal to the party of Lincoln: 40% of black voters voted for Dwight Eisenhower in 1956, and 32% cast their ballots for Richard Nixon in 1960. The black middle class, eager to associate itself with a message of self-sufficiency, was even more Republican: In some prosperous areas, Republicans were getting nearly 50% of the black vote as late as 1960.

Then Lyndon Johnson—who accomplished more for blacks legislatively than any president in American history—enacted his historic civil rights acts. Disgruntled Southern whites defected to the Republicans in the 1961 election, enabling Barry Goldwater to win such once-solid Democratic states as Mississippi, Georgia, Louisiana, South Carolina and Alabama. Tempted by these votes, the Republicans adopted a "Southern strategy," which has carried them to the White House in all but one of the elections since then. The strategy, as expounded in "The Emerging Republican Majority" by Kevin Phillips, demonstrated how Republicans could profit from racial polarization with code words like "law and order." The insidious idea behind this "Willie Hortonism"[1] was to gain anti-black votes without appearing racist in the old Deep South style.

Today's near-unanimous perception among blacks that all white Republicans are racists is born out of that history—and the subsequent extension of the Southern strategy into Northern suburbs and ethnic enclaves. As a result, blacks have almost completely deserted the Republicans: In 1988, just 1% of the votes cast in the Republican presidential primaries were cast by blacks.   6

The absence of blacks from the Republican Party spells disaster for the black community. Between 1936 and 1964, when blacks voted roughly 65% Democratic to 35% Republican, both parties had to compete for their votes. Today, however, because blacks vote overwhelmingly Democratic, the Democrats can offer lip service and still count on the black vote. And because blacks have become an almost nonexistent force in the GOP, Republicans can ignore them altogether.   7

But the absence of blacks from the Republican Party also spells long-term economic ruin for our country. We must adapt to cultural diversity as the foundation of our economic competitiveness. And it spells long-term political danger for the Republicans themselves: What the GOP is doing, or not doing, in the black ghettoes can have consequences in the white suburbs. White suburbanites could defect from the Republican fold if the party becomes stigmatized as racist. That's what moves Republicans like Sen. John Danforth (R., Mo.) to criticize the way some Republicans are exploiting the quota issue. That's why the Ripon Republicans in the 1960s warned of the danger of a strategy of racial divisiveness and promoted racial inclusion instead.   8

So, no matter how great the risk to some of us personally, we cannot allow black America to remain a one-party community in a two-party system. Nor can we permit the Republican Party to become a lily-white enclave in a heterogeneous country.   9

At one stage in history, the Democratic Party may have been the best choice for blacks. However, the Democratic poli-   10

---

[1] Willie Hortonism (5)   The act of creating conflicting views by distorting facts; named for a Massachusetts African American prison inmate, who committed a crime while on a weekend furlough. Distorting this story, Republicans were successful in polarizing voters and contributing to the Massachusetts governor (Michael Dukakis) losing the 1988 presidential race.

cies of exclusive reliance on government programs evidently has not brought economic success to black America. As Martin Luther King, Jr., said more than 20 years ago: "New laws are not enough. The emergency we now face is economic." Blacks have an abiding faith in the philosophy of self-sufficiency, but are stuck, out of perverse necessity, with the something-for-nothing entitlement dogma of the Democrats. But the problem with depending on government is that you cannot depend on it.

Racism is a problem, but poverty is the primary problem 11 facing blacks. Blacks need economic solutions. And self-help is a time-tested economic solution.

For example, the 350 black organizations that spend $16 12 billion in white-owned hotels each summer ($500 million at the Congressional Black Caucus meeting alone) discussing white racism and black poverty could cancel their 1992 conventions and use that $16 billion as a capital fund to buy hotels (at the moment, not one major hotel in America is owned by blacks) start new companies, create jobs for the poor and fund social programs in the black community.

In September, I am launching an effort to start 50,000 13 small companies in the next five years through a telephone-based loan program, using a state-of-the-art telecommunications system. Profits from calls to the businesses on the Buy Freedom 900 network will be used to provide the loans.

A community of 30 million people who emphasize civil 14 rights over economic power will never have equal rights. Both civil rights and economic power are equally necessary. Neither can a black community earning $300 billion a year, the equivalent of the GNP of the ninth-richest nation in the free world, spend 95% of its money with other groups and blame them for 100% of its problems.

The color of freedom is green. As Adam Smith taught in 15 "The Wealth of Nations," true freedom can come only from an intelligent and humane use of the free market system. And the party of free enterprise, despite all its potentially reversible shortcomings, is the Republican Party. If blacks want to return the Republican Party to its tradition of inclusion, they will have to join it and work from within.

Ideological Diversity

Since I announced my affiliation with the Republicans, a 16 surprising number of blacks have told me they will follow my example. And all of the blacks who have spoken to me like the idea of greater ideological diversity within the black community. The statement that best typified the reaction to my becoming a Republican came from a woman at the Apollo Theater in Harlem, following my interview on WLIB, New York's black radio station.

"When I first heard the news, I thought you had sold out.   17 So I had to hear an explanation from you personally. After hearing you explain, I agree with you and admire your courage. We do have to rely on self-help and we do have to be involved in both parties. But I'm not ready to become a Republican yet. I don't trust the Republican Party, but I trust Tony Brown."

Discussion Questions

1. Why did Brown become a Republican?
2. After the abolition of slavery, why did blacks join the Republican Party? When did blacks begin to join the Democratic Party? Why?
3. According to Brown, why can we not allow "Black Americans to remain a one-party community in a two-party community"?
4. Brown feels that the color of freedom is green. What is the significance of this idea to blacks joining the Republican Party?
5. How does Brown prove that self-help is a time-tested economic solution?
6. To what extent do you agree or disagree with Brown's argument for becoming a Republican?
7. How does the use of comparison and contrast and cause and effect strengthen Brown's argument?
8. Does Brown provide sufficient examples to develop the thesis?

Writing Assignments

1. Write an essay in which you contrast your political viewpoint with that of someone you know.
2. If you disagree with Brown's view, write an essay arguing why African Americans should not join the Republican Party.
3. Write an essay in which you explain one of your philosophical, moral, or religious views.

Student Essay:
THE BLACK PANTHER PARTY

Khadijah A. Mayo

Vocabulary

turbulent   (1)   stormy
immeasurable   (9)   unable to be determined

The civil rights era was a very turbulent period in the United   1
States. The country was battling over whether or not black people should receive racial equality. At the forefront of the movement in the early 1960s were Martin Luther King, Jr., and Malcolm X. After both of these black leaders were assassinated,
black people were left with a major sense of loss. The Black
Panther Party played a positive and greatly needed role in fulfilling this loss during the civil rights era.

In 1966, the Black Panther Party officially began in Oak-   2
land, California. Bobby Seale was the national chairman, Huey
P. Newton was the minister of defense, and Eldridge Cleaver
was the minister of information. The party was made up of a
wide cross section of individuals, including college graduates. It
was founded because the needs of the black community were
simply not being met. For instance, there was a lack of jobs,
and, as a result, the ghettos were saturated with sick, poor,
and hungry black people.

Although some of the party's ideas were not well planned,   3
many of them were positive and progressive. Most of its demands were related, directly and indirectly, to the economic
treatment of black people. These demands helped the Panthers
to awaken a consciousness in black people that made them realize there were problems in society. Unfortunately, many of
the people that opposed the Panthers were not familiar with the
positive work they did.

One of the most beneficial activities of the Panthers was   4
the Free Breakfast Program in Oakland, California. Many students were not eating breakfast and their hunger led to poor
progress in school. The goal of the program was to ensure that
black children did not go to school hungry. Parents and volunteers prepared and served the breakfasts, washed dishes, and
cleaned the facility. The Panthers solicited donations of food

and supplies from the community. These donations were the backbone of the program. Once the program began, teachers noted the improvement in the students' work. This program was the parent to the breakfast and lunch programs now in public and private schools.

To further aid the community, the Panthers founded Lib-   5
eration Schools, which were open in the summer for students ages two to thirteen. The schools trained students to be revolutionary leaders. It also taught the students African and African American history.

Perhaps the most notable contribution of the Black Pan-   6
thers was the People's Free Medical Care Center. The centers were located throughout the United States. They provided health care for people who would otherwise go without medical attention. The doctors and nurses volunteered their services. They went out into the community to look for people with illnesses. This service was a vital one because many could not afford medical care.

The Panthers did many other things for the black commu-   7
nity that went unrecognized. For example, they registered blacks to vote and held community discussions. Huey Newton issued the "Pocket Lawyer," which informed people of their rights when arrested. It listed the number of the nearest Black Panther chapter so people could call for legal aid.

The *Black Panther* was a grassroots newspaper in which   8
black people told news stories from a black person's perspective. The information for the paper was pooled from the various Black Panther Party chapters around the country. The first issue was printed in 1967 and was called the "Voice of the Party."

Regardless of the Panthers' shortcomings, their benefit to   9
the black community was immeasurable. Black power was more than a phrase; it was an experience. Positive community activities may not have made the newspapers, but that omission was not necessary for the many people who benefited from the party's existence.

Discussion Questions

1. When was the Black Panther Party founded and why?
2. What were some of the positive programs started by the party?
3. Considering the type of contributions the Black Panther Party made, what assumptions can you make about the party's beliefs?

4. According to Mayo, why were some people opposed to the Panthers?

5. How effective is Mayo's use of illustration in her essay?

6. How effective is the writer's use of transitions?

Writing Assignments

1. Write an essay about the contributions made by some organization you know of or are affiliated with.

2. Write an essay about some of the improvements that are being made (or are needed) in the African American community. Discuss the source of these improvements and the significance of each.

17

Black Dialect • Language

PARAPOETICS

Eugene Redmond

Eugene Redmond (1937–), poet, editor, critic, and teacher, was born in St. Louis, Missouri, and graduated from Southern Illinois University and Washington University in St. Louis. He was a senior consultant to Katherine Dunham's Performing Arts Training Center at Southern Illinois University and has been writer-in-residence at Southern University, Oberlin College, and Sacramento State College. His works, which have appeared in a number of anthologies and journals, include A Tale of Two Toms *(1968),* Songs from an Afro/Phone *(1972),* In a Time of Rain and Desire *(1973), and* There's a Wiretap in My Soup *(1974). In the following poem, from* Sentry of the Four Golden Pillars *(1970), Redmond explores the process of poetry writing.*

Vocabulary

eloquented	(1)	vivid, forceful
cellular	(1)	having a small hollow space
gestate	(2)	to conceive and develop
lode	(5)	rich source or supply

(For my former students and writing friends in East St. Louis, Illinois)

Poetry is an *applied science:*   1
   Re-wrapped corner rap;
   Rootly-eloquented, cellular, soulular sermons.
   Grit reincarnations of
   Lady Day[1]
   Bird[2]
   & Otis;[3]
   Silk songs pitched on 'round and rhythmic rumps;
   Carved halos (for heroes) and asserted maleness:
   Sounds and sights of fire-tongues
   Leaping from lips of flame-stricken buildings in the night.

Directions: apply poetry as needed.   2
   Envision.
   Visualize.
   Violate!
   Wring minds.
   Shout!
   Right words.
   Rite!!
   Cohabitate.
   Gestate.
   Pregnate your vocabulary.
   Dig, a parapoet!

[1] Lady Day (1)   Nickname of 1940s African American jazz singer Eleanor "Billie" Holiday.
[2] Bird (1)   Nickname of African American 1950s jazz alto saxophonist Charles Christopher "Charlie" Parker, Jr.
[3] Otis (1)   1960s African American rhythm and blues singer Otis Redding.

Parenthesis: Replace winter with spring, move Mississippi   3
to New York, Oberlin (Ohio) to East St. Louis, Harlem
to the summer whitehouse. Carve candles and flintstones
for flashlights.

Carry your poems.   4
Grit teeth. Bear labor-love pains.
Have twins and triplets.
Furtilize poem-farms with after-birth,
Before birth and dung [rearrange old words];
Study/strike tradition.

Caution to parapoets: 5
Carry the weight of your own poem.
. . . it's a *heavy lode.*

Discussion Questions

1. "Para" means "beyond" or "similar to." How significant is the poem's title to its message?
2. In what way does the second line suggest that poetry is not a new art form?
3. An applied science is one that is practiced or used. Why do you think Redmond writes that poetry is an applied science?
4. The "Parenthesis" section of the poem is a good example of the revising process. What do you think this section means?
5. How does Redmond convince the reader that writing in general and poetry writing in particular is hard work?
6. How does Redmond's use of process help the reader understand the definition of parapoetics?
7. Redmond uses interesting words to spark various reactions from the reader. Why do you think he uses unusual spellings of words such as *soulular* and *furtilize*?

Writing Assignments

1. Write an essay on a topic of your choice. Rewrite the essay several times, keeping in mind Redmond's suggestions for revision.
2. Write an essay that explains a familiar process.
3. A large part of writing is revision. Write an essay describing your process of revision.

AFRICAN AMERICAN YOUTH RESIST STANDARD ENGLISH

Felicia R. Lee

The following excerpt was first published in the New York
Times *on January 5, 1994, under the title, "Grappling with
How to Teach Young Speakers of Black Dialect." Its focus is
the widespread and persistent use of black dialect, an occurrence that seems to be the result of the resistance of
African American youth to those things associated with
white people and white culture.*

Vocabulary

linguists	(2)	language specialists
diverged	(2)	departed from
assimilate	(3)	adapt, conform
cynicism	(3)	a distrustful attitude
exquisitely	(11)	very, intensely
vernacular	(11)	language commonly spoken by members of a particular group; language considered non-standard

More than a decade after educators first grappled with the 1
issue, school districts in New York and elsewhere are still seeking the best way to teach standard English to students who
usually use black dialect. A few districts have a policy to teach
standard English like a second language, but in most, as in
New York, the approach is scattershot, varying from school to
school and classroom to classroom.

During this time, linguists say, the black vernacular has 2
steadily diverged from standard English and become more
widespread in poor, urban neighborhoods. Educators once predicted that as more black people entered the mainstream, the
dialect would fade not only among the middle class, as it has,
but also among the poor. Linguists say, however, that the current generation of inner-city youth rely more heavily on black
vernacular than ever.

The persistence of the dialect reflects, in part, the growing 3
resistance of some black young people to assimilate and their
efforts to use language as part of a value system that prizes

cultural distinction. It also stems from the increasing isolation of black inner-city residents from both whites and middle-class blacks, and stems as well from a deep cynicism about the pay-offs of conforming.

While the dialect is used as a kind of in-group code among many black people of all stations, educators worry about those young people who never master standard English at all.   4

Some teachers say they are uncertain about how to in-struct students who use the dialect, and in the absence of clear policy, they are largely left to devise their own methods.   5

Mr. Halperin, who teaches at the Richard Green High School for Teaching, said that many of his students become fu-rious and shout "Who are you trying to be?" when a student uses standard English in class. His strategy is to work around the hostility with things like the bilingual dictionary, dramatic presentations and reading aloud.   6

In some neighborhoods, young people acknowledge an ele-ment of resistance, and even a stigma, to using standard Eng-lish or "talking proper."   7

"English is not our language," said Takiyah Hudson, a 17-year-old high school senior who lives in Harlem. She said her mother and sister correct her English when she slips into a black dialect, which she does not use in formal situations.   8

"Our language has more rhythmic tones," Ms. Hudson said. "To some people, 'she be going' just flows, it's just a nat-ural thing."   9

Ms. Hudson acknowledges that students have to use stan-dard English in some settings. "It's like going to France and speaking English and getting mad at them. Such and such cor-poration isn't going to hire me. That's realistic thinking."   10

The issue is exquisitely sensitive, going beyond nouns and verbs to questions of racial identity and class, as well as the politics of education. There is some sentiment among the black middle class that the vernacular legitimizes poor grammar. Others blame schools for not teaching standard English better because teachers have low expectations of black students. Lin-guists, having seen acknowledgement by educators of the di-alect, say it is time to become more sophisticated in the class-room.   11

"When we were in the 60's to the 80's, we were trying to get recognition for the language, that it had rules, it has a system, it has a pattern," said Geneva Smitherman, a Michigan State University linguist and English professor whose book on black   12 vernacular is to be published in June. "Now we are at the point where we need a multilingual policy that means that everybody would learn one other language or one other dialect. . . ."

Linguists say the dialect represents the remnants of West [13] African languages used by American slaves and the efforts of those slaves—denied formal education—to mimic white people. Ironically, the dialect has contributed richly to standard English, influencing everything from advertising to slang. The dialect has such features as dropping the verb "to be" or the lack of subject-verb agreement, resulting in "She sick" and "He like ice cream."

Jo-Ann Graham, chairwoman of the department of com- [14] munications at the Bronx Community College, said teaching standard English is not simply cleaning up grammatical lapses. "It is not just saying, 'You don't say "they is" you say "they are,"'" she said. "You have to teach the structure, the vocabulary, the sound system, the grammar just as if you were teaching another language."

The country's largest school system to use such an ap- [15] proach is Los Angeles. Its "Proficiency in English" program, started in 1978, uses methods like repetitive drills to teach standard English like a second language. Several other California school districts, including Oakland, Sacramento and Vallejo, use similar programs.

Individual school districts in cities with large black popu- [16] lations, like Baltimore, Detroit and Philadelphia, are using programs to teach students who use black vernacular.

Most programs use something called "contrastive analy- [17] sis," which attempts to get students to hear and see the differences between what they say and write and what is said and written in standard English.

There is also role-playing for different audiences, so stu- [18] dents learn the time and place for their vernacular and for formal speech.

"The problem is, this is not in any textbook," said Ms. [19] Wright-Lewis, a teacher at Boys and Girls High School in the Bedford-Stuyvesant section of Brooklyn. "I had to make up my own curriculum. No one asks teachers 'What would you put in a textbook?'"

Ms. Wright-Lewis has students write and rewrite assign- [20] ments. She makes them give oral presentations and participate in discussions that she privately assesses for syntax and grammar. She writes her own stories for students, in which characters switch back and forth between standard and non-standard English. And she corrects her students in private to help protect their fragile self-esteem.

Frank Mickens, the principal of Boys and Girls, believes   21 that the issue is not as pressing as other concerns, like the safety of his students, who come from some of the toughest housing projects in the nation. Most students, he said, already use both standard English and the vernacular.

Discussion Questions

1. What are the two reasons given for the persistence of the black vernacular?
2. What are some major features of black dialect?
3. Why is the use of black dialect considered a problem by educators?
4. Why has there been growing resistance by African American youth to using standard English?
5. What is the origin of black dialect?
6. How does Lee use cause and effect to explain the title of her essay?
7. How effective is the ending of Lee's essay? Explain your answer.

Writing Assignments

1. Write an essay discussing the use of dialect or slang in your family, group, or community.
2. In an essay, argue for or against the need for bilingual classes for African Americans.
3. Write an essay telling how teachers treat African American students who do not use standard English.

BLACK TALK

Geneva Smitherman

Geneva Smitherman (1940–) is University Distinguished Professor of English and director of the African-American Language and Literacy Programs at Michigan State University in East Lansing. She is also director of My Brother's Keeper Program in Detroit. Known for her passionate defense of black English, Smitherman was one of the expert witnesses in the so-called black English trial of 1977 in Ann Arbor, Michigan. Her works include Talkin and Testifyin: The Language of Black America *(1977),* Black English and the Education of Black Children and Youth *(1981),* Discourse and Discrimination *(1988), and* Black Talk: Words and Phrases from the Hood to the Amen Corner *(1994), from which this excerpt is taken. Here Smitherman discusses the crossover of black language into white America.*

Vocabulary

implicitly	(2)	by suggestion
sigged on	(3)	talked about
confrontational	(3)	face to face
adheres	(3)	sticks
deem	(3)	believe to be
dynamism	(4)	energy, force
potent	(4)	powerful
counterforce	(4)	opposition
generically	(5)	in general
wary	(5)	careful, cautious
Lexicon	(5)	vocabulary
exploitation	(6)	taking advantage of
sterile	(7)	uninteresting, lifeless
phenomenon	(7)	extremely unusual happening
deterioration	(7)	conditions becoming worse

A 1993 article by a European American used the title "A New Way to Talk that Talk" (small capitals added) to describe a new talk show. *The American Heritage Dictionary,* Third Edition, lists bug and grapevine as just plain old words, with no label indicating "slang" or "Black." Merriam-Webster's latest (tenth) edition of its Collegiate Dictionary lists boom box the

1

same way. A lengthy 1993 article in the *New York Times Magazine,* entitled "Talking Trash," discussed this ancient Black verbal tradition as the "art of conversation in the N.B.A." And in his first year in office, the nation's new "baby boomer" President was taken to task for "terminal HIPness."

The absorption of African American English into Eurocentric culture masks its true origin and reason for being. It is a language born from a culture of struggle, a way of talking that has taken surviving African language elements as the base for self-expression in an alien tongue. Through various processes such as "Semantic Inversion" (taking words and turning them into their opposites), African Americans stake our claim to the English language, and at the same time, reflect distinct Black values that are often at odds with Eurocentric standards. "Fat," spelled *phat* in Hip Hop, refers to a person or thing that is excellent and desirable, reflecting the traditional African value that human body weight is a good thing, and implicitly rejecting the Euro-American mainstream, where skinny, not fat, is valued and everybody is on a diet. Senior Blacks convey the same value with the expression, "Don't nobody want no BONE." By the process of giving negative words positive meanings, BAD means "good," STUPID means "excellent," and even the word DOPE becomes positive in Hip Hop, meaning "very good" or "superb."

The blunt, coded language of enslavement SIGged on Christian slaveholders with the expression, "Everybody talkin bout Heaven ain goin there." Hip Hop language, too, is bold and confrontational. It uses obscenities, graphic depictions of the sex act, oral and otherwise, and it adheres to the pronunciation and grammar of African American English (which the uninformed deem "poor English") . . .

The dynamism and creativity in African American Language revitalizes and re-energizes bland Euro-talk. There's electricity and excitement in PLAYERS and FLY girls who wear GEAR. The metaphors, images, and poetry in Black Talk make the ordinary ALL THAT, AND THEN SOME. African American English is a dramatic, potent counterforce to verbal deadness and emptiness. One is not simply accepted by a group, one is IN LIKE FLIN. Fraternities and sororities don't merely march; they perform a STEP SHOW. And when folk get AMP, they don't fight the feeling, they TESTIFY. For whites, there is a certain magnetism in the African American use of English because it seems to make the impossible possible. I bet you a FAT MAN AGAINST THE HOLE IN A DOUGHNUT. . . .

For *wiggas*[1] and other white folk latching onto Black   5
Talk, that's the good news. The bad news is that there's a reality check in African American English. Its terms and expressions keep you grounded, catch you just as you are taking
flight and bring you right back down to the NITTY GRITTY of
African American Life. There are rare flights of fancy in this poetry, no chance of getting so carried away that you don't know
yo ASS FROM A HOLE IN THE GROUND. Unh-unh. Words like NIGGA reinforce Blackness since, whether used positively, generically, or
negatively, the term can refer only to people of African descent.
DEVIL, a negative reference to the white man, reminds Blacks to
be on the lookout for HYPE. RUN AND TELL THAT, historically referring to Blacks who snitched to white folks, is a cultural caution
to those planning Black affairs to be wary of the Judases[2]
among them. Such words in the Black Lexicon are constant reminders of race and the Black Struggle. And when you TALK
THAT TALK, you must be loyal to Blackness, or as Ice Cube[3]
would say, be true to the GAME.

There are words and expressions in Black Talk like TWO-   6
MINUTE BROTHA, describing a man who completes the sex act in a
few seconds, and it's all over for the woman. Both in RAP and in
everyday talk, the words B (bitch) and HO (whore) are generic
references to Black women. GOT HIS/HER NOSE OPEN describes a
male or female so deeply in love that he or she is ripe for exploitation. Terms like these in Black Language are continuing
reminders that, despite all the talk about Black passion and
SOUL, despite all the sixty-minute-man myths, despite all the
WOOFin and TALKin SHIT, at bottom, the man-woman Thang
among African Americans is just as problematic as it is among
other groups.

Some African Americans see crossover as positive because   7
of its possibilities for reducing racial tension. Fashion journalist Robin D. Givhan, writing in the *Detroit Free Press* (June 21,
1993), asserts that she is "optimistic about wiggers":

> Appreciating someone else's culture is good. An increased level of
> interest among whites in what makes some African Americans
> groove can only be helpful to improved race relations.

[1] wiggas (5)   Whites who adopt African American dress, language, and culture.
[1] Judas(es) (5)   Disciple who betrayed Jesus; used here to refer to African
Americans who betray their race.
[3] Ice Cube (5)   African American rapper.

Yet the reality of race, racism, and personal conflicts, which are often intensified by racism, does make crossover problematic. Whites pay no dues, but reap the psychological, social, and economic benefits of a language and culture born out of struggle and hard times. In his "We Use Words Like 'Mackadocious,'" Upski characterizes the "white rap audience" thus: "When they say they like rap, they usually have in mind a *certain* kind of rap, one that spits back what they already believe or lends an escape from their limited lives." And Ledbetter's "Imitation of Life" yields this conclusion: "By listening to rap and tapping into its extra-musical expressions, then, whites are attempting to bear witness to—even correct—their own often sterile, oppressive culture." Yet it is also the case that not only Rap, but other forms of Black Language and Culture, are attractive because of the dynamism, creativity, and excitement in these forms. However one accounts for the crossover phenomenon, one thing is certain: today we are witnessing a multi-billion-dollar industry based on this Language-Culture while there is continued underdevelopment and deterioration in the HOOD that produces it. In Ralph Wiley's collection of essays *Why Black People Tend to Shout*, which contains his *signifyin*[4] piece, "Why Black People Have No Culture," he states: "Black people have no culture because most of it is out on loan to white people. With no interest."

Discussion Questions

1. What are some characteristics of African American language described by Smitherman?
2. According to Smitherman, what is it about European Americans' lives that causes black language to cross over into mainstream use?
3. What is the "reality check" in African American English and what is its purpose?
4. What are some positive aspects of the crossover of African American English as seen by some African Americans?
5. According to Smitherman, what are some problems related to the crossover of African American English?
6. How does Smitherman use illustration to describe African American English?
7. What is the tone of this excerpt?

[4] signifyin (7)   African American verbal game of insults, usually played for fun and with humor.

Writing Assignments

1. Write an essay in which you illustrate some popular words or phrases used by you or your friends.
2. Write an essay in which you agree or disagree with the statement "Black people have no culture because most of it is out on loan to white people."
3. Write an essay illustrating and explaining the use of language in a particular rap song or in some other type of popular music.

IF BLACK ENGLISH ISN'T A LANGUAGE, THEN TELL ME, WHAT IS?

James Baldwin

James Baldwin (1924–1987) was born and raised in Harlem, New York. Most of his writings describe racial conflict and prejudice in the United States. His works include two books of autobiographical essays, Notes of a Native Son *(1955) and* Nobody Knows My Name *(1961); a nonfiction work,* The Fire Next Time *(1963); novels,* Go Tell It on the Mountain *(1953),* Another Country *(1962), and* Just Above My Head *(1979); and plays,* Blues for Mister Charlie *(1964) and* The Amen Corner *(1965). The following excerpt is from "If Black English Isn't a Language, Then Tell Me, What Is?" and was published in the* New York Times *in 1979. In it, Baldwin offers evidence to support the idea that black English, just like American English, is not a dialect but a language.*

Vocabulary

antecedents	(1)	ancestors
phenomenon	(2)	event
despairing	(2)	hopeless, desperate
skirmish	(4)	a minor dispute or fight
diaspora	(4)	areas where African Americans live outside of their homeland, Africa
chattel slavery	(4)	legal slavery
alchemy	(4)	process of changing from one form to another
unassailable	(6)	unquestionable
patronizingly	(7)	with an air of superiority
inarticulate	(7)	not able to express clearly
repudiate	(8)	refuse to recognize, reject
sustenance	(8)	nourishment, support
limbo	(8)	the state of being in between, neither here nor there
mediocrities	(9)	average abilities or achievements

It goes without saying, then, that language is also a political 1 instrument, means, and proof of power. It is the most vivid and crucial key to identity: It reveals the private identity, and connects one with, or divorces one from, the larger public, or communal identity. There have been, and are, times, and places, when to speak a certain language could be dangerous, even fatal. Or, one may speak the same language, but in such a way that one's antecedents are revealed, or (one hopes) hidden. This is true in France, and is absolutely true in England. The range (and reign) of accents on that damp little island make England coherent for the English and totally incomprehensible for everyone else. To open your mouth in England is (if I may use black English) to "put your business in the street": You have confessed your parents, your youth, your school, your salary, your self-esteem, and, alas, your future.

Now, I do not know what white Americans would sound   2
like if there had never been any black people in the United States, but they would not sound the way they sound. *Jazz*, for example, is a very specific sexual term, as in *jazz me, baby*, but white people purified it into the Jazz Age. *Sock it to me*, which means, roughly, the same thing, has been adopted by Nathaniel Hawthorne's descendants with no qualms or hesitations at all, along with *let it all hang out* and *right on! Beat to his socks*, which was once the black's most total and despairing image of poverty, was transformed into a thing called the Beat Generation, which phenomenon was, largely, composed of *uptight*, middle-class white people, imitating poverty, trying to *get down*, to get *with it*, doing their *thing*, doing their despairing best to be *funky*, which we, the blacks, never dreamed of doing—we *were* funky, baby, like *funk* was going out of style.

Now, no one can eat his cake, and have it, too, and it is   3
late in the day to attempt to penalize black people for having created a language that permits the nation its only glimpse of reality, a language without which the nation would be even more *whipped* than it is.

I say that this present skirmish is rooted in American his-   4
tory, and it is. Black English is the creation of the black diaspora. Blacks came to the United States chained to each other, but from different tribes: Neither could speak the other's language. If two black people, at that bitter hour of the world's history, had been able to speak to each other, the institution of chattel slavery could never have lasted as long as it did. Subsequently, the slave was given, under the eye, and the gun, of his master, Congo Square, and the Bible—or, in other words, and under these conditions, the slave began the formation of the black church, and it is within this unprecedented tabernacle

that black English began to be formed. This was not, merely, as in the European example, the adoption of a foreign tongue, but an alchemy that transformed ancient elements into new language: *A language comes into existence by means of brutal necessity, and the rules of the language are dictated by what the language must convey.*

There was a moment, in time, and in this place, when my brother, or my mother, or my father, or my sister, had to convey to me, for example, the danger in which I was standing from the white man standing just behind me, and to convey this with a speed, and in a language, that the white man could not possibly understand, and that, indeed, he cannot understand, until today. He cannot afford to understand it. This understanding would reveal to him too much about himself, and smash that mirror before which he has been frozen for so long.

Now, if this passion, this skill, this (to quote Toni Morrison) "sheer intelligence," this incredible music, the mighty achievement of having brought a people utterly unknown to, or despised by "history"—to have brought this people to their present, troubled, troubling, and unassailable and unanswerable place—if this absolutely unprecedented journey does not indicate that black English is a language, I am curious to know what definition of language is to be trusted.

A people at the center of the Western world, and in the midst of so hostile a population, has not endured and transcended by means of what is patronizingly called a "dialect." We, the blacks, are in trouble, certainly, but we are not doomed, and we are not inarticulate because we are not compelled to defend a morality that we know to be a lie.

The brutal truth is that the bulk of the white people in America never had any interest in educating black people, except as this could serve white purposes. It is not the black child's language that is in question, it is not his language that is despised: It is his experience. A child cannot be taught by anyone who despises him, and a child cannot afford to be fooled. A child cannot be taught by anyone whose demand, essentially, is that the child repudiate his experience, and all that gives him sustenance, and enter a limbo in which he will no longer be black, and in which he knows that he can never become white. Black people have lost too many black children that way.

And, after all, finally, in a country with standards so untrustworthy, a country that makes heroes of so many criminal mediocrities, a country unable to face why so many of the non-white are in prison, or on the needle, or standing, futureless, in the streets—it may very well be that both the child, and his elder, have concluded that they have nothing whatever to learn from the people of a country that has managed to learn so little.

Discussion Questions

1. According to Baldwin, what is the role of language? How does it come into existence?
2. Why does Baldwin feel that black English is a language, not a dialect?
3. Why does Baldwin say that white Americans would not sound the way they do had there never been any black people in the United States?
4. What evidence does Baldwin offer to prove that black English developed as a result of the African American's attempt to retain a sense of identity and morality?
5. According to Baldwin, who cannot teach a child?
6. In the last paragraph, how does Baldwin describe the United States?
7. How does the title suggest the dominant rhetorical strategy that Baldwin uses in this essay?
8. How effective is Baldwin's technique of using the word *Now* to begin three of his paragraphs?

Writing Assignments

1. Certain words and expressions are peculiar to a particular experience or culture. Write an essay exploring a word or an expression that you feel few people know.
2. Write an essay classifying the various types of English dialects in the United States.
3. In an essay, argue the usefulness of slang.

Student Essay:
THE QUESTION OF NAME:
AFRICAN OR AFRICAN AMERICAN?

Cyril Austin Greene

Vocabulary

blatant	(5)	obvious
proscribe	(5)	to express disapproval of, to prohibit
goaded	(9)	urged

What's in a name? There are those who feel a name is just 1
a word; others feel a name defines who one is, and what he or
she stands for. Does a name have the power to mentally enslave an entire race of people? Or is a race, regardless of what
it is called, as strong as its members?

Since the early seventeenth century when Africans were 2
taken from their native land and placed into this foreign country, they have undergone an identity crisis. They could no
longer consider Africa their homeland, so could they call themselves Africans? They were in another world, which would soon
become known as America, but could they really call themselves Americans? They were here against their will, and they
were treated with total disregard for their humanity. Their enslavers took control of everything, even the right of these people
to define themselves. Hence, a 350-year history of an entire
race of people along with their identity was dictated by someone else.

Now, in the late twentieth century we as people of African 3
descent are breaking free of the hold that our enslavers have
had on us. Within the past fifty years, we people of color in
America have taken control of our destiny and part of that has
been a decision on what to call ourselves.

On the outside, the term *African American* seems so per- 4
fect. It acknowledges our current status of American citizenship and our former homeland of Africa. But why do we cling
so tightly to the idea of being American? Yes, according to our
birth certificates, we are American citizens, and we do reap certain benefits by living here, but we also went through slavery,

Jim Crow,[1] and civil rights, which are only giant umbrellas that enclose millions of personalized cases of hardships, torture, poverty, racism, and death. Maybe it is the fact that I do not forget the past as easily as others, but I refuse to associate myself with the name of a country that was built on exploitation, lies, rape, and murder.

To this day, Africans living here face discrimination, blatant and hidden. They must compete to survive, to attain human rights that were denied to them for so long. They were attacked by dogs, sprayed with hoses and shot in the streets a mere thirty years ago for trying to obtain the rights that were granted to them as human beings. Many lost their lives in a battle with the white majority, a battle for something that no one ever has the right to take from another: human rights. People died so that words could be printed on paper stating where our grandparents could eat and drink and sleep and walk. It still puzzles me the way in which one person can proscribe and prescribe the actions of another. Regardless of that fact, the battle against racism has been long and hard, and it is not over.   5

I believe this country will never accept me as it accepts the white majority. I am content with referring to myself as an African living in America. I have no desire to conform to this American culture and society; therefore, I choose not to recognize it in how I call myself.   6

Contrastingly, there are those who would argue that I cannot possibly call myself African, for I have never stepped foot on the continent of Africa. True, I am not an African citizen, nor have I ever been there. But does this mean that my heritage can be denied? I strongly feel that I am what my forefathers were. I doubt that Africans would be in this country were it not for the slave trade. It is unfortunate that some citizens of Africa look down on any attempts on the part of people of color from the United States to associate themselves with African citizenship, but I know where my heart lies.   7

Further opposition points out the fact that since this country was essentially built on slave labor, that gives us the right to call ourselves Americans, for in essence, we built this country. In theory, this sounds good, but the same people who forced us to build this country now own it, and they do not   8

[1] Jim Crow (4)   Legal and systematic practice of segregating, suppressing, and discriminating against African Americans.

plan to give up what is due to us. We may have the right to call ourselves American, but those in power will see to it that that is all we do, call ourselves American.

This society has a way of whitewashing situations so they   9
do not seem so bad. If one were not careful, he or she could be goaded into believing this is truly the land of the free. The virtue, strength, and freedom of America is propagandized to cover up the racism and the hate of this biased country, but the past is not easily forgotten.

The argument of being considered African or African   10
American continues. I believe the future holds other terms that we will use to define ourselves. I also see a split in our community. There will be those who try to refute their American heritage, as well as those who continue to search for a correct name to describe their mix of American and African backgrounds. As for me, I consider myself African. What do you consider yourself?

Discussion Questions

1. According to Greene, how long have African Americans experienced an identity crisis? Why have they experienced this crisis?
2. What are the major points presented to support Greene's position? Which do you think is his most convincing point?
3. What opposing points does Greene present? Can you think of others?
4. Why does Greene question the use of the term *African American?*
5. How does Greene address the following statement that some African Americans make: "Since this country was essentially built on slave labor, that gives us the right to call ourselves Americans"?
6. Does Greene use sufficient illustrations to make his argument convincing?
7. How effective is Greene's use of a question to end the essay?

Writing Assignments

1. Write an essay supporting the use of *African American* (or some other term) as an appropriate name for those we now call African Americans.
2. Write an essay examining the following question: Who is an American?

18

Folklore

I GET BORN

Zora Neale Hurston

Writer and folklorist Zora Neale Hurston (1907–1960) was born in Eatonville, Florida, and is the author of three novels: Jonah's Gourd Vine (1934), Their Eyes Were Watching God (1937), and Seraph on the Suwanee (1948). Her works also include her autobiography, Dust Tracks on the Road (1943), from which this excerpt is taken, and several volumes of folklore. In this selection, Hurston recounts events surrounding her birth and early childhood.

Vocabulary

shoat	(5)	young pig
gourd vine	(10)	vine of the bulb-shaped fruit of the squash, melon, and pumpkin family

This is all hear-say. Maybe some of the details of my birth   1
as told me might be a little inaccurate, but it is pretty well established that I really did get born.

The saying goes like this. My mother's time had come and my father was not there. Being a carpenter, successful enough to have other helpers on some jobs, he was away often on building business, as well as preaching. It seems that my father was away from home for months this time. I have never been told why. But I did hear that he threatened to cut his throat when he got the news. It seems that one daughter was all that he figured he could stand. My sister, Sarah, was his favorite child, but that one girl was enough. Plenty more sons, but no more girl babies to wear out shoes and bring in nothing. I don't think he ever got over the trick he felt that I played on him by getting born a girl, and while he was off from home at that. A little of my sugar used to sweeten his coffee right now. This is a Negro way of saying his patience was short with me. Let me change a few words with him—and I am of the word changing kind—and he was ready to change ends. Still and all, I looked more like him than any child in the house. Of course, by the time I got born, it was too late to make any suggestions, so the old man had to put up with me. He was nice about it in a way. He didn't tie me in a sack and drop me in the lake, as he probably felt like doing.

People were digging sweet potatoes, and then it was hog-killing time. Not at our house, but it was going on in general over the country like, being January and a bit cool. Most people were either butchering for themselves, or off helping other folks do their butchering, which was almost just as good. It is a gay time. A big pot of hasslits[1] cooking with plenty of seasoning, lean slabs of fresh-killed pork frying for the helpers to refresh themselves after the work is done. Over and above being neighborly and giving aid, there is the food, the drinks and the fun of getting together.

So there was no grown folks close around when Mama's water broke. She sent one of the smaller children to fetch Aunt Judy, the mid-wife, but she was gone to Woodbridge, a mile and a half away, to eat at a hog-killing. The child was told to go over there and tell Aunt Judy to come. But nature, being indifferent to human arrangements, was impatient. My mother had to make it alone. She was too weak after I rushed out to do anything for herself, so she just was lying there, sick in the body, and worried in mind, wondering what would become of

[1] hasslits   (3)   Variety of leafy plants used as a vegetable.

her, as well as me. She was so weak, she couldn't even reach down to where I was. She had one consolation. She knew I wasn't dead, because I was crying strong.

Help came from where she never would have thought to 5 look for it. A white man of many acres and things, who knew the family well, had butchered the day before. Knowing that Papa was not at home, and that consequently there would be no fresh meat in our house, he decided to drive the five miles and bring a half of a shoat, sweet potatoes, and other garden stuff along. He was standing there a few minutes after I was born. Seeing the front standing open, he came on in, and hollered, "Hello, there! Call your dogs!" That is the regular way to call in the country because nearly everybody who has anything to watch has biting dogs.

Nobody answered, but he claimed later that he heard me 6 spreading my lungs all over Orange County, so he shoved the door open and bolted on into the house.

He followed the noise and then he saw how things were, 7 and, being the kind of man he was, he took out his Barlow Knife and cut the navel cord, then he did the best he could about other things. When the mid-wife, locally known as a granny, arrived about an hour later, there was a fire in the stove and plenty of hot water on. I had been sponged off in some sort of a way, and Mama was holding me in her arms.

As soon as the old woman got there, the white man un- 8 loaded what he had brought, and drove off cussing about some blankety-blank people never being where you could put your hands on them when they were needed. He got no thanks from Aunt Judy. She grumbled for years about it. She complained that the cord had not been cut just right, and the bellyband had not been put on tight enough. She was mighty scared I was going to have a weak back, and that I would have trouble holding my water until I reached puberty. I did.

The next day or so a Mrs. Neale, a friend of Mama's, came 9 in and reminded her that she had promised to let her name the baby in case it was a girl. She had picked up a name somewhere which she thought was very pretty. Perhaps she had read it somewhere, or somebody back in those woods was smoking Turkish cigarettes. So I became Zora Neale Hurston.

There is nothing to make you like other human beings so 10 much as doing things for them. Therefore, the man who grannied me was back next day to see how I was coming along. Maybe it was a pride in his own handiwork, and his resourcefulness in a pinch, that made him want to see it through. He remarked that I was a God-damned fine baby, fat and plenty of lung-power. As time went on, he came infrequently, but somehow kept a pinch of interest in my welfare. It seemed that I was spying noble, growing like a gourd vine, and yelling bass like a gator. He was the kind of man that had no use for puny things, so I was all to the good with him. He thought my mother was justified in keeping me.

But nine months rolled around, and I just would not get   11
on with the walking business. I was strong, crawling well, but showed no inclination to use my feet. I might remark in passing, that I still don't like to walk. Then I was over a year old, but still I would not walk. They made allowances for my weight, but yet, that was no real reason for my not trying.

They tell me that an old sow-hog taught me how to walk.   12
That is, she didn't instruct me in detail, but she convinced me that I really ought to try. It was like this. My mother was going to have collard greens for dinner, so she took the dishpan and went down to the spring to wash the greens. She left me sitting on the floor, and gave me a hunk of cornbread to keep me quiet. Everything was going along all right, until the sow with her litter of pigs in convoy came abreast of the door. She must have smelled the cornbread I was messing with and scattering crumbs about the floor. So, she came right on in, and began to nuzzle around.

My mother heard my screams and came running. Her   13
heart must have stood still when she saw the sow in there, because hogs have been known to eat human flesh.

But I was not taking this thing sitting down. I had been   14
placed by a chair, and when my mother got inside the door, I had pulled myself up by that chair and was getting around it right smart.

As for the sow, poor misunderstood lady, she had no inter-   15
est in me except my bread. I lost that in scrambling to my feet and she was eating it. She had much less intention of eating Mama's baby, than Mama had of eating hers. With no more suggestions from the sow or anybody else, it seems that I just took to walking and kept the thing a-going. The strangest thing about it was that once I found the use of my feet, they took to wandering. I always wanted to go. I would wander off in the woods all alone, following some inside urge to go places. This alarmed my mother a great deal. She used to say that she believed a woman who was an enemy of hers had sprinkled

"travel dust" around the doorstep the day I was born. That was the only explanation she could find. I don't know why it never occurred to her to connect my tendency with my father, who didn't have a thing on his mind but this town and the next one. That should have given her a sort of hint. Some children are just bound to take after their fathers in spite of women's prayers.

Discussion Questions

1. Why was Hurston's father disappointed in her birth?
2. Why does Hurston describe hog-killing time as a "gay time"?
3. Why did the white man take a special interest in Hurston?
4. According to Hurston, how did she learn to walk?
5. What are some of the folk sayings mentioned in the story? Explain each.
6. What are some of the folk myths surrounding Hurston's birth?
7. How does Hurston's use of cause and effect add to the interest of the story?
8. What is the main idea of this story?

Writing Assignments

1. Write an essay describing the circumstances of your birth and how you got your name.
2. Write an essay recounting a story about your early childhood, for example, speaking your first words, making your first steps, learning to ride a bike.
3. Write an essay about some of the sayings or superstitions you have heard in your family.

THE GHOST OF ORION

John Edgar Wideman

*John Edgar Wideman (1941–) was born in Washington,
D.C., and educated at the University of Pennsylvania,
where he was an outstanding basketball player and
scholar, and at Oxford University, where he was a Rhodes
Scholar. He is professor of English at the University of
Massachusetts at Amherst. Wideman has written several
books, including* Brothers and Keepers *(1984), about his
brother who is serving a life term in prison, and* Philadelphia Fire *(1990). His* Homewood Trilogy *(named for the
Homewood section of Pittsburgh where he grew up) consists
of* Hiding Place *(1981),* Damballah *(1981), and* Sent for You
Yesterday *(1983). His most recent work is* Fatheralong
(1994). This excerpt from Damballah *is the story of a slave
who maintains dignity and pride in his African heritage in
spite of the consequences.*

Vocabulary

vaunted	(4)	boastful, extravagant
docility	(4)	obedience, submissiveness
tractability	(4)	ease with which one is managed or controlled
disparity	(4)	difference
accrued	(4)	accumulated
temporal	(4)	worldly
droning	(12)	humming

Damballah was the word. Said it to Aunt Lissy and she   1
went upside his head, harder than she had ever slapped him.
Felt like crumpling right there in the dust of the yard it hurt so
bad but he bit his lip and didn't cry out, held his ground and
said the word again and again silently to himself, pretending
nothing but a bug on his burning cheek and twitched and sent
it flying. Damballah. Be strong as he needed to be. Nothing
touch him if he don't want. Before long they'd cut him from the
herd of pickaninnies.[1] No more chasing flies from the table, no
more silver spoons to get shiny, no fat, old woman telling him

---

[1] pickaninnies (1)   Negative term for African American children.

what to do. He'd go to the fields each morning with the men. Holler like they did before the sun rose to burn off the mist. Work like they did from can to caint. From first crack of light to dusk when the puddles of shadow deepened and spread so you couldn't see your hands or feet or the sharp tools hacking at the cane.

He was already taller than the others, a stork among   2
the chicks scurrying behind Aunt Lissy. Soon he'd rise with the conch horn[2] and do a man's share so he had let the fire rage on half his face and thought of the nothing always there to think of. In the spoon, his face long and thin as a finger. He looked for the print of Lissy's black hand on his cheek, but the image would not stay still. Dancing like his face reflected in the river. Damballah. "Don't you ever, you hear me, ever let me hear that heathen talk no more. You hear me, boy? You talk Merican, boy." Lissy's voice like chicken cackle. And his head a barn packed with animal noise and animal smell. His own head but he had to sneak round in it. Too many others crowded in there with him. His head so crowded and noisy lots of time don't hear his own voice with all them braying and cackling.

Orion squatted the way the boy had seen the other old   3
men collapse on their haunches and go still as a stump. Their bony knees poking up and their backsides resting on their ankles. Looked like they could sit that way all day, legs folded under them like wings. Orion drew a cross in the dust. Damballah. When Orion passed his hands over the cross the air seemed to shimmer like it does above a flame or like it does when the sun so hot you can see waves of heat rising off the fields. Orion talked to the emptiness he shaped with his long black fingers. His eyes were closed. Orion wasn't speaking but sounds came from inside him the boy had never heard before, strange words, clicks, whistles and grunts. A singsong moan that rose and fell and floated like the old man's busy hands above the cross. Damballah like a drum beat in the chant. Damballah a place the boy could enter, a familiar sound he began to anticipate, a sound outside of him which slowly forced its way inside, a sound measuring his heartbeat then one with the pumping surge of his blood.

[2] conch horn   (2)   A spiral one-piece seashell, often blown to call slaves to work.

The boy heard part of what Lissy saying to Primus in the   4
cooking shed: "Ryan he yell that heathen word right in the middle of Jim talking bout Sweet Jesus the Son of God. Jump up
like he snake bit and scream that word so everybody hushed,
even the white folks that came to hear Jim preach. Simple
Ryan standing there at the back of the chapel like a knot poked
out on somebody's forehead. Lookin like a nigger caught wid
his hand in the chicken coop. Screeching like some crazy hoot
owl while Preacher Jim praying the word of the Lord. They gon
kill that simple nigger one day."

> Dear Sir:
>   The nigger Orion which I purchased of you in good faith
> sight unseen on your promise that he was of sound constitution
> "a full grown and able-bodied house servant who can read, write,
> do sums and cipher" to recite the exact words of your letter
> dated April 17, 1852, has proved to be a burden, a deficit to the
> economy of my plantation rather than the asset I fully believed I
> was receiving when I agreed to pay the price you asked. Of the
> vaunted intelligence so rare in his kind, I have seen nothing. Not
> an English word has passed through his mouth since he arrived.
> Of his docility and tractability I have seen only the willingness
> with which he bares his leatherish back to receive the stripes
> constant misconduct earn him. He is a creature whose brutish
> habits would shame me were he quartered in my kennels. I find
> it odd that I should write at such length about any nigger, but
> seldom have I have been so struck by the disparity between
> promise and performance. As I have accrued nothing but ex-
> pense and inconvenience as a result of his presence, I think it
> only just that you return the full amount I paid for this flawed
> *piece of the Indies.*
>   You know me as an honest and fair man and my regard for
> those same qualities in you prompts me to write this letter. I am
> not a harsh master. I concern myself with the spiritual as well as
> the temporal needs of my slaves. My nigger Jim is renowned in
> this county as a preacher. Many say I am foolish, that the words
> of scripture are wasted on these savage blacks. I fear you have
> sent me a living argument to support the critics of my Christian-
> izing project. Among other absences of truly human qualities I
> have observed in this Orion is the utter lack of a soul.

She said it time for Orion to die. Broke half the overseer's   5
bones knocking him off his horse this morning and everybody
thought Ryan done run away sure but Mistress come upon the
crazy nigger at suppertime on the big house porch naked as
the day he born and he just sat there staring into her eyes till
Mistress screamed and run away. Aunt Lissy said Ryan ain't
studying no women, ain't gone near to woman since he been

here and she say his ain't the first black butt Mistress done seen all them nearly grown boys walkin round summer in the onliest shirt Master give em barely come down to they knees and niggers man nor woman don't get drawers the first. Mistress and Master both seen plenty. Wasn't what she saw scared her less she see the ghost leaving out Ryan's body.

The ghost wouldn't steam out the top of Orion's head. The   6
boy remembered the sweaty men come in from the fields at dusk when the nights start to cool early, remembered them with the drinking gourds[3] in they hands scooping up water from the wooden barrel he filled, how they throw they heads back and the water trickles from the sides of they mouth and down they chin and they let it roll on down they chests, and the smoky steam curling off they shoulders. Orion's spirit would not rise up like that but wiggle out of his skin and swim off up the river.

The boy knew many kinds of ghosts and learned the ways   7
you get round their tricks. Some spirits almost good company and he filled the nothing with jingles and whistles and took roundabout paths and sang to them when he walked up on a crossroads and yoo-hooed at doors. No way you fool the haunts if a spell conjured strong on you, no way to miss a beating if it your day to get beat, but the ghosts had everything in they hands, even the white folks in they hands. You know they there, you know they floating up in the air watching and counting and remembering them strokes Ole Master laying cross your back.

They dragged Orion across the yard. He didn't buck or   8
kick but it seemed as if the four men carrying him were struggling with a giant stone rather than a black bag of bones. His ashy nigger weight swung between the two pairs of white men like a lazy hammock but the faces of the men all red and twisted. They huffed and puffed and sweated through they clothes carrying Ryan's bones to the barn. The dry spell had layered the yard with a coat of dust. Little squalls of yellow spurted from under the men's boots. Trudging steps heavy as if each man carried seven Orions on his shoulders. Four grown men struggling with one string of black flesh. The boy had never seen so many white folks dealing with one nigger. Aunt Lissy had said it time to die and the boy wondered what Ryan's

[3] drinking gourds (6)   The dried, hollowed-out shells of the bulb-shaped fruit of the squash, melon, and pumpkin family, used as drinking cups or dippers.

ghost would think dropping onto the dust surrounded by the scowling faces of the Master and his overseers.

One scream that night. Like a bull when they cut off his 9 maleness. Couldn't tell who it was. A bull screaming once that night and torches burning in the barn and Master and the men coming out and no Ryan.

Mistress crying behind a locked door and Master messing 10 with Patty down the quarters.

In the morning light the barn swelling and rising and tee- 11 tering in the yellow dust, moving the way you could catch the ghost of something in a spoon and play with it, bending it, twisting it. That goldish ash on everybody's bare shins. Nobody talking. No cries nor hollers from the fields. The boy watched till his eyes hurt, waiting for a moment when he could slip unseen into the shivering barn. On his hands and knees hiding under a wagon, then edging sideways through the loose boards and wedge of space where the weathered door hung crooked on its hinge.

The interior of the barn lay in shadows. Once beyond the 12 sliver of light coming in at the cracked door the boy stood still till his eyes adjusted to the darkness. First he could pick out the stacks of hay, the rough partitions dividing the animals. The smells, the choking heat there like always, but rising above these familiar sensations the buzz of flies, unnaturally loud, as if the barn breathing and each breath shook the wooden walls. Then the boy's eyes followed the sound to an open space at the center of the far wall. A black shape there. Orion there, floating in his own blood. The boy ran at the blanket of flies. When he stomped, some of the flies buzzed up from the carcass. Others too drunk on the shimmering blood ignored him except to join the ones hovering above the body in a sudden droning peal of annoyance. He could keep the flies stirring but they always returned from the recesses of the high ceiling, the dark corners of the building, to gather in a cloud above the body. The boy looked for something to throw. Heard his breath, heavy and threatening like the sound of the flies. He sank to the dirt floor, sitting cross-legged where he had stood. He moved only once, ten slow paces away from Orion and back again, near enough to be sure, to see again how the head had been cleaved from the rest of the body, to see how the ax and tongs, branding iron and other tools were scattered around the corpse, to see how one man's hat and another's shirt, a letter that must have come from someone's pocket lay about in a helter-skelter way as if the men had suddenly bolted before they had finished with Orion.

Forgive him, Father. I tried to the end of my patience to re-   13
store his lost soul. I made a mighty effort to bring him to the Ark of Salvation but he had walked in darkness too long. He mocked Your Grace. He denied Your Word. Have mercy on him and forgive his heathen ways as you forgive the soulless beasts of the fields and birds of the air.

She say Master still down slave row. She say everybody   14
fraid to go down and get him. Everybody fraid to open the barn door. Overseer half dead and the Mistress still crying in her locked room and that barn starting to stink already with crazy Ryan and nobody gon get him.

And the boy knew his legs were moving and he knew they   15
would carry him where they needed to go and he knew the legs belonged to him but he could not feel them, he had been sitting too long thinking on nothing for too long and he felt the sweat running on his body but his mind off somewhere cool and quiet and hard and he knew the space between his body and mind could not be crossed by anything, knew you mize well try to stick the head back on Ryan as try to cross that space. So he took what he needed out of the barn, unfolding, getting his gangly crane's legs together under him and shouldered open the creaking double doors and walked through the flame in the center where he had to go.

Damballah said it be a long way a ghost be going and Jor-   16
dan chilly and wide and a new ghost take his time getting his wings together. Long way to go so you can sit and listen till the ghost ready to go on home. The boy wiped his wet hands on his knees and drew the cross and said the word and settled down and listened to Orion tell the stories again. Orion talked and he listened and couldn't stop listening till he saw Orion's eyes rise up through the back of the severed skull and lips rise up through the skull and the wings of the ghost measure out the rhythm of one last word.

Late afternoon and the river slept dark at its edges like it   17
did in the mornings. The boy threw the head as far as he could and he knew the fish would hear it and swim to it and welcome it. He knew they had been waiting. He knew the ripples would touch him when he entered.

Discussion Questions

1. What type of person is Orion? Why is he also called Ryan?
2. What effect does the word *Damballah* have on Aunt Lissy? Why does she want the boy to speak "Merican"?
3. Why is it significant that Orion could read and write but would not speak English?
4. Why does Orion's master decide to kill him?
5. Why is everyone afraid to bury Orion?
6. What are some of the mystical or supernatural occurrences in this story?
7. How does Wideman use classification to tell the story of Orion?
8. What is the main idea of this story?

Writing Assignments

1. Write an essay about someone you know who held on to his or her convictions in spite of the consequences.
2. Write an essay explaining the importance of maintaining one's heritage by observing its customs, traditions, or rituals.
3. Write an essay retelling one of your favorite ghost stories.

STRANGE THINGS OF 1923

Toni Morrison

Born Chloe Anthony Wofford in Lorain, Ohio, Toni Morrison (1931–) graduated from Howard University and Cornell University. She is the author of the following novels: The Bluest Eye *(1969),* Sula *(1973),* Song of Solomon *(1977),* Tar Baby *(1981),* Beloved *(1987), winner of the Pulitzer Prize in 1988, and being written into a screenplay by Oprah Winfrey's Harpo Productions, and* Jazz *(1992). Her work encompasses the total African American experience, from slavery to segregation to today. In 1993, Morrison won the Nobel Prize for Literature, becoming the first African American and only the second American woman so honored. She currently teaches creative writing at Princeton University. In this selection from* Sula, *set in 1923, Morrison describes supernatural events in the life of the Peace family.*

Vocabulary

splaying	(29)	spreading out
spigot	(34)	faucet
trundled	(41)	rolled along

1923

The second strange thing was Hannah's coming into her   1
mother's room with an empty bowl and a peck of Kentucky
Wonders and saying, "Mamma, did you ever love us?" She sang
the words like a small child saying a piece at Easter, then knelt
to spread a newspaper on the floor and set the basket on it; the
bowl she tucked in the space between her legs. Eva, who was
just sitting there fanning herself with the cardboard fan from
Mr. Hodges' funeral parlor, listened to the silence that followed
Hannah's words, then said, "Scat!" to the deweys[1] who were
playing chain gang near the window. With the shoelaces of
each of them tied to the laces of the others, they stumbled and
tumbled out of Eva's room.

---

[1] deweys (1)   Three boys adopted by Eva.

"Now," Eva looked up across from her wagon at her   2
daughter. "Give me that again. Flat out to fit my head."

"I mean, did you? You know. When we was little."   3

Eva's hand moved snail-like down her thigh toward her   4
stump, but stopped short of it to realign a pleat. "No. I don't
reckon I did. Not the way you thinkin'.'"

"Oh, well. I was just wonderin'.'" Hannah appeared to be   5
through with the subject.

"An evil wonderin' if I ever heard one." Eva was not   6
through.

"I didn't mean nothing by it, Mamma."   7

"What you mean you didn't *mean* nothing by it? How you   8
gone not mean something by it?"

Hannah pinched the tips off the Kentucky Wonders and   9
snapped their long pods. What with the sound of the cracking
and snapping and her swift-fingered movements, she seemed to
be playing a complicated instrument. Eva watched her a moment and then said, "You gone can them?"

"No. They for tonight."   10

"Thought you was gone can some."   11

"Uncle Paul ain't brought me none yet. A peck ain't   12
enough to can. He say he got two bushels for me."

"Triflin'."   13

"Oh, he all right."   14

"Sho he all right. Everybody all right. 'Cept Mamma.   15
Mamma the only one ain't all right. Cause she didn't *love* us."

"Awww, Mamma."   16

"Awww, Mamma? Awww, Mamma? You settin' here with   17
your healthy-ass self and ax me did I love you? Them big old
eyes in your head would a been two holes full of maggots if I
hadn't."

"I didn't mean that, Mamma. I know you fed us and all. I   18
was talkin' 'bout something else. Like. Like. Playin' with us. Did
you ever, you know, play with us?"

"Play? Wasn't nobody playin' in 1895. Just 'cause you got   19
it good now you think it was always this good? 1895 was a
killer, girl. Things was bad. Niggers was dying like flies. Stepping tall, ain't you? Uncle Paul gone bring me *two* bushels. Yeh.
And they's a melon downstairs, ain't they? And I bake every
Saturday, and Shad brings fish on Friday, and they's a pork
barrel full of meal, and we float eggs in a crock of vinegar . . ."

"Mamma, what you talkin' 'bout?"   20

"I'm talking 'bout 18 and 95 when I set in that house five   21

days with you and Pearl and Plum and three beets, you snake-
eyed ungrateful hussy. What would I look like leapin' 'round
that little old room playin' with youngins with three beets to my
name?"

"I know 'bout them beets, Mamma. You told us that a mil-   22
lion times."

"Yeah? Well? Don't that count? Ain't that love? You want   23
me to tinkle you under the jaw and forget 'bout them sores in
your mouth? Pearl was shittin' worms and I was supposed to
play rang-around-the-rosie?"

"But Mamma, they had to be some time when you wasn't   24
thinkin' 'bout . . . "

"No time. They wasn't no time. Not none. Soon as I got one   25
day done here come a night. With you all coughin' and me
watchin' so TB wouldn't take you off and if you was sleepin'
quiet I thought, O Lord, they dead and put my hand over your
mouth to feel if the breath was comin' what you talkin' 'bout
did I love you girl I stayed alive for you can't you get that
through your thick head or what is that between your ears,
heifer?"

Hannah had enough beans now. With some tomatoes and   26
hot bread, she thought, that would be enough for everybody,
especially since the deweys didn't eat vegetables no how and
Eva never made them and Tar Baby was living off air and music these days. She picked up the basket and stood with it and
the bowl of beans over her mother. Eva's face was still asking
her last question. Hannah looked into her mother's eyes.

"But what about Plum? What'd you kill Plum for,   27
Mamma?"

It was a Wednesday in August and the ice wagon was com-   28
ing and coming. You could hear bits of the driver's song. Now
Mrs. Jackson would be tipping down her porch steps. "Jes a
piece. You got a lil ole piece layin' 'round in there you could
spare?" And as he had since the time of the pigeons, the ice-
man would hand her a lump of ice saying, "Watch it now, Mrs.
Jackson. That straw'll tickle your pretty neck to death."

Eva listened to the wagon coming and thought about what   29
it must be like in the icehouse. She leaned back a little and
closed her eyes trying to see the insides of the icehouse. It was
a dark, lovely picture in this heat, until it reminded her of that
winter night in the outhouse holding her baby in the dark, her
fingers searching for his asshole and the last bit of lard
scooped from the sides of the can, held deliberately on the tip

of her middle finger, the last bit of lard to keep from hurting him when she slid her finger in and all because she had broken the slop jar[2] and the rags had frozen. The last food staple in the house she had rammed up her baby's behind to keep from hurting him too much when she opened up his bowels to pull the stools out. He had been screaming fit to kill, but when she found his hole at last and struck her finger up in it, the shock was so great he was suddenly quiet. Even now on the hottest day anyone in Medallion could remember—a day so hot flies slept and cats were splaying their fur like quills, a day so hot pregnant wives leaned up against trees and cried, and women remembering some three-month-old hurt put ground glass in their lovers' food and the men looked at the food and wondered if there was glass in it and ate it anyway because it was too hot to resist eating it—even on this hottest of days in the hot spell, Eva shivered from the biting cold and stench of that outhouse.

Hannah was waiting. Watching her mother's eyelids. When Eva spoke at last it was with two voices. Like two people were talking at the same time, saying the same thing, one a fraction of a second behind the other.   30

"He give me such a time. Such a time. Look like he didn't   31 even want to be born. But he come on out. Boys is hard to bear. You wouldn't know that but they is. It was such a carryin' on to get him born and to keep him alive. Just to keep his little heart beating and his little old lungs cleared and look like when he came back from that war he wanted to git back in. After all that carryin' on, just gettin' him out and keepin' him alive, he wanted to crawl back in my womb and well . . . I ain't got the room no more even if he could do it. There wasn't space for him in my womb. And he was crawlin' back. Being helpless and thinking baby thoughts and dreaming baby dreams and messing up his pants again and smiling all the time. I had room enough in my heart, but not in my womb, not no more. I birthed him once. I couldn't do it again. He was growed, a big old thing. Godhavemercy, I couldn't birth him twice. I'd be laying here at night and he be downstairs in that room, but when I closed my eyes I'd see him . . . six feet tall smilin' and crawlin' up the stairs quietlike so I wouldn't hear and opening the door soft so I wouldn't hear and he'd be creepin' to the bed trying to spread my legs trying to get back up in my womb. He was a man, girl, a big old growed-up man. I didn't have that

[2] slop jar (29)   A metal pot used as a toilet.

much room. I kept on dreaming it. Dreaming it and I knowed it was true. One night it wouldn't be no dream. It'd be true and I would have done it, would have let him if I'd've had the room but a big man can't be a baby all wrapped up inside his mamma no more; he suffocate. I done everything I could to make him leave me and go on and live and be a man but he wouldn't and I had to keep him out so I just thought of a way he could die like a man not all scrunched up inside my womb, but like a man."

Eva couldn't see Hannah clearly for the tears, but she looked up at her anyway and said, by way of apology or explanation or perhaps just by way of neatness, "But I held him close first. Real close. Sweet Plum. My baby boy."

Long after Hannah turned and walked out of the room, Eva continued to call his name while her fingers lined up the pleats in her dress.

Hannah went off to the kitchen, her old man's slippers plopping down the stairs and over the hardwood floors. She turned the spigot on, letting water break up the tight knots of Kentucky Wonders and float them to the top of the bowl. She swirled them about with her fingers, poured the water off and repeated the process. Each time the green tubes rose to the surface she felt elated and collected whole handfuls at a time to drop in twos and threes back into the water.

Through the window over the sink she could see the deweys still playing chain gang; their ankles bound one to the other, they tumbled, struggled back to their feet and tried to walk single file. Hens strutted by with one suspicious eye on the deweys, another on the brick fireplace where sheets and mason jars were boiled. Only the deweys could play in this heat. Hannah put the Kentucky Wonders over the fire and, struck by a sudden sleepiness, she went off to lie down in the front room. It was even hotter there, for the windows were shut to keep out the sunlight. Hannah straightened the shawl that draped the couch and lay down. She dreamed of a wedding in a red bridal gown until Sula came in and woke her.

But before the second strange thing, there had been the wind, which was the first. The very night before the day Hannah had asked Eva if she had ever loved them, the wind tore over the hills rattling roofs and loosening doors. Everything shook, and although the people were frightened they thought it meant rain and welcomed it. Windows fell out and trees lost arms. People waited up half the night for the first crack of lightning. Some had even uncovered barrels to catch the rain water, which they loved to drink and cook in. They waited in vain, for no lightning no thunder no rain came. The wind just swept through, took what dampness there was out of the air, messed up the yards, and went on. The hills of the Bottom, as always, protected the valley part of town where the white people lived, and the next morning all the people were grateful because there was a dryer heat. So they set about their work early, for it was canning time, and who knew but what the wind would come back this time with a cooling rain. The men who worked in the valley got up at four thirty in the morning and looked at the sky where the sun was already rising like a hot white bitch. They beat the brims of their hats against their legs before putting them on and trudged down the road like old promises nobody wanted kept.

On Thursday, when Hannah brought Eva her fried tomatoes and soft scrambled eggs with the white left out for good luck, she mentioned her dream of the wedding in the red dress. Neither one bothered to look it up for they both knew the number was 522. Eva said she'd play it when Mr. Buckland Reed came by. Later she would remember it as the third strange thing. She had thought it odd even then, but the red in the dream confused her. But she wasn't certain that it was third or not because Sula was acting up, fretting the deweys and meddling the newly married couple. Because she was thirteen, everybody supposed her nature was coming down, but it was hard to put up with her sulking and irritation. The birthmark over her eye was getting darker and looked more and more like a stem and rose. She was dropping things and eating food that belonged to the newly married couple and started in to worrying everybody that the deweys needed a bath and she was going to give it to them. The deweys, who went wild at the thought of water, were crying and thundering all over the house like colts. 37

"We ain't got to, do we? Do we got to do what she says? It ain't Saturday." They even woke up Tar Baby, who came out of his room to look at them and then left the house in search of music. 38

Hannah ignored them and kept on bringing mason jars out of the cellar and washing them. Eva banged on the floor with her stick but nobody came. By noon it was quiet. The deweys had escaped, Sula was either in her room or gone off somewhere. The newly married couple, energized by their 39 morning lovemaking, had gone to look for a day's work happily certain that they would find none.

The air all over the Bottom got heavy with peeled fruit and   40 boiling vegetables. Fresh corn, tomatoes, string beans, melon rinds. The women, the children and the old men who had no jobs were putting up for a winter they understood so well. Peaches were stuffed into jars and black cherries (later, when it got cooler, they would put up jellies and preserves). The greedy canned as many as forty-two a day even though some of them, like Mrs. Jackson, who ate ice, had jars from 1920.

Before she trundled her wagon over to the dresser to get   41 her comb, Eva looked out the window and saw Hannah bending to light the yard fire. And that was the fifth (or fourth, if you didn't count Sula's craziness) strange thing. She couldn't find her comb. Nobody moved stuff in Eva's room except to clean and then they put everything right back. But Eva couldn't find it anywhere. One hand pulling her braids loose, the other searching the dresser drawers, she had just begun to get irritated when she felt it in her blouse drawer. Then she trundled back to the window to catch a breeze, if one took a mind to come by, while she combed her hair. She rolled up to the window and it was then she saw Hannah burning. The flames from the yard fire were licking the blue cotton dress, making her dance. Eva knew there was time for nothing in this world other than the time it took to get there and cover her daughter's body with her own. She lifted her heavy frame up on her good leg, and with fists and arms smashed the windowpane. Using her stump as a support on the window sill, her good leg as a lever, she threw herself out of the window. Cut and bleeding she clawed the air trying to aim her body toward the flaming, dancing figure. She missed and came crashing down some twelve feet from Hannah's smoke. Stunned but still conscious, Eva dragged herself toward her firstborn, but Hannah, her senses lost, went flying out of the yard gesturing and bobbing like a sprung jack-in-the-box.

Mr. and Mrs. Suggs, who had set up their canning appara-   42 tus in their front yard, saw her running, dancing toward them. They whispered, "Jesus, Jesus," and together hoisted up their tub of water in which tight red tomatoes floated and threw it on the smoke-and-flame-bound woman. The water did put out the flames, but it also made steam, which seared to sealing all that was left of the beautiful Hannah Peace. She lay there on the wooden sidewalk planks, twitching lightly among the smashed tomatoes, her face a mask of agony so intense that for years the people who gathered 'round would shake their heads at the recollection of it.

Somebody covered her legs with a shirt. A woman un-   43 wrapped her head rag and placed it on Hannah's shoulder. Somebody else ran to Dick's Fresh Food and Sundries to call the ambulance. The rest stood there as helpless as sunflowers leaning on a fence. The deweys came and stepped in the tomatoes, their eyes raked with wonder. Two cats sidled through the legs of the crowd, sniffing the burned flesh. The vomiting of a young girl finally broke the profound silence and caused the women to talk to each other and to God. In the midst of calling Jesus they heard the hollow clang of the ambulance bell struggling up the hill, but not the "Help me, ya'll" that the dying woman whispered. Then somebody remembered to go and see about Eva. They found her on her stomach by the forsythia bushes calling Hannah's name and dragging her body through the sweet peas and clover that grew under the forsythia by the side of the house. Mother and daughter were placed on stretchers and carried to the ambulance. Eva was wide awake. The blood from her face cuts filled her eyes so she could not see, could only smell the familiar odor of cooked flesh.

Hannah died on the way to the hospital. Or so they said.   44 In any case, she had already begun to bubble and blister so badly that the coffin had to be kept closed at the funeral and the women who washed the body and dressed it for death wept for her burned hair and wrinkled breasts as though they themselves had been her lovers.

When Eva got to the hospital they put her stretcher on the   45 floor, so preoccupied with the hot and bubbling flesh of the other (some of them had never seen so extreme a burn case before) they forgot Eva, who would have bled to death except Old Willy Fields, the orderly, saw blood staining his just-mopped floors and went to find out where it was coming from. Recognizing Eva at once he shouted to a nurse, who came to see if the bloody one-legged black woman was alive or dead. From then on Willy boasted that he had saved Eva's life—an indisputable fact which she herself admitted and for which she cursed him every day for thirty-seven years thereafter and would have cursed him for the rest of her life except by then she was already ninety years old and forgot things.

Lying in the colored ward of the hospital, which was a   46 screened corner of a larger ward, Eva mused over the perfection of the judgment against her. She remembered the wedding dream and recalled that weddings always meant death. And the red gown, well that was the fire, as she should have known. She remembered something else too, and try as she might to deny it, she knew that as she lay on the ground trying to drag herself through the sweet peas and clover to get to Hannah, she had seen Sula standing on the back porch just looking. When Eva, who was never one to hide the faults of her children, mentioned what she thought she'd seen to a few friends, they said it was natural. Sula was probably struck dumb, as anybody would be who saw her own mamma burn up. Eva said yes, but inside she disagreed and remained convinced that Sula had watched Hannah burn not because she was paralyzed, but because she was interested.

Discussion Questions

1. What seems to be the relationship between Hannah and her mother Eva?
2. What proof does Eva offer of her love for her children? How could you argue that Eva's killing of Plum was an act of love?
3. What are the five "strange things" that occur in 1923?
4. Why does Eva have trouble saving Hannah from the fire?
5. What is significant about Eva's thought that "Sula had watched Hannah burn not because she was paralyzed, but because she was interested"?
6. There are several examples of folk beliefs in this selection. One is that a dream of a wedding in a red bridal gown suggests death by fire. What are other examples of superstitions?
7. How is Morrison's use of description especially effective in this story?
8. Why do you think Morrison chose to begin her story with the second strange thing instead of the first?

Writing Assignments

1. Write an essay about some of the superstitions you have heard most of your life.
2. Write an essay about a time when you had a feeling or a dream that something good or bad was going to happen.
3. Write an essay about a time when you felt helpless in a situation.

Student Essay:
FOLKTALES: AN AFRICAN-AMERICAN TREASURE

Elizabeth Mitchell

Vocabulary

inexplicable	(2)	unexplainable
phenomena	(2)	events, circumstances
rites of passage	(2)	significant events in one's life that indicate a change from one stage to another (e.g., first car, marriage)
rivals	(3)	competitors, enemies

I can still remember how embarrassed I was when Aunt 1
Jennie would corner my friends when they stopped by to see
me and tell them one of her many folktales. Living with Aunt
Jennie all of my life, I had taken her stories for granted and
had come to resent her choosing inconvenient times to retell
them to me and my friends. It took someone outside of my family to make me appreciate the value of her tales.

When I went away to summer camp school, I took a 2
course entitled "African-American Folk Tradition." One day
when I was only half listening to Mr. Dawson, he began talking
about the value of African American folktales. He said that
these tales, of unknown origin, have been passed from generation to generation. According to Mr. Dawson, they serve important functions: (1) to give encouragement, (2) to explain inexplicable phenomena, for example, why is the sky blue? (3) to
teach moral lessons, (4) to help youth understand rites of passage, and (5) to provide entertainment. He said African American folktales are considered a cultural treasure.

After that afternoon session, I began to think about Aunt 3
Jennie and all of the stories she had told me. I remembered an
evening I had come home crying because my childhood rivals,
who were bigger and stronger than I, were constantly picking
on me. I remembered her telling me about a slave who learned
to outsmart his master by being more clever. I also remembered how impatient I was then, having to listen to Aunt Jennie
talk about slaves. Now I see that Aunt Jennie was giving me
just what I needed, but I was too dumb to see it.

After summer camp school, I was anxious to share all that   4
I had learned about folktales with Aunt Jennie. "I don't know
nothing about all that stuff you're talking about," she grinned.
"I just know that my stories always make people feel better."

After finishing lunch, Aunt Jennie and I went into the   5
family room. Before she sank into her big Lazy Boy, she peered
out of the window to see the sun brightly beaming as the rain
continued to fall. "Do you know why the sun shines while it's
raining?" she asked.

"No," I smiled. "Tell me."   6

Then with a faraway look, Aunt Jennie began to explain.   7
"It all started a long, long time ago . . ." I inched closer to her
as she talked. And perhaps for the very first time, I heard her.

Discussion Questions

1. Why do you think that Mitchell was embarrassed by Aunt Jennie's tales before she left home?
2. How would you characterize Aunt Jennie?
3. According to Mitchell, what are the functions of African American folktales? Can you think of others?
4. Why do you think that Aunt Jennie did not try to explain the folktales to Mitchell?
5. What do you think the author means when she said, "And perhaps for the very first time, I heard her"?
6. How effective is Mitchell's use of the narrative within the narrative?
7. How effective is the conclusion?

Writing Assignments

1. Write an essay in which you discuss the significance of a folktale you have heard or read.
2. Write an essay in which you discuss how your exposure to other folk traditions, for example, music, medicine, or superstition influenced you or someone you know.

19

Racism • Discrimination

INCIDENT

Countee Cullen

Poet, editor, dramatist, Countee Cullen (1903–1946) was born in Baltimore, Maryland. He studied at New York University, where he earned the Phi Beta Kappa key, and completed his graduate work at Harvard. One of the best known of the artists of the Harlem Renaissance, Cullen wrote several volumes of poetry: Color *(1925),* Cooper Sun *(1927),* The Ballad of the Brown Girl *(1927), and* On These I Stand *(1947), published after his death. In the following poem, from his last collection, Cullen shares a memorable Baltimore experience with racism.*

(For Eric Walrond)

Once riding in old Baltimore,   1
  Heart-filled, head-filled with glee,
I saw a Baltimorean
  Keep looking straight at me.

Now I was eight and very small,   2
  And he was no whit bigger,

And so I smiled, but he poked out
   His tongue, and called me, "Nigger."

I saw the whole of Baltimore   3
   From May until December;
Of all the things that happened there
   That's all that I remember.

Discussion Questions

1. Why do you think that "the incident" is all the speaker remembers from his experience in Baltimore?
2. What assumption can the reader make about the young Baltimorean who called the speaker "nigger"?
3. Why do you think the author decided not to describe the speaker's immediate reaction to being called "nigger"?
4. What was the speaker's mood before the incident? What do you think it was after the incident?
5. How does Cullen use description and illustration to help the reader understand the differences between the two boys?
6. What is the tone of the poem?

Writing Assignments

1. Write an essay detailing your reaction to an incident when you were called an unpleasant name.
2. Write an essay about a childhood memory that is still vivid today.
3. Write an essay about something you did that you wish you could undo.

A DIFFERENCE OF OPINION

Toni Morrison

Born Chloe Anthony Wofford, Toni Morrison (1931–   ), editor, dramatist, and Pulitzer Prize–winning novelist, is hailed by many as having become the most accomplished African American writer. She is the author of six critically acclaimed novels: The Bluest Eye *(1969),* Sula *(1973),* Song of Solomon *(1977),* Tar Baby *(1981),* Beloved *(1987), and* Jazz *(1992). In 1993, Morrison won the Nobel Prize for Literature, becoming the first African American and only the second American woman so honored. She currently teaches creative writing at Princeton University. In the following selection, first published in the* New York Times Magazine *in 1976, Morrison contrasts how her grandparents felt about racism in the United States.*

Vocabulary

rancor	(1)	bitterness
lobotomized	(3)	deprived of sensitivity or intelligence
virility	(5)	manhood
irrevocable	(5)	unchangeable, binding

His name was John Solomon Willis, and when at age 5 he heard from the old folks that "the Emancipation Proclamation was coming," he crawled under the bed. It was his earliest recollection of what was to be his habitual response to the promise of white people: horror and an instinctive yearning for safety. He was my grandfather, a musician who managed to hold on to his violin but not his land. He lost all 88 acres of his Indian mother's inheritance to legal predators who built their fortunes on the likes of him. He was an unreconstructed black pessimist who, in spite of or because of emancipation, was convinced for 85 years that there was no hope whatever for black people in this country. His rancor was legitimate, for he, John Solomon, was not only an artist but a first-rate carpenter and farmer, reduced to sending home to his family money he had made playing the violin because he was not able to find work. And this during the years when almost half the black male population were skilled craftsmen who lost their jobs to white ex-convicts and immigrant farmers.

His wife, however, was of a quite different frame of mind   2
and believed that all things could be improved by faith in Jesus and an effort of the will. So it was she, Ardelia Willis, who sneaked her seven children out of the back window into the darkness, rather than permit the patron of their sharecropper's existence to become their executioner as well, and headed north in 1912, when 99.2 percent of all black people in the U.S. were native-born and only 60 percent of white Americans were. And it was Ardelia who told her husband that they could not stay in the Kentucky town they ended up in because the teacher didn't know long division.

They have been dead now for 30 years and more and I still   3
don't know which of them came closer to the truth about the possibilities of life for black people in this country. One of their grandchildren is a tenured professor at Princeton. Another, who suffered from what the Peruvian poet called "anger that breaks a man into children," was picked up just as he entered his teens and emotionally lobotomized by the reformatories and mental institutions specifically designed to serve him. Neither John Solomon nor Ardelia lived long enough to despair over one or swell with pride over the other. But if they were alive today each would have selected and collected enough evidence to support the accuracy of the other's original point of view. And it would be difficult to convince either one that the other was right.

Some of the monstrous events that took place in John   4
Solomon's America have been duplicated in alarming detail in my own America. There was the public murder of a President in a theater in 1865 and the public murder of another President on television in 1963. The Civil War of 1861 had its encore as the civil-rights movement of 1960. The torture and mutilation of a black West Point Cadet (Cadet Johnson Whittaker) in 1880 had its rerun with the 1970's murders of students at Jackson State College, Texas Southern and Southern University in Baton Rouge. And in 1976 we watch for what must be the thousandth time a pitched battle between the children of slaves and the children of immigrants—only this time, it is not the New York draft riots of 1863, but the busing turmoil in Paul Revere's home town, Boston.

Hopeless, he'd said. Hopeless. For he was certain that   5
white people of every political, religious, geographical and eco-

nomic background would band together against black people everywhere when they felt the threat of our progress. And a hundred years after he sought safety from the white man's "promise," somebody put a bullet in Martin Luther King's brain. And not long before that some excellent samples of the master race demonstrated their courage and virility by dynamiting some little black girls to death. If he were here now, my grandfather, he would shake his head, close his eyes and pull out his violin—too polite to say, "I told you so." And his wife would pay attention to the music but not to the sadness in her husband's eyes, for she would see what she expected to see— not the occasional historical repetition, but, *like the slow walk of certain species of trees from the flatlands up into the mountains,* she would see the signs of irrevocable and permanent change. She, who pulled her girls out of an inadequate school in the Cumberland Mountains, knew all along that the gentlemen from Alabama who had killed the little girls would be rounded up. And it wouldn't surprise her in the least to know that the number of black college graduates jumped 12 percent in the last three years: 47 percent in 20 years. That there are 140 black mayors in this country; 14 black judges in the District Circuit, 4 in the Court of Appeals and one on the Supreme Court. That there are 17 blacks in Congress, one in the Senate; 276 in state legislatures—223 in state houses, 53 in state senates. That there are 112 elected black police chiefs and sheriffs, 1 Pulitzer Prize winner; 1 winner of the Prix de Rome; a dozen or so winners of the Guggenheim; 4 deans of predominantly white colleges. . . . Oh, her list would go on and on. But so would John Solomon's sweet sad music.

Discussion Questions

1. How would you characterize Morrison's grandfather and grandmother?

2. What was John Solomon Willis's view of life in the United States for African Americans? How did Willis's wife view life in the United States for African Americans?

3. What evidence does Morrison provide to support her grandfather's view? Her grandmother's?

4. Do you think Morrison's life was complicated or complemented by her grandparents' different views? Why or why not?

5. Why is comparison and contrast an ideal organization to use in developing the main idea of this essay?

6. What is the main idea that Morrison develops?

Writing Assignments

1. Write an essay contrasting two different views that your parents or grandparents had (or have) about race, religion, or culture.

2. Write an essay explaining what you would do if you received conflicting advice from two people who are both very close to you.

3. Write an essay exploring conflicting views on a subject that is both controversial and complex.

FOR MY PEOPLE

Margaret Walker

*Born in Birmingham, Alabama, Margaret Walker (1915–   )
completed her undergraduate work at Northwestern University in Evanston, Illinois. Perhaps Walker is best known for
her poem "For My People" (1942), which appears here, and
for her historical novel on slavery,* Jubilee *(1966). Her other
books include* Prophets for a New Day *(1970),* October
Journey *(1973), and* How I Wrote Jubilee and Other Essays on Life and Literature *(1990). In the following poem,
the narrator longs for "another world" that would relieve
blacks of racist oppression.*

Vocabulary

dirges	(1)	funeral hymns
ditties	(1)	simple songs
jubilees	(1)	celebrations
consumption	(5)	tuberculosis
omnisciently	(7)	with all knowledge
facile	(8)	effortless, simple
martial	(10)	military

For my people everywhere singing their slave songs repeatedly: 1
  their dirges and their ditties and their blues and jubilees,
  praying their prayers nightly to an unknown god, bending
  their knees humbly to an unseen power;
For my people lending their strength to the years: to the gone 2
  years and the now years and the maybe years, washing ironing cooking scrubbing sewing mending hoeing plowing digging planting pruning patching dragging along never gaining
  never reaping never knowing and never understanding;
For my playmates in the clay and dust and sand of Alabama 3
  backyards playing baptizing and preaching, and doctor and
  jail and soldier and school and mama and cooking and play-
  house and concert and store and Miss Choomby and hair
  and company;
For the cramped bewildered years we went to school to learn to 4
  know the reasons why and the answers to and the people
  who and the places where and the days when, in memory of
  the bitter hours when we discovered we were black and poor

and small and different and nobody wondered and nobody
understood;

For the boys and girls who grew in spite of these things to be   5
Man and Woman, to laugh and dance and sing and play and
drink their wine and religion and success, to marry their
playmates and bear children and then die of consumption
and anemia and lynching;

For my people thronging 47th Street in Chicago and Lenox Av-   6
enue in New York and Rampart Street in New Orleans, lost
disinherited dispossessed and HAPPY people filling the
cabarets and taverns and other people's pockets needing
bread and shoes and milk and land and money and Something—Something all our own;

For my people walking blindly, spreading joy, losing time being   7
lazy, sleeping when hungry, shouting when burdened, drinking when hopeless, tied and shackled and tangled among
ourselves by the unseen creatures who tower over us omni-
sciently and laugh;

For my people blundering and groping and floundering in the   8
dark of churches and schools and clubs and societies, associations and councils and committees and conventions, distressed and disturbed and deceived and devoured by money-
hungry glory-craving leeches, preyed on by facile force of
state and fad and novelty by false prophet and holy believer;

For my people standing staring trying to fashion a better way   9
from confusion from hypocrisy and misunderstanding, trying
to fashion a world that will hold all the people all the faces all
the adams and eves and their countless generations;

Let a new earth rise. Let another world be born. Let a bloody   10
peace be written in the sky. Let a second generation full of
courage issue forth, let a people loving freedom come to
growth, let a beauty full of healing and a strength of final
clenching be the pulsing in our spirits and our blood. Let the
martial songs be written, let the dirges disappear. Let a race
of men now rise and take control!

Discussion Questions

1. Why was the speaker's discovery of being black and poor "bitter
hours"?

2. In what geographical setting do the first five stanzas occur? Why
do you think the setting changes in the sixth stanza?

3. What are some of the obstacles that Walker sees as preventing African Americans from taking control of their lives?
4. Why does Walker refer to her people as HAPPY people despite the unhappy and unpleasant aspects of their lives?
5. What is the speaker's attitude about prejudice and the hardships of growing up?
6. What is the significance of the last line?
7. Why is Walker's use of description important to the reader's recognition of blacks as victims and victors?
8. What is the tone of the poem?

Writing Assignments

1. Write an essay illustrating what you believe to be a current problem and propose a solution to it.
2. Write an essay in which you show how a popular solution to a social problem may not be a workable solution at all.
3. Write a letter to someone or to an organization in which you call for some type of action.

MY LIFE IN BLACK AND WHITE

Pauli Murray

Born in Baltimore, Maryland, Pauli Murray (1910–1985) was a writer, attorney, law professor, and the first African American woman ordained Episcopal priest. Murray gradu- ated first in her Howard University law class, earning her a fellowship to Harvard Law School. Ironically, Harvard re- jected her because of her gender. Refusing to be discour- aged, she continued her studies and received her doctorate from Yale University in 1965. Her major works include Proud Shoes: The Story of an American Family *(1956), from which the following selection is taken, and* Dark Tes- tament and Other Poems *(1970). In the following selection, Murray describes life growing up under segregation.*

Vocabulary

turrets	(4)	tower-shaped projections on a building
gables	(4)	triangular sections formed by two roof slopes
piazza	(4)	a roof or arcaded passageway
brickbat	(11)	piece of brick, especially one used as a weapon

As I look back on those years at Grandfather's house, I see that 1 I inhabited a world of unbelievable contradictions. There were the disciplines of study, of doing one's duty at all costs, of walking up to fear and conquering it. Against these were the imagined terrors of the cemetery and its dead and the equally disconcerting fear of the living—that unknown white world with which I had little or no contact but which surrounded and stifled me, a great amorphous mass without personality about which I had much curiosity but dared not investigate in the in- terests of maintaining my dignity and pride. There were the ex- hortations of Grandfather and my aunts as teachers to bring out the best in people and there were Grandmother's gloomy prophecies warning of the worst. There were competing prides and loyalties—Grandfather's loyalty to his Union cause and Grandmother's to her Smiths—and while each sprang from widely different sources, both, it seemed to me, in the long run ended up in near poverty and isolation between the Bottoms and the cemetery.

For me all this could only end in rebellion. I do not know   2
which generated the greater revolt in me: the talk I heard about
the Smiths or stories of the Fitzgeralds. Each played its part.
Listening to my elders tell of the old days in North Carolina, it
sometimes appeared that the world my aunts and mother grew
up in bore little resemblance to the one in which I lived only a
few decades later.

When the Fitzgeralds had gone south, there were no rigid   3
Jim Crow laws as I knew them in my time and there was still
room to breathe. Durham was a village without pre-Civil War
history or strong ante-bellum traditions. In some ways it was
like a frontier town. There was considerable prejudice, of
course, but there were recognition of individual worth and
bridges of mutual respect between the older white and colored
families of the town which persisted into the twentieth century.
Robert and Richard Fitzgerald were respected as builders of
this tobacco center and their families were held in high esteem.

Everyone knew the Fitzgerald daughters and what their   4
families stood for. Uncle Richard Fitzgerald was known as the
town's leading brick manufacturer and was considered
wealthy. He owned a great deal of property all over town and
was president of the first Negro bank organized in Durham. He
and his family lived in a fine eighteen-room slate-roofed house
of many turrets and gables and a wide piazza, set in a large
maple-and-magnolia grove and surrounded by white sandy
drives and terraced lawns. Grandfather lived in much humbler
surroundings but was equally respected for his integrity and
stubbornness in the face of many odds. People sometimes distinguished the two families as the "rich Fitzgeralds" and "poor
Fitzgeralds," but treated them all with deference and courtesy.
When my aunts went to town men of good breeding tipped their
hats and used courtesy titles in their business transactions.
They went where they pleased with little restraint and were all
grown women before the first law requiring separation on
trains and streetcars appeared in North Carolina.

They regarded these laws disdainfully as a temporary evil,   5
perhaps, and often ignored them, but they were never crushed
by them. They had known better times and were closer to the
triumphs of Grandfather's youth. I could only look
forward to a time when I could complete Grandfather's work,
which had been so violently interrupted during Reconstruction.

Mary Ruffin Smith had sown seeds of rebellion in dispos-   6
ing of her wealth. She had done what she thought was best ac-

cording to her lights, but we thought differently. She gave the balance of her estate, which consisted mostly of heavily wooded land worth around $50,000, to the Western Diocese of the Protestant Episcopal Church in the state and the University of North Carolina. The University got the Jones's Grove tract with the stipulation that it be converted into a permanent trust fund in memory of her late brother who once owned it. The fund was to be used for the education of students at the University and is known as the Francis Jones Smith Scholarships.

Grandmother and her children owned property almost in   7
the shadow of the University with whose history and traditions they were well acquainted. It did not take her daughters long to ask why she must pay taxes to support an institution which they could not attend. It was a burning issue in our family, kindled as much by feelings of personal injustice as by group discrimination. I heard it so often at home that it was only natural that I should be among the first to hammer on the doors of the University and demand the right to enter.

Then there was the fact of Grandfather's pension check   8
and what it symbolized. I used to lead him to town each month when he went to cash it. He seemed to walk straighter on those days. He was the Robert Fitzgerald of old before blindness and infirmity had slowed his steps and interrupted his work. His check was his government's recognition of honored service and of the disability he had suffered in his country's cause.

But I saw the things which Grandfather could not see—in   9
fact had never seen—the signs which literally screamed at me from every side—on streetcars, over drinking fountains, on doorways: FOR WHITE ONLY, FOR COLORED ONLY, WHITE LADIES, COLORED WOMEN, WHITE, COLORED. If I missed the signs I had only to follow my nose to the dirtiest, smelliest, most neglected accommodations or they were pointed out to me by a heavily armed, invariably mountainous red-faced policeman who to me seemed more a signal of calamity than of protection. I saw the names of telephone subscribers conspicuously starred "(C)" in the telephone directory and the equally conspicuous space given to crimes of Negroes by the newspapers, the inconspicuous space given to public recognition and always with the ignominious and insulting "negro" or "negress."

When Grandfather came south to teach, the little Negro   10
freedmen and the poor white children were more or less on an equal footing, shared an abysmal ignorance and went to log cabin schools. A half century later the crusade against starving

the colored schools was a feeble whimper. Each morning I passed white children as poor as I going in the opposite direction on their way to school. We never had fights; I don't recall their ever having called me a single insulting name. It was worse than that. They passed me as if I weren't there! They looked through me and beyond me with unseeing eyes. Their school was a beautiful red-and-white brick building on a wide paved street. Its lawn was large and green and watered every day and flower beds were everywhere. Their playground, a wonderland of iron swings, sand slides, see-saws, crossbars and a basketball court, was barred from us by a strong eight-foot-high fence topped by barbed wire. We could only press our noses against the wire and watch them playing on the other side.

I went to West End where Aunt Pauline taught, on Ferrell Street, a dirt road which began at a lumberyard and ended in a dump. On one side of this road were long low warehouses where huge barrels of tobacco shavings and tobacco dust were stored. All day long our nostrils sucked in the brown silt like fine snuff in the air. West End looked more like a warehouse than a school. It was a dilapidated, rickety, two-story wooden building which creaked and swayed in the wind as if it might collapse. Outside it was scarred with peeling paint from many winters of rain and snow. Inside the floors were bare and splintery, the plumbing was leaky, the drinking fountains broken and the toilets in the basement smelly and constantly out of order. We'd have to wade through pools of foul water to get to them. At recess we herded into a yard of cracked clay, barren of tree or bush, and played what games we could improvise like hopscotch or springboard, which we contrived by pulling rotted palings off the wooden fence and placing them on brickbats. 11

It was never the hardship which hurt so much as the contrast between what we had and what the white children had. We got the greasy, torn, dog-eared books; they got the new ones. They had field day in the city park; we had it on a furrowed stubbly hillside. They got wide mention in the newspaper; we got a paragraph at the bottom. The entire city officialdom from the mayor down turned out to review their pageantry; we got a solitary official. 12

Our seedy run-down school told us that if we had any place at all in the scheme of things it was a separate place, marked off, proscribed and unwanted by the white people. We 13 were bottled up and labeled and set aside—sent to the Jim Crow car, the back of the bus, the side door of the theater, the side window of a restaurant. We came to know that whatever we had was always inferior. We came to understand that no matter how neat and clean, how law abiding, submissive and polite, how studious in school, how churchgoing and moral, how scrupulous in paying our bills and taxes we were, it made no essential difference in our place.

It seemed as if there were only two kinds of people in the   14
world—*They* and *We*—*White* and *Colored.* The world revolved on color and variations in color. It pervaded the air I breathed. I lcarned it in hundreds of ways. I picked it up from grown folks round me. I heard it in the house, on the playground, in the streets, everywhere. The tide of color beat upon me ceaselessly, relentlessly.

Always the same tune, played like a broken record, rob-   15
bing one of personal identity. Always the shifting sands of color so that there was no solid ground under one's feet. It was color, color, color all the time, color, features and hair. Folks were never just folks. They were white folks! Black folks! Poor white crackers! No-count niggers! Red necks! Darkies! Peckerwoods! Coons!

Two shades lighter! Two shades darker! Dead white! Coal   16
black! High yaller! Mariny! Good hair! Bad hair! Stringy hair! Nappy hair! Thin lips! Thick lips! Red lips! Liver lips! Blue veined! Blue gummed! Straight nosed! Flat nosed!

Brush your hair, child, don't let it get kinky! Cold-cream   17
your face, child, don't let it get sunburned! Don't suck your lips, child, you'll make them too niggerish! Black is evil, don't mix with mean niggers! Black is honest, you half-white bastard. I always said a little black and a little white sure do make a pretty sight! He's black as sin and evil in the bargain. The blacker the berry, the sweeter the juice!

Discussion Questions

1. How did the Jim Crow laws affect the life of blacks in North Carolina in 1956?

2. Why was color such a dominant issue for black people during that time?

3. How did the author's living conditions differ from those of her grandparents?

4. What do you think the author means by the expression, "the blacker the berry, the sweeter the juice"?

5. How does the author use illustration to show the extent of discrimination in the town?

6. What is the narrator's tone?

Writing Assignments

1. Write an essay comparing or contrasting your neighborhood with one that is significantly different from yours.

2. Write an essay recalling a childhood incident that led you to reach a new awareness of something.

3. Write an essay describing a time when you became stronger when confronting difficulty.

Student Essay:
POVERTY AND EDUCATION

Melinda Elaine Edmond

"One out of every twenty-one black American males will be murdered in their lifetime. Most will die at the hands of another black male." Many moviegoers and I first set eyes on that caption when watching John Singleton's *Boyz N The Hood* in July 1991. In August of that same year, my brother became a part of that statistic. Too often one opens the newspaper or turns on the nightly news and is informed about the death of another black male. Too often the victim of violence is also a victim of poverty. What can be done to stop it? Poverty is preventing America's ghetto youth from obtaining a decent education, and a lack of education is pulling the trigger of the guns that are murdering our black men.   1

Families living in poverty are deprived of a satisfactory education for several reasons. Schools in poor urban areas do not receive enough funding to compete with today's modern technology. These schools are not equipped with adequate materials to teach children about the changing world. For example, books and other learning aids are used and outdated; the word *computer* is almost foreign to students in these poor schools. If our children are not educated to use modern technology, they will be unable to compete in school, and as adults, unable to compete at work.   2

Along with inadequate resources in school, poor children face obstacles at home. For instance, poor families may not have enough food in the house; therefore, some children go to school on empty stomachs. When a child is hungry, he or she cannot focus and learn properly. His or her attention is on eating the free lunch the school provides, which, in some cases, is the only meal the child receives.   3

When children do not learn properly, the chances for their going on to higher education is almost impossible. Many of our black males think the only job available to them after graduation from high school (if they are lucky) is at a gas station or at McDonald's. Therefore, many turn to selling drugs for "fast cash." Desperate youths see the wealth gap between a legal and illegal job, and many choose the one that provides them   4 with the most money: drugs. As a result, black males are killing each other over drug money, trying to rob another drug dealer for his valuables, or over a deal gone wrong.

Lack of education can also lead to gang violence. Gang violence is another source of black-on-black crime. When black males are living in poverty, they often have no sense of family. They turn to gangs because of the unity and love they do not receive from home. Gangs provide young men with everything they feel they need to survive: family, money, and protection. The members' unity goes as far as killing for one another. 5

Youth today do not know enough about their own culture, and do not know the contributions blacks have made to this society. Today's young blacks do not understand the struggle their grandparents and parents went through during the civil rights movement. They do not know the power of black people. 6

The key to understanding is in education—education that the black poor in this country seldom achieve. Education provides an opportunity for blacks to compete for better jobs and, thus, to improve their economic condition, closing the gap that poverty has kept so wide for so long. 7

Discussion Questions

1. Why is poverty the enemy of the black male?
2. Why do you think the writer refers to poverty and education as being hopelessly linked?
3. Why is selling drugs a more attractive "job" for some young black males?
4. According to Edmond, why do young people turn to gangs?
5. How could knowledge of black history help solve some of the problems experienced by black youth?
6. What makes Edmond's argument an effective one?
7. The author chose to introduce her essay by using remarkable statistics. What other types of introductions might she have used?

Writing Assignments

1. Write an essay in which you discuss the "effects of _____."
2. Write an essay in which you show the positive contributions of today's African American youth.

20

Interracial Relationships

BECKY

Jean Toomer

Born Nathan Eugene Toomer in Washington, D.C., Jean Toomer (1894–1967) is best known for Cane *(1923), a book of poems, short stories, and a novella about African Americans frustrated by their conflicts in society and within themselves. This work established Toomer as a leading writer of the 1920s and inspired writers of the Harlem Renaissance. His other works include* Essentials *(1931) and* The Wayward and the Seeking, *published in 1980 after his death. In this short story from* Cane, *Toomer describes a tragic result of racial prejudice.*

Vocabulary

rustle	(1)	a soft whispering sound
mound	(1)	grave
listless	(4)	with a lack of energy or interest
snuff	(4)	powdered tobacco sniffed into the nose or applied to the gums
sullen	(5)	gloomy
cunning	(5)	sly

wraith	(5)	ghost
hant	(5)	ghost
stock-still	(6)	perfectly motionless
whinnied	(6)	whined
uncanny	(6)	mysterious, weird

Becky was the white woman who had two Negro sons. She's   1
dead; they've gone away. The pines whisper to Jesus. The Bible
flaps its leaves with an aimless rustle on her mound.

Becky had one Negro son. Who gave it to her? Damn buck   2
nigger, said the white folks' mouths. She wouldnt tell. Common, God-forsaken, insane white shameless wench, said the
white folks' mouths. Her eyes were sunken, her neck stringy,
her breasts fallen, till then. Taking their words, they filled her,
like a bubble rising—then she broke. Mouth setting in a twist
that held her eyes, harsh, vacant, staring . . . Who gave it to
her? Low-down nigger with no self-respect, said the black folks'
mouths. She wouldnt tell. Poor Catholic poor-white crazy
woman, said the black folks' mouths. White folks and black
folks built her cabin, fed her and her growing baby, prayed secretly to God who'd put His cross upon her and cast her out.

When the first was born, the white folks said they'd have   3
no more to do with her. And black folks, they too joined hands
to cast her out . . . The pines whispered to Jesus . . . The
railroad boss said not to say he said it, but she could live, if
she wanted to, on the narrow strip of land between the railroad
and the road. John Stone, who owned the lumber and the
bricks, would have shot the man who told he gave the stuff to
Lonnie Deacon, who stole out there at night and built the
cabin. A single room held down to earth . . . O fly away to Jesus . . . by a leaning chimney . . .

Six trains each day rumbled past and shook the ground   4
under her cabin. Fords, and horse- and mule-drawn buggies
went back and forth along the road. No one ever saw her.
Trainmen, and passengers who'd heard about her, threw out
papers and food. Threw out little crumpled slips of paper scribbled with prayers, as they passed her eye-shaped piece of
sandy ground. Ground islandized between the road and railroad track. Pushed up where a blue-sheen God with listless
eyes could look at it. Folks from the town took turns, unknown, of course, to each other, in bringing corn and meat and
sweet potatoes. Even sometimes snuff . . . O thank y Jesus

. . . Old David Georgia, grinding cane and boiling syrup, never went her way without some sugar sap. No one ever saw her. The boy grew up and ran around. When he was five years old as folks reckoned it, Hugh Jourdon saw him carrying a baby. "Becky has another son," was what the whole town knew. But nothing was said, for the part of man that says things to the likes of that had told itself that if there was a Becky, that Becky now was dead.

The two boys grew. Sullen and cunning . . . O pines,   5
whisper to Jesus; tell Him to come and press sweet Jesus-lips against their lips and eyes . . . It seemed as though with those two big fellows there, there could be no room for Becky. The part that prayed wondered if perhaps she'd really died, and they had buried her. No one dared ask. They'd beat and cut a man who meant nothing at all in mentioning that they lived along the road. White or colored? No one knew, and least of all themselves. They drifted around from job to job. We, who had cast out their mother because of them, could we take them in? They answered black and white folks by shooting up two men and leaving town. "Godam the white folks; godam the niggers," they shouted as they left town. Becky? Smoke curled up from her chimney; she must be there. Trains passing shook the ground. The ground shook the leaning chimney. Nobody noticed it. A creepy feeling came over all who saw that thin wraith of smoke and felt the trembling of the ground. Folks began to take her food again. They quit it soon because they had a fear. Becky if dead might be a hant, and if alive—it took some nerve even to mention it . . . O pines, whisper to Jesus . . .

It was Sunday. Our congregation had been visiting at Pul-   6
verton, and were coming home. There was no wind. The autumn sun, the bell from Ebenezer Church, listless and heavy. Even the pines were stale, sticky, like the smell of food that makes you sick. Before we turned the bend of the road that would show us the Becky cabin, the horses stopped stock-still, pushed back their ears, and nervously whinnied. We urged, then whipped them on. Quarter of a mile away thin smoke curled up from the leaning chimney . . . O pines, whisper to Jesus . . . Goose-flesh came on my skin though there still was neither chill nor wind. Eyes left their sockets for the cabin. Ears burned and throbbed. Uncanny eclipse! fear closed my mind. We were just about to pass . . . Pines shout to Jesus! . . . the ground trembled as a ghost train rumbled by. The

chimney fell into the cabin. Its thud was like a hollow report, ages having passed since it went off. Barlo and I were pulled out of our seats. Dragged to the door that had swung open. Through the dust we saw the bricks in a mound upon the floor. Becky, if she was there, lay under them. I thought I heard a groan. Barlo, mumbling something, threw his Bible on the pile. (No one has ever touched it.) Somehow we got away. My buggy was still on the road. The last thing that I remember was whipping old Dan like fury; I remember nothing after that—that is, until I reached town and folks crowded round to get the true word of it.

> Becky was the white woman who had two Negro sons. She's   7
> dead; they've gone away. The pines whisper to Jesus. The Bible
> flaps its leaves with an aimless rustle on her mound.

Discussion Questions

1. Why was Becky abandoned by both the whites and the blacks?

2. What type of person do you think Becky was? Explain your answer.

3. What attitudes did Becky's sons have toward the whites and the blacks?

4. Why do you think the townspeople brought food to Becky and her sons "unknown to each other"? Why did they soon stop bringing food the second time?

5. How did Becky die?

6. What effect does the author's repetition of the phrase "O pines, whisper to Jesus" have on the reading of the story?

7. How does Toomer use cause and effect to illustrate the plight of Becky?

8. Toomer uses the same paragraph for both the opening and the ending of the story. What effect, if any, does this have on the tone of the story?

Writing Assignments

1. Write an essay about someone you know who died in a strange way.

2. Write an essay about a time when you or someone you know was treated badly because of prejudice.

3. Write an essay describing a situation in which you or someone you know learned something positive from an interracial relationship.

BETRAYAL? WHEN BLACK MEN DATE WHITE WOMEN

Bebe Moore Campbell

Bebe Moore Campbell (1950–   ) is a free-lance writer and novelist. She is a frequent contributor to Morning Edition *on National Public Radio (NPR) and has also contributed to the* New York Times, *the* Washington Post, *and the* Los Angeles Times. *She has written several books:* Successful Women, Angry Men: Backlash in the Two-Career Marriage *(1987),* Sweet Summer: Growing Up With and Without My Dad *(1989),* Your Blues Ain't Like Mine *(1992), and* Brothers and Sisters *(1994). In the following article, which appeared in the* New York Times Magazine *in 1992, Campbell expresses her feelings about interracial dating.*

Vocabulary

restrained	(2)	held back
surreptitiously	(2)	discreetly, without calling attention to
iota	(2)	very small amount
lamented	(5)	expressed deep sorrow
perfidy	(5)	betrayal of trust
fervor	(6)	intense feeling
rendition	(6)	performance
internecine	(11)	mutually destructive or deadly
proprietary	(15)	ownership
testosterone	(16)	male hormone
psyches	(33)	souls, spirits

Not long ago some friends and I, all African-American 1
women, were sitting in a trendy Beverly Hills restaurant having
lunch when a good-looking, popular black actor strolled in.

As an audible buzz of recognition traveled from table to 2
table, my group, restrained stargazers all, managed to surreptitiously turn our heads toward the handsome celebrity without
sacrificing one iota of our collective cool.

That is, until we saw the blonde trailing behind him. 3

Our forks hit the plates on the first beat. An invisible choir 4
director only we could see raised her hands: All together now.
In unison, we moaned, we groaned, we rolled our eyes heavenward. We gnashed our teeth in harmony and made ugly faces.

The altos sang, Umph! Umph! Umph!, then we all shook 5

our heads as we lamented for the 10,000th time the perfidy of black men and cursed trespassing white women who dared to "take our men."

The fact that I am married to my second black husband did-   6
n't lessen the fervor of my rendition of this same old song one bit.

Had Spike Lee ventured in with a camera and recorder he   7
would have had the footage and soundtrack for "Jungle Fever, Parts II, III and IV."

Before lunch was over I had a headache, indigestion and   8
probably elevated blood pressure. In retrospect, I think I may have shortened my life considerably.

For many African-American women, the thought of black   9
men, particularly those who are successful, dating or marrying white women is like being passed over for the prom by the boy we consider our steady date, causing us pain, rage and an overwhelming sense of betrayal and personal rejection.

When asked why they are with white women, most black   10
men explain that they just happened to fall in love. Others say that they consider white women more docile and obedient than feisty black women. And some refuse to answer the question.

Whatever the real reasons may be, many black women   11
perceive a hurtful mixture of blatant sexism and eerie internecine racism: If you were good enough (if you looked like white women and didn't give me so much back talk) I wouldn't choose someone else.

For sisters, the message that we don't measure up is the   12
nightmare side of integration.

We can't get even, so we get mad.   13

I once believed that if I could just lock my rolling eyes onto   14
those of some wayward brothers, somehow I could will them to return to black women where they belong.

But as I drove home from lunch with my head pounding   15
and my heart racing, I slowly came to a conclusion I've been avoiding for three decades, out of pride, sisterly solidarity and just plain stubbornness: In the multiracial society we Americans live in, to feel one has exclusive, proprietary rights to the members of the opposite sex of one's race is a one-way ticket to Migraine City.

Let me be clear: I'm not ashamed of my fury. The resent-   16
ment and even hostility I harbor are perfectly normal, and I believe my sisters and I have conducted ourselves with ladylike dignity and enormous restraint; we don't have enough testosterone to do anybody harm.

I haven't slashed one brother's tire; I don't have any blond   17
ponytails hanging on my bedroom walls. I've just been obsessing.

And I'm in good company. Asian men, when their women   18
marry whites; Jewish women, when their men pick "shiksas";
and Latinas, when Latinos choose white women—all rant and
rave just as I do.

But if my anger is within the range of predictable and ac-   19
ceptable norms, it is increasingly uncomfortable for me personally. Anger has become an addiction.

There are, of course, black women who couldn't care less   20
about any man besides the man they are seeing. Still, almost
every time I get together with two or more African-American
women, the topic turns to "the problem."

We're disgusted; we're depressed. We're obsessing; we're   21
PMS-ing. I'm tired of putting my mood at the mercy of
strangers.

Yes, I want my people to date and marry each other and I   22
don't think it will ever give me pleasure to see black men with
white women, but my being angry isn't going to make these
couples stop choosing each other.

The only thing I can control regarding this phenomenon is   23
my response to it.

What I'm striving for is the same feeling I get whenever I   24
run into my ex-husband: neutrality. I can acknowledge the
man without giving up any negative energy or emotions. I
worked for years to achieve that kind of peace of mind; it is a
wonderful blessing.

Many sisters say black women's pain comes from black   25
men abandoning them for other women. I used to believe that,
but I no longer do.

I can't speak for other women, but when my thinking isn't   26
clouded by anger I am forced to recognize that my pain isn't
coming from black men and white women. It is coming from
within. Therein lies my healing.

I remember sitting in my bedroom in the dark with a hair   27
clip on my nose, trying to reduce the size of my wide nostrils.

When the teenage parties I attended grew hot and my   28
pageboy turned "nappy" I'd dash into the bathroom and attempt to comb it so the boys wouldn't see how ugly I was.

---

[1] "shiksas"   (18)   Non-Jewish girls or young women.

While I was growing up I recall watching my grandmother 29
make pancakes and seeing Aunt Jemima's smiling face on the
box.

Aunt Jemima has a new, modern hairdo now, but she is 30
still on the pancake box, a sturdy, sensible woman, not unpleasant to look at, but clearly one who is meant for servitude
and not adoration.

And what I knew then, I know now: When some people 31
look at me, or any black woman, they see Aunt Jemima—a
mammy, built to serve, not to adore. A few of those people are
my men.

I can't change anyone's perception of me, but I can hold 32
all the facets of me in high esteem. The thing I like about Sister
Jemima is this: She's a survivor.

Some black men may need to ask themselves why they are 33
with white women, particularly those who use them as emotional props to soothe wounded psyches and maybe even those
who are truly in love. It isn't my responsibility to conduct the
interrogation.

I don't want to be held hostage by my own rage. Aunt 34
Jemima is a survivor. Like her, I want to endure through the
decades with a smile on my face, knowing that no one can reject me unless I give them permission to do so.

If, like me, my brothers need to embark upon the path 35
that leads to the resurrection of their damaged souls, then I
urge them to read the books, attend the seminars or choose the
therapists and begin their journey.

I forgive black men for hurting me; I forgive me for letting 36
them.

I am moving toward peace. 37

Discussion Questions

1. How would you describe Campbell's attitude toward black men
   who date white women?
2. According to Campbell, what reasons do most black men give for
   dating white women?
3. What is Campbell's attitude toward Aunt Jemima?
4. How has Campbell learned to soothe her anger and to heal her
   hurt?
5. What is the tone of this article?
6. What makes Campbell's argument a persuasive one?

7. Which sentence seems to state the thesis of this article? Explain your answer.

Writing Assignments

1. Write an essay expressing your feelings on interracial relationships.
2. Write an essay in which you explore reasons why some people have difficulty accepting interracial relationships.
3. Write an essay describing a positive or a negative interracial relationship that you have experienced or observed. Explain why you consider it positive or negative.

NOTES OF A NATIVE SON

James Baldwin

James Baldwin (1924–1987) was born and reared in Harlem, New York. Most of his writings describe racial conflict and prejudice in the United States. His works include two books of autobiographical essays, Notes of a Native Son *(1955) and* Nobody Knows My Name *(1961); a nonfiction work,* The Fire Next Time *(1963); novels,* Go Tell It on the Mountain *(1953),* Another Country *(1962), and* Just Above My Head *(1979); and plays,* Blues for Mister Charlie *(1964) and* The Amen Corner *(1965). This excerpt is taken from Baldwin's essay "Stranger in the Village," which was first published in* Notes of a Native Son. *Here Baldwin reflects on American black-white race relations.*

Vocabulary

sporadically	(2)	occassionally
ambivalence	(2)	conflicting feelings
subtle	(2)	hard to detect
sustenance	(2)	nourishment, food
estrangement	(3)	keeping apart
perpetual	(4)	continuing indefinitely

At the root of the American Negro problem is the necessity of the American white man to find a way of living with the Negro in order to be able to live with himself. And the history of this problem can be reduced to the means used by Americans—lynch law and law, segregation and legal acceptance, terrorization and concession—either to come to terms with this necessity, or to find a way around it, or (most usually) to find a way of doing both these things at once. The resulting spectacle, at once foolish and dreadful, led someone to make the quite accurate observation that "the Negro-in-America is a form of insanity which overtakes white men." 1

In this long battle, a battle by no means finished, the unforeseeable effects of which will be felt by many future generations, the white man's motive was the protection of his identity; the black man was motivated by the need to establish an identity. And despite the terrorization which the Negro in America endured and endures sporadically until today, despite the cruel 2 and totally inescapable ambivalence of his status in his country, the battle for his identity has long ago been won. He is not a visitor to the West, but a citizen there, an American; as American as the Americans who despise him, the Americans who fear him, the Americans who love him—the Americans who became less than themselves, or rose to be greater than themselves by virtue of the fact that the challenge he represented was inescapable. He is perhaps the only black man in the world whose relationship to white men is more terrible, more subtle, and more meaningful than the relationship of bitter possessed to uncertain possessors. His survival depended, and his development depends, on his ability to turn his peculiar status in the Western world to his own advantage and, it may be, to the very great advantage of that world. It remains for him to fashion out of his experience that which will give him sustenance, and a voice. . . .

Yet, if the American Negro has arrived at his identity by   3
virtue of the absoluteness of his estrangement from his past, American white men still nourish the illusion that there is some means of recovering the European innocence, of returning to a state in which black men do not exist. This is one of the greatest errors Americans can make. The identity they fought so hard to protect has, by virtue of that battle, undergone a change: Americans are as unlike any other white people in the world as it is possible to be. I do not think, for example, that it is too much to suggest that the American vision of the world—which allows so little reality, generally speaking, for any of the darker forces in human life, which tends until today to paint moral issues in glaring black and white—owes a great deal to the battle waged by Americans to maintain between themselves and black men a human separation which could not be bridged. It is only now beginning to be borne in on us— very faintly, it must be admitted, very slowly, and very much against our will—that this vision of the world is dangerously inaccurate, and perfectly useless. For it protects our moral high-mindedness at the terrible expense of weakening our grasp of reality. People who shut their eyes to reality simply invite their own destruction, and anyone who insists on remaining in a state of innocence long after that innocence is dead turns himself into a monster.

The time has come to realize that the interracial drama   4
acted out on the American continent has not only created a new black man, it has created a new white man, too. No road

whatever will lead Americans back to the simplicity of this European village where white men still have the luxury of looking on me as a stranger. I am not, really, a stranger any longer for any American alive. One of the things that distinguishes Americans from other people is that no other people has ever been so deeply involved in the lives of black men, and vice versa. This fact faced, with all its implications, it can be seen that the history of the American Negro problem is not merely shameful, it is also something of an achievement. For even when the worst has been said, it must also be added that the perpetual challenge posed by this problem was always, somehow, perpetually met. It is precisely this black-white experience which may prove of indispensable value to us in the world we face today. This world is white no longer, and it will never be white again.

Discussion Questions

1. According to Baldwin, what is the root of the "American Negro problem"?
2. Why does Baldwin say that "Americans are as unlike as any other white people in the world as it is possible to be"?
3. Why do you think Baldwin feels he is a stranger in Europe and not in America?
4. How does Baldwin use comparison and contrast, description, and illustration to develop his argument?
5. For what audience do you think this selection is written? Explain your answer.

Writing Assignments

1. Write an essay expressing your hope or lack of hope for improvement in race relations in America.
2. Write an essay describing a time when you felt like a stranger.
3. Write an essay responding to Baldwin's statement: "This world is white no longer, and it will never be white again."

WHAT'S AMERICAN ABOUT AMERICA?

Ishmael Reed

*Ishmael Reed (1938–) was born in Chattanooga, Ten-
nessee, but grew up in Buffalo, New York. He attended the
University of Buffalo, was an activist in the Civil Rights
Movement, and worked for several newspapers. Reed is
best known for his many novels, which not only attack economic exploitation, racism, and sexism, but also poke fun at
Western literary standards. Some of his novels include* The
Free-Lance Pallbearers *(1967),* Yellow Back Radio Broke-
Down *(1971),* Mumbo Jumbo *(1972), and* Reckless Eye-
balling *(1986). "What's American About America?" originally appeared as a longer version in Reed's collection of
essays,* Writin' Is Fightin': Thirty-Seven Years of Boxing on
Paper *(1988). This shortened version of the essay highlights
the many serious social problems present in the United
States and emphasizes that the nation has always been
considered more like a bowl of stew or salad rather than a
melting pot.*

Vocabulary

ostracism	(3)	exclusion from a group; rejection
mythological	(4)	imaginary
monolithic	(5)	always the same, unchanging
dissidents	(6)	those who disagree
patriarchs	(9)	father figures
razed	(9)	tore down, destroyed
meticulous	(11)	extremely careful and precise
repository	(14)	a place where things are put for safekeeping

On the day before Memorial Day, 1983, a poet called me to   1
describe a city he had just visited. He said that one section included mosques, built by the Islamic people who dwelled there.
Attending his reading, he said, were large numbers of Hispanic
people, 40,000 of whom lived in the same city. He was not talking about a fabled city located in some mysterious region of the
world. The city he'd visited was Detroit.

A few months before, as I was visiting Texas, I heard the   2
taped voice used to guide passengers to their connections at
the Dallas Airport announcing items in both Spanish and Eng-

lish. This trend is likely to continue; after all, for some south-western states like Texas, where the largest minority is now Mexican-American, Spanish was the first written language and the Spanish style lives on in the western way of life.

Shortly after my Texas trip, I sat in a campus auditorium   3
at the University of Wisconsin at Milwaukee as a Yale profes-sor—whose original work on the influence of African cultures upon those of the Americas has led to his ostracism from some intellectual circles—walked up and down the aisle like an old-time Southern evangelist, dancing and drumming the top of the lectern, illustrating his points before some Afro-American intel-lectuals and artists who cheered and applauded his perfor-mance. The professor was "white." After his lecture, he con-versed with a group of Milwaukeeans—all who spoke Yoruban,[1] though only the professor had ever traveled to Africa.

One of the artists there told me that his paintings, which   4
included African and Afro-American mythological symbols and imagery, were hanging in the local McDonald's restaurant. The next day I went to McDonald's and snapped pictures of smiling youngsters eating hamburgers below paintings that could grace the walls of any of the country's leading museums. The man-ager of the local McDonald's said, "I don't know what you boys are doing, but I like it," as he commissioned the local painters to exhibit in his restaurant.

Such blurring of cultural styles occurs in everyday life in   5
the United States to a greater extent than anyone can imagine. The result is what the above-mentioned Yale professor, Robert Thompson, referred to as a cultural bouillabaisse.[2] Yet mem-bers of the nation's present educational and cultural elect still cling to the notion that the United States belongs to some vaguely defined entity they refer to as "Western civilization," by which they mean, presumably, a civilization created by people of Europe, as if Europe can even be viewed in monolithic terms. Is Beethoven's Ninth Symphony, which includes Turkish marches, a part of Western civilization? Or the late-nineteenth- and twentieth-century French paintings, whose creators were

---

[1] Yoruban   (3)   An African language spoken in Nigeria.
[2] cultural bouillabaisse   (5)   Refers to the coexistence of several cultures in one society; "bouillabaisse" is a stew made up of different types of fish and shellfish.

influenced by Japanese art? And what of the cubists,[3] through whom the influence of African art changed modern painting? Or the surrealists[4] who were so impressed with the art of the Pacific Northwest Indians that, in their map of North America, Alaska dwarfs the lower forty-eight states in size?

Are the Russians, who are often criticized for their adoption   6
of "Western" ways by Tsarist[5] dissidents in exile, members of Western civilization? And what of the millions of Europeans who have black African and Asian ancestry, black Africans having occupied several European countries for hundreds of years? Are these "Europeans" a part of Western civilization? Or the Hungarians, who originated across the Urals in a place called Greater Hungary? Or the Irish, who came from the Iberian Peninsula?

Even the notion that North America is part of Western civi-   7
lization because our "system of government" is derived from Europe is being challenged by Native American historians who say that the founding fathers, Benjamin Franklin especially, were actually influenced by the system of government that had been adopted by the Iroquois hundreds of years prior to the arrival of Europeans.

Western civilization, then, becomes another confusing cat-   8
egory—like Third World, or Judeo-Christian culture—as humanity attempts to impose its small-screen view of political and cultural reality upon a complex world. Our most publicized novelist recently said that Western civilization was the greatest achievement of mankind—an attitude that flourishes on the street level as scribbles in public restrooms: "White Power," "Niggers and Spics Suck," or "Hitler was a prophet." Where did such an attitude, which has caused so much misery and depression in our national life, which has tainted even our noblest achievements, begin? An attitude that caused the incarceration of Japanese-American citizens during World War II, the persecution of Chicanos and Chinese Americans, the near-extermination of the Indians, and the murder and lynchings of thousands of Afro-Americans.

---

[3] cubists   (5)   Those representing a school of painting and sculpture that reflects geometric shapes.
[4] surrealists   (5)   Those representing a literacy and artistic movement that proclaims the changing of social, scientific, and philosophical values through the freeing of the unconscious.
[5] Tsarist   (6)   Sometimes spelled *czarist;* characterized by a system of absolute authority or monarchy.

The Puritans of New England are idealized in our school-   9
books as the first Americans, "a hardy band" of no-nonsense
patriarchs whose discipline razed the forest and brought order
to the New World (a term that annoys Native American historians). Industrious, responsible, it was their "Yankee ingenuity"
and practicality that created the work ethic.

The Puritans, however, had a mean streak. They hated the   10
theater and banned Christmas. They punished people in a
cruel and inhuman manner. They killed children who dis-
obeyed their parents. They exterminated the Indians, who had
taught them how to survive in a world unknown to them. And
their encounter with calypso culture, in the form of a servant
from Barbados working in a Salem minister's household, resulted in the witchcraft hysteria.

The Puritan legacy of hard work and meticulous account-   11
ing led to the establishment of a great industrial society, but
there was the other side—the strange and paranoid attitudes
of that society toward those different from the elect.

The cultural attitudes of that early elect continue to   12
be voiced in everyday life in the United States; the president of
a distinguished university, writing a letter to the *Times,* belit-
tling the study of African civilizations; the television network
that promoted its show on the Vatican art with the boast that
this art represented "the finest achievements of the human
spirit."

When I heard a schoolteacher warn the other night about   13
the invasion of the American educational system by foreign
curricula, I wanted to yell at the television set, "Lady, they're
already here." It has already begun because the world is here.
The world has been arriving at these shores for at least 10,000
years from Europe, Africa, and Asia. In the late nineteenth and
early twentieth centuries, large numbers of Europeans arrived,
adding their cultures to those of the European, African, and
Asian settlers who were already here, and recently millions
have been entering the country from South America and the
Caribbean, making Robert Thompson's bouillabaisse richer and
thicker.

North America deserves a more exciting destiny than as a   14
repository of "Western civilization." We can become a place
where the cultures of the world crisscross. This is possible because the United States and Canada are unique in the world:
The world is here.

Discussion Questions

1. How does Reed show that the notion of Western civilization is not only confusing, but also leads to racist attitudes?
2. According to Reed, what mean streak did the Puritans possess? Give examples.
3. What does Reed mean when he says, "North America deserves a more exciting destiny than to be a repository of 'Western civilization'"?
4. According to Reed, what kind of place can North America become?
5. How effective is Reed's use of description? Support your answer.
6. Why do you think Reed chooses to use a question for the title of his essay? How effective is this choice?

Writing Assignments

1. Write an essay explaining the difference between the following two terms used to describe the United States: *melting pot* and *cultural bouillabaisse.*
2. Write an essay describing your culture's contribution to civilization.
3. Write an essay arguing for a North America that is better in some way.

Student Essay:
SOCIETY REJECTS MIXED CHILDREN

Mia Elliott

Though their numbers have significantly increased over 1
the past decade, interracial marriages still constitute only a
small percentage of the U.S. population. Until 1967, marriages
between whites and nonwhites were against the law. Though
these marriages are not illegal today, interracial couples and
their offspring still are often not accepted by society. Because
society is slow to accept them, many mixed children suffer psychologically.

Many mixed children experience psychological problems 2
such as a loss of identity. For instance, children with one white
parent and one parent of color will generally be identified with
the parent of color; their biracial identity is ignored. Likewise,
children with one black parent and one parent of color from
another race are still perceived as black. Racial identity is influenced not only by the perceptions of white society, but also
by the tendency of cultures of color to be more accepting of
children of interracial unions than are those in white society.
Peer pressure is also a factor that contributes to psychological
problems. Names such as "zebra," "oreo," and "cream-in-coffee"
are often targeted at mixed children by their peers. Not surprisingly, mixed children, particularly during the teen years, face
many discomforts because they want to fit into their peer
group. For example, a young man, half black and half Chinese,
felt as if his mixed blood was a curse. He lived in a neighborhood where the majority was black, the group with whom he
seemed to relate. One day he met a Chinese girl in a store and
decided to get acquainted. As he began to approach her, his
black friends commented, "Don't tell me you're a chink lover."
Though the young man abandoned his intentions, he was hurt
that in doing so, he had rejected part of himself.

Despite many encounters with racism, mixed children are 3
learning to cope with it, to take pride in being themselves, and
to form friendships with people of diverse cultures. After all,
the world is changing and in order to survive, everyone must
learn to accept differences.

Discussion Questions

1. According to Elliott, what are some of the psychological problems suffered by mixed children?
2. What determines whether or not a mixed child is identified as belonging to one racial group or another?
3. The author says that society has difficulty in accepting mixed children. Why do you think this is the case?
4. Elliott has relied primarily on illustration in developing her essay. How does her use of narration and cause and effect also support her thesis?
5. Do you think this relatively short essay contains adequate details to support its thesis? Why or why not?

Writing Assignments

1. Write an essay in which you discuss another group that in your opinion has been rejected by society.
2. In an essay relate a time when you felt caught between two different groups, cultures, religions, or beliefs.

21

Intraracial Prejudice

IF YOU'RE LIGHT AND HAVE LONG HAIR

Gwendolyn Brooks

Gwendolyn Brooks (1917–) is still on the lecture circuit, conducting creative writing workshops at colleges and universities throughout the United States. Perhaps what is most remarkable about this African American poet is not her ability to learn and to grow from younger poets such as Haki R. Madhubuti (don l. lee), but her untiring, selfless efforts to spark young people to write creatively. Since the publication of her A Street in Bronzeville *(1945),* Brooks *has published many volumes of poetry, including* Annie Allen *(1949),* Riot *(1969),* Becomings *(1975),* Primer for Blacks *(1980), and* Blacks *(1987). In all of her volumes, she offers snapshot descriptions of poor, frustrated, or troubled African Americans living in urban areas in the North. In 1950, she became the first African American to receive the Pulitzer Prize for poetry. In 1994, she received the National Book Lifetime Achievement Award. Currently, she directs the Gwendolyn Brooks Center for Black Literature and Creative Writing in Chicago. The following selection is taken from Brooks's novel,* Maud Martha *(1953), and describes the problem that some African Americans face when they apply the beauty standards of white America to themselves.*

Vocabulary

elucidation	(1)	explanation
bid	(2)	invitation
supercilious	(10)	a feeling of contempt based on a sense of superiority
surreptitiously	(10)	secretly
superimposed	(10)	placed over something, covering
reeked	(21)	smelled strongly of

Came the invitation that Paul recognized as an honor of the 1
first water, and as sufficient indication that he was, at last, a
social somebody. The invitation was from the Foxy Cats Club,
the club of clubs. He was to be present, in formal dress, at the
Annual Foxy Cats Dawn Ball. No chances were taken: "Top hat,
white tie and tails" hastily followed the "Formal dress," and
that elucidation was in bold type.

Twenty men were in the Foxy Cats Club. All were good- 2
looking. All wore clothes that were rich and suave. All "handled
money," for their number consisted of well-located barbers, policemen, "government men," and men with a lucky touch at the
tracks. Certainly the Foxy Cats Club was not a representative
of that growing group of South Side organizations devoted to
moral and civic improvements, or to literary or other cultural
pursuits. If that had been so, Paul would have chucked his bid
(which was black and silver, decorated with winking cat faces)
down the toilet with a yawn. "That kind of stuff" was hardly
understood by Paul, and was always dismissed with an airy
"dicty," "hincty," or "highfalutin." But no. The Foxy Cats devoted themselves solely to the business of being "hep," and
each year they spent hundreds of dollars on their wonderful
Dawn Ball, which did not begin at dawn, but was scheduled to
end at dawn. "Ball," they called the frolic, but it served also the
purposes of party, feast, and fashion show. Maud Martha,
watching him study his invitation, watching him lift his chin,
could see that he considered himself one of the blessed.

Who—what kind soul had recommended him! 3

"He'll have to take me," thought Maud Martha. "For the 4
envelope is addressed 'Mr. and Mrs.,' and I opened it. I guess
he'd like to leave me home. At the Ball, there will be only beautiful girls, or real stylish ones. There won't be more than a
handful like me. My type is not a Foxy Cat favorite. But he
can't avoid taking me—since he hasn't yet thought of words or
ways strong enough, and at the same time soft enough—for
he's kind; he doesn't like to injure—to carry across to me the

news that he is not to be held permanently by my type, and that he can go on with this marriage only if I put no ropes or questions around him. Also, he'll want to humor me, now that I'm pregnant."

She would need a good dress. That, she knew, could be a 5 problem, on his grocery clerk's pay. He would have his own expenses. He would have to rent his topper and tails, and he would have to buy a fine tie, and really excellent shoes. She knew he was thinking that on the strength of his appearance and sophisticated behavior at this Ball might depend his future admission (for why not dream?) to *membership*, actually, in the Foxy Cats Club!

"I'll settle," decided Maud Martha, "on a plain white 6 princess-style thing and some blue and black satin ribbon. I'll go to my mother's. I'll work miracles at the sewing machine.

"On that night, I'll wave my hair. I'll smell faintly of lily of 7 the valley."

The main room of the Club 99, where the Ball was held, 8 was hung with green and yellow and red balloons, and the thick pillars, painted to give an effect of marble, and stretching from floor to ceiling, were draped with green and red and yellow crepe paper. Huge ferns, rubber plants, and bowls of flowers were at every corner. The floor itself was a decoration, golden, glazed. There was no overhead light; only wall lamps, and the bulbs in these were romantically dim. At the back of the room, standing on a furry white rug, was the long banquet table, dressed in damask, accented by groups of thin silver candlesticks bearing white candles, and laden with lovely food: cold chicken, lobster, candied ham fruit combinations, potato salad in a great gold dish, corn sticks, a cheese fluff in spiked tomato cups, fruit cake, angel cake, sunshine cake. The drinks were at a smaller table nearby, behind which stood a genial mixologist, quick with maraschino cherries, and with lemon, ice, and liquor. Wines were there, and whisky, and rum, and eggnog made with pure cream.

Paul and Maud Martha arrived rather late, on purpose. 9 Rid of their wraps, they approached the glittering floor. Bunny Bates's orchestra was playing Ellington's "Solitude."

Paul, royal in rented finery, was flushed with excitement. 10 Maud Martha looked at him. Not very tall. Not very handsomely made. But there was that extraordinary quality of maleness. Hiding in the body that was not *too* yellow, waiting to spring, out at her, surround her (she liked to think)—that maleness. The Ball stirred her. The Beauties, in their gorgeous gowns, bustling, supercilious; the young men, who at other times most unpleasantly blew their noses, and darted surreptitiously into alleys to relieve themselves, and sweated and swore at their jobs, and scratched their more intimate parts, now smiling, smooth, overgallant; the drowsy lights; the smells of food and flowers, the smell of Murray's pomade, the body perfumes, natural and superimposed; the sensuous heaviness of the wine-colored draperies at the many windows; the music, now steamy and slow, now as clear and fragile as glass, now raging, passionate, now moaning and thickly gray. The Ball made toys of her emotions, stirred her variously. But she was anxious to have it end, she was anxious to be at home again, with the door closed behind herself and her husband. Then, he might be warm. There might be more than the absent courtesy he had been giving her of late. Then, he might be the tree she had a great need to lean against, in this "emergency." There was no telling what dear thing he might say to her, what little gem let fall.

But, to tell the truth, his behavior now was not very 11 promising of gems to come. After their second dance he escorted her to a bench by the wall, left her. Trying to look nonchalant, she sat. She sat, trying not to show the inferiority she did not feel. When the music struck up again, he began to dance with someone red-haired and curved, and white as a white. Who was she? He had approached her easily, he had taken her confidently, he held her and conversed with her as though he had known her well for a long, long time. The girl smiled up at him. Her gold-spangled bosom was pressed—was pressed against that maleness—

A man asked Maud Martha to dance. He was dark, too. 12 His mustache was small.

"Is this your first Foxy Cats?" he asked. 13

"What?" Paul's cheek was on that of Gold-Spangles. 14

"First Cats?" 15

"Oh. Yes." Paul and Gold-Spangles were weaving through 16 the noisy twisting couples, were trying, apparently, to get to the reception hall.

"Do you know that girl? What's her name?" Maud Martha 17 asked her partner, pointing to Gold-Spangles. Her partner looked, nodded. He pressed her closer.

"That's Maella. That's Maella." 18

"Pretty, isn't she?" She wanted him to keep talking about   19
Maella. He nodded again.

"Yep. She has 'em howling along the stroll, all right, all   20
right."

Another man, dancing past with an artificial redhead,   21
threw a whispered word at Maud Martha's partner, who caught
it eagerly, winked. "Solid, ol' man," he said. "Solid, Jack." He
pressed Maud Martha closer. "You're a babe," he said. "You're a
real babe." He reeked excitingly of tobacco, liquor, pinesoap,
toilet water, and Sen Sen.[1]

Maud Martha thought of her parents' back yard. Fresh.   22
Clean. Smokeless. In her childhood, a snowball bush had
shone there, big above the dandelions. The snowballs had been
big, healthy. Once, she and her sister and brother had waited
in the back yard for their parents to finish readying themselves
for a trip to Milwaukee. The snowballs had been so beautiful,
so fat and startlingly white in the sunlight, that she had suddenly loved home a thousand times more than ever before, and
had not wanted to go to Milwaukee. But as the children grew,
the bush sickened. Each year, the snowballs were smaller and
more dispirited. Finally a summer came when there were no
blossoms at all. Maud Martha wondered what had become of
the bush. For it was not there now. Yet she, at least, had never
seen it go.

"Not," thought Maud Martha, "that they love each other. It   23
oughta be that simple. Then I could like it. It oughta be that
easy. But it's my color that makes him mad. I try to shut my
eyes to that, but it's no good. What I am inside, what is really
me, he likes okay. But he keeps looking at my color, which is
like a wall. He has to jump over it in order to meet and touch
what I've got for him. He has to jump away up high in order to
see it. He gets awful tired of all that jumping."

Paul came back from the reception hall. Maella was cling-   24
ing to his arm. A final cry of the saxophone finished that particular slice of the blues. Maud Martha's partner bowed, escorted her to a chair by a rubber plant, bowed again, left.

"I could," considered Maud Martha, "go over there and   25
scratch her upsweep down. I could spit on her back. I could
scream. 'Listen,' I could scream, 'I'm making a baby for this
man and I mean to do it in peace.' "

---

[1] Sen Sen   (21)   Breath freshener.

But if the root was sour what business did she have up   26
there hacking at a leaf?

Discussion Questions

1. What kind of club is the Foxy Cats Club?
2. What is the meaning of the phrase, "trying not to show the inferiority she did not feel"?
3. What is the significance of the snowball bush?
4. What is the problem between Paul and Maud Martha?
5. What is the significance of the question at the end of the story?
6. How does Brooks use comparison and contrast in the story?
7. Why do you think Brooks uses a subordinate clause for the title of her story?

Writing Assignments

1. Write an essay relating an experience in which you felt embarrassed or ashamed.
2. Write an essay in which you discuss the types of people you have dated.
3. In an essay, compare and contrast two people you know who have different physical features, but who are both physically attractive.

THE REVOLT OF THE EVIL FAIRIES

Ted Poston

Theodore Roosevelt (Ted) Poston (1906–1974) was born in Hopkinsville, Kentucky, graduated from Tennessee State University, and did additional study at New York University. He was a pullman car porter before becoming a journalist with the New Amsterdam News *and the* Pittsburgh Courier. *Poston was among the first African American reporters to write for the* New York Post, *where he worked for over thirty-three years and demonstrated that an African American reporter could cover general stories. He won numerous awards for his coverage of World War II and was a member of Franklin Roosevelt's "Black Cabinet." Among Poston's most popular articles are "My Most Humiliating Jim Crow Experience" (1944), "New York Vs. Chicago: Which Is [the] Better Place for Negroes?" (1952), and "The Simple World of Langston Hughes" (1957). In this selection, which was first published in the* New Republic *(1944), Poston describes his experiences with intraracial prejudice as a student at the Booker T. Washington Colored Grammar School.*

Vocabulary

ferment	(5)	excitement
scion	(7)	descendant
skulking	(8)	moving in a sly, shifty manner
vanquished	(8)	conquered
inconsolable	(12)	not able to be comforted
fervent	(15)	with warm feelings, intense
purloined	(16)	stole
fettle	(22)	condition
slunk	(22)	moved in a sneaking manner

The grand dramatic offering of the Booker T. Washington Colored Grammar School was the biggest event of the year in our social life in Hopkinsville, Kentucky. It was the one occasion on which they let us use the old Cooper Opera House, and even some of the white folks came out yearly to applaud our presentation. The first two rows of the orchestra were always reserved for our white friends, and our leading colored citizens sat right behind them—with an empty row intervening, of course.

Mr. Ed Smith, our local undertaker, invariably occupied a   2
box to the left of the house and wore his cutaway coat and
striped breeches. This distinctive garb was usually reserved for
those rare occasions when he officiated at the funerals of our
most prominent colored citizens. Mr. Thaddeus Long, our colored mailman, once rented a tuxedo and bought a box too. But
nobody paid him much mind. We knew he was just showing
off.

The title of our play never varied. It was always Prince   3
Charming and the Sleeping Beauty but no two presentations
were ever the same. Miss H. Belle LaPrade, our sixth-grade
teacher, rewrote the script every season, and it was never like
anything you read in the storybooks.

Miss LaPrade called it "a modern morality play of conflict   4
between the forces of good and evil." And the forces of evil, of
course, always came off second best.

The Booker T. Washington Colored Grammar School was   5
in a state of ferment from Christmas until February, for this
was the period when parts were assigned. First there was the
selection of the Good Fairies and the Evil Fairies. This was very
important, because the Good Fairies wore white costumes and
the Evil Fairies black. And strangely enough most of the Good
Fairies usually turned out to be extremely light in complexion,
with straight hair and white folks' features. On rare occasions a
darkskinned girl might be lucky enough to be a Good Fairy, but
not one with a speaking part.

There was never any doubt about Prince Charming and   6
the Sleeping Beauty. They were always lightskinned. And
though nobody ever discussed those things openly, it was an
accepted fact that a lack of pigmentation was a decided advantage in the Prince Charming and Sleeping Beauty sweepstakes.

And therein lay my personal tragedy. I made the best   7
grades in my class. I was the leading debater, and the scion of
a respected family in the community. But I could never be
Prince Charming, because I was black.

In fact, every year when they started casting our grand   8
dramatic offering my family started pricing black cheesecloth at
Franklin's Department Store. For they knew that I would be
leading the forces of darkness and skulking back in the shadows—waiting to be vanquished in the third act. Mamma had
experience with this sort of thing. All my brothers had finished
Booker T. before me.

Not that I was alone in my disappointment. Many of my   9

classmates felt it too. I probably just took it more to heart. Rat Joiner, for instance, could rationalize the situation. Rat was not only black; he lived on Billy Goat Hill. But Rat summed it up like this:

"If you black, you black." 10

I should have been able to regard the matter calmly too. 11 For our grand dramatic offering was only a reflection of our daily community life in Hopkinsville. The yallers had the best of everything. They held most of the teaching jobs in Booker T. Washington Colored Grammar School. They were the Negro doctors, the lawyers, the insurance men. They even had a "Blue Vein Society," and if your dark skin obscured your throbbing pulse you were hardly a member of the elite.

Yet I was inconsolable the first time they turned me down 12 for Prince Charming. That was the year they picked Roger Jackson. Roger was not only dumb; he stuttered. But he was light enough to pass for white, and that was apparently sufficient.

In all fairness, however, it must be admitted that Roger 13 had other qualifications. His father owned the only colored saloon in town and was quite a power in local politics. In fact, Mr. Clinton Jackson had a lot to say about just who taught in the Booker T. Washington Colored Grammar School. So it was understandable that Roger should have been picked for Prince Charming.

My real heartbreak, however, came the year they picked 14 Sarah Williams for Sleeping Beauty. I had been in love with Sarah since kindergarten. She had soft light hair, bluish-gray eyes, and a dimple which stayed in her left cheek whether she was smiling or not.

Of course Sarah never encouraged me much. She never 15 answered any of my fervent love letters, and Rat was very scornful of my one-sided love affairs. "As long as she don't call you a black baboon," he sneered, "you'll keep on hanging around."

After Sarah was chosen for Sleeping Beauty, I went out for 16 the Prince Charming role with all my heart. If I had declaimed boldly in previous contests, I was matchless now. If I had bothered Mamma with rehearsals at home before, I pestered her to death this time. Yes, and I purloined my sister's can of Palmer's Skin Success.

I knew the Prince's role from start to finish, having played 17 the Head Evil Fairy opposite it for two seasons. And Prince

Charming was one character whose lines Miss LaPrade never varied much in her many versions. But although I never admitted it, even to myself, I knew I was doomed from the start. They gave the part to Leonardius Wright. Leonardius, of course, was yaller.

The teachers sensed my resentment. They were most 18
apologetic. They pointed out that I had been such a splendid Head Evil Fairy for two seasons that it would be a crime to let anybody else try the role. They reminded me that Mamma wouldn't have to buy any more cheesecloth because I could use my same old costume. They insisted that the Head Evil Fairy was even more important than Prince Charming because he was the one who cast the spell on Sleeping Beauty. So what could I do but accept?

I had never liked Leonardius Wright. He was a goody- 19
goody, and even Mamma was always throwing him up to me. But, above all, he too was in love with Sarah Williams. And now he got a chance to kiss Sarah every day in rehearsing the awakening scene.

Well, the show must go on, even for little black boys. So I 20
threw my soul into my part and made the Head Evil Fairy a character to be remembered. When I drew back from the couch of Sleeping Beauty and slunk away into the shadows at the approach of Prince Charming, my facial expression was indeed something to behold. When I was vanquished by the shining sword of Prince Charming in the last act, I was a little hammy perhaps—but terrific!

The attendance at our grand dramatic offering that year 21
was the best in its history. Even the white folks overflowed the two rows reserved for them, and a few were forced to sit in the intervening one. This created a delicate situation, but everybody tactfully ignored it.

When the curtain went up on the last act, the audience 22
was in fine fettle. Everything had gone well for me too—except for one spot in the second act. That was where Leonardius unexpectedly rapped me over the head with his sword as I slunk off into the shadows. That was not in the script, but Miss LaPrade quieted me down by saying it made a nice touch anyway. Rat said Leonardius did it on purpose.

The third act went on smoothly, though, until we came to 23
the vanquishing scene. That was where I slunk from the shadows for the last time and challenged Prince Charming to mortal combat. The hero reached for his shining sword—a bit un-

sportsmanlike, I always thought, since Miss LaPrade consistently left the Head Evil Fairy unarmed—and then it happened!

Later I protested loudly—but in vain—that it was a case of self-defense. I pointed out that Leonardius had a mean look in his eye. I cited the impromptu rapping he had given my head in the second act. But nobody would listen. They just wouldn't believe that Leonardius really intended to brain me when he reached for his sword.   24

Anyway, he didn't succeed. For the minute I saw that evil gleam in his eye—or was it my own?—I cut loose with a right to the chin, and Prince Charming dropped his shining sword and staggered back. His astonishment lasted only a minute, though, for he lowered his head and came charging in, fists flailing. There was nothing yellow about Leonardius but his skin.   25

The audience thought the scrap was something new Miss LaPrade had written in. They might have kept on thinking so if Miss LaPrade hadn't been screaming so hysterically from the sidelines. And if Rat Joiner hadn't decided that this was as good a time as any to settle old scores. So he turned around and took a sock at the male Good Fairy nearest him.   26

When the curtain rang down, the forces of Good and Evil were locked in combat. And Sleeping Beauty was wide awake and streaking for the wings.   27

They rang the curtain back up fifteen minutes later, and we finished the play. I lay down and expired according to specifications but Prince Charming will probably remember my sneering corpse to his dying day. They wouldn't let me appear in the grand dramatic offering at all the next year. But I didn't care. I couldn't have been Prince Charming anyway.   28

Discussion Questions

1. Why does Poston say that the Prince Charming presentation was only a reflection of the daily community life in Hopkinsville?

2. How would you characterize the narrator?

3. Why was the narrator not given the role of Prince Charming although he was qualified for the part?

4. From the context of the story, can you explain the meaning of the Blue Vein Society (paragraph 11) and Palmer's Skin Success (paragraph 16)?

5. What do you think led to the fight between the narrator and Prince Charming?

6. What does the casting of the roles reveal about the attitudes of the teachers, the students, and the parents?

7. How does Poston use cause and effect to illustrate the story's theme?

8. For what audience is this story written?

Writing Assignments

1. Write an essay analyzing the story's symbolic meanings of good and evil. Compare or contrast these meanings with society's view of them.

2. Write an essay about your experiences of discrimination because of ethnic, gender, or other differences.

3. Write an essay analyzing the causes and/or the effects of intraracial prejudice.

DEBUT

Kristin Hunter

Novelist Kristin Hunter (1931–) was born in Philadelphia and graduated from the University of Pennsylvania. She has worked as an elementary school teacher, an advertising copywriter, a television scriptwriter, and a professor of creative writing at the University of Pennsylvania. Her novels include God Bless the Child *(1964),* The Landlord *(1966),* The Survivors *(1975), and* The Lakestown Rebellion *(1978). She has also written several young adult books:* The Soul Brothers and Sister Lou *(1968),* Boss Cat *(1971), and* Lou in the Limelight *(1981). In this selection, which first appeared in* Negro Digest *(1968), a young girl examines her feelings while preparing for her debutante ball.*

Vocabulary

tattered	(9)	ragged, torn
ingratiated	(16)	brought into favor
precipitate	(19)	hasten
brazen	(23)	shameless, harsh
guffawed	(38)	laughed loudly
tapestry	(55)	a woven design
awe	(56)	wonder, respect
diffidence	(56)	lack of confidence, shyness
grating	(84)	irritating

"Hold *still,* Judy," Mrs. Simmons said around the spray of pins   1
that protruded dangerously from her mouth. She gave the thirtieth tug to the tight sash at the waist of the dress. "Now walk over there and turn around slowly."

The dress, Judy's first long one, was white organdy over   2
taffeta, with spaghetti straps that bared her round brown shoulders and a floating skirt and a wide sash that cascaded in a butterfly effect behind. It was a dream, but Judy was sick and tired of the endless fittings she had endured so that she might wear it at the Debutantes' Ball. Her thoughts leaped ahead to the Ball itself . . .

"*Slowly,* I said!" Mrs. Simmons' dark, angular face was al-   3
ways grim, but now it was screwed into an expression resembling a prune. Judy, starting nervously, began to revolve by moving her feet an inch at a time.

Her mother watched her critically. "No, it's still not right.   4
I'll just have to rip out that waistline seam again."

"Oh, Mother!" Judy's impatience slipped out at last. "No-   5
body's going to notice all those little details."

"They will too. They'll be watching you every minute, hop-   6
ing to see something wrong. You've got to be the *best.* Can't you
get that through your head?" Mrs. Simmons gave a sigh of despair. "You better start noticin' 'all those little details' yourself. I
can't do it for you all your life. Now turn around and stand up
straight."

"Oh, Mother," Judy said, close to tears from being made to   7
turn and pose while her feet itched to be dancing, "I can't stand
it any more!"

"You can't stand it, huh? How do you think *I* feel?" Mrs.   8
Simmons said in her harshest tone.

Judy was immediately ashamed, remembering the weeks   9
her mother had spent at the sewing machine, pricking her already tattered fingers with needles and pins, and the great
weight of sacrifice that had been borne on Mrs. Simmons'
shoulders for the past two years so that Judy might bare hers
at the Ball.

"All right, take it off," her mother said. "I'm going to take it   10
up the street to Mrs. Luby and let her help me. It's got to be
right or I won't let you leave the house."

"Can't we just leave it the way it is, Mother?" Judy pleaded   11
without hope of success. "I think it's perfect."

"You would," Mrs. Simmons said tartly as she folded the   12
dress and prepared to bear it out of the room. "Sometimes I
think I'll never get it through your head. You got to look just
right and act just right. That Rose Griffin and those other girls
can afford to be careless, maybe, but you can't. You're gonna
be the darkest, poorest one there."

Judy shivered in her new lace strapless bra and her old,   13
childish knit snuggies.[1] "You make it sound like a battle I'm
going to instead of just a dance."

"It is a battle," her mother said firmly. "It starts tonight   14
and it goes on for the rest of your life. The battle to hold your
head up and get someplace and be somebody. We've done all
we can for you, your father and I. Now you've got to start fighting some on your own." She gave Judy a slight smile; her voice

---

[1] snuggies (13)   Thigh-length cotton underwear worn for extra warmth.

softened a little. "You'll do all right, don't worry. Try and get some rest this afternoon. Just don't mess up your hair."

"All right, Mother," Judy said listlessly.   15

She did not really think her father had much to do with   16
anything that happened to her. It was her mother who had in-
gratiated her way into the Gay Charmers two years ago, taking
all sorts of humiliation from the better-dressed, better-off,
lighter-skinned women, humbly making and mending their
dresses, fixing food for their meetings, addressing more mail and
selling more tickets than anyone else. The club had put it off as
long as they could, but finally they had to admit Mrs. Simmons
to membership because she worked so hard. And that meant, of
course, that Judy would be on the list for this year's Ball.

Her father, a quiet carpenter who had given up any other   17
ambitions years ago, did not think much of Negro society or his
wife's fierce determination to launch Judy into it. "Just keep
clean and be decent," he would say. "That's all anybody has to
do."

Her mother always answered, "If that's all *I* did we'd still   18
be on relief," and he would shut up with shame over the years
when he had been laid off repeatedly and her days' work and
sewing had kept them going. Now he had steady work but she
refused to quit, as if she expected it to end at any moment. The
intense energy that burned in Mrs. Simmons' large dark eyes
had scorched her features into permanent irony. She worked
day and night and spent her spare time scheming and planning. Whatever her personal ambitions had been, Judy knew
she blamed Mr. Simmons for their failure; now all her schemes
revolved around their only child.

Judy went to her mother's window and watched her stride   19
down the street with the dress until she was hidden by the
high brick wall that went around two sides of their house. Then
she returned to her own room. She did not get dressed because
she was afraid of pulling a sweater over her hair—her mother
would notice the difference even if it looked all right to Judy—
and because she was afraid that doing anything, even getting
dressed, might precipitate her into the battle. She drew a stool
up to her window and looked out. She had no real view, but
she liked her room. The wall hid the crowded tenement houses
beyond the alley, and from its cracks and bumps and depres-
sions she could construct any imaginary landscape she chose.
It was how she had spent most of the free hours of her dreamy
adolescence.

"Hey, can I go?"   20

It was the voice of an invisible boy in the alley. As another   21
boy chuckled, Judy recognized the familiar ritual; if you said
yes, they said, "Can I go with you?" It had been tried on her
dozens of times. She always walked past, head in the air, as if
she had not heard. Her mother said that was the only thing to
do; if they knew she was a lady, they wouldn't dare bother her.
But this time a girl's voice, cool and assured, answered.

"If you think you're big enough," it said.   22

It was Lucy Mae Watkins; Judy could picture her standing   23
there in a tight dress with bright, brazen eyes.

"I'm big enough to give you a baby," the boy answered.   24

Judy would die if a boy every spoke to her like that, but   25
she knew Lucy Mae could handle it. Lucy Mae could handle all
the boys, even if they ganged up on her, because she had been
born knowing something other girls had to learn.

"Aw, you ain't big enough to give me a shoe-shine," she   26
told him.

"Come here and I'll show you how big I am," the boy said.   27

"Yeah, Lucy Mae, what's happenin'?" another, younger boy   28
said. "Come here and tell us."

Lucy Mae laughed. "What I'm puttin' down is too strong   29
for little boys like you."

"Come here a minute, baby," the first boy said. "I got a cig-   30
arette for you."

"Aw, I ain't studyin' your cigarettes," Lucy Mae answered.   31
But her voice was closer, directly below Judy. There were the
sounds of a scuffle and Lucy Mae's muffled laughter. When she
spoke her voice sounded raw and cross. "Come on now, boy.
Cut it out and give me the damn cigarette." There was more
scuffling, and the sharp crack of a slap, and then Lucy Mae
said, "Cut it out, I said. Just for that I'm gonna take 'em all."
The clack of high heels rang down the sidewalk with a boy's
clumsy shoes in pursuit.

Judy realized that there were three of them down there.   32
"Let her go, Buster," one said. "You can't catch her now."

"Aw, hell, man, she took the whole damn pack," the one   33
called Buster complained.

"That'll learn you!" Lucy Mae's voice mocked from down   34
the street. "Don't mess with nothin' you can't handle."

"Hey, Lucy Mae. Hey, I heard Rudy Grant already gave you   35
a baby," a second boy called out.

"Yeah. Is that true, Lucy Mae?" the youngest one yelled.   36

There was no answer. She must be a block away by now. 37

For a moment the hidden boys were silent; then one of 38
them guffawed directly below Judy, and the other two joined in
the secret male laughter that was oddly high-pitched and feminine.

"Aw, man, I don't know what you all laughin' about," 39
Buster finally grumbled. "That girl took all my cigarettes. You
got some, Leroy?"

"Naw," the second boy said. 40

"Me neither," the third one said. 41

"What we gonna do? I ain't got but fifteen cent. Hell, man, 42
I want more than a feel for a pack of cigarettes." There was an
unpleasant whine in Buster's voice. "Hell, for a pack of cigarettes I want a bitch to come across."

"She will next time, man," the boy called Leroy said. 43

"She better," Buster said. "You know she better. If she 44
pass by here again, we gonna jump her, you hear?"

"Sure, man," Leroy said. "The three of us can grab her 45
easy."

"Then we can all three of us have some fun. Oh, *yeah*, 46
man," the youngest boy said. He sounded as if he might be
about 14.

Leroy said, "We oughta get Roland and J.T. too. For a 47
whole pack of cigarettes she oughta treat all five of us."

"Aw, man, why tell Roland and J.T.?" the youngest voice 48
whined. "They ain't in it. Them was *our* cigarettes."

"They was *my* cigarettes, you mean," Buster said with au- 49
thority. "You guys better quit it before I decide to cut you out."

"Oh, man, don't do that. We with you, you know that." 50

"Sure, Buster, we your aces, man." 51

"All right, that's better." There was a minute of silence. 52

Then, "What we gonna do with the girl, Buster?" the 53
youngest one wanted to know.

"When she come back we gonna jump the bitch, man. We 54
gonna jump her and grab her. Then we gonna turn her every
way but loose." He went on, spinning a crude fantasy that got
wilder each time he retold it, until it became so secretive that
their voices dropped to a low indistinct murmur punctuated by
guffaws. Now and then Judy could distinguish the word "girl"
or the other word they used for it; these words always produced the loudest guffaws of all. She shook off her fear with
the thought that Lucy Mae was too smart to pass there again
today. She had heard them at their dirty talk in the alley before

and had always been successful in ignoring it; it had nothing to do with her, the wall protected her from their kind. All the ugliness was on their side of it, and this side was hers to fill with beauty.

She turned on her radio to shut them out completely and   55
began to weave her tapestry to its music. More for practice than anything else, she started by picturing the maps of the places to which she intended to travel, then went on to the faces of her friends. Rose Griffin's sharp, Indian profile appeared on the wall. Her coloring was like an Indian's too and her hair was straight and black and glossy. Judy's hair, naturally none of these things, had been "done" four days ago so that tonight it would be "old" enough to have a gloss as natural-looking as Rose's. But Rose, despite her handsome looks, was silly; her voice broke constantly into high-pitched giggles and she became even sillier and more nervous around boys.

Judy was not sure that she knew how to act around boys   56
either. The sisters kept boys and girls apart at the Catholic high school where her parents sent her to keep her away from low-class kids. But she felt that she knew a secret; tonight, in that dress, with her hair in a sophisticated upsweep, she would be transformed into a poised princess. Tonight all the college boys her mother described so eagerly would rush to dance with her, and then from somewhere *the boy* would appear. She did not know his name; she neither knew nor cared whether he went to college, but she imagined that he would be as dark as she was, and that there would be awe and diffidence in his manner as he bent to kiss her hand . . .

A waltz swelled from the radio; the wall, turning blue in   57
deepening twilight, came alive with whirling figures. Judy rose and began to go through the steps she had rehearsed for so many weeks. She swirled with a practiced smile on her face, holding an imaginary skirt at her side; turned, dipped, and flicked on her bedside lamp without missing a fraction of the beat. Faster and faster she danced with her imaginary partner, to an inner music that was better than the sounds on the radio. She was "coming out," and tonight the world would discover what it had been waiting for all these years.

"Aw, git it, baby." She ignored it as she would ignore the   58
crowds that lined the streets to watch her pass on her way to the Ball.

"Aw, do your number." She waltzed on, safe and secure on   59
her side of the wall.

"Can I come up there and do it with you?" 60

At this she stopped, paralyzed. Somehow they had come 61
over the wall or around it and into her room.

"Man, I sure like the view from here," the youngest boy 62
said. "How come we never tried this view before?"

She came to life, ran quickly to the lamp and turned it off, 63
but not before Buster said, "Yeah, and the back view is fine,
too."

"Aw, she turned off the light," a voice complained. 64

"Put it on again, baby, we don't mean no harm." 65

"Let us see you dance some more. I bet you can really do 66
it."

"Yeah, I bet she can shimmy on down." 67

"You know it, man." 68

"Come on down here, baby," Buster's voice urged softly 69
dangerously. "I got a cigarette for you."

"Yeah, and he got something else for you, too." 70

Judy flattened against her closet door, gradually lost her 71
urge to scream. She realized that she was shivering in her underwear. Taking a deep breath, she opened the closet door and
found her robe. She thought of going to the window and yelling
down, "You don't have a thing I want. Do you understand?" But
she had more important things to do.

Wrapping her hair in protective plastic, she ran a full 72
steaming tub and dumped in half a bottle of her mother's favorite cologne. At first she scrubbed herself furiously, irritating
her skin. But finally she stopped, knowing she would never be
able to get cleaner than this again. She could not wash away
the thing they considered dirty, the thing that made them pronounce "girl" in the same way as the other four-letter words
they wrote on the wall in the alley; it was part of her, just as it
was part of her mother and Rose Griffin and Lucy Mae. She relaxed then because it was true that the boys in the alley did not
have a thing she wanted. She had what they wanted, and the
knowledge replaced her shame with a strange, calm feeling of
power.

After her bath she splashed on more cologne and spent 40 73
minutes on her makeup, erasing and retracing her eyebrows
six times until she was satisfied. She went to her mother's
room then and found the dress, finished and freshly pressed,
on its hanger.

When Mrs. Simmons came upstairs to help her daughter 74
she found her sitting on the bench before the vanity mirror as

if it were a throne. She looked young and arrogant and beautiful and perfect and cold.

"Why, you're dressed already," Mrs. Simmons said in surprise. While she stared, Judy rose with perfect, icy grace and glided to the center of the room. She stood there motionless as a mannequin.   75

"I want you to fix the hem, Mother," she directed. "It's still uneven in back."   76

Her mother went down obediently on her knees muttering, "It looks all right to me." She put in a couple of pins. "That better?"   77

"Yes," Judy said with a brief glance at the mirror. "You'll have to sew it on me, Mother. I can't take it off now. I'd ruin my hair."   78

Mrs. Simmons went to fetch her sewing things, returned, and surveyed her daughter. "You sure did a good job on yourself, I must say," she admitted grudgingly. "Can't find a thing to complain about. You'll look as good as anybody there."   79

"Of course, Mother," Judy said as Mrs. Simmons knelt and sewed. "I don't know what you were so worried about." Her secret feeling of confidence had returned, stronger than ever, but the evening ahead was no longer the vague girlish fantasy she had pictured on the wall; it had hard, clear outlines leading up to a definite goal. She would be the belle of the Ball because she knew more than Rose Griffin and her silly friends; more than her mother; more, even, than Lucy Mae, because she knew better than to settle for a mere pack of cigarettes.   80

"There," her mother said, breaking the thread. She got up. "I never expected to get you ready this early. Ernest Lee won't be here for another hour."   81

"That silly Ernest Lee," Judy said, with a new contempt in her young voice. Until tonight she had been pleased by the thought of going to the dance with Ernest Lee; he was nice, she felt comfortable with him, and he might even be the awe-struck boy of her dream. He was a dark, serious neighborhood boy who could not afford to go to college; Mrs. Simmons had reluctantly selected him to take Judy to the dance because all the Gay Charmers' sons were spoken for. Now, with an undertone of excitement, Judy said, "I'm going to ditch him after the first dance, Mother. You'll see. I'm going to come home with one of the college boys."   82

"It's very nice, Ernest Lee," she told him an hour later when he handed her the white orchid, "but it's rather small. I'm   83 gong to wear it on my wrist, if you don't mind." And then, dazzling him with a smile of sweetest cruelty, she stepped back and waited while he fumbled with the door.

"You know, Edward, I'm not worried about her any more," 84 Mrs. Simmons said to her husband after the children were gone. Her voice became harsh and grating. "Put down that paper and listen to me! Aren't you interested in your child?— That's better," she said as he complied meekly. "I was saying, I do believe she's learned what I've been trying to teach her, after all."

Discussion Questions

1. What type of person is Mrs. Simmons? What had she been trying to teach Judy?
2. What are the Gay Charmers? Why was it so important for Mrs. Simmons to join them?
3. What is Mrs. Simmons's relationship with her husband?
4. What effect does the boys' conversation with and about Lucy Mae have on Judy? How does Lucy Mae differ from Judy?
5. What is the significance of the wall?
6. What are the intraracial prejudices reflected in the story? What prejudice of her own does Judy acquire at the end of the story?
7. How does Hunter's use of comparison and contrast help the reader understand Judy's change in attitude?
8. To what extent does Hunter's use of dialogue add to the reader's understanding of the characters?

Writing Assignments

1. Write an essay describing a time when you gained a new awareness of something.
2. Write an essay comparing and/or contrasting your views on an issue with those of your parent(s).
3. Write an essay about your experiences with intraracial prejudice.

TRUE LOVE LOST AND FOUND

Charles W. Chesnutt

Charles Waddell Chesnutt (1858–1932), born in Cleveland, Ohio, and primarily self-educated, was a teacher and a principal in the public schools of North Carolina. He was admitted to the Ohio bar in 1887 and worked as a court reporter and a commercial stenographer. Hailed as a master craftsman of the short story, Chesnutt's works consist of two collections of short stories: The Conjure Woman *(1899) and* The Wife of His Youth and Other Stories of the Color Line *(1899), from which this excerpt is taken. He also wrote three novels:* The House Behind the Cedars *(1900),* The Marrow of Tradition *(1901), and* The Colonel's Dream *(1905). Chesnutt, considered the first African American writer of fiction whose work was generally critiqued without regard to race, wrote about the complexities of class and color during the Reconstruction period. A major theme of Chesnutt's works, as illustrated in the following excerpt, is the tragic situation of intraracial prejudice.*

Vocabulary

affinity	(2)	similarity, likeness
assail	(3)	attack
bulwark	(3)	defense, protection
prerequisite	(3)	required beforehand
servile	(3)	like slaves or servants
grosser	(3)	more wrong, more obscene
irreproachable	(5)	faultless
vivacity	(6)	liveliness
epoch	(7)	period of time
laxity	(7)	slackness
nether	(8)	lower
buxom	(10)	healthily plump and ample
brooch	(12)	ornamental pin with a clasp
countenance	(28)	face
emphatically	(33)	forcibly
incredulously	(39)	disbelievingly
mincing	(45)	dainty, short

I

Mr. Ryder was going to give a ball. There were several reasons   1
why this was an opportune time for such an event.

Mr. Ryder might aptly be called the dean of the Blue   2
Veins. The original Blue Veins were a little society of colored
persons organized in a certain Northern city shortly after the
war. Its purpose was to establish and maintain correct social
standards among a people whose social condition presented almost unlimited room for improvement. By accident, combined
perhaps with some natural affinity, the society consisted of individuals who were, generally speaking, more white than black.
Some envious outsider made the suggestion that no one was eligible for membership who was not white enough to show blue
veins. The suggestion was readily adopted by those who were
not of the favored few, and since that time the society, though
possessing a longer and more pretentious name, had been
known far and wide as the "Blue Vein Society," and its members as the "Blue Veins."

The Blue Veins did not allow that any such requirement   3
existed for admission to their circle, but, on the contrary, declared that character and culture were the only things considered; and that if most of their members were light-colored, it
was because such persons, as a rule, had had better opportunities to qualify themselves for membership. Opinions differed,
too, as to the usefulness of the society. There were those who
had been known to assail it violently as a glaring example of
the very prejudice from which the colored race had suffered
most; and later, when such critics had succeeded in getting on
the inside, they had been heard to maintain with zeal and
earnestness that the society was a lifeboat, an anchor, a bul-
wark and a shield,—a pillar of cloud by day and of fire by night,
to guide their people through the social wilderness. Another alleged prerequisite for Blue Vein membership was that of free
birth; and while there was really no such requirement, it is
doubtless true that very few of the members would have been
unable to meet it if there had been. If there were one or two of
the older members who had come up from the South and from
slavery, their history presented enough romantic circumstances to rob their servile origin of its grosser aspects.

While there were no such tests of eligibility, it is true   4
that the Blue Veins had their notions on these subjects, and

that not all of them were equally liberal in regard to the things they collectively disclaimed. Mr. Ryder was one of the most conservative. Though he had not been among the founders of the society, but had come in some years later, his genius for social leadership was such that he had speedily become its recognized adviser and head, the custodian of its standards, and the preserver of its traditions. He shaped its social policy, was active in providing for its entertainment, and when the interest fell off, as it sometimes did, he fanned the embers until they burst again into a cheerful flame.

There were still other reasons for his popularity. While he   5
was not as white as some of the Blue Veins, his appearance was such as to confer distinction upon them. His features were of a refined type, his hair was almost straight; he was always neatly dressed; his manners were irreproachable, and his morals above suspicion. He had come to Groveland a young man, and obtaining employment in the office of a railroad company as messenger had in time worked himself up to the position of stationery clerk, having charge of the distribution of the office supplies for the whole company. Although the lack of early training had hindered the orderly development of a naturally fine mind, it had not prevented him from doing a great deal of reading or from forming decidedly literary tastes. Poetry was his passion. He could repeat whole pages of the great English poets; and if his pronunciation was sometimes faulty, his eye, his voice, his gestures, would respond to the changing sentiment with a precision that revealed a poetic soul and disarmed criticism. He was economical, and had saved money; he owned and occupied a very comfortable house on a respectable street. His residence was handsomely furnished, containing among other things a good library, especially rich in poetry, a piano, and some choice engravings. He generally shared his house with some young couple, who looked after his wants and were company for him; for Mr. Ryder was a single man. In the early days of his connection with the Blue Veins he had been regarded as quite a catch, and young ladies and their mothers had manoeuvred with much ingenuity to capture him. Not, however, until Mrs. Molly Dixon visited Groveland had any woman ever made him wish to change his condition to that of a married man.

Mrs. Dixon had come to Groveland from Washington in the   6
spring, and before the summer was over she had won Mr. Ryder's heart. She possessed many attractive qualities. She was much younger than he; in fact, he was old enough to have been

her father, though no one knew exactly how old he was. She was whiter than he, and better educated. She had moved in the best colored society of the country, at Washington, and had taught in the schools of that city. Such a superior person had been eagerly welcomed to the Blue Vein Society, and had taken a leading part in its activities. Mr. Ryder had at first been attracted by her charms of person, for she was very good looking and not over twenty-five; then by her refined manners and the vivacity of her wit. Her husband had been a government clerk and at his death had left a considerable life insurance. She was visiting friends in Groveland, and, finding the town and the people to her liking, had prolonged her stay indefinitely. She had not seemed displeased at Mr. Ryder's attentions, but on the contrary had given him every proper encouragement; indeed, a younger and less cautious man would long since have spoken. But he had made up his mind, and had only to determine the time when he would ask her to be his wife. He decided to give a ball in her honor, and at some time during the evening of the ball to offer her his heart and hand. He had no special fears about the outcome, but, with a little touch of romance, he wanted the surroundings to be in harmony with his own feelings when he should have received the answer he expected.

Mr. Ryder resolved that this ball should mark an epoch in the social history of Groveland. He knew, of course,—no one could know better,—the entertainments that had taken place in past years, and what must be done to surpass them. His ball must be worthy of the lady whose honor it was to be given, and must, by the quality of its guests, set an example for the future. He had observed of late a growing liberality, almost a laxity, in social matters, even among members of his own set, and had several times been forced to meet in a social way persons whose complexions and callings in life were hardly up to the standard which he considered proper for the society to maintain. He had a theory of his own. 7

"I have no race prejudice," he would say, "but we people of mixed blood are ground between the upper and the nether millstone. Our fate lies between absorption by the white race and extinction in the black. The one doesn't want us yet, but may take us in time. The other would welcome us, but it would be for us a backward step. 'With malice towards none, with charity for all,' we must do the best we can for ourselves and those who are to follow us. Self-preservation is the first law of nature." 8

His ball would serve by its exclusiveness to counteract lev-   9
eling tendencies, and his marriage with Mrs. Dixon would help
to further the upward process of absorption he had been wishing and waiting for.

II

The ball was to take place on Friday night. The house had been   10
put in order, the carpets covered with canvas, the halls and
stairs decorated with palms and potted plants; and in the afternoon Mr. Ryder sat on his front porch, which the shade of a
vine running up over a wire netting made a cool and pleasant
lounging place. He expected to respond to the toast "The
Ladies" at the supper, and from a volume of Tennyson—his favorite poet—was fortifying himself with apt quotations. The volume was open at "A Dream of Fair Women." His eyes fell on
these lines, and he read them aloud to judge better of their effect:—

> At length I saw a lady within call,
>   Stiller than chisell'd marble, standing there;
> A daughter of the gods, divinely tall,
>   And most divinely fair.

He marked the verse, and turning the page read the stanza beginning,—

> O sweet pale Margaret,
> O rare pale Margaret.

He weighed the passage a moment, and decided that it would
not do. Mrs. Dixon was the palest lady he expected at the ball,
and she was of a rather ruddy complexion, and of lively disposition and buxom build. So he ran over the leaves until his eye
rested on the description of Queen Guinevere:—

> She seem'd a part of joyous Spring:
> A gown of grass-green silk she wore,
> Buckled with golden clasps before;
> A light-green tuft of plumes she bore
> Closed in a golden ring.

• • •

She look'd so lovely, as she sway'd
The rein with dainty finger-tips,
A man had given all other bliss,
And all his worldly worth for this,
To waste his whole heart in one kiss
Upon her perfect lips.

As Mr. Ryder murmured these words audibly, with an ap- 11
preciative thrill, he heard the latch of his gate click, and a light
footfall sounding on the steps. He turned his head, and saw a
woman standing before his door.

She was a little woman, not five feet tall, and proportioned 12
to her height. Although she stood erect, and looked around her
with very bright and restless eyes, she seemed quite old; for her
face was crossed and recrossed with a hundred wrinkles, and
around the edges of her bonnet could be seen protruding here
and there a tuft of short gray wool. She wore a blue calico gown
of ancient cut, a little red shawl fastened around her shoulders
with an old-fashioned brass brooch, and a large bonnet profusely ornamented with faded red and yellow artificial flowers.
And she was very black,—so black that her toothless gums, revealed when she opened her mouth to speak, were not red, but
blue. She looked like a bit of the old plantation life, summoned
up from the past by the wave of a magician's wand, as the
poet's fancy had called into being the gracious shapes of which
Mr. Ryder had just been reading.

He rose from his chair and came over to where she stood. 13
"Good-afternoon, madam," he said. 14
"Good-evenin', suh," she answered, ducking suddenly with 15
a quaint curtsy. Her voice was shrill and piping, but softened
somewhat by age. "Is dis yere whar Mistuh Ryduh lib, suh?"
she asked, looking around her doubtfully, and glancing into the
open windows, through which some of the preparations for the
evening were visible.

"Yes," he replied, with an air of kindly patronage, uncon- 16
sciously flattered by her manner. "I am Mr. Ryder. Did you
want to see me?"

"Yas, suh, ef I ain't 'sturbin' of you too much." 17

"Not at all. Have a seat over here behind the vine, where it 18
is cool. What can I do for you?"

"'Scuse me, suh," she continued, when she had sat down 19
on the edge of a chair, "'scuse me, suh. I's lookin' for my hus-

ban'. I heerd you wuz a big man an' had libbed heah a long
time, an' I 'lowed you wouldn't min' ef I'd come roun' an' ax you
ef you'd ever heerd of a merlatter man by de name er Sam Taylor 'quirin' roun' in de chu'ches ermongs' de people fer his wife
'Liza Jane?"

Mr. Ryder seemed to think for a moment.   20

"There used to be many such cases right after the war," he   21
said, "but it has been so long that I have forgotten them. There
are very few now. But tell me your story, and it may refresh my
memory."

She sat back farther in her chair so as to be more comfort-   22
able, and folded her withered hands in her lap.

"My name's 'Liza," she began, "'Liza Jane. W'en I wuz   23
young I us'ter b'long ter Marse Bob Smif, down in ole Missoura.
I wuz bawn down dere. W'en I wuz a gal I wuz married ter a
man named Jim. But Jim died, an' after dat I married a merlatter man named Sam Taylor. Sam wuz free-bawn, but his
mammy and daddy died, an' de w'ite folks 'prenticed him ter
my marster fer ter work fer 'im 'tel he wuz growed up. Sam
worked in de fiel', an' I wuz de cook. One day Ma'y Ann, ole
miss's maid, came rushin' out ter de kitchen, an' says she,
''Liza Jane, ole marse gwine sell yo' Sam down de ribber.'

"'Go way f'm yere,' says I; 'my husban' 's free!'   24

"'Don' make no diff'ence. I heerd ole marse tell ole miss he   25
wuz gwine take yo' Sam 'way wid 'im ter-morrow, fer he needed
money, an' he knowed whar he could git a t'ousan' dollats fer
Sam an' no questions axed.'

"W'en Sam come home f'm de fiel' dat night, I tole him   26
bout ole marse gwine steal 'im, an' Sam run erway. His time
wuz mos' up, an' he swo' dat w'en he wuz twenty-one he would
come back an' he'p me run erway, er else save up de money ter
buy my freedom. An' I know he'd 'a' done it, fer he thought a
heap er me, Sam did. But w'en he come back he didn' fin' me,
fer I wuzn' dere. Ole marse had heerd dat I warned Sam, so he
had me whip' an' sol' down de ribber.

"Den de wah broke out, an' w'en it wuz ober de cullud   27
folks wuz scattered. I went back ter de ole home; but Sam
wuzn' dere, an' I could n' l'arn nuffin' 'bout 'im. But I knowed
he'd be'n dere to look fer me an' had n' foun' me, an' had gone
erway ter hunt fer me.

"I's be'n lookin' fer 'im eber sence," she added simply, as   28
though twenty-five years were but a couple of weeks, "an' I
knows he's be'n lookin' fer me. Fer he sot a heap er sto' by me,

Sam did, an' I know he's be'n huntin' fer me all dese years,— 'less'n he's be'n sick er sump'n, so he could n' work er out'n his head, so he could n' 'member his promise. I went back down de ribber, fer I 'lowed he'd gone down dere lookin' for me. I's be'n ter Noo Orleens, an' Atlanty an' Charleston, an' Richmon'; an' w'en I'd be'n all ober de Souf I come ter de Norf. Fer I knows I'll fin' 'im some er dese days," she added softly, "'er he'll fin' me, an' den we'll bofe be as happy in freedom as we wuz in de ole days befo' de wah." A smile stole over her withered countenance as she paused a moment, and her bright eyes softened into a faraway look.

This was the substance of the old woman's story. She had 29
wandered a little here and there. Mr. Ryder was looking at her curiously when she finished.

"How have you lived all these years?" he asked. 30

"Cookin', suh. I's a good cook. Does you know anybody 31
w'at needs a good cook, suh? I's stoppin wid a cullud fam'ly roun' de corner yonder 'tel I kin git a place."

"Do you really expect to find your husband? He may be 32
dead long ago."

She shook her head emphatically. "Oh no, he ain't dead. 33
De signs an' de token tells me. I dremp three nights runnin' on'y dis las' week dat I foun' him."

"He may have married another woman. Your slave mar- 34
riage would not have prevented him, for you never lived with him after the war, and without that your marriage doesn't count."

"Wouldn' make no diff'ence wid Sam. He would n' marry 35
no yuther 'ooman 'tel he foun' out 'bout me. I knows it," she added. "Sump'n 's be'n tellin' me all dese years dat I's gwine fin' Sam 'fo' I dies."

"Perhaps he's outgrown you, and climbed up in the world 36
where he wouldn't care to have you find him."

"No, indeed, suh," she replied, "Sam ain' dat kin' er man. 37
He wuz good ter me, Sam wuz, but he wuzn' much good ter nobody e'se, fer he wuz one er de triflin'es' han's on de plantation. I 'spec's ter haf ter suppo't 'im w'en I fin' 'im, fer he nebber would work 'less'n he had ter. But den he wuz free, an' he didn' git no pay fer his work, an' I don' blame 'im much. Mebbe he's done better sence he run erway, but I ain' 'spectin' much."

"You may have passed him on the street a hundred times 38
during the twenty-five years and not have known him; time works great changes."

She smiled incredulously. "I'd know 'im 'mongs' a hund'ed   39
men. Fer dey wuzn' no yuther merlatter man like my man Sam,
an' I couldn' be mistook. I's toted his picture roun' wid me
twenty-five years."

"May I see it?" asked Mr. Ryder. "It might help me to re-   40
member whether I have seen the original."

As she drew a small parcel from her bosom he saw that it   41
was fastened to a string that went around her neck. Removing
several wrappers, she brought to light an old-fashioned daguerreotype[1] in a black case. He looked long and intently at
the portrait. It was faded with time, but the features were still
distinct, and it was easy to see what manner of man it had represented.

He closed the case, and with a slow movement handed it   42
back to her.

"I don't know of any man in town who goes by that name,"   43
he said, "nor have I heard of any one making such inquiries.
But if you will leave me your address, I will give the matter
some attention, and if I find out anything I will let you know."

She gave him the number of a house in the neighborhood,   44
and went away, after thanking him warmly.

He wrote the address on the fly-leaf of the volume of Ten-   45
nyson, and, when she had gone, rose to his feet and stood looking after her curiously. As she walked down the street with
mincing step, he saw several persons whom she passed turn
and look back at her with a smile of kindly amusement. When
she had turned the corner, he went upstairs to his bedroom,
and stood for a long time before the mirror of his dressing-case,
gazing thoughtfully at the reflection of his own face.

Discussion Questions

1. What was the Blue Vein Society? Why do you think Chesnutt
provides so much information about this society?
2. What type of person is Mr. Ryder?
3. What role did skin color play in the lives of African Americans
during this time? Has this role changed today? Why or why not?
4. Is it significant that Liza Jane has searched for her husband for
twenty-five years? Explain your answer.

---

[1] daguerreotype   (41)   A photograph made by an early method on a plate of
chemically treated metal or glass, named for French inventor L.J.M. Daguerre
(1789–1851).

5. How does Liza Jane characterize Sam? Can you guess who Sam really is?

6. To what extent does Chesnutt use comparison and contrast to develop the theme of the story?

7. To what extent does black dialect help the reader understand the character of Liza Jane?

Writing Assignments

1. Write an essay that describes how you treated someone after a long separation or how someone treated you after a long separation.

2. Write an essay illustrating the existence or nonexistence of intraracial prejudice today.

3. Write an essay about an incident you viewed one way in the past and have come to view differently now. Explain why you think your views have changed.

Student Essay:
BLACK IS BEAUTIFUL—ALL SHADES

Andrea Providence Robinson

Vocabulary

preferential (3)   showing that one favors something or someone
                        over another
illustrious (4)   brilliantly outstanding

Recently, while sitting in my doctor's waiting room, two dark-   1
skinned sisters were engaged in conversation. I overheard one
woman say, "I don't want my children to come out light." After
hearing this statement, I swelled with so much anger that I
could no longer bear to hear another word of their conversation. Without thinking, I immediately sprang up from my seat
and walked away. I was upset over the ignorance that still exists within our culture.

It really puzzles me, how we have gone as far as to create   2
stereotypes about one another—stereotypes that include making up such myths as "the blacker the berry, the sweeter the
juice," or as some women would believe, "All that men are interested in is light skin and long hair."

Many of the stereotypes of today date back to slavery   3
when the light-skinned slave children received preferential
treatment over the dark-skinned slave children. In the 1940s
anthropologists conducted studies to answer the question,
"Why are African American men seeking to marry lighter com-
plexioned women?" Well, times have certainly changed. We are
now more culturally aware of our history and have more pride
in it. Also, color barriers have become less a factor in entertainment, sports, and the workplace. But I ask, if times have
changed so much, then why is dark-skinned vs. light-skinned
still an issue? In today's black music videos, for example, the
love interest is usually a fair-skinned, long-haired, hazel-eyed
black woman. We watch these videos and subconsciously allow
them to arouse resentment against each other's skin color.

We cannot allow the media and others to have such a pro-   4
found impression on our feelings about one another. Instead of
indulging ourselves in insignificant concerns such as skin
color, we must embrace our rich and illustrious culture and

celebrate the beauty of the variety of shades our culture has to offer—like that little chocolate-complexioned boy who lives down the street, that caramel cream–colored teenage girl who works at the mall, or that eggshell-complexioned woman who watches the neighborhood children.

Let us not engage in name calling, such as "high-yellow," 5
"redbone," "jiggaboo," and "wannabee." These names, whether we choose to realize it or not, can be degrading. Put simply, they can hurt.

We must educate our children that no matter what shade 6
their skin is, they are beautiful, because "black is beautiful." Let us teach them to be proud of their culture and to show respect for one another, regardless of complexion. Let us teach them love, instead of hate; for it is this love that will unite our communities and make them stand strong.

So now I would ask that woman in the doctor's waiting 7
room, "Would you sell yourself short by passing up a nice light-skinned brother who would love you and respect you just as a dark-skinned brother would? If it happens that you have a light-skinned child, would you love him or her any less than if he or she were dark-skinned?" Well, my sister, I can answer that question, for in the final analysis, color makes no difference because "black *is* beautiful—all shades."

Discussion Questions

1. What is the author's primary argument?
2. What are some stereotypes that exist concerning African American skin color?
3. According to the author, where do these stereotypes originate?
4. Why is skin color still an issue among African Americans?
5. What solution does the author propose?
6. What rhetorical strategies does Robinson use in this essay? Support your answer.
7. Why is the title an effective one for this essay?

Writing Assignments

1. Write an essay describing an incident of color discrimination that happened to you or to someone you know.
2. In an essay, explain your own observations regarding color prejudice.

22

Supplemental Readings

LETTER TO THOMAS JEFFERSON

Benjamin Banneker

The son of ex-slave parents, Benjamin Banneker (1731–1806) was born free in Baltimore County, Maryland. His grandmother taught him to read, and he went on to become a mathematician, naturalist, astronomer, inventor, poet, and urban planner. With his knowledge of astronomy, Banneker compiled an almanac for the year 1792. Because of his knowledge of civil engineering, President George Washington appointed him to a commission to lay out the city of Washington, D.C. Despite all of his accomplishments, and those of other African Americans, there were prominent white statesmen and philosophers who spoke and wrote about the African American's intellectual inferiority. One of these statesmen was Thomas Jefferson, who in his "Notes on Virginia" wrote that "in reason" African Americans were "much inferior." It is in response to Jefferson's "Notes" that Banneker wrote the following letter to Jefferson on August 19, 1791.

Vocabulary

prepossession	(1)	attitude
attested	(2)	affirmed, proven to be true
censure	(2)	an expression of blame or disapproval
calamities	(3)	disasters
eradicate	(4)	erase
concurrent	(4)	in agreement with
solicitous	(6)	anxious and concerned
diffusion	(6)	the act of pouring out or scattering about
degradation	(6)	disgrace
thraldom	(7)	enslavement
fruition	(7)	pleasure
fortitude	(8)	endurance or courage
abhorrence	(9)	hatred
benevolence	(10)	goodwill
impartial	(10)	unprejudiced
imbibed	(11)	absorbed into the mind
ardently	(12)	eagerly, enthusiastically
assiduous	(13)	hardworking, devoted

Maryland, Baltimore County
Near Ellicotts' Lower Mills, August 19th, 1791

Thomas Jefferson, Secretary of State,

Sir:—I am fully sensible of the greatness of that freedom, 1
which I take with you on the present occasion, a liberty which
seemed to me scarcely allowable, when I reflected on that distinguished and dignified station in which you stand, and the
almost general prejudice and prepossession which is so prevalent in the world against those of my complexion.

I suppose it is a truth too well attested to you, to need a 2
proof here, that we are a race of beings who have long laboured
under the abuse and censure of the world, that we have long
been considered rather as brutish than human, and scarcely
capable of mental endowments.

Sir, I hope I may safely admit, in consequence of that re- 3
port which hath reached me, that you are a man far less inflex-
ible in sentiments of this nature than many others, that you
are measurably friendly and well disposed towards us, and that
you are willing and ready to lend your aid and assistance to
our relief, from those many distresses and numerous calami-
ties, to which we are reduced.

Now, sir, if this is founded in truth, I apprehend you will 4
readily embrace every opportunity to eradicate that train of

absurd and false ideas and opinions, which so generally prevails with respect to us, and that your sentiments are concurrent with mine, which are that one universal Father hath given Being to us all, and that he hath not only made us all of one flesh, but that he hath also without partiality afforded us all the same sensations, and endued us all with the same faculties, and that however variable we may be in society or religion, however diversified in situation or colour, we are all of the same family, and stand in the same relation to him.

Sir, if these are sentiments of which you are fully persuaded, I hope you cannot but acknowledge, that it is the indispensable duty of those who maintain for themselves the rights of human nature, and who profess the obligations of christianity, to extend their power and influence to the relief of every part of the human race, from whatever burden or oppression they may unjustly labour under, and this I apprehend a full conviction of the truth and obligation of these principles should lead all to. 5

Sir, I have long been convinced that if your love for yourselves and for those inesteemable laws, which preserve to you the rights of human nature, was found on sincerity, you could not but be solicitous that every individual of whatever rank or distinction, might with you equally enjoy the blessings thereof, neither could you rest satisfied, short of the most active diffusion of your exertions in order to their promotions from any state of degradation, to which the unjustifiable cruelty and barbarism of men have reduced them. 6

Sir, I freely and cheerfully acknowledge that I am of the African race, and in that colour which is natural to them of the deepest dye, and it is under a sense of the most profound gratitude to the Supreme Ruler of the universe that I now confess to you that I am not under that state of tyrannical thraldom and inhuman captivity to which too many of my brethren are doomed; but that I have abundantly tasted of the fruition of those blessings which proceed from that free and unequalled liberty with which you are favoured and which, I hope you will willingly allow you have received from the immediate hand of that Being, from whom proceedeth every good and perfect gift. 7

Sir, suffer me to recall to your mind that time in which the arms and tyranny of the British Crown were exerted with every powerful effort in order to reduce you to a State of Servitude, look back I entreat you on the variety of dangers to which you were exposed; reflect on that time in which every human aid 8 appeared unavailable, and in which even hope and fortitude wore the aspect of inability to the conflict and you cannot but be led to a serious and grateful sense of your miraculous and providential preservation; you cannot but acknowledge that the present freedom and tranquility which you enjoy you have mercifully received and that it is the peculiar blessing of Heaven.

This sir, was a time in which you clearly saw into the injustice of a state of slavery and in which you had just apprehensions of the horrors of its condition, it was now, sir, that your abhorrence thereof was so excited, that you publicly held forth this true and valuable doctrine, which is worthy to be recorded and remembered in all succeeding ages. "We hold these truths to be self-evident, that all men are created equal, and that they are endowed by their creator with certain unalienable rights, that among these are life, liberty and the pursuit of happiness." 9

Here, sir, was a time in which your tender feelings for yourselves had engaged you thus to declare, you were then impressed with proper ideas of the great valuation of liberty and the free possession of those blessings to which you were entitled by nature; but, sir, how pitiable is it to reflect that although you were so fully convinced of the benevolence of the Father of mankind and of his equal and impartial distribution of those rights and privileges which he had conferred upon them, that you should at the same time counteract his mercies in detaining by fraud and violence so numerous a part of my brethren under groaning captivity and cruel oppression, that you should at the same time be found guilty of that most criminal act which you professedly detested in others with respect to yourselves. 10

Sir, I suppose that your knowledge of the situation of my brethren is too extensive to need a recital here; neither shall I presume to prescribe methods by which they may be relieved, otherwise than by recommending to you and all others to wean yourselves from those narrow prejudices which you have imbibed with respect to them and as Job proposed to his friends, "put your souls in their souls stead," thus shall your hearts be enlarged with kindness and benevolence towards them, and thus shall you need neither the direction of myself or others, in what manner to proceed herein. 11

And now, sir, although my sympathy and affection for my brethren hath caused my enlargement thus far, I ardently hope that your candour and generosity will plead with you in my 12 behalf when I make known to you that it was not originally my design; but that having taken up my pen in order to direct to you as a present, a copy of an almanac, which I have calculated for the succeeding year, I was unexpectedly and unavoidably led thereto.

This calculation, sir, is the production of my arduous 13 study in this my advanced stage of life; for having long had unbounded desires to become acquainted with the secrets of nature, I have had to gratify my curiosity herein through my own assiduous application to astronomical study, in which I need not to recount to you the many difficulties and disadvantages which I have had to encounter.

And although I had almost declined to make my calcula- 14 tion for the ensuing year, in consequence of that time which I had allotted therefor being taken up at the Federal Territory by the request of Mr. Andrew Ellicott, yet finding myself under several engagements to printers of this state, to whom I had communicated my design, on my return to my place of residence I industriously applied myself thereto which I hope I have accomplished with correctness and accuracy, a copy of which I have taken the liberty to direct to you and which I humbly request you will favorably receive. Although you may have the opportunity of perusing it after its publication yet I chose to send it to you in manuscript previous thereto that you might not only have an earlier inspection but that you might also view it in my own handwriting.

And now, sir, I shall conclude and subscribe myself, with 15 the most profound respect, your most obedient humble servant.

B. Banneker

Discussion Questions

1. What is the purpose of Benjamin Banneker's letter to Thomas Jefferson?
2. Why does Banneker ask Jefferson to remember the time when Jefferson and the other colonists were considered British subjects?
3. Why does Banneker remind Jefferson that all humankind is created by God?
4. Why did Banneker give Jefferson an almanac that Banneker had written?

5. Why does Banneker make reference to the Declaration of Independence?

6. What is the tone of Banneker's letter?

7. How does Banneker's use of illustration and comparison and contrast help strengthen his argument?

8. What do you think of the letter format as a structural device for conveying Banneker's ideas?

Writing Assignments

1. Write an essay arguing that intelligence is determined primarily by opportunities and environment, not by one's race.

2. Write a letter to a friend, group, or newspaper editor voicing your concern about a particular issue.

3. In an essay, discuss the ways in which racism is rationalized or accepted.

RLACK COMEDY, WHITE REALITY

Jannette Dates

Jannette Dates (1939–   ) is associate dean of the Howard University School of Communications. She is co-author of Split Image: African-Americans in the Mass Media *(1990), from which this excerpt is taken. In this selection, Dates analyzes African American television shows of the 1970s and how white Americans perceived them.*

Vocabulary

frugal	(1)	thrifty
vignette	(2)	sketch, picture
outlandish	(3)	absurd, bizarre
racy	(3)	coarse, suggestive
satirical	(3)	sarcastic, mocking
infused	(4)	filled
nuances	(4)	subtle changes
nouveau riche	(5)	the recent rich
acumen	(5)	mental sharpness
redressing	(5)	making up for
palatable	(5)	acceptable
jaded	(5)	tired, worn out
protagonists	(6)	main characters
aberration	(6)	departure from the normal
innocuous	(7)	harmless
emasculated	(7)	weak, powerless
subversive	(7)	intending to overthrow
quintessential	(7)	ultimate
apex	(7)	peak
culmination	(7)	highest point
subliminal	(8)	subconscious
peripheral	(9)	outside, external

1

Television viewers' perceptions about African Americans changed during the 1960s as the civil rights story unfolded at dinnertime each day. Moreover, law and order and the "silent" majority were much discussed by those in the Nixon White House of the late 1960s and early 1970s. Then, between 1972 and 1979, Richard Nixon was forced to resign as president of the country, Gerald Ford served out Nixon's term, and Jimmy Carter was elected to a single term in office. When "Good Times" first aired at this point, the civil rights era was drawing to a close. The series was introduced to American viewers by its producers as a sympathetic, "authentic," and realistic portrayal of the black man's plight. The setting in the series established the environment as a lower-class, housing projects apartment, where the frugal, conscientious mother, Florida (played by Esther Rolle, who was formerly the maid on "Maude"), used curtains behind which she hid clothes and household items. One room served this family as the entrance area, living room, and the dining-kitchen area. The three bedrooms were out of most camera shots, as large windows allowed suggestions of daylight or nighttime into the living room-kitchen area. A desk and chair in one corner were surrounded by boxes, probably used to store family belongings. When the series premiered, Esther Rolle was the star. As the scripts developed, however, Jimmie Walker (J.J.), the older son, eclipsed Rolle (Florida) and John Amos (James), as he caught on with teenage viewers who often influenced their parents' viewing patterns.

Though the setting was a lower-class, poor neighborhood, the values and beliefs expressed in "Good Times" were from middle America. In the segment "J.J.'s Eighteenth Birthday," for example, the worldly character Willona, with snapping fingers and "I know the score" glances, stated, "When I was twenty-five, I decided to blow out the candles, freeze the cake, and stop the clock," as J.J.'s parents manipulated their plastic money to try to give him a worthy eighteenth-birthday celebration. Willona, established as good-hearted, represented a lower-class figure, but in her the writers created a contradictory image. Viewers were never quite sure whether she was a swinger or a middle-class striver fallen on bad times, who was forced to live in "the projects." The "J.J.'s Eighteenth Birthday" episode could have evolved into an authentic vignette about black culture at the lower socioeconomic level, but instead the plot developed in the "usual" (white, middle-class) style. For example, for this celebration everyone came in changed clothes, "dressed up" for the occasion, and helped prepare J.J's favorite foods. After eating, they "moved to the living room," which was two steps from the kitchen table, for coffee and cake. Few people would act this way in this setting.

The comedy of "Sanford and Son" was based on the assumption that the characters lacked intelligence. It was a modern version of "Amos 'n' Andy," featuring outlandish (though often funny) plots and one-dimensional clown characters. Redd Foxx was a well-known stand-up comedian from the nightclub circuit. He had built up a strong following among black audiences. His material often featured racy, off-color humor with much profanity. Like Nipsey Russell, a comedian who played minor roles in other television programs and was Foxx's contemporary, and Richard Pryor, another major comedian from television and film, Foxx had used racial incidents as a basis for much of his satirical humor. When he was signed to play Fred on "Sanford and Sons," black viewers anticipated and received the type of performances from Foxx that they expected, with some important alterations.

Fred Sanford was a stubborn bully who dominated others 4 with his sharp tongue and ever-present anger. Sanford seemed to be angry at anyone who intruded on his turf, from his dead wife's sister to any nonblack who entered his domain, a junkyard where he and his son acquired and recycled society's discards. This series was not original to America, however. The story concept was imported from a popular British series entitled "Steptoe and Son." The American story lines were sometimes infused with African American cultural nuances, but the basic themes were created by white producers and writers, based on the British model. Again, viewers saw African American characters whose values and outlook were shaped and designed by outsiders to their culture.

"The Jeffersons" began as a spinoff from "All in the Family." George Jefferson was cast in the mold of the freed, corrupt, black legislators of the film "Birth of a Nation," who were depicted as arrogant and idiotic. The audience is asked to laugh at Jefferson's antics and his basic insecurity without unconsciously making an association with his blackness. Obviously this is a difficult feat to accomplish. "The Jeffersons" dealt with middle-class strivers who happened to be black. When it was originally broadcast, the theme celebrated the arrival of the nouveau riche black middle class. George Jefferson, characterized by producers as a loudmouthed braggart, spoke a great deal about "honkies" and "whities" while Louise, his wife, tried to appease him and smooth the ruffled feathers of others. Usually, the plots centered on George's attempts to climb the social ladder or make more money, with some note made of how difficult it was for those of African descent to move up in American society. The humor and warmth of the show often came from Louise's methods of controlling George and the problems he caused. Louise Jefferson, though submissive to a degree, exercised great influence over George because, no matter what the conflict, George was never right. Even in the early episodes, though George was recognized as having exceptional business acumen, those skills were never transferred into his personal family relationships. This family was seldom portrayed as engaging in group activities or working toward a collective goal. In a 1983 article in the journal *Channels*, columnist William Henry noted that "The Jeffersons" appealed to white Americans because they represented African Americans who had "made it." "The Jeffersons" was the fulfillment of the American dream. Henry thought that viewers "yearned to believe that a social revolution had been won," and that this somehow freed white Americans from redressing any more grievances which African Americans might have said were due. He went on to argue that though George Jefferson was a counterpart to Archie Bunker, the distinct difference between the two men's situations made George a palatable character to white viewers. He noted that Archie was the master in his own home while George was not ("George's wife outmaneuvered, out foxed and out whoofed him, constantly"). Archie was taken seriously whereas George was not (other characters tried to reason with Archie about his bigotry, while George was ignored or laughed at), and Archie had the respect of his household, while George did not. For example, George constantly battled with his maid over who was really master. In the early years of "The Jeffersons," Lear developed George's character in the manner described above in an attempt to bring to viewers' consciousness some of the same social issues generated by the Archie Bunker character, seen this time through the eyes of a counterpart in the black community—George Jefferson. The Jefferson character, like Bunker, was a flawed person who tried to live life on his own terms, marching to his own drummer and subject to insecurities and human frailties. Lear thus attempted to make viewers empathize and identify with a black person similar in human strengths and failings to themselves. He succeeded with both characters, by touching the pulse of an America that had become jaded by post-Vietnam blues—partially because of ambivalent feelings about the conflict itself and partially because of their loss of faith in the country's leadership. Americans were no longer idealistic about the nation. Thus, Lear's comedies reflected a "tell it like it is" philosophy of life that featured imperfect characters and realistic problems.

A 1974 article by Eugenia Collier, a college professor and   6
writer, entitled "Black Shows for White Viewers," compared two
of the highly rated television series featuring African Americans
in prime time. She concluded that "Sanford and Son" was appealing because viewers could laugh *at* weak people in order to
feel good about themselves, whereas viewers of "Good Times"
laughed *with* strong survivors. She argued that "Good Times"
had appeal because of the universal attractiveness of protagonists pitted against strong outside forces that make courage,
resourcefulness, and intelligence essential to survival. She believed that viewers were enriched, made wiser and more humane, by their experiences with "Good Times" but were diminished by their experiences with "Sanford and Son" because the
latter program focused on the baser instincts—trickery, ignorance, naïveté, and mental aberration.

"Benson" fit the pattern that scripted African American   7
male characters as innocuous true-believers in the system,
who supported, defended, and nurtured mainstream, middle-
class American values, interests, concerns, and even faults.
Benson was thus an emasculated, nonthreatening, "acceptable" black male. A spinoff from the highly successful series of
the seventies, "Soap," the "Benson" series featured Robert Guillaume as Benson Dubois, a witty and quietly subversive but
dependable confidant of the governor of some mythical state.
Benson began the series as the head housekeeper but was later
promoted to a position of Lieutenant Governor. According to sociologist Herman Gray, Robert Guillaume was "attractive and
likeable, cool under pressure, and perhaps the quintessential
black middle class professional." The Benson character was the
apex of all the servant and helping roles that black actors had
played historically in television and the movies. There was,
however, one major qualification—"Benson was uniquely modern—sophisticated, competent and arrogant! He openly maintained his integrity and his pride week after week [though] . . .
the posture of servitude was maintained." In this sense, Gray
believed, Benson represented the culmination of a white view of
acceptable African American males.

The adoption of black male children into middle-class   8
white American homes on television allowed creators opportunities to send conscious and subconscious messages to viewers
about molding and controlling the minds and hearts of young
African American males, possibly to make them more acceptable to whites. In the situation comedy "Webster," Emmanuel

Lewis played the black adopted son of a white couple in a cross between a kid show and a family comedy. Like "Different Strokes," the hit NBC series with a similar theme, the subliminal message the "Webster" series sent out was that black people did not involve themselves with their own people's children when their parents died. This circumstance could be seen as an advantage since white foster parents could then socialize the youngsters into the "real" American way. Even visits from grandparents or cousins, or any evidence of their concern about the youngsters' welfare, were not central to the theme of either of these two series during their first season. Beginning with the second season, Ben Vereen was featured as Webster's uncle, who vainly attempted to adopt the youngster and visited him on occasion. In reality, however, the black extended family often had black women who reared generation after generation of other people's children—grandchildren, cousins, nephews and nieces, and so on—"because their own folks were gone or dead."

"The White Shadow," an earlier series that had aired from 1979 to 1981, had featured a white basketball coach/physical education teacher and his predominantly black high-school team. "The White Shadow," "Webster," and "Different Strokes" each treated the issue of race as peripheral, as the frame of reference for addressing other issues where race was simply another individual difference rather than a social or public issue. Race as a central theme of concern in American society was ignored or broken down into simplified components and then resolved with ease. Like early television series such as "East Side, West Side," usually the problems raised on television, even those involving African Americans and particularly evident in these programs, were resolved by a white male problem-solver. 9

Discussion Questions

1. Why did television viewers' perceptions of African Americans change during the 1960s?

2. According to Dates, how did *Good Times* represent middle-class values, even though it featured a poor, lower-class family?

3. What was the assumption on which the comedy of *Sanford and Son* was based?

4. According to Dates, what was the appeal of *The Jeffersons* to white America?

5. Why does Dates describe Benson as "an emasculated, nonthreatening, 'acceptable' black male"?

6. What was the subliminal message sent out by *Webster* and *Different Strokes*?

7. How does Dates use classification to discuss the various television shows?

8. Dates chose not to write a formal conclusion to this essay. What type of ending would you suggest for this essay?

Writing Assignments

1. Write an essay in which you disagree with one of Dates's theories about one or more of the television shows discussed in the essay.

2. Write an essay comparing one of the shows discussed in the essay with a current African American television show.

3. Write an essay analyzing one or more current African American television shows, and discuss the basis for your analysis.

REQUIEM BEFORE REVIVAL

Gwendolyn Brooks

At seventy-seven, Gwendolyn Brooks (1917–   ) is still on the lecture circuit, conducting creative writing workshops at colleges and universities throughout the United States. Perhaps what is most remarkable about the African American poet is not her ability to learn and to grow from younger poets such as Haki R. Madhubuti (don l. lee), but her untiring, selfless efforts to spark young people to write creatively. Since the publication of her A Street in Bronzeville *(1945),* Brooks *has published many volumes of poetry, including* Annie Allen *(1949),* Riot *(1969),* Becomings *(1975),* Primer for Blacks *(1980), and* Blacks *(1987). In all of her volumes, she offers snapshot descriptions of poor, frustrated, or troubled African Americans living in urban areas in the North. In 1950, she became the first African American to receive the Pulitzer Prize for poetry. Currently, she directs the Gwendolyn Brooks Center for Black Literature and Creative Writing in Chicago. In the following selection, Brooks attempts to persuade African Americans that they must reclaim their identity as a proud and powerful people.*

Vocabulary

assimilationist	(1)	one who adapts himself or herself to a particular society without any protest
inarticulate	(1)	unable to express oneself
befuddles	(3)	thoroughly confuses
mesmerized	(6)	fascinated or hypnotized by something or someone
fervently	(6)	eagerly, intensely
iterated	(6)	repeated
efficacy	(6)	effectiveness; the power to bring about a desired result
vertigo	(6)	confusion

We still need the essential Black statement of defense and definition. Of course, we are happiest when that statement is not dulled by assimilationist urges, secret or overt. However,   1 there is in "the souls of Black Folk"—even when inarticulate and crippled—a yearning toward Black validation.

To be Black is rich, is subtle, is nourishing and a nutrient 2 in the universe. What could be nourishing about aiming against your nature?

I give whites big credit. They have never tried to be any- 3 thing but what they are. They have been and will be everlastingly proud proud proud to be white. It has never occurred to them that there has been or ever will be ANYthing better than, nor one zillionth as good as, being white. They have an overwhelming belief in their validity. Not in their "virtue," for they are shrewdly capable of a very cold view of *that*. But their validity they salute with an amazing innocence—yes, a genuine innocence, the brass of which befuddles most of the rest of us in the world because we have allowed ourselves to be hypnotized by its shine.

In the throat of the Town Crier throbs the Power. 4

If you yell long enough and shrilly enough "I'M GREAT!," 5 ultimately you will convince your listeners. Or you will be thrown into the insane asylum. The scant Caucasian race has escaped the insane asylum and has gone on to *virtually* unquestioned "glory"—has achieved virtually unchallenged italics.

Swarms of Blacks have not understood the mechanics of 6 the proceeding, and they trot along to the rear of Pied Piper whites, their strange gazes fixed on, and worshiping, each switch of the white rear, their mesmerized mentalities fervently and firmly convinced that there is nothing better than quaking in that tail's wake. They do not see that the secret of Supremacy success is—you just go ahead and impress yourself on the world whether the world wants you or not. They have not seen some Announcements register just *because* they are iterated and iterated and iterated—the oppressed consciousness finally sinking back and accepting the burden of relentless assault. Though eager to imitate any other property of the white compulsion, much of the Black swarm has refused to imitate the efficacy of Iteration; and the fruit of that Black refusal is chaos, is vertigo, is self-swallow, or self-shrivel and decline.

I continue my old optimism. In spite of all the disappoint- 7 ment and disillusionment and befuddlement out there, I go on believing that the Weak among us will, finally, perceive the impressiveness of our numbers, perceive the quality and legitimacy of our essence, and take sufficient, indicated steps toward definition, clarification.

Discussion Questions

1. How does Brooks describe African Americans?
2. What do you think is the meaning of the following line: "In the throat of the Town Crier throbs the Power"?
3. Why do you think Brooks capitalizes words such as "Power" and "Folk"? Why do you think some words are in all capital letters?
4. What does Brooks see as the main strength of white America?
5. What does Brooks say is the secret of supremacy?
6. What is the meaning of the title?
7. How does Brooks use comparison and contrast to strengthen her argument?
8. What is thesis? Is it stated or implied?

Writing Assignments

1. Write an essay describing what it means to be a part of your racial or ethnic group.
2. There is an old proverb: "As one thinks, so is he [or she]." Write an essay in which you agree or disagree with the proverb. Explain why or why not.
3. Write an essay discussing a particular strength you have observed in some racial or ethnic group other than your own.

WITHOUT DAD

Bebe Moore Campbell

Bebe Moore Campbell (1950–   ) is an essayist, novelist, and free-lance writer. She is a frequent contributor to Morning Edition *on National Public Radio (NPR) and has also contributed to the* New York Times, *the* Washington Post *and the* Los Angeles Times. *She has written the following books:* Successful Women, Angry Men: Backlash in the Two-Career Marriage *(1987);* Sweet Summer: Growing Up With and Without My Dad *(1989), from which the following excerpt was taken;* Your Blues Ain't Like Mine *(1992); and* Brothers and Sisters *(1994). The following selection shows how deeply a young girl is affected by the absence of a father in her home.*

Vocabulary

allure	(5)	charm, glamour
cajoled	(6)	urged
distaff	(6)	female, maternal
hapless	(9)	unfortunate, pitiful
cootie	(10)	slang for lice
buttressed	(11)	reinforced
hordes	(11)	crowds
unremitting	(12)	constant, unending
nonplussed	(35)	amazed, dumbfounded

The red bricks of 2239 North 16th Street melded into the uniformity of look-alike doors, windows, and brownstone-steps. From the outside our rowhouse looked the same as any other. When I was a toddler, the similarity was unsettling. The family story was that my mother and I were out walking on the street one day when panic rumbled through me. "Where's our house? Where's our house?" I cried, grabbing my mother's hand.

My mother walked me to our house, pointed to the numbers painted next to the door. "Twenty-two thirty-nine," she said, slapping the wall. "This is our house."

Much later I learned that the real difference was inside. 3

In my house there was no morning stubble, no long johns 4
or Fruit of the Loom on the clothesline, no baritone hollering
for keys that were sitting on the table. There was no beer in the
refrigerator, no ball game on TV, no loud cussing. After dark
the snores that emanated from the bedrooms were subtle, ladylike, little moans really.

Growing up, I could have died from overexposure to femi- 5
ninity. Women ruled at 2239. A grandmother, a mother, occasionally an aunt, grown-up girlfriends from at least two generations, all the time rubbing up against me, fixing my food,
running my bathwater, telling me to sit still and be good in
those grown-up, girly-girl voices. Chanel and Prince Matcha-
belli wafting through the bedrooms. Bubble bath and Jergens
came from the bathroom, scents unbroken by aftershave, macho beer breath, a good he-man funk. I remember a house full
of 'do rags and rollers, the soft, sweet allure of Dixie peach and
bergamot;[1] brown-skinned queens wearing pastel housecoats
and worn-out size six-and-a-half flip-flops that slapped softly
against the wood as the royal women climbed the stairs at
night carrying their paperbacks to bed.

The outside world offered no retreat. School was taught by 6
stern, old-maid white women with age spots and merciless gray
eyes; ballet lessons, piano lessons, Sunday school, and choir
were all led by colored sisters with a hands-on-their-hips attitude who cajoled and screeched in distaff tongues.

And what did they want from me, these Bosoms? Achieve- 7
ment! This desire had nothing to do with the pittance they collected from the Philadelphia Board of Education or the few dollars my mother paid them. Pushing little colored girls forward
was in their blood. They made it clear: a life of white picket
fences and teas was for other girls to aspire to. I was to *do*
something. And if I didn't climb willingly up their ladder, they'd
drag me to the top. Rap my knuckles hard for not practicing.
Make me lift my leg until I wanted to die. Stay after school and
write "I will listen to the teacher" five hundred times. They were
not playing. "Obey them," my mother commanded.

When I entered 2B—the Philadelphia school system di- 8
vided grades into A and B—in September 1957, I sensed immediately that Miss Bradley was not a woman to be challenged.

[1]Dixie peach and bergamot　　(5)　　Refers to African American hair conditioning products.

She looked like one of those evil old spinsters Shirley Temple[2] was always getting shipped off to live with; she was kind of hefty, but so tightly corseted that if she happened to grab you or if you fell against her during recess, it felt as if you were bouncing into a steel wall. In reality she was a sweet lady who was probably a good five years past her retirement age when I wound up in her class. Miss Bradley remained at Logan for one reason and one reason only: she was dedicated. She wanted her students to learn! learn! learn! Miss Bradley was halfway sick, hacking and coughing her lungs out through every lesson, spitting the phlegm into fluffy white tissues from the box on her desk, but she was *never* absent. Each day at three o'clock she kissed each one of her "little pupils" on the cheek, sending a faint scent of Emeraude home with us. Her rules for teaching children seemed to be: love them; discipline them; reward them; and make sure they are clean.

Every morning she ran a hygiene check on the entire   9
class. She marched down the aisle like a stormtrooper, rummaging through the ears of hapless students, checking for embedded wax. She looked under our fingernails for dirt. Too bad on you if she found any. Once she made David, a stringy-haired white boy who thought Elvis Presley was a living deity and who was the most notorious booger-eater in the entire school, go the the nurse's office to have the dirt cleaned from under his fingernails. Everybody knew that what was under David's fingernails was most likely dried-up boogies and not dirt, but nobody said anything.

If she was death on dirt and earwax, Miss Bradley's spe-   10
cialty was head-lice patrol. Down the aisles she stomped in her black Enna Jettick shoes,[3] stopping at each student to part strands of blond, brown, or dark hair, looking for cooties. Miss Bradley would flip through plaits, curls, kinks—the woman was relentless. I always passed inspection. Nana put enough Nu Nile in my hair to suffocate any living creature that had the nerve to come tipping up on my scalp. Nu Nile was the official cootie killer. I was clean, wax-free, bug-free, and smart. The folder inside my desk contained a stack of spelling and arith- metic papers with A's emblazoned across the top, gold stars in

---

[2]Shirley Temple   (8)   Famous child actor of the 1930s and 1940s.
[3]Enna Jettick shoes   (10)   Brand name of women's shoes.

the corner. Miss Bradley always called on me. She sent me to run errands for her too. I was her pet.

When Mrs. Clark, my piano teacher and my mother's good friend, told my mother that Logan Elementary School was accepting children who didn't live in the neighborhood, my mother immediately enrolled Michael and later me. "It's not crowded and it's mixed," she told a nodding, smiling Nana. The fact that Logan was integrated was the main reason Michael and I were sent there. Nana and Mommy, like most upwardly mobile colored women, believed that to have the same education as a white child was the first step up the rocky road to success. This viewpoint was buttressed by the fact that George Washington Carver, my neighborhood school, was severely overcrowded. Logan was just barely integrated, with only a handful of black kids thrown in with hordes of square-jawed, pale-eyed second-generation Ukrainians whose immigrant parents and grandparents populated the neighborhood near the school. There were a few dark-haired Jews and aristocratic-looking WASPs too. My first day in kindergarten it was Nana who enthusiastically grabbed Michael's and my hands, pulling us away from North Philly's stacked-up rowhouses, from the hucksters whose wagons bounced down the streets with trucks full of ripe fruits and vegetables, from the street-corner singers and jitterbugs who filled my block with all-day doo-wahs. It was Nana who resolutely walked me past the early-morning hordes of colored kids heading two blocks away to Carver Elementary School, Nana who pulled me by the hand and led me in another direction.

We went underground at the Susquehanna and Dauphin subway station, leaving behind the unremitting asphalt and bricks and the bits of paper strewn in the streets above us. We emerged at Logan station, where sunlight, brilliant red and pink roses and yellow chrysanthemums, and neatly clipped lawns and clean streets startled me. There were robins and blue jays flying overhead. The only birds in my neighborhood were sparrows and pigeons. Delivering me at the schoolyard, Nana firmly cupped my chin with her hand as she bent down to instruct me. "Your mother's sending you up here to learn, so you do everything your teacher tells you to, okay?" To Michael she turned and said, "You're not up here to be a monkey on a stick." Then to both of us: "Don't talk. Listen. Act like you've got some home training. You've got as much brains as anybody

11

12

up here. Do you know that? All right now. Make Nana proud of you."

A month after I returned from Pasquotank County,[4] I sat   13
in Miss Bradley's classroom on a rainy Monday watching her
write spelling words on the blackboard. The harsh sccurr,
sccurr of Miss Bradley's chalk and the tinny sound the rain
made against the window took my mind to faraway places. I
couldn't get as far away as I wanted. Wallace, the bane of the
whole class, had only moments earlier laid the most gigunda[5]
fart in history, one in a never-ending series, and the air was
just clearing. His farts were silent wonders. Not a hint, not the
slightest sound. You could be in the middle of a sentence and
then wham! bam! Mystery Funk would knock you down.

Two seats ahead of me was Leonard, a lean colored boy   14
from West Philly who always wore suits and ties to school, waving his hand like a crazy man. A showoff if ever there was one.

I was bored that day. I looked around at the walls. Miss   15
Bradley had decorated the room with pictures of the ABCs in
cursive. Portraits of the presidents were hanging in a row on
one wall above the blackboard. On the bulletin board there was
a display of the Russian satellite, *Sputnik I,* and the American
satellite, *Explorer I.* Miss Bradley was satellite-crazy. She
thought it was just wonderful that America was in the "space
race" and she constantly filled our heads with space fantasies.
"Boys and girls," she told us, "one day man will walk on the
moon." In the far corner on another bulletin board there was a
Thanksgiving scene of turkeys and pilgrims. And stuck in the
corner was a picture of Sacajawea.[6] Sacajewea, Indian Woman
Guide. I preferred looking at Sacajawea over satellites any day.

Thinking about the bubble gum that lay in my pocket, I   16
decided to sneak a piece, even though gum chewing was
strictly forbidden. I rarely broke the rules. Could anyone hear
the loud drumming of my heart, I wondered, as I slid my hand
into my skirt pocket and felt for the Double Bubble? I peeked
cautiously to either side of me. Then I managed to unwrap it
without even rustling the paper; I drew my hand to my lips,

[4]Pasquotank County	(13)	North Carolina county where Campbell's father lived.
[5]gigunda	(13)	Slang for gigantic.
[6]Sacajawea	(15)	a Shoshone Native American woman (1786–1812) who was captured and sold to a white man. She became a famous guide of the 1804 Lewis and Clark expedition.

coughed, and popped the gum in my mouth. Ahhh! Miss Bradley's back was to the class. I chomped down hard on the Double Bubble. Miss Bradley turned around. I quickly packed the gum under my tongue. My hands were folded on top of my desk. "Who can give me a sentence for 'birthday'?" Leonard just about went nuts. Miss Bradley ignored him, which she did a lot. "Sandra," Miss Bradley called.

A petite white girl rose obediently. I liked Sandra. She had   17
shared her crayons with me once when I left mine at home. I remember her drawing: a white house with smoke coming out of the chimney, a little girl with yellow hair like hers, a mommy, a daddy, a little boy, and a dog standing in front of the house in a yard full of flowers. Her voice was crystal clear when she spoke. There were smiles in that voice. She said, "My father made me a beautiful dollhouse for my birthday."

The lump under my tongue was suddenly a stone and   18
when I swallowed, the taste was bitter. I coughed into a piece of tablet paper, spit out the bubble gum, and crumpled up the wad and pushed it inside my desk. The center of my chest was burning. I breathed deeply and slowly. Sandra sat down as demurely as a princess. She crossed her ankles. Her words came back to me in a rush. "Muuuy fatha made me a bee-yoo-tee-ful dollhouse." Miss Bradley said, "Very good," and moved on to the next word. Around me hands were waving, waving. Pick me! Pick me! Behind me I could hear David softly crooning, "You ain't nothin' but a hound dog, cryin' all the time." Sometimes he would stick his head inside his desk, sing Elvis songs, and pick his boogies at the same time. Somebody was jabbing pins in my chest. Ping! Ping! Ping! I wanted to holler, "Yowee! Stop!" as loud as I could, but I pressed my lips together hard.

"Now who can give me a sentence?" Miss Bradley asked. I   19
put my head down on my desk and when Miss Bradley asked me what was wrong I told her that I didn't feel well and that I didn't want to be chosen. When Leonard collected the homework, I shoved mine at him so hard all the papers he was carrying fell on the floor.

Bile was still clogging my throat when Miss Bradley sent   20
me into the cloakroom to get my lunchbox. The rule was, only one student in the cloakroom at a time. When the second one came in, the first one had to leave. I was still rummaging around in my bookbag when I saw Sandra.

"Miss Bradley said for you to come out," she said. She was   21
smiling. That dollhouse girl was always smiling. I glared at her.

"Leave when I get ready to," I said, my words full of   22
venom.

Sandra's eyes darted around in confusion. "Miss Bradley   23
said . . . " she began again, still trying to smile as if she expected somebody to crown her Miss America or something and
come take her picture any minute.

In my head a dam broke. Terrible waters rushed out. "I   24
don't care about any Miss Bradley. If she messes with me I'll,
I'll . . . I'll take my butcher knife and stab her until she
bleeds." What I lacked in props I made up for in drama. My
balled-up hand swung menacingly in the air. I aimed the invisible dagger toward Sandra. Her Miss America smile faded instantly. Her eyes grew round and frightened as she blinked
rapidly. "Think I won't, huh? Huh?" I whispered, enjoying my
meanness, liking the scared look on Sandra's face. Scaredy cat!
Scaredy cat! Muuuy fatha made me a bee-yoo-tee-full dollhouse. "What do you think about that?" I added viciously, looking into her eyes to see the total effect of my daring words.

But Sandra wasn't looking at me. Upon closer inspection,   25
I realized that she was looking *over* me with sudden relief in
her face. I turned to see what was so interesting, and my chin
jammed smack into the Emeraude-scented iron bosom of Miss
Bradley. Even as my mind scrambled for an excuse, I knew I
was lost.

Miss Bradley had a look of horror on her face. For a   26
minute she didn't say anything, just stood there looking as
though someone had slapped her across the face. Sandra didn't
say anything. I didn't move. Finally, "Would you mind repeating
what you just said, Bebe."

"I didn't say anything, Miss Bradley." I could feel my dress   27
sticking to my body.

"Sandra, what did Bebe say?"   28

Sandra was crying softly, little delicate tears streaming   29
down her face. For just a second she paused, giving a tiny shudder. I rubbed my ear vigorously, thinking, "Oh, please . . ."

"She said, she said, if you bothered with her she would   30
cut you with her knife."

"Unh unh, Miss Bradley, I didn't say that. I didn't. I didn't   31
say anything like that."

Miss Bradley's gray eyes penetrated mine. She locked me   32
into her gaze until I looked down at the floor. Then she looked
at Sandra.

"Bebe, you and I had better go see the principal." 33

The floor blurred. The principal! Jennie G., the students 34
called her with awe and fear. As Miss Bradley wrapped her
thick knuckles around my forearm and dutifully steered me
from the cloakroom and out the classroom door, I completely
lost what little cool I had left. I began to cry, a jerky hiccuping,
snot-filled cry for mercy. "I didn't say it. I didn't say it," I
moaned.

Miss Bradley was nonplussed. Dedication and duty over- 35
ruled compassion. Always. "Too late for that now," she said
grimly.

Jennie G.'s office was small, neat, and dim. The principal 36
was dwarfed by the large brown desk she sat behind, and when
she stood up she wasn't much bigger than I. But she was big
enough to make me tremble as I stood in front of her, listening
to Miss Bradley recount the sordid details of my downfall. Jennie G. was one of those pale, pale vein-showing white women.
She had a vocabulary of about six horrible phrases, designed to
send chills of despair down the spine of any young transgres-
sor. Phrases like "We'll just see about that" or "Come with me,
young lady," spoken ominously. Her face was impassive as she
listened to Miss Bradley. I'd been told that she had a six-foot
paddle in her office used solely to beat young transgressors.
Suppose she tried to beat me? My heart gave a lurch. I tugged
rapidly at my ears. I longed to suck my thumb.

"Well, Bebe, I think we'll have to call your mother." 37

My mother! I wanted the floor to swallow me up and take 38
me whole. My mother! As Jennie G. dialed the number, I envisioned my mother's face, clouded with disappointment and
shame. I started crying again as I listened to the principal
telling my mother what had happened. They talked for a pretty
long time. When she hung up, ole Jennie G. flipped through
some paper on her desk before looking at me sternly.

"You go back to class and watch your mouth, young lady." 39

As I was closing the door to her office I heard her say to 40
Miss Bradley, "What can you expect?"

Discussion Questions

1. Why does the narrator feel she was "overexposed to femininity"
when she was growing up?

2. Who are the "Bosoms" to whom Campbell refers?

3. Do you think Bebe's feelings about a household of women are generally shared by other young girls who grow up in a similar situation? Why or why not?

4. Why did Bebe get angry at Sandra?

5. Why is Bebe taken to the principal's office?

6. What does the principal mean when she says "What do you expect"?

7. To what extent does Campbell's use of cause and effect support the theme of the story?

8. How would this story be different if it were told by a character other than the main character?

Writing Assignments

1. Write an essay describing an incident in which you took out your frustration on someone who didn't deserve it.

2. Write an essay describing your childhood relationship with a person or persons who had a major influence on your life.

3. Write an essay in which you explore some stereotypic beliefs about the roles of men and women.

Student Essay:
FEMALE GENITAL MUTILATION AND CASTRATION

Anika Yetunde

Vocabulary

genital (1) of, relating to, or being a sexual organ
mutilated (1) cut off or crippled
retention (3) the act of keeping
obsolete (6) no longer useful

African women throughout the world have a common op- 1
pressor: female genital mutilation and castration. The woman
suffers from this oppression because of racism, sexism, and
classism. Because she suffers from all of these forms of oppression, the woman of African descent has been the one most affected by this practice throughout the world. For example,
6,000 young girls are mutilated daily, many of them African
women. Since the early 1980s, over 100 million young girls and
women have been mutilated. Yet organizations such as
UNICEF[1] have only recently acknowledged that this practice
still exists. How can you ignore 100 million mutilated women?
It has a lot to do with the fact that the majority of these women
are poor and African.

Female genital mutilation is the collective name given to the 2
several different traditional practices that involve the cutting and
mutilating of female genitals. There are many different forms of
female genital mutilation, and they vary from region to region
and continent to continent, but they all fall into three broad categories. The first is called "sunna" circumcision and is the
mildest type. It consists of removing only the tip of the prepuce[2]
of the clitoris.[2] The next type is called "clitoridectomy" which

---

[1]UNICEF (1) United Nations International Children's Emergency
Fund founded in 1946.
[2]prepuce, clitoris, (2) Biological names for parts of the female genital or-
labia minora, labia gan.
majora

consists of the removal of the entire clitoris, usually together with the adjacent parts of the labia minora.[2] The last type is called "infibulation," which includes removing the entire clitoris, some or all of the labia minora, and making incisions on the labia majora[2] to create raw surfaces. These raw surfaces are either stitched together or kept in contact by pressure until they heal as a "hood of skin" that covers the urethra[3] and most of the vagina. Since a physical barrier to sexual intercourse is created as a result, a small hole must be reconstructed for the flow of urine and menstrual blood. Also, recutting and stitching is performed after each childbirth. This means a woman may average six to eight reinfibulations in her lifetime!

Many complications are associated with female genital   3
mutilation: excessive bleeding, infection, continuous pain, urine retention, damage to the urethra, and stress. In the infibulation case, there is an excessive growth of scar tissue and severe complications during childbirth. The majority of these practices are performed in rural areas where anesthesia is difficult to obtain. Despite these complications, the psychological and emotional side effects of female genital mutilation have never been investigated and recorded.

Myths concerning the origin of the practice are numerous.   4
Most of the myths trace the practice to Africa, others to ancient Rome. Some believe it is associated with Islam; others say it predates Islam.

Why does the practice persist? Many women have said   5
that female genital mutilation represents a spiritual bond that they share with their ancestors; in other words, it is a custom or a tradition. Many also have stated that they fear the ancestors would seek vengeance if they abandon this practice. The vast majority who are Islamic believe it is a requirement. Moreover, African men in Islamic societies place a great deal of emphasis on women being virgins upon marriage, so the majority of the men will not marry a woman if she is not circumcised. In the societies where female genital mutilation is allowed, there is an obsession with controlling a woman's virginity. Many people in these societies believe that if a woman is not circumcised she will become a sex delinquent. Then, too, many myths and superstitions surround this practice, such as circumcision increases fertility; an uncircumcised woman is dirty and masculine; and an uncircumcised woman will kill her firstborn.

---

[3]urethra   (3)   The body part through which urine is eliminated.

Female genital mutilation and male circumcision used to 3
have one similarity. Both of these practices were performed on
boys and girls in the same age group and were a part of the
rites of passage into adulthood. Today, these rites of passage
are almost obsolete, yet the mutilation continues. It appears as
if female genital mutilation has only continued to be practiced,
on women of African descent in particular, because of the triple
oppression that they confront. This practice must be abolished.

Discussion Questions

1. How does the author account for the reluctance of some health
   organizations to acknowledge the practice of female genital mutilation?
2. What are the three types of circumcision? How are they different?
3. Why does the practice persist?
4. Of the many reasons given by the author to discontinue female
   circumcision, which do you consider the most convincing? Why?
5. How effective is Yetunde's use of classification in educating the
   reader on female genital mutilation and castration?
6. How can you argue that the last sentence of the essay is
   Yetunde's thesis statement?

Writing Assignments

1. In an essay, offer reasons why you think female (or male) circumcision should (or should not) be abolished.
2. Write an essay in which you argue that some type of other societal or environmental practice should be abolished.

Literary and Writing Terms

audience   person or group to whom a piece of writing is addressed

body   in writing, the central part of an essay where ideas supporting the thesis are presented

brainstorming   prewriting strategy whereby words or phrases are listed as quickly as they come to mind

cause and effect   organizing strategy that examines the reasons for a certain condition or event (causes) or examines the results a certain condition or event has had on something or someone else (effects)

central idea   main point of a piece of writing; thesis

character   person in a story, poem, or play

classification   method of defining whereby one places various people, ideas, or things into separate and distinct categories

climax   highest or most dramatic point of a story

comparison and contrast   technique of analyzing two topics or works in order to determine similarities and/or differences

complex sentence   consisting of only one independent clause and at least one dependent clause

Example: Since traffic was so heavy, Rashida walked to the park.

compound-complex sentence   consisting of at least two independent clauses and at least one dependent clause

Example: Since traffic was so heavy, Rashida walked to the park, but she took the bus home.

compound sentence   consisting of two independent clauses and no dependent clauses

Example: Rashida walked to the park, but she took the bus home.

conflict   clash between or within characters and/or society

connotation   what a word suggests beyond its dictionary meaning

   Example: I was impressed by her *childlike* behavior. [Whereas *child-like* connotates positive behavior, *childish* connotates negative behavior.]

denotation   the dictionary meaning of a word

definition   organizing strategy that emphasizes the meanings of word(s) to develop a major point

description   organizing strategy that focuses on sensory details (sight, sound, touch, taste, smell)

dialect   speech of a particular region or social group

dialogue   speech between two (or more) characters

diction   choice and/or use of words in an essay

dilemma   choices a character faces in resolving a problem

drama   a play

editing   process of correcting spelling, grammar, punctuation, or changing sentence structure and word choice; also see *revising*

essay   group of paragraphs that develops a single idea

explication   detailed analysis of a literary work

fiction   writing based on an author's imagination

figurative language   words and expressions that often attempt to compare unlike things

first-person narrator   when a character in the story narrates it, using first-person singular (*I*) and plural (*we*) pronouns

flashback   part in a story, play, or film, showing events that happened at an earlier time

folklore   songs, stories, myths, and proverbs of a people or cultural group with no known origin that are handed down from generation to generation

freewriting   process of writing down your thoughts on paper, freely and continuously for a set period of time

genre   type of literature, for example, fiction, nonfiction, drama, or poetry

hyperbole   exaggerated speech

   Example: Her heart is as big as Texas.

idiom   phrase (particularly to a group, race, nation, or class) that does not make sense taken literally

   Example: *green thumb* or *sweet tooth*

illustration   organizing strategy that relies on specific examples or reasons to develop an idea

imagery   vivid language that appeals to the senses of sight, sound, taste, smell, and touch

irony   something said or done, but something else meant or expected

jargon   language characteristic of a particular profession or activity

   Example: Kwame has downloaded the file he received from Jamal.

journal   notebook in which one writes on a regular basis; unlike a diary in which one records the day's events, a journal reflects the writer's feelings on a given subject

loose sentence   sentence in which the main idea comes at the beginning
> Example: *Carolyn had played her best although she lost the triathlon.*

metaphor   comparison of two things by substituting one for the other
> Example: Dante, the smart new reporter, thinks he is a *firecracker* of the well-known national newspaper.

mood   writer's attitude in a piece of writing

narrative   organizing strategy that tells a story to make a point

narrator   the one who tells the story; sometimes referred to as the speaker

nonfiction   writing that is factual rather than imaginary

nonstandard English   language that does not conform to standards of American edited English

novel   long work of fiction

onomatopoeia   consonant and vowel sounds used to imitate or suggest the activity being described
> Example: The mother grew tired of listening to the *bangs* and *booms* of her six-year-old son.

parable   story designed to illustrate a truth, often associated with the stories of Jesus

paradox   statement that is seemingly contradictory yet true
> Example: The weary parent said she had just about loved her young teenage daughter to death.

paraphrase   rewording of someone else's ideas in a piece of writing to fit the style of the writer

periodic sentence   sentence in which the main idea comes at the end of the sentence
> Example: Although she tried her best, *Carolyn lost the triathlon.*

persona   speaker of a poem

personification   expression that gives human qualities to nonhuman things
> Example: The *tree's branches danced* in the wind.

persuasion   organizing strategy designed to convince readers to accept or seriously consider the writer's viewpoint

plot   sequence of incidents in a story or play

poetry   literature characterized by rhythmic language

point of view   perspective from which a story is told, for example, first-person or third-person narrator

précis   *in literature*, a short paraphrased summary of a narrative; *in writing*, a summary that captures the overall style and tone of the source

process   organizing strategy that focuses on how something works or is done

proofreading   reviewing an essay for both revision and editing concerns

prose   the ordinary form of written language, not arranged in verse

protagonist   main character in a story or play

pun   play on words

Example: The owner of the butcher shop *cut* his losses by laying off two workers.

purpose   writer's chief reason for communicating something about a topic, for example, to inform, to persuade, to express feelings

resolution   final stage of a story in which conflicts are resolved

revising   reconsidering the whole paper as well as its individual parts, including assessing purpose, audience, main idea, and perhaps reordering supporting paragraphs and sentences

rhetorical strategies   methods used to organize an essay (See section on "Planning Your Essay.")

setting   time and place in which a story occurs

sexist language   language that excludes or offends men or women

short story   short fictional work

simile   comparison of unlike objects using "like" or "as"

Example: His eyes twinkled *like* the stars.

simple sentence   consisting of only one independent clause and no dependent clauses

Example: Rashida walked to the park.

slang   informal language that is short lived and used by those within a particular group

speaker   See *persona* and *narrator.*

stanza   In a poem, lines that are grouped together

structure   arrangement of material in a story

style   overall characteristic of a writer's work that gives the work its particular flavor

symbol   word or object that stands for something other than itself

syntax   word order and sentence structure

theme   main idea of a piece of writing

thesis   generally, a specific sentence that reflects the central point of an essay; however, a thesis may also be implied.

third-person narrator   speaker who tells the story, but is not a character in it

tone   writer's attitude toward his or her ideas and toward the audience

topic sentence   sentence that reflects the main idea of a paragraph

understatement   sentence that by design undervalues something

writing process   mental and physical activities that go into producing a piece of writing

Suggested Bibliography

SLAVERY

COOPER, J. CALIFORNIA. *Family: A Novel.* New York: Doubleday, 1991.

HARRIS, MIDDLETON. *The Black Book.* New York: Random House, 1974.

HAYDEN, ROBERT. "Middle Passage." In Arthur P. Davis, J. Saunders Redding and Joyce Ann Joyce (eds), *The New Cavalcade.* 2 vols. Washington, DC: Howard University Press, 1991. 1:846–851.

HORTON, MOSES. "On Liberty and Slavery." In Arthur P. Davis, J. Saunders Redding and Joyce Ann Joyce (eds.), *The New Cavalcade.* 2 vols. Washington, DC: Howard University Press, 1991. 1:50–51.

JOHNSON, CHARLES. *Middle Passage.* New York: Atheneum, 1990.

MORRISON, TONI. *Beloved.* New York: Knopf, 1987.

"Raise a Ruckus Tonight." In Richard K. Barksdale and Keneth Kinnamon (eds.), *Black Writers of America.* New York: Macmillan, 1972.

"Swapping Dreams." In Richard K. Barksdale and Keneth Kinnamon (eds.), *Black Writers of America.* New York: Macmillan, 1972.

WALKER, DAVID. *Appeal.* New York: Hill and Wang, 1965.

WALKER, MARGARET. *Jubilee.* New York: Bantam, 1975.

WILLIAMS, SHERLEY ANNE. *Dessa Rose.* New York: Berkley, 1987.

AFRICAN AMERICAN WOMEN

ANGELOU, MAYA. *I Know Why the Caged Bird Sings.* New York: Random House, 1969.

CLIFTON, LUCILLE. "for her." In Amiri and Amina Baraka (eds.), *Confirmation: An Anthology of African American Women.* New York: Quill, 1983.

CORTEZ, JAYNE. "Rape." In Amiri and Amina Baraka (eds.), *Confirmation: An Anthology of African American Women.* New York: Quill, 1983.

HUDSON-WEEMS, CLENORA. *Africana Womanism.* Troy, MI: Bedford, 1993.

JONES, GAYL. "Asylum." In Mary Helen Washington (ed.), *Midnight Birds.* New York: Anchor Press/Doubleday, 1980.

LEWIS-THORNTON, RAE. "Facing AIDS." *Essence,* December 1994: 62–64, 124, 126, 130.

NAYLOR, GLORIA. *The Women of Brewster Place.* New York: Penguin, 1983.

NELSON, JILL. "Doing Time: Our Women in Prison." *Essence,* May 1994: 83–84, 86, 158, 160.

MORRISON, TONI. *The Bluest Eye.* New York: Holt, Rinehart & Winston, 1970.

TRUTH, SOJOURNER. "And Arn't I a Woman?" In Arthur P. Davis, J. Saunders Redding and Joyce Ann Joyce (eds.), *The New Cavalcade.* 2 vols. Washington, DC: Howard University Press, 1991. 1:101–104.

WALKER, ALICE. *The Color Purple.* New York: Harcourt, 1982.

WHETSTONE, MURIEL L. "New AIDS Scare for Heterosexuals: The Increasing Threat to Black Women." *Ebony,* April 1994: 118, 120.

AFRICAN AMERICAN MEN

BROWN, CLAUDE. *Manchild in the Promised Land.* New York: Macmillan, 1965.

BROWN, WILLIAM WELLS. "from *The Negro in the American Rebellion: His Heroism and His Fidelity.*" Richard K. Barksdale and Keneth Kinnamon (eds.), *Black Writers of America.* New York: Macmillan, 1972.

DANIELS, LEE. "Targeting Black Boys for Failure." *Emerge,* May 1994: 58–61.

HODGES, FRENCHY. "Requiem for Willie Lee." In Mary Helen Washington (ed.), *Midnight Birds.* New York: Anchor Press/Doubleday, 1980.

KILLENS, JOHN. *And Then We Heard the Thunder.* Washington, DC: Howard University Press, 1982.

MORRISON, TONI. *Song of Solomon.* New York: Knopf, 1977.

WIDEMAN, JOHN EDGAR. "Tommy." In *Damballah.* New York: Vintage, 1988.

WILLIAMS, JOHN. *The Man Who Cried I Am.* New York: Little, Brown, 1967.

WRIGHT, RICHARD. *Black Boy.* New York: Harper, 1945.

CHILDHOOD • ADOLESCENCE • GROWING UP

BALDWIN, JAMES. *Go Tell It on the Mountain.* New York: Dell, 1953.

CHILDRESS, ALICE. *A Hero Ain't Nothin But a Sandwich.* New York: Coward, McCann and Geoghegan, 1973.

DEVEAUX, ALEXIS. "The Riddles of Egypt Brownstone." In Mary Helen Washington (ed.), *Midnight Birds.* New York: Anchor Press/Doubleday, 1980.

JOHNSON, KIRK. "Alive and Well." *Essence,* December 1993: 74, 83.

MERIWETHER, LOUISE. *Daddy Was a Number Runner.* New York: Feminist Press, 1986.

MORRISON, TONI. *The Bluest Eye.* New York: Holt, Rinehart & Winston, 1970.

PARKS, GORDON. *The Learning Tree.* New York: Fawcett Crest, 1963.

FAMILY

BALDWIN, JAMES. *Go Tell It on the Mountain.* New York: Dell, 1953.

"The Black Family Nobody Knows." *Ebony,* August 1993: 28, 30–31.

COOPER, J. CALIFORNIA. "Swimming to the Top of the Rain." *Homemade Love.* New York: St. Martin's Press, 1987.

JEWELL, K. SUE. *Survival of the Black Family.* New York: Praeger, 1989.

MALCOLM X. "Nightmare." In *The Autobiography of Malcolm X.* New York: Grove Press, 1965.

MORRISON, TONI. *The Bluest Eye.* New York: Holt, Rinehart & Winston, 1970.

MURRAY, PAULI. *Proud Shoes.* New York: Harper, 1956.

RUSSELL, SANDI. "Sister." In Margaret Bugsby (ed.), *Daughters of Africa.* New York: Pantheon Books, 1992.

SCOTT-JONES, DIANE, A. DAVIS, M. FOSTER, and P. HUGHES. "Sexual Activity, Pregnancy and Childbearing Among African-American Youth." In Ronald L. Taylor. *African-American Youth: Their Social and Economic Status in the U.S.* New York: Praeger, 1994.

SHANGE, NTOZAKE. *Sassafrass, Cypress & Indigo.* New York: St. Martin's Press, 1982.

TAYLOR, MILDRED. *Roll of Thunder, Hear My Cry.* New York: Dial, 1976.

MALE-FEMALE RELATIONSHIPS

"Date Rape: The Tyson Syndrome." *Emerge,* May 1992: 43–44.

DOVE, RITA. "The Zulus." In Margaret Bugsby (ed.), *Daughters of Africa.* New York: Pantheon Books, 1992.

GRIMES, NIKKI. "Fragments: Mousetrap." Amiri and Amina Baraka (eds.), *Confirmation.* New York: Quill, 1983.

HURSTON, ZORA NEALE. "The Gilded Six-Bits." John Henrik Clarke (ed.), In *American Negro Short Stories.* New York: Hill and Wang, 1966.

———. *Their Eyes Were Watching God.* Urbana: University of Illinois Press, 1978.

KARENGA, MAULANA. "Black Male-Female Relationships." In *Introduction to Black Studies.* Los Angeles: University of Sankore Press, 1992.

MCMILLAN, TERRY. *Disappearing Acts.* New York: Washington Square Press, 1989.

———. *Waiting to Exhale.* New York: Viking, 1992.

MORRISON, TONI. *Tar Baby.* New York: Knopf, 1981.

SHANGE, NTOZAKE. "comin to terms." Mary Helen Washington (ed.), In *Midnight Birds.* New York: Anchor Press/Doubleday, 1980.

CIVIL RIGHTS

BALDWIN, JAMES. "Blues for Mister Charlie." Clinton F. Oliver and Stephanie Sills (eds.), *Contemporary Black Drama.* New York: Scribner's, 1971.

Campbell, Bebe Moore. *Your Blues Ain't Like Mine.* New York: Ballantine, 1992.

Gaines, Ernest J. *The Autobiography of Miss Jane Pittman.* New York: Doubleday, 1987.

King, Martin Luther, Jr. *Stride Toward Freedom: The Montgomery Story.* New York: Harper & Row, 1958.

Lowe, Walter, Jr. "Civil Rights: 25 Years After Martin's Death." *Emerge,* April 1993: 32–39.

Walker, Alice. *Meridian.* New York: Harcourt, 1976.

Zinn, Howard. *SNCC: The New Abolitionists.* Boston: Beacon Press, 1964.

FREEDOM • EQUALITY • UNITY • PROTEST

Aptheker, Herbert. *American Negro Slave Revolts.* New York: International, 1963.

Baraka, Amina. "Soweto Song." Amiri and Amina Baraka (eds.), *Confirmation.* New York: Quill, 1983.

"Beyond Rodney King: Unequal Justice in America." *Emerge,* December 1992: 38–40.

Giovanni, Nikki. "For Saundra." Dudley Randall (ed.), *The Black Poets.* New York: Bantam, 1971.

Greenlee, Sam. *The Spook Who Sat by the Door.* New York: Kayode Publishers, 1991.

Harding, Vincent. "Power from Our People." *The Black Scholar* 18(1) Jan./Feb. 1987, pp. 41–51.

Ismaili, Rashidah. "Dialogue." Amiri and Amina Baraka (eds.), *Confirmation.* New York: Quill, 1983.

Sanchez, Sonia. *The Bronx Is Next. The Drama Review* 12(4) (T40), Summer 1968.

Wheatley, Phillis. "To the Right Honorable William, Earl of Dartmouth." Margaret Bugsby (ed.), *Daughters of Africa.* New York: Pantheon Books, 1992.

ARTS • SCIENCES • MEDIA

Baraka, Amiri. "Black Art." *The Black Scholar* 18(1), Jan./Feb. 1987, pp. 23–30.

"Guinea Pigs: Secret Medical Experiments on Blacks." *Emerge,* October 1994: 24–35.

Jewell, K. Sue. *From Mammy to Miss America and Beyond: Cultural Images and the Shaping of U.S. Social Policy.* New York: Routledge, 1993.

Kennedy, Shawn. "Prime-Time Sister." *Emerge,* April 1994: 46–49.

Neal, Larry. "The Social Background of the Black Arts Movement." *The Black Scholar* 18(1), Jan./Feb. 1987, pp. 11–22.

Walker, Alice. "In Search of Our Mother's Gardens." In *In Search of Our Mother's Gardens.* New York: Harcourt Brace Jovanovich, 1983.

RELIGION • CHURCH

BALDWIN, JAMES. *Go Tell It on the Mountain.* New York: Dell, 1953.

——. *The Amen Corner.* New York: Dial, 1968.

BATTLE, V. DuWAYNE. "The Influence of Al-Islam in America on the Black Community." *The Black Scholar* 19(1), Jan./Feb. 1988, pp. 33–41.

CLARKE, JOHN HENRIK. "The Boy Who Painted Christ Black." In *American Negro Short Stories.* New York: Hill and Wang, 1966.

HAYNES, REV. LEMUEL B. "Universal Salvation—A Very Ancient Doctrine." In Richard K. Barksdale and Keneth Kinnamon (eds.), *Black Writers of America.* New York: Macmillan, 1972.

HUGHES, LANGSTON. *Tambourines to Glory.* New York: Hill and Wang, 1958.

JONES, LISA. "Blacks in the Bible." *Ebony,* February 1994: 60, 62, 66.

MONROE, SYLVESTER. "The Fruits of Islam: Muslim Faith Grows in Followers and Respect." *Emerge,* March 1994: 38–43.

WHEATLEY, PHILLIS. "On Being Brought from Africa to America." Richard K. Barksdale and Keneth Kinnamon (eds.), *Black Writers of America.* New York: Macmillan, 1972.

HERITAGE • IDENTITY

CARMICHAEL, STOKELY. "From Black Power Back to Pan-Africanism." In *Stokely Speaks.* New York: Vintage, 1971.

CULLEN, COUNTEE. "Heritage." In Richard K. Barksdale and Keneth Kinnamon (eds.), *Black Writers of America.* New York: Macmillan, 1972.

DuBois, W.E.B. *The World and Africa.* New York: International, 1965.

DUNBAR, PAUL LAURENCE. "Ode to Ethiopia." In Arthur P. Davis, J. Saunders Redding, and Joyce Ann Joyce (eds.), *The New Cavalcade.* 2 vols. Washington, DC: Howard University Press, 1991. 1: 304–305.

ELLISON, RALPH. *Invisible Man.* New York: Vintage, 1972.

HALEY, ALEX. *Roots.* New York: Doubleday, 1976.

KILLENS, JOHN. "Yoruba." In Arthur P. Davis, J. Saunders Redding, and Joyce Ann Joyce (eds.), *The New Cavalcade.* 2 vols. Washington, DC: Howard University Press, 1991. 2: 29–44.

MARSHALL, PAULE. *Praisesong for the Widow.* New York: Putnam, 1983.

VAN SERTIMA, IVAN. *They Came Before Columbus: The African Presence in Ancient America.* New York: Random House, 1976.

WILLIAMS, CHANCELLOR. *The Destruction of Black Civilization.* Chicago: Third World Press, 1987.

READING • WRITING • EDUCATION

IRVINE, JACQUELINE J. *Black Students and School Failure.* New York: Praeger, 1991.

MADGETT, NAOMI LONG. "Writing a Poem." In Arthur P. Davis, J. Saunders Redding, and Joyce Ann Joyce (eds.), *The New Cavalcade.* 2 vols. Washington, DC: Howard University Press, 1991. 2: 175.

"Separate and Unequal: The Education of Blacks 40 Years After Brown." *Emerge,* May 1994: 25–52.

"Toni Morrison," In Claudia Tate (ed.), *Black Women Writers at Work.* New York: Continuum, 1985.

WILLIE, CHARLES V. (ed.). *The Education of African-Americans.* New York: Praeger, 1991.

WOODSON, CARTER G. *The Mis-Education of the Negro.* Nashville, TN: Winston-Derek, 1940.

POLITICAL PHILOSOPHIES

AKADE, MAURICE. "A New Call: Reparations for Africa." *Emerge,* October 1992: 20.

CARMICHAEL, STOKELY, and CHARLES V. HAMILTON. *Black Power: The Politics of Liberation in America.* New York: Vintage, 1967.

CRUMMELL, ALEXANDER. "The Relations and Duties of Free Colored Men in America to Africa." In Richard K. Barksdale and Keneth Kinnamon (eds.), *Black Writers of America.* New York: Macmillan, 1972.

DAVIS, ANGELA Y. *Angela Davis: An Autobiography.* New York: International Publishers, 1988.

DOUGLASS, FREDERICK. "Oration, Delivered in Corinthian Hall, Rochester, July 5, 1852." In Richard K. Barksdale and Keneth Kinnamon (eds.), *Black Writers of America.* New York: Macmillan, 1972.

DuBois, W.E.B. *The Souls of Black Folk.* A.C. McClurg, 1903. Mattituck, New York: Amereon Ltd.

GARVEY, MARCUS. *The Philosophy and Opinions of Marcus Garvey.* 2 vols. Amy Jacques Garvey (ed.), New York: Atheneum, 1973.

KING, MARTIN LUTHER, JR. *Why We Can't Wait.* New York: Harper & Row, 1964.

MALCOLM X. *Malcolm X Speaks.* New York: Grove Press, 1965.

MUHAMMAD, ELIJAH. *Message to the Black Man in America.* Chicago: Muhammad Mosque of Islam No. 2, 1965.

SHAKUR, ASSATA. *Assata: An Autobiography.* Westport, CT: Lawrence Hill, 1987.

WASHINGTON, BOOKER T. *Up from Slavery.* New York: Doubleday, 1901.

BLACK ENGLISH • DIALECT

CHESNUTT, CHARLES W. *The Conjure Woman.* New York: Houghton Mifflin, 1969.

DANIEL, JACK L., and GENEVA SMITHERMAN. "How I Got Over: Communication Dynamics in the Black Community." *Quarterly Journal of Speech* 62, 1976, pp. 26–39.

DILLARD, JOEY L. *Black English: Its History and Usage in the U.S.* New York: Random House, 1972.

DUNBAR, PAUL Laurence "The Party." In Richard K. Barksdale and Keneth Kinnamon (eds.), *Black Writers of America.* New York: Macmillan, 1972.

HOLT, GRACE SIMS. "Stylin' Outta the Black Pulpit." In Thomas Kochman (ed.), *Rappin' and Stylin' Out.* Urbana: University of Illinois Press, 1972.

MAJOR, CLARENCE (ed.). *Juba to Jive: A Dictionary of African-American Slang.* New York: Penguin, 1994.

SMITHERMAN, GENEVA. *Talkin and Testifyin: The Language of Black America.* Boston: Houghton Mifflin, 1977.

———. *Black Talk: Words and Phrases from the Hood to the Amen Corner.* Boston: Houghton-Mifflin, 1994.

FOLKLORE

BUTLER, OCTAVIA. *Wild Seed.* New York: Doubleday, 1980.

———. *Kindred.* New York: Beacon Press, 1988.

CAMPBELL, JAMES EDWIN. "De Cunjah Man." In Arthur P. Davis, J. Saunders Redding, and Joyce Ann Joyce (eds.), *The New Cavalcade.* 2 vols. Washington, DC: Howard University Press, 1991. 1:287–288.

CHESNUTT, CHARLES W. *The Conjure Woman.* New York: Houghton Mifflin, 1969.

HURSTON, ZORA NEALE. *Mules and Men.* Bloomington: Indiana University Press, 1978.

———. *Their Eyes Were Watching God.* Urbana: University of Illinois Press, 1978.

MARSHALL, PAULE. "Ibo Landing." In Chapter 3, *Praisesong for the Widow.* New York: Plume, 1983.

MORRISON, TONI. *Song of Solomon.* New York: Knopf, 1977.

NAYLOR, GLORIA. *Mama Day.* New York: Vintage, 1989.

REED, ISHMAEL. *Yellow Back Radio Broke-Down.* New York: Doubleday, 1971.

RACISM • DISCRIMINATION

DULA, ANNETTE (ed.). *"It Just Ain't Fair": The Ethics of Health Care for African Americans.* New York: Praeger, 1994.

DUMAS, HENRY. *Ark of Bones, and Other Stories.* Carbondale: Southern Illinois University Press, 1974.

KILLENS, JOHN OLIVER. *Black Man's Burden.* New York: Simon & Schuster, 1965.

KING, MARTIN LUTHER, JR. *Why I Can't Wait.* New York: Harper & Row, 1964.

MCKAY, CLAUDE. "America." In Richard K. Barksdale and Keneth Kinnamon (eds.), *Black Writers of America.* New York: Macmillan, 1972.

NICHOLS, CHARLES H. *Many Thousand Gone: The Ex-Slaves' Account of Their Bondage and Freedom.* Bloomington: Indiana Univ. Press, 1969.

WELLS, IDA B. *Crusade for Justice.* Chicago: University of Chicago Press, 1970.

WHITE, WALTER. "I Investigate Lynchings." In Richard K. Barksdale and Keneth Kinnamon (eds.), *Black Writers of America.* New York: Macmillan, 1972.

WRIGHT, RICHARD. *Uncle Tom's Children.* New York: Harper, 1969.

INTERRACIAL RELATIONSHIPS

ANGELOU, MAYA. "The Reunion." In Amiri and Amina Baraka (eds.), *Confirmation.* New York: Quill, 1983.

BALDWIN, JAMES. "Going to Meet the Man." In *Going to Meet the Man.* New York: Doubleday, 1965.

CAMPBELL, BEBE MOORE. *Your Blues Ain't Like Mine.* New York: Ballantine, 1992.

DUMAS, HENRY. "Double Nigger." In *Goodbye, Sweetwater.* New York: Thunder's Mouth Press, 1988.

FAUSET, JESSIE. *There Is Confusion.* New York: Boni & Liveright, 1924.

JONES, LEROI. "Dutchman." Clinton F. Oliver and Stephanie Sills (eds.), *Contemporary Black Drama.* New York: Scribner's, 1971.

JONES, LISA, and HETTIE JONES. "Mama's White." *Essence,* May 1994: 78–80, 150–152, 154, 158.

KILLENS, JOHN OLIVER. "God Bless America." John Henrik Clarke (ed.), In *American Negro Short Stories.* New York: Hill and Wang, 1966.

INTERRACIAL PREJUDICE

BATES, KAREN GRIGSBY. "The Color Thing." *Essence,* September 1994: 79–30, 132, 134–135.

BROOKS, GWENDOLYN. *Maud Martha.* New York: Farrar, Straus & Giroux, 1969.

CHESNUTT, CHARLES. *The Wife of His Youth, and Other Stories of the Color Line.* New York: Houghton Mifflin, 1899.

FAUSET, JESSIE. *Comedy: American Style.* Stokes, 1933.

LARSEN, NELLA. *Passing.* New York: Collier, 1971.

MORRISON, TONI. "Geraldine." *The Bluest Eye.* New York: Holt, Rinehart and Winston, 1970.

THURMAN, WALLACE. *The Blacker the Berry.* New York: Macaulay, 1929.

Video List to Supplement Readings

(Unless otherwise noted, all video cassettes may be rented from your local video store or borrowed from your local public library. Where film length and ratings were available, they have been provided.)

Slavery

Skin Game. 102 min. 1971 (Color) (PG).
Roots. 540 min. 1977 (Color).
Roots: The Next Generation. 480 min. 1978 (Color).
Presenting Mr. Frederick Douglass: "The Lesson of the Hour." 60 min. (Color) Films for the Humanities and Sciences.
Unearthing the Slave Trade. 28 min. (Color) Films for the Humanities and Sciences.
Race to Freedom: The Underground Railroad. 90 min. 1993 (Color).
Brother Future. A Wonderworks Family Movie. 60 min.
Half Slave, Half Free (a.k.a. *Solomon Northrop's Odyssey*). 113 min. 1984.
Half Slave, Half Free 2 (a.k.a. *Charlotte Forten's Mission: Experiment in Freedom*). 120 min. 1985.
Sankofa. 120 min. 1993 (Color).

African American Women

Lady Sings the Blues. 144 min. 1972 (Color) (R).
Happy Birthday, Mrs. Craig. 55 min. Filmakers Library.
Two Dollars and A Dream: Madame C.J. Walker. 56 min. Filmakers Library.
Freedom Bags. 32 min. Filmakers Library.
Ida B. Wells: A Passion for Justice. 60 min.
The Women of Brewster Place. 180 min. 1988 (Color).
Fundi: The Story of Ella Baker. 45 min. 1986 (Color). First Run/Icarus Films.

Wilma: The Wilma Rudolph Story. 100 min. (Color) (PG-13).
Mrs. Fannie Lou Hamer. 52 min. 1983 (Color).

African American Men

Jo Jo Dancer, Your Life Is Calling. 97 min. 1986 (Color) (R).
Native Son. 111 min. 1987 (Color).
Black Boy. 86 min. 1994. The African-American Video Library.
Almos' A Man. 51 min. (Color).
Tuskegee Airmen. 23 min.
The "Rodney King" Case: What The Jury Saw in California v. Powell. 1992
   (Color).
Menace II Society. 104 min. 1993 (Color) (R).
Negro Soldier. 49 min. 1943.
Glory. 122 min. 1989 (Color) (R).

Childhood • Adolescence • Growing Up

I Know Why the Caged Bird Sings. 96 min. 1979 (Color).
The Learning Tree. 107 min. 1969 (Color) (PG).
Bustin' Loose. 94 min. 1981 (Color) (R).
The Kid from Left Field. 99 min. 1979 (Color) (G).
The Breeding of Impotence. 55 min. 1993 (Color). The Cinema Guild, Inc.
Hardwood Dreams. 47 min. 1993 (Color).
Tell Them Who We Are: African-American Drill Teams. 29 min. New Day Film
   Library.
A Hero Ain't Nothin' But a Sandwich. 1977 (PG).
South Central. 99 min. 1992 (Color) (R).
Runaway. 58 min. (Color).
Fresh. 112 min. 1994 (Color) (R).

Family

A Raisin in the Sun. 128 min. 1961 (B & W).
The River Niger. 104 min. 1978 (Color) (R).
Sounder. 105 min. 1972 (Color) (G).
Crooklyn. 112 min. 1994 (Color) (PG-13).
In Search of Our Fathers. 55 min. Filmakers Library.
Goin Back to T-Town: African-Americans in Oklahoma. 60 min.
Go Tell It on the Mountain. 100 min. 1985 (Color).
The River Niger. 104 min. 1978 (R).
The Sky Is Gray. 46 min. 1980.

Male-Female Relationships

Mahogany. 110 min. 1975 (Color) (PG).
Pipe Dreams. 89 min. 1976 (Color).
Poetic Justice. 109 min. (Color) (R).
The Color Purple. 154 min. 1985 (Color) (PG-13).
What's Love Got to Do with It. 118 min. (Color) (R).
*The Honorable Louis Farrakhan: The Role of Women and Their Relationship
   with God and Man.* 1990.
Jawanza Kunjufu on Black Male-Female Relationships. 1992.
Porgy and Bess. 138 min. 1959.
Waiting to Exhale. 127 min. 1996 (Color) (R).

Civil Rights

King. 245 min. 1978 (Color).
The Autobiography of Miss Jane Pittman. 110 min. 1974 (Color).
The Freedom Train. 28 min. Filmakers Library.
Last Breeze of Summer. (bussing).
The Ernest Green Story. (desegregation).
For Us the Living: The Story of Medgar Evers. 84 min. 1984 (Color).
Mississippi Burning. 127 min. 1988 (Color) (R).

Freedom • Equality • Unity • Protest

Eyes on the Prize, Pts. I and II. 50 min. segments.
Roll of Thunder, Hear My Cry. 115 min. 1978 (Color) (PG).
Freedom on My Mind. 115 min. (Color). Clarity Educational Productions, Inc.
Words by Heart. A Wonderworks Family Movie.
Dark Exodus. 28 min. (B & W).
The Spook Who Sat by the Door. 102 min. 1973 (Color) (PG).
Attica. 97 min. 1980.
Cornbread, Earl and Me. 95 min. 1975 (PG).
Meteor Man. 99 min. 1993 (Color) (PG).
A Gathering of Old Men. 100 min. 1987 (Color).
Heat Wave. 94 min. 1990 (Color).

Arts • Sciences • Media

The Deadly Deception: The Tuskegee Study of Untreated Syphilis in the Negro Male. 58 min. (Color). Films for the Humanities and Sciences.
Jessye Norman, Singer. 74 min. Filmakers Library.
Didn't We Ramble On: The Black Marching Band. 14 min. Filmakers Library.
African-American Art: Past and Present. 90 min. Reading & O'Reilly, Inc.
Race Against Prime Time. 58 min. 1985. California Newsreel.
Color Adjustment. 88 min. 1991. California Newsreel.

Religion • Church

God's Alcatraz. 36 min. (B & W). Filmakers Library.
Saturday Night, Sunday Morning. 70 min. 1992. California Newsreel.
Let the Church Say Amen. 60 min. 1973 (Color). First Run/Icarus Films.
King James Version. 91 min. 1988 (Color). First Run/Icarus Films.
Religion and Race in America: Martin L. King's Lament. 60 min. (Color). Films for the Humanities and Sciences.
Go Down Death. 54 min. 1944.
Africentric Spirituality: A Lecture by Dr. Akbar. 1993.
Say Amen Somebody. 120 min. (Color). GTN Productions.

Heritage • Identity

Roots. 540 min. 1977 (Color).
Speak It! From the Heart Nova Scotia. 29 min. Filmakers Library.
Kwanzaa: A Cultural Celebration. 29 min. (Color). Films for the Humanities and Sciences.

Black Is . . . Black Ain't. 87 min. 1995. California Newsreel.
Bernice Johnson Reagon: The Songs Are Free. 58 min. 1991 (Color).
Daughters of the Dust. 113 min. 1991 (Color).

Reading • Writing • Education

Something with Me. 55 min. 1992. Filmakers Library.
Toni Morrison: A Writer's Work. 52 min. (Color). Films for the Humanities
and Sciences.
Facing the Facade. 60 min. 1994 (Color). The Cinema Guild.
Clarence and Angel. 75 min. 1980 (Color) (G).
The George McKenna Story. 95 min. 1993 (Color).
Cooley High. 107 min. 1975 (PG).
The Marva Collins Story. 100 min. 1981 (Color).
The Mighty Pawns. 58 min. 1987 (Color).
To Be Popular or Smart: The Black Peer Group. (Jawanza Kunjufu) 1988.

Political Philosophies

Malcolm X. 201 min. 1992 (Color) (PG-13).
Marcus Garvey: Toward Black Nationhood. 42 min. (Color). Films for the Hu-
manities and Sciences.
Ida B. Wells: A Passion for Justice. 60 min. Public Broadcasting System.
King: A Filmed Record . . . Montgomery to Memphis. 153 min. 1970.
Black Conservatives. 28 min. (Color). Films for the Humanities and Sci-
ences.
Paul Robeson. 118 min. 1977.

Black Dialect • Language

The Darker Side of Black. 59 min. 1966. Filmakers Library.
Straight Up Rappin'. 29 min. Filmakers Library.
Rap, Race and Equality. 58 min. Filmakers Library.
The Story of English: Black on White. Public Broadcasting System.

Folklore

Aesop's Fables. 30 min. (Color).
Zajota and the Boogie Spirit. 20 min. Filmakers Library.
When the Animals Talked. 28 min. 1982.
Juba: How Stories Came to Be. 15 min. (Color).
Juba: Brer Rabbit Stories. 15 min. (Color).
Juba: Why Stories. 15 min. (Color).

Racism • Discrimination

To Kill a Mockingbird. 129 min. 1962 (B & W).
The Watermelon Man. 97 min. 1970 (Color) (R).
Black Like Me. 110 min. 1964 (B & W).
Ethnic Notions. 56 min. 1987. California Newsreel.
The Road to Brown. 56 min. 1990. California Newsreel.
The Klansman. 112 min. 1974 (Color) (R).

Tarzan, the Ape Man. 104 min. 1932.
Jawanza Kunjufu: From Miseducation to Education: The Psychological Effects of Racism on African-Americans. 1992.

Interracial Relationships

In the Heat of the Night. 111 min. 1967 (Color).
Guess Who's Coming to Dinner. 108 min. 1967 (Color).
The Adventures of Huckleberry Finn. 74 min. 1975 (Color) (G).
Are We Different? 27 min. Filmakers Library.
Just Black? 57 min. Filmakers Library.
Dutchman. 55 min. 1967. Insight Media.
Separate But Equal. 193 min. 1991 (Color) (PG).
Do the Right Thing. 120 min. 1989 (Color) (R).
The Sky Is Gray. 46 min. 1980.

Intraracial Prejudice

School Daze. 114 min. 1987 (Color) (R).
A Question of Color. 56 min. 1993. California Newsreel.
I Passed for White. 93 min. 1960.
Imitation of Life. 124 min. 1959.
The Colored Museum. 60 min. (Color). Public Broadcasting System.

Additional Videos

Fire Eyes: Female Circumcision. 60 min. Filmakers Library. (African-American Women).
The Defiant Ones. 97 min. 1958 (B & W). (Interracial).
The Call of the Jitterbug. 30 min. Filmakers Library. (Arts/Sciences/Media).
South Central. 99 min. 1992 (Color) (R). (Childhood/Adolescence/ Growing Up).
Wild Women Don't Have the Blues. 58 min. 1989. California Newsreel. (Racism/Discrimination).
Kindred Spirits: Contemporary African-American Artists. 30 min. 1992 (Color). (Arts/Sciences/Media).
A Patch of Blue. 106 min. 1965 (Interracial Relationships).
To Sir With Love. 105 min. 1967 (Color). (Reading/Writing/Education).

Acknowledgments

ELIJAH ANDERSON, "Respect of the Streets" (editors' title), excerpt from "The Code of the Streets" from *The Code of the Streets*. Originally in *The Atlantic Monthly* 273, no. 5 (May 1994). Copyright © 1994 by Elijah Anderson. Reprinted with the permission of W.W. Norton & Company, Inc.

MAYA ANGELOU, "Marguerite's Graduation" (editors' title) from *I Know Why the Caged Bird Sings*. Copyright © 1969 by Maya Angelou. Reprinted with the permission of Random House, Inc.

ARTHUR ASHE, "Send Your Children to the Libraries," *The New York Times* (February 6, 1977). Copyright © 1977 by The New York Times Company. Reprinted with the permission of *The New York Times*.

JAMES BALDWIN, "If Black English Isn't a Language, Then Tell Me, What Is?," *The New York Times* (July 29, 1979). Copyright © 1979 by The New York Times Company. Reprinted with the permission of *The New York Times*.

JAMES BALDWIN, "The Stranger in the Village" from *Notes of a Native Son*. Copyright © 1953, 1955 by James Baldwin. Reprinted with the permission of Beacon Press.

TONI CADE BAMBARA, "Gorilla, My Love" from *Gorilla, My Love*. Copyright © 1972 by Toni Cade Bambara. Reprinted with the permission of Random House, Inc.

MICHAEL A. BATTLE, SR., "The Dynamic Tension in the Black Church" from *The African-American Church at Work*. Reprinted with the permission of Hodale Press, Inc.

ARNA BONTEMPS, "A Summer Tragedy" from *The Old South: "A Summer Tragedy" and Other Stories of the Thirties* (New York: Dodd, Mead, 1973). Copyright 1933 by Arna Bontemps. Reprinted with the permission of Harold Ober Associates, Inc.

GWENDOLYN BROOKS, "To Those Of My Sisters Who Kept Their Naturals" from *Blacks* (Chicago: Third World Press, 1987). Copyright © 1991 by Gwendolyn Brooks. Reprinted with the permission of the author. "Requiem

Before Revival" from *Primer for Blacks* (Chicago: Third World Press, 1991). Copyright © 1991 by Gwendolyn Brooks. Reprinted with the permission of the author. "if you're light and have long hair" from *Maud Martha,* reprinted in *Blacks* (Chicago: Third World Press, 1987). Copyright © 1991 by Gwendolyn Brooks. Reprinted with the permission of the author.

TONY BROWN, "Becoming a Republican," *The Wall Street Journal* (August 5, 1991). Copyright © 1991 by Dow Jones & Company, Inc. Reprinted with the permission of *The Wall Street Journal.*

EARL CALDWELL, "Shining light of a poet & pioneer," *Amsterdam News* (August 21, 1993). Reprinted by permission.

BEBE MOORE CAMPBELL, "Without Dad" (editors' title) from *Sweet Summer: Growing Up With and Without My Dad.* Copyright © 1989 by Bebe Moore Campbell. Reprinted with the permission of The Putnam Publishing Group. "Betrayal? When black men date white women," The New York Times Magazine (August 29, 1992). Copyright © 1992 by Bebe Moore Campbell. Reprinted with the permission of *The New York Times.*

JOHN HENRIK CLARKE, "To Know One's History Is To Know Oneself" (editors' title, originally titled and excerpted from "A Search for Identity"), *Social Casework* (May 1970). Copyright © 1970 by Family Services Association of America. Reprinted with the permission of Families International, Inc.

BILL COSBY, "A Fling on the Track" from *Love and Marriage.* Copyright © 1989 by William H. Cosby, Jr. Reprinted with the permission of Doubleday, a division of Bantam Doubleday Dell Publishing Group, Inc.

COUNTEE CULLEN, "Incident" from *On These I Stand* (New York: Harper & Brothers, 1925). Copyright 1925 by Harper & Brothers, renewed 1953 by Ida M. Cullen. Reprinted with the permission of GRM Associates as agents for the Estate of Ida M. Cullen.

JANNETTE LAKE DATES and WILLIAM BARLOW, "Crossover Dreams and Racial Realities" (editors' title, originally titled "Conclusion: Crossover Dreams and Racial Realities") and "Black Comedy, White Reality" (editors' title, originally titled "Commercial Television"), both from *Split Image: African Americans in the Mass Media.* Copyright © 1990 by Janette Lake Dates and William Barlow. Reprinted with the permission of Howard University Press.

ANGELA DAVIS, "Slavery and Womanhood" (editors' title) from *Women, Race and Class.* Copyright © 1983 by Angela Carter. Reprinted with the permission of Random House, Inc.

MELINDA ELAINE EDMOND, "Poverty and Education" (previously unpublished student essay). Reprinted with the permission of the author.

MIA ELLIOTT, "Society Rejects Mixed Children" (previously unpublished student essay). Reprinted with the permission of the author.

MARI EVANS, "Who I Am and How I Work" (editors' title, originally titled "My Father's Passage") from *Black Women Writers (1950–1980): A Critical Evaluation,* edited by Mari Evans. Copyright © 1983 by Mari Evans. Reprinted with the permission of Doubleday, a division of Bantam Doubleday Dell Publishing Group, Inc. "I Am a Black Woman" from *I Am A Black Woman* (New York: William Morrow & Company, 1970). Copyright © 1970 by Mari Evans. Reprinted with the permission of the author.

ERNEST GAINES, "The Sky is Gray" (excerpt) from *Bloodline.* Copyright © 1963 by Ernest Gaines. Reprinted with the permission of Doubleday, a division of Bantam Doubleday Dell Publishing Group, Inc.

MARCUS GARVEY, "Garvey Speaks at Madison Square Garden" (editors' title, originally titled "Speech Delivered at Madison Square Garden, March 1924"). Reprinted by permission.

HENRY LOUIS GATES, JR., "TV's Black World," (editors' title, originally titled "TV's Black World Turns—But Stays Unreal"), *The New York Times* (November 12, 1989). Copyright © 1989 by Henry Louis Gates, Jr. Reprinted with the permission of Brandt & Brandt Literary Agents, Inc.

CAMILLE GRAY, "The Positive Environment in Black Female-Headed Families" (previously unpublished student essay). Reprinted with the permission of the author.

CYRIL AUSTIN GREENE, "The Question of Name: African or African-American?" (previously unpublished student essay). Reprinted with the permission of the author.

HAKIMAH A. GREGORY, "Fruits of Labor, Fruits of Sorrow, Fruits of Love" (previously unpublished student essay). Reprinted with the permission of the author.

DWAYNE GRIFFIN, "Are Black Males Becoming An Endangered Species?" (previously unpublished student essay). Reprinted with the permission of the author.

ALEX HALEY, "Kunta Kinte Is Born" (editors' title) from *Roots*. Copyright © 1976 by Alex Haley. Reprinted with the permission of Doubleday, a division of Bantam Doubleday Dell Publishing Group, Inc.

VIRGINIA HAMILTON, "The People Could Fly" from *The People Could Fly: American Black Folktales*. Copyright © 1985 by Virginia Hamilton. Reprinted with the permission of Alfred A. Knopf, Inc.

LORRAINE HANSBERRY, "A Raisin in the Sun" (excerpt). Copyright © 1958, 1959, 1966, 1984 by Robert Nemiroff. Reprinted with the permission of Random House, Inc.

ROBERT HAYDEN, "Those Winter Sundays" from *Angle of Ascent: New and Selected Poems*. Copyright © 1966 by Robert Hayden. Reprinted with the permission of Liveright Publishing Corporation.

LANGSTON HUGHES, "Mother to Son" and "The Negro Speaks of Rivers" from *Selected Poems*. Copyright 1926 by Alfred A. Knopf, Inc., renewed 1954 by Langston Hughes. Reprinted with the permission of the publisher. "Salvation" from *The Big Sea*. Copyright 1940 by Langston Hughes, renewed © 1968 by Arna Bontemps and George Houston Bass. Reprinted with the permission of Hill & Wang, a division of Farrar, Straus & Giroux, Inc.

KRISTIN HUNTER, "Debut," *Negro Digest* 17 (June 1968). Copyright © 1968 by Kristin Hunter. Reprinted with the permission of the author, c/o Jane Dystel Literary Management.

ZORA NEALE HURSTON, "Tea Cake and Janie" (editors' title) from *Their Eyes Were Watching God*. Copyright 1937 by Zora Neale Hurston, renewed © 1965 by John C. Hurston and Joel Hurston. Reprinted with the permission of HarperCollins Publishers, Inc. "I Get Born" from *Dust Tracks on a Road* (New York: J.B. Lippincott, 1971). Copyright 1942 by Zora Neale Hurston, renewed © 1970 by John C. Hurston. Reprinted with the permission of HarperCollins Publishers, Inc.

PORTIA P. JAMES, "The Slave Inventors" (editors' title, originally titled "Enslaved Inventors: Hidden Contributions") from *The Real McCoy: African American Invention and Innovation 1619–1930*. Copyright © 1989. Reprinted with the permission of Smithsonian Institution Press.

JOYCE M. JARRETT, "Freedom" from *Between Worlds* (1988). Reprinted in *Pathways: A Text for Developing Writers* by Joyce Jarrett, Doreatha Mbalia and Margaret Lee (New York: Macmillan Publishing Company, 1990). Copyright © 1988 by Joyce Jarrett. Reprinted with the permission of the author.

LANCE JEFFERS, "My Blackness is the Beauty of this Land" from *My Blackness is the Beauty of this Land.* Copyright © 1970 by Lance Jeffers. Reprinted with the permission of Broadside Press.

JAMES WELDON JOHNSON, "The Creation" from *God's Trombones.* Copyright 1927 by The Viking Press, Inc., renewed © 1955 by Grace Nail Johnson. Reprinted with the permission of Viking Penguin, a division of Penguin Books USA Inc.

JAMAICA KINCAID, "The Circling Hand" from *Annie John.* Copyright © 1985 by Jamaica Kincaid. Reprinted with the permission of Farrar, Straus & Giroux, Inc.

MARTIN LUTHER KING, JR., "I Have a Dream." Copyright © 1962 by Martin Luther King, Jr., renewed 1990 by Coretta Scott King, Dexter King, Martin Luther King III, Yolanda King and Bernice King. Reprinted with the permission of the Joan Daves Agency.

FELICIA R. LEE, "African-American Youth Resist Using Standard English" (editors' title, originally titled "Grappling With How to Teach Young Speakers of Black Dialect"), *The New York Times* (January 5, 1994). Copyright © 1994 by The New York Times Company. Reprinted with the permission of *The New York Times.*

JEROME MASON, "Stone City" (previously unpublished student essay). Reprinted with the permission of the author.

KHADIJAH A. MAYO, "The Black Panther Party" (previously unpublished student essay). Reprinted with the permission of the author.

CLAUDE McKAY, "If We Must Die" from *Home to Harlem* (New York: Harper & Brothers, 1928). Copyright 1928 by Harper & Brothers, Inc., renewed © 1956 by Hope McKay Virtue. Reprinted with the permission of Carl Cowl, Administrator, The Archives of Claude McKay.

TERRY McMILLAN, "Discovering the Writer In Me" (editors' title) from "Introduction" to *Breaking Ice.* Copyright © 1990 by Terry McMillan. Reprinted with the permission of Viking Penguin, a division of Penguin Books USA Inc.

MARSHALL MERCY, "The Criminal Justice System and Poor Blacks" (previously unpublished student essay). Reprinted with the permission of the author.

JAMES MITCHENER, "Affirmative Action: The Controversial Topic" (previously unpublished student essay). Reprinted with the permission of the author.

ANNE MOODY, Chapter X from *Coming of Age in Mississippi.* Copyright © 1968 by Anne Moody. Reprinted with the permission of Doubleday, a division of Bantam Doubleday Dell Publishing Group, Inc.

TONI MORRISON, "A Difference of Opinion" (editors' title, originally titled "A Slow Walk of Trees"), *The New York Times Magazine* (July 4, 1976). Copyright © 1976 by Toni Morrison. Reprinted with the permission of International Creative Management, Inc. "1923" from *Sula* (New York: Alfred A. Knopf, 1974). Copyright © 1973 by Toni Morrison. Reprinted with the permission of International Creative Management, Inc.

ROBERT W. MULLEN, "Blacks in Vietnam" (editors' title) from *Blacks in America's Wars.* Copyright © 1973 by Dr. Robert W. Mullen. Reprinted with the permission of the author.

VERNELL MUNADI, "Islam and African-American Women" (previously unpublished student essay). Reprinted with the permission of the author.

PAULI MURRAY, "My Life in Black and White" (editors' title) from *Proud Shoes:*

JEAN TOOMER, "Becky" from *Cane.* Copyright 1923 by Boni & Liveright, renewed 1951 by Jean Toomer. Reprinted with the permission of Liveright Publishing Corporation.

MALCOLM X, "Learning to Read" (editors' title, originally titled "Learning To Read") from *The Autobiography of Malcolm X* by Malcolm X with the assistance of Alex Haley. Copyright © 1964 by Alex Haley and Malcolm X. Copyright © 1965 by Alex Haley and Malcolm X, copyright © 1965 by Alex Haley and Betty Shabazz. Reprinted with the permission of Random House, Inc.

MARGARET WALKER, "For My People" from *This is My Century: New and Collected Poems.* Copyright 1942 by Margaret Walker Alexander. Reprinted with the permission of The University of Georgia Press.

WILLIAM WEIR, "Kwanzaa" (previously unpublished student essay). Reprinted with the permission of the author.

KARIE WERMELING, "The Eugenics Sterilization Movement" (previously unpublished student essay). Reprinted with the permission of the author.

PAULETTE CHILDRESS WHITE, "Alice" from *Essence* (January 1977). Copyright © 1977 by Paulette Childress White. Reprinted by permission.

JOHN EDGAR WIDEMAN, "The Ghost of Orion" (editors' title) from *Damballah.* Copyright © 1988 by John Edgar Wideman. Reprinted with the permission of Vintage Books, a Division of Random House, Inc.

RICHARD WRIGHT, "Living Jim Crow" (editors' title, originally titled "The Ethics of Living Jim Crow: An Autobiographical Sketch," parts I-III), from *Uncle Tom's Children* (New York: Harper, 1937). Copyright 1937 by Richard Wright, renewed © 1965 by Ellen Wright. Reprinted with the permission of HarperCollins Publishers, Inc.

ANIKA YETUNDE, "Female Genital Mutilation and Castration" (previously unpublished student essay). Reprinted with the permission of the author.

Index

MW00754816

JUDAS ISLAND

Also by Kathryn R. Wall

In for a Penny

And Not a Penny More

Perdition House

JUDAS ISLAND

A BAY TANNER MYSTERY

KATHRYN R. WALL

ST. MARTIN'S MINOTAUR ⚲ NEW YORK

www.minotaurbooks.com

ISBN 0-312-31387-X
EAN 978-0312-31387-6

First Edition: May 2004
10   9   8   7   6   5   4   3   2   1

For Norman
Here's to seventy-five more!

ACKNOWLEDGMENTS

A perceptive, caring, and dedicated editor is every writer's dream, and I have one in the person of Linda McFall. It helps that we share a somewhat quirky sense of humor because I've found you need one in this business. Publicity and marketing are twin monsters that scare most authors to death, and again Linda McFall, along with Rachel Ekstrom, has helped me navigate those treacherous waters. Thanks as well to PJ Nunn and her staff at Breakthrough Promotions for their work on my behalf.

In the course of researching *Judas Island,* I had the good fortune of being permitted to pick the brains of two very knowledgeable men: Jack Keller enlightened me on the subject of the local waterways and Coast Guard procedure, while John Dukes shared insight and information about the Port of Charleston. Any factual errors are the result of either my own misunderstanding or intentional fictional license. Thanks also to Captain Mark Poindexter and Ken Bell for a chilly but fascinating ride up the creeks and rivers that surround my island.

There are so many bookstore owners and their personnel to thank, I can't begin to name them all here, but you know who you are. There are no words to thank you for your enthusiasm and support. The same is true of my fellow writers, both published and aspiring. It really is a community in the truest sense of that word.

And finally I want to acknowledge the next two generations of my family: Kristin, Gretchen, Erik, Jennifer, and Doug; Liam, Elinor, Benjamin, and Brendan; and Josh, Taylor, and Carli. Thanks, kids. You've kept us young.

JUDAS ISLAND

PROLOGUE

THE FLAT BOTTOM OF THE JOHNBOAT SCRAPED ACROSS
the narrow shingle as the young man leaped out into the shallows and waded ashore. The tide was on the turn, rising for the next few hours, so he tugged the wooden boat up into the scrub palmetto and hawthorn growing nearly down to the water's edge. Though without shoes, he did not feel the sharp edges of the oyster and clam shells strewn along the barely perceptible path he followed toward the interior. As a boy he had fished and shrimped and crabbed the marsh creeks and mud flats of these islands, toughening his feet as well as his spirit. Even without the light of a three-quarter moon he could have found his way unerringly to the site of the gathering.

Fifteen minutes later he paused on the edge of the clearing, surprised to find the fire circle dead and cold, the stumps and logs scattered around it empty. He had feared he would be late, Mr. Clymer having kept him beyond closing time at the Red 'n White to sweep out the storeroom and stack the last of the day's shipments. Today it had been cabbages from one of the big truck farms out near Ridgeland. He hated the smell and the way their slimy leaves stuck to the concrete of the loading dock.

So he had expected the others to have arrived before him, the fire to be already beating off the October chill, the bottle to have been passed back and forth between them at least a couple of times. And tonight he couldn't dawdle. She'd have his hide if he kept her waiting again.

The young man settled back onto his haunches in the thick underbrush, unsure of what had stirred this faint whisper of unease that prickled at the back of his neck. He sat unmoving for a long while, his still form melting into the gray and black shadows, his breath indistinguishable from the rhythmic soughing of the wind high up in the swaying pines.

A soft footfall on the carpet of needles off to his right. He tensed in alarm a second before the suffocating hood dropped over his head. He had a moment to register the unmistakable *click* of a hammer being pulled back before the heft of the rope settled around his neck.

"This is the last of them, gentlemen."

He recognized the voice immediately, low and ugly just a few inches from his ear, and he knew that he was dead.

CHAPTER ONE

I FLUNG MY ARM ACROSS THE WIDE EXPANSE OF BED,
but my fingers encountered only rumpled, silky emptiness. I
cracked open one eye against the shaft of sunlight seeping into the room
through a chink in the wooden shutters. When I had verified that he
was in fact gone, I hitched the duvet up around my bare shoulders and
snuggled back down into the warmth he'd left behind.

Probably picking up the papers. I stretched and rolled over onto my side,
picturing Darnay passing the time with Madame Srabian and her son over
a demitasse of the thick Algerian coffee he loved. As I drifted back into a
light doze, I hoped he'd remember to bring me the English-language version of the *New York Times* along with one or two of Madame's croissants.
Though my French was fast improving, I still couldn't manage *Le Monde,*
especially on an empty stomach . . .

It could have been an hour or only minutes later when the sharp
rapping on the outside door finally penetrated my sluggish brain. I
rolled out, snatching up the shirt Darnay had left draped on the bedpost
the night before. Not much in the way of a robe, but at least it covered
the important parts. Besides, I expected my caller would prove to be
Darnay himself.

As I padded down the hallway and across the worn Aubusson carpet
covering the front room of the vast apartment, I could envision him just

on the other side of the massive old door: the newspapers, a huge box of pastries, and a net bag full of fruit from the little stand on the corner clutched to his chest as he fumbled for his keys.

We never had visitors except, occasionally, his chic, sour-faced sister Madeleine, and she, thank God, was spending the month at the house in Provençe.

But the smile of welcome died on my lips when I flung open the door to a young man in yellow-and-black spandex, his long orange hair flowing from beneath a bullet-shaped bicycle helmet. Unconsciously I took a step back, my fingers working of their own accord to fasten the top button of the wrinkled white shirt.

"M. Darnay, *s'il vous plaît.*"

I watched him check out the long expanse of bare leg that constituted a good part of my five-foot, ten-inch frame, his gaze lingering in a couple of places along the way, before his knowing eyes finally fastened on my face. The grin was pure French; and, because I had grown used to their frankness in my four months of living in Paris, I tried not to take offense. "*Il n'est pas chez nous. Puis-je vous aider?*"

I was pretty sure I'd gotten it right, and Darnay swore my pronunciation improved daily.

"*Êtes-vous sa femme?*"

"*Non, seulement une amie. Pourquoi?*"

Now that we'd established that Darnay was not there, and that I was not his wife but merely a friend, the courier seemed at a loss. He consulted his watch then flipped through some papers attached to a metal clipboard. Finally, with a shrug that exemplified the live-and-let-live attitude of almost everyone in this marvelous city, he thrust a pen into my hand. "*Nombre sept, mademoiselle.*"

I scratched *Bay Tanner* on line seven and accepted the bulky envelope. It bore no return address, but the label looked as if it had been computer-generated. *Perhaps something he's ordered,* I thought, although a catalogue shipment would have come through the mail or by one of the overnight delivery services, not a special courier. I turned the package over in my hand then looked up, surprised to see my admirer still studying me intently. I was trying to formulate a stinging rebuke he might possibly understand when it dawned on me he was waiting for a tip.

Since I so obviously had no pockets, I left him standing in the doorway as I dropped the envelope onto the Louis XIV console table and sprinted back into the bedroom. I snatched a few francs from my wallet and paused long enough to pull on a pair of black leggings before returning to thrust the bills into the messenger's hand. He looked disappointed, whether from the size of the tip or from my more modest state of attire, I couldn't tell.

Again I studied the package, squeezing it gently in an effort to determine exactly what it might contain. It felt like a thick wad of paper, although that could have been padding for something fragile or easily crushed. Which might explain the courier. The French postal service was no better than its American counterpart when it came to complying with such optimistic requests as "Handle with Care." With a shrug I propped the envelope up against one of the heavy brass candlesticks on the console.

I was heading down the hall to our one bathroom, visions of a long soak in the mammoth, claw-footed tub sending little murmurs of anticipation vibrating in my throat, when I heard the click of the lock. Alain Darnay, burdened much as I had imagined him just a few minutes before, sidled into the entryway and pushed the door closed with a sharp thrust of his right hip. I hurried to meet him, laughing as I disentangled his long fingers from the string bag of oranges and peaches dangling from his hand.

"Thank God!" he exclaimed and dropped a brief kiss on the end of my nose. "I thought I might not make that last flight of stairs." He hurried into the narrow kitchen to deposit his other treasures on the old oak table. We took most of our meals there, despite the magnificence of the formal dining room just a few steps away.

"Here, let me help." I stacked the heavy newspapers off to one side, drew a sharp paring knife from the old wooden block on the counter, and cut the twine on the pastry box while Darnay shrugged out of his jacket.

Even in the bulky fisherman's sweater and baggy corduroy pants, he looked too thin. I had made it my mission over the past few months to feed him back into the vigorous health he had enjoyed before an encounter with a bullet nearly ended our burgeoning love affair, along with his life. That my amateur investigation into a series of gruesome murders had been the cause of this misery still lay like a hard kernel of guilt in my chest.

"Jean sends his regards," he said, rubbing his hands together to warm them as I set the kettle on for tea. Despite the time-worn words of the old song, April in Paris was turning out to be gray and decidedly cold. "He wants to know when you'll be available for his next lesson."

Madame's twelve-year-old son and I had worked out a mutual assistance pact, he for his English and I for my French. We met as often as his schoolwork allowed, usually while exploring the markets, shops, and parks which abounded in our little neighborhood of tree-lined boulevards.

"I nearly forgot," Darnay said, pausing in the midst of peeling and slicing the fruit to reach for the jacket he had slung over the back of a chair. "I picked up the *poste* on my way up. There seems to be something for you." He grinned as he waved the white envelope. "From the colonies, I believe." I snatched it from his hand just as the kettle set up its insistent whistle. "Go ahead and read it, *ma petite*. I'll make the tea."

The letter was from my father. Retired Judge Talbot Simpson, wheelchair-bound after a series of strokes, steadfastly refused to succumb to such modern conveniences as e-mail or the trans-Atlantic telephone system. While I kept in close touch with most of my friends and acquaintances via the Internet, I was still forced to wait upon the whims and vagaries of the international postal service for word from the Judge.

I spread the pages out on the table while Darnay poured tea. I marveled at the steadiness of my father's handwriting, despite his infirmity and the fact that his eightieth birthday was fast approaching. Absently I slathered butter on a still-warm croissant, smiling to myself at the gossip which had become the lifeblood of the Judge's existence in the small town of Beaufort, South Carolina, just up the road from my own home on Hilton Head Island.

Home, I thought, my eyes darting to Alain Darnay.

He had spread out the newspaper *Le Monde* across the old wooden table and sat hunched over it, absorbed by some article, while he sucked the sweet juice from a dripping section of orange.

I sighed and blew across the rim of my cup, then sipped the hot, strong tea.

As soon as he had been pronounced healed by his bosses at Interpol, who had spirited their best undercover agent away immediately after his wounding, I had sped to Paris. To this apartment, this life. Widowed nearly two years before by my husband Rob's murder, it had seemed imperative to find out if I could find it in myself to commit to another man. To Darnay. Four months later, I still didn't have an answer.

I flipped to the second page of the letter, smiling despite myself at my father's seemingly endless store of anecdotes about his old cronies in local politics and law enforcement. Including my brother-in-law, Beaufort County Sheriff's Sergeant Red Tanner, a younger, shorter version of my dead husband. Red occupied a special place in my life, the spot I would have reserved for an annoying but well-loved brother if my parents had seen fit to provide me with one. I missed him, too.

The paper rattled as Darnay turned to a new section. I looked up to find his steel-blue eyes fixed on mine. "Everything all right?"

"Fine," I answered and popped the remaining bite of croissant into my mouth.

"Bien." He bent again to his newspaper.

I read through the remaining few paragraphs, pleased to find that Lavinia Smalls, our family's housekeeper through most of my childhood and now my father's caregiver and companion, had added a few lines at the bottom. She conveyed news of my longtime friend Bitsy and her children, reported on the health and well-being of her own son and his family, and asked when I thought I might be coming home. Twice.

"Bay?" Once again I found Darnay staring at me from across the table. "Are you sure everything is fine? You look troubled, *ma petite.*"

I smiled and shook my head, confused and embarrassed at the wave of longing that swept over me at Lavinia's question. *Home?* Of course it was. But Darnay's life was here. Despite having retired from Interpol, he was bound to France, not only by his father's heritage, but by the land. The small vineyard would be his as soon as his health permitted him to claim it. His sister Madeleine could barely wait to take possession of the sprawling Paris apartment.

At first we did not discuss our life together any farther than the next day, the next outing—to the palace at Versailles, to the marvelous castle at Chenonçeaux, to Monet's gardens at Giverny, no doubt bursting soon, in spite of the cold, into glorious spring color. We had both been content to let the days of rediscovering each other drift from one week into the next, both of us fearful of planning too far ahead. Life had taught us the futility of that, but sooner or later we would have to decide.

I would have to decide.

Absorbed in my own thoughts, I hadn't registered his moving until I felt his warm breath against the side of my neck. I leaned back into his arms.

"You are homesick, *n'est-ce pas?* Would you like to go for a visit?"

"Could we?" I tried to keep the excitement out of my voice, but all of a sudden the idea of it seemed to consume me. "Are you sure you're up to it? I mean, you are nearly finished with the doctors, but what about therapy? Are you strong . . . ?"

"*Sshhh! Tais-toi!*" He pressed one finger against my lips. "Why don't you check the Internet for flights, see what can be arranged? Go on, let me finish my newspaper in peace."

I kissed the hand that trailed across my cheek then flew toward the bedroom where Alain's laptop computer rested incongruously on an ornately gilded little bureau. I could be booking flights in a matter of minutes. *By this time tomorrow,* I thought, *we could be stepping off the plane in Savannah into warmth and sunshine and the sweet scents of home.*

I checked my headlong dash down the hallway as I passed the console beneath the heavy gilt mirror. I scooped up the package and reversed my steps back into the kitchen.

"Alain, I completely forgot! This came for you by messenger just before you got home."

I slid it onto the table, startled by his grunt of surprise and a barely perceptible recoil, as if the padded envelope were alive—and dangerous.

For a moment he stared, his hands still gripping the edges of *Le Monde,* his cheeks drained of even the faint color the chill April sun had given him during his morning walk.

"What is it? Alain?" I prodded when he didn't reply.

With leaden arms, he lowered the paper and ran his fingers lightly across the address label. He turned it over, testing the contents much as I had done when it had been placed into my hands. Then with a sigh he said, *"Un couteau, s'il vous plaît."*

I handed him the same small knife I had used for the string on the pastry box, and he slit open the envelope. It *was* paper, several sheets of computer printout, with a handwritten note clipped to the upper left-hand corner. I could make out nothing of the heavy script except for the signature: *LeBrun.*

I didn't need a translator. The guilty excitement in Alain's eyes told me all I needed to know. LeBrun ran Interpol. Darnay had indeed recovered enough to travel.

And they wanted him back.

CHAPTER TWO

THE AIRPORT LIMOUSINE NEGOTIATED THE LAST OF THE ruts in the dusty dirt road and eased into the circular drive in front of Presqu'isle. I'd had the window rolled down during the entire one-hour trip from Savannah, and I leaned out to reacquaint myself with the sight of my childhood home. The tall, square-columned house sat high on its arched foundation of tabby, its split staircase gleaming with a fresh coat of white paint in the late afternoon sun.

The driver shut off the engine then moved around to the back of the vehicle to fling open the trunk. Behind me I heard his grunts as he hefted the luggage onto the ground. I sat, my chin resting on my arms, savoring the familiar smell of pluff mud and decay drifting up from the narrow strip of marsh that bordered St. Helena Sound at the rear of the property. In the warm silence of April in the Lowcountry I heard the muted cries of the curlews and ibis, the drumlike cadence of a woodpecker attacking the bole of a loblolly pine, and the high scream of a solitary gull as he skimmed along the shoreline in search of food and his fellows.

The driver paused, one highly polished black shoe resting on the first of the sixteen steps leading up to the verandah. "Ma'am," he called, indicating with a nod the two oversized suitcases he struggled with, "you want them all up here?"

"What?" I mumbled, startled by the sharp interruption of my

dreamy reverie, then, "Oh, the bags. Sure. Up on the porch is fine. I'll be right there."

I retrieved my tote from the floor next to my feet and pulled a twenty from my wallet, glancing to the empty seat beside me. With a brief shake of my head to clear the tears I felt rising in my throat, I pushed open the car door. I slung the jacket of my rumpled suit over one arm and followed the driver up the steps.

I leaned against the railing and gazed out across the front lawn. A carpet of pink and white petals lay strewn beneath the line of shrubs bordering the road, evidence that I had missed the azaleas in bloom. If the weather gods smiled, spring almost always came early to this south-ernmost tip of the Carolinas, bathed in soft breezes out of Florida and nudged gently by the warmth of the Gulf Stream as it meandered by off shore.

"I can take these inside if you like."

I turned at his voice, the nasal twang and harsh vowels betraying him as a Yankee transplant, one of thousands who swelled our already exploding population every month.

"No thanks, that's fine." I reached to hand him the twenty as he set the last two smaller cases next to the larger ones, arranging them so that all the edges were perfectly aligned.

An obsessive-compulsive Yankee, no less, I thought and smiled at his nod of thanks. He'd go far in this land of "Fiddle-dee-dee, I'll just worry about that tomorrow." No doubt he'd own the limousine company one day.

The longing for a cigarette jolted me, and I actually felt my hand reaching into my bag before my conscious mind ordered it to halt. I had quit, with only a little help from the various nicotine-replacement aids, as soon as it became apparent that Darnay's damaged lung could not tol-erate the intrusion of smoke—his own or anyone else's. With that kind of incentive it had been much less stressful than I'd ever imagined. Strangely emancipating as well, and not just because I was no longer burdened with the paraphernalia of smoking. For the most part I had conquered the need. Incredible, too, that I had found the commitment so easy to keep in a country where everyone lit up everywhere, and no-smoking signs were as rare as restaurants that didn't serve wine.

Darnay's image shimmered before my eyes in the waning afternoon sun, and I pushed it away with an angry twist of my head. I had known what his decision would be—would *have* to be—the moment I recognized the signature on the background material LeBrun had sent to entice him back into their deadly game. Twenty-four hours of pleading and shouting had not altered his grim determination. Nor had it changed my own.

I had watched him hover near death once before. I couldn't do it again.

"Bay?"

I hadn't heard the heavy front door swing open on its well-oiled hinges. I turned to find Lavinia Smalls, her worn hands the color of polished oak folded primly against the starched blue apron. Her deep brown eyes regarded me solemnly. We stood staring at each other for a long moment, a lifetime of shared memory hovering between us on the still air of the wide verandah.

Then she smiled and opened her once-strong arms, and I rushed into her welcoming embrace, knowing as I laid my cheek against her face that I was truly home.

If my father felt any joy at the return of the prodigal daughter, he managed to conceal it well behind a cloud of smoke from his contraband Cuban cigar. I found him ensconced in his favorite spot on the verandah at the rear of the restored antebellum mansion. He had settled his wheelchair in the shade to the left of the ramp leading out from his old study which we had converted into a bedroom after his last stroke.

"Hello, Daddy." I pulled up my assigned rocker and kicked off my low-heeled pumps.

"About time you quit gallivantin' all over the damn world and came back where you belong." He cast a sidelong glance at me from the corner of his clear gray eyes and lifted his glass of bourbon and lemonade from the wicker table between us.

I made no attempt to embrace my father. Ours had never been a *touching* family, and we abhorred naked displays of emotion, which was why his lack of enthusiasm didn't particularly bother me. I hitched a footstool over in front of me, propped up my stockinged feet, and let the warmth and the birdsong and the soft breeze off the Sound settle around me. Again I breathed deeply of the dank odor of the marsh.

We sat that way for some time, the near silence and the familiar serenity of the Lowcountry afternoon lulling me into a peaceful half-doze until the Judge's words jerked me awake.

"You really quit smoking?"

I rubbed a hand across my face, willing myself back into consciousness. "Yes, sir. I've been clean for three months now."

His snort spoke volumes. "Well, don't think you're gonna start in on me about it. It's bad enough havin' Vinnie dole out my cigars and measure the level in the whiskey decanter every damn day. I won't tolerate any such nonsense from you."

"No, Your Honor."

I caught the twitch at the corner of his mouth just before he turned to face me.

"You look tired," he said, his voice softening now that he'd reestablished the chain of command to his satisfaction. "Bad flight?"

"No, just long. But I'm going to have to force myself to stay awake until something resembling a normal bedtime, or I'll never get reoriented."

I waited for him to ask the obvious question. Instead he resumed his contemplation of the wide lawn rolling down to the short dock and the soft lavender of evening creeping across the water. I realized I would have to be the one to raise the painful subject and get it out of the way.

"Darnay's going back to work."

"I figured as much." He rattled the melting ice cubes around in his glass before swallowing the last of his diluted drink. "Can't expect a man to retire at his age."

The breeze had freshened, bringing with it the lingering remnants of winter's chill, and I shivered. "He wouldn't have been idle," I said, rubbing my hands along the silken sleeves of my thin blouse. "He has the house, the farm in Provençe . . ."

On the fading smoke from the Judge's cigar I drifted back to the cold Paris nights, Darnay and I wrapped in the duvet, curled on the Empire sofa before a blazing fire. Heads close together, we had pored over his sketchpad filled with drawings, designs, and landscapes. He would transform *Le Manoir d'Or* from a drafty, seventeenth-century cottage into a comfortable, modern home surrounded by a few acres of vines. In my mind we walked there, arm in arm, as the last light of a summer evening burnished the golden stone of the manor house, and sea-eyed children with dimples in their tiny chins protested the call to bed.

"Bay?" Lavinia's soft tread on the old boards of the verandah had failed to penetrate my reverie, and I jumped. "Sorry. Telephone," she said.

"Is it . . . ?"

"No, it's Erik. Callin' to welcome you home, I expect. Shall I take a message?"

"No, thanks. I'll get it." I swiped my thumbs across the corners of my eyes and forced my swollen feet back into my pumps.

"Are you staying the night?" Lavinia asked as I followed her down the ramp and into the Judge's study.

"If it's okay," I answered, unable to contemplate the cold, yawning emptiness of the beach house on Hilton Head. Without Dolores and the cat, there was nothing and no one to care if I ever returned.

"Dinner in about an hour," she said over her shoulder as she made her way toward the kitchen. "Get changed and you can give me a hand."

As if she needed my help, I thought. My culinary skills, though vastly improved during my sojourn in the land that invented haute cuisine, were still rudimentary at best. I forced a smile into my voice and picked up the receiver.

"Hey, Erik! What's up?"

"So the long-lost Bay Tanner returns! Welcome home, partner."

Erik Whiteside was the third member, along with the Judge and me, of the loose confederation we had dubbed Simpson & Tanner, Inquiry Agents. The manager of an electronics store in Charlotte, Erik brought a sharp intellect and an encyclopedic knowledge of computers and the Internet to our fledgling enterprise which so far had failed to attract a single paying client. At least so far as I knew. I had been out of circulation for nearly five months.

"Thanks. It's good to be back," I said.

The silence grew as Erik fumbled for some way to inquire about what had sent me scurrying back to the old homestead. My e-mail to him had merely announced my intentions and approximate arrival time without offering any explanation as to the reasons for my abrupt departure from the City of Light.

I decided to let him off the hook. I was going to have to get used to answering the unasked question. "Darnay had some business to take care of, family stuff, so I decided to spend a little time at home." I lied with an ease that made me just a little uncomfortable.

"Great! So how about getting together? We could run down there this weekend, if it's okay with you."

"We?"

"Well, you know, Mercer and I. We've sort of been seeing each other now and then."

I could visualize the color creeping slowly up toward his pale blond hair, and it brought me the first genuine pleasure I'd felt in a number of days. That my flaky half fifth cousin, Mercer Mary Prescott, and my rock-solid partner had hit it off still amazed and delighted me. At least someone's love life was on track.

"Sure, that would be great. When do you think you'll head out?"

"I'll check on hotels and see what we can work out for Friday night. If I leave here around noon, I can pick Merce up at the farm on the way down."

My cousin and her mother rented a small place about halfway between Orangeburg and Walterboro. I was surprised to hear that, despite their newfound wealth, they still lived in the ramshackle old farmhouse where I had sought refuge just before Christmas last year. I turned at the hiss of the tires on the Judge's motorized wheelchair as he rolled down the ramp.

"Forget about hotels, Erik," I said, recalling the mass of humanity pressing around the carousels on the lower level of the Savannah Airport

as I'd claimed my bags. "It's Heritage week. You'd better plan on staying with me at the beach house."

The annual PGA tournament, contested on the famous Harbour
Town golf course in Sea Pines on the south end of Hilton Head, swelled
our population to overflowing every April.

"You sure? We wouldn't want to impose."

"Not at all," I replied with false confidence. *Friday!* Which left me
only a couple of days to get the house opened up and in some kind of
condition to receive visitors. And then there were groceries to buy and
flowers and . . . But it beat the hell out of sitting around alone and
brooding. "I'm looking forward to it," I said with a conviction I almost
believed.

"It won't just be all pleasure, either," Erik said with the hint of a
smile in his voice. "I think we might have a client."

"Oh, really?"

"Yeah, this guy I know in Charleston called and asked if I could help
him find some stuff on the Web, maybe teach him how to get into some
places he couldn't access." Erik's prowess in penetrating secure servers
and databases had been well established during our initial collaboration
in tracking down a vicious serial killer. "It sounded pretty weird, so I
pressed him for details. I know it's not exactly what we set out to do, but
he doesn't want to go to the cops, and his dad's got plenty of money, so
that won't be a problem. I told him all about you and the Judge, and he
wants to hire us, but I told him I'd have to run it by you guys first."

Despite myself, I was intrigued. "So what is it he wants to know?"

The pause lasted just long enough to achieve the effect Erik intended. "He dug up a body, and he wants us to find out who it was."

CHAPTER
THREE

I SHUT OFF THE IGNITION AND SAT FOR A MOMENT IN MY driveway, savoring the silence. The house looked much the same, the boards replaced after the explosion already weathering into the same muted, silvery tan of the original wood siding. The shrubs were neatly trimmed, and the ever-present pine straw had been blown from the concrete pad into neat piles along its edges. Apparently the maintenance company I'd hired before dashing off to Paris had been earning its fees in my absence.

I slammed the door on the rented car then paused to allow the low murmur of the ocean to wash over me. The rhythmic *whoosh* and roll of the breakers soothed some of the chaotic jumble rattling around in my head: *Rob, Dolores, fire, explosion, Mr. Bones, pain, death . . . Darnay.*

I shook off the ghosts and began wrestling my bags from the shallow trunk. If I kept myself busy, perhaps I could hold the memories at bay. Slamming the lid, I decided the first order of business was transportation. I hated the thought of having to shop for a vehicle again, but it was something I had to face up to soon. Considering the fact I had demolished two perfectly good automobiles in a matter of six months, I hoped I would still be able to get insurance.

The stale, heavy air hit me like a slap when I stepped through into the foyer. Without hesitating I strode across the great room and flung open the French doors onto the deck, moving purposefully then from room to room until every window in the house stood wide to the cool breeze drifting over the dunes from the beach.

Two hours later I had slid the last of my French silk lingerie into the dresser drawers, stowed the suitcases in the attic, and stood leaning against the railing on the deck outside my bedroom. The evening sky over the ocean had deepened to a rich purple, and against this darkening backdrop, the lights of a freighter passing by on its way to the Port of Savannah sparkled on the horizon. Below, the rustling of the night creatures accompanied the cries of hungry gulls and the soft rattling of the wind in the palmettos.

I was home, and I wanted a cigarette so badly I could have screamed.

By the time I set the last pots of bright red geraniums and scarlet-throated hibiscus along the edges of the back deck on Friday night, the smoking urge had subsided to manageable proportions, and I had amazed myself at what I had accomplished in two short days. The refrigerator and larder overflowed with the results of my extended excursion to Publix; the cleaning ladies had helped me banish the accumulated dust of four months of neglect from furniture, walls, and carpets; and a call to Carolyn's Nursery on the north end of the island had brought an efficient crew to transform my winter-brown flowerbeds into spring magnificence.

I turned at the sound of a powerful engine easing up the driveway and went to greet my guests, the first I had allowed to storm the walls of my hideout without Dolores for backup. The idea of facing this weekend without my former housekeeper suddenly overwhelmed me, and I had to wipe my damp palms on the seat of my khaki pants before reaching for the handle to pull open the front door.

They looked almost like parent and child standing there hand-in-hand on my porch. Erik Whiteside, blond and tanned and well over six feet tall, towered above my diminutive half fifth cousin, Mercer Mary Prescott, whose dress and personal hygiene had taken a decided turn for the better since our last meeting. I flashed back to the first time we'd encountered each other, through the bulletproof partition of the visitor's room in the Beaufort County Jail, and marveled at the changes a few short months and an unexpected infusion of cash could make in a girl's appearance. Her mousy brown hair now sported pale gold highlights and curved softly around her narrow face. The grungy, black-rimmed glasses had obviously been replaced by contacts, and I thought I detected a hint of deftly applied makeup, especially around her eyes. The short denim jumper and white T-shirt were pressed and spotless, and I was pretty certain the navy blue Birkenstock sandals were new.

Not a hole or a rip anywhere. *How very un-Mercer-like,* I thought.

"Is there a secret password, partner, or can we come in now?"

I reached quickly to unlatch the screen. "Of course! Sorry. It's just . . . well, damn it, Mercer, I wouldn't have recognized you! Come in, both of you. I'm so glad you're here."

The moment I said the words I knew they were true. During the long Paris winter with Darnay, I had finally been able to shed the mantle of grief and guilt which seemed to have been hanging over me for years. Coming home—*alone*—had threatened to plunge me back into that pit of despair. These two would bring youth and life and happiness into this place of ghosts and bad memories, dispel the aura of sadness that seemed to permeate the walls of the beach house.

I flung open the door and embraced them both.

"So tell me about this client of ours," I said as I poured coffee into one of the mismatched mugs and passed it over to Erik.

Mercer had decided to join me in after-dinner tea, and the kettle had yet to whistle its readiness. I stacked the dirty dishes on the counter and returned to the table where the three of us lounged in companionable informality.

"That was quite a meal, by the way," Erik said, raising his cup in acknowledgment. "Sure didn't take you long to pick up on this cooking thing. Did you learn all that in Paris?"

"Thanks," I replied, unexpectedly shy under his frank compliments. For years my inability to do more than punch the buttons on the microwave had been the subject of good-natured ribbing from practically everyone I knew. "I did take a couple of classes while I was there. It's hard not to get caught up in the whole culinary thing. Food and wine are some of the most frequent topics of conversation. I sort of had to get in the game or find myself with nothing to contribute."

The teakettle shrieked, and Mercer Mary Prescott leaped from her chair. "I'll get it," she offered as she crossed to the range top on the center island.

I pointed out the cupboard which held the tea bags then turned back to Erik. "Okay, enough stalling. Let's hear it."

He grinned at me and sipped his coffee, heavily laden with milk and sweetener. "Well, it's not that I'm stalling, exactly. It's just the whole thing's sort of weird, as I told you on the phone, and I'm beginning to think we might want to take a pass."

"Why? I thought this guy was a friend of yours."

"Not exactly a friend. We went to college together, at N.C. State. We had some of the same classes, and we sort of hit it off, used to meet for a few beers on the weekends, hang out at the same parties. You know."

Mercer set a mug of tea in front of me then carried her own back to her place next to Erik. The smile they exchanged sent a stab of loneliness straight through my chest. *Damn you, Darnay!* I thought for about the millionth time since I'd boarded the huge jet at Orly Airport an ocean away. *Damn you!*

I jerked my mind back to the matter at hand. I was having difficulty understanding Erik's sudden reluctance to give me the details of this supposed new case. He had sounded so upbeat on the telephone. "Why don't you just tell me what this guy wants us to do, and let's talk about it. You said he found some bones. Where? When? Why does he think they might be human? And why didn't he just go to the police?"

Erik's deep brown eyes held mine for a moment then flicked briefly toward Mercer, and it dawned on me he didn't want to discuss details in front of her.

Too gruesome? I asked myself and almost laughed aloud at how ridiculous the idea sounded. Mercer Mary Prescott had been in her share of scrapes with the law, had even spent time in jail. She'd done some

pretty disgusting things in support of her obsession with our shared ancestors, so I really didn't think hearing the details about the discovery of
a few old bones would send her into a fit of the vapors or whatever else
Erik feared might happen. Still, it was his story, his call . . .

I was racking my brain for some excuse to send her out of the room
when she apparently caught the vibes and rose from the table. "I think
I'll check in on Cat, see how she's doing on her own," my cousin said. "Is
there a phone I can use?"

Mercer Mary's mother, Catherine, had a long history of mental instability, supposedly now kept under control by a new miracle drug, but
I was glad to know my cousin was keeping close tabs on her.

"There's one in your room."

I turned back to Erik, remembering with a smile my dread as I'd
pulled long-unused linens from the cupboard and carried sheets and
towels into the guest room. I hadn't a clue of how to approach the awk-
wardness of determining if I needed to make up the sleeper sofa or if
these two planned on sharing a bed. They had solved the dilemma before I even had an opportunity to ask by tossing both bags into the
guest room and emptying two sets of toiletries onto the counters of the
adjoining bath.

"So you really quit smoking," Erik said, a statement rather than a
question, but I answered him anyway, my eyes following my cousin's
progress toward the hallway.

"Yes, I did. Why is everyone so amazed? I thought at least some of
my friends might have had a little more confidence in me."

Erik pointed at the small pile of blue paper littering the table in
front of me. Without thinking, I had taken the empty packet of artificial sweetener and systematically torn it into tiny squares. "Oh, I don't
know . . . Maybe something to do with your obsessive-compulsive nature?" His bright laugh took any sting from the words. "You should
think about taking up knitting."

"Go to hell," I said, returning his smile then sobering. "Tell me
about the bones."

Erik straightened around in his chair and planted his elbows firmly
on the glass-topped table. "Gray—that's my buddy, Gray Palmer—was

doing some digging on this island, and he came across a skull. Human. At first he thought it might be Indian, maybe the site of an old burial ground or something, but then he realized it couldn't be."

He paused and glanced toward the hallway. I followed his gaze. Over the low hum of the air conditioning I could hear Mercer Mary Prescott's voice through the open door of the bedroom.

"Where was this?" I asked. I rose to refresh Erik's coffee, then my own tea, and settled back into my chair.

"Well, that's just it, he doesn't want to say. I guess he could be in trouble for even being there, so he's keeping that to himself for the time being."

"Why was he digging? Did he tell you that?"

"No. He's working with this group, but . . ."

"But he can't say who they are," I finished for him, and Erik nodded.

I flashed back to my previous involvement with one gang of pseudo-environmentalists and another of anti-nuke wackos and shook my head. "No way. I don't want any part of some bunch of nuts with an agenda. I vote for running as fast as we can in the opposite direction of whatever this guy's up to."

"How do you know they're nuts?" There was an edge to his voice I hadn't heard before, a hint of anger.

"Erik, think back to what we just went through a little more than five months ago, what happened to Mercer. We almost got ourselves killed, if you recall."

He shrugged and studied the picture of the Harbour Town Light-house emblazoned on the side of his coffee mug. I watched his wide shoulders relax before his face lifted to mine. The old smile was back. "But we didn't, did we? Get killed, I mean."

"That's not the point. Look, tell me everything you know about this guy and the mess he's gotten himself into. Then we can make a semi-intelligent decision."

"Okay. He found the skull, kept digging, found the rest of the skeleton. When he realized what he'd stumbled on, he covered it back up, marked it so he could find the spot again, and got the hell out of there. He won't say where he found it, and he won't say why he was there. What he wants from us is to find a way to determine who the dead guy is without alerting the authorities."

"Well that's just ridiculous! How would either one of us know a thing like that? The only way to determine the identity of a body, so far as I'm aware, is for a coroner or a forensic pathologist to examine the remains. To do that, they need to have access to the corpse. And something to compare it with, like dental records."

I turned at the sound of the toilet flushing in the guest bath and realized Mercer must be finished with her call. "I don't see how we can help him, do you? Besides I really don't like all this secrecy stuff."

Erik had heard the water running as well and rushed to finish. "He took one of the bones. He wants us to find someone willing to examine it and try to find out at least how old the skeleton is. He'll take it from there."

I sighed and shook my head. This sounded *exactly* like a case I wanted nothing to do with. "How does he know it isn't what he first suggested, an old Indian burial ground? Why does he think the corpse can even be identified?"

Erik smiled as Mercer crossed the great room and started up the three steps into the kitchen. In a voice so low I had to strain to hear him, he said, "Because he found a wristwatch still strapped to the guy's arm."

CHAPTER
FOUR

THE NEXT MORNING WE ENJOYED A LEISURELY BREAKFAST then joined the long line of vehicles snaking their way around the infamous traffic circle on the south end of Hilton Head Island. As we crawled toward the main entrance to Sea Pines, I reached across from my place in the backseat of Erik Whiteside's massive Ford Expedition and handed him our tickets.

"You'll need to show these at the security gate," I said.

When Erik had expressed an interest the night before in experiencing the Heritage golf tournament in person, I had scrambled around to come up with passes to the always sold-out event. Big Cal Elliott, my best friend Bitsy's husband and a man I thoroughly detested, grudgingly parted with some spares he had not yet handed out to political cronies or potential customers of his vast used-car empire. Bits and I shared a brief hug and a promise to get together soon when I breezed by to pick up the tickets. Although she was too much of a friend to ask right then, I saw the questions about Darnay reflected in her soft blue eyes, and I knew I'd be in for an intensive interrogation over our next lunch.

Better get used to it, I warned myself. *She won't be the only one.*

We pulled up to the gate, and a guard in full Scottish regalia, from tam-o'-shanter to kilt and patterned knee socks, glanced briefly at the tickets Erik held out the window and waved us through. We crept along the two-lane road leading into the heart of the late Charles Fraser's visionary development, the first on this once-deserted island which now ranked as one of the poshest resort destinations on the eastern seaboard. Having lived in the area all my life except for my last few years of college, spent at Northwestern on the frigid shores of Lake Michigan, I sometimes forgot that this explosion of population and tourism had happened over a relatively short period of time.

"Is the traffic always like this?" Mercer Mary Prescott asked, turning in the passenger seat to face me.

"This isn't bad at all," I said as we approached the first of the designated parking areas roped off beyond a line of trees to our left. "Tomorrow, for the final round, we'd be lucky to get in the gate unless we started out a lot earlier."

"I didn't realize there were this many people so crazy about golf." Erik cranked the air conditioning up a notch as the uniformed parking attendant waved the line of cars past the overflowing lot and on toward the next.

"It's the biggest event on the island, since the Family Circle tennis tournament moved up to Charleston," I replied. "Some locals plan their vacations for this time every year and get out of town, while others consider it the social highpoint and spend the whole week partying."

Rob and I had been frequent guests over the years at the rolling parties throughout the Sea Pines community, often spending the night with friends on Calibogue Cay just to avoid having to deal with the traffic.

"Maybe this wasn't such a good idea," Mercer mumbled from the front seat, and Erik reached over to pat her tanned thigh.

Again I smiled to myself at this unlikely alliance.

Within twenty minutes, we had wound our way up to the big open area next to Lawton Stables, followed the direction of one of the many volunteers into a tight parking space, and joined the short line awaiting one of the many motor coaches pressed into service from as far away as Charleston. Using buses was an efficient method of handling the thousands who flocked to the tournament each year, and in a short time we were whisked off in air-conditioned comfort and deposited in the heart of Harbour Town.

We followed the throng around the curve of the harbor lined with everything from small motor boats to massive, multimillion-dollar yachts. Mercer Mary Prescott's gold-tinted hair flipped from side to side as her head swiveled in an effort to take in the elegantly dressed people, the quaint shops and restaurants, and the magnificent condominiums flanking this tiny jewel of a marina.

Without conscious thought, my eyes strayed to the windows of the penthouse apartment at the far end of the promenade. For an instant, the noise and jostle of the crowd faded, and in my mind I lay again in the arms of Geoffrey Anderson, gazing out at the lights of the harbor below us. In spite of the warm midday sun, I shuddered, reliving in a kaleidoscopic flash those days of longing, fear, betrayal . . .

"Bay, is something wrong?"

I felt Erik's hand on my shoulder a second before his words registered, and I shook myself as if waking from a nasty dream.

"No, sorry. I'm fine."

His look said he thought otherwise, but I pasted a reassuring smile on my face and moved out into the lead.

"Come on, let's move up by the clubhouse. That way we can see the players on both the first tee and the ninth green without having to walk too far."

I strode off, leaving Mercer and Erik to trail along behind, weaving my way at a brisk pace through the slow-moving crowd.

Will I ever be free of the ghosts? I wondered as we stopped to have our passes inspected at the entrance to the golf course area. *So much misery and death in the past couple of years, and yet . . .*

A roar went up from the tightly packed group pressed along the edge of the number one tee to our left. Mercer's, "Oh my God, there's Greg Norman!" was followed by Erik's laughing, "I thought you didn't know anything about golf," and I was thankfully back in the sunlight of the present once again.

I carried my hot dog, loaded with ketchup and onions, and an icy can of Diet Coke to a vacant table and settled gratefully into the matching white plastic chair. Despite the canopy of shade provided by the inter-lacing branches of the little grove of trees, sweat streaked my face and trickled down between my breasts. I popped the top on the soda and guzzled half of it down.

After giving them a quick orientation on the layout of the various holes, I had sent Erik and Mercer off to explore on their own and wandered down the concrete path to this spot where Rob and I had often rested our feet during previous tournaments. Situated between the fifteenth green and the sixteenth tee, the welcome oasis provided the perfect place to relax and watch the golfers parade by in their groups of two or three, caddies trailing behind lugging the heavy bags of clubs. Sooner or later, every one of them had to pass this spot. Besides which, S.H.A.R.E., the local senior center, manned the concession booth right behind me, and they cooked up the best hot dogs on the grounds.

I'd arranged to meet the youngsters there in a couple of hours.

Youngsters. I smiled to myself and wiped a dribble of ketchup from the corner of my mouth. Erik was only ten or twelve years my junior, while Mercer was at least in her early twenties. June would find me turning thirty-nine, with the ominous watershed of forty lurking right behind. If I ever expected to have children . . .

I glanced up as a cheer erupted from the stands surrounding the green to my left. I propped my feet up on the chair next to me, wadded my napkin and the empty hot dog wrapper into a ball, and tossed them in a long arc toward the nearby trash can. I snapped my fingers when my makeshift missile landed cleanly in the center of the opening.

"She shoots—she scores!"

I turned at the laugh which followed this announcement to find a man towering over me, his face lost in a sliver of sunlight filtering through a gap in the leaves. I tilted my head to avoid the glare just as he removed his sunglasses and moved closer.

"I thought it was you, but I wasn't certain. How are you, Bay? When did you get back? I thought I heard you'd decided to stay in Europe."

It took me a moment to place the eager, open smile and boyish countenance of the young Beaufort attorney who had handled the affairs of the Herrington family. I suffered a brief flash of guilt for not having

been in touch lately with Jordan von Brandt. One of the three Herrington offspring who had inherited their late parents' hardware stores, Jordan had set in motion the chain of events that led me to Darnay.

"Chris. Chris Brandon," he said, extending his hand. "Maybe you
don't . . ."

"Of course I remember. It's good to see you." I shook his hand, lowered my feet, and gestured toward the empty chair. "Have a seat. Tell
me what's been happening in the old hometown."

His answering smile was out of all proportion to my casual invitation. "Thanks! Gosh, you look great," he said, running his hand through
his wavy brown hair in a nervous gesture which would have identified
him to me even if I couldn't have seen his face.

"Thank you." I acknowledged the compliment, recalling with dis-
comfort that the awkward young lawyer had displayed something resembling a crush on me during our brief encounters over the Bi-Rite
Hardware fiasco. "You look different though, somehow. I can't quite put
my finger on it, but definitely different."

The blush started at his chin and worked its way in seconds to the
roots of his unruly hair. "Laser surgery on my eyes. I finally got rid of the
glasses."

"Good for you," I said, refraining from telling him the loss of his
wire-rimmed spectacles made him look even younger and more vulnerable, not necessarily desirable traits in a practicing attorney. "It suits
you," I lied.

"Thanks. So what brings you back? I hope the Judge isn't . . ."

I waved away his concern, although not before a little ripple of fear
ran along my nerve endings. He'd been okay a couple of days before,
ornery and overbearing as ever. And surely Lavinia would have said . . .
I flinched, suddenly remembering the repeated questions in her letters
about when I was coming home.

"Bay? Is something wrong?"

"Oh, no, Chris. Sorry. The Judge is fine. I guess I just got homesick.
Paris is wonderful, but it's so hard to get a decent glass of sweet tea."

He smiled. "I can see how that would be a major problem."

Conversation halted all around as Phil Mickelson and David Duval hurried by us, their cleats clacking against the concrete of the cart path. When their respective fans and entourages had clustered around the edges of the next tee box, Chris resumed.

"Listen, this is really funny, my running into you this way. I was thinking about you just the other day, wishing you were still around." My face must have betrayed the apprehension this statement engendered in me because he stammered a bit before going on. "I mean, you know, it's really great you're back and all, and I know the Judge must be thrilled and . . . well, it's just . . . I have this client." The rambling sentence stumbled to a conclusion, and he regarded me expectantly across the table.

I waited for him to continue, unsure what sort of response I was supposed to make.

"The case is right up your alley, a possible embezzlement or at least some hanky-panky with the books, and I was thinking it would be great if you could take a look at it for me." When I failed to answer, he mumbled, "You know, like you did for the Herringtons."

The offer took me completely by surprise. I had given no thought to what I would do to occupy my time once I was back in my old neighborhood. All I had been able to think of was getting out of Paris, away from the anger and disappointment I read in Darnay's eyes every time we passed each other in the hallway or tripped over each other on the way to the bathroom. I really hadn't planned any farther ahead than the next few days. Chris's proposal had reminded me with a jolt that I would have to find something to do or I'd die of boredom. One thing was certain: I was *not* getting involved with Erik's friend and his dismembered skeleton.

"I might have time to take a look at it for you," I heard myself saying. "Yes, I think I'd like that. When can we get together?"

"Great! How about Monday at my office? Is ten good for you?"

"Sure . . ." I began when I felt a presence at my back, and a shadow fell across the white table between us.

Chris Brandon jumped immediately to his feet. "Oh, good, you're here. I want you to meet a friend of mine," he said.

The shadow moved around and resolved itself into a pretty young woman in a white sundress, her long, light brown hair topped by a wide-brimmed straw hat. She snaked one tanned arm around Chris's waist and smiled tentatively up into his face.

"Amy, I'd like you to meet Bay Tanner. I know I've spoken to you about her. She helped me with the Herrington estate last year. Bay, this is Amy Fleming. My fiancée."

I suppose the shock must have registered on my face, and I found myself uncharacteristically at a loss for words. Amy struggled to keep the self-satisfied smirk of the newly affianced from lifting one corner of her generous mouth. I waited for her to waggle an impossibly huge diamond under my nose, and she didn't disappoint.

Okay, so maybe I *had* gotten just a little too used to Chris Brandon dancing attendance on me, too smug about regarding him as a fawning puppy trotting obediently at my heels.

When I recovered my voice, I immediately wished I hadn't. "How lovely to meet you," I heard myself gushing. "Congratulations! It's strange we've never met before. Are your people from the County?"

God, I thought, *I do not believe I said that!* Mama would have been proud.

"Amy's father's in the service." Chris broke in before his soon-to-be-bride had a chance to respond. "Career Marine. Colonel Harlan Fleming?"

He left the sentence hanging, as if I should be nodding sagely in recognition. The truth was I had no idea who Colonel Fleming was and frankly didn't care to. Except for the fact that Red, my sheriff's deputy brother-in-law, had once been a Marine, I had no connection whatsoever to the military and planned to keep it that way. Over the years I'd had more than enough experience with Citadel graduates, including my own father. The arrogance seemed to linger long after the uniform had been folded away.

"So you must have moved around a lot," I ventured, twisting in my chair to avoid the slanting beam of sunlight.

I was beginning to think the child couldn't speak as Chris replied, "All over the world. Amy was actually born in Turkey, can you imagine?"

He patted her hand, now tucked possessively into the crook of his arm, and she smiled up into his naked eyes.

"Not much different really from being born in the States," she said, the sweetness of her face now evident since she'd dropped the simper of triumph. "Except I have two birth certificates, and one of them is written in Turkish."

I was trying to think of some tactful way to extricate myself from the inevitable next act of this already-scripted exchange in which I would be expected to inquire into the details of the wedding—date, location, number of attendants, an exhaustive description of the gown, etc., etc., etc.

As if in answer to prayer, I heard a familiar voice call, "There she is!"

We all turned as Erik strode up to the table, Mercer trotting along behind. I could tell by his expression that something was very wrong, and my cousin's normally pale skin had gone ashen.

"What is it?" I asked, jumping to my feet. "What's happened?"

Erik stood awkwardly, his head swiveling from Chris and Amy to me and back again. I managed to stutter out perfunctory introductions, and everyone smiled and nodded, but the tension level had to be evident even to someone as generally oblivious as Chris Brandon.

"Well, nice to have met you both," Chris finally said, steering his fiancée toward the sixteenth hole. "Bay, I'll see you on Monday?" he called over his shoulder.

For a moment I had no idea what he could be talking about, then our pre-Amy discussion came back to me, and I nodded. "Sure. Monday. At ten."

Erik immediately sank into the chair across from me.

"What?" I demanded for the second time in as many minutes.

"I just got a call on my cell, from someone named Mindy . . . something, I don't remember now. The name's not important."

"Slow down . . ." I began, but he cut me off.

"She's a friend of . . . works with . . . Gray Palmer. Remember the guy I told you about?"

"The one who found the bones?" A shiver of fear skittered across my scalp and down my back.

"Yeah, him." Erik paused to run a hand over his sweating face. "They just pulled him out of the water south of Charleston. He's dead."

CHAPTER FIVE

BACK AT THE BEACH HOUSE, I ABANDONED MY NEWLY acquired passion for culinary experimentation, and we called Giuseppi's for pizza. Once again Mercer was on the phone checking up on Cat, and Erik and I sat huddled together over the kitchen table.

"Tell me again what this Mindy person said," I urged him. "Word for word if you can remember."

"Why? I mean, what does it matter?"

I had never seen my partner so downcast. Even in the darkest times—his grandmother's murder, the incredible scene high in the three-story house where it seemed as if we might watch each other die—Erik Whiteside had been confident, upbeat, optimistic. This was my first experience with his sullen, defeated side, and I didn't know how to react to it. So far I'd tried cajolery, sympathy, and businesslike brusqueness. Nothing had worked. Time to try another tack.

"What does it matter?" I parroted his question. "It matters because I want to know! Now quit acting like a baby and answer me!"

His head snapped up at the anger in my voice, and his response was just as intense. "You didn't want to help him in the first place! What the hell difference does it make what his moronic girlfriend said? Dead is dead. End of story. Case closed."

Erik dropped his face into his hands in a gesture at once exasperated and pathetic. In spite of his recent brushes with death, the drowning of his old college drinking buddy seemed to have unnerved him completely. I reached to lay a hand on his muscled forearm and forced him to look at me.

"What has you so upset?" I asked softly. "It's a shock, of course, especially since you just talked with him a few days ago. But you weren't that close, were you?"

I didn't notice Mercer had slipped into the chair next to his until her thin, childlike hand joined mine on Erik's arm. The possessive look my cousin shot me stirred the simmering resentment I usually managed to control whenever she was around. In my mind I knew her dropping into our lives on that stormy night the previous November had not directly caused the misery that followed it, but my gut blamed her anyway.

Erik slid his arm out from under our hands and crossed the kitchen to throw open the refrigerator door. "I need a beer." He twisted off the cap, tilted a slug down his throat, and flopped back down in his chair.

"Look," I said as he studied the wet rings the sweating bottle left on the shimmering glass tabletop, "I understand it's not pleasant when someone you know dies." I gulped a little at that masterpiece of understatement. "But it's not as if you could have done anything . . ."

"How do we know that?" he asked, some of the anger easing out of his face. "I mean, God! We . . . we made fun of him, almost. Like he was some sort of kook or . . ."

"Hey!" I interrupted him. "That wasn't *we*. That was *me*. So if you want to beat someone up about it, get the guilty party." I paused to let some more of the tension drain out of the air. "If you like, we can step outside and go a couple of rounds."

He almost smiled. "Nah. I guess I'm being a jerk. I just wish . . ."

"You wish you could change things. You can't." I knew I didn't have to explain to Erik Whiteside why this had become the bedrock of my personal philosophy. He understood. He proved it by nodding gently; and his eyes, when he raised them to meet my own, were clear and steady.

I opened my mouth to ask again for the story of the phone call when the peal of the doorbell interrupted. I grabbed my wallet, and traded money for pizza in the time-honored tradition of my pre-Paris days. I sent Mercer scurrying for plates, napkins, and cutlery as I set the large box in the center of the table. Whatever Erik had to tell me, it would sit better on a full stomach. At least that's what I told myself as I licked dripping mozzarella off my fingers and tried to turn the conversation to something suitable for the dinner table.

"Did you guys enjoy the golf today?" I pulled an errant slice of pepperoni from the bottom of the box and popped it into my mouth. When neither of them responded, I pressed on, determined to keep us away from unpalatable topics. "I've always thought it was a boring game to watch. Especially on television. I put it right up there with billiards and bowling as far as spectator sports are concerned."

Again I got no response. Mercer crossed to the refrigerator and returned with two cans of Diet Coke. She set one in front of me and popped the other open. The silence settled around us. I forced myself to finish another slice before I slid the last of the pizza onto Erik's plate and carried the empty box to the counter. I busied myself with tidying up around the sink while Mercer brought the used plates and silverware to the counter. Over the racks of the dishwasher I saw her nod.

In for a penny, in for a pound, I told myself, not for the first time in the past several months, and sat back down at the table across from my partner. I felt the nervous flutter just beneath my breastbone which signaled my body's craving for nicotine, and I pushed it viciously away. "Okay, tell me about the phone call."

"It's pretty gruesome," Erik said, his eyes darting to Mercer.

"I figured that. You up for it?" I asked her.

"I can handle it," my cousin said firmly, tossing the dish towel onto the counter as she crossed back to the table. "Y'all need to quit treating me like a baby."

"Fair enough. Go ahead, Erik."

"You sure?" He reached for her slender hand.

"God sakes, I used to work in a nut house! You really think you can shock me?"

I winced, but her candor had apparently made its point.

Erik shrugged. "Okay. Mindy Albright. She and Gray work . . .
worked on some kind of project that involved the Sea Islands, up and
down the coast, from Charleston to Jacksonville. She didn't say what
they did or what they were looking for. She just wanted me to know that
Gray . . . that Gray had gone out yesterday on his boat, to check something out, she said. When he didn't come home last night—I got the
idea they lived together—she didn't panic at first because he's apparently
done this before, gotten on the trail of something and lost track of time."

Erik paused and swiped his napkin across his upper lip. He did look
flushed even though the air conditioning was blowing full blast. Mercer
seemed on the verge of asking something, but I quelled her with a
pointed look.

"Go on," I said.

"The police showed up at her door around noon to tell her . . . tell
her someone had spotted his boat running in circles and called the Coast
Guard. It had run out of gas by the time they got a patrol out there."

He didn't flinch, but I could tell it pained him to relate the rest of
the story told to him by a perfect stranger over the phone. The Coast
Guard had boarded the drifting boat and found it empty, although a local fisherman had reported seeing the seventeen-foot Sea Pro spinning in
circles just an hour or so before. While Erik confessed to knowing absolutely nothing about boats—an ignorance I shared—apparently the
professionals took to wondering why someone would have abandoned a
craft with the throttle set at full, especially since a rope dangling over
the side seemed to indicate the anchor might have been deployed.
When they hauled up the line, they found their answer.

Gray Palmer had somehow become entangled in the rope and gone
overboard. Dangling helplessly underwater, he had come in contact
with the propeller. Repeatedly.

Erik stopped, and the air seemed to vibrate with the ugly picture
his words had conjured up. Mercer and I exchanged looks of horror.

"Do you mean . . . ?" I began.

"Yes," he said between clenched teeth. "The props nearly chewed his
face off. The only way they could identify him was by his clothes and his
wallet."

The silence lasted several minutes. Mercer quietly left the table, passing her hand gently across Erik's shoulder before trotting down the steps and disappearing into the hallway. I hoped she wasn't in the bathroom, losing her pizza, which was exactly what *I* felt like doing. I swallowed hard and asked the question that had been nagging at me almost from the first.

"Why did this Mindy person call you?"

"What?"

"Mindy Albright. Gray's girlfriend or whatever. Where'd she get your number? Why did she call *you*?"

Erik shrugged. "I don't really know for sure. She was pretty upset. I didn't want to press her."

"But surely the question occurred to you, too?"

"Sure it did. All she said was Gray had told her about the . . . bones and all, and that he'd been in touch with me about identifying them. She found my numbers in his Day-Timer, tried the store, then my cell. She said she thought I'd want to know."

"Strange behavior for a woman whose boyfriend just died. I mean, you'd think she'd be out of her mind with grief or whatever, wouldn't you?"

An image so vivid it nearly took my breath away flashed briefly in front of my eyes: *Rob's plane exploded in a thunderous roar . . . flaming debris and body parts littered the small country airstrip . . . my own flesh smoldered under the assault of white-hot metal falling from the sky . . .* Without conscious thought my hand moved to touch the scars on my left shoulder, the ridges of the mangled tissue discernible to my fingers through the thin fabric of my cotton shirt.

Erik shrugged again. "I suppose. Her voice was pretty rough, as if she might have been crying a lot. But she wasn't babbling or anything. Gave me all the details in logical order."

The details. I shivered, praying Gray Palmer had drowned or at least been unconscious long before his face ever made contact with the deadly propellers.

"So did she say *why* she thought you'd want to know? Aside from the fact that you and Gray knew each other?"

Erik fidgeted, tapping his fingers in rhythmic succession against the glass table. The sound sent little shivers of annoyance up my spine, and I reached across to still his hand.

"Erik?"

The look he gave me was half apology, half defiance. "She thinks it might not have been an accident, and she's afraid. She asked me to help her." He paused and leveled his clear brown eyes at my face. "And I told her I would."

None of us had the heart for any more detailed discussion of the horror of Gray Palmer's death, but we kicked it around in generalities awhile before deciding to call it a night. Sometimes Scarlett O'Hara's method of dealing with trouble—*I'll just worry about that tomorrow*—seemed the best course of action. I sent the young people off to their room, tidied up the kitchen, and carried a steaming cup of Earl Grey with me out onto the deck.

I shivered a little in the salty breeze floating in off the Atlantic and curled myself onto the brightly flowered cushion of the chaise. I half expected Mr. Bones, the scruffy tomcat I'd adopted after Rob's murder, to come bounding up into my lap as he had on so many other soft nights when I'd taken my problems to the solitude of the stars and the ocean. But, like so much else in my life, he was gone, disappearing into the palmettos as unexpectedly as he'd once emerged. He was a good hunter, as the tiny skeletons that once littered my yard could attest, so I knew he would survive. I missed the warmth of his sturdy body, the reassurance that here at least was one creature who demanded nothing of me except my presence and an occasional scratch behind his battle-scarred ears. I could almost feel his full-throated purr against my chest . . .

I must have dozed in the late-night stillness, because the shrill of the phone inside the house took a long time to register. When at last I came fully awake, I could hear my voice on the answering machine inviting the caller to leave a message. I kicked over the half-empty mug of tea in my haste and sprinted through the French doors just as I heard the unmistakable *click* of a receiver being replaced.

Darnay? I wondered, staring at the silent telephone as if it might somehow reveal its secrets.

How many nights had I waited for his call, for some acknowledgment that he had survived his wounds? I'd never fully understood his bosses' insistence on restricting their most valued undercover agent's contact with me during the period of his convalescence. Had they seen his involvement with me as a threat to their plans? Had they even then anticipated luring him back into their dangerous game, knowing a lover—a *wife*—would be an entanglement from which they might not be able to woo him?

I wandered the house, securing doors, shutting off lights, and setting the alarm system before padding wearily down the hallway to my empty bed. I peeled off my clothes and burrowed under the sheets. With my mind full of death and loss, I expected to fight for sleep, but exhaustion won out.

Sometime in the night I dreamed of Darnay, floating peacefully on a teal-green sea, his arms outflung in a mockery of joy, his slashed, ruined face staring sightlessly into a boundless sky . . .

CHAPTER SIX

I SNEAKED OUT EARLY ON SUNDAY MORNING FOR QUICK stops at the French bakery and the pharmacy, returning laden with warm croissants and the local papers. I made coffee, another lesson learned at the feet of Madame Srabian in Paris, and arranged sliced strawberries and melon on a serving platter. I was just setting the basket of fragrant pastry on the round table in the screened-in area of the deck when Erik and Mercer emerged, hand-in-hand, from the guest room. The softness of my cousin's face and the tender manner in which Erik gazed down at her made me pretty sure they'd just had sex.

The little ripple of annoyance that rose in my chest was tinged, I had to admit, with just a hint of envy. "Good morning," I said, forcing myself into a cheerfulness I didn't feel. "Your timing is perfect. There's coffee or tea, take your pick."

Erik's fingers trailed across my cousin's arm as he seated her, then flopped himself into a chair. "Coffee, please," he said, flashing me his devastating smile. "And quickly."

Mercer reached to pick up the carafe and serve him, then pour tea for herself. "Bay?" She extended the flowered teapot toward me, and I lifted my cup.

"Thanks."

It may just have been my imagination, but her simpering look from beneath partly lowered lashes seemed mocking and more than a little smug. For a moment she reminded me of Amy Fleming, Chris Brandon's fiancée. Did every female on the planet—except me—have an actual functioning love life? And were they all determined to rub my nose in it?

I checked that descent into rampant paranoia and offered my cousin a croissant. "Sleep well?" I asked sweetly.

"Fine," they answered in unison, grinning at each other.

"Speaking for myself, I should have stopped about two beers before I did," Erik said, blowing gently across the top of his cup. "I must be getting old. In college, Gray and I used to . . ."

The introduction of his former drinking buddy, the late Gray Palmer, brought conversation to a screeching halt. We ate and sipped in silence, avoiding each other's eyes, and pretending to be absorbed by the doings of the town council and the school board as enumerated in the Sunday *Island Packet*. When we'd been reduced to picking pastry crumbs from the napkin in the bottom of the basket and passing around the advertising inserts and classifieds, I reasserted myself as hostess.

"What's on your agenda for today? Do you have to head back early or can you stay for lunch?"

My two houseguests exchanged a look which told me they'd already had this discussion.

"We thought we'd get going pretty soon," Erik said, glancing at Mercer, but failing to meet my eyes. "It's a long drive, and I want to spend some time with Cat when I drop Merce off."

Erik Whiteside is a wonderful, caring young man, kind and considerate, and a really lousy liar. It was the main reason his contributions to our investigative enterprise were designed to keep him in front of the computer screen and away from contact with actual clients. Every thought that passed through his mind found expression on his face.

I, on the other hand, was getting depressingly good at lying.

"You're stopping in Charleston," I said, freshening my cup from the teapot. I tried hard to keep anything resembling disapproval out of my voice. "Have you been in touch with this Mindy person to arrange a place to meet? You probably should, you know. It's a confusing town if you're not familiar with all the twists and turns of the old streets. I can help if you need directions. We . . . I used to live there."

His smile of chagrin told me I'd hit the mark. "In the lobby of the Fort Charles Hotel downtown. Shouldn't be too hard to find, should it?"

"We didn't mean . . ." Mercer began, but I cut her off with a wave of my hand.

"Not to worry. I know you both mean well, but have you really thought this through? I won't bore you with lectures about the police and the Coast Guard being far better equipped than we are to investigate Gray's death. You know that already. What I will say . . ." Again I forestalled my cousin's attempt to interrupt, this time with a finger pointed squarely in her face. "What I will say is your assumption that Mindy Albright's fears may be valid is precisely the reason you should *not* get involved."

"I don't get it," Mercer said.

"I do." Erik spoke before I could launch into my well-reasoned argument. "Bay is saying that, if Mindy is correct about Gray's death not being an accident, we'll be hanging out with someone who may be another target."

"You'll be adding yourselves to the list," I said. "Assuming, of course, this girl isn't just paranoid, or some kind of nut case. Either way, it's a bad idea. You're walking into what could be a dangerous situation, with a person about whom you know absolutely nothing, in a setting with which you're completely unfamiliar. Sounds to me like a recipe for disaster."

I rose and began gathering the loose newspaper pages. Mercer stacked plates and cups, Erik picked up the two pots, and we carried the silence along with us into the kitchen. I knew he was giving serious consideration to everything I'd just said, while my cousin was barely containing her desire to tell me to mind my own business. As I filled the dishwasher, Erik cleared his throat.

"Okay, what you say makes good sense." He offered me his killer smile. "But I promised I'd at least talk to her. She's pretty shaken, and it sounds as if she doesn't have anybody else to rely on. What can I do?"

I turned to face him and leaned back against the sink. "You can go back to Charlotte, run your business, take Mercer out to dinner on Friday nights, and put this out of your mind."

"And what about Mindy Albright?" he asked.

"Oh, don't worry about Mindy," I said brightly, wiping my hands on the dish towel. "I'll just tell her you couldn't make it."

"*You'll* tell her?"

"Sure," I said, patting his arm gently. "When I see her this afternoon. Now what time is my appointment at the Fort Charles?"

I decided to take the back way, jumping off I-95 at Point South and skirting Beaufort on Route 17. Traffic sped along at well over seventy until we reached the spot where the road narrows to two lanes near Gardens Corner. From there, the way meandered on toward Charleston, the blacktop seeming to dance in the alternate dappling of shadow and sunlight filtered through swaying pines and sweet gums overhanging the road.

Erik Whiteside and Mercer Mary Prescott had finally left the beach house some time around noon, refusing my offer of lunch, saying they'd grab a sandwich on the way back to Charlotte. I knew my partner didn't like handing over the job of interviewing Mindy Albright to me, but I'd given him little choice.

Something about the whole episode rang false, although I couldn't have said exactly what at the time. Perhaps it was our ready acceptance of everything this unknown young woman had told us. We had no reason to trust her, and yet here I was dashing off to meet someone whose motives might not be entirely pure. *She* believed Gray Palmer's death might not have been an accident. *She* expressed fear that she herself might somehow be in danger. No proof, just feelings. Since I had never spoken to her myself, I wondered how much Mindy Albright had preyed on Erik's sympathy, his innate sense of honor. I wondered how she'd react to encountering, not a chivalrous young man ready to ride to her defense, but a pragmatic woman who'd been led down way too many garden paths in her lifetime. A few snuffling tears and a little-girl-lost look were not going to get her far with me.

I decided I'd find those answers soon enough. As I moseyed my way north in the dowdy four-door sedan, I forced myself to put out of my mind any expectation of what my meeting with Mindy Albright would bring. As it turned out, that was probably a good thing.

Crossing the bridge into the outskirts of Charleston brought such an unanticipated flood of memory washing over me I almost had to stop the car in the middle of the highway. As I navigated through the surprisingly light weekend traffic, everywhere I looked brought flashes of Rob and our life here in this treasure of the antebellum South. Even something so mundane as the Exxon gas station, devoid of customers in the lull of midafternoon, brought a vision of my dead husband, filling the tank and checking under the hood before sliding back into the seat of the white convertible.

In my mind I reach again to wipe the smudge of oil from his tanned cheek, and he captures my fingers in his hand, bringing them to his lips with a mischievous grin . . .

Bad idea, bad idea. The words reverberated in my brain. Nearly two years since I'd tossed everything we owned into the back of a rental truck and raced out of the city we had both loved so well. Two years, one brief, disastrous love affair, and the joy of finding Darnay—and still the pain of Rob's memory held the power to reduce me to this state of ragged breathing, racing heart, and . . .

Screeeeech! Without conscious thought I stood on the brakes, sliding to a stop with the front of the car just nosing out into the intersection. Horns blared as angry drivers mouthed obscenities at the idiot woman who had almost run the red light.

For the nine millionth time since returning from France, I reached toward my bag with the intention of grabbing a cigarette, only to recall, just in time, that I no longer smoked. I wondered how long it would be before I ceased thinking about nicotine as the panacea for all my nervous reactions.

Instead I drew a long, shuddering breath and eased sedately across Coburg Road when the light changed. I ordered myself not to think about Rob, to concentrate on negotiating the narrow, one-way streets that drive visitors to Charleston frantic with frustration, and pulled up ten minutes later into the courtyard of the Fort Charles Hotel. Leaving the car with a smiling attendant, I made my way past the statue of rearing stallions and into the stately magnificence of the downtown landmark.

Scanning the clusters of chairs and tables drawn up into intimate groupings scattered around the lobby, it occurred to me neither Erik nor I had thought to request a description of our potential client. My gaze lighted on a young woman, her long blond hair splayed out across the back of a maroon-and-green-flowered wing chair, her eyes closed in either boredom or sleep. But as I watched, a dashing young son of old Charleston, dressed in the approved uniform of blue oxford cloth shirt, sharply pressed khakis, and Topsiders, approached the girl and swept her into an exuberant embrace. Arm in arm they wandered toward the exit onto King Street.

I took a leisurely stroll, examining the displays in the windows of the shops lining the long hallway while at the same time surreptitiously checking out my fellow browsers, eliminating them one by one by reason of age or gender. And my quarry would be looking for a handsome young man about the age of her dead boyfriend, so there was no use expecting her to leap up and announce herself to me.

I wandered back into the resplendent lobby, admiring the split spiral staircase rising elegantly to the second floor. Above me, two huge crystal chandeliers cast a glow over the green marble counters of the reception desk, as well as a pair of perfectly formed topiaries flanking the main entrance, and a stunning flower arrangement in a mammoth Chinese vase.

When the tap came on my shoulder, I jumped about a foot off the Italian marble tiles.

"May I be of some assistance?"

He wore the livery of the hotel—white dress shirt, black pants, and a deep green blazer with a discreet logo. His name tag proclaimed him to be Robert . . . *something,* whose native language contained way too many consonants and apostrophes and a decided dearth of vowels.

"Uh, yes," I stammered, "perhaps you can. My friend was supposed to meet someone here . . . in your lobby, but he couldn't make it, so

I came instead." The brilliant white smile never wavered, and his brown eyes regarded me expectantly. But I could tell he was thinking about calling security to have this nut case removed from his hotel. "So, you see, the young lady would not be expecting me, and I don't . . ."

"Ah, it is a young lady you seek, no doubt the one from the foundation."

Foundation? I had no idea what he was talking about, but I had no opportunity to voice a question, for he had turned and was moving across the expanse of tile. "This way, madam, if you please. She will be waiting in the lounge, which you see there before you. Please to go up."

The formal, almost British cadence of his voice and manner of speech made questioning his statement seem unconscionably rude, so I nodded my thanks and stepped around him toward an elevated area marked off by a polished brass railing. Dimly lit, the lounge was dominated by a baby grand piano. High-backed leather chairs were drawn up around both dining- and coffee-type tables creating a variety of groupings where one might take Sunday afternoon tea with the family or enjoy an intimate tête-à-tête without fear of interruption.

As I stepped up, I noticed only one occupant, and she turned to stare. It took me a moment to adjust to the dimness, but the woman had already returned her attention to her book. I moved around the table for two at which she sat, just in front of a lacquered Chinese screen, and laid my hand on the back of the chair across from her.

"Mindy? Mindy Albright?"

The young woman raised her head from the paperback novel and regarded me solemnly. "Yes?"

"I'm Erik Whiteside's partner. He couldn't make it this afternoon, so I've come in his stead. May I sit down?"

A nod of the regal head was followed by the extension of a slender arm bound from wrist to elbow in a winding coil of gold.

"Araminda Albright," she said, shaking my hand and flicking aside a fall of straight, blue-black hair.

"Bay Tanner," I replied, and stared into the clear gray eyes of one of the most stunningly beautiful women I had ever encountered.

CHAPTER SEVEN

RAMINDA ALBRIGHT DEFINITELY CAME FROM A VARIED lineage, as evidenced by the straight, aristocratic nose and a slight up-tilt at the corners of her unusual eyes, heavily outlined in black like those of an Egyptian goddess. I hooked my bag over the arm of my chair and ordered a soda from the waitress who had materialized at my shoulder.

I crossed my legs, adjusting the crease in my tan linen trousers, decidedly uncomfortable with the poise of this striking young woman now regarding me coolly from across the table. I cleared my throat, unsure how to begin the interview. I had envisioned some puffy-eyed beach girl with a mane of sun-bleached hair and a head as empty as her wallet. Instead I found myself the subject of a frank appraisal by a woman whose mixed heritage had given her not only an astonishing beauty but a studied confidence as well.

"I'm sorry about your friend," I began as soon as the waitress had deposited my soda and departed.

"Thank you." Araminda Albright adjusted the bracelet twisting its way up her arm, and I realized it was in the form of a serpent. If it were in fact real gold, and if its sparkling eyes—one red, one blue—were real stones, the piece had to be worth more than the price of my last car.

Curiouser and curiouser.

"Erik sends his condolences as well, although he and Gray hadn't seen each other in some time." When my companion failed to respond, I continued, "Miss Albright, I'm a bit confused . . ."

"Mindy," she interrupted, her husky voice inviting intimacy. "Please call me Mindy."

"Mindy," I echoed, although I couldn't help thinking how inappropriate a nickname it was for such an exotic creature. *Araminda* suited her much better. "At any rate, as I said, I'm confused as to what it is you think Erik—or I—can do for you."

Again I felt myself being inspected—*assessed*—by those knowing eyes. Her next words told me I had passed whatever unspoken test she had set for me.

"I want to hire you to find out who murdered Gray. And to keep them from killing me."

I followed the bright yellow PT Cruiser through the winding streets of old Charleston. Araminda Albright had given me just enough information to pique my curiosity without divulging any specifics. Despite my warnings to Erik, I found myself trailing along behind this stranger to an undisclosed location, without so much as a nail file for protection or a phone call to let someone know where to start looking for my body. I tried to find that last thought outrageous and managed only limited success.

We skirted the Slave Market and the Four Corners of Law, including the grandeur of St. Michael's Church. This symbol of the old Confederacy had just recently been restored to splendor from its devastation during Hurricane Hugo. When we finally gained the highway, I realized she had taken me on a roundabout tour of the downtown area in order to head back south, exactly the way I had come in. I made a mental note to ask her if the maneuver had been intended to confuse me or to throw off a possible tail. If she was seriously worried about the latter, she needed to find herself a less conspicuous vehicle. Like mine.

We took the turn toward the beach and a short time later pulled up in the sandy yard of an ancient but well-maintained cottage whose boards had been weathered to a silver patina by the relentless assault of sun and ocean spray. I maneuvered the rental car in beside her and stepped out into a brisk, on-shore breeze and the smell of dead fish.

Shaded by one stately live oak and surrounded by a tangle of sea grape, oleander, and crape myrtle run wild, the old single-story house stood wrapped in porches and the silence of the late Sunday afternoon. I trekked through the loose sand behind Araminda Albright, pausing to shade my eyes from the glare off the ocean. A few yards away, a narrow strip of beach lay littered with seaweed-draped driftwood and the usual debris abandoned by a retreating tide.

I turned toward the sound of jangling keys then followed my hostess across the wide, open verandah and into the cool dimness of the house. The tap of her high-heeled sandals and the *clunk* of my tasseled loafers on the worn pine floor broke the stillness. In the sparse light filtering through narrow slats of bamboo, I could just make out the shapes of bulky sofas and overstuffed chairs scattered around the single, large room. When Mindy moved to raise the blinds on the front windows, I smiled in pleasure at the eclectic chaos of her home.

"Would you like a tea?" she asked, dropping her keys into a sweet-grass basket perched atop a mahogany console table against the near wall.

"That would be great," I said, and she disappeared through a curtain of glass beads that rattled softly as she passed into what must have been the kitchen at the back of the house.

I wandered the room, amazed at the extent and variety of the objects displayed across the surfaces of a hodgepodge of furniture periods and styles. Rattan sat coolly alongside Queen Anne; the stark beauty of a Shaker chair nestled against the gilt magnificence of a French armoire which reminded me of the Paris apartment. Intricately carved jade figurines shared space with bleached sand dollars; a ruby-and-sapphire cloisonné egg on a filigreed stand lay nested within a collection of feathers. Book-filled shelves lined one entire wall, and an antique, hand-crank Victrola cabinet served as the stand for an ultramodern metal sculpture, twisted ingeniously into the shape of a dolphin.

Nothing matched, and yet everything fit, as if each piece had been chosen for the particular spot it now occupied and would have looked jarringly out of place in any other.

Encouraged in my snooping by the *clink* of ice still emanating from the kitchen, I inspected the spines of some of the books. Most appeared to be used, outdated textbooks, at least on the shelf I was studying, and I pulled out a few to riffle the mildewed pages. Several dealing with archaeology and anthropology had large blocks of text underlined in heavy black ink. Biology, philosophy, medicine. Jane Goodall's book on primates, one of the few that looked as if it might have been bought new and not at some flea market. No light bedtime reading here. There wasn't a John Grisham or Stephen King in the lot.

"Here we are."

Araminda glided soundlessly into the room on bare feet, her voice causing me to jump like a burglar interrupted in the act of sliding the jewel case out of the safe.

"Sorry," I said, accepting the tall frosted glass as I slid a volume back into its slot. "I have this thing for old books."

Mindy set the tray on the sideboard. Carrying her drink she settled herself into a rocker draped with a colorful Southwestern throw. "No need to apologize," she said.

I sank onto soft chintz and waited for her to begin. When she didn't, turning her elegant head to stare out the windows toward the ocean, I said, "You have a wonderful variety of things here. Are you a collector?"

"My parents," she replied, her gaze still locked on the soft rollers washing up against her private beach. "They traveled all over the world. My father was a professor of archaeology at the University of Edinburgh, and my mother taught English literature. She was Lebanese."

The short genealogy explained both her strange name and exotic face.

Her gold-wrapped arm gestured to encompass the array of treasures scattered around the room. "They planned to retire here. This was their refuge, the place they retreated to when things got . . ."

She let the sentence trail off, and once again her wondrous eyes sought the sea. I itched to press her for details, but the tone of her words held me back. Her continued use of the past tense made it pretty obvious her parents were dead, and I didn't want to add to her sorrow. Somewhere, between the hotel bar and this isolated beach cottage, the haughty, confident Araminda Albright had disappeared, replaced by a young, vulnerable, and intensely sad girl called Mindy.

"Look," I began, hoping to break the mesmerizing effect of the heat and the silence and the strange woman rocking rhythmically across from me, "I can appreciate how upsetting Gray's death has been for you." When she looked up, as if to challenge me, I hurried on. "Believe me, I do. My husband was . . . killed a couple of years ago, and I spent a good bit of time trying to find someone to punish. I even proved, at least to my own satisfaction, who was responsible. But that's as far as it's gone. I've had to resign myself to living without retribution."

I paused, brought up short by that statement which had slipped from my mouth without conscious thought. *Could it be true? Had I finally come to terms with never seeing Rob's murderers brought to justice?*

"You think that's what I'm after? Vengeance?"

Her gray eyes flashed, and the force of her emotion brought a blush of color to her sculpted cheeks. It was the first hint of any strong emotion I'd seen her display since we entered her sanctuary, and it gave me hope. I'd begun to wonder if she were on some sort of downers.

"I don't know. Maybe not. But you haven't been very forthcoming, at least not so far. As I told you at the hotel, I came up here to meet you in person and tell you that our firm . . ." I almost choked, on the idea as much as on the word itself. Considering our only investigation so far had ended in dismal failure, it sounded pretty damn presumptuous to refer to Erik, the Judge, and me as a *firm*. "That our firm is not equipped to investigate a murder, if that's in fact what this is."

"You think I'm lying?" With a flip of her ebony hair, she rose from the rocker, her fist clenched so tightly around the iced tea glass I flinched in anticipation of its splintering in her hand.

I tried for a calm, nonthreatening tone of voice as I said, "Well, look at it from my point of view. The Coast Guard tells you your boyfriend died in a tragic boating accident, and the first thing you do is ask complete strangers to investigate the death as a homicide."

"I didn't call *you*." *Araminda* had resurfaced, her voice icy with contempt. "I asked for help from Gray's friend, someone he trusted. Whether Erik doesn't have the balls for the job, or you decided to butt into it on your own, I don't really care. But if you aren't interested in hearing my side of things, if you're convinced I'm a liar—or a lunatic— then feel free to haul your arrogant ass back where you came from. I'll handle it on my own."

Araminda Albright glared at me across the wide expanse of pine floor, her proud head jutting out defiantly on her slender neck, and promptly burst into tears.

Half a box of tissues later, I pulled on my navy blazer and joined Mindy on the beach. I left my shoes on the backseat of the rental car, rolled up my pants legs, and swung into step beside her. We turned south, keeping the wind at our backs. Though the young woman was a few inches shorter than my five-foot ten, I had to lengthen my stride to keep up with her determined pace.

We rounded a small headland, having encountered no one but the ever-present sandpipers skittering across the hard-packed beach. As we approached a narrow copse of palmettos a few yards up from the tide line, my companion veered away from the edge of the water and led the way toward a weathered wooden bench nestled in among the trees. I flopped down beside her, breathing a little more heavily than I would have liked to admit. The months in Paris—the languid decadence of rich food and good sex—had taken their toll on my physical fitness. A new regimen was definitely in order.

"Okay," I said, as we watched the sky deepening to a rosy purple out over the water, "tell me everything you know. No snap judgments until I've heard you out."

Araminda peered out at me from around her curtain of hair and nodded.

"But no promises, either," I added, digging my bare toes into the loose sand and wishing I had a cigarette.

"Gray and I work . . . *worked* for his father," Mindy began, stumbling a little over the past tense. "He's Gray Palmer, too. Senior. He owns boats—container ships, actually. His offices and warehouses are down at the Port of Charleston."

"Palmer Shipping," I said, surprised at not having made the connection before.

"Right. But we didn't work for the company."

I remembered then that the man at the hotel had referred to Mindy as the young lady from *the foundation*. "What's the purpose of his foundation?"

If my knowledge of Gray Palmer's other interest surprised her, she didn't let on. "Lots of things. Archaeology, history, ecology. He's especially interested in native cultures, the Indians and then the Gullah, the descendants of the West African slaves. How they lived, how they're being affected by all the development and the loss of their family lands."

"Why?"

The question seemed to unnerve her, and she leaned back to study my face in the gathering dusk. "What do you mean?" she asked.

"Why is he interested enough in this subject to fund an organization and hire people to gather data for him? It must cost a great deal of money."

"I guess. Although he doesn't pay us much. Gray had to move in with me because he couldn't afford his own place anymore."

"He lived with you here? At the beach?" When Araminda nodded, I hurried on. "Are his things still intact? I mean, the police or the Coast Guard or somebody hasn't already been through them?"

Her puzzled frown lasted only a moment. "No, of course not. They're all convinced he just got drunk and fell off his boat. No one official is going to do anything about whoever killed him."

I still didn't understand her willingness—hell, it was almost *eagerness*—to believe her boyfriend had been murdered. "So tell me why you're so certain it wasn't an accident."

"It's the grave. The skeleton," she said. "Gray knew it wasn't an old Indian burial, because of the watch. And he said there was some material in there that didn't jibe with a death which would have occurred over two hundred and fifty years ago."

"What kind of material?"

"He didn't tell me. He thought the information might be dangerous, that someone wouldn't want him out there digging around where he wasn't supposed to be in the first place." She swallowed hard and rubbed her hands across her glistening, almond-shaped eyes.

"Out where?"

"I don't know! Don't you get it? He . . . he went out on his own that day, said he had something he wanted to check out. I didn't think much about it—he's done that before. But when he came back, he was . . . I don't know, *excited* isn't the right word. He was nervous, scared almost, but exhilarated, too. He told me about the grave, about the skeleton, then went right in and called Erik. He said this was too big for him to handle on his own, and his old college pal was 'in the business.' That's what he'd heard, anyway."

I could read in her eyes that some or all of what she'd just said had been a lie. How much or which part I couldn't tell.

"Why didn't Gray just go to the police if he thought there was something fishy about the corpse?"

"I don't know!"

"Did he tell his father what he'd found?" It seemed to me it would have been the next logical step if the young man felt threatened and believed he couldn't trust the authorities. Why call someone you hadn't been in touch with in years, someone you'd known primarily as a college drinking buddy?

Araminda shook her head as if I were a backward child. "Gray hated his father. You remember you asked me why GS . . ."

"GS?" I interrupted her.

"Gray Senior. That's what my Gray called him. You wanted to know why GS was spending all this money investigating abandoned islands and the remains of old cultures? Well, Gray wanted to know that, too. He took his father's money and did the work, because it's what he was trained to do. But he didn't understand it, either." She sighed and pulled the sweater more tightly around her slim body. "GS never did anything that didn't make him a buck. That's what Gray always said."

I filed the son's bitterness toward his father away for future reference, but I didn't think it probably meant much. Name me a young person who hasn't at one time or another despised one or both of his parents.

The thought hit a little too close to home, and I changed the subject.

"So you know absolutely nothing more about where this skeleton is located or what else Gray might have found in the grave. Does that about sum it up?"

"He went back out there on Friday to get more proof, but he wouldn't tell me anything more about it until he had solid evidence. He said he didn't want me to be vulnerable, too."

"But you still think you are."

She snuffled, pulled a wad of tissues out of the sleeve of her baggy sweater, and wiped her leaking eyes and nose. "Listen. Gray Palmer grew up on the water. He knew more about boats than anyone else I've ever met. There is no way he got tangled in the lines and fell overboard. There is no way he would have tried to set the anchor with the throttle running full-open. Someone else did that, someone who didn't want him to get to the gravesite. Or didn't want him to get back." She stuffed the sodden Kleenex into her pocket and stood up. "Come on. I'll let you see his room, although I don't think it will do much good. I've already been through it all myself. But I'm sure he didn't put anything on paper. There was no entry in his site journal. I'm sure he kept it all in his head."

The image of the damage done to that head by the boat's propellers sent a shiver through me which had absolutely nothing to do with the falling temperature, nor with the freshening wind off the ocean. In silent agreement we turned back toward the cottage.

The one thing I had going for me was the fact that Araminda apparently knew nothing about the bone. Gray Palmer had told Erik he'd removed a bone from the gravesite. If it were in his room, surely she would have found it. So her boyfriend had stashed his grisly find somewhere for safekeeping and taken the secret of that location to his death. Or someone had taken it from him.

Araminda, walking slightly ahead of me, sighed deeply and straightened her shoulders, not only physically, but—it seemed to me—emotionally as well. I remember thinking I wouldn't be surprised if those were the last tears, the last display of weakness I would see from Araminda Albright.

I wish to hell I hadn't been so wrong.

CHAPTER EIGHT

HE DRIVE BACK FROM CHARLESTON SEEMED TO DISAP-
pear in a whirl of speculation, my conscious mind worrying
away at the thin threads of Gray and Araminda's story, while some instinctive portion of my brain kept the car on the road and my speed
somewhere under eighty.

I hadn't found the bone. I hadn't found much of anything other
than the usual assortment of clutter one would expect to encounter in
the room of a young man who had neither mother nor wife to pick up
after him. Clothes were strewn across the unmade bed, and papers and
notebooks littered every flat surface. I glanced through a couple of
them, but Gray's shorthand defeated me. Araminda claimed he hadn't
made any notes about his most recent discovery, and I couldn't find anything to contradict her statement. I checked his camera—an expensive
Nikon with a telephoto lens attached—but there was no film in it. I also
recognized one of the handheld GPS gizmos Erik had introduced me to
the past winter. All in all, the search had pretty much been a waste of
time.

Both Erik and I had made the assumption that Gray and Araminda
had been more than friends—*why*, I couldn't exactly put my finger on
right then—but the evidence in his room and the girl's own demeanor
seemed to indicate she had taken on a boarder rather than a lover.

Darkness had fallen completely by the time I turned onto Route 17, and the headlights of the small car cut only a narrow swath through the gloom of the nearly deserted roadway. For long stretches I appeared to be the only one alive as I hurtled down the smooth macadam hemmed in on both sides by endless stands of towering pines. I was grateful for the sudden appearance of the occasional hamlets with their clusters of roadside amenities and scattered houses which disappeared into the distance behind me in a matter of seconds.

Reception was terrible in the no-man's land between Charleston and Savannah, so I switched off the radio and tried making a mental list of exactly what I knew. The enumeration was pitifully inadequate. From Mindy I had learned the foundation set up by Gray Palmer, Senior, was a nonprofit organization funded entirely by Palmer's shipping company. Basically, he was studying the history, ecology, and fauna of the small islands dotting the coastline between Charleston and Jacksonville, Florida. Not the developed ones like Hilton Head or St. Simon's or Amelia, where most remnants of the previous tenants had disappeared under the foundations of sprawling resort complexes and the feet of millions of tourists.

The goal was to determine how these inaccessible little tufts of land had first become inhabited, how the animal population was introduced, and how life there progressed. I'd never given much thought as to how places we now routinely visited had supported life, human and otherwise, before the advent of causeways and humpbacked bridges. I guess I'd just assumed that Indians in canoes and the Gullah in their flat-bottomed boats had traveled easily from the mainland, and that deer, rabbits, bobcats, and the other denizens had simply swum over.

Obviously my assumptions were way too simplistic, otherwise what was the point of investigating? In a way I admired Gray Palmer, Senior's willingness to expend some of his accumulated wealth on a purely academic pursuit, in spite of the son's conviction that the father's motives had to be monetary rather than altruistic.

I hadn't managed to ferret out exactly what Araminda's educational background was, but Gray Palmer had earned his degree from N.C. State in archaeology, with a minor in biology. He and Mindy—along with several other young people the foundation employed—traveled by boat to these isolated islands, gathering spoor, observing and recording the various animal populations, and taking soil and plant samples. They also searched for evidence of past human habitation, sometimes encountering the foundations of abandoned houses or the rotted remains of old cabins. Occasionally they recovered artifacts—arrowheads and rusted implements along with more modern leavings such as tin cans and beer bottles.

At any rate, they recorded their findings, labeled their samples, and turned them over to the foundation for analysis and classification. Sounded pretty mundane, perhaps even boring, at least to me. Why anyone would find these two young people a threat still eluded me. And yet, Gray Palmer was dead, and Araminda Albright was scared she might be next. I knew I had already made up my mind to pursue it, even though I had no real idea of where to begin. Or even of what a satisfactory resolution might look like.

It was an intriguing enough puzzle to keep me from spending every waking moment obsessing about Alain Darnay and his return to active duty in Interpol.

At least I hoped it was.

I had nearly forgotten my commitment to meet with Chris Brandon.

It dawned on me as I puttered in the kitchen next morning, trying to decide where to begin my investigation into the death of Gray Palmer. I'd reported in to Erik the night before, downplaying my stupidity in allowing myself to be lured to Mindy Albright's beach cottage, telling myself it didn't matter because nothing bad had happened. Still, I made a mental note to get my head in the game if I were serious about pursuing this case.

I should probably think about retrieving the 9 mm Glock from its nesting place in the floor safe in my bedroom closet, I thought, as I split an English muffin and dropped the halves into either side of the toaster. I assumed my permit was still valid, although I hadn't had occasion to carry the weapon in the last several months, most of which I had spent in Paris.

Erik committed to gleaning as much information about Palmer Shipping and its CEO's strange foundation as he could coax from the Internet, as well as any background material about Palmer, his son, and the girl. He sounded resentful that I had pretty much shanghaied the legwork and left him only the butt-in-the-chair part of the job, but he finally agreed we each had our own individual area of expertise.

What mine was, exactly, I had yet to figure out.

We hung up, our relationship frayed a little around the edges, but basically intact, with a promise to get together online and compare notes in a day or so. Though Mindy had more than once expressed fear her own life might also be in danger, I had a difficult time accepting that in my gut. I'd been in enough tight situations lately that I'd learned to trust my instincts, at least to a certain extent, and I just couldn't work up any real urgency in regard to this investigation. We didn't have anywhere near enough information to make a rational decision at this point, so I decided to defer judgment until we did.

It was after eight-thirty when some random electrical impulse in the back of my brain kicked the Chris Brandon appointment up into my consciousness, so I had to scramble. I tossed on a slim black skirt and white silk blouse and forced my protesting feet into pumps. I hadn't wanted to bother with stockings, but my painfully white, pasty legs sent me digging into the lingerie drawer. I definitely needed sun, the sooner the better. I resurrected my old briefcase from the back of the closet, tossed in a faded legal pad and a couple of pens, then slathered peanut butter on the cold English muffin and hit the road.

The golf tournament crowds had scattered back to their homes and offices, and traffic was just the usual mayhem of a Monday morning in the Lowcountry. The worst stretch, as always, was from the foot of the Cross Island Parkway to just past the intersection at Moss Creek. As I idled in my drab rental car at the traffic signal at Spanish Wells Road, the image of Dolores Santiago flashed into my head.

How many times had I turned left at this light, following the meandering two-lane road back to the Santiagos' neatly kept home on the marsh?

Not nearly enough, I chided myself, drumming my fingers on the

steering wheel while visions of my friend and housekeeper unrolled behind my suddenly misty eyes . . . *Dolores huddled in a pool of blood in the
hallway of the beach house . . . tiny Dolores swallowed up by the paraphernalia of the hospital room, her shattered leg suspended from a tangle of wires and
pulleys . . .*

I tried to shake off the guilt which overwhelmed me whenever
thoughts of her crept past my defenses. Five months ago I had forced her
out of my mind, fleeing to Paris and my waiting lover. In his infrequent
letters, the Judge had hinted at progress in Dolores's recovery but had
not provided details. And I hadn't asked. I had been home now for close
to a week, and still I had not called. The truth was I couldn't face it if
the outcome had been bad. Better not to know. I clung to my ignorance
like a security blanket.

An ominous *whoosh* as the driver of the big concrete truck behind
me released his air brakes gave me a blessed excuse to shove the guilt
back into its mental storage compartment. I stomped on the accelerator,
and the car lurched ahead, leaving Dolores and memory behind.

In fits and starts dictated by the flood of vehicles choking Route 278, I
finally gained the turn onto 170, only to be stopped a few miles later
by the construction at the new bridge rising inexorably over the Broad
River. Only one lane of traffic was open in each direction, and I cranked
up the radio and sang along to keep my mind from drifting again into
painful territory. When I finally pulled into a parking space along Bay
Street in front of Chris Brandon's building, the white numerals of
the digital clock on the dashboard had just rolled over to *10:00* on the
button.

The office décor, spare and modern, hadn't been changed since my
last visit, nor had the officious little snot at the receptionist's desk.
Cheryl something, if memory served, and her one-word acknowledgment and pointed glance at the round clock face hanging over her desk
told me her attitude hadn't undergone any serious adjustment, either.
Back in the days when Chris had been making half-hearted attempts to
interest me in easing our relationship into something more romantic,

Cheryl had developed an intense antipathy to my person and presence, no doubt seeing me as a threat to her own plans for the eminently eligible young attorney.

I wondered how she was dealing with the reality of a fiancée in the person of little Amy Fleming.

This thought buoyed me as Cheryl pointed me silently toward a chair in the waiting area and lifted the phone to announce my arrival. I barely had time to settle myself in the black leather chair and cross my legs before Chris Brandon popped out of the door leading to his office and waved me forward.

"Bay! Good to see you again. Gosh, you look wonderful. Please, come in."

"Why, thank you, Chris," I replied and edged past him through the doorway, unable to resist casting a smirk of satisfaction over my shoulder at the glowering Cheryl.

It was childish and unkind, and I ordered myself to grow up as I stepped into Chris's office and seated myself in one of the client chairs drawn up in front of his glass-topped desk. As on previous visits, I marveled at the dearth of paper and clutter. My mother would have said an orderly environment indicated an orderly mind, or some such twaddle. She had a cliché for every occasion, and I shuddered, thinking she would probably have applauded my attitude toward the unfortunate secretary instead of condemning it. Sometimes genes have a way of sneaking past your better judgment. At least mine seem to.

"So, what's up?" I asked, pulling my bag onto my lap and rummaging for my reading glasses. "You said something about a possible embezzlement?" I finally located the rimless, John Lennon–style frames and settled them onto my nose. "Have the police been notified?"

"Oh, no, nothing's gone that far yet. These are clients who're convinced they're being ripped off, but don't have enough accounting knowledge to prove it."

"Have they contacted their outside accountant? Their CPA?" It was generally the first course of action in cases like this. Because of his familiarity with the books, the person doing the taxes is more inclined to pick up on anything hinky, especially if he's been alerted to the possibility.

Chris paused, a look of uncertainty passing across his expressive face, and I frowned. "Wait, this isn't another of those fiascos like the Bi-Rite Hardware thing, is it? Please tell me these people at least *employed* an outside auditor."

The fact that the managers of the Herrington family's hardware empire had been doing all the taxes as well as keeping the day-to-day books had led to an embezzlement scheme so sloppily obvious, a first-year accounting student could have tumbled to it inside of half a day's investigation. The biggest problem had been sorting through the tons of useless paper we had been bombarded with. Strange as it might have sounded, I hoped these next folks had been a little creative, could at least provide a challenge while I nailed them to the wall. My former partners in the CPA firm in Charleston had always looked somewhat askance whenever I'd voiced my preference for at least mildly intelligent crooks and tax evaders instead of the stumbling stupidity of most of the ones we encountered.

"Chris? Is there an accountant of record?"

"Well, yes and no."

"That clears everything right up."

"Sorry. It's a little complicated." He pulled one of the gold-plated pens from his onyx desk set and leaned back in his chair, his fingers twirling the slim metal cylinder like a miniature baton. "I don't suppose you've been keeping up with the local scandals while you've been in France, have you?"

I settled myself more comfortably into the client's chair, prepared now for an extended story in the hallowed Southern tradition. "Only the gossip the Judge occasionally passed on in his letters," I said. "What member—or former member—of the profession has run afoul of the law this time?"

His rueful smile told me I'd nailed it in one. "Remember Worthy Foxworth?"

"No!" I shot upright in the chair, my astonishment genuine. Whether in accounting, real estate, or the law, the name Foxworth had always been synonymous with honor and fair dealing in our little corner of the world. Even my mother had been unable to find fault with anyone in the family, all the way back to their original immigrant ancestors fleeing religious persecution in England. "No," I repeated, "not Foxy! I don't believe it."

"Neither did anyone else until the State Accountancy Board revoked his license to practice. Seems he had a little problem differentiating between the money his clients had designated for their tax bills and his own investment account. The market slide last fall hit him hard."

"Worthy Foxworth." I shook my head, still staggered by the fall from grace of one of my early mentors and puzzled by my father's failure to pass along such a juicy item. Maybe he'd thought it would distress me too much. He would have been right.

"Yeah, it kind of took everyone that way. He pled guilty to embezzlement, liquidated everything he had in order to make restitution, and still fell way short. He's doing three-to-five upstate."

"And this is the 'little matter' you wanted me to look into? There's no way . . ."

"No, no," he hastened to assure me. "That's all in the hands of the state boys. Worthy's client list reads like a who's who of Hilton Head money and power. I have a feeling it's going to take years before that mess gets squared away. No, my client is a much smaller fish, so to speak. Mitchell Seafood." He smiled at his own clever turn of phrase.

"You mean the Shack? Those Mitchells?"

Damon "Bubba" Mitchell, an all-pro defensive tackle before blowing out a knee, and his equally massive brother Dwight ran Hilton Head's oldest fishing and shrimping business from a series of docks on Skull Creek. Their dilapidated, four-table bar and restaurant, appropriately named the Shack, squatted next door to their fleet of boats and was one of the most popular seafood places in the area. We locals guarded its secret from the tourists with almost religious fanaticism.

It was all beginning to make sense now. "They were Worthy's clients?"

"Right. Just for taxes. Dwight and Bubba's mother kept the books until she got sick last fall. Cancer. Sad."

I vaguely remembered Delia Mitchell, a taciturn woman with weather-worn brown skin and a slender frame so compact it was hard to believe she could have brought forth the giants her two sons had grown into. "Did she . . . ?" I began, but Chris was already shaking his head.

"No, she pulled through. Had to have a mastectomy, and the chemo pretty well ate her up, but she made it. Problem is the boys had to hire someone to take over the office work, and that's where the trouble started."

It was a story familiar to every accountant who dealt with small business: proprietors or partners whose expertise didn't extend to the mysteries of double-entry bookkeeping entrusting their financial well-being to a stranger who seemed to know what she was doing, only to find out too late their faith had been misplaced. If Worthy Foxworth had had any inkling the Mitchells' employee was helping herself to the profits, he had apparently been too embroiled in his own troubles to do anything about it.

"So what is it you want me to do?" I asked with a decided lack of enthusiasm. Visions of mangled boxes overflowing with random receipts and ledgers, à la the Bi-Rite Hardware mess, sent a shiver of revulsion along my arms, and my mind began searching for some plausible excuse to renege on my commitment.

"Take over for Worthy. The girl has to be thinking she's all set, what with him in jail and no one lookin' over her shoulder. The boys just want you to go in, like you would if you were doing the taxes, and see if you can spot how she's getting the money out. It's almost time to file their return anyway, so it shouldn't arouse any suspicion."

"Are they incorporated? If so, they're already past the March fifteenth deadline."

"No, it's still a proprietorship, just the same as when their granddaddy started it up right after the war. That makes them good until the end of this week. April fifteenth, right?"

"Doesn't give me much time to operate. First thing I'll have to do is file an extension. Where are the records?"

"Most of them are at the docks. Delia kept an office in the back of the retail store. But I did put together a few things for you to look over."

Chris handed me a brown accordion file fastened with a matching elastic band. The label on the front had MITCHELL SEAFOOD typed neatly beneath the imprint of the Foxworth & Company accounting firm.

"Where'd you get this?" I asked, accepting the package and tucking it into my briefcase. "I would have thought all Foxy's files would be in the hands of the auditors."

Chris Brandon's smile spoke volumes about favors, connections, and the good-ol'-boy network, a concept that not only flourished, but probably originated, in the South.

I stood and brushed at the creases in the front of my skirt. "I won't ask. Do Dwight and Bubba know I'm coming?"

Chris rose and moved around to the front of the desk. He cupped a hand under my elbow and guided me toward the door. "Yes. I tentatively set you up for tomorrow at ten, but we can change that if it's not convenient."

"Nope, ten tomorrow is fine."

"Great! I'll call them and confirm. They're really happy it's you, someone they already know. It's going to be awkward for them, especially if you find out she really is skimming funds out of the business."

"Awkward?" I asked, one hand on the doorknob. "Why would they be uncomfortable about exposing someone who's stealing from them?"

"Didn't I tell you? The woman they hired to take their mother's place is Tamika Jessup. Used to be a Mitchell. She's Dwight and Bubba's cousin."

I toyed with the idea of running out to Presqu'isle and checking up on the Judge then changed my mind. Too many things to do, and Lavinia would insist on feeding me. Instead I headed back through the construction nightmare toward Hilton Head.

I stopped at an office supply store in one of the many shopping clusters springing up almost daily along the 278 corridor in Bluffton and replenished my depleted stock in preparation for my assault on the Mitchell Seafood books. I spent considerable time in the electronics section, astonished by the advances achieved since I'd last shopped for a computer. The sleek laptops were already lighter, smaller, and faster, and a smooth-talking youngster who couldn't have been long out of high school nearly sent me from the store with one tucked under my arm.

I resisted both his grinning charm and the lure of cutting-edge technology, at least temporarily, and settled for the boring, but functional aisles offering calculators, mechanical pens and pencils with fine points, and pale green pads lined in comforting, orderly rows and columns. These last required a dedicated search, no doubt a result of the proliferation of spreadsheet programs. But, despite my familiarity with these wonders of efficiency and convenience, I still preferred the scratch of lead on paper when it came to puzzling out the kind of accounting conundrums I expected to find at Mitchell Seafood. There was something about the activity of writing it all down that stimulated my brain in a way pounding on keys never could.

As I pulled back out into the streaming noontime traffic, I felt a familiar stirring of anticipation, not unlike the feeling you get in the pit of your stomach just before you toe the starting line or step out onto the court for a singles match against a highly ranked opponent. I certainly didn't miss advising recently retired fat cats about how to invest their millions for maximum tax advantage, or dueling with arrogant, belligerent IRS agents over the legitimacy of a charitable deduction. Those were facets of my days as a Certified Public Accountant I had cheerfully consigned to the file marked *Never Again*. But I did miss the challenge of the puzzle, the beauty and precision of the numbers. All these years and still I craved the inevitability, the predictability . . .

The certainty of the outcome, I said to myself with a mocking smile.

I gave a thought to stopping in at the Shack for lunch then decided against it as I zipped past the light at Squire Pope Road. Instead I joined the line of cars snaking its way through the Wendy's drive-up lane, and ordered a Number 7 chicken combo to go. Ironically, one of the things I'd missed most during my sojourn in France had been French fries, and I pulled a few from the bag to nibble on as I drove.

Ten minutes later, I pulled into my driveway and stopped dead, all thoughts of food evaporating in a heartbeat. I swallowed hard against the fist squeezing the air from my lungs, the knot of dread rising in my throat.

Tucked in among the trees sat a dented blue Hyundai. Dolores Santiago's spot. Dolores Santiago's car.

I shook my head to clear the paralyzing wave of *déjà vu* washing over me, eased the rental car the rest of the way up to the garage, and switched off the engine.

My day of reckoning had come, and I was not prepared.

With leaden fingers I grabbed the door latch, the chicken sandwich and my office supplies forgotten on the seat beside me. I had only one foot on the ground when I heard the kitchen window slide open above me, and a voice I thought I might never hear again called loudly, *"Señora! Gracias a Dios!* Come quick or your lunch, it will be cold."

CHAPTER NINE

I DON'T REMEMBER WHAT WE ATE OR WHAT WE SAID, exactly. My strongest memory of that afternoon is one of joy— at Dolores's almost complete recovery, at her strong, sure gait with only a barely perceptible limp, at finding my worst fears unrealized. After my initial outburst, we never spoke of the past again, not about the attack nor its terrible aftermath. God had smiled, and now we were both back where we belonged. That was good enough for Dolores Santiago, and she insisted it be good enough for me.

The only topic relating to our previous lives over which we did linger was the unexpected bounty of the cupboards and pantry. I downplayed my newly acquired cooking skills as best I could, laying it off on the necessity of providing for my recently departed guests. Whether or not Dolores entirely bought my stumbling excuses, we both knew we needed her to accept them in order for us to resume our old relationship: Bay Tanner, inept bumbler in all things culinary, saved from starvation of both body and spirit by her dear friend and housekeeper, Dolores Santiago.

I allowed myself to be chased from the kitchen, retrieved my soggy lunch bag and office purchases from the front seat of the car, and carried the latter into the third bedroom. What had once been Rob's and my shared office still housed the desktop computer, printer, and a couple of filing cabinets and had now become the Hilton Head branch of Simpson

& Tanner, Inquiry Agents. I selected a manila file folder from the package I'd purchased that morning, resurrected my favorite Waterford pen from the center desk drawer, and printed PALMER/ALBRIGHT neatly on the tab.

If we were going to run this as a legitimate business, I needed to start treating it like one.

For the next couple of hours I lost myself in the familiar routine of organizing a project while Dolores's soft humming, interrupted occasionally by the drone of the vacuum cleaner, provided sweet background music. I used the word processing program to type up a detailed report on my encounter with Araminda Albright, including all my speculations, and printed it out for the file.

Next I prepared a series of forms using the green columnar pads in anticipation of my meeting with the Mitchell brothers the following morning. Though it had been several years since I had fully utilized my accounting and auditing skills, the routine felt familiar, almost comforting.

Like riding a bike, I thought, leaning back in the chair. My hand shot out, automatically seeking a nonexistent pack of cigarettes and a lighter. The need seemed as much a part of the process as the paper or the computer.

The soft knock on the partially opened door behind me checked the impulse, and I turned to face Dolores, who had a blouse and two pairs of slacks draped over her arm.

"I have finished the cleaning, *Señora.* The carpet, she is *muy sucio,*" she added, shaking her head. "I call the men who do the cleaning, *sí?*"

"Fine. I don't know how soon you can get someone, but I'll be out most of tomorrow morning."

"Mañana, Señora?"

Her brief laugh, the sparkle in her black eyes, made me smile in gratitude for the unexpected gift of her return.

"You're right," I said. "Tomorrow is definitely a fantasy. Whenever you can arrange it is fine with me. I'll work around them." Dolores nodded, turning toward the hallway when I called, "Wait! Where are you going with the clothes, *amiga?*"

One of our agreements before her injury had been that I took care of my own laundry. While that generally meant hauling anything which needed ironing down to the local cleaners, I handled the mundane things like jeans and underwear on my own. However, that hadn't kept Dolores from trying to sneak it by me in the past. She had often expressed her horror at the cost of professional cleaning.

"*Los botóns, Señora.*" At my bewildered look she fingered the buttons on her own gaily striped blouse. "I fix for you."

"Buttons! Oh, okay, that'll be great. Thanks."

"*De nada. Miércoles?*"

Over lunch we had discussed a schedule which would accommodate Dolores's physical therapy sessions and keep her from overdoing on her still fragile leg. I had to fight to keep her from insisting on returning to her regular daily schedule. We'd start with two days a week and go from there, I'd insisted, and finally received grudging agreement.

"Wednesday it is," I replied. "Just give me a call when you can get a commitment from the carpet cleaners."

"*Si, bueno. Adios, Señora.*"

"Goodbye, my friend. And welcome back."

Dolores ducked her head in embarrassment at the emotion I couldn't keep from my voice. A few moments later I heard the spluttering cough of the Hyundai as she cranked it over, and I allowed a few tears of relief and thanksgiving to spill over onto the desk.

I spent the rest of the afternoon assembling my financial "detective" kit and arranging everything in the calfskin briefcase which had been Rob's last Christmas gift to me. The memory brought a more manageable twinge of pain than usual, and I considered the possibility that I was finally coming to terms with his death. It was way past time to stop allowing grief to govern my life, to release the hard core of guilt and anger that had been my constant companion in the years since my husband's murder . . .

The welcome interruption to these gloomy reminiscences came in the form of the pealing doorbell, and I slid my bare feet back into my loafers before heading down the hallway. I glanced quickly out the front window, surprised and pleased to find a white Beaufort County sheriff's cruiser pulled up in the driveway. I flung open the door to the slightly shorter, slightly younger version of my dead husband standing stiffly on the wide porch.

"Red," I cried, "how great to see you! Come in."

Sergeant Redmond Tanner, handsome and tanned as always in his crisply pressed khaki uniform, remained in place, legs apart, hands clasped behind his back, in the formal stance of "parade rest."

I faltered, checking my natural impulse to grasp him in a sisterly embrace. "Red? What's the matter? Is something wrong?"

My mind flew immediately to my father, to Lavinia's persistent questions at the tail end of his letters about when I was coming home from Paris. I'd put them out of my mind once I'd been able to see for myself that the Judge seemed his usual irascible, hearty self. Had I been wrong? Had I missed some sign of frailty or impending collapse? I could feel my heart kick into overdrive as I stood staring into the implacable face of my brother-in-law, imagining the worst possible scenarios of heart attack, stroke . . .

"Back nearly a week and I have to hear it through the grapevine. When were you going to be in touch, when you got yourself ass-deep in trouble again and needed a cop to bail you out?"

I swallowed the flare of anger, tinged with relief, as I watched his face break into a mischievous grin.

"Bastard!" I laughed and punched him hard, just above the gold star and nameplate pinned to his chest. "You scared me to death with that damned funeral face of yours."

"Hey, that hurt! When did you stop hitting like a girl?"

I grabbed his arm and pulled him inside the house where we finally managed the awkward, fraternal hug. Rob's murder, which had come right on the heels of Red and Sarah's painful divorce, had left him reeling, and I soon became aware his feelings for me could become more than brotherly if I gave him any indication I was interested. It had created a gulf between us I sincerely hoped my escape to Paris and the intervening months had healed.

"You on or off duty?" I asked, leading Red up the three steps and into the kitchen. "Want a beer?"

"Nope, thanks. I'm on at seven."

"How about a tea?"

"Sure."

I retrieved the ever-present pitcher from the refrigerator, dumped ice into a pair of tall glasses, and set it all on the table. "You hungry?" I asked, pulling out the chair across from my brother-in-law and dropping into it.

"If I was, I wouldn't be looking for relief here." His grin took any sting from his accustomed jibes at my lack of cooking skills.

"I could whip up a spinach quiche make you think you'd died and gone to Paris," I said, my sarcasm matching his own. "I wasn't exactly idle all those months in France, *mon ami.*"

"So what are you doing back here? What happened?"

The directness of his questions wiped the smile from my face and quelled the stock lies hovering on my tongue. Like my father, Red deserved the truth.

"Darnay's back in the game. His old boss whistled, and he went running." With my index finger I traced the pattern of blue lilies on the linen place mat in front of me and avoided Red's gaze. "Or maybe I should say he went limping back. He isn't completely healed yet. He has no business getting involved with all that . . . that *crap* again!"

I could feel the heat of my anger, rising again to engulf me. Red's next words didn't help any.

"So you just ran off and left him?"

I flung back my chair, crossed the room in three strides, and dumped the remains of my tea into the sink. I fought hard to control the anger Red's question had sent surging into my throat. "I wasn't going to sit around by myself in a strange country and wait for a knock on the door, for some officious little man to bring me the news that Darnay has been shot again. Or worse. I won't do it. I won't!"

I hate tears, almost more than anything. In the fine tradition of my Tattnall-Baynard ancestors, I pride myself on being able to control my emotions. But anger seems to be the one which most often creeps past my defenses. I swiped a hand across my eyes, aware that Red had moved quietly across the floor to stand directly behind me. I sensed a hand hovering just above my shoulder, felt his need to comfort and console as if it were a tangible presence in the room. I swallowed tightly and edged away, out of his reach.

"You love him?"

The question, loaded with all sorts of implications for both of us, hung in the air for a long time before I shrugged. "I don't know for sure. I think. Maybe."

The smile that always made my heart ache for Rob worked its way across his brother's face. "Then get your butt back to Paris," he said. "Now."

After he left, I remembered I'd meant to ask Red about Gray Palmer's death, about who had jurisdiction and which agency would be in possession of the reports. *Later,* I told myself. *Mañana, demain. Yes, Miss Scarlett, tomorrow is another day.*

I found the chicken breast nestled in its bed of wild rice in a casserole dish in the refrigerator, followed Dolores's directions for reheating it in the microwave, and made myself a salad. The silence seemed almost overwhelming in the rambling beach house as I picked at my dinner. So different from meals taken around the ancient kitchen table, with Darnay insisting I speak French, then correcting my syntax and pronunciation at every turn; the two of us giggling like children when my barbarian's tongue mutilated the beauty of his language, turning the name of the French Minister of Finance into a slimy toad with the mere misplacement of an *accent grave.*

I retrieved the remote control from the counter and flipped on the small television set suspended under the corner cabinet. Dolores hated to miss her afternoon soaps, broadcast in Spanish on one of the cable channels, so the placement of the TV had been an integral part of our plans when we remodeled the kitchen. I surfed to one of the local stations and let the chattering newscasters provide diversion to my gloomy thoughts until a familiar name snapped me back to attention.

". . . held a news conference this afternoon at the headquarters of his shipping empire here in Charleston. The sixty-one-year-old Palmer, whose rags-to-riches story was the subject of a recent series of articles in *The Post and Courier,* pleaded for information regarding the tragic drowning death of his only son early last Saturday morning."

The scene switched from the studio to what looked to be the lobby of a large hotel or office building. The camera focused on a tall, good-looking man in an impeccable navy blue suit and maroon tie, who leaned into the bank of microphones sprouting from a polished mahogany lectern. His dark brown hair, streaked with gray, had been combed straight back from a broad forehead. The picture zoomed in on a face dominated by an aristocratic nose. Hazel eyes squinted against the glare of the lights, and a mouth which was probably generous when he smiled was clenched in a tight grimace that might have been pain. Or anger. When he spoke, his voice carried a hint of his Southern origins, subdued but not entirely eradicated by either a Northern education or dedicated effort.

Much like my own.

The videotape editor had picked up his speech somewhere in the middle.

"While I have every confidence in the ability of the local authorities, as well as the Coast Guard and the Department of Natural Resources, I am convinced my son's death was not an accident. Therefore, I am offering a reward of twenty-five thousand dollars for information leading to the arrest and conviction of those responsible for this heinous crime. Anyone with knowledge of my son's whereabouts or activities on the night of his death should contact the special toll-free number you see on your screen. For those of you in the print media, a copy of my remarks will be available immediately following this press conference. Thank you."

I lifted the remote, my finger poised on the channel selector to check out the other local stations' coverage, when the camera pulled back from the determined face of the grieving father. A slender hand lay clasped in his. The ruby and sapphire eyes of the serpent winked in the strobe of still camera flashes, and its gold body wound up the olive-skinned arm.

"Despite Mr. Palmer's eloquent plea and generous offer, a Charleston police spokesman reiterated the department's belief young Gray Palmer was a victim of an accidental drowning. The autopsy, due by the end of the week, will determine if alcohol or drugs played any part in the tragedy.

In other news, the stock market edged up today . . ."

I mentally tuned out the voices, my mind racing with the implications of the fade-out shot of Gray Palmer, Senior, comforting a weeping Araminda Albright.

CHAPTER
TEN

$\mathcal{T}$HE NEXT MORNING BEGAN WELL ENOUGH. I ARRIVED, laden with briefcase and calculator, at the docks on Skull Creek at precisely ten o'clock to be engulfed in a bear hug that might have shattered bones on a daintier woman. Damon "Bubba" Mitchell and I had known each other a long time, his hole-in-the-wall eatery a regular stop whenever Rob and I had traveled down from our home in Charleston to the beach house for the weekend. It wasn't the type of greeting I usually got from my clients, but the Mitchell brothers and I had broken bread together, and that created a special bond.

"Damn, Bay, it's been too long. Where the hell you been keepin'?"

Bubba's huge black hand engulfed my upper arm as he steered me up the rickety steps and into the cramped little room which served as the office for his business. Tucked in behind the converted single-wide containing the retail shrimp and fish store, the narrow space was clean and orderly and held a surprising amount of modern equipment: computer, printer, fax machine, copier. Neatly labeled file folders stood aligned in a rack on the scarred oak desktop, and a pristine calendar lay open to the day's date.

I set my briefcase on the floor and turned to Damon Mitchell. "I've actually been out of the country for a few months," I said, shrugging out of my linen blazer and draping it across the back of the swivel chair tucked in to the desk. "Just got back last week."

"What you want to do a damn-fool thing like that for? Ain't nowhere better than the good ol' U. S. of A."

"Business," I replied, cutting short any additional questions about my temporary defection to the hinterlands of Europe. "How about you? How's Delia getting along?"

Bubba's naturally genial countenance darkened, and he shook his head. "I tell ya, Bay, that cancer's the Devil's work. Mama was a skinny little thing to start off with, but now . . . Well, she looks plain deathly, and that's the truth of it."

"But she's feeling better? Chris Brandon said . . ."

"Oh, yeah, they say they got it all. But all them chemicals sucked the life right out of her. Just lays around most days, watching the TV and readin' some. Now you know that don't sound like my mama."

"It sure doesn't." Delia Mitchell had been the driving force in holding together her father-in-law's business over the years. As I recalled, her late husband hadn't been good for much except fishing, and that more for pleasure than for producing income. "But she's earned her rest, don't you think?"

"Oh, surely. I'd just like to see some spark in them eyes again, hear her threaten to switch me and Dwight for cussin' like she used to."

I smiled at the picture of the reed-thin matriarch of the Mitchells taking on her mammoth offspring with a hazel branch. I had been emptying the contents of the briefcase onto the desk as we chatted and decided we needed to get down to business. I settled myself into the chair and pulled my reading glasses from my bag.

"So, what's been going on here, Bubba? Chris says you think your cousin has been stealing from you?"

Damon Mitchell perched his massive bulk precariously on a wooden chair which disappeared beneath him and shook his head. "I don't wanna believe it, but it seems like she must be."

"What does your mother say?"

"Mama don't know nothin' about it! I won't have her worryin', hear?"

"Sure, Bubba, no problem. Just between us. I promise." It would have been helpful to have Delia's take on the situation from her unique perspective of having kept the books all those years, but her son had a point. Recovering from cancer and a mastectomy was burden enough, especially for a woman no longer young. "So what roused your suspicion in the first place?"

The former pro-football tackle told his story with a minimum of words. In a nutshell, the catches had been of near record proportions lately, the boats requiring remarkably few major repairs, the longtime employees working hard and efficiently. They'd even had to take on some high school kids to help out on the weekends. Like this morning the parking lot in front of the retail store was almost always full, and it was not a rare occurrence for folks who arrived late in the afternoon to go away empty handed because the day's catch had been sold out.

"And yet every week seems we're scramblin' to make payroll, pay the bills," Damon Mitchell concluded. "Tamika says we're doin' fine, not to worry. But I call the bank every once in a while, to check the balance, and it just keeps goin' down. Seems like we can't get ahead of the game no matter what. It just don't seem right to me." He shook his large, shaved head at the perplexity of the situation and raised his troubled eyes to my own. "Just don't seem right."

"Calling Chris Brandon was the smart thing to do, although I'm sure Mr. Foxworth would have brought it to your attention if he had noticed anything untoward."

"Ol' Foxy's got his own troubles," Bubba said with another head shake and a rueful grin. "Though maybe he woulda been a good one for it. Set a thief to catch a thief, ain't that what they say?"

I smiled back and nodded. "Could be. Well, let me get started here and see what I can find. Is there anything locked up here in the office? Any cabinets or cupboards I'll need keys for, or maybe a safe?"

"I opened it all up this mornin', first thing. Safe is over there underneath that lamp and the cloth Mama crocheted for it. It's closed, but not locked. Same with the files and such. Anything you need you can't find, you just give a holler. I need to be gettin' the lunch started. Folks start showin' up at the Shack sometimes right after eleven."

"What about your cousin?" I asked as I unbuttoned the cuffs on my long-sleeved shirt and rolled them up in anticipation of getting down to work. "Where's she today?"

I didn't relish the idea of an irate Mitchell woman storming in on me in the middle of my investigation, particularly if she carried any portion of her cousins' girth and height.

"Tamika don't come in on Tuesdays," Bubba replied, hoisting his three hundred-plus pounds out of the chair. "Monday, Wednesday, and Friday, that's it."

"Does she know I'm going to be looking at the books?"

"Sure. I told her you were takin' over for Foxy, I mean Mr. Foxworth. For the taxes and all. You don't have to worry about puttin' things back exactly like they was."

I nodded again at Bubba's insight. Folks who assumed he was just another washed up ex-athlete seriously underestimated his native intelligence and savvy.

"Well, I'll let you get to it. You holler if you need anythin'. I'll be just across the way there, gettin' the pots boiling."

"Thanks," I called as he lumbered down the steps.

I pulled open the bottom drawer on the right side of the desk—the one with the lock and the place I'd keep the checkbook if I were arranging things in the office—and smiled as I lifted out the black binder with blank, three-to-a-page checks and the green stubs of those already written. I plugged in the calculator, arranged my spreadsheets, wished for about the millionth time I hadn't quit smoking, and got busy.

Tamika Jessup wasn't nearly as clever as she undoubtedly thought she was, nor as inept as I'd imagined her to be. I found the legitimate work she'd done to be neat, orderly, and precise. Her printing was legible; her math, accurate. Problem was, she was skimming money at such an alarming rate I wondered if she had a gambling debt or a drug habit she was financing. Damon and Dwight paid her a good salary, especially for a part-time employee, and they picked up her medical insurance as well.

Ungrateful little wretch, I thought, leaning back and tossing my pencil onto the pile of paper strewn across the desk.

I had taken a quick break around one o'clock and wandered across the driveway where the lunch activity at the Shack's four tables and cramped bar was still in full swing. I'd carried a plate of steaming shrimp and a diet Coke, none of which Bubba would let me pay for, out to an old-fashioned park bench set beneath the sheltering branches of an ancient live oak. I ate looking out over the docks and the creek to the green serenity of uninhabited Pinckney Island just across the way. The mid-April sun, filtered down through leaves quivering in a light breeze off the water, felt warm against my upturned face. The peace and beauty of my Lowcountry settled over me as gulls and pelicans swooped and called, and I had to force myself back to the task at hand.

By the end of the day, I was pretty confident I had Tamika's scam nailed. I gathered up my work papers and notes, made several copies of cancelled checks and some other pertinent documents, and returned it all to my briefcase. I would write up a complete analysis of my findings at home then deliver the report to Chris Brandon. It would be up to the Mitchell family to decide if they wanted to involve the sheriff.

I would have liked to avoid Bubba, but I couldn't. My affection for him and his brother, as well as Delia, made confirming their fears more difficult than if they had been simply clients, strangers. No one likes to hear they've been cheated and robbed, especially when the perpetrator is one of their own. But despite my reluctance to be the messenger who brings the bad news, I had to discuss the tax situation with someone. I would have preferred Delia, but Bubba had let me know in no uncertain terms she was off-limits.

He came after I called to him across the driveway, his shaved head glistening in the combined heat of the spring afternoon and several hours spent over boiling kettles of seafood. He took the news surprisingly well, asking only a few questions. I was more convinced than ever he must have known the answer before he asked the question, simply needing someone from outside to confirm his fears.

"I'll put it all in writing, and you can discuss your next move with Chris Brandon," I said as the huge man mopped sweat from his face with a crumpled white handkerchief. "What I do need is for someone to write a check to the IRS and get it in the mail ASAP. I've prepared a 4868 for you—that's an extension of time to file the tax return—but you can't get an extension for payment of the tax. I've estimated the amount due based on the prior years' Schedule C's from your mother's returns I got from Chris, so this may not be all of it. It's hard to tell when the books are in this state. You're going to need a full-blown audit and a reconstruction of the records before you can file an accurate return."

"Can't you do it?" Bubba's voice seemed diminished, lacking its usual force and timbre.

"I don't have the time to devote to it," I said honestly, my thoughts running to the press conference I'd witnessed on television the night before. Erik Whiteside had committed us to an investigation, and Gray Palmer's performance had kicked my curiosity level up a few notches. I had a feeling I might be spending a lot of time in Charleston over the next few weeks.

"Chris can recommend a competent firm to do the reconstruction for you." I had to suppress the urge to pat the former tackle on the head, so forlorn did he look at the news. "You also need to find someone to replace Tamika. There are a couple of good temp agencies here locally. I can give you a few names . . ."

"You want me to fire Tamika?"

It took me a moment to comprehend the question. "Of course. Why wouldn't you?"

"She's family," Bubba said simply.

"But she's been stealing from you! She created false employees and phony vendors, recorded that information on the stubs then made the checks out to herself. Or to cash. She's been averaging at least a thousand dollars a week, sometimes more. Why on earth would you *not* fire her?"

His look held genuine puzzlement. "She's Uncle T's daughter. Daddy's brother's girl."

"And?"

Again Bubba wagged his bald black head at me. "You don't understand, Bay. Family don't fire family. Tamika musta needed the money for somethin' important. I'll just ask her what it is, and we'll give her whatever she needs." His final statement seemed to settle it, at least in his mind. "That's what families do."

"Of course, it's up to you," I said, unrolling my sleeves and slipping on my blazer. "I'll give my report to your attorney, and you can take it from there. I'll send my bill to him as well. Be sure and get the extension and the check in the mail by Friday."

I could tell by the look on Bubba's face that my brusqueness had hurt him in some way, but I couldn't help it, and I wasn't sure why. Anger at a criminal's getting away with it? The feeling that my efforts had been for nothing?

Honesty compelled me to consider the emotion rolling around in the pit of my stomach just might be envy. How many people in this world had the luxury of knowing their families would forgive them anything, even stealing from their own kin? Not many I knew of, that was certain. Maybe not even my own.

Bubba Mitchell and I finally parted on an upbeat note, my genuine smile and firm handshake apparently erasing any bad feelings. He insisted Red and I stop in soon for some oysters and shrimp or maybe a bowl of his renowned Frogmore stew, and he promised to give his mother my best regards.

As I pulled out of the bumpy dirt driveway onto Squire Pope Road, I wondered if Tamika Mitchell Jessup had any idea how lucky she was.

I set the carryout bag on the counter next to the telephone and punched the message playback key. I brought a plate from the cupboard and emptied the foam container of grilled chicken Caesar salad onto it as I listened to a honey-voiced woman try to sell me on the joys of time-share investment in Myrtle Beach, and a fast-talking guy who promised to improve my golf game in just three short lessons. I had arranged the slices of garlic pita bread along the edge of the dish and poured myself a glass of tea before we finally got to the good stuff.

I recognized Gray Palmer's voice from his television appearance the night before. For some reason, I wasn't surprised to hear from him.

"Ms. Tanner," the message began, and I noticed his non–press conference voice held more of the South in it. "This is Gray Palmer, Senior, of Charleston. My late son's roommate has informed me that Gray had

engaged your, uh, firm to do some investigative work for him. She is unaware of the nature of that work, but I did want to make it clear any relationship you may think you have with my family has, of course, been
rendered null and void by my son's unfortunate death. If you will present your bill to my office here in Charleston, I'll be happy to see that
you're properly reimbursed. I trust this will effectively terminate any
contract, either implied or written, which my son may have entered
into. I look forward to receiving your invoice. Have a pleasant day."

Whew! I thought, mopping up the last remnants of the Caesar
dressing with the remaining sliver of pita bread. *That was interesting.*

I carried the plate to the dishwasher, added my fork, and tossed the
foam container into the trash. In the bedroom I pulled out my favorite
sweats, which had lain neglected in the dresser since my defection to
France. The pants felt a little tight around the waist and hips, a condition I intended to remedy immediately. I laced up my battered, disrep-
utable Nikes, did ten minutes of intense stretching, and ran down the
steps from the deck and onto the beach.

A light breeze lifted my hair as I turned left, away from the Westin
Hotel and its early spring tourists, and set out in a light jog. Despite
my warm-up, I could feel the long unused muscles in my legs and back
protesting as I picked up the pace. When I had finally gained my
rhythm, settling into a comfortable lope, I turned my mind loose on the
puzzle of Gray Palmer's message.

First off, poor little Araminda Albright, grieving friend of the deceased, had lied through her teeth, either to me or to her employer.
Palmer had said his son's roommate had no idea why Gray had hired
us, yet she had been perfectly lucid on the subject as we'd sat together on
the beach near her house. She had stated unequivocally Gray's discovery
of the skeleton on one of the islands he'd been investigating for his father
had been the cause of his murder. And might endanger her, as well.

What had happened to change her mind? And where had this sudden allegiance, evidenced by her appearance at the press conference with
Gray Senior, come from? She had told me in no uncertain terms that
Gray hated his father, even though he worked for him and took his
money. She hadn't seemed to be his biggest fan, either. Then why the

public display of support? Had she run to her employer after our meeting, or had he somehow found out about it on his own? What was the game here, and who exactly were the players?

I tuned back in to my breathing and the light burn beginning in the backs of my calves and decided to head toward home. My watch told me I'd been out for a little over twenty minutes, and the soft graying of the light across the ocean signaled that nightfall was fast encroaching. I cut the return trip by five minutes, sprinting the last hundred yards just to prove I wasn't completely out of shape, knowing I would pay a price for it the next day.

Still, it felt good to have worked up a sweat, although it was rapidly cooling in the darkening twilight as I plodded up the steps onto the deck. The interior lights, connected to a sensor, popped on just as I inserted my key, and I felt again the stab of loneliness I'd experienced when I'd stepped back into my home after the long months away. The house looked warm, inviting, and yet I would walk inside to yawning emptiness, with only the comfort of the TV to banish the silence.

Quit whining, I ordered myself. Dolores was almost fully recovered and back in my life, and for that I would be eternally grateful to whatever Power had made it so. I had friends, family, financial security, and an interesting new career, if I could ever manage to get the damned thing off the ground.

This newest case had proved to be a bust, Gray Palmer, Senior, blowing us off with a brusque determination couched in Southern gentility, and Araminda Albright proving herself to be a beautiful, charming liar. The picture of her exotic, multiethnic face, strained with what I had believed to be genuine grief and fear, floated ahead of me down the hallway to my bathroom where I stripped off my running clothes and tossed them into the hamper.

I had been wrong about a lot of things lately . . . about a lot of *people,* actually.

Which is why you should stick to numbers, my girl, I told myself, setting the hot water to run in the whirlpool tub and pulling on my old chenille robe. In the kitchen I nuked a cup of hot water, dropped in a tea bag, and carried it back with me. The aroma of eucalyptus steaming in the bath was already easing the strain in my unused muscles when the telephone interrupted.

I gave thought to letting the machine pick up, until another face—last seen glowering in anger as I handed my bags to the Parisian taxi driver—materialized inside my head. I dropped onto the closed lid of the toilet and picked up the extension from the marble vanity.

"Bay," an excited Erik Whiteside shouted into my ear, "you'll never guess what I just got in the mail!"

I swallowed my disappointment, forcing my mind away from a thousand images the thoughts of Darnay had conjured up, and said, "Hey, partner! Before you tell me, I have to give you some news, too."

"Wait, mine's better."

I laughed. "You sound like some kid who just got a new bike. This is business. I had a message on my machine tonight from Gray Palmer, the father. Apparently the lovely Araminda spilled her guts to him about his son hiring us and all, and he called to bounce us off the case. Pretty adamant about it, too. Told me to send him a bill and basically take a hike. I'm sorry, but . . ."

"Well, you can tell him to take a walk, too."

"What do you mean?"

"I'm trying to tell you. This package. It was waiting outside my door when I got home tonight. It's from Gray." He sobered suddenly, and my breath quickened. "And guess what I found inside?"

It took only a moment to figure out what was the one thing which could have engendered this much excitement in my young associate.

"A bone," I said, the implications of it sending all thoughts of a long, soothing soak whirling away with the steam.

CHAPTER ELEVEN

AS THE WATER IN THE TUB COOLED AND MY MUSCLES tightened, we wrestled with what to do about the strange contents of the package dropped by the door of Erik Whiteside's apartment.

"Does it . . . smell?" I asked at one point.

"No, not at all. Well, just kind of musty. Sort of like a damp basement, or the ground under a rock when you roll it over. You know."

Actually, I didn't. No one in his right mind would build a house with a basement in the marshy, flood-prone area in which I'd lived most of my life, and I hadn't had many occasions to be turning over rocks, at least not literally. My late husband's passion for *Law and Order* reruns had given me my only insight into dead bodies and how they deteriorated. I was pretty certain the local bugs and worms would have quickly stripped the body of any tissue or ligament, but we had no idea how long the remains had been in the ground.

I ventured another grisly question. "There isn't anything attached to it, is there?"

"You mean like flesh or anything? No. It's pretty clean, except for some dirt and a few leaves. It came wrapped in a material sort of like oilcloth and then canvas, maybe from a sail or something else nautical."

"Nothing else? No note or letter of explanation?"

"Nope." Erik cleared his throat, stumbling a little over his next words. "I guess he figured he'd explain everything when he saw me."

I gave him a moment to get himself back together. I had to keep reminding myself this was his friend we were discussing.

"About the bone. How big is it? Can you tell what part of the body it's from?"

I couldn't believe I was sitting there on the lid of my toilet discussing human remains over the telephone. Perhaps I needed to rethink this new profession of mine.

"Well, I don't know squat about biology, but I got onto a Web site that had a detailed diagram of the human skeleton. The bone is long and narrow, so it looks like it could be from either the arm or the leg. Humerus or femur, maybe. Sucker's heavy at any rate."

I swallowed against the sudden image of young Gray Palmer gently extricating the bone from the disturbed gravesite, carefully wrapping and packing it, then trotting down to the nearest FedEx location to ship it off to Erik. The smile hovering on my lips disappeared, however, when I remembered this boy lay dead in the Charleston County morgue, his face slashed beyond recognition. That grim thought triggered an idea which had been hovering in the back of my mind, just out of reach, since we'd heard the details of his death.

"How do you suppose they identified him?" I asked, as much to myself as to Erik, whose quick response surprised me.

"You mean Gray? Yeah, I wondered that, too. Maybe by clothes or jewelry? I guess they could have assumed it was him because it was his boat. Or they could have done dental records."

Again my television training leaped to the fore. "But they'd already said it was him immediately after they pulled the body out of the water. They wouldn't have had time to do any dental comparisons, even if they could have contacted his dentist on a Saturday afternoon. When was the package mailed? You don't suppose . . . ?"

"I thought of that, too. No, the date on the shipping label is Friday, just after nine A.M. A Mailboxes office in downtown Charleston. He probably dropped it off on his way to the boat."

We both digested the implications of the timing. According to

Araminda Albright, Gray Palmer set off on Friday to revisit the name-less island where he had discovered the skeleton. And never returned. Of course, she hadn't proved herself to be the most reliable of infor-mants, and I said so to Erik.

"You think there's something fishy about her relationship with the old man?"

"I really don't give a damn if she's sleeping with him or anyone else. My point is she lied about it, which makes me wonder how much of her story we can rely on at all."

"Well, it's kind of pointless to worry about it now, don't you think? I mean, if she's gone over to the enemy and GS doesn't want to fork over any fees to find out what his son was involved in, we're sort of up the creek without a client, aren't we?"

"Technically speaking. But you're forgetting about the bone. What do we do about that?"

"We could always turn it over to the authorities."

I sensed a hesitation in his voice which mirrored my own thoughts. "Do you really want to do that?"

"No, but I don't see how we have any choice."

"No one knows we have it, so I don't suppose we need to make a de-cision on it right this minute. Do you have a safe place for it?"

His laugh brought a welcome break in the gruesome conversation. "You bet. Ever since I was a teenager and Mom started making me do my own laundry, I've always stashed stuff in the bottom of my dirty clothes hamper. So far it's been better than a safe. I figure if anyone's brave enough to dig through my sweaty socks and used under . . ."

"Okay, I get the picture."

"So then what? I mean, what's the plan?"

I stood and stretched, easing the stiffness in my back and thighs. "I don't have a game plan. Yet. Sit tight and let me think this through. I'll get back to you tomorrow."

"Okay, you're the boss. I'd feel kind of bad just letting it drop, though. Because of Gray and all."

"I understand. By the way, they said something on the newscast yesterday, the one that had Palmer's press conference, about an article the Charleston paper did on him not long ago. Would something like that be on-line?"

"Should be. Want me to check it out?"

"No, thanks. I think it's time I learned a little more about how to navigate my way around the Internet. What should I do?"

I heard the disappointment in his voice, but I felt strongly about not relying entirely on my young partner whenever something needed to be checked out on the Web. He had a full-time job and responsibilities and an actual functioning love life, none of which troubled my existence at the moment.

"Just do a Google search for the name. Or better yet, find the Web site of the paper and search the archives. Most larger papers have their primary articles out there."

"Google?" I hadn't even started and already I was behind the curve.

"Google dot com. It's a search engine, probably the best one."

"Okay, I'm on it. Come to think of it, I may not get back to you for a day or two. I have to do something about getting myself a car. I can't keep running around in this little cracker box forever."

"Got any particular model in mind?"

"Not really. Maybe something a little bigger than the Zeemer. But definitely a convertible."

"You should check out the new Jags."

"Thanks, pal. Maybe if I hit the lottery." I thought of Worthy Foxworth, cooling his heels in a state prison for appropriating client funds to cover his own investment losses. The stock market had not been entirely kind to me, either, during the past few months. I leaned over to let some of the tepid water out of the tub then turned the hot tap back on full blast. "You're sure you're okay with holding onto the . . . thing?"

"Don't worry. It'll probably improve the smell in the hamper. Talk to you soon."

I hung up laughing, peeled off the robe, and slipped into the steaming whirlpool, marveling at the progress I had made in becoming a real private eye. I could joke about bones. Maybe I just might succeed at this after all.

Instead of relaxing me, the half hour in the tub seemed to rejuvenate both mind and body. I pulled on my old flannel pajamas, made a pot of tea, and hunkered down in front of the computer. My initial intention was to dive into the quest for more background information on Gray Palmer and his shipping empire, but first I forced myself to type up my report on the Mitchell Seafood embezzlement. I printed it out and slipped the pages, along with an invoice, into an oversized brown envelope. I slid my feet into sandals and pulled my robe back on, then trotted out to the mailbox at the end of my driveway. A choir of tree frogs serenaded me in their piercing voices as I hurried back into the house.

Back at the computer, I tried *The Post and Courier* first and struck pay dirt almost immediately. Apparently the paper had run a series of articles on local movers and shakers during the February tourist doldrums, and Gray Palmer's had required two successive Sunday feature pages to do him justice.

I scanned the columns, interested to learn he hailed from Yemassee, a tiny crossroads town northwest of Beaufort famous for its old gas-station-turned-steakhouse restaurant. After a brief stint in the Marine Corps, Palmer blasted through the business curriculum of the University of South Carolina, graduating with honors in less than three years. After two failed attempts to start his own enterprises—a nautical supplies store and an ill-fated excursion boat venture whose principal asset sank before the first tourist ever stepped on board—Gray Palmer found the perfect solution to his entrepreneurial ambitions.

He married money.

Anne Compton Whitley's family rose from relative financial and social obscurity to incredible wealth and power on the polished decks of their sleek sailing ships. Not nearly as dashing as Scarlett's Rhett, to judge by the grainy photos accompanying the *Post* article, the Whitley blockade runners bribed and fought their way to glory by regularly penetrating the nets thrown up around vital Confederate ports such as Charleston. Ironically, their wealth grew in direct proportion to the misery and deprivation of the local populations whose desperation for foodstuffs and other goods drove prices to dizzying heights. Despite this, they earned themselves the everlasting admiration of their countrymen and untold riches with which to begin a new life when the South had finally been reduced to ashes.

Apparently the heroes had not been as adept at procreating as they had been at slipping past gunboats in the dead of night. Anne had been the last Whitley, her only brother having died in infancy. Enter Gray Palmer—charming, handsome, ambitious. Whitley Maritime became Palmer Shipping, and everyone's problems were solved.

I printed out the pages, scanning them as they slipped from the printer. The only other item of immediate interest I found was the mention of another child, a married daughter living in California, and the sudden death of Anne Compton Whitley Palmer when Gray the younger was in his teens. No mention of cause of death, which I found curious, and I made a note in the margin to see if I could track down her obituary. Not that it probably had any bearing on anything, but the omission intrigued me. I added the sheets to the thin PALMER/ALBRIGHT file and went to make more tea.

I settled on the white sofa in front of the television in the great room and tried to give my brain a respite. I surfed idly through the dozens of channels, finally coming to rest on a PBS rerun of an old *Mystery* episode. While Jeremy Brett had always seemed to me the quintessential Holmes, I couldn't seem to concentrate on his crisp delivery of the familiar lines, his scathing repartee with the bumbling Watson. My mind kept wandering, my outer gaze drifting to the deep gloom just outside the partially closed drapes, and my inner eye to the darker void around my heart.

Damn it, Darnay, where are you?

CHAPTER TWELVE

J HAVE NO IDEA WHAT POSSESSED ME TO SOLICIT MY
father's advice on the subject of a new car, but I knew it had
been a serious tactical error the moment the words were out of my
mouth.

We sat glowering at each other across the scarred oak table in the
kitchen, our hands and arms washed in patterned warmth from the late
morning sunlight streaming through the mullioned windows. Lavinia,
neutral as usual in the silly confrontations which erupted regularly between the Judge and me, ignored us, humming softly to herself as she
worked biscuit dough with her strong brown hands. Something redo-
lent with garlic and sea creatures bubbled gently on the stove.

"Just borrowin' someone else's miseries," my father said for what I
seriously believed might have been the tenth time in as many minutes.
"I have never bought a used vehicle. Buy new and buy American, that's
been my credo, and it's stood me in good stead, daughter. All these
damned Germans and Japanese dumpin' their inferior products on our
markets, that's what's wrong with the whole country!"

I'd tried to point out earlier that his thinking was about thirty years
out of date, that some of the finest automobiles now rolled off American
assembly lines with foreign nameplates decorating their trunk lids. My
beloved little BMW Z-3 had been put together right up the interstate

from us in Greer, South Carolina. Besides which, since his last stroke had rendered his left side virtually useless he hadn't even been a passenger in a car, let alone a driver. Rob and I had ordered and equipped the handicapped accessible van which sat out in the driveway, the one Lavinia used for shopping and errands. The number of times my father had even set foot or wheel inside of it could be counted on the fingers of two hands. But the Judge never let facts stand in the way of his firmly entrenched opinions, so I sipped tea and let him rant until he finally had to stop for breath.

"I'm going to buy an American car, Your Honor, so save the closing arguments. And I've decided it's going to be one of the new T-Birds. But the company seems to be restricting production, no doubt to keep the demand up, and the only one the dealer has is a program vehicle." As the young female salesperson at Island Ford had explained it to me, these were cars driven briefly by company bigwigs then sold to dealers at closed auctions. "It's only got six thousand miles on it."

And it's yellow, I wanted to add, a beautiful, creamy, butter-yellow with a tan leather interior whose bucket seats and retro styling fit me perfectly. Admitting to my father that the color of the car was influencing my decision would have been like pouring gasoline on an already roaring blaze. Instead I had been enumerating the many safety and engineering features of the resurrected classic of the late fifties, rattling off crash-test and performance statistics I'd memorized from the brochure.

"Besides," I added, saving my most devastating salvo for last, "it's almost eight thousand dollars less than the sticker price on a new one."

I had rendered him speechless. I sat back in my chair and crossed my arms over my chest in satisfied triumph. I so seldom won an argument with the Judge.

He *harrumphed* a couple of times, cleared his throat noisily, and reached for another of the blueberry bran muffins from the plate we'd been working on.

"No more of those. Lunch will be ready in less than an hour."

Lavinia's voice, though soft, crackled with the authority she had exercised in this house since before I was born. Emmaline Baynard Simpson had found the perfect housekeeper in Lavinia Smalls not long after she inherited Presqu'isle, and the calm, stately black woman had ruled as a benign dictator ever since. Not that my mother didn't run the show. Her autocratic demands for perfection echoed throughout the massive old mansion, her pride of heritage and its trappings evidenced in every room. But it was always Lavinia, subservient but never servile, who carried out the commands from on high, administering justice and keeping the wheels greased amid the day-to-day messiness of raising a child. If anything about my early years resembled a normal home life, it was due to Lavinia.

"You stayin'?" she said to me, sliding out an oven rack and setting on it the pan of biscuits she'd rolled out.

"What's in the pot?"

"A gumbo. I had some shrimp and a few other things I needed to use up. Thad and Isaiah brought us over a mess of oysters, but I'm saving those for supper."

Lavinia's only child, Thaddeus, worked for the post office and lived in Bluffton. Although my mother had always addressed her as *Mrs.* Smalls, I had never once heard either of them refer to Thad's father, and the mysterious progenitor of the boy who had shared my childhood remained a subject about which we did not speak. Her grandson, along with my best friend Bitsy's son CJ, was a star athlete for Hilton Head High. Both boys would be graduating this year, if memory served me right. A light shiver traveled down my arms as I recalled how close they had both come to spending this past year in jail instead of piling up touchdown statistics.

"Is there okra in it?" I asked, getting back to the topic of lunch.

"Of course there's okra in it. Wouldn't be a gumbo without okra." Lavinia shook her head at my aversion to all things green.

"Just pick it out, like you do the peas." My father had apparently recovered from his humiliating defeat in the auto wars.

"Okay," I said. "Thanks."

"You can set the table then," Lavinia replied, wiping her floury hands on her ever-present apron.

"Yes, ma'am."

"I'll go wash up." The Judge toggled his wheelchair controls and

beat a hasty retreat out into the hallway. Over the soft whirring of the
motor, I heard him mutter, "'Any coward can fight a battle when he's
sure of winning.'"

I stepped into the doorway and called, "George Eliot. Pen name of
Mary Ann Evans. No doubt the coward she was referring to was a man."

He stopped and maneuvered his chair around to face me. "'Winning isn't everything . . .'" he began.

"'. . . it's the only thing!'" I crowed. "Vince Lombardi. Two for
two, ladies and gentlemen, the little lady is two for two!" I pumped my
fist in victory, and my father shrugged good-naturedly as he swiveled
back around toward his study.

"I don't know why the two of you can't be in the same room for
more than thirty seconds without getting into some kind of hoop-de-
do." Lavinia sprinkled herbs over the surface of the pot and stirred them
in while inhaling the fragrant steam which rose in a cloud around her
face.

"*Hoop-de-do?* What the hell kind of word is that?" I laughed as I
popped back into the kitchen and began distributing place mats and the
everyday china and silver around the table.

"You know what I mean. And there's no need for profanity."

I suffered the oft-repeated rebuke in silence, finished laying out the
table, and dropped back into my chair. "Anything else I can do?"

Lavinia turned from the stove. The look she cast over my head and
out to the doorway brought me snapping to attention. She was obviously checking on the whereabouts of the Judge, and there was something furtive, almost conspiratorial in her eyes. The memory of her
postscripts to my father's letters surfaced again in my consciousness, and
I was suddenly afraid.

"What?" I demanded in a forced whisper.

"I've been wanting to talk to you, but I don't quite know how to . . ."

"Is he sick?"

"No, nothing like that." She said it offhandedly, a throwaway line
that made anger rise into my throat.

"Well, it's not exactly an unwarranted fear. He is pushing eighty, if
you recall, and you certainly planted enough hints in his letters."

My sharp tone surprised her, and I watched comprehension, then remorse chase each other across her face. She dropped into a chair and reached for my hands.

"Oh, Bay, I'm so sorry! What a fool I am! I had no idea you'd interpret my words that way. And I should have." She shook her elegant head in dismay. "I surely should have."

It was my turn to feel bad, for challenging her, for doubting for a moment that, if the Judge had serious medical problems, she would have called me in Paris and demanded my immediate return to the States.

"It's okay," I said, patting her hand where it lay next to mine on the table. "I shouldn't have jumped to conclusions. So what is the problem?"

Again she stared past me, her head cocked to one side, listening for the soft *whoosh* of tires on the heart pine floor which would announce my father's return.

"Do you know anyone named Felicity Baronne?"

I studied Lavinia's face, wrinkled in worry, and shook my head. "No, not that I'm aware of." *Felicity* did scratch a little at the back of my memory, but it may have been because it was an unusual name, anachronistic in a pleasant sort of way. "Why?" I asked.

"She's been coming here. To the house."

The statement itself wouldn't have caused an eyebrow to twitch in most homes in Beaufort County, but it made mine rise almost to my hairline.

"Here? To Presqu'isle?"

When I told people my father had become housebound after his strokes, it was something of an under-exaggeration. He had, in fact, become a virtual hermit, refusing to allow any but his most intimate friends of very long standing see him brought to the sorry physical state to which he had been reduced. Lavinia and I had become accustomed to his left hand lying curled and useless in his lap, his once powerful legs shriveled to sticks. Although he retained his full head of thick white hair and the sparkle in his piercing gray eyes, he was most distressed by the flaccid, drooping left side of his face. I had said on more than one occasion he should be thankful his mammoth intellect had been unaffected, as evidenced just a few minutes before with his rattling off obscure quotations without a moment's hesitation.

It was a concession to good fortune I could never get him to acknowledge.

"He never mentioned her in his letters," I went on in the face of Lavinia's silence. "Who is she?"

"She called one day, right after the first of the year, and asked to speak to your father. Referred to him as 'Tally.'"

Lavinia paused to let that sink in. Again, no one but people he had known for dogs' years called him by that nickname. To most residents of Beaufort, he had been simply "the Judge" for as long as I could remember.

I caught some of her apprehension, glancing quickly over my shoulder at the empty hallway. "What did you do?"

"Told her he wasn't available, just like I always do, unless I recognize who it is. She said if there was a more convenient time she'd be glad to call back. I asked her what her business was with him, because you know these days we get so many of those annoying people wanting to sell stocks or vacations or whatnot."

"What did she say?"

Lavinia pulled her narrow lips into the line of disapproval I remembered so well from my childhood and said, "Personal."

"That's it? Just 'personal'?"

"All I could get out of her. Said to give your father her name, even spelled it out for me as if I was some illiterate high school dropout, and then said she'd call back later in the day."

"And did you? Tell him, I mean?"

"Of course I did. And the look on his face! As if he'd seen the ghost of one of his dead ancestors or something. 'I'll talk to her.' That's all he said. So when she rang again, about four that afternoon, I took him in the phone and left him to it. Next thing I know, he's telling me she's coming to visit, the following day, and would I be so kind as to make certain we had some refreshment to offer her." The snort of derision was pure Lavinia. "Would I be so kind! I wanted to shake him until his teeth rattled!"

I had no idea where this story was going, but I was beginning to get an inkling. Lavinia had ruled Presqu'isle—and my father's life—for the more than fifteen years since my mother's death. That their relationship might have been more than employer and housekeeper had been brought home to me in a very poignant way last summer, and the shock of it had strained my relationship with Lavinia for some time afterwards. We had promised each other a long talk, but the truth of it was I hadn't really wanted to know. I preferred that both Lavinia and my father stick to their assigned roles as I perceived them, and counted myself happy in my ignorance. Over time, our avoidance of any direct reference to our confrontation on the back verandah those many months ago had allowed us to drift easily back into our old relationship without looking too closely at what the new one should be.

Of course, the truly adult part of me recognized this situation couldn't go on forever without some clearing of the air between Lavinia and me. But, despite Plato's warning, both of us seemed content, at least for the moment, to find our unexamined lives quite worth living.

"What happened when she showed up? What was she like?"

I figured it was the appearance of an attractive female which had so rattled Lavinia, especially one who had obviously once known my father well enough to call him Tally.

"White. Pretty, in a hard sort of way, lots of makeup and clothes way too young for her. But still in decent shape, considering her age."

I nearly laughed at Lavinia's grudging description until I noticed the anger in her eyes. Both our heads snapped up at the creaking of the floorboards at the far end of the hall. The Judge's tuneless humming could be heard just over the whirring of the wheelchair mechanism as he neared the door to the kitchen.

"Quick! Tell me what happened! Did he say where he knew her from?"

"No," Lavinia whispered, leaning in so close our noses almost touched. "But I did eventually find out what she came for."

"What?" I urged.

"Money," she announced triumphantly. "Your father is giving this floozy money!"

Apparently the strain of getting through lunch after that bombshell didn't register at all on my father. He chattered away about local gossip, culled from the many phone conversations he had with his old cronies over the course of a day. Several times I opened my mouth to bring up the subject of the *floozy,* only to be quelled by a dagger stare from Lavinia. I'd hoped for the opportunity to pump him once we'd left the table for his customary post-meal cigar and bourbon on the verandah, but he expressed himself tired after a restless night and whirred off to his afternoon nap.

I cleaned up the dishes while Lavinia got him settled. I managed to scrape into the garbage the untouched okra, which I'd cleverly camouflaged under a partially eaten biscuit, before she returned. I dried while she washed; and, though I questioned her at length, she had seemingly given me all the information she possessed.

"How do you know about the money?" I asked, vigorously attacking one of the silver knives with the dish towel to insure against water spots as I'd been taught at Lavinia's knee.

She transferred soapy dishwater from the sink to the big cooking pot and set it on the counter to soak. When she didn't meet my eyes, I was pretty sure she had been doing a little old-fashioned snooping of her own.

"It's okay," I said. "Whatever you did, I know it was done out of loyalty and . . ." I was about to add *love* and thought better of it.

"It's just that he kept giving me envelopes to mail, the small kind, like you use for checks. They were addressed to her at a post-office box in Hilton Head."

"How many?" I asked.

"Six, so far, that I know of."

"How much money?"

Lavinia ducked her head and scrubbed unnecessarily hard on the pan she'd used for the biscuits. "How would I . . ." she began, but I wasn't having any of that nonsense.

"You would know by going through the bank statements when

they came and adding up the cancelled checks made out to her," I said matter-of-factly. "Now don't try to BS me, Mrs. Smalls. I know you have access to the statements, and it's what any concerned person would do. So how much?"

She straightened her shoulders and looked me squarely in the eye. "Three thousand dollars. Six checks for five hundred each. Since the middle of January, and the last one bein' about two weeks ago."

"And you asked him about it? Asked him what was going on?"

"Of course I did no such thing! Is it any of my business what he spends his money on?"

"Come on, Lavinia, this is crazy! You've been worrying yourself into a decline about this mystery woman, and you haven't just come out and asked him?"

"No, and you won't either. I mean it, Bay Tanner, I won't have you pickin' at him about this."

"Then why the hell did you tell me about it in the first place?" My voice rose, and she shushed me with a wave of her hand. "I swear I don't understand either one of you most of the time."

Lavinia sighed and finally turned from the sink to face me squarely. "If he wanted me to know, he would have told me right away. He knows it's gnawing at me. I can tell when I glance up sometimes, sudden-like, and find him looking at me in that way he has. You know, as if he's trying to read my mind."

"Yes, I know what you mean. But answer my question. What was the point of all the hints in the letters and the whispered conversation before lunch if you don't want me to confront him about it?"

She nodded her head, as if coming to some conclusion. "I want to hire you. To investigate." I opened my mouth to point out the utter stupidity of her statement, but she overrode me. "Yes, and I want you to charge me, just like you would anyone else."

"Don't be ridiculous! First of all, I wouldn't take your money if you held me down and stuffed it in my pockets, and secondly this is my father we're talking about. If he's gotten himself into some kind of mess, I'll get him out of it. Free. Gratis. No charge. Are we clear?"

It might have been the first time I'd ever really asserted myself with

Lavinia Smalls, and I watched grudging admiration dawn in her eyes. "As you like, Bay. Thank you."

"Get me the address and the cancelled checks and I'll see if I can track this woman down."

"Why do you need the checks?"

"To see where she cashed them or deposited them. When's the last time you saw Ms. Felicity Baronne?"

"A few days before you came home. I served them tea and carrot cake in his study." Amazingly there were tears forming in Lavinia's deep brown eyes. "He asked me to close the door behind me."

I resisted the urge to put my arms around this wonderful woman who had been my refuge and my salvation, but I knew she'd soon regret her moment of weakness and resent my witnessing of it. Instead I slid the last of the silver into its lined drawers and hung the dish towel on the hook next to the sink

"Okay, then," I said, "go find me that information, and I'll get busy."

Lavinia Smalls gave me a watery smile and bustled out of the kitchen.

"Lord help me," I muttered and collapsed into a chair.

CHAPTER
THIRTEEN

I HAD TO HUSTLE TO GET BACK TO THE CAR DEALERSHIP before they closed for the evening, but I made it with about half an hour to spare. After dropping off the rental car in Beaufort, I'd paid them an additional fee to be ferried back to Bluffton just ahead of the nightly rush hour. The young man who delivered me safely to the front door of Island Ford said his company had a policy against accepting tips, but I folded a ten and slipped it into the pocket of his crisp blue oxford shirt anyway.

I had made all the arrangements with the young saleswoman by phone from the Judge's house, and she had the T-Bird shined up and waiting just outside the showroom. I wrote out the check, wincing a little at the dent it put in my brokerage cash account and signed more papers than I thought could possibly be necessary for a relatively simple transaction. But, shortly before six, the convertible top stored neatly under the boot, I roared onto Route 278 in my fabulous new wheels.

The bean counter in me acknowledged I should have done more research, considered more options. Done a few test drives, whipped up some lists, and made detailed comparisons. But there's something visceral about vehicles, at least to me. Maybe it harks back to the days when our personal mode of transportation was a living, breathing creature, with a face, a personality, a name. The car simply replaced the horse, and I still needed a connection in my gut with whatever pile of steel and fiberglass and plastic was going to haul me from place to place. Not exactly logical, but there you are.

We caught a lot of stares, this sleek yellow beauty and I. My dark brown hair had regained some of its reddish-gold highlights after a few days' exposure to the Lowcountry sun and had grown back in enough to stream out behind me when we finally got up to speed. The sheer joy of it lifted my spirits to a level I hadn't experienced since I'd fled Paris.

As we idled at the stoplight at Moss Creek, my words to Lavinia came back to me, and I realized I needed to take my own advice.

And you asked him about it? I'd demanded, and been astounded to find the answer was no. I had been waiting for more than a week for Alain Darnay to call, for him to come to his senses, realize the folly of his decision, and beg me to return. Obviously that wasn't going to happen. So, unless I intended to spend the rest of my life waiting and wondering, I was going to have to make the first move.

If I remembered correctly, the time difference between Hilton Head and Paris would be five hours now that Daylight Savings Time had gone into effect, so it would be well past midnight there by the time I got home. Still, if I stayed up late enough, I could catch him before he left the apartment next morning for . . . well, for wherever he was spending his time now. The decision made, I cruised on over the bridges, delighting in the glistening mud of the marshes at low tide and the reflection of pristine sailboats in the clear waters of the Intracoastal Waterway.

My bridge, my ocean, my island. The old, familiar litany ran through my head, and I wondered again what it was about Hilton Head that had made it home, despite my many years in Charleston and my growing up on St. Helena.

When I stepped into the house, I realized Dolores had worked her magic with the carpet cleaners. The whole place smelled fresh and slightly damp, and I found several of her wonderful bilingual notes tacked up at the entrance to almost every room: *Is no dry. Not walking hasta noche.*

I slipped off my shoes and tested the condition of the great room rug, finding it satisfactory. In the bedroom it was still a little squishy, but I changed quickly and headed back to the kitchen. I had consumed enough biscuits and gumbo at Lavinia's table to live off for at least a couple of days, so I threw together a salad and ate it standing at the counter. One bowl and one fork into the dishwasher and I was done.

I slid onto the chair at the built-in desk and lifted the local phone directory from the center drawer. I felt a little foolish as I thumbed my way to the beginning pages, but stranger things had happened. I ran my finger down the tightly packed names. There were several one-*n* Barones listed, but none with two. If it had been that easy, Lavinia would have found the woman herself, but it had been worth a try.

I carried tea into the office and settled myself in front of the computer. I signed on and typed in *www.google.com,* the search engine Erik had suggested I try when I had been looking for information on Gray Palmer. *Felicity Baronne* kicked up a couple hundred responses, but most of them had to do with street names in New Orleans and other obscure references. I gave up after scanning through the first thirty.

So apparently Felicity Baronne hadn't done anything to warrant mention on any of the gazillions of Web sites out there in the great void. Just for fun I typed in my own name and was astounded by the number of references. Upon investigation I discovered that many came from articles in the local papers, mostly to do with the Judge rather than with my own infamous exploits. I resisted the temptation to explore further and logged off.

The next order of business would be the cancelled checks. Lavinia had slipped me the packet after rifling my father's desk while he napped. She'd also enclosed the post-office box address to which she'd sent the envelopes, and I noticed the ZIP was 29938, indicating the box was at the branch on the south end of the island. The handwriting on the endorsement looked ordinary enough, neither flowery and flowing nor cramped or illegible. They had all been cashed at Bank of America.

I pulled the desk lamp closer and examined the jumble of numbers encoded on the back of the first check. There was no indication of which branch of the huge financial conglomerate she had used, and there were at least three or four on the island. One thing was certain, though: she had an account there. I'd stood in line at my own bank many times waiting while non-account holders produced their identification and inked their thumbs to place an impression on the document they were presenting. There was nothing resembling a smudgy thumbprint on the face of these checks.

And there was no way Bank of America or any other financial institution was going to give me information about an account holder. Good thing, too, since I'd be the first one screaming bloody murder if accessing my own personal records were as easy for some stranger as simply inquiring. The only real clue of any value to me was the date stamped on the reverse. By comparing that with the day the check was drawn in my father's spidery handwriting on the face of the document, I realized Ms. Baronne must hotfoot it to the bank the same day she picked up the envelope. Every check had been cashed within two days of its having been mailed.

I leaned back in the chair and stretched to loosen the kinks settling into my shoulders from hunching over the desk. A sore back and a cramped neck had been occupational hazards back in my full-time accounting days, but I'd been relatively free of those pains since I'd given up my practice and begun exercising regularly. I touched the ridges of scar tissue on my left shoulder through the fabric of my shirt. I worked hard to keep the shiny, ugly skin loose with special creams and lotions, but it still seemed to be stretched too tightly across the flesh beneath. Nearly two years, and the healing was not yet complete.

I shook my head to chase those gloomy thoughts away and contemplated the six checks spread out across my desk. I had exhausted just about every avenue for identifying my father's mystery woman short of asking Erik Whiteside to hack into the bank's computers. I smiled at the idea. Erik would no doubt jump at the challenge, but I had no intention of putting him into a position to get nailed by what had to be an extremely sophisticated firewall system. I could envision his being hauled out of his apartment by two burly Treasury agents and carted off to federal prison.

No, I told myself, *we'd have to do it the hard way.* I'd advise Lavinia to alert me the next time she mailed a check to the elusive Felicity

Baronne, and I'd stake out the post office. Though how I'd manage to make myself inconspicuous in that relatively small area for extended periods of time escaped me at the moment. And I had just purchased a vehicle which would attract attention wherever it was parked.

I carried my empty glass back toward the kitchen, detouring on the way to peer through the gap in the great room drapes out into the fading light. The outdoor thermometer attached to the railing directly across from the French doors hovered just a little below seventy degrees. I opened the door a crack, sniffing the air like a bloodhound seeking his quarry. It smelled like spring: warm, damp, loamy. Too pleasant an evening to be shut up inside.

I put my glass in the top rack of the dishwasher, grabbed a sweatshirt and my bag, and trotted down the steps into the garage.

There really wasn't anyplace other than a few stretches on the interstate to let my new baby have her head, so I settled for roaming up and down the island, top down, heater cranked up to drive off the chill breeze blowing in off the ocean. I cruised 278 from end to end, the traffic sparse on a weekday night. I cut down side roads I hadn't been on in years: Union Cemetery, Dillon, Fish Haul, Baygall. I explored some of the new condominium and apartment complexes which had sprung up in the months I'd spent in Paris. They seemed to explode from the stands of palmettos and chinaberry trees, all natural wood and muted trim, low-impact lighting and carefully camouflaged parking lots. They were well conceived and every attempt had been made to make them blend in with their environment, but nothing could disguise the fact that progress was slowly eating away at the natural beauty of my island.

I tried not to let it depress me, turning back onto 278 and eventually onto the Cross Island Parkway, another blight on the landscape which nonetheless helped keep the hordes of tourist invaders moving along during the summer. I paid my dollar at the toll booth. Cresting the bridge over Broad Creek, I slowed to take in the breathtaking beauty of the vista spreading away on either side of me: the vast expanse of star-studded sky arching overhead; the smooth flow of the waterway as it

widened into Calibogue Sound; the lights of Shelter Cove Harbor twin-
kling in the distance off to my left and those of the smaller, snugger
Palmetto Bay Marina casting a soft glow on my right.

Tourists be damned, I thought, *it's still a wonderful place to live.*

Approaching the traffic signal at the foot of the bridge, I suddenly
remembered Miss Addie. Adelaide Boyce Hammond. Thanks to her
having been duped into a shady investment the past summer, I had
found the courage to slink from my hiding place at the beach and face
the world again after Rob's murder. I had been unable to refuse the plea
of one of my late mother's oldest and dearest friends, and it had been the
saving of me. I checked the clock on the dashboard and realized it was
much too late to go calling on octogenarian ladies. Besides, the upscale
retirement community where she resided, just down the road, had a
twenty-four-hour security gate. Tomorrow would have to do.

I pulled through the light and headed for home, making a mental
note to call Miss Addie first thing in the morning. If anyone knew what
Felicity Baronne had once been to my father, it would likely be Adelaide
Boyce Hammond.

The baseball season had just gotten underway, and many of the games
were being postponed due to cold, rainy weather in the northern cities,
so I had to content myself with a re-viewing of *Raiders of the Lost Ark* for
about the hundredth time on one of the movie channels. I dozed off
somewhere after Indiana Jones's famous gun-versus-scimitar scene in
the marketplace and woke just as the Nazis were being consumed and
melted by the guardian spirits. Thankfully I'd missed the part with the
snakes.

I rubbed my eyes, squinted blearily at my watch, and swore. Almost
two o'clock, approaching seven in Paris, and Darnay might already have
been up and about his business. Still, I didn't want to make such an important call with only half my brain engaged, so I stumbled into my
bathroom and threw a few handfuls of cold water over my face.

I needn't have bothered.

I sat on the sofa listening to the hollow ringing, imagining the shrill sound echoing off the silk-covered walls and the wonderful old fireplace framed by original Delft tiles, the sound sliding across the Empress Eugénie chaise longue and the faded green Aubusson carpet beneath the old casement windows.

I don't know how long I huddled there before the realization hit me, and I finally brought my thumb up to depress the off button on the portable handset.

No answering machine had picked up; no bright, *"Allô, je ne suis pas chez moi maintenant"* in Darnay's soft, rolling French had invited me to leave a message.

"Gone," I murmured into the dead telephone and dropped it into my lap.

Somewhere I had written the number for the manor house in Provençe. No doubt his sister, Madeleine, had been given a way to reach him in an emergency. But I had neither the will nor the desire to run the gauntlet of her haughty demeanor and obvious disapproval. It would probably give her a great deal of pleasure for me to come begging for a way to contact her brother, and I'd be damned if I'd give her the satisfaction of refusing.

No, the painful truth was Darnay had disappeared once again into the great void of his undercover world, and he'd gone without a word to me.

Bien. Fine. So be it.

CHAPTER
FOURTEEN

I TRIED TO SLEEP, FAILED MISERABLY, AND SPENT THE remainder of the night tossing on the wide cushions of the sofa in the great room, staring through the open drapes toward the sea. As soon as the first soft glints of dawn touched the horizon, I pulled on my running clothes and punished my body for the better part of an hour.

One of the things you have to develop in the accounting business is the ability to compartmentalize. You have to learn to put away all the numbers associated with the current project running around in your head and clear the mental decks for the next one. By the time I came pounding back over the dune and up the steps onto the deck, my mind had constructed a steel-walled chamber, shoved the memories of Darnay's loving smiles, sweet caresses, and lying words inside, and slammed the stout door firmly shut.

If I occasionally heard him scratching faintly to get out, I promised myself to ignore it.

Ravenous after a steaming shower, I dressed hurriedly and wolfed down a huge mushroom-and-cheese omelet accompanied by English muffins slathered in blackberry jelly. I left the dirty dishes on the table and dialed Adelaide Boyce Hammond.

Her soft, tentative, "Hello?" brought a smile.

"Miss Addie? It's Bay. Bay Tanner."

"Oh, Lydia . . . I mean, Bay, how delightful to hear from you, my dear."

"It's good to talk to you, too."

"Surely you're not calling me from France, are you? Does this mean you have some word about Win?"

Oh, God, I thought, and mentally smacked my forehead. How could I have been so stupid!

What now seemed a lifetime ago, Miss Addie had asked me to help her locate her brother, Edwin Hollister Hammond, who had disappeared more than twenty years before. During her recent troubles the past summer, she had received a cryptic postcard from Win, indicating he had been aware of all the news from the old hometown, but neglecting—intentionally or otherwise—to disclose his whereabouts. Miss Addie had professed a desire to find him before, as she put it, he had to come home for her funeral.

I'd set Erik Whiteside on his trail, figuring he, with all his computer skills, would have a better chance than I of tracking down a man who apparently didn't want to be found. In the chaos which had been my life in the months preceding my pilgrimage to Paris, neither one of us had given the task the slightest priority. Now it was time to pay the piper for that neglect.

"No, Miss Addie, I'm sorry. I don't have any news about Win." I heard her soft sigh of disappointment, and I added, "But we're still working on it." The lie only made me feel worse.

"Well, I always knew it was a long shot, as Daddy used to say. And how is Paris, my dear? I was there once, in my girlhood. Did I ever tell you?"

"No, I don't believe you ever did," I replied, settling onto the chaise at the edge of the deck. This could be a long story, and I owed Miss Addie the chance to tell it to me. I had no trains to catch. In fact, I had nothing now but time.

Her rambling tale of a pre–World War II Paris delighted me, and I let her reminisce to her heart's content. I did manage to squeeze in a couple of comments in an attempt to make clear that I was back in the States, but I'm not sure she heard me. Her voice had taken on a girlish quality, and just for those few moments, she seemed to have slipped back into a time when the idea of love, husband, and a family of her own had still been very real possibilities in her life.

Eventually she wound down, and I said into a brief silence, "Thank you so much for sharing that with me. When . . . if I return, I'll be able to look at things in a vastly different way now."

"You're quite welcome, my dear. It's so rare these days for young people to have the slightest interest in the memories of an old woman. Thank you for taking the time."

"No problem. Listen, Miss Addie, I wonder if you could answer a question for me."

"I'll certainly try."

"Do you know someone named Felicity Baronne? A friend of the Judge's from the old days, I'm guessing. Or maybe an acquaintance of my mother's. Does the name do anything for you?"

She was quiet for so long I thought we might have been cut off.

"Miss Addie? Are you still there?"

"Yes, of course, Lydia. I'm sorry. *Felicity.* Lord help me, I haven't heard that name in years! At least thirty, maybe more. It quite took me back."

"Who was she? *Is* she, I mean."

Again Miss Addie hesitated.

"Oh, come on now," I wheedled. "If Felicity was a former flame of my father's, an old girlfriend or something, it can't really matter now."

"Why are you asking?"

All the teasing and sweetness was gone from her voice, and the simple question hung in the air for the few moments it took me to decide how much of the present situation to reveal to my mother's oldest friend.

Tough call. I settled on, "She's been in touch with the Judge recently, and Lavinia is concerned."

"I don't wonder," I thought she said, but the murmur had been so low I wasn't positive I'd heard her correctly.

"Excuse me?"

"Oh, it's nothing, my dear. I'm not quite clear on why you're asking me about this. Your father knows perfectly well who—and what—Felicity is, although I believe her name was Starks in those days. Strange, I can't believe she married." The pause was infinitesimal, but laden with meaning. "Is there some reason you're hesitant to ask him yourself?"

Again I faltered, unsure how much of this Lavinia would be comfortable with my sharing. Then, though no one could see me, I shrugged in a what-the-hell manner and plunged in. "He's being very secretive about it, offering no explanations whatsoever. And he's giving her money."

I was expecting a shocked gasp of dismay, but Miss Addie disappointed me. Instead—inexplicably—she laughed, a dry chuckle I couldn't quite interpret.

"You find it amusing?" I asked with perhaps a little more acerbity than I should have.

"I'm sorry, my dear. Of course I don't find it amusing if it upsets you and Mrs. Smalls. But really, it is ironic. 'The more things change . . .'" she began and let the rest of the quotation dribble off into silence.

"It could be blackmail."

It was what Lavinia had been hinting at and the idea which had first sprung into my own mind when she'd first broached the subject. It wouldn't have been the first time someone tried to hold past or even recent indiscretions over my father's head.

"No, Lydia, I don't think it's blackmail, at least not in the sense you're implying. Why don't you just ask the Judge? I'm quite sure he'll tell you anything you want to know."

"And if he doesn't?"

"Well then he must have an excellent reason, and it would be most improper of me to gossip with you about personal matters he prefers to keep private. I'm sure you understand."

Of course I didn't understand, but I could tell it wasn't going to make a damned bit of difference to Miss Addie. I mustered up my early childhood training, thanked her graciously for her time, and promised to stay in touch regarding the search for her brother. Mad as I was at her old woman's coyness, I still owed her that.

The phone rang almost the second after I hung it up.

"Mrs. Tanner?" a bright female voice I didn't recognize chirped into my ear. "Mrs. *Bay* Tanner?"

"Yes?"

"Please hold for Mr. Palmer."

Before I had a chance to stutter out any response, the line switched to canned hold music, something Broadway and innocuous, with lots of strings. I swallowed my surprise along with the last of the tea in my glass, moved back through the house and up the steps into the kitchen. I dropped into the chair which matched the built-in desk and pulled a small pad and a pen in front of me. I had no idea what this was all about, but I had a feeling note-taking might be in order. I'd straightened and aligned every item on the granite surface and was starting in on the drawers when the remembered voice from my answering machine cut into a haunting rendition of "If I Loved You."

"Mrs. Tanner? Sorry to keep you waiting. Had to take an emergency call from one of our overseas offices. This is Gray Palmer. Senior."

The last was added in a tone which made me swallow hard, recalling that the other person entitled to the use of those names no longer existed.

"Yes, Mr. Palmer. How may I help you?"

I kept it strictly business, the memory of his message basically telling me to butt out of his son's affairs still fresh in my mind. If he was calling to rant some more, I'd cut him off in a second. But kindly, of course. Allowances had to be made for grief.

"I hope my previous communication didn't offend you. I certainly meant no disrespect."

"None taken, Mr. Palmer. While my partner was initially contacted by your son, the relationship necessarily terminated upon his unfortunate death." I had no intention of revealing anything about the strange contents of the package Erik had received. If Araminda Albright had spilled everything to GS, as she referred to him, I'd let him broach the subject first. "So you had no real need for concern, and there will of course be no bill."

"The money is of no concern to me, Mrs. Tanner," he snapped.

"Then I'm afraid I don't quite understand the purpose of your call," I replied in a voice frosty enough to match his own.

The pause lasted several seconds. When next he spoke, his tone had softened considerably. "Again, let me apologize. I'm sure you of all people must understand how something like this . . ."

He let it hang there, inviting me to comment on his unfinished thought. Two things flashed immediately across my mind: he was trying hard to elicit my sympathy, and he had checked me out. His oblique reference had to be about Rob's murder.

"Of course."

Two could play the waiting game, and I felt certain I was at least as good at it as Gray Palmer, Senior.

"I seem to have made a complete muddle of this," he finally said. "Could we start over?"

"Of course," I repeated.

"Look, Mrs. Tanner, I understand from Miss Albright that she spoke with you at some length last weekend about my son and the circumstances surrounding his death. She told me you expressed an interest in helping her to some resolution of her concerns."

I thought that a strange way to put it, but I got his drift. And this would have been the perfect time for him to mention the bone. I waited a few seconds to give him a chance to jump in, but he didn't. "What Miss Albright and I discussed is confidential, Mr. Palmer. If she chose to reveal the particulars to you, that is certainly her right. I'm afraid I cannot."

Again I had given him the perfect lead-in, but he ignored it. Perhaps, for some inexplicable reason, Mindy had held out on him about his son's grisly find. What the hell was her game?

"Understood. What I'm calling for is to take back the condescending message I left for you, and to engage your services on my son's behalf."

That took me by surprise. "To what end?" I asked.

"You may be aware from the local news coverage that I am firmly convinced my son's death was not an accident."

"Yes. I did happen to see your news conference the other night."

"Good. Then you know I've offered a substantial reward for anyone with information concerning his death to come forward."

"Yes."

"I'm afraid I've been inundated with calls and messages, at both my office and my home, although I installed a special toll-free line to deal with any responses. How these . . . these *maniacs* managed to track me down I don't know, but I'm being harassed day and night by people claiming all sorts of bizarre things."

"Bizarre?"

"Absolutely! Everything from his having been zapped by an alien death ray to being executed by some paramilitary group, to someone claiming he was killed by drug dealers because he owed them fifty thousand dollars."

"And they wanted you to settle the debt?"

"Exactly. I had no idea my offer would engender these kinds of cruel hoaxes. I suppose I should have, but I didn't."

He had my sympathy now. "What can we do to help?"

"I'd like to hire your firm to track down all these people and weed out the obvious crackpots. I know you probably think I'm incredibly naïve, but I can't help believing there just might be a legitimate lead somewhere in all this madness." He paused for effect, and it worked. He had my complete attention. "I'm determined to find out what happened to my son, and I don't care how long it takes or how much it costs. Will you do it? Will you help me?"

Without the first idea of how Erik, the Judge, and I could possibly live up to the commitment, I said, "Of course."

CHAPTER
FIFTEEN

SAT FOR A LONG TIME STARING AT THE WALL BEHIND my desk after Gray Palmer hung up.

He had a record of all the call-back numbers left by the reward-seekers, whether on the toll-free line or his private and business numbers. He promised to have his secretary fax me the information as soon as he could have it collated into a useable list. I had no idea how to go about putting names and addresses with them, but I was pretty sure Erik Whiteside would.

My sleepless night had begun to creep up on me, and I stifled a yawn as I carried my scribbled notes into the office. I opened the Word program and transcribed them, printing out a copy and adding it to the file. Then I picked up the phone and dialed Chris Brandon's office.

Of course Gray Palmer had forced me to discuss money, and I didn't want it to appear as if this were our first legitimate case, even though it was. So I'd quoted him a daily rate gleaned from countless PI novels and television episodes, and he hadn't flinched. What I needed now was a contract. I wondered if there was a standard document for engaging the services of an accountant-turned-gumshoe. The thought made me smile, even through the ill-tempered Cheryl's veiled attempts to make me go away. In a matter of moments, Chris came on the line.

"Bay, good to hear from you. How goes the investigation?"

That stopped me in midsentence. How the hell did he know about the new case? Then I realized he must be talking about the Mitchells.

"Oh, fine. All done. Didn't you get my report?"

"No, I didn't. Maybe it's languishing in the mail somewhere. I swear, sometimes I think it would be faster just to walk the paperwork from town to town."

"Well, I'll give you the thumbnail version. Tamika is definitely embezzling, creating phony employees and vendors then cashing the checks herself. Not very original, but she's draining a lot of money out of the business."

"That's too bad. How did Bubba react?"

"He doesn't want to prosecute, says families don't treat each other that way. I don't agree, but it's not my call. Maybe you can convince him. At any rate, they're going to need a complete audit. First priority would be the payroll taxes. With nonexistent employees, they're going to be totally inaccurate and will need to be re-filed."

"Can you do it?" I started to enumerate the reasons for my inability to oblige him when I heard him say, "Oh, hi, sweetheart! Come on in. I'll be done in a minute." Then, "Sorry about that, Bay. Amy's here. We're headed for lunch with her mother and the Colonel. Wedding plans, you know?"

"Sure, no problem. We can finish this up . . ."

"No, go ahead. We've got plenty of time."

"Okay. I was just saying I don't have time to take on that extensive an operation. How about the firm that did the Bi-Rite audit?"

"I'm sure they'll be glad to help. I'll give them a call after I get your report."

"Great. Listen, Chris, I need to retain your services to draw up a contract for me. It's kind of complicated, so maybe we should make it another time if you're in a rush to get to lunch."

"What kind of contract?"

I don't know why I hesitated to reveal the nature of my new venture to Chris Brandon. Now that the formerly amorphous idea had actually become reality, I suppose I felt a little silly about my decision to become a full-fledged investigator. In the cold light of day, it seemed somehow childish, a game I'd decided to play to keep myself busy. Not unlike an old widow-woman's learning bridge. Or taking a lover.

"Personal services," I replied, hoping the generic term would keep him from probing any more deeply into specifics. "Is there some standard form I could use, maybe a fill-in-the-blanks kind of thing?"

"Well, I don't see why you couldn't use whatever you had for the old accounting practice. You'd have to change the names and all, but it should work. Are you going back into business?"

"In a manner of speaking. So you think that would fly?"

"I don't see why not. If you like, I could look it over for you, make sure there aren't any ugly loopholes for potential deadbeats to wriggle through. The main goal is to protect you from unnecessary liability. If the contract was vetted by your attorneys before, I think you'd be pretty safe in using it again."

I hadn't thought of that, and it seemed a good suggestion. Change some wording, print it out from the computer, and I'd be in business. Literally.

"Thanks, Chris. It's a great idea. I'll give you a holler if I run into anything I can't figure out."

"Not much chance of that," he said, and once again I basked in the glow of his boyish admiration. "Did you include an invoice for the Mitchell thing in with your report?"

"Yup. Hope it's okay with you, but I took it easy on them. I'm not looking to make money on these kinds of things, and Bubba is my friend. If I thought he'd let me get away with doing it for nothing, I would."

"Understood. Thanks again for taking it on."

"No problem. Thank you for the referral and the advice. Be sure to bill me."

"Don't hold your breath. Best to your father."

"And tell Amy I said hello."

"Will do. She wants the two of you to get together sometime soon. I'll have her call you for lunch."

What the hell for? I asked myself, but upbringing won out again. "Lovely! I'll wait to hear from her," is what came out of my mouth.

In a pig's ear! I thought, hanging up the phone. Why on earth would Chris Brandon's fiancée want a cozy little tête-à-tête with me? I vowed to use every excuse in my considerable arsenal to avoid having to sit across the table from a simpering Amy Fleming and her massive engagement ring.

I signed on again to my Word program, located a copy of my old contract, and spent the next two hours cutting and pasting until I had a document I thought would be sufficient to mollify Gray Palmer. I also played with a couple of graphics programs I found lurking on the hard drive, and ended up designing a logo for Simpson & Tanner, Inquiry Agents I thought was pretty damned clever. I had no idea how my father and Erik would feel about it, but since I seemed to be doing all the grunt work they'd just have to live with it.

I printed off two copies of the contract onto the new letterhead, filled in the appropriate blanks, and signed them. Then I whipped out a cover letter asking Palmer to return one signed copy to me, along with a retainer, and slid it all into a manila envelope. If we really decided to go full steam ahead with this business, we were going to need clerical help. And someplace for her to operate.

I pushed those unpleasant thoughts aside and went to the kitchen for a sandwich. By two o'clock I was back in the office watching several pages of phone numbers and reproduced messages roll off my fax machine. Gray Palmer's secretary was not only accurate, she was fast. Maybe I should think about luring her away to man the imaginary office which was taking shape and form in the back of my mind. I tapped the pages to straighten the edges and dropped into the chair in front of the computer.

There were sixteen entries in all, far fewer than I had been led to believe. The three Palmer had mentioned were there, along with a couple who might be legitimate. A weekend father, out fishing with his sons, thought he had seen young Gray's boat anchored just about dawn on Saturday morning. The vessel looked abandoned, no one visible on deck as he and his boys passed by about thirty yards off his stern. He couldn't be positive until he'd verified the name of Gray's craft. One of the kids remarked on the unusual name, although the father hadn't seen it himself: *Arky Olly Jist.* The man had been forced to think about it himself, until he finally caught on and explained it to his son.

"Clever," I muttered, although it seemed like something you'd put on a vanity license plate rather than a name for a boat. Still, Gray Palmer, Senior, should certainly have recognized it.

I circled that entry. The Good Samaritan and reward-seeker had left his name—Delbert Pidgen—as well as home, work, and cell phone numbers and an e-mail address. I could tackle him myself, though how I would go about verifying his story escaped me for the moment.

The other intriguing message came from another weekend boater, this one a woman traveling from Hilton Head up the Intracoastal Waterway to Charleston. She had left Skull Creek Marina well before first light in order to rendezvous with some friends and had observed a craft matching the description of the *Arky Olly Jist* pulled up alongside another boat. Young Gray, if in fact that's who it was, seemed to be carrying on a conversation with two men. Although they had to shout to be heard above their respective idling engines, she couldn't make out what was being said. Her impression, however, had been that the exchange of words being hurled across the narrow gap between the two boats had been angry. She had not observed the name on either vessel, opting to give them a wide berth. Ms. Cynthia Sellers professed herself completely disinterested in the reward, her only goal to be of some assistance to the grieving father.

Right. There are a lot of wealthy people on Hilton Head, but I couldn't seriously envision anyone turning down twenty-five grand. That kind of money would buy an awful lot of gas or finance a few barnacle-scrapings—or whatever it was one did with boats. Or maybe Ms. Sellers had discovered Gray Palmer was a widower—a wealthy widower. Maybe her game was passing up the little fish in order to land the big tuna.

The remainder of the list consisted of numbers left without name or detailed message attached, except that most of the callers had hinted at valuable information to be imparted, but only if Palmer coughed up some good-faith cash in advance. I thought we'd probably check these out, but not until we'd eliminated the quasi-legitimate ones.

The alien death-ray guy intrigued me, but he'd no doubt turn out to be one of those fruitcakes who think the CIA is stealing their thoughts through microwave towers or radio antennae. The drug deal gone bad theory didn't sound so far-fetched now that I'd read Ms. Sellers's account. This had possibilities on two fronts. The paramilitary hit I dismissed out of hand. We would probably check it out, just to be thorough, but I felt it probably ranked right up there with the Venusian laser-zapper guy.

I typed it all into a file, organizing and prioritizing as I went. It occurred to me that if I had one of those scanner thingys I wouldn't have to keep re-entering this kind of information. I'd have to ask Erik. It was also probably time I caved in to his repeated insistence I avail myself of a cell phone. I supposed if we were actually going to get this enterprise off the ground, it would become a necessity rather than a nuisance.

By four-fifteen, I'd had it with playing secretary/typist. I saved all my files after printing hardcopy and placed a call to Erik Whiteside in Charlotte. It was time to let someone else's fingers do the walking.

The call came as I stood before the open refrigerator door trying to muster up some enthusiasm for defrosting something for dinner. But it wasn't Erik, back from whatever errand had lured him out of the store. It was a very agitated Lavinia.

"Bay! She's here!" Her words, urgent and excited, came through in a tight whisper. "I just left them in the study—with the door closed!" I knew immediately who "she" was: the mysterious Felicity Baronne. "Can you come?" The plaintive voice cut straight into my heart.

I glanced at the clock over the sink. Just after five. Rush hour. Even if I made every traffic light, and there were no major pileups, it would still take me the better part of an hour to make it to Presqu'isle.

"How long does she usually stay?" I asked.

"It varies. Sometimes fifteen or twenty minutes. Never more than an hour."

"There's no way I can make it there in time, Lavinia." I paused, hesitant to make the suggestion. "Have you tried eavesdropping?"

Her own hesitation confirmed my suspicion that this idea might already have occurred, even to the painfully honest Lavinia Smalls. "The door is over a hundred years old and solid oak. Don't be ridiculous, child."

"Well, I don't see any way I can get there before she leaves."

"I know. I can't think what's gotten into me."

"You're worried about the Judge, that's what's gotten into you. And I have to admit you're making me pretty damned nervous, too. Do you seriously think this woman can harm my father in some way?"

"I'm telling you, I just don't know! It's the sneaking around, closing doors, and pretending like everything's just like normal that worries me. I don't for one second think your father has to tell me every last detail of his personal life. But we . . . that is, we've shared most everything in these last years, and I have to believe it's something he thinks will hurt me in some way. And the only thing that could do that is if it's something that could hurt him!"

I promised myself I'd examine this extraordinary outburst when I had the opportunity to think about it more clearly. What I did recognize was that this was about as much revelation on the subject of her relationship with my father as I'd heard her divulge—ever.

"Let me think a minute," I said to cover my own confusion.

A sharp click followed by a deep humming made me realize I'd been carrying on this conversation with the freezer door hanging open. I pushed it closed and settled myself onto one of the chairs ranged around the glass-topped table in the bay of the kitchen window. I glanced out toward my shiny new T-Bird pulled up in the drive, and inspiration struck.

"How did she arrive?" I asked.

"What do you mean?"

"By cab, or did she drive herself?"

"She drove. I saw the car when I opened the door for her."

"What kind is it?"

"Lord, girl, I don't know anything about cars!" I could feel Lavinia's frustration level rising. Then, "Wait!" I heard her whisper. "She's comin' out!"

"Don't hang up!" I ordered. I found myself lowering my own voice, though I had no idea why. "Follow her outside and get the color and make of her car. License plate number, too, if you can manage it."

She hesitated for only a moment. "I understand. I'll call you back just as soon as she's gone."

I hung up the phone, abandoning all thoughts of an early dinner. As I passed down the hall to my bedroom, I found myself smiling.

You're in this investigating thing up to your neck now, my girl, I told myself while I stripped out of my clothes and surveyed the contents of my walk-in closet. I had about half an hour to select an appropriate outfit for my first genuine stakeout and figure out the best place to lie in wait for the unsuspecting Felicity Baronne.

CHAPTER
SIXTEEN

I PULLED THE SWEATING CAN OF DIET COKE AND A
handful of pretzels out of the brown paper bag beside me and
shifted around again in the seat. A glance at the dashboard clock told
me it was a little after six, and I was beginning to worry.

I'd settled the T-Bird under the canopy of a spreading sweet gum
just inside the driveway of the Gullah Flea Market on the north end of the
island. Carolyn's Nursery next door would have offered more cover, but
they had closed and locked their gates sometime before I arrived. A few
stragglers had still been wandering the colorful stalls of the long rambling market which housed everything from native island crafts to used
lawn furniture and exercise bikes, but by five-thirty most of the customers had headed off. The wide wooden doors had been lowered across
the open-air building, and mine had become the only car in the lot.

I'd left the motor running, the local oldies station playing softly
during the first half hour of my inaugural stakeout, in order to be able to
jump into traffic the moment I spotted Felicity Baronne's car. The problem was I had spotted *dozens* of white Ford Escorts, most flying through
the intersection at such a clip I had no time to check out license plate
numbers. I'd considered the Gullah Market a good choice because it sat
right at a traffic signal where vehicles would be slowing in anticipation
of having to stop. Apparently I'd been in Paris too long. I'd forgotten no

one on Hilton Head obeys the forty-five mile per hour speed limit, and the lights on 278, especially during rush hour, turn red only about once every half hour.

I grabbed another handful of pretzels without taking my eyes from the road. A Beaufort County sheriff's cruiser leading a parade of suddenly law-abiding motorists rolled sedately through the light just as it changed. I saw the officer glance briefly over at me then continue on his way.

Admiring the T-Bird, I thought, then gasped as I realized the car I had been seeking had landed practically in my lap. The little white four-door sedan sat almost directly in front of me on the inside lane. The profile of the driver was partially concealed by a mass of red-gold hair teased into the kind of bouffant you only see in old Gidget and Elvis Presley movies. Exactly as Lavinia had described her to me. As I watched, she leaned over toward the center of the dash then straightened to touch the car's round lighter to an impossibly long cigarette.

Another clue confirmed. "Smells like you used to." Lavinia's terse description of my quarry's reeking clothes had made me blush in embarrassment.

I shook off my astonishment and put my plan into action. I jerked the gearshift into drive, turned right onto the main drag, and eased over into the middle lane. I let my speed settle in at about thirty-five, slow enough for everyone behind me to pull around and ahead, and not so turtle-like that I risked getting myself rear-ended. At least I hoped not. I had to stay flexible because Ms. Baronne could make one of several moves at the next intersection, the one at Spanish Wells Road, and I had to be ready for any eventuality.

Behind me the light changed, and vehicles shot past like drag racers coming off the line. Felicity Baronne moved more sedately by me on the left. I let a couple of cars get between us, after noting with satisfaction that her license plate number jibed with my information, then darted into the left lane in front of a minivan from Ohio. The poor guy at the wheel was so confused by all the road signs dangling overhead he didn't even take the time to blow his horn at me.

I followed the Escort through the light and onto the Cross Island

Parkway. Another guess confirmed. If she used the south end post office, Felicity probably lived in that vicinity as well. I stayed behind her through the toll gates, handing over my dollar through a rolling stop which earned me a glare from the lady in the glass-enclosed booth. At the foot of the bridge she again moved to the left. By this time only one car separated us, and I tried to hang back. But when she flipped on her signal at the light, I had no choice but to move right up behind her in the turn lane. When she made another hard left, I breathed a sigh of relief. This road dead-ended at Palmetto Bay Marina, and there were a limited number of places she could be heading. I slowed enough to let her get a little ahead then watched as she eased into the parking lot of the high-rise condominium building in the heart of the marina.

I pulled into the area reserved for guests of the Chart House restaurant and got out of the car. I slung my bag over my shoulder and stuck my hands in the pockets of my jeans. Felicity Baronne was a small woman, dwarfed even more by her riotous hair which made her easy to keep an eye on as she tottered on three-inch heels toward the glass entrance doors. Her bright purple knit top strained across an ample bosom which may or may not have been real, and her white stretch Capri pants revealed way too many bumps and bulges.

A floozy indeed, I thought, at least to judge by outward appearances.

I lurked outside while she waited for the elevator to arrive then stepped in to watch the indicator until it stopped on the third floor. I searched the foyer for the bank of mailboxes, but Felicity's name appeared on none of the little slots. Of course, she had a post office box, so I supposed she had no need of a receptacle on site, although that, too, seemed a little odd.

I debated whether or not to hang around to see if she went out again, but my rumbling stomach decided me against it. Besides, I knew where she lived, and I had her box number. What good it was doing me I hadn't quite worked out yet, although I supposed a confrontation would be inevitable. If Lavinia refused to let me ask my father why he was paying off this woman, I would have to get it from the horse's mouth. Now that I knew where to find her, it didn't seem quite so imperative.

I turned back toward the restaurant, realizing with sadness the name had been changed to Eugene's. Another landmark altered. I wandered inside anyway to find to my delight that the spectacular view of the sunset over the marsh and the wonderful food had both survived the change intact.

I awoke Friday morning to lowering skies and a pounding headache. I'd stayed up late waiting for Erik to return my call but had heard nothing from him. No messages, no e-mails, nothing. My first thought was he'd gone down to visit Mercer Mary Prescott, but he was usually so paranoid about checking his answering machine from his cell phone I couldn't quite shake a feeling of unease. Especially when I remembered he had a human bone, recently stolen from a disturbed gravesite, stashed in his clothes hamper.

I popped three aspirin, showered, and tried Erik's home number again. The machine engaged after only one ring, so there had to be a lot of messages waiting for him. It was too early for him to be at the store, and I realized I'd never gotten his cell number from him. Lots of things needed to be much better organized if we ever hoped to pull off running an investigation agency.

I made tea and studied the weather from the comfort of the great room. A line of gray clouds hung along the horizon, and the ocean looked dark and angry. I paced, craving a cigarette, frustrated by my inability to formulate a coherent agenda for dealing with Gray Palmer's death or my father's duplicity. I flopped down onto the sofa and promptly fell asleep.

"*Señora? Señora!*"

I waved a hand in front of my face, trying to ward off the annoying intrusion into my fractured dreams of Darnay standing in the doorway of the house in Provençe, sunlight bathing the golden stone and his wonderful blue eyes . . .

"*Señora, qué pasa?* You are ill?"

I rolled onto my back and forced my gummy eyes open to find

Dolores leaning over me, concern deep in her voice. I stretched and forced a reassuring smile.

"A headache, is all. I must have needed a little catnap." I sat up and rolled my head on my stiff shoulders. "What time is it?"

"*A las cuatro.*"

"Four o'clock? In the afternoon?" I swung my legs to the floor as Dolores stepped back. "How is that possible? I've been asleep the entire day!"

"*Necesario,*" she replied, nodding, which I took to mean something like, "You must have needed it."

The storm appeared to have passed, because sharp needles of light were bombarding my eyes through the shimmering glass of the French doors. I groaned and dropped my head into my hands.

"Is good I come," Dolores said, patting my back reassuringly before turning toward the kitchen. "I bring *la cena* for you, *Señora*. Roberto and Alejandro, they catch many shrimps."

I didn't want to think about dinner or eating or anything which required dragging my butt off the sofa at that moment, but I knew I needed to break the lethargy that lay over me like a sopping blanket. I pinched my cheeks a couple of times and forced myself to my feet.

"What is it?" I asked, trying to fake some enthusiasm as I staggered up the steps.

"Ah, you will like. The garlic, the *vino blanco*. Many things *muy bueno*."

"Thank you," I said, mustering a smile. "Just put it in the fridge."

"I fix for you?" Dolores stood in the middle of the kitchen, the casserole dish held out to me like an offering to an angry god.

"Later," I said as I punched the play button on the answering machine. "I need to take a shower."

The messages were all junk, and I deleted them immediately, amazed the phone had rung that many times and I had failed to hear it.

Dolores slid the dish into the refrigerator and lifted her worn black handbag from the counter.

"Thank you," I repeated, with genuine feeling this time.

"*De nada.*"

"I'll see you on Monday then?"

"Si, Señora. A lunes."

I followed her out to the door, then reset the alarm and hurried into the office. I signed on and scrolled through more spam, but found no message from Erik.

"Damn you!" I said aloud.

I peeled off my sweaty, wrinkled slacks and sweater and headed for the shower, hoping I'd be able to wash away the growing knot of anxiety which seemed to have taken up permanent residence in the bottom of my stomach.

CHAPTER
SEVENTEEN

OLORES HAD BEEN RIGHT ABOUT THE SHRIMP CASSE-role—*muy bueno*. In the spirit of my grumpy mood, I ate it straight out of the dish while standing on the deck staring out toward the ocean. Wisps of mauve-and-orange-tinted cloud drifted out from the mainland along with the deepening twilight. The line of demarcation between sky and water slowly blurred, then disappeared altogether into the night.

The lights in the house clicked on behind me, the timers connected to the security system performing their assigned task as I lowered myself onto the chaise. I tucked my hands behind my head and tried to force myself to relax.

In the years since Rob's murder, I had learned how to be alone. Not the kind of solitude I used to crave when the demands of my own business and my husband's relentless drive to nail every drug dealer in the state had seemed to occupy us twenty hours a day. Back then I would simply toss my handbag into the front seat of the car, let down the top, and take myself off to the beach. I had favorite spots, secluded inlets and tiny strips of sand unknown and often inaccessible to the casual visitor. For a stolen hour or so I'd simply toss aside my shoes and my harried life and contemplate the water, the sand, the sky.

But since the day I had watched my husband's plane explode on takeoff, had felt the hot metal pieces striking my own cowering body, I had resigned myself to being alone. True, there had been that one, unguarded moment of passion, dying quickly when it became apparent I was only being used. With Darnay I had been more cautious, testing, yearning forward, only to draw back at the point of intimacy, of real connection. Paris had been a test, not only of his feelings for me, but of my ability to accept them, as well. And again I had failed. At the first sign of stress, both of us had bolted—he to the work that defined him, and I . . .

To this, I told myself, *this place, this life. This loneliness.*

I never cry. Well, almost never. It seems to me a pointless exercise, messy and not the least productive. I sniffed loudly in the darkness and was saved the ignominy of making a liar out of myself by the sharp ringing of the telephone.

I sprinted across the great room and snatched up the handset.

"Hey, partner, it's me."

I bit down hard on the stream of invective waiting to leap from my lips, the natural outlet for all the day's miserable frustration. Instead I forced myself to say calmly, "Hey yourself. Where have you been? I've been trying to reach you."

"Have you? Sorry. Something's wrong with the damn cell, and I've been out of touch for the last few hours. What's up?"

"Where have you been?" I repeated.

"On the road."

"To where?"

"Well, right now I'm parked outside your security gate. The guy inside let me use his phone. Can you tell him it's okay to let me in?"

"Here? You're here?"

Erik Whiteside hesitated a moment before replying. "It's okay, isn't it? I mean, you don't have company or anything, right? I would have called first, but the cell . . ."

"Don't worry about it," I interrupted, the idea of sharing the lonely night with another living, breathing, human being overriding all the annoyance I had been building up against my partner and friend. "Let me talk to the security officer."

I authorized Erik's entrance into the sanctity of Port Royal Plantation, then scurried around plumping up the cushions on the sofa,
crushed and dented from my day-long sleep, and tossing the morning
paper into the trash. In the bathroom I slapped on a little lipstick and
mascara and ran a brush through the usual tangle of my hair. By the
time the sweep of the headlights on the monstrous SUV finally cut
across the kitchen, I had glasses of beer and iced tea poured and waiting
on the table.

"So it just made sense to come straight down here and talk it all out
with you. If you agree, we can run over there tomorrow." Erik leaned
back in his chair and wiped his mouth with the blue linen napkin.
"Thanks," he added, "that was great."

I'd thrown together an omelet when he'd finally confessed to being
hungry, and I had sat listening to his story between bites.

"So this guy, this retired professor, lives on Hilton Head?"

"Not exactly. It's another island, he said, close by. Some place called
Daufuskie?"

"Right. It's just off the 'toe' of Hilton Head, between us and Savannah." I carried his plate and silverware to the dishwasher and poured
myself more tea. "Ready for that beer now?" It had seemed not entirely
the correct accompaniment to the eggs.

"Sure. So how do we get over there? Is there a bridge?"

"Nope. You have to go by ferry. The landing's down at the south
end, by Palmetto Bay Marina."

"So that's what he meant when he said he'd make arrangements for
us. We have an appointment tomorrow morning at ten."

"Why the rush?" I asked. I still didn't understand the urgency
which had sent Erik tearing down from Charlotte, turning the operation of his computer store over to the assistant he usually claimed didn't
have the brains God gave a goat. And this would make twice in one
week he'd done so.

"Doctor Douglass and his wife are leaving for Asheville on Monday.

Something to do with one of their grandkids. Anyway, he agreed to run some preliminary tests for us before he goes. I just thought we should take advantage of the opportunity."

Erik had apparently not been idle in the days since receiving the grisly package from young Gray Palmer. Through some alumni contacts and a good deal of Internet sleuthing, he had discovered Dr. Denton Douglass, late of the anthropology department of Erik's alma mater and currently an occasional consultant to various police agencies on matters of forensic pathology. I didn't quite understand how my partner had convinced this obviously upright citizen to involve himself with a gruesome artifact from a robbed grave. Then again, perhaps he hadn't.

"Does he know the circumstances?" I asked.

"Not exactly," he said, dipping his head in that way he had when he'd been caught out in some fib or obfuscation.

"So what parts did you leave out?"

Erik fidgeted with his glass, tilting it at various angles and sloshing the beer around inside. I had to force myself not to reach over and take it away from him. Finally he glanced up to find my gaze fixed on him, and he grinned.

"Just about all of them," he said.

"I can't wait to hear the story myself."

"A variation on the truth, a lesson I learned at an early age. I told him I used to be one of his students."

"And were you?"

"Yeah, technically. At least for a week or so. See, Gray talked me into taking the course. It was required for him because he was an archaeology major, and he convinced me it would be cool to learn about bones and all that."

"No doubt in the midst of one of your drinking dates." I smiled to take the sting out of my words.

"Probably. Anyway, I was already up to my eyeballs, and I just couldn't cut it. Tons of reading and fieldwork. I dropped the class and picked up a management course instead. I figured, since he's taught there for so many years, he wouldn't remember me one way or the other."

"So what yarn did you spin him?"

"I said I'd dug it up while gardening in my backyard. Just the one bone, not a whole skeleton. I said it was probably a dog or some other animal, and I didn't want to look like a fool by calling in the cops. At first he said I should just send him a picture and he could tell from that, but I told him I was going to be on Hilton Head visiting a friend for the weekend and couldn't I just run over and show it to him. I offered him a hundred dollars for his time. He said okay."

Erik looked tired as he worked his head and neck around on his shoulders as if to ease some tension that had settled there.

"And what do you expect to happen when he confirms that it's human?" I asked. "Assuming that Gray's story is true."

"Why would you think it wasn't?" There was a clear challenge in his voice, an edge I seldom heard. "Do you think he was lying about finding the grave? Why would he? Besides, didn't his girlfriend confirm it?"

I sighed and shook my head. "She was only repeating what she heard from Gray. You can't use her as any kind of confirmation of his story."

"You think he was involved in some sort of crime?"

I held up my hands in a gesture of peace. "No, Erik, I don't believe Gray had anything to do with this person's death. But you have to stop making assumptions based on nothing more than wishful thinking. You haven't heard from this kid in a lot of years. You're drawing conclusions which may have no basis in fact now. Today. People change."

"Not that much. Listen, if you're dead set against this, I'll just get a hotel tonight and go see the doc myself in the morning. I don't want you involved in something you're not comfortable with. I can pay his fee, no problem. I just can't drop this thing, do you understand that? I just can't."

All of a sudden I realized we'd been so busy discussing Erik's bombshell I hadn't had an opportunity to relate my own news.

"Don't be silly," I said. "We're in this together. And you won't have to foot the bill for the good doctor's expertise. We have a client again."

"Mindy Albright?"

"Nope," I said with just a hint of smugness, "better than that. Gray Palmer, Senior, himself. Contracts are in the mail."

Once we got Erik's things settled in the guest room, we adjourned to the office where we pored over the file I had compiled and especially over the list of reward-seekers. Though we chewed on the possibilities, neither of us could come up with any plausible explanation for why young Gray had kept his gruesome discovery from his father or why Araminda Albright continued to do so as well.

"Why wouldn't she just have told the old man about the bone and the grave?" Erik rose from the futon on one end of the converted bedroom and stretched.

"I have no idea. I've tried several scenarios on for size, but none of them fits. The only possible explanation is there's something in it for her, something she hopes to gain from keeping the knowledge to herself. But that doesn't wash, either, because she knows that *we* know. She has no guarantee we won't tell GS the whole story. In fact, she hasn't even asked us to keep it quiet."

"Right." Erik prowled around the room, picking up objects, tossing them from hand to hand, then replacing them on the desk in a nervous ritual that was beginning to irritate me. "What's up with this?" he asked abruptly, thrusting the heavy crystal cigarette lighter under my nose. His accusatory tone made my response more waspish than I'd intended.

"Put that down, would you? And go park it. You're making me dizzy."

"Sore subject?" he asked with that grin that could always totally disarm me.

"No," I said, returning his smile. "And no, I haven't been backsliding, though God knows I've been tempted often enough in the last week. The lighter is a way of reminding myself of how well I'm doing at holding the devil at bay."

"Sort of like a recovering alcoholic keeping an inch or so of gin in a bottle in the cupboard?"

"I suppose. Anyway, back to the matter at hand. How long were you planning on staying? Any chance you could hang on past the weekend?"

"I guess," he said, somewhat reluctantly. "I've got about a year of vacation days saved up. I suppose I could use a couple of them. What do you have in mind?"

"I thought we could tackle this list of people trying to claim the reward. If we split them up, we could eliminate a lot of them right off the bat and be able to concentrate on the real possibles."

"Sounds like a plan. Let me call Jackie and see if she can cover for me."

I tried unsuccessfully to stifle a gaping yawn. "Great," I mumbled.

"Guess we'd better turn in. Big day tomorrow." Erik extended a hand and hauled me from the chair.

As I reached to flip off the lights, I shot a glance over my shoulder at the innocuous-looking file cabinet nestled up against the computer desk. I hesitated, then crossed back over and pushed in the lock. No one probably had the least interest in my meager files, but past experience had shown me you just never knew what could happen.

Still, a casual burglar would have to share my warped sense of humor if he intended to make off with the looted bone.

I'd filed it under "G" for Ghastly.

Saturday morning should have been bottled and saved, to be opened on one of those occasional dreary days in mid-December or January when it seems as if the sun will never appear again. Very little humidity, a light breeze, and a pristine sky greeted us as we walked from the parking area to the embarkation point for the ferry. I'd heard somewhere that vehicles—except for golf carts—were prohibited on Daufuskie, and this seemed to be attested to by the number of cars shrouded in tarps and hunkered down in the tree-shaded lot.

The main building resembled a typical Lowcountry–style house with wide porches, the one facing the water complete with several rocking chairs. Inside, the reception area echoed the attempt to recreate a feel of days gone by with painted wainscoting, scattered imitation Oriental rugs, and dark green wing-backed chairs. The cherry desk was unoccupied. A discreet sign requested us to pick up our boarding passes at the small building where golfers left their bags to be transported in the closed metal containers we'd seen lined up just outside. I assumed these were also used for carrying mail and supplies to the isolated residents of Daufuskie Island.

The boat, sparkling white against the glistening water of Broad Creek, sat waiting as we made our way down the long gangway. A sign informed us the ferry left every hour on the half hour. A uniformed attendant offered us a hand as we stepped aboard and entered a snug salon carpeted in dark green with matching upholstery on wide benches. Some flanked tables, while others sat back-to-back down the center of the cabin. Several copies of the morning's *Island Packet* were scattered around, and an overhead TV set, sound off, was tuned to CNN.

We nodded greetings to several people already seated, many of whom carried shopping bags, apparently from early morning excursions to the Food Lion and Publix stores on Palmetto Bay Road. We plopped onto seats facing the open water.

"This is pretty cool," Erik whispered to me. "I mean, these people *really* live on an island."

"I'm not sure I'd like it," I said, shedding the light jacket I'd thrown on over my cotton sweater.

"Why not? Just think, you'd never have uninvited guests if you lived like this."

"True, but what happens in an evacuation? If a hurricane hit, you'd have no other way to escape except on this little boat. I don't know how many people live over there, but it seems to me it would take a lot of trips to get everyone off."

My watch read 9:29 when a man who appeared to be the captain passed through the cabin and headed forward. Lines were cast off, and the ferry edged away from the concrete dock. Erik hitched himself around to watch the land slipping away as we moved out into Broad Creek. Once we'd passed beneath the Cross Island bridge and rounded the little point on which the Palmetto Bay Marina sat, Erik turned back toward the elegant homes of Spanish Wells sliding by the wide, square windows.

"Beautiful places," he said, shifting around in an effort to accommodate his long legs in the narrow aisle.

"Bram's Point. It's not a spot for the faint of pocketbook," I replied.

"The founders and heads of some of the biggest companies in America have homes over there."

" 'Them that has, gets', or so my grandmother used to say."

"Granny Pen?" I shivered, recalling with sadness the woman whose brutal murder had first brought Erik and me together.

"No, my mom's mother, Grandmother Kingman. No *Gran* or *Granny* for her. It was strictly *Grandmother* or heads were sure to roll."

I smiled, lapsing into silence while we cruised past Buck Island and out into Calibogue Sound. Off to our left the red-and-white-striped column of the Harbour Town Lighthouse rose into the clear warm air. Beside me, Erik maneuvered the black nylon case he'd had slung over his shoulder until it settled on his knees. He wrapped both arms around the carryall and pulled it close to his chest.

I tried hard to pretend I didn't know what lay tucked in the bottom of the innocuous-looking bag. We'd rolled the bone in some old towels and packed others around it in an effort not only to conceal the grisly thing, but hopefully to insure no telltale smell would escape. I wasn't sure exactly how the owners of this well-maintained little craft would react to our bringing human remains aboard, but I was pretty sure it wouldn't be pleasant.

Shaking off the chilling feeling we were also breaking about a dozen state and local laws, I lowered my voice and edged myself closer to Erik's side. "What do you expect to gain from this excursion?" I asked. "I mean, what can this Dr. Douglass tell us we don't already know?" I ducked my head as the man across from us lowered his newspaper and glanced across the aisle.

"Besides confirm it's human? He can take measurements and do some tests to determine . . ."

Again our nosy companion peered over the top of the sports section, this time fixing me with an oily smile. I nodded and turned back to Erik who said softly, "This isn't the place."

"You're right. Sorry."

I reached behind me and snagged an abandoned copy of the *Packet*, snapping it open to the editorial page. Erik levered himself around again and watched the approaching outline of Daufuskie Island growing larger as we neared the ferry terminal. I forced myself to become en-grossed in a spate of letters both for and against a proposed dredging project in South Beach when the voice cut through the hum of the en-gines and the low murmur of conversation around me.

"Excuse me, but aren't you Bay Tanner?"

I rattled the paper, hoping the thin sheets of newsprint would pro-tect me from this unwanted intrusion. No such luck.

"I'm sorry, but I'm pretty sure I remember you from Beaufort. Well, St. Helena, actually."

I drew a deep breath and lowered the paper. Beside me I felt Erik stiffen and turn back around on the bench.

"Harry. Harry Simon," the man said, one hand extended across the aisle which separated us. "Beachside Realty. I'm workin' outta Hilton Head now."

"I'm sorry, but I don't remember you."

"Oh, sure ya do! We used to run into each other a lot at your daddy's political rallies. Back in the old days, when he was runnin' for solicitor and then judge. I swear your mama could flat-out throw a party! Why, I remember one time . . ."

I tuned out the good-ol'-boy rhetoric, noting the rustling of those around us as the ferry sidled up to the landing on Daufuskie Island. I gathered my jacket and bag, nodding all the while at this fool man's scattered reminiscences. I still had no idea who the hell he was.

". . . and then Law Merriweather chucked the whole damn thing right off the dock and into the Sound!" He slapped his thigh, but the hearty laugh which accompanied it never reached his eyes. "Remem-ber?" he prompted me.

"No, sorry, can't say that I do."

My curt response didn't slow him up at all. "You by any chance lookin' for property over here? I have some great listings . . ."

"No. Thanks."

"Visiting friends?"

"Something like that. Nice to see you again."

I grabbed Erik's arm and jerked him to his feet, sliding around in front to place his not inconsiderable bulk between me and Harry Simon.

We moved in single file through the narrow doorway and onto the dock. I set a brisk pace up the slight incline of the gangway, and soon we had left the garrulous, overweight real estate agent puffing some distance behind us.

"How do we get to this Doctor Douglass's place?" I asked as we passed the enclosed waiting room at the top of the walkway.

"He said he'd meet us."

Several people hoisted their grocery bags and other purchases into waiting golf carts and sped away, while others boarded what looked to be a converted school bus. I glanced back over my shoulder, pleased to find Harry Simon had stopped to chat with one of the uniformed crew members off the ferry.

"What's up with that guy?" Erik asked as he hefted the bag containing the bone up onto his shoulder.

"Beats the hell out of me. So far as I know, I've never met him before. But some of those fund-raisers for the Judge's campaigns used to be real madhouses. Sometimes two hundred people or more would show up for one of his barbecues or oyster roasts. Simon couldn't have been much of a player, though, or I'd remember him. I used to keep all the financial records of my father's contributors."

We moved up toward what appeared to be an inn or some sort of restaurant as the last of the passengers on the 9:30 ferry climbed onto the bus which then lumbered slowly out onto the road. There didn't seem to be anyone waiting for the return trip.

"Hello there! Are you the folks from Hilton Head?"

The man approaching wore green plaid golf pants and a brilliant yellow shirt. Beneath a white billed cap with the Nike swoosh emblazoned across the front, a few wisps of curly gray hair fluttered in the light breeze. "I'm Denton Douglass."

"Erik Whiteside. This is my friend, Bay Tanner."

We shook hands all around.

"Pleased to meet you. Sorry I'm a little late. Tried to get in a quick nine holes this morning and had a bunch of hackers in front of me the whole way. We're over here."

The retired anthropologist bustled off toward one of the ubiquitous golf carts with a gleaming set of clubs strapped onto the back ledge. He moved with the energy of a much younger man, a testament no doubt to the benefits of regular exercise on the Haig Point course. A little below average height, with the deep tan and spreading crow's feet of someone who spent a lot of time in the Lowcountry sun, Denton Douglass seemed an unlikely candidate for a career spent carving up dead bodies in the bowels of some dingy science building.

"You'll have to take the rumble seat, young man," he said, offering me his hand as I slid into the passenger side of the compact vehicle. "It won't take us but a couple of minutes to the house. Martha will have the coffee on, and maybe some of her special cinnamon buns. She does love to bake, that woman. Amazing I don't weigh three hundred pounds."

The doctor kept up this running commentary as we circled around and headed out in the same direction the bus had taken. Almost immediately we were into heavy stands of live oak, the resurrection fern clinging to their twisted limbs glistening bright green after the recent rains. Pines and sweet gums and cedars concealed massive homes, the sweep of their front entrances merely a flash of color as the cart chugged down the path. More houses, no doubt much less expensive, many with the distinctive porches and dormers of Lowcountry architecture, nestled closer to the road. It was into the short driveway of one of these, pale yellow with gleaming white trim, that our host pulled to a stop.

"Here we are," he announced, sliding from the golf cart. "Mmmm. Smell that? Fresh rolls. Lord, I love that woman!"

We followed Dr. Denton Douglass up the steps and into a high-ceilinged great room furnished comfortably with loveseats and over-stuffed chairs which had probably made the trip with them from their college housing back in North Carolina. Wide windows across the back wall overlooked a small lagoon. In a brilliant patch of sunshine filtering down through the limbs of the shade trees surrounding the house, a baby alligator took his ease along the near bank.

The doctor followed the direction of my gaze. "Ah, Freddie! He shows up just about every morning, at least when the sun's out. He's cute now, but Martha won't be so inclined to coo over him when he gets to be eight feet long! Martha!" he yelled, making both of us jump. "Where are you, woman? Company's here!"

Mrs. Douglass bustled in, wiping her hands on the dish towel tucked into the waistband of her polyester pants. As wide as her husband was narrow, she beamed and held out her hands.

"Young people! How wonderful! Everything's set up on the back porch. Just come right on out."

We followed Mrs. Douglass onto a screened-in room furnished with obviously new rattan furniture with brightly flowered cushions. The yeasty smell of something not long out of the oven mingled with the pungent aromas of pine and newly mown grass.

"Sit," Mrs. Douglass ordered then turned to her husband. "Denton, you pour. I have more buns ready to come out." She showered us all with her smile and turned back into the kitchen.

I declined coffee, and the professor filled bright blue mugs for himself and Erik before settling back in his chair. "Can't say that I remember you, young fella. Sorry. But then I was at N.C. State for the better part of twenty years, so I guess it's not surprising. Archaeology major or pre-med?"

The question took Erik by surprise, and he stumbled a little over his answer. "I changed majors a lot, sir. Couldn't seem to make up my mind."

"Always a lot of that goin' on back then, though not so much these days. Lots of kids come in hell-bent on getting into business or computers or some other such nonsense. Know exactly what they want to do. Only interest is in making a bundle of money. Hardly anyone cares about science anymore."

He paused, although neither of us had a clue what he expected us to say. Erik slurped coffee, and I stuffed a section of the delectable cinnamon roll into my mouth to avoid answering.

But apparently the former professor was used to carrying on conversations with himself. "So let's see it," he said abruptly, with an air of anticipation which sounded, at least to me, a little too gleeful.

I selected another of the warm buns from a cloth-draped basket and rose to stand looking out the screened window. The nylon bag rustled as

Erik handed it to the professor. I forced myself to tune out the low conversation of the doctor's murmured questions and my partner's well-rehearsed story.

"Well, let's see what we can do."

I turned as Denton Douglass disappeared through the door, the black bag swinging jauntily from his hand.

"Shouldn't take too long," he called over his shoulder. "Make yourself at home."

Erik and I exchanged looks as he crossed his long legs and settled back into his chair.

Though we could hear the professor's wife humming tunelessly in the kitchen, she never reappeared during the half hour or so we cooled our heels on the porch. I ate enough cinnamon rolls to wipe out at least a week's worth of beach runs while Erik became engrossed in several back issues of the N.C. State alumni magazine spread out on a side table. Neither of us seemed inclined to break the silence of the warm South Carolina morning. The atmosphere felt like that of a surgical waiting room, hushed anticipation mixed with large doses of dread.

When the doctor finally spoke from the doorway, his voice sounded like a crack of thunder.

"Where in hell did this really come from?" he barked, all trace of the mild-mannered, bumbling professor wiped from his tone. "And I'd better like the answer, or I'm going to be on the phone to the authorities before you can spit."

CHAPTER
EIGHTEEN

B Y THE TIME WE STEPPED OFF THE FERRY ONTO THE
dock at Hilton Head, the sun had retreated behind a bank of
clouds building up off toward the mainland, and the temperature had
dropped considerably. A chilly breeze lifted the strands of hair that had
curled and frizzed against my neck in the dank humidity of Daufuskie.

We had remained silent throughout most of the ride back, the import of the doctor's revelations and the crowded salon of the small boat
combining to thwart conversation. As we trudged up the gangway toward the parking lot, Erik voiced my thoughts as if he could read them
inside my head.

"We've gotten ourselves into a real mess this time, haven't we?" He
stood alongside the T-Bird as I unlocked the doors. "Or rather, *I've* gotten us into a real mess. What the hell was I thinking? We should have
turned the damned thing over to the cops the minute it landed on my
doorstep. If Dr. Douglass decides . . ."

"Quit beating yourself up," I said, unconsciously parroting Red
Tanner's oft-repeated order to me whenever I'd stuck my nose into
something which had the potential to turn into a disaster. I slid behind
the wheel and cranked the powerful engine to life. "What's done is
done. We've got a window of opportunity here, although a pretty narrow one, and we need to take advantage of it."

I negotiated the roundabout at the entrance to the Haig Point facility, made a couple of turns past the new Crossings Park, and pulled out onto Palmetto Bay Road before adding, "We're fortunate the good professor took a shine to you. I think it's what tipped the scales in our favor."

"I think it has more to do with the fact he's enamored of Indiana Jones movies. I think he fancies himself in the Sean Connery role as Indy's father."

I turned to smile at Erik whose optimism could never be squelched for long, and a lot of the tension evaporated.

The retired anthropologist's findings shouldn't have been as shocking as they seemed when you applied a little logic to the situation, but we had both reacted with dismay when he announced his conclusions. I was particularly astounded to hear all he had been able to determine during his brief examination in the small lab he had set up in his garage.

In a nutshell, Gray Palmer, Junior, had shipped us a human femur, the long bone between the knee and the hip and the largest, heaviest one in the skeleton. It was also the one from which the most information could be gleaned. As an archaeologist, he would have known that. Gray's selection had not been a random one.

The corpse was a male, probably African-American, approximately twenty to thirty years of age at the time of his death, and somewhere in the neighborhood of six feet tall. Of course Dr. Douglass had no access to any really sophisticated equipment, so his estimate as to how long the body had been interred was a guess at best. He did seem fairly certain burial would have taken place somewhere within the past fifty years.

How the body came to be where Gray had discovered it and how the unfortunate young man had died were topics of complete conjecture at this point.

Early afternoon traffic was heavy as we negotiated the Sea Pines Circle, and I spared a moment to lament once again the annual onslaught of tourists this congestion heralded. In a matter of weeks we permanent residents would be back to scheduling our trips and errands around the least likely times for our tens of thousands of visitors to be on the road. My months abroad, where Darnay and I had used the Mètro to avoid the clogged streets of Paris, seemed even more like a distant memory.

I gunned the T-Bird into the narrow gap between two vanloads of bewildered Northerners before replying.

"When he challenged you about there being just the one bone, I almost fainted. He could actually tell it hadn't been . . . What was the
word he used?"

"Disarticulated," Erik replied.

"Right. Disarticulated more than a few days ago."

"Apparently it wasn't as clean as we thought. He managed to detect
enough cartilage or ligament or whatever to tell it had been discon-
nected from the other bones only a short time ago." He paused, thinking something through. "I'm surprised there was any of that left, if he's
right about it being in the ground for fifty years."

My stomach did a few flips, and I swallowed hard against it. "No
more than fifty, he said. Could be less. We're just damned lucky he's heading out of town tomorrow, or I'm convinced he would have insisted on
turning the blasted thing over to the coroner's office. He's basically given
us until next weekend to come up with a valid reason for him not to, and
I haven't a clue what our next move should be. Any brilliant ideas?"

"Any place along here to get something to eat? I'm starving."

The non sequitur stopped me for a moment. "Sure." I flipped on my
left turn signal and waited for a long line of cars to clear before turning
into the entrance to the Hilton Head Diner. "This okay?"

"Great." I caught his glance and smiled back. Apparently all our
talk of cartilage and disarticulated bones hadn't affected his appetite. "I
know, I know," he said. "I ate practically my weight in those fabulous
cinnamon buns, but what can I say? I'm a growing boy."

When we were settled in a booth and Erik had ordered his second
complete breakfast of the day, I leaned toward him across the wide expanse of Formica. "Okay, I'm still soliciting brilliant ideas about how to
proceed."

"I think we need to make one of your famous lists. Let's get down
everything we know about the . . . *item*," he said, checking the area for
potential eavesdroppers. "Got any paper?"

I rummaged in the oversized canvas tote which doubled as my
handbag and pulled out the small notebook I used for my grocery lists.

Locating a pen in the jumble of used tissues, loose change, and stale peppermints took a while longer.

"Okay, shoot."

We were interrupted by the arrival of two heaping platters bearing Erik's eggs, pancakes, sausage, grits, and various other accompaniments along with my English muffin and hot tea. While he attacked the mountain of food, I took notes.

The result was a pathetic enumeration of just how little we had to go on. It could be condensed into a couple of simple sentences: On an island, probably isolated and uninhabited, located somewhere between Beaufort and Charleston, Gray Palmer the younger had uncovered the grave of a black man, approximately six feet tall and between twenty and thirty years old at the time of his death. He had been buried hurriedly and without benefit of casket or formal service. Artifacts found in the grave would no doubt confirm Dr. Denton's assumption he had been dead no more than fifty years.

That his death had been the result of foul play of some sort seemed to be without question, although Erik hesitated a bit over this last conclusion.

"Why?" I asked, watching him use his last sliver of toast to mop up the bright yellow and amber swirl of egg yolk mixed with maple syrup.

"You're always telling me not to assume," he replied. He wiped the corners of his mouth then held out his cup for the approaching waitress to refill with steaming coffee.

I waited until she'd cleared the table and set the bill down in front of Erik. "I don't think it's any kind of leap in logic. Araminda Albright said their research involved the undeveloped islands along the coast, so Gray didn't stumble onto some kind of illegal family burial plot. The fact that the corpse was apparently fully clothed, including a watch, when it went into the ground seems to indicate a certain amount of desperation on the part of whoever did the burying, don't you think?"

"Yes and no."

"That's helpful."

"What I mean is, the grave had to be pretty deep or animals would have disturbed it long before now. So that says to me the gravedigger spent a lot of time making sure no one would stumble across it accidentally. That doesn't square with someone in a panic to conceal a murder."

"Maybe he wasn't in a panic. Maybe he chose that spot to kill our guy because he knew he'd have lots of time to work and no fear of being interrupted. He could do the job right."

"Then how did Gray find it?"

"Good question."

Erik reached for the bill, but I snatched it out from under his fingers then fished a credit card from my wallet. "Business lunch," I said as we slid out of the booth. "Deductible, at least partially."

Outside, the clouds had moved off over the ocean, and a surprisingly warm sun beat down once again. I put the top down and eased us back onto Route 278. Erik studied our meager list and picked up the conversation.

"Then we appear to have a contradiction in our assumptions."

"Elaborate."

"I see one of two scenarios. Either the death was accidental and whoever was responsible panicked and tried to conceal it by burying the corpse on the spot, or it was a cold-blooded murder, and the killer meticulously planned to make certain no one would ever find the body. You can't have it both ways."

"Why not?" I waved to Jim, the guard on duty at the entrance to Port Royal Plantation, and eased through the checkpoint. "We're theorizing based on way too little concrete evidence, projecting logic onto a situation which by its very nature defies rational explanation." I eased into my driveway and turned toward Erik as I hit the button on the garage door opener. "I suppose even Jeffrey Dahmer or those two dolts who shot up the Washington, D.C. area had some sort of rationale, at least in their own twisted minds, but it isn't something a normal person could probably deduce."

"Did you see that?" Erik shot up in the bucket seat, his finger pointing at the open garage beneath the house.

"What?" The sudden edge to his voice sent memories of fire and devastation on this very spot tumbling through my head. "What?" I repeated, more urgently this time.

"There was something written on the door. Didn't you see it before you hit the button?"

"No. What kind of writing?"

"Looked like spray paint. Put it back down."

How we had missed it that morning I couldn't imagine, except I had probably backed the T-Bird around and headed out before lowering the garage door. Some of the red letters had run, long swirling blobs of paint giving the whole thing a cartoonish, written-in-blood look. However, the message, though lacking the finer points of spelling and syntax, certainly managed to convey the sentiments of its author in a concise and very convincing manner.

The words *WHITE BITCH* covered the top half, while I thought the bottom line intended to label me a racist whore. I wasn't positive, because the wielder of the spray can had left the W off the final word, and the E was truncated where he—or she—apparently ran out of room, failing to heed that age-old admonition to plan ahead.

"Jesus!" Erik expelled a breath and jumped out of the car. He approached the door and gingerly pressed a finger into the paint. "Dry, except for the globs. Must have been done last night. Jesus!" he repeated.

I turned off the engine and slid out of my seat, moving around the front of the car to stand next to Erik. "A pretty sad commentary on the state of our educational system, don't you think?" I remarked, mimicking his gesture by touching my own index finger onto the paint. "Stupid bastard can't even spell 'whore.'"

"You think this is funny?"

"Not particularly."

"You're awfully damned calm about it. Doesn't the thought of some lowlife skulking around here last night while we were sleeping a few feet away give you just a little chill?"

I couldn't explain my lack of surprise or indignation to myself, let alone to the earnest young man standing beside me. I suppose it had something to do with the complete lack of any validity to the charge, the fact that the whole idea of my being either racist or a whore was so completely ludicrous I had a hard time taking the whole thing seriously.

"You going to notify the cops?"

"And tell them what? That some kids defaced my garage door? That I heard nothing, saw nothing, have absolutely no idea who or why?"

"You can't just let it slide." Indignation vibrated in Erik White-side's voice. "You should file a police report."

"What for? Repairing this won't even make a blip on my home-owner's deductible. I'll call maintenance and see if they can come by and slap a couple of coats of something over it until I can get a painting con-tractor in here next week." I retreated to the T-Bird and depressed the button on the opener. "Relax. The morons obviously got the wrong house."

I lifted my bag from the seat as the bizarre epithets slid out of sight on silent rollers.

"I hope to hell you're right," I heard Erik mutter as he followed me into the house.

In honor of the gift of a warm, sunny afternoon, we moved our office out onto the deck. I hunkered down onto the chaise with my favorite Waterford pen and a supply of yellow legal pads, while Erik balanced a state-of-the-art laptop on his knees. An extra-long modem cable snaked its way through the open French doors and into the phone jack in the great room so we could access the Internet when necessary. The file la-beled PALMER/ALBRIGHT lay spread out on a low rattan table between us.

We systematically worked our way down the list of Gray Palmer, Senior's reward seekers, chewing over the possible legitimate ones for later contact while attempting to eliminate the kooks and the weirdoes. Erik managed to coax his recalcitrant cell phone back into service while I used the portable from the kitchen. In the space of two hours we had reduced the list to a manageable few by virtue of the criteria we had de-cided upon, primarily insisting on a description of Gray's boat and the unusual name painted on its stern. Erik proved surprisingly good at this game of trap-the-liars, and we had a couple of laughs at the expense of some of the more inventive claimants to the twenty-five-thousand-dollar jackpot.

Two of our possibles weren't at the numbers they'd provided, so my partner used his expertise to tease addresses from the Internet. The woman who had provided the information about a verbal altercation between Gray and two men in a boat pulled up alongside his lived only a few streets away in Port Royal Plantation. The second had been added to our follow-up list over my protests, but Erik had a gut feeling it had possibilities, so I deferred to his instincts. I felt certain the paramilitary angle would prove to be a dead end, but my partner stood his ground.

"There's an awful lot of bases around here, aren't there?" he asked as I returned from the kitchen with our second pitcher of iced tea. "Parris Island, the Marine Air Station. A couple in Savannah. And isn't there a Navy base in Charleston?"

I refilled our glasses and added melting ice from the bowl I'd carried out earlier. "I think the big one in Charleston got shut down in the last round of Defense Department closings, but I'm not certain. I haven't been around there much lately, except for that last trip to meet Mindy Albright."

"Well, I'm not ready to dismiss it out of hand just yet. There's something about the story which speaks to me. I'd like for us to talk to the guy before we write him off."

"Fair enough. So where are we with this thing? Any closer to finding out what really happened to Gray?"

"Not that I can see." The admission brought a frown to Erik's normally cheerful countenance. "You know," he added, "there's something else bothering me about this whole scenario. A couple of things, actually."

"What's that?"

"Well, why are we going through all this when the authorities obviously think Gray's death was an accident? Why are his father and the Albright girl so convinced he was murdered? It seems a strange thing for a father to fixate on, don't you think? I mean, I sort of understand how he feels, because of, you know, Granny Pen. No one believed me either when I insisted she'd been . . . a victim. Everyone thought I was just delusional, overcome by grief, not able to accept her death. You know?"

I did indeed, and Erik's speech startled me into admitting I had been thinking exactly the same things about Gray Palmer, Senior. I had

leaped at the opportunity to take on this case, to get our infant enterprise up on its feet and underway, but the small voice inside my head
had been whispering that it was a fool's errand. Young Gray had fallen
overboard, whether by sheer bad luck or from the stupidity of trying to
handle a boat while drunk or stoned. We wouldn't really know which
until the autopsy report was finalized. But there was absolutely no indication, at least from anything we knew for certain, that foul play had
been involved. Just a father's insistence and a friend/lover's conviction.
And Erik Whiteside's gut instinct. That's the one that would keep me
in the game until we discovered the truth.

I glanced up to find him studying me, and I realized I had left his
rhetorical question dangling. "Yes, Erik, I understand. So we'll keep going. It occurs to me we should see if Red can get hold of the official police report."

"I wonder who actually conducted the investigation."

"Good point. I suppose it could have been the local police, the sheriff's office, or even the Coast Guard. How can we find out who would
have jurisdiction?"

"I suppose it would depend on exactly where the . . . accident or
whatever occurred. I really don't know that much about territorial limits or any of that stuff. Would your brother-in-law?"

"Let's call and find out. If he doesn't, I'm sure the Judge knows
someone connected with the Coast Guard who could help us. It's probably time we let him in on this anyway. He's going to be madder than
hell if we cut him out of our first real investigation."

"Want me to give him a call? I think he's less likely to ream me out
than he is if you're the one who announces we've been sleuthing behind
his back."

"Good idea."

The mention of my father brought the problem of his mysterious
visitor whirling back into my head. I was on the verge of soliciting
Erik's advice on the best way to ferret out some information on the elusive Felicity Baronne when the sounds of a heavy truck sent me down
the steps and around to the driveway.

The uniformed maintenance men, both of whom were black, made no comment on the accusation dripping from my garage door in the fading afternoon sun, but set to work silently with rollers and brushes. I felt as if I should offer some explanation, some defense against the stark red words, but I turned instead and retreated back onto the deck.

What, after all, could I have said?

Seeing the shock register in their dark, somber eyes forced me to rethink my earlier, cavalier dismissal of this attack on my property. What if it wasn't a mistake? What if the denunciation had, in fact, been intended for me?

I shook off the bizarre notion and rejoined Erik, who was just terminating a cell call when I plopped back onto the chaise. "The Judge is not a happy camper, but I think I got him calmed down. Anyway, we're invited, or rather commanded, to appear for dinner tonight at precisely six thirty. No excuses, or so I was instructed. And we're to bring all the paperwork with us."

We exchanged smiles. Erik was beginning to understand how to deal with my father, a lesson it had taken me many years to learn: acquiescence was the only acceptable response to his pronouncements, and giving in immediately rather than putting up a fight made everyone's life a whole lot easier.

As we began to gather our things together, I remembered the thread of the conversation the arrival of the painters had interrupted. "You said there were a couple of things about the case that bothered you. What's the other?"

Erik stopped midway in the process of disconnecting the modem cable and fixed me with an intent stare.

"Just this," he said, and his tone made me sit up straighter. "Suppose the father is right. I keep coming back to Mindy Albright's idea there's a connection between these two deaths, Gray's and the poor guy he dug up."

The shiver that raised gooseflesh along my arms had nothing to do with the cool breeze off the ocean. "What do you mean, exactly?"

"What I mean is, did Gray Palmer die because he found that body? Or did someone kill him to shut him up about something else entirely?"

CHAPTER
NINETEEN

E LET THE TOPIC OF BOTH GRAY PALMERS SIMMER AS
the cool wind whipped around us. We'd bundled up a little in
deference to the inevitable drop in temperature which would accom-
pany encroaching twilight, but we'd agreed the top should definitely
stay down. I'd spared a glance in the rearview mirror as we pulled out of
the driveway, relieved to be able to discern only the barest shadow of the
red letters of hatred some unknown moron had spray-painted on my
garage door.

That was also a subject I had forcefully put off-limits.

So we listened to the Saturday oldies show on the local radio station
while I picked Erik Whiteside's brain about how to track down the
scoop on Felicity Baronne, and the beauty of the Lowcountry afternoon
whizzed by our open windows.

"So you did a Google search?" Erik asked, reaching down to lower
the volume on the radio. "And nothing at all popped up?"

"Sure, I got lots of hits, but nothing related to this woman."

"Did you try enclosing her name in quotation marks?"

"What good would that do?" I slowed as we approached the construction area on the road-widening project which seemed to have been
defacing the lovely Chechessee River area for decades. I still couldn't get

used to the openness of the roadside where huge swaths of trees had been leveled to make way for the addition of two more lanes.

"It keeps you from getting hits with only one of the names in them, or from having the search engine find the first name in one part of an article and the last name in another."

"I didn't know that."

"I'll give it a try when we get back to your place. In the meantime, there are other things we can check out."

"Like what?"

"Genealogy sites, land records, Social Security. I've been doing a lot of study on this ever since your friend Miss Hammond asked us to find her brother."

The reminder stacked another layer of guilt on my already overburdened pile of regrets. "We really have to get on that, Erik," I said, then quickly added, "not that you haven't already done a ton of work. It's just I feel so damned bad about letting her down. And the truth is I pretty much blew the whole thing off while I was . . ."

I realized the trap the moment the words were out of my mouth, but it was too late to call them back. Erik pounced on the opening with both feet.

"Just what exactly happened over there, Bay?" I started to interrupt, but he cut me off. "Yeah, I know what you told me in the e-mail, about Alain having family business to attend to, or some such crap. I didn't buy it then, and I'm sure as hell not buying it now. You haven't once mentioned the guy's name since you've been back. Unless you're holding out on me, you haven't even talked to him. What gives?"

I toyed with the idea of telling him it was none of his damned business, which was technically correct, but he was my friend. I could hear the genuine concern in his voice. What I didn't hear was the naked curiosity I expected from other of my acquaintances, especially the female ones, so I made a snap decision to tell him the truth.

"He's back in the game," I said in what I hoped was a calm, rational statement of fact. "The big boys at Interpol sent him the background on a case they've been trying to crack for months, something related to smuggling. Supposedly they wanted his 'take' on their operation, but what they were really after was enticing him into another undercover assignment."

"And he agreed? I thought he was . . . you know, still banged up from being shot. I thought he couldn't . . ."

"Me, too." I forced the anger back into its little compartment and continued, "But you don't know Darnay. Once he had the details, once he'd gotten his head into the case, it was all over. He couldn't resist the challenge, missed the excitement, I guess. At any rate, I decided I didn't want to sit around Paris waiting for the phone to ring or worse yet, have him disappear into that world and never know what really happened to him. We weren't married. They would have no obligation to inform me of his death."

The last word hung between us as we eased down Carteret Street in Beaufort, swooped over the bridge onto Lady's Island, and sped on toward St. Helena. Around us, the afternoon had softened into the pale, hazy glow that presages evening in the Lowcountry spring. Wherever the wide expanse of water met the limitless sky, opalescent streaks of pink and lavender tinged the wispy clouds hovering on the horizon.

Erik mistook my sigh of contentment at the incredible beauty for one of despair.

"Want me to go over there and beat the crap out of him? Bring the man to his senses?"

It was exactly the right tone, exactly what I needed, and I laughed out loud.

"No, but thanks for the thought." Sobering, I added, "He'll come on his own, or not at all. That's what I've decided. It's his life, and he has to live it."

We lapsed into silence then, and I forced my thoughts to the upcoming confrontation with my father. I had no doubt it would be a battle. I could almost predict his reaction to our running around the countryside with a leg bone stolen from an illicit grave. He might have been inclined to bend the rules a little, especially when it involved his friends and cronies, but concealing evidence of a possible homicide would be stretching his understanding way past the breaking point.

As we pulled into the circular drive in front of Presqu'isle's stately grandeur, I drew a deep breath and strapped on my proverbial sword.

" 'There is no sin except stupidity.' "

It was the last straw for me, although Erik had maintained his equilibrium remarkably well during the long tirade we'd been subjected to from the moment we'd leaned back from the dinner table. Lavinia, ever the woman of wisdom and sound judgment, had retreated to the kitchen, refusing all offers of help and leaving us, in effect, defenseless against the Judge's rant.

By the time that particularly scurrilous salvo had been fired off, the party had moved out onto the back verandah where my father was performing his nightly cigar ritual. In a fit of pique, I at first refused to help him. But after watching him struggle to manipulate the cutter with only one good hand, I finally gave in and came to his rescue. I received only a grudging nod for my efforts.

When smoke was billowing around his head and swirling away into the deep night, I said, " 'There is no sin except stupidity.' Oscar Wilde, *The Picture of Dorian Gray.* I'll take two points. And that remark was totally uncalled for. While it may be part of my job description as your daughter to put up with your ill humors and bad temper, Erik is not similarly burdened. That was an insult which he certainly doesn't deserve."

The Judge fidgeted around in his wheelchair, apparently fascinated by the glowing end of his panatela, and harrumphed a little before replying. "Perhaps it was a bit harsh. I apologize, young man. No offense intended."

"None taken, Your Honor," Erik said, and I could hear the smile in his voice.

I gave a thought to playacting a heart attack, brought on from the shock of actually witnessing my father's apologizing to someone, but the darkness would have rendered my performance something less than effective. Instead I remarked, "I notice you're not including me in this magnanimous reprieve."

"He's young and hasn't had the benefit of my tutelage over the course of his lifetime. You, on the other hand . . ."

"Do you guys always talk like this?" Erik interrupted him in mid-sentence. " 'Magnanimous reprieve'? 'Tutelage'? You make me feel like I should carry a dictionary around with me just so I can follow the thread of the conversation."

"Sorry," I said, settling into my favorite rocking chair and setting it in motion. I couldn't begin to explain to an outsider the depth of the competition that existed between my father and me on all kinds of levels, not just the vastness of our respective vocabularies or our ability to reference obscure quotations.

"The point is," the Judge continued as if the last exchange had not taken place, "you have both acted foolishly in not turning this bone over to the police or at least to the coroner. Not only is it possible evidence in the crime in which its unfortunate owner met his death, it could also have bearing on the investigation into the demise of Erik's friend. Evidence tampering is not something the authorities take lightly. I myself have imposed jail terms as well as onerous fines in a number of such cases which came before me when I was on the bench."

It was my father at his pompous best, and I could tell he was cranking up for another lengthy diatribe, so I cut him off at the pass. "Spilled milk, water over the dam, et cetera, et cetera," I said into the hushed night air. Down by the end of the dock, a fish jumped, slapping the water with a loud smack. "What do you suggest we do about it now?" Behind me, in the depths of the entry hall, I heard the muted peal of the doorbell.

"Ah, perhaps some of the answers are about to be made known. Follow my lead."

The Judge negotiated the tangle of legs and chairs and glided down the ramp into his room. I strained to recognize the voice responding to Lavinia's inquiries. It did sound familiar, as if I had heard the deep drawl before, but I couldn't put a name to it. Erik and I exchanged looks as the soft whirr of the Judge's chair grew louder, and the conversation came into focus.

". . . out here on the verandah," my father was saying, slightly

muted, as if he spoke over his shoulder. "Lavinia will bring us some refreshment in just a moment."

He rolled onto the porch, followed by a bulky presence whose features were lost in the backlight from the doorway. But as the visitor
moved onto the shadowy deck, my father said, "I believe you know my
daughter, Bay Tanner? And this is our friend, Erik Whiteside."

Before my father could complete the introductions, I found myself
staring into the hard eyes and oily smile of the Daufuskie real estate
salesman, Harry Simon.

My father had given us no hint about what he was up to prior to the arrival of his guest. He'd probably intended to, but he'd wasted too much
time showing off for Erik. Still, we managed to pick away at Simon
without anyone's divulging the real reasons for our questions. No one
mentioned the bone or the grave or the mysterious island. Instead, we
concentrated on learning as much as we could about the workings of
the Coast Guard in general and their response to the call about Gray
Palmer in particular. Because, inexplicably, this overweight, unctuous
man turned out to be a member of the reserve and had served in that capacity for a number of years. He also claimed to have been in the Marine
Corps in his youth. Looking at the paunch that overflowed the waistband
of his wrinkled black trousers, I found this assertion difficult to believe.

Over outrageously expensive cigars and a steady flow of bourbon diluted with the merest trickle of soda, we squeezed him dry of every drop
of information which could prove useful to us in our investigation of
young Gray Palmer's death. We learned the Coast Guard has primary
jurisdiction over any crime which occurs over three miles from the
shore. If such an incident involved murder, they would no doubt turn
the case over to the FBI to continue the investigation.

Inside that three-mile limit, however, things got a little murky.
Harry Simon pointed out that it's the natural inclination of most
boaters to call the Coast Guard, regardless of where they encountered
trouble. It made sense the average guy wouldn't think about exactly
where he was in relation to some arbitrarily proscribed limit. Crime

on the water equals the Coast Guard, at least in most people's minds.

"That's what happened with your friend," Simon offered as I splashed more Kentucky bourbon over the melting ice cubes in his tumbler. "Mostly the Intracoastal Waterway—that's where your boy was spotted—is state-controlled water, but that don't . . . doesn't register with most folks." Harry's careful syntax had deteriorated in direct proportion to the level of whiskey in his glass.

"So who does the Coast Guard hand off to?" I asked.

"State boys," he responded promptly. "Department of Natural Resources."

"I thought they just ticketed speeding boaters and checked for fishing licenses, things like that," Erik offered.

"Nope. Lots of folks make that mistake. Them boys got it all, same as the police. They can investigate stuff, got arrest powers, all that. Some of 'em even carry guns."

I detected a note of wistfulness in Harry Simon's voice, and I shuddered at the thought of this blustering salesman climbing aboard a boat, brandishing a weapon like some modern-day pirate.

"I seem to recall, though, that this particular incident ended up in the hands of the local authorities. The Charleston police, I believe." My father spoke with the careful enunciation one uses for very small children and fools. Or drunks.

"True, true. Far as I can recollect, the boat was drifting somewhere between the two juri . . . juris . . . you know, and they took it over 'cause the kid was from there. Somethin' like that. Anyway, it don't really make any difference, 'cause everyone says it was just a stupid accident. Boy shoulda known better 'n to be drinkin' while runnin' full-out in a boat like that. Stupid accident," he repeated.

"Did you or any of your buddies get in on the investigation?" I asked. "Did you interview any witnesses, collect any physical evidence?"

"None to be found, far as we could tell. Poor kid was pretty chewed up by the prop, though. Glad I wasn't one of the guys who had to pull him out. I ain't real good with blood."

"So no signs of foul play? No open bottles or drug paraphernalia found on the boat?"

The Judge's question got no immediate response, so he leaned in toward Harry Simon, lowering his tone to a conspiratorial level. "I realize this may be privileged information, but you can trust us to respect the confidence. We're just trying to find out what happened so young Erik here can gain some closure on his friend's death. I'm sure you understand."

The Judge's voice exuded respect and gratitude. Harry Simon seemed to lap it up.

"Sure, Judge, sure. Jack Kelly, who heads our reserve unit, he told me they had a devil of a time even identifyin' the kid. The props, you know. But the boat had this kinda weird name, and the kid's old man confirmed it. The girlfriend said the clothes on the corpse were the ones the kid was wearin' when he took off the day before. So . . ." Harry tried for a wink, but the coordination of his facial muscles had been compromised by the booze. "Course, that's just between us chickens, if you get my drift."

"Of course, of course. That goes without saying. But no signs of foul play, so far as the Coast Guard is aware."

"Nope, Judge, not a thing. The kid was prob'ly drunk. Maybe stood up to take a leak off the side of the boat and fell in. Or got tangled up in the line and lost his balance. Lots o' stupid accidents happen out there on the water. People got no respect for how dangerous it can be."

"Well, thanks, Harry. You've been very helpful. I surely do appreciate it."

As if on cue, Lavinia appeared with coffee and tea along with thin slivers of her famous carrot cake, and we set about sobering up our guest. Harry Simon's fawning abated as the bourbon worked itself out of his system until, by the time the Judge maneuvered his chair out of the rough circle we had formed around the low table, the man had become only marginally obnoxious. It took him a couple of minutes to realize this was the signal the meeting was over, but finally he rose and offered his hand all around. His palm was sweaty, and I resisted the urge to wipe my own on the leg of my slacks once Harry had reluctantly returned it to me.

"Glad I could be of help. Any time, you just call on ol' Harry.

A pleasure, yessir, a real pleasure." He turned and the Judge followed him down the ramp and into the house.

The door had barely eased shut behind them before Erik whirled to face me. "That's the same guy who was on the boat out to Daufuskie, isn't it? The one you didn't want to talk to?"

"Yup. Good ol' Harry. God, he gives me the creeps."

"And you don't think it's strange he turns out to be involved in investigating Gray's death?"

I stood and stretched then leaned my elbows atop the railing of the verandah and studied the blackness out over the Sound. "You keep forgetting this isn't Charlotte. Beaufort, Hilton Head, Bluffton—they're all basically small towns when you factor out the tourists."

"I suppose." Erik joined me at the railing. "So that's it then. They're going to write this off as an accident."

"There's still the autopsy report," I reminded him. "If the tox screen and blood tests come back clean, how are they going to justify labeling it an accident without investigating it further?"

"Because somebody wants them to," he murmured, "and I'm damned if I can figure out exactly who. Or why."

CHAPTER TWENTY

UT ALL DURING THE DRIVE BACK TO HILTON HEAD I kept worrying at the idea of Harry Simon's appearance on the Daufuskie ferry that morning as a coincidence.

"They do happen," Erik reminded me in a complete reversal of his earlier position.

"I know that!"

"And the Judge just happened to decide to pick Simon's brain when he couldn't get hold of this Jack Kelly guy. I don't see anything sinister about it."

"Just serendipity, is that what you're saying?"

Erik studied the empty road cut by the twin beams of the T-Bird's headlights before answering. I knew the sharpness of his words was engendered, in part anyway, by my own sarcastic tone. "Yeah, that's what I'm saying. And I think they call it paranoia when you see conspiracies behind every tree."

I let the silence deepen while I fought my own fear and resentment for control of my emotions. "You're right," I said, finally expelling some of the tightness in my chest with a long, slow breath. "Sorry."

I caught the edges of Erik's answering smile out of the corner of my eye. "Me, too." He shifted his long legs into a more comfortable configuration before adding, "You know what I think?"

"What?"

"I think this thing with the graffiti has you more bugged than you're willing to admit. Why don't you let me call your brother-in-law and see what he has to say? Give me the number, and I'll try to raise him on my cell."

He pulled the slim phone from his pocket and flipped it open.

I didn't like the idea Erik Whiteside could read me quite so well. And I wasn't paranoid. Circumstances over the past few years of my life had taught me that assumptions could not only be foolish, they could be deadly. Taking things for granted had gotten me and those I loved into some dangerous situations. I was trying to learn from my mistakes.

I relayed Red's number to Erik who punched it in as I negotiated the on-ramp leading to Route 278. We tried him on his personal cell first. I could never keep track of Sergeant Red Tanner's changing shift schedule, so I had an entire repertoire of phone numbers to access whenever I needed to contact him. We lucked out. He picked up after only three rings, and Erik extended the little gadget in my direction.

"No way," I said, shooing his hand away. "I'm always cursing at drivers who talk on those damned things while they're behind the wheel. You tell him."

The recitation took only a couple of minutes, and I could tell from Erik's side of the conversation Red was taking him seriously. "He'll meet us at the house. Should be there about the same time we are." He tucked the phone back in his pocket. "I'm actually looking forward to meeting the guy."

"You and Red have never met? Are you sure?"

I racked my brain trying to remember. It was inconceivable to me these two men who had both played such enormous roles in my life were virtual strangers.

"Nope," Erik confirmed. "I've heard you talk about him enough times, and I did meet his ex-wife Sarah, of course. But I don't know the sergeant except by reputation."

I mulled this strange situation over in my head as we sped along through sparse traffic past several new golf course housing developments which had sprouted seemingly overnight while I'd been in Paris.

Soon there wouldn't be an open expanse of trees between Hilton Head and Beaufort. I was ruminating about the old days, back when 278 had been a two-lane road and there had been nothing to interrupt the green except an occasional cottage or trailer tucked back into the woods.

"Look out!"

The wheel jerked in my hand at Erik's shout. Then the deer came sailing into my vision from the right, soaring in a leap that cleared the hood of the T-Bird before I had a chance to react. By the time I'd stomped on the brakes and sent the car swerving toward the shoulder, the graceful creature had bounded across the remaining three lanes of the divided highway and disappeared into the blackness. Behind me I heard the blare of horns and the screech of protesting tires, but thankfully no tearing or crash of metal. I eased to a stop on the grass verge and shoved the gearshift into park before dropping my head onto hands still locked to the steering wheel in a death grip.

"Jesus!" Erik exclaimed, then I felt his touch on my shoulder. "Are you okay?"

"Sure," I managed to say around the fear constricting my throat and the roar of blood rushing in my ears. I exhaled deeply and turned toward him. "You?"

"Fine. Although I should probably check my pants."

He smiled and ran a hand through his short blond hair. I was afraid the laughter bubbling up inside me might have been hysteria, but I gave in to it anyway, and soon both of us were roaring. Anyone stopping to offer assistance would have found two seemingly normal adults whooping and gasping, tears streaming down their faces.

When I had finally hiccuped my way back to some semblance of normalcy, I accepted Erik's proffered handkerchief and rubbed at my mascara-stained cheeks. As I handed it back, he said, "You look like a giant raccoon," threatening to send me back into another laughing jag, but I forced myself to gain control.

"Live with it until we get home," I replied, checking the side mirror for traffic and easing back onto the highway.

"Nice bit of driving," Erik remarked as he searched for a clean spot on his hanky to blow his nose.

"I had nothing to do with it. All the credit for avoiding an accident belongs to the deer. Did you see if it was a buck or a doe?"

"Female, I think. At least I didn't see any big rack of antlers, although I wasn't really at my most observant in those couple of seconds."

"If we didn't keep building all these damned projects and bulldozing their habitat into oblivion, the poor things wouldn't have to keep risking their lives and ours crossing major highways."

It was probably a good thing Erik didn't reply. It was a subject about which I could speak for hours with a fine degree of passion.

The near-disaster finally sobered us into a silence that lasted until I pulled into the driveway of my brightly lit beach house. Two things immediately caught my attention. The first was the white Beaufort County sheriff's cruiser pulled up on the pine straw beneath the towering trees.

The second was the bright red letters sprayed across my garage door.

I made coffee, thick and strong the way Madame Srabian had taught me in Paris, and carried the pot to the breakfast alcove where Red Tanner and Erik Whiteside sat eyeing each other across the glass-topped table. I returned for cream and sugar and my own mug of steaming tea before seating myself between the two men.

After my hurried introductions beneath the light of the outdoor vapor lamp which bathed the driveway in a soft blue glow, the two men had shaken hands warily, then joined me in contemplating the new message from my nocturnal accuser. This time the sentiment was less complex, though repetitious, and actually spelled correctly: the word *BITCH* scrawled three times in foot-high letters.

"Simple, but effective," Red had remarked, unwittingly mimicking Erik's actions of a few hours before by touching a finger to the center of one of the Bs. He rubbed the stickiness against his thumb. "Fresh. Can't say for sure how long ago, especially because it's damp tonight. But I'd guess not more than an hour or two. How long you been gone?"

I had checked my watch, surprised to find it only a little past ten thirty. The day had somehow taken on the feel of an endless loop of trouble and anxiety, from the early morning boat ride and the professor's revelations, to my father's tirades and the reappearance of Harry Simon, to the deer and the return of the midnight scribbler.

Déjà vu all over again, as Yogi used to say.

"Since five or so." I had answered Red's question, then suggested we adjourn inside. I'd felt somehow strangely vulnerable standing out there in the driveway, like a target in a brightly lit shooting gallery at a carnival sideshow.

"So what have you stuck your nose into this time?" Red asked when we'd all finished our individual drink rituals. Erik and I exchanged a look which no doubt spoke volumes to my brother-in-law. "Spill it, Tanner. Stop trying to figure out how you can fudge or manipulate or manage to tell me just enough to get me off your back for a while." He held up a hand at my grunt of protest. "Save it! For once just give me the truth, the whole truth, and nothing but the truth the first time out and spare us all a lot of grief in the long run. It's been a hell of a day, and I'm not in the mood to play your games."

It was perhaps as long and as harsh a dressing-down as I'd ever gotten from Red, and I had a sneaking suspicion it had something to do with his having an audience in the person of Erik Whiteside. Although Red was well aware of my business relationship with the handsome young computer expert, I also hadn't imagined the look of distaste that flitted across his face when Erik trotted down the hallway to "his room" to leave his jacket and use the john.

"Thanks for stopping by, Officer," I said, rising from the table with such force I nearly toppled my own chair. "If I could have a copy of the report for my insurance company, I'd be grateful."

"Knock it off, Bay." Red's voice now held more resignation than anger.

"Go to hell," I snapped, not the least bit mollified by his change of tone. "It wasn't my idea to drag you into this, and I sure as hell don't need you waltzing in here and reprimanding me as if I were some naughty child. God, you sound just like my father!"

I dumped the remains of my tea into the sink, banging the mug against the stainless steel side.

"Maybe it would be a good idea to have Red's input on our other . . . problem," Erik ventured in the kind of voice usually reserved for skittish horses or snarling dogs.

"Bad idea, in my obviously flawed judgment. But you spill your guts if you want to. I'm going to bed."

I stomped down the steps into the great room, took the length of the hallway in three angry strides, and slammed my bedroom door behind me.

Though I didn't expect to, I fell asleep fairly soon after stepping from a long, hot shower and arose Sunday morning feeling a little ashamed at my outburst of the night before. I brushed my teeth and threw on a pair of shorts and a T-shirt before padding barefoot into the hall. Erik's door was still closed, and a glissando of snores worked its way up and down the scale as I passed.

I had no idea what time the party had broken up, but the boys had at least cleaned up the kitchen. I made tea, slid my feet into the beaten-up pair of Birkenstock sandals I kept by the door, and carried the mug with me down the steps and outside. The wind off the ocean smelled clean and sweet as I moved around to the driveway and stood contemplating last night's message.

What in the hell is this all about? I asked myself. I had no clue as to what actions or words of mine might have prompted someone to take such extreme measures to chastise me, nor did any names suggest themselves while I stood lost in thought in the cool, bright morning.

Obviously there was no way I could dismiss this second attack as a mistake, unless the perpetrator was incredibly stupid. I suppose he could have gotten the wrong house twice in a row, but something now told me the accusation was in fact meant for me. I wandered over to the yard and slid down next to the base of one of the massive live oaks which guarded my property from the curious eyes of random beach walkers and my widely scattered neighbors. I settled onto the soft bed of pine straw, my back supported by the trunk of a tree which had probably sprouted when only Indians and wild pigs roamed the island. As much as I loved my home on the ocean, I tried never to forget what price had been paid in the loss of trees, plants, and habitat for the deer and other creatures in order to grant me the peace and pleasure I always found here.

The thoughts took me back to my conversation with Araminda Albright. It astounded me when I realized it had been only one week ago that I had sat in her home on another stretch of beach and listened to her halting tale of the death of Gray Palmer and her fears for her own life. I tried to pinpoint exactly what part of her story had triggered this connection in my memory. I let my eyes drift closed as I sipped my cooling tea and tried to let my mind float back to that afternoon. Overhead a jay squawked, and a mockingbird took up the cry . . .

We had been discussing the foundation Gray's father ran in addition to his shipping empire. Araminda was telling me that she and Gray spent their time exploring uninhabited islands up and down the Atlantic coast, from the Carolinas to Florida, studying the old cultures and the habitats of animals and their migration from the mainland, how . . .

"I hope you didn't spend the night out here." Erik's voice sent tea sloshing out of the cup and across my hand. "Sorry! You okay?"

I shook the tepid drops from my fingers and squinted up at him. "Yes, I'm fine. It's pretty much cooled off. But try to avoid scaring the . . . scaring me like that, okay? I'm getting way too old to have to keep restarting my heart on any regular basis."

"Sorry," he repeated and extended his hand. I allowed him to help me up. "Get any more ideas about who might have done it?"

For a moment I didn't follow his thread then I realized he was talking about the graffiti on the garage door. "No, not really. Actually I was thinking about something else entirely. You up for a walk?"

His bare feet and long, muscular legs were topped by a pair of gray athletic shorts and a ratty Carolina Panthers T-shirt. He carried a mug of what smelled like really strong coffee.

"I haven't showered yet," he said, his free hand trying to tame a stubborn cowlick that stood up on the back of his head.

"I can stand it if you can," I said, and he shrugged in what I took to be acquiescence.

I turned and headed around the side of the house, pausing to set my cup on the steps up to the deck as we passed. I took the boardwalk over the dune and in minutes stepped out onto the wide, deserted beach. Sandpipers scurried frantically across the packed sand, alternately chasing and fleeing the rhythmic ebb and flow of the tide. I turned away from the Westin Hotel, its pristine whiteness visible in the soft morning glow off to my right, a cluster of early rising tourists milling around in the surf in front of the beachside pool. We walked in silence at first, Erik matching my long stride with ease.

"So how did it go with Red last night?" I finally asked without looking at him.

"Fine. He got a call not long after you . . . left us and had to take off." When I didn't comment, he continued, "He said to tell you there wasn't much he could do about your midnight prowler. He said you should spend some time thinking about who you might have pissed off recently. Should be a fairly short list this time, since you've only been back in town for a couple of weeks." Erik raised his hands in a protestation of innocence. "His words, not mine." I could tell he was struggling to control a bubble of laughter.

"I'm thrilled to find you two had so much in common. Like your biting wit, for example."

"Seriously," Erik went on, lowering his voice as we passed a slower moving tourist couple in hideously matching Hawaiian shirts, "Red said you shouldn't get the door repainted for a couple of days. See what happens."

"He thinks if the artist is deprived of his canvas he'll just go away? That's pretty stupid. All he'll do is get busy on the rest of the house."

I paused to watch a flock of geese holding formation in a perfect V that pointed dead north. *Heading home for the summer,* I thought.

I let several minutes go by before changing the subject. I found it difficult to break the serenity of the morning with talk of death.

"I've been thinking," I began.

"Always a good start."

"Thank you. Did you decide to run any of our current problems past my charming brother-in-law?"

"Nope. As I said, he got called out to an accident just a few minutes after you went to bed. And besides, I'd already figured you were probably right and we should wait until we had more to go on."

"Good call. As I was saying, I've been thinking about this whole thing, trying to lay it out in my mind in some sort of order, and it seems to me we may be going about this investigation all wrong."

"Enlighten me."

"Well, you said it first, yesterday I think, when we got back from Daufuskie."

"Hold that thought." Erik paused to flip the dregs of his coffee into the Atlantic then jogged back up to settle the empty mug into the sea oats waving along the top of the dune. "I'll pick it up on the way back," he said, falling again into step beside me. "Go ahead."

"Actually, it was two things. First, you wondered if Araminda was right that the two deaths were connected somehow. You know, Gray's and whoever was buried in the grave. And then last night, you mumbled something about why was everyone except her and Gray's father so hell-bent on believing it was just a boating accident."

"Look!"

I turned toward the water, in the direction of Erik's outstretched arm. A few yards off shore, shining gray fins broke the surface of the placid ocean.

"Dolphins," I replied.

As we watched, three of the graceful water mammals cruised along beside us, like a family out for a leisurely stroll after breakfast. Rising to take air into the breathing holes in the tops of their heads, they dived again, only to reappear moments later in a rhythmic dance which held Erik transfixed.

"They're spectacular," he whispered, and I smiled.

"I guess we have a tendency to take them for granted here."

The trio rose once more, as if in farewell then headed back out to sea.

"That was worth the price of admission." Erik grinned and turned as we resumed our walk. "Sorry for the interruption. You were just about to give me credit for some brilliant, but unintentional deduction, I believe."

I knew his flip attitude was a cover for his sadness and frustration.

Erik Whiteside didn't like displaying his emotions any more than I did.

"Let's say you and Mindy are right. Assume there's a connection. Now let's look at how the timeline of events plays out." I hadn't really given this much thought, contrary to what I'd told Erik. Somehow the connection between my bemoaning the loss of the habitat on Hilton Head Island and Araminda Albright's story last Sunday had fired off synapses in my brain.

"Sometime before last Friday, a week ago I mean, Gray Palmer was digging on some unnamed island between Charleston and Beaufort when he unearthed a grave. The contents led him to believe it was not an ancient site. For some unknown reason, he decided to remove a bone from the corpse and carry it away with him after doing his best to conceal the evidence of his tampering. So far so good?"

"I'm with you." Erik picked up the recitation. "So then he gets back to Charleston, shares his bizarre find with his co-worker/girlfriend, but not his father, and calls me. At the time, you asked me why, I mean, why he called *me,* and I just blew it off. And how did he know how to find me? Or that I would even be able to help him?"

"Albright said he'd heard you were 'in the business' or something like that."

"Who would know that? I mean, it's not as if we've been advertising in the paper or sending out announcements or anything."

"True. I don't know."

We had reached a long spit of land, actually a large sandbar only exposed when the tide was at its lowest, and I paused there to settle onto the beach out of reach of the water. Erik dropped down beside me.

"Anyway," I went on, "on Friday he told Mindy he was going back to the island to have another look. But before he left on the boat, he took the time to package up the bone and ship it off to you at your home address. You're sure there was no note or any other kind of explanation in the box?"

"Positive. I literally tore the thing apart. There was only the bone and the wrappings, the canvas or whatever. And some newspapers stuffed down inside to keep it from rattling, I guess."

"Did you check them out?"

"The newspapers? I opened them up and spread them out, just to make sure nothing was written on them."

I stretched and pulled my legs up into a modified yoga position. "How did you know the package was from Gray?" I asked, squinting into the glare of the rising sun.

"It had his name on the shipping label. Besides, once I heard the girlfriend's story from you, I assumed it had to be Gray. I don't know too many other people who would be sending me parts of dead people by FedEx."

I ignored the sarcasm. "And you never got another call from him? He didn't try to get in touch to tell you about the package or anything else?"

"No. He didn't leave a message anywhere—the store, the apartment, my cell. I checked them all again after I got the delivery, but there was nothing."

"Strange. But we're getting sidetracked here," I said. "I'm trying to nail down the timeline. So Gray mails the package on Friday, heads out on the boat—presumably back to the island where he found the body—and the next thing anyone knows about him is when he turns up dead Saturday morning." I glanced at Erik, but he was staring out across the expanse of the ocean. "So my conclusion is we have to start where the whole thing began. We have to locate that island and find that grave. It's the key to everything."

"Why do you say that?"

"Logic." I worked my feet up a little higher, trying for a perfect Lotus position, something I'd not yet been able to achieve. "If you accept my timeline, then there are huge gaps unaccounted for, as well as a ton of unanswered questions." I began to tick them off on my fingers. "First, the grave. He told Araminda it wasn't an archaeological site, and I think we can take his word for that. After all, it was his field. But what could he have seen to make him so sure the man had been murdered?"

Erik opened his mouth to speculate, but I cut him off. "These are just rhetorical questions for now. Hear me out. Secondly, he felt compelled to go back out there just a couple of days after he talked with you. Why? Supposedly he wanted information about who the buried guy was, but he didn't wait for you to get that for him. Hell, he didn't even wait long enough for you to get the package before he went tearing off in his boat."

"Okay, I'm with you," Erik said, and I took more than a little pride in the admiration I heard in his voice. "Wait, though," he added. "Here's another thing."

"What?"

"You just said archaeology was his field. He'd probably already drawn some conclusions on his own. Why did he send it to me? Why didn't he just track down someone like Dr. Douglass in the first place?"

"Maybe you're right, and he already knew all the things Douglass told us. About it being a black male and all that. Didn't he say he wanted to find out how to hack into some databases?"

"Then why did he send me the bone? I had no need for it."

"I don't know. But if he got scared, spooked by something or someone, he might have just wanted it out of his possession. Which leads me to the next question. Who else did he tell about his discovery?"

"His girlfriend said he didn't tell anyone, except her. And me."

"That doesn't make sense. If we're operating on the assumption Gray was murdered because he stumbled onto this grave, then someone else had to find out about it between whenever he unearthed the thing and Saturday morning when he turned up dead." I paused as another thought struck me. They seemed to be coming faster than I could give them voice. "What day did he call you?"

Erik didn't reply for a moment, then said, "I think it must have been Tuesday. What day did you get home from Paris?"

"Wednesday."

"Okay, then it was Tuesday. I was going to contact the Judge about what I should do about Gray's call, but then I got your e-mail, so I decided to wait until I could talk to you."

"Good! Now we're getting somewhere. I wish to hell I had some paper to take notes on. Anyway, so sometime between Tuesday and Friday, something—or someone—made Gray so nervous he decided to ship you the bone and take off for the gravesite. We have to find out who that is. And I still think we won't have a clue how to go about finding the person until we find the grave and discover whatever it is that made Gray somebody's target. Assuming they don't find anything in the autopsy that would render the whole thing pointless. See anything wrong with the logic?"

Erik whistled. "No, I think you've absolutely nailed it. God, you're really good at this."

"Thanks," I said, again glowing under his praise. "Comes from all those years of working with numbers. You can't get much more logical than numbers."

"But I think you might have left out a couple of things that could be crucial to finding the place."

"Like what?"

"Like all those people who are claiming Gray Senior's reward. If one of them did in fact see Gray alive on his boat on Saturday morning, then that should help us concentrate the search for where he was coming from. Or at least give us a good chance at narrowing down the field."

"Good point. There are lots of little hummocks and islets out there. It could take weeks to investigate them all, and I don't think we'd have a prayer in hell of keeping our interest under wraps."

"Which would be a good idea if we don't want to end up dangling from the end of a rope underneath a boat somewhere."

I shook off the fear his suggestion engendered. If we were going to become legitimate investigators, I had to learn to deal with danger.

"So how do you suggest we proceed?"

I rose as I spoke, and Erik joined me. "I think we need to track down those couple of people from Mr. Palmer's list we haven't talked to yet, then maybe re-interview the others and get a fix on just where they claim to have seen Gray's boat. Do you have access to a marine map or whatever you call it? We could do like they do on TV and put markers in all the spots where he was supposedly seen. Maybe we can triangulate from there and pinpoint the spot."

"Great idea. And your mother probably thinks you wasted all those hours glued to the tube." He laughed and stretched his tanned arms over his head. "And then I think we have one more task that will help us get off dead center on this investigation," I added.

"What's that?"

"I think we need to have another talk with Miss Araminda Albright. I have a feeling she didn't give me the whole story the last time we met. She never really explained to me why she thinks her own life might be in danger, or why she's so willing to accept the idea of murder. Maybe she can help us fill in those missing gaps."

"If she's as gorgeous as you described her, I'd like to volunteer for that duty."

"I'd watch myself if I were you. Mercer Mary Prescott has demonstrated she's not a woman to be trifled with."

I meant it as a joke, but some of the light went out of Erik's eyes. I opened my mouth to ask about the reasons for his traveling alone this time, but he cut me off.

"Care to work some of these kinks out? Let's jog a ways to get loosened up then I'll challenge you to a race back to your place."

"You're dead meat," I called, but he had already set off in an easy lope, and I had to break into a trot to catch up with him. By the time we had moved past a number of other runners getting in their morning exercise, the moment to pursue his relationship had passed, and a short while later all my concentration was centered on leaving him in the dust on our mad sprint for home.

CHAPTER
TWENTY-ONE

*C*YNTHIA SELLERS WAS ALMOST A NEIGHBOR, IF YOU calculated it as the crow flies, but it took us close to ten minutes of twisting and turning through the streets of Port Royal Plantation before I finally pulled the T-Bird up in front of her two-story home. Obviously one of the older sections of the sprawling development, most of the houses along the narrow lane had been built of natural wood which had weathered to a mellow patina in the salt and humidity of the winds off the ocean. We pulled into the semicircular curve of driveway and stopped behind a gleaming red Miata convertible.

After showering and wolfing down a quick breakfast, Erik and I had decided to spend the day trying to hook up with the few reward claimants we felt might be at least marginally legitimate. We had an appointment for later in the morning with Delbert Pidgen, the weekend father, at his condo in Shelter Cove. While we didn't expect to get much more information from him about the actual sighting, we did hope to be able to use his knowledge of the local waters to pinpoint the exact location. We didn't have an official chart yet, but I had managed to unearth a map of Beaufort which showed many of the outlying islands and waterways in some detail. It was at least a place to start.

"Looks like she's home," Erik remarked as I cut the engine.

We'd been unsuccessful once again in getting Cynthia Sellers to answer her phone that morning.

"Unless she has a husband. Or a roommate," I replied, sliding out of the bucket seat. "You want to take the lead?"

Erik shrugged. "Sure. You think my boyish charm will work on the ladies better than your more direct approach?"

"Something like that," I said, smiling. "Remember, we're here as representatives of Gray Palmer. Don't mention anything about our being investigators."

"I wouldn't have the nerve."

We climbed the front steps to a wide porch devoid of plants or chairs or any other concession to decoration, and I rang the bell next to the open screen door. Peeking inside, I looked past a short entryway directly into the living room. A little to the right, a staircase rose to a small landing, disappearing quickly in a sharp left angle toward the second story. The carpet appeared to be a soft blue, faded a little, and I could just discern the delicately curved legs of a table when my vision was cut off by the sudden appearance of a presence blocking the doorway. I hadn't heard anyone approach.

"I don't mean to be rude," a woman's voice said as I stepped back away from the door, "but I've asked you people not to bother me, especially on a Sunday morning."

"I beg your pardon, but . . ." I began, but got cut off immediately.

"I'm perfectly willing to allow you the right to your religious views. Please grant me the same privilege."

Erik caught on to it a split-second before I did. "I'm Erik Whiteside and this is Bay Tanner. We're not Jehovah's Witnesses, ma'am," he said softly, reliability and trustworthiness almost oozing from his pores. "And we did try to call first. I'm sorry if we startled you."

Cynthia Sellers paused in the act of pushing the inside door closed. I took another step backward, and her face and form came more into focus. Relatively small, perhaps five-feet four or five, her blond hair was pulled up into a ponytail tied jauntily with a bright red ribbon. Compact and well-muscled, she looked to be the kind of woman who works hard at keeping in shape. Or has the kind of job that does it for her. In a white tank top and light blue denim shorts, she could have been anywhere from thirty to fifty. I needed to see her eyes more clearly to make that judgment.

"We represent Gray Palmer of Palmer Shipping," I said before she could change her mind again and swing the door shut. "You contacted him about a reward?"

"Why didn't you say so? Come in."

She stepped out of the way, and we filed into the small entry. Without a word, our hostess turned to her right and led us through an elegantly furnished dining room and pristine kitchen, then out a set of French doors onto a spacious screened porch.

"Sit." It sounded more like a command to a pair of ill-behaved dogs than an invitation to guests.

"Thank you." Erik dropped into one of a pair of cushioned, wicker chairs, and I settled myself on the matching loveseat. Cynthia Sellers took what looked to be her usual seat in a rocker drawn up beside a round table littered with magazines, books, and a tall, sweating glass of an amber-colored liquid I took to be iced tea.

"So you've come about the reward. I said in my message I wasn't interested in that. Just trying to help. So what do you want?"

Erik and I exchanged a look, and I nodded slightly. "We have a few questions, a few points we'd like to clarify," he began, correctly interpreting my intention. I could already see how our hostess relaxed when Erik held her attention.

"So you work for him? For Mr. Palmer?" She leaned over her tanned legs, crossed at the knees, to expose a nicely rounded cleavage above the edge of her tank top. The move looked far too practiced to have been accidental.

"Yes. He's asked us to follow up on the leads he received after his news conference. We did try to call, as I said before, but we never got an answer."

"Caller ID. If I don't recognize the number, I don't pick up the phone. Usually the answering machine gets it. Damned thing must be on the fritz again."

"Of course I understand. A young woman living alone can't be too careful."

Cynthia leaned over a little farther, displaying a few more of her charms, and I knew Erik had her.

"Ask me anything you like. I really don't know much more than I told them on the phone, but I'm more than willing . . ." Like the lean, I didn't think the pause had been unintentional. ". . . to help you. And Mr. Palmer, too, of course."

I had been looking out over the backyard, enclosed in a fence which matched the siding on the house and ringed with bright pink, red, and orange blooms when inspiration struck. "May I see your roses?" I interrupted Erik's reply without a qualm. "I believe you have some unusual varieties." I answered her quizzical look with an enthusiasm entirely false but apparently convincing. "I'm something of a rose gardener myself."

"By all means," Cynthia answered, her face puzzled. "Help yourself."

"Thank you. I won't be a moment."

I let myself out the narrow screen door, down two steps, and out into the yard. I actually didn't give two damns about flowers, except to admire their beauty from afar. It had been my late mother who owned the passion for exotic rosebushes and who could rattle off the names of hundreds of hybrids just by sight and smell. I knew, however, that whatever information we would be able to wrench from the reluctant Ms. Sellers would best be extracted by my charming partner—on his own, without any other female around to cramp the lady's style.

I made two complete rounds of the small area, bending and sniffing and examining each bud or bloom with what I hoped looked like genuine fascination. I needn't have bothered with the charade. Every time I glanced back up toward the screened-in porch area, Cynthia Sellers had my partner locked in her gaze. I could have dug up the damned bushes and carted them off, and she'd never have noticed.

I was just beginning to get seriously annoyed when I heard Erik call my name. As I approached them, Cynthia laid her hand on Erik's forearm and tilted her head to one side in a way I was certain she thought provocative.

"You'll call me?" I heard her ask in a little-girl-lost voice so phony I was surprised my partner could keep a straight face. "With any news? I'm so concerned about poor Mr. Palmer. All this must be just dreadful for him."

"We'll certainly be in touch if we need any additional information." Erik gently disengaged himself as I pulled open the screen door.

"Are you sure I can't offer you a drink? Or lunch?"

He shot me a look of helplessness, and I had to choke back a laugh. If Erik was going to be an active participant in Simpson & Tanner, Inquiry Agents, I was going to have to sign him up for Extricating from Predatory Females 101.

"We really do have to run, or we'll be late for our next appointment. But thanks so much." I didn't pause, but kept right on walking into the kitchen and through to the entryway. They had no choice but to follow. "Thanks again, Ms. Sellers," I said as I marched through the front door and down the steps while Erik turned to shake hands.

"Yes, thanks, Ms. . . ."

"Cynthia, remember?" She interrupted him with a dazzling smile and that restraining hand again on his arm.

"Cynthia," he mumbled, pulling away and all but sprinting to the passenger door of the T-Bird. "Thanks again."

"Bye-bye," she chirped.

The red-painted nails on the ends of her blunt fingers were still wiggling in the breeze as we eased out of her driveway.

I waited until we were well away from the Sellers house before allowing the shout of laughter to burst from my lips.

"What?" Erik demanded, his expression so perplexed it sent me off into another fit of giggles.

"I half expected to come back up on the porch to find she had you down on the floor, trussed and tied up like a calf in a roping contest. You do have a way with the ladies, partner, I'll certainly give you that."

"Okay, wise guy, let's see how you make out with ol' Delbert," he retorted, his natural good humor once again rising to the fore. "And don't expect me to bail you out if the guy decides he wants to grab you by the hair and drag you off to his harem."

"You mean you wouldn't defend my honor? Hell, I was ready to go toe-to-toe with Ms. Sellers back there. I would have taken her on to protect your virtue."

"Who said I wanted to be protected?" he retorted.

"The look of absolute and total panic on your face was a clue."

We rode a ways in silence, both of us enjoying the soft breeze and gentle sun. The traffic on Route 278 was sparse, not surprising for a late Sunday morning, and we pulled into the parking lot in front of the Anchorage at Shelter Cove barely ten minutes after leaving Port Royal Plantation.

"So what did you find out?" I asked, turning in my seat to face Erik. "You did take notes I trust?"

"Of course." He slipped the narrow pad from the breast pocket of his pullover and flipped back a couple of pages. "Well, nothing really more than what she said in the message she left. She's quite an accomplished sailor, you know. One of the few, men or women, who can actually parallel park her boat at the dock without any help."

"I'm impressed all to hell," I replied. As a confirmed landlubber, I hadn't the foggiest notion what that meant, except it probably sounded good when she was on the prowl for men. Some might be intimidated by the feisty Cynthia Sellers, but a lot would no doubt find her nautical proficiency attractive. No accounting for taste.

"She said she recognized the kind of boat those guys were in." He consulted his notebook. "A Grady White. About twenty-four feet. And she did give me a more precise idea of the location of her sighting." He had apparently decided to ignore my sarcasm. "I wrote down everything she told me, although I have to admit it doesn't mean anything to me. Maybe when we get that map up and working it will start to come together."

"So you stuck your head in the lion's mouth for nothing." I checked my watch, then pulled my bag from the floor of the car and slid out. "Let's go find Mr. Delbert Pidgen and see if he's any more help."

"Wait. There is something else."

I stopped and leaned over the door. "What?"

"Cynthia said she thought the men she saw arguing with Gray might have been in uniform."

"Uniform? As in what?" The suggestion by one of the callers that Gray had been killed by a paramilitary group popped into my head.

"She didn't know. She thought it was more like camouflage, you know, the kind of T-shirts and pants kids like to wear to be cool."

"Doesn't sound like the sort of thing you'd put on to go fishing, though, does it? Isn't that used more for hunting?"

Erik tucked the notepad back in his pocket. "Maybe. But then what I don't know about either one would fill an encyclopedia. It could mean nothing."

I shrugged and slung my bag over my shoulder. "Come on. Let's go see if we can pump anything useful out of our next reward-seeker."

Following the directions we found tacked to the door of his apartment, we located him, along with his sons, cleaning fish on the pier that ran alongside the swanky Harbourmaster restaurant. Mid-thirties, the beginnings of a serious paunch just inching over the waistband of his stained khaki shorts, Delbert Pidgen proved to be the soul of cooperation. He answered our questions in a straightforward manner.

We retreated to one of the benches bolted to the concrete pier zigzagging its way along the harbor. The adjoining docks were lined with small pleasure craft as well as several large yachts and a couple of dolphin-sighting excursion boats. Behind us the condominiums of Shelter Cove rose in long stretches of glass made opaque by the relentless reflection of the sun off the water. The ones on the third story no doubt provided a spectacular view across the Disney timeshare complex and straight out to Broad Creek.

Thankfully Delbert Pidgen didn't offer to shake hands, and he apologized several times for the smell clinging to his clothes and person. "We just got back from fishing," he explained, "and the boys wanted to cook these up for lunch so we had to get them gutted and filleted. I need to have them back to their mother by six." At my quizzical look he added, "The boys, not the fish."

This time I pumped, and Erik made himself scarce, with about the same results. No actual coordinates, but we did get a clearer picture of exactly where the *Arky Olly Jist* had been when Delbert and his sons passed by. At one point he called to the older boy who verified his father's recollection that it had been just around seven thirty A.M.

"If you had a chart, I could show you," Delbert Pidgen offered.

I rooted around in my bag and came up with the Beaufort County map I'd pulled from a drawer in my kitchen just before we'd set out. "Will this be of any help?" I unfolded it and spread it across my lap.

Delbert studied it for a moment then flipped it over. "Ah, this'll work."

The reverse side had a detailed outline of the city of Beaufort itself as well as its immediate environs, including the larger outlying islands. He paused, running his finger along what I thought was an imaginary line from the downtown docks, up between the western edge of Lady's Island and the U.S. Marine Corps Air Station on Chisolm Island, and out into the Coosaw River. On closer inspection, aided by my having perched my reading glasses on the end of my nose, I saw that in fact the route was marked by a faint, dotted red line.

"What's that?" I asked, pointing to the dots.

"Intracoastal Waterway," Delbert replied promptly. "Runs all the way up the East Coast. You can start in Florida and go pretty much up to Maine if you follow this route."

"And this is where you saw the Palmer boat?"

"No," he said, "not exactly. Farther out into St. Helena Sound. Not too far off Monkey Island."

"Monkey Island?" I watched his finger where it tapped against the pale blue color indicating waterways on the map. "I don't see that."

"Oh, sorry. That's what the locals call Judas Island. Right here."

Something tickled at the back of my memory, an article in the paper, or a conversation with someone, but I couldn't pull it up. "Why do they call it Monkey Island?" I asked.

Erik, who had been chatting with the boys as they split the bellies of the unfortunate fish and tossed their gleaming insides into a bucket at their feet, wandered back at that point and stood gazing down at the map. "I read about that not too long ago," he said. "Isn't that the place where they raise the rhesus macaques for research?"

"Right," Delbert Pidgen said, squinting up into the sun to nod at Erik. "Get them from Indonesia or the Philippines, or somewhere like that, and breed them over here for government labs, the CDC in Atlanta, places like that. Big scandal about it a couple of years back as I recall, but I don't remember exactly what."

The whole story sounded vaguely familiar, but I couldn't have said why. Since Rob and I had divided our time between work in Charleston and weekends on Hilton Head, I had gotten woefully out of touch with a lot of the local gossip and goings-on in Beaufort during those years. You could bet my father would have all the gory details, though, I thought.

"Good fishing spot?" Erik asked.

"Probably, but you can't get anywhere near the island itself. All kinds of warning signs about givin' it a wide berth. No one's allowed to set foot on the place except the people who feed the monkeys."

"Why not? Are they afraid of disease or something?" I asked.

"Maybe, I'm not sure. Main reason, I guess, is the monkeys roam free. Don't keep 'em in cages or anything. I guess it makes it easier for them to breed. Hey, you kids about done over there?" Delbert called to his sons.

"Yeah, Dad, last one," the older boy replied.

"So do you think I have a chance of collecting any of this reward?" the father asked, turning back to me.

I liked the honesty of his question. Unlike Cynthia Sellers, he had no qualms about claiming his interest in the money. "I really can't say," I answered, just as honestly. "All we're doing is gathering information for Mr. Palmer. The final decision will be up to him."

"Understood. But what with alimony and child support and keeping two households going . . ." He let the thought trail off as the boys, both lean and tanned and impossibly good-looking, sidled up, one carrying the shiny silver filets on the lid of a plastic cooler. "All done?"

their father asked, then added, "Good job. Take them on up to the condo, and I'll be right there."

They nodded and scampered off.

"Nice kids," I said, and their father smiled.

"Thanks. They're the primary reason I'm even getting involved in this thing, you know? By the time they're ready for college, it's going to cost the damn national debt to get them through."

I rose and refolded the map. "I certainly understand. Thanks for your help, Mr. Pidgen. Someone from Mr. Palmer's office will be in touch."

"I hope so," he said, favoring us again with his open smile. "The little one thinks he wants to go to med school."

We left him dealing with the bucket of fish guts his boys had left behind and made our way back to the car.

"What do you think?" Erik asked as we slid into the T-Bird.

"I hope to hell he's the one who ends up with the money," I said. I backed the car around and headed out toward 278. "And I think I'd like to know a little more about this Monkey Island."

"Why?"

"Because it sounds like just the kind of place that might have proved irresistible to your friend Gray Palmer."

CHAPTER
TWENTY-TWO

I MANAGED TO CONVINCE ERIK TO STICK AROUND FOR A couple more days by the simple act of saying I needed him. I'd been prepared for an argument, the usual one about his having to get back to the store in Charlotte because he couldn't trust anyone to keep things going in his absence. But, after a long talk with his assistant, a conversation which was punctuated by about a dozen admonitions for her to call if she ran into any trouble, he finally agreed to stay.

I defrosted a couple of T-bones and fired up the gas grill in celebration of my victory, and we ate dinner at the round table in the screened-in area of the deck. Though we were protected from the annual invasion of mosquitoes and no-see-ums, I lit a few citronella candles for ambiance. As we licked the last of the double-chocolate almond fudge ice cream from our dessert spoons, I thought how nice it was to have someone to cook for.

"So did you find anything interesting on the 'net?" I asked, stacking the ice cream bowls on the pile of dirty plates and silverware at the edge of the table. I'd made tea in the electric coffeepot and plugged it in outside. I poured for myself, though Erik held up his hand.

"None for me, thanks."

"Shall I make you some coffee? Won't take a moment."

"No, I'm fine. To answer your question, I found lots of interesting stuff, although I don't know how much use it's going to be to us. Do you know why the place was originally named Judas Island?"

"Something to do with the slave trade if memory serves."

"Right. I found this article about it. Seems some enterprising sea captains convinced runaway slaves they'd help them escape to the North. This was in about 1850 or so, right after the Fugitive Slave Act was passed."

"I remember now. Didn't they lure the poor slaves to the island, then actually take them farther south and resell them?"

Erik nodded. "Alabama and Mississippi mostly."

"Bastards. They finally got caught and hanged, right?"

"Actually it was the local planters who meted out the justice. It never got to a trial."

"Well, that's one lynching I find it hard to object to." I stirred sweetener into my tea and settled more comfortably into my chair. "So I take it you don't share my theory."

"That Gray might have found the body on Judas Island? I don't necessarily disagree, but I don't see any proof. And from the other stuff I found on-line, we're going to need a dispensation from the Pope to gain access to that place. There's no way we could do it in secret."

"If our assumptions are correct, Gray managed it."

Erik's cocked eyebrow brought me back to the crux of our problem.

"And he got killed. I hear you." I blew across the top of my teacup before saying, "But we don't know that his death came from his just being on the island. Our working hypothesis is that it was what—or who—was in the grave that got him in trouble."

"Maybe they're related," Erik offered.

"What, the grave and the island, or the grave and the monkeys?"

In the extended twilight afforded us by the recent onset of Daylight Savings Time, I saw him shrug. "I don't know. Insufficient data, as we say in the computer biz."

"Well at least tell me what you found out on-line, and I'll fill you in on what the Judge had to contribute." I knew my father would be a fount of information on whatever local political scandal there might have been, and he proved me right.

"I ran across several articles, most of them from the local newspapers. There were a couple, too, from some animal rights groups who want to see the whole thing shut down. From what I can gather, they're the reason for all the mystery and security around the place. The people who run the facility are paranoid about PETA and something called the IPPO organizing protests. Considering what they do out there, I don't blame either side."

"I'm familiar with People for the Ethical Treatment of Animals, but what's the other acronym stand for?" I asked.

"International Primate Protection Organization. Seems they were involved with a lawsuit a few years back because the company that runs the facility was importing pregnant monkeys caught in the wild in Indonesia. Apparently that's a no-no."

I poured myself another cup of tea. Outside, the night creatures had begun to slip from their daytime hiding places as evidenced by the increased rustling among the sharp-edged leaves of the palmettos and the occasional screech of an owl.

"According to the Judge," I said, "that was the cause of the scandal Delbert Pidgen referred to this afternoon. Seems one of our local politicos was also an officer of the company which operates the facility. He and some others got sued. My father said most of them resigned. He also said this thing with raising the monkeys has been going on for more than twenty years, and he can't see any reason why Gray's being in the area should have had anything to do with his death. Lots of folks like to take their boats out there and try to spot the monkeys. Some have even gotten in close enough to toss them potato chips. Feeders come out every day to leave them food, so they're pretty used to humans."

Erik stretched and recrossed his long legs. "And eventually someone has to go out there and catch them, right? I mean, the whole point of the exercise is to sell them to research labs and make a buck. Did you know they get about five thousand dollars a head?"

I whistled. "That much? How many are there at any one time?"

"One article I found said about three thousand. You know, I'm not much of a joiner, but I think I could work up some enthusiasm for hooking up with whatever organizations are trying to put a stop to this."

"I don't like the idea of using animals for research, especially ones who exhibit a high degree of intelligence, like monkeys and dolphins, any more than you do. But let's face it: most of the strides in curing some pretty hideous diseases have resulted from animal research."

"I know." Erik leaned in toward the table, his earnest conviction evident in his wide brown eyes. "But, it doesn't seem right to let animals breed, create offspring, and then take them away to be infected with Parkinson's or cancer or AIDS. Intellectually I understand the necessity of it, but it bothers me. Here." He touched his chest in the general vicinity of his heart.

"You'll get no argument from me. I hate cruelty to animals as much as the next guy. But that's a philosophical discussion we're not likely to resolve tonight. I'm more interested in what—if anything—this has to do with Gray Palmer's death. The Judge said the Department of Natural Resources just bought a portion of the island and agreed to allow the monkey facility to keep operating. There's even talk about opening up part of the land for public use. He seemed to think that pretty much ruled out any connection, although I'm not sure I'm buying it."

"I'm inclined to agree with him." He forestalled my interruption with a raised hand. "But I'm not entirely convinced you're wrong, either. There's still the little matter of the grave. If we assume Monkey Island is where Gray stumbled across the skeleton, then we still have no idea who it was or why he was buried out there. It could have something to do with the breeding operation. We just don't know."

"Insufficient data."

"Exactly," he answered.

"I think we need to hit the road," I said, rising.

"Now? Where?" Erik stood as well.

"No, not now. Tomorrow. We need to get over to that island and check it out for ourselves."

Erik slid the door open with his foot as we both balanced dirty dishes and glasses. In the kitchen, he scraped while I stacked the dishwasher.

"And just how do you propose we do that?" he asked, resuming our interrupted conversation. "It's supposedly off-limits, isn't it?"

"Not if you know the right people," I replied. I wiped my hands on the dish towel and mopped up a few water spots from the granite counter. "I've got the name of someone who can get us in close. I swear, sometimes it amazes even me how many connections my father has. I have to give the guy a call and set it up. I think it should be tomorrow, as long as you're here, if I can work it out. And the weather cooperates."

Erik pulled a beer from the refrigerator and settled himself at the kitchen table in the alcove. "I think you're jumping the gun," he said after a few moments' hesitation.

"Why?" I leaned against the cabinets, my arms crossed over my chest in what even I recognized as a defensive position.

"Don't get your back up, partner. I'm not saying you're wrong. I'm just advising caution." The smile took any sting from his words. "You know how you bean-counters can be, running off half-cocked, doing crazy, impulsive things."

"Yeah, right. Look, I don't say we storm the island and begin hunting for disturbed graves. I just think it would be a good opportunity to check the place out, see what kind of security they have, how difficult it would really be to land a boat there undetected. The map did pretty strongly suggest Judas Island could be where Gray found the skeleton."

When we returned from Shelter Cove, Erik and I had spread out the map of Beaufort and marked as best we could the three spots we knew about: the sightings by Cynthia Sellers and Delbert Pidgen, and the approximate final location of the boat off Edisto Beach where it was found by the Coast Guard. I had used a ruler to connect the three small dots then extended the line back through St. Helena Sound toward Beaufort. Judas, alias Monkey Island, was directly in the path of that line. It had also amazed me how close it was to Presqu'isle at the tip of St. Helena.

" 'Could be' are the operative words here." Again Erik checked my attempted interruption with his hand. "I know you think that little exercise in map-plotting proved something, but I don't believe we know enough about what we're doing to jump to that big a conclusion. There are lots of other little islands out there. It could just as easily be one of those."

"It could also be in the middle of Waterfront Park in downtown Beaufort, but I'd bet it's not."

I turned my back and busied myself with pouring out a large glass of Diet Coke over a lot of ice and tried to analyze why Erik's sudden opposition was pushing all my buttons. Maybe I had gotten way too used to the idea he was just a minor player in this new enterprise, someone I could use to track down information when I needed him to and then fade away into the woodwork when I didn't. It wasn't a very pleasant discovery about myself, but I had a sneaking suspicion it might be true. After all, in my initial planning, in drawing up the contracts, and even in designing the company logo, the name *Whiteside* hadn't appeared anywhere.

Maybe I had gotten too damned used to running the show.

I turned back to him with a genuine smile. "You could be right. Let's sleep on that and talk about it again tomorrow. We can arrange the trip almost anytime, at least according to the Judge. And we need to get back up to Charleston, as well. I still think we need to talk to Araminda Albright again in person. Maybe you can work your Cynthia Sellers number on her and get her to tell us the whole truth."

His answering grin made me feel a lot better. "Don't you think it's time we met up with Gray's father, too? After all, we do have some concrete information to share with him about the reward, so requesting a meeting would be perfectly legitimate. I'd like to get a handle on the guy, see if I can figure out why Gray hated him so much."

"Did you manage to get a line on the other caller you were trying to track down?" I asked.

The report of a paramilitary group's being after Gray had seemed far-fetched to me until Ms. Sellers's revelation that the men she had seen arguing with him might have been wearing camouflage.

"No luck. The number is for a cell phone, and none of my directories can cross-reference an address to that. I left him another message. I guess we'll just have to wait and see if he calls us back."

"Do we know for certain it's a man?"

"Well, no, I guess we don't. My assumption. I'd still like to talk to whoever it is."

We compromised on a plan to make appointments with both Araminda and Gray's father, hopefully for Tuesday. We'd spend Monday in Beaufort, perhaps hooking up with the guy who could take us out to Monkey Island, then head on up to Charleston the next day. We could spend the night at Presqu'isle. I headed for the office to make the calls.

"I'm going to take a quick walk up the beach," Erik said, dumping his empty beer bottle in the wastebasket. "Got a flashlight I can use?"

I cast him a quizzical look. "At this time of night? There's not much of a moon. You won't be able to see your hand in front of your face."

He shrugged. "I know. That's kind of the lure of it. Living in the middle of all the city lights you don't get much of a chance to see the stars. Or the ocean. Besides, in the heat of our mad race up the beach this morning . . ."

"Which I won, if you recall."

"Only because I'm such a gentleman," he shot back.

"Right."

"Anyway, I left your coffee mug sitting out there on the dune." He managed to look sheepish and about four years old.

"For heaven's sake don't worry about it. I've got tons of them. Besides, the tide's probably taken it halfway to Africa by now."

"I'd still like to take that walk. And if I find the mug, I'll sleep better."

"Suit yourself," I said. "Flashlight's in the left-hand drawer under the desk."

I had already given him the security code as well as a key so he could come and go as he pleased. "Just make sure you set the alarm and lock up when you come back in. Have fun."

"I won't be gone that long," he said, heading for the French doors, the ancient Eveready in his hand.

But nearly two hours later, Erik had still not returned. I had made arrangements with Gray Palmer, Senior, to meet him at his office and had settled on a tentative time for our boat tour around Judas Island. Araminda Albright did not answer despite the lateness of the hour, so I told her machine we'd be in the area on Tuesday and I'd touch base with her when we got to town. I left a light on in the great room, washed up, and climbed beneath the sheets. I fully expected Erik's return to waken me, but I heard nothing until the scream right underneath my window sent me rocketing from the bed.

No one could say I hadn't learned my lesson.

Despite the fear that threatened to choke off my breath, already coming in short, heaving gasps, I took the time to fumble open the safe hidden in the floor of my closet, retrieve the Glock, and ram home the clip. I grabbed a pair of sweat pants and a rumpled T-shirt to cover my nakedness then eased out into the hallway.

I stood for a moment trying to quiet my thudding heart and heard muffled *whumps* up against the outside wall, followed by garbled shouting. I crept to the kitchen, snatching up the cordless phone on my way by and dialing 911. I told the operator there was a disturbance outside my house, and she promised to dispatch a unit immediately.

Satisfied that I had acted in as rational a manner as I could muster under the circumstances, I disengaged the alarm and eased open the French doors. Out on the deck I could tell immediately the ruckus was coming from the side of the house facing the ocean. With the gun held slightly in front of me I crept around in that direction. What sounded like a staged fistfight from an old western was going on just beneath me. I peered over the edge of the railing just as the dim outline of a body went racing past, down the path over the dune, and out toward the beach.

"Hey, you son of a bitch! Come back here!"

The voice belonged to Erik Whiteside. I had no idea who he might be grappling with.

"Stop! I'm armed!" I tried to sound sure and forceful, but I heard the fear quivering in my words. I probably sounded hysterical, but I thought that might actually work in my favor. I couldn't imagine too many people wanting to get tangled up with a crazy woman waving a loaded gun around. Although I had proved I could use it—and accurately—when I had to, there was no way I would fire with no clear target other than the thrashing bodies on the ground beside the deck and a dim shadow running away from me into the night.

"Stay where you are! The police are on their way!"

I sprinted for the steps and bounded down them two at a time, my bare feet stumbling a little at the bottom. By the time I righted myself, the noise had stopped. I hesitated, unsure what this sudden silence might mean. I crept forward on the scratchy pine straw, whipping my head from side to side, the gun still held in the ready position as Red had taught me. Once before someone had attacked me from behind, and I wasn't about to let that happen again. Back then I had been unarmed and a whole lot more ignorant about how criminals operate.

I stopped again as a low groaning drifted out to me on the cool night air. "Erik?" I ventured in a taut whisper, but got no response.

"Erik?" I tried again, inching forward into the blackness beneath the shadow of the house.

The sound seemed closer. Again I checked to the sides and rear. *Where the hell are the damned cops?* I wondered as I strained to distinguish the outlines of shrubs and bushes which might lie in my path.

He broke from cover right at my elbow, like a pheasant flushed by a well-trained bird dog, so close I could smell the sweat of fear drenching his dark shirt. The glancing blow sent the Glock spinning from my hand and knocked me sideways onto my left knee. The pain took my breath away and forced me to roll onto my side. The toe of one of his sneakers caught my right arm as he leaped over me and sprinted away into the palmettos. For a few seconds I heard him thrashing through the razor-edged plants, then he broke free, and the sounds of his escape died in the loose sand of the dune.

I remember thinking he'd be a mass of cuts. If we ever caught up to him, he wouldn't be hard to identify.

I rubbed the spot on my forearm and felt a knot beginning to rise there. I turned back onto my knees and put my hands out to lever myself to my feet. My fingers sank into a thick puddle of something wet and sticky, and I had to clamp my teeth down over the scream hovering low in my throat.

I scrambled up, took two steps in the wide pool of wetness, and stumbled over the body of Erik Whiteside.

CHAPTER
TWENTY-THREE

ESUS, WOMAN, TAKE IT EASY!"

I nearly fainted with the relief of hearing his voice, drowned out almost immediately by the welcome commotion of slamming doors and booted feet pounding on the driveway. The slashing beam of a powerful flashlight cut through the night, and a commanding voice ordered us to stay where we were.

"I'm Bay Tanner," I called, rising slowly with both hands clearly visible out to my sides. I knew how the police operated, and I didn't want to give them any reason to see me as a danger to them. "This is my house."

Blinded by the glare, I couldn't make out who was advancing cautiously toward us, but there was no mistaking the business end of the pistol pointing directly at me.

"Stay where you are," he repeated, "hands where I can see them."

One officer approached from the side, making a wide berth around the puddle with Erik's inert form stretched out in the middle of it while the other held us in the circle of light.

"Okay," I said, "okay. But my friend is hurt. We need to get an ambulance in here."

"I don't need an ambulance." Erik rose to a sitting position and reached up to touch the side of his face.

Immediately the officer with the gun pointed at us took a step back and yelled, "Don't move! Hands on the back of your head! Do it!"

It seemed as if I'd been in this exact position before, being threatened by the very people who were supposed to be helping me. I bit back the tide of fury which had overtaken my initial fear.

"He's not the intruder. There were two of them. They ran away over the dune and onto the beach. Quit wasting time! This man needs medical attention."

"Shut up, Bay! I don't need medical attention. Nothing's hurt but my pride."

"Sir, I want to see those hands on the back of your head, fingers locked. Now!"

"Just do it," I hissed down at Erik who glared back at me but finally complied.

The light advanced again in our direction as the officer with his gun drawn moved toward us. The other one pulled his flashlight from his belt and began playing the beam over the ground.

"Weapon here," I heard him say as the light fell on my Glock gleaming black against the pine straw.

"It's mine," I said. "One of them knocked it out of my hand when he ran into me. I have a permit."

Although that carry permit had been illegally obtained thanks to my father's connections, I didn't think that was a piece of information I really needed to share. At least not at the moment.

"Anybody got any I.D. on them?" the gun-toting deputy asked.

"I do," Erik replied promptly. "Wallet in the back pocket of my jeans."

"Okay, stand up. But slowly."

I stepped back a little to give him room to maneuver. It's tough getting to your feet from a sitting position without using your hands for leverage.

"Turn around," the officer ordered him. "Left hand down, slowly, and pull the wallet out."

Erik did as instructed, and the second deputy reached out to take it from his outstretched hand.

"Erik," I said into the silence as the two men came together to study the contents of the slim, black wallet. "If you're okay, where did all the blood come from? Did you get one of them?"

"I'd like to know the answer to that one, too, Mr. Whiteside." He spoke from much closer this time and had thankfully redirected the beam of the flashlight from my face to the squishy mess around us.

"It's not blood. It's paint," Erik said, sounding almost apologetic. "I came back up from the beach and caught the two of them leaving you another love letter, this time on the side of the house."

He gestured with his head toward the deck, and one of them slid a light over it. The still-dripping red *B* could be seen quite clearly against the weathered boards.

"Did you say your name was Tanner?" the first deputy asked.

I felt enormous relief his tone had retreated from powerfully commanding to something more conversational.

"Yes. Bay Tanner. My brother-in-law is Sergeant Red Tanner."

"Okay then." He lowered his gun and the tension level along with it. "You can put your hands down now," he added, almost as an afterthought, and holstered his weapon. "What happened here?"

I could feel the anger rolling off Erik, and I stepped up to nudge him gently. I had, on several occasions, given voice to my frustration with the tactics of local law enforcement and had been forced to acknowledge the futility of it. They had their methods, no doubt intended to protect them as well as innocent citizens from imminent harm. I didn't like their rules, but I understood their necessity.

So I gave them the gist of the previous two graffiti incidents, and Erik finished up with his own account of the night's adventure. In a nutshell, he had encountered two people slopping paint on the side of my house as he came up the beach path. He'd crept up on them, counting on his size and the element of surprise to corral at least one of them and wring an explanation from his prisoner before alerting me to call the police. He hated admitting to it, but they had gotten the better of him, which resulted in the fistfight and assorted grunts and screams I'd heard from my bedroom. He felt pretty certain one of them had struck him in the side of his head with the old flashlight he'd dropped in the scuffle.

And he'd been doubly certain one of them was a girl.

———————

After the cops left, Erik and I took turns using the outside shower I'd had installed for the purpose of washing off the salt and sand of the beach. It worked just as well for paint. When we finally located the little hoodlums who had decided to use my beautiful house for a billboard, I made a note to thank them for choosing the latex rather than the oil-based variety. I don't think I would have felt quite so magnanimous if I'd been forced to douse myself in turpentine.

Over coffee and tea, we chewed on the events of the night which was even then beginning to pass into morning.

"So you have no idea what this could be about?" Erik slouched in the chair at the kitchen table, his long legs and bare feet stretched out in front of him.

"No. Why do I have to keep answering the same damned question? Doesn't anyone believe me?"

The deputies had pounded on that theme for quite some time, but I didn't have any better answer for them than the one I'd just given Erik. I personally remained convinced it was a case of mistaken identity, but no one else seemed willing to accept that. Taking into account the bizarre things that had happened to me over the past year or so, I supposed I couldn't entirely blame them.

"I believe that's what *you* believe," he answered, "but not necessarily that it's the right explanation. Isn't there anyone you can think of with a grudge to do something like this?"

I truly couldn't and said so. The problem was, this whole thing was more an annoyance than a genuine threat. The people I had tangled with in the past had been more interested in plastering *me* all over the countryside than in just defacing my house. I seriously couldn't see any of them resorting to something so childish.

That thought struck a chord. "You said to the cops you were certain one of the two was a girl."

"Either that, or it was a guy with a really big set of boobs."

He blushed and ducked his head, and I smiled. "It's okay, Erik. I've

actually heard the word 'boobs' before. But what I'm getting at is, you
didn't say 'woman.' Do you think they were both kids?"

"Now that you say it, I guess I did sort of have that impression. Not
that I got a look at either of them. Too damned dark. Maybe it was the
voices while we were wrestling around. I don't know. It's just a feeling.
Although the guy was plenty big enough. Sucker tackled me like a
linebacker."

The solution hit me with the same force.

"The piece of cloth they found out there in the paint. The deputy
said it looked as if it had been torn from a shirt pocket or something.
What were the letters on it?"

The officers, Erik, and I had examined the small strip under the
flashlight beam after one of them had picked it up out of the muck.

"It looked like a *t* and an *o* to me. That's what they thought, too.
Why?"

"Could the second letter have been a *c*?"

"I suppose so. What difference does it make?"

"Nothing," I answered. "Never mind."

I found I wasn't ready to give voice to my theory, at least not right
then. I felt certain I had the cause of this graffiti business figured out,
but I was damned if I knew what to do about it.

By the time I'd fixed us some breakfast and tossed a few things into an
overnight bag, Erik had pronounced himself packed up and ready to
roll. I left a note for Dolores, explaining my absence and telling her to
take the rest of the week off. Not that she'd probably listen to me. My
housekeeper/friend had a way of smiling beneficently and nodding
agreement when she had no intention of complying. I would no doubt
return to find she'd cleaned all the closets or the cupboards or done up
all the stored linens or taken down and rehung all the drapes. I wanted
her to take it easy on her still unhealed leg, but I knew she wouldn't.

She had the Judge's number, and I added that of Erik's cell phone to
the note.

The morning had broken on a high overcast, not exactly cloudy, but not the brilliant sunshine we natives of the Lowcountry generally take for granted except during the dreary days of late December and early January. We had decided to take Erik's hulking Expedition rather than my Thunderbird, primarily because my companion didn't particularly like being a passenger. I shared his aversion to abdicating control of anything to someone else, but I decided he deserved his turn in the driver's seat. In more ways than one.

"How's the face?" I asked as we pulled out of Port Royal Plantation and merged into the heavy Monday morning traffic on Route 278. The small cut just beneath his right eye rode atop a welling lump which had begun to take on a royal purple tinge. Despite my attempts to play nurse, fussing at him with antiseptic cream, Band-Aids, and ice packs, he was going to have one hell of a shiner.

"Fine."

Erik's terse reply let me know that subject was still off-limits. He had consistently refused to discuss his injury, even as I was trying to minister to him in the early morning hours. He couldn't get past the fact that a couple of teenagers—and one of them probably a *girl*—had gotten the better of him.

We rode in silence then for the next couple of miles, managing to hit the red on every one of the traffic lights. As we approached Squire Pope Road which branches off to the right just opposite the Gullah Market, another of the loose threads which seemed to be tangling my life snapped into my head.

"Did you ever get a chance to check out Felicity Baronne on the Internet?" I asked, glancing to the left and the large tree under which I had conducted my stakeout a few days before. The woman who seemed to regard my father as her own personal cash cow had pretty much slipped my mind in the chaos of the Gray Palmer investigation.

"Damn it, yes I did! I'm sorry, Bay. I just completely forgot, what with everything else going on."

"What did you find?"

"Not a whole lot, but I printed the stuff out. It's in the pocket of my laptop case in the backseat."

I unhooked my shoulder harness and squirmed around to unzip the black leather carrier.

"Three sheets, I think. Should be right in the front."

I pulled the papers out, closed the case, and buckled back up.

"What is all this?" I asked while I dug my reading glasses out of my bag.

Erik sped up as we crossed the first bridge and left the town limits of Hilton Head behind. "A couple of credit reports which aren't too favorable, a notation of a lawsuit she was involved in as the result of an accident . . ." He glanced at the tightly packed printing on the single-spaced pages and pointed to an item about a third of the way down the second sheet. "And this. This one is what I thought you would find most interesting."

I began reading where he indicated and stopped short after the first sentence. "Felicity Baronne is a prostitute?" I don't know what I had expected, but it certainly wasn't that.

"Keep reading," Erik said.

"She's been arrested several times in towns all over the Southeast: Tallahassee, Jacksonville, Charlotte, Greenville. I don't believe this! The last time was six months ago in Atlanta."

"So maybe she's decided to move her business interests to Hilton Head."

"But that's not the point. Six months ago? You haven't seen her, Erik. The woman must be pushing sixty!"

"And you think guys over sixty aren't interested in sex anymore? Boy, you're going to have a rude awakening by the time you're eligible for Social Security. I bet the Judge would find that downright insulting."

His grin invited me to share the joke, but I couldn't bring myself to see anything the least bit amusing about it. Not only was the whole idea repugnant to me, I also felt a fleeting sympathy for a woman who had apparently spent her entire adult life selling herself to men for money. And the sudden implications this information evoked about the nature of her involvement with my father . . .

"Are you implying Felicity Baronne and the Judge . . . ? While Lavinia cooks his dinner in the kitchen? That he's paying her for . . . ?"

If he hadn't been driving I would have added another black eye to his collection.

Erik seemed genuinely shocked. "Of course not! I didn't mean any such thing, and you know it! I have nothing but complete respect and admiration for your father. I would never suggest . . ."

"Then knock off the wise-ass remarks about prostitutes and old men. It may be a subject you and your buddies can wink and jab each other about over a few beers, but I don't find anything funny about it at all. In fact, it's pretty damned pathetic, if you ask me, from both sides of the coin."

"I didn't . . . oh, hell, let's just drop it."

Which we did for about the next ten miles. I studied all the information Erik had gleaned about Felicity Baronne, and gradually a picture began to form of a transient life lived on the fringes of society: no home, no apparent family, no connections. Why had she suddenly decided to return to her hometown? Didn't the woman have any shame? And why was my father paying her off?

As the big SUV slowed entering the road-widening construction area, I sneaked a glance at Erik's profile, his lips set in a hard line, his chin jutting out pugnaciously. Sometimes I wish I would just think a moment before I open my mouth. I took a deep breath and let it out slowly.

"I'm sorry," I said, meaning it.

He paused just long enough to make me fear he wasn't going to accept my apology. "Yeah," he answered, and I could feel him relax. "I know."

"Can I blame it on the case and last night and almost no sleep?"

"You can try." The smile removed any sting from the words.

"So how did you find out all this stuff? What was I doing wrong that I couldn't get anything to come up on my search?"

We came to a complete stop while a lumbering dump truck, piled high with dirt, backed around from beneath a huge shovel mounted on caterpillar tracks and ground its way down the highway.

"I didn't have much luck either on a standard Google search, but

I have some resources the average person doesn't have access to," he replied.

"Like what?"

"Like a locator service I pay to do background checks on prospective employees and vendors. For a fee, they can find out just about anything about anybody."

"Is that legal?"

"From my end it certainly is. They guarantee they break no laws, so I'm covered no matter what. Mostly it's just a matter of having access to huge databases, newspaper files, public records. Finding out that Ms. Baronne has been arrested numerous times for prostitution isn't violating her civil rights or anything."

"She might feel differently about it," I remarked, and we fell silent again.

And so might the Judge, I thought and added a very unpleasant confrontation with my father to what was quickly becoming a seemingly endless list of things to do. As we inched along in the clogged traffic, I leaned back in the high bucket seat and planned my attack.

CHAPTER
TWENTY-FOUR

THE *WANDERER* SAT HIGH IN THE WATER, ITS ONCE white hull faded to a mellow cream as it rubbed against the weathered dock in downtown Beaufort. As we climbed the gangplank and stepped aboard the large sightseeing vessel, a brisk wind off the Beaufort River lifted my hair and sent goose bumps racing along my arms. Above us, the sun struggled to break through the overcast.

"Glad you convinced me to throw my windbreaker in the car," Erik said, helping me shrug into Rob's worn bomber jacket.

"Sixty-five degrees on land can feel a whole lot colder on the water." I didn't remember from what part of my distant past I had dredged up that tidbit of information. I only knew it to be true.

Ron Singleton stepped out of the forward wheelhouse and raised a hand in greeting. "Bay!" he called. "Welcome aboard."

His warm brown hand clasped mine, and I introduced him to Erik. Ron and I had known each other since middle school, although I'd had no idea prior to my father's announcement that he ran this tourist service.

"I really appreciate your taking us out this morning," I said as we followed the short, compact sailor into the cabin and mercifully out of the wind.

"Not a problem," he said. "I always run a couple of shakedown cruises before tourist season gets into full swing. Another two weeks, and we'll be doing three trips a day with a full load."

"At least let me pay for the gas," I said, moving up beside him to stare out toward the bridge arcing over the river on its way to Lady's Island. Somehow from down here the span looked much more impressive than it did from a car.

"Nope," he replied. The big diesel engines roared to life at his touch on the control panel, and I felt the deck begin to vibrate under my feet. "I was goin' out anyways. And besides, after what the Judge did for my mama, there aren't enough ways I could repay him. This one doesn't even count."

I had no idea what service my father might have rendered to Ron's mother, or in what capacity, and it seemed ill-mannered to ask. So I simply nodded my thanks and stepped back out of his way as he leaned out to call to one of the dockhands who cast off the ropes looped around the pilings in the front and back of the boat. Or fore and aft, I supposed, if you wanted to get technical about it.

We eased out into the river, and Erik and I settled ourselves in the spacious cabin lined with cushion-covered benches and wide windows, not unlike the much smaller ferry we had taken over to Daufuskie Island a few days before. This boat was built to accommodate many more people and included a snack bar in one corner which no doubt did a brisk summer trade in soft drinks. The vibrations increased as we glided under the massive bridge and rounded the Point where the cluster of magnificent summer homes built by antebellum planters sat tall and proud in the thin morning light.

"I still don't know what you hope to accomplish by this." Erik had to raise his voice to be heard over the thrumming of the engines as we picked up speed.

"I just want to see the place," I answered, "get some feel for what it looks like and how difficult it would be to get close. We can also check out some of those other islands you mentioned, all the little ones with no names on our map. I'm not ruling out the possibility one of them might be the place."

"But you're still pretty convinced this Monkey Island is our spot."

"Gut feeling. I can't explain it. Call it woman's intuition, though, and I'll belt you one."

He grinned and shrugged then turned back to his observation of the river sliding by on the right side of the boat.

Once the pillars and porches of the homes on the Point and the austerity of the land comprising the Marine Corps Air Station had slipped behind us, I found myself completely disoriented. The river twisted and turned along marshy bottoms filled with birds swooping or wading in search of food, and here and there a glimpse of the shimmering green of a golf course or the pitched roof of a Lowcountry mansion could be seen through the thick screen of trees lining the banks.

I stepped up toward the front of the boat where Ron stood with his hands resting lightly on the wheel. "Do you have any charts or maps I might have a prayer of reading?" I asked.

He turned briefly and nodded toward a wooden locker built into the side of the wheelhouse. "In there. Help yourself."

"What am I looking for?" I lifted the lid to uncover a stack of spiral-bound books which appeared to be about a foot and a half square, along with several laminated charts rolled up and fastened with rubber bands.

"One of those books, the big ones. Get out the one that says Norfolk to Jacksonville on the top."

I located it and pulled the cumbersome thing out onto the floor.

"There's an index," Ron said, "on the back. You want the page for the Beaufort River."

"Thanks."

I carried the bulky book back into the passenger cabin and spread it out on one of the benches. Erik moved across from the other side to stand over me. I flipped to the indicated page and located Beaufort with no problem. With my finger I traced our route up the Intracoastal Waterway.

"Where are we now?" I called to Ron.

"Just turning into the Coosaw River," he yelled over his shoulder.

I located the spot and glanced up as we moved right into a much wider expanse of water. "Lady's Island," I said confidently and pointed to the land visible out the windows behind Erik. "Next comes Coosaw Island, then Judas. Shouldn't be too much longer."

I lowered the chart book onto the floor, and we settled back to enjoy the ride.

"Comin' up on it," Ron Singleton called about twenty minutes later, snapping me out of a half-doze.

The rhythmic humming of the engines and the beauty of the scenery had combined with the warmth from a strengthening sun to lull me into complete relaxation. I felt the boat slow as Ron eased back on the throttle. I shook myself awake and reached in my bag for the compact binoculars I'd tossed in before we'd left the house.

"Come on," I said to Erik, "let's head out on deck."

We pushed open the heavy door and stepped over the raised threshold. Outside, the wind hit us, chilly after the drowsy warmth of the cabin. We climbed the steep stairs up to the top deck. Folding chairs were stacked neatly on one end and lashed with a series of ropes to keep them secure. I could imagine a horde of pasty-faced Northerners packed into them on a mid-July afternoon, their pink skin blistering under a relentless sun. We moved to the rail on the right side, and I trained the glasses toward the green canopy spread out before us.

"See anything?" Erik asked after a couple of minutes, and I shook my head.

"Just trees." I handed over the glasses, and he scanned the endless stands of fir and hardwoods.

"Did you tell your friend down there what we were looking for?" He lowered the binoculars and leaned his forearms on the rail.

"No. And I don't know exactly what the Judge told him, either. Maybe we should let him in on our interest in how someone would go about landing on the island. I could make it seem like just idle curiosity."

"He doesn't appear to be a stupid man. I think he might make a few connections we don't exactly want him to."

"And if he did, he'd keep them to himself. Especially if I asked him to."

"Your call." Erik raised the glasses again and made a smooth sweep from left to right.

We were edging in closer to the shore, and even with my naked eye I could make out indentations in the thick canopy where small streams and rivulets cut into the interior. We had already passed Parrot Creek which formed the western boundary of the island. I had my hand on the railing, ready to descend the steps to the wheelhouse when I heard Erik cry out.

"Bay! I see them! Come here!"

I whirled to take the binoculars from his outstretched hand and aimed them in the direction of his pointing finger.

And there they were. From a distance the motion had appeared to be natural, the ever-present wind in the tops of the oaks and pines. But abruptly the movements took on shape and definition, and I realized we were looking at hundreds of rhesus monkeys, darting from tree to tree, clambering up and down the trunks, and scrambling across the floor of the island forest.

"Amazing," I breathed, completely captivated. "Look! On that live oak limb hanging out over the water."

I thrust the glasses back at Erik who trained them on the branch. A mother nestled a tiny infant in one arm, while with the fingers of her hand she picked at the shock of hair standing straight up on the tiny monkey's head. As we drifted along in the slow-moving river, the sounds of their screeching gradually drifted across the water to us.

Erik and I exchanged a look, and I said again, "Amazing."

"It's like *Jurassic Park*," he murmured, as awestruck as I. From the pocket of his windbreaker he pulled a small video camera and trained it on the island. "I've got it set on maximum zoom, so we should get some good images."

I could tell by the sun which now shone directly into my eyes we were rounding the eastern side of the island when the noise level rose dramatically. Ahead I could see a small dock jutting out into the narrow channel. As we neared it, dozens of monkeys swarmed out of the forest and across the hard-packed earth of a small clearing next to the landing. Through the binoculars I could see several of the larger ones, probably territorial males, jumping up and down in excited agitation, their lips pulled back in menacing sneers. They kept back from the dock, though, as if they knew precisely where their boundaries lay, despite the lack of fences or any kind of barrier.

I left Erik topside, his little camera running continuously, and climbed back down to where Ron lounged comfortably in a high swivel chair, one hand carelessly on the wheel, the other clutching a long, thin cigar. The heavy smoke drifting out of the wheelhouse seemed sweet and familiar.

"Those smell just like the Judge's," I said, then, "Sorry," as he jumped in his seat.

"I can put it out if it bothers you," Ron offered, but I waved the suggestion away.

"I've recently become reformed, but I'm not above satisfying my cravings with a little secondhand smoke. Just blow a few puffs over in my direction once in a while, and I'll be fine."

He laughed and turned his attention back to the river. "This what you wanted to see?" he asked.

There was just a hint of challenge in his voice, an invitation to share what this trip was really all about, but he didn't press me when I failed to rise to the bait. I decided to risk probing a little more.

"Pretty much," I said and moved into the narrow cabin. "Who uses the dock?"

I kept my gaze on the island, hoping my question would be taken as polite curiosity, but out of the corner of my eye I saw his head swivel in my direction.

"The feeders," he said. "Come around eight every morning to leave some sort of special food for them."

"Who?" I asked. "Who comes to feed them?"

"Company that owns the place, owns the monkeys. Some bunch of *scientists.*" He said the word as if it were a profanity.

"I take it you don't approve."

He drew long on the cigar before answering, his words floating out on a cloud of smoke. "It doesn't seem right to me, raisin' these creatures just so some other folks in white coats can infect 'em with AIDS or TB or some other god-awful disease, and then cut 'em open to see what made 'em die. It's not right."

His response mirrored the discussion Erik and I had gotten into the night before. It had been easy then to debate such concepts in the abstract, yet quite another to envision that tiny baby I'd seen cradled in its mother's arms dying in agony in some laboratory in Atlanta or Washington, D.C. As much as I could accept the necessity of it intellectually, my heart still cringed at the innate cruelty.

I shook off the morbid thoughts. We weren't here to get tangled up in a dialogue on animal rights. "Can just anyone dock there?" I asked, and again Ron Singleton fixed me with that curious gaze.

"See those signs?"

I followed his pointing finger. I didn't need the binoculars to read the large posters, the ones Delbert Pidgen had referred to: WARNING! PROPERTY OF U.S. GOVERNMENT. NO TRESPASSING! It would have taken a moron not to get the message that unauthorized persons were not welcome on the island.

"Do they have security?" I asked, hoping Erik was getting the panorama drifting by us on tape.

"Naw. Nothing 'cept the usual, you know, DNR and sheriff's patrol boats. 'Course kids used to try to use it for beer parties and such, but they prosecuted a few of 'em, and the fines were stiff enough to discourage the rest. Once in a while you hear tell of some of the Marines from Parris Island havin' a few too many and tryin' to practice their landing tactics." He laughed and rolled his large brown eyes. "Military doesn't take too kindly to that, either."

"So the company that runs the place, they don't have any guards or anything like that?"

We were moving past the landing area, and the acres of tightly packed live oaks and palmettos were closing in again.

"Not that I know of. They run the thing out of Yemassee, so they're not exactly right next door."

Yemassee, I thought. Where had I heard mention of the little crossroads town just recently?

My head snapped up at Erik's shout, barely heard above the idling engines. "Bay! Get up here!"

I heard the sound as I climbed the steps, a boat motor running full out. As I stepped out onto the upper deck, Erik motioned me to join him at the rail. I noticed his hands were empty, so he must have stashed both the binoculars and his video camera in the pockets of his windbreaker. The boat roared toward us from around a headland, its two occupants standing upright in the well. As they neared the *Wanderer,* the pitch of the motor changed, and the smaller craft slowed. Below us, Ron Singleton gave a single blast on the horn in what sounded more like a greeting than a warning of our presence. The big excursion boat would be hard to miss.

Erik and I exchanged glances. "Be a tourist," I said, and he nodded.

The glint of light reflected off lenses told me we were being observed through field glasses. Erik must have caught it, too. He raised his hand in a friendly wave, and I joined him as the boat slowed still more and moved in closer. The driver lifted his arm in acknowledgment while his passenger kept us in his binoculars. I saw them exchange a few words, and the craft suddenly accelerated and veered away in a long arc, pounding off in the direction from which it had first appeared.

Below us, Ron Singleton increased power to his engines and began a wide turn of his own, heading back toward Beaufort.

"Did you get the name on their boat?" I asked. "Did it fit Cynthia Sellers's description?"

Erik leaned down toward a chair I hadn't noticed he'd opened in front of the rail and came back up with the video camera in his hand.

"Was that running?" I asked, and he nodded. "Way to go! We've got the bastards on tape."

Neither of us had any doubt that Monkey Island held the key to what had happened to Gray Palmer. The video would be helpful if it ever came to a prosecution, but we already had enough information to satisfy us.

Both of the men in the fishing boat had been wearing camouflage fatigues.

CHAPTER
TWENTY-FIVE

WE PULLED INTO THE SEMICIRCULAR DRIVEWAY IN front of Presqu'isle just before one in the afternoon. Since we'd finished our boat tour so early, I had been agitating to head on up to Charleston, get a couple of hotel rooms, and hit the ground running. Erik wanted to mull things over with my father, map out a plan of action, and make the one-hour drive first thing in the morning. I was having a really difficult time getting used to being the fly-by-the-seat-of-your-pants member of this organization.

We carried our overnight bags with us up the steps and through the massive oak door into the entryway. The beautiful proportions of this central hall, neatly bisected by the grand sweep of the freestanding staircase, never failed to inspire my admiration for the incredible talent of the craftsmen, both free and slave, who had achieved such perfection without benefit of modern tools.

I dropped my case on the first step and turned at Lavinia's voice as she emerged from the kitchen. "There you are! Lunch has been ready for more than half an hour. Good thing I decided on a cold collation. Welcome back, young man." The disapproving frown she had been directing at me softened into a warm smile as her gaze swung around to my partner.

"Thank you, Mrs. Smalls, ma'am. It's good to be back."

"Now, I thought we had decided you were to call me Lavinia, just like everyone else around here. You're practically family, leastwise in all the ways that matter."

Erik grinned. "Sorry. Thank you, Lavinia."

"Now set those things down and get yourselves in there. Bay, your father has been fidgeting all morning waiting to hear what you have to tell him. Man has liked to drive me crazy."

We followed her retreating back down the hall and into the hazy warmth of the kitchen, its round oak table set for four. My father's wheelchair was already pulled up in his usual place, and I could tell by the glower on his face I was in for one of his infamous tongue-lashings.

"First Alexander Graham Bell and then generations of folks after him spent their entire lives perfecting a technology so you could call and let folks know where the hell you are," he began even before I'd had a chance to sit down. "Hello, Erik," he added, barely pausing for breath. "I know he carries one of those damned fool cellular things around with him. Thirty seconds, that's all . . ."

"Oh, stuff a sock in it, Daddy," I said, with more humor than rancor. "I'm thirsty and hungry. If I'm going to be forced to listen to any more of this nonsense from you, at least let me do it on a full stomach."

We gnawed on cold chicken legs and redskin potato salad along with an assortment of pickles and sliced vegetables. Into the uncomfortable silence, broken only by the clatter of our respective silverware against the everyday plates, Lavinia finally spoke.

"Have you returned your R.S.V.P. to Mrs. Quintard yet, Bay?"

I had no idea what she was talking about, and said so.

"For the bridal shower? Now, quit scowling at me like an angry dog. I know you received an invitation because Mrs. Quintard called and specifically requested your address in Hilton Head."

"Why would Bitsy's mother be giving a bridal shower?" My best friend since first grade, Elizabeth "Bitsy" Quintard, the only daughter of the house, had been married to the detestable Big Cal Elliott for nearly twenty years. And, to the best of my recollection, her own two daughters were way too young even to be contemplating the big plunge.

"For Amy Fleming, of course," my father chimed in. "She's marrying the Brandon boy, the one you got mixed up with in that Herrington mess last fall."

"I didn't get 'mixed up' with Chris Brandon." I could hear the defensiveness in my own voice, but I didn't care. "He hired me to do a job, which I did very well, thank you, and for which I was paid quite handsomely."

When he stuffed a forkful of potato salad into his mouth instead of whipping off a snappy retort, I knew he'd exhausted his vitriol on that particular subject. I glanced at Erik in time to see him trying unsuccessfully to stifle a grin.

"Why would anyone think I had the slightest interest in *any* bridal shower, let alone one being held in honor of someone I don't even know and given by a woman who has hated my guts since I was in grade school?"

"Really, Bay, such talk. Mrs. Quintard always speaks very highly of you." Lavinia had almost perfected my father's disapproving scowl. She still needed a little work on the scrunching eyebrows part, but it was pretty close.

"We had quite an interesting boat ride this morning," Erik began, and I flashed him a smile for his gallant effort at changing the subject and thereby rescuing me from being battered to a verbal pulp from all sides. I could have told him it was pointless.

"Mrs. Quintard and Regina Fleming, young Amy's mother, became fast friends during the Colonel's second tour of duty at Parris Island," the Judge chimed in, uninvited. "They were part of your mother's circle of acquaintance for a time if I recall."

I looked to Lavinia who nodded in agreement. "Well, sorry, I don't remember any of them. I met Amy with Chris at the Heritage Golf Tournament last weekend, but only for a couple of minutes. She doesn't know me from Adam. I'm sure my presence will not be missed."

"You will go."

The bald statement brought everyone up short, even Lavinia. While we had both gotten used to my father's peremptory commands over the years, not many of them were delivered with such force and assertion. He tended to favor sly manipulation when he really wanted something.

"Why should I?"

"I had a lot of dealings with Colonel Fleming back in the early days when he was at Parris Island. Basically a fine officer. Sometimes overly harsh with the men of color under his command . . ." He glanced obliquely at Lavinia as if in unspoken apology. "An unfortunate symptom of the times, I'm afraid. Occasionally the local law enforcement community had to make allowances for the military's priorities regarding certain . . . incidents. But I always found him to be a man I could work with, a man who understood how the world operates."

"In other words, you and he would put your heads together and circumvent the law when it served your mutual purpose," I said.

His chin trembled with the effort to control his irritation with me. "As you say. At any rate, I want you to represent the family."

"Why?" I repeated.

His anger-management exercise failed. "Because I owe him that courtesy," he snapped. "And because I asked you to."

"I didn't hear anything resembling a request," I said, tossing my napkin on the table. "It sounded to me like an order. And I'm not going to spend an eternity with a bunch of simpering girl-children and doddering old ladies over weak tea and cucumber sandwiches just to placate your sense of honor. If it means so damned much to you, go yourself."

I pushed back from the table and stomped from the room. I flung myself out the front door and dropped onto the top step of the verandah, my chest heaving in righteous indignation.

I would have sold my soul for a cigarette.

When Erik emerged about half an hour later, he found me wandering the hedge of azaleas which bordered the edge of the lawn where it ran alongside the rutted lane. I'd been pacing the perimeter of the property, front to back, calming my inner self while working up a considerable sweat in the afternoon sun.

"All clear," he called as he approached in that languid stride of his, loose-jointed, hands thrust in the pockets of his Dockers. "The other combatants have retired from the field, so it's safe to come back in."

I smiled and shook my head, more at my own foolishness than anyone else's. "I have no idea why I let him do that to me," I said, tossing
aside the twig I'd been chewing on. As a substitute cigarette it was
pretty useless. "I'm pushing forty years old, and he still has the power to
reduce me to a snotty teenager."

"Genes," he said, and I turned to face him. "Too many of his in you,
would be my guess."

"You could be right. Or maybe too many of Emmaline's. I notice
lately that a lot of our arguments have that *déjà vu* quality, as if I've
heard them before." I shivered in the sunlight. "God, what if I'm turning into my mother? I'll have to shoot myself."

Erik dropped into stride beside me as I set off on another circuit of
the grounds. "I filled the Judge in on what we discovered this morning," he said.

"And?"

"And he pretty much agrees with you, much as it pained him to admit it. He thinks we should concentrate on Judas Island. He says Ron
Singleton would take us over there, but he can't think how we'd go
about pinpointing the exact site of the grave."

"We need Araminda Albright to cough up what she knows," I
said. "I just don't believe Gray Palmer made this fantastic find and kept
it all to himself. Did he strike you as that kind of guy? From what you
remember?"

We wandered down toward the marsh and the short dock which
jutted out into St. Helena Sound. I wondered if the line of green, barely
visible on the horizon off to our left, could be Judas Island. I'd never
paid much attention to it before. I settled onto an old wooden bench,
and Erik dropped down beside me. We contemplated the placid water,
broken occasionally by a diving pelican, each absorbed in our own
thoughts. He took a long time to answer.

"Gray wasn't above a little cheating, if it got him what he wanted.
And he was always eager to impress the girls. I suppose, unless there
was a good, sound reason not to, he wouldn't have been able to resist
bragging to his current woman about his big find. Of course, he could

have become a completely different person by now. But that would be my best guess."

"So why would she be keeping quiet about it? That's the part of this whole scenario I just can't get a handle on. I'm willing to bet just about anything Gray Senior knows nothing about the grave and the bone his son removed from it. Unless he betrays something when we meet him face to face. But Araminda knows. Why hasn't she told him? If that is, in fact, the reason Gray died, why hasn't she told his father?"

As if on cue, both of us slouched down against the back of the bench, our legs stretched out in front of us. I peeled a little more bark off the twig with my thumbnail and stuck it back in my mouth.

"Well, let's run that down," Erik said, clasping his hands behind his head. "What kind of motive could she have?"

"Okay, good plan. Let's see. If Monkey Island was off-limits, as I'm certain it was, she could be afraid of losing her job. Except, judging by her cozy little scene with her employer after his press conference, I don't think there's any danger of that."

"You think she and Gray's dad are . . . you know?"

Even after everything we'd been through together, Erik Whiteside still felt a need to protect my feminine sensibilities. You just had to love the kid.

"What? Shacking up? Sleeping together? You can say it out loud. I think it's a possibility."

"I thought she was Gray's, I mean my Gray's, girl."

"I could have been wrong about that. There really wasn't any evidence at her place they were anything other than roommates. I guess I got the impression they were more than that to each other by her passion about finding out what happened to him. Maybe I misread her. I did feel all that hand-wringing about being afraid she was next was just a trifle overdone."

Erik kicked off his deck shoes and ran his bare feet through the soft grass.

"So you think she's really just worrying about losing her job with this foundation? But that doesn't wash because *she* didn't break the rules, Gray did."

I shot upright on the bench. "But what if she *did*? We only have her word for it Gray was alone when he found the body! What if she was there, too? That would explain everything—her fear, her staying close to his father, all of it."

Erik turned to face me, his brow wrinkled in concentration. "And that's why she called me. She knew Gray had been in touch with me after his first trip to the island, and that he was trying to get me to help him find someone who could identify the body, to date when it might have gone into the ground."

"And after he was killed, she couldn't find it. The bone, I mean. So she jumped to the logical conclusion he had somehow gotten it to you. What she's really been after all along is finding out how much *we* know, not providing us with information herself."

"And that also explains why she hasn't told the old man. She truly doesn't know who to trust."

I saw my own elation at this epiphany mirrored on Erik's face. Both of us were grinning widely. Then another thought sobered me. "But that means I did misread her. She is afraid for her life. And with good cause, it would seem."

"It also means she thinks Gray's father could be involved. We need to get up there," Erik said, and I nodded.

He slipped his shoes back on, and we headed for the house.

The Fort Charles was completely booked, so we settled for a chain motel just a few blocks away in downtown Charleston. The adjoining rooms, while certainly not opulent, were clean and well-appointed and about one-third the price of the landmark hotel where I'd first met Araminda Albright. We settled in quickly since neither of us had brought more than a change of clothes and a few toiletries.

It was close to five by the time we'd checked in, and a quick call verified Gray Palmer had left for the day. But we had an appointment for ten the next morning; and besides, the dead boy's father wasn't our prime objective anyway. I tried Araminda twice from the room phone, but again got no answer. Her lack of response didn't yet have me alarmed, but I had to admit, at least to myself, that her silence was making me a little apprehensive.

I voted for jumping right back in the car and trying to locate her beach cottage while it was still light. I knew I could find my way to the general vicinity, but I was pretty certain I'd need time to locate the precise house.

"Let's grab a bite to eat first," Erik suggested as we stood alongside his black Expedition in the motel parking lot. "If she's working, she won't be home for a while. Besides, it's going to stay light outside for at least another two or three hours. We've got time."

I fussed and argued a little, but finally gave in to the insistent rumblings of my partner's stomach. I tried to sell him on a quick burger, but he was having none of that.

"You must know tons of places around here," he said. "Let's go somewhere really local, somewhere we can walk to."

I figured the sooner I got him fed and watered the sooner we could get underway, so I set off at a brisk pace in the direction of the old slave market a few blocks over. The long brick buildings which today house rows of vendors of every kind of souvenir and trinket imaginable had at one point, a couple of centuries before, served exactly the function its name implied. Despite the throngs of chattering tourists who regularly packed its narrow aisles, I always found the place depressing.

Thankfully its doors were shuttered for the evening, so we took the narrow sidewalk alongside, stepping shortly up to a maitre d's stand set out in front of an old building whose entrance rose a couple of steps up from the street. A pretty blonde armed with menus asked if we were interested in being seated for dinner, and I nodded.

"Follow me," she said, glancing slyly up at Erik from interesting hazel eyes.

I probably only imagined her swaying walk, emphasized by a tight black miniskirt, was being exaggerated for his benefit.

"We'd like the roof," I called as she led us inside, up a steep flight of stairs next to the bar, then out onto a wide seating area to a small table near the balustrade.

"This okay?" she asked Erik.

"Fine," I answered for him, amazed at how invisible I became to young, attractive females whenever I was in his company.

Erik studied the tall menu while I set mine aside without glancing at it. Rob and I had eaten here many times in years past, and I always ordered the same meal. If the wait staff didn't change with every season, someone here would surely have remembered.

"What's good?" he asked over the top of the bill of fare.

"Everything. Anything seafood. I'm having she-crab soup and a Caesar salad."

Thankfully our server turned out to be a male, making the ordering process a little speedier. Erik mimicked my selections, adding a pound of peel-and-eat shrimp and an order of fried oysters.

The view from the second-floor dining area was impeded by roofs and steeples, but still provided a nice panorama of the old city whose charming, other-century ambiance was guarded with fervor by several historical and preservation societies. Very little changed in Charleston, primarily because gaining a variance from the strict codes for restoration on any of the antebellum buildings could take a lifetime.

I wolfed down the creamy chowder and attacked my salad. Across from me, Erik savored every bite of his meal. When I had speared the last bit of romaine out of the large white bowl in front of me, the little patience I had been clinging to evaporated.

"Come on, Erik, it's almost six. We're going to be caught in the rush-hour traffic now, and I'm not really sure how long it'll take to get out to the beach. We need to get moving."

"They have a rush hour? I haven't seen anybody move beyond a slow amble since we got here."

"Cute. In case you hadn't noticed, the whole damn place is full of narrow one-way streets. It doesn't make for a quick exit from the city." I signaled our waiter who wandered over to clear. "I'll take the check, please," I said, and he nodded.

When he returned, I handed over my platinum card then added a tip and scribbled my name on the ticket he brought back. All that, and Erik still picked the pale, translucent shells from his plate of rosy shrimp.

"Okay, okay," he said, cleaning his messy fingers on the wet-wipe provided with his dinner. "You sure do make it difficult to enjoy a meal."

"We're not here to eat," I snapped, more worried about Araminda Albright than I cared to admit. "Let's hit it."

I rose without giving him a chance to reply and led the way back onto the street. The hazy glow of late afternoon bathed everything in a gold mist which made even the most desolate of buildings on the side streets seem to reflect the radiance of this wonderful old city. I fidgeted beside the Expedition while Erik released the locks, then scrambled up into the high passenger seat and buckled up. I could feel his annoyance at me, but I brushed off any guilt I might have felt. With each passing minute, my anxiety grew. If pressed, I couldn't have said why I felt such urgency.

In fairness, most of the evening traffic had dissipated, and it took us only fifteen minutes to gain the turnoff which led to the beaches and the outer islands which guarded Charleston. I tried my best to gauge the distance I had followed Araminda down this narrow road on that Sunday afternoon. Twice I had Erik slow so I could peer out the open window at a home tucked back in among riotous bushes and a single live oak. We were the subject of more than one horn blast and barrage of angry words as the vehicles behind swerved out and around us.

We hit it on the third try.

Erik pulled in beside the bright yellow PT Cruiser. As he cut the engine, he leaned across to lay a hand on my arm. "Before we go bursting in on her, can we at least agree we need to go slowly? She has no real cause to trust us, and there has to be some legitimate reason she didn't level with you before."

I gritted my teeth and told myself not to get upset just because my formerly silent partner had decided to step into a more vocal role in our detecting enterprise. I told myself that, but I didn't listen.

"No, Erik, I think I'll just throw her down on the carpet and beat the truth out of her, okay?"

Wisely, he didn't dignify my outburst with an answer. I resisted the urge to slam the heavy door closed, and he followed me through the loose sand and onto the porch. There were no lights burning, despite the deepening of the twilight out over the ocean a few yards away. I rapped lightly on the silvered wood panel, and a few seconds later knocked again. Erik and I exchanged a look.

"What do you think?" he asked. "Maybe sleeping?"

"Or out walking."

"You'd think she'd leave a lamp on for herself."

"I know." I tried the ancient metal doorknob. It turned in my hand, but the door remained tightly closed. "Always works in the movies," I said and earned a smile.

"What now?" he asked, leaving my side to peer into the long, narrow window beside the door.

"See anything?"

"Nope," he replied. "It's completely dark in there. Want me to try around back?"

I had no idea if there was another entrance to the ramshackle old place, but I shrugged and nodded. "Sure. In the meantime, I'll take a look down the beach, see if I can spot her."

We each set out on our appointed tasks, both of us moving carefully down the front steps. Perhaps it was the silence, broken only by the wash of the waves against the sand and a light breeze ruffling the tops of the pines, but we both seemed to feel the need for stealth. Erik disappeared around the back of the house as I followed the well-used path over the low dune and onto the beach.

At first I thought it might have been a dolphin, although I'd never known one to beach itself, the long body draped in seaweed. As I stepped closer, I realized it wasn't seaweed, but hair.

Long, shining, black hair.

In the last slanting rays of the sun, one red eye gleamed at me from a tangled coil of gold.

CHAPTER
TWENTY-SIX

I DIDN'T HEAR ERIK'S APPROACH IN THE SOFT SAND, AND his startled yell finally forced my frozen legs into motion. I knelt beside the body, unsure of what to do. With trembling hands, I rolled Araminda Albright onto her back and pushed the wild mass of hair away from her face. I gasped at the sight of the purpling bruise that covered one entire cheek.

"Is she dead?" I could barely hear Erik's whispered words above the *shushing* of the waves that lapped at the girl's feet and splashed up over her ankles.

"No," I said, removing my fingers from her neck where the pulse beat steadily. "Help me get her out of the water."

Her clothes were sodden and stuck to her body, and it took both of us to half-carry, half-drag her dead weight back to the higher ground of the dune. "We need to get her warm," I said. The slender body trembled, and a low moan escaped her salt-caked lips. "We have to get in the house. Break a window if you have to, but find a blanket."

"I don't have to break in," Erik said softly, "someone already did that. The back door is standing wide open, and the whole place has been ransacked."

"Are you sure they're gone? Whoever did this?"

"Positive. I checked all the rooms."

"Then you'd better go get that blanket. And call an ambulance."

I gasped as icy fingers suddenly closed around my wrist. Araminda Albright coughed once, and her eyes flicked open. "No," she managed to croak.

"No what?" I asked, my head bent low over hers in an effort to make out her garbled words.

"No doctors," I thought she said.

"You're hurt. You need medical attention." Erik had squatted next to me, his tone calm, but firm. "I'll get on my cell. It's in the car."

"No! Wait!" Strength was fast returning, both to her voice and to her limbs. She struggled to sit up, but I held her down.

"Araminda—Mindy—you have to stay still. You have a head wound. We need to call an ambulance. And the police."

Her gaze kept wandering in and out of focus, and I was certain this was a sign of concussion. But she managed to shake her head with such vehemence I thought she might pass out again. "No! No police!"

I looked at Erik who shrugged and sat back on his haunches. "We can't force her," he said.

"The hell we can't," I began, then caught myself up short, flashing back to my own near brush with death. I saw myself strapped to a gurney, staring at the ruins of my car and one side of my house. Heard Red and the paramedics urging me to get checked out at the hospital and my own stubborn refusal to be driven from my home by the animals who had attacked me. I of all people should have some sympathy for Araminda Albright's position.

"Okay," I said, more calmly, "okay. It's your call." Araminda seemed to relax at my words. I turned to my partner. "Get a couple of blankets. It'll make it easier to carry her."

"I can walk." She pushed my hand away and rolled onto her knees then used my shoulder to lever herself to her feet. She swayed a little, and Erik reached to grasp her around the waist. She struggled in his arms for a moment then let him take her weight as they hobbled back toward the cottage.

———

In her bedroom, I stripped her of the remnants of her shorts and T-shirt, helped her peel off her underwear and bra, and supported her as she stood for what seemed to me like an eternity under the needle spray of the shower. I was pleased to see some pinkness returning to her skin as the hot water cascaded over her slender body and sluiced away bits of kelp and sand from her luxuriant hair. I left her alone long enough to make an ice pack then returned to help her into a fiery red kimono I found amid a pile of clothes someone had dumped from her bureau and closet onto the floor. I tried to insist she should climb into bed, but the haughty Araminda Albright surfaced again, and I was forced to follow her out onto the chintz sofa in the living area where she collapsed onto a pile of cushions with the ice bag held firmly against her badly bruised cheek. I pulled the Southwestern throw from where it lay crumpled under the rocking chair, tucked it around her, and earned a fierce scowl for my trouble.

Erik came in from the kitchen carrying a tray heavy with mugs of steaming tea and a sugar bowl. I accepted mine gratefully, although Araminda made only a token effort at sipping from her cup. I settled myself in the rocker she herself had occupied just a little more than a week before, and Erik pushed aside a few scattered books and papers and sprawled on the floor next to the raised hearth of the fireplace.

"So let's have it," I said when several moments had passed in silence.

"I don't have to tell you anything."

I gave thought to resurrecting my plan to throw her on the floor and pound the truth out of her, but it looked as if someone had beaten me to it. Literally.

"Who did this to you?" Erik spoke softly, but there was steel there as well. I had a feeling his sympathies were being exhausted about as fast as mine. When he got no response, he sat up a little straighter and fixed our patient with an unflinching stare. "You can tell us or you can tell the police. Your decision."

Something in his posture or his tone must have penetrated Araminda's defenses. "I can't tell you! They'll come back!"

"What makes you say that?"

Erik continued to speak in a firm, but soothing voice. He seemed to

have her attention, and perhaps her confidence, so I sat back in the
rocker and let him take the lead.

"They tried to kill me! I want them to think I'm dead. If they find
out I'm not, they'll come back and finish the job."

"Who?"

That seemed to make one question too many. Araminda turned her
head away, cushioning her cheek against the melting ice pack. Erik
looked at me and nodded as if tossing the ball into my court.

"How did you escape?" I asked. "What happened, exactly?"

Strangely, this was apparently firmer ground. "They just burst
through the back door. Around six o'clock tonight. Two of them. They
wanted . . . something. They never said what, just kept insisting I knew
what they were after. But I didn't! I told them! But they wouldn't believe
me. I tried to run, but the big one grabbed me and hit me with some sort
of . . . I don't know. It looked like a sock filled with something heavy. It
didn't knock me out, but I pretended it did. I thought if . . . I figured if
I just played dead, they'd find what they were looking for and go away."

The monotone in which this horrible tale was delivered made me
question again whether Araminda might have a serious head injury.

"Then how did you end up . . . ?" I began.

"When they went into my bedroom, I jumped up and ran outside
and into the water. They thought I was out cold, and I took them by
surprise. I swam straight out from the shore, and I could hear them
cursing and trying to start the boat. I'm a strong swimmer, and I can
hold my breath for a long time. I'd stay under until I couldn't take another second, then surface to grab a breath. They looked for me for a
long time."

She paused in her tale of playing cat-and-mouse with a speedboat
and took a sip of tea from her mug. I wondered if, like me, she was
thinking of Gray and his poor face, mutilated by the propeller of his
own boat.

"Then what?" I prodded her.

"Finally I surfaced once more and realized the boat was moving
away. By then I was really dizzy, but I kept swimming underwater, coming back up until I couldn't see them anymore. Then I struck out toward

shore. But I ran out of energy. In the end I just floated on my back, hoping the tide would take me in. I don't remember landing, but I must have been tossed far enough up on the beach to keep me from getting pulled back in. That's all I can remember."

"Do you think these are the same people who killed Gray?" I asked. She took a long time to answer. "Yes," she murmured into the back of the sofa.

"And it's because you were with him, weren't you? You saw the skeleton as well."

The fight went out of her then, and she nodded once before turning her back to us.

I motioned for Erik to follow, and we stepped out onto the front porch. The moon had risen, casting a shimmering glow across the gently rolling ocean.

"She needs to see a doctor," I said, wrapping my arms around one of the thick balusters which supported the roof of the verandah and laying my cheek against the roughness of its peeling paint.

"And the cops." Erik sat on the top step and let his hands dangle between his knees. "Jesus, Bay, that's an incredible story. It's a miracle she survived." When I didn't answer immediately, he said, "Isn't it?"

"I'm not sure I'm buying it."

"What? You think she's making it up?"

"*Sshh!* Keep your voice down," I whispered.

"She sure as hell didn't imagine that bruise on the side of her face. And we found her down there by the water, just like she said."

I knew it would take more than I had to offer to convince even myself of my suspicions, but something about the story didn't scan for me. I had no idea what it was exactly. Maybe too pat, too rehearsed. Only a couple of pauses for breath, no shudders of remembered fear. I'd been in her situation before. I had to admit I'd been pretty calm in the thick of things, some inner strength I never knew I had rising to take control of my brain and my actions. But when it was over . . .

And maybe that wasn't fair, I told myself, swinging away from the baluster to join Erik on the top step. Mindy Albright wasn't me. Wasn't I. Whatever.

"I could be full of it, Erik," I said. "Who knows? Maybe after she
has a chance to sleep and heal a little we'll be able to get more out of
her." I sighed and ran a hand through the tangled mess of my hair, beginning to curl around my face in the dampness of the night air. "What
are we going to do with her in the meantime?"

"What do you mean?"

"We can't leave her here alone! And I don't think it's a good plan for
any of us to stick around. She could be right. Her pals could come calling again."

"They'd have no reason, would they? If they think she's dead?"

"Unless they're watching the house. Even from pretty far out in a
boat, they could see the lights on here." I rose and dusted off the seat of
my pants. "And she says they didn't tell her what it was they were looking for. I'm not buying that. You know as well as I do the only thing
they could have been after, and so does she."

"The bone," he said.

"And, if they're convinced she doesn't have it, and they spot us
here, where do you think they'll look next?"

I had a difficult time convincing Araminda Albright her safest course
was to come with us. In the end I gave up arguing with her about getting dressed. We wrapped her in the Indian throw, and Erik wrestled
her out to his car while I gathered up what necessities I could find, including her purse and keys, and tossed it all in a grocery bag. In ten
minutes we were back on the road to Charleston.

"What about my car?" Mindy asked as we sped off into the night.

"It's locked. Besides, you won't be going anywhere for a while without us."

I'd given thought to driving her Cruiser into town myself, but we
decided it was too distinctive. Even in the crowded parking lot of the
motel, anyone familiar with Mindy and her bright yellow wagon
would have no trouble finding it. And her. Besides, if we left everything just as we had found it, they might just be convinced they'd
succeeded in killing her. Moving the car would be a sure sign they

needed to give it another try. If she was telling the truth. If, if, if . . .

We bundled her inside with a minimum of fuss and settled her in one of the two double beds in my room. While I spread her meager toiletries on the shelf in the bathroom, Erik made a run to the nearby convenience store for aspirin and ice packs. He returned laden with those as well as sodas, an assortment of chips, and a bag of apples.

Araminda had dozed during the short trip to the motel and now seemed restored, so it seemed like a good time to push her for more answers. I perched on the end of the bed in a pose I hoped would remind her of middle-school sleepovers where the girls stay up all night and reveal their darkest secrets while sipping Coca-Colas and stuffing themselves with junk food. The ugly bruise darkening on her face reminded me this game was a lot more serious.

"Tell me about how you and Gray found the grave," I began, sliding off my shoes and tucking my feet up under me.

Erik had tactfully retreated to his own room, but I noticed he'd left the connecting door open.

I confronted Araminda's stony silence and pulled a handful of corn chips out of the bag. I extended the package to her, but she shook her head. I washed the chips down with a swig of soda and pressed ahead.

"Okay, fine. I'll tell you what I think happened. Feel free to jump in and correct any errors." Again I met the stubborn set of her mouth which remained firmly shut. "In your investigation on behalf of the foundation you encountered Judas Island, or Monkey Island as the locals have dubbed it. I'm guessing you were warned off it by Gray's father because it's government property. Even without that, it could have taken you only about two minutes to realize from all the signs the place was off-limits. But from what I know of your partner, both those things probably only served to egg him on."

The thin smile softened Mindy's solemn face. "Gray hated to be told no."

I nodded. "You probably argued against it, because you seem like a nice, law-abiding kind of girl—" I broke off at her ladylike snort of derision. "Okay," I said, "you could be right. At any rate, the challenge was just too much for Gray to resist."

I paused, hoping she'd pick up the tale. Again I extended the chips, and this time she reached into the bag. Not wanting to break the tenuous truce, I held my silence. Araminda Albright licked salt from her fingers and leaned back into the pillows bunched against the headboard.

"We hung around until just before dusk, checking out some of the other little islets in the area." Her voice sounded small, almost childlike in the chill air of the impersonal motel room. "I was tired and hungry, and I wanted to go home, but Gray was determined to go snooping around Judas. He'd located this little creek on the back side and decided we could land there, poke around some, and be out before dark, before anyone knew we'd been there. Could I have a drink?"

I jumped at the unexpected change of subject. "Certainly. Glass? Ice?" I popped the top on a can of soda.

"No thanks. This is fine." She took it from me and swallowed delicately before continuing. "Gray hauled out the metal detector and all the other equipment, and we followed this narrow path toward the interior." She paused to sip again from the can. "Spooky. The animals . . . Anyway, we stopped at this clearing because he thought the ground didn't look natural. He had a real talent for that, you know. An instinct or something. And then the detector indicated metal, and he got excited, so we started digging . . ."

When she seemed hesitant to continue, I prompted, "So you found a skeleton. What on earth made Gray take the bone away? I know you said the body had remnants of clothing intact, and of course there's the wristwatch. Probably what set off the detector. But what so intrigued him he would disturb the remains?"

I felt as if she wanted to tell me, as if she needed to be relieved of the knowledge of whatever horror she'd witnessed on Monkey Island. "Come on, Mindy. One way or the other we're going to find out. We have a meeting with Gray's father tomorrow. Don't you think he has a right to know why his son died?"

At the mention of Gray Palmer, Senior, her face crumpled, and I watched tears well up and spill over onto her bruised cheek.

"Mindy? What is it?"

Her whole body began to tremble. She reached out a hand, and I grasped it tightly.

"Tell me," I said.

And she did.

CHAPTER
TWENTY-SEVEN

I WAITED UNTIL AN HOUR AFTER I HEARD ERIK SWITCH off ESPN and saw the thin band of light disappear from the crack in the connecting door we'd decided to leave partially open. In the bed beside me, Araminda Albright slept quietly, her injured cheek cradled in her cupped hand. I flung back the sheet and slipped on my sneakers, then eased into the adjoining room. As I'd hoped, Erik had left his keys, along with his wallet and the change from his pocket, lying in plain view on the low bureau. I scooped up the keys, leaving a brief note to explain my absence, then tiptoed back into my own room and out into the dark.

The dashboard clock glowed 3:11 as I cranked over the Expedition's powerful engine. Its roar sounded like a jet landing in the hushed stillness of the motel parking lot. Once on the street, I was surprised by the number of vehicles cruising along with me at this ungodly hour. I wondered if any of my fellow travelers were on missions as clandestine as mine.

We whizzed through traffic signals blinking yellow in the predawn blackness, and in less than half an hour I pulled up into the sand next to Mindy Albright's darkened cottage. I sat for a long time, my eyes focused on the shadows cast by the bushes hugging the porch and the sides of the house, my ears straining through the open car window for any sign I was not alone. The motor ticked loudly as it cooled in the light breeze off the ocean.

Satisfied as I could be, I pulled Mindy's house keys from the pocket of my jacket. After her revelations, I'd had no compunction about lifting them from her purse as soon as she'd finally dropped off to sleep. On the other hand, I felt bad about deceiving Erik, but I knew what his reaction would be to my plan. As I clicked on the pocket flashlight I'd also found in Mindy's cluttered handbag, I paused to consider again the irony of my having somehow become the risk-taker in this venture. Older, supposedly wiser, and conservative both by nature and profession, I had nonetheless slipped easily into the role. Maybe Bay the Wonder Woman had been lurking all along under the placid façade of Lydia Baynard Simpson Tanner, girl accountant. I chuckled to myself as I mounted the steps, crossed the porch, and inserted the worn key into the lock. Somehow I couldn't quite picture myself in tights and bullet-deflecting bracelets, though God knew the latter would have come in handy a couple of times in the past year.

The door opened silently, and I slipped inside. I flicked off the flashlight and let my eyes become accustomed to the dim interior. We had done nothing in the way of righting overturned chairs or cleaning up the mess left by the invaders. If they came back, I wanted them to see things exactly as they'd left them. As I picked my way gingerly through the debris, I hoped Araminda wouldn't be too crushed when she realized how much of her parents' wonderful collection had been damaged or destroyed.

I used brief bursts from the flashlight to guide me to the bookcases, although the pearly rose of dawn had already begun to push against the night-dark still hovering over the ocean. I made a quick check of the few books the would-be thieves had tossed onto the floor, but the one I sought wasn't among them. If they had been after the bone, as we suspected, they would have been looking for a safe or some other hidey-hole concealed by the thick volumes.

But Gray Palmer had been smarter than that. He'd gotten the bone out of his possession and in such a way it would have taken a lot of manpower and luck to track it down. Next he'd made certain someone would be able to relocate his grisly find in case anything happened to him. And he'd done it in such a way Araminda Albright could have truthfully sworn not to know the details, although I had every confidence she would have eventually figured out the cryptic clue on her own.

I knew I'd passed over the worn spine of the book I sought during my perusal of Mindy's library that Sunday afternoon more than a week ago. Where exactly I couldn't be certain, but I knew I'd seen it. I felt along each row, stopping to flash the light on anything that felt wide enough. My frustration level grew as I worked my way around the room, only checking those shelves at or near my eye level. I didn't remember having done any reaching up or bending down during my previous snooping.

I finally located it to the right of the fireplace, a massive volume which required both hands to lift it from its shelf. I tucked the flashlight in my pocket and carried the book to the chintz-covered sofa. I ran my hand along the top edge, feeling for any irregularity that might indicate something had been slipped inside. When that failed, I riffled the pages, but again found nothing.

For a moment I wavered. I'd been so sure I had the hiding place figured out. When Mindy had finished pouring out her bizarre story, I'd latched onto the one verifiable piece of information she'd given me. Before venturing out on his ill-fated return trip to Judas Island, Gray had left her a strange message: a biblical citation he'd told her to memorize and then destroy.

I'd immediately snatched up the nearly pristine Gideon Bible from the drawer in the motel nightstand and verified my recollection of Genesis 2:23 which detailed the creation of Eve from Adam's rib. I wondered if the Judge could be badgered into giving me a couple of points since I'd remembered it exactly: "Bone of my bones, and flesh of my flesh . . ."

The solution had seemed so clear to me in that moment I'd dashed off in the middle of the night, returning to a scene of recent violence with little fear of danger. The pressure of the Glock in the right-hand pocket of my jacket gave me some comfort, but if I'd had any sense at all I would have taken the damned book with me back to the motel. I decided to give myself five more minutes before admitting defeat.

I risked clicking on the flashlight again and this time ran my finger down the index. Gray Palmer was an intelligent man. If he'd used this book as his hiding place, he wouldn't have made it easy for potential searchers like those who had attacked Mindy. My finger seemed to stop of its own accord, although my eyes must have registered the faint pencil mark, nearly invisible in the soft circle of light. I flipped to page 612, and there it was: a tiny scrap of paper with one set of coordinates— longitude and latitude in degrees, minutes, and seconds—clearly marking the location of the mysterious grave on Judas Island.

It had been tucked into the section on the human femur in an outdated copy of the bible of both medicine and archaeology, *Gray's Anatomy*.

Not only was he smart, but the boy definitely had a sense of humor. I wished I could have known him.

"I don't know whether to congratulate you or throttle you."

"I wouldn't try the latter, my friend. I'm armed." I tried to keep it light as I perched on the edge of the desk chair in Erik's room. I'd sneaked back in just before five and gone immediately to waken him. Perhaps it was just a bit of showing off, but I couldn't even contemplate keeping the news to myself until he had come to on his own.

I'd crept back to my own room while he pulled on a pair of pants. I slipped Mindy's keys and flashlight back into her purse, relieved to see the gentle rise and fall of her chest beneath the sheet. By the time I'd splashed some cold water on my face, he had coffee going in the miniature two-cup pot thoughtfully provided by the motel. I brought a warm can of Diet Coke along with the remains of the bag of corn chips. And Gray Palmer's ingeniously hidden coordinates.

"So is that what the creeps who beat up Mindy were looking for?" Erik asked as I settled onto the foot of his rumpled bed and popped the top on the soda. He poured coffee into a Styrofoam cup and took the desk chair.

"I don't think so. According to Mindy, they really didn't know *what* they were looking for. It was actually our fault she got beaten up. At least that's my working theory at the moment."

"How do you figure that?"

"We got spotted yesterday morning, if you recall. The way I see it, those guys in the boat reported it to someone. I don't think it can be a coincidence they left her alone for more than a week after they killed Gray then all of a sudden decided to go after her only a few hours after we stupidly let them know we had an interest in the island."

I gave him the chance to remind me it had been *my* stupidity, my eagerness to prove myself right that had put us on the *Wanderer* off Judas Island on Monday morning. Ever the gentleman, Erik let the opportunity pass.

Instead he asked, "You think they followed us up here? That they knew about our trying to get in touch with her?" He rubbed his hand across his face in a gesture which told me he'd had way too little sleep. Maybe the coffee would help. As if reading my mind, he crossed the room to refill his cup and start another pot going.

"No, I can't see that unless there are a whole lot more of them than we know about. Mindy said they came by boat. From her description they sound like the same two who checked us out yesterday."

"So you're saying our snooping around Monkey Island set off some sort of alarm bells with whoever is behind all this."

"Exactly. Somebody put two and two together and got five. They figured Mindy must have told me something which sent us to that specific spot. How else could we have latched on to it? So they sent their goons to beat it out of her and ransack her place. They really didn't know what they were looking for. I think they were counting on making her give it up if they couldn't find it on their own."

I swigged down more warm Coke, waiting for my partner to make the next logical leap of deduction. He took a couple of detours, but in the end he didn't disappoint.

"So you went out there, knowing full well they could come back at any minute to continue their search."

"Not likely. They didn't know what they were looking for. Without Araminda, they didn't have much hope. I think they just busted up her place to scare her into talking."

Again I waited. I wanted him to reach the same conclusion without any prompting from me. He blew across the steaming cup and stared at the sliver of light seeping through a crack in the dark blue drapes. When he finally spoke, his words could have come straight from my own lips.

"Then as soon as they figure out who and where we are, we're next up on the list."

The motel provided a continental breakfast, served in a small room just off the lobby. Erik and I loaded up with croissants, bagels, fruit, and juice and carried it all back upstairs. I could hear the shower running next door when we stepped back into Erik's room and spread the goodies out on his dresser. I moved through the connecting door and stuck my head in the bathroom.

"Breakfast is served," I called into the cloud of steam drifting out of the enclosed tub area, but got no response.

I shrugged and pulled the door closed behind me and filled a paper plate with a warm bagel which I slathered with cream cheese squeezed from a small packet. I peeled a banana and lifted the lid from a container of orange juice. Settled at the desk, I talked around mouthfuls to answer Erik's questions.

"What exactly did she tell you last night?" he asked when he'd perched on the end of the bed with his own laden plate.

"I think it would be better if you heard it directly from her," I said. "Some of it sounds really far-fetched. I think she and Gray may have jumped to a whole lot of conclusions based on pretty flimsy evidence. Their scenario certainly explains some of what's been going on, but there's one big stumbling block I just can't get past."

"What's that?"

"Wait until you hear her story. I don't want to influence your judgment."

He shrugged, and I could tell he wasn't happy about my reticence, but I really believed he should get the unfiltered version. I licked cream cheese from my fingers and wiped them on the paper napkins we'd brought up with us. Erik flipped on the television, and we watched the latest from the turmoil in the Middle East. Engrossed in the live broadcast from reporters in the field, it was some time before it dawned on me Araminda Albright had not yet appeared.

I eased open the connecting door. The sounds from the shower had not abated. I stepped into the room and did a quick sweep before dashing back to the bathroom and flinging open the sliding door on the tub.

"All her things are gone," I reported to Erik after my shout of frustration brought him running next door.

"What the hell is the matter with her?"

I knew he didn't expect an answer to the rhetorical question, and I didn't offer one. "Okay, let's think this out. Her car's out at the house, so she's either walking or she called a cab."

"Or a friend," Erik offered.

"Good point." I picked up the phone and dialed the front desk. The clerk on duty sounded way too chirpy for a little after seven o'clock in the morning. "Hi," I said, "this is Mrs. Tanner in 206. Did my friend get her cab okay?"

"I'm sorry?"

"My friend. Tall, beautiful, long black hair? She called a cab a while ago, and I wondered if she got picked up okay. I was down at breakfast when she left."

If the pleasant young man on the other end of the phone found my request strange, he had been too well trained to let it show. "Why, yes, ma'am, she did. About fifteen minutes ago."

I wanted to ask if the helpful desk clerk knew which way she'd headed, but I thought that might be pushing his cooperation just a bit too far. "Thanks," I said and hung up.

"Where could she have gone?" Erik ran a hand through his tousled hair.

"I don't think we'll be able to find that out," I said, flopping myself down on the bed again. "I know the cops can get info from cab companies about where they took their fares, but there's no way anyone's going to share that with us."

"You're probably right. Do you think she went back to her house?"

"Maybe. If she did, I'd bet she's only there long enough to throw some things in a bag and hit the road. The girl is seriously frightened."

"So you've given up on your idea her story about the break-in was a fabrication?"

"Pretty much. From what she told me last night, she probably has reason to be afraid, if everything she and Gray suspected is true."

"You ready to share the fruits of last night's little tête-à-tête with me?" he asked.

"Absolutely. Let's get packed up first. I need to make a couple of calls, then we can get out of here and find someplace to plan our strategy. I don't think we should stay in one place too long, and we need to have it together before we meet with Gray, Senior."

"Why? What's he got to do with last night?"

I paused in the doorway before I spoke. "Araminda Albright thinks he might be responsible for his son's death."

CHAPTER
TWENTY-EIGHT

WE TOOK A COUPLE OF WRONG TURNS, PRIMARILY because it had been a number of years since I'd had any reason to visit the Port of Charleston. Rob and I had always intended to check out the new aquarium and the nearby IMAX theater, but our weekends always seemed to have been spent at the beach house on Hilton Head rather than exploring the attractions of the town in which we lived the rest of the week.

As we approached the actual harbor, Erik let out a low whistle. "Wow! Look at the size of those cranes!"

Off-loaded containers were stacked all along the wide concrete dock near the towering blue-and-white behemoths rising almost a hundred feet in the clear morning air. Palmer Shipping's vessels were container ships, the goods they carried already packed into the large metal boxes which could be hooked up to tractor-trailer rigs and sent on the way to their ultimate destinations without further handling.

"Look there," I said, pointing to one of the giant ships lumbering its way from the ocean up the sparkling Cooper River and on to a terminal farther up the waterway. Erik slowed the car, and we watched the huge yet graceful vessel glide toward the massive bridge which connected the peninsula that was Charleston to the mainland. It was a route I generally refused to take, my obsessive fear of bridges with any kind of superstructure making my driving across it completely impossible. In fact, even as a mere passenger, I had to keep my eyes closed until the wheels of the car had rolled onto solid ground once again.

"That's it," I said, indicating a tall, modern building sitting incongruously next to the brick debarkation terminal for the boats which carried tourists out to Fort Sumter. Every school child knew cannonballs crashing into the walls of the federal garrison on that tiny island had been the flashpoint for the start of our bloody Civil War.

Erik, however, found the present-day wonders more engrossing. "Think what it must be like driving one of those things," he said. His eyes were still fixed on the giant container ship moving past the decommissioned World War II aircraft carrier *Yorktown* moored just across the way at Patriots Point, a poignant reminder of yet another conflict. Despite its beauty and serenity, Charleston seemed to be steeped in monuments to war.

He pulled into the parking lot in front of the office building and cut the engine.

"The captain doesn't actually get to 'drive' the ship in here," I said as we both climbed down from the Expedition.

"What do you mean?" Erik shaded his eyes against the brilliant glare of sun on water.

"Rob had a good friend who's a harbor pilot. They take a small boat out to those big boys and guide them in."

"Sounds like a cool job."

"It takes a long time to get certified, around six years I think, at least until you can work on something that size. They have to bring in over fifteen hundred ships or some incredible number before they're considered qualified."

We fell silent then, neither of us making a move toward the building which housed Gray Palmer's office. I knew Erik was dreading this encounter as much as I was.

I had made my phone calls—one fruitful, one not—and we'd checked out of the motel around seven thirty. I directed Erik to a small coffee shop in the heart of the historic district down near the Battery and its stately antebellum mansions facing the water. Amazingly most of these pastel-colored monuments to a long-dead Southern aristocracy showed no scars from the pounding they'd taken during Hurricane Hugo.

The narrow café was nearly deserted, but we asked for the last booth in the back just to be safe. Once the waitress had deposited our respective cups of tea and coffee in front of us, I leaned in and began my story.

Or rather Araminda Albright's story, for I related it as best I could without embellishment or comment. Erik, sensing the importance of letting me get it out, refrained from interruptions. When I finally sat back, he shook his head as if to clear it.

"That's just nuts," was his initial assessment, and I had to nod.

It had been my first reaction as well. Still, the girl and Gray had been a lot more intimately involved in the situation than either of us. And we had the added disadvantage of not knowing all the players. But that was about to change. We had had less than two hours at that point before we would be confronted with the supposedly grieving father, and Araminda's revelations had tossed all our carefully planned strategies into the toilet.

"She seriously believes Gray Palmer had his own son murdered?"

I shushed him with a wave of my hand. "You have to admit there's a certain logic. If young Gray had become convinced his father was involved in smuggling and had stumbled across the debarkation point on Judas Island, his father might have panicked. Or maybe his associates took it into their own heads the kid was a danger to the operation. It's possible Gray, Senior, had nothing to do with it."

"I can't believe a father could order a hit on his own kid. I know the damned world has gone crazy lately, but I'm just not prepared to believe that until there's irrefutable proof."

"I'm inclined to agree. But Mindy has herself convinced that's what happened. Her Gray's theory was that this foundation thing was just a cover to have them scout out possible new locations for the drop sites. A lot of those little islands we sailed past yesterday morning used to be havens for pirates and slavers back in the old days. When the State of South Carolina bought Judas Island, there was all kind of talk about developing the place. They figured GS needed to find another spot before that happened."

"But why not pick someplace completely deserted? Why Monkey Island in the first place?"

"Maybe that was the point. Someone goes over there every day to feed the macaques. And they must have to mount some kind of expedition to round up the ones they've sold. It wouldn't be as noticeable for boats to be hanging around that area as it would for the totally uninhabited ones. The fact the place is off-limits to the general public would also prevent their being surprised in the act, so to speak, by some fisherman or tourist."

"I suppose that makes sense. What is he supposedly smuggling? I assume we're talking drugs."

"No. She told me Gray thought it might be people."

"People?" Again I had to quiet Erik down. The waitress ambled by and offered him a refill. When she'd moved off, he said, "You mean like illegal aliens? Foreigners? Terrorists? And the grave they found was supposed to be one of these guys who died or got killed in the process?"

"God, Erik, I don't know, and neither did she. I never said this made a whole lot of sense. I just believe they took a bunch of circumstances and came to a set of conclusions that fit the evidence they thought they'd gathered. If it weren't so tragic, this entire thing could be classified as a comedy of errors."

"Okay, wait." His forehead furrowed in concentration. "Here's what shoots that whole idea out of the water. Doctor Douglass told us the bone had been in the ground for forty or fifty years, so there's no way it could have been some victim of this supposed smuggling operation."

"Exactly my point this morning when I told you there was one big stumbling block in their whole scenario. But Gray didn't know that. He was dead before you ever got the bone in the mail."

"But wouldn't he have figured it out? The same way Dr. Douglass did? He had the background."

"I don't think so. As I said before, he might have tagged the gender and race, but he didn't have any equipment for the other tests."

It felt as if the temperature had dropped ten degrees in the cozy restaurant as we both contemplated the validity of my statement. We'd fallen silent then. I had sipped my cold tea while Erik tapped his spoon against the side of his cup. When I couldn't stand the rhythmic banging any longer, I reached across to still his hand with my own.

"I still won't believe Gray Senior had anything to do with killing his own son," he said for what must have been the third or fourth time. "What reason did Mindy have for buying into something so disgusting?"

This had been another revelation I'd had trouble swallowing, but again I had no way to dispute their conclusions. "Apparently Gray blames his father for his mother's death. I suppose that's when he first began hating him, and it doesn't appear to have abated over the intervening years."

When Mindy had floated this explanation for Gray's hatred of his father, my mind flashed back to my Internet research on the elder Palmer and the lack of any mention of his late wife's cause of death. "According to Mindy," I went on, "Gray's mother committed suicide. He blames his father. She seems to think it isn't much of a leap from driving someone to kill herself and being capable of ordering the murder of your own child."

"God," was Erik's only reaction.

"Did he ever mention any of this to you? About his father, I mean?"

"No. All he ever said was his old man was a rich bastard and his mother was dead."

"Anything about a sister? The article I read mentioned she lived in California."

Erik shook his head. "Not that I can remember. Is it important?"

"Probably not. It's just another bit of confusion. I swear I don't know what to believe."

I had checked my watch then and realized we had only a short time before our appointment with this man whose son's friend was convinced he was a smuggler and a murderer.

"Listen," I had said, leaning in toward Erik again, "this is what I think we have to do . . ."

I realized with a start I had been standing frozen next to the front fender of the Expedition, mentally rehashing earlier conversations, for quite some time. I glanced across the expanse of gleaming black hood to find Erik studying my face.

"Cold feet?" he asked, and I shook my head.

"Just gathering my thoughts. Ready?"

In answer he pushed himself away from the car and walked resolutely toward the building.

Our plan, devised hurriedly in the short time we had, was basically to operate without a plan. We could hardly charge into Gray Palmer, Senior's office and accuse him of having ordered a hit on his own son. Conversely, we certainly couldn't spill our guts to him about everything we had actually learned in the brief course of our investigation. We decided to play it by ear, to give him the report on the reward seekers, trying our best to ignore Araminda Albright's contention that the posting of the offer and his subsequent hiring of our neophyte firm to follow up had simply been a smoke screen to divert attention from himself and his illegal activities. While I still couldn't bring myself to believe her wild story completely, parts of it had enough ring of truth to make me tread cautiously. The opening lines of our script had been planned, but from there on we were pretty much going to have to wing it.

The reception area had the expected nautical theme, with framed color photographs of what I assumed were the ships of the line taking up one entire wall of the spacious room. To the left, a small antique desk, empty at the moment of our entrance, was shaded by several tall tropical plants in large clay pots. The ubiquitous computer screen sat in a matching hutch over a beautifully carved cherry credenza, and the multiline telephone *chirruped* softly as we stood waiting on a muted red carpet which looked to be either a genuine Persian or an excellent reproduction. The phone call must have been automatically transferred over to voice mail because the measured ringing abruptly stopped.

I was studying a chart of the local waters hanging just in front of us when the door next to it slid open. A compact woman who looked to be about my age pulled it closed behind her and moved around behind the desk.

"I'm so sorry to keep you waiting," she said in a voice mellow with the honey of the South. "You must be Mrs. Tanner and Mr. Whiteside. I'm Linda Marean, Mr. Palmer's secretary."

Ah, I thought, *the efficient one who faxed me the list of names.* In her tailored navy blue suit and prim white blouse, she appeared perfectly cast for the role.

"Nice to meet you," I said.

"Won't you have a seat? Mr. Palmer is running a little late this morning, but I'm sure he'll be with you very shortly."

"Thanks."

We sank down into matching overstuffed chairs upholstered in dark blue. Linda Marean pulled a slim file from a drawer next to her and swiveled her chair around to face the computer. Erik reached for the current copy of *Time* from the neat stack of magazines on the low table beside him while I fidgeted.

I had to admit I was having serious doubts. Not just about trying to bluff our way through a meeting with a man we seriously considered capable of causing his own son's death, but about the whole idea of being an investigator. Who did we think we were? A kid who knew his way around computers and a widowed accountant. What business did we have snooping into things that might have gotten people killed? I had to admit I loved the idea of solving the puzzle, but this wasn't some mystery novel or made-for-TV movie. If any part of Araminda Albright's story came even close to the truth, our butts should be planted in chairs across from the nearest police detective, not parked primly outside the office of a man who could be responsible for smuggling illegal aliens into the country and God knew what else.

I had almost made the decision to offer Ms. Marean some generic excuse, grab Erik, and bolt when the door to the inner office suddenly banged open. It bounced off the wall and rattled the framed photographs of the Palmer Line's ships. I jumped to my feet as if I'd been yanked from the chair.

The man who nearly bowled me over was in full military uniform, his peaked cap tucked under his arm. Behind him, framed in the doorway to the office, a figure I recognized from his television appearance as Gray Palmer, Senior, carried a look I couldn't quite identify. Something between anger and fear, I decided. His skin had that blotchy red color you associate with high blood pressure. Or someone about to have a heart attack.

"Harlan, wait!" he called to the stiff, retreating back.

Erik and I might have been invisible for all the attention anyone paid to us.

"Mr. Palmer . . ." Ms. Marean began, but she, too, was ignored.

"Pardon me," the military man said as he brushed by me, but he didn't slow his determined stride. I had a brief glimpse of blazing blue eyes under closely cropped gray hair before he pushed through the outer door and disappeared.

Employer and secretary exchanged a look I couldn't quite interpret before Palmer closed the door, much more gently than his visitor had opened it. He hadn't once acknowledged our presence. I collapsed back into the chair like a deflated balloon.

"I'm so sorry." Linda Marean had moved from behind her desk and stood guard before the entrance to Gray Palmer's office. "The Colonel just popped in for a minute. They're old friends, and . . ." Her explanation was cut short by the buzzing of the intercom. "Excuse me," she murmured and scurried back to her station.

I watched her listen and nod, then pull a pad of paper toward her and begin scribbling hurriedly. Once or twice she tried to interrupt, but her employer apparently cut her off in midsentence.

"What was that all about?" Erik whispered, his head bent close to mine.

Across the room I saw Palmer's secretary hang up the phone and turn back to the computer. In a few moments, the printer whirred into life.

"Beats me," I replied, but my brain was spinning.

What possible connection could there be between Gray Palmer and Colonel Harlan Fleming? I had no doubt this was the identity of the man who'd barely missed running me down, even though I'd never laid eyes on him before. The combination of his rank and his unusual first name made the deduction less than brilliant. But what was the father of the smug Amy, Chris Brandon's fiancée, doing here? Coincidence or . . . ?

I didn't have time to finish the thought.

"Mrs. Tanner?" Linda Marean beckoned. I rose to stand in front of her desk. "I'm so sorry, but Mr. Palmer is unable to keep his appointment with you. An emergency with one of the ships. I'm sure you understand."

I glanced over my shoulder at Erik, who had also risen from his comfortable chair to join me.

"That's okay. We'll wait," I said. Some part of my subconscious had apparently decided to ignore all my good intentions of just a few minutes before.

"I'm sorry, but that won't be possible."

Linda Marean drew herself up and took my stare without flinching. She couldn't begin to match me in height, but I had a feeling we'd rank dead even on the stubborn scale. The moment of silent confrontation held until Erik cleared his throat.

"Could we reschedule, ma'am? Perhaps for later in the day? Or maybe tomorrow?"

Erik's soft voice and calm demeanor melted some of the tension. The line of her shoulders eased, and her smile made it to just short of pleasant. "I don't think so. Mr. Palmer asked me to give you this." She thrust a sealed white envelope into my hand. "I apologize as well for any inconvenience. Please have a safe trip home."

With that Linda Marean took her seat, deliberately turned her back, and resumed her rhythmic attack on the keyboard.

Erik's face mirrored my own confusion, but there seemed little we could do outside of physically storming Gray Palmer's office. I shrugged, and he turned to follow me out of the building and into a glaring sun.

"Don't even ask," I said, holding up a hand to forestall the questions ready to burst from my young partner. "I don't have a clue what's going on. Maybe this will prove enlightening."

I pried up a corner of the envelope flap and ripped it open. The single sheet of paper was folded in thirds as proper correspondence etiquette required. The message was terse and unequivocal. I summarized for Erik as I read.

"He's firing us again. He says the autopsy report indicates young Gray had alcohol in his system, so Daddy thinks he's been wrong all along. Looks like it was just a stupid accident. 'Thank you for . . .' blah, blah, blah. He hopes we haven't been *terribly* inconvenienced. Yeah, right."

I shook my head in disbelief at the effrontery of the man. " 'The attached should cover your time and expenses. If not, please submit an invoice for any balance, and I will be happy to . . .' This guy sure has balls."

Erik winced at the crudity, then gasped as I turned the paper around for him to see.

The company check neatly stapled to the bottom of the letter was made out to Simpson & Tanner in the amount of ten thousand dollars.

CHAPTER
TWENTY-NINE

E HELD OUR COUNCIL OF WAR OVER CHEESEBURGERS and fries in a McDonald's on the way out of Charleston. I'd deliberately chosen a table next to the brightly colored playground equipment where any conversation we didn't want overheard would be drowned out by the squeals of half a dozen kids clambering over slides and swings.

We had taken a detour after getting bounced out of Gray Palmer's office, but that too proved fruitless. Araminda Albright's house stood empty, the bright yellow splash of her PT Cruiser gone from the sandy yard. The place was locked up tight, so we'd walked the perimeter, peering into cracks in the blinds and drapes, able to see enough to convince us she'd probably thrown some necessities together and bolted. Neither of us had the foggiest idea where she might have flown to, no clue as to what friends or relatives she might have sought refuge with. Although I knew she had all my contact numbers, I had added Erik's cell phone to the list and slid the piece of paper under the crack beneath the front door.

"So, back to square one," Erik said, wiping mustard from the corner of his mouth.

"Not exactly. We know a lot of things we didn't know yesterday. The trouble is, I'm damned if I can figure out exactly what to do with them."

"But I'm sure you're working on it. Refill?" he asked, rising from the molded plastic chair affixed to the table. At my nod, he carried our cups to the row of self-serve drink dispensers.

Despite my earlier misgivings, I wasn't yet ready to admit defeat in the matter of the two Gray Palmers. I had the distinct feeling my partner had already begun to tire of the game, but was hanging on because of some sort of warped idea that I needed protecting. I thanked him when he set the brimming container of icy soda back in front of me.

We continued eating in silence for a few minutes, my racing mind proposing and rejecting possible scenarios. I knew the one I kept coming back to wouldn't sit well with my partner. I was right. Before the entire plan was even out of my mouth, he had rendered his decision.

"You're nuts," he said, the oozing sandwich hovering halfway between the table and his mouth.

"You're dripping that on your shirt," I pointed out. "And I'm not nuts. If you just apply a little logic to the process, you'll see I'm right."

Erik dabbed at the combination mustard/mayo stain on his blue denim shirt and shook his head. "If *you* apply a little logic to the process," he mocked me, "you'll see that our mounting some sort of daring midnight raid on an island crawling with wild monkeys and patrolled by a couple of armed goons in a speedboat ranks right up there with some of your all-time stupider ideas."

I tried to make light of our disagreement. "Come on. Where's your spirit of adventure?"

"Where's your spirit of self-preservation?" he countered.

We left it there and slipped the remains of our wrapped and boxed meals into the trash container before climbing back into the Expedition. We had left most of the midday traffic behind us by the time Erik spoke again.

"I didn't mean to say 'stupider,'" he said.

"What are you apologizing for, the insult or the bad grammar?"

He laughed. "Both, I guess. But are you really serious? How would we get out there?"

I was tempted to give him a smart-ass reply, but I knew he wasn't really questioning the method of transport. "Ron Singleton will take us.

There isn't anyone who knows the waters any better. And he does seem to feel beholden to the Judge."

"We can't go cruising up to Monkey Island in that huge tourist boat of his."

"I agree," I said, "but I'm sure Ron will arrange to get something smaller. We can even rent one for him if we have to. And I'm thinking we'll leave from Presqu'isle."

"Why?"

"Because I checked out the map. It's a lot closer to Judas Island than the Beaufort marina. Ron can tie the boat up at our little dock, and we can approach the island from the back side. I'd be willing to bet that's where Gray landed."

I watched him mull it over. His eyes kept jumping to the rearview mirror, and I turned in my seat to see what was occupying so much of his attention. The road stretched clear behind us except for an SUV almost identical to ours a few hundred yards back.

"Something the matter?" I asked.

"I don't know. That big Chevy has been behind us ever since we left McDonald's."

"You think he's following us?" I stared out the rear window. "You know, except for the Interstate, this is the most direct route between Charleston and Beaufort. Anyone making the trip would normally come this way."

"You're probably right," he said, but I noticed he didn't stop checking the mirror every few seconds.

"So what do you think?" I asked, attempting to steer us back on topic.

"Let me see if I have this straight." An eighteen-wheeler zoomed by us heading north, the wash of its passing rocking us just a little. "You propose we hire this guy Ron to take us from Presqu'isle in a small boat, land us on Monkey Island, and wait to take us back. You and I will use the coordinates you found in that anatomy book and my GPS unit to locate the spot where Gray found the skeleton, dig it up, and . . ."

"What?" I asked when he paused, his gaze intent on the road behind us again.

"I've slowed down to fifty and speeded back up to seventy, and we haven't lost him."

Again I looked at the huge vehicle, its massive chrome grille gleaming in the afternoon sunlight. "Forget about him," I said, turning back around in my seat. "Finish your thought."

"I was finished. I can't get past the part where we dig up the body."

"We're not going to dig it up. Well, I guess we are, technically, but I don't intend for us to load it up and cart it away with us."

"I'm relieved to hear that."

"We just need to see whatever it was Gray saw. Maybe take some pictures."

"Why do I have the feeling this is already a done deal?"

I sat demurely in the passenger seat, my hands folded in my lap. "What do you mean?"

"Oh, please! Don't play Little Miss Innocent with me. Those phone calls you made this morning. Was one of them by chance to our intrepid captain of the *Wanderer*?" When I didn't reply, he went on. "No, wait. You wouldn't have wasted time trying to arrange this yourself. You talked to your father."

"Let's just say we explored the possibilities."

"You really are crazy, you know?" He smiled to take the sting out of his words. "Okay, so when is the big expedition set for?"

"Tonight."

"And after we locate this skeleton, assuming of course those numbers you found in Gray's book weren't just the coordinates of a great fishing spot, then what?"

"Like I said, we take a few pictures and get the hell out of there. And then we turn the whole thing over to the authorities."

"I know you love this sort of thing, this skulking around and playing detective, but why don't we do that right now? Give all this information to your brother-in-law and bow out?"

"Think about Judas Island," I said. "Part of it's privately owned, the rest just acquired by the State of South Carolina. Even if we could convince the authorities there's anything to investigate, how long do you think it would take to get permissions or warrants? Whoever is involved in killing Gray Palmer could remove the skeleton, cover their tracks. This might be our only chance."

Erik sighed and nodded. "I see your point. Okay, good."

I understood the abrupt change of subject as the vehicle which had been trailing us suddenly sped up and moved out to the left. Because of the glare off the watery marsh bordering both edges of the road, I couldn't see the driver through the windshield. All the side windows were deeply tinted, although the passenger one appeared to be sliding down as the vehicle roared past.

"Satisfied?" I asked.

Erik turned to shrug just as the big vehicle pulled back into the right-hand lane. Neither of us recognized the distant popping sound that preceded the Expedition's lurch to the left, but the bright flash of brake lights registered on my brain a split-second before it did on Erik's.

"Watch out!" I screamed.

Erik stomped hard on his own brake pedal. The huge vehicle jerked under his hands as he fought for control, but it was already too late. The car began a long, lazy slide into the opposite lane. I had a brief glimpse of our former pursuers speeding away just before the grille of the on-coming cement truck filled my vision and the world exploded in a cacophony of air horns and screeching metal.

I credit the driver of the cement truck as much as Erik with saving our lives.

His reactions bordered on incredible. He registered the road behind us was empty and, by flinging his mammoth vehicle to the left, avoided slamming us broadside. His rig did catch the right rear of the Expedition's bumper, ripping it completely off and sending us into a series of spins. We came to rest pointing back toward Charleston, our front wheels buried in the soft mud at the edge of the marsh.

The sudden stop had hit me like the punch of a giant hand, slamming me back against the seat. Dazed, I don't really remember anything for the next few minutes except black eyes round with fear and the gentle pressure of even blacker hands unhooking my shoulder harness and easing me out of the car. Other vehicles and other concerned faces swam before me as passing motorists pulled over to offer assistance.

Other than what I was certain would turn out to be massive bruising over every square inch of my body, I appeared to be unhurt, as was Erik, who came quickly around to join me on the narrow grass verge. The truck driver kept insisting we had to lie down, but neither of us complied. When it became apparent no one required immediate medical attention, many of the drivers who had stopped to help moved off. In the distance, the muted wail of a siren drifted across the expanse of swampy water.

Two hours later we had been checked over by the EMS unit and pronounced fit enough to travel. After an efficient tow truck driver from AAA had cranked the vehicle out of the mud and replaced the blown tire with Erik's spare, we remounted the Expedition and moved sedately on toward Beaufort. I had the name and address of our savior in the cement truck, and I had vowed to myself his children would never want for anything. Tons of paperwork had been filled out, and heads had been shaken over the vagaries of Fate which had allowed us to come through the blowout and subsequent accident without a scratch.

Neither Erik nor I ever mentioned the popping noises just before the crash, but both of us knew exactly what they had been.

CHAPTER THIRTY

E DIDN'T DISCUSS THE PALMERS OR OUR BRUSH WITH death. Erik found the classical music station, something soothing with a lot of strings drifting softly from the speakers, and I lay my head back and feigned sleep. Though I kept my eyes firmly closed, I could feel his head move to check on me from time to time.

I tried to wipe all the violence of the past two days out of my mind, but images still played out against the inside of my eyelids like a bad dream. I could tell by the firm set of Erik's jaw as we'd climbed back into the car that I would have no more problems convincing him of the rightness of our cause. Having people trying to kill you can be a sobering experience. It can also seriously piss you off.

I came close to suggesting we postpone our planned excursion, but then thought better of it. The sooner we got the evidence, the sooner we could remove ourselves from Gray Palmer's radar. I squirmed in the seat trying to relieve some of the soreness in my neck, and Erik took it as a sign I had awakened for good.

"Almost there," he said, and I opened my eyes to glance at him.

We had passed over the Lady's Island bridge and were moving toward the causeway out to St. Helena.

"Good," I said, pushing myself into the full upright and locked position. "You're sure you're okay?"

He smiled. "Yup, I'm fine. You?"

"I'll make it." I paused, unsure how to open the discussion. "Hell of a job back there," I said, staring straight ahead at the soft green of spring unfolding along either side of the narrow road. The serenity of the scene belied the turmoil of the past few hours.

"Not any better than you and the deer," he replied.

I cleared my throat nervously. "The deer didn't shoot out our left front tire."

"So you noticed that, did you?"

I looked over to find him grinning like a child. A laugh bubbled up from deep inside me, again part hysteria, part relief, but I bit it back down. I had a feeling this one might turn into sobs before I could catch hold of it.

"Why didn't you say anything to the sheriff's deputy?"

"Why didn't you?"

I had the answer to that one ready. "Because we would have been there till this time tomorrow trying to make them believe us. We probably would have spent the night in the psych ward."

"Agreed. So now what? You think it's time to bring Red in on this?"

I eyed him as he made the turn into the rutted lane that passed for a road up to Presqu'isle. "No. We go ahead as planned tonight, get our evidence, and then let Red and his pals have at it. Even with the grave we've still got nothing like actual proof, but I think it will go a long way toward validating our theories. There might still not be enough for a prosecutor to take to a judge. Especially with the autopsy report stating young Gray had alcohol in his blood. I'm trusting Daddy will be able to enlighten us on that point."

He looked at me then in a peculiar way, as if he were appraising me or seeing me in a different light. Maybe he'd never heard me refer to my father as *Daddy* before. I only tend to do that in moments of stress. It isn't necessarily a term of endearment. At least that's what I tell myself.

I ignored him and plunged ahead. "No, I think we have to have something to make them sit up and take notice, something they won't be able to sweep under the carpet. Don't forget Gray Palmer is a prominent citizen in Charleston. No one's going to investigate him for murder, attempted murder, smuggling, and whatever else he's been up to just on our say-so."

"You know we only have his word on the coroner's report."

Even a close brush with death couldn't dull the quickness of his mind. "Right. You know the other phone call I made this morning?"

"You mean besides the one to arrange tonight's rendezvous?"

"Yes. I called Red and asked him to get us a copy of the autopsy findings."

"Why? We hadn't even heard Gray's father's version then."

"I was hoping to use it for ammunition, but Red told me it would take a few hours to process the request. He wasn't even sure if the Charleston police would release it to him. I asked him to leave a message with the Judge."

"Good."

I winced as the right wheel bounced out of one of the innumerable holes in the sandy dirt road. Everything hurt. I hoped a hot shower would restore me enough to get me through what we had to do in just a few hours' time. "So are we on? For tonight?"

"Okay." His capitulation seemed too easy, and he correctly read the suspicion in my eyes. "Hey, I don't like getting shot at any more than the next guy. I got into this whole mess to try and help out a friend. Then, when he died, I wanted to find out what really happened to him. Now it's personal. I want to nail that lying bastard father of his as much as you do."

"Okay." I softened my mockery with a smile. "I'll get the Judge to confirm things with Ron, see if he's found a suitable boat, and we'll . . . Son of a bitch!"

"What is it?" Erik asked as he pulled into the semicircular driveway behind a small white car parked just in front of the steps.

"Felicity Baronne."

"The hooker?"

"Yeah, the hooker." I closed my eyes, drew a deep breath, and stumbled out of the mud-spattered truck.

———————

Lavinia pulled the door open just as I placed my hand on the knob, nearly jerking me off my feet. I saw her eyes flash past our shoulders to the Expedition.

"Lord, son, what happened to your car?"

Her remarks came out in a rushed whisper. Before he could respond, I grabbed his hand and pulled him after me down the hall and into the kitchen, Lavinia on our heels.

"How long has she been here?" I asked before Lavinia could start in on her own inquisition. The less we said about our afternoon's adventures, the less grief I would be subjected to.

The question served to divert her attention, as I had intended it should. "About half an hour."

The anger in her voice made Erik take a step backward, then decide on a total retreat. "I'll go wash up, if I may?"

Lavinia nodded and waved her hand in his general direction as if she were swatting at a pesky insect. "Guest bath, upstairs, second door on your right."

"Thank you. I remember." Erik shot me a look mingled with compassion and confusion and bolted.

"If things run true to form, she'll sashay out of here in a few minutes, and your father will have another check for me to mail."

"Why doesn't he just give them to her while she's here?" It hadn't occurred to me before, but it seemed a legitimate question.

"Why is grass green? Why don't you ask me something I might possibly know the answer to, you silly child?"

Lavinia was so rarely given to sarcasm or nasty temper I simply stared at her in disbelief. I couldn't remember a time when I had seen her this upset, not even during the chaos of my mother's sudden death or the agony of my father's strokes.

It was the last thing in the world I wanted to do, but I couldn't let her suffer any longer. "I'm going in there and find out what's going on."

"Bay, wait!" The hand she laid on my arm was as strong and firm as it had been in the remembered days of my childhood, but I shook her off and stomped toward my father's study. Enough was enough.

I nearly collided with Felicity Baronne as she emerged from the

Judge's study. Resplendent this time in an emerald green silk sheath which had seen better days, she tottered toward the front door on stiletto heels that had to be leaving deep scars on the boards of the heart pine floor. Without a word she brushed past me.

"Wait!" I called, but she kept on moving away. "Felicity, wait!"

I didn't hear the wheelchair until the footrest bumped against the back of my legs, almost sending me sprawling. By the time I righted myself, my quarry had clattered across the verandah and stumbled down the steps, leaving the front door wide open. Our eyes met for a brief instant as she wrenched open the door of her little car. Then she ground the engine to life and sped off toward the lane in a shower of pebbles and dust.

I whirled to find my father glaring up at me. I could feel him gathering himself for an attack, but this time I was not having any of it. I grabbed one of the handles on the back of his wheelchair and spun him around. Without a word I propelled him across the faded Aubusson carpet and down the hall to his study. I pushed him into the room and kicked the door shut behind me. When I turned him again to face me, his look held both astonishment and anger.

"Okay," I said, my chest heaving with the effort to control my own fury, "that's enough! You're not putting Lavinia through any more of this crap. Spill it! Now! And I'm telling you, Father, it had better be a damned good story!"

Erik had the good sense to make himself scarce. Either he was hiding in the bathroom, or he had sneaked out the front door while I had gone to drag a protesting Lavinia from the kitchen. Either way, I felt relieved not to have to deal with him for the hour or so it took me to wring the truth out of my father.

We assembled in his study, the Judge's wheelchair pulled up in front of the cold fireplace, Lavinia in one of the wing chairs to the right, facing him. I found I couldn't settle, so I spent the time pacing back and forth, ignoring both their entreaties for me to park myself somewhere. An observer might have thought the scene resembled an abbreviated courtroom, with my father as the accused, Lavinia the jury, and myself as the prosecuting attorney. If so, the roles had been fairly allotted.

"Bay, this isn't necessary," Lavinia said for about the third time. Ankles crossed primly in front of her, her back ramrod straight as usual, only her worn brown hands twisting a handkerchief in her lap betrayed her agitation.

"Yes, it is," I replied. I paused then to gather my thoughts, and what came out of my mouth surprised me as much as it did my listeners. "This house has always been about secrets. At least in the years I spent in it. And it's time it stopped."

I waved off the Judge's attempt to interrupt me. Now that I had begun, I realized I had an opportunity to say some things I hadn't even acknowledged to myself.

"As a child, I always felt left out of everything, as if I were an outsider and not a real member of the family. Conversations stopped when I came into rooms. Looks were exchanged . . ."

This time my father did manage to cut me off. "That's ridiculous! You were a child. You had no right to be privy to grown-up talk."

"No right. Yes, that pretty much sums it up. But it didn't stop after I grew up, Daddy. You still act as if I'm seven and need to be sent from the room because the adults are discussing sex."

The response fell short of his usual bark of contempt. "Nonsense."

"It doesn't matter whether you believe it or not. It's what I felt. What I *feel*. For God's sakes, I'm nearly forty years old! I watched my husband and two other people die in front of me! Haven't I earned the right to be treated like an equal?"

The muted ticking of the grandfather clock provided the only background. A tiny voice in the back of my head told me to leave it alone, not to open the Pandora's box of our family's history. *Maybe secrets aren't such a bad thing,* it whispered, and I faltered.

"Your father has a right to his privacy," Lavinia said softly. "We all do."

As reprimands go, it was pretty mild, but it had the desired effect. I felt the anger seep out of me like a long, slow exhalation of held breath. "Okay," I said, turning to my father. "Okay. But you do owe us an explanation about this woman and why you're paying her money." In a courtroom tactic I knew he had perfected, I paused for effect. "If not me, then you certainly owe it to Lavinia."

He tried for his usual bluster and again fell a little short. He would tell us. It just had to be on his terms.

"Forty years ago," he began, wiping the corners of his mouth with a pristine white handkerchief, "Felicity Baronne was a stunningly beautiful teenager."

He looked at Lavinia and me, defying us to contradict him. I nodded for him to continue, though it was hard to associate that description with the ravaged woman who'd just fled Presqu'isle.

"But wild," he went on. "Her daddy had run out on the family years before, and she had several brothers and sisters. The mother took in laundry, as I recall, or maybe cleaned houses. It doesn't matter. The point is there was no money. They were on the county a good part of Felicity's life."

"So she became a hooker?" This trite, maudlin tale grated on my nerves. A lot of people grew up in poverty and went on to make something of themselves. It seemed fairly obvious what Felicity Baronne had chosen to do with her life.

I couldn't quite read my father's stare. A mixture of sadness and disappointment, perhaps. "You can be as hard as your mother sometimes, Lydia." Two insults in one sentence. I had definitely angered him.

"Were you one of her clients? Is she blackmailing you? It seems a little late for that, don't you think? I mean, why should you worry about it now? No one's going to give a damn after forty years."

"Hush, Bay," Lavinia said from across the room. "Let him tell it in his own way."

I dropped onto the loveseat and wished for a cigarette. "Fine. Let's just move it along, okay? I have things to do tonight."

He knew exactly what I meant. We locked stares for nearly a full minute before he shook his head. "No, I was not one of her 'clients.'" The pause this time came from reticence, not from calculation. "But others were."

"Who?"

"That is none of your concern. Suffice it to say there are those whose families are still intact, men who don't wish to bring disgrace and unhappiness upon their wives."

A lot of candidates flashed through my mind, cronies and lifelong friends of the Judge who might call on him to rescue them from this dilemma: Law Merriweather, the attorney who had helped us with Mercer Mary Prescott; Charlie Seldon, the former county solicitor; Boyd Allison, whose daughter and son-in-law still operated the East Bay Book Emporium he had founded. These were just the first who leaped to mind, probably because they had been my father's poker buddies up until the last few months when the ill health of several members had forced them to disband their Thursday night ritual. But my father knew hundreds of people. It could have been any number of them, names I might not even recognize.

"So this has all been done out of altruism? You're paying this woman thousands of dollars of your own money to keep her from blackmailing your friends?"

He shook his head, and again I thought I detected disappointment in his eyes. "It's not blackmail, daughter. It's . . ."

He hesitated, and it struck me how old and frail he looked. I opened my mouth to stop him, to call a halt to the inquisition. But I glanced quickly at Lavinia and remembered why I had started this in the first place.

"It's what?" I prompted.

He took a long time to answer. "There was a child."

CHAPTER
THIRTY-ONE

WENTY MINUTES LATER I LEFT THEM ALONE AND DRAGGED myself up the steps to my old room. I stopped on the way by in what had become my private bathroom to set the plug in the old claw-footed tub and turn the hot water tap on full. I dropped my wrinkled clothes on the floor next to my four-poster and pulled on the threadbare chenille robe I kept hanging on a hook behind the door before padding back to the bathroom. I eased myself into the soothing, scented water and lay back against the cushioned headrest.

Secrets, I thought, feeling my battered muscles begin to relax, *always secrets.*

In those days before DNA testing, no one could be certain who had fathered Felicity Baronne's child, my father had said, so several of her regular customers discreetly provided a substantial stake and sent her on her way. Perhaps there was a spark of honor or conscience in the girl, for she had gone willingly and never looked back. If the child was born or aborted, no one ever knew for certain. Until now.

I lifted the bar of lavender soap from the wire holder hanging on the rim of the tub and lathered my body.

Lavinia believed him, although I wasn't sure I did. If Felicity Baronne had indeed come back to ask for help for her daughter—as alone as her mother and ravaged by ovarian cancer—why hadn't the

Judge just quietly canvassed the likely candidates and come up with another joint payoff? Why did the woman continue to haunt Presqu'isle? Once she'd made her pitch, my father or the others could just as easily have given her a lump sum and sent her packing again.

"She isn't good with money," my father had replied when I'd posed the question. "This way she's assured of its being available when she needs it."

He had a ready answer, too, for why Felicity made the hour-long drive to St. Helena rather than simply telephoning and asking for a payment.

"Because it's more . . . civilized. She enjoys talking about the old days. As do I."

His eyes had gone wistful then, some of the ravages of the years and the strokes slipping away from his drooping face, and again I'd wondered if I could trust his insistence that he had not been involved with the wild, beautiful teenager. Hadn't Lavinia said Felicity called him Tally? No one but his wife and his intimates had ever referred to him by that name. Why should my then vigorous, handsome father have been immune to the girl's charms? God knew his home life hadn't been any bed of roses.

"Then why didn't you just give her the money while she was here? Why involve Lavinia in something that was certain to upset her?" I'd asked.

"Handing her a check would have been . . . demeaning to her. Believe it or not, Felicity Baronne is a woman of considerable dignity."

My laugh of derision had gone unchallenged, although my father had shaken his head sadly.

You can be as hard as your mother sometimes, he'd said to me. I shivered in the cooling bathwater. Tough to escape genetics, but I had spent a lot of years trying. Maybe you couldn't. Maybe those twisted little strands of DNA were bound to win out in the end no matter what you did.

I rinsed out my hair and pulled the plug. As I wrapped my head in one towel and dried my aching body with the other, I could at least smile at the picture on which I had closed the study door: Lavinia's sturdy brown hand clasped in my father's, their heads close together as she knelt on the floor by his chair. It was the first time they'd ever let me see a display of physical affection between them. I sincerely hoped it wouldn't be the last.

Apparently I was the only one feeling the least uncomfortable as we gathered around the kitchen table. Lavinia had recovered her old, brusque efficiency. Never given to overt displays of any emotion, I could tell nonetheless that she was happy again by the way she bullied my father and by her insistence that Erik fill his plate a second time. I ate mechanically, my mind on the upcoming expedition, and to this day I couldn't say for certain what we had for dinner that night.

Over coffee and tea we talked about the case. No one suggested Lavinia leave the room, and she bustled around behind us, arranging the few leftovers in plastic containers and washing up the dishes.

The Judge had been as astounded as Erik and I by Gray Palmer's check. Like us, he interpreted the inappropriate size of it as an admission he seriously wanted us to drop the investigation and go away. Red's phone call while I had been drowsing in the tub only added more substantiation.

"Point-oh-two," my father said. "That's what the boy's blood alcohol level was. I'm no expert on the matter, but I wouldn't think that would be much more than a beer or two. You have to hit point-one-zero to be considered legally intoxicated in this state. And no sign of drugs."

"What does Red think?"

"I didn't pursue the matter with him, daughter. The less he knows about your scheme, the less likely he is to come charging to your rescue."

I had to admit this new attitude surprised me. Usually my father stood in the forefront of those warning me off my more harebrained ideas. If he were going to become a fully engaged partner, we just might get this detecting enterprise off the ground after all.

"So what time will Ron get here?" I asked as Lavinia refilled Erik's coffee cup, poured one for herself, and joined us again at the table.

"Around midnight," he said. "That should get you to the island sometime after one. I figured that would give you plenty of time to find the . . . uh, location, take your pictures, and get away well before first light." I smiled, and he raised an eyebrow. "What?" he asked.

"I have to say, Your Honor, I'm really enjoying having you as a co-conspirator instead of a nagging, overprotective father."

"I'll take that as the compliment I'm sure it was intended to be."

He had obviously forgiven me for my inquisition earlier in the study. Perhaps he was even glad I had taken the initiative in forcing him to tell Lavinia the truth about Felicity Baronne. Both his honor and his happiness had been well-served.

"Well, young man," my father said, turning to Erik, "are you prepared for this adventure?"

"I guess so, Judge Simpson," Erik replied. "I've got film in the Nikon and fresh batteries in the GPS unit. Bay says you have a couple of powerful flashlights." My father nodded. "I guess the only thing I'm missing is a warm jacket and a way to get these damned knots out of my stomach."

We laughed, but I knew exactly what he meant. Like so many other things in life, contemplating this trip intellectually had been exciting. Now that the time for action was drawing near, my mind kept dwelling on all the things that could go wrong.

"Ron Singleton will have a radio in case you run into trouble. He's sworn to me he won't leave the island without you, and at the first hint of trouble he'll call in reinforcements." A note of something I thought might be fear had crept into his voice. "You'll take your pictures and get the hell out of there as fast as you can."

"No argument here," I said. I hugged my arms as a chill ran up them.

We sipped our drinks in silence for a few moments, each of us no doubt wondering what revelations the night's work might bring. I sent up a short prayer we would all be sitting here discussing it like this come morning.

My father broke into our thoughts. "Vinnie, would you be so kind as to fetch me that box from the top of my desk?"

I loved the look which passed between them as Lavinia rose and left the room. He turned then to Erik.

"Tell me again what this professor friend of yours had to say."

"About the bone?" Erik looked at me, but I could only shrug. I had no idea where the Judge was going.

"Yes. He said it had probably been in the ground for how many years?"

"Forty, maybe fifty. Somewhere around that. He said he couldn't be certain without running some further tests."

We waited for a response, but my father seemed deep in thought. Finally he mumbled, "Hmm. That would be about right."

"What are you getting at?" I asked, leaning toward him. "Do you have some idea about who it could be?"

Lavinia's return forestalled his immediate response. She set a small wooden box in front of him and resumed her seat.

All eyes focused on the Judge as he made a ceremony of raising the lid. The small leather holster he lifted out fit neatly in the palm of his hand, as did the miniature weapon he slid from it.

"Tally! Dear God, put that thing away!" Lavinia leaped to her feet, backing up until the sink stopped her.

"Vinnie, hush now. It isn't loaded. Come on, sit back down here."

Reluctantly she obeyed. Erik and I exchanged a look of surprise.

"It's for you, Bay," my father said, turning the little pistol over and handing it to me, grip first.

"Why? I have the Glock."

He raised an eyebrow in unspoken question.

"Yes, I carry it. Especially since . . ." I let the thought trail off. No sense in bringing up unpleasant memories. Much as I had resisted his first insistence that I learn to shoot, the weapon had been instrumental in the fact I was still here to talk about it.

"You'll give that to Erik. Can you handle a gun, young man?"

"No, sir. And with all due respect, I won't carry one. I'd probably shoot myself rather than a bad guy."

"As you wish, although I'd feel much better if you were both armed."

"Why can't I just use the Glock?" I asked, fingering the miniature weapon.

"Smaller, easier to fire, single-action. It can fit in your pocket, and no one will even know you have it."

I had to admit the gun felt comfortable in my hand. I tried not to think too much about what that said.

"I'll load it up for you and give you a quick lesson. It's a Seecamp, completely handmade. They're very rare. And very expensive."

"Where . . . ?"

"A friend of mine gave it to me. I was able to help him out with a small problem some years back. A barber named Len over on Hilton Head. He's also a registered gun dealer."

He paused and extended his hand to me. Reluctantly I surrendered the weapon. In those few short minutes it seemed to have become mine in a way the Glock never had. He placed the pistol back in its holster.

"I hate all this talk of guns. I'm going to make sure Erik's room is in good order." Lavinia rose and marched out.

"Sometimes unpleasant things are necessary," my father mumbled to no one in particular. He paused to follow the sound of Lavinia's soft tread as she mounted the staircase, and I thought I detected a look of relief on his face. Before I had a chance to examine that too closely, he hurried on. "Listen to me now. After you told me what the professor had to say about that bone, I had Law Merriweather do a little checking for me."

"About what?" I asked.

"Missing persons cases, still open. From the late fifties, early sixties."

"Did he find anything?"

"He came up with quite a few possibilities, I'm afraid."

"How many?"

"Eleven which were suspicious over a period of five years or so."

"Really?" I asked, surprised. "I wouldn't have thought there would be that many in this little area. Anyone who fits the professor's profile?"

"Three," he answered, and cast a look over his shoulder. I could feel the tension in his voice. "That's the only reason I'm giving my sanction to this scheme of yours, Bay. Because I have a terrible feeling there might be more than one grave over there."

"You think all three could be buried on Judas Island? But why? What could they possibly have to do with Gray's death or his father's smuggling? And you don't even know if these people are actually dead. They could be anywhere."

"You're right," he said, "but the coincidence is just too much to ignore. All of them were young black men in their early twenties. They all disappeared on the same night, and I'm very afraid one of them may be . . ."

I whirled at the low moan.

Lavinia stood in the doorway, her face a mask of fear and stunned disbelief. "Dear God, you don't think . . ." she began, but her words were cut off by the crash of the crystal vase of wilted roses as it slipped from her trembling hand and shattered against the gleaming wood floor.

CHAPTER
THIRTY-TWO

 RON SINGLETON OFFERED ME HIS HAND AS I STEPPED down into the narrow aluminum boat and crawled toward the cushioned seat at the bow. I felt the rocking as Erik clambered in after me. He carried a backpack, resurrected by Lavinia from some storage box in the far reaches of the attic. It seemed familiar, as if it might have been the one I toted around with me at Northwestern half a lifetime ago. Into it we had stuffed the flashlights, camera, a couple of spare jackets, and a few other things we'd need to complete the night's work. At the last minute, I'd shoved in the Glock.

"All set?"

At our nods, Ron slipped the single rope from the piling at the end of our small fishing dock. The scream of the outboard motor as it roared to life seemed loud enough to be heard in Charleston. As we eased out into St. Helena Sound, I looked back toward Presqu'isle. Silhouetted in the spill of light from the Judge's study, Lavinia stood on the back verandah, arms folded across her chest, a solitary sentinel to our departure. I felt as if her gaze held mine, even though her face was lost in the shadows, and mine could have been no more than a blur in the meager light of a thin moon. Nonetheless, I kept my eyes fastened on her retreating figure until we rounded a small headland and the house was lost to view.

The outcome of our expedition had become as important to her as it was to us. Maybe more so.

Ron revved the engine, and we moved out into the current, headed directly for Judas Island. With the tide coming in, the trip should take no more than twenty minutes. It was one of the reasons for waiting until after midnight to set out. The other had been the belief that any patrols might be relaxed in the hours when most sane people were in their beds.

Erik had voiced the concern that the attack on Araminda Albright— and the senior Gray Palmer's sudden about-face regarding our employment—might have engendered a heightened presence in the area. My father and I were of the opinion just the opposite might be the case. Again, normal people would have taken the not-too-subtle hints and moved on. They also had no way of knowing if their attempt on Erik and me earlier that day had been successful or not. For all Palmer's murderous associates knew, we might be lying in the hospital. Or the morgue. At any rate, if things went according to plan, we'd be in and out of there too fast to alert anyone to our presence. If . . .

In spite of our heavy sweatshirts and jeans and the warmth of the evening breeze as we'd waited for Ron, the air out on the open water cut through to my bones. In only a few minutes of running flat-out in the small motorboat, with no screen to cut the bite of the wind, my eyes were streaming and my teeth chattering. I hung on as long as I could.

I had just turned to ask Erik to pull one of the fleece jackets out of his pack when the engine speed dropped. I glanced past him to Ron Singleton, seated at the tiller, and he gestured with his free hand. I followed the direction of his finger and saw a solid bank of trees rising off to our right. He cut the engine altogether. It amazed me how fast the temperature of my skin rose once the wind no longer buffeted me.

I righted myself and watched the island loom closer as we drifted silently on the incoming tide. I couldn't believe how fast we were moving without the motor. As we drew nearer, I saw a narrow ribbon of water open up to our right. Parrot Creek, if I remembered correctly from our brief study of the charts during our first trip out with Ron.

He reached under the seat and pulled out two long oars. Mutely he fitted them into the locks on either side of the boat and signaled Erik to change places with him. Our captain positioned himself on the center seat and dug the oars into the water. We glided into the stream, the only sound an occasional grunt as Ron moved us closer. I saw Erik remove the GPS unit from his pocket and tap the button to illuminate its face. In answer, I patted the Seecamp tucked snugly against my right hip.

The next shallow creek seemed little more than a trickle as Ron maneuvered us into its channel. Again we drifted on an unseen current. A few hundred yards in, the boat nosed its way toward the barely perceptible shore then bumped against solid ground. Ron leaped out, his tall rubber boots making sucking sounds in the mud as he grabbed the painter and pulled us farther up onto land. Erik and I scrambled out, our own shoes immediately soaked through.

"You got our location marked on that thing?" Ron's whisper cut through the eerie stillness.

"Got it," Erik replied in an equally hushed voice.

We took the flashlights from his pack and tested them briefly against the marshy ground.

"Look!" I said softly, pointing to the area immediately in front of us.

Several sets of footprints, confirming our guess about this being Gray and Araminda's own landing site, led away from where we stood and disappeared into the trees, many of their trunks stripped bare of bark. I remembered seeing that on our initial reconnaissance of the island and wondered if the monkeys had wrought the destruction. At the exact moment the thought flashed through my head, one solitary, high-pitched scream split the air.

"Jesus!" I whispered, and beside me I heard Ron's low chuckle.

"Just the locals," he said, and his gleaming white teeth flashed in the nearly invisible black of his face. "Avoid 'em if you can. Nasty-tempered little bastards, or so they say. I'll be just offshore here, in among this marsh grass. I'll give you two hours, then I'm callin' in the Marines."

"Thanks," I said, and touched Erik on the arm. "Let's go."

He flicked on the global positioning unit, set off along a barely perceptible path, and was almost immediately swallowed up by the dense woods.

With a last look over my shoulder at the small boat drifting slowly out into the creek, I trotted in after Erik.

I felt rather than saw the presence of the monkeys. At first it was hard to tell their furtive movements from the natural rustling of the trees in the light breeze. But as we moved farther into the interior of the island, I could sense dozens of pairs of eyes on us. It was as creepy a feeling as I've ever had. Only an occasional squeak or chatter betrayed it was not humans who monitored our slow progress.

We hadn't wanted to risk using the flashlights until we had no choice in the matter, and that point arrived within seconds. Without the sure, steady beams to guide us, we would have sprawled facedown on the squishy floor of the woods any number of times. Twisted tree roots hidden beneath a carpet of brown pine needles and decomposing leaves could easily have been our undoing.

I judged we had been walking in nearly a straight line for the better part of ten minutes when Erik stopped.

"What is it?" I moved up close behind him before speaking softly.

"The unit indicates we should move off to the right." He pointed in a direction at about a forty-five degree angle to where we stood.

"So let's do it."

"It doesn't make sense," he said, and I could hear, rather than see, his concern.

"Why? Isn't that the reason we brought the damn thing? What's the point if we don't go where it tells us to?"

"Flash your light over there."

Again I followed his pointing finger. The beam seemed to bounce right back at me.

"That underbrush is almost a solid wall. And look here," he said, scanning his own light across the tangle of thorny bushes and weeds. "There's no break anywhere along here. If Gray forced his way through here, there would be broken branches. Some of this undergrowth would be trampled. And it's not."

"So what do we do?" I surprised myself by the depth of my calm.

But once before I had put myself in the hands of Erik and his magical gadget, and he had proved its worth beyond any doubt. Of course that had been in broad daylight with half a dozen people around. Still . . .

"I say we keep following this track," he said. "I'll bet it twists around and comes back to the direction we want to go. I think it's what Gray would have done."

"Fine. Let's try it."

He nodded, and we moved off. Overhead the rattling of branches grew louder, as if the monkeys leaped from tree to tree, keeping tabs on us. I tried to shut the images out of my mind and keep my eyes on the muddy path in front of me. So deep was my concentration I nearly stumbled into Erik who had come to a dead stop. I put out a hand to brace myself against his back then followed the direction of his light.

The bracken on the right side of the path opened up to a small clearing. If you weren't looking for it, the slight mound in the center would have been indiscernible from the bumpy terrain around it. I added my beam to Erik's, and together we swept the area. An attempt had been made to disguise the disturbance by scattering leaves and debris randomly across the top of the grave. Gray had done a pretty good job, and again a casual passerby would probably never have given the place a second glance.

In the dim glow reflected up from the illuminated ground we exchanged a look of satisfaction. Then Erik lowered the backpack and began removing its contents. He set the Nikon carefully to one side along with the Glock then pulled out the two folding shovels. I knelt on one of the unused jackets and brushed away the thin covering of leaves and twigs. The ground was so loosely packed we could almost have used our hands, but I took the shovel Erik held out to me, and together we began the disinterment.

I sent up a silent prayer that I wouldn't disgrace myself by doing something female, like throwing up or passing out when we finally reached the body.

I stopped once to stretch out my back and pull the sweatshirt over my head. I pushed up the sleeves of the turtleneck which constituted my second layer. We had to go slowly since we had no idea how close to the surface the remains might lie, and we didn't want to destroy anything vital by being careless. Still, as I paused to catch my breath and check my watch, I found we had been on Judas Island just under an hour.

Beside me, Erik kept up his rhythmic motion, gently loosening the soil and setting it aside. The grim lines of his face told me he might share some of my own misgivings about what we were doing, but that, like me, he would see it through. I set back in, matching my movements to his. In the glow of the flashlights, positioned on the ground to illuminate our work area, I finally saw a flicker of color beneath the next layer of soil.

"Wait," I whispered, but Erik had seen it too.

We tossed the shovels aside and began scooping the dirt away with our hands.

It was a lot less frightening than I had imagined. The bones, though caked with dirt, seemed no more alarming than the model of a skeleton Mr. Baylor had brought in for our tenth-grade biology class. We cleared away as much of the soil as we could, my eyes avoiding the gap in the right leg where Gray Palmer had removed the femur.

"There's the watch," Erik said.

Some trick of decomposition had left the watch face stuck to the left wrist bone. We played the light over it, and I thought I could detect a few strands of what had probably been a leather band. In unspoken agreement, we set the lights back on the ground and resumed our grisly task.

Erik worked at the head and I at the feet. I felt the dirt caking my nails and imbedding itself in the pores and creases of my skin. In our careful planning we had neglected to think of gloves. Even a brush would have been of some help.

Overhead, I could again feel the eyes of the monkeys on us. The level of their chattering and screeching had increased as if they discussed this invasion of their sleep by their oversized primate cousins. I wondered if somewhere, deep in their nonhuman brains, they associated our presence with the regular disappearance of their mates and offspring.

In a few more minutes we had the skeleton completely exposed, and Erik reached for the camera. As he fussed with the lenses and attached the flash, I ran my light over the entire grave. Dark blue remnants of what must once have been a pair of jeans clung to the lower torso. It— or rather *he*—must have been barefooted, for I could detect no sign of shoes. Nothing remained of anything resembling a shirt, but there did seem to be some material near the head. Thin strands of what looked like burlap had adhered themselves to the skull, and other fibers stuck out from behind the neck. I tried, but couldn't bring myself to touch them.

"Erik," I whispered.

He slung the strap of the Nikon around his neck and knelt beside me.

"See this stuff?" I pointed to the few frayed strands. "What do you think that is?"

"I don't know. Let me get some pictures first. We really shouldn't touch anything until we get a record of how it looked when we first uncovered it. Keep the light low so it doesn't interfere with the flash."

I moved over opposite him and trained the flashlight on the head. The strobe of the camera almost blinded me, and I looked away. Erik stepped methodically around the open grave, snapping continuously.

"There, I think that's got it," he finally said, setting the Nikon aside. "Now let's see what we've got here."

Again I fixed the upper part of the skeleton in the light. The fibers were clearly visible on both sides of the neck. I leaned in, still afraid to touch the remains. "It almost looks like . . ."

"Rope," a voice said behind me.

The flashlight tumbled from my hand into the open grave, clattering against the stark white ribs of the body, and plunging us into darkness.

CHAPTER
THIRTY-THREE

I KNOW I DIDN'T FAINT. I'VE NEVER FAINTED IN MY life. But there were at least a few minutes unaccounted for by the time I had recovered my senses enough to realize what was happening.

I found myself seated on the ground next to Erik, our backs pressed up against the scratchy trunk of a pine tree unscathed by the monkeys. Across the gaping hole we'd just dug, the blinding beams of their flashlights kept the men's faces indistinguishable. I knew there were two of them only by the matching sets of black boots visible just outside the arc of the light. And by the yawning holes in the barrels of the guns they pointed at us.

I glanced immediately to the contents of the pack spread just out of reach to my right, but the Glock was gone.

"I regret I needed to confiscate that, Mrs. Tanner."

The deep, masculine voice carried a hint of an accent, and I strained in an effort to recognize it. Nothing came. I'd almost swear I'd never encountered this man before. His companion remained mute. It didn't take much of a leap of logic to figure out who they must be. And that gave me hope. The two men who had broken into Araminda Albright's house could have killed her right off if they'd wanted to. Perhaps this was only meant to frighten us off. If so, it was working admirably.

"My father knows where we are," I said, surprised by my own calm. "If we're not back . . ."

"Screw your father! Too damn bad the old goat isn't here, too. I'd love . . ."

"Shut up! Now!"

The second man fell silent at this command, but not before I'd recognized his slightly slurred voice. I knew I was right, but it made absolutely no sense.

"You're a long way from the real estate office, Harry," I said in as conversational a tone as I could muster. Beside me I felt Erik's head whip around in my direction. "I'm surprised you could haul your fat, sorry ass this far into the woods without dropping dead of a heart attack."

Harry Simon growled low in his throat, and I saw a camouflaged arm reach out to restrain him.

Camouflage! And yet I couldn't begin to imagine balding, overweight Harry Simon crawling in and out of boats, beating up young women, murdering . . .

"It will do you no good to annoy my friend here any further, Mrs. Tanner. You and your father are not exactly his favorite people to begin with. Though I was actually quite amused by his account of the evening he spent in your charming company." His laugh made my stomach knot. "If you'd ever seen Harry drink, you'd know it would take more than a few watered-down bourbons to pry anything out of him we didn't want you to know." He paused to let this information sink in then flicked the flashlight at us. "Up now. Both of you. Nice and slow."

Erik helped me to stand. The stiffness screamed in every part of my body, and I wasn't certain my legs would hold me. Strangely I felt no fear, or very little at any rate. That might have had something to do with the sharp stab of the little Seecamp pistol against my right hip as I scrambled to my feet. Removed from its holster and tucked into the pocket of my jeans, its presence was invisible. Neither of them had frisked me. Even if they had, the tiny weapon would probably have gone undetected.

Once before someone had assumed I—a mere woman—would be unarmed, an assumption they lived awhile to regret.

"We're going for a little hike," the non-Harry man said, and again he used the light to motion us forward.

"Who's in there?" I asked, my eyes dropping to the gaping hole of the uncovered grave. "Is he the reason you had to kill Gray Palmer?"

"Little bastard just couldn't leave it alone," Harry began. "We tried to warn him off, but . . ."

"Shut up, Corporal! That's an order!"

Corporal? The barked command could have come straight off the parade ground. But Harry Simon hadn't been in the military for at least thirty or forty years.

"Move! You first, Mrs. Tanner."

The man jerked his light toward the path we'd taken up from the landing, and I suddenly wondered what had happened to Ron Singleton. Surely they wouldn't have . . .

But he motioned us in the opposite direction. Harry moved out in front, his waddling bulk nearly obscuring the beam of his flashlight on the rough track. Behind me I could hear Erik's measured breathing over the crackle of our feet on the underbrush. The second man brought up the rear. I glanced back over my shoulder, but again the light kept me from seeing anything of his face.

The monkeys tracked us, their excited chattering growing in volume as we moved farther away from the grave. I stumbled frequently, my hand brushing against my pocket each time I righted myself. As we trekked farther into the dark interior of the island, I became more and more convinced the concealed pistol might represent our only hope.

I couldn't read my watch face, so I had no idea how long we marched single-file along the narrow path. It could have been ten minutes or an hour before we finally stumbled into a clearing. I thought I could make out the dim outlines of a building off to one side, and just beyond I could hear the gentle lapping of water against the shore. In my first glimpse of the sky since we'd entered the woods on the other end of the island, I noticed a small bank of clouds had obscured the waning moon.

Harry Simon lighted himself to a bench and flopped down, breathing heavily. His companion snapped off his own flashlight, leaving Erik and me standing disoriented in the open space.

"Sit," the voice ordered from behind us, and we lowered ourselves to the rough, uneven ground.

Erik shifted himself until his left leg brushed against mine. I felt his arm move to encircle my shoulders, but I shrugged him off. I knew he only meant to offer comfort, but I wanted to keep my right hand free, just in case I got a chance to go for the pistol. I squirmed around, trying for the position which would allow me the quickest access to the gun.

"Quit fidgeting, Mrs. Tanner." His conversational tone and the way he kept repeating my name were beginning to grate on me in a way Harry Simon's snarling nastiness hadn't.

"What now?" I asked, making no effort to keep the contempt out of my own voice. "If you're going to kill us, it would have made more sense to do it back there. You could have used the grave we'd already opened for you."

"Bay . . ." Erik began, but our captor's low chuckle interrupted his protest.

"I must say I do admire your sang-froid, Mrs. Tanner. You would have made a formidable soldier."

The way he spoke to me . . . The mocking, formal address . . . It was almost as if he knew me. And yet I had no clue as to his identity. In the silence that followed, I let my mind range back over the events of the past two weeks. *Nothing.* Unless . . . His use of the word "corporal." The aura of command in his voice. And that last remark about my making a good solider . . . *No! But why?*

"I can feel the heat from your mental processes all the way over here," he said. Had there been enough light, I felt certain I would have seen him smiling. "Have you figured it out yet? The Judge was always bragging about how clever you are."

So he knew my father, too. Another possible confirmation of the wild idea rattling around in my head. I had nothing to lose. And it almost seemed as if he *wanted* me to . . .

"Well, Colonel, I'd hate to think my father might be accused of hubris on my behalf."

"Colonel?" Erik mumbled beside me, but our captor's laugh drowned him out.

"Bravo, my dear, bravo! What gave me away? My unfortunate slip in addressing poor Harry here by his former rank? Or was it our accidental meeting yesterday in Gray's office? It's what I always tell my junior officers: even the most careful planning has to allow for the element of circumstance. That you and I should be in that particular place at that particular time . . . Well, who could have factored in such a twist of fate?"

"What the hell is he talking about?" Erik's voice held anger, although I couldn't be certain at whom it was directed.

I knew now how the game would have to be played. "Erik Whiteside meet Harlan Fleming, Colonel, United States Marine Corps."

"I'm truly sorry for this, young man." He sounded almost sincere. "I had hoped we could avoid further bloodshed."

"So you did kill Gray Palmer! But Gray Senior is your friend! The secretary said you'd known each other . . ."

I stopped myself, names and images tumbling around in my brain faster than I could sort them out. Harry Simon on the Judge's verandah . . . The newspaper article on Palmer . . . The connection, when it clicked into place, seemed so obvious.

"You were all in the service together. You and Harry and Gray's father. All here, I'll bet, at Parris Island." When he didn't reply, I took a second to do the math. "You would all have been what—twenty or so? In the early sixties. Just about the time that body went into its grave."

"You killed him," Erik said beside me, the wonder in his voice tinged with outrage. "You hanged a black man—or strangled him—and buried him on this deserted island."

I recalled then the Judge's remark over lunch the previous day. *Sometimes overly harsh with the men of color under his command . . .* Maybe that explained why he'd never risen any higher in the Corps. A man with his years of service should have been a general by now. Thank God there was little tolerance in the modern armed forces for men like . . .

"They deserved it." Harry Simon had been silent for so long, his sudden interruption made me jump. "Always interferin' with us. Damned King and them others riling 'em up, making 'em think they were as good as us." He spat loudly onto the hard ground at his feet. " '*I have a dream.*' Shit! We gave 'em somethin' to dream about, didn't we, Colonel?"

"Shut up, Harry." Fleming's tone remained conversational, but the air of command still crackled in every word. Simon fell silent. "Go down to the dock and make certain everything is in readiness. Then contact the others and tell them we're ready to proceed."

Harry Simon moved off, using the flashlight to illuminate the path. Fleming clicked his back on, the beam pointed loosely in our direction from several yards away. In the near blackness I found Erik's face and felt my own fear reflected in his eyes. *Others.* Two on two, we had a chance. With reinforcements, the odds dropped considerably. Before I could begin to think about some way to get us out of there alive, Harlan Fleming took up the tale.

"I want you to understand, Mrs. Tanner, that all of this could have been avoided if only people would have listened to reason. I told the others there was no need to harm young Palmer. I was certain his father could make him understand the necessity of forgetting about what he'd stumbled upon." He paused, and I thought I could see him shaking his head in the dim light of the sliver of moon exposed as the clouds moved off to the east. "So tragic, really. I'm afraid Gray is devastated."

"I can tell you're all broken up," I said, then hurried on before he could comment. "So are you telling me Gray Palmer had nothing to do with his son's death?"

"Of course he didn't! And neither did I! What kind of men do you think we are?"

I knew he didn't really want the answer to that question. "Then who . . . ?"

"As I said, I'm afraid the remaining members of our little band didn't trust Gray's influence. Apparently father and son have had some difficulties in the past."

Like believing his father had driven his mother to suicide, for one. Then another thought struck me. "Why would Palmer have been using this island for his smuggling operation when he knew full well this was the scene of your . . ." I wanted to say "killing spree," then thought better of it. ". . . of your secrets?"

His laugh, coming out of the darkness, sounded like that of a madman, and yet I couldn't bring myself to believe Colonel Harlan Fleming deranged. A racist, yes. A cold-blooded murderer, probably. But not crazy. Not unless bigotry and arrogance were mental disorders.

"Gray Palmer a smuggler? Where on earth did you get such a notion? Ah, from the young lady, no doubt. I understand the boy never quite believed his father's altruistic motives for the work of the foundation, but I assure you they were quite genuine. Poor Gray has suffered more than any of us for that night's work in 'sixty-three. I believe he's tried to atone in a number of ways. Too bad he assumed all the warning signs and threats of prosecution posted here on the island would be enough to curb his son's curiosity."

"How did you know he'd been here? Young Gray, I mean. His girlfriend says he didn't tell anyone but us."

I felt rather than saw Harlan Fleming rise. Beside me, Erik stiffened as he, too, sensed the movement. The light flickered away. In the darkness that seemed to weigh down on us like a shroud, I shifted as if seeking a more comfortable position and slid my hand into the right pocket of my jeans. I couldn't quite wrap my fingers around the pistol, but the cold metal against my skin felt incredibly reassuring.

"We keep an eye on Judas Island," the Colonel said, and I remembered the men who had checked us out as we cruised by with Ron Singleton Monday morning.

"You've been watching the place for forty years?" Erik voiced the question that had leaped immediately into my own mind.

"Of course not. We were a little concerned when they located the monkey colony here, but it soon became evident the handlers had no interest in exploring the island itself."

"Then why . . ." I couldn't believe the Colonel was being so forthcoming.

"Politics and progress, my dear, the twin banes of Beaufort County. When the State of South Carolina bought Judas, we feared they might decide to develop it in some way. Unfortunately our governments are so susceptible to the temptation to make money. I've served a long time in this area. Former subordinates are always willing to do an old commander a favor, no questions asked."

So some old buddies had alerted the Colonel to Gray's incursion onto the scene of their crime. "But why . . . ?" I began when our captor interrupted. He seemed to be tiring of the interrogation.

"One visit can be construed as happenstance. Two . . . well, I'm sure you can see our dilemma."

So calm. So reasonable. Gray Palmer had made a second visit to Judas Island and sealed his doom. His confrontation with Fleming's cohorts had ended in his death. We'd probably never know what actually transpired, if Gray had scoffed or resisted or threatened. What little I knew of him made me think he probably hadn't been intimidated.

Then I realized the import of exactly what Fleming had said. *Two* visits. Just like us. If I'd had any doubts as to just what they intended for Erik and me, that throwaway line had pretty much eliminated them. I didn't think they'd shoot us there. It wouldn't do to have two more graves to worry about. Development meant bulldozers and digging . . .

"You're moving the bodies, aren't you?" The words tumbled out the moment the thought took shape in my mind. "You didn't expect us. You were as surprised as we were."

"Actually, Mrs. Tanner, I thought you might be dead. Kramer and Parelli assured me your, uh, accident was quite spectacular." In the dim light of the moon I saw Colonel Harlan Fleming shrug. "Ironic, is it not? Another few days and there would have been nothing for young Palmer to find. Tragic, really, when you think of it. All these casualties because of a simple matter of timing."

I had a sudden, overwhelming desire to smash in the face of this smug, arrogant bastard. I coughed to cover my movement and managed to get a firm grip on the pistol. I nudged Erik gently with my elbow, but there was no way to communicate my intentions to him. I could only hope he'd sense when it was time to move.

Again I coughed and shifted my legs. If I could just get my feet under me! I felt Erik stiffen as if the call to action had somehow communicated itself from my tensing muscles to his own. With Harry Simon out of the picture for the moment, there was no time to waste.

"Sit still!" Harlan Fleming commanded, and I could feel him take a couple of steps in our direction. The light of the thin moon glinted off the barrel of his pistol.

"I'm cold," I said, raising my closed left hand to blow on my fingers.

"My apologies, Mrs. Tanner. Perhaps you'd be more comfortable on the bench?" Erik began to rise, but the Colonel waved him back down with a flick of his gun. "No! You stay where you are!"

I scrambled to my feet at his invitation. I'd never have a better chance. I shoved my free hand into the left pocket of my jeans as if to warm it and began gently easing the gun from the right, but it snagged on the seam! I slowed my steps, trying desperately to pull the pistol out without giving myself away. In the distance I could hear the crackling of twigs underfoot as Harry Simon tromped back from his mission. It had to be now!

With one final tug, my hand and the pistol jerked free.

"Erik, down!" I shouted at the same moment I spun and sighted on the splinter of light thrown off by the gun barrel across the clearing.

The two explosions came almost simultaneously.

I don't think I screamed, but any sound either of us might have made was immediately swallowed up in the reverberating echoes of the gunshots and the frenzied screeching of three thousand terrified monkeys.

I remember thanking God I hadn't hit him when I recognized Erik's face bending over me. I remember the stabbing pain in my eyes as the clearing was suddenly bathed in searchlights, and scrambling men shouted orders.

I remember thinking how odd it was that the rest of me should be so cold when my left arm felt bathed in a warm, sticky flow.

And then I don't remember anything.

CHAPTER
THIRTY-FOUR

At least this time they didn't have to cut off my hair in the emergency room. But I did have to spend three days in the hospital, mostly to make sure the bullet had caused no more nerve damage to my already mangled left shoulder.

I felt truly touched by the steady parade of visitors who trickled in by ones and twos.

My best friend Bitsy Elliott tried hard not to cry, but lost the battle. I could tell she wanted desperately to hug me, but the stiff white sling made it awkward. She settled for a gentle kiss on my forehead and my promise to visit with her and the children as soon as I felt able to get around.

"You've lost entirely too much weight," she admonished me, swiping at the tears marring her careful makeup. "What you need is some feeding up."

Dr. Nedra Halloran, my old college roommate and one of Savannah's premier child psychologists, didn't let me off so lightly. Dear Neddie had seen me through my other brushes with violence and sat quietly next to the bed studying my face.

"What?" I'd finally said when the silence threatened to become uncomfortable.

"You've changed," she said, and I didn't think she meant it as a compliment.

"Why, because I'm not hiding out, mourning for Rob anymore? I thought that's what you wanted me to do."

"You used to be afraid," she'd said.

"And now I'm not. Isn't that a good thing?"

She'd taken a long time to answer. "I'm not so sure. Come see me when you're up to it. Or I can come to you." She, too, planted a soft kiss on my temple before pausing to turn back at the door. "Fear of death and injury is normal, Bay. Not caring if you . . ." She shrugged. "We'll talk," she said and was gone.

Erik came every day. The bullet which had struck Colonel Harlan Fleming had whistled just inches over my partner's head as he hit the ground. He tried to make light of it, but I could tell the experience had shaken him to his core. From him I first learned the details of the timely arrival of both the Coast Guard and the Sheriff's Department. Summoned by Ron Singleton, they had intercepted both Harry Simon and the two men approaching Judas Island by boat.

"Who were they?" I asked as Erik handed me the cheeseburger oozing with ketchup and mayonnaise I'd begged him to smuggle into the hospital. A girl can tolerate just so much meat loaf and lime Jell-O.

"The ones in the boat? Kramer and Parelli, the other two remaining guys from the squad that murdered those black men back in 'sixty-three."

"Why?"

"You mean why did they kill them?" Erik fished a paper napkin out of the bag and wiped a dribble of grease from my chin.

"Thanks. Yes."

"They were locals, probably the ones the Judge told us about. Your pal Harry Simon spilled his guts. Gray Palmer is standing firm, but I think he'll end up admitting his involvement. Back in the late fifties, early sixties the Marines used the island to practice amphibious landings. That was a long time before the monkeys got there. Seems the recruits got in the habit of using it for parties when they had leave time—drinking, maybe women. Harry wasn't real specific."

"Did you get all this from Red?" I asked, handing him the empty wrapper and wiping my good hand surreptitiously on the sheet. "Thanks, that was great," I added.

"You're welcome. Yeah, pretty much. He knew you'd be driving yourself crazy stuck here without any information. He said he'd be up to see you soon."

I could hardly wait. No doubt he'd rail at me for having gone off half-cocked again, for bumbling into danger, into things I had no business being involved in. There'd be the usual ranting about leaving things like this to the professionals. I'd have to promise not to leave him out in the cold on future cases.

Assuming there were any.

"So what did the black kids do, crash the party?"

"Something like that. Apparently they had been hanging out on Judas Island since they were teenagers. They'd smoke and pass around a bottle and talk about stuff. The Civil Rights movement was just getting started then, and maybe that gave them courage. Or maybe it was the booze. Anyway, they clashed with the recruits more than once. According to Simon, the recruits just got pissed one night and decided to teach them a lesson. He says Fleming was the ringleader. Who knows? They all took part."

"There were four of them? Recruits, I mean?"

"Actually there were eight. Including Gray Palmer. Harry Simon confirms that Gray was the one who tried to 'wuss out,' as Harry put it. One guy died of cancer just a few years ago. One was killed in Vietnam, and a third was shot up pretty bad over there. Never walked again. Apparently none of them still has any use for blacks."

"Jesus," I murmured, "when will it end?"

"Pretty soon for that bunch."

"Is Fleming here? In the hospital?"

I knew he'd survived the .32 slug which passed through his side. My aim had been low and too far right.

"No. They patched him up and took him away. I don't know where they're holding him."

"Poor Amy," I said. "I hope Chris Brandon stands by her."

"He will. The Judge says there's talk around town he may help with Fleming's defense. Providing of course it comes to a trial."

"What do you mean, *if?* Surely they're not going to let . . ."

I had jerked myself upright and the sudden motion sent waves of pain shooting down my left arm. I yelped, and Erik jumped to his feet.

"Don't do that! What the hell is the matter with you?"

I didn't need his yelling at me to realize it wasn't a good idea to be bouncing around just yet. I lay back, panting.

"Okay," he said, resuming his seat. "Take it easy. Nobody's going to get away with anything. It's just a question of who has jurisdiction. Fleming's still on active duty, you know. It may be a court-martial instead of a trial."

"Just so long as somebody nails the bastards." I rang for a pain pill and lay back, exhausted.

The morning of my release I tried to sneak out the back way, but the nursing staff was having none of that. They forced me to take the required wheelchair ride in the elevator, across the lobby, and out to the Judge's van which Erik had been using while his Expedition underwent repairs.

Though I had been badgered by reporters throughout my stay, no one lurked nearby as Erik handed me into the passenger seat and clipped the shoulder harness around me. I held the strap away from my injured arm.

"Sure you won't change your mind?"

I shook my head. "No. I want to go home."

Both my father and Lavinia had insisted I come to them at Presqu'isle for a few days, to recuperate and be pampered, but I'd refused. I wanted to be home. A phone call from Dolores had assured me I could expect no more loving care and attention than I would receive at the beach house. She was prepared to spend as much time with me as I needed. *Déjà vu.*

"I think they're a little hurt by your refusal," Erik said. He maneuvered the van into traffic, traveling much more slowly than he usually did in deference to my injury.

"They understand."

When I had awakened on my second day in the hospital to find Lavinia standing over me, I had at first been alarmed. She looked ten years older, her normally squared shoulders slumped, her narrow face creased with new lines.

"I didn't mean to disturb you, honey," she said.

The endearment startled me as much as her appearance.

"That's okay. All I do is sleep. Is everything okay? You look . . ."

"We're fine," she had replied, automatically including my father.

"Did they find . . . anything yet?"

She'd shaken her head, the air of sadness deepening around her. "It should take about two weeks before the results come back." The pause nearly broke my heart. "But I'm sure it's him." She touched her worn brown hand to her chest. "In here."

Confirming the fate of Eugene Smalls, the purported husband whose name was never mentioned, whose very existence many questioned, lay in the hands of a DNA lab in northern Virginia. Armed with a sample from Lavinia's son, Thaddeus, they would determine if any of the graves on Judas Island held an answer which might ease the uncertainty of forty years.

Eugene Smalls had disappeared in late October of 1963, along with two of his friends, leaving behind a pregnant bride-to-be who took his name and gave it to their son. Over time, few questioned her right to do both. During the four agonizing decades which followed she had believed he had run away, lured by high-paying jobs in the north or perhaps by the rhetoric of those who preached violence in answer to a legacy of oppression. Or even worse in Lavinia's mind, by another woman. Whatever the reason, he had left her alone to raise a bastard child, and she had hated him for it, had wiped his face from her memory—and that of his son. Never once had she considered he might be dead. Never once had she looked out from the back verandah toward the small dot of Judas Island and thought she might be looking at her lover's grave.

Even with the help of Dr. Denton Douglass who had agreed to expedite the DNA tests as much as he was able, it would still be weeks before we had a definitive answer. I couldn't spend those days watching her pain. She wouldn't want me to, for her own sake as well as for mine. And so I was going home.

"I understand," Erik replied when I finished my explanation. "I'm just surprised no one made a connection with the Smalls name."

"It's fairly common in these parts. There was no real reason for Law Merriweather to link the old missing person's case with Lavinia."

"I suppose not. Forty years is a long time. But your father did."

"Even he couldn't be sure. I still believe it's the only reason he encouraged us to go. He wanted to find the answer, spare Lavinia from having to hear the news from strangers."

Erik eased the van into the wide turn at the on-ramp for Route 278, and I braced myself with my good hand. I wondered what my mother would have done if she'd known the real story. She'd dropped hints over the years, about the elusive Mr. Smalls and whether or not he actually existed. Thank God that, in spite of her own doubts, she'd still taken on the proud black woman and her bastard son. I shuddered at the thought of my childhood without Lavinia . . .

I dozed a little, the warmth of the sun beating through the windows and the rhythmic motion of the van lulling me into sleep. I awoke with a start as we slowed for the guard house at the entrance to Port Royal Plantation. I forced my mind into gear and leaned across Erik to assure Jim it was okay to let us in.

"What happened to your arm, Miz Tanner?" he asked.

"Nothing serious," I replied and waved with my right hand as Erik pulled on through.

We rolled past the golf course, and Erik caught me studying his profile. He looked embarrassed, and I realized we'd never talked about his role in the incident on Judas Island.

"How are you holding up?" I asked.

"Fine." He replied without thinking then added, "I guess."

"This is the second time I've put your life at risk. I don't mean to do it, you know. It's not that I don't care . . ."

"I know that," he cut in. He cleared his throat nervously. "But . . ."

"But it's happened just the same," I finished for him. "Look, if you want out, I'll certainly understand. I don't think this is exactly what you signed on for last fall."

I expected him to protest, to contradict me. I was surprised how much it hurt when he didn't. We were only a few hundred yards from my driveway when he finally spoke.

"I think maybe I need some time to think about it. Not that I've made a decision. It's just . . ."

"You don't owe me any explanation," I said, mustering a cheerful tone from some reserve I didn't know I had. "When you've made up your mind, just let me know. I'll understand. Either way."

He shot me his heart-stopping smile and nodded. "Okay. Thanks."

I would miss him.

As I swallowed against the pain I felt rising in my throat, we took the right turn into my driveway and pulled up in front of my gleaming white garage door. I smiled, and Erik grinned back. All traces of the graffiti were gone.

"Dolores took care of it," he said. "Got the side of the house cleaned up, too. By the way, Red told me to tell you that you were right. It was someone from the seafood place."

I had been convinced the scrap of cloth with the small *t* and *c,* found on the night Erik tangled with the two vandals, probably had something to do with the Mitchells. I couldn't think of anyone else associated with those two letters who might have had a grudge against me.

"Who was it?" I asked.

"Tamika Jessup's daughter and her boyfriend. The kid works for your friend Bubba on the boats on weekends. Red wanted to know if you're going to press charges."

I shook my head and waited for him to come around and open my door. A week ago I would have answered a resounding "Of course!" even though I understood the girl's anger at having her mother's embezzlement exposed. On that day, after everything that had happened, it didn't seem important.

"Did anyone say why she was stealing the money?" I asked, fumbling with the seat belt release.

"Gambling. Started out a few years back with those video poker machines they've outlawed and then just escalated. The family's getting her some help," Erik added, giving me his hand as I stepped down from the van. "By the way, the Mitchells took care of the cost of repairs on the door and the siding. And the kids are going to be over here every weekend for the next six months keeping your yard in shape."

Bubba Mitchell is a very wise man, I thought.

Erik pulled my overnight bag from behind the seat, and I leaned on him as he ushered me toward the front door. Dolores didn't wait for me to make it to the top of the steps before her sweet smile engulfed me.

"Come, *Señora.* Let Dolores help you. I know you will not stay in the bed, so I make up the sofa for you. Is good, no? *Poco a poco, Señora.*"

I eased myself onto the pillows Dolores had stacked up and leaned back gratefully. She slipped off my shoes and covered my legs with a light blanket.

"I bring the tea now," she said, glancing toward the front entryway before bustling off toward the kitchen. Erik excused himself and wandered down the hallway to the guest room.

I closed my eyes for a moment, grateful to be back. Strangely enough, despite all the terrors of the past year, I felt safe here. And at peace. No longer Rob's and my house, no longer the repository of bitter memories of what might have been. Just my home. *Mine.*

"*Señora,* many messages have come. I write them down for you." Dolores set the teacup and saucer on the coffee table along with a pad covered in her delightful if sometimes indecipherable phonetic English. "And there is the lunch soon." Again I saw her eyes dart toward the door. "You rest. *Dormirse, mi señora.* Sleep. Dolores keep watch."

"Keep watch for what?" I asked but she scurried away without answering.

I settled myself more comfortably into the warmth of the soft cushions and moments later felt my eyelids beginning to droop. I wasn't certain how long I dozed before the sound of muted voices penetrated my half-sleep, and I sensed someone hovering over me.

"*Ma pauvre petite.*"

His clothes were rumpled, and his face looked drawn with fatigue and worry.

Alain Darnay dropped to one knee beside the sofa and gently pressed his lips to my cheek.

"You need a shave," I said, and he laughed.

Behind him I saw Dolores beaming as Erik hefted the two huge suitcases and carried them down the hallway toward my room.

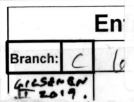
Chosen as ~~book~~ of the ~~Year~~ in the *Economist*, ~~Independent~~
and *Daily Telegraph*

'Jason Burke is a major authority on the politics and organization
of Islamic extremism and a talented writer with the rare gift of
joining effortless prose to challenging scholarship. He marshals
both talents in this latest book . . . It is a magnificent achievement'
Bill McSweeney, *Irish Times*

'This remarkably balanced, well-sourced and very well-written
book will be turned to in the future . . . [He] has demonstrated
impressive expertise as a historian who has had the
advantage of having been present on many of the battlefields
he describes' Andrew Roberts, *Evening Standard*

'Essential for understanding the past decade'
Sherard Cowper-Coles, *Sunday Times*

'Burke's book provides much sober information and analysis . . .
The long patient sentences of *The 9/11 Wars* are suffused with the
melancholy of a man who has learned a great deal from long
exposure to atrocity and folly' Pankaj Mishra, *Guardian*

'A reader wanting a more dispassionate survey of how 9/11, and the
response to it, may have shaped parts of the world will do no better
than invest in [this] brilliant book' David Aaronovitch, *The Times*

'At a time when there are more books out on terrorism than
ever before . . . this is likely to be among the best'
Colin Freeman, *Sunday Telegraph*

'A comprehensive summing up of the past decade's violent events . . .
Throughout, Burke's concern is to insist any accurate rendering must
show the murky, convoluted nature of Western nations imposing one
good-bad narrative on frequently unrelated local conflicts' *Metro*

'The joy of Jason Burke's book is that his account of people and
places caught up in complex and ferocious struggles is based on
long personal experience . . . Burke's account is by far the best to
appear on the intertwined battles sparked off by 9/11'
Patrick Cockburn, *Mail on Sunday*

'Insightful, thorough, and at times fascinating . . . leaves the reader more informed, though often appalled by policymakers' ignorance and furious when well-intentioned policies backfire' Daniel Byman, *Foreign Policy*

'At a time when more books than ever have been published about terrorism, *The 9/11 Wars* must certainly be considered one of the best' al-Sharq al-Awsat

'For the sheer pleasure of reading top-notch journalism, this is the one book about the last decade you can't fail to read' Arun J Nair, *Hindustan Times*

'Burke's book may never be bettered as a holistic account of what followed from the 9/11 attacks' Whit Mason, *The Australian*

'His is a history from below, not of the kind written by court historians, academics or parachuted journalists who make episodic visits to the war zone. He has been, and remains, a reporter who has spent a great deal of time the field, and it tells in the work' Manoj Joshi, *Mail Today*, India

ABOUT THE AUTHOR

Jason Burke is the South Asia correspondent for the *Guardian*. He has reported around the world for both the *Guardian* and the *Observer*. He is the author of two other widely praised books, both published by Penguin: *Al-Qaeda* and *On the Road to Kandahar*. He lives in New Delhi.

JASON BURKE

The 9/11 Wars

PENGUIN BOOKS

PENGUIN BOOKS

Published by the Penguin Group
Penguin Books Ltd, 80 Strand, London WC2R ORL, England
Penguin Group (USA), Inc., 375 Hudson Street, New York, New York 10014, USA
Penguin Group (Canada), 90 Eglinton Avenue East, Suite 700, Toronto, Ontario, Canada M4P 2Y3
(a division of Pearson Penguin Canada Inc.)
Penguin Ireland, 25 St Stephen's Green, Dublin 2, Ireland (a division of Penguin Books Ltd)
Penguin Group (Australia), 250 Camberwell Road, Camberwell, Victoria 3124, Australia
(a division of Pearson Australia Group Pty Ltd)
Penguin Books India Pvt Ltd, 11 Community Centre, Panchsheel Park, New Delhi – 110 017, India
Penguin Group (NZ), 67 Apollo Drive, Rosedale, Auckland 0632, New Zealand
(a division of Pearson New Zealand Ltd)
Penguin Books (South Africa) (Pty) Ltd, Block D, Rosebank Office Park,
181 Jan Smuts Avenue, Parktown North, Gauteng 2193, South Africa

Penguin Books Ltd, Registered Offices: 80 Strand, London WC2R ORL, England

www.penguin.com

First published by Allen Lane 2011
Published in Penguin Books 2012
001

Copyright © Jason Burke, 2011

Typeset by Jouve (UK), Milton Keynes
Printed in Great Britain by Clays Ltd, St Ives plc

A CIP catalogue record for this book is available from the British Library

ISBN: 978-0-141-04459-0

www.greenpenguin.co.uk

ALWAYS LEARNING   **PEARSON**

To Anne-Sophie and to Victor

Contents

PART FIVE
Afghanistan, Pakistan and Al-Qaeda: 2008

PART SIX
Endgames: 2009–11

List of Illustrations

Endpages: Taliban marching through a village (*Ghaith Abdul-Ahad / Guardian*)

All images reproduced with the permission of Corbis except for 9, copyright © Jason Howe, and 20, 24, 25 and 26, copyright © Jason Burke.

Acknowledgements

A long book means a long list of people to thank. First of all, there are all my various editors who, over the last fifteen years of foreign reporting, have sent me around the world on assignments that have been sometimes testing, always fascinating and often hugely enjoyable. Roger Alton, Paul Webster and John Mulholland at the *Observer* and Harriet Sherwood at the *Guardian* all funded trips, found me space and, equally important, gave me time to travel, to talk, to listen and to write.

Years of reporting means years of accumulated favours owed. There are many hundreds of fellow journalists, translators, fixers, drivers, experts, soldiers, bureaucrats, diplomats and others, too many to mention individually, to whom I am genuinely indebted for their generosity, company, learning, advice and assistance.

As for the writing of *The 9/11 Wars* itself, I would like particularly to thank Paul Harris and Marc Thibodeau for their helpful criticism of early drafts. I am particularly grateful to Iain King for his careful reading and to Toby Dodge, Owen Bennett-Jones, John Boone and Alexander Evans for agreeing to look over drafts. Owen's comments, astute and informed as ever, were of particular help.

Nadja Korinth, Aashish Jethra and Kailash Prasad all helped enthusiastically and competently with research and fact checking. A series of major events in 2011 meant scant time for final verifications. All errors are, of course, my own.

As ever, without the advice, inspiration, competence, drive and perspicacity of Toby Eady, my agent, and Simon Winder, my editor, this book would never have come to be. My thanks to them and all who work with them, especially David Watson for his fine work on the text.

My thanks too to my parents-in-law for their hospitality during long weeks at Lancieux and, of course, to my own parents, brothers and sisters for their forbearance and support for a stressed son or sibling.

But most of all my thanks to my wife, Anne-Sophie, for her love, understanding and encouragement and to Victor for his laugh.

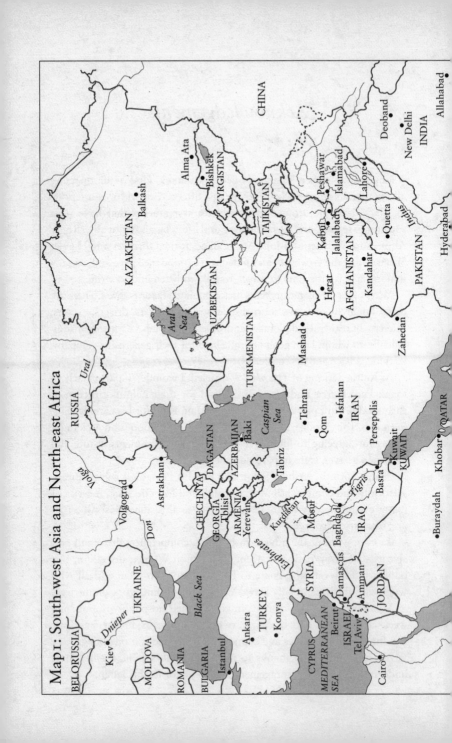

Map 1: South-west Asia and North-east Africa

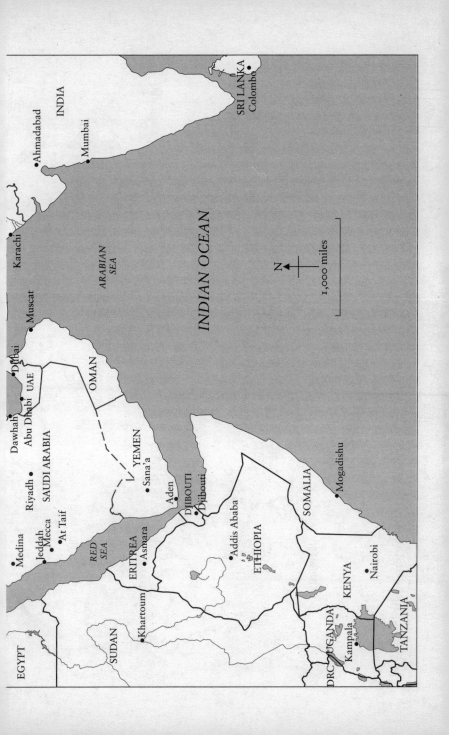

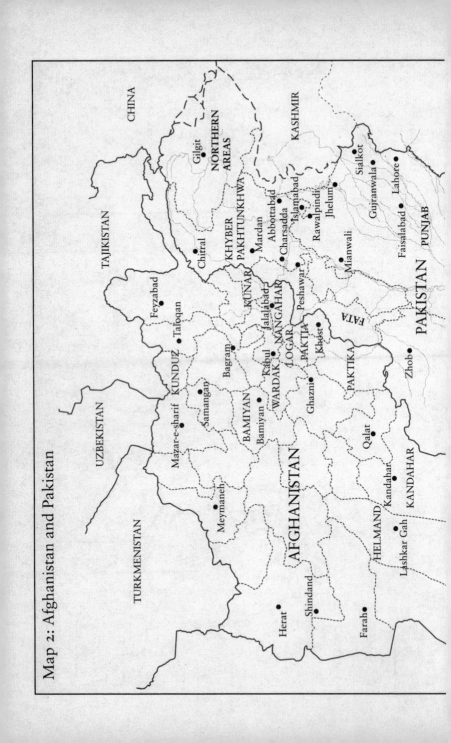

Map 2: Afghanistan and Pakistan

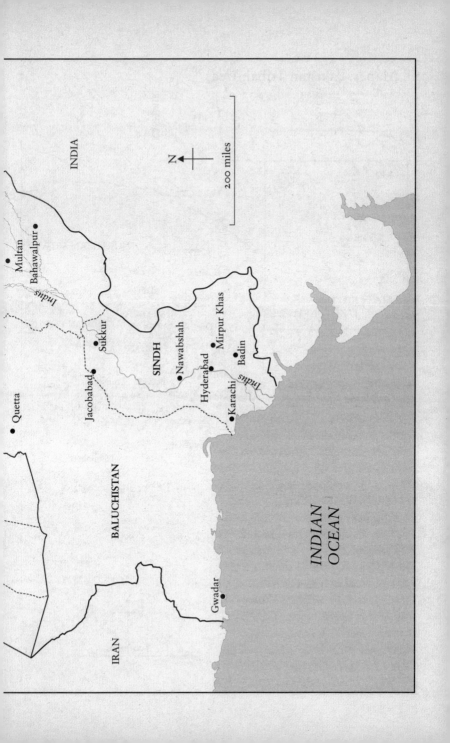

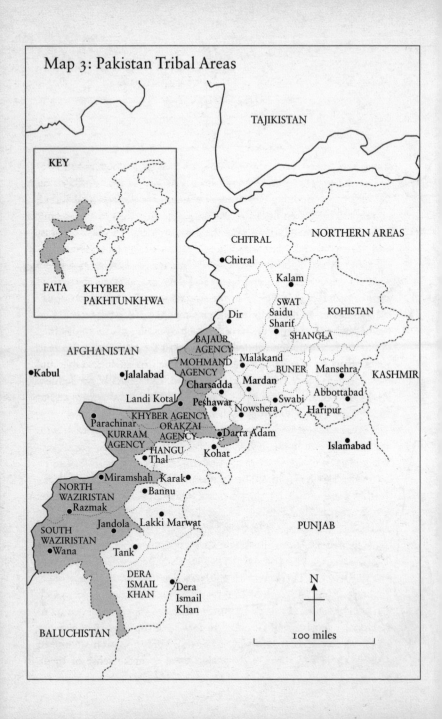

Map 3: Pakistan Tribal Areas

KEY

FATA

KHYBER
PAKHTUNKHWA

TAJIKISTAN

CHITRAL

NORTHERN AREAS

•Chitral

Kalam•

SWAT
Saidu
Sharif•

KOHISTAN

SHANGLA

Dir•

AFGHANISTAN

BAJAUR
AGENCY

MOHMAND
AGENCY

Malakand•

BUNER

Mansehra•

KASHMIR

•Kabul

•Jalalabad

Charsadda•

Mardan•

Swabi•

Abbottabad•

Landi Kotal•

Peshawar•

Nowshera•

Haripur•

KHYBER AGENCY

Parachinar•

ORAKZAI
AGENCY

KURRAM
AGENCY

Darra Adam•

Islamabad•

HANGU
Thal•

Kohat•

•Miramshah

Karak•

NORTH
WAZIRISTAN

•Bannu

Razmak•

PUNJAB

SOUTH
WAZIRISTAN

Jandola•

Lakki Marwat•

•Wana

Tank•

N

DERA
ISMAIL
KHAN

•Dera
Ismail
Khan

BALUCHISTAN

100 miles

Introduction

If you had looked down through binoculars on to the battered runway of Bagram in the summer of 1998 from frontline Taliban positions on the heights overlooking the Shomali plains, 30 miles north of Kabul, you would have seen little that indicated the role the old Soviet-built airbase could possibly play over the coming years. Through the dust and haze, you would have made out a cluster of ruined buildings surrounded by broad zones of overgrown land strewn with rusting metal stakes, a single battered jeep and no actual aircraft at all on the scarred strip of concrete shimmering in the Afghan sun. The group of scruffy Taliban fighters in filthy clothes who manned the makeshift trenches on the heights would probably have served grapes and tea to you as they did to the rare reporters who wandered up to the frontline in the dead years when no one was interested very much in an intractable and incomprehensible civil war in a far-off land. Occasionally, the fighters fired a rusty artillery piece in the general direction of the airstrip and of their enemies, usually hitting neither.

If you had come back four years later, say in the spring of 2002, you would have seen a startling difference. With the Taliban apparently defeated and dispersed, a bright new era for Afghanistan seemed to be dawning. The once-ruined airstrip down on the plains had become the fulcrum of a build-up of American and other international forces in the country that would continue inexorably over the next years. The bulldozers, the tents going up in the sand and the jets and helicopters lined up in serried ranks on the newly surfaced runway gave a sense that something extraordinary was happening, something of genuine historical importance. The only problem was that the exact nature of its importance was still very unclear. Now, many years on, though much inevitably remains obscured by the immediacy of events, something of that nature has become clearer. The form and the flow of events are beginning to emerge from the chaos of war. This book is an attempt to describe them and through describing them to make sense of them.

Bagram is now a small town of around 10,000 people, with its own shopping centres, gyms, evening classes, pizza parlour, Burger King, multi-denominational places of worship and mess halls all protected by treble rows of razor wire and electrified fences. The Taliban are in the hills around, though not yet back in their former positions from where they fired their poorly aimed shells and shared their tea and grapes.

As this book is rooted in many years of ground reporting, it has a different perspective from many of the works written about the events of the years since the attacks of September 11, 2001. Its focus is not the decisions taken in Western capitals but the effects of those decisions. Its aim is to suggest a grubby view from below, rather than a lofty view from above. It is primarily about people rather than about power, particularly people for whom life has changed in ways that no one could have predicted a decade ago. Occasionally these changes have been for the better; sometimes it is still too early to tell what they will bring; often these changes have been, savagely and brutally, for the worse. Sometimes these individuals and communities are passive victims. Often they are actors. Either way, they are not those whose decisions and motivations dominate many accounts. It is out of this intricate web of individuals, communities and events, however, that the story of the conflicts which we have watched, been touched by, even participated in directly or indirectly, is inevitably woven.

This account does not pretend to be objective. Though one aim of the book is to provide a historical record, it does not pretend to be comprehensive either. Such a work, even if practically realizable, would probably be unreadable. Too much has happened in too many places to too many people in too complex a way for it to be compressed and explained even in some 500 pages. The path this narrative takes is thus not necessarily the most direct or the most obvious. The places it visits are not always the most central. In journalism, analysis and academia there is a natural trend to the general, the global and the aggregated. The complex and often messy reality of history as it happens is reduced to single explanations or overarching theories. Though without synthesis nothing is comprehensible, there is a risk that, in reducing the complexity to find an answer, that answer is wrong. The devil is very often in the detail. Much of this book is devoted to exploring this detail.

The dangers of relying on broad generalizations or analyses that ignore the specificities of place, history, personality, culture and identity is very evident in the pages that follow. One early and costly error was a fundamental failure to properly understand the phenomenon of 'al-Qaeda'. This took years to right. A broader mistake which also proved tragically expensive in lives and resources was the insistence that the violence suddenly sweeping two, even three, continents was the product of a single, unitary conflict pitting good against evil, the West against Islam, the modern against the retrograde. For the last decade has not seen one conflict but many. Inevitably, a multi-polar, multifaceted, chaotic world without overarching ideological narratives generates conflicts in its own image. The events described in this book can only be understood as part of a matrix of ongoing, overlaid, interlinked and overlapping conflicts, some of which ended during the ten years since 9/11 and some of which started; some of which worsened and some of which died away; some of which have roots going back decades if not centuries and some of which are relatively recent in origin.

This is not a unique characteristic of the current crisis but is certainly one of its essential distinguishing qualities.[1] The wars that make up this most recent conflict span the globe geographically – from Indonesia in the east to the Atlantic-Mediterranean coastline in the west, from south-west China to south-west Spain, from small-town America to small-town Pakistan – as well as culturally, politically and ideologically. With no obvious starting point and no obvious end, with no sense of what might constitute victory or defeat, their chronological span is impossible to determine. No soldiers at the battle of Castillon in 1453 knew they were fighting in the last major engagement of the Hundred Years War. No one fighting at Waterloo could have known they were taking part in what turned out to be the ultimate confrontation of the Napoleonic Wars. The First World War was the Great War until the Second World War came along. Inevitably perhaps, this present conflict is currently without a name. In decades or centuries to come historians will no doubt find one – or several, as is usually the case. In the interim, given the one event that, in the Western public consciousness at least, saw hostilities commence, 'the 9/11 Wars' seems an apt working title for a conflict in progress.

Another major theme running through this work is inevitably that of religious extremism. What motivates the militants? How are they radicalized and mobilized? Why do they and how can they commit such terrible acts? The answer, as this narrative seeks to make clear, does not appear to lie in poverty, insanity or innate evil. Nor does it lie in Islam, though Islam, like all great religions, has a wide range of resources within it that can be deployed for a variety of functions including encouraging or legitimizing violence. The problem is not Islam but a particularly complex fusion of the secular and the religious that is extremely difficult to counter. The critical question is why this ideology, itself continually evolving, appeals to any given individual or community at a given moment. The answer, as one would expect, varies hugely over time and space. All ideologies are rooted in a context, and radical Islamic militancy is no different. These contexts inevitably change, and charting those shifts is one of the aims of this book.

Looking at violence leads into other major themes. It is now a commonplace to say that recent years have seen a hardening of identities based around ethnic, faith or other communities in response to the supposed 'flattening' of local difference by a process of globalization based in a heavily European or American market capitalist system. This is undoubtedly the case and has been consistently underestimated by policy-makers in London and Washington, who remain convinced of the universal attraction of the liberal democratic, liberal economic model in spite of much evidence to the contrary. But a key element missed by many analyses is the degree to which radical Islam is in itself as hostile to local specificity as anything that has come out of the West. One major current running through the pages that follow is the constant tug of war between 'the global' and 'the local', the general and the particular, the ideological and the individual. It is this tension that has defined much of the form and the course of the 9/11 Wars. The conflict was launched in the name of global ideologies. It was the rejection of global ideologies by key Muslim populations in the middle years of the decade that changed the course of the conflict. Ironically after years of vaunting the merits of the global, the West's greatest ally at a critical moment was its opposite: bloody-minded local particularism. The same force was also to work in less favourable ways elsewhere however.

This book ends with an account of the more recent phases of the conflict, where, even if cause for great concern still exists, the more apocalyptic predictions of a decade or so ago remain unfulfilled. This relative stabilization of the situation is precarious, however. Only a close examination of the previous course of 'the 9/11 Wars' and their antecedents can tell us whether what we are currently witnessing is simply a pause before a new cycle of violence or the uncertain early days of a definitive and positive trend towards something that resembles peace.

This book remains, however, primarily a work of journalism and not of history. It aims, in the long tradition of reportage, to reveal and communicate something about the world and about key events through the voices and views of those who participate in them and are affected by them. Its main aim is to provoke and inform discussion of vital questions rather than confidently lay out certitudes. As new material becomes available, others will improve the accounts of many of the events contained in the pages that follow. Overall I have tried to catch something of the nature of the conflict that has gripped and affected billions of people in recent years. Watching the aerial bombing of Tora Bora in the mountains of eastern Afghanistan in December 2001, with vapour trails from B-52s slicing across the pale sky above the snowy peaks and row upon row of rocky ridges successively lit by the slanting rising sun, a fellow journalist commented as a scene of untold horror and violence and extraordinary aesthetic beauty unfolded before us that only a vast novel really could make sense of what was happening. He was probably right.

PART ONE

Afghanistan, America, Al-Qaeda: 2001–3

I

The Buddhas

ALI SHAH

The winter had been hard, and in March 2001 the snow still lay thick on the passes. The only road open into the valley was a thin trace of black meltwater and icy mud. The small Afghan town of Bamiyan was virtually deserted. Men of working or fighting age had either fled or been forced out by the fighters who now walked down the single street of the bazaar, squatted by their pick-up trucks or sat on the grubby, threadbare carpets of the *chaikhana*.[1] The sky was an icy blue overhead, and it was still very cold.[2] To the south of the town, in a shallow river valley, almond orchards and slender silver-leaved poplars lay below low hills covered in cemeteries and fields desiccated as much by the freezing winter nights as by the summer heat. Behind, stretching to the horizon, were the higher mountains of Afghanistan's central highlands banded in different shades of brown, ochre and sand like a beach at low tide and ending in snow. Through the slats of a stable door beside one small mud-brick and wood home in a stand of trees near the river, a young man, sixteen years old, carefully watched the fighters walking through the streets.

Ali Shah had left with his parents, two sisters and two brothers when the Taliban had first arrived in Bamiyan weeks earlier but had returned to check on the family home. He had slipped back, easily evading sentries on the paths through the hills. Years of guarding sheep on the hills around had given the teenager a deep knowledge of the remote tracks that crossed the apparently barren peaks. He watched through the slatted doors of the stables beside the locked house and waited.[3]

The town of Bamiyan lies at the intersection of four roads, 9,200 feet up on an outlying spur of the Himalayan mountains. One leads west across the snowy peaks and ridges of Afghanistan's central highlands to the city of Herat and on to the Iranian frontier. A second leads southeast, across a high pass and through a narrow valley studded with small fortified villages and ribbed by terraced fields of wheat before dropping down to a shallow and fertile plain, where it joins the main road that runs from the Afghan capital Kabul down to Kandahar, the southern city that was the cultural and administrative centre of the Taliban. As this road drops off the high plateau of Bamiyan, it crosses the religious, ethnic, cultural and linguistic divide between the lands of the Shia Muslim Hazara, of central Asian ancestry, and the southern and eastern regions, where the ethnic Pashtuns, almost all Sunni Muslims, dominate.[4] The third road that leads out of Bamiyan runs north to the grassy steppes and eventually to the Amu Darya river and the frontier with the former Soviet Republics of Uzbekistan and Tajikistan. The fourth and final road leads east over yet another pass and down through a deep gorge to the fertile Shomali plains and the frontlines across which the fighters of the Taliban confronted the ragged troops of the Northern Alliance, the last remaining opposition to their rule over Afghanistan, firing desultory shells at Bagram airport and serving tea to the occasional visiting reporter.

Though in one of the poorest and most isolated provinces of Afghanistan, Bamiyan had once been a thriving and prosperous centre of trade and religion. In the fourth century, two huge Buddhas, one 175 feet high, the other 120, had been built into cavities hewn from the sandstone of the cliffs just to the north of the present-day town of Bamiyan. The statues themselves were not carved directly from the rock face but made of successive layers of mud and straw and finally painted plaster laid over a rock core. Beyond their religious purpose, they served too as giant landmarks for travellers on one of Asia's great trade routes.[5] With the vast statues, a monastery had been constructed, a mixture of wooden scaffolding built against the cliff face and caves. The Buddhist monks and believers who had once lived and studied there had long gone, as had the wooden passageways and façades, but even in 2001 the caves were still inhabited. The families who lived there were mainly destitute refugees who survived on thin earnings as shepherds and day labourers and ate stale bread scraps left over by the inhabitants of the town below their barely accessible and uncomfortable homes. The frescoes and murals on the inside of the monastic cells and pilgrims' accommodation had long since been defaced in waves of iconoclasm or simply obscured by the soot from decades of cooking fires. It was these giant Buddhas that the Taliban had come to destroy. Ali Shah waited until nightfall and slipped away.

THE TALIBAN

In successive campaigns the Taliban had brought 80 per cent of Afghanistan under their nominal rule. The movement had its origins in a vigilante group founded by a mullah, the equivalent of a country priest or parson in clerical terms, near Kandahar in September 1994. The very fact that it was the mullahs, traditionally lowly figures in Afghan society, who were in charge signalled the revolutionary nature of the new movement. The new group's innovatory style of fighting, which involved night combat and highly mobile 'charges' on the back of pick-up trucks, was another radical change.[6] Though often described as 'medieval', the Taliban were thus profoundly contemporary. Ideologically they were radical too and 'revolutionary' in the sense of the word that would have been understood by rebels seeking a return to an imagined earlier era of social justice across the ages. A worldview and language heavily informed by a utopian vision of an idealized past hid the fact that they actually sought to create something that had never existed: an Afghan state and society that resembled in culture, government and religious practice the idea they had of a perfect Pashtun village. That idea may have been a myth, but it was very real to them, and so was the political project of creating it.

At the beginning the Taliban's aim had simply been to end the anarchy and civil war into which Afghanistan had been plunged at the end of the decade-long Soviet intervention in 1989.[7] But the movement very rapidly acquired a variety of different and sometimes contradictory agendas, each representing one of the myriad fracture lines of an Afghan society fragmented by decades of war and uneven development. Ethnic splits, cultural divides, resentments nurtured through a conflict in which the bulk of the fighting had pitted Afghans against other Afghans, as well as a host of external interests came rapidly into play. The name Taliban, an Arabo-Persian word which means seekers of knowledge or religious students, reflected the origins, leadership and project of the new movement.[8] Initially welcomed in many parts by a population tired of war and insecurity, the Taliban had advanced rapidly, aided by their opponents' lack of unity, by local traditions which encouraged rather than stigmatized changing sides at the right moment and, at critical moments, by logistic and technical aid from the main Pakistani military intelligence service, the Inter-Services Intelligence Directorate (ISI).[9] Skilfully exploiting all the fracture lines of Afghan society, Taliban leaders ignored urban areas and institutions and instigated an extremely effective rural grass-roots outreach programme.[10] Using networks of association built up through family or tribal connections, in the refugee camps of Pakistan or among fellow veterans of the Soviet war, they approached tribal leaders, militia commanders, anyone who they felt could be co-opted, offering security, moral certainty, a restoration of social justice and order and personal advancement.[11] Their uncompromising message was nonetheless carefully tailored to fit local needs and identities. Those Taliban leaders with particular knowledge of a specific district's customs, history and dialects were sent there. Where a little encouragement was still needed, intimidation and selective violence usually sufficed.

Yet not only were the Taliban unable to turn their vision into reality but they proved incapable even of beginning to tackle the myriad problems of the country. In September 1996 the Taliban had captured Kabul, where their conception of an ideal Afghanistan and their literal reading of the Islamic holy texts was very alien to the better-educated urbanites of the city, many of whom had lived well under the Soviets.[12] The latter, at least for the better-off and better-educated, had been modern and liberal rulers who cleared slums, built schools and polytechnics and offered employment in a new, sprawling bureaucracy and military. Though the depredations of the post-Soviet period when the various *mujahideen* factions had fought over the capital meant that the Taliban seizure of the city was welcomed by some Kabulis, the five years that followed had seen increasing repression, haphazard government, growing violence against opponents and dissidents, and, apart from the booming drugs industry, a moribund economy. It had also seen the failure of the Taliban's early attempts to distance themselves from the rest of the world. Partly this was due to their own need for weapons, manpower and instruction, much of which came from across the border in Pakistan. Partly this was due to the fact that, as had been the case through the nineteenth century and before, Afghanistan was a ground across which the rivalries of bigger powers played out.

Some of these powers were formal states recognized by international law. The security establishment and successive governments of Pakistan had seen the Taliban as the perfect vehicle to project their own interests in Afghanistan and funnelled money, fuel, food, advice and ammunition to these new actors on the Afghan scene.[13] Very significant numbers of young fighters came from the religious schools of Pakistan's north-west frontier, where many Afghans, refugees or otherwise, were educated. Others sent over from the religious schools in Pakistan's eastern province of the Punjab were easily recognizable. The author found squads of them doing star jumps on the frontline north of Kabul in 1999. Other overseas allies were non-state actors, though powerful nonetheless. Much of the movement's money came through donations from clerical networks in Pakistan and further afield. Rich donors in the Gulf, devout and deeply conservative Muslim businessmen or royalty, contributed significant funds, happy to help to further the spread of the rigorous strands of Sunni Islam that they themselves followed.

If the web of alliances, funding streams and ideological strands drawn together in the Taliban was complicated so too were the networks that centred on the various factions opposed to their rule. Limited to the north and north-east of the country, denuded of material and men, each broadly representing a different ethnic minority, these groups were dependent on different regional sponsors for money and weapons and connected to different drugs or smuggling networks. The Hazara minority, for example, made up between 10 and 15 per cent of the overall Afghan population, and their factions were backed by the Iranians. This created a Shia axis that was a counterpart to the informal Taliban–Pakistani Sunni alliance on Afghanistan's other flank. The Uzbeks constituted 5 to 15 per cent, and their militia were supported by Uzbekistan. The Tajiks, who made up around 20 or 25 per cent, got funding and weapons from Tajikistan and from India.[14]

Amidst all these frames of geopolitical and regional alignment, the enormous majority of Afghans simply tried to survive. A measure of the plight of the Afghan people was that in 2001 nobody knew how many of them there were as there had been no census since 1979. Around 5 million were estimated to be living outside the country, largely in refugee camps in Iran and Pakistan, and perhaps 15 million remained in

Afghanistan. The population of Kabul was around half a million and, though it was by far the biggest Afghan city, its streets were empty, bazaars were bare, fuel was scarce and electricity rarer still. The only entertainments were executions and occasional football matches in the city's sports stadium, woefully ill-equipped gyms and boxing clubs, which provided an outlet for jobless teenagers, and a motorcyclist who set up a 'wall of death' in the central Ariana Square. That most of the spectators at the executions the author attended were there simply because there was nothing else to do was ample testament to the desperation and meanness of their lives. Many hours each day were devoted to procuring enough fuel in the winter and clean water in the summer. Ministers with little more than a basic religious education sat in the corner of decrepit offices warmed by Chinese-made bar heaters. A handful of students walked through the derelict halls of the university and the polytechnic was too heavily mined to be used. On the wall of the offices of the religious police, who were largely composed of young men armed with sticks or lengths of rubber hose who harassed women whom they deemed immodestly dressed or men whose beards were under the regulation length of the width of a fist, a scrawled slogan read: 'Throw reason to the dogs, it stinks of corruption.' The rural areas were worse. In the north-eastern Badakshan province, communities stockpiled animal fodder for human consumption. Life expectancy was around forty-two years (one year more than it had been in 1990), literacy rates were no more than 30 per cent, and 18 in every thousand women who gave birth died, the highest rate in the world. The word that featured most frequently in conversation with ordinary Afghans in the years before 9/11 was *mushkil*, difficult. This was the backdrop against which the first encounters of the 9/11 Wars were fought.[15]

BAMIYAN

The way into Bamiyan for the Taliban had been opened when a local commander had swapped sides in the classic Afghan fashion to allow his erstwhile enemies across the northern passes into the valley. Desultory fighting had continued for some months, however, and finally a specially constituted Taliban 'taskforce' was dispatched in January 2001 with the aim of subduing the central highlands and the Hazaras once and for all. Its young commander was Mullah Dadaullah Akhund, who had already acquired a reputation for brutality, atrocity and violence.[16] Charged with establishing full Taliban control in Bamiyan, Dadaullah set to work with terrible efficiency. In two days alone, his troops, reinforced by international militants and hundreds of teenagers from religious schools in Pakistan, used bulldozers, explosives and their bare hands to destroy villages, schools, mosques, clinics and orchards, effectively replicating what the Soviets had done to much of the Afghan countryside in the 1980s. Around two-thirds of the local population fled. The family of Ali Shah, the young shepherd, was among them.[17]

With Bamiyan now securely in Taliban hands, the question of the future of the Buddhas was raised. A meeting of senior ministers was convened to decide their fate.[18] It was not the first time that demolishing the great Buddhas of Bamiyan had been envisaged. The 'destruction of icons' in Afghanistan had been discussed for many decades in the conservative Islamic circles from which the Taliban drew their religious inspiration and had always provoked fierce debate. Early on the Taliban had seemed to value the cultural heritage of Afghanistan, allowing themselves to be convinced that they should protect the Buddhas and other remnants of Afghanistan's pre-Islamic past just as Egypt had worked to preserve the pyramids, and when Dadaullah's request reached the Taliban ministers in Kabul many argued that the Buddhas should be left as they were as 'cultural monuments'.[19] But such voices had powerful opponents.[20] There had long been bitter arguments between moderates and conservatives within the Taliban over a variety of issues: tactics of ethnic cleansing, the education of girls, engagement with the international community, the ban on opium that had been successfully implemented in 2000.[21] This time the hardliners outmanoeuvred their opponents by the simple expedient of making sure the question of the Buddhas was referred to their supreme leader, Mullah Mohammed Omar.

In the spring of 2001 Mullah Omar was forty-two years old. Tall, dark-skinned, reclusive, of limited literacy, relatively inarticulate, he had recently swapped the cheap mass-produced Pakistani-made *shalwar kameez* he had worn previously for a higher-quality local version with traditional embroidery. His eye-patch had been replaced by a foreign-made glass eye.[22] Yet these small concessions to comfort barely countered the overall impression of asceticism. Omar rarely appeared in public and gave few interviews but did not need to be seen or heard to keep command. The authority of the Taliban leader depended instead on his reputation for fierce probity, his war record from the days the Soviet occupation and his subsequent success at leading the movement to control much of his country.[23] Whether receiving visitors sitting on a cheap prayer rug in the mud mosque of his village home or in the run-down residence of the governor in Kandahar, Omar, despite his modest appearance, remained unpredictable and independent-minded. The self-styled *amir-ul momineen*, leader of the faithful, was a charismatic and instinctive leader with a natural talent for spectacular symbolic gestures such as publicly wrapping himself in the cloak of the Prophet Mohammed, a relic kept for more than 200 years in Kandahar and rarely shown in public.[24] Even after several years in power, as the Taliban more generally had begun to lose the support of many of their key constituencies in the east and south of the country, Mullah Omar himself retained significant personal authority.[25]

Presented with the demand from Mullah Dadaullah for permission to destroy the Buddhas, Omar requested a judgement from the Afghan Supreme Court, which comprised senior religious scholars, or *ulema*. Courts were perhaps the only functioning institution in Afghanistan. They applied, with relative honesty, efficiency and speed, a rigorous and literalist interpretation of the Shariat, the body of law based on the Koran, the sayings and deeds of the prophets and centuries of interpretation, exegesis and precedent. The clerics of the Supreme Court, all extreme conservatives and all appointed by Omar, unsurprisingly ruled that the destruction of the Buddhas was not only in accordance with the teachings of Islam but also strongly recommended. On February 24 Omar personally radioed Dadaullah in Bamiyan with the news and personally gave his instructions for the statues to be levelled.[26]

Many different strands – from the cosmic to the brutally practical, from the parochial to the international – determined the decision. On one level, the destruction of the Buddhas was a carefully weighed and calculated political act which to many of Mullah Omar's followers at the time seemed a logical response to the strategic and tactical challenges facing them. From this perspective, it was fanatical, perhaps, but far from irrational.[27] Omar had many very mundane reasons to destroy the Buddhas. The first was rooted in the internal dynamics of the Taliban. In the months before the demolition, Omar had increasingly found himself under pressure from a faction of committed extremists among the senior ranks and the younger generation of extremely violent new leaders rising through middle ranks best represented by Mullah Dadaullah. Destroying the Buddhas was thus a useful way for Omar to marginalize any moderate challengers while rallying the hardliners behind him. Equally, with a new fighting season about to start and complete victory still distant even after nearly seven years of gruelling warfare, the destruction of the Buddhas would energize and radicalize a movement which was losing momentum in the face of growing discontent with their rule, even among constituencies which had previously supported them.[28] Also, the demolition of the Buddhas was an act of communication in a predominantly illiterate land used to such public spectacles of violence. Successive rulers in Afghanistan recognized the importance of such gestures. The Mughals in the sixteenth century had built 'pyramids of skulls' of their enemies and made sure that potential opponents were kept well informed of the extreme violence they risked if they resisted. Abdur Rahman, known as the Iron Emir and widely credited with building the basis of Afghanistan as a nation state in the late nineteenth century, had publicized rather than hidden the excesses associated with his repeated campaigns of ethnic cleansing.[29] The Taliban had always understood and exploited the symbolic and the ritual. Their public hanging of a corrupt, child-abusing warlord-cum-bandit in 1994 near Kandahar and subsequent dismantling of the 'chains', the roadblocks where armed groups extorted money and abused local traders and travellers, had been the foundational acts of the movement. With their delivery of justice haphazard, the Taliban relied on the visibility and violence of punishment rather than its inevitability to discourage crime. To have the desired deterrent effect, that violence had to be seen or, as very few Afghans had access to televisions, at least imagined.

Then there was a more mystic element. The destruction of the Buddhas was part of a continued violent campaign prosecuted by the Taliban to extirpate all that they saw as counter to their vision of the authentically 'Afghan' Afghanistan, whether that involved pre-Islamic artefacts, the presence of Shia Muslims such as the population in Bamiyan or on the Shomali plains, heresy and 'modern' or Western influences. The destruction of the Buddhas was also an act by which they would be doing God's work. The order to demolish, Mullah Omar told some interlocutors, had come to him in a dream.[30] 'If on Judgement Day I stand before Allah, I'll see those two statues floating before me, and I know that Allah will ask me why, when I had the power, I did not destroy them,' he told one visitor.[31]

Finally, there was the influence of the various international extremists who were based in Afghanistan in the late 1990s. The most prominent among them was the al-Qaeda group led by Osama bin Laden, who had arrived in Afghanistan in 1996 after being forced out of Sudan and who had, as the years had passed, become increasingly close to Omar.

Bin Laden's relationship with Omar and other senior Taliban has been the subject of much debate. Often described as close, in fact it appears to have been characterized more by ambivalence and tension than complicity.[32] The Taliban were constantly torn. On the one hand they admired the Saudi-born extremist's apparent grasp of global politics, respected his piety and needed the money he could bring them through his contacts in the Gulf as well as the fighters he could supply. But they nonetheless remained irritated by the lack of respect this foreigner frequently showed them, their people and, despite his occasional praise, their country. Continually concerned about the damage that his ambitions might do to their own campaigns, senior Taliban figures repeatedly described bin Laden, whose arrival in Afghanistan had been the result of an invitation extended by a group of warlords who had been their opponents, as 'a problem inherited from the days of the civil war'.[33] The tensions were rooted too in the mutual wariness between the Afghans and the largely Arab international militants of al-Qaeda – predominantly Egyptian, Yemeni, Saudi or Algerian – and exacerbated by profound differences of outlook, worldview, religious practice and strategy.[34] Bin Laden's enemy was different from that of the Taliban, who were focused on conquering the pockets of resistance to their rule in Afghanistan. Bin Laden and his associate, the veteran Egyptian militant Ayman al-Zawahiri, saw their primary targets as the regimes of the Middle East, particularly those ruling in their native lands, or, as they announced in a series of public statements, America. Few among the Taliban knew or cared much about the USA or were particularly preoccupied by the political situation in Egypt or Saudi Arabia.[35] A second difference was theological. The Taliban had been raised in the hierarchical Deobandi school of conservative Islam, a discrete south-west Asian strand of Islamic thinking and practices very different in crucial aspects from the Gulf-based schools of the international militants. One reason Omar had turned to the judges for a decision on the Bamiyan Buddhas was that, in the fiercely hierarchical tradition of Deobandism, a mere mullah such as the Taliban leader was simply not qualified to pass judgement on such a question. He and other senior Taliban figures were thus shocked and angered to see bin Laden giving interviews on television, which was banned in Afghanistan, and issuing *fatawa*, scholastic opinions which they believed should only be given by senior religious scholars, not autodidacts who had trained as civil engineers.[36]

Nonetheless the international extremists did have an influence. From late 1998 onwards, there is much evidence of a more internationalized outlook among the Taliban leadership. For the first time, their propaganda began to refer to Zionist spies and American Crusaders, phrases borrowed directly from men like bin Laden. If Mullah Omar had his own reasons, cosmic and mundane, for assenting to Dadaullah's request to destroy the Buddhas he was at the very least encouraged by the foreign extremists who increasingly determined his perception of the world beyond the borders of his homeland.

THE WORLD TO THE RESCUE

The news of Omar's decision broke rapidly, and, one after another, a whole range of international actors set out to dissuade the Taliban. The first to fail were the Americans. Though to start with Washington welcomed the Taliban as a potential stabilizing force, that initial positive sentiment towards the movement was rapidly dissipated. First, there was increasing concern over human rights abuses. Then came the double bombing in 1998 of two US embassies in east Africa by al-Qaeda teams sent from Afghanistan and the subsequent refusal of the Taliban to withdraw their protection of bin Laden. The attack and the shelter offered to the perpetrators had provoked unilateral American sanctions in 1999 and a series of acrimonious exchanges through 2000. The affable Taliban ambassador in Islamabad, the capital of neighbouring Pakistan, continued to be received at the embassy – 'No one recognizes us but everyone recognizes me,' he explained – but apart from frequent demands made by State Department officials that bin Laden be handed over and occasional conversations it was a dialogue of the deaf.[37]

With no leverage on the Taliban the Americans were forced to rely on the Pakistanis. Islamabad sent both formal and informal deputations to

Kandahar and Kabul. Yet, though diplomatic as well as military assistance continued, Pakistan's leverage over the Taliban was less than was often thought, particularly following al-Qaeda's bombing of the embassies in east Africa and the messy battles around Mazar-e-Sharif in 1998 and 1999, during which widespread atrocities by both sides were widely reported.[38] A series of incidents – such as the beating of the Pakistani youth football team, who had made the mistake of wearing shorts to play in Kandahar, by the Taliban's religious police – had reinforced the impression that Islamabad was losing any grip it had once had on the movement.

By 2000, many in Pakistan's foreign ministry were expressing grave concerns about the diplomatic damage being done by their country's support for their increasingly unpredictable and extreme allies.[39] The Pakistani efforts to convince the Taliban to leave the Buddhas intact met with no success. Neither the interior minister nor retired senior Pakistani soldiers who had personally contributed to the movement's early victories were able to influence their former students to change their mind.

Relations with the Saudi Arabians had also soured long before. Along with Pakistan and the United Arab Emirates, Saudi Arabia had recognized the Taliban as the legitimate rulers of Afghanistan by 1997, seeing the movement as one of many vehicles for the propagation of the kingdom's brand of rigorous Sunni Islam across the Islamic world that merited financial and diplomatic support. This early enthusiasm had quickly evaporated, however. Again it was the presence of bin Laden and other militants that most angered Riyadh. After a particularly ill-tempered exchange following the bombings of 1998, official support for the Taliban ceased, though of course private Saudi Arabian supporters of the movement and their project remained numerous.[40] Unsurprisingly, Riyadh's efforts to influence the Taliban when news of the decision to destroy the Buddhas broke met with no success either. Given the propensity of the Saudi religious establishment for iconoclasm within the kingdom, that such efforts were relatively feeble surprised few.

For a time, there was hope that where the Pakistanis and Saudis could not or would not succeed the United Nations might. The UN had been present in Afghanistan for many years, and the Taliban, recognizing that the humanitarian work done by the organization at the very least spared them the trouble and expense of trying to feed and house hundreds of thousands of urban and rural poor, had initially cooperated relatively well with senior international officials. But the United Nations' values had often been difficult to reconcile with the Taliban's vision of Afghanistan. The idea that the organization represented some kind of benign 'international community' had little currency in a country where, at least in living memory, almost everything from abroad, and particularly from beyond the Islamic world, represented a threat. Senior Taliban figures, unsurprisingly given the widespread view among them that the UN was a Trojan horse for moral corruption and an assault on 'traditional' Afghan and Islamic values, had always showed profound hostility to UN staff, and relations only deteriorated further as time passed.[41] There continued to be contacts between the special United Nations envoy, veteran Spanish diplomat Francesc Vendrell, and high-ranking Taliban moderates with a more worldly outlook, but none of Vendrell's interlocutors had any real influence on Mullah Omar or on the direction the movement was taking. One of the last attempts to win a reprieve for the Buddhas saw an extraordinary meeting, organized by Vendrell, between Wakil Ahmed Muttawakel, the Taliban foreign minister, and Kofi Annan, the UN secretary general. It took place in the five-star Marriott Hotel in Islamabad. Few encounters better encapsulate the gulf between the Taliban and the developed, Westernized world than this between the urbane New-York-based Ghanaian diplomat and the envoy from Kabul. The meeting was polite, indeed relatively convivial. But even as Muttawakel pledged on behalf of his government that no harm would befall the Buddhas, preparations for their destruction were underway.[42]

The final attempt to save the Buddhas came from within the mainstream conservative Muslim community, in the person of the senior Qatar-based Egyptian cleric Yusuf al-Qaradawi. This could perhaps have been expected to stand a greater chance of success. Known throughout much of the Islamic world for his extremely popular and influential television programme in which he drew on his deep religious knowledge to issue instant *fatawa* in answer to viewers' queries about the correct Islamic response to topics as varied as oral sex and the plight of the Palestinians, al-Qaradawi travelled to Kandahar with a group of very senior conservative clerics intending to convince Mullah Omar to spare the Buddhas through a careful argument based on key Islamic texts, quotations and precedents. Classic diplomatic means involving bilateral relations and multilateral organizations had failed and this was an attempt founded in a long tradition in the Islamic world of debate and argument. However, not only were al-Qaradawi's ideological roots very different from the neo-traditional revivalism of the Taliban's religious culture but he was also seen as having 'sold out' to 'apostate' governments in the Arab world, not only by the international extremist clerics but also by their local Deobandi counterparts, to whom Omar was prone to listen for spiritual guidance. In many ways, al-Qaradawi's world, that of the major Islamic universities, of televised religious advice with audiences of millions, of the core Arab Middle East, was as alien to the Taliban as that of Kofi Annan. From the start the visit went badly with the eminent cleric's party ordered out of the cars bringing them from Kandahar airport and forced to pray in the sand by the side of the road by excited young Taliban fighters. Omar showed little interest in al-Qaradawi's sophisticated, learned and utterly pragmatic argument that, though the Taliban were justified in their belief that the Buddhas should be destroyed, there was an equally strong argument that the act, though undoubtedly legitimate, should be postponed until a more favourable conjuncture of political circumstances. Al-Qaradawi and his delegation left empty-handed, vocally complaining about their hosts' political immaturity.[43]

However, despite his apparent parochialism and mysticism, Omar sensed what effect the destruction of the Buddhas would have on the international community. Steps were taken to make sure that the audience overseas understood what was being said. His edict announcing the demolition was distributed to international journalists, the act itself was filmed by a cameraman, and its aftermath was later proudly shown to the international press.[44] To underline the message, Taliban spokesmen briefed reporters, claiming that the rest of the world had no right to complain. 'They give us nothing . . . Why should we listen to them?' one senior Taliban official in Islamabad said. 'They care more about old statues than Afghans starving.'

The destruction of the Buddhas started at dawn on March 1 and took at least ten days. The practical difficulties of demolishing such enormous objects, built on to a cliff face, had been grossly underestimated. Tank shells and rockets fired had little effect, simply sending showers of splinters into the air. The Taliban, who had originally thought they could destroy the statues in a few hours, were forced to resort to other means, eventually stacking shells and loose explosives found in the stocks held by the warlords they had defeated or co-opted in the valley around the base of the statues. This too failed, however. On the morning of the third day, Taliban fighters and coerced local men were lowered on ropes from the galleries around the sculptures and, dangling above the void, drilled holes into the now rock-hard ancient clay and straw mix into which they introduced explosives prised out of mines. This had more effect, and repeated blasts over the next twenty-four hours slowly reduced the two giant edifices to piles of yellow rubble. Footage showed huge explosions blasting dust out of the cavities housing the Buddhas high into the air as turbaned Taliban fighters cheered with shouts of 'Allahu akbar' (God is great). Two great plumes of yellow dust and black smoke hung in the clear blue sky for many hours after the statues had ceased to exist.[45]

THE BAMIYAN BUDDHAS
AND THE 9/11 WARS

The episode had given an early glimpse of a multitude of key strands that would mark the future course of the 9/11 Wars. First of all, there was the complexity of the environment, a thick matrix of overlaid and interwoven legacies of scores of conflicts over previous decades and indeed centuries, meshing the local, national and geopolitical with the tribal, ethnic and individual. It showed too the variety and division within entities often seen from the outside as relatively monolithic, whether that be the Taliban or even 'Islam'. The episode had revealed at least five different tendencies within Muslim practice – the Taliban's Deobandi neo-traditionalism, Gulf-style Wahhabism, the radically contemporary fusion of political Islam with ultra-conservatism of al-Qaeda, the internationalized orthodoxy of al-Qaradawi, the more moderate folksy traditions of the Hazara in Afghanistan – all competing for ideological and often physical space. All these elements, apart from the last, could be termed 'Salafi', in that they sought inspiration from the earliest generations, the *salaf*, of Islam and were part of a project to reproduce today the (imagined) society of the first Muslims on earth.[46] But as the destruction of the Buddhas showed, their internal differences of practice and outlook were vast. The episode had demonstrated how Islam is no more a 'religion of peace' than any other faith but a repository of resources which can be creative and destructive, positive and negative, depending on how they are instrumentalized. The episode had also shown the uses of spectacular violence, something else that was to mark the course of the conflict to come. The Taliban's iconoclasm was 'shock and awe' in a pure and raw form. It was a form of intimidation and of communication too, of 'propaganda by deed'. It was effectively an act of terrorism, though directed at inanimate if valued objects, not living people. Then there was the agency of key actors. Mullah Omar had not acted because he was mad, in thrall to someone else or simply reacting to the West but had made independent decisions based on his own perception of his best interests in the situation in which he found himself. And the episode had also shown the deficiencies of the West in understanding, shaping and genuinely seeing what was happening elsewhere. The response to the destruction of the Buddhas also revealed something else that would be frequently apparent over the coming years: the international community's chronic inability to focus on any one problem for a significant period. For after a week of well-ventilated shock and anger, attention drifted. Very quickly political leaders, reporters and editors turned to other stories, and politicians looked to other issues. There were suicide bombings in Israel and a riot in Bosnia-Herzegovina, Tony Blair won a second term as prime minister in the UK and in the US President George W. Bush, who had taken office in January after a contentious election, saw his package of massive tax cuts signed into law. A G8 summit in Genoa, Italy, was marred by violence, and the United Nations sanctions imposed on Iraq in the wake of the 1991 Gulf War were extended amid acrimonious debates. Afghanistan was no longer news.

In April Ahmed Shah Massood, the Afghan opposition leader famous for his long and effective guerrilla war against the Soviets and resistance to the Taliban, travelled to France to raise funds and his profile but had little success with either goal. Others who made the trip to Europe included Hamid Karzai, a young Afghan exile whose father, leader of the southern Pashtun Popalzai tribe, had been murdered by the Taliban in 1999. Karzai visited London with two older experienced Pashtun leaders from the days of 'the jihad' against the Soviets but received a relatively frosty reception from senior officials at MI6, Britain's foreign security service, who, though concerned about the situation in Afghanistan, were unconvinced of the need for urgent action.[47] Another visitor to MI6 was Mahmud Ahmed, director of the Pakistani ISI spy agency, who made repeated attempts to convince both Richard Dearlove, head of MI6, and his deputy, Nigel Inkster, to help get British diplomatic recognition for the Taliban despite the recent 'fuss' over the destruction of the Buddhas. Over dinner one evening Ahmed insisted that Dearlove should travel to Afghanistan to meet Mullah Omar, whom he described as 'a political visionary'. Dearlove declined.[48]

9/11

As the Taliban had been preparing to destroy the Buddhas, a thirty-one-year-old Yemeni called Ali al-Bahlul was putting the finishing touches to a video. Watching it on a laptop computer in a house in Kandahar, he was proud of his handiwork. Carefully edited on a laptop computer with pirated software, the images flowed smoothly one after the other. In the longest sequence, a young, bespectacled, bearded man, with a red and white *keffiyeh* scarf around his shoulders vivid against a backdrop of dusty southern Afghan hills, poured bile on the West, Israel, Saudi Arabia and the 'apostate regimes' of the Islamic world, occasionally waving his finger at the viewer.[49] The video had been specially commissioned, and though al-Bahlul had made many videos in the previous eighteen months none had been like this. He knew the young man on the screen personally as they had shared a house in Kandahar for many months the year before. Al-Bahlul did not know exactly what the video was for, though he was aware it was the last statement of someone who had been chosen to die for the cause. Al-Bahlul had left his home in the Yemeni region of the Hadramawt two years earlier, making his way to Afghanistan via Pakistan. It was his second trip to Afghanistan. On his first, like many such volunteers, his intention had simply been to find and fight for the Taliban. This time, inspired by the bombings in east Africa the year before, he wanted to find Osama bin Laden and, if possible, join al-Qaeda.[50]

Al-Qaeda had been founded by bin Laden and fourteen associates in a series of long meetings at a rented house in a western suburb of the noisy, dusty Pakistani frontier city of Peshawar in August 1988.[51] The meetings had stretched into the small hours as discussions ranged over the aims of the group, its composition and hierarchy. The 'organized Islamic faction' that was eventually created was not big – of its fifteen members, nine sat on the leading council – but it had grand ambitions.[52] Little thought appears to have been given to the name the founders chose for their group, but it was an appropriate and useful one nonetheless. 'Al-Qaeda' is a commonly used word in Arabic and, though often simply translated as 'the base', in fact has a range of other meanings too. This variety and consequent flexibility, itself a departure from the style of names adopted previously by militant groups, was to prove key in the coming years.

Bin Laden was thirty-one in the summer of 1988 and had spent the preceding years shuttling between his native Saudi Arabia and Pakistan, raising funds and organizing everything from medical care to earthmoving equipment for the Afghan *mujahideen*. In around 1987 he had actually seen combat in a series of skirmishes, later vastly mythologized, around the village of Jaji in Afghanistan. The legend of bin Laden's warrior prowess is linked to another myth: that the war against Soviets was fought and won by men like him who were backed – even 'created' – by the CIA. In fact, with tens of thousands of Afghans in the field at any one time and only a few hundred Arabs, the contribution of the latter, especially as they were largely inexperienced and untrained, was negligible. As for the support, the CIA did not enter Afghanistan nor instruct any Arab fighters nor disburse funds or weapons to them. Any US contact with *mujahideen* of any background was indirect, as the Pakistani ISI acted as intermediaries for all assistance, deciding which of the seven Afghan factions would receive what proportion of aid. Techniques taught by the ISI on the basis of US manuals and instruction from the CIA did bleed into the world of the Arab volunteers, but no direct contact took place. Indeed, the foundation of al-Qaeda was not the consequence of American intervention in any way but of bin Laden's frustration with the deep parochialism, national chauvinism, jealousy and feuding that marked relations between different Arab – as well as Afghan – factions during the war against the Soviets.

For what marked Al-Qaeda out among the multitude of other militant groups active across the Islamic world at the time was its avowed internationalism. Its founders' aim was to unite the disparate groups of militants who had fought in the war in Afghanistan to focus their collective energies on new targets. The fragmented factions that composed the world of radical Islamic activism would not restrict their activities to 'liberating' their respective homelands from 'despotic, hypocrite, apostate rulers' but would fight together, directed, coordinated and assisted by al-Qaeda. Their campaign would take two main forms: irregular warfare waged against the 'enemies of Islam' on 'open fronts of conflict', effectively guerrilla wars like that that had defeated the Soviets, and a series of spectacular and violent actions which would radicalize and mobilize all those who had hitherto shunned the call to arms, eventually provoking a mass uprising that would lead to a new era for the world's Muslims. The two strategies would be mutually reinforcing.

Though focused on the contemporary 'plight' of the world's Muslim community, the founders of al-Qaeda were drawing heavily on a long chain of militant scholars and strategists. Each had attempted to formulate a response adapted to his time. They included key Middle Eastern thinkers from the colonial period as well as strategists from the 1960s and 70s such as the Egyptians Syed Qutb and Abdelsalam al-Farraj. However, the most significant was Abdullah Azzam, the Palestinan ideologue, organizer and propagandist who had become the key point of reference for international radicals drawn to the war in Afghanistan during the 1980s. Azzam had not just theorized the duty of each individual Muslim to wage jihad, in this context defined as a violent effort to defend Muslims under attack, but had also been able to practically put it into effect too. As Soviet troops prepared to pull out of Afghanistan, Azzam had called for 'a vanguard that gives everything it possesses in order to achieve victory . . . [and] constitutes the solid base [*al-qaeda al-sulbah*] for the expected society'.[53] The founders of al-Qaeda aimed to be that vanguard and that base.

When al-Bahlul arrived in Afghanistan in 1999 al-Qaeda was reaching the peak of its capabilities. The eleven years since its foundation had not been without trouble. In 1990, with the war in Afghanistan descending into chaos, bin Laden, like the vast bulk of the foreign militants who had been fighting there, had gone home, returning to the city of Jeddah, where he had passed a comfortable youth as the seventeenth son of an immensely wealthy construction magnate. His welcome there was chilly, however, and, after a personal offer to the Saudi royal family to raise an international militant army to defend the kingdom from invasion by Saddam Hussein had been peremptorily rejected, it became clear that if he was to stay he would have to abandon his radical activities.[54] Bin Laden headed for Sudan, where the Islamist regime of Hassan ul-Turabi was in power. Khartoum was the destination of choice for those Arab veterans of the Afghan war who were increasingly unwelcome in Pakistan or in their native lands. Re-creating the atmosphere of Peshawar during the 1980s, Algerian, Libyan, Tunisian, Lebanese, Palestinian, Yemeni and other groups all co-existed in a constant stew of petty jealousies, temporary alliances and noisy boasting. Few among the groups and activists in Sudan at the time had heard of bin Laden, even fewer of al-Qaeda. Their attention was captured by developments elsewhere: the 1993 attack on the World Trade Center orchestrated by Pakistani-born militant Ramzi Yousef, the 'Black Hawk Down' episode in Somalia, which saw the effective defeat of US forces sent to secure the delivery of humanitarian assistance in the country, the terrible violence of the campaign by local militants against authorities in Algeria, the fighting in Bosnia-Herzegovina, Chechnya, the Philippines and in Egypt.[55]

In 1996, bin Laden had been expelled from Sudan when the regime decided that offering a haven to international militants was doing them more harm than good and had fled to Afghanistan. The next years finally saw al-Qaeda, already the vanguard, finally become the 'base' or 'foundation' too, as originally envisaged. Working with a growing group of experienced collaborators, bin Laden and al-Zawahiri set up or appropriated dozens of training camps, guesthouses and other facilities which provided them with a pool of ready volunteers for various ongoing projects. At the same time they launched a sophisticated outreach programme, sending emissaries to groups throughout the Islamic world offering cash and technical help in return for a degree of fealty. Such bids were often unsuccessful, with groups in Algeria, Indonesia, Chechnya, Uzbekistan and elsewhere jealously guarding their independence, but they were accepted frequently enough for a 'network of networks' to begin to emerge. The basic strategy remained the same: a series of spectacular violent actions to radicalize and mobilize potential recruits, to weaken the enemy economically and morally and to eventually provoke a mass uprising that would lead to a new era for the world's Muslims.

The idea for the September 11 attacks originally came from Khaled Sheikh Mohammed, an experienced and capable Kuwait-born Pakistani militant who travelled to seek out bin Laden shortly after the latter's arrival in Afghanistan.[56] Building on schemes he had tried to implement in the Far East, Mohammed's ambitious plans for hijacking dozens of aircraft to strike American targets was initially rejected by bin Laden, but then dusted off, revised and finally accepted after a series of heated meetings of al-Qaeda's senior leadership in the spring of 1999.[57]

The volunteers for the plan could be found simply by scouring the various training camps, either those offering basic training for foreigners arriving to fight with the Taliban or those where more advanced candidates were being trained by al-Qaeda instructors in techniques of urban terrorism. Though most in the camps were there simply to gain combat skills for battles elsewhere in the Islamic world, senior al-Qaeda leaders had little difficulty in finding suitable candidates for a spectacular martyrdom mission. Many recruits were found in one particular camp – al-Farooq near Kandahar – where around 100 volunteers were undergoing basic and advanced training. Investigators later said that al-Farooq was where al-Qaeda sent its top operatives to be prepared for their missions, but for David Hicks, an Australian convert who spent time in the camp in 2001, it was where 'all the oddbods' who did not already belong to any particular group ended up and thus was full of more cosmopolitan, Westernized militants of diverse origins. The proof, he said, was the ease with which he found fellow English-speakers. It was in al-Farooq that a team of volunteers who would be able to evade detection in America was assembled and trained.[58] One of them, a highly committed Egyptian called Mohammed Atta, was designated the operational commander of the attack in the USA. The video that Ali al-Bahlul was so proud of was the 'will' of another team member, his former housemate Ziad Samir Jarrah.

The summer of 2001 passed in final preparations as the hijacking teams arrived in America. By the end of August Atta signalled that the attacks were planned for the second week of September. In his compound in Kandahar bin Laden warned his entourage to prepare to move as an operation was imminent and ordered the evacuation of al-Qaeda's training camps.[59]

One preparatory strike by al-Qaeda, repeatedly postponed, was finally carried out with only forty-eight hours left before the operation in America was due to be launched. On September 9, two Tunisians killed both themselves and Ahmed Shah Massood, the main military leader of the Afghan opposition, with a bomb hidden in a TV camera during an interview at the veteran guerrilla leader's headquarters in the northern town of Taloqan.[60] The delay had largely been due to the target's busy schedule.[61]

On the day of the assassination of Massood, bin Laden and a handful of trusted and well-armed followers left Kandahar in a convoy of four ordinary cars and headed north to Kabul. On the 11th, they left the Afghan capital early and headed east, towards the Pakistani border, and by three o'clock were high in the hills of Logar province, not far from the villages where bin Laden had fought the Soviets over a decade before. Ali al-Bahlul, now appointed bin Laden's personal media technician, was driving a beige Toyota minibus that he had converted into a mobile media centre, fitting it with a satellite receiver, a monitor, a Toshiba computer, a VCR and a video camera. By late afternoon, the van was parked with the other vehicles in the convoy in a remote complex of run-down houses and cement buildings in one of the less-well-known training camps.[62]

Before leaving Kabul, bin Laden had told al-Bahlul that 'it is very important to see the news today' and had asked if he could get US networks on the satellite receiver. In the hills of Logar, however, the mountainous terrain blocked the signal. Instead al-Bahlul tuned a short-wave radio to the BBC Arabic Service. The presenter finished a report and then broke off scheduled programming. A plane, he said, had just crashed into the World Trade Center in New York. Bin Laden's entourage erupted into cheers, some prostrating themselves on the ground. It was 8:48 a.m. New York time, 17.18 in Afghanistan. Bin Laden held up a hand to quiet them. Half an hour later came the news, broadcast immediately this time, that another plane had hit the second of the twin towers. Again bin Laden calmed those around, this time holding up three fingers. The men wept and prayed. Almost exactly an hour later came news of a third strike, this time on the Pentagon. Bin Laden held up four fingers.[63] The final attack never came. A fourth plane, aiming for Washington's Capitol Hill, had crashed into a field in Shanksville, Pennsylvania, after a desperate attempt by passengers to wrest back control. The final death toll from the attacks would be just under 3,000. By nightfall, bin Laden and his followers and al-Bahlul's media van were gone.[64]

2

9/11, Before and After

THE REACTION TO 9/11

In the hours after the attacks world leaders received briefings from their security agencies about who might be responsible and what threats the perpetrators might still pose. The immediate fear was of a second or even third wave of strikes. Before the third plane had even hit the Pentagon, the White House 'counter-terrorism coordinator', Richard Clarke, had told Condoleezza Rice, the former academic who was national security adviser to the Bush administration, and Dick Cheney, the vice president, that America had been attacked by al-Qaeda. By early afternoon, individuals known to have links with bin Laden's organization had been identified on the passenger manifests of the hijacked planes.[1] In London, 'everyone seemed to think it was bin Laden'.[2] Blair was briefed by Stephen Lander, the head of MI5, the domestic intelligence service, and John Scarlett, the Chairman of the Joint Intelligence Committee, the government body tasked with aggregating the product of the British intelligence community for decision-makers. Both made it clear that bin Laden and al-Qaeda were the only people capable of such an attack. Scarlett pointed out that the strike was 'less about technology and more about skill and nerve'. Lander stressed that the US would be under enormous pressure to respond quickly and that Iran, Iraq and Libya were potential targets as well as Afghanistan. Both men told Blair that they ruled out 'the involvement of any other governments'.

Many TV networks had trained cameras on the Twin Towers after the impact of the first plane and thus captured both the arrival of the second plane and the eventual collapse of the entire complex. The strikes had been conceived to exploit the capabilities of new communications technology and in this had succeeded perfectly. The events and the live broadcasting of images of it were without historical parallel.

Though there were to be many more terrorist attacks over the coming decade – as there had been over previous centuries – none would come close to being as individually striking as the 9/11 attacks. Though over coming years terrorists would inflict many more casualties than the 2,977 victims who died in New York, Washington and Pennsylvania, no one incident would break so dramatically with previous examples of spectacular political or religious violence. The impact of the 9/11 attacks was inevitably magnified by their sheer unexpectedness. Many later accounts refer to the 'clear blue sky' from which the planes came, a metaphor for an imagined pre-war calm supposedly shattered by the strike. That the victims were in the middle of such mundane rituals as settling at a desk in the morning before a day's work, so well known to so many in the West, also amplified its effect, as did the extraordinary scale of the attack. There was the almost unimaginable sight of the collapse of two 110-floor towers but simultaneously there were the individuals caught up in the tragedy: the husbands ringing wives from their offices as the floors below burned, the 200 men and women forced to chose between fire or falling as a mode of death and who opted for the latter, the calls from the passengers before their ill-fated bid to retake control of the fourth hijacked plane, the firemen who continued to search empty floors in the doomed towers unaware because of faulty radios that orders had been given to evacuate the burning buildings and who perished as a result. The dead came from sixty different nations and represented almost every religion on the planet. Apart from fifty-five service men and women who died in the Pentagon, they were all civilians. They were bankers and postmen, short order chefs and stock-brokers, cleaners and artists, aspirant writers and out-of-work actors, senior counter-terrorism officials and tourists. Over 400 were emergency workers. The youngest victim was two-year-old Christine Hanson of Groton, Massachusetts, who was with her parents aboard the plane that crashed into the South Tower. The oldest was eighty-five-year-old Robert Grant Norton of Lubec, Maine, on the plane that struck the North Tower. 'Today is obviously one of the most difficult days in the history of the city,' Rudy Giuliani, the mayor of New York, told reporters at a hastily arranged press conference hours after the towers had collapsed, with the air still thick with ash and acrid smoke. 'The number of casualties will be more than any of us can bear ultimately.'[3]

Reactions around the world were instant and, as the attacks had been, were broadcast live. They naturally comprised, in those early instants of horror and shock, automatic, instinctive expressions of sympathy for the bereaved and solidarity with the American people. Early estimates of casualties ran higher than 15,000 – the number of people who were thought to be working in the World Trade Center at the time. 'We are all traumatized by this terrible tragedy,' Kofi Annan, the United Nations secretary general, said as the organization's headquarters building in New York was evacuated. In London, the national anthem at the Changing of the Guard was replaced by 'The Stars and Stripes'. Queen Elizabeth herself expressed 'growing disbelief and total shock' at the events. *Le Monde*, the French newspaper, declared, 'we are all Americans now'. The prime minister of New Zealand spoke of 'the sort of thing the worst movie scenario wouldn't dream up'. Many spoke of the 'barbarity' of those responsible. Gerhard Schroeder, the German chancellor, said the attacks were 'a declaration of war against the civilized world'. The European Union's external relations commissioner, Chris Patten, called the attacks 'the work of a madman'.

Within twenty-four hours NATO had unanimously invoked Article Five of the North Atlantic Treaty, which describes an attack on one member as an attack on all, and diplomats were calling for the United Nations Security Council to impose sanctions on any governments or groups found to be responsible. European foreign ministers scheduled a rare emergency meeting to discuss a joint response. Around the world, government installations and tall buildings were evacuated amid widespread fear of imminent further strikes. Information on supposed plots, on sleeper cells waiting to be activated poured in as intelligence services, stunned by their collective failure, scanned every last file for any hint of a potential danger. President Bush, who had spent much of the previous day in the air or in protected bunkers far from Washington, was told on the morning of the 12th that the CIA believed there were more 'al-Qaeda operatives' within the USA and that they wanted to attack with biological, chemical or nuclear weapons.[4] The ambient fear deepened and spread. Each public reaction provoked its own reaction, sparking a chain of accelerating, proliferating live commentary on an event the scale and significance of which no one knew quite how to gauge.

But even as their aides issued their statements of sympathy and grief, many world leaders saw immediately how the 9/11 attacks could be exploited to their own personal advantage and that of the nations they led. In public President Vladimir V. Putin publicly supported a tough response to the 'barbaric acts'. Privately, speaking to Blair on the afternoon of the attacks, the Russian premier lectured the British prime minister about how the world had long ignored his warnings about 'the threat of Islamic fundamentalism' and hoped that would now change.[5] Putin, who had been the first foreign head of state to call the White House on September 11 itself, repeated his message to Bush on the day after the disaster. For several years Putin had sought to cast the brutal war in the southern breakaway republic of Chechnya as a battle against Islamic radicalism rather than the latest manifestation in a centuries-old conflict between local irredentist tendencies and the Russian state. He had astutely sensed the shift that would now come in the perception of any conflict that could be said to involve Islamic militants. Ariel Sharon, the hawkish prime minister of Israel, was also equally quick to realize that the attacks, whatever the immediate calls by statesmen across the world for reconciliation and moderation, signalled a paradigm shift that would allow Israel greater freedom of action in combating Palestinian militant groups in Gaza and the West Bank and in consolidating the Israeli hold on the Occupied Territories.[6] Sharon immediately declared a national day of mourning in solidarity with the United States while urging the world to fight all terrorism. The coming weeks would see politicians ranging from David Trimble, the Northern Irish Unionist leader, to Robert Mugabe, the dictatorial ruler of Zimbabwe, all proclaiming that their long-term domestic or international enemies were in fact the equivalents of the terrorists who had struck the US.[7] Efforts to misrepresent domestic enemies or long-standing local conflicts as generated by or at the very least exacerbated by al-Qaeda were to become systematic over coming years, becoming a key element of the 9/11 Wars.

Across the Islamic world, there were effectively three different types of reaction: those of heads of state, those of the clergy and those of the general population. Figures like President Mubarak of Egypt and King Abdullah of Jordan, favoured allies of the USA and recipients of significant American aid, all expressed sympathy and offered cooperation with America, refraining, at least in the first instance, from any attempt to exploit the attacks. This was largely predictable. Whatever their views in private, such leaders understood how poorly a wounded America would view any disloyalty. More surprising was the strong condemnation of the attack by President Mohammad Khatami of Iran and Libya's Colonel Muammar Gaddafi. Khatami went as far as describing the strikes as 'terrorist', and Gaddafi offered aid to the American people. Only the Taliban and Saddam Hussein's Iraq broke ranks. Spokesmen in the former denied bin Laden was responsible. State television in the latter hailed the attacks as the 'operation of the century' which the United States deserved because of its 'crimes against humanity'.[8]

Clerics in the Islamic world had a more delicate path to tread. The fact that their influence depended not so much on any formal qualifications or positions but largely on the number of people who accepted and acted on their *fatawa* made them naturally more responsive to public opinion. A compromise needed to be found between the strongly pro-American position taken by rulers and the much more ambivalent sentiment of the street. Clergy close to or protected by governments, like Mohammed Tantawi, the Grand Mufti of the hugely prestigious al-Azhar university in Cairo, and Abdul Aziz Abdullah al-Sheikh in Saudi Arabia, could call the strikes 'stupid', 'forbidden' and underline that they constituted a 'grave sin' that would be 'punished on judgement day', but other religious figures needed to be more nuanced in their response.[9] So although Yusuf al-Qaradawi, the cleric who had attempted to dissuade the Taliban from destroying the Bamiyan Buddhas, denounced the attacks, particularly on those simply 'earning their daily bread', as a 'heinous crime' and urged Muslims to donate blood for the victims, he made a point of simultaneously stressing the United States' 'political bias towards Israel' as a reason for the strike and went as far as implicitly criticizing its perpetrators for mistaking their target. Instead, he said, Muslims should 'concentrate on facing the occupying enemy directly' inside Gaza and the West Bank.[10] This was to recur as a key argument – and a dynamic debate – in the decade that followed.

Beyond the clergy and the rulers came the genuine popular reaction. It was deeply conflicted. Horror, shock, genuine sympathy for individual victims was mixed in much of the Islamic world with a strong sense that the attacks were, if not legitimate in themselves, at least justified by the perceived misdeeds of America and Americans over recent decades. Bin Laden had previously been careful to pick targets that would have some popular resonance – the strike which had immediately preceded the

9/11 attacks was against a US warship anchored off the Yemeni port of Aden in October 2000 – and there can be no doubt that levels of anti-American sentiment in the Islamic world in the late summer of 2001 were high. Certainly this had been abundantly clear to anyone travelling in the Middle East, Pakistan or the Muslim majority countries of the Far East. The author spent the week before the September 11 attacks in Algeria, passing several evenings in the garden of one local human rights activist whose friends, most of whom would have been described as 'cultural' rather than practising Muslims, took American enmity towards the Islamic world as an indisputable given, barely worthy of discussion. The same had been the case in Jordan and in Morocco, as well as among many Muslims living in the West.[11] Yet such sentiments were far from straightforward. Few remained unmoved before the images of those forced to jump to their deaths.[12] Nor was the sense that the USA had somehow 'got what it deserved' limited to the Muslim world.

These various tensions were one of the reasons for the astonishing rapidity with which conspiracy theories sprang up, spread and became embedded in the public consciousness in the Islamic world and beyond. Within days of the attacks al-Manar, the satellite chain run by the Lebanese Hezbollah militant Islamist organization broadcasting from Beirut was reporting that 4,000 Jews 'remarkably did not show up in their jobs' on September 11, clearly implying that responsibility for them lay with some kind of global Jewish conspiracy rather than with the nineteen hijackers and their organizers.[13] Rooted in longstanding and widespread anti-Semitic stereotypes, some imported from Europe, such ideas, often strongly encouraged by governments and carefully fused with anti-Zionist rhetoric, had become a part of general daily discourse in much of the Middle East over previous decades. Others strands of conspiracy theory and denial, such as the idea that 'it must have been the Jews or the Americans' as it was impossible that Arabs could organize such a complicated operation, revealed a noxious mix of psychological evasion of the hard questions posed to Muslims by the 9/11 strikes and to a lesser extent the internalization of centuries of Western statements about the incapacity of Muslims or Arabs. Sitting at dinner with American Under Secretary of Defense Douglas Feith in Riyadh during a short tour of the Gulf and central Asia by Defense Secretary Donald Rumsfeld, Prince Saud al-Faisal, the Saudi foreign minister, wondered aloud who indeed was behind such a sophisticated operation given it was inconceivable that 'cave dwellers in Afghanistan' were responsible. As America was now at war with the Islamic world, al-Faisal mused, the answer surely would be found by seeking out who stood to benefit the most. After all, he continued, he had read press stories that Israel had warned Jews who worked in the Twin Towers not to go to the office on the day of the attacks.[14] Overall, one poll found, only 18 per cent in the Middle East as a whole, 4 per cent of Pakistanis and just one in ten Kuwaitis believed that Arabs were responsible for 9/11.[15] A poll in November 2001 showed that, while 81 per cent of British Muslims felt the 9/11 strikes were unjustified, 60 per cent felt that America was wrong to blame them on al-Qaeda.[16] Conspiracy theories also spread rapidly among non-Muslim populations, especially among the extreme left or in countries like France with a long history of anti-Americanism.

A FAILURE OF INTELLIGENCE

Key to the speed at which the conspiracy theories spread was incredulity that Western security services could not have prevented the attacks. Much has now been written about this failure, one of the greatest of the many intelligence failures of recent decades. There is no space here to tell once again the long story of administrative squabbles, petty bureaucratic feuds and institutional failings that allowed the 9/11 hijackers to avoid the attention of American law-enforcement agencies despite the plethora of individual clues to their presence and plans that were uncovered through the spring and summer of 2001. In very simple terms, the 9/11 hijackers slipped through the gap between domestic security services looking for American citizens attacking in America and overseas security services, mainly the CIA, looking for foreign citizens attacking US interests overseas. Though it was understood that a third scenario – foreign citizens attacking in the US – was increasingly likely, the systems to deal with such an eventuality were not in place. The CIA picked up the trail of key individuals in the 9/11 plot in Malaysia but was unable to exploit the opportunity they were given to unravel the conspiracy. When the 9/11 teams did arrive in the US, a series of errors, avoidable delays and bad luck meant they evaded detection and capture. Finally no one had imagined terrorists ever using tactics like those that the hijackers were to adopt.

There is no space either to retell the story of the failure of various attempts to eliminate bin Laden in the late 1990s. What appears clear, however, is that, though American decision-makers undoubtedly recognized the threat bin Laden and his associates posed to US and other nations' interests, certainly from 1998 onwards, they simply did not have the mental, legal, technical and cultural equipment to formulate and execute an effective policy to counter that threat.[17] One reason for this was the lack of a legal framework to deal with an amorphous, dynamic and fragmented movement based more on personal relations and a shared worldview than on formal membership of an organization. So when in 2001 the perpetrators of the 1998 embassy bombings went on trial in New York, al-Qaeda was represented in the courtroom as a classic hierarchical terrorist group. Prosecutors and investigators were constrained both by their training and the legal tools at their disposal to fit this radically new phenomenon into a pre-existing schema, deploying laws designed to fight serious crime in order to obtain convictions. Equally, the nature of Islamic militant activism posed difficulties when it came to pre-emptive action to stop a plot. At what point and against whom, senior Clinton administration figures asked, could one intervene with military force before an attack took place? Was it justified to assassinate bin Laden when there was no direct evidence linking a conspiracy to him?[18] One result of this ongoing debate was a lack of concrete purpose. 'No one said kill him. The word used was "neutralized", which covers a multitude of sins,' remembered Jack Cloonan, who was a special agent for the FBI's Osama bin Laden unit from 1996 to 2002.[19]

A further problem was finding a way of using military force against these irregular fighters in a distant country who, despite their unconventional structure and behaviour, nonetheless threatened attacks that could incur levels of physical destruction and casualties which had previously been the monopoly of states. American defence spending in 2000 was budgeted at $267 billion, with intelligence agencies receiving significant resources too, but this did not mean the right tools had been developed for such a technically difficult task.[20] A project to mount missiles on the new unmanned surveillance drones being developed was being held up by squabbles between government departments and intelligence agencies over its funding. There were also problems with putting 'boots on the ground', i.e. combat troops into Afghanistan. The military, suited by habit, doctrine and equipment to fight single, strategically critical battles against conventional enemies, showed both an innate conservatism and an understandable reluctance to get involved with unorthodox plans often hatched by civilians whom they saw as dangerous amateurs.[21] The missile strikes on Afghanistan and in the Sudan following the 1998 east African bombings had been an embarrassing failure, missing all major targets, killing a few recruits from Pakistani-based militant organizations who had camps in Afghanistan that were independent of those of al-Qaeda, incinerating a few tents and destroying what appeared to be a factory for making veterinary antibiotics at a total cost of more than $50 million.

Through 1999 and 2000 many alternative plans for 'neutralizing' bin Laden were discussed and rejected. Complicating the situation was an absence of actionable intelligence. This was inevitable given the lack of cultural resources suffered by Western intelligence services and the weaknesses in the relations with their counterparts in the Islamic world. The CIA and counterparts elsewhere in the West, with the possible exception of the French DGSE, had a very limited number of Arabists, and almost no one who spoke the languages of Afghanistan or Pakistan with any proficiency. MI6 did not have a single Pashto-speaker on its staff in 2001.[22]

The consequences of this lack of both a ground presence and detailed understanding were exacerbated by an increasing reliance on high technology and communications intercepts in place of so-called HUMINT, intelligence gathered by live human beings on the ground. Then there were the tight restrictions under which the CIA in particular worked. Often living in diplomatic compounds, sometimes not even speaking local languages, hedged round by security restrictions, intelligence operatives found even the most banal of relations with their local counterparts difficult. Developing the kind of range of contacts they needed for a genuine understanding of any given society, culture, country or community and the various forms of militancy and extremism it could produce was almost impossible. Many stations had been shut down in the early 1990s, and often the US agencies simply had no permanent physical presence. In Tajikistan, marginal in global terms perhaps but crucial for Afghanistan, the level of lawlessness and street violence was deemed 'simply too great to allow CIA officers to visit there for more than a day or two at a time ... once a month'.[23] The CIA had few high-quality assets in Afghanistan, though they had developed a range of basic tribal contacts, and none within the senior ranks of the Taliban or circles close to bin Laden.

The degree of ignorance of local conditions was illustrated by a plan during the summer of 2001 to use Ahmed Shah Massood's northern troops to attack or capture bin Laden, despite the fact that their target spent most of his time hundreds of miles from the dwindling pocket of territory Massood and his allies held. Massood's men were predominantly Tajik and thus instantly recognizable outside parts of the north-east and Kabul. This posed an evident tactical problem. To show willing, Massood sent a detachment to fire some rockets into a training camp near Darunta when it was thought bin Laden might be in the vicinity.[24] Predictably the strike had no effect. In the capital, a series of attempts were made to find out where bin Laden stayed and when he would be there. These too came to nothing.[25] In the end it was al-Qaeda who, with lethal consequences, penetrated Massood's security, killing the best asset America had in the country.

Another major obstacle was poor intelligence passed on by those who did have a better handle on what was going on than their Western counterparts. Despite relatively close relations with the Americans, information flowing from services in countries such as Jordan, Egypt and Algeria was designed primarily to convince the US government of the bona fides, stability and competence of the organization and government supplying it, not to give the recipient a fair and accurate assessment of distinctly sensitive issues such as international extremism or their own problems with domestic radical Muslim activism. Equally, key potential allies like the Pakistanis or the Saudi Arabians simply could not be trusted. Though it was in fact a variety of factors (including a last-minute decision by a driver) that had saved bin Laden from the missiles fired at eastern Afghanistan by Clinton in the wake of the 1998 east African bombings, US intelligence officials were convinced that their target had been tipped off by Pakistani security services.[26] Following blasts targeting American troops in Saudi Arabia in the 1990s, Riyadh's security services had done as much to hinder American agencies' investigations as to aid them. As for Yemeni authorities supposedly assisting Americans tracking those behind the attack on the USS *Cole* in 2000 they were 'worse than a joke', according to US officials working on the file at the time.[27] Indian intelligence fed a steady stream of highly politicized 'findings' to American counterparts throughout this period. These were largely focused on proving Osama bin Laden's connection to, or even presence in, the disputed Himalayan territory of Kashmir.[28] A variety of Middle Eastern intelligence services insisted that the Saudi was seriously ill from a kidney disease, a falsehood that was to surface regularly over the following years.[29]

Despite the obstacles, an understanding of what was happening in Afghanistan did gradually emerge. The CIA had set up a special unit to track bin Laden in 1996, which, after a difficult start, had begun to formulate a more accurate vision of the man and his operations.[30] When it came to individual threats, formidable resources could be deployed. Following the 1998 east African attacks an extraordinary and very successful investigation led by the FBI saw the rapid detention of many of the key individuals involved. When it was feared that Islamic militants were planning a series of attacks on the eve of the new millennium, a vast worldwide operation of intelligence gathering, analysis and interdiction was launched. Hundreds of CIA officials worked round the clock through the last weeks of December 2000, checking every lead, trawling through vast banks of intercepted communications or reports received from overseas stations and foreign services. 'It was extremely intense. There were rows of people sitting in jeans and sweatshirts all day and all night, all through the weekends,' remembered Art Keller, a junior CIA official involved in the effort. 'There was a genuine sense of urgency and threat.'[31] But despite the growing body of knowledge about what was going on in Afghanistan, the true nature of the threat posed by al-Qaeda and Islamic militancy as it evolved in the last years of the twentieth century still seemed to escape many senior intelligence and counter-terrorist officials and, more importantly perhaps, their political masters. The shrill warnings from the CIA's bin Laden unit – Alec Station – earned its staff a reputation as fanatics who suffered from a lack of perspective.[32] Just a year or so before the September 11 attacks, researching the international militants in Pakistan was the job of the most junior member of the MI6 station in Islamabad.[33]

One key weakness was intelligence on exactly who was travelling to the camps in Afghanistan. In the years following the attacks counter-terrorist agencies would make massive efforts to fill this gap, working feverishly to understand the identity of those attracted in such numbers by the structures that al-Qaeda and a multitude of other groups had created there in the late 1990s. 'In retrospect, there was one question we simply never really tried hard enough to answer,' remembered one former MI6 officer. 'Who were the volunteers?'[34]

THE VOLUNTEERS

Male, young, Muslim but otherwise very varied, those in the camps were the products of various broad trends affecting Islamic communities across a vast stretch of territory from Morocco to Malaysia, via Europe, the Balkans and central Asia.[35] Though some were from developed Western countries, often second-generation immigrants or converts, most came from Egypt, Saudi Arabia, the Yemen and Algeria.[36] There were, the Pakistani ambassador to Kabul at the time cabled home, also hundreds of central Asians, Bangladeshis and a hundred or so Uighurs.[37]

Three elements were immediately striking. The first was the age of the volunteers – eighteen to twenty-eight for the most part, which placed them firmly in the 'youth bulge' seen across the Islamic world in the late 1990s. They were the children of the economic boom in the Middle East fuelled by the oil price hikes that followed the 1973 Arab–Israeli war. Each stage of their relatively short lives had been marked by a new broad ideological development. Their first memories would have been of a time when the secular pan-Arab or nationalist ideas which had been dominant since the colonial powers left the region were being questioned in an unprecedented way following decades of economic mismanagement and graft. They had grown up during the 1980s, a decade which saw political Islamism come of age as a mass ideology in their countries of origin, particularly when left-wing ideologies were fatally undermined by the collapse of the Soviet Union. They were teenagers at precisely the time when political Islamism itself had began to lose momentum in the face of intransigent regimes and a failure to broaden its appeal beyond sections of the conservative urban middle and upper working class. And they reached adulthood at exactly the moment when the violent insurgencies of the early 1990s which had followed the failure of the Islamist project themselves began to run into difficulties as their indiscriminate brutality alienated potential supporters.

In their short lives, therefore, the young men who ended up in the camps in Afghanistan between 1998 and 2001 had seen the failure of the nationalism of the first mid-twentieth-century postcolonial regimes, the socialism or pan-Arabism of their largely incompetent successors, the moderate Islamism of the opposition groups in many of their home-lands and finally the violent extremism targeting local regimes. The new internationalist extremism of men like bin Laden was, at the very least, untried.[38]

The second macro-factor evident was that a very large number of the volunteers making their way to Afghanistan in the late 1990s were either immigrants themselves or the children of immigrants. This immi-gration might be international, in the case of Ziad Samir Jarrah, Atta and the rest of the 'Hamburg cell' who led the 9/11 hijackers, or internal, from rural areas to urban areas. The family of al-Bahlul, the young man who had struggled to set up the television for bin Laden to watch the 9/11 attacks live, had, like tens of millions of others in the Islamic world over previous decades, made the transition from the countryside to the town, in its case from a small village in the Yemen to Sana'a, the capital, before subsequently living in Saudi Arabia. Bin Laden's father had made a similar journey, leaving the Hadramawt region of Yemen for Saudi Arabia's most cosmopolitan city, Jeddah. Three of the 9/11 pilots had emigrated from their homeland to the West. There were myriad other examples. In every case, such displacement implied a significant change in terms of environment and of social codes and traditions and the necessity of finding a new set of values and modes of behaviour and of integration.

The third obvious macro-factor was the new wave of anti-Americanism that coursed through the Islamic world in the 1990s. There had been previous such waves, of course, but post-Cold-War American hegemony had focused resentment on the new 'hyper-power' in a new and urgent way, sharpening the two-centuries-old dilemma in the Islamic world of how to confront, deal with, profit from, learn from or indeed influence the West. This anti-Western sentiment, which had often provoked a var-iety of revivalist religious sentiments, was reinforced by the new media technology emerging in the 1990s which allowed someone like bin Laden to reach an audience directly without risking years of dangerous activism on the ground. It also accelerated a process, seen outside the

Islamic world too, of the construction and consolidation of new, often deeply conservative, communal and sectarian identities, in this case an unprecedented sense of solidarity with Muslims elsewhere in the world.

Al-Jazeera, the feisty satellite TV channel launched from the gas-rich Gulf emirate of Qatar in 1996, played a part in this, along with its many emulators. The channel pioneered a new, sharper style that broke with the stolid traditions of heavily censored state broadcasters in the Middle East and tried to represent the views and interests of ordinary people. This, however, meant that the channel's programming often reflected and reinforced prejudices rather than challenging them. News bulletins from Gaza, southern Lebanon, Chechnya, Kashmir or elsewhere played into a generalized narrative of victimhood. Simultaneously Western soap operas and documentaries, beamed directly into tens of millions of homes, raised expectations and aspirations as well as resentment at the economic success of the West and the Far East. The internet, which more than any other medium allows individuals to construct their own personal worlds of information without being challenged, also spread rapidly despite many governments' attempts to control its use. By 2001, even Saudi Arabia with its then restrictive media regulations had 100,000 net subscribers.[39]

Exacerbating this, of course, was Western policy. By omission as much as commission, successive American and European governments through the mid and late 1990s failed to engage with the tough core issues that had long troubled their relations with the multiple communities and countries that constitute the Islamic world. The Arab–Israeli peace process, so promising at the beginning of the decade, was allowed to fail, and longstanding strategies to secure the stable flow of strategic resources such as oil to world markets and key short-term domestic factors were allowed to continue to determine policy. European powers and Washington appeared to be, at the very least, insensitive to the plight of Muslim communities during the wars in the former Yugoslavia. A Cold War legacy of support for repressive regimes was continued with the new enemy becoming the Islamists rather than the Communists. The bulk of the volunteers flowing into Afghanistan came from countries – Saudi Arabia, Jordan, Egypt, Algeria – whose governments received significant support from the West. Even if the West was by no means at the root of all troubles, as often argued, the policies and language of Western countries did help militants 'frame' the world's problems and their own grievances within a simple and persuasive single narrative of Muslims suffering at the hands of a belligerent, rapacious America and, to a lesser extent, its allies. This may not have been true but was nonetheless convincing to many.

The volunteers making their way to Afghanistan were, however, a minority of a minority. Of a global population of around 1.2 billion Muslims and a population of perhaps 300 million in the Arab world, perhaps between 10,000 and 20,000 individuals travelled to Afghanistan through the 1990s and underwent some kind of militant training or experience of combat there.[40] One thing that is certain is that they were not mad, poverty-stricken or stupid. There is no evidence that levels of mental illness exceeded those of the population in general. Also, though volunteers from central Asia were often much less well off, the vast bulk of those from the Middle East, and indeed the handful from the West, were from families that were, if not wealthy, then far from poor.[41] Any link with poverty was thus indirect. As was to be seen again throughout the course of the 9/11 Wars, a lack of means was a poor predictor of radicalism. Equally, though some were of below-average education, particularly in terms of their theological knowledge, most were of a normal or often superior intellectual capacity. Those in the camps had travelled for a wide variety of reasons: political, religious and personal. Though some were motivated by a specific desire to meet Osama bin Laden, the main aim of most was to get training to fight in Kashmir (especially for those from the British Pakistani community), Chechnya (for Saudi Arabians, Algerians and Egyptians) or in Afghanistan itself against the Northern Alliance, who were seen as enemies of Islam.[42] Some were outraged at the second Chechen war of 1999 or events in Israel-Palestine. Some travelled for religious reasons stemming from genuine conviction: to fulfil a religious duty of jihad and potentially to achieve martyrdom without the political context being particularly important. Many were motivated by more personal factors: a genuine desire for adventure, to flee 'family problems' or to go in the footsteps of relatives or friends who had previously travelled. A relatively high number had suffered educational or business failures. Some came from jihadi families with numerous examples of volunteers. Fathers of others had fought in wars of independence against Western colonizers in Algeria, Libya or elsewhere.[43] Often motives were mixed within the groups who set off. There were even brothers who travelled together but for different reasons – one out of a genuine sense of religious duty, the other almost as a 'lifestyle choice'.[44] Those who facilitated the passage of the young men to Afghanistan tended to be older, part of the generation of militants formed during the 1980s. There is no evidence to suggest anyone was 'brainwashed', however. A few were genuinely 'groomed' to travel by recruiters who carefully targeted vulnerable and suggestible individuals and drew them into activities that they appear never to have fully understood. To the unskilled and jobless, jihad was presented as an alternative employment, an extension of the charity work at home that many were already involved in.[45] But the vast proportion actively sought out the networks which could help them fulfil a relatively mature ambition. Certainly few hid their destinations or ambitions from friends, families or even their governments. As during the war against the Soviets, videos of 'atrocities' and feats of arms were effective means of sensitizing, mobilizing and radicalizing individuals already rendered receptive by other factors.

In Afghanistan, separated from their home environment, their radicalization accelerated. A whole range of key concepts embodied in Islamic history and holy texts were deployed in the camps to reinforce the sense that the volunteers were engaged on a righteous, rational path. Often early weeks of instruction were dominated by lessons in theology. The idea of *hijra*, the flight from an unholy, ignorant and barbaric environment to a remote place where a true community of believers, the *jemaa islamiya*, could be constituted before returning to establish a new golden age convincingly reformulated the story of the Prophet Mohammed to better fit it to the 'reality' of the current situation of Muslims. The cosmic single narrative of the age-old war between good and evil, belief and unbelief could be further embedded, the 'enemy' could be dehumanized, fellow Muslims of insufficient piety deemed unworthy of the faith, an extreme and minority interpretation of jihad could be reinforced, and a powerful sentiment of belonging to an elite vanguard encouraged. The theological and psychological indoctrination was, of course, backed up by the practical excitement of weapons training and the team-building effect of physical hardship.[46]

The process was far from universally effective. Letters from volunteers and later testimony speaks of disappointment at the quality of teaching, at the lack of solidarity between groups of students (who were taught according to language or nationality) and at the food.[47] Around a quarter to a third of volunteers, few of whom had ever travelled before, suffered gastro-intestinal problems or other illnesses, and few camps had even rudimentary medical facilities.[48] But volunteers were never prevented from leaving, and many dropped out, returning home or simply hanging around in Jalalabad or Kabul, living in the many guesthouses established by the various groups or funded by the major Islamic NGOs or missionaries in Afghanistan at the time. 'I never at any moment felt I couldn't leave. It was all very casual. You could walk in and walk out,' David Hicks, the Australian convert who ended up in al-Farooq camp in 2001 after fighting in Kashmir, said.[49]

Nonetheless, as the 9/11 attacks revealed, the system, if more chaotic and ramshackle than often thought, worked. And not just for al-Qaeda either. By the late years of the decade, militant organizations ranging from the Islamic Movement of Uzbekistan through to fragmented groups such as the Jordanians who had established camps in the west of Afghanistan to the Algerians who had their guesthouses in Jalalabad were all receiving more recruits that ever before. There were so many that those trying to administrate the scores of guesthouses, camps and training centres in Afghanistan frequently complained of the sheer numbers.[50]

LONDONISTAN

The final problem for those seeking to protect the West against the new threat that radical Islam posed was thus one of imagination: the failure of so many, particularly in America, to understand what globalization actually meant and what kind of new menace it could generate.[51]

This failure was not restricted to the US. It was certainly evident in the UK, where the true role of key individuals based in London through the late 1990s almost entirely escaped British security services.[52] The importance of the city as a secure base from which to organize fund-raising, propaganda and recruitment for the international militant movement was consistently missed by officers from Special Branch and MI5, who were more used to dealing with Irish republican terrorism. Hundreds of militants wanted in their own countries for a range of activities had arrived in the UK in two broad waves between the end of the 1980s and the mid 1990s. Some were relatively harmless, relatively moderate political Islamists. But others posed a much more serious risk to Britain and its allies which was seriously underestimated.

Nothing shows the confusion of this period clearly more than the question of a 'Londonistan deal' by which militants were allegedly allowed to stay in the UK as long as they refrained from targeting British interests. For many militants, such a pact undoubtedly existed. Omar Mahmoud Othman, better known as Abu Qutada, a Jordanian Palestinian and radical scholar who was both a key ideological reference and a key organizer for al-Qaeda, had several meetings with MI5 soon after his arrival in the UK during which he offered to report on anyone harming *British* interests.[53] Other key militants in the UK at the time later spoke of how British security services had told them that they would be guaranteed the rights of the 'British constitution' as long as they refrained from fighting each other on UK soil, from targeting the UK itself or from using UK territory as a base from which to attack other countries.[54] A third militant activist later linked to the radicalization of perpetrators of terrorist attacks, a Syrian-born preacher based in north London called Omar Mohammed Bakri Fostok, frequently told prayer meetings that the Koran teaches that covenants exist between believers and non-Muslim authorities who give them shelter. He even on one occasion made the argument to British viewers of a middlebrow afternoon television show.[55] When Algerian militants in London passed a message to operational commanders waging a vicious war in their home country that their presence would be tolerated in the UK provided they did not break any laws, the then leader of the main militant group in Algeria, Djamel Zitouni of the Groupe Islamique Armée, responded by offering not to harm Britons anywhere.[56] British officials and politicians have always denied coming to any arrangement with any activists. 'They were told their rights and the legal position was explained, nothing more,' said one senior British police officer.[57] The likelihood is thus that the 'deal' was more a product of cultural misunderstanding than any conspiracy. The militants, coming from repressive states of the Middle East, naturally saw things differently from the British police, whose legalistic position – if you break no laws we can't touch you – would have seemed nonsensical unless part of a bargain. That the anti-terrorism laws in effect at the time in the UK did not cover conspiracies to attack overseas must also have escaped the comprehension of the new arrivals – as they escaped that even of close allies like the French.

Deal or no deal, what is certain is that British security agencies had difficulty tracking the shift in the orientation of militants in the UK over the decade. Whereas early arrivals had been largely focused on the 'near enemy', the regimes of their home countries, later on in the decade it was the 'far enemy' of the US and by extension its allies that had become the target for London-based militants. In this, of course, activists in the UK were following the broader trend across the Muslim world that had seen the 'internationalization' of Islamic radical activism over the decade. But such esoteric technicalities largely escaped those tasked with monitoring Britain's radical population and there was trouble quantifying quite who threatened whom. Another strand that went virtually ignored was what was to eventually come to be called 'home-grown militancy'. Throughout the 1990s, young British men of Pakistani origin made their way to Kashmir to fight with local groups there. Their activities were monitored by the security service but again were not seen as a potential threat to UK interests even when British citizens died in suicidal assaults on Indian troops or paramilitaries. Funds destined for Kashmiri groups, often collected in mosques in the Midlands or the north of the UK, were seized frequently, but logistic support networks were more or less tolerated.[58] In general, however, security services were too busy with other issues raised in the chaos of the collapse of Communism to think too much about the apparently fringe problem of radical Islamist activism. A third of the 1,800 staff of MI5 was focused on Irish republican violence. Turkish groups such as the PKK or Dev Sol, which ran rackets in north London and were actively involved in criminal activities, were a significant concern. One major problem was that the service had very few offices outside London and none at all in the areas where much of the British Muslim population was concentrated.[59] As relations with local police were often poor, this meant very limited visibility on the ground.

'[Islamic radicalism] was a concern but far from a real priority,' one senior MI6 official said later. 'We had a lot going on [and] had suffered significant cuts in resources in the search for a post-Cold-War peace dividend. But we were not approaching the problem in the right way or digging in the right places. We were looking but simply not seeing.'[60] Parliament's Intelligence and Security Committee later said that the British JIC had in fact warned Blair in its weekly intelligence assessment of July 16 that al-Qaeda – operating from bases in Afghanistan – was in the 'final stages' of preparing a terrorist attack on the West, probably targeting Israelis or Americans, though the details, timings and methods of attack were not known. The nature of the threat was not 'understood' at the time, the Committee noted, 'due to a failure of imagination'.[61]

A GLOBAL WAR ON TERROR

In the eight months between taking power and the attacks of 9/11 the president, Condoleezza Rice, the national security adviser, and Colin Powell, the former general who had been appointed secretary of state, had shown little interest in the Middle East in general and in Islamic terrorism in particular, preferring to focus on more traditional sources of danger such as Russia and China or states with long records of hostility towards the US such as Iraq. One major preoccupation was the question of missile defence.

Rice later mounted a spirited rebuttal of the criticisms of the Bush team's record in the months before 9/11, saying that their priorities were in line with briefings by the outgoing administration which had emphasized North Korea, Iran and the Balkans. Rice claimed too that a major strategy aiming to deny sanctuary to al-Qaeda and its various offshoots and affiliates in Afghanistan and to freeze the assets of the group and those of its benefactors was being put into action by the late summer of 2001.[62] Much of the acrimonious argument after the 9/11 strikes revolved around a series of warnings received by the Bush administration during the summer of 2001. In his memoirs, Bush recalled that CIA intelligence before 9/11 had first pointed to an attack 'overseas' and that during the late spring security had been 'hardened' at embassies abroad, cooperation with foreign services increased and warnings issued to domestic American authorities about potential hijackings on internal flights. In early August Bush was briefed that bin Laden intended to strike in the US. Though the possibility of a hijack was raised, concrete details of what form that strike might take were thin.[63] A meeting of the top-ranking 'Principals Committee' to discuss the terrorist threat – repeatedly postponed through the Bush administration's first eight months in office – finally took place on September 4.[64] By the time it met, it was, of course, far too late to do anything. 'On 9/11 it was obvious the intelligence community had missed something big,' the president later wrote.[65] It is hard to escape the impression that, even if the warnings reaching him were vague, Bush, who had taken a vacation of record length through the summer, was at the very least guilty himself of a degree of slackness that bordered on the negligent.

Even more has been written since September 2001 on the internal workings of the Bush administration in the days and weeks following the September 11 attacks than on the failure to prevent the 9/11 plot. The immediate reactions to 9/11 on the part of key individuals in the Bush administration were clearly crucial in setting the broad lines along which US strategy would at least initially evolve and in 'framing' the conflict more generally for nearly 400 million Americans and many more people around the globe. The major long-term significance of the 9/11 attacks lay to a very large extent in the reactions they provoked.

Though privately the reaction of President Bush himself to the attacks was unequivocal – 'my blood was boiling. We were going to find out who did this and kick their ass' – his initial public response was hesitant.[66] It was only at his third attempt that he began to deliver the simple, reassuring and confident rhetoric that the hurt, frightened and angry US population expected, needed and appreciated. In his first major address, broadcast at 8.30 on the evening of the attacks, Bush said no American would ever forget 'this day', that 'our fellow citizens, our way of life, our very freedom' had come under attack, that America had been targeted because it was 'the brightest beacon for freedom and opportunity in the world'. He quoted Psalm 23: 'though I walk through the valley of death'. No distinction would be made between terrorists and those that harbour them, he said. The perpetrators of the attack would be hunted down and brought to justice.[67]

With each further speech, the narrative of righteous vengeance, of a new era dawning and of religiosity, became better defined. Bush's prose, terse and folksy as it may have been, was soaked in a sense of American exceptionalism, the 'manifest destiny', two centuries of American belief in its own role in the world as a beacon of enlightenment and progress, the sense of an existential battle between freedom and repression. 'This will be a monumental struggle of good versus evil. But good will prevail,' Bush told Americans on September 12.

The president's chosen strategy – the Global War on Terror – took around a week to be clearly formulated. Though often seen as a simple and instinctive product of a simple and instinctive view of the world, this is to underestimate its intellectual coherence and internal logic. The thinking among many in the American Department of Defense is revealed by the account of a lengthy debate among senior Pentagon political appointees on the day after the attacks. Related by Douglas Feith, the under secretary of defense for policy, the conversation involved General John Abizaid, who was to take command of US forces in the key theatres of the war on terror within two years and who would start to develop the American military's thinking on 'the 9/11 Wars'.[68] It took place on board a military transport plane bringing the Americans back to Washington from Moscow, where they had been discussing the abrogation of Cold-War-era missile control agreements.

The president had already told his most senior intelligence officials that their mission was now to 'disrupt attacks before they had happened' and stressed the need for deterrence.[69] Starting from the principle that their primary task was not to punish those responsible for 9/11 but to prevent such attacks happening again, the men on the plane talked for many hours about how best to target the shadowy and elusive group of individuals responsible. The answer lay in the nature of the enemy, which, Feith argued, comprised two main elements: a network of interlinked terrorist groups apparently including al-Qaeda, Hezbollah in Lebanon, Hamas in the Gaza Strip, the Indonesian Jemaa Islamiya and many others and the states which supported them. These latter included, *inter alia*, Pakistan, Iraq, Iran and Taliban Afghanistan. If America was to be protected in the future – especially from the threat of chemical, biological or nuclear weapons – then this network needed to be broken up and these states – and potentially others such as North Korea and Libya – needed to be made to cease their sponsorship of terrorists. It followed that any strike on Afghanistan could only therefore be a component of a much broader effort against multiple targets. One key element of any campaign would be the necessity to intimidate actual or potential sponsors of terror around the world.[70] Indeed, the operations in Afghanistan against al-Qaeda – part of the network – and the Taliban – the sponsoring regime – would have to be the first demonstration of the new strategy but far from the last. For if intimidation did not work, then forcing regime change needed to be considered too. America's future safety lay in the resolve with which this new policy of prevention by deterrence was prosecuted. There had to be a definitive end to the drift and indecision that had so gravely weakened the USA over previous years. Otherwise, the logic ran, there would be another September 11.[71]

Over the coming weeks, despite the protest of many other loud voices in the administration who favoured a much narrower 'law enforcement' approach focusing on the perpetrators of 9/11, this reasoning would prevail. The thinking of senior figures such as Cheney and Rumsfeld as well as the input of less important but nonetheless ideological influential figures such as Feith and Paul Wolfowitz, a brilliant career academic and diplomat who had been appointed deputy defense secretary, would be condensed into the Defense Department's strategic plan for what had become, after the idea of declaring 'a War on Radical Islam' or 'a War on Islamic Extremism' were both rejected, a 'Global War on Terror'. Five days after 9/11, Bush was promising to rid the world of 'evil doers'.[72] Before two weeks had passed, he promised that 'our war begins with al-Qaeda but it does not end there'. Instead, 'it will not end until every terrorist group of global reach has been found, stopped and defeated'.[73] All the major figures in the administration stressed repeatedly that this new conflict would last a long time.

OPERATION ENDURING FREEDOM

By the end of September 2001 the US war plan for the first action of the Global War on Terror, the attack on Afghanistan, had been finalized. The aim of Operation Enduring Freedom was both to capture or otherwise eliminate al-Qaeda and to depose the Taliban.[74] Difficult negotiations with Uzbekistan to secure basing rights for American planes had been successfully concluded. More crucially, General Pervez Musharraf, the army general who had seized power in Pakistan in a bloodless coup in 1999, had agreed to a list of seven demands including full intelligence sharing, the use of two small airstrips and a halt to his nation's support for the Taliban.[75] The close, if tense and unstable, working relationship that successive Pakistani governments and the Pakistani security and military establishment had established with the USA through the Cold War had soured through the 1990s, and the relative ease with which Musharraf's acquiescence appeared to have been obtained through a mixture of cajolery and threat heartened the White

House. Offers of assistance or cooperation from more than seventy countries ranging from the Republic of the Congo to South Korea had been received and, on the whole, politely rejected. Congress had appropriated $40 billion for the coming campaign.[76]

The strategy for Afghanistan decided on by Bush, Rumsfeld, Cheney and the military was determined by a variety of considerations. One key element was the desire of the president to 'change the impression' he felt had been left by successive withdrawals in the face of threat over the previous twenty years. This had been an invitation to ever more brazen attacks. Only 'the most aggressive' of responses would suffice to deter the enemy.[77] That did not mean huge numbers of troops, however. Both Bush and Rumsfeld believed that modern wars could be won by forces 'defined less by size and more by mobility [and which] rely more heavily on stealth, precision weaponry and information technologies'.[78] They thus explicitly rejected the 'Powell Doctrine', named after the administration's secretary of state, who as an army general had commanded coalition forces in the First Gulf War. That doctrine had meant only going to war with massive and overwhelming numbers and was deemed outdated or, at the very least, unsuitable to Afghanistan. No one had any desire to end up where the Soviets had found themselves, and the key to this was seen as keeping a 'light footprint' to avoid becoming an army of occupation and sparking a generalized insurrection. There was also the wish, particularly of Wolfowitz, who had been heavily influenced by his direct experience of relatively successful processes of democratization in south-east Asia, to see 'the Afghans liberate themselves'.[79] Finally, there were longstanding American conservative suspicions, nurtured through the Clinton era, of the use of military forces for 'soft' liberal humanitarian-type tasks.

Equally, though Bush had said that the White House would 'rally the world', Afghanistan would be an American campaign. Tony Blair, who had immediately offered to supply any help the US required, was told that joining the coalition involved 'accepting the doctrine' and that though 'the wider the coalition the better, [we] are going to do this anyway'.[80] The Bush administration, and especially Rumsfeld, was determined to avoid any repetition of the 'war by committee' that had been seen during the Kosovo campaign of 1999 and, they felt, had severely hampered the use of US military power. When NATO invoked Article Five of its charter, summoning all members to the aid of one who had been attacked, the gesture went unacknowledged by the White House. Building a coalition, Rumsfeld insisted, should not become an end in itself as conditions posed by participants risked 'limiting the ability of the president ... to protect the United States'. The coalition should not be allowed to define the mission, he told subordinates and wrote in the *New York Times*.[81]

Once it had been decided to avoid the use of large numbers of American troops on the ground, the question of the military capacities of the Northern Alliance, the rough coalition of the various militia which made up the opposition to the Taliban in Afghanistan, became critical. The CIA's poor view of their competence and reliability was shared by General Tommy Franks, the commander of the US military operation, and was only reinforced as more was learned about General Mohammed Fahim, the late Massood's uninspiring and uncharismatic successor. The State Department also had serious concerns about the consequences for a post-war Afghanistan if the opposition groups ended up with too much power. The Pakistanis had made their own reservations about the disparate factions of the anti-Taliban opposition taking power abundantly clear to the Americans, enlisting the Saudis in a fairly unsubtle lobbying campaign, and important voices within the CIA were 'sensitive to Islamabad's concerns'.[82] This led to a natural tendency in the intelligence community to favour the strategy of undermining the Taliban's hold on the south and the east of Afghanistan by exploiting tribal splits and discontents rather than throwing American military and diplomatic weight entirely behind the rag-tag anti-Taliban forces in the north. The senior leadership at the Department of Defense disagreed, and the result was a compromise. Though the first option remained the 'southern strategy' of provoking a rebellion among the Pashtun populations who provided the bedrock support for the Taliban, measures were taken to prepare a 'northern strategy' if it proved necessary. Teams of CIA operatives were thus airdropped into the north of Afghanistan to link up with the Northern Alliance.

The first American boots arrived on the ground in Afghanistan at about the time when, after convincing the army high command that his decision to offer full cooperation to the US was the only viable option, President Musharraf went on Pakistani state television to explain that he had acted in his nation's interests by accepting American demands. In Washington the reaction to his announcement was watched warily, as it was clear from secret polling that support in Pakistan for Mullah Omar's regime had actually hardened after 9/11.[83] There was, however, little real opposition to Musharraf's decision. Religious parties organized a few relatively small rallies around the country. In Peshawar police baton-charged students from the religious schools around the city, but the anger seemed half-hearted. At most rallies the police exercised restraint. A pair of fingers that the author saw lying in the road had been severed from the hand of a demonstrator by a simple tear gas canister. Other protests, however, degenerated, and authorities, fearful of a wider breakdown of law and order, ordered the use of live rounds. Inevitably, a handful of demonstrators were shot and killed. They became the first victims of the 9/11 Wars outside America.[84]

3
War in Afghanistan

FIRST STRIKES

On the eve of war Mullah Omar addressed his followers. He told them
that they were facing an extremely powerful enemy and that defeat and
death were probable – though the forces of Islam would eventually prevail over the very long term. He admitted his own very human fear at
the prospect of losing his family, his friends, position, privileges and,
quite probably, his life. However, his reasons for fighting were clear.
Omar said he 'did not want to become a friend of the non-Muslims for
[they] are against all my beliefs and my religion' and was thus 'ready to
lose everything'. He would trust, he told his troops, only 'in Islam' and
his own 'Afghan bravery'.[1] There was no reason to doubt the sincerity
of the Taliban leader's words. The chances that Mullah Omar would
even discuss agreeing to US demands and handing over the Saudi-born
militant who was theoretically his guest, however poor relations often
were between Afghans and the Arabs living in their country, were always
extremely slim. However, beyond the rhetoric and the genuine emotion
was another purely rational calculation. If Omar had surrendered bin
Laden even to a 'third country', his credibility and thus authority within
the Taliban would have been destroyed, and the movement would have
most likely disintegrated. If he refused to hand over bin Laden, however,
the Taliban would probably be defeated but not necessarily decisively.
Certainly the movement's ideological credentials would remain untar-
nished, as would Mullah Omar's own moral authority. His refusal of
the American ultimatum and of Pakistani attempts to mediate some
kind of deal was thus predictable.[2] 'Try as we did we could not persuade
Mullah Omar to let go of bin Laden in the window available before the

deadline imposed by President Bush,' General Musharraf later recalled. With the cursory diplomacy over, the war could start.[3] The bombing began on October 7.

To start with, there was little in the way of 'shock and awe', as Rumsfeld had originally wanted. Sorties were flown against fifty-three targets in the first twenty-four hours and continued through the following days at the same relatively low intensity.[4] To the frustration of the defense secretary, the strikes were steered deliberately away from frontline positions by General Tommy Franks, the military commander in charge of the campaign, to allow the CIA's 'southern strategy' to develop. Bob Grenier, the CIA chief in Pakistan, had twice met one of the Taliban's most senior military commanders in the luxurious surroundings of the Serena hotel in the western Pakistani city of Quetta, only 110 miles from Kandahar itself, first to reiterate the American offer of negotiations if bin Laden was handed over and, at the second meeting, to suggest a possibility of an internal coup against Mullah Omar.[5] Elsewhere, the CIA and to a lesser extent MI6 were handing out dozens of satellite phones accompanied by packets of $10,000 to warlords and tribal chiefs within Afghanistan and approaching scores more.[6] Many took the cash and handed the telephone to the Taliban. Others simply rejected the CIA's offer. The Taliban themselves had a rudimentary but effective intelligence system and made scores of arrests in Jalalabad, in Kabul and in the eastern city of Khost, where, at least before the US-led air strikes started, local tribes had looked to be wavering.[7] The bombing continued, largely ineffectually, with Taliban commanders mocking the American efforts, for a second week and then a third. Early bombing had been directed at the sort of rear area targets that would have been useful when fighting a more conventional enemy – supplies depots, vehicle parks – but anyone who knew Afghanistan at the time knew that talk in Pentagon press conferences of 'degrading command and control systems' and suppressing anti-aircraft defences was nonsense. The local version of the former was a man sitting on a rug with a radio, of the latter Soviet-era heavy machine guns that needed to be manually sighted. 'We are not running out of targets . . . Afghanistan is,' General Richard Myers, chairman of America's joint chiefs of staff, said.[8] But this was a problem. With no sign of any significant movement against the Taliban among the tribes in the south and the east, frustration in Washington and among the teams of American operatives in the north mounted. The latter sent back cables pleading for more resources. The Islamabad CIA station insisted their strategy would work if given sufficient time.[9]

ABDUL HAQ

The coming war did not just pose challenges to states and their security services, however.

A few days after September 11 a portly forty-three-year-old Afghan flew into Peshawar from Dubai. His name was Abdul Rauf Humayun Arsala, but everyone called him Abdul Haq. His life had been profoundly intertwined with the conflicts that had racked south-west Asia over previous decades, and his death would be too. Though a very minor player in the great scheme of what was happening in late September 2001, Haq's story was a useful reminder of the reality on the ground in the places where the 9/11 Wars were to be fought over the coming months and years. For in places like Peshawar or Jalalabad and for men like Haq the grand rhetoric of a 'global war on terrorism' meant very little.

A Pashtun from a landowning family from the eastern Afghan province of Nangahar with a long history of serving their country's monarchs, Abdul Haq and his two elder brothers had been among the first to start fighting the Afghan Communists who had seized power in 1973, ending the thirty-year-long rule of King Zahir Shah. His brothers, Abdul Qadir and Din Mohammed, had both been influenced by new Islamist doctrines coming from the Middle East, and Abdul Haq, a rebel by temperament, quickly found himself involved in active violence.[10] Haq's entry into the world of violent political dissidence showed many of the factors that would prove later so common among militants of a different stamp: the example of respected peers or family members; a temperamental disposition to adventure or practical action; generalized support among his community for the cause in the name of which he was acting; a particular incident which triggered the transition from talk to execution – in Haq's case a public reprimand from a detested Communist teacher at school.[11]

Across Afghanistan at the time there were thousands of other local leaders launching similar attacks by similar bands of rebels against efforts of the committed Marxists of the People's Democratic Party of Afghanistan to forcibly haul their country out of its 'feudal torpor' and into the bright new era of revolutionary Socialism.[12] By 1978 the tiny clique of hardline Communists in Kabul had lost control of vast swathes of the Afghan countryside, and Moscow began to contemplate a 'temporary' armed intervention. When the Soviets invaded to bolster the tottering regime in December 1979, aiming to stay only for a few months, Haq and his brothers found themselves fighting a new enemy.

Haq had a good war. Active in the faction of the Hezb-e-Islami party loyal to the senior cleric Younis Khalis, boisterous, charismatic, energetic, with moderate political views, good English and, at least early on in the conflict, a relatively impressive combat record, he got on well with representatives of Western intelligence agencies and journalists.[13] He got on less well, however, with the ISI, who favoured hardliners such as Gulbuddin Hekmatyar, an Islamist former engineering student with whom they had had an ongoing relationship since the early 1970s and who now headed the main Hezb-e-Islami, or Abdul Rasul Sayyaf, whose group was mainly bankrolled by the Saudi Arabians. By 1992, with the Soviets gone, the regime they had left deposed, the various *mujahideen* factions in Kabul and the country plunging towards a vicious civil war, Haq had left for exile in Dubai, where he had contented himself with a series of minor business ventures in the United Arab Emirates. His taste for political manoeuvring had never left him, however. He kept up contacts with British intelligence developed during the war against the Soviets and had been one of the Afghans who had walked through the twin gates and airlock doors of the headquarters of MI6 in London's Vauxhall with the much younger Hamid Karzai in the months before the 9/11 attacks.[14] For Haq the 9/11 attacks, which he watched on a television screen in the internet café he ran in Dubai, were not an 'attack on freedom', as President Bush described them, nor was the reaction to them 'the new Jewish crusade campaign on the soil of Pakistan and Afghanistan', as bin Laden described it in his first public communication after 9/11.[15] Instead, they signified the latest phase in the ever-shifting matrix of Afghan politics and, crucially, an opportunity to return to his native land and, potentially, to wealth and possibly power. Haq, however, had underestimated the complexity of the game currently being played out by the Pakistanis, their intelligence services, the CIA, those directing the war from Washington and a variety of local actors in Afghanistan.[16]

This time, Haq was not backed by Western intelligence services. The CIA did not believe that he was a credible candidate to raise the eastern tribes and had offered him only derisory help.[17] Nor did the Pakistani security establishment have any intention of seeing one of their former enemies, a moderate with excellent connections in the West who was close to the viscerally anti-Pakistani exiled Afghan king in Italy, at the head of a broad-based revolt that might place a new leader in Kabul. So, though Haq's men had found themselves hindered and even attacked by local tribesmen when buying weapons, they found the road to the border mysteriously clear of checkpoints when they finally headed into Afghanistan to lead what they hoped would become the revolt that would overthrow the Taliban.[18] Haq's operational security had been lamentable, with the whole of Peshawar aware that he had ordered leaflets and paper flags from local printers in preparation for an expedition across the border. The Taliban, who had their own spies moving throughout the frontier region, were naturally waiting for him. Within days of entering Afghanistan, Haq was in trouble, tracked by superior forces across the scruffy hills south-west of Jalalabad. Though the area was his tribal homeland, the communities Haq had hoped to raise remained uncommitted. Frantic calls by his backers in the US alerted the CIA and the Pentagon to his plight, but missiles launched from a CIA Predator drone – now finally operational – did little to hold back the Taliban fighters closing on his small band. Out of ammunition, outnumbered and cut off, cornered in a dry gorge that had once been one of the *mujahideen*'s favourite spots for ambushing Soviets, pinned down for most of a day, Haq eventually had no choice but to surrender. Within hours, Din Mohammed, Haq's brother, received a call in Peshawar. It came from the satellite phone his brother had taken into Afghanistan three days earlier. The Taliban were on the line. They had captured his brother alive. Within twenty-four hours Haq's mutilated corpse was hanging from a makeshift gibbet in Jalalabad bazaar.[19]

THE NORTHERN STRATEGY WINS OUT, THE FIRST VICTORIES AND THE RACE IN THE EAST

In Washington, Haq's death did not help the protagonists of the 'southern strategy'. By the end of October the senior members of the administration were beginning to worry about the approach of the brutal Afghan winter, the growing anger in the Islamic world sparked by a number of recent incidents involving civilian casualties killed by US bombs and the increasingly negative domestic press coverage. Much to the irritation of Bush, some pundits spoke of a 'quagmire' and even invoked the dreaded 'Vietnam'.[20] An attempted raid on a deserted airbase in the southern Afghan deserts had descended into farce, with special forces troops wounding themselves with their own demolition blasts. Bin Laden had not only succeeded in having a pre-recorded video broadcast by al-Jazeera within hours of the first raids on October 7, in which he made a series of points about the 'humiliation' the Islamic world had suffered for decades at the hands of the West, that resonated widely but also successfully met journalists subsequently. At home, the US population remained febrile, frightened, hurt and angry. Sales of flags soared. People stockpiled food. On October 17, a detector at the White House apparently found traces of a biological toxin known as botulinum. For twenty-four hours, the president and his top officials awaited the results of tests on mice that, if positive, could mean their own imminent deaths. The results were negative. Robert Mueller, the director of the FBI, told Bush that there were 331 potential al-Qaeda operatives inside the United States.[21] Successive scares of new attacks, misinformed and exaggerated reporting (as it later proved) of al-Qaeda's destructive potential and the appearance of fatal anthrax-filled letters believed erroneously to have been sent by Islamic militants or even Saddam Hussein's intelligence services to congressmen and media organizations all combined to increase the pressure.[22]

The emphasis thus began to shift. There was no sudden rejection of the 'southern strategy', but, once the Northern Alliance had promised the president himself not to enter Kabul, Rumsfeld asked General Franks to step up bombing of the Taliban frontlines in the north. Concerns about the consequences for the long-term stability of Afghanistan were brushed aside.[23] Within a week 90 to 120 sorties a day were being flown, of which the vast proportion were in direct support of the opposition troops. Now guided in by small groups of American special forces operatives who, after being delayed by poor weather, had reached the northern end of the Shomali plains 40 miles from Kabul and the rolling steppe around Mazar-e-Sharif, the strikes quickly brought more impressive results.[24]

On November 10, Northern Alliance forces, who used some of the tens of millions of crisp new dollar bills given to them by the CIA to buy off key commanders around the northern city of Mazar-e-Sharif and open a way through its defences, took the city after air strikes which saw B-52s using some of the heaviest arms in the American sub-nuclear arsenal on Taliban trenches. The next day, massive strikes broke the resistance of the Taliban troops defending Kabul, allowing opposition troops to surge across the battered villages, derelict orchards and mine-strewn fields of the Shomali plains. Though everyone along the decision-making chain from the Shomali to the White House was aware that theoretically it would be better to stop the Northern Alliance short of Kabul, the plans carefully drawn up to balance Pakistani and Afghan Pashtun sensibilities with those of the factions now advancing towards the capital were rapidly forgotten in the excitement and relief. The senior CIA man on the ground had raised no objections when told of their allies' plans to advance into the city, and by the evening of November 13, the Northern Alliance was in possession of Kabul. A few Arabs were shot around the city, but the major force of foreign *mujahideen* which some feared would defend the city simply did not exist. Their putative commander, a senior Libyan militant known as Abu Laith, had spent the previous weeks arguing with the al-Qaeda senior commanders for more troops. First he had been promised 200 men, then told to make do with only fifty. When even these did not arrive, Abu Laith complained again, only to be told there were now no spare troops as the bulk of the Arab fighters were already heading east towards the Pakistani border.[25] There was no resistance from the Taliban either. The vast bulk of the movement's forces withdrew from Kabul the evening before the arrival of the Northern Alliance in long convoys of their trademark pick-up trucks. 'We left at night like frightened women. It was a disgrace. We left in small groups and in any vehicle we could find. We did not know where we were going and we were scared of the missiles,' remembered later one young Pakistani volunteer with the Taliban at the time.[26]

The Northern Alliance commanders would argue that, as they could not have left Kabul without any government whatsoever, there was no alternative but to move in. Their case had a certain logic – at least the capital was temporarily secure – but their seizure of the city was to cause major problems later on.[27] The primary casualties of the war so far had been those civilians who had been unable to flee. Stray missiles and bombs in the capital had killed somewhere between 50 and 150 people. The family of Ali Shah, the young shepherd who had watched the preparation of the destruction of the Buddhas, had had a narrow escape. They had fled to Kabul and were lucky enough to find a room in a home of wealthier relatives. In one of the early strikes on the capital, bombs fell only a 100 metres or so away, hitting an old warehouse near by, where a small detachment of Taliban was based. The Taliban were killed, but so were a dozen refugees sheltering alongside them.

The most immediate effect of the fall of Kabul was to deprive Afghanistan of any kind of formal authority. The Taliban regime had been ramshackle but had provided a degree of overall government. Even if traditional tribal structures now filled the breach in many areas, the situation was fluid and chaotic. In the south fighting was continuing around Kandahar. In the centre, Hamid Karzai, the young exile who had travelled into Afghanistan with the CIA's blessing early in the campaign and was protected by American special forces, was steadily overcoming the initial reluctance of local tribes in Oruzgan province to commit to a rebellion against the Taliban. But though he was gaining support, Karzai controlled no ground, and his position was tenuous.[28] Towards the Pakistani border, in provinces such as Paktia, there was a confused struggle between former warlords and tribal leaders. In the north-east, Taliban and foreign fighters from various groups which had been based in Afghanistan prior to 9/11 – al-Qaeda, the Pakistani Harkat-ul-Mujahideen, the Islamic Movement of Uzbekistan and others – were still fighting hard but were cut off from supplies and surrounded. In the west, Ismail Khan, one of the best-known veterans of the war against the Soviets and the subsequent civil conflict, was back in the city of Herat. Bamiyan had reverted to the Hazaran militias. All around the country, American airpower was now simply hitting any target of opportunity that presented itself. When accurate, their strikes were of devastating power and lethality, killing hundreds of Taliban fighters in hours.

In the east, three different forces were racing for Jalalabad. The main contenders in the race were Hazrat Ali, an illiterate and brutish minor warlord known for his involvement in the drugs trade and a brief alliance with the Taliban who had recently joined the Northern Alliance, and Haji Zaman Gamsharik, a Pashtun who had been expelled from a comfortable and lucrative position in eastern Afghanistan by the Taliban and forced into exile in France. Like Abdul Haq, he too had returned to try his luck after September 11. The only things Hazrat Ali and

Gamsharik had in common were that they were both veterans of the jihad against the Soviets and were both receiving weapons, cash and logistic assistance from the Pakistani ISI, which was trying desperately to salvage something from the wreckage of its Afghan policy. Having lost both Mazar-e-Sharif and Kabul to the Northern Alliance, the Pakistanis were now determined not to lose influence over Jalalabad. As ever, local competition for power and resources became overlaid with multiple regional – and in this instance global – dimensions.

The third contender in the race, Abdul Qadir, was the outsider. He was the late Abdul Haq's second brother, and for him the new turn of events in Afghanistan represented an opportunity to return to power, wealth and influence. He too had fled the Taliban, to Germany, and was unwilling to travel to Pakistan and place himself under the dubious protection of the ISI. Instead he had entrusted his twenty-seven-year-old son, known as Haji Zaheer, with the task of spearheading his re-entry into the rude game of Afghan politics. Haji Zaheer, already a hardened veteran of the vagaries of Afghan politics and well aware of the price of failure even before the death of his uncle, was on a plane to Zahedan, the south-eastern Iranian desert city, within hours of his receiving his father's orders.

Zahedan is one of the great smuggling centres of the Middle East and Asia, a key hub for the passage of narcotics to Europe. Zaheer knew that the ISI would be looking for him and was unwilling to risk the conventional border crossing. Instead he had himself smuggled over the Iranian border into the south-western corner of Afghanistan before cutting back into Pakistan across the unguarded desert. Keeping to remote back roads running across the arid mountain wastes of the Pakistani province of Baluchistan, he headed east and then swung north, following much of the length of the 1,600-mile-long frontier and finally reaching Peshawar, at the foot of the Khyber Pass and just 25 miles from the Afghan border and 120 miles from his destination, Jalalabad, after three days of solid travelling. The already substantial population of Afghan refugees, parked for a decade or more in sprawling refugee camps on the outskirts of the city, had been swollen by new arrivals fleeing the American bombing, but otherwise little had changed since Zaheer had last been in the city five years before.

Zaheer's father was one of the best-known and respected of all the local warlords, and his son was thus able to rapidly rally a makeshift force. Each local commander brought in a dozen or so men who themselves could answer for another score or so. Equally important, Zaheer was able to arm them too. Each commander, of whatever power and influence, knew that at some stage in the future his loyalty would be rewarded with cash, in drugs, a lucrative official post or in some other way. Each of their men expected the same: a few thousand rupees, a weapon, further employment.

One of the legacies of the Khyber region's role in the 1980s as a rear area for the Afghan *mujahideen* were the numerous arms factories and dealers. When Zaheer cited his father's name to one merchant in the town of Landi Kotal, high in the Khyber Pass, the man simply opened his warehouse doors and handed over 450 Kalashnikovs, rocket-propelled grenade launchers, light machine guns and ammunition. After receiving an admonitory call from his father, Zaheer led his men at night across a smugglers' track from the top of the Khyber Pass and on to the main road leading from the official border crossing to Jalalabad, 10 miles inside Afghanistan. The march took until dawn. When the fighters reached the main road to the city, they easily routed a unit of fifty Taliban, teenagers mostly, still cleaning their teeth with neem sticks and making tea for breakfast when Zaheer's men found them. The Taliban in Jalalabad itself had already melted away and Zaheer took control of the city. His father, having travelled from Germany on planes, helicopters and finally in a jeep, arrived at dawn. The other contenders in the race, Hazrat Ali and Gamsharik, drove in twelve hours later, each accompanied by thousands more fighters. Under pressure from the ISI and with significant amounts of Western cash on the table, the three commanders came to an uneasy power-sharing agreement, though the city rang with undisciplined gunfire for forty-eight hours.[29] Jalalabad too had now fallen. Only Kandahar remained in Taliban hands.

Lying in a crook in the Kabul river and surrounded by glades of palm trees, well-irrigated fields, with busy bazaars and a famous university, Jalalabad had always been one of the most cultured and wealthy cities of Afghanistan. Yet the fall of the Taliban – or rather the arrival of the various militia forces from Pakistan – brought mixed reactions that surprised many of the Western, especially American, reporters who drove in from Pakistan and gave an early indication that reality on the ground might be more complex than the simple narrative of liberation repeated in Western capitals suggested. 'I am sick when I see what is happening.

There is no discipline here. There is no police, no army, no government. Everyone has a Kalashnikov,' said Rehmat Ali Khan, a spice trader in the once busy bazaar, eyeing the militia men who had flooded the city. 'Thank you, Britain and America, for allowing these men [Gamsharik, Hazrat Ali and Qadir] to come back and rob and beat us again,' another man shouted. Others worried loudly about the presence of Northern Alliance troops. 'We are Pashtuns,' one man said. 'The Tajiks have never been good to us.' At the filthy and battered local hospital where more than 300 civilian victims of the bombing raids had been treated in the last two months, Waly Yad, a twenty-four-year-old doctor, was unafraid to voice his support for the Taliban. 'They followed Islamic law, and that is the only way to resist America's tyranny . . . Osama is a very good Muslim. This is all wrong now.'[30]

'THE BASE' DISINTEGRATES
AND TORA BORA

Bin Laden himself had spent the first weeks of the war moving between Kandahar, Kabul and Khost, where he took time to meet local villagers and hand out cash.[31] Though constantly mobile, he had nonetheless found time to receive a veteran Saudi Arabian militant cleric. Though bin Laden had given at least two major interviews during the war and issued two communiqués, he had hitherto avoided claiming direct responsibility for the attacks, possibly wanting to see what the reaction in the Muslim world to them would be before admitting or boasting that they were his work. Sitting in what appeared to be the guestroom of an ostensibly ordinary Afghan middle-class home with his visitor, however, he happily described how he had always been convinced that the impact of planes loaded with fuel would bring down the Twin Towers. A video of their conversation later found by the CIA and released by the White House furnished the first indisputable proof of bin Laden's responsibility for the 9/11 attacks.[32]

On November 8, bin Laden and al-Zawahiri were in Kabul, where they attended a memorial service for the Uzbek militant leader Juma Khan Namangani, who had been killed in a US air strike a day or so before, and met a Pakistani journalist.[33] The next day the pair set out for Jalalabad, where bin Laden had lived on his arrival in Afghanistan from the Sudan five years before. Four days later, Jalalabad itself was to fall to the forces led by Haji Zaheer and his rivals but with Kabul clearly on the point of being lost, must have nonetheless seemed relatively safe to the al-Qaeda leaders. Their small convoy shunned the direct route from the capital to the eastern city, itself a bone-shaking five-hour drive, and instead took smaller, even worse roads further south, where sympathetic local tribes provided greater security. After a night spent near Jagdallak, the al-Qaeda senior commanders had arrived at their destination on November 10.[34] There was rout in the air, and Jalalabad's streets were full of refugees and demoralized Taliban fighters. The city had been home to a large population of older international militants and workers with Islamic NGOs, who now choked the streets as they loaded their families into buses or pick-up trucks heading for supposed safety to the east. Large contingents from Pakistani militant groups or the tribal militias raised by radical Pakistani clerics slept on the floors of mosques or in the gardens of the run-down governor's residence, resting briefly on their way back to their home villages across the border. On the evening of November 11, local tribal leaders and Taliban notables from the area gathered in an Islamic centre in the city to hear bin Laden make a rousing speech about resistance.[35] The al-Qaeda leader handed out $100,000 and then left the next day in a small group of vehicles, crossing over the old metal bridge that marks Jalalabad's southern limits, climbing the short, steep slope off the river plain and heading due south towards the mountains lining the horizon 30 miles away.[36]

The convoy drove up the increasingly poor roads and on towards the small village of Ghani Khel, a cluster of mud-walled homes, a couple of mulberry trees and a small run-down concrete mosque, tucked in among the foothills of the ranges behind. Arriving at the village in the late evening, the occupants then left their vehicles and walked higher still towards Tora Bora, the name given by local people to the shelf of wooded hills below the final high snowy ridges of the White Mountains that mark the border with Pakistan.[37] A day after bin Laden's flight, a second convoy left Jalalabad. It too headed south, carrying the local Taliban leadership and several hundred fighters, and also passed by Ghani Khel before working its way up the slopes above the village and then stopping where four or five cars were drawn up in a heavily guarded clearing. The Taliban sent fighters to learn what was happening. They returned angry. Bin Laden was there, recently returned from a brief reconnaissance of the rocky slopes above, and his guards had warned them away. Mullah Jan Mohammed, the private secretary of the governor of Taliban Nangahar, remembered his irritation. 'It was our country. How could they tell us where to go?' he said. Overhead, B-52s were already leaving their distinctive traces in the sky.[38]

The two convoys in mid-November were only a minute part of a vast exodus which saw tens of thousands of people moving across Afghanistan's western frontier by foot, motorbike, in SUVs, buses and trucks in the last six weeks of 2001. Some fugitives even travelled by plane. The most northern element of this chaotic retreat was the flight of several thousand militant fighters from combat zones around Mazar-e-Sharif, Kunduz and Taloqan, many hundred of whom were transported in an extraordinary airlift organized by the Pakistani secret services. Others, including Mullah Dadaullah Akhund, the brutal Taliban leader who had overseen the destruction of the Bamiyan Buddhas, slipped into north-western Pakistan after paying off local Northern Alliance commanders.[39] Further south, either side of Jalalabad, scores of tracks and dirt roads along a long stretch of frontier saw heavy traffic of fugitives from mid-November onwards. Malik Habib Gul, a tribal elder, described how he arranged mule trains for over 600 militants in the first two weeks of December, charging between 5,000 and 50,000 Pakistani rupees to lead them out, not over the high mountain ridge behind Tora Bora itself but by longer but more practicable routes to the east and north.[40] One local smuggler on the Pakistani side of the mountains described leading 100 fighters to safety across these passes in five separate trips through late November.[41] Rehmat Ali, a farmer from Ghani Khel, spoke of accompanying 'sixty or seventy foreigners' over the same period.[42] Other fighters slipped out by crossing the Kabul river and then heading east into Pakistan through the deforested hills and steep valleys of Kunar province along tracks that had been used by Alexander the Great's army as it fought its way down to the Indus more than two millennia before. There, a single local commander helped up to seventy-five to escape – after relieving them of vehicles and valuables.[43] Finally there was the exodus along the roads around the Afghan city of Khost and across the long unguarded frontier running down to the official border post at Chaman. Most of those who had left Kabul on the eve of its fall had driven across eastern Afghanistan and crossed without difficulty into Pakistan. The foreigners in Afghanistan had a tougher time than the locals. The Pakistanis arrested somewhere between 600 and 700 of them.[44] They included Ali al-Bahlul, the al-Qaeda media specialist who had listened to the news of the 9/11 attacks with bin Laden, who was detained at the frontier near Khost on December 15. Bin Laden's three current wives and dozen or so children, however, crossed the border without incident.[45]

Reports of the fighting at Tora Bora gave the impression of a pitched battle, the Americans and the Afghans below, bin Laden and his men on the high ridges above. But the accounts that have emerged over recent years point to something much more chaotic and much more dispersed. The fighting at Tora Bora was scrappy in the extreme. Though there was a hardcore of militants determined to seek martyrdom, many of those who filled the defences scraped in the mountainsides stayed only for a couple of days, sometimes even a few hours, before once more moving on through the wooded peaks on their way out of Afghanistan. One was Mohammed Umr, a young Afghan-born militant who had been raised in Saudi Arabia and who, despite a budding career as a professional footballer, had left his home in the Saudi city of Medina to get training in the militant camps in Afghanistan.[46] When the 9/11 attacks took place, Umr had left his camp when warned about likely bombing and had crossed the country on buses, passing through Kabul a day or so before its fall and arriving in Jalalabad just a few days after bin Laden had left. After hearing that 'the sheikh' was in the mountains to the south of the city, he too had got a lift to Ghani Khel and then walked on up into the hills, finally finding a small group of other Saudis who were fortifying an old stone shepherd's shelter built around a shallow cave. All over the hillsides around the small band Umr had joined were other groups, a random selection from the various extremist groups which had been present in Afghanistan under the Taliban. All were building up positions as best they could to resist the assault they knew was coming. 'The trenches were all hand-dug, not linked and poorly defended,' one twenty-two-year-old Algerian who shared a foxhole with four others later recalled.[47] Arms and ammunition had been brought in on donkeys but were still in short supply. 'There were sixteen Kalashnikovs for two hundred people,' said another survivor of the battle. 'There was no one in charge.'[48]

According to the official American military history of the campaign, analysts within both the CIA and US Central Command (CentCom) had been speculating for several weeks that bin Laden would make a stand along the northern peaks of the Spin Ghar mountains at a place they called 'Tora Gora'.[49] It took some time, however, for a significant force to be deployed, with the first special forces units arriving in Jalalabad on December 2.[50] Eventually, around ninety American special forces troops supplemented by a handful of their British and Australian counterparts had taken up positions on the lower slopes. As auxiliaries they had recruited several thousand Afghan fighters under the command of Hazrat Ali, Zaman Gamsharik and Haji Zaheer, the three commanders who had raced for Jalalabad three weeks earlier and who were now being paid by the CIA. The plan was for the Afghans to act as beaters moving up the northern slopes of the Spin Ghar mountains while other Afghans blocked the escape routes to the east and west. As the opposing militants revealed their positions to the special forces accompanying the lightly armed irregulars, air strikes would then be called in with the laser guiding technology used over previous weeks. After some debate, the idea of using American troops – 1,000 Marines had recently arrived in the south of Afghanistan – to block the southern escape routes over the back of the mountain range behind Tora Bora was rejected by the White House and Tommy Franks, the commanding general directing the operation from the headquarters of CentCom in Florida. So too were suggestions from the field to parachute in special forces. The task fell to the Pakistanis instead.[51] The assault was launched on December 8.

After just forty-eight hours of fighting, American special forces commanders were confident they were closing in on their target. Though they had had great difficulty getting the local forces to close with the enemy – or indeed preventing them from returning to their bases below the mountain when dusk fell – the air strikes were beginning to tell on the militants high on the mountain. On the 12th a communication was heard by the American troops indicating that bin Laden was joining one of the groups of fugitives that continued to pour over or around the mountain range.[52] On December 14, bin Laden appears to have completed his last will and testament on a laptop computer. 'Allah bears witness that the love of jihad and death in the cause of Allah has dominated my life,' the al-Qaeda leader wrote, adding that 'if it were not for treachery, the situation would not be what it is now'.[53] Around December 15, bin Laden's voice was heard over the radio, giving permission for a general withdrawal to his troops.[54] By the 16th or 17th, more than a month after they had passed through Jalalabad and thirteen days since the start of the battle, bin Laden and al-Zawahiri were gone, leaving subordinates to lead any remaining fighters to safety. Their departure was precipitate and inglorious. [Bin Laden] even 'left his bodyguards in Tora Bora', one captured militant later told interrogators. '[He] suddenly departed Tora Bora with a few individuals [he] selected,' another remembered. A third said bin Laden left owing one local commander $7,000, a debt only paid ten months later. Though many Taliban fugitives, including the convoy of leaders that had been irritated by being warned off by the al-Qaeda leadership's guards at Ghani Khel, headed south from Tora Bora into the narrow salient of Pakistani land that extends into Afghanistan, bin Laden and al-Zawahiri appear to have headed in the other direction, north and away from the Pakistani border, slipping through the lines of the special forces and their Afghan auxiliaries, lying low in the house of an Afghan sympathizer near Jalalabad for a few days before heading on into the rough and remote Kunar on little-known trails, probably on horseback. Then, deep in the mountains, they disappeared.[55]

The battle at Tora Bora was declared over on December 16, when the three Afghan commanders hired by the CIA paraded an unimpressive bunch of fifty-seven shell-shocked and half-starved Afghan and Arab prisoners before local journalists. Equally unimpressive were the famous 'cave complexes'. These had been repeatedly described in Western media as vast bunkers with floor after floor of armoured gun positions, bedrooms, offices and ammunition stores all equipped with electrics and computer systems, sanitation and even power plants. There was not just one but many of these constructions, Donald Rumsfeld told a television interviewer, after being shown an astonishing graphic featuring a hollowed-out mountain fortress in the London *Sunday Times*.[56] The reality was more mundane. Only simple caves existed. They offered some protection, however. 'I remember the Afghans below and the American planes above,' Mohammed Umr said later. 'We got used to the bombing even when it was near us. Sometimes we got bombed when we were cooking so we had to keep moving the pot all the time. But otherwise it was OK.' However, the total absence of interconnecting passages between the caves naturally cast some doubt on the lurid accounts of Western soldiers clearing cavern after cavern in vicious hand-to-hand fights as they advanced deeper and deeper into bin Laden's lair in a real-life video game. Nor were there any extensive catering or medical facilities. 'There was no normal food,' said Abdullah al-Batarfi, a doctor who ended up at Tora Bora during the fighting. 'I did a hand amputation with a knife ... a finger amputation with scissors.'[57] After the battle, reporters searching the caves found little more than basic field dressings, some petrol camping stoves and tin after tin of baby food and jam.[58]

The total number of militants actually killed at Tora Bora is unknown. Some estimates run into the low hundreds.[59] 'Dalton Fury', the leader of the American special forces during the fighting, says that 220 militants were killed and 52 fighters captured.[60] Few bodies were found, however, though several dozen dead militants appear to have been buried in rapid makeshift graves during the battle by local tribesmen or their comrades. Some survivors spoke of dozens more being buried alive in caves by bombs.[61] A few score died on the high passes on the way into Pakistan. One, Djamel Loiseau, had made his way to Afghanistan from Paris' eleventh arrondissement and died of hypothermia high amid the ice and snow of the frontier ridge after volunteering to wait on the summit to guide groups of fugitives still making their way up the mountain in the dark.[62] Several of the columns of fighters organized by the subordinate al-Qaeda leaders were badly shot up.[63] But most of those defending Tora Bora escaped alive. Bin Laden himself claimed that only sixteen of a force of 300 had been killed.[64] The truth probably lies somewhere between this claim and those of the US-led coalition. Either way the numbers of fighters who actually resisted the oncoming Afghan and American forces would appear to be substantially lower than often imagined. So too is the number who died.

Mohammed Umr was one of the last to leave. Around December 17, probably after the departure of bin Laden, Umr was told by the senior al-Qaeda commanders 'to go to Pakistan', make his way home to Saudi Arabia and wait to be contacted. For Umr, the only option for escape was to follow the most risky of the many routes that fugitives had taken the previous month. With around 100 others, most of the remainder of fighters then at Tora Bora, he walked for a night and most of a day through pine forests and then through snow fields at between 10,000 and 14,000 feet, before crossing into Pakistan. The group was found and then betrayed by local tribesmen, who revealed their location to the Pakistani army. Umr was eventually handed over to the Americans.[65]

Soon after the end of the fighting, recriminations over the failure to capture bin Laden began. If it had been hard to read rapidly evolving events – senior British intelligence officials later spoke of 'a fast-moving and confused situation' on which 'it was very difficult to get a real handle' without the satellite surveillance capabilities that would later become almost banal – there was little excuse for the decision to believe that local auxiliaries could do as effective a job at Tora Bora as they had done around Mazar-e-Sharif or on the Shomali plains. Western troops and their commanders clearly had enormous trouble simply grasping the nature of the war they were fighting, of their allies and of their enemies. For the Americans, this was a just war of righteous vengeance to eliminate a group of evil men opposed to all that was good in the world, summed up rhetorically as 'freedom'. To the Afghan commanders, this was another round in a continual contest for power, influence and resources pitting individuals who had been competing for decades and communities that had been competing for centuries against one another. The Americans were new actors in this game, undoubtedly the richest and the best-armed to date, but, everyone suspected, unlikely to be playing too long.

The commander of the US special forces at Tora Bora later complained that all his Afghan allies would do was 'go up, get into a skirmish, lose a guy or two, maybe kill an al-Qaeda guy or two and then leave', adding that 'it was almost like it was an agreement or an understanding between the two forces [to] put on a good show and then leave'. Unwittingly 'Fury' had nicely summed up the traditional style of Afghan combat. In a society where reaching adulthood was already an achievement and where communities were unwilling to waste precious lives, war was more often a negotiating tool in the perpetual bargaining for scarce resources rather than a means of annihilating opponents. The 1980s had taught the Afghans a bitter lesson about fully industrialized warfare and at Tora Bora they had logically reverted to older customs designed to preserve life more than take it. Most of the Afghan troops were neither professionals nor ideologically motivated. One fighter, returning to his makeshift camp at the end of the day, described the day's fighting to the author as 'work', using the Pashto word for repetitive agricultural labour. Being a soldier was just a better-paid and more dangerous alternative to farming. And if there were other opportunities for further self-enrichment, all the better. The sub-commander designated to cut off one key escape route, paid $10,000 to do so, was simply paid more by escaping Arabs. Though a principal ally of the Americans, Hazrat Ali himself was overheard by reporters in the Spin Ghar hotel in Jalalabad negotiating the safe passage of senior militants.[66] Some of his men appear to have attempted to levy money at checkpoints from the American special forces themselves.[67] Such men were certainly unlikely, as one US officer angrily exhorted them, to 'destroy, destroy, destroy', not least because they were the ones who would have to live with the consequences of any destruction.[68]

The Pakistanis also had their own interests. Contrary to what is often said, the Pakistanis did in fact move large numbers of troops, both regular and paramilitary, up to the border behind Tora Bora and even ferried Bob Grenier, the Islamabad CIA station chief, up to the frontier to review them on two occasions.[69] But coordination had been poor, and the senior Pakistani civilian and military leadership claim to have been unaware of what was happening at Tora Bora until very late. Maleeha Lodhi, the Pakistani ambassador in Washington at the time, remembers that the precise timing of American actions on the other side of the mountains was never communicated to the Pakistanis. General Ali Mohammed Jan Orakzai, the officer who commanded the deployment of the two Pakistani brigades to the frontier behind Tora Bora, claims to have learned of the December 8 offensive from CNN.[70] Even once their troops were mobilized, Pakistani commanders had to negotiate access to the high valleys behind the Tora Bora massif with the local tribal elders, or the troops would have been attacked themselves. The result was that the Pakistani troops took up their positions several days after the American special forces and their Afghan auxiliaries had started pushing up the slopes of the mountains from the northern side. Even when they were in position, Afghan members of the Taliban were allowed to pass through their positions. President Musharraf had already made his position clear to Wendy Chamberlain, the US ambassador in Islamabad, telling her days after 9/11 that 'we will hand over AQ but handle Pakistanis and other locals ourselves'.[71] The troops who deployed behind Tora Bora were accompanied by ISI officers, who made sure that it was international militants who were detained while potentially useful proxies who might help the Pakistanis rebuild their Afghan strategy in the future were allowed to go free.[72] In any case, the senior Pakistani generals and President Musharraf were, true to the historic prioritization of threats by Pakistani strategists, much more concerned by the reaction of India to a spectacular and bloody attack on the national assembly in New Delhi launched on December 13 by a group based in Pakistan than what was happening on their western borders.

Like the destruction of the Bamiyan Buddhas, Tora Bora was one of those episodes which, though misunderstood at the time, gave a very clear indication of what kind of conflict was coming. The fighting there had revealed how combat in the 9/11 Wars was going to be. Hugely complex, it involved at least five different forces all fighting for different reasons. Often referred to as a battle, it was in fact more of a long-drawn-out sequence of inconclusive skirmishes than a climactic strategic event. Difficult to define in terms of time or space, simplified and mythologized in the popular imagination, Tora Bora was about small groups of militants scattered across a very large area of very broken terrain fighting a series of disjointed and chaotic actions of varying intensity with Western troops and their local auxiliaries, who had enormous difficulty bringing their massively superior firepower to bear. It was thus less the final engagement of the 2001 Afghan war and more the first major action of the conflict to come. Equally, the highest casualties may well have been among civilians. Within two days of bin Laden's convoy passing through, the village of Ghani Khel had been virtually flattened by a massive bombing raid which, though it had killed at least forty Arabs, had also left an equal number of non-combatants, including the children of several of the elders of the village, dead. A second air strike days later on the nearby village of Pacheer Agam missed its intended target – a reported intermediary between al-Qaeda and local Afghans – and killed around seventy civilians.[73] Other similar incidents went unreported, but the 300 civilians that doctors at Jalalabad's hospital said they had treated indicated they were numerous.

While Tora Bora had been unfolding, the Taliban's last redoubts had fallen. In the south Mullah Omar had been tracked by American special forces to a valley in the province of Helmand, west of Kandahar but predictably escaped an operation to capture him that, as at Tora Bora, relied on the use of local forces as auxiliaries to secure the village where he was believed to be hiding. The Taliban leader was last seen heading towards the southern Dasht-e-Margo, the Desert of Death, on a motor-bike.[74] On December 7, Kandahar was secured by American special forces soldiers, who had as much trouble with skirmishes between rival 'liberating' groups as they did with the remnants of the Taliban and international militants. On December 11, Hamid Karzai, who had emerged as a consensus candidate among the various Afghan factions collected by the Americans under the auspices of the United Nations at a hotel near Bonn in Germany, received the news that he was to be the new leader of his country. Eleven days later, he was sworn in as chairman of the Interim Government in Afghanistan. The White House was careful to steer away from any triumphalism, but the new 'coalition information centers' that had been set up in London, Washington and Islamabad, where hundreds of journalists had gathered, issued a rousing pamphlet entitled 'The Global War on Terrorism: The First 100 Days', which boasted of how fewer than 3,000 troops had brought 'broad military success'.[75] The campaign had been cheap, short and apparently successful, a 'bargain' in the words of President Bush.[76] In all, beyond the massive airpower deployed, the US commitment to overthrow the Taliban on the ground had been about 110 CIA officers and 316 special forces personnel.[77] The former had distributed $70 million.[78] Though eleven reporters had died, the military had not suffered a single combat fatality. When a soldier had been shot in the arm on December 4 it was front-page news.[79] It had almost been too easy.

There were, however, various worrying postscripts to the war other than the escape of the al-Qaeda leadership from Tora Bora and Mullah Omar from Kandahar. The first was the secret airlift that had brought hundreds of Pakistani militants who had been fighting alongside the Taliban in Kunduz back home. With the carefully leaked news that the ISI had continued supplying arms and ammunition to the Taliban after the bombing had started on October 7 and the blind eye turned to the arrival of Taliban fugitives on their soil, this indicated that the Pakistanis' reversal of their previous policy in Afghanistan clearly had limits.[80]

The second worrying postscript involved reports of further air strikes that had caused significant civilian casualties. One incident saw a party of tribal elders on their way to Kabul for the inauguration of the new president methodically annihilated by US navy jets and gunships. Fifty were killed in their vehicles on the road, and more died as the survivors tried to find refuge in two nearby villages. American authorities first denied that the attack had taken place and then claimed the dead were Taliban. In fact the strike had been based on information that had come from Bacha Khan Zadran, a Pashtun anti-Taliban warlord who had exploited the anarchy following the fall of the Taliban regime to claim effective rule over a chunk of eastern Afghanistan after being recruited as part of the CIA's 'southern strategy'. Zadran, having learned that the elders travelling in the convoy opposed his claim to rule three provinces, had cynically exploited American ignorance of local conditions to eliminate his personal political opponents by telling the CIA that they were hostile to the coalition.[81] The final incident saw a village in Paktia province destroyed and ten men, seventeen women and twenty-seven children killed. The Americans claimed this time that the village was a weapons depot. Again, the information was out of date. The Taliban were long gone. These were the incidents that were sufficiently egregious to come to the notice of reporters or NGOs. There were many other deaths that went unreported. Near Gardez a father who had lost three daughters to an American bomb showed the author their shredded clothes, hung on a line to dry when the missiles had struck. 'The Taliban were in the town but they left days ago,' he told the author. 'Why do they bomb us?'

In retrospect another worrying postscript could be added. Within twenty-four hours of the September 11 attacks, senior officials in Washington had suggested that Saddam Hussein was involved. On the orders of the president, Franks and his Centcom staff had begun planning for a potential invasion of Iraq shortly after the fall of Kabul in the fourth week of November.[82] On December 20, little noticed among the chaos of Tora Bora's aftermath and the inauguration of Karzai, the *New York Times* published an article by Judith Miller, a reporter at the paper. 'An Iraqi defector who described himself as a civil engineer said he personally worked on renovations of secret facilities for biological, chemical and nuclear weapons,' it began.[83] The broader aims of the Global War on Terror remained unchanged. Less than a month after Tora Bora, President Bush had used his State of the Union speech to further flesh out his doctrine of pre-emptive intervention against entities posing an actual or potential threat to the USA and had named three – Iran, Iraq and North Korea – as comprising an 'Axis of Evil'. The next phase of the 9/11 Wars was already underway.

4

The Calm before the Storm

THE PHONEY WAR

Looking back, the fifteen months following Tora Bora, seem, given the sudden and extreme violence that preceded them and the escalation that followed them, like a moment of relative calm. This calm was tempered by profound anxiety but was coloured too by a suspicion that perhaps, despite the extraordinary events unfolding across the planet and the enduring trauma of 9/11, the world had not changed quite as much as many had thought on that day in early autumn 2001 when the planes had arrived from the clear blue sky in New York and Washington. As the first phase of the 9/11 Wars – the immediate aftermath of 9/11 – shaded into the second phase of the conflict, it appeared more and more likely that the apocalypse that many had thought imminent a few months previously had at the very least been postponed. The institutions of Western and Middle Eastern societies appeared stronger than many had thought. Those seeking to undermine them seemed weaker. And the critical middle ground – the hundreds of millions in the Islamic world whom bin Laden had hoped to radicalize and mobilize – remained at the very least uncommitted.

Certainly the war in Afghanistan had not provoked the violence across the Islamic world that some had predicted. Operations there appeared to be going relatively well, and Pakistan, where General Musharraf successfully managed elections to keep hold of power partly by co-opting local Islamist parties and partly by ensuring that the country's most prominent democratic political leaders stayed in exile, remained more or less calm. Musharraf himself remained relatively popular domestically, and his speeches announcing a policy of 'enlightened moderation' in religion and neoliberal economic reforms reassured much of the international community. Tensions in Europe between Muslim communities and the broader population remained negligible. Counter-terrorist authorities in the UK and elsewhere were still directing the bulk of their efforts at rounding up foreigners rather than focusing on the far more worrying threat that their own citizens might pose. The attacks that did occur – though spectacular and bloody and though often targeting Westerners – were in places that appeared very distant from Europe or the USA.

Equally, the hunt for bin Laden, though there were no definitive leads on its principal target, appeared to be making progress. Many of those foreign volunteers and militants who had fled Afghanistan in November and December 2001 had first sought security in cities in Pakistan, exploiting the relationships with local groups they had made over previous years. But urban centres had proved far from safe, and with cooperation between American agencies and the Pakistani ISI better than it had ever been before – senior CIA officers in Islamabad met their ISI counterparts almost daily to exchange information and plan operations – a series of raids rounded up many of the most senior or at least most notorious al-Qaeda figures.[1] Ramzi bin al-Shibh, a young Yemeni who had been a key planner and aspirant hijacker in the 9/11 conspiracy, was detained in Karachi, and Khaled Sheikh Mohammed, the overall mastermind of the plot, was found in Rawalpindi. 'There was a sense we were closing in,' remembered Bruce Riedel, a senior CIA analyst at the time.[2]

Though large numbers of fugitive militants were concentrating in and around towns like Shakai in the tribal agency of South Waziristan or further north in Miram Shah and Mir Ali in North Waziristan, their arrival had gone largely unnoticed and thus did little to mar the overall impression of progress.[3] Elsewhere, the seizure of a theatre in Moscow by Chechen groups was a spectacular and horrifying reminder of the variety and dynamism of terrorism but had little broader impact, and though the stand-off between a nuclear-armed India and Pakistan sparked by the Islamic militant attack on the Indian parliament in December 2001 was worrying, the tension it provoked was hardly something new in the region. Violence in Gaza and the West Bank, especially an alleged massacre at Jenin during the summer, continued to rouse passions across the Islamic world, further sensitizing potential audiences to extremist messages, and a spate of suicide bombs hit Israel in an all too familiar way, but if or how such events played into the bigger picture of modern Islamic militancy in the post-9/11 era was unclear.[4]

In the shadows, the CIA was already well engaged on an extensive programme of kidnapping suspects overseas, illegal detention, collusion and direct participation in torture, but little had yet become public, and little was yet known about abuse at bases in Afghanistan. The extension of electronic surveillance in America without warrants remained secret, and the passing of the Uniting and Strengthening America by Providing Appropriate Tools to Intercept and Obstruct Terrorism, or USA PATRIOT Act, which, among other provisions, gave new powers of surveillance to investigators, was achieved with minimal opposition. A new 'Department for Homeland Security' was also created. Most of the public outrage was directed at the establishment of a detention centre for supposed high-level 'enemy combatants' on the 45 acre site of a former coaling station leased from Cuba under a treaty from 1903 and known as Guantanamo Bay. For some time in the autumn of 2001, detainees had been held on navy ships in the Arabian Sea, but transferring them to American territory could mean they would receive protection under the US constitution. The right to silence they would then be able to invoke particularly worried Bush administration officials. Guantanamo Bay – or 'Gitmo' as the centre became known – was the 'least worst choice' available for holding such men, they claimed.[5] That there was not a greater outcry was a mark of quite how exceptional the atmosphere in the immediate aftermath of the 9/11 attacks was. As so often in the 9/11 Wars it was an image – of the first inmates wearing orange jump suits, ear defenders, blindfolds and wrist and ankle shackles kneeling in fenced-off pens shortly after arriving at the camp – which provoked the greatest reaction.

And at least through most of 2002, until the press campaigns to crank up support for the Iraq war started in earnest and the overall temperature began to rise, levels of enthusiasm for bin Laden in the Islamic world or negative Western feelings about Muslims barely changed.[6] Indeed polls in the months following the strikes and the Afghan campaign in fact showed remarkably positive views of Islam among many Americans and Europeans. One revealed that Americans saw Muslim neighbours more favourably than they did before the September 11 terrorist attacks, a trend analysts attributed to the average American's increased familiarity with the religion over the previous three months.[7] A study of discussions of terrorism in US newspapers revealed that early coverage tended in general to be relatively generous towards 'Islam'.[8] Teenagers in the US even felt confident enough to appropriate the vocabulary of the new conflict, describing a messy bedroom as 'ground zero', something out of date as 'so September 10th' and using 'terrorist', 'fundamentalist' and 'Osama' as terms of abuse.[9] In the Islamic world, though broad views of the USA had gone from bad to worse, a relatively low 28 per cent, 35 per cent and 33 per cent of respondents in Pakistan, Turkey and Indonesia respectively told pollsters that the West posed a general threat to Islam.[10] Nearly 80 per cent of Pakistanis saw terrorism as a major problem.[11] Surveys such as Zogby International's 'Arab nations' impressions of America' poll or the Pew Research Centre's 'How global publics view their lives, their country, the world' showed that a profound belief in values seen as typically American (elected government, personal liberty, educational opportunity and economic choice) co-existed with visceral anti-Americanism. Work by the University of Michigan's Institute for Social Research found that the most positive attitudes to American culture in the Arab world were found among young adults, regardless of their religious feeling.[12] The sharpening in rhetoric and radicalism on both sides was to come later, particularly in the months before the war on Iraq and when that campaign began to go badly wrong.

Nonetheless, many elements that would come to define the 9/11 Wars had in fact begun to reveal themselves. It was just too early to know how characteristic of the conflict – and its many sub-conflicts – they were to be.

The polyvalence of the 9/11 Wars has already been mentioned. But that the conflict has many dimensions is self-evident. Already we have seen how for different people – Abdul Haq, Zaheer Arsala, Mohammed Umr, Dalton Fury – the war sparked by the 9/11 attacks meant different things. Most major conflicts are complex affairs, subsuming many sub-conflicts, and it would be surprising if, despite attempts by many to minimize this vast diversity, the 9/11 Wars somehow were an exception. Yet even the most multidimensional of conflicts have distinctive qualities which give them a particular character and significance that mean they are more than simply the sum of their various parts. As the Wars continued, the common elements naturally became more pronounced. Cross-fertilization of tactics among all the protagonists, the simple movement of individuals from one theatre to another, public discussion and communication all helped stitch together the mesh which made up the conflict. At Tora Bora something of its chaotic nature had become clear. Through 2002 and into the early months of 2003, a variety of other elements also emerged. All evolved over the years that followed and all were important in defining the nature of the 9/11 Wars. This chapter examines two of those characteristics, both in evidence during the campaign in Afghanistan in 2001. One was the odd mix of ideology, blithe optimism and lack of judgement which characterized the approach of Western governments to extremely difficult and delicate interventions in foreign lands, at least for the first five years of the conflict. The second is the problems Western militaries, and in particular the American army, had in understanding the challenges the fighting posed and in evolving effective responses to it.

IDEALISM, IDEOLOGY AND HARD CASH: HAPPY EARLY DAYS IN AFGHANISTAN

In Afghanistan, by the spring of 2002, the fighting of a few months previously and the 'quiet of the grave' under the Taliban was a distant memory. Under the trees in a dusty courtyard in the southern suburbs of Jalalabad, slates on their knees, books shared between three, latecomers searching for their friends among the rows of blue headscarves before the blackboards, the 800 girls of a newly reopened school were starting a new year. Pupils of all ages sat together in classes, the cheerful, flustered headmistress said, because many had missed several years of schooling under the Taliban. Now thousands sought to make up the time they had lost.

In Jalalabad itself the bazaars were lively, the restaurants full. Saif Shezad, a businessman who had spent eighteen years in Pakistan, said he was 'very happy' with how things had turned out. He ran Jalalabad's biggest music and video shop. All his music, let alone the Indian 'Bollywood' movies that were his clients' favourites, had been banned by the Taliban, and now Shezad sold 200 videos each week. Next door was a pharmacy run by Sikhs. They too were content. Not just because, as one of Afghanistan's religious minorities, they had faced discrimination under the previous regime but, Gurmut Singh said, because now they could play billiards and computer games at an arcade near by.[13] Near the former militant training camp of Darunta, there were rows of new cars waiting to be sold. Every day scores of taxis bounced along the road west, too dangerous to travel without a heavily armed escort just six months previously, weaving among the over-laden lorries ferrying goods to and from the Afghan capital.

Kabul too was transformed with hundreds of new businesses and restaurants now open. There was an internet café and a mobile phone network in a city where a single satellite phone at the general post office once provided the only public international phone connection. There were even traffic jams. A huge fruit market had opened on the city's outskirts, and a new hotel or guesthouse appeared every week. One or two of the most daring and most liberal-minded women had substituted a headscarf for the *burqa* when they left home.[14]

It is easy to forget the heady days in Afghanistan in the wake of the Taliban's fall from power, especially given the violence and disillusion that came later. Yet through 2002 the worry among the vast proportion of Afghans, including much of the deeply conservative south and east where the Pashtun ethnic tribes dominated, was not that foreign troops would stay too long in their country but that they might prematurely leave. Many spoke of the country's collective experience after the Soviet war to justify their anxiety. Polls said that 80 to 90 per cent of Afghans supported the presence of the ISAF troops.[15] This may have been an exaggeration, but everywhere one travelled – and for around eighteen months it was possible to travel anywhere without concern for anything other than the appalling state of the roads – one found the expectation that a new era of security, stability and prosperity was dawning. The failure to manage these expectations was arguably the first major non-military strategic error made by the international community.

But few at the time thought expectations even needed to be managed. The soldiers of the newly formed International Security Assistance Force, led to start with by the British and then the Turks, were popular in Kabul and successfully achieved their limited aims of ensuring security in the city and protecting the new government and the thousands of Westerners who had arrived there to assist with the nation's reconstruction. An emergency *loya jirga* (grand assembly or council) involving 1,501 indirectly elected delegates including 160 women was held, the president inaugurated with a two-year term, a constitution and eventual 'free, fair and representative' elections prepared. At Tokyo in January 2002 the international community had pledged $4.5 billion of redevelopment funds which, though about half of what the World Bank said was necessary, was seen at the time as a sufficient sum.

By the end of the year a substantial proportion of the 4.5 million Afghans living as refugees in Pakistan and Iran had returned to their homeland under the auspices of international agencies working through the newly created United Nations Assistance Mission in Afghanistan (UNAMA) in what was one of the biggest peaceful voluntary transfers of populations in recent history. A significant number of educated and capable Afghans from the US and Europe had returned too. A single and stable currency was created, banks and banking systems were set up, ministries were created, equipped and staffed (albeit fairly rudimentarily compared to the resources available to the new offices of the international organizations or the UN), and a British team collated, compiled and revised the nation's maps. After President Bush personally resolved a year-long internal stand-off between the American government development agency USAID, who wanted to prioritize rural development, and those in the administration who favoured using the money to hire (foreign) contractors to start road-building projects, work finally began on resurfacing the Kabul–Kandahar highway.[16] Tens of thousands of weapons were collected in a rolling programme to disarm militias. Many of the arms were old, and huge stocks remained, but it was a start nonetheless. Corruption, astonishingly, was actually reduced, with Afghanistan improving its rating by Transparency International, the international NGO that monitors the problem.[17] Private investment flowed in – from the Gulf, from the Afghan diaspora, from China. A media sector of great energy and very variable quality sprung up almost overnight. Foreign reporters working in Afghanistan split into those who were seeing the country for the first time and were surprised by its poverty and the apparent lack of progress and those who had known Kabul and other cities under the Taliban and for whom the change was dramatic. There was much talk of 'the international community'.

For the 'international community' had certainly arrived in Afghanistan – or in Kabul at least. Journalists filled the coffee-shop-cum-bar at the Mustafa Hotel in Shar-e-Nau, watching DVDs of Russell Crowe in *Gladiator* on a new flat-screen brought over from Dubai, and held impromptu parties on the roof that provoked complaints about late-night noise from the newly refurbished Interior Ministry. NGOs poured in international staff, many coming direct from the Balkans, Africa or Pakistan. Thousands of often young, usually highly educated, largely white Western people arrived. Many were serious, experienced and highly qualified experts in their fields; others were not. There were ex-British army engineers, wide-eyed American college graduates, Italian jurists, Californian water specialists, polylingual veterans of a dozen anti-narcotics campaigns from everywhere between central Asia and Latin America. One new 'adviser' cheerfully confessed to having been hired on a Tuesday and arriving in Afghanistan, a country he had never visited before, the following Sunday. Hundreds of brand new luxury four-wheel-drive vehicles jammed the streets – white for the United Nations and the diplomats, black for the private security companies also arriving en masse, khaki for the militaries. Inevitably, an infrastructure sprang up to serve this large and wealthy new population – courier companies, fixers, translators, workmen, drivers, cleaners and bars such as 'L'Atmosphère', where steaks, imported bottles of French wine, a swimming pool and the thrill of being in a supposed conflict-zone encouraged a holiday atmosphere. Visiting dignitaries haggled over carpets and 'genuine' Gandharan relics made in sweatshops in Pakistan. Rents rose five- or tenfold in desirable parts of the city such as Wazir Akbar Khan, the upmarket northern suburb undamaged during the civil war of the early 1990s. One evening in 2002, as off-duty Italian soldiers, Dutch and French NGO workers, British anti-narcotics experts, American journalists and a gaggle of recently hired consultants to the newly created ministries drank and danced, the author was offered ecstasy by a development specialist who had flown in that day from Frankfurt.

These were not the first representatives of the developed West to arrive in Afghanistan in recent decades, of course. Apart from isolated travellers or academics, the first wave had been the hippies during the 1960s. But these visitors were few and minimal in terms of their social impact. There had also been the limited number of American development experts and contractors who had arrived to oversee the spending of the aid that both superpowers used in a proxy competition for influence in Afghanistan. The Soviet military intervention had seen another kind of foreign presence, of course. In the 1990s, Afghanistan had been a backwater. This latest influx was thus unprecedented.

Quite when the intervention in Afghanistan was expanded from a pure security operation aimed at dismantling Osama bin Laden's terrorist infrastructure first to a relatively limited nation-building project and finally to an extremely ambitious bid to reconstruct and develop Afghanistan in the image of a liberal, democratic and pluralistic Western state is unclear. Certainly many of the more hard-working and sensible development workers or consultants were as surprised and concerned by it as anyone else. As with so many such phenomena, it was the result of a range of different factors, each unremarkable in itself but together almost irresistible.

One was the background. The intervention in Afghanistan came at the end of a long run of other 'peace' or 'nation-building' operations in Somalia, the Balkans, East Timor, Sierra Leone and elsewhere. It was thus a culmination of the forward momentum these had generated, in terms of action both on the ground and the new philosophies – moral, legal and political – that informed them. A second factor was the dynamic generated by those arriving in Kabul themselves. Usually Western or Westernized in outlook, they were, whatever their personal politics, representatives of a new and powerful industry of humanitarian assistance and activism that had grown enormously through the 1990s. Though total financial assistance to the developing world had diminished in quantitative terms since the end of the Cold War, with governments ceasing to fund massive politically inspired infrastructural projects such as those seen in Afghanistan or across much of the Middle East in the 1960s and 1970s, the numbers of people engaged in the 'third sector' of non-governmental aid had increased exponentially. Along with the military and national foreign services they had become a major player deeply engaged in post-conflict environments, a diverse but nonetheless clearly identifiable institution with its own norms, interests, lobbying, capacity and desire for resources, funding, exposure and employment. Finally, there was public consciousness in the West. Since the 1980s, a new awareness among citizens of their ability to 'aid' the miserable and suffering, encouraged by a series of international landmark legal agreements such as those banning the use of landmines and reinforced by unprecedented levels of individual activism, had created a new and potent global force recognized and reinforced by politicians and the media. Every new intervention or emergency operation through the 1990s had intensified this new sense of empowerment and zeal. Rebuilding Afghanistan, however, was a very different prospect from a famine-relief operation, separating rival groups in the Balkans or protecting breakaway republics.

One key element that had become rapidly woven into the post-war project for Afghanistan was the issue of women and women's rights. This continued the dialogue initiated during the autumn when the repression of Afghan women under Taliban rule had been an important part of the political rhetoric of leaders in America and in Europe to the point of almost becoming a *casus belli* in itself. Laura Bush, the president's wife, had bluntly stated that the 'fight against terrorism is also a fight for the rights and dignity of women', and in the days after the fall of Kabul, Blair, watching television in Downing Street, had pointed to images of women without *burqas* in the streets of the capital as a vindication of the war and how it had been conducted.[18] The fact that the *burqa* was worn by Afghan women long before the Taliban came to power and owed as much to the detribalization and urbanization of Afghan society than reactionary rule in itself was ignored.[19]

The 'liberation of women' thus became a key element of the new enlarged project for Afghanistan's future too.[20] Quite what this would entail or how it would be achieved was never fully defined. Bianca Jagger, the human rights campaigner, flew in to Kabul for an International Women's Day organized by the United Nations and spoke of the 'passive resistance of Afghan women' over decades.[21] Such an event would have been 'unthinkable under the oppressive Taliban regime', said a British Ministry of Defence press release. One difficult and revealing moment came when a young Afghan woman, Vida Samadzai, who had been living in the USA since 1996, controversially took part in the Miss World beauty pageant. Habiba Surabi, the minister for women, told reporters that Samadzai 'is not representing Afghanistan's women ... and appearing naked before a camera or television to entertain men is not women's freedom'. When the twenty-three-year-old, the first Afghan in three decades to take part in a beauty contest, confessed her own unease during the beachwear round of the contest and then failed to make the semi-finals, the judges announced that, for the first time, they were giving her a new 'beauty for a cause' prize for 'representing the victory of women's rights and various social, personal and religious struggles'.[22]

Such sentiments betrayed at the very least a certain naivety. With the vast bulk of the international community rarely travelling beyond Kabul and certainly having little contact with rural communities, the deep conservatism of much of Afghan society, which the Taliban in part represented, was obscured. Instead, with their interlocutors selected from educated and highly Westernized returning exiles or exceptional women such as the unique (and much-interviewed) former TV news presenter, the vision of the visiting dignitaries who flew in for a short period or of some journalists of Afghanistan as a country ripe for 'modernization' and Westernization, the two being increasingly projected as synonymous, went largely unchallenged.[23] Even if the core issue remained development, the concentration on the rights of women had the effect of establishing the '*burqa* ratio', as one senior European diplomat in Kabul cynically put it, as a key metric for success in Afghanistan with domestic public opinion in the West. History, however, argued that any effort to radically change Afghanistan needed very careful thought. Change was not impossible, but if any measure came to be seen as alien or imposed efforts could badly backfire. As early as the late nineteenth century, bids to change by force the customary relations of rural Afghan communities had provoked violent revolts. Efforts by King Amanullah during the 1920s to follow the example of Kemal Ataturk in Turkey and force Western-style modernity on reactionary rural populations had provoked a rebellion that eventually led to his deposition. Along with the imposition of secular curricula in schools, the primacy of state law and the reduction of the autonomy of the clergy, it was the issue of female education that had been a particular flashpoint. The same issues led to revolts in the late 1950s and, particularly when allied to land reform, to the protracted and extensive violence in the 1970s which had seen men like Abdul Haq take up arms and had so weakened the Marxist regime of the 1970s that Moscow had felt obliged to intervene.[24]

Many Westerners in Afghanistan at the time knew this and were wary of the expanded project for the country and the values with which it was loaded. Some of the better constructed aid programmes were designed to encourage a slow change in mentalities through empowering women by obliging men to allow them take part in the decision-making process that might trigger the delivery of funds to the village and in the management of the money.[25] These projects encouraged basic economic activity – and thus often literacy – among women and were very successful. But such schemes were all too rare. Though Lakhdar Brahimi, the UN special envoy, had recruited many of the most informed people, often long-term residents who spoke local languages, as political officers, they were sidelined relatively rapidly by the new arrivals. So too were many of the more capable and aware local Afghan operators. The project in Afghanistan could have benefited from their deep knowledge and pragmatism. Instead, often following mission statements drafted in distant Western capitals, everything began to take a strongly ideological turn.

As so often, tensions became condensed in individual figures. One had been the aspirant Miss World, Vida Samadzai. Another was Malalai Kakar, one of Afghanistan's rare female police officers. Small, active, sharp-featured, Kakar was undoubtedly both impressive and brave. She looked after the Kandahar Department of Crimes against Women, a tough and valuable job in an extremely dangerous environment.[26] Her work, she explained, usually involved 'family clashes' or 'boy and girl friendships where they run away'. Her days were spent trying to stop young women being killed by relatives for having 'shamed' their families by exercising a small degree of independent choice. Few such elopements ended in a sexual relationship. Many, however, ended in death. Kakar spoke about her work but was not interested in answering questions about the 1980s, when, having been inducted into the police in the footsteps of her father, she had served the Communist government. 'I was a police officer before the Taliban came and I joined again to serve the people,' she said drily, standing in the courtyard of Kandahar's main prison with a mobile phone in one hand and a *burqa* thrown over her arm. Seen with some justification as a courageous campaigner for women's rights in the West, Malalai Kakar was viewed rather differently locally. In her person, many local fault lines were reunited: urban and educated versus rural and illiterate, 'modernizing' and Westernized versus what was locally perceived to be authentically 'Afghan' or 'Pashtun', secular versus religious. For many around Kandahar, perhaps the most conservative part of the country and a zone where the Soviet war had seen huge destruction, displacement and loss of life in rural areas, Kakar represented memories of an earlier experience of a reforming project under the auspices of the 'international community' and of those who had collaborated with it. They hated her as a result.

THE 'GREEN MACHINE'

Major Hilferty took as long a view of the conflict as anyone. Throughout most of 2002 the American reservist officer started every day by giving reporters a reminder of why they, he and around 4,000 other soldiers from a dozen or so countries were at Bagram airbase. 'Today is the two hundred and thirty-third day since al-Qaeda terrorists murdered three thousand innocent people when they attacked the World Trade Center in New York,' he said at 9 a.m. one morning in early May as he briefed journalists. He then read out another short obituary of one of the victims of the 9/11 attacks culled from the *New York Times*. On one morning it was 'Robert McCarthy, thirty-three, a trader with Cantor Fitzgerald who gave his wife six dozen roses on their anniversary. Five for each year they had been married and a dozen for her colleagues. Every time she looks into the eyes of her son Shane she sees her husband.' The next it was 'Ricardo Quinn, forty, a paramedic who loved to make life-size sand sculptures on Jones Beach, where he loved to go with his family.' Hilferty used the same formula – the time elapsed since 9/11, the obituary – every day. He ended every briefing with: 'The hunt goes on. The war on terrorism in Afghanistan continues.'

By May 2002, nearly 13,000 foreign troops had been deployed in Afghanistan, including 8,000 Americans involved in the ongoing Operation Enduring Freedom (OEF) and 4,650 of the newly established International Security Assistance Force (ISAF). The aims of the OEF troops were, as Hilferty said, to find and kill or capture American enemies in Afghanistan now usually labelled 'AQT', or 'Al-Qaeda-Taliban'. Their task thus differed dramatically from that of ISAF, which, as the name suggested, was to ensure basic security in the zones where it was deployed and thus to assist stabilization operations and eventual reconstruction. Bagram was the main OEF base, and the specific task of the troops there was to be ready to be airlifted to wherever they might be needed as reinforcements for the special forces soldiers who were out in the hills trying to physically catch the fugitives. The one major engagement in previous months had been a bloody fiasco with eight dead American soldiers after planners had grossly underestimated the strength of a force of international militants and former Taliban fighters who had taken them on amid the mountains of Shah-e-Kot in the east of the country. Since then, the 'Green Machine', as its soldiers called the US military, was having trouble finding anyone to fight, and conventional military activities had largely been restricted to what Colonel Patrick Fetterman, commanding officer of the 187th Battalion of the 101st Airborne, called 'clean and sweep' operations.

Fetterman, a small, wiry forty-year-old, described the one contact his unit had had with the enemy in the last ten weeks. Four Afghan men had been killed after they opened fire on an Australian special forces patrol who had then called in support. Two hundred men from the 187th were airlifted in when the shooting started: 'We landed on a hard LZ [landing zone] in very steep terrain above a village. We moved down into it and found blood traces and three large caches of ammunition. We had overwhelming force and, though some villagers were not very happy about it, we asked them to unlock their doors and we went through the village. Sometimes we had to break down doors, and that was hard for my guys, who are going from strong sunlight into interiors that could be hostile. Any AQT elements would not have been able to flee because we had air [support].' His men had fired just one shot, to kill a dog that had attacked a soldier. 'It was a pity, but better than one of my guys getting rabies,' the colonel told the author.[27]

Fetterman's statement encapsulated the flaws of the American military effort in Afghanistan at the time. The colonel, an intelligent graduate from West Point, was operating at battalion level, but the failures of the tactics he was employing were reproduced all the way up to the very highest levels of military and civilian leadership. The fundamental problem was that the American army, an extraordinary force of 1.8 million men and women funded by a defence budget in 2002 of $328 billion, had misconceived its mission.[28] Instead of framing its operations as counter-insurgency, with a consequent emphasis on protecting the population from the enemy and on creating an environment propitious to the development of security and progressively stronger governance, the American army, from the top of the Pentagon to the lowest footsoldier, saw its job as 'killing bad guys, not protecting good guys'.[29] US commanders and the CIA were under orders not to refer to their task as fighting insurgents but as counter-terrorism.[30] If villagers were upset by their operations, so be it.

Not that US troops would be around to see the consequences of the offence they caused. Strategy and doctrine called for the amount of time troops spent among Afghans to be minimized. Troops launched rapid raids from heavily fortified bases before returning as soon as possible to their Cheesy Nachos, beef jerky teriyaki, Pop-Tarts and bibles in tactical camouflage covers. Until the summer of 2002, food for the troops in Bagram was cooked at US bases in Ramstein, Germany, then flown 4,000 miles, reheated and served. The isolation meant, as conversations with US soldiers made absolutely clear, the environment 'outside the wire' was seen as populated by people who were at best picturesque, at worst evil. This created an inevitable vicious circle, making any contact with local communities much less likely, leading in turn to the reinforcement of the isolation. One soldier said that he liked going on patrol because it was like 'being on safari'. Within weeks local trucks were known by the soldiers as 'jinglies', a reference to their jangling metallic decorations, and local people were called 'habibis' or, more disrespectfully, 'hajis'.[31] Both the latter terms were, of course, Arabic in origin and had come, like the military's taste for huge walled-off bases with all home comforts, from earlier deployments in the Gulf and the tedious task of flying enforcement missions over Iraq through the 1990s.

The consequences of this mix of physical and cultural isolation and ill-adapted tactics were exacerbated by the low number of troops committed to Afghanistan. At the end of 2002 the twin operations of ISAF and the American Operation Enduring Freedom, the former still restricted to the capital Kabul and 'peacekeeping' while the latter hunted for AQT targets, still only totalled around 14,000, which worked out at well under one soldier per thousand inhabitants. This compared unfavourably with the ration of 9.8 per thousand inhabitants in East Timor, 19.3 in Kosovo, 17.5 in Bosnia, 20 in Northern Ireland and a massive 89.3 per thousand in Germany after the Second World War.[32]

For political leaders such as Rumsfeld, who were committed to a continuing and broader Global War on Terror, it made sense to hold back as many resources as possible, partly to have more for further operations but also to enhance the deterrent effect that operations in Afghanistan were designed to have on others who might sponsor terrorism. The lesser the fraction of total available resources America deployed, the more impressive the operation would be. There was also the continuing desire to avoid the fate of the Soviets and not get bogged down in a country with such a long history of resisting outside interventions. A large army was not only slow, unwieldy and hugely expensive, but its presence would almost inevitably spark a national uprising, men like Wolfowitz and Feith still argued.[33] Strong pressure from allies such as Tony Blair and from within the State Department to increase the size and extend the remit of ISAF to allow a physical permanent presence of up to 25,000 'peacekeeping' troops across much of Afghanistan was therefore stubbornly resisted by Rumsfeld and the Pentagon.[34]

Senior British military officers also resisted proposals by British diplomats to station the country's first 'Provincial Reconstruction Team', a joint base of soldiers and development and aid specialists, in Kandahar, arguing that the area was 'too large and dangerous'.[35] This meant that large parts of the country, such as the strategically critical south and south-west, remained without anything but the smallest presence of foreign troops throughout 2002 and 2003, frontiers went unsecured and the use of local proxies was continued and indeed expanded despite the problems experienced at Tora Bora and elsewhere.[36] It was not just the return to prominent positions of warlords such as Rashid Dostum, Mohammed Fahim and Gul Agha Sherzai (the veteran and broadly feared commander who had won the race for Kandahar the previous autumn with the help of US special forces) that shocked many Afghans. They were also horrified by the emergence as local powerbrokers of a multitude of less high-profile figures. Around two-thirds of provincial governors appointed in 2002 led armed groups, and the sight of such men – especially when physically protected by American soldiers or clearly benefiting financially from a relationship with international powers – undermined the fledgling Afghan government's attempts to re-establish some kind of central authority. Even down at district level, the best-armed and the best-connected were able to capture key elements of local government. The most sought-after posts were naturally those which commanded considerable opportunities for corruption, such as chief of police. Entire militias, often tribal in organization, were inducted into local security forces. Not only did this damage the credibility of the Western intervention but it also fuelled the usual Afghan competition between powerbrokers at every level from province to village across the entire country.[37]

PRISONER ABUSE STARTS

Alongside the 'ideological turn', the mistaken tactics and the 'light footprint' approach, another element that emerged very rapidly and then subsequently flowed on to other theatres was the abuse of captives. This occurred early in the conflict and continued in a systematic way throughout almost all of it. Of course, atrocities are a feature of most wars, and there seems no reason why this one should be any different. But the particular quality of the abuse, its odd uniformity across theatres and protagonists, is nonetheless striking. It is also significant that, though the mistreatment of prisoners in American-run facilities was to climax in 2004 and 2005, it was already widespread even before senior White House officials met to construct a legal framework that would officially determine procedure for prisoners captured during 'the Global War on Terror'. This suggests the abuse was thus both a 'ground-up' and a 'top-down' phenomenon and thus deeply representative in a profoundly worrying way of the essence of the broader conflict. Along with images from live executions of detainees by militants, the abuse of prisoners by US troops would produce many of the starkest and most memorable visual images of the 9/11 Wars.

The precursor to the abuse in American facilities was the inaction of American special forces and CIA personnel who witnessed, or were made aware of, torture, abuse and mass executions without trial during or following the collapse of the Taliban. This was particularly widespread in the north of Afghanistan, where several thousand prisoners, a mixed bag of Pakistanis, Afghans and international volunteers, had been taken by General Dostum, alongside whom American military and CIA operatives had been fighting for several weeks in and around Kunduz. Many hundreds, if not thousands, were murdered, some apparently buried alive, others driven long distances loaded into container trucks from which, one of the drivers recalled, the bodies 'spilled out like fish' when they were later opened.[38] US special forces at the very least knew this was happening even if they may not have been directly involved.

The most famous detainee in the north was John Walker Lindh, a young American who, after a long journey from California through radical Yemeni and Pakistani religious schools, had ended up fighting with the Taliban. Captured, he was refused medical treatment, was blindfolded with a rag with 'shithead' scrawled on it by soldiers, who, in another precursor of what was to come much later, then posed around him for a photograph.[39] In Pakistan, American personnel were visiting prisons and holding centres established to handle the fugitives caught crossing the border and taking part in interrogations where their Pakistani counterparts beat detainees badly, denied them sleep or placed them in stress positions for many hours at a stretch.[40] By December, CIA personnel in Bagram were forcing captives to stand for hours on end and wear spray-painted goggles with the deliberate aim of inflicting severe sensory deprivation to facilitate interrogation. By January, concerned British intelligence officers on the ground in Afghanistan were reporting mistreatment to their superiors, and assaults that would incur lengthy prison sentences in most nations were becoming widespread.[41] In February President Bush made public his decision that captured al-Qaeda or Taliban suspects would be treated as non-combatants rather than prisoners of war and denied the protection of the Geneva Convention and thus subjected to an arbitrary regime that would allow the US military to hold and interrogate them for as long as was desired. This breached almost every broadly established standard of international law. What by most standards would be defined as cruel and unnatural was now enshrined as official policy.[42] Bush's announcement undoubtedly had an aggravating effect – one interrogator who served in Afghanistan told the *New York Times* that 'giving [detainees] the [status] of soldier would have changed our attitudes toward them' – but also simply legitimized something that was already happening.[43]

Kandahar prison, established at the airport 10 miles east of the city, had opened in early December and received its first major batch of detainees just as the fighting in Tora Bora was winding up and a few days before the inauguration of Hamid Karzai. For the next three months it would be the main holding centre for prisoners in Afghanistan. The interrogators at Kandahar had three tasks: to obtain 'actionable intelligence' to be passed to the special forces units and the CIA to initiate immediate operations in Afghanistan or elsewhere; to elicit information that would fill the vast gaps in the American understanding of the enemy they faced; and to ascertain whether detainees were the high-level al-Qaeda and Taliban figures they were believed to be and thus worthy of transfer to the new facility being constructed at Guantanamo Bay. The pressure to get information was very high, especially as it was believed that some of the detainees probably knew about forthcoming or planned terrorist attacks.

Kandahar was brutal from the start. On planes to the prison in December, detainees were locked down in painful positions, hit with rifle butts and verbally abused. On arrival they were, according to one military interrogator, 'bound together in long chains', marched down a ramp, screamed at by military policemen shouting 'commands and obscenities audible even over the roar of the plane' and 'hurled' to the ground. Screaming and struggling, anticipating rape or execution, the detainees then had their clothes, often soiled with excrement or urine during the flight, cut away. Naked, hooded and still in chains they then underwent a full intrusive medical examination, were interrogated rapidly to establish a provisional identity and then locked, twenty-five at a time, into tents equipped with a single toilet bucket and little else. Ringed with barbed wire, open sided, the tents were unprotected from the fierce cold of a southern Afghan desert winter night. If the detainees tried to communicate with each other, they were beaten.[44]

The early 'rough treatment' soon escalated. Detainees later claimed that guards and interrogators at Kandahar had assaulted them, made death threats, deprived them of sleep, urinated on them, burned them with cigarettes, inserted sticks or poured petrol into their anuses and, again in ways that would become all too familiar later, 'took photographs of [them] completely naked' and 'stripped and piled [them] naked on each other while soldiers in full uniform took pictures and laughed'. One military translator complained to his hierarchy that special forces soldiers had used some kind of 'electric device' on one detainee. As the vast bulk of detainees were neither senior al-Qaeda nor senior Taliban and sometimes totally innocent of any involvement in violence, their interrogators inevitably failed to obtain any useful intelligence from them. Increasingly frustrated, they intensified their efforts to 'get a result'.[45]

What was happening on the ground in Afghanistan was happening elsewhere. Through late 2001 and 2002 the CIA set up a system of secret prisons across the Middle East and Asia – with some facilities in Europe or on board ships in international waters too. Within this and the parallel military detention system practices flowed from one prison to another, from one theatre to another, sometimes passing through the White House or the Pentagon, where senior administration figures effectively signed off on what was already happening, sometimes simply transferring horizontally among those involved in the interrogations at a lower level.[46]

The treatment of Zayn al-Abidin Mohammed Hussein, a thirty-year-old Saudi-Arabian-born Palestinian better known as Abu Zubaydah and alleged to be a key militant, illustrates the steady intensification of violence in this period and the way, as each new level of abuse was reached in one location, it affected behaviour elsewhere. Detained in a joint local and American operation in Faisalabad, the sprawling eastern Pakistani industrial city in March 28, 2002, Abu Zubaydah was first transferred to a secret prison in Thailand and then passed through a series of facilities in eastern Europe before finally arriving in Guantanamo Bay. As such he was one of the first few dozen detainees in the 9/11 Wars to be subject to a 'rendition', a covert transfer to third countries or into US custody by the CIA of an individual seized overseas and one of the first to be shipped around the world through the new networks being established at the time. These saw planes flying suspects from Egypt to Azerbaijan, from Thailand to Libya, from Italy to Germany via Egypt, from Tanzania to Djibouti, from Zimbabwe to the Sudan.[47] Abu Zubaydah's itinerary was relatively mundane by comparison. The treatment he received was not, however. Though his interrogation was initially handled by the FBI, it was taken over by the CIA, who were convinced that more robust measures were needed to get significant information out of their prisoner. One problem may well have been that Abu Zubaydah was simply nowhere near as knowledgeable of al-Qaeda's inner workings as he was believed to be. Over the next months he would be subjected to the full range of interrogation techniques seen in Afghanistan in previous months including dousing with freezing water, sensory and sleep deprivation, forced nudity and stress positions and the rediscovered practice of 'waterboarding', the repeated near drowning of a subject of interrogation by placing a cloth over the face and pouring water into the mouth.[48] The introduction of waterboarding has been attributed to specialist private consultants who had researched Soviet, Chinese, Korean and Vietnamese techniques and who were hired by the CIA to direct Abu Zubaydah's questioning.[49] Despite claims to the contrary such practices and thinking may have been relatively widespread. At least one former detainee in Afghanistan told the author he had undergone waterboarding – or a form of waterboarding – while in

American detention shortly after being arrested near Jalalabad in October 2002.[50]

Once abuse had reached the level of nearly killing prisoners, it did not take long before the inevitable next stage of escalation was reached, and by late December 2002 detainees had begun to die. In Afghanistan, the first was Mullah Habibullah, a big, confident man wrongly accused of links to a Taliban commander from Oruzgan who died in his cell at Bagram after six days of violent beatings. The second fatal casualty was a taxi driver called Dilawar, detained with three other men on information from Bacha Khan Zadran, the warlord who had provided the false information which had led to the bombing of the convoy of elders near Gardez a year before, who, though he had been dumped as a political ally, was still being used as an intelligence source. Dilawar, a small, frail man innocent of any involvement in violence, was subjected to a series of assaults of extreme brutality. In the last sessions, as his legs were already so damaged, he was thrown against a wall. Dilawar too died in his cell.[51] It is almost certain that there were other deaths that went unrecorded. Omar Deghayes, a Libyan NGO worker detained in Pakistan who ended up in Bagram in late 2002, claimed to have witnessed at least one murder, saying he saw 'a prisoner shot dead after he had gone to the aid of an inmate who was being beaten and kicked by the guards' and another 'beaten until [he] heard no sound of him after the screaming'. Deghayes said the incident was followed by 'panic in prison and the guards running about in fear saying to each other "the Arab has died"'.[52]

Such events were but a way point on a continuing descent. In addition to Bagram and Kandahar and the various unofficial prisons on various smaller bases across the country, there was the network of secret detention centres in Afghanistan run by the CIA. Details of two are now known: the 'Salt Pit' and the 'Dark Prison', both apparently operational early in 2002 and both key facilities of the international system of 'ghost' prisons that the CIA had established across the world. Conditions in these were even worse than in Bagram. Cells measuring 2 by 3 metres contained ten men. Prisoners were kept for months in pitch-black cells, fed once a day. The use of extreme cold or heat to 'prepare' a subject for interrogation was routine.[53] At least one, possibly half a dozen, detainees died in these two prisons. At least three others were killed elsewhere in Afghanistan at different forward operating bases in Gardez, in Kunar and in Gereshk in Helmand. In Gardez, the victim was an eighteen-year-old Afghan army recruit who died after being beaten with hoses and cables, immersed in cold water and subjected to electric shocks. In Kunar, it was a twenty-eight-year-old who approached American troops with information after a rocket attack and was beaten to death over a two-day period by a private contractor using 'his hands and feet and a large flashlight'.[54]

The spiral of escalation and abuse throughout the global network being established by the CIA was to continue over coming years. Much would slowly become public, provoking horror and anger even among allies. Senior officials at MI6 later described, disingenuously given that British intelligence officers were happy to receive information from some of the 'more muscular' interrogations and indeed may have facilitated a number of them, being 'as shocked as anybody'.[55]

In Afghanistan the detention, humiliation and abuse of thousands of often respected men was to have predictable consequences. Many of those rounded up in raids like those of Colonel Fetterman, by special forces or delivered by warlords' militia to the CIA were innocent; some were allies who were playing key roles in stabilizing the country smeared by rivals in complex local Afghan politics; all were linked into extended familial and tribal networks which meant that violence against one was seen as violence against scores or even hundreds.[56] One interrogator at Bagram said he felt he was on the receiving end of an invisible war, with barely identified individuals brought to him from out 'beyond the wire' by special forces teams and CIA operatives fighting a shadowy conflict that he knew little about. The same, however, could be said of the men out on the raids themselves, who appear to have had almost no understanding of who and what they were looking for. The three locations that had seen fatal beatings – Gardez, Asadabad and Gereshk – were among the first where violence against the coalition would start to surge. One village elder from near Kandahar who was accused wrongly of being a senior Taliban commander told his jailers shortly before his release after two years in Guantanamo Bay: 'This is just me you brought [here] but I have six sons [and] ten uncles who will be against you . . . I don't care about myself but have 300 male members of my family there in my country . . . If you want to build Afghanistan you can't build it this way . . . I will tell anybody who asks me this is *zulm* [arbitrary rule or tyranny].'[57]

PART TWO

Escalation: 2003–4

5

The War in Iraq I: Threats, Falsehoods and Dead Men

The fifteen months between January 2002 and March 2003, if something of a phoney war, had seen a series of visual elements emerging that would come to represent the 9/11 Wars. All conflicts have their iconic images. These are often based on newly introduced technology or newly evolved tactics. The helicopter in Vietnam is one example. The trenches of the First World War is another. The tank or possibly the nuclear bomb are icons of the Second World War. If the characteristic tactic of the 9/11 Wars was the suicide bomb, it was the defences erected to defend against such strikes which became the marker of this new conflict. Before 9/11, few had ever seen the inverted Ts of concrete from which the newly necessary blast walls were constructed. By the end of 2002, placed in long lines to form instant walls of astonishing ugliness, it was increasingly difficult to escape them.

After that first period of relative calm, the 9/11 Wars would escalate massively. That escalation was to bring many new elements to them as well as embedding, magnifying, amplifying and extending existing characteristics. Not only did the war in Iraq flow naturally out of the campaign in Afghanistan – the ease with which that conflict appeared to have been won bred a confidence in the White House and a more general sense of opportunity in America that greatly informed the decision to press ahead – but much of what had been seen in the earlier fighting would be repeated in this new theatre. There was the same chaotic, indefinite new form of warfare seen at Tora Bora, the lack of genuine comprehension on the part of Western militaries of the tactics necessary to successfully fulfil the tasks they had been assigned and their vision of the population as a battlefield across which the shadowy insurgents were to be fought. There was also the violence dealt to civilians by all parties, the brutalization of prisoners, the continuing importance of the image and of spectacular violence broadcast to as large an audience as possible, the critical interplay between the local identities and global narratives and ideologies, and the systematic use of misinformation. All have been seen in previous chapters and were to feature, often on a far greater scale, in Iraq.

'TWO IRAQIS, THREE SECTS'

One key quality that the Iraq conflict shared with that in Afghanistan was the long roots of the various sub-conflicts of which it was composed. Few states, even in the rough neighbourhood of the central Middle East, could claim as turbulent and brutal a history, recent or otherwise, as Iraq. From its early origins as three frontier provinces established by the Ottoman Turks on the rich lands along the Tigris and Euphrates rivers on their frontier with Persia, through its forced birth as a nation under the British, through the turbulent years that followed the end of the Hashemite monarchy in 1958 and on through the early years of Ba'athist rule and the dictatorship of Saddam Hussein and the Iran–Iraq war of the 1980s, Iraq had been racked by violence, competition and instability. It had also, however, been relatively wealthy – in the 1970s Iraq was one of the most developed of all Arab states – and the drastic retreat from affluence was arguably more damaging to social fabric and attitudes than poverty alone ever could have been. There had also been the quarter of a million casualties in the war against Iran,[1] the huge financial cost of that conflict and then the economic and military catastrophe that had followed the invasion of Kuwait in 1990. The Iraq that Western forces and civilians found in the aftermath of the invasion of 2003 was thus bitter, disillusioned and brutalized. A national identity that was stronger than many believed bred a sense of wounded pride and a xenophobia that complemented rather than countered strong sectarian or ethnic identities.

The 1990s had seen a low-intensity war between Saddam Hussein and the West and a higher-intensity if unwitting war between the West and the Iraqi people in the shape of the United Nations sanctions imposed in 1991. These brutally punished ordinary Iraqis without harming the regime. In Baghdad expensive restaurants were full while over half the country's children were malnourished, many critically.[2] The wounds of the country were hidden, not least because no one risked speaking frankly to reporters. Almost everyone in Iraq lived in fear.

The country was divided into three. In the mountainous north were the 4 million Kurds, semi-autonomous under the umbrella of the northern no-fly zone patrolled by US and British aircraft since 1991 and set on defending their precarious liberty not just from Baghdad but from Ankara too. Below Mosul and the contested, mixed city of Kirkuk with its surrounding oil fields, the majority of the population across the central belt of the country was Sunni Arab. These were the four provinces that had remained loyal to Saddam during the bloodily suppressed revolts that had followed the Gulf War. Overall the Sunnis made up another 4 or 5 million. Then came the Shia south, scarred by war, violent repression and deep poverty.

Two roads led south from Baghdad to the southern port city of Basra. One took you down the Tigris, through rough towns like Amarah, across the old battlefields of the Iran–Iraq war and past the famous marshes that Saddam had drained to deny shelter to insurgent bands fighting his rule. The other followed the Euphrates past the shrine cities of Najaf and Karbala, the holiest sites in Shia Islam, and through seething cities like Nasariyah. Both skirted the vast oil fields and entered Basra through slums composed of row after row of decrepit single-storey brick and concrete homes with scant electricity, limited sanitation and borderline starvation. Largely purged from the Ba'ath Party, particularly after Saddam Hussein and his fellow Tikritis took power in 1979, one element that all Iraqi Shia shared was a desire to see the end of centuries of Sunni monopoly of central power.[3]

These apparently homogeneous communities – Kurd, Shia Arab and Sunni Arab – were, however, internally deeply divided. Though the northern zone was increasingly prosperous and stable, the Kurds had ended a vicious civil war only a few years previously. The Sunni community itself was split between those who benefited from a direct collaboration with the regime – these, of course, included Saddam's own tribesmen from his hometown of Tikrit but other major tribes too as well as others co-opted into the state military, security or bureaucratic establishments – and those who did not. The Sunnis were also split along class lines between urban and rural populations and between the educated middle class that had seen their wealth and status destroyed by war and sanctions and the newly enriched businessmen who had made money from smuggling. The Shia majority – 65 per cent of the population by some estimates – were far from a homogeneous body either. They too were fragmented along tribal lines, culturally between urban and rural or previously rural communities and divided religiously too. Baghdad itself condensed all these various fractures.[4]

Iraq also lay at the centre of an extraordinarily complex regional picture. Around its borders lay six states – Turkey, Iran, Saudi Arabia, Jordan, Kuwait and Syria – which each had its own distinctive governmental system, popular culture, worldview and history and which each had its own interests to pursue in Iraq. To the old local proverb 'two Iraqis, three sects' could be added four classes, five regional backers and six different strands of religious observance. The author, working in Iraq from 1999 to 2002, found as in Afghanistan, the sense of a multiplicity of interwoven, overlaid conflicts almost overwhelming.

THE USE AND ABUSE OF INFORMATION BEFORE THE WAR

The process of preparing public opinion for the conflict which had started with the selective leaks of raw intelligence to newspapers such as the *New York Times* towards the end of 2001 reached its climax with the United Nations presentation made in February 2003 by Colin Powell. The only member of the Bush administration to have sufficient broad credibility to convince those doubtful of the White House's case for war, Powell, who had spent days closeted at CIA headquarters before his speech going over the intelligence, claimed that Saddam Hussein's regime was trying to acquire nuclear weapons capability and that there was 'no doubt' that Iraq both possessed and was prepared to use biological and chemical weapons of mass destruction (WMD).[5] None of these statements proved correct.[6] David Kay, the man charged by the Bush administration with running the Iraq Survey Group to find the evidence of WMD after the invasion, later said bluntly: 'We were almost all wrong.' Kay's successor, Charles Duelfer, concurred. The resulting ISG report said 'with high confidence' that there were no chemical weapons on Iraq soil.[7] None has ever been found, and President Bush himself has admitted that this failure gives him 'a sickening feeling' whenever he thinks about it.[8]

The key problem for any analyst was that, particularly following the departure of United Nations inspectors from Iraq in December 1998, reliable information was very thin on the ground. In the absence of any alternative sources, the reports of the United Nations Special Commission (UNSCOM) had provided the basis for almost all intelligence estimations of Saddam's capacity and intentions. But their data were swiftly out of date. In 1999 the CIA had acknowledged it was receiving very little that was new and was forced to hedge its bets over whether Iraqi stocks of components for WMD had been reconstituted from the enormous WMD programme developed by Saddam before the first Gulf War. This lack of certainty continued through 2000 and 2001, with American agencies raising the possibility that some 'non-weaponized' components for weapons might exist but admitting that there was no real evidence that this was the case.[9]

By late 2002, however, the qualifications had disappeared. In the USA, and in virtually every Western nation, intelligence agencies, undoubtedly aware of the importance of avoiding another grotesque failure such as that which had resulted in 9/11 and unwilling to risk a damaging row with political masters, began to issue much more alarming analyses of the potential threat that Saddam posed. What had been speculation rapidly became fact, buttressed by a stream of falsehoods transmitted by defectors close to the Iraqi exiles lobbying for the invasion. Material that had once been discarded as unreliable was re-examined and, often after have been laundered through a series of different agencies across the world, became the basis for new and more aggressive threat assessments. Not only was information from the Iraqi National Congress (INC), the opposition group led by Iraqi dissident and former banker Ahmed Chalabi, the source for over 100 individual news stories in major publications ranging from *Vanity Fair* to *The Sunday Times* (and subsequently syndicated to, or reproduced in, thousands more) but it was also fed directly to senior officials at the Department of Defense and in the office of the vice president.[10] Beyond recounting Saddam's debauchery, many of these stories reported that Iraq had mobile biological warfare facilities disguised as yogurt and milk trucks or hid banned weapons production and storage facilities beneath hospitals, fake lead-lined wells and Saddam's palaces. Others revealed that Iraq had the capacity to launch toxin-armed Scud missiles at Israel. Several such tales, often embellished with convincing detail, came from an Iraqi refugee in Germany codenamed Curveball, who later confessed to trying 'to fabricate something to topple the regime'.[11] The truth, however, appears to have been that, though he may well have still harboured a strong desire to possess such arms, Saddam had halted production and destroyed almost all WMD stocks in stages between 1991 and 1999. In a fatal miscalculation, he continued to obfuscate out of fear of being seen as vulnerable by regional enemies, in particular Iran. His failure to fully cooperate with the returning United Nations inspectors as the war drew closer was therefore due to a misreading of where the true threat to his regime lay. The last weeks before the Iraq war thus saw a miasma of untruth, myth and miscalculation on all sides.[12]

Further sources for the erroneous claims about Iraq's WMD was testimony from detainees. These included Abu Zubaydah, the detainee who had been waterboarded after capture in Pakistan, and Ibn al-Shaykh al-Libi, another senior al-Qaeda detainee who in early 2002 was tortured in Egypt at the CIA's request.[13] These two men appeared to corroborate the INC's defectors' allegations that al-Qaeda had received assistance for a WMD programme from Saddam Hussein's regime. Information also came from a smuggler imprisoned in a Kurdish jail who told interrogators (and journalists) stories of phials of chemicals being transferred from Baghdad to Kandahar. However, the smuggler, whose claims were widely disseminated in the American press, was a fantasist, unable to even accurately describe Kandahar to the author when interviewed in northern Iraq in August 2002 and al-Libi later retracted his own statement as having been procured under duress.[14]

Such claims naturally played into the question of far broader links between bin Laden's organization and Saddam Hussein's regime. In his speech to the United Nations Powell had described a close and long-standing relationship between al-Qaeda and Saddam Hussein. His claims were conservative in comparison with many of those made by senior White House figures who had repeatedly suggested that the 9/11 attacks had depended on Iraqi assistance or even been an Iraqi plan from the beginning. These ideas were based on a highly selective mix of unverified, false or misinterpreted intelligence stripped of all context.[15]

The picture built up from these various scraps of information was only convincing if, either through genuine 'cognitive dissonance' or deliberate mendacity, any contradictory evidence or contextual analysis was screened out. So when Powell told the UN that there had been contacts between representatives of bin Laden and Iraqi intelligence agents, he was not actually lying. There had indeed been around a dozen such meetings, and though most dated largely from the early and mid 1990s, when bin Laden had been based in Sudan, at least one had occurred more recently, in 1998 in Afghanistan.[16] But, as classified CIA assessments in June 2002 had already concluded, none of these meetings had succeeded in doing anything other than confirming the profound differences between the two parties concerned. This crucial qualification did not feature in the secretary of state's speech.[17]

The same was the case with the idea that al-Qaeda fugitives making their way to Iraq were being sheltered and co-opted by Saddam. Again Powell was right in saying that militants had reached Iraq from Afghanistan. However, he failed to make clear that almost all were heading for the Kurdish zones outside the control of Saddam Hussein at the time. This was not just misleading but revealed once again the fundamental misunderstanding of the real nature of Islamic militancy that had crippled the American response to the threat revealed by the 9/11 attacks hitherto. The whole concept of a link between Saddam and bin Laden was underpinned by the belief that radical Muslim activism could (a) only exist with the support of an individual state or of a shadowy coalition of states and (b) was largely the result of the activities of bin Laden himself or those around him. Yet the situation in northern Iraq in 2002 clearly demonstrated how badly wrong both those presumptions were. Though some militants did make their way to Baghdad, they did not do so at the invitation of Saddam, nor were they welcomed by the Iraqi regime. Indeed, a letter found after the invasion revealed that Saddam was not aware of the arrival of the militants in the Iraqi capital nor particularly happy about it when he did finally learn of their presence. Concerned about the potential threat the new arrivals posed, his intelligence chiefs had in August 2002 been ordered to comb the city to find them as a 'top priority'.[18] Equally, militancy in northern Iraq dated back to the early 1990s and, like almost all such activism at the time, had developed entirely independently of any contact with bin Laden or his associates. Its roots lay in factors as diverse as the civil war between secular Kurdish factions in the middle of the decade, the rejection of radicals at elections in the Kurdish enclave in northern Iraq in the early 1990s and a long tradition of political Islamism in cities such as Mosul and Arbil.[19] Contact between the various groups operating in northern Iraq and bin Laden had come very much later.

In 2000 two of the three largest groups based in the enclave they had been able to create north of the town of Halabjah had sent emissaries to bin Laden in Afghanistan to solicit logistical aid and training. Bin Laden had provided some meagre resources but exploited the opportunity to first establish relations with the third group and then finally, months before September 11, seal a union between the three factions. The group created was called Ansar ul Islam but could in no sense be considered a creation of bin Laden comprising as it did local militants already active in some cases for decades.[20] Powell also claimed that the group had constructed a chemical and biological weapons facility in the mountains of north-eastern Iraq, where they had carved out an enclave. Again, when the author was able to visit the site in April 2003, there was little evidence to back up the statement. An exhaustive investigation by American intelligence agencies found indications that experiments with poison such as cyanide had taken place but nothing to support any claim of any link with al-Qaeda.[21]

A final element that had fed the claim that al-Qaeda and Saddam had cooperated was a report filed by the CIA on September 17, 2001, noting that 'a foreign intelligence service' – in fact the Czechs – had reported that the leader of the 9/11 hijackers, Mohammed Atta, had met 'the local Iraqi intelligence service chief' in Prague in April 2001. Subsequently, this too was contradicted by both the FBI and the CIA after analysis of Atta's cell and bank card records in the USA during the relevant period.

The British MI6 had remained consistently sceptical of efforts to link al-Qaeda and Saddam throughout the run-up to war and their stance was reflected in the public positions taken by UK politicians. Even Blair avoided any direct claims of an actual current relationship, though he did raise on a number of occasions the possibility that one could be formed in the future.[22] The British government issued a series of dossiers, first to MPs and then to a larger audience, in which a mix of intelligence material and public information was presented to argue that the Iraqi leader and his regime represented a clear and urgent danger to global security in general, to the West and to the UK in particular. They focused on the supposed threat posed by WMD. Such dossiers had long been a favoured means by which Downing Street influenced public opinion and had been presented to parliamentarians and journalists during the NATO intervention in Kosovo in 1999 and more recently to set out the case that bin Laden had been responsible for 9/11. Increasingly controversial, they were discontinued after the third prepared during the run-up to the Iraq war was revealed to be largely based not on secret intelligence at all but on hastily cut and pasted information from an out-of-date doctoral thesis found on the internet.[23]

One point worth stressing is that the debate about the potential threat from Iraq took place in a context where abuses of information had become almost banal. Reports of allied and civilian casualties in Afghanistan had been systematically proved to be inaccurate. The British government dossier on bin Laden issued in the autumn of 2001 had included a reference to al-Qaeda's involvement in the narcotics trade, which was known by British officials at the time to be at the very least doubtful.[24] (The 9/11 Commission was later to conclude there was 'no reliable evidence that bin Ladin [sic] was involved [in] or made money through drug trafficking'.[25]) More broadly there was the flagrant abuse of the patchy public understanding of what al-Qaeda was and what threat it posed. By early 2003, the list of governments seeking to exploit the atmosphere of fear inspired by the 9/11 attacks was long. States from Uzbekistan to the Philippines had claimed – without real challenge – that local Islamic militant movements owed their existence to the agency of Osama bin Laden rather than their own repressive, self-serving and incompetent policies. India, Russia and China labelled longstanding local separatist conflicts with roots dating back decades if not centuries as 'al-Qaeda-led' or at the very least 'al-Qaeda-linked'.[26] In Macedonia, senior elected officials went as far as staging a shoot-out with supposed al-Qaeda fighters set on attacking embassies 'to impress the international community'. The victims were in fact entirely innocent Pakistani economic migrants whose bodies had been dressed in combat uniforms by officials before being displayed to the press.[27]

In the UK, as in the USA and many other nations, legislation granting radically enhanced powers to police and security services had been passed in an atmosphere of profound anxiety exacerbated by a series of high-profile arrests of terrorist suspects and a stream of sensationally reported alleged threats from terrorists, ranging from plots to release gas on the London Underground to schemes to plant a series of bombs at Old Trafford football ground, the home of Manchester United.[28] Many turned out to be hugely inflated if not downright fantasy. Though police announced that ricin, a poison made from pounded castor beans, had been found in a raid in which a group of alleged Algerian militants had been arrested in a flat in north London, specialist scientists from Porton Down, the British government biological weapons centre, found that none had actually been manufactured. This did not stop the non-existent ricin being cited in Powell's United Nations speech as a potential link between al-Qaeda, Iraq and Europe.[29] The alleged plot to attack Old Trafford ran across front pages and led bulletins in Britain for two days but turned out to have been entirely based on the discovery by investigating policemen of a couple of ticket stubs and a scarf in the homes of one of the accused, who, ironically, were Iraqi Kurdish refugees who had fled Saddam Hussein's regime.[30] When in August 2002 a man was arrested in Stockholm's Västerås airport with a gun in his toilet bag the mere fact that he had been travelling on a plane with a group of Muslims who were on their way to a conference on the Salafi strand of Islam in the British city of Birmingham was enough for UK newspapers to splash a 'bin Laden link' on their front pages. Prosecutors found no such connection or indeed any terrorist intent at all.[31]

In America, there was much talk of 'dirty bombs', devices laced with sub-explosive radioactive material, largely based on the interrogation under torture of Abu Zubaydah and of an American Hispanic former gang member and convert detained in 2002.[32] One major scare, which led to flights to the USA from Britain and France being cancelled and warnings from officials of a looming 'spectacular attack' to rival 9/11, was based on an elaborate confidence trick by a compulsive gambler who claimed to have developed software that allowed him to decrypt messages to al-Qaeda sleeper cells buried deep in America hidden in al-Jazeera broadcasts.[33] Official statements, such as the leaked intelligence estimates that there were as many as 5,000 'al-Qaeda terrorists and supporters' and warnings by FBI director Robert Mueller of a 'support infrastructure' in America 'which would allow the network to mount another attack on US soil', stoked further fears.[34] The strand of extremist ideology that bin Laden had propagated over previous years had indeed penetrated some American communities – a group of young men of Yemeni origin from the nondescript New York state town of Lacka-wanna who had travelled to an Afghan training camp before 9/11 were arrested amid massive publicity – but its purchase was extremely limited. The impression that a few deliberately fuelled the fear of many to build support for a deeply divisive policy is strong.

For though Bush's memoirs and other similar accounts emphasize the supposed threat posed by Saddam's weapons of mass destruction, the idea that Iraq posed a clear and present danger to the United States or more broadly to world security was only one of the reasons for going to war. It was the most prominent in the run-up to the conflict because, as Paul Wolfowitz later admitted, 'it was the one reason everyone could agree on'.[35] There was never a single instant when a categoric decision was taken to militarily depose Saddam Hussein but rather a growing consensus within the inner circle of the Bush administration that built on the original impulses of key individuals like Cheney and Rumsfeld in the immediate aftermath of 9/11 and made conflict inevitable.

This consensus comprised many strands. There was the original logic of the Global War on Terror: that only through aggressive, forceful and pre-emptive action by the US could potential aggressors be dissuaded and future terrorist attacks averted. There was also a strong sense that, after what was now felt to be aimless drift and weakness under Bill Clinton, a moment had come to radically change the status quo in the Middle East region in America's favour. Here both ideological visions of an invasion of Iraq triggering a wave of liberal-democratic and free-market capitalist reform in the region, forever draining the 'terrorist swamp', and more realist views based on securing the long-term future of Israel, implanting American power in the Middle East region more fully and assuring that key strategic resources such as oil flowed freely on to the world market for the foreseeable future came together.[36] Iraq, after all, had the second-largest oil reserves in the world. The human rights record of Saddam Hussein played a role too, though very much a secondary one, in the collective thinking at senior levels of the Bush administration, as did the Iraqi dictator's earlier attempt to kill Presi-dent Bush's father. A desire to eliminate or at least severely weaken a perceived threat to Israel, carefully focused and reinforced by senior Israeli politicians and army officers in repeated interactions with admin-istration officials, also contributed. One element that was notable in all these calculations was the degree to which they were 'driven by theory – general ideas about what might or could happen'.[37] Like the intelligence about whether Saddam Hussein had WMD or a relationship with bin Laden or the strength of the regime's popular support, few of these theses could be tested in a definitive fashion other than, as historian Lawrence Freedman pointed out, by the supreme empirical test of a war and, more importantly, whatever would follow it.[38] This apparent unwillingness to consider or analyse potential negative outcomes and their consequences when so much was at stake was rooted in a deliberate attempt to deal with risk at a strategic level in a radically new way. 'We don't exactly deal in "expectations" ... and ... we're not comfortable with predictions. It is one of the big strategic premises of the work that we do,' Douglas Feith at the Department of Defense explained.[39] Historical precedents were thus dismissed as irrelevant. So instead of viewing the war in Vietnam as an example of the limits of American power, the earlier conflict was seen instead as a warning that policymakers had to have enormous determination and dedication to a given policy to achieve victory. Nor was the example of British rule in Iraq – or Western rule more generally in the region in the first half of the twentieth century – considered worthwhile of study. Doubt was seen as likely to lead to self-fulfilling failure.[40]

Much of the post-invasion criticism focused on this blithe optimism. Several members of the Bush administration have defended their record, saying that they in fact spent a significant amount of time pondering possible outcomes post-invasion and planning for them. President Bush himself has said that he spent 'hours' talking over a possible humanitarian crisis.[41] However, it is clear that any planning that did occur was based on assumptions about the post-invasion situation that were entirely wrong. The Pentagon, charged by the president with managing the post-war phase, worked on the basis that following the deposition of Saddam Hussein there would be large numbers of Iraqi security personnel willing and able to support the occupation, that 'significant support' from the 'other nations, international organizations and non-governmental organizations' would be forthcoming and that an Iraqi government would rapidly emerge, allowing a 'quick hand off to [an] Iraqi interim administration with [a] UN mandate'.[42] The latter would, it was imagined by officials such as Feith and Wolfowitz, be largely composed of the Iraqi exiles who had spent the last decade or so in the

UK, US and elsewhere. These central assumptions were shared by more in the vast apparatus of the US government than was later admitted.[43]

Another key principle was that the invaders would be greeted broadly as liberators. Senior administration figures quoted American professor Fouad Ajami, who foresaw that the streets of Baghdad and Basra were 'sure to erupt in joy in the same way the throngs in Kabul greeted the Americans'.[44] Dick Cheney, the vice president, explained that there was 'no question' but that the Iraqi people would see the United States as 'liberators'.[45] Such views were echoed by many exiles too. Kanan Makiya, author of the much-read and harrowing denunciation of Saddam's regime *The Republic of Fear*, spoke of a welcome with 'flowers and sweets'.[46]

THE WAR AND EARLY DRIFT

The war of March and April 2003 was over quickly and, as journalist Thomas Ricks has astutely commented, is now chiefly of interest for the problems it bequeathed. It had started earlier than had been planned as last-minute intelligence suggested that Saddam Hussein was at a compound on the outskirts of Baghdad. A hastily programmed missile strike missed him, however. The next day the 145,000 troops massed in Kuwait over previous months crossed the border prepared for a campaign of three months.[47] A British armoured division advanced to secure the crucial oil infrastructure on the Fao Peninsula and to surround Basra while the American forces pushed rapidly north. Resistance did not come from conventional Iraqi army forces – even from the 70,000 elite Republican Guard and the 20,000 strong Special Republican Guard – but was offered in key cities on the invasion route by swarms of irregular *fedayeen*. One of the first American soldiers to die was Platoon Sergeant Anthony Broomhead, riding in a tank in the vanguard of the advancing 3rd Infantry Division. When he waved at a group of Iraqis as his troop drove towards a bridge over the Tigris 60 miles from the city of Nasariyah they did not wave back but launched RPGs instead. 'For the first but not the last time well-armed paramilitary forces, indistinguishable except by their weapons from civilians, attacked,' the army's official history of the invasion said.[48] The idea that the attackers might in fact have been civilians does not seem to have occurred to the author.

Notwithstanding sandstorms and logistical hold-ups, Baghdad was reached relatively easily, and the city's defences, such as they were, collapsed after two American armoured columns pulled off daring raids into the heart of the city and to the airport.[49] A supposed 100-day campaign had lasted just over three weeks and had cost the coalition 133 US and 32 British soldiers. Between 3,000 and 11,000 Iraqi soldiers and between 4,000 and 7,000 Iraqi civilians are thought to have lost their lives.[50] One element that would be important later was the extremely graphic images of the fighting, casualties and destruction broadcast by Arabic-language satellite channels and to a very much lesser extent their Western counterparts. As Saddam's regime had crumbled, satellite dishes had proliferated throughout Iraq, and so much of the population was able to watch the invasion of their own country effectively live on TV, a probable historic first.[51]

For a few weeks after the collapse of the regime, most of Iraq was relatively quiet. Once the spasm of looting, conducted in front of American troops who had no orders to intervene, had subsided Baghdad and other cities were left tense but calm. The expected humanitarian crisis had not occurred, but then nor was there any functioning government. Even if anyone had wanted to try to run the country, most of the ministries were now gutted shells. The Office of Reconstruction and Humanitarian Assistance (ORHA), set up under a retired general to oversee transition to a new Iraqi government and deal with millions of refugees, thus found itself largely redundant. Most of the population, as had been the case in Afghanistan in the immediate aftermath of the deposition of the Taliban, fell back on local social mechanisms, particularly tribal or clerical systems of authority, justice and distribution of resources. The occupier was, for the moment, largely ignored.[52]

The late spring and early summer months also saw febrile political activity. A whole range of groups had emerged to manoeuvre for power. Many had existed in exile in the UK, the US or Iran for decades. There were the revolutionary Iraqi nationalist Islamists of Dawa, the more pro-Iran Islamists of the Supreme Council for Islamic Revolution in Iraq (SCIRI), the relatively secular Iraqi National Congress of the smooth Ahmed Chalabi with his Pentagon connections and the dissident Ba'athists of Ayad Allawi's Iraqi National Alliance (INA), who had been based in London. Once in 'liberated' Baghdad, the various groups jostled and argued, appropriating houses, villas, archives and offices, largely isolated from their own communities and the concerns of the moment. That they would clash with the 'indigeneous' groups that had emerged during the 1990s inside Iraq and which profoundly resented the arrival and presumption of the returning exiles was inevitable. One of the earliest such confrontations saw the moderate cleric Sayid Majid al-Khoie killed in Najaf by a mob of supporters of a young and relatively unknown militant cleric called Muqtada al-Sadr who were apparently incensed by al-Khoie's presence in the city's main shrine in company of a well-known local official seen as a collaborator with the regime.[53]

Yet, despite the sudden and largely spontaneous outbreaks of extreme violence, the general atmosphere across most of Iraq in the immediate aftermath of the invasion was not of bloody chaos but of drift and uncertainty mixed with a degree of jubilation that the largely hated regime had gone. In the capital, the restaurants were open in the upmarket neighbourhood of al-Mansour, shops selling satellite dishes and air-conditioners did excellent business in the middle-class Karada, and the famous fish cafés along Abu Nawas street on the banks of the Tigris were full all through the balmy evenings and late into the night. American soldiers lounged on their tanks or patrolled in their armoured Bradley fighting vehicles leaving a trail of empty Gatorade sports drink bottles in the dust and potholes behind them. With electricity very limited – the acute pre-war lack of power had been exacerbated by the disruption and destruction of the fighting – millions of people simply spent much of their time trying to avoid the searing heat of the Iraqi summer. No power meant not just no fans or fridges in temperatures above 45 centigrade but often no sanitation or irrigation pumps either. The temperatures were a significant disincentive to any activity, insurgency included. Basra and the south were also relatively quiet. An apparently impressive number of wanted members of the old regime were being found and arrested. Saddam's sons Qusay and Uday had been killed in the northern city of Mosul. As in Afghanistan, something of a honeymoon period had followed the actual invasion. In Iraq, however, it was to be very short.[54]

THE COALITION PROVISIONAL
AUTHORITY

The summer and autumn of 2003 are seen as the time when the White House, having won a short war in Iraq, then lost the peace. It is certainly the case that, if the Bush administration's project in Iraq had ever been realizable, the errors made in the space of a few short, hot months ended any chance of success. When it became clear that no new government was going to emerge to replace the state that had disintegrated with the deposition of Saddam, the White House decided to replace the ineffective Office for Reconstruction and Humanitarian Assistance (ORHA) with a much more powerful Coalition Provisional Authority (CPA). They thus, with their allies in the 'coalition of the willing', effectively accepted the role of occupying power, a situation recognized by the United Nations Security Council in mid May.[55]

After four other candidates refused the post, a retired diplomat and businessman with no prior experience of Iraq or the region, Paul Bremer, was appointed as the CPA's head vested with extraordinary plenipotentiary power.[56] Bremer swiftly implemented three measures which together made what was already going to be a very hard job almost impossible. The first was the disbanding of the 385,000-strong Iraqi army along with a wide range of other state entities including large chunks of the Ministry of the Interior. The second was a radical 'de-Ba'athification' decree designed to make the rupture with the previous regime both irreversible and evident. The third was the postponement of elections until an undefined date in the future. Quite why these measures were taken with such alacrity has been long debated, but one answer may be that senior CPA officials were taking what they believed had worked in post-1945 Germany as a useful template. This was so much the case that a twelve-page draft of orders to be presented to Bremer for signature included the phrase 'the only currencies that will be used shall be dollars and Reichsmarks'.[57] A second reason may have been the simple necessity to be seen to be taking charge of a country already sliding into anarchy. A third was that the true impact of these policies was not fully understood. Officials from CPA said that they expected 70 per cent of soldiers from the old army would join the new army – when it was set up.[58] Equally the aim was only to remove the elite – the senior four levels – of the 600,000-strong Ba'ath Party. Officials were therefore surprised when, largely due to the zeal with which de-Ba'athification was pursued by the US allies entrusted with executing the policy, many more were expelled from positions than they had anticipated.[59] The problem was exacerbated by Saddam having devalued rank in the party in recent years to bolster support. Bremer later claimed that he had been told by Douglas Feith, the acutely ideological under-secretary at the Pentagon, that de-Ba'athification should be completed 'even if it causes administrative inconvenience'.[60] The British deputy ambassador in Baghdad described the de-Ba'athification decree as prompted by popular opinion after 'an intense period of listening to Iraqis'.[61] Quite whom they had listened to was unclear.

Together, the dissolution of the army and the aggressive de-Ba'athification programme denied jobs, pensions and what remained of an often already very battered sense of personal dignity to several hundred thousand soldiers, policemen and bureaucrats.[62] They also eradicated the only institutions that provided a genuine unifying structure to the country and stripped those that remained of their entire management. Even headmasters and senior doctors found themselves unemployed.[63] A third of the staff of the Health Ministry simply gave up work.[64] The secondary effects of such mass enforced redundancy – the loss of revenue for the main breadwinner in a household for example – affected many millions of people. In writing in a memo that he wanted his arrival in Iraq 'to be marked by clear, public and decisive steps' which would 'reassure Iraqis' that Saddamism would be eradicated, Bremer was falling into the classic trap of so many senior figures in the 9/11 Wars.[65] He could not see the situation in Iraq through any other eyes than his own or those, in very general terms, of his compatriots.

Then there was the decision to postpone elections indefinitely, effectively to allow a suitably pro-American, moderate, pro-free-market, relatively secular Iraqi political class some time to emerge.[66] Rumsfeld had already warned that the United States would not allow Iraq to become like Iran, confusing the idea of including *sharia* in Iraq's new constitution with creating a theocracy.[67] A CPA spokesman justified the postponement by the lack of a census and the fact that 'rejectionist and religious parties' were the most organized.[68] However, delaying the polls simply confirmed the worst suspicions of millions. One of the points missed in the West was the degree to which the nearly forty-year-old Israeli occupation of the West Bank and Gaza influenced views in Iraq of the length of time it was believed the Americans might remain there. 'Why if the US just want to leave have they cancelled the elections? This is a kind of tyranny,' said Haider Abdul Numin, a money-changer in

Najaf.[69] A weak 'Iraqi Governing Council' was created, packed with pro-American exiles and then largely ignored.

AN INSURGENCY GETS UNDERWAY

As the spring had passed and the long, hot summer months went on, violence began to rise steadily. Much of it remained the work of unco-ordinated groups who took direction, if at all, from local clerics or from former senior regime members. These groups were bands of friends or former colleagues, men who prayed at the same mosque, went to the same café or even, in the case of one group of insurgents the author interviewed in Baghdad, half a dozen fathers whose children went to the same school.[70] Some were former professional soldiers, almost all knew how to handle weapons though not usually place bombs or fire mortars. They were professors, businessmen, civil servants, mechanics and the unemployed.[71]

They included men like 'Abu Mujahed', as he called himself, a thirty-year-old bureaucrat. A Sunni from the big Baghdad neighbourhood of Adhamiyah, Abu Mujahed had never been a member of the Ba'ath Party and said he had been 'very happy' to hear that the Americans were coming to 'liberate Iraq'. American culture had symbolized freedom, meritocracy and opportunity and Bon Jovi, the stadium rock band, he remembered. The process of disillusionment was rapid, however. First came the images of civilian casualties broadcast by Arabic-language sat-ellite channels and watched on an illicit dish during the war itself. Then there was the sight of Americans troops doing nothing to stop the loot-ing of Baghdad. The latter, Abu Mujahed said, had convinced him that the Americans were not here to help the Iraqis but 'to destroy them'. This was not enough in itself to push Abu Mujahed into violent mili-tancy. Over several months other factors each furthered his progression towards taking up arms. One significant moment, he remembered, came when the Americans started 'killing and arresting' his 'own people'. Another was when he realized that, with food prices rising rapidly since the invasion, his pay as a minor government functionary was no longer sufficient to feed his family decently. 'I could no longer afford a chicken to put on the table in the evening,' he said. In addition, he said, none of the advantages he had hoped for from the invasion had come to pass.

There was no democracy, he claimed, especially for Iraq's Sunni Muslim minority, and no electricity or proper sanitation either.

It would have been difficult to describe Abu Mujahed as an 'Islamic militant'. Certainly his beliefs and values had little in common with those of a reactionary cleric or an autodidact extremist organizer and propagandist like bin Laden. He only went to mosque on a Friday and rarely prayed five times a day except during Ramadan. However, religion clearly played a significant part in his worldview and was particularly important in unifying his group and, crucially, legitimizing its actions. 'Always we discuss what we are going to do in religious terms so we can say we are fighting for the sake of religion,' he said. 'We have formed our group to fight for religion, and the main thing for our group is religion.' Abu Mujahed said that above all he felt 'humiliated'.

Over a period of weeks a group of six or seven like-minded men came together. There was no major effort at recruitment, certainly no direction from above or outside, just a band of people sharing a fairly indistinct goal and similar sentiments. The group contained, Abu Mujahed said, 'one man fighting for his nation, another fighting for a principle', as well as someone who was 'very religious'. He was the leader but not through any formal mechanism. More because 'someone has to organize things a bit', he said. Nor was the process by which his group sourced the various basic elements that all militants and terrorists require – weapons, expertise and somewhere to train and rest and hide – any less amateurish or haphazard. Careful if casual inquiries established that there was an underground network of arms suppliers already in existence. Saddam had distributed vast numbers of weapons, and the locations of dumps – often left untouched and unsecured by American troops for fear of lethal chemical or biological weapons – were known to many. Finding people who had the specialized knowledge that the group needed to use the arms that were available took longer, but step by step Abu Mujahed and his friends were able to locate experts in weapons, concealment and communications among demobilized members of the Iraqi army. 'They would help us out as a favour and did things like show us how to use a mortar in the front room of someone's house,' he said. 'Bit by bit, we learned what we needed to know.' One former army officer joined the group.

Abu Mujahed and his friends soon began establishing contacts with other similar groups, all of which paid nominal allegiance to a single tribal sheikh. There were no specific commands as such but merely broad direction from more senior tribal leaders. Over the next months the group tried various tactics: sniping at Americans, learning about remote-controlled bombs, laying mines where they knew patrols would pass and using mortars.

In every way, Abu Mujahed's operations were typical of those of such men in Iraq and in many other theatres of the 9/11 Wars. His motivations or those of the others in his group – a mixture of disappointed expectations, wounded pride, concepts of tribal and national honour, socio-economic hardship and a desire to avenge killed, injured or humiliated loved ones or associates, the smooth fusion of global Islamic narratives with local nationalist or sectarian ones – were broadly representative. The emergence and instrumentalization of religion was classic too as Islam, as we have seen in early chapters, has consistently played a role as a rallying flag and a discourse to concentrate, express and unify diverse grievances. The deteriorating economic situation of the last years of Saddam Hussein's regime had also seen a strengthening of kinship and tribal ties. These tribal and family associations sometimes clashed with more nationalist and religious identities but were often easily combined – as in the case of Abu Mujahed's band.

However, the activities of men like Abu Mujahed were still of little strategic significance in the summer of 2003. There were others who were much more organized and who targeted their efforts much more carefully. Before the war, defence officials in London and Washington had briefed reporters on the new form of warfare that the conflict in Iraq would demonstrate. The intention was to reinforce domestic support for the war while simultaneously undermining morale in Iraq. One aide to the British secretary of state for defence explained to the author over lunch off Trafalgar Square how 'networkcentric' warfare would incapacitate the key internal communications systems of an opposing force, effectively ending its ability to respond to orders, manoeuvre and fight. A key element of networkcentric warfare, he said, involved getting inside the enemy's 'decision loop' or more technically 'Observation-Orientation-Decision-Action time' (OODA), effectively acting repeatedly before the opponent had had time to react and thus, like a boxer with a winning combination, landing a flurry of blows of such power and rapidity that the total collapse of all opposition was assured. In the event, it was the insurgents who successfully got inside the OODA of the coalition forces and seized the tactical and strategic initiative. They were to hold it for at least three, arguably four, years.

Within only a few weeks of the invasion powerful bombs began to go off. The attacks, largely massive suicide blasts, could have directly targeted the Americans. Instead, they were focused on all other actors whose presence in Iraq could render the occupation of Iraq more legitimate in the eyes of locals and the international community. The massive bomb that destroyed much of the United Nations' Canal Road headquarters and killed twenty-three, including Sergio Viera de Mello, the UN's well-liked and competent special envoy to Iraq, on August 19 was just the most spectacular of the series. The target was justified in the eyes of many Iraqis as the UN's role in administering the sanctions that limited medicine and other essentials all the while keeping Saddam in power (and providing good jobs to hundreds of foreigners) during the 1990s meant that it was widely disliked. One poll in 2003 revealed that 69 per cent of Iraqis thought the UN would hurt rather than help Iraq over the next five years.[72] Senior UN staff were blissfully unaware of this, and the bombing effectively removed any major United Nations presence from Iraq and prompted other major multilateral entities like the World Bank and the International Monetary Fund to leave too.[73] A series of attacks on NGOs such as the Red Cross and Save the Children had a similar effect.

Ayatollah Mohammed Baqr al-Hakim – head of SCIRI and the most senior Iraqi political figure to publicly back the occupation – died in a massive blast that sent a very clear message about what was likely to happen to anyone contemplating taking a similar stance. Other attacks hit diplomatic representations – such as those of the Turks and the Jordanians – whose presence might too have been seen to legitimize the occupiers' presence in the Arab or Muslim worlds. American coalition allies, such as the Italians, were also targeted. The tactic was an old one, familiar to Saddam's intelligence services. Rather than directly attack an individual, particularly one who might still have some residual ability to cause harm, Saddam's intelligence services would pick off those around him, threatening, abducting, raping, beating family members and associates, leaving their real target more and more exposed and weaker and weaker until finally little effort was needed to finish him off. Though the background hum of violence might have been the work of men like Abu Mujahed, the string of major 'headline' attacks throughout the summer of 2003 was the work of senior and middle-ranking officials from within the security establishment of the former regime. They used both Iraqi and foreign volunteers as suicide bombers to deliver the bombs, an example of the 'odd couples' the 9/11 Wars sometimes threw together. The bombs progressively isolated the Americans as all those around them who could lend legitimacy and capacity to their rule fell away.

As autumn approached, a second series of targets began to be developed too: the Shia community and anything that could possibly provide any nascent government with an effective security infrastructure. Shia targets and security targets often coincided as few Sunni policemen had remained at their posts. Those standing for hours in the unprotected recruitment queues were almost all Shia too. When the Red Cross had been attacked, three police stations were hit with it. And when SCIRI leader al-Hakim died so did nearly 100 others, all Shia, in Najaf, the holy city. That those behind the attacks knew exactly what they were doing was evident. Their identity, however, was still a mystery to the coalition.

SIX DEAD MEN

If Afghanistan was a war of far hills and valleys, Iraq was going to be a war of scruffy streets in hard-scrabble towns. Their names would become depressingly familiar over the coming years. One such place was Majjar al-Kabir, a chaos of cement-and-brick tenements, houses and slums by the Tigris 100 miles north of Basra and 250 miles southeast of Baghdad, which was the site of a short and brutal engagement in late June 2003 typical of much of the fighting that was to come.[74] As such, it is worth looking at in some detail.

Majjar al-Kabir, home to around 35,000, had been one of the many places in Iraq to liberate itself during the invasion. When American troops had arrived in the town they had found it already under the control of former anti-Saddam fighters. The US units had none too diplomatically sidelined the locals and had then handed over to the British troops moving up from the south. By June, it was a senior soldier, a British Parachute Regiment colonel, who was, despite the presence of the newly created Coalition Provisional Authority and a variety of now fairly disgruntled local actors, the de facto authority in the town.

The British decided that the priority needed to be establishing a 'secure' environment and that this aim could not be achieved without disarming the local population. Every rural household in Iraq has at least one small arm and many have heavier weapons too. Majjar al-Kabir had been close to the battle fronts of the Iran–Iraq war, had seen an anti-Saddam insurgency as well as decades of internecine tribal warfare, widespread banditry and smuggling and as a result was heavily armed even by local standards. As the population was not going to hand in their weapons voluntarily, the troops had to search for them. This they did in the same way as they had done in Afghanistan and with similar results. It did not take long for locals to make their anger at the disarmament operations very clear. At the small village of Abu Ala, a collection of breeze-block homesteads ringed with thorn bushes, thin-ribbed sheep and filthy children on the outskirts of Majjar al-Kabir, there were scuffles as locals reacted angrily to British troops entering women's quarters and using dogs, seen as unclean in many Islamic societies. 'They came into our houses with no respect,' Mohammed Ayub, a forty-five-year-old farmer, told the author.[75]

The incensed villagers organized a demonstration in the main town which degenerated into a small riot ending with British troops, pelted with stones, firing into the air. To calm tempers, a long meeting was held between British officers and local representatives, mainly elders and clerics, and an agreement drawn up. The locals would hand in their heavy weapons within a month, and the British would stop the searches. In the meantime, there would be no British presence in the town.[76]

The problem lay in differing interpretations of the latter phrase. The British took it to mean *permanent* presence, locals thought it meant *any* presence. When the British sent a patrol through Majjar al-Kabir the day after the agreement it encountered no trouble. When twenty-four hours later another patrol set out it quickly found itself hemmed in by an angry, rock-throwing crowd. The troops fired rubber bullets and then, when they had no more non-lethal ammunition, fired live rounds into the air. The crowd withdrew a little, allowing the British soldiers to reach the town's marketplace, at which point someone opened fire from a top-floor window of a nearby building. The gunman was shot dead, but two others started shooting from another direction. These too were hit, but soon, in the laconic description of the official report into the events, 'numerous members of the crowd were firing on the patrol'. For the next hour there was a chaotic street battle as more and more locals joined the fight, and the cornered British troops tried to defend themselves.[77] A Chinook helicopter carrying reinforcements was badly shot up as it flew over the town and, with half a dozen of the troops it was carrying seriously wounded, had to return to the British forces' base at Amarah 'pissing blood and oil', in the words of Lieutenant Colonel Stuart Tootal, in the operations room at the main base of the British force outside the town of Amarah, 15 miles away. 'We looked at each other. We thought the wheels were coming off, that this was our Blackhawk Down,' Tootal remembered.

Eventually reinforcements from Amarah arrived and brought sufficient firepower to bear on the gunmen – now hundreds strong – to allow the British troops to be extricated. It was only then that it was realized that the paratroopers' patrol had not been the only British military presence in Majjar al-Kabir. At 10 a.m., half an hour after the patrol had reached the town, six military policemen, or 'Redcaps', assigned to the rather thankless task of trying to rebuild and reform the town's police force had also arrived to talk to the newly appointed police chief about renovating the local station – a 'reconstruction' mission typical of those assigned to thousands of British soldiers at the time.

The men were under the command of Sergeant Simon Hamilton-Jewell from Thames Ditton in southern England. A mechanic and judo black belt, he had first joined the army as a reservist in 1979 aged twenty-eight, before enlisting in the regular forces. Hamilton-Jewell had served with British special forces for six years before joining the Royal Military Police and still described himself as 'sixteen stone of romping, stomping airborne fury'.[78] Respected and liked by the much younger men in his detachment, 'HJ' was known as a competent, experienced and motivated soldier.

It had taken nearly an hour for the group to drive slowly in two open-top landrovers from the base at Amarah to Majjar al-Kabir. Forty-five minutes after the six soldiers arrived at their destination – the battered single-storey police station 100 metres or so down a turn-off from the main road out of town – they heard gunfire from the town centre. They had no idea that the Parachute Regiment patrol was there, let alone that it had come under attack. Very soon, groups of armed Iraqis started appearing in the streets around them.

Newspaper reports in Britain later spoke of a 'last stand', as if Hamilton-Jewell and his men were cornered imperial soldiers resisting the onslaught of natives.[79] In fact, events were messier than the image suggested. The gunmen surging out of Majjar al-Kabir following the retreating paratroopers moved into buildings around the police station and started firing on the Redcaps, quickly wounding two. The soldiers abandoned their positions around their vehicles in front of the police station and moved indoors, taking up positions at windows and around the small internal courtyard, levelling their SA80 automatic rifles at the oncoming attackers.[80] With their only radios on their now burning Land Rovers, Hamilton-Jewell turned to one of the policemen who had remained in the station and asked if he had any means of communication. He did not and implored the Redcaps to flee through a window at the rear of the building.[81] It was, however, too late. The station was surrounded. After another brief exchange of fire, a local elder forced his way through the crowd around the station and convinced the gunmen outside to let him negotiate. Entering the station, he found one British soldier apparently dying and three others propped wounded against the walls of one of the storerooms. But the crowd had followed him in. The elder was pulled out of the way, Hamilton-Jewell shot and then the other soldiers, though they held out pictures of their children and wives and pleaded for their lives, executed.[82]

The violence at Majjar al-Kabir appeared to defy explanation. The men who fought the British in the town were not 'foreign fighters' nor 'regime dead-enders' but from the southern Shia populations who had suffered most under the regime and were rightly thought most likely to support the invasion and deposition of Saddam. 'We all hated the dictator and his terrorists,' Talal Abid Ahmed Zubaida, a local tribal chief and militia leader said the day after the killings of the Redcaps.[83] The local power was Karim Mahoud aka Abu Hatem, aka 'the Lord of the Marshes', a charismatic, brave, effective, ruthless and unscrupulous former guerrilla leader, who had taken charge locally after the invasion until forced to bow before the new powers in the land, but he had no immediate interest in provoking a confrontation.[84] The economy, the provision of jobs or the supply of electricity were not major factors as most locals understood that any economic improvements would take months to be seen. Indeed, electricity provision to Abu Ala, the village where the trouble had started, had actually improved in previous weeks as power that was once reserved for Baghdad was more equitably distributed.[85] The impact of the dissolution of the army and the purging of the bureaucracy of all supposed regime loyalists had also been limited in a rural, poor, relatively remote Shia area. Even the struggle for power between militia loyal to the (very) relatively secular and moderate Abu Hatem and networks loyal to the young militant cleric Muqtada al-Sadr was at an embryonic phase, and though the local supporters of the latter had an interest in disrupting the city, later arrests of the presumed murderers revealed that they were not behind the killings of the Redcaps.

There is, however, one explanation for the violence that was barely cited in the weeks that followed the fighting in Majjar al-Kabir. Two months after the killings there a senior aide to the British minister of defence told the author that, unlike the Americans, 'the British are not intrinsically viewed as an occupying force in Iraq'.[86] He was wrong. Many have spoken of the 'antibody' theory by which any foreign troops are inevitably attacked, particularly in Arab or Islamic lands. Such generalizations are of little use, however. As subsequent events in Iraq and elsewhere were to show, all depends on the role foreign troops are expected to play, their actions and the context. In Majjar al-Kabbir foreign troops were attacked because of a fundamental problem of legitimacy which fed a visceral emotional reaction. The fact that the people of both the town and the city of Amarah had liberated themselves during the campaign in March, pre-empting the arrival of coalition troops, made the perceived humiliation of the weapons searches, itself symbolic of the broader humiliation of occupation, even sharper.[87] There was a practical issue too. With the elections postponed indefinitely, local people believed the British wanted the arms to ensure there could be no serious resistance to their long-term projects for 'occupying Iraq and stealing its oil'. 'During Saddam's time, people reacted in the same way when they searched for weapons,' said Hamid Shagambi, one of the local elders sitting on the town's council.

Some of those who had opened fire in the marketplace had been waiting to do so. But they were few. Once the fighting had started, scores, if not hundreds, fetched their weapons. Mohammed Nasr Amari was one. In Baghdad fourteen months after the events in Majjar al-Kabir, he explained to the author: 'Some people started fighting the soldiers when they were there in the town. Perhaps they had organized it like some kind of ambush, I don't know, but when it started we all went and got our guns. Of course everyone joined in. Who would want to be without honour? Who would want to be the one who did not take up his gun? If they hadn't been there we wouldn't have shot at them.'[88] Majjar al-Kabir would remain effectively outside the control of the coalition forces and successive Iraqi governments for years to come.[89]

Hamilton-Jewell had written a letter to his mother to be opened in the event of his death:

> Dear Mum, If you receive this, then I have been killed in the conflict. Don't be sad for me because I died doing the job I enjoy. I have had a good life and that was thanks to my upbringing. I valued right from wrong and I believe what I was doing was for the purpose of good and my life is a small price to pay for peace. Just because I didn't always show that I cared doesn't mean that was the case. I always cared and appreciated you and how you were always there for me. It is just that I am not always good at showing my emotions. I hope you are proud of me and realise that there is nothing to regret in my passing, because my life has been good and my ambitions fulfilled. I don't really know what else to say other than I love you and I don't want you to be sad because I did my duty and loved life. There are a lot of people in the world who have not been blessed with the great life I have had. Love, Simon. Army number 2447779.[90]

6

War in Iraq II: Losing It

THE SUNNIS AND THE FIRST
BATTLE OF FALLUJA

Saddam Hussein was pulled from a small underground hiding place in the village of al-Auda on December 14, 2003 and definitively identified by the tribal tattoo of three dots on his wrist.[1] 'We got him,' a triumphant Paul Bremer announced at a hastily arranged press conference a few hours later. He and others pronounced themselves confident that any resistance to the occupation would wither away. Instead it intensified, and the year of 2004 would be one in which it all went very badly wrong in Iraq. Why did the insurgency not die when Saddam had been captured? The answers to the question lay, as so often in the 9/11 Wars, in the deep-rooted historical factors that determined the context.

One major factor was demographic. The March 2003 war plan had been focused on decapitating Saddam's regime. Its targets were Baghdad and the senior ranks of the Ba'ath Party or Saddam's own clique. The areas that in many ways were much more critical – the western provinces, the fertile belt of farmland surrounding Baghdad and stretching away up the Euphrates valley towards Syria and the string of tough towns along the highways radiating out from the capital – were largely ignored. These areas, however, were the heartland of Iraq's Sunnis, who for five centuries had been the ruling caste and received the largest share of resources. Saddam had not broken with this tradition. Travellers driving down from the northern Iraqi city of Mosul in the late 1990s knew when they had reached Tikrit, the dictator's home town, because the road widened, and rows of brand new strip lights appeared along either side interspersed with giant, very well-watered trees. But the hard demographic logic of Iraq was clear to all. If the country was to be a democracy – as the Americans and their coalition partners repeatedly proclaimed – then the Sunnis would be the losers. The dissolution of the army, the de-Ba'athification campaign and a range of other measures made it very clear very early what being a loser looked like. If the 22 per cent of Iraqis who were Sunnis were going to keep at least some of their privileges they were going to have to fight.[2]

Secondly, both modern and traditional strands of Islam were much stronger than many outside the region – indeed outside the country – thought. The modernity of Iraq during the 1970s, the image projected both by the secular leadership and allies such as America during the war against the 'fanatics' of Iran and the difficulties involved in reporting the true sentiments of Iraqis during the 1990s had combined to embed the sense that Islam played a less important role in the culture and politics of the country than elsewhere. Nothing could be further from the truth. Though not as overtly politically religious as Iran nor as religiously political as Saudi Arabia, faith remained as deeply ingrained in the lives and worldviews of most Iraqis, particularly the poorer and rural communities, as it did in other countries across the region. Nor had Iraq been immune to the broad ideological shifts affecting other nations in the region over previous decades. In every other Arab nation, the opposition to the kind of discredited Socialist, nationalist or pan-Arab ideologies that many regimes had originally espoused had been Islamist since the mid 1980s at the very latest. In Iraq too the same conditions existed that had led to the popularization of Islamism elsewhere and also to the growth of Salafi tendencies. Throughout the 1990s, Saddam himself had tried to co-opt this tendency by launching his own 'Islamification' drive. Bars and clubs had been shut down, a once-thriving gay scene repressed, hundreds of mosques built and a new Islamic slogan placed on the national flag. Saddam was pictured at prayer on many of his newer portraits, readings of the Koran were introduced on state television, and the construction of a vast mosque was started which was to house a Koran supposedly written in the blood of the nation's 'Great Uncle' or 'Anointed Leader', as he called himself.[3] But Saddam's new-found piety was far from credible. As he was broadcasting his spurious religious credentials, clandestine preachers from the Gulf were moving through his country, funded by private donors and wealthy foundations in Saudi Arabia, Kuwait and elsewhere.

Local Iraqi activists of the Muslim Brotherhood were also at work. Both they and the Salafis focused on the same social and geographic terrain. Avoiding the cities where Saddam's security services would have easily discovered their activities and the remote rural areas where there was insufficient population for their purposes, they concentrated their efforts on the proud, independent-minded Sunni communities of the agricultural or semi-urban hinterland of the capital, towns like Baqubah, Ramadi, Muhammadiya, Balad and Samarra, where they found a welcome in once-thriving farming communities for whom Ba'athist nationalism had meant war and repression and for whom the West meant support for Israel and sanctions.[4] The radical, austere but coherent message spread by the travelling clerics and activists fell on fertile ground. It was not surprising that one of first bits of graffiti the author encountered on the road running south-west from the central city of Kirkuk into the Sunni-Arab-dominated zones days after the fall of Saddam was the slogan of the Brotherhood: 'Islam is the solution'.[5] Nor was it surprising that the bomber who had killed himself destroying the United Nations headquarters and mission in August 2003 had been a young man who had been both a Ba'ath Party member enrolled in Saddam's *fedayeen* militia and a member of radical Islamic circles in his small home town just south of Baghdad.[6]

A third major factor was the simple conservatism and xenophobia of the Sunni communities beyond the elite circles from amongst whom the majority of Western interlocutors were drawn. Falluja, a city of 400,000 at a strategic crossing point on the Euphrates surrounded by rich farmland which was to become the centre of the Sunni insurgency during 2004, had always been one of the most conservative communities in Iraq. Unlike somewhere like Tikrit, where the tribes were relatively urbanized, the tribes of Falluja were concentrated in the rural areas surrounding the city and were still heavily influenced by decades or centuries-old tribal traditions and customs.[7] Like so many towns, Falluja had also liberated itself, with local sheikhs and clerics establishing a series of management councils largely based in the many mosques in the city after the fall of the regime. These had successfully prevented any looting and made sure that if anyone was going to raid traffic on the major highways leading west which passed the city it was locals.[8] 'We all know one another here, there were no problems,' said shopkeeper Abdul Kadeer.[9] Falluja was thus another one of those cities like

Majjar al-Kabir whose inhabitants did not consider themselves to have been defeated and who believed that they had a right to govern themselves according to their own customs. Powerful and well-armed local tribes with their own wealth from agriculture and smuggling such as the al-Dulaimi had been treated warily by Saddam Hussein even as they remained one of his most important bases of support.[10] Though some experts made efforts to point out these crucial elements to key individuals in the Pentagon or the White House itself – some featured in the vast multi-volume work produced by the State Department before the invasion – their warnings were largely dismissed. American strategic thinking was conventional. Objectives were seen in terms of individuals – particularly those with political power such as Saddam and his clique – or geography – crucial terrain features or facilities such as airports or roads. As had been the case in Afghanistan, there was no concept of populations like the Sunnis of the western provinces or the Baghdad hinterland as objectives in their own right. Such communities nonetheless constituted 'terrain' of the highest strategic importance.

This inevitably contributed to a final factor: the counter-productive behaviour of the occupiers. It was not just the well-reported civilian casualties or the looting of the invasion itself. Within weeks of the invasion, there had been a series of incidents in or around Falluja in which American troops had killed significant numbers of local people. American commanders denied frequent accusations that they were trigger-happy, but anyone accompanying their troops on raids could see the impact their tactics had on local populations. When men from the 3rd Armoured Cavalry Regiment in Falluja and its nearby smaller twin Ramadi set out on an operation to round up suspected insurgents in June 2003 they blasted the doors of the suspects' homes off their hinges with explosives, ransacked rooms and forced scores of men to squat with bags over their heads for hours in the sun waiting to be 'processed'. Returning to their base in a commandeered palace outside Ramadi, troops played gangster rap at high volume through speakers mounted on their armoured vehicles. 'It's good for morale,' Lieutenant Colonel Hector Mirabile explained to the author. On patrol at night the soldiers, mainly reservists from Florida, came under sniper and mortar fire while locals made mock howling noises in the dark and shouted that the 'amriki' would 'die like dogs'. The soldiers replied with insults they had picked from interpreters. On the streets that had been raided the anger was palpable. Few hid their sentiments. 'I am not sorry for the US dead. They cross the ocean to come here to plunder our wealth not to help us,' said Jamal Nawaf, a sixty-year-old shopkeeper. 'They don't respect old people. I can't sleep because of the helicopters. If even the kids throw stones they shoot. They have taken my Kalashnikov, they have taken money from my house, they have taken my pride.'[11]

Yet it would be a mistake to see the growing insurgency in Iraq as either homogeneous or particularly organized. General John Abizaid, appointed commander of US Central Command in the aftermath of the campaign of 2003, described the conflict in Iraq his troops were engaged on in Iraq as a 'classical guerrilla-type campaign'.[12] In fact, the opposite was true. As Professor Bruce Hoffman pointed out after a visit to Iraq, what the US and their allies were facing there was anything but classical. Hoffman observed that the Iraq insurgency had no center of gravity, no clear leader or leadership, made no attempt to seize and actually hold territory, had no single, defined, or unifying ideology or identifiable organization. Iraq, Hoffman argued, was a 'loose, ambiguous, and constantly shifting environment, [where] constellations of cells or collections of individuals gravitate toward one another to carry out armed attacks, exchange intelligence, trade weapons, or engage in joint training and then disperse at times never to operate together again.'[13]

What this structure, or lack of structure, brought the insurgents was a formidable ability to adapt and evolve. Networks of fighters were not only able to form but to change their tactics, adapting to unpredictable events and unforeseen opportunities with extraordinary rapidity. Their evolution was more the result of fragmentary connections between semi-autonomous parts or 'localized tinkering' than hierarchical command and control or intelligent design and was thus much better suited to fast-changing local circumstances than the ponderous and structured organizations, whether military or other, trying to eliminate them.[14] The insurgency was adaptive, social, informal and dynamic. It was perfectly suited to and a perfect product of the first decade of the twenty-first century. Nothing illustrated this better than the rapid adoption of Improvised Explosive Devices (IEDs) as a weapon of choice. That the IEDs became the preferred arm of the insurgents was, unless one believed the rhetoric about 'loving death more than you love life', hardly surprising. Insurgents soon worked out that IEDs, though once disdained as somehow unmanly, gave them a much better chance of causing casualties and of escaping unscathed than taking on heavily armed allied soldiers conventionally. The tactic thus combined the two qualities sought by all those who use political violence: capability, in that they were effective, and resilience, in that they did not expose those using them to excessive risk.[15] But no one commander in chief took a decision to adopt the use of IEDs as a primary tactic. The process by which cells came together to build and place IEDs was chaotic and haphazard. This was one reason it was so hard to counter. If the militants themselves did not know where they were to meet or when an attack was to take place, it was inevitably impossible for those hunting them to focus the undoubted firepower they had at their disposal. During 2003 an average of less than a dozen US troops had been killed by roadside or other bombs detonated from a distance each month. In 2004 every single month saw at least twenty killed by such devices with significant spikes in such attacks (and resultant casualties) whenever a major conventional operation was underway.[16]

In Falluja particularly, any vision of a broader, united, strategically directed movement broke down entirely. The growing insurgency against the occupiers developed in tandem with growing civil conflict in which the Americans had only a background role. The city was rent by the firefights and score-settling that went with the ferocious and fast-moving manoeuvring for power between sheikhs and a variety of tribal and political factions all looking to exploit the collapse of Saddam's regime. Among the contenders were the Association of Muslim Clerics, who represented the extremist neo-traditionalist 'Salafist' tendency closest to al-Qaeda's or the Taliban's style of Islam, and the Iraqi Islamic Party, who were the local branch of the Islamist Muslim Brotherhood. These two tendencies clashed repeatedly. What Hoffman had seen among insurgents attacking American forces was equally true of groups of Iraqis attacking one another. Tribal groups formed, launched an attack against their rivals and then dispersed with bewildering rapidity. Some tribes showed themselves more amenable to the occupiers, often looking for lucrative contracts for reconstruction work. Others shot, kidnapped or threatened anyone cooperating with the Americans or their allies. It was difficult to tell exactly who was in charge in Falluja, though it was evident that it was not the CPA or the American army. As it became obvious that Saddam's capture had not ended the insurgency, Falluja began to shift to the forefront of American strategic thinking about Iraq. Dealing with Falluja, it was reasoned by Abizaid and others, would definitively end the resistance in the country. Months before the first battle for the city it was clear a major confrontation was inevitable.

The American commanders were not, however, able to choose the moment of that confrontation. A division of US Marines, better trained for lighter, faster expeditionary and irregular warfare than their regular army counterparts, had taken over responsibility for Anbar, the western province that was becoming the heart of the insurgency, in March 2004, and their commander on the ground, Major General James Mattis, a loud-talking but deep-thinking bachelor with a passion for military history, had drawn up a careful and long-term strategy based on sound counter-insurgency theory that he hoped would allow him to win over the city and its hinterland through a careful mixture of big, 'kinetic' stick and financial and developmental carrot.[17] The strategy required a long period of preparation and a slow and steady approach once launched. Mattis' plan was overtaken by events when, on March 31, 2004, four private contractors working for an American security company were ambushed in Falluja, lynched, and their bodies dragged through the streets, mutilated and then torched amid scenes of celebration. The ambush had been the work of insurgents, the lynching was a spontaneous reaction by locals led by day labourers waiting with their tools in the central marketplace to be hired.[18]

In previous conflicts, perhaps, the violent deaths of four civilians would have had little effect. But the ritualized violence in Falluja was filmed and uploaded on to the internet, and images of the unrecognizable remains of the contractors swinging from a bridge were broadcast by almost all major media outlets within hours. 'The moment we saw it we knew this was going to be a problem. Everyone from the president down were all shouting "sort this out",' Andrew Rathmell, a senior British diplomat attached to the CPA in Baghdad, remembered. Bremer, the British and the CPA's political officers were all initially against any precipitate action, Rathmell said, some arguing that they had 'interlocutors' in the city, others simply pushing for Falluja to be 'isolated'.[19] But no one in the US military, the Pentagon and the White House was interested in 'half-measures'. Early plans that involved 'more or less carpet-bombing Falluja' were shelved after strenuous protests from Downing Street, the British Foreign Office and senior British officers in Baghdad – as well as some American officers on the ground in Iraq – and instead Mattis and his Marines were ordered to move immediately into the city, re-establish order, hunt down the culprits of the killing and expel the insurgents.[20] It was a tall order. The Marines had 'little idea how well organized, armed and determined the insurgents were', and though they had set out with the intention of avoiding reducing the city to rubble they were eventually forced to call in intensive artillery bombardment of civilian neighbourhoods.[21] The fighting was dirty, tough and extremely dangerous work, involving close-quarter combat of a rarely seen intensity. The insurgents, not unreasonably, concluded that the battle was 'of great importance because the Americans wanted to make an exemplary punishment of all cities', according to one senior leader, and resisted with determination.[22] The Marines, surprised by the sophistication and defences of the 1,000 or so combatants who faced them, took significant casualties as they advanced very gradually into the city. After three weeks of inconclusive urban fighting the Marines were ordered to halt their advance. The American troops had suffered 26 killed and 90 wounded, an estimated 200 insurgents had died. So too had as many as 600 civilians, including at least 300 women and children.[23] Though deeply unpopular with troops on the ground, the ceasefire appears to have been agreed by senior military commanders in Iraq, Bremer and the White House.[24] Control of the city was ceded to a hastily created 'Falluja Brigade' commanded by a former general of Saddam's Republican Guard, and the Marines pulled out, having failed to fulfil any of their original objectives. This was described by coalition spokesmen as 'handing over to Iraqi partners'. The 'Falluja Brigade' disintegrated a few weeks later, its 800 US-issued AK-47s soon in the hands of the insurgents.

Whatever the spin placed on the outcome, Falluja I was a victory for the insurgents.[25] It had been a pitched battle, one of the very few that took place during the 9/11 Wars, and in strategic terms a major check for the occupying authorities. It inspired insurgents all over Iraq, provoking what one officer called 'a jihad wildfire, spreading mosque to mosque from the Syrian border to Baghdad'.[26] Hastily produced DVDs of the fighting, edited to mournful music and melodramatic soundtracks, flooded local markets. With saturation coverage of the fighting across the Islamic world, Falluja had become a household name, a byword for successful Arab and Islamic resistance against the 'neoimperialist crusading Americans and their Jewish manipulators'.[27] It was equally clear to all parties that a second battle for the city was inevitable. Until that moment, Falluja was left more or less to its own devices, an unofficial 'free capital' of the growing Sunni insurgency.

ABU GHRAIB

The need to gather intelligence on the networks responsible for the increasingly lethal and increasingly numerous IED attacks was stressed by a number of high-level US army reviews during 2004.[28] But the American intelligence operation in Iraq, as in Afghanistan, was hobbled by a lack of local knowledge and cultural understanding and an over-reliance on 'SIGINT' or technical communications intercepts.[29]. The response of ground commanders – with one or two notable exceptions – was to fall back on the same tactics as were being employed in Afghanistan: 'cordon and sweep' operations designed to hoover up potential insurgents. Through early 2004, the tempo of such raids had accelerated. They were indiscriminate and resulted in huge numbers of suspects being sent into the American military-run prison system. On one raid the author joined in Tikrit shortly after the fighting had ended in Falluja, troops first knocked down the door of the wrong home and then detained a suspected financier on the basis that, as a professed taxi driver, he could not afford the china on display in his dining room. The suspect affected a studied insouciance, sniffing a flower from his garden, which prompted Captain Eric Coombs, thirty and in charge of the operation, to comment disgustedly, 'It's like he's French or something,' and take him into custody.[30] Back at Coombs' base, a solitary tank fired shells at irregular intervals into a patch of open ground a mile or so away from which mortar attacks were occasionally launched. There was no evidence of any insurgent movement at the site, which was taken as proof that the 'terrain-denial' operation was working. 'No one is going to shoot anything at us from that bit of Iraq,' said the tank's gunner. A day later, news of what had been happening at Abu Ghraib prison west of Baghdad broke.

In the short term the scandal at Abu Ghraib resulted from the huge flow of detainees from units on the ground like that of Coombs or Hector Mirabile in Ramadi conducting their vast dragnets. These sent tens of thousands of detainees into the creaking system set up by the coalition. As there was never meant to be an occupation let alone an insurgency, no one had thought about what might need to be done with captured Iraqis and hastily created facilities, chronically undermanned and under-resourced, were quickly swamped.

Abu Ghraib itself, one of the most notorious jails under Saddam Hussein and a symbol of the violence of the past regime, had been reopened by the Americans in August 2003 as a holding centre for captured former regime figures and common criminals, the two mixed together in contravention of the Geneva Conventions. Looting after the invasion had not just gutted the ministries but had rendered most of Iraq's extensive prison system unusable too. Some 75,000 secure prison places were needed, experts estimated. A few thousand were available.[31] By the end of the year, however, Abu Ghraib alone had a population of 7,000. Poorly defended, situated between the hardline Sunni suburbs of western Baghdad and the rough towns of Falluja and Ramadi, the complex was an obvious target and was soon being regularly mortared. The servicemen posted there had little training for running a detention facility and lived among decomposing rubbish, ate monotonous and unhealthy combat rations and showered under drums of cold water. The prisoners and 'security detainees', the new term usefully blurring their exact legal status, lived in abject squalor, many exposed to the elements, to insects, rabid dogs and the fire of the insurgents. Others, in the rehabilitated Saddam-era concrete cell blocks, had marginally better physical conditions but were exposed to the worst of the mistreatment perpetrated by the gaolers. There were frequent power and water cuts. Unsurprisingly, there were also riots, some of which were put down with live ammunition. The commanding officer, a reservist brigadier general, tried to raise these issues with her higher command but without success.[32]

However, if the abuse occurred for a variety of specifically local reasons the forms it took were those that had evolved so early in the conflict in Afghanistan. Many American interrogators and prison guards in Iraq had served in facilities like Kandahar or Bagram, where interrogators had faced the same circumstances and similar pressures for results. Indeed some of those now in Iraq had already been implicated in serious abuse. One, Captain Carolyn Wood of the 519th Military Intelligence Battalion, considered herself 'very knowledgeable of interrogation techniques'. At Bagram, Wood had issued a list of recommended techniques – from sensory deprivation to the use of dogs – without precedent in American army history and it was under her command that the three deaths detailed in chapter 3 had occurred. Decorated for her service in Afghanistan, she was appointed head of interrogations at Abu Ghraib in August 2003 and immediately issued a new list of techniques more appropriate for 'the Arab mind-set'.[33] When American military interrogators across Iraq were told by superiors that 'the gloves were coming off regarding ... detainees ... we want these individuals broken', the suggestions as to how this might be done revealed how extensive the influence of the first major campaign after 9/11 had been.[34] One soldier answered the memo outlining the new, tougher approach, saying he had 'spent several months ... interrogating the Taliban and al-Qaeda' and as a result recommended 'open-handed facial slaps from a distance of ... about two feet and back handed blows to the mid-section from ... about 18 inches' as well as exploiting 'fear of dogs and snakes'. Another respondent to the memo recommended using closed fists and 'low voltage electrocution', also practised in Kandahar.[35] Indeed, almost all the abuses in Abu Ghraib – stripping prisoners naked, low-voltage shocks, humiliating sexual practices, stress positions, cold and heat, chaining to bars or walls, beatings and the compulsive photographing or filming of such acts – had already been seen in Afghanistan.

A second influence was the example of practices in the broader network of US prison facilities that had been constructed over the previous two years. The idea of exploiting the psychological fears of those under interrogation had been suggested with Abu Zubaydah, the supposed al-Qaeda senior leader detained the previous year in Pakistan and subsequently waterboarded. In August 2003, General Geoffrey Miller, who as commander of detainee operations at the Guantanamo Bay prison camp had introduced a much harsher regime there, visited Iraq as part of a review of intelligence-gathering operations and recommended charging prison guards with preparing, i.e. softening up, detainees for questioning.[36] This new definition of the role of the guards in American prisons in Iraq undoubtedly exacerbated the deterioration in conditions at Abu Ghraib. Staff Sergeant Ivan L. Frederick II, a member of the 372nd Military Police Company and a central figure in the Abu Ghraib scandal, wrote home describing how he had 'questioned some of the things' that he had seen such as leaving inmates in their cell naked or dressed in female underwear, handcuffing them to the cell door, isolating them with no clothes, toilet facilities, ventilation or running water for up to three days but had been told that 'this is how military intelligence (MI) wants it done'.[37]

As in Afghanistan an interesting question is whether the abuse was driven from the bottom or from the top. Did it evolve endogeneously or as a result of directives from the most senior levels of political and military leadership?[38] Certainly in Abu Ghraib – as well as in the prison at Camp Bucca in the south and countless smaller facilities – detainees were often seen as terrorists responsible for 9/11 and treated as such. An example of how language percolated through all those involved in a mission was the memo referred to above which used words – 'the gloves coming off' – borrowed directly from the Bush administration's 'point man' on counter-terrorism, Cofer Black.[39] Also, the connections between theatres, units, individuals and policies make it hard to argue either that the handful of low-ranking soldiers disciplined for the Abu Ghraib abuse were simply the proverbial bad apples or, as Pentagon undersecretary Douglas Feith claimed, that their actions were 'a matter of personal sadism by a small number of individuals'.[40]

Abuse was of course far from universal – the American soldiers the author was with when the scandal broke were horrified – but it had become an integral part of the American military and counter-terrorist effort. For example, interrogators at Camp Nama at Baghdad International Airport had also systematically stripped prisoners, employed stress positions and sleep deprivation, had punched and kicked them and, according to one report, added a new technique of shooting them with paintballs.[41] Nor was such behaviour restricted merely to the Americans. Abuse by the British in Basra and other parts of the province was astonishingly similar to that practised elsewhere. Though smaller in scale, abuse by British troops too featured ritualized sexual humiliation, beatings, exposure to heat, thirst, stress positions and it too saw soldiers, some eventually implicated in the deaths of a series of detainees between 2003 and 2004, film or photograph their actions with careful attention to the *mise en scène*.[42] The conclusion must be that such behaviour was at the very least a phenomenon that had both a 'top-down' and 'bottom-up' element. The Bush administration encouraged and aggravated problems that had, from the very earliest days of the war, been evident. In Abu Ghraib itself, the role that interrogators from Military Intelligence played in driving the abuse was paradoxically underplayed by the photographs that eventually emerged which showed only low-ranking military police personnel.[43] Whether directed from above or the result of the independent actions of hundreds, if not thousands, of individuals, the result was the same. The abuse of prisoners by all sides rapidly became one of the defining characteristics of the 9/11 Wars, somehow integral to the very nature of the conflict. Certainly the images that depicted the abuse at Abu Ghraib – the hooded man, the leashed man, the slavering dog inches from the face of a terrified detainee – became some of the Wars' most recognizable and enduring icons.[44]

One of the most worrying elements of the Abu Ghraib scandal was the lack of reaction it provoked in Iraq. Among those waiting outside the prison the day after the scandal broke was Zacaria Falah, from the northern city of Mosul, who had spent seventy days in Abu Ghraib. His older brother was still imprisoned. Both had been accused of helping 'the resistance' – a charge they denied. Falah said he had been taken from his home, which was ransacked during the raid, in the middle of the night and transported to a base in the northern city of Mosul known as 'Camp Disco' to Iraqis because of the habit of the guards of putting on loud music and making the detainees 'dance' for hours on end. From there he was taken to Abu Ghraib, where he was housed in a tent, sleeping on the floor with thirty-four other men. 'Of course, everything that you are now talking about was happening,' he said. 'That is what the Americans are like. We have known for years. We have always been angry. Why be more angry now?'[45]

THE GREEN ZONE

Saddam had walled off a city within a city along the Tigris in the centre of Baghdad, where he had built a vast palace, rows of villas for members of his extended clan and senior officials, guardhouses, even hospitals and schools. It was here that the Coalition Provisional Authority was based. This was the Green Zone, named after the shading on Coalition security maps, where red marked danger and green its opposite. At night, with much of the city plunged into steaming darkness due to power cuts, the Baghdadis sleeping on their roofs to avoid the heat could see the ten hectares of the Green Zone 'lit up like a wedding in an Indian musical', as Bashem Jaffar, a hairdresser in the upmarket Karada area, put it. Joining the CPA in its heavily defended enclave was most of the diplomatic community. As had happened in Kabul eighteen months earlier, the British had reopened their colonial-era embassy, realized it was indefensible and then, as the security situation deteriorated, been forced to leave the garden and the colonnade and retreat to a new complex behind the blastwalls.[46] Elsewhere in the capital, long lines of concrete T-blocks were beginning to block off streets, bridges, a view of the sky.

Like the huge military bases going up around the country (and in Afghanistan) the Green Zone was profoundly isolated. The food in the vast mess hall was all imported and included an extraordinarily high proportion of pork products.[47] A variety of bars, licit or otherwise, provided often hard-working and stressed CPA officials the chance to blow off steam. Women went jogging in singlets and shorts. The scene in the ballroom nightclub of the al-Rashid hotel in the centre of the Green Zone was surreal – a frenetic decadence fuelled by cheap whiskey and recent broken marriages. Identical SUVs, Humvees and shuttle buses ferried people around. Most staff were on short-term contracts, and very few spoke any Arabic.[48] Visiting the Green Zone involved crossing at least three checkpoints manned variously by American troops, a range of coalition allies and private security guards. Reporters had to do this often – it regularly took an hour or more – if they wanted to attend the press briefings held at the convention centre opposite the al-Rashid hotel. At the briefings they would be told about the latest initiatives taken by the CPA, and occasionally there would be some details of military operations. There was a café and a board on which press releases detailing events such as 'ribbon-cutting ceremony al-Nathana bridge, 9am saturday' were posted alongside the latest casualties, increasingly from IED attacks. 'Every single one haunts us but we are not wavering,' said the American military spokesman. Another notice announced that 'several planned reconstruction projects have been suspended due to the non-permissive environment posed by terrorists'. In one briefing an Iraqi reporter asked what he should tell his frightened children woken by the sound of low-flying military helicopters. 'Tell them that is the sound of freedom,' came the response. General Ricardo Sanchez, the US commander in Iraq, told assembled reporters that he was 'very optimistic' and was sure that he had the 'combat forces' to prevail. A banner hung above the new Iraqi Business Development Center: 'Peace and best wishes from the children of America to the children of Iraq'.[49]

Bremer and the most senior CPA officials had their offices in the giant palace, which was still adorned with vast busts of the former dictator. Between 1,000 and 1,500 – the CPA was permanently understaffed – people worked there. Supposedly international, the operation was '99 per cent American, half a per cent British, half a per cent the rest,' remembered Andy Bearpark, the CPA's director of operations.[50] They were an odd bunch. Some were grizzled veterans of nation-building efforts hired by the CPA who had come direct from Afghanistan or, like Bearpark, from Kosovo. The rest were either drawn from America's best and brightest or knew someone in the Republican Party or both. They were often extremely young. The mixture of jaded pragmatism, can-do naivety and starry-eyed ideology was striking. 'The CPA is having to invent this day by day,' said Mark Kennon, the authority's coordinator for Salahuddin province. Contacts with the local population were limited. When people did travel they ended up 'looking at Iraq through armoured glass surrounded by guns,' in the words of Rory Stewart, deputy governer in Maysan province and then in Nasariyah.[51] In the provinces, moving three CPA engineers involved a convoy of seven Humvees, two with .50 calibre machine guns and seven squad-level weapons. The atmosphere was rendered even more surreal by two enormous disconnects: between official language and reality 'beyond the wire' and between what was expected of the CPA and what it could deliver. One reporter turned his mobile back on after sitting through a long briefing on how security was excellent around the country to find messages reporting a series of car bombs.[52] As in Afghanistan, 'there was a crisis of expectations', according to Bearpark. Tom Parker, a Briton who headed the CPA's Crimes against Humanity Investigation Unit, was blunter. 'First impressions count, and the first three months were a disaster,' he said.[53]

If talking to the Iraqis was tough, so was talking to other CPA officials. Links with the offices in the various provinces, set up several months into the CPA's rule, were haphazard at best.[54] Emails from distant governorates went unanswered or unreceived. Cash was distributed in thick wads of plastic-wrapped new dollar bills.[55] With nearly $10 billion owed to Iraq under the Oil for Food programme that had been languishing in United Nations accounts, money was not short, but finding a sensible and productive way to spend it was complicated.[56] With the twin hierarchies of civilian and military command meeting only in Washington at stratospherically high levels, coordination of effort was almost impossible. Enormous amounts were lost through corruption or simply accounting incompetence. The consequences were evident to anyone travelling around the country.[57] Before the overthrow of Saddam, 95 per cent of urban Iraqis and 75 per cent of those living in rural zones had access to clean drinking water, according to needs assessments by the United Nations. By 2003, these levels had declined to 60 per cent and 50 per cent respectively. By the end of 2005, the figure had dropped to 32 per cent.[58] When the CPA was criticized for missing the target of generating 4,400 Kw of power in July 2003, the target was then achieved two months later by the simple expedient of switching on all the facilities in the country for twenty-four hours. Many were then shut down for 'maintenance' and remained closed. In much of Baghdad water supply was down to three hours per day by the end of the year. Though hospitals were receiving a better supply of basics such as insulin or antibiotics, often provided by independent NGOs such as the Red Cross or Médecins Sans Frontières, there were no drugs for any more advanced treatments.[59]

It was not the cultural inappropriateness nor the dysfunctional administrative systems – which many of the bright, experienced and hardworking officials eventually got to work – nor even the isolation of most of those who lived, ate, drank and breathed only in the Green Zone that crippled the CPA. It was what it was trying to do. The mission statement of the CPA appeared relatively uncontroversial. The aim was to reach an endstate defined as 'a durable peace for a united and stable, democratic Iraq that provides effective and representative government for and by the Iraqi people; is underpinned by new and protected freedoms and a growing market economy; and no longer poses a threat to its neighbours or international security and is able to defend itself.'[60] Yet the ideological roots of the project were obvious. When a year after the 9/11 attacks the Bush administration had published a National Security Strategy, its first page had included the pledge: 'We will actively work to bring the hope of democracy, development, free markets and free trade to every corner of the world.'[61] Across most of the globe, the obstacles to fulfilling this were manifest. However, post-invasion Iraq, both for those with little interest in the history of the local communities or for those who were well-informed but ideologically committed, appeared to be the perfect place to realize that promise. The mission statement of the CPA was a wish-list drawn up by people who were absolutely certain that their values and models were applicable and attractive to other societies and cultures *whatever the circumstances*. The latter qualification is of critical importance as it traces a path between essentialist arguments that 'Muslims' or 'Arabs' cannot ever be receptive to 'Western' ideas of democracy, free-market capitalism, human rights and so forth and the equally problematic argument, favoured by so many within the Bush administration, that such ideas were a universally applicable panacea. In fact, as the 9/11 Wars were to demonstrate again and again, any culture, taken to mean the totality of values, norms, learned behaviours and worldviews of any community, is infinitely flexible and dynamic all while evolving within inherited boundaries set over time. Unlike in Afghanistan, where the security project had seen an ideological component grafted on to it, the project in Iraq had been ideological from the start. It was not rooted in a continuing, sensitive and informed appraisal of the measures best suited to bring security, stability and prosperity to Iraq in 2003 or early 2004 but in a utopian, universalizing vision which, as the National Security Strategy had made clear, served American interests. It suffered enormously as a result.

For the primary obstacle to the American plan to re-create Iraq rapidly became the paradox of many such attempts by one community to change the behaviour and nature of another: the values that the powerful foreigners hoped to encourage, support or, if they had to, impose were fatally tarnished by the indelible fact that they were those of the occupiers or at least those the occupiers preferred. Though a significant minority of Iraqis still saw a Westernized future for their nation as preferable, vast swathes of the population had come to see such values as foreign. When asked if 'democracy can work well in Iraq', 51 per cent said, 'No, it is a Western way of doing things and will not work here.' All that was conservative, religious and nationalistic was thus naturally vested with a new sense of being 'Iraqi' and acquired a powerful legitimacy as culturally authentic. Whether or not this had been the case before the invasion was immaterial.[62] The invasion and the subsequent acts of the CPA had triggered vast change. Any predictions based on anything other than the finest knowledge of pre-war conditions were now unreliable at best. Often they were entirely redundant.

By the spring of 2004, as the CPA began to prepare for an eventual handover to restore sovereignty to Iraq and to transfer its responsibilities to a nominally independent government, it had long become clear to most observers that the 'endstate' originally envisaged in Washington and elsewhere was a long way off. This was made very evident when Bremer had postponed elections and hinted strongly he envisaged a process of undetermined length, possibly up to two years according to one British diplomat, to design a constitution.[63] Eventually, in June 2004, the CPA handed over to an interim government led by Ayad Allawi, an exile, a moderate Shia and former Ba'athist dissident with good Western intelligence connections who, though he had a narrow support base within Iraq limited to educated secularists, was seen as at least relatively pro-American. Three elections were scheduled: in January 2005 for a new transitional assembly which would elect itself a new prime minister, a referendum to ratify a constitution and finally, at the end of the year, for a government that would sit for a four-year term. There was no public leaving ceremony for Bremer, and the CPA was dissolved in some disorder. On June 28, Condoleezza Rice scribbled a note which Donald Rumsfeld then passed to President Bush at the NATO summit in Turkey, informing him that Iraq was sovereign. 'Let freedom reign,' the president wrote across it and turned to shake hands with the man on his right, Tony Blair.[64]

THE ROAD TO NAJAF

The new Iraqi government's first real test came in August 2004 with a fresh round of fighting between American and allied military forces and the al-Mahdi Army militia of the young cleric Muqtada al-Sadr.[65] This second strand to the insurgency in Iraq had emerged in the spring. Very different in its origins, structure and aims from the Sunni insurgency, being far closer to an organized religious, cultural and political movement like the Taliban in Afghanistan in the 1990s, Hezbollah in Lebanon or Hamas in the Gaza Strip, it nonetheless shared some qualities of other insurgents in Iraq. There was the same pattern of recruitment through association, the same often chaotic reliance on self-forming communities, the same capability to rapidly adapt to changing contexts and challenges. There was also the same rapid development of a capability to cause serious harm and to pose a significant threat to the stability of Iraq.

Muqtada al-Sadr and the al-Mahdi Army were the product of the intersection of the major historical trends which have already marked much of this narrative: demography, Islamism, nationalism and cultural revivalism. The demographic element had two elements, both with significant political consequences. Firstly, the Shia, a minority in Iraq when it had been ruled by the Sunni Ottomans, had been a majority since the southern desert tribes had converted in the eighteenth and nineteenth centuries and thus collectively felt that Saddam's deposition would inevitably lead to their domination of any subsequent political set-up. Secondly, Saddam's Iraq had seen the same explosive population growth rates as the rest of the Middle East in the 1970s and 1980s. This meant a huge number of potentially troublesome young men by the first decade of the twenty-first century. Naturally, then, in the aftermath of the invasion, it was likely that Shia male youth would be a source of trouble.

Like the young men who had made their way to the Afghan camps, their counterparts in the slums of Basra, Nasariyah or Baghdad had also seen a series of different ideologies fail in their short lives. Pan-Arab secular Socialist nationalism was clearly associated with their oppressor, Saddam Hussein, and brutal Sunni repression and discrimination; their only real experience of Western liberal democracy had been the betrayal of the Iraqi Shias in the aftermath of the 1991 war, when hundreds of thousands who had revolted against the government were butchered without any Western intervention, and then the punishing sanctions that had followed; the fall of Communism had discredited left-wing thought and Saddam's highly effective purges had destroyed any left-wing activism. All that was left was religion in its various politicized and non-politicized forms.

Here Muqtada al-Sadr had a unique advantage: the two great dissident Islamist leaders in recent decades in Iraq had been his father, Ayatollah Mohammed Sadeq al-Sadr, and his father-in-law, Ayatollah Mohammed Baqr al-Sadr.[66] Both had been killed by Saddam Hussein and were popularly venerated as martyrs. They were known as al-Sadr I and al-Sadr II. The first had been one of the key thinkers of the wave of new radical ideology that emerged in the 1960s among Shia Muslims. This matched strains of Sunni political Islamism being developed elsewhere and found its most obvious expression in the 1979 Iranian revolution. Men like al-Sadr I and his contemporary Ayatollah Ruhollah

Khomeini in Iran developed the radical new concept of *wilayat al faqih* or 'the guardianship of the jurist' and challenged the long-established Shia tradition that the clergy should remain aloof from 'corrupting' secular politics.[67] Both saw mass activism as the only way to realize their respective theocratic visions.[68] Despite their assassinations and the ruthless repression of activists both older al-Sadrs had retained a following that was still extensive in Saddam's final years.[69]

The young Muqtada al-Sadr was careful, however, to combine the appeal of this activist Islamism with an appeal to Iraqi nationalism. Like their religious identity, the national identity of the Iraqi Shia had always been stronger than many, especially relatively Westernized exiles, had given them credit for. Their perpetual grievance was that they had been deprived of a fair share of power in the Iraqi state – not that the state itself was somehow illegitimate. It was their senior clerics who had hoisted the banner of jihad in the great Iraqi revolt against the British in 1920, and when the question of national allegiance had been posed sharply during the Iran–Iraq war of 1980 to 1988 the Iraqi Shia troops who made up the bulk of the rank and file fought, often bravely.[70] The posters pasted to walls all over the slum suburb of Baghdad once called Saddam City and now universally known as Sadr City showed Muqtada al-Sadr's chubby, acned face in the foreground, his respected forebears and the Iraqi national flag behind.

Another element that al-Sadr was able to exploit was a resurgent revivalist Shia identity which overlapped both with Islamism and nationalism, reinforcing and amplifying both to create a potent vision of a conservative, Islamist, Shia-dominated Iraq. Though part of the broader surge in such identities through the 1990s across much of the Islamic (and indeed non-Islamic) world, the new piety and identification of the Shia in Iraq can be explained also by the way in which long Shia traditions of martyrdom and suffering, of passive resistance to tyranny and of internal spiritual renewal and questioning were perfectly adapted to the poverty, frustration, anger and brutal repression experienced by the community under Saddam Hussein. The strong social revolutionary strand within Shia thought, traditionally if somewhat simplistically seen as a faith of the underdogs and of the poor, also lent longstanding religious and historic myths an immediate relevance that they might not otherwise have had. By the late 1990s, in homes across Iraq, the garish pictures of Ali, the son-in-law of the Prophet Mohammed assassinated in AD 661, and his son Hussein, killed in battle fighting against overwhelming odds by forces loyal to the dictatorial caliph Yazid, went back up on the walls of Shia households. Immediately after the invasion, millions took part in ritual pilgrimages that had been banned for many decades.[71]

Finally there was a very specific social and economic dynamic too. Muqtada al-Sadr was not able to garner support among the broad masses of Shia society – most people remained loyal to the revered Grand Ayatollah Ali al-Sistani and the college of clerics, the *hawza*, that he led – but was able to make significant inroads among the young unemployed urban working-class men from the seething slums of cities like Baghdad, Basra, Nasariyah, Kut and others. Beyond the broad structural trends, such men joined the movement for a typical range of more immediate factors. It was here where there was some overlap with the young men flowing into the networks of Sunni insurgents. Years of anti-Western propaganda, the lived experience of the consequences of United-Nations-sponsored and American-backed sanctions and the rhetoric both of resurgent Islamic extremism and of the mainstream Arabic-language media, all encouraged a profound antipathy to the invaders and made the idea of taking up arms more attractive too. The Shia community too was affected by the looting that followed the invasion or the insecurity that it brought. Though initially many services improved for Iraq's Shias as Saddam's discriminatory policies were reversed by the new rulers, they soon deteriorated. So the continuing failure to provide power, sanitation, medical services and jobs also fuelled discontent.

Nor was the fact that these young men, often only a decade younger than Muqtada al-Sadr himself, were also joining a revolt against the traditional Shia authorities, the *hawza*, insignificant. If they rejected the automatic authority accorded to Grand Ayatollah Ali al-Sistani, it was not just in a spirit of adolescent rebellion but also because his quietist message matched neither their aspirations nor their instincts. Angry young men in desperate times demanded desperate and angry measures. That said, most joined not for ideological or religious reasons but through personal associations, because in the microcommunities that structured life in the overcrowded slums where most lived, joining the al-Mahdi Army was encouraged or was simply what most of their peers were doing. The al-Mahdi Army offered adventure, comradeship, social mobility and a clear, certain, lucid dogma that made sense of a world turned upside down. Most of the young activists of the al-Mahdi Army had nothing else to do and understandably preferred carrying weapons, enforcing local order or simply contributing to the various social activities that Muqtada al-Sadr's office sponsored to hanging around on street corners watching American patrols go by.

Muqtada al-Sadr, thirty years old in 2003, was also helped by the way in which coalition leaders, political advisers and military intelligence officers consistently underestimated him in the way that they underestimated so many opponents in the early years of the 9/11 Wars.[72] Few in the West had ever heard of al-Sadr before the invasion – he did not feature in any of the cursory briefings received by Hilary Synnott, the British diplomat sent to Basra to be the CPA representative in the south, before leaving the UK in July 2003 – and no one anticipated his extraordinarily rapid rise from unknown junior cleric to major power-broker.[73] Though he admitted that the self-styled 'Sadr III' represented a genuine popular constituency, David Richmond, the British special representative in Iraq, professed 'reasonable confidence' in March 2004 that al-Sadr would be 'wound down and put back in his box' without too much trouble.[74] For Brigadier Kimmitt, chief US military spokesman, al-Sadr led an 'illegal mob'. One US intelligence officer described the cleric to the author in March 2004 as 'a fucking punk, an opportunistic little bastard'.[75] A week later the al-Mahdi Army launched an armed insurrection against occupation forces which plunged much of Iraq into chaos and would take six months to suppress.

The spring fighting saw the ragged and untrained teenagers of the al-Mahdi Army fighting coalition troops, attacking CPA offices and attempting to eliminate rivals within the Shia community. Many of the major routes to the capital – such as the huge supply lines the Americans had constructed across the desert or through remote villages and farmland so they could avoid the main arteries – were rapidly rendered unusable. Others were made extremely dangerous by the breakdown in law and order that was a consequence of the fighting. Driving to Karbala to cover the fighting, a car carrying other journalists only a few minutes ahead of the author's own vehicle was ambushed and its occupants shot dead, their corpses spread in the dirt by the side of the road. Civilian traffic from Jordan and Kuwait was cut off. The CPA even started drawing up plans for rationing in Baghdad's Green Zone. Across a swathe of southern Iraq, in towns such as Amarah, Kut and Nasari-yah, the half-trained teenagers from urban slums brushed aside Western troops whose political leaders and generals had never anticipated their soldiers participating in real fighting. In Nasariyah an Italian contingent lost control of the city, refusing to engage the mortars set up by the al-Mahdi Army that were bombarding the CPA's offices. In Kut, the Ukrainians, who had a reputation locally for taking bribes at their checkpoints, tried to run away.[76] In Najaf, Spanish troops refused to leave their base.

Al-Sadr's initial success did not last, however, and as more American troops entered the fight, it had rapidly become clear that the al-Mahdi Army's undoubted zeal was no match for a modern professional mili-tary, especially one with the firepower the US army could muster. In Sadr City, support for the militia had remained relatively solid. But the com-mercial and educated classes of the Shia community were contemptuous and fearful of al-Sadr's predominantly working-class fighters, and any backing outside the tougher suburbs of Baghdad or the southern cities rapidly fell away as the fighting continued. In the holy city of Najaf, leaflets had denounced the al-Mahdi Army as 'thieves, robbers and per-verts under the command of a one-eyed charlatan'.[77] Nor had al-Sadr himself mapped out a broader political strategy to take advantage of his military gains. By the end of May, much of the south had been retaken by coalition troops, and the *hawza* had made their disapproval of al-Sadr very clear. Al-Sadr called off the fight, the CPA dropped demands for the dissolution of his militia and, like the Sunnis in Falluja, everyone began to prepare for round two. Al-Sadr had much to show for his efforts, however. He had emerged as a player in the new post-invasion Iraqi politics – aided in no little way by the largely uncritical saturation coverage he had received from al-Jazeera and other Arabic-language sat-ellite channels. Polls showed the impact the fighting had had on al-Sadr's profile. When asked in February 2004, 'Which national leader do you trust the most?' only 1.5 per cent of respondents had mentioned al-Sadr's name. Four months later that figure was 7.4 per cent, still low in overall terms but the highest jump in popularity for any Iraqi political figure.[78]

Over the summer, as the political situation more generally in the country evolved rapidly, al-Sadr embedded his organization still further in his bastion of Baghdad's Sadr City. There his office set up judges, unofficial police forces, organized food distribution – in short did everything that the government could not or would not do. The social movement began to evolve into a genuine social force as al-Sadr attempted to organize and discipline his followers. There is also some evidence of contacts at this point with elements within the Iranian government. The Iranians may have supplied weapons or at least training and technical advice to parts of the still fairly fragmented al-Mahdi Army, but their aid was probably less substantial than alleged by many at the time.[79] The militia's leaders had learned from experience, and by August, when al-Sadr moved again to take control of Najaf and the vast wealth its pilgrim trade generated, the force was more than the collection of carloads of young gunmen that it had been earlier in the year and easily occupied the key religious sites there and in nearby Kerbala, once again forcing government forces and those loyal to the traditional clerical authorities into flight or hiding. A force of newly arrived US Marines decided to deal immediately and aggressively with the new threat and attacked.

Again the fighting was intense, particularly in Najaf. Over ten days the American troops forced the militia back through the vast cemeteries around the city to positions around the main shrine itself. The scene in Najaf's centre was one of devastation. Whole blocks of homes, shops, hotels and restaurants had been reduced to a mass of rubble, twisted iron and hanging wires. Helicopters circled overhead, air strikes were called in, tanks inched their way down the narrow lanes with infantry crouching in the dust behind. American snipers had ringed the city and picked off anyone bringing supplies in to the centre, shooting the donkeys that carried them. Al-Sadr's men had turned their office in the city into a torture centre, and its courtyard was filled with dozens of rotting bodies, opponents who had been executed over previous weeks. The wounded were dragged in sheets to a makeshift dressing station inside the shrine, where scores of young men from Baghdad, Nasariyah, Basra and elsewhere lay moaning on tiling slick with blood. 'We are here to defend our leader, our country and Islam against the invaders,' Haider Abbas, an unemployed nineteen-year-old from Sadr City who had been in Najaf for months, told the author. 'Our weapon is faith. They have tried to kill us with everything but not suceeded,' said Khalid Hada, twenty-three, who had been a soldier in Saddam's army until it was demobilized. The young men spoke of death, of angels, of how the bodies of martyrs smelt of musk, all images and ideas common to their counterparts in Pakistan,

Afghanistan and elsewhere. With the militia entrenched in the houses around the main shrine, difficult to dislodge, the Americans were unwilling to risk an all-out attack. Iraqi troops were neither sufficiently well armed nor trained nor motivated to fight their way in alone, and there appeared no obvious way of rapidly ending the violence. Al-Sadr remained defiant. Those local people who had stayed were resigned to the destruction of their town and livelihood. Salah Alawi Jassm, fifty-eight, had remained in his home for fear of looters. Down a side street strewn with debris, paper, spent ammunition, wire, dead dogs and all the other detritus of battle, the house had largely escaped damage. Over the hammering of automatic weapons a few hundred metres away and the screech of shells he told the author that the people of Najaf had two enemies: 'the Americans and the Mahdi militia'. At the city's main hospital, tired doctors did what they could for children suffering from dehydration or diarrhoea. In lulls in the fighting, civilians picked their way through the rubble and the rubbish to get water. The scenes that had so gripped Iraq and the Islamic world more generally five months earlier in Falluja were being repeated.

Eventually it was not the Marines but Grand Ayatollah Ali al-Sistani who broke the deadlock by telling his followers to march peacefully on Najaf and reclaim the shrine. It was a powerful demonstration of his continuing authority over Iraq's 14 million Shias. With elections now looming in January, the *hawza* did not want their political strategy derailed by the young radical al-Sadr though they recognized his new appeal as a figurehead for resistance for significant parts of their community. For his part, al-Sadr could not confront al-Sistani, even if some of his followers rejected the authority of the ageing scholar and even if the wealth of Najaf was at stake. At dawn on a Friday morning, with the low sun glinting off the golden dome of the shrine, the pilgrims marched along the pocked roads through the ruined city centre and to the shrine. Al-Sadr's men loaded their weapons on to carts and slipped away.[80] In the vast cemetery where much of the fiercest fighting had taken place over previous weeks, exhausted US soldiers, their uniforms stained with sweat, hollow-eyed and pale with fatigue, sat or lay in the shade of the tombs with their weapons beside them. Many were sleeping for the first time in days, one officer said. A sergeant questioned passing journalists on events elsewhere. He was pleased to hear that the country was now mostly quiet. 'Do you think we are going to have to do this all over again?' he asked.

Al-Sadr was not to appear again in public for many months and was never again to directly engage coalition troops on such a scale. Recognizing that at the very least al-Sistani's policy of conditional cooperation with the occupation authorities was leading to polls which would inevitably imply a vast shift of power to the Shia, al-Sadr made a strategic choice. 'The Sadrist movement first resorted to peaceful resistance, then to armed resistance and finally to political resistance. This does not present a problem: every situation requires its own response,' he told one interviewer.[81] For the national assembly elections in January 2005 al-Sadr joined the United Iraqi Alliance (UIA), a grand coalition of Shia parties supported by al-Sistani. The ayatollah told his millions of followers: 'Voting is a religious duty like prayers and fasting and your abstention constitutes disobedience of God Almighty.' An aged Iran-born senior cleric who had always refused to meet any representatives of the occupying powers and had simply insisted on nothing more than a rapid move to polls had become American's greatest helper in the effort to bring democracy to Iraq.[82] Al-Sistani's assistance was far from unconditional however. His message to Bremer had been simple, acutely pertinent and unanswerable in its logic: 'You are an American, I am Iranian. Why not let the Iraqi people decide?'

The Shia UIA coalition won 48 per cent of the vote and 140 of the 275 seats available. A total of 23 were won by candidates linked to Muqtada al-Sadr, who, as a self-styled senior cleric, distanced himself from active involvement in electioneering.[83] The respectable moderates of incumbent prime minister Ayad Allawi received 14 per cent of ballots cast. The turn-out was higher than expected even if scores of polling stations were attacked, and the pictures of patient Iraqis standing in long lines protected by local security forces provided a welcome morale boost for increasingly concerned Western populations and politicians. But Iraq's Sunnis had largely boycotted the vote. In Anbar, less than 2 per cent of those eligible participated. Whether this was from fear or from a genuine disaffection with a process which many Sunnis felt was dominated by their ethnic rivals was unclear. The newly elected body now had to form a government and draft a constitution in an increasingly divided country that continued to slide towards yet worse chaos and violence.

7

Al-Qaeda and the 9/11 Wars

THE 9/11 WARS EXPAND

The invasion of Iraq saw the extension of the 9/11 Wars to an entirely new theatre that previously, if not at peace, certainly had not been an integral part of the conflict. It resulted too in a higher level of overall daily violence, conventional or otherwise, than had yet been seen anywhere or at any time since September 11, 2001. By the end of 2004 more people were dying every month in Iraq than had been killed in any of the bloodiest terrorist attacks of the period excepting those of 9/11 itself.[1] But the war in Iraq saw more than simply the expansion of the 9/11 Wars in geographic terms to include both south-west Asia and a major state in the core of the Middle East. It provoked a wave of radicalization and mobilization in the Middle East not seen since the Arab–Israeli conflicts of 1967 and 1973. This wave of heightened political consciousness, anger and frustration did not just affect the countries close to Iraq but extended throughout almost the entire Islamic world, exacerbating many of the trends which had contributed to the surge of militancy through the 1990s and the broadening radicalization seen since the 9/11 attacks. It also reinforced the credibility of the extremists' key message that a belligerent West led by America was set on the subordination, exploitation and humiliation of Muslim lands and it boosted further the image of the extremists as the legitimate defender of a beleaguered community. The images of American tanks in front of mosques in Baghdad, the seat of the caliphate for half a millennium and the scene of some of the most glorious chapters in Islamic history, had enormous emotional impact.[2] According to the Pew Global Attitudes survey, in Pakistan the proportion of Muslims seeing Islam as threatened – often by the West – more than doubled in twelve months to reach a level of 64 per cent in March 2003, in Indonesia the proportion went from 33 to 59 per cent, in Turkey from 35 to 50 per cent. The same poll found that 77 per cent of Moroccans said they felt 'more solidarity with other Muslims these days' and 49 per cent said they had confidence in bin Laden to 'do the right thing in world affairs'.[3]

Yet if this new anger was welcome to the senior leadership of al-Qaeda, the situation emerging in the aftermath of the loss of their haven in Afghanistan and the invasion of Iraq posed serious challenges as well as opportunities. Militant thinkers and leaders, like Western policy-makers and strategists, found themselves struggling desperately to grasp the contours and dynamics of the complex and chaotic new circum-stances. The 9/11 attacks had been controversial among extremists, with many within al-Qaeda itself concerned that, by risking the safe haven the group had secured in Afghanistan, they could prove counter-productive. Outside al-Qaeda, the strikes had been by no means universally welcomed, with many long-term militants deeply concerned that the attacks might jeopardize any gains that the extremist movement had made over previous years. When in the aftermath of the Afghan cam-paign the fractious community of foreign militants in Afghanistan had dispersed they had divided often along ideological lines. A febrile debate was already underway by the summer of 2002 over how best to deal with the coming invasion of Iraq – a development that no extremist ideologue, strategist or propagandist had actually predicted. Though the arrival of large numbers of Western troops to fight a war in the core of the Middle East, particularly in a part of the region with as long and resonant a history as Iraq, was a chance for many radicals to realize long-held strategic aims, the new situation was not without its potential pitfalls. Equally, the new radicalization provoked by the war needed to be successfully managed if it was to benefit the jihadis. In these changed circumstances the thinking that had evolved during the 1990s was clearly no longer relevant. The period of 2002 to 2004 was thus one of particular intellectual activity within militant circles as major ideo-logues and strategists tried to formulate and impose different responses to the rapidly evolving situation.

The most obvious tension among them pitted once again the global against the local. Two broad schools of thought developed among radi-cals, with bin Laden and Ayman al-Zawahiri, faithful to their vision of al-Qaeda as an overarching, unifying and directing structure for disparate groups and strands, trying to find middle ground and struggling continually to overcome personality clashes, deep ideological divisions, reluctance among many to accept their leadership and the very real practical problems posed even by communicating with other major figures and thinkers in the world of Islamic militancy. The most prominent advocate of the 'global' approach, which rejected attempts to carve out actual chunks of 'liberated' territory in favour of launching the ultimate decentralized campaign based on individuals and self-radicalizing and self-organizing cells, was the Syrian Mustafa Setmariam Nasar, better known as Abu Musab al-Suri. Those who held true to a more 'local' strategy which sought to find, fight for, clear and hold physical bases for jihad and eventually for a new caliphate, were best represented by Jordanian-born Ahmad Fadeel al-Nazal al-Khalayleh, who was to become infamous across the globe under the *nom de guerre* of Abu Musab al-Zarqawi.[4] Both men had been among those who had escaped Afghanistan at the end of 2001, and the ideological contest between them was to be critical in shaping the form of Islamic militancy and thus of the 9/11 Wars over the coming years.

ABU MUSAB AL-SURI

As the bombs had fallen on Tora Bora, al-Suri, forty-three in 2001, had headed west into Iran before looping back to reach the dry mountains and valleys north of the Pakistani city of Quetta by the end of the year.[5] Al-Suri appears to have been convinced he was likely to be either captured or killed in the imminent future and thus spent much of his time in an unspecified 'mountainous retreat' finishing a huge volume distilling decades of strategic criticism, historical analysis and theory that he hoped would be a template for a new form of structure for the radical Islamic militant movement. The work, *The Call for Global Islamic Resistance*, was finally published on extremist websites in late 2004. It was only then that al-Suri's significance as one of the primary strategists of contemporary Islamic militancy was genuinely understood in the West.

Al-Suri never fitted the standard stereotype of the extremist, though his route into radicalism was relatively typical of his generation. His long career took him through many of the most significant locations of late twentieth-century Islamic extremism. Born in Aleppo, Syria, in 1958 to a well-off, socially conservative and religious family whose economic and social status as well as cultural values were threatened by the new modernizing nationalist, secular Ba'athist regime, al-Suri became involved in underground 'Islamic resistance' groups when young.[6] Trained as an engineer like so many militants at the time, he escaped the bloody crushing of Syrian Islamists in 1982 and fled first to France and then to Spain, where he married a convert and had three children. By 1988, he was in Peshawar, where, he later claimed, he became involved in the foundation of al-Qaeda and worked as a trainer in camps for the 'Arab Afghan' *mujahideen*.[7] Even at this early stage, his relations with bin Laden were cool. Al-Suri did not like leaders of any type, and his own intellectual curiosity and contrarian spirit contrasted strongly with bin Laden's carefully cultivated asceticism and dogmatic rigour. After four years spent instructing militants in explosives and urban guerrilla warfare techniques, he left for Spain, where he spent three years in the southern city of Granada before finally arriving in London in 1995.[8] In the British capital, he collaborated with Algerian militants and the Jordanian-born radical scholar Abu Qutada, running propaganda operations for the Groupe Islamique Armée (GIA), whose battle against Algerian security forces was reaching a climax.[9] Al-Suri, however, broke with GIA leaders over their policy of sowing terror through indiscriminate massacres and started working for other groups active at the time, including al-Qaeda. The decision appears to have been based as much on personal pique as anything else.[10] By 1998, after a brief incarceration by British police when his involvement with senior active militants including bin Laden was revealed, al-Suri moved with his family to Afghanistan, which he described as 'the best example of a Muslim state on earth today'.[11] There, he appears to have become close to Mullah Omar. Confident of his own understanding of the West after fifteen years living in Europe and of his standing among fellow militants, al-Suri established his own training camp, prepared propaganda tracts for the Taliban, ran a rudimentary think-tank in Kabul and 'wrote thousands of pages in ideology, political, military and martial science and sharia studies'.[12] He kept away from bin Laden and, he claimed, was unaware of the 9/11 plot. This distance from al-Qaeda was not due to any moderation. In his lectures in Afghanistan he told listeners: 'Kill wherever and don't make a distinction between men, women and children.'[13] One of the many criticisms he subsequently levelled at the 9/11 attacks was that, if they were going to be done at all, they should have been done properly, i.e. with weapons of mass destruction.[14] Neither a gifted organizer nor an orator nor a particularly experienced fighter, al-Suri theorized the evolution of al-Qaeda post-9/11 into something much more contemporary, much less conventional and much more effective. 'Al-Qaeda is not an organization, it is not a group, nor do we want it to be,' he wrote in his 1,600-page final magnum opus. 'It is a call, a reference, a methodology.'

As mentioned briefly in Chapter 1, al-Qaeda had always been in part a 'methodology'. The word al-Qaeda itself comes from the Arabic root *qaf-ayn-dal* and, though it can mean 'a base', as in a camp or a home, a military installation, a foundation such as that beneath a house or a pedestal that supports a column, it has a range of other meanings as well.[15] It can, for example, be used to indicate the revolutionary vanguard envisaged by early thinkers and activists – the *al-qaeda al-sulbah* – and, crucially, can also mean a precept, rule, principle, maxim, model or even pattern.[16] The al-Qaeda phenomenon had always incorporated these three elements, a physical base, the vanguard or leadership element and a free-floating worldview and ideology. These elements had interacted with each other in a dynamic way, each becoming more dominant depending on the circumstances, each influencing the others' evolution. In the 1988–96 period, without a base or a coherent ideology, al-Qaeda had largely meant its senior leadership, the vanguard. From the return to Afghanistan until the end of 2001, as al-Qaeda acquired a geographical base, this latter physical element came to acquire much greater significance. Through this period too the ideology of al-Qaeda was honed and then disseminated, first through press conferences, tapes and press releases and then increasingly through acts of spectacular violence such as the strikes against American embassies in east Africa, on the USS *Cole* and finally in America in September 2001. In 2002, 2003 and 2004, with the physical structures of the group overrun and the leadership scattered, it was logical that the ideological component of al-Qaeda would take its turn as dominant. Al-Suri's thinking not only shaped the evolution of al-Qaeda or international violent Islamic extremism in the early years of the twenty-first century but described it too.

Al-Suri's argument was radically modern and relatively simple. His motto was '*nizam la tanzim*' or 'system not organization', and his vision was of a broad, self-organizing popular uprising that would have no leaders, no organizations but simply like-minded highly motivated activists 'swarming' together for specific attacks.[17] These would be on targets which, after having consulted his own writings, everybody understood to be legitimate and which would cumulatively, particularly through their propaganda value, advance the overall cause. One of al-Suri's sources for this vision was his own largely inaccurate reading of the second Palestinian Intifada, still ongoing as he worked on early drafts of his work and receiving easily as much coverage on Arab-language satellite television as anything al-Qaeda was doing. He understood the Intifada to be the sort of 'strategic phenomenon', a bottom-up spontaneous mass participation leaderless revolt, which he wanted to see across 'all corners of the Islamic world'.[18] But al-Suri was also a realist. He saw the Islamic militant movement as on the defensive, with huge and potent forces ranged against it. One advantage of al-Suri's strategy would thus be the increased resilience it would give militant networks, albeit at the cost of their capacity to organize major strikes against distant targets.[19] At his Afghan camp, al-Suri had advised his protégés to form no cells bigger than ten members for, 'if you are caught, they are all caught'.[20] Logistics would be dealt with locally and communications kept to a minimum. Autonomous local units would be empowered to act along broad strategic guidelines without seeking further authority, and there would be no oath of allegiance to an *emir*.[21]

In addition to boosting security, al-Suri hoped to end the 'disunity' or *fitna* that he, like bin Laden, saw as the greatest threat to the movement by dissolving all difference in a single, 'flat' ideology that took no account of local specificity. There would be an end to the previously incessant arguments about which country would be the base of the new caliphate because no country would be. His book, accessible to everyone via the internet, would provide the guidance formerly provided by a central leadership. Al-Suri's vision thus combined the local – individuals doing what they could where they could – with the global – a common goal and style of all the combined efforts. Like the 9/11 Wars themselves, al-Suri's jihad would be composed of an infinitely complex matrix of sub-conflicts the sum of which would be greater than the parts. One thing for al-Suri was certain: open confrontation with superior 'Crusader-Zionist forces' must be avoided unless victory was absolutely assured. The 9/11 attacks had been a catastrophic strategic error, he felt, casting 'jihadists into the fiery furnace ... a hellfire which consumed most of their leaders, fighters and bases, leaving only a very few to escape either capture or death'.[22]

Through 2003 and 2004 more and more evidence began to emerge that something approaching al-Suri's vision of individual militants acting individually according to a universal template was actually already happening. One area was in the Far East, specifically in Indonesia, where a series of new networks evolved in the immediate aftermath of the war in Afghanistan and the invasion of Iraq. These successfully launched a series of attacks on Western targets, particularly Australian interests, and on local people or groups associated with the West.[23] The most shocking and ruthless was the strike on nightclubs in the resort town of Kuta beach in Bali in October 2002 in which more than 200 people, including many tourists, lost their lives. In August 2003, the Marriott hotel was attacked in Jakarta, and just over a year later it was the turn of the Australian embassy in the Indonesian capital.

As ever, the violence in Indonesia had long roots, stretching back to resistance by revivalist Islamic groups to Dutch colonizers and then the various governments that had followed them.[24] Local Salafis had also received large amounts of Saudi Arabian money in the 1980s.[25] Sectarian unrest in the 1990s and in 2000 had fuelled the growth of radical Islamic ideologies, and by the turn of the millennium Indonesia had developed a thriving and relatively large and heavily politicized extremist Islamist movement, Jemaa Islamiya (JI), which was rooted in an extensive network of religious schools across the country. As elsewhere, the Indonesian government went to some lengths to stress the international connections of many of JI's senior members and ignored the longer and much darker purely national history that lay behind its emergence.[26]

The JI organization became the focus of attention following the Bali attacks and their successors. It had certainly provided the organizers of the strikes with a reservoir of manpower for the recruitment of many of those involved. Yet organizationally it was not linked to al-Qaeda. The leading players in the Bali plot had been in Pakistan in the late 1980s and early 1990s and had attended what were effectively terrorist training camps, but the facilities where they had learned about bombing, counter-surveillance and so on had been run by Abdul Rasul Sayyaf, an Afghan cleric with strong Saudi connections who led his own '*muja-hideen* faction' and who was a rival of bin Laden rather than an associate. Ten of the score or so individuals closely involved with the Bali bombing were alumni of Sayyaf's Sadda camp near Peshawar.[27] There were a handful of key individuals, often operating outside the structure of JI, who acted as go betweens with al-Qaeda at the time of the Bali plot. They exploited personal relationships with al-Qaeda leaders established before 9/11 during the period when the group was fully established and operational in Afghanistan to source some assistance for their campaign. But their role was less than has often been said. The test came following the arrest of Riduan Isamuddin, aka Hambali, in Thailand in August 2003, the man said to be key link between al-Qaeda and operational groups in south-east Asia, who had, according to local and American intelligence, brought cash from bin Laden as one-off funding for the Bali attack.[28] Despite his removal from the scene, the bombs continued. The man behind them, Noordin Top, had never travelled to Afghanistan and was not in contact with the al-Qaeda leadership – though he nonetheless called his group Tanzim Qaidat ul Jihad. He also translated documents from al-Qaeda's online magazines and took the *nom de guerre* of 'Ayman', almost certainly after Ayman al-Zawahiri, whom he had never met. Top, an extremely effective, ruthless and dedicated operator who would continue to launch a series of attacks throughout much of the decade, was an example of how al-Suri's vision was already being realized by the time the Syrian strategist was putting pen to paper in his mountain hide-out.[29]

Other attacks provided further apparent proof. Many occurred on the other side of the world, testament itself to the apparently global relevance of al-Suri's strategy. Three in particular – in Casablanca, Morocco, in March 2003, in Istanbul eight months later and in Madrid in March 2004 – showed this very clearly. The Casablanca attacks, which killed twenty-nine people, were organized by two men who had recently been in training camps in Afghanistan but were carried out by fourteen suicide bombers recruited locally. All were young men, all aged between twenty and twenty-four, from the sprawling Casablanca slum of Sidi Moumin. For several years radical preachers in these slums, often educated in, or influenced by, Saudi Arabian religious schools and foundations, had been attracting a growing following among the offspring of immigrants who had arrived from poor rural communities over the previous three decades.[30] Such groups tapped into similar local conditions to those that were leading to the growth of al-Sadr's militia in Iraq and, like the al-Mahdi Army, provided a coherent set of values, aspirations, explanations and an identity to young men growing up in communities largely marginalized from mainstream social, cultural and political life in Morocco, including from the officially sanctioned Islamist parties.[31] Also like in Iraq, they formed semi-criminal gangs, enforcing their own law and even carrying out scores, possibly hundreds, of executions. Almost all those who killed themselves in the Casablanca bombing were unmarried, unemployed, poorly educated and so unworldly that their failure to find the targets they were aiming for in the centre of the city revealed not just their amateurism but the fact that many had barely travelled further than the edge of the violent slum that was home. Only one, a substitute teacher, had graduated from high school and been to college. None were previously known to the authorities, none had any previous known involvement in Islamic activism, and all were recruited during the four months it took one or two senior activists to plan the attack. The attacks came two months after the invasion of Iraq, an event cited as critical in almost all the interrogations of the survivors of the cell once they were rounded up by Moroccan security services. They had no connection to anyone among the senior leaders of al-Qaeda.[32]

The bombings in Istanbul in November 2003 came against a similarly febrile background. In few places was the radicalization and the concomitant aggravation of anti-Americanism caused by the Iraq war more evident than in Turkey, a majority Muslim nation but a secular, historically pro-Western state. Though bin Laden remained deeply unpopular, not least because he was an Arab, as many as 31 per cent of Turks nonetheless said that suicide attacks against Americans and other Westerners in Iraq were justified, a sentiment that undoubtedly encouraged domestic militants to see bombing campaigns as likely to be approved by a significant proportion of their own community.[33] In spring of 2003, the Americans had made huge efforts to negotiate passage for 15,000 crucial troops across the territory of their NATO ally into northern Iraq for the invasion of Iraq, sending Zalmay Khalilzad, the urbane Afghan-born special emissary of the White House, to spend days in Ankara negotiating with Recep Tayyip Erdogan, leader of the moderate Islamist Justice and Development Party (AKP). Erdogan, who had just been appointed prime minister after clearing legal hardles following a landslide victory in 2002, got the consent of his cabinet to a deal worth $6 billion in grants and $20 billion in credit guarantees but ultimately failed to convince parliament.[34] The rejection of the American offer was acclaimed almost unanimously by a Turkish public which polls said was 94 per cent against the US invasion plan.[35]

Of a very similar nature to those in Casablanca, the Istanbul bombings too revealed both the impact of the new diaspora of Afghan veterans and the ease with which they recruited new volunteers for the cause. One of bin Laden's last acts before 9/11 had been to receive a deputation of Turkish militants and approve their request for $10,000 to fund operations in their homeland.[36] The attacks, which targeted two synagogues, a British-owned bank and the British consulate, left fifty-eight people dead, generated worldwide media coverage and were considered a success. Though two of the most senior militants involved escaped to Iraq, most of those they had recruited were rounded up. One explained his vision of the group's activity to Turkish police. 'We are different from al-Qaeda in terms of structure,' said Yusuf Polat, who admitted serving as a lookout for the bombers. 'But our views and our actions are in harmony.' The quote summed up al-Suri's vision of militant activism perfectly. The passive acquiescence of the 400 people who investigators calculated knew something about the planned strike but had said nothing indicated the degree to which, by the end of 2003, many of the precepts underpinning the extremists' worldview were taking hold on a much wider population.[37]

That the violence was going to spill over into mainland Europe was probably always inevitable, though few anticipated quite how spectacular the first attacks on European soil would be. They came on March 11, 2004 between 7.38 and 7.43 in the morning when eleven bombs detonated almost simultaneously on commuter trains pulling into Madrid's Atocha station and two suburban stations. The death toll eventually reached 191 and one of the most appalling scenes of the 9/11 Wars must be the shattered trains with, as rescue workers fought to free casualties and corpses, the constant ringing of mobile phones called by anxious relatives who had heard the news of the blasts and whose loved ones would never answer. About a third of the dead were immigrants from eleven different countries.[38] Once again these attacks seemed to show that al-Suri's vision of a genuine popular uprising spearheaded by self-radicalizing militants was being realized.

The Madrid strikes were very different from many previous such actions. The bombers did not die in the attack itself, thus failing to demonstrate the supposed faith of those behind the attack as the attacks over previous years had so often sought to do. Martyrdom or *shahadhah*, as the etymology of the word in both English and in Arabic implies, involves the act of bearing witness by one's voluntary death before a real or imagined audience, and this, contrary to standard al-Qaeda practice, the Madrid bombers did not do.[39] Neither, on the whole, had previous strikes been conducted in such a way as to kill and maim hundreds of ordinary people without even the pretence of attacking a military, administrative, political or commercial target. The targets in Casablanca – a restaurant frequented by tourists and the elite, a Jewish-owned hotel, a synagogue – had been at least representative of the standard enemies of radical Islamists. The same was true of the bombings in Istanbul. Bin Laden, al-Suri and others understood that they needed to justify civilian deaths as part of a broader defensive effort against a bigger target, such as Israel or America. Even tourists could, at a push, be portrayed as 'ambassadors of depravity, corruption, immorality and decadence', in al-Suri's words. But killing crowds of ordinary commuters on their way to work was far harder to 'sell' to potential sympathizers and thus risked delegitimizing the cause as a whole.

The reasons for this series of ideological and tactical differences became clear as investigations into the attacks in Madrid progressed. The attackers were not experienced al-Qaeda operatives parachuted in from overseas as initially suspected but were first-generation Moroccan and Tunisian immigrants who had been living in Spain for some time.[40] Neither was it directed by some kind of shadowy al-Qaeda 'head of operations' from afar. The group had largely formed in 2001 and 2002, drawing on a base established largely by Syrian activists fleeing persecution in their own country who had arrived in the mid-1990s. It had, however, evolved fast as new members were drawn into or left the overlapping networks of friends, family and associates that it comprised. No one recruited its members or brought them deliberately together with the aim of creating a terror cell. They formed like any unorganized social group. A police informer, the cleric at one of the mosques they frequented, described the men meeting at apartments to chant jihadi songs and watch videos of jihadi preaching 'clandestinely, with no regularity or fixed place, by oral agreement and without any schedule, though usually on Fridays'.[41] Soon, most had 'reached the conclusion that they had to undertake jihad'. If there was a leader it was Abd al-Majid al-Fakhet, an intelligent thirty-five-year-old Tunisian-born economist with Spanish citizenship. His key associate was an energetic and violent BMW-driving drug dealer of Moroccan origin, Jamal Ahmidan, who was known as 'the Chinaman' on account of his large oval eyes and diminutive stature. The latter, whose commitment to radical Islam had come after addiction to alcohol and crack, was still involved in the heroin trade, though no longer a user himself, and provided the bulk of €55,000 needed for the attacks. Most of the rest of those in the various sets of social networks – 'childhood friends, teenage buddies, neighborhood pals, prison cellmates, siblings, cousins' – that formed the group were poor, ill-educated and marginalized.[42] Only one marginal member of the group had ever travelled to Afghanistan, and though the web of connections around the group was vastly complex, touching the UK, Morocco and Italy, no clear direct connection to the al-Qaeda senior leadership has ever emerged. After several years of investigation, Spanish intelligence and police investigators concluded that the bombers were acting largely on their own. There were, officials said, 'no phone calls to al-Qaeda and no money transfers' nor any solid evidence of any direction from bin Laden other than the portraits of him some of the bombers had on the screens of their mobile phones.[43]

One much-debated question has been whether or not the Madrid attacks were timed to achieve the specific short-term political gain of swinging the imminent Spanish election to ensure the withdrawal of Spanish troops from Iraq. According to Spanish court documents, the intentions and plans of its leaders only began to become concrete following the invasion of Iraq.[44] The earliest ambitions of the group, discussed at length in various apartments or on picnics by the banks of the Navalcarnero river outside Madrid in between games of soccer and while children ran around and wives prepared food, had been to travel to Afghanistan to fight.[45] However, by late 2002, a new member of the group, an Egyptian called Rabei Ousmane Sayed, suggested that instead of travelling all the way to Afghanistan or Chechnya they should focus their efforts closer to home. According to the police informer, Sayed told the others: 'We need martyrs who are ready where they are. If one lives in France, then he's prepared for France; if one lives in Spain, then he's prepared for Spain.' Sayed then asked who was 'prepared' for martyrdom. 'Everybody raised their hand,' the informer said.[46]

Yet there was still no focus on who or what to attack or the timing of any strike. In late December 2003, a document entitled 'Iraqi Jihad, Hopes and Risks' was circulated on the internet. Of uncertain origin, it nonetheless summed up contemporary thinking in extremist circles about how to force the retreat of Western troops from Iraq by attacking 'weak links' in the US-led coalition.[47] Spain, where 90 per cent of the population were opposed to the conservative government's decision to dispatch Spanish troops to Iraq, was designated as vulnerable. The tract gave the key figures in the Madrid group – 'the Chinaman' and the Tunisian al-Fakhet – the idea of launching an attack before general elections due in Spain in March 2004. The plot itself was largely organized from a farmhouse outside Madrid that belonged to a relative of one of the group. Explosives were sourced through a Spanish ex-convict working in a quarry whom the Chinaman knew through criminal contacts. The bombs were prepared, placed in bags and dropped off on the trains. If the Atocha train had not been running late, the devices hidden aboard would have exploded in the station itself, killing at least several hundred more.

The influence of Iraq rapidly became very clear. On the day of the bombing, with the government still insisting the attack was the work of ETA, the Basque separatist organization, a Madrid television station received an anonymous statement from a man speaking Arabic with a Moroccan accent who said the attacks were revenge for Spain's 'collaboration with the criminal Bush and his allies'. More attacks would follow if the injustices did not end, the man, later identified as the Chinaman, said. 'You want life and we want death,' he added, echoing a phrase bin Laden and other radical propagandists had used repeatedly.[48] One key element that the invasion of Iraq provided in the eyes of the extremists was a justification for such an attack on ordinary commuters. The support of the Spanish administration for the invasion had strengthened the Islamic militant argument that the group's proposed victims were not mere civilians but, because they had voted at elections for those who had dispatched the Spanish troops, complicit in military attacks on Muslims. The war in Iraq, like the broader 'War on Terror', also allowed the militants to imagine themselves as glorious defenders of the Islamic faith, tapping into the powerful psychological resources of a highly selective and martial version of Islamic history. One of the videos found in the ruins of the apartment in a suburb of Madrid where seven of the group blew themselves up when surrounded by police three weeks after the attacks refers to 'the Spanish Crusade against the Muslims . . . the expulsion [of the Muslims] from Andalusia and the tribunals of the Inquisition'.[49] Such arguments, though theologically weak and morally repugnant, were emotionally very powerful and by the spring of 2004 attractive not just to a handful of young alienated immigrants in a run-down inner-city district of Madrid but to many other young men among Muslim communities elsewhere in Europe and elsewhere in the Islamic world. As every month passed and 24 million Iraqis, through little fault of their own, lurched further away from the path towards stability, prosperity and democracy that the White House had hoped they would pursue and further towards a grim future on what was now dubbed 'the central front of the War on Terror', they grew that much more convincing.[50] If there was no sign yet of a generalized 'Intifada' across the entire Islamic world and among European Muslims as al-Suri had hoped, the appalling events in Madrid showed the trend was very clearly towards greater radicalization, a greater degree of autonomy on the part of individual militants, greater resilience of terrorist networks and, almost inevitably, a greater extent of violence as a consequence.

AL-ZARQAWI AND ANOTHER VIEW OF VIOLENCE

Of course, al-Suri was not formulating his theories in a vacuum. He was attempting to explain and guide fast-moving events on the ground. He was doing so from some distance. Others were much closer to the gritty reality of 'the struggle' and held rather different views. So when, ten days before the first battle of Falluja in April 2004, a group of senior militants had met in the western Iraqi city 'to review the situation', they had little time for any strategy of 'leaderless jihad' as advocated by al-Suri. Their priorities and interests were much more concrete. Settling down to 'study recent accomplishments', their conclusions were far from edifying, recorded Abu Anas al-Shami, a Jordanian Palestinian cleric who was the group's religious adviser and a fighter and present at the meeting. 'We realized that after a year of jihad we still had achieved nothing on the ground,' Abu Anas wrote in a diary published on the internet a few months later. 'None of us had even a palm-sized lot of earth on which to reside, no place to find a refuge at home in peace amongst his own . . . We had all abandoned our homes, our families, to become wanderers.'[51] The outlook, the militant leaders unanimously agreed, was bleak. All felt they had 'failed resoundingly' and that a change of plan was needed. The new approach would involve a reaffirmation of a familiar strategy. What was needed was territory, fortifications, bunkers, a physical front; in short, a base that would be a home, a haven and, of course, a springboard for further expansion once the immediate defensive phase of fighting, so like the early trials faced by the Prophet himself with his small band of followers, was over. 'So we decided to make Falluja a safe and impregnable refuge for Muslims and an inviolable and dangerous territory for the Americans, which they would enter in fear and leave in shock, burdened by their dead and wounded,' Abu Anas wrote.[52]

If Falluja came to be the city which embodied the insurgency, then the individual who became the face of the violence in Iraq in 2004 and on into 2005 was Abu Musab al-Zarqawi. Born, as his *nisbah* suggested, in the rough industrial city of Zarqa in Jordan in 1966, al-Zarqawi had grown up in relative poverty. A violent petty criminal as a youth, he travelled to Afghanistan around 1989, probably influenced by propaganda videos and stories of glorious battles retold in his local mosque. He had, however, at least according to some reports, arrived too late for the fighting against the Soviets and became a reporter for a Pakistan-based radical newspaper instead.[53] On his return to Jordan, al-Zarqawi became involved in a militant plot, was arrested, imprisoned and then released in an amnesty in 1999. Free again, he returned to Pakistan and then crossed into Afghanistan, where he established his own very basic training camp in the west of the country near to Herat. Despite his lack of facilities and funds, al-Zarqawi rejected the patronage of bin Laden after a meeting with the Saudi in mid 2000. Like al-Suri he was unaware of the September 11 attacks before they occurred but nonetheless was able to successfully evacuate his camp and the families of his followers to Iran in their aftermath, a feat which, though he still remained little known outside certain tight circles of Jordanian militants, undoubtedly added to his status.[54] It is likely that al-Zarqawi reached northern Iraq towards the end of 2002, probably passing through Iran clandestinely, and established himself in an enclave in the hills of the north-east corner of the Kurdish-ruled autonomous parts of northern Iraq held at the time by Ansar ul Islam, the group of local and international militants who had succeeded over the previous decade in securing themselves a chunk of mountainous territory and who had developed some links with al-Qaeda itself in the year or so before the 9/11 attacks.[55] Al-Zarqawi's entry into the lists of top wanted militants came a month before the 2003 invasion, when he played a starring role in US Secretary of State Colin Powell's speech to the United Nations setting out the American case for attacking Iraq. In the speech al-Zarqawi was described as an 'associated collaborator' of bin Laden and blamed for a range of attacks – including the supposed 'ricin' plots in the UK. This was simply untrue. Like al-Suri, al-Zarqawi saw himself as a rival of bin Laden and had never made any formal alliance with bin Laden or any of his close associates.[56] Obviously, Powell also failed to make clear that al-Zarqawi, if present in Iraq at all, was one of those militants based in a zone outside Baghdad's control, telling the Security Council simply that Iraq 'harbours a deadly terrorist network' that al-Zarqawi 'headed', which may have been a factually accurate statement but was grossly misleading.[57] Claims that al-Zarqawi had visited Baghdad for medical treatment after losing a leg fighting in Afghanistan were also tendentious in the extreme, as was amply demonstrated when he eventually surfaced with both lower limbs very much intact.[58]

As the American tank columns advanced from Kuwait in the south, US special forces and Kurdish *peshmerga* irregulars had flushed out the Ansar al Islam fighters from their bases in eastern Iraqi Kurdistan. The militants had then dispersed.[59] Some had headed into Iran, others set off south. Having escaped the bombing and the dragnet, al-Zarqawi worked his way down into the heartlands of the Sunni insurgency. Over the months to come he was joined there by hundreds of other fighters. Some were fleeing the north like him, others were fugitives direct from Afghanistan, many were from core Middle Eastern countries and had come to Iraq to fight as *fedayeen* irregulars during the fighting in the spring and had stayed on. Renaming his group Tawhid wal Jihad (Unity and Jihad), al-Zarqawi showed both extreme brutality – himself executing by knife several hostages – and a talent for media manipulation – rapidly and effectively ensuring the broadcast of the atrocious images of the executions by internet and video. Some of these videos were produced in terrible makeshift studios-cum-torture chambers in Falluja and else-where and were thick with instinctively but adeptly chosen symbolic touches such as dressing prisoners in orange overalls like those worn by detainees in Guantanamo Bay.[60] They were viewed by extraordinary numbers of people across the Middle East and the world – the video showing the beheading of the kidnapped American contractor Nicholas Berg was downloaded half a million times in the first twenty-four hours it was online – and together with the continuing bomb attacks he was able to launch both against American troops and Iraqi government forces rapidly made him by far the best-known foreign Islamic militant fighting in Iraq.[61] It was also al-Zarqawi who had been responsible for many of the attacks on Shia in the summer and autumn of 2003. At the time the identity of those behind the growing carnage among the Iraqi Shia population had been unclear. Al-Zarqawi, however, had made little secret of his hatred for those he called 'snakes', and the attacks escalated through the early months of 2004, becoming a new bloody strand of the violence seizing Iraq.[62] Another reason for the extraordinary profile that al-Zarqawi enjoyed as the first anniversary of the invasion approached was the concerted effort by the American military to focus media atten-tion on him in the hope that projecting the Jordanian extremist as the leader of 'the resistance' would provoke a xenophobic reaction from Iraqis, splitting the insurgents. In weekly briefings for reporters in Bagh-dad, US spokesmen regularly displayed slides showing his face, generals mentioned him as often as possible in public, and a variety of steps were taken to 'boost the Zarqawi factor' in local coverage of any violence whether directed against American or local forces. This effort was, one of its instigators was later reported to have said, extremely effective.[63]

Al-Zarqawi's strategic thinking – inasmuch as there was any – differed profoundly from that of al-Suri. The two had very different personali-ties and very different experiences of militancy too, and this showed in their vision of how 'the jihad' should be fought. Al-Suri's formative experience was the destruction of his fellow Syrian Islamists after their revolt against the Syrian regime in 1982. President Hafz al-Assad had acted without pity, razing much of the city of Hama, their base, and giv-ing al-Suri an early and profound lesson in what too great an attachment to controlling physical territory might bring. Al-Zarqawi's formative experiences were the opposite. He had ended up in prison because he had had no base and nowhere to hide when the Jordanian security services came looking for him in the early 1990s. He thus saw the establishment of physical enclaves as the key goal of any militant movement. This was a more traditional vision of guerrilla warfare, involving the creation of secure havens where insurgents could plot, train and rule, preparing for the major conflicts to come but also drawing on a whole range of theological resources such as the concept of the pure 'Islamic community', living as an isolated example in a sea of barbaric ignorance, *jahiliya*, that was recurrent in both recent radical Islamic thought, such as the works of thinkers such as Syed Qutb, and in its antecedents stretching back to the righteous community of the Prophet Mohammed himself. This perfect imagined Islamic community could be realized both metaphysically – in terms of a personal spiritual withdrawal – and physically – as militants had done in Egypt in the 1970s. A related concept was that of *takfir*.[64] Being a *takfiri* meant assuming the right to designate others who called themselves Muslims as *kufr*, or non-believers, and was an integral and controversial part of the ideology of al-Zarqawi, his associates and their spiritual mentors. So, for example, Abu Anas al-Shami, the militant Falluja-based cleric, said in a radio message in July 2004, that anyone collaborating with the coalition in Iraq was an unbeliever and it was permitted, indeed encouraged, to kill them.[65] But *takfir* also implied a separation from the corrupt, the hypocritical and the apostate which true believers should attempt to realize in real concrete terms. It was not enough merely to try to engineer a righteous community, but territory needed to be defined, seized, sacralized, Islamicized and purged.

The last decades had seen attempts to do this at all levels within the Islamic militant movement. The history of the 9/11 plot itself was replete with examples. From the Hamburg flat of the hijacker pilots to the Islamic centres where they met and the prayer rooms they established in the universities they attended through to the training camps in Afghanistan and finally the Islamicized Taliban Emirate, purged of impure objects and influences such as the Bamiyan Buddhas, the concept of finding, controlling, defining and occupying space had been key. The aim of al-Zarqawi and his followers was to re-create the Taliban's Afghanistan in Iraq.[66] The 'home' that they had said they missed so much, the patch of land where they could unfurl their prayer mats, had to be rigorously policed if it was going to be held against the huge forces ranged against them. So in Falluja, the men of al-Zarqawi's group spent much of the summer and early autumn of 2004 trying to eradicate everything in the city that contravened this radical vision. In the run-up to the battle of November 2004 the effort they made to enforce a strict code of personal behaviour on local populations who did not share their rigorous interpretation of Islam – in part by subjecting them to the sight (or experience) of spectacular public violence involving torture, beatings and videoed humiliation – was at least as great as the energy they dedicated to constructing bunkers to resist American troops. Al-Shami, head of al-Zarqawi's *fatwa* committee, declared both equally valid and necessary ways of preparing the defence of the city.

FROM SAUDI TO IRAQ, THE FOREIGNERS ARRIVE

In the early autumn of 2004, as the fighters in Falluja dug in physically and spiritually, Hizam al-Ghatani, a softly spoken twenty-six-year-old shopkeeper from the south-eastern Saudi Arabian port town of Jizan, left his home, his wife and small son and set out for Iraq. No one told him to do so, no one 'brainwashed him', he was not 'recruited' in the conventional sense of the word. A thin, bespectacled orphan with poor educational qualifications who had scrabbled to support his family, al-Ghatani found his own way into militancy, overcoming significant obstacles to reach his destination. He did not expect any material rewards. Indeed, he was not even sure of what he expected at all. But he travelled willingly, even if anxiously.[67]

Al-Ghatani was not alone. Many hundreds – possibly many thousands – of volunteers were arriving in Iraq through the late spring, summer and autumn of 2004. Their numbers were often exaggerated as was their importance in what remained a predominantly local insurgency. But that they came is beyond doubt. An analysis in early 2005 of fatal casualties among such *mujahideen* recorded on Arabic-language extremist websites over the previous six months found mentions of 154 non-Iraqi Arabs killed in the country.[68] Very few had any combat experience at all.

There was nothing inevitable about al-Ghatani's transition from shopkeeper to *mujahed*. He had been shocked and upset by the 9/11 attacks. 'I was not happy because all those people were civilians,' he remembered, admitting that he 'was not clear about al-Qaeda or their ideology'. He had also been horrified by the violence in his own country, where returning Afghan veterans had built networks, recruited volunteers and eventually launched a series of increasingly bloody attacks from May 2003. But for al-Ghatani, as for most Saudis, Iraq was different. 'I saw the TV, al-Jazeera, the internet news websites and I was angry at the aggression against civilians, the children being killed, the air attacks . . . I wanted to be of service . . . They were at war, I was at peace. I wanted to do something to help them,' he said. 'I knew nothing about the criteria for a jihad. I just thought it was simple: you fought unfair aggression.'

In Mecca in mid 2004, the young man met a band of Iraqis who described the situation in their homeland in graphic terms. Al-Ghatani needed no further convincing. The group put him in touch with a smuggler in Kuwait. He paid the man $1,000, and together they walked and drove across the shifting rock and sand of the desert frontier with Iraq before another car picked him up and drove him to Baghdad.[69] The Iraqis he had met in Mecca were waiting for him in a house in the city's al-Doura district, a stronghold of the insurgency. 'I was thinking more of being a stretcher bearer or a medic, but they convinced me to become a fighter,' al-Ghatani said. The young man was told he was going to Falluja. He had never used a gun before and was apprehensive.

The highest proportion of foreign militants in Iraq – up to two-thirds by some estimates – came from Saudi Arabia, and most had reached Iraq not via Kuwait like al-Ghatani but through Syria. This Syria–Saudi nexus was not foreseen by Western pre-war planners but, admittedly with hindsight, seems eminently logical. It evolved organically and rapidly, because it suited ground realities as well as the interests of the individuals and states involved. It is a perfect example of the sort of secondary effects the confident and ambitious American project in Iraq could generate in such a complex region and of the kind of transient phenomenon that characterized much of the continually evolving internal dynamics of the 9/11 Wars.

That a number of Saudi citizens – a small fraction of the Kingdom's 23 million perhaps but significant nonetheless – would be motivated to fight in Iraq was always probable. Even in 2003 and 2004 the power and legitimacy of the ruling Saudi royal family still rested on two pillars: the pact established with the kingdom's religious establishment at the foundation of the state more than seventy years before and the generous disbursement of the country's vast oil revenue via jobs and welfare. Both of those pillars were unsteady. The pact – by which the descendants of Ibn Saud would exercise temporal power and be permitted to appropriate a very large proportion of the kingdom's immense wealth in return for allowing the clergy control over education, enormous financial resources themselves and relative autonomy – had been strained by the nation's continuing alliance with the United States and by elements within the royal family's continued attempts to gradually lead a profoundly conservative society in a more Westernized, less rigorous direction. Simultaneously the buying of social peace was threatened by a whole series of parlous economic indicators: per capita oil revenue was lower than it was in the 1980s, unemployment was up to 20 per cent.[70] None of this necessarily guaranteed a flow of militants to Iraq, but against the background of decades of the intense propagation of a particularly conservative strand of Islam and coming on top of almost all the factors seen elsewhere – such as massive rural–urban drift, a huge youth bulge and a powerful narrative of Muslim solidarity in the face of a supposedly belligerent and anti-Islamic West – it did make it much more likely.[71] One significant factor which undoubtedly encouraged many to travel to Iraq was the strong support of local clerics. Again, though, along with the macro-factors there were the micro-factors: low-level, 'flat' social networks played an important role too, with most volunteers making their way to war in groups of friends, neighbours or worshippers at the same mosque.[72] Significantly, the networks through which volunteers came together and then travelled were entirely distinct from those of al-Qaeda in Saudi Arabia. The rapid rise and abrupt fall of 'Al-Qaeda in the Arabian Peninsula' (AQAP) is explored further in later chapters. For the moment, it is simply worth stressing that, however much their ideology and rhetoric may have seemed superficially similar, AQAP remained operationally and organizationally distinct from the much broader movement of volunteers from the kingdom to Iraq.

The Syrian connection owed more to the longstanding poor relations between Damascus and Washington. A brief period of optimism following the accession of Bashar al-Assad as president in July 2000 had been rapidly followed by a new nadir in relations as the Syrian security establishment reasserted its grip on power and continued its support for Hezbollah in Lebanon and other Islamic militants across the region.

A complicating factor in an already complex situation was that, though they watched over a predominantly Sunni country, the Syrian security establishment was dominated by Shia from the tiny Allawite sect, including the ruling family. Tolerating, if not actively assisting, the passage of volunteers across their territory served several of the Syrian intelligence services' interests: it fuelled the insurgency in Iraq and therefore made a US intervention against Damascus less likely, it provided a useful card to play in any potential negotiations with Western states or even Israel and, as Saudis and other foreigners paid considerable sums to smugglers and to border tribes who often had connections with the security services, it made them money too. Finally it also diverted the attention of anyone who might otherwise be tempted to take up arms against the Syrian regime, which, as secular Ba'athist and in large part Shia, represented two of contemporary Sunni militancy's priority targets. The necessity for such a safety valve was shown, not only by the rising number of incidents within Syria, but also by statistics on the origins of the volunteers arriving in Iraq. Up to a fifth were Syrian, their homeland naturally no more immune to the broad currents of radicalization coursing through the Islamic world than anywhere else in the region.[73]

The journey was not always simple. Mohammed al-Fawzan, a thirty-five-year-old from the wealthy al-Shifa neighbourhood of Riyadh, was an example not just of how any inevitable link between poverty and violent activism is difficult to construct but also of the obstacles those who set out for Iraq had to overcome to reach their goal. Al-Fawzan too blamed al-Jazeera and 'the TV' for his decision to try to become a *mujahed*. A self-confessed partygoer more interested in football than religion, al-Fawzan, sixth of nine sons of a rich businessman, said that neither the al-Aqsa Intifada nor the war in Afghanistan had 'meant much' to him, but the images from Abu Ghraib in particular and from Iraq more generally, as they had done with al-Ghatani, created 'a kind of mental shock'. 'When I saw those pictures, it came into my mind that I had to do something,' he recalled. Al-Fawzan, who had a secure and relatively well-paid government job in the Transport Ministry, sought out a relative in Mecca who was already sending volunteers to Iraq and was despatched, after some basic training in the Yemen, to Damascus, where he was hidden by a 'coordinator', a fellow Saudi, in an apartment and furnished with false ID papers. After a month, however, with no sign of an imminent departure and unable to leave the safehouse, al-Fawzan lost patience, decided to try another way to reach Iraq, returned to Saudi Arabia and was arrested.[74] Others, such as Abu Thar, a Yemeni taxi driver and religious student who also said he had left his home after seeing the images from Abu Ghraib, were more determined. Abu Thar described spending weeks moving between cheap hotel rooms, mosques, rooms above religious schools in Damascus, Aleppo and elsewhere as he waited to cross into Iraq from Syria. In each, he said, he found another dozen young volunteers.[75] Finally, he was taken to a village on the Syrian side of the border close to a checkpoint where the police had been bribed and, after a frightening trek through the desert, was led into Iraq and to Falluja.[76]

Al-Ghatani the shopkeeper had arrived in Baghdad in October, dropped off in a safehouse in the rough Sunni-dominated al-Doura neighbourhood of the city. There he had handed over more cash to another group of militants-cum-criminals – documents later seized by US troops confirmed that $1,000 was more or less what the smugglers to whom insurgents tended to subcontract the task of bringing in recruits charged Saudis – who drove him to the outskirts of Falluja and left him by the roadside.[77] Al-Ghatani, who had travelled without any introduction from any known figure in Saudi Arabia, failed to convince the *mujahideen* in the city of his bona fides. He was not discouraged, however, and instead spent the next four months fighting with 'the tribes', as he called them, along the short stretch of road between Falluja, Ramadi and Baghdad. 'They taught me to use an AK-47. I shot at the Americans when they attacked us,' al-Ghatani said. 'They would use planes, and I saw old women and children killed, and I buried them myself and I let the anger out by shooting and fighting.'

FALLUJA TWO

The long-awaited American offensive into Falluja started on November 7, 2004. There had been sustained fighting across the Sunni Triangle through most of the summer and early autumn. Weeks of raids, firefights and occasional air strikes were punctuated by more conventional engagements. Several took place around Abu Ghraib, as al-Zarqawi's fighters from Falluja and local tribes mounted sustained attacks on American positions. 'I've got to tell you, we've killed a lot of people carrying weapons this week . . . I'm talking hundreds,' Brigadier General Hertling, deputy commander of the 1st US Armoured Division, had told reporters in Baghdad in late September. Among them was Abu Anas al-Shami, the *takfiri* cleric, head of al-Zarqawi's *fatwa* committee and occasional diarist.[78]

For the second battle of Falluja, General Mattis deployed 9,000 troops, four times as many as in the first battle seven months before. They included 2,000 Iraqis. In the spring the vast bulk of local troops and police deployed in Falluja had deserted or refused to fight, so this new engagement would be a key test of the US strategy of building up local security forces.[79] Eleven million rounds of ammunition had been stockpiled and efforts made to close the Syrian border to halt the flow of foreign militant volunteers.[80] The city's defenders were estimated to number around 2,000, of whom perhaps a quarter were foreign nationals.

This time the American troops pushed right through the city. After ten days of fighting, several hundred insurgents, fifty-four Americans and eight Iraqi soldiers had been killed. The latter had performed marginally better than before, though they were still far from being able to operate independently. The fighting was possibly the most intense seen by American troops in recent decades, a succession of vicious house-to-house fights with tanks firing from a few metres away into buildings, protracted artillery bombardment and air strikes. It was the apogee of the kind of 'kinetic' warfare the Marines had originally hoped to avoid. In a sense it was the climactic battle that the initial campaign of March 2003 had lacked.

Though the 'international' or 'foreign' fighters were outnumbered at least three to one by Iraqi fighters in the opening stages of the battle, many of the latter slipped away as combat intensified, returning to their homes in the farmland around the city or going to ground elsewhere in the country and leaving a higher and higher concentration of foreigners in the city. By the final stages of the battle, American troops fought a heterogeneous force of militants from outside Iraq in the ruins of an Iraqi city largely deserted by the Iraqis themselves.

A month before the battle came, al-Zarqawi had finally pledged allegiance to bin Laden and accepted his role as an 'al-Qaeda affiliate', the local representative of the global brand. In so doing he made the second battle of Falluja the only conventional confrontation on such a scale between a force at the very least nominally loyal to al-Qaeda and troops fielded by the US or their allies in the whole of the 9/11 Wars.[81] What was supposed to be a battle for territory – for the safe haven and few square metres of ground that the militants had said they so desired – had become invested with a new significance. For many of the combatants Falluja – and by extension Iraq – had been reduced simply to a stage on which a titanic struggle between the forces of good and evil, belief and non-belief, would take place. 'We are not here to liberate Iraq, we're here to fight the infidels,' Abu Osama, a Tunisian, told one reporter bluntly days before the fighting began.[82] The people of Falluja – few of whom took part in the actual fighting in the city – had little role in this great imagined drama of cosmic conflict between faiths, cultures and civilizations.

BIN LADEN REDUX

Shortly after the end of the fighting in Falluja, four days before the American presidential elections, a video was released by bin Laden, his first for eighteen months. It directly addressed the 'People of America', advising them on 'how to prevent another [9/11]'.[83] There was little new in bin Laden's rhetoric, though the careful *mise en scène* – a lectern, no weapon, the robe of a respected statesman and scholar – indicated that the leader of al-Qaeda sought to project a more nuanced image than had hitherto been the case. In the tape, bin Laden suggested that it was what America did, not what it was, that provoked the attacks against it, pointing out that al-Qaeda did not target Sweden.[84] Bin Laden almost certainly sought to influence the American poll – or at least exploit the opportunity for further publicity it provided. It is less clear that the forty-seven-year-old fugitive wanted Bush to win, however. In the event, the incumbent was re-elected with ease.

The video dominated headlines and news bulletins on the eve of the elections, a powerful reminder of bin Laden's ability to project himself globally and of who, after all the interest in al-Zarqawi and others, still remained the pre-eminent leader of the global jihad. It was also a reminder of the very obvious failure of the most expensive manhunt in history to make any evident progress. Since the al-Qaeda senior leadership had disappeared after Tora Bora, Western intelligence services had been unable to obtain any solid lead as to where they might be.[85]

Most of the militants who had fled Afghanistan had ended up in South Waziristan, the most southerly of Pakistan's Federally Administered Tribal Areas (FATA), so the working theory among Western intelligence that bin Laden was there too was, though little more than informed speculation, reasonable. Mahmood Shah, the chief civilian administrator of the FATA from 2001 to 2005, remembered that the foreigners had begun arriving in Shakai, an impoverished area of pine forests, mountains and valleys close to the border, in early 2002.[86] Secret American intelligence reports later used in the compilation of dossiers on detainees at Guantanamo Bay contained repeated references to meetings of the al-Qaeda leadership in Shakai in late 2003 and 2004. One report even implied that, after the capture of Khaled Sheikh Mohammed in Rawalpindi, al-Zawahiri himself had moved to the area from an unspecified urban area.

But it was not actually clear if 'high value target one', as the al-Qaeda leader was known to the teams tracking him in Pakistan, Afghanistan and from America, was even in the frontier zone at all. With little fresh human or technical intelligence coming in, the hunters adopted some unusual methods of analysis. In 2003 it was rock types in the background of one video that featured the al-Qaeda leaders that were scrutinized closely. A year later trees pictured in another video led investigators to believe bin Laden might be in the valleys of Chitral, hundreds of miles or more north of Shakai and South Waziristan. But if his references to current events and people showed the fugitive leader had access to some kind of news media, there was little else to go on. Hundreds of leads were being developed by the CIA. There was a particular interest in finding and tracking the couriers bin Laden was known to use. His extensive close family – three current wives, a dozen or more children – was a possible weakness. But beyond that, there was nothing.

Yet, despite the problems of their pursuers, the situation of any senior militants in Pakistan remained precarious. Once the presence of hundreds, possibly thousands, of international militants in South Waziristan had been detected by Western intelligence services, pressure had been put on President Musharraf to launch a series of military offensives to deny al-Qaeda any secure base there.[87] A first effort in 2003 had concentrated on a 30 square mile area in South Waziristan under the control of local Pakistani militants suspected of harbouring 'foreign terrorists', and, even if this was a bloody fiasco as local and foreign militants ambushed ill-prepared troops and inflicted heavy losses, other offensives had followed.

These made clear that, though the senior al-Qaeda leadership had seen their ideology propagated across the world through spectacular violent acts such as 9/11 or the various strikes it had subsequently inspired, they were still a long way from finding a replacement for the secure base they had once enjoyed in Afghanistan.[88] If the attractions of a strategy based on a decentralized 'global, leaderless jihad' were strong, the late 1990s had amply proven how useful a genuine safe haven could be. As a result, bin Laden had carefully followed a middle road in strategic terms in his statements over the previous eighteen months, seeing his role as being 'inciter-in-chief' along lines closer to the thinking of al-Suri without entirely renouncing al-Zarqawi's strategy of creating a physical base from which to launch the great campaign to build the new Islamic caliphate.[89]

If the testing ground for al-Zarqawi's ideas was to be the campaign in Iraq, the testing ground for al-Suri's strategy of incitement of a decentralized, leaderless jihad would not be in the traditional lands where Islam has been the dominant religion for centuries, the *dar ul Islam*, the land of peace, however. Instead, it would be in a new zone of conflict: in the *dar ul kufr*, the land of unbelief, and more specifically in Europe, where 20 million Muslims living in the heart of the unbelievers' societies constituted an immense potential strategic asset for the global militant movement.[90]

PART THREE

Europe, the Darkest Days: 2005–6

8

The 9/11 Wars Reach Europe

A MURDER IN HOLLAND

Sitting on a sofa upstairs in an open-plan office off a quiet street in an unfashionable part of Amsterdam, Gijs van de Westelaken was talking about his dead friend and business associate, the film-maker and professional controversialist Theo van Gogh. 'He was provocative but never just for the sake of provocation. He wanted to know what made people tick,' de Westelaken said. 'He always said he would go on saying what he wanted to say whatever the threats.'[1] A few yards away, two tall blonde Dutch women in long denim skirts stood sipping warm white wine out of plastic cups and spoke in low voices. Some children played under desks, between architects' design tables and coiled cables of state-of-the-art computers. This was van Gogh's wake. A day earlier, on November 2, 2004, the forty-seven-year-old director had been cycling along Linnaeus Straat a few miles away from where de Westelaken was talking when he was stopped by a young man in a hooded sweater. A brief altercation followed, shots rang out, van Gogh collapsed, his attacker bent over his body, cutting, stabbing, then running. Panicked passers-by crowded round the corpse, a note pinned to its chest by a knife. Van Gogh's last words were: 'Surely we can talk about this?'[2]

The death of van Gogh, notwithstanding the bombings in Madrid seven months earlier, revealed to a shocked public in Holland, Germany, France, the UK and elsewhere that the 9/11 Wars had reached Europe. The strike in Spain had involved first-generation immigrants, most still barely integrated, many of whom elected to speak Arabic in court as their Spanish was too limited. Mohammed Bouyeri was very different. The 2,000-word note he had left was written in good Dutch, which was unsurprising as its twenty-six-year-old author had been born, raised and educated only a few miles away and at least in legal terms was as Dutch as his victim. It was in fact addressed not to Van Gogh but to Ayaan Hirsi Ali, a Somali-born refugee and member of the Dutch parliament with whom the director had been working on a film about Islam and domestic violence called *Submission*, which featured lines from the Koran projected over a semi-naked woman. The letter was in part a screed of incoherent apocalyptic poetry and in part a distillation of the familiar radical Islamic worldview. Hirsi Ali, who had made a series of controversial and uncompromising public statements criticizing Islam as a backward religion that encouraged violence to women, was an apostate, it said, working for hidden Jewish masters who ran Dutch and global politics. Those to blame for the terrible current situation of the world's Muslims were all those supposed believers who failed to act in the face of such clear provocation. Bouyeri's origins, act and views, especially as it became clear that he was connected to a much wider circle of radicalized young Dutch Muslims, thus apparently signalled that the scenario most feared by the counter-terrorist community, policy-makers and the general population – the radicalization and mobilization of the Muslims of Europe – was being realized. For major countries with large Muslim communities such as France, Germany and the UK, the killing of van Gogh meant that the war they had found themselves caught up in since 2001 no longer solely involved battles or bombs in far-off, dusty, hot countries but had reached them, their homes, their places of work, their friends and family.

For ordinary people in London, Amsterdam, Copenhagen, Rome, Stuttgart or any number of smaller cities and towns across Europe, the coming years would be marked by anxiety, anger and deep pessimism. Every day brought news of further attacks. The world seemed launched on an ineluctable course towards a dark and violent future. The 'Clash of Civilizations' appeared not just to be inevitable but a reality. Nor were such impressions entirely without foundation. Iraq continued to slide deeper into chaos, public debate globally became increasingly bitter and polarized, relations deteriorated between Western countries and a series of Muslim majority states, polls recorded more and more extreme positions becoming increasingly widespread among huge swathes of populations who had often previously shown themselves largely uninterested in politics or activism. There was a deep, and possibly well-founded, fear that the world would soon become divided into two warring camps. These years, from 2004 to 2007, saw the 9/11 Wars reach a new level of intensity, touching, irrevocably altering, indeed sometimes destroying, the lives of hundreds of millions of people across the entire planet. It was in this period that the 9/11 Wars came closest to being a genuine global conflict.

In this new and violent phase, Europe was crucial. The wars had expanded from south-west Asia to Iraq and had inflamed much of the Middle East. As al-Suri and bin Laden had both recognized, what happened in Europe would determine whether the wars would continue to broaden and deepen as a conflict or whether its hitherto apparently inexorable expansion would falter, opening up the possibility that the slide towards a deeper and broader chaos could be slowed, possibly halted and even, perhaps, reversed.

EUROPE AND ITS MUSLIMS

The problem with even the most cursory overview of relations between 'Europe' and 'the Islamic world' is that defining either entity is difficult and sketching a single history impossible. If Europe has a geographic unity, encompassing more or less the tract of land bordered by the Atlantic, the Mediterranean and an imaginary line somewhere between the Vistula river and the Ural mountains, there exists no consensus among its infinitely diverse communities as to what being a 'European' actually entails. Equally, though the 'Islamic world' is supposedly defined by faith, the definition of 'Islamic' varies so dramatically as to almost invalidate the very concept of a global community of Muslims. This, as the previous chapters have explored, was the fundamental problem for al-Qaeda from the outset. It is unsurprising that it poses challenges for historians too. It is thus also inevitable that readings of the last 1,300 years of relations between these two already poorly defined and largely imaginary blocs are so often highly subjective and politicized.

So while some readings emphasize the rich cultural exchange between, for example, Muslim Moorish Spain and more northern Christian interlocutors in the early medieval period, others emphasize the violence that occurred at the same time. While some prefer to emphasize how the eleventh and thirteenth centuries saw European crusaders fighting and sacking their way across the Holy Land with an extraordinary and often indiscriminate brutality, others stress how trading contacts thrived despite the hostilities and underline the constant flow of words, ideas, tastes and practices from the Islamic world – algebra, admiral, coffee, guitar – into Europe and vice versa. Some see the first battle of Poitiers in 732 as the moment when a united Christendom successfully repelled a concerted attempt by Islamic armies to subdue and colonize northern Europe, others portray it as nothing more than the heading-off of a raid by Moorish armies set on gathering gold rather than spreading the faith.[3] Some prefer to emphasize the long centuries of strife between a newly potent Ottoman Empire and 'European' Christian powers following the 1453 fall of Constantinople, while others point out that Francis I of France allied with Sultan Suleiman the Magnificent to fight his rival, the Holy Roman Emperor Charles V, and that Queen Elizabeth I of England asked one of Suleiman's successors for naval assistance to defeat the Spanish Armada.[4]

What is certain is that the view that Europeans have had of the Moor, Saracen, Turk or Mohammedan has often been determined by the potential threat the latter have been thought to pose.[5] With Muslim armies advancing on Constantinople and Ottoman navies surging into the Mediterranean, commentators and writers such as Nicetas Byzantios or Dante Alighieri reserved the worst of their bile for 'the bad and noxious' religion of Islam with Mohammed 'the Antichrist' at its head. With the Ottomans on the defensive after the failed siege of Vienna in 1683, the Turk was seen instead as exotic and eccentric but not necessarily dangerous.[6] The Crimean War of 1853 to 1856 saw Anglican Christian Britain and Roman Catholic France allied with the Ottomans to defend Constantinople against a Russian (Orthodox) Empire demonized by Western European clergy as 'impure, demoralising and intolerant'.[7] As European colonial armies pushed deeper into the Islamic world – the French into what was to become Algeria, the Spanish into Morocco, the British into the Asian subcontinent and the Dutch into what was to become Indonesia – Muslims, Turks or Moors became decadent, sensual, poetic, representative of the supposed simplicity, honesty and 'honour' that an industrializing West was leaving behind.[8] When the 'Oriental' was depicted as violent, the violence was usually directed at others of his type through exotic punishments, duels, incomprehensible tribal wars. In all cases, the Western viewer could rest assured that these heroic warriors' picturesque *jezzail* muskets and long curved *yatagans* were no match for well-drilled troops with contemporary Western armaments. The superb duelling Arab or Berber horsemen painted by Eugène Delacroix to the acclaim of Parisians through the middle of the nineteenth century were being wiped out by modern armies armed with modern weapons even as the artist's canvases dried.[9] When a threat surfaced, however, so did the old stereotypes. So during the Indian Mutiny or War of Independence of 1857 'proud, vengeful and fanatical . . . cunning and cruel' Muslims were blamed in Britain for the trouble even though 90 per cent of the mutineers were Hindu.[10] A decade or so later, when the immediate scare had passed, a less negative vision of 'the Mohammedan' returned to dominate literature, popular journalism and art.

The myths woven through this vexed and complex history of representation and misrepresentation have permanently marked imaginations and identities. Few of the clichés bear much relation to reality. Early Islamic armies fought on foot with spears, not waving scimitars from Arab stallions as popularly imagined, not least because they tended to be composed of poor desert tribesmen who could not afford a mount.[11] The great Christian knight Roland, the paragon of medieval chivalry, died fighting Basque bandits who had lain in ambush in a Pyrenean mountain pass, not 'the Moors' as recounted in later literature. The sensuality of the East so dear to nineteenth-century travelling (or indeed sedentary) French poets revealed more about the conservative contemporary mores of their homeland than about the Levant. More recently a series of commentators and analysts have opposed 'Oriental' and 'Western' styles of warfare, unconsciously reproducing the old stereotypes of the wily, highly mobile Saracen with the sharp scimitar trying to outwit the manly, slightly plodding but fundamentally honest and upstanding Western warrior with his heavy broadsword that featured in primary school history books even in the 1970s.[12]

But if there is Orientalism, a false and romanticized vision of 'the East' informed as much by the prejudices and complexes of 'the West', there has also been Occidentalism, the equally distorted vision of 'the West' in the Muslim world (and elsewhere) too.[13] Many of the prejudices so tediously trotted out by radical Islamic militants such as Bouyeri have roots as deep as any of those of 'European' visions of Muslims. They too have been embedded by successive decades of representation in literature and films. The vision of the European in much of the Islamic world has been as heavily mythologized as any representation of the sensual or violent Moor in Europe and has also depended to a considerable degree on the degree of perceived threat posed by the West at a given time. The resilience of such stereotypes is striking too. During the eleventh and twelfth centuries Muslims 'regarded the Franks ... as little better than animals in manners of sexual propriety' and Crusaders were, like American troops today, seen as dirty, polluting, indelicate and bestial.[14] 'All those who were well informed about the Franks saw them as animals who are superior in strength and aggression,' said Usama ibn Munqidh in 1095. And Saladin himself is meant to have commented on the 'obstinacy' with which the 'Franks ... fight for religion'.[15] In the eighteenth century, the famous Ottoman scholar Naima compared contemporary European states to those of the Crusaders and concluded that they were so backward and barbaric as to not be 'worthy of his attention'.[16] Concepts of infection or corruption by a decadent and depraved West go back to anti-colonial rhetoric from the first half of the last century and well beyond. There are the key texts of radical Islamic militancy such as those of Sayyid Qutb, who, after a short voyage in America in the late 1940s, dismissed Western civilization as lascivious, materialist and base, citing it as the modern version of pre-Islamic ignorance and barbarism, *jahiliya*.[17] Another solidly rooted generalization is that Westerners in general and Western soldiers in particular are cowards, afraid to fight man to man but who rely instead on their technological superiority. Interrogations of aides of the dictator revealed that the latter presumption was one reason why Saddam Hussein – who distributed videos of the film *Blackhawk Down* to his generals – failed to avail himself of the various possible options that might conceivably have averted the war of 2003.[18] It was also one reason why bin Laden took the enormous strategic gamble of 9/11, though better informed associates warned the US would react like 'a wounded bear'. Such ideas have bled into mainstream political, public and private conversation in much of the Islamic world, which is often marked by a depressing level of ignorance and prejudice.

Another important part of Occidentalism has long been a crude anti-Semitism. As the writings of Qutb show, negative images of the Jew have long been associated with urbanity and thus a 'decadent' modernity.

Hatred of Jews in many Muslim countries, despite some historic examples of peaceful and fruitful coexistence, was extremely widespread even before the foundation of Israel. Since the establishment of the Jewish state, the fusion of the political and the religious has given rise to an anti-Semitism that is impressive in its vitriol. 'Read history,' Sheikh Abdur-Rahman al-Sudais, the imam of the Grand mosque in Mecca and a controversial figure who has also been seen by some as a proponent of moderation, preached in 2004, 'and you will understand that the Jews of yesterday are the evil fathers of the Jews of today, who are evil offspring, infidels ... calf-worshippers, prophet-murderers, prophecy-deniers ... the scum of the human race whom Allah cursed and turned into apes and pigs ... These are the Jews, a continuous lineage of meanness, cunning, obstinacy, tyranny, licentiousness, evil, and corruption.'[19] A favourite theme of soap operas in Egypt, Jordan, Turkey and elsewhere is the shadowy Zionist-Semitic conspiracy and its brutal American accomplices.[20] *The Protocols of the Elders of Zion*, a tract first published in 1903 supposedly outlining a Jewish conspiracy to take over the world and exposed many years ago as a fake by the Tsarist secret police, has long been on sale throughout the Middle East and beyond.[21] The tract's claims, which featured prominently in the foundational literature of groups such as Hamas that were increasingly popular with European Muslims and others from the 1990s onwards, were seen as entirely uncontroversial by many hundreds of millions of people in the Islamic world and in Muslim communities in Western Europe by the end of the twentieth century.[22]

Such stereotypes – the Frank, the Moor, the Saracen, the European colonizer, the American neo-imperialist – had rarely survived contact with reality. Until very recently, the distance that allowed them to persist unchallenged remained. But in Europe in the last forty years that distance has vanished. Communities that were once free to imagine the worst of one another without such preconceptions being challenged – or having direct effects on everyday life – live intermingled. New and difficult questions of integration and assimilation are being posed that a thousand years' worth of myths and misrepresentations aggravate rather than resolve. As it was meant to do, the Islamic extremist violence of the middle years of the decade revealed the tensions this new proximity has generated in a cruel and effective way.

THE MECHANICS OF IMMIGRATION

As the American conservative commentator Christopher Caldwell has usefully pointed out, Europe acquired a large immigrant population of which a substantial proportion define themselves as Muslim 'in a fit of absence of mind'. Though a provocative formulation, Caldwell's phrase nicely encapsulates the lack of foresight, management or even recognition of large-scale immigration through the latter half of the last century.[23] Few had ever predicted that Europe would become home to tens of millions of Muslims in less than fifty years, and therefore little forward planning was ever done to deal with an eventuality that many could neither envisage nor countenance.[24] That influx has naturally created a number of difficult issues specific to the continent.

Immigration to Europe from colonies had grown steadily, especially towards the end of the nineteenth century as European nations began to industrialize. That increase was minimal, however, compared with that which came after the Second World War when, denuded of manpower and money by the conflict, Western nations looked to their former overseas possessions, many still in the process of gaining their independence, for cheap labour. For the French this was mainly Algeria, theoretically part of France until 1962; for the British it was the Caribbean, India, Pakistan (particularly rural areas in the north-eastern lowland regions adjacent to Kashmir which had long supplied recruits to the Merchant Navy) and from the Sylhet region of Bangladesh which also had a long tradition of providing labour. Where former colonial links did not suffice, other sources were found. Germany and Holland, as well as several Scandinavian countries, looked to Turkey. The Dutch brought in substantial numbers of Moroccan workers.

At first, it was intended that such workers would spend only a couple of years in their new host nations, living in relatively isolated communities often on the outskirts or in run-down central neighbourhoods of cities, before returning home. Most did just that. However, not least because employers preferred to avoid the complicated and expensive process of refreshing their diligent, cheap and compliant labour force every couple of years, many ended up staying. Wives and other family members were allowed to join them and communities became, often literally, more concrete as local authorities recognized that having tens of thousands living in shantytowns was a hazard both to public order and to health and replaced makeshift accommodation with more permanent structures. This was done with little genuine planning and as cheaply as possible.

The sites where the earliest workers were more or less dumped had been chosen to maximize ease of access to the heavy industries where most of them worked and minimize their impact on 'native' communities. However, it did not take long before there was a strong reaction from local populations, who felt their jobs and, to a lesser extent, lifestyles threatened. By the 1960s governments were beginning to limit entry to family members of existing settled migrants and a relatively small number of asylum-seekers. These restrictions were progressively tightened, particularly as the post-war economic boom gave way to the downturn of the 1970s and mass unemployment. Yet such efforts to restrict the new migration came late.[25] By the later 1990s, the population referred to or declaring itself as Muslim in the UK numbered 1.6 million (out of a total of around 60 million), in France around 5 to 6 million (8 to 9.5 per cent), in Germany 4 million and in Holland around 800,000 (5 and 6 per cent of total populations respectively). In all, if the centuries-old 6-million-strong Muslim communities in the Balkans were included, it was thus thought that at the time of the 9/11 attacks just over 20 million Muslims lived in Europe.[26]

All these communities had three things in common. Firstly, in every country, an increasing proportion of the so-called immigrant population, Muslim or otherwise, had been born locally.[27] Secondly, though their conditions varied, almost all the communities designated Muslim in Western Europe scored significantly lower on most social and economic indicators than their 'host communities' and many non-Muslim immigrant communities. So, in Holland, at the time of the murder of van Gogh, 27 per cent of Dutch Moroccans and 21 per cent of Dutch Turks were unemployed in contrast to a rate of only 9 per cent among 'native' Dutch.[28] In the UK, the 2001 census found that Muslims had the poorest health and lowest educational qualifications of all British communities. In 2003 and 2004, British Muslims also suffered the highest unemployment rate, topping 14 per cent, around three times the national average, and young Muslims from sixteen to twenty-four had the highest unemployment rates of anyone at 22 per cent, twice as high as their non-Muslim counterparts.[29] In Germany and France, where data are not broken down according to religion, extrapolating from existing statistics indicated that a similar situation prevailed. According to the 2005 data from the National Institute for Statistics and Economic Studies (INSEE), unemployment among people of French origin was 9.2 per cent while for those of foreign backgrounds, the rate was 14 per cent. More importantly perhaps, in comparison to a 5 per cent overall employment rate for people of French origin, 26.5 per cent of university graduates with North African backgrounds were unemployed.[30] Thirdly, the communities themselves were immensely varied and often remained separated internally between Moroccan Berbers and Arabs, Pakistani Punjabis, Mirpuris and Pashtuns, between the various Kurds who speak the mutually unintelligible Kermanji and Sohrani dialects, and so on. Marriages between immigrants and 'native-born' French, German, Danish, Dutch or British men and women often outnumbered those between members of communities portrayed as homogeneous monoliths by outsiders.[31]

As the profile of such communities evolved, so models developed or discussed by policy-makers to deal with issues of integration and assimilation – the two being far from the same thing – did so too. These also predictably varied enormously between European countries. In the UK, policies were largely based on a strong belief that different cultures could coexist in relative harmony without imposed overarching narratives of national identity as long as the bedrock principles of British society was observed. Given the rather grand name of multiculturalism, seen as irresponsible and naive laissez faire by its critics and as a tolerant celebration of an economically and culturally enriching diversity by its supporters, this model had been under significant strain since the late 1980s. The controversy following the publication of Salman Rushdie's *Satanic Verses* in 1988 had revealed deep tensions. Subsequent rows over faith schooling, scares over the number of *medressas* and clashes over arranged marriages continued to expose and exacerbate them. One of the problems was that no one was very clear about exactly what the British model actually implied. Did it involve a 'pure multiculturalism', in which no single culture was seen as more valid or more 'native' than any other, or a softer version, where minorities were allowed very considerable autonomy within a dominant culture? One interpretation, rooted in a rejection of assimilation in the 1960s and heavily influenced by left-wing thinking from the 1980s that had been particularly dominant among those running many of Britain's inner-city municipal councils, was based on a complicated argument that as citizens had 'differing needs' equal treatment meant taking 'full account ... of their differences' and that 'equality' needed therefore to be defined in a culturally sensitive way that was 'discriminating' but not 'discriminatory'.[32] Others, such as Trevor Phillips, the head of the Commission for Racial Equality and a former television executive and presenter, demanded the opposite: that there should be more 'Britishness'. But what was Britishness? For Phillips, it was 'an inclusive culture which allows you to be all sorts of strange and eccentric things as long as the core values are accepted'.[33] Others defined Britishness very differently, appealing to ideas of island nations, green and pleasant lands, warm beer and even, in the title of one book, the 'Warrior Race' that the British apparently constituted.[34] In fact, the most British quality of the concept of Britishness appeared to be not only that it was so undefined but that most people were happy for that to be the case. British multiculturalism as a model tended in practice to be a compromise of the sort only acceptable in a country where there is no perceived need for either a fully codified law or a constitution.[35]

The French model of *laïcité*, an imposed theoretical equality before the law and before a rigorously secular state, had deeper ideological roots than the British model and a more coherent intellectual structure and came in for less criticism within France through the middle years of the decade, though it was often attacked externally. Different models had developed in Germany, Spain, Italy and the Scandinavian countries. In Holland, the system was known as the 'pillars' and was based on a denominational segregation where each community had its own schools, trade unions, social associations, even hospitals. Though the system, originally designed to manage the nation's numerous churches, had largely broken down by the time of van Gogh's murder, it still allowed, indeed encouraged, Muslim communities to live with a significant degree of separation from the rest of Dutch society and culture. 'We've had a tolerant tradition since the seventeenth century ... but a lot of difficult issues here were never discussed. The dark side of multiculturalism has been taboo,' said van de Westelaken, the late van Gogh's friend.

Equally, the immigrants themselves developed their own models of integration or assimilation. Often seen as the passive subject of policies or attitudes in their host countries, in fact immigrant communities dynamically developed their own ways of dealing with the situations that they found themselves in. The encounter with the West had been one of the primary drivers for reflection and for religious and political activism throughout the Muslim world from the nineteenth century onwards, and life in late twentieth-century Europe provoked a similar range of responses among immigrant communities. As they had done in countries from Morocco to Indonesia over the previous two centuries, these responses included outright rejection, an attempt to appropriate certain elements deemed compatible with a given vision of culture and belief, wholesale and enthusiastic acceptance and pretty much every possible shade in between. One important determining factor was, of course, conditions in the countries of origin. Turkish immigrants in Germany who came from developed Western Anatolian cities had advantages that arrivals in the UK from poor rural Pakistani villages did not. The difference between the opportunities open to savvy Moroccan townsmen and Berbers from the Rif mountains was huge. So too was the difference in social outlook. Immigrants from Pashtun communities on the northwest frontier of Pakistan were much more conservative as a general rule than those from much more literate and broad-minded Kurdish villages of northern Iraq, for example.

Also significant, despite the heterogeneity of the various immigrant communities, was the political evolution of their countries of origin. Complexes and conflicts from 'the old country' were often imported, and new emerging problems in states many thousands of miles away could have a significant effect in Bradford, Rotterdam, Hamburg or elsewhere. With most Dutch Muslim communities coming from relatively stable states such as Turkey and Morocco, Holland was spared some of the backwash of radicalism that troubled other nations. However, parts of the French immigrant population were deeply affected by the savage civil war in Algeria during the 1990s.[36] In Britain, in a much less evident way, the radicalization of the Kashmir conflict in the same period led to thousands of young men from communities in the west and north of England travelling to Pakistan not just, as many hundreds of thousands did every year, for family visits but to actively participate in a violent insurgency led by increasingly extremist groups. Another important example of this transfer between immigrants' countries of origin and the West was the composition of the various organizations that sprang up through the late 1980s and 1990s as representatives of newly vocal communities. Some British groups were close to Saudi Arabia, others to

Iran.[37] The Muslim Council of Britain which was founded in 1997 and would become the privileged interlocutor of the Labour government elected in that year had strong links to Pakistani Islamist organizations.[38] National and ethnic splits riddled the various representative bodies in France. Already in the 1990s European Muslims had become a prize in the internal battle for influence, power and worshippers between the various opposed strands of religious practice seen in the Islamic world with Gulf states, notably Saudi Arabia, pouring funds into bursaries, mosque construction, preaching and public meetings to further the reach of their own rigorously conservative brand of Islam. The contest between various strands of Islamic observance within Europe in the key period of 2004 to 2007 must thus be seen as an extension of both an ongoing struggle within the Islamic world more broadly and the longstanding competition between Muslim states for the loyalty of European Muslim communities. As ever, the 9/11 Wars played out within a framework of older conflicts. As ever, they involved the subtle interplay of a huge range of global and local factors and trends.

Many of these global trends have already been explored earlier, when discussing the flow of young volunteers from the Middle East to the militant training camps set up in Afghanistan by bin Laden, al-Zarqawi, al-Suri and others for example. They included a 'youth bulge' and immigration from the countryside to the cities or internationally. There was the discrediting of left-wing, nationalist or other ideologies and the subsequent wave of religious revivalism that had swept the Middle East in the 1980s. There was the surge of politics based on religious or sectarian identities around the globe in the 1990s and the construction of a new more global Islamic identity and narrative infused with a strong anti-American or anti-Western sentiment. Looking back, it is clear that Britain and Europe were far from immune to these broad historical trends affecting the Islamic world more generally.[39] There was also the impact of events such as the war in the former Yugoslavia, the conflict in Chechnya and the Second Palestinian Intifada. All of these episodes – especially the war in the Balkans – could be portrayed as evidence that Christian Europe did not care about Muslims.

Many felt the tensions coursing underneath. There were clues to what was happening. French authorities began recording a rise in anti-Semitic attacks – after years of decline – that were largely perpetrated by young men from Muslim immigrant communities.[40] In the UK, violent riots in

Bradford in 2001 had revealed deep social problems. Whereas once young 'British-Pakistanis' had experienced outrage at 'racism', seeing themselves as 'black', many now saw themselves as victims of Islamophobia, defining themselves as Muslims.[41] The success of radical Islamist groups such as Hezb-ut-Tahrir and of other similar organizations on university campuses showed how easily such ideologies could attract significant numbers of young people. In October 2001, two young Britons from families of Pakistani origin who had joined the Taliban in Afghanistan were killed in Kabul in a missile strike.[42] Two months later, a young British convert tried to blow himself up on a transatlantic jet. In April 2003, two Britons tried to bomb a Tel Aviv nightclub 'for the sake of Allah and to get revenge against the Jews and Crusaders', according to a videoed will in a rare example of the 9/11 Wars suddenly surging into the otherwise largely autonomous conflict in Israel-Palestine. One of the pair detonated his device outside the club, killing three and wounding more than fifty.[43] The other, whose bomb failed to detonate, turned up dead on a beach ten days later.[44] In Holland, 'a different political wind [had been] blowing since the 9/11 attacks', Mohammed al-Aissati, of the Dutch Association of Moroccan Immigrants, told the author on the day after van Gogh's death.[45] 'We all had a good feeling about how we were doing here in terms of tolerance but 9/11 changed all that. This murder could not have come at a worse time.'

EUROPEAN INTELLIGENCE SERVICES ON THE BACK FOOT

In the early years of the 9/11 Wars, with a poor understanding of the nature of the problem, creaking structures better adapted to Cold War enemies or more traditional terrorist groups and limited resources, intelligence services in Europe rapidly found themselves on the back foot. By early 2004, though it was clear that the conflict would almost inevitably come to the continent, few had grasped the nature or scale of the threat. A series of meetings the author had with senior British security officials at the time was salutary. The officials privately expressed their concern at the lack of 'handle' they had on the problem and worried about the possibility both of a major attack and of lower-level violence by 'self-radicalizing' freelance militants. They frankly admitted that their knowledge of processes of radicalization and of the workings of modern Islamic militancy was superficial and worried that the terms with which they described their 'clients' – their analysis was based on groups, cells, operatives – did not adequately capture the nature of the phenomenon they were trying to grasp. Though some of the discussion was about so-called 'cleanskins' – 'It is not the ones we know about who worry us but the ones we don't,' the head of the militant Islam desk of the Metropolitan Police's Special Branch said over a drink in one of the pubs around Scotland Yard – the focus was more on 'sleeper cells' implanted by al-Qaeda over previous years which could be activated when needed. According to Stella Rimington, former head of MI5, these were 'networks of individuals ... that blend into society ... who live normal, routine lives until called upon for specific tasks by another part of the network.' One of the lessons learned from other modern terrorist conflicts, Rimington explained, was that terrorists aimed 'to hide in plain sight, to be seen but not noticed and to all intents and purposes to live a law-abiding existence'. One of the key targets of her service's efforts, she said, were people who might offer logistic help from the UK to overseas militants to strike abroad. In this Rimington revealed quite how far from fully comprehending the nature of the threat she and her service were.[46] The biggest danger, as events would shortly reveal, was in fact posed by militants who were very much British *receiving* aid from overseas to strike *locally*. The individuals involved in radical Islamic militancy 'blended into society' and 'lived normal, routine lives' for the very simple reason that they *were* normal members of society.

This, of course, meant that a preventive strategy based on the idea that it was possible to find potentially dangerous individuals through 'profiling', i.e. seeking those whose qualities might indicate a vulnerability or a tendency towards violent militancy, was unlikely to meet with much success. It was swiftly clear that being young, male, Muslim, anti-Semitic, pro-Palestinian, anti-American, of immigrant background, with conflicted identity issues and poor relations with one's parents in, say, late 2003 was not particularly useful as a predictor of any terrorist activity. The sheer number of those sharing some or all of those qualities was in the hundreds of thousands in Britain alone. A government report later found that during 2004, MI5, though one of the better resourced European intelligence services, was unable to watch even the fifty-two suspects classed as 'essential targets' and could only provide 'reasonable' surveillance coverage of about one in twenty terror suspects.[47] Outgoing Metropolitan Police commissioner Sir John Stevens spoke of 2,000 'al-Qaeda-trained' militants stalking British streets only a few months after the killing in Amsterdam, clumsily ratcheting tensions higher for little obvious purpose.[48] In Germany, local services found 31,000 individuals who they believed posed a significant security risk.[49] One potential solution suggested in the UK was the introduction of identity cards. That classic visual symbol of the 9/11 Wars – the concrete barrier – began to appear outside key London sites such as the Houses of Parliament and the American embassy like outriders of the coming storm.

In Holland, local authorities had been wrestling with the same issues. In late 2001 and early 2002 Dutch security services had begun monitoring Salafist mosques and prayer halls suspected of acting as centres of recruitment and logistics hubs for young Muslims hoping to travel to a variety of 'theatres of jihad'. One criterion for focusing their efforts was whether a given institution had financial links to Saudi religious foundations such as al-Haramain International, which had been blacklisted for its links to militant Islam. This led them to the al-Tauheed mosque in the north of Eindhoven, where they identified a group of young Dutch Muslims, largely the children of immigrants of Moroccan origin, who had gathered around a Syrian-born cleric. One, a seventeen-year-old still at school, set off for Chechnya in January 2003. He was arrested. Another travelled to Spain to seek out a radical cleric tangentially connected to the Casablanca bombings which had occurred a few months before.[50] Two or three others actually made it to Pakistan. Another had discussed jihad and training with al-Qaeda sympathizers on the internet. A fifth is believed to have been in the process of making multiple plans for terrorist attacks in Holland. But the Dutch services had failed to pay any serious attention to the group's self-appointed 'media coordinator', apparently only a peripheral member who after the 9/11 attacks had been making public pleas for intercultural dialogue and tolerance.[51] He was deemed to be relatively harmless. This was Mohammed Bouyeri, the killer of van Gogh.

THE PROCESS

The various factors described above are important but can only be a part of any explanation of what lay behind Islamic militancy in Europe or indeed elsewhere in this period. One problem with the classic approach employed by security services in the early years of the conflict was that it was based on seeing radicalization as a consequence of an accumulation of the right elements at the right time. In fact, it is also possible to see radicalization as a process which itself often generated the conditions or qualities that led an individual to extremism and eventually violence. The key was not necessarily in the 'who' – essential character traits or profile of an individual – nor even in the 'why' – the sense of injustice or the attraction of a cause – but was to be found very often in the 'how'. It is this dynamic, complex and often chaotic interplay of environment and agency that, through the stories of a range of British militants of varying extremism who were active in the UK between the 9/11 attacks and the 7/7 bombings of 2005, the rest of this chapter sets out to explore.

If the process started anywhere it started not in the backroom of a radical-run mosque but in the frontroom of a family home. Ed Husain, who once held a senior position in Hezb-ut-Tahrir, the international Islamist organization that aims to overturn the alleged Western dominance of Muslims by forming Islamic states in what are seen as historically Muslim countries and is banned in many countries, remembered how as a teenager, despite years spent intensively studying with a traditional Pakistani Islamic spiritual leader, he had become increasingly distant from his conservative family.[52] They were steeped in the religious and social customs of Pakistan, which no longer interested him. A self-confessed 'misfit' at school, Husain soon found himself at the centre of the tension between the old systems of religious observance imported by first-generation migrants, which saw politics as something to be shunned, and newer styles of worship, often heavily influenced by Saudi Arabia and other Gulf countries, which adopted an aggressively political stance and were boosted by a massive, well-funded propaganda campaign. The latter had a strong appeal for Husain. 'What they [Hezb-ut-Tahrir] were saying seemed more relevant, more contemporary,' he said. 'They answered my questions.'[53]

Other catalysts for a shift towards involvement in radical organizations or towards an interest in more extreme strands of Islam were arguments over choices of sexual or marital partner, going out late at night, drinking, using soft drugs. Most of these would be familiar to many teenagers but were exacerbated in the context of the British

Pakistani community by a deep cultural generation gap which extended to almost all aspects of social relations within Britain's Muslim communities, from education to employment. The *biraderi* social system of north-eastern Pakistan, by which the interests of the individual are always subordinated to those of the extended family and broader social group or tribe, was difficult to reconcile with Western and urban values of individualism and personal empowerment. Under the system, communities were informally run by elders whose authority could not be challenged without risking total ostracism.[54] One response to this was radical secularism and rejection, another extreme religiosity.[55]

But the paths into radicalization were as many and varied as the responses to such tensions. Minor events such as incidents of racism or petty humiliations played a role. Major events could create the critical 'cognitive opening' that could lead to a radical change of direction. Shiraz Maher, then a history student at Leeds University, had never been attracted to any kind of activism before 9/11. His family had never been observant, he drank, smoked and 'was a normal first-year student'. And though in the summer of 2001 Maher had started seeing a more observant Muslim girl who had encouraged him to go to mosque more often and chided him for his lack of religious rigour, he was still far from any form of extremism. The 9/11 attacks, however, 'forced a choice', Maher said.[56] 'The rules of the game were clearly changing. You had to decide where you stood. I suddenly started asking questions that I had never asked before about Islam, about my identity, about the world.' A few days after the attacks in New York and Washington, outside the mosque where he prayed, Maher was approached by a Hezb-ut-Tahrir activist. The man, an Arabic and politics graduate from Maher's own university, was just a few years older, knew the Koran by heart but wore a suit and was clean-shaven. He 'seemed to have the answers' to the questions that Maher was now asking and was convincing too. 'I thought, here is someone who is successful and who talks my language,' Maher said. Within months Maher was meeting his mentor two or three times a week. The older man suggested ideas, leading rather than dragging his target in a certain direction. 'I felt he understood me,' said Maher. 'When I said, "I've been clubbing, I've smoked some weed," he was cool. At a traditional mosque in the Pakistani community [in Britain] they would have told me I was going to Hell, but he just said, "If it wasn't fun people wouldn't do it," and suggested that there were more rewarding and important things in life.' None of the conversations between Maher and his recruiter took place in mosques, which after 9/11 were under close scrutiny either by the security services or by local communities. This was typical. Apart from during the earliest years after 9/11, recruitment and the subsequent activism in the UK took place in independent Islamic centres, in private homes, in cafés, not in obvious locations such as the infamous mosque at Finsbury Park in north London. All the major terrorist plots in the UK in this period took shape in zones that are outside traditional established authority, religious or secular. Typically too, Maher was profoundly ignorant of Islam at the time of his recruitment. In this he was similar to the bombers in Madrid and to Bouyeri, all of whom had relatively poor and superficial under-standings of the faith's teachings and doctrines. Maher went on to spend four years in the Hezb-ut-Tahrir group, rising up the ranks and recruiting scores of new activists himself.[57] Maher and Husain's respective routes into radical activism show many common elements found elsewhere but were atypical in one important aspect: both men were, at least in part, radicalized within a large organization. Most militants in the UK – or for that matter France, Holland, Germany or elsewhere – had never been part of any other group but were 'self-starters'.

THE SELF-STARTERS

As security services in the UK began to make significant efforts to ana-lyse militants and their behaviour they informally grouped them into various categories.[58] There were the 'followers' – people who were vul-nerable to the right approach from the right person at the right moment, particularly if they were already partly radicalized by a particular event that made them question their identity or their own cultural back-ground for the first time. Then there were the 'seekers', those who actively went looking for people with authority, knowledge and the cru-cial contacts who could help them get to where they wanted to go and often used the internet if there was no other option. One example in 2006 was an eighteen-year-old school boy who became attracted to radical Islam – he was known as 'the terrorist' at school because of his frequent statements of support for terrorists and his avowed anti-Semitism – and then got in touch via the internet with a group of students at Bradford university who were themselves planning trips to training camps in Pakistan. He was arrested after his mother called the police after finding a suicide note, a library of extremist videos and a desktop icon that played a song about martyrdom on his computer.[59]

Another category, however, were the self-starters, the natural leaders, those who were motivated and active and wanted, through their own actions, to change things. Again, many such figures have featured in previous pages: Ali al-Bahlul, for example, the Yemeni who sought out bin Laden and became his media secretary; Abu Thar, who left his family to fight in Iraq was another; Al-Fakhet, the Tunisian-born Spanish immigrant who led the Madrid bombers, was a third; Mohammed Bouyeri, deeply involved in local community work and profoundly frustrated and bitter when his projects did not receive government funding, had the same profile. A classic 'self-starter' was Hanif Qadir, a successful British small businessman in his forties who became involved in radical activism in 2002 and who spoke to the author shortly after deciding to end his involvement. Never particularly bothered by politics previously, Qadir had, however, followed the typical path from practising the traditional Barelvi Islam of his Pakistani-born parents to the Saudi-style Salafi rigorous conservatism which had spread from Pakistan into many of Britain's Pakistani-origin communities in the 1990s.[60] As with so many others, the 9/11 attacks were critical in focusing his growing new political and religious consciousness. Qadir began fundraising 'for the jihad', as he described it, in 2002.[61] 'I had always been involved in charity work, in helping out in the community, in doing stuff, and for me it was just an extension of that,' he said. 'It was like stepping in to help someone out who is being beaten up. There was no question in my mind that I was on the right side. I watched the news, saw what was happening over there [in Afghanistan] and got going.' Qadir started off simply asking friends, relatives and clients for donations for 'the jihad'. He made little effort to hide what he was doing. The money was passed to an Afghan refugee in London, who sent it via Pakistan to be used to buy weapons and equipment for the Taliban. On one occasion Qadir's contact presented him with a letter that was said to come from Mullah Omar, the leader of the Taliban, thanking him for his support. 'I was blown away. I was on cloud nine. I saw what I was doing as my duty, as the only thing I could do in the circumstances, but that was a true reward,' Qadir said. 'The fact that I was funding people who were killing British soldiers did not bother me at all.' Finally, after raising tens of thousands of pounds to help others to fight, Qadir decided to see action himself. Using his fundraising contacts, he travelled to Pakistan and to Peshawar with the aim of joining the Taliban. There, after briefly being vetted, the London-based businessman was packed into a bus with dozens of other volunteers for the journey into Afghanistan. Qadir never reached the frontline. After seeing wounded men coming back from the fighting and experiencing the way local fighters treated the international volunteers as 'cannon fodder', Qadir turned back. Many others did not.[62]

OPERATION CREVICE

On October 22, 2003, a nineteen-year-old British student called Jawad Akbar was talking with an old school friend, a twenty-one-year-old college drop-out called Omar Khyam, at Akbar's small flat in a university hall of residence in Uxbridge, a nondescript commuter town west of London. The conversation was recorded by MI5 and subsequently produced as evidence in court. 'You're thinking airports, yeah, [but] what about easy stuff where you don't need no experience,' Akbar said. 'You could get a job like, for example, [in] the biggest nightclub in central London, where now no one can even turn around and say "Oh, they were innocent, those slags dancing around" . . . then you will really get the public talking . . . if you went for where every Tom, Dick and Harry goes on a Saturday night then that would be crazy.'

'If you got a job in a bar or club, say the Ministry of Sound,' said Khyam. 'What are you planning to do then?'

'Blow the whole thing up,' said Akbar. 'The best thing you can do is put terror in their hearts. There is no doubt, that is the best thing, there is nothing better than that.'[63]

The conversation could have been dismissed as youthful bravado were it not for the fact that the men had recently spent time in a training camp in Pakistan, at least one of the pair had met senior militants of al-Qaeda, and both were involved in the purchase of 600 kg of ingredients for rudimentary if powerful explosives less than a month after their talk about potential targets.[64] In April 2004, Akbar and Khyam were both arrested along with five other men aged between nineteen and thirty-five from south and west London and charged with being the ringleaders of the so-called 'Operation Crevice' plot, one of the biggest terrorist conspiracies uncovered in the UK in the years following 9/11. Named after the law-enforcement operation which foiled it, the plot involved a complex network of dozens of individuals, many of whom were dedicated to committing a string of violent attacks in the UK. Their trial revealed an enormous amount about the way those involved in the plot were drawn into violent extremism and how they changed from angry young men into potential mass murderers.

The five men eventually convicted for their roles in the plot were as representative as anyone else of the young men who were becoming radicalized in the UK at the time. Four were of Pakistani origin, either first- or second-generation immigrants, one was born in Algeria but raised in Britain. The average age of those in the group when they were sentenced was 28.4, almost the exact average of British militants.[65] The sprawling nature of the cell, with its multiple links and indistinct hierarchy, was also typical. A chart drawn of the links between the terrorists was an astonishingly complex maze of common connections – a far cry from the clear organogrammes traditionally used to depict the structure of militant groups and movements. In more general terms, 'Operation Crevice' also revealed the degree to which, even by 2003, Western Muslim populations had begun to produce violent radicals whose major drawback, much to the authorities' relief, was their glaring lack of technical skill and inexperience, not a lack of commitment.

Those involved had met each other at school or socially: through mutual friends, through relatives, at Luton mosque, at an Islamic fair at the University of East London or at religious discussion groups. These 'horizontal' patterns of recruitment have often featured in previous chapters – in the bombings in Madrid and Casablanca, to take just two examples. The backgrounds of the men were entirely familiar too. A couple came from broken homes. Some came from observant families, the others were raised in homes where the family Koran literally gathered dust on a shelf. Few were religiously observant as teenagers. None came from genuinely deprived backgrounds, most had got GCSEs or 'A' levels. Though at least one was an academic high-achiever, several were college drop-outs, and at least two could be described as disappointments to families with high aspirations. Some enjoyed sport, others preferred nightclubbing. The 'Crevice' plotters also showed evidence of profound identity issues, with surveillance tapes revealing them insulting Pakistan and 'Pakis' and referring appreciatively to 'the good old

British police' while simultaneously talking about blowing up a British Airways jet or a shopping centre. One of the defendants, the Algerian-born Anthony Garcia, had anglicized his real name, Rahman Benouis, to give it a 'better ring' in the modelling business where he hoped to make money, some of which he planned to use to finance 'the jihad'. None showed any evidence of mental illness. As with so many militants, none had anything but the most superficial knowledge of Islamic theology or, for that matter, of world politics.[66] The men were recorded arguing over whether Chad and the Sudan were Muslim-majority countries. They decided they were not. They are.

The paths taken to radicalization by the dozens of men involved in the Crevice plot had been typically varied too. For some, the process took years, for others just months. In some instances, videos – including one of attacks on Muslims in India and others of Taliban or Kashmiri fighters in action – played a key part. For others, the court heard, it was taped sermons by extremist clerics or television images of 'Muslims suffering' that had played an important role. At least two involved had had contact with an extremist breakaway faction of Hezb-ut-Tahrir. One senior policeman described them as 'a pretty fair broad cross-section of young British working-class Muslim males', adding that 'there was nothing particularly noteworthy about any of them'.[67]

The first stage of almost all the plots featured in the previous chapters had involved a loose group of individuals with a strong interest in becoming involved in jihad coalescing around an individual with a degree of authority and leadership capacity, a 'self-starter'. Khyam had credibility because in 2000 he had travelled to Pakistan to train in a militant camp in Kashmir and had made a second journey, this time into Afghanistan, a year later. By the time the group began coming together in Luton, Uxbridge and south-west London he had spent many years fundraising for fighters both in Kashmir and in Afghanistan and thus had connections and kudos. The next stage, once a group has formed, is the hardening of the bonds that bind together its members and the focusing of their resolve to act. Social workers in east London pointed out the parallels between local radical extremists and criminal or teenage gangs they saw on a daily basis.[68] The clusters the militants formed often showed the same structure as gangs, the social workers said, with a leader, his close circle, the one who does the finance, the 'one who makes them all laugh, the hangers-on who don't really know what to do or why they are there'. Then there are rituals and coded jargon. Ed Husain recalled how the first Islamist organization he had joined – the Young Muslim Organization based at the East London Mosque – had a reputation of being 'tougher than the toughest gangsters . . . They were as bad and cool as the other street gangs, just without the drugs, drinking and womanizing.'[69] The Crevice defendants spoke to each other of 'the cause' or 'the thing', meaning militant Islam, of Israel as 'Yahudi land', using the Arabic for Jews, and of non-believers as 'kuffs', short for *kufr*, or unbelief. They also revealed deep rivalry between different groups of militants, who referred to each other as 'crews', as do British gangs. Members of both gangs and militant Islamic organizations and groups referred to each other as 'brother' too. A fairly well-defined sartorial code became current for young 'Islamic militants', a mixture of military-style Western gear, Pakistani traditional clothing and 'streetwear'.[70] 'Jihad' had also become a relatively glamorous alternative lifestyle choice for some young men, symbolizing adventure, rebellion, clandestinity, and this was reflected in their 'jihadic chic'.[71] Several militants in this period indiscreetly boasted of their exploits to women they were seeking to impress, in one instance an undercover female police officer. Others recorded raps. But gangs, groups and even families need to be tightly bonded together and, as any army drill sergeant knows, the best way to develop solidarity is through shared pain, adventure, fear and fun.

SUMMER CAMP

Three months before the conversation about potential targets that had been recorded by MI5, a small minivan had pulled out from in front of the Avari hotel in the centre of the eastern Pakistani city of Lahore and headed off into the choking traffic. In it were all the key Crevice plotters – Omar Khyam, Jawad Akbar, Anthony Garcia – and a handful of others. Posing as tourists, they broke up the seventeen-hour drive into the mountains along Pakistan's frontier with Afghanistan with stops to photograph each other. Instead of heading into the rugged tribal areas south of Peshawar, where Osama bin Laden was hiding and where al-Qaeda fugitives had been able to set up makeshift training camps since fleeing Afghanistan just over eighteen months earlier, the group turned north as they approached the Afghan frontier, heading up into the picturesque Swat valley, a jumble of high valleys and pine forests which was then still a major tourist destination for wealthy Pakistanis and an area renowned for its natural beauty. Khyam had organized the trip after raising £3,500 through collections among sympathizers in the UK. Most of the money was to pay a local tribal leader and businessman to run a training camp for him and his band of friends. Khyam's aim was not to teach Akbar, Garcia and the others how to make bombs but to draw them together as a unit. The minivan dropped them at Kalam, a trekking and trout-fishing resort at the northern end of the valley.[72]

Kalam is surrounded by high mountains, difficult terrain where government authority is virtually non-existent. The only roads are dirt tracks. After resting in a cheap hotel, the group of Britons, equipped with only rudimentary hiking gear, set off towards the camp. It was tough going, and, unused to the exercise, the group went so slowly that they had to spend a night in the open. With the altitude and the heat, at least one collapsed. When they reached the camp, it was not quite what they had expected. 'I was thinking about something with ranges and assault courses, like I'd seen on TV,' one of the group said later. 'But it wasn't that at all.' Instead, the cash raised by Khyam had bought them two tents – one for the local men who ran the camp and the other for everyone else – and a field. The group had to dig a hole for their own latrine. The first day was spent doing physical exercises, then, on day two, the local men brought out some AK-47s, a light machine gun and a rocket launcher, and the young men, 'scared but excited' according to later testimony, took turns to fire the weapons. 'It was wicked,' one recalled. Eight days later, the men walked back down to the valley, drove back to Lahore and, apart from Khyam, who remained to continue practising his bomb-making skills in the back garden of a house in the city, flew back to the UK. Though makeshift, the camp was effective. Junaid Babar, one of the group, later told the FBI, 'After attending the camp . . . the guys were much more serious. [Before] they were joking around and using slang. After the camp the guys were talking jihad, praying and quoting the Koran. They would say, "One day of jihad is better than eighty days of praying." By the end of the camp they were saying, "Let's go kill the non-believer." '[73]

Such episodes were common to almost all plots in the UK at this time. Some went hiking in the Lake District, others went white-water canoeing. As one MI5 analyst commented: 'The moment when someone put himself

in danger for another member of the group or took on an additional burden, when he reached out of a canoe or picked up someone else's rucksack
to help them over the last few miles, was worth more than years of propaganda.'[74] But it was not just the new solidarity within a terrorist cell that
was important. It was also the way the group began to see others. Ed
Husain and Shiraz Maher, the two former members of Hezb-ut-Tahrir,
both described how they had been very quickly sucked into a world that
was entirely closed off from the rest of society. 'Almost all my social contacts were within the movement,' said Maher. For some, Husain said, the
group provided 'an entire existence': food, lodging, employment and company, even wives or husbands. This phase of 'isolation' appears to have
been critical. Hardline Islamic websites consulted by British militants in
this period were dominated by advice given to those asking about 'true
Muslim practice' in any given situation. Often the sites quoted the Koran
or senior clerics to reinforce the idea of a separation from society more
generally, a version of the *takfiri* ideology of al-Zarqawi and his fellow
international militants in Iraq. As the groups like the Crevice plotters
became more and more bound together the outside world and those who
lived in it retreated, merging as they did so into an undistinguishable mass
devoid of the characteristics that mark them as living, talking, walking,
feeling people. This process of 'dehumanizing' potential victims – an
integral part of all genocides or massacres over the decades – was key to
moving the group to the final stages of radicalization, where preparations
for executing acts of extreme violence began. So the end of the Crevice
plotters' summer training camp did not mean that Omar Khyam's work
was finished. The ten-day trip in the Pakistani mountains had been useful
to bind the group together, but there was more for its leader to do. A week
after the rest of the group had flown home, Khyam set off from his Lahore
base once again, this time to meet al-Qaeda.[75]

AL-QAEDA

Khyam had met senior al-Qaeda figures before. When he had arrived in
Pakistan in the spring of 2003, a few months before organizing the summer training camp, he had apparently hoped to join the Taliban to fight
against allied troops in Afghanistan. He was not, his lawyers said later,
planning attacks on the UK at that stage. However, when friends in

Lahore, part of the loose network of British militants linking Pakistan and the UK, put the twenty-one-year-old in touch with contacts in Pakistani extremist groups who themselves would lead him to the Taliban, his plans started to change. One of the 'British brothers' in Lahore had already established contact with Abdul Hadi al-Iraqi, al-Qaeda's 'number three' or 'director of external operations' at the time. Al-Iraqi's role was to do what bin Laden, al-Zawahiri and others had done in the late 1990s in Afghanistan: to receive the delegations from overseas coming to request logistical aid with a variety of projects as well as the young volunteers arriving in search of assistance or direction.[76] Despite the limited facilities available at the time – only the most makeshift of training camps could be set up, and many of the best instructors had been killed – the al-Qaeda senior leadership could still try to exploit the raw material that reached them. The primary attribute young Europeans had for the group was not their ardent if unfocused desire for 'action' in Afghanistan or any other theatre of jihad – a relatively mundane contribution to the cause – but their passports and lack of criminal records. These made them ideal candidates for much more valuable projects. When al-Iraqi met Khyam he apparently told the young Briton that, praiseworthy though his ambition to fight for the Taliban was, 'if he was serious', he should 'do something' back home.[77] This marked a turning point in the Crevice conspiracy. Rather than introduce Khyam to the Taliban, al-Iraqi arranged for him to spend a weekend in a house in the dusty western Pakistani town of Kohat learning more about bomb-making. The al-Qaeda militants' suggestion to strike at home had apparently fallen on fertile ground. One witness described how Khyam came back from the Kohat camp convinced that 'the UK should be hit because of its support for the US in Afghanistan and Iraq and because, [as] nothing has ever happened in the UK, the UK is unscathed'. Previously he had expressed the view that the coalition campaign in Afghanistan had been 'more or less' justified. Now his views had hardened considerably. 'Khyam said we need to do more, we should hit . . . pubs, trains and nightclubs,' the witness continued. '[Khyam said] targets in the UK are legitimate because British soldiers are killing Muslims and because military targets are too difficult to hit.'[78]

This was the critical contribution that, from the autumn of 2002 on, al-Qaeda was in a position to make. The hardcore leadership clustered around bin Laden in the zone along the Afghan–Pakistani frontier gave the volunteers who sought them out crucial direction, focusing their violent ambitions to fit in with the broader global strategy the al-Qaeda senior leadership were trying, not without some difficulty, to orchestrate. This was neither 'top-down' nor 'bottom-up' activism, neither vertical nor horizontal models of militancy. Instead it was hybrid, a mixture of both. Young men who had by themselves formed a group set on violence and who were convinced that they were to be soldiers in a global war in defence of Islam were taken a few vital steps further down that path by senior militants with prestige and authority. Men like Abdul Hadi al-Iraqi used a carefully honed message that exploited key elements in Islam – such as concepts of an enlightened and embattled elite, the idea of a world split into a domain of faith and peace and a domain of war and unbelief or a particular interpretation of jihad – to harden the resolve of the young volunteers. The 'who' and the 'why' were important in bringing them this far. The 'how' – the dynamics within the groups of extremists and the inputs from outside – was crucial in taking the next step.

There was another crucial dynamic at work. The recruits had come seeking to participate in the international jihad with their heads full of rhetoric about pan-Islamic solidarity. Their missions, however, were to be local, using their local knowledge, difference and cultural specificity as British or German or Belgian or other Muslims to successfully execute attacks that would take place at most a few hours' travelling from their homes or even where they were born. The global was fused with the local with devastating efficacy.

There were three other contributions – more practical – that al-Qaeda could make to a homegrown plot between 2002 and 2005. There was guidance on the nature of the strike: Khyam also apparently came back from that meeting saying that his instructions were to work towards 'multiple, simultaneous' attacks, an al-Qaeda hallmark.[79] There was technical assistance. And finally there was help in turning volunteers into the weapon so characteristic of the 9/11 Wars: suicide bombers.

THE MARTYRS

Personal accounts from successful suicide bombers that go beyond banal propaganda are rare – for obvious reasons. Statements by failed suicide bombers elsewhere – such as in Israel or Afghanistan – are often highly unreliable. However, they do exist, and suicide bombers who at the last minute decided not to blow themselves up interviewed by the author in Iraq, Afghanistan and Pakistan give some indication of the state of mind of individuals on the point of killing themselves and dozens of others. The process of radicalization that most described was typically gradual. In the case of the Iraqi it started with prayer meetings at a mosque and then moved deeper into radical militancy. It took many months before the young man, aged nineteen, began contemplating a suicide attack.[80] He was a 'follower' rather than a 'self-starter', deeply admiring of a more confident and more radical friend, and was susceptible to suggestion. 'Martyrdom operations' were introduced as an idea after many months of discussion and only raised seriously when the young man had made his way to a remote training camp far from his hometown. There, along with the physical exercise and small-arms training, he was exposed to hours of videos showing Muslims as victims of violence in Afghanistan, Iraq, Kashmir or elsewhere and to lectures from senior clerics on the rewards of martyrdom in the afterlife and the fame and glory such a sacrifice would attract. The friend said he would conduct a similar attack simultaneously. A critical element, the young man said, was that he was absolutely convinced that his action would be seen as praiseworthy by his family, his peers and the community as a whole. So much so, that when his mother located him and came to get him at the camp, he turned her away in tears. What was most important, he stressed, was the gradual way in which he had been led down the path towards 'martyrdom'. 'Each step logically seemed to follow from the next one,' he said. 'I ended up somewhere I had no intention to go without really knowing how I had got there.' He also, he added, did not want to let his friend down. The Pakistani interviewees described similar experiences. One had been recruited through 'friends', another through the militant organization that he belonged to. Both had then been isolated for long months and exposed to long hours of heavily slanted religious instruction interspersed with emotive videos before finally being judged ready to carry out their tasks.[81]

Before the actual attack, the young Iraqi spoke of being 'calm', of 'thinking about nothing', and of 'not wanting to fail' by refusing to go through with the bombing. The youngest of the Pakistanis, twenty-one at the time of the attack, spoke of a 'numbness' as he drove his heavily loaded truck towards its target listening to Koranic chants on the stereo.

He gave himself up when he saw there were no Americans at the checkpoint he was supposed to attack. The Iraqi only decided not to detonate his device when, in the seconds before he flicked the switch around his belt, he heard his potential victims talking with the accent of his hometown. In that instant, those he was about to kill became human once again, he said, and he could go no further and surrendered. Again, however, though many chose not to make the ultimate gesture and chose another path, others continued, right to the bitter end.

9

Bombs, Riots and Cartoons

7/7

At 8.24 on the morning of July 7, 2005, four men had said goodbye in front of the Boots chemist's shop at King's Cross station. They had huddled for a moment, hugged each other, and then, 'euphoric, as if they were celebrating something', had split up.[1] At 8.50 three set off simultaneous bombs, killing themselves and thirty-nine others, on the London Underground. At 9.27 the fourth, delayed by a defective battery on his bomb, had boarded a number 30 bus outside King's Cross station and taken a seat on the top deck. He sat there for twenty minutes as the bus edged its way through the chaotic London traffic, nervously fiddling with a rucksack at his feet.[2] Earlier he had called the phones of the three others, who he must have suspected were already dead, leaving the message 'I can't get on the Northern Line' and asking what he should do. It is unclear whether he meant that his resolve had failed – at the time of the call much of the Northern Line was in fact still open – or whether he was merely looking for last-minute instructions.[3] At 9.47, when the bus reached Tavistock Square, possibly because he mistook a traffic warden talking to the bus driver for a policeman, he set the fourth bomb off. It killed him and thirteen others and injured dozens more. The total dead in the 7/7 bombings eventually reached fifty-six, counting the bombers, with around 700 wounded. The four bombers were rapidly identified. They were: Mohammed Sidique Khan, a thirty-one-year-old former social worker who grew up in a suburb of the northern English city Leeds called Beeston; Shehzad Tanweer, also from Beeston, and the twenty-two-year-old son of a local businessman; Germaine Lindsay, a nineteen-year-old Jamaican-born convert raised by his mother in Huddersfield, another grim northern British town with deep social and economic problems and a large population of Pakistani immigrant origin;[4] and Hasib Hussain, the bomber on the bus, an eighteen-year-old from Leeds.

The respective journeys into violent radicalism of the four were, as ever, unique to each individual while nonetheless showing elements common to very many radicals in the UK, in the Middle East and elsewhere in areas affected by the 9/11 Wars. The route taken by Mohammed Sidique Khan, the 7/7 leader, showed almost all the factors that were explored in the previous chapter: he faced a variety of problems in his home town of Beeston, itself a community that was physically and culturally isolated from mainstream British social, political and economic life; the conservative, folksy Pakistani religious traditions of his parents were not, he felt, relevant to the present time; Khan had become alienated from his family when he refused a traditional arranged marriage, choosing instead a girl he had met and fallen in love with while studying at the vast Leeds Metropolitan University and turning to more modern and politicized Islamic ideologies at the same time.[5] However, Khan's biography reveals that many of the factors often cited as predictors of violent extremism are only at best indirectly responsible. Khan was not poor, and in no sense can poverty, relative or absolute, been seen as a motivation for his actions. Nor was he badly educated – he was a graduate – nor particularly well educated either – his business studies degree from a far from prestigious establishment was hardly a guarantee of a broad range of opportunities for a fulfilling and satisfying professional career.[6] Like so many other radicals too, Khan was a man of projects and action. A professional youth worker, he and other strongly religious individuals in Beeston had once formed a gang called the 'Mullah Boys', who took on drug dealers in their neighbourhood and forced addicts in the Pakistani community to go 'cold turkey'. He was thus in a good position to recruit others when the time came. One of the primary ways he did so was by offering to organize ceremonies for marriages that were outlawed by the traditional community. Married himself with a young child, he was a peer but a peer with standing and confidence.[7] He was very much a self-starter.

In the years after 9/11 – which he initially opposed as an unjustified attack on civilians – Khan had come to share the classic 'single-narrative' view of the world common to Islamic militants. In a video released after his death, he explained to the people of Britain that, just as their role in voting for governments who 'perpetuate atrocities against [his] people' made them 'directly responsible', he was 'directly responsible for protecting and avenging [his] Muslim brothers and sisters'.[8] The text, it was later realized, drew heavily on the published will of a young Briton killed at Tora Bora who came from a similar background to Khan.[9] Also in the video, in a section that was not broadcast by most mainstream media outlets, Khan criticized 'corrupt and incompetent' traditional Muslim clerics in Britain.[10] The tape, in a major innovation, had English-language subtitles which emphasized that its key audience was intended to be the UK, the USA and, to an extent, Europe.

As for the three younger men who joined Khan in his scheme to kill and maim hundreds in London, while their own backgrounds show once again the factors seen elsewhere, they equally demonstrate the sheer variety of paths into militancy. All four were young immigrants or the children of immigrants. Germaine Lindsay was a convert, an increasingly present subset of militants through the period. One came from a broken home, one was an under-achiever at school, two appear to have enjoyed happy and relatively stable backgrounds. Typically, too, they were not recruited in mosques but through personal contacts, people they happened to know or happened to meet. There was certainly little in the lives or characters of the 7/7 bombers that made them radically different from hundreds of thousands of young British or European men, Muslim or otherwise.

The four men followed the course of those involved in the Crevice plot, going whitewater rafting together to build solidarity, living in virtual isolation from the *kufr*, 'who they gradually came to see as less and less human'. Like Khyam, indeed probably with Khyam, Khan had travelled to the tribal areas of Pakistan to meet senior al-Qaeda figures who convinced him to launch attacks in the UK rather than fulfil his own ambition to fight alongside the Taliban.[11] The 7/7 plotters showed more professionalism than the Crevice group, however, making technically more complex devices and successfully hiding their preparations from the security services. On the morning of the attacks, they took a train from Luton station, where an image from a surveillance camera shows them walking through the ticket gates in jeans and jackets at 07.21 with the rucksacks containing their bombs, packed with nails, over their shoulders. Commuters on the 07.23 Luton to Brighton train, on which the bombers travelled to London, later described them as 'smiling, laughing and generally relaxed'.[12]

What is the significance of the 7/7 attacks in the 9/11 Wars? That the 7/7 attacks showed the polyvalence or multidimensionality so typical of the conflict was evident. They were the result of short-term factors such as the effects of the invasion of Iraq catalysing a whole range of broader trends which have frequently been seen in previous pages. As elsewhere too, the key question was how easily the ideology of contemporary international militancy would be grafted onto a pre-existing local situations of tension, if not open conflict. The project that al-Qaeda had proposed to Khan in the tribal areas of Pakistan had been another perfect example of thinking globally – i.e. in terms of a cosmic struggle between faiths, communities, good and evil – but acting locally. The 7/7 attacks also saw one of the defining tactics of the 9/11 Wars – suicide bombing – extended to an entirely new theatre. Finally, they, or at least their aftermath, provided another example of the politicization of intelligence and debate so characteristic of the conflict so far.[13] But the real significance of the 7/7 attacks was not the degree to which they were representative of the various established qualities of the 9/11 Wars but what they threatened for the future. Exactly two weeks after the bombings came another round of attempted attacks on London's public transport system. Though they were all young Muslim men, the profile of those responsible was different from that of the 7/7 attackers. They were first-generation immigrants of East African origin, most living marginal lives, poorly educated, inadequate, ill-equipped for making their way in London. Their leader, Muktar Said Ibrahim, was the twenty-seven-year-old Eritrean-born son of asylum-seekers with a police record for sexual assault and disorderly conduct. Ibrahim had swapped a life of petty crime for radical Islam while incarcerated in a young offenders institution and, a classic 'self-starter', actively sought out training and combat experience on his release. In December 2004, Special Branch officers stopped him at Heathrow and discovered thousands of pounds in cash, cold-weather camping gear, a military first-aid kit and a manual on ballistics in his baggage. Though he was questioned for three hours, Ibrahim had not committed any crime and was thus allowed to board a plane to Islamabad.[14] Ibrahim was in Pakistan at around the same time as Mohammed Sidique Khan and Omar Khyam of the Crevice plot and is thought to have received some training there. Indeed, it is possible all three trained together and that the '21/7 attacks' had been planned as a second wave by the al-Qaeda leadership themselves. However, whatever skills Ibrahim had learned were insufficient – another example of poor tradecraft among militants – and the bombs at three London Underground stations and on a bus all failed to explode. Nonetheless, the attempt created panic in the UK and provoked excited reactions from militant leaders and thinkers.

Taken together, the two attacks in London seemed to indicate that the strategy of Abu Musab al-Suri might be succeeding. Five years previously no one would have dreamed that a strike on the London Underground could be successful, let alone one followed up by a separate wave of attempted bombings. Now it appeared a fire had been lit in Western Europe that would be hard to extinguish. Al-Suri, whose name had been mentioned as a possible 'mastermind' of the London attack, posted a long statement on the internet immediately after the bombings in which he described how, 'when the attacks on the historic stronghold of oppression and darkness [London] took place', he had been among 'the hundreds of millions of Muslims who joyfully watched the events unfold'. Al-Suri denied any personal connection to the attacks and called 'upon the *mujahideen* in Europe . . . to act quickly and strike'. His strategy of provoking a global 'leaderless jihad' was bearing fruit, and victory, he clearly believed, was at hand. 'We are at the height of the war, and the enemy is on the verge of defeat, as many signs clearly indicate,' he boasted. 'Whoever stays asleep now might not be able to participate upon finally waking up.'[15] In the event, al-Suri's own participation was cut short not long after he posted his 'message to the British and the Europeans' when he was captured after a shoot-out with local security forces near the Pakistani city of Quetta.[16] But though al-Suri had been permanently removed from the scene – the Pakistanis had handed him over to the Americans by the end of 2005 – the fear that he had correctly read the broad strategic situation remained.

THE AFTERMATH

On the afternoon of the 7/7 attacks, in the perfect summer sunshine, Londoners stood in long queues for telephone boxes because their mobile phones had been rendered useless by the overloaded networks, sat on the grass in parks, drank on benches outside pubs, waited to go back to their homes. 'What do you feel about those who did this?' one television reporter asked a wounded survivor. 'Contempt. No anger. Just contempt,' he replied. Down below, in the shattered wreck of the three tube trains, rescue teams worked among the twisted metal, charred corpses and body parts. The attack, said Ken Livingstone, the mayor of London, was 'not . . . against the mighty and the powerful', not 'aimed at presidents or prime ministers' but at 'ordinary, working-class Londoners, black and white, Muslim and Christian, Hindu and Jew, young and old'. Livingstone, himself a controversial figure criticized for talking a soft line with Islamists and accused of anti-Semitism, had caught the mood of the city. One blogger posted that, whatever Londoners might think of the government's policy in Iraq or elsewhere, as a community they had their own ways of dealing with things, and these did not include blowing people up. Livingstone said that the strikes were not 'just an indiscriminate attempt at mass murder'. Their objectives were instead 'to divide Londoners . . . to turn Londoners against each other'.[17]

In fact, the exact objectives of the 7/7 bombers have never been made entirely clear. The videoed testaments broadcast after the attack revealed why, in their own minds, Khan and Tanweer felt such an act was necessary and justified but not what they hoped to achieve by it. Nor has the targeting of the strikes ever been satisfactorily explained – though the timing was probably determined by a desire to coincide with the summit of the G8 nations – Canada, France, Germany, Italy, Japan, Russia, UK and the US – in Scotland. No one knew where Hasib Hussain, the bus bomber, was actually meant to detonate his device. All that was obvious was that the three locations hit had no evident political, military or broader symbolic importance. It may be that they were determined simply by timing, and the three bombers had set out in different directions from King's Cross itself to blow themselves up at exactly the same moment wherever they might have been. It may be that to search for overt symbolism in the targets would be wrong. For many such attackers it is after all simply their violent suicide that, as a statement of will and faith, is as important as any direct consequence of an attack. One quality that did link the sites of the explosions was that each one was strongly representative of the cosmopolitan nature of the UK's capital city. Tanweer detonated his bomb at Aldgate East, the historic heart of successive waves of immigration to the city including, most recently, Pakistani and Bangladeshi communities. Khan detonated his device at

Edgware Road, centre of one of London's major Middle Eastern Arab communities, and King's Cross itself, as the casualty lists showed, is one of the most cosmopolitan places in one of the most cosmopolitan cities on the planet. In 2005, a third of Londoners had been born outside the UK, and some 300 languages were regularly spoken in the city.[18] Those who died in the explosions included Ojara Ikeagwu, Shahara Islam, Anat Rosenberg, Karolina Gluck, Ciaran Cassidy, Rachelle Chung For Yuen and Benedetta Ciaccia, who, from a distinguished Italian family, had come to London to work as an au pair ten years before and, engaged to a Muslim, was preparing for a wedding ceremony in Rome which would have united Catholic and Islamic rites.[19] Even the upmarket Tavistock Square, where Hasib had detonated his device, is a neighbourhood given a distinctly international character by high numbers of foreign students and tourists. Consciously or otherwise, it seems likely that, as Livingstone suspected, the 7/7 bombings were an attack on the ideas of integration and assimilation as much as anything else. The last thing the bombers would have seen before exploding their devices would have been a crowded tube train or a bus full of scores of people of all races, colours and creeds coexisting in relative harmony as they started another day.

In addition to the role and nature of al-Qaeda and the effects of the Iraq war, the 7/7 attacks thus naturally focused attention on the British model of multiculturalism. Much of the debate picked up on themes broached following the murder of Theo van Gogh in Amsterdam nine months previously. This time the debate took place in an extremely polarized environment that left very little room for reasonable commentary. It was perhaps inevitable that during a period of intense violence – or at least fear of intense violence – the debate was dominated by aggressive and extreme voices and characterized by an astonishing disregard for facts. This was the case on all sides. Iqbal Sacranie, the general secretary of the Muslim Council of Great Britain, repeatedly claimed that '95 to 98 per cent of those stopped and searched under new anti-terror laws are Muslims', though the true total was around 15 per cent.[20] Others compared the situation of Muslims in Europe to that of the Jews in pre-Holocaust Germany, an ugly and insulting exaggeration. Diatribes of extraordinary vitriol, many soaked in a primary anti-Americanism or sophomoric analyses of American imperialism, were directed at President Bush and Blair. Conspiracy theories were rife.

In France a book by a Marxist polemicist called Thierry Meyssan which argued that 9/11 was set up by the American 'military-industrial complex' was a bestseller. Similarly, in the UK such views were not simply restricted to the 45 per cent of the British Muslims who thought that 9/11 was a conspiracy between the USA and Israel but bled inexorably into the mainstream.[21] Even usually relatively sensible newspapers like the centre-left *Guardian* printed a 2,000-word comment piece by Michael Meacher, a former government environment minister, which suggested that the Bush administration had, at the very least, allowed 9/11 to happen so as to be able to execute a new strategy of global domination formulated by American conservatives in the late 1990s. The US were not seriously pursuing bin Laden as he was too useful a pretext for their plans to seize key strategic resources across half the Middle East, Meacher argued, and implied that the response to the hijacking of the planes that would go on to strike the Twin Towers had been deliberately slowed to allow them to reach their targets.[22]

There was no shortage of extreme voices on the right either. For conservatives, attacks on multiculturalism blurred with criticism of welfarism and the general moral decadence of the West. If many left-wing voices lapsed into uninformed rhetoric about 'the Americans', the right reverted to the most basic essentialist vision of a monolithic and unchanging Islam and a weak and emasculated Europe. For many of these commentators, Arabs and Muslims were conflated into a single body of civilizational enemies whose millennium-old war against the West was an historical fact rejected only by those who were at best naive and at worst criminally negligent collaborators. In Italy Oriana Fallaci's *The Rage and the Pride*, replete with descriptions of Muslim immigrants as 'terrorists, thieves, rapists. Ex-convicts, prostitutes, beggars. Drug-dealers, contagiously ill' and of 'Arab men' as 'disgusting to women of good taste' sold over 1.5 million copies.[23] The oldest stereotypes of the Turk, Mohammedan, Saracen and Muslim were recycled and, as was usual in a time of perceived threat, it was the most negative representations that prevailed. Other popular works on similar themes included Bruce Bawer's *While Europe Slept: How Radical Islam Is Destroying the West from Within*, Mark Steyn's *America Alone* and Melanie Phillips' *Londonistan*.[24]

Much of the argument of these books, particularly those from American authors, was based on the idea of Europe being 'flooded' by Islamic populations. This idea had already been proposed at various moments of ethnic tension since the mid-1960s but had been focused most recently on Europe's Muslim communities by right-wing politicians such as Holland's Fritz Bolkestein and the populist maverick Pim Fortuyn. 'Current trends allow only one conclusion: the USA will remain the only superpower. China is becoming an economic giant. Europe is being Islamicized,' Bolkestein said in Leiden in September 2004.[25] Bernard Lewis, the highly respected conservative American historian of the Ottoman Empire and the Arab world, breezily told one audience a month or so later that within a few decades Europe would 'be part of the Arabic west, of the Maghreb'.[26] For one columnist in the neo-conservative *Washington Times*, writing shortly after the 7/7 bombings, 'the threat of the radical Islamists taking over Europe is every bit as great to the United States as was the threat of the Nazis taking over Europe in the 1940s'. Europe, he wrote, would soon become pockmarked with 'little Fallujahs ... effectively ... impenetrable by anything much short of a U.S. Marine division'.[27] Nor was this kind of rhetoric limited to cranky or partisan publications. The prestigious *Foreign Affairs* spoke of 'distinctive, bitter and cohesive' European Muslims forming 'colonies' on the continent.[28] Charles Krauthammer wrote in *Time* of 'this civilizational struggle taking place in France'.[29] In the *New York Times*, Niall Ferguson, the conservative British historian, posed once more the great counterfactual questions asked by his Georgian predecessor Edward Gibbon: 'If the French had failed to defeat an invading Muslim army at the Battle of Poitiers in A.D. 732, would all of Western Europe have succumbed to Islam?' Back in 1788, Ferguson wrote, 'the idea could scarcely have seemed more fanciful ... Today, however, the idea seems somewhat less risible.'[30] Ferguson spoke of how 'a youthful Muslim society to the south and east of the Mediterranean is poised to colonize ... a senescent Europe'[31] and, along with conservative commentator Barbara Amiel, approvingly cited the Egyptian-born writer Bat Ye'or. Bat Ye'or's book *Eurabia: The Euro-Arab Axis*, published in 2005, had outlined an extraordinary conspiracy theory by which a secret organization known as 'The Euro-Arab Dialogue' at the heart of the European Union has 'engineered Europe's irreversible transformation through hidden channels' into 'a fundamentally anti-Christian, anti-Western and anti-Semitic ... cultural appendage of the Arab/Muslim world'.[32] That even the concept of 'Eurabia' could be taken seriously let alone seep into the mainstream conversation was a sign of the times. *The Economist* even devoted a cover story to exploring Bat Ye'or's propositions, though happily decided that her thesis was 'alarmist'.[33]

The al-Qaeda senior leadership, from the distant Pakistani tribal areas, exploited the febrile atmosphere as far as they could. The various communications released by al-Zawahiri and bin Laden at this time have a far more confident air than a year previously. Four weeks after the July 7 London bombing and two weeks after the so-called 21/7 abortive attacks that had followed them, al-Zawahiri, on a videotape broadcast on al-Jazeera, explained that the 'volcanoes of wrath' were the consequence of Britain rejecting an earlier offer of a truce from bin Laden that was conditional on the withdrawal of its troops from Iraq. 'Blair's policies will bring more destruction to Britons after the London explosions, God willing,' he promised.[34]

A RIOT OF MY OWN

Four months after the London bombings, a banal incident in the outer suburbs of Paris sparked rioting, predominantly involving French immigrants of 'Arab or African origin' and of nominally Muslim denomination, which continued for three weeks. The disturbances were of a violence and extent unprecedented in recent decades and seemed to support all the most alarming predictions of the conservative commentators, Ayman al-Zawahiri and Abu Musab al-Suri alike.

Late in the afternoon of October 27, 2005, three teenagers were coming home from a game of football in the run-down, overcrowded town of Clichy-sous-Bois, 10 miles north-east of Paris, when they heard police sirens and saw other youths running. Worried about being late home for the *iftar* dinner which breaks the fast of Ramadan and because they did not have their identity papers on them as French law requires, the teenagers ran too and then decided to hide. Scaling the gates of a local electricity transformer, they waited thirty minutes, hearing the voices of police officers, barking dogs and more sirens outside. In trying to climb back out, they received massive electric shocks. Two, fifteen-year-old Zyed Benna and seventeen-year-old Bouna Traoré, whose parents came from Tunisia and Mauritania respectively, were killed. The third, also

1. Bamiyan, Afghanistan. The Taliban's destruction of the ancient statues of Buddha in March 2001 was not simple fanaticism but a carefully judged act of spectacular violence designed to send a message to various local and international audiences and thus a sign of what was to come.

2. The folksy language and faith of George W. Bush connected with Middle America – whatever people thought overseas. The forty-third US president remained committed to a radical and ideological foreign policy throughout his time in office. In his memoirs, he said history would vindicate his decisions.

3. The key aim of Saudi Arabian-born Osama bin Laden was to radicalize the world's 1.2 billion Muslims and thus mobilize them to revive their faith and fight 'injustice', tyranny and the West. But his ideology – a selective mix of politics, religion and myth – showed little respect for local cultural differences or identities and eventually failed to attract mass support.

(*opposite*) 4. The ruins of the World Trade Center. Nearly 3,000 died in the September 11 attacks on New York and Washington. Rooted in a strategy of 'propaganda by deed', viewed by hundreds of millions of people, their significance would be defined as much by the reaction to the strategy as by the number of people it killed or the economic damage it caused.

5. The fighting at Tora Bora in eastern Afghanistan in December 2001 was less the last stand portrayed by Western media than a chaotic fighting retreat by international militants. With its lack of clear frontlines, blurring of civilians and soldiers and the conflicting agendas even of allies, it presaged much of the combat in the 9/11 Wars.

6. The aftermath of the Bali bombing. Through 2002, veterans of the al-Qaeda training camps in Afghanistan and existing militant networks around the Islamic world launched attacks from Morocco to Indonesia. Some strikes could be directly attributed to bin Laden or associates; others were the work of independent groups. The blasts in Bali killed more than 200 and were the bloodiest.

7. Anti-war march, London. The invasion of Iraq – at least without a specific United Nations resolution – was opposed by the vast majority of Europeans and many Americans too. It took the 9/11 Wars into new territory, bringing an extension and an intensification of the violence as well as sparking a wave of anger in the Muslim world not seen since the 1970s.

8. The Iraq War. The invasion campaign was supposed to last 100 days. In the end Saddam Hussein's detested and brutal regime collapsed much more quickly. But errors made in the spring and summer of 2003 – most rooted in a grave lack of preparedness and huge overconfidence – soon saw the situation in the country deteriorating very quickly.

9. The Iraq War. Heavy-handed coalition tactics, indiscriminate raids such as this one in search of an elusive enemy and deep ignorance of Iraqi society all helped fuel an insurgency. Within months, it was the fast-adapting networks of irregular Iraqi fighters that had seized the initiative from the slow-moving American army.

10. After the invasion, the Iraqi Shia population experienced a potent cultural revival. For young, unemployed, uneducated urban men, the attraction of populist revolutionary Islamism was strong. Here, followers of the young cleric Moqtada al-Sadr carry his picture and chant under a banner of his father-in-law and father, both murdered by Saddam Hussein's regime. Tens of thousands joined his al-Mahdi Army.

11. Murals on a Tehran street. The abuse of Iraqi prisoners by US soldiers at Abu Ghraib prison in western Baghdad revealed in March 2004 was cited by militants everywhere as a key in convincing them to participate in the 'jihad'. Though there was much abuse elsewhere, the image of a hooded prisoner threatened with a mock electrocution became an icon of the 9/11 Wars.

12. Jordanian-born Abu Musab al-Zarqawi was a former petty criminal and veteran militant who only reluctantly joined al-Qaeda in late 2004. A believer in seizing territory as a base for 'jihad', his taste for extreme and indiscriminate violence as well as his lack of respect for local Iraqi tribal leaders eventually alienated local and international supporters.

13. The aftermath of the Madrid train bombing. In March 2004 a series of bombs exploded on commuter trains in Madrid, Spain. Planted by a group of recent immigrants with no links to al-Qaeda who had been living in Spain for some time, it signalled the arrival of the 9/11 Wars in Europe and was a step towards 'home-grown' terrorism.

14. 7/7. On July 7, 2005, three suicide bombers exploded devices on tube trains and one on a bus in London. They had been born or had grown up in Britain. Key to the attack was the combination of the UK's links with Pakistan, where al-Qaeda had reconstituted a basic infrastructure, and the radicalization of some parts of the country's immigrant population.

seventeen, was badly injured but managed to call for help. For decades in the *cités* – as the vast complexes of public housing built around urban edges in the 1950s and 1960s are known in France – such incidents have been followed by riots. Usually disturbances follow a fairly well-worn pattern. Cars are burned, there may be some minor looting and arson and, though warm weather may prolong the fairly ritualized confrontation longer, everything is over after three days and two nights.[35] At first, it seemed like the riots – *émeutes* in French – sparked by the deaths of Benna and Traoré would follow the normal course. On the first weekend after the deaths a silent march was organized through Clichy-sous-Bois, and the following night was relatively calm. But then the rioting started again, shifting up a gear in intensity after a tear-gas canister fired by the police landed in the forecourt of a mosque in the town during prayers, and spread over subsequent nights across much of the Seine et Saint-Denis department, an area north-east of Paris with a population of nearly 1.5 million packed into 95 square miles. It then flared in Yvelines, 40 miles to the south-west, an area with broadly similar social and economic characteristics, and then spread out across much of the Ile de France region, home to around 15 to 20 million people and of course the economic, cultural and political centre of France. Soon hundreds of vehicles were being burned every night, and there were long and violent clashes with the police as well as attacks on public transport and firemen. The centre of Paris itself – with a largely wealthy population of 2 million – was almost untouched with a very small amount of violence in the relatively poor and mixed eighteenth, nineteenth and twentieth arrondissements in the north and east of the city. But as the rioting died away in the belt of *cités* around the capital it flared up elsewhere, starting during the night of November 3 and 4 in Lyon, in the western cities of Rouen and Rennes and in the northern former mining and steel towns along the Belgian border. The peak of the rioting came three days later, when 1,500 cars were burned in a single night in around 300 cities and towns.[36] For the first time in the contemporary history of France, a riot in one town had sparked similar events hundreds of miles away.[37] Only Marseille, where one in four of the population was born outside France and which has a huge Muslim population living in vast expanses of tough public housing projects, remained calm. No one appeared entirely certain why.

The *émeutes* provoked two totally different debates inside France and overseas. Domestically, the argument was about whether or not the rioters were '70 to 80 per cent' hardened criminals fomenting trouble the better to protect the 'no go areas' which they needed to continue their cocaine and cannabis businesses as Nicolas Sarkozy, the then minister of the interior, claimed.[38] The row continued for a week or two but died down when Sarkozy modified his language as it became clear that his denigration of the rioters as criminals had an immediate inflammatory effect and after judges told the press that in fact the vast majority of those the police brought before them were first offenders.[39] In fact, later detailed studies revealed a complex picture of three types of rioters: a hardcore with criminal records (though not for serious offences) who took the initiative, then a larger number of youths mainly without records who refrained from active involvement in the more spectacular criminal acts such as arson but did join in when it came to attacking the police, and a third group, by far the most numerous, who simply enjoyed 'le spectacle', running when the police charged, taunting them from afar but not actually engaging in any confrontation or destructive acts.[40]

Outside the country, the debate was framed very differently. It revolved, fairly predictably given the febrile atmosphere at the time, around religion. That it was France that appeared to have a problem with its Muslim minority – the largest such minority in Europe – provoked an extraordinary outpouring of bile from right-wing commentators who immediately linked the rioting with French opposition to war in Iraq, theorizing that France had tried to block the conflict to avoid angering its Muslim minority. Thrown into the mix was further criticism of French welfarism, which was now seen as a way of buying off a truculent and violent Muslim population, and a series of reheated and long-established stereotypes of French decadence, double-dealing, laziness and lack of virility. The end result was a perfect morality fable of the 'cheese-eating surrender monkeys' facing at home the very threat against which they had actively impeded the Americans fighting abroad.[41] That the riots were indeed 'Islamic' in origin and nature was taken as a given. That they were part of a broader uprising or potential rebellion by Europe's Muslim population was apparently evident. 'What we are seeing is, in effect, a French intifada: an uprising by French Muslims against the state,' said Melanie Phillips in the Daily Mail.[42] 'The Eurabian civil war appears to have started some years ahead of schedule,' Mark Steyn told readers of the *Chicago Sun Times*.[43] Some terrorism experts even argued that the rioting was 'jihad' by other means.[44]

One reason for the violence of the reaction to the *émeutes* overseas was the very real and important question they posed. If the French riots of November 2005 had indeed been motivated by radical Islamic ideologies, organized by extremists or justified by an appeal to a global Islamic identity, they would have indicated not just that al-Qaeda had succeeded in mobilizing and radicalizing an entirely new population in the heart of Europe far beyond its usual constituency but equally that the ideas and the violence that the group had set out to popularize more than fifteen years previously were no longer restricted to an extremist fringe prepared to use terrorist violence but had for the first time sparked a genuine popular mass uprising. This would have taken the 9/11 Wars into entirely new territory and marked a critical turning for the worst. Previously the conflict had not seen the emergence of a single genuinely popular Islamist movement or at least not one that involved more than a fraction of a nation's population. Even the Sunni militancy in Iraq had comprised a minority of a minority. The followers of Muqtada al-Sadr were a few hundred thousand strong at best. Jemaa Islamiyya in Indonesia was minuscule compared to the major local Islamist parties. Even Pakistani extremists, despite their visibility, were still small in number, though their social roots ran deep. The same went for Morocco and Turkey, where those who had been responsible for bomb attacks, even if they had benefited from the tacit support of many, were still shunned even by mainstream Islamist parties. The Madrid bombings had been perpetrated by a dozen or so individuals linked to networks which, at an absolute maximum, had a membership in the low hundreds. In none of these societies, nor in any other, had the increased political consciousness, popular anger, ambient anti-Americanism, radicalism and mobilization of the late 1990s and the years since 2001 yet been translated into a mass popular movement. Only in the specific circumstances of the Lebanon and the Gaza Strip did groups such as Hezbollah and Hamas – both bitter enemies of al-Qaeda – have a mass following. But if tens if not hundreds of thousands of young Frenchmen – and most of the rioters were indeed born in France – were now taking to the streets, then that signalled an intensification and aggravation of violence which went well beyond anything seen before. This would mean that mobilizing

European Muslim populations had been relatively easy for al-Qaeda and that, instead of offering resistance to its expansion to the Atlantic or beyond, Europe's 20 million Muslims would have acted to accelerate the process of the broadening and deepening the conflict. And if it happened in France, it could happen in Germany, the UK, Holland and eventually, despite the differences in background and socio-economic achievement of American Muslims, even in the USA. If this was indeed occurring, as al-Suri, the al-Qaeda senior leadership and the right-wing commentators apparently all believed, then the Madrid attacks, 7/7, even 9/11 would be rapidly forgotten in a civil war of appalling violence which would tear apart half the planet. Pinpointing the exact reasons for the rioting in France in November 2005 and the real motivations of those involved, obscured beneath the layers of heated rhetoric at the time, was thus critical.

The first clues as to how the immediate and most worrying reading of the *émeutes* might not have been entirely justified were clear, as is so often the case, to anyone who witnessed them at first hand. Firstly, there was little in the 'uprising of Europe's Muslims' which actually indicated that the disturbances were in any way more 'religious' than any other that Europe had seen over previous decades. In three weeks of reporting the rioting, the author heard no slogans, saw no graffiti and read no demands that were in any way related to faith. The firing of a tear-gas canister into a mosque in Clichy-sous-Bois may – though this is disputed – have led to shouts of 'Allahu akbar' (God is great), but otherwise there was nothing. In all the ground reporting of the riots, by foreign or French journalists, religious imagery, vocabulary or ideas had a negligible presence. References to Iraq or Palestine or any expression indicating that the rioters were acting or saw themselves as acting out of some kind of solidarity with Muslims elsewhere in the world were extremely rare – though one *émeutier* did confess to wanting to create 'a bit of Baghdad'.[45] Rioters mentioned a range of grievances when interviewed, but these were almost all restricted to immediate issues touching their daily lives, particularly alleged racial discrimination. All displayed a profound animosity towards the French state and its various manifestations. The most dominant theme was that hardy perennial of urban violence: Fuck the police, *nique la police*.[46] A large proportion were still in school, which may in part explain why the primary targets of arson and vandalism were educational establishments which were, with the police, the strongest state presence in their lives. 'Me, what I wanted to do during the rioting was burn the high school, because they are the ones that fucked my future,' said one nineteen-year-old small-time cannabis dealer.

What was also notable by its absence from the *émeutes* was anti-Semitic violence.[47] Anti-Semitism in immigrant communities in France was undoubtedly a serious and growing problem. Until 2004 the spikes in anti-Semitic violence had largely come at times of increased tension in Israel-Palestine and the Middle East more broadly, such as during the Second Intifada of October 2000, the 'battle of Jenin' in the West Bank in April 2002 and during the 2003 invasion of Iraq. However, from 2004 the correlation had broken down as what appeared to be a structurally greater level of anti-Semitic violence became the norm.[48] In 2004, nearly 1,000 attacks on French Jews took place, with, as previously mentioned, the proportion of the perpetrators from 'Muslim' immigrant communities much larger than previously seen. The total number of attacks dropped significantly the following year but remained high.[49] The abduction, torture and murder of a young Jewish salesman, targeted by a gang of young immigrants of mixed backgrounds led by a self-confessed 'Salafist', in January 2006, was thus part of a broad trend.[50] However, alarming though these tendencies undoubtedly were, there was no suggestion that Jewish or Israeli targets were targeted in France during the *émeutes*. Indeed, all religious sites were largely ignored. The targets of the rioters, like their language, were non-sectarian.

A second element of importance was the identity, in both senses of the word, of the rioters. Not all the rioters were 'Muslims', however defined.[51] A number were of non-immigrant background or, as their Spanish, Italian or Portuguese names indicated, from earlier waves of immigration. A larger number were relatively recent arrivals from sub-Saharan African countries, especially the Democratic Republic of the Congo, Cameroon, Equatorial Guinea and Cape Verde. These largely non-Muslim populations were among the most active in the riots according to later studies.[52] One acquaintance of the author was typical: a twenty-seven-year-old aspirant rapper from the twentieth arrondissement of Paris whose Congolese parents worked double shifts as cleaners to support four children and went to church every Sunday. Certainly French authorities did not frame the troubles in a religious narrative. According to a leaked confidential report by the Direction

Centrale of the Renseignements Généraux, the intelligence service of the French police, the *émeutes* were 'a form of unorganized urban insurrection', a 'popular revolt of the *cités*, without leaders or demands' led by youths 'full of a sense of identity based not only on their ethnic or geographic origin but on the condition of social exclusion from French society'.[53]

That identity was in fact the opposite of the globalized Islamic one, being extremely local. French expert Olivier Roy later referred to it as 'le nationalisme du quartier' (neighbourhood nationalism). Others spoke of the ambivalent relationship of pride and resentment rioters displayed for where they lived.[54] Rioters talked of their 'shitty neighbourhoods' all the while boasting how they had vied with other nearby housing projects for the highest number of cars burned – even though the cars belonged to their neighbours. 'I just wanted to get on the evening news like them in Montfermeil,' said Rabat Sifaoui, fifteen, mentioning a well-known *cité* 7 miles away from his home on the fifth floor of a rundown block in Bobigny. One rioter from the rough northern part of the town of Aulnay-sous-Bois spoke of how seeing the slightly less rough eastern part on TV had motivated him and his friends to go out on the streets to defend their own neighbourhood's long-established reputation for confronting the forces of order.[55] As ever, even this local identity had multiple layers. At the most specific or particular it was based on individual housing estates. When asked where they 'came from', most rioters named the projects – 'Cité des 4000' at La Courneuve; 'La Madeleine' at Evreux; 'Val Fourré' at Mantes-la-Jolie; 'Les Minguettes' at Vénissieux, near Lyon – where they lived. At its most general level the young rioters' identity was merely that of coming from a département. The most infamous of these was Seine et Saint-Denis, which was known colloquially by its number, ninety-three, though given as 'Neuf Trois', not *quatre-vingt-treize*, as it should be in correct French. 'Neuf Trois' was known throughout France for being the toughest of all departments and thus had a name to live up to. 'When I say us, I mean the kids from round here, from Aulnay, from Neuf Trois,' twenty-two-year-old Mehdi in Aulnay-sous-Bois told one interviewer.[56] There was no evidence of any broader national, international, ethnic or religious identities. There was no tension between the global and the local as so often seen elsewhere in the 9/11 Wars for the simple reason that the global was not present.

Another problem for the 'Intifada' thesis of either al-Suri or the right-wing commentators was that no Islamists, al-Qaeda-type militants or members of France's community of rigorous Islamic conservatives from quietist traditions were involved in the violence. This was despite a substantial population of all three. Islamic militant violence in France, with a few specificities of its own such as a tradition of cooperation between armed robbers and Islamic militants and the origins of its Muslim immigrant populations largely in the Maghreb rather than south Asia, had its roots in the same causes and catalysts as did violence in the UK.[57] Though French radicals lacked the ease of access to Pakistan and thus to the al-Qaeda senior leadership that their British counterparts enjoyed, patterns of radicalization in France had been broadly the same as across the Channel with, at least in the 2001–5 period, recruits drawn from the same social strata of the marginally better-off, better-educated, relatively well-integrated working classes. There was also the same pattern of family tensions and generational difficulties and recruitment by peers, brothers and friends rather than older clerics. This occurred, as in the UK, around rather than in mosques or in Islamic centres, in homes and in prison, where in some French institutions upwards of 60 per cent of detainees were self-declared Muslims, even if few were particularly observant.[58] The same processes of the evolution and radicalization of cells were also evident: the outward-bound trips, the bonding sessions, the same role for images – especially of the abuse in Abu Ghraib – and the internet.[59] At least four Frenchmen had died in or around Falluja in 2004, and several dozen others were said to have travelled to Iraq.[60] One issue that concerned French security agencies, as it did their British counterparts, was the constant flow of young men to Riyadh, Cairo or radical religious schools in Pakistan for instruction in extremely conservative if pacific broadly 'Salafi' strands of Islam. Significant subsidies from the Saudi government facilitated the trips and between 2004 and 2005 around 250 travelled, not enough to be a mass phenomenon, as one French intelligence officer commented, but enough to be worrying.[61]

Salafi movements such as the Jamaat Tabligh, a vast network dedicated to preaching and good works that professes to shun violence, had recruited tens of thousands from all walks of life in France as in the UK. French intelligence services had been watching such groups as well as freelance preachers often sponsored by Gulf-based religious organizations for many years. But, instead of causing trouble themselves during the *émeutes*, senior French Salafis suspected of involvement in militant activities were heard by eavesdropping security operatives complaining that the rioting caused problems for their recruiting by attracting unwelcome police attention. The neighbourhoods where the Salafis (both those suspected of involvement in radicalism and those known to be law-abiding) had the most influence remained quiet.[62] Of the 3,000 rioters arrested in the Paris region, not one was previously known to the French security services. Instead surveillance revealed genuine violent extremists going to ground, suspending efforts to send new volunteers to Iraq or leaving areas for fear of major security operations.[63] There was certainly no evidence of any involvement by anyone associated with al-Qaeda in the rioting. Nor was there any surge in recruitment to radical Muslim groups or networks either, security agencies found.[64] Instead, the weeks after the *émeutes*, due to a high-profile campaign led by figures respected locally such as the rapper Joey Starr, saw a significant surge in registrations to vote in the forthcoming 2007 presidential elections in the *cités*.[65]

Finally, and more fundamentally, describing the revolt as 'Muslim' or by Muslims was misleading because it reduced the nature of religious identity to a 'one size fits all' that took no account of the range of what it meant to be 'Muslim' in France – or elsewhere for that matter – in the autumn 2005. This went beyond a simple challenge of describing the vast diversity of the Muslim community – Arab, non-Arab, black African, practising, non-practising, 'cultural Muslims', 'street Muslims', theological Muslims, political Muslims and so on – and to the heart of a difficult problem of terminology that caused grave problems for all discussions of the issue at the time. Identity is not only multiple – age, educational background, marital status, gender, life course, ethnic or geographic origin, interests, profession, aspirations, tastes – all furnishing a potential identity or elements of an identity but profoundly dynamic as well. 'I am French one day, of "Algerian origin" the next, a Muslim the third,' one demonstrator protesting the lack of public recognition of the deaths of scores of Algerians in Paris at the hands of French police in the 1960s told the author in late 2005. 'It depends who I am talking to.'[66] The particular element that is dominant at any one time depends on the situation and, crucially, the interlocutor. Identity is thus a conversation, a dialectic and never static. Defining the *émeutes* as 'Muslim revolts' was not only factually misleading and counterproductive but hindered a balanced, more nuanced and more accurate analysis. This is not to say that religion does not play a role in the *banlieues* – often a troubled one – and is not sometimes deeply important to young men like those who rioted in France in November 2005, but it was not the reason that they went out and threw stones and petrol bombs at policemen. So what were the reasons?

The *cités* where the rioters lived and where the riots took place were – if not true ghettos – a 'ghetto phenomenon' with a rare combination of severe social and economic problems.[67] Many were extremely physically isolated, built on the edges of cities with little public transport where the heavy industry that had once required their presence was long gone. Around Paris, the *cités* were separated from the twenty arrondissements of the city itself by a strong symbolic and administrative frontier that ran along the line once traced by the nineteenth-century city defences that was now the route of the six-lane orbital highway known as *le périphérique*.[68] The physical environment of the *cités* was often severely degraded. In the famous Neuf Trois – the département of Seine et Saint-Denis – over a third of the population were foreign-born and 18 per cent lived below the poverty line.[69] Nearly 20 per cent had no hot water, and a quarter of housing units had no indoor shower or bathroom.[70] Then there was unemployment – rising through the 1990s to reach levels of over 40 per cent for young unqualified men nationally.[71] Jobs that were available were often of extremely low quality, partly due to some genuine discrimination based on colour, name or religion, but also partly due to the strong negative image associated with the *banlieusard*, an image which the subject consciously or unconsciously reinforced through immediately recognizable speech patterns, clothing and so on. Often the perceived deficiencies in social skills, language competence and so forth were real. Schools were under-funded and staffed by often young teachers ill equipped to deal with the range of social problems with which they were confronted.[72] Two in five male pupils from north African backgrounds left school without any qualification at all.[73]

Though such areas were far from being zones of '*non-droit*' or 'no-go areas', as so often claimed, they were places where the presence and authority of the République Française was undoubtedly contested and weak. A report by domestic intelligence services a year before the *émeutes* spoke of hundreds of 'sensitive neighbourhoods' where 'populations conserve cultural traditions and ways of life and parallel institutions for social regulation and conflict'.[74] Political representation was almost non-existent. There were no Muslim members of parliament, very few of first-generation immigrant origin and a minimal representation in mainstream parties. The Communist Party's hold on the working-class population of towns in the north, the east or the Paris region had disappeared along with the heavy industry, and the weak French Socialists, whose senior and middle ranks showed even less ethnic and religious diversity than their right-wing opponents, had no real support among a largely depoliticized immigrant population. The main presence of the state in the *cités* was a police force whose philosophy of law enforcement has always favoured the coercive over the consensual and was heavily resistant to ideas of community or neighbourhood policing.[75] Policing of the *cités* was thus extremely confrontational, with almost exclusively white officers in riot gear patrolling or mounting raids from heavily protected individual bases. None of the local police were from the places they patrolled, and banter with local youth was limited and often abusive.[76]

Along with the political and the physical exclusion went cultural exclusion. The vision of France promoted by the elite internally and largely accepted externally is of a country of fine wine, good cheeses, *saucisson*, stunning mountains, the beaches of St Tropez, an immensely rich literary and intellectual heritage, fashion, elegance and history. Little of any of this is to be found in the *cités*. Faiza Guène, a young and popular author from a *cité* on the northern rim of Paris, explained how the France in which she had grown up was very different. Her mother, born in Morocco, had only ever seen the Eiffel Tower once and would not normally have been able to afford her own daughter's highly successful, ironic book on life in the *banlieues*, she said. The French Republic – one, indivisible and secular according to the constitution – accepted new arrivals often with a singular generosity but on its own terms. One reason for the success of Guène's book, *Kiffe Kiffe Demain*, was an ending in which republican France triumphed, largely resolving the problems faced by the characters in the *cité* as they accepted its values, myths and institutions.[77] Anis Bouabsa, a baker in Paris' twentieth arrondissement appointed to supply the daily bread for the president's table, was also seen as an example of successful integration. But Bouabsa, whose parents had been born in Tunisia, had earned the contract by being more classically French than any Frenchman, winning an award for Paris' finest baguette.[78] Chefs of Moroccan cuisine, though their dishes were enormously popular, did not win any of the myriad prizes for *gastronomie* awarded every year. One problem was the very high goals the French Republic set for itself. More often than sometimes thought overseas, the system did assure a measure of *liberté*, some *égalité* and, to a lesser extent, *fraternité*. But not in Aulnay, Clichy, Sevran, La Courneuve and so on.[79] The *émeutes* saw non-sectarian political violence involving a ritualized and low-casualty confrontation with the forces of order which was in fact one of the few quintessentially French activities, generally accepted and approved of, in which the young men who comprised the rioters could actually participate.[80] The riots were a demand for more integration, not a rejection of integration.

Within weeks of the riots, the profile of the *émeutier* was thus fairly clear. He was a minority of a minority of a minority. Aged between twelve and twenty-five, a first- or second-generation immigrant, interested more in Air Max and 'le polo Lacoste' or mobile phones than religion or politics, bored, alienated, resentful, full of complex identity issues, desperate to 'get on TV' to get some attention, however fleeting. If asked, he might have called himself a Muslim, though not in the sense meant either by conservative commentators or by Abu Musab al-Suri. Within days of the end of the violence, the people who had rioted could be seen again, either in their neighbourhoods or in specific favoured zones within Paris such as the shopping mall at the Gare du Nord or Les Halles, chatting up girls, comparing phones, arguing with the police. Such young men were a problem certainly, potentially a very serious one. But they were not part of a global radical Islamic militant network. If European Muslims were on the brink of an uprising, it had still to come.

THE CARTOONS

Hardly had the French *émeutes* died away, however, when a new confrontation blew up, international rather than local this time, which again, not least through the striking images it generated, forced all the same issues raised by the rioting back on to the front pages of the world's newspapers and into the lead of global television bulletins.

Its origin lay in the publication by a little-known Danish newspaper,

Jyllands-Posten, of some not particularly amusing cartoons of the Prophet Mohammed. One showed him with a bomb tucked in a fold of his turban; in another he was greeting suicide bombers in heaven, saying, 'Stop, Stop! We have run out of virgins!' An accompanying text, written by the newspaper's forty-six-year-old culture editor, Flemming Rose, shortly before the crucial pages went to press explained: 'Some Muslims reject modern, secular society. They demand a special position, insisting on special consideration of their own religious feelings. It is incompatible with secular democracy and freedom of expression, where one has to be ready to put up with scorn, mockery and ridicule.' The cartoons were published on September 30, 2005. The 'crisis' they caused occurred almost five months later. The intervening months had been filled by the concerted efforts of individual clerics seeking personal advancement and of states to manufacture a confrontation.

The cartoons crisis had its origin in a story reported in Denmark about the difficulties faced by an author who wanted to find an illustrator for his children's book on the life of the Prophet Mohammed which had struck editors at *Jyllands-Posten*. The author concerned had found that potential illustrators systematically refused the commission, and the only one who accepted insisted on anonymity. The story tied in with a series of other incidents in Denmark, Sweden and elsewhere in Europe which appeared to reveal a widespread trend of artists, museum directors or creators avoiding controversial subjects or withdrawing works from exhibition to pre-empt any threat of violence from Muslim extremists. Searching for a way to follow up the story with empirical evidence that such self-censorship was widespread, the *Jyllands-Posten* editors hit upon the idea of asking several dozen Danish cartoonists to send in images depicting the Prophet 'as they saw him' for publication to see how many would accept. A dozen did so, and their work was published. Several of the images mocked the *Jyllands-Posten* itself. These, however, were ignored in the controversy that was to follow, and it was the three depicting Mohammed negatively that were to receive all the attention. 'It never occurred to me that there could be a problem. We were not focused on Muslim reaction but on the problem of self-censorship within the artistic community in Denmark,' Rose recalled.[81] Two of the cartoons' authors were to receive anonymous death threats within a fortnight.

The initial public reaction to the publication of the cartoons had been muted, though editors at the *Jyllands-Posten* were aware that they had created a stir. On the day the cartoons came out, Rose received a telephone call from an irate vendor in Copenhagen who said he would never sell the newspaper again. But there was little anger expressed publicly, and journalists of the *Jyllands-Posten* were forced eventually to contact a number of local clerics for their response to the cartoons to get a follow-up story.[82] Among them was a former mechanical engineer turned cleric called Ahmad Abu Laban, who had come to Denmark in 1984 after being expelled from Egypt and the United Arab Emirates. He had already become something of a 'rent-a-quote' for Danish journalists, having called bin Laden a 'businessman and freedom fighter'. Once alerted to the cartoons' publication, Laban saw a clear opportunity to boost his profile and garner support, donations and influence. Hitherto, the group of Islamists he led had numbered only a few thousand despite inflated claims of a much greater strength.[83] Abu Laban and other Muslim religious leaders in Denmark therefore called loudly for the *Jyllands-Posten* to make an apology and, when none was forthcoming, organized a demonstration in Copenhagen that was attended by between 3,000 and 5,000 people. There was some further local anger when the Danish government refused to intervene.[84] Then the affair appeared to die away. Even when the cartoons were reprinted in an Egyptian newspaper alongside an incendiary editorial, no one took to the streets either in the Middle East or in Europe. There the matter might have rested.

Abu Laban did not give up, however. He and a group of other Danish clerics put together a dossier including the cartoons published by the *Jyllands-Posten*, three far more offensive images of Mohammed from an unidentified source, clippings and hate-mail allegedly sent to Muslims in Denmark and travelled to the meeting of the Organization of the Islamic Conference (OIC) that was being held in Mecca. The clerics then passed around their file, calling for action. With no alternative, the OIC issued a condemnation and demanded United Nations action against Denmark. Still not satisfied, a new delegation of Danish clerics then set off around Middle Eastern capitals, presenting their dossier to religious and political leaders, claiming, as they had done before, that all the cartoons it contained had been published repeatedly in the Western press. On January 10, 2006, a Christian publication in Norway reprinted the three original images, allowing the clerics to claim a concerted campaign in the West to slight Islam. With this new publication, Abu Laban and his associates began finally to make some progress. Saudi Arabia recalled its ambassador from Denmark and declared a consumer boycott. On January 30, the Danish prime minister and the *Jyllands-Posten* tried to defuse the growing row by expressing their regret at any offence caused to Muslims. Their carefully worded semi-apology – 'we learned that in Arabic "regret" isn't very easily understood, so we made a semantic change, but nothing changed in substance because we could not apologize for something we did not believe was wrong,' said Rose – triggered a backlash in Europe, and a number of newspapers in France, Spain, Germany, Holland and Italy republished the images.[85] The cycle of escalation soon developed a momentum of its own, helped by reporting of the story in the Middle East in particular that was often inflammatory and inaccurate.

Within a few days, there were riots in Pakistan, Afghanistan, Lebanon, Syria, Libya, Nigeria and elsewhere. In the West, the row was once more cited as evidence of a clash of civilizations and an augur of violence on the streets of Europe. In the Muslim world, it was seen as further proof that a belligerent and aggressive West was incapable of 'respecting' Islamic faith and culture. Once more, however, there were deeper forces at work. A close look at the demonstrations organized around the world and at the origins of the more inflammatory statements that fuelled the cycle of escalation reveals that those hurling stones, burning flags and chanting slogans may have been less representative of entire communities than they might have looked at the time. For, as had been the case during the Rushdie affair seventeen years before, different Middle Eastern governments, religious leaders and movements all sought to exploit events, seeking to outdo each other in indignation and to use the opportunity offered by the crisis to reinforce their otherwise often shaky religious credentials. After the local Danish clerics, it was the turn of the major international religious figures. Following relatively moderate early statements, the immensely influential Egyptian university of al-Azhar issued a statement signed by its Grand Sheikh, Mohammed Tantawi, which said the cartoons showed 'contempt [for] the religious beliefs of more than one billion Muslims around the world'. Yusuf al-Qaradawi, the conservative Islamist scholar who had tried to dissuade the Taliban from destroying the Buddhas almost exactly five years earlier and who had a following of tens of millions, used his programme on al-Jazeera to call for secular rulers to keep on stoking 'the awakening of the Muslim nation' after various rivals used their own broadcasts to voice more extreme statements.[86] Clerics in Saudi Arabia, particularly aware of the importance of not letting the government take the lead in the campaign against the cartoons, told their congregations to 'rise up ... grab swords ... they have trampled on the Prophet'.[87]

If there was competition between clerics, it was nothing in comparison to that between states. The Rushdie affair had been played out in a context of vicious rivalry between Saudi Arabia and Iran for the symbolic leadership of Islam. Nearly twenty years later, that rivalry still existed along, of course, with many others. Few states in the Middle East or further afield could allow themselves to be seen as soft on those who insulted the Prophet. In Syria, where any unauthorized political demonstration would have faced violent repression, 'spontaneous' crowds sacked the Danish and Norwegian embassies in Damascus. Denmark's embassy in Tehran was attacked by another 'spontaneous' crowd hours after the Iranian government announced a suspension of trade links with Denmark. Kuwait and Egypt organized a consumer boycott and allowed demonstrations of a violence that would normally have brought a crushing police response. In the Palestinian Occupied Territories elements of the more secular Fatah, fresh from a heavy defeat in elections in January 2006, made statements far more inflammatory than those of their victorious electoral opponents, the Islamists of Hamas.[88] In Lebanon, as ever, a more complicated agenda fuelled events. In Beirut, Christian shops were sacked and the Danish consulate attacked by a crowd containing significant numbers of Syrian citizens, prompting observers to point out how Damascus had an interest in destabilizing the incumbent Lebanese prime minister.[89] The cycle continued for several weeks until well over 100 people had been killed (mainly by police firing on crowds), the al-Qaeda senior leadership had issued a statement threatening reprisals against Denmark, and, according to polls in the West, several tens of millions more Europeans and Americans had been convinced that Islam was either a threat or incompatible with democracy or both.[90] The issues raised by the cartoons affair – of free speech in largely secular societies, of the place of Muslims within European nations – were important and difficult ones. They were also unlikely to find an easy resolution in the near future. 'We found ourselves involved in a story where people had to make tough choices about what they believed was right and take the consequences,'

Flemming Rose told the author. Abu Laban, the man who had fuelled the furore in the first place, explained that 'though these riots were not on our agenda . . . it might be good for the West to know what happens when you insult Mohammed.'[91]

TOUCHING THE BOTTOM

If you had marked with a red spot every violent incident justifiably linked to radical Islam on a map of the world in 2001, most would have been clustered on Afghanistan with a sprinkling elsewhere and four key markers on the east cost of the USA. In 2003, the affected areas would have been much greater. Though there would have been nothing in America, a thick red line would have stretched across North Africa, broadening into a bloody smear across Iraq and the Arabian peninsula, before arcing across south-west Asia and on into the Far East. The map would have shown a noticeable and worrying increase on 2001. Yet this increase would be nothing compared to what was coming. By late summer 2006, as the fifth anniversary of 9/11 approached, whole swathes of the globe would have been covered in red: red across parts of the UK; red across parts of western Europe; red across the Maghreb, where counter-terrorism services and newly re-energized radical movements in Morocco, Libya and Algeria played a deadly game of survival, torture, conspiracy and killing; red across Lebanon, where hopes of a democratic revolution had rapidly faded to be replaced by a vicious and hard-fought short war between Hezbollah and Israel; red across Gaza, where Hamas was increasingly powerful; red across Saudi Arabia, where authorities continued to round up militants responsible for a series of bloody attacks and from where hundreds continued to head for jihad in an Iraq that itself was apparently plunging deeper and deeper into a terrible savage violence; red across the Yemen, where senior militants planned attacks on oil refineries and Western interests; red across Pakistan and Afghanistan and into India, where for the first time in recent decades there were indications of problems of extremism among the nation's 150-million-strong Muslim minority. More than 200 had died in bombings in Mumbai, the country's commercial centre, organized by Pakistani-based groups and the local Students Islamic Movement of India working together. There was red too in Africa, where in the dust and gravel of the great empty wastes of the central Sahara troops from Mauritania and Niger backed by American special forces fought a running battle with a growing number of semi-criminal militants and where, in Somalia, Islamic militias in part inspired by the Taliban fleetingly seized Mogadishu before being forced out by Ethiopian troops. As for the Far East, in Thailand a long-running insurgency pitting Muslims of Malay ethnic stock against an often brutal and exploitative government seen as representing only the interests of the Buddhist majority population had flared back into life with radical Islam now replacing revolutionary Marxism as the dominant discourse. And in Indonesia, the world's largest Muslim-majority state, Jemaa Islamiya, though weakened, was still dangerous, and violence continued. Australian security services were extremely nervous and there were even reports – ludicrously overblown as it turned out – of activity in South America. It was a picture grimmer than had been seen for many decades, and little augured well for the future.

There had, of course, been a few glimmers of something more positive – or at least less negative. Actually quantifying the menace al-Qaeda posed was very hard, and the numbers involved in radical activism remained a minuscule fraction of Muslim communities, particularly in the West, and of the world's Muslim population. In the USA, despite a few isolated influences, the better-integrated, -educated and -accepted Muslim community posed no obvious problem for the moment despite the febrile atmosphere. As more became known about the real reasons for the French riots of the autumn before and about the machinations of clerics and Middle Eastern regimes during the cartoons crisis, more measured analyses of what the two episodes meant for Europe began to roll back some of the hysteria. After all, the riots had led to only two deaths, and in Europe the cartoon crisis had seen nothing but largely legal protests through traditional channels.[92] But the bad outweighed the good. The French riots may not have seen the worst predictions fulfilled, but community relations across much of Europe had nonetheless reached a long-term low, with evidence of a growing and potent trend of the consolidation of sectarian and ethnic identities. The cartoon crisis had shown the power of crowd violence and crowd psychology, how hysterical populism could resonate among anxious and insecure populations and the ease with which rumours and myths could become the received wisdom for millions. A major initiative launched by the Bush administration in 2004 to promote democracy in an overconfident bid to 'drain the swamp' of support for terrorism in the 'Greater Middle East' had foundered on the entrenched interests of local regimes and those who benefited from them and on the gap between what the Americans were promising and what was being delivered in Iraq, Afghanistan and elsewhere. In Cairo in June 2005, Condoleezza Rice, now secretary of state, had pledged a new era in relations with the Muslim world. For too long, Rice told her audience, the United States had pursued 'stability at the expense of democracy in the Middle East'. In the future, she said, 'supporting the democratic aspirations of all people would be the touchstone of the administration's policies in the region'.[93] However, exactly what had been happening in Guantanamo, Bagram, Kandahar and in secret 'black prisons' was increasingly clear as was the true extent of the CIA's rendition programme, and when it came to a genuine choice between supporting a long-favoured ally such as Hosni Mubarak or backing a nascent reform movement, it was fairly clear where the White House's priorities lay. Polls showed that around 7 per cent of the global Muslim population – 100 million or so people – believed the 9/11 attacks were '*completely justified*'.[94] Security authorities appeared at best nervous, at worst trigger-happy and paranoid. A young Brazilian called Jean Charles de Menezes had been shot dead by British anti-terror police at a tube station in London the day after the abortive 21/7 attacks – they mistook him for a fugitive bomber – and hundreds of innocent citizens continued to be caught in massive dragnets in the US and in Europe. And all the while the steady background drumbeat of increased and more extreme violence, horrific videos of executions viewed by hundreds of thousands and communiqués from the senior al-Qaeda leadership continued.[95] As 2006 ground on, the 9/11 Wars seemed to be showing no signs of doing anything other than broadening to new parts of the globe, deepening further in terms of their intensity and intractability and causing more pain, destruction and hate all while inflicting long-term scars that would take decades to heal if they were to heal at all. As autumn turned to winter and the end of 2006 approached, there was one faint light just visible in the gloom. It shone from a very unlikely direction: Iraq.

PART FOUR

Iraq and the Turning:
2005–7

IO

The Awakening

A BAD YEAR, A BOMB IN A SHRINE . . . AND CIVIL WAR

On the night of February 21, 2006, six men wearing police uniforms entered the huge al-Askariya shrine in the town of Samarra, 70 miles north of Baghdad.[1] The leader of the group was a local Islamic extremist called Hathim al-Badri. With him were four Saudis and a Tunisian. The men rapidly overpowered the policemen guarding the complex, tied them up and then set about wiring several large bombs underneath its gilded main dome.[2]

The next morning two American infantry officers embedded with a force of new Iraqi 'special police commandos' in Samarra left their base at around 6.30 a.m. to set up a cordon and search operation in the neighbourhood adjacent to the mosque. It was the third such operation in three days. Though they had received no intelligence that the shrine might be attacked, they had been repeatedly told ammunition and explosives were being stored inside the rambling complex of buildings around the edifice of the main mosque. It was not clear, however, who was storing what, and as regulations prevented them searching religious sites without solid evidence the Americans had started combing the surrounding districts instead.[3] The two operations the previous mornings had turned up nothing. This time, even before the search could begin, there was an explosion. Then came silence and then a second blast, much bigger than the first. 'You blink and shudder and hunch down. You're thinking: "What the heck happened there?"' Major Jeremy Lewis, one of the two US officers at the scene, later recalled. 'My gunner says, "Sir, it's fucking gone! It's gone." I'm like, "No it's not gone, it's not gone." But then the wind carried the plume of smoke away.'[4] The entire main dome of the shrine had indeed disappeared.

The Shia police commandos, Lewis remembered, were 'very, very upset ... like when one of them had died'. The al-Askariya mosque complex contained a shrine to the twelfth 'hidden' imam, 'Muhammed al-Mahdi', the ultimate saviour of human kind, kept from the world by God until the day of his return. It also contained the tombs of the tenth and eleventh of the Shia imams, the ultimate Mahdi's immediate predecessors. A site of immense importance for all Shias, though particularly for those of the 'Twelver' strand, the Samarra shrine had been carefully chosen as a target to provoke a violent sectarian response. For a short period, almost as if people did not want to accept the implications of the act, the attack was blamed on the 'Jews' and 'Americans'. But the bombing came at the end of a long series of similar strikes directed at the Shia by extremists in networks run by Abu Musab al-Zarqawi which had killed hundreds of people over previous months and wounded thousands more.[5] Only six weeks earlier around sixty had died when suicide bombers had hit a shrine in Karbala, and the culprits of this latest attack were fairly obvious even before the yellow dust of the ninth-century mosque had settled.[6] Within hours, carloads of gunmen from the al-Mahdi Army were pouring out of Sadr City, the huge Shia slum in east Baghdad, and shooting up Sunni parts of the city. Across the country thirty Sunni mosques were rocketed, sprayed with automatic fire or incinerated. The next day, just to stoke the fires further, Sunni militants in police uniforms set up false roadblocks a few miles south of Sadr City and executed forty-five Shias.[7] Similar incidents were occurring wherever Shia and Sunni communities lived close to one another, each designed to accelerate the plunge into all-out sectarian warfare. Over the next weeks, the pace of such killings picked up. 'The day [the Samarra shrine] blew up every last one of us said it was the beginning of the civil war in Iraq,' Major Lewis remembered in his post-tour interview.[8]

The signs of the impending civil war had been plain for some time. The conflict was partly a result of the longstanding tensions within Iraq and partly due to the total failure of the coalition's military and political strategies from the second Falluja battle of November 2004 through to the summer of 2006. On the political front, the three national polls held during the period which had been supposed to provide the political architecture that would lead Iraq into a new era of democratic progress, multi-ethnic harmony and non-sectarian stability had instead exacerbated rather than healed the divisions between Iraq's main communities. Largely boycotted by the Sunnis, they had resulted in successive victories for Iraq's Shia. The big electoral gains of the United Iraqi Alliance, which broadly reflected the popular will and culture of the religiously and socially conservative Shia masses, meant control of most of the government apparatus was in Shia hands, and with the Sunni stranglehold on political power broken for ever, many in the Shia community felt there was no longer any need for the restraint once counselled by conservative religious leaders such as Grand Ayatollah Ali al-Sistani. If anything, they believed, Shia dominance needed to be reinforced to ensure that there was no chance of the beaten Sunnis returning to power. Many simply sought power and money. Ibrahim Jafaari, the weak and incompetent compromise candidate eventually chosen as prime minister after months of negotiation, proved both unable and unwilling to rein in the growing excesses of either those loyal to Muqtada al-Sadr, whose representatives had done well enough in the polls to be rewarded with effective control of the Ministry of Health, or the hardline Islamists of the Iran-linked SCIRI, who had got the Ministry of the Interior, from which they ousted all Sunnis before turning the police into an armed Shia militia that collaborated in sectarian killings. With no effective administration or law enforcement and a legacy of graft from the days of the Coalition Provisional Authority, corruption had flourished on an astonishing scale. Inevitably the meagre services that had been restored or maintained in 2004 had collapsed across much of the country, though Sunni areas suffered worse as resources were diverted to Shia communities by the now largely Shia-run central government. If, towards the end of the year, the flow of refugees from Iraq eased up, it was only because all those who could leave had already done so.[9]

Militarily, too, the situation had deteriorated. The American generals, driven by an administration whose policy was to make the Iraqis 'stand up' so American troops could 'stand down' and leave, were caught in vicious circle.[10] Aiming to weaken the insurgents sufficiently to allow a handover to the still under-equipped, poorly trained, demoralized and politicized Iraqi security forces, they launched successive efforts with names like Operation Dagger, Sword, Spear, Quick Strike, Iron Fist and Steel Curtain in a bid to clear the crucial Anbar province.

But the gruelling and resource-intensive battles fought along the Euphrates valley towards the Syrian border merely fuelled the insurgency. In 2004 the Americans had lost 848 dead and 7,989 wounded. In 2005 their casualties remained as high.[11] Iraqi security forces lost many more, and at the end of the year were no nearer acquiring the capabilities to take over from the Americans than at the beginning. The US strategy was fundamentally flawed. It was based on handing over to a government that could both militarily defeat the insurgents and work towards national reconciliation. However, not only were the Iraqi government and its forces incapable of defeating anyone, but, certainly after the elections of 2005, their collective sectarian bias was probably the primary obstacle to any national unity.

Worse, in preparation for an eventual handover and departure, US troops were pulled back from city centres into huge Forward Operating Bases (FOBs) with massive defences behind which soldiers could sleep in air-conditioned barrack blocks, eat imported steaks and lobster tails in the vast dining facilities, buy DVDs, phone home and go to the gym. Relations with the local population for the bulk of the 140,000-odd American troops in Iraq were limited to relatively hostile encounters while on patrol. The US military existed in Iraq like some kind of hermetic circulatory system within the body of the country. Servicemen flew from the US, arrived in Iraq from Kuwait in army planes, drove in armoured vehicles, lived and ate behind triple blast walls in bases supplied by huge convoys that arrived from Kuwait or Turkey, carrying even water and salad. Flying over the truck parks of the huge logistic base at Balad, effectively the beating heart of the American military effort in Iraq, was the only way to appreciate the size of the undertaking and the degree to which it was self-sufficient. Hundreds and hundreds of vehicles needed to ferry the supplies consumed by the vast apparatus of the army formed queues for miles around the base, ready to be emptied or refilled. Returning to the base from a twelve-hour patrol with one unit, the author witnessed a grimly amusing argument between infantrymen and the military traffic policeman who tried to book them for speeding. The only Iraqis were menial staff, a few advisers, a handful of translators and an unknown number of detainees. The special forces units, who were supposed to show a degree of cultural sensitivity that was not expected from the average infantryman, were paradoxically among the most isolated as they were charged with picking up 'high-value targets' on night raids, an activity unlikely to engender any relations at all, let alone cordial ones, with local people. One special forces officer commented that he had never met an Iraqi who was not in handcuffs.[12]

Bases like that at Balad were the result of various factors. First was the weight of decades of previous practice. Back in Bagram in Afghanistan in 2002 there had never been any questions over what sort of base was going to be built there. It was always going to be a small corner of America transplanted to a foreign field. One influence, as mentioned earlier, was the example of the bases constructed in the Middle East for operations over Iraq in the 1990s. In Saudi Arabia, due to the sensitivity of the American presence in the Land of the Two Holy Places, all troops had effectively been confined to their bases even if, given the cultural gulf between most American servicemen and women and the societies around them, there had been limited reasons why any of the 10,000 or so who were stationed in the region would mix at all with locals.[13] A second influence was the autonomy that had so marked American military communities based overseas in Europe or east Asia through much of the Cold War. The historic isolation of American forces deployed abroad thus had long roots. It reached, however, an entirely new scale with the deployments of the 9/11 Wars.

A second logic was that of General John P. Abizaid and other senior officers and officials in the US government. Abizaid, the commander of the US Central Command from 2003 to 2007 and one of the most intellectually able and aware of the American higher military command, had a Lebanese Christian Arab father and had learned Arabic and this, rightly or wrongly, gave his opinions significantly more weight than they might otherwise have had. Abizaid's 'antibody theory' held that societies, especially Muslim and Arab societies, inevitably reject the foreign. The profile of American soldiers in Iraqi towns – as in Afghan towns – should thus be as low as possible. Their presence on the streets and amid the people should be minimized to avoid provoking automatic rejection due to wounded personal pride, a sense of national, religious or ethnic identity or simple misunderstanding. This had influenced strategic thinking in Afghanistan and, by 2005, coincided perfectly with the desire of the increasingly troubled Bush administration to limit casualties and its avowed belief that, when it comes to democracy, too much care can kill the patient. Again and again, the mantra 'we will stand down as they stand up' was repeated and the American military withdrew further, out of towns and major cities, into their huge bases, sending ever more optimistic assessments up their chain of command.

But the reality of war in Ramadi, Tal Afar, Kut and hundreds of other Iraqi towns and cities was very different, and the seemingly aimless and endless combat, the mounting casualties and of course the isolation inevitably took their toll on morale and discipline. While the second Falluja battle had been winding down, a unit of American marines in the upper Euphrates town of Haditha had shot dead twenty-four Iraqis in the aftermath of an IED attack that had killed a well-liked twenty-year-old corporal. At least fifteen of the casualties were unarmed Iraqis killed in their homes, including seven women and three children. 'I couldn't see their faces very well – only their guns sticking into the doorway. I watched them shoot my grandfather, first in the chest and then in the head. Then they killed my granny,' Eman Waleed, a nine-year-old child, told Tim McGirk of *Time* magazine.[14] An old man in a wheelchair had been shot nine times.[15] As bad as the incident itself was the profound lack of interest of the Marines' senior officers. The killings, which provoked uproar in the USA when they were revealed, were indicative of a much broader malaise. A US army survey at the time showed 40 per cent of soldiers disliked the Iraqis and 38 per cent believed they did not have to treat them with respect.[16] About two-thirds of Marines and about half of army troops said they would not report a team member for mistreating a civilian and 10 per cent admitted they had personally been involved in abuse.[17] In the south, British confidence in their 'softer' touch, cultural sensitivity and discipline had long looked somewhat misplaced. The cheery 'salaamaleikums' and waves from the back of open-top Land Rovers of 2003 were a distant memory. Through 2005 British troops progressively withdrew into fortified bases in Basra and other southern cities which, if less luxurious than their American counterparts, were every bit as cut off from local populations. Their positions came under constant rocket and mortar fire, the local police were almost entirely infiltrated by various Shia Islamist groups and gangs fighting each other and foreign troops and central government control was nominal. Graffiti seen by the author on the inside of a bunker on one British post was telling: 'I am in a world of shit,' it read, a quote from Stanley Kubrick's 1987 Vietnam war film *Full Metal Jacket*. The isolation of the troops had predictable consequences. These were compounded by the farcical idea that British forces somehow understood their environment better than their American counterparts. In September 2005 two British special forces soldiers were taken captive as they attempted to drive around Basra 'undercover' on a mission to build up a 'pattern of life picture'.[18] Astonishingly, the soldiers had believed that darkening their skins, wearing cheap local shirts and driving a local car would allow them to 'blend in'. They were naturally as obvious as a group of Iraqi special forces trying to do something similar in a major British city would have been and were swiftly spotted and detained by Iraqi police. It took a full-scale armoured assault to free them.[19] Over the next two years, the British troops would gradually leave Basra entirely, ending up cantoned out in a big base at the airport, from where they launched occasional raids into the city but otherwise did little.

So 2005 thus ended as it had begun. In Washington and London, politicians continued to insist that progress was being made. That Iraqis voted 'yes' in the referendum on the constitution in October and had gone to the polls, again relatively peacefully, to elect a new full-term government in December was cited as evidence of political maturity and nascent stability. However, Sunnis had voted overwhelmingly against the constitution, which they believed would deny them a fair share of central political power and the immense oil wealth that went with it.[20] Many, both inside and outside Iraq, felt an explosion of violence was imminent. One senior British diplomat, speaking off the record shortly after returning from a long posting in Baghdad, dully summed up his time in Iraq in the first weeks of 2006. 'I think we will look back and say that 2005 was a bad year,' he said. 'I hope to God that the next one brings us something better.' In Baghdad's upmarket Karada, the barber Jaffar, who had grumbled about the Green Zone being lit up 'like in an Indian musical' two years previously had other things to worry about. No one came now to have their hair cut. Half the neighbourhood was deserted. Robberies were common. Bodies were turning up in the streets. Most were Shia, killed by Sunnis. Some were Sunnis, killed by Shia. At his local bakery, the young men sweating over the dough kept AK-47s close by. Most bakers were Shia and thus, like the queues of police recruits, easy and identifiable targets. 'I spend a lot of time praying,' Jaffar said. [21] Less than a month later came the al-Askariya mosque explosion and a further slide into terrible violence became inevitable.

AL-QAEDA IN MESOPOTAMIA AND THE 9/11 WARS

When, in October 2004, Abu Musab al-Zarqawi had finally overcome his reluctance to enter into a close relationship with al-Qaeda and had sworn allegiance to Osama bin Laden, the name he chose for his network was 'Tanzim Qaedat al-Jihad fi Bilad al Rafidayn', usually translated as 'the Al-Qaeda Jihad Organization in the Land of the Two Rivers' or 'Al-Qaeda in Mesopotamia' or, becoming progressively more distant from the original, 'al-Qaeda in Iraq', or 'AQI'.[22] The problem with the repeated reduction of the admittedly long-winded original title to the snappier 'AQI' was that it obscured the group's independent origins, the nature of its project, its fragmented nature and its place within the broader 'jihadi' movement. For though al-Zarqawi was now nominally loyal to bin Laden, the name he had taken for his organization was in fact a clear statement that his 'territorialist' philosophy and local strategy remained very much intact. Firstly, there was his use of the word *tanzim*, which meant organization or armed militia in the context of an insurgency. This showed the difference between al-Zarqawi's approach, based on the establishment of a coherent and organized armed group, and that of strategists such as Abu Musab al-Suri. The latter's very motto was '*nizam, la tanzim*', 'system not organization'.[23] Secondly, there was the reference to a real, physical, identifiable place, the patch of ground that the militants meeting in Falluja had yearned for. This place, for al-Zarqawi, was 'the land of the two rivers', i.e. the fertile strip watered by the Tigris and the Euphrates, the cradle of human civilization. By using such an archaic name, al-Zarqawi avoided recognition of the existence of a nation state known as Iraq and, by extension, the 'unIslamic' concept of any nation other than the *ummah*, the community or nation of all believers. The insistence on place indicated too al-Zarqawi's practical attachment to the establishment of a physical geographic base for the radical Islamic movement from which a broader campaign to bring the rest of the Middle East and potentially the Islamic world within the boundaries of a new caliphate could be waged. The problem for al-Zarqawi was, of course, that he was not Iraqi and was thus attempting to appropriate territory to which he had no evident right and a war that was not his own.

This was not an unfamiliar problem for leaders of international Islamic extremist groups. Indeed the original *raison d'être* of al-Qaeda back in the late 1980s had been to draw together various different national strands of Islamic militant activity under a single umbrella, co-opting local campaigns with limited local objectives into one global strategy with global objectives. The foundation of the group had been one of the consequences of the bitter debate between thinkers who favoured a return to a fight against the 'near enemy', Israel and the 'hypocrite, apostate' Middle Eastern regimes governing at the time, and others who saw the defeat of the Soviet Union as showing the way forward. For the latter, the time had come for a global battle in which a key foe and target would be the 'far enemy' of the West and more specifically the USA. It was American support, they argued, that propped up regimes in Egypt and in Saudi Arabia (as well as Israel), and the only way to bring down President Mubarak or the House of Saud would be through attacks on the USA, which would force Washington to abandon its allies in the region. Through the 1990s, Al-Qaeda offered local groups resources and tried to draw together a web of networked militant movements. However, alliance with al-Qaeda was something of a Faustian pact, requiring the surrender of varying degrees of autonomy and an internationalization of what had usually only been seen as a local battle hitherto. By entering into a relationship with al-Qaeda with its globalized message and objectives local groups thus risked support in their own communities, where there may have been a desire for change in people's immediate circumstances but there was often much less enthusiasm for a war against the much more abstract 'Crusader-Zionist' alliance.

The 1990s had shown quite how resistant local communities often were to attempts to mobilize them for a greater cause. Despite the violence of the fighting on the ground, broadly moderate local Muslim populations in the Balkans and the Caucasus had unequivocally rejected pan-Islamic global 'jihadi' ideologies.[24] Initial attempts by Osama bin Laden in the early 1990s to co-opt the Groupe Islamique Armée in Algeria into his nascent global network had been angrily rebuffed.[25] Attempts a few years later to build links with Indonesian organizations such as the Lashkar Jihad involved primarily in local sectarian violence had also failed. An effort in the Philippines to co-opt the Abu Sayyaf group had had only very limited success. When radicals had succeeded in making inroads, their successes were more due to political manoeuvring among the local groups or the states (or even superpowers) that were backing them than any significant support among local people. By the end of the decade, the huge resources amassed by al-Qaeda were certainly proving attractive – leaders of Iraqi Kurdish groups had after all sought out bin Laden to ask for funds and training as did a range of other militants – but none of those making the trip to Afghanistan in the hope of obtaining financial or other aid had anything like a mass popular constituency. Even the relationship between the Taliban in Afghanistan and their foreign guests remained extremely complex, and support for the project of bin Laden and his associates among ordinary Afghans, where memories of the extremism and lack of respect to local cultures showed by largely Arab international fighters during the war of the 1980s remained fresh, was negligible.[26]

Bin Laden, al-Zawahiri and others were, of course, aware of this. After all, the whole point of the 9/11 attacks had been to broaden the support base of both al-Qaeda and its affiliates by sparking a wave of radicalization and mobilization across the Islamic world. In this, al-Qaeda had, as previous chapters have shown, met with some success. The question was whether in the extraordinary circumstances that existed by 2005, created as much by the actions of America and its allies as by al-Qaeda's various initiatives, this success would be consolidated and expanded. Would the resistance offered by broad populations to global radical ideologies through the 1990s be finally overcome? Or would the global ideology and culture of contemporary militant Islam, stripped as it was of much of its local specificity and context, once again have great difficulty in convincing local communities that their best hopes of salvation, however defined, lay in extremism? After four years of conflict, the most obvious test case was Iraq, where these exact questions were being posed at a local level in a very immediate way. If the battle in Europe would determine how far radical Islam would be allowed to spread in geographic terms across the world, the battle in Iraq would indicate how deep into societies extremism could penetrate. If al-Qaeda's brand of militant activism and ideology failed to attract mass support in Iraq, given the chaos, the violence and the American-led occupation, it was unlikely to do so elsewhere.

In retrospect there had been many early signs indicating what turn events in Iraq were likely to take. The foreign volunteers who arrived through 2003 and early 2004 had been neither universally nor unconditionally welcomed. In some instances the more nationalist, more secular insurgents steeped in Ba'athist pan-Arab ideologies called the newcomers *irhabeen*, or terrorists, and either avoided them or tried simply to exploit their willingness to participate in suicide operations. And though the first battle of Falluja in April 2004 had seen locals and foreigners fighting alongside one another, strains had emerged relatively soon both among the different elements within the insurgents and between local people and the foreign militants.[27] This was lost in the chaos, confusion and hyperbole surrounding events at the time and received little attention. But it was there nonetheless. Many points of difference were cultural. Though the footsoldiers of the new al-Qaeda-affiliated groups were often young local men, the leaders were largely foreigners who enforced a form of ultra-rigorous Salafi orthodoxy entirely stripped of any local cultural context. Militants connected to one group in Falluja stopped locals smoking, for example, though getting through a packet of cigarettes a day was almost as much a part of being an adult Iraqi male as being able to use an AK-47 or liking Egyptian soap operas (which were also now banned). Others attempted to force women to wear the full head-to-toe coverings traditional in the Gulf but alien even in conservative Anbar.[28] Other tensions were social. As had been the case with Arab volunteers in Afghanistan during the 1980s and in Bosnia in the 1990s, newcomers wanted relationships with local women. In part this was a deliberate strategy to build connections among local tribes and communities but also a simple consequence of the inevitable desires of young men at war. One aspect in which traditional society in Anbar resembles that in much of Afghanistan is the degree to which the honour of a man, a family or a community is vested in its women and so the demands of the newcomers, often backed by force, caused immediate clashes, often fatal. Again as in Afghanistan during the war against the Soviets, there were arguments over styles of prayer and worshipping at tombs, seen as polytheism or *shirq* by many raised in strict Gulf Salafi traditions. One Falluja resident was reported to have shot dead a Kuwaiti who told him he could not pray at the grave of his ancestors.[29] Then there were political divergences, particularly over the future or indeed concept of any Iraqi nation. Local fighters identified themselves both as defenders of Islam and of 'Iraq'. As the name of al-Zarqawi's group indicated with its reference to ancient Mesopotamia, the land of the two rivers, the foreigners saw the concept of the nation state as unIslamic. They were there to 'kill infidels' not liberate Iraq, as the young Yemeni fighter Abu Thar had said in Falluja in late 2004.[30] Then there were tensions over more mundane issues of basic local politics. The new leaders of the Islamic militants, whether foreign or Iraqi, were competing with the traditional local tribal sheikhs for power and resources. The new groups were unwitting social revolutionaries, attracting elements who previously had little status in traditional Iraqi rural society. One of the most notorious leaders of the militant groups which emerged in Falluja in the summer of 2004 was a former Baghdad electrician.[31] Then, there were economic reasons for tensions. Much of the local tribes' wealth was based on smuggling. By mid-2005, many of the more lucrative routes were in the hands of militants who, Iraqi or otherwise, diverted the funds away from local communities and their traditional leaders, denying the latter what was usually their most important source of patronage. Finally, there were simple military reasons for the growing disaffection. Though full of zeal, the foreign militants, as in Afghanistan in the 1980s, were untrained and unpredictable.[32] Though their operations often grabbed the headlines, the vast proportion of the IEDs and ambushes directed at coalition troops were the work of Iraqis for whom the insurgency remained first a local war against a foreign occupying force before being a global religious jihad.

By spring of 2005, armed clashes were being reported between tribesmen and foreign militants across Anbar province and elsewhere.[33] These intensified as the year went on. To make up for their loss of genuine popular support, militants of groups such as al-Zarqawi's were forced to rely increasingly on simple murder and intimidation. This violence, which was often deliberately public, took more and more baroque forms such as tying people to burning tyres, boiling them alive or killing them by drilling holes through their limbs.[34] Even by the tough standards of Anbar and Saddam Hussein's Iraq the brutality was shocking.[35] In Anbar, every such act sparked a new series of blood feuds, setting militants against families and tribes, leading to further alienation of local people and thus to even more killings and intimidation. One important moment was reached when a significant number of Sunni leaders in Iraq recognized that two and a half years of fighting had gained them very little, that the demographic superiority and consequent political dominance of the Shia was now an established fact and that they needed to participate in elections if they were going to have a chance of retaining any stake in central government. Such thinking naturally led to a direct clash between their local aims and the global, universal ideologies of the foreigners, who had no interest whatsoever in any accommodation with the new authorities in Iraq let alone their American allies.

The result was that when some Sunni communities in Anbar had decided to vote in the December 2005 national assembly elections they found themselves shot at and bombed on polling day by the militant groups who eighteen months earlier they had welcomed, albeit warily, as protectors. Their assailants justified the killings on the basis that participating in democratic elections was a challenge to the unique authority of God and therefore polytheism and therefore *takfir*. Old ladies voting were thus excommunicable and as apostates were legitimate targets.[36] This kind of uncompromising extremism and the sophistic arguments which purported to provide its intellectual underpinning were spectacularly ill-suited to running an insurgent campaign. A key moment came when, during the polls, nationalist insurgent Iraqi groups ended up fighting to protect Sunni voters alongside, though not in formal alliance with, American troops engaged in the same task.

This was a breakthrough. A second came in January of 2006, only a month before the bombing of the al-Askariya mosque in Samarra, when the tribes of Ramadi, the city where Colonel Hector Mirabile's men had blasted gansta rap on dawn raids in 2003, sent their sons to enlist in the police force to start a drive to force out al-Qaeda. Seventy were killed by a suicide bomber, and the leaders of the initiative were systematically assassinated over subsequent weeks. Despite the ongoing carnage, however, the balance was shifting.[37] The sheiks in Ramadi announced that they were 'withdrawing protection' from foreign extremists and those who fought alongside them. Clashes between tribal fighters and radical Islamic militants broke out in Falluja, Samarra and in the anarchic towns of Latifiya and Mahmoudiya on the main highway south-west of Baghdad.[38] Casualties among foreign militants mounted.

More experienced extremist strategists had tried to warn al-Zarqawi of how a loss of popular support could jeopardize his project in Iraq. Through 2005 and early 2006 the extremist leader had received a stream of communications from senior al-Qaeda militants in Pakistan and other senior figures in the jihadi movement. One, from al-Zawahiri, had thanked al-Zarqawi for 'his efforts and sacrifices' but reminded the younger man that 'popular support would be a decisive factor between victory and defeat'. Telling al-Zarqawi to be mindful that 'the mujahed movement must avoid any action that the masses do not understand or approve', the Egyptian explained that 'in a race for the hearts and minds of our Ummah ... more than half of this battle is taking place in the battlefield of the media'.[39] Significantly, the letter had pointed to the rout of the Algerian extremists in the 1990s as an example of what happens if popular support and legitimacy are lost.[40] A second admonishment, also citing Algeria, came from Atiyah Abd al-Rahman, a senior Libyan militant based in Pakistan who had watched events there at first hand having been sent to the Maghreb as an envoy of bin Laden in the late 1990s. Atiyah, as he signed himself, reminded al-Zarqawi of how 'at the height of their power and capabilities' the Algerian militants had 'destroyed themselves with their own hands by their alienation of the population with their lack of reason ... oppression, deviance and ruthlessness' and called on him to avoid 'things that are perilous and ruinous' such as killing tribal leaders or religious scholars. 'Their enemy did not defeat them,' Atiyah had said of the extremists in Algeria, stressing his credentials as an eyewitness. 'They defeated themselves, were consumed and fell.'[41]

In June, five months after the al-Askariya attack and as Iraq's slide into the Shia–Sunni civil war accelerated, al-Zarqawi was killed by two 500 lb bombs dropped by American aircraft on a farmhouse north-east of Baghdad in Diyala province, where he had apparently been hiding for six weeks.

A TURNING

The beginning of the end for the leader of al-Qaeda in Iraq (AQI) can be dated to a night the previous November when suicide bombers blew themselves up in three luxury hotels in Amman, the Jordanian capital, killing sixty people, including thirty-eight members of a wedding party.[42] The attacks had been organized by al-Zarqawi, who claimed responsibility.

Almost all the victims were Jordanian, and the images of the bloodied and torn bodies of the revellers, broadcast continually for days by local TV channels, provoked an outcry locally with scores of well-attended and genuinely spontaneous demonstrations against such violence taking place over the days after the attacks. The extended family of al-Zarqawi took out advertisements in Jordan's three main newspapers to announce that 'the sons of the al-Khalayleh tribe' would 'sever links' with their kinsman 'until doomsday'.[43]

Subsequent polls revealed that the effect the November hotel bombings had on Jordanian public opinion. The kingdom had always been in a delicate position with its moderate religious and cultural tradition, frequently pro-American foreign policy and Westernized elite coexisting uneasily with a deep and popular Islamist sentiment. With its proximity to Israel and very substantial population of Palestinian refugees, Jordan had also always played a pivotal role in the core Middle East and for a long time support for Osama bin Laden and for suicide bombing had been higher there than elsewhere. This phenomenon was no doubt due in part to the sensitivity of the Palestinian issue in the kingdom and to the distinction between suicide attacks in Israel and elsewhere made by most local clerics and many local people. Support for the Iraqi insurgents had been even greater. From 2002 to 2005 support in Jordan for violence against civilians in 'the defense of Islam' had increased from 43 per cent to 57 per cent according to successive polls by the American Pew Centre. Another survey conducted by the Center for Strategic Studies at the University of Jordan in the second half of 2005 indicated that 70 per cent of the Jordanian public considered al-Qaeda an 'armed resistance organization' and not a 'terrorist group'. A further secret study by the Jordanian authorities confirmed the results.[44] Yet the November 9 bombings totally changed the dynamic. A public opinion poll conducted by Ipsos Stat for the Jordan-based *al-Ghad* newspaper in the aftermath of the attack revealed that 64 per cent of the respondents now had a negative view of bin Laden's group and only 2.1 per cent a positive view. When asked, 'Do you think al-Qaeda is a terrorist organization?' nearly 90 per cent answered 'yes'.[45] Polling by Pew six months after the attacks confirmed that the change was not simply a knee-jerk response: support for violence against civilians in Jordan had halved to 29 per cent. Confidence in bin Laden 'to do the right thing in world affairs', 64 per cent in 2005, had dropped to 24 per cent in 2006.[46]

The shift in public sentiment had an immediate tactical impact. Al-Zarqawi's networks in Iraq had a long logistical tail stretching back to hundreds of radical activists and extremist clerics in his native land who had promoted him as a true believer and *mujahed* and supplied significant practical, theological and financial support throughout 2004 and 2005. These had proved resistant to attempts by intelligence services to penetrate them.[47] Yet in the aftermath of the Amman bombings, new sources of information began to open up. In May 2006, an official serving on the western border was arrested by the Jordanian police. A key figure in the transfer of weapons, money and material to al-Zarqawi's fighters in Iraq from Jordan, he had been betrayed by associates who had been disgusted by the hotel attacks.[48] The details his interrogation furnished were fed through to the American teams in Iraq running the hunt for the fugitive leader of al-Qaeda in Mesopotamia. Clever and patient questioning – far removed from the atrocities of Abu Ghraib – by US interrogators of an ever-lengthening list of close associates through the spring and summer of 2006 and information volunteered by senior figures, many still active in the insurgency, within major Anbar tribes, meant that the identities of most of those in al-Zarqawi's inner circle were now known.[49]

By the early summer of 2006, the animosity towards al-Zarqawi and his foreign militants in Anbar meant the province was no longer safe for the AQI leader. Effectively on the run, moving from safehouse to safehouse, the forty-year-old traversed the semi-rural belt to the north of Baghdad and ended up in a small village in Diyala province, not far from the tough mixed Sunni and Shia town of Baqubah. When a former associate of al-Zarqawi, 'turned' by Jordanian security forces after being betrayed by a suspicious hotel owner and arrested early in the year, provided a key telephone number, this lead, together with the work of the interrogators in Iraq, allowed al-Zarqawi's spiritual adviser, Sheikh Rahman, to be physically located and put under surveillance. A Predator drone then followed the cleric to the farmhouse where al-Zarqawi himself was believed to be staying. The two men and two or three women and children also staying in the building died almost immediately in the ensuing strike.[50] In addition to the new sophistication of American methods, key to the capture of the militant leader were thus two critical phenomena: the alienation of the tribes from the foreign extremists within Iraq, forcing al-Zarqawi to leave Anbar, and the changing attitude of ordinary people in Jordan towards a man whom many had once seen as a heroic resistance fighter which had led to crucial leads reaching the Jordanian intelligence services. But the real significance of the plunging support for radical Islamic violence and senior militant leaders in Jordan had ramifications much more wide-ranging than the death of a single militant, albeit one of the notoriety of al-Zarqawi. If the same phenomenon was reproduced elsewhere then it was clear that it would signal a genuine strategic shift in the evolution of the 9/11 Wars.

It had been obvious for a long time to anyone working or living in Muslim-majority countries that support for bin Laden or for radical Islamic militants was far from universal and that, by the middle of the decade, more and more people were beginning to question al-Qaeda's means and message. In a barber shop in the Sabra and Shatila refugee camp in Beirut, the site of the infamous massacres of 1982 and as likely a location for support for radical Islam as one could hope to find in the region, three brothers gave three different answers – 'Yes, it is justified', 'No it is never justified', 'It depends on the circumstances' – when questioned by the author about suicide bombings and executions of civilians in Iraq in late 2005. Similar responses were heard in living rooms, shops and restaurants in Indonesia, Pakistan and Qatar, in Morocco in January 2006 and among British, French, German and Dutch Muslims. Along with the indication of the beginning of a reaction against extremist violence came a clue as to why and where this emerging trend might be strongest. There was good evidence, though at that time still only anecdotal, of a strong correlation between the proximity of any violence and the degree of support for the perpetrators of violence.

By the spring of 2006, however, starting with the surveys in Jordan, a wealth of polling had begun to put flesh on the anecdotal bones. In Indonesia support for radical violence had dropped in the wake of the first Bali bombing in 2002 from the already low level of 26 per cent to 20 per cent and then continued to drop further to 11 per cent after a further round of bombings in 2005.[51] The most dramatic drop in support for terrorism had been seen in Morocco, where fully 79 per cent of those surveyed said that support for suicide bombing and violence against civilians was never justified – more than double the percentage (38 per cent) who had expressed this view in 2004.[52] In Turkey, despite the growing chaos in Iraq, confidence in bin Laden to 'do the right thing in world affairs' dropped from 15 per cent before the Istanbul bombing of 2002 to 7 per cent a year after it and to 3 per cent by 2005.[53] In

Egypt, the attacks, in the holiday town of Taba in the autumn of 2004, Cairo in April 2005 and then in the Red Sea resort of Sharm-el-Sheikh in July of that year contributed to 68 per cent of people remaining 'very or somewhat concerned' about the rise of Islamic extremism in 2006.[54] One of the key reasons for the collapse of support for the militants of Islamic Jihad and Gamaa al-Islamiyya in Egypt in the 1990s had been the combination of local casualties and the economic damage done, especially to the crucial tourist trade, which had particularly hit the middle class, and the 2005 strikes in the country appeared to have a similar effect, with a decline in support for suicide bombing from 28 per cent to 8 per cent in 2007.[55]

In Saudi Arabia high levels of support for bin Laden and his violent tactics and for suicide bombing in general had plunged the instant that the first bombs had exploded on Saudi streets and the reality of what such attacks meant became clear. Though the shift in public sentiment was reinforced by the deliberate dissemination of graphic images by the Saudi authorities and statements against violence made by clerics once known for their radical stance, the reaction against the extremists was a genuine and deep one. 'When we hear bin Laden railing against the West, pointing out the corruption and incompetence of the Arab governments and the suffering of the Palestinians, it is like being transported to a dream, [but] when we see the images of innocent people murdered for this ideology, it's as if we've entered a nightmare,' one poll subject in a conservative southern Saudi town explained.[56] When violence remained abstract, something that happened over there to those people, it could be supported. But when it was local men, women and children who were blown apart, and local economies that suffered, and local governments who were undermined, the response was very different. Only one conclusion could be drawn: the moment communities started seeing close up what radical Islamic militancy genuinely meant, they turned against it. What had happened on a small scale in Anbar Province in Iraq was indeed happening on a much wider scale across the Islamic world.

This drop in support did not indicate lower levels of animosity towards 'the West', America, Bush, Israel and Jews, or lower levels of belief in conspiracy theories attributing the September 11 attacks to Mossad or the CIA. Large majorities in the Muslim world remained convinced that there was a widespread lack of respect for Islam in the

West and that any American rhetoric about spreading democracy was, like the 'Global War on Terror', simply a cover for a neo-imperialist strategy to divide and exploit.[57] But the polls did apparently show that, even as the apparently unstoppable wave of violence had broken across the Middle East and Europe over previous years, there had been a counter-current, a riptide, that had been difficult to see for what it was but was now finally making itself felt. The picture was messy. There was certainly little uniformity; visibility on a whole range of issues was very poor and a counter-example could be found for every more positive sign.

There was certainly much evidence that very serious problems remained. In August of 2006. a new plot had been uncovered in the UK centred on a group of young British Pakistanis in Walthamstow, east London. Very similar to the conspiracies that had preceded it except in its ambition, it would have seen suicide attackers mix liquid components to form explosives inside a series of airborne transatlantic jets, potentially causing the deaths of as many as had died in the 9/11 attacks.[58] Shortly afterwards had come another wave of global controversy sparked by a speech made by the newly elected conservative Pope Benedict XVI, who unhelpfully quoted a fourteenth-century Byzantine Emperor, saying that the Prophet Mohammed had brought 'things only evil and inhuman such as his command to spread by the sword the faith he preached'.[59] Muslim leaders, clerics and activists responded as they had before, demanding once again why the West was set on the humiliation and subordination of Islam and calling again on 'the faithful' to show their anger. But as 2006 wore on, it became clear that for the first time since 9/11 not all the dials had their needles deep in the red zone. There were even grounds for, if not optimism, then at least a nuancing of the previous deep pessimism.

Two months after the death of al-Zarqawi, in August 2006, militants linked to 'al-Qaeda in Iraq' assassinated a senior sheikh in Ramadi and dumped his body in undergrowth rather than return it for immediate burial as tribal and Muslim custom demanded. The incident provoked a young middle-ranking local sheikh called Abdul Sattar Buzaigh Albu Risha to organize a meeting to proclaim the formation of the Sahwa or 'Awakening' Council and to publicly call on the tribes to rise up against al-Qaeda. Sattar, who had had several relatives killed by the extremists, contacted the press in Baghdad to announce he had the support of twenty-five of the thirty-one tribes in Anbar and a strength of 30,000 armed men. It was a ludicrously inflated claim but that wasn't the point. One significant difference to previous such initiatives was that Sattar, who made up for what he lacked in genuine tribal status with charisma and drive, had secured a promise of support and, most importantly, protection from a far-sighted local American commander.[60] Over the following months, the tribes and the US forces began working closely together in Ramadi, gradually clearing the city of foreigners and extremists. Thousands of tribesmen were enrolled in the police or, if illiterate, into a range of auxiliary forces. As the US forces went from block to block, forcing out insurgents, these new reinforcements secured the areas they cleared. The rapid flow of large sums of cash disbursed by the local US senior officers for immediate reconstruction and development projects helped further consolidate the hold the new combined US and Iraqi regular and irregular forces had on any given neighbourhood and provided space for more durable political and administrative structures to be set up.

The motivations of Sattar and the tribes may not have been as altruistic or traditional as sometimes said. The murdered relatives for which Sattar sought vengeance had been executed after negotiating with coalition authorities for a slice of the vast reconstruction budgets available to local contractors. One reason for the Albu Risha, the clan to which Abdul Sattar belonged, turning against the foreign militants was that the latter had appropriated many of the lucrative smuggling, theft and extortion rackets focused around the main Baghdad–Amman highway which had provided much of the tribe's income for several decades.[61] But the exact motives of those picking up their AK-47s to fight beside the US and Iraqi government troops was not important. As the winter of 2006 came on, similar initiatives to that of the Albu Risha, all a result of a combination of similar micro-factors, had gained momentum in the town of Khalidiyah, where an al-Qaeda group had irritated local sheikhs by taking charge of the local distribution of smuggled petrol, in Haditha, scene of the massacre perpetrated by US Marines a year previously, and in a dozen other small towns across western Iraq.[62] Given the still generalized mayhem in Iraq, where levels of violence were as high as they had ever been across the entire country and there was an unprecedented degree of political chaos, it was not surprising that the apparently very minor bits of good news were missed. A change in the evolution of a phenomenon as complex and as diverse as either the war in Iraq or the 9/11 Wars more generally would not come from a single event, a single new trend, a single development but from the accumulated effect of scores of different factors which together would alter its path. But out in the scruffy, battered towns and the fields and date orchards of the upper Euphrates valley, as much as in the bazaars, cafés, living rooms and mosques of Jordan, Egypt, Turkey and elsewhere, another of the elements that together would begin a new evolution of the local conflict and the broader global one had fallen into place.

'THE LONG WAR'

If this key turn looked in any way possible it was in spite of, rather than because of, anything Washington was doing. In February 2006, a couple of weeks before the Samarra bombing, the Pentagon had published a 'Strategic Defense Review', its third such comprehensive assessment of how best to shape America's military forces to cope with the challenges that would face them over the coming two decades. The previous review, completed before the 9/11 attacks and published after them, had been largely obsolete by the time it had come out. The new version started with the unequivocal words: 'The United States is a nation engaged in what will be a long war.'[63] It went further than the simple reiteration of a fact that was clear to everyone, however. The document's first chapter was entitled 'Fighting the Long War' and set about defining a conflict that, it said, saw 350,000 American servicemen and women engaged in 130 different countries.

The term 'the Long War' had emerged in military circles at least two years before it made its public debut. The man credited with first using it to describe the ensemble of ongoing operations undertaken by the US army was General Abizaid. He had spoken of the Long War 'to underscore the long-term challenge posed by al Qaeda and other Islamic extremist groups' and had had his staff prepare presentations on 'The Long War 2006 to 2016'.[64] At the time his thinking was a radical departure from the vision that had previously dominated. Though only days after 9/11 Bush had warned America to expect a different kind of conflict, there was in fact more continuity than change. America's wars were still expected to be rapid and relatively cheap. The 'full spectrum dominance' which the US military believed it had attained, its huge technological advance on the rest of the planet and its energy, 'warrior spirit' and will were perceived as largely invincible. By 2005, mired in a hideous war of attrition for which they were neither trained nor equipped, senior American commanders were thus left groping for new conceptual tools to allow them to construct an appropriate strategic framework. The idea of the Long War, as evolved by Abizaid, with its implication of generational struggle, marathon effort and the interdependency of the various theatres in which the US military was engaged, appeared to explain the conflict in a new and potentially useful way.[65]

But there was another strand of thinking which had also sought to define the ongoing struggle and also used the term 'the Long War'. Developed by senior officials in the Bush administration and in intellectual circles close to them, it was more controversial. For the politicians and several highly influential conservative thinkers the phrase 'the Long War' became, in part, a replacement for the increasingly discredited concept of a 'Global War on Terrorism'.[66] More broadly, it framed the various contemporary conflicts as the successors to those fought by the West through the twentieth century against Nazism and Fascism and then Communism.[67] The National Strategy for Combating Terrorism of September 2006 clearly stated that al-Qaeda's 'ideology of oppression, violence and hate' was a 'form of totalitarianism following in the path of Fascism and Nazism'.[68] Such a view undoubtedly reflected the collective historical vision of the senior Bush administration and their view of the current conflict – indeed it reiterated almost word for word phrases used in the president's first address to Congress and the American nation nine days after 9/11. It also had clear political utility.[69] By extending the timescale in which results could be expected in this new conflict, the vision of 'the Long War' explained the apparent failure to achieve rapid victory in Afghanistan and Iraq, justified the continued commitment of very significant resources to what was perceived as a fight for the survival of the American nation and of American values – 'freedom' – and provided a rationale for the continuation of extraordinary legal measures and presidential powers for the foreseeable future.

Thinkers such as Samuel Huntingdon, author of *The Clash of Civilizations*, and Bernard Lewis, the scholar of Islam and the Middle East, were both widely cited to provide intellectual ballast. Underlying such analyses was the perception of the Long War as being a single conflict against a single, united and uniform foe. In an editorial called 'The Long War: the radical Islamists are on the offensive. Will we defeat them?' in the *Weekly Standard* journal in March 2006 William Kristol, one of the most prominent American neo-conservatives, posed a simple question: 'Does [the Bush administration] have the will ... to lead the nation toward victory in the long war against radical Islamism.' In this 'Long War' the enemy was aggregated. If it was not 'Islam' itself, as some argued, it was 'Islamism' or 'Islamofascism' or 'jihadism'. As the emphasis on states as sponsors of terrorism lessened so a new stress on the uniformity and unity of the non-state groups who constituted the enemy emerged. The bombing of the al-Askariya shrine, to take one example, was thus described as 'another indication of the worldwide jihadist offensive against the West', an odd description of an attack on a Muslim holy place by other Muslims.[70]

The problem with this highly ideological vision of the Long War was that it perpetuated one of the fundamental attribution errors that had underpinned the conceptualization and execution of the entire 'Global War on Terrorism'. Men like Abizaid within the military may have instinctively sensed that for their soldiers facing complex situations involving militancy on the ground such generalized responses were inadequate. But the development of any new strategies that might take local context into account or attempt to mitigate the violent reaction that efforts to impose wide-ranging political, social and customary changes on societies appeared often to provoke was politically very difficult. So though the Pentagon's review argued that there was no 'one size fits all' approach and that solutions needed to be 'tailored to local conditions and differentiated worldwide', the conflict was still compared directly to the Cold War. Though the review was careful to explain that victory would be elusive and would depend 'on information, perception, and how and what we communicate as much as application of kinetic effects', i.e. firepower, the enemy was described as 'global non-state terrorist networks'. Finally, though the review called for a new brand of warriors with deep cultural knowledge of the societies in which they operated. American soldiers were described bluntly as 'a force for good' and the enemy as opposing 'globalization and the expansion of freedom it brings'.[71] This tension ran through almost all American strategic thinking at the time. In his last press conference as chairman of the American Joint Chiefs of Staff in September 2005, General Richard Myers had picked up on a variety of semantic changes introduced by Abizaid – such as referring to 'violent extremists' rather than 'terrorists' – but nonetheless described the conflict as 'the long war against terrorism'. A seminar organized by the Pentagon on 'Defining the Long War' shortly after the publication of the review failed to come up with a satisfactory formula to describe and define the conflict.

Taken together this meant that, in the spring of 2006, little looked likely to change on the ground in Iraq or elsewhere in the near future. For authors of the Pentagon review the aims in Iraq remained those of 2003, 'a democratic [nation] that will be able to defend itself, that will not be a safe haven for terrorists, that will not be a threat to its neighbours, and that can serve as a model of freedom for the Middle East'. The means of achieving that goal were also unaltered. Having been successful in 'defeating the Iraqi military and liberating the Iraqi people', the effort remained focused on 'building up Iraqi security forces and local institutions and transitioning responsibility for security to the Iraqis'.[72] If anything was going to change in Iraq and if the more positive developments there and elsewhere were to be exploited strategically, the thinking that would allow that to happen was clearly not going to come from the White House or the upper levels of the Pentagon. As had so often been the case in the course of the 9/11 Wars, the crucial shifts occurred much lower down, much closer to the dusty and bloody ground, where some soldiers and specialists were realizing that real communities have histories, aspirations, resentments, myths, views, hopes and hates which cannot be reduced to simple single-sentence slogans.

II

The Turning

FIELD MANUAL 3-24

On the day of the bombing of the al-Askariya shrine in Samarra, an eclectic group of soldiers, experts, intelligence specialists, civilian analysts, human rights campaigners, anthropologists, historians and journalists were sitting around tables and half-empty cups of coffee in a nondescript meeting room in the American army staff college of Leavenworth, Kansas.[1] They were a very long way from Iraq, but the conflict was very much present.[2]

The meeting had been convened by General David Petraeus, the fifty-four-year-old senior officer in charge of the college who after serving in Iraq had seized the opportunity offered by his new tenure to formally reshape the American military's understanding of how to fight non-conventional operations. The various experts were there to discuss the draft of a new US military field manual on fighting counter-insurgency warfare. Politically adept, ambitious and driven, Petraeus had served as commander of the 101st Airborne Division during and after the 2003 invasion, where he had employed classic counter-insurgency doctrine to achieve a reasonable level of calm and stability in the difficult northern city of Mosul, a Sunni and Ba'athist bastion. A second tour in charge of training Iraqi security forces had been less successful but had nonetheless reinforced the reputation Petraeus had acquired for combining intellectual acumen and curiosity with practical effectiveness. A series of glowing media reports boosted his public profile and sparked some jealousy among the notoriously competitive senior ranks of the US military. Known to have been sceptical of the American involvement in Iraq from the beginning, famously asking 'how does this end?' during the invasion,

Petraeus represented a maverick minority strand of thinkers that had been largely marginalized within the American armed forces over the four years since 2003.[3] Within ten months of the Samarra bombing and the Leavenworth meeting, this minority would be determining US strategy in Iraq.

The writing of the manual, the sessions in Leavenworth, the debate sparked by successive drafts of the manual amounted to a huge and public self-criticism session for the American military. First, the flaws in the strategy and tactics implemented in Afghanistan in 2002 and 2003 were unpicked. The failure to secure borders, the raiding from big, heavily defended bases, the isolation from local people, the counterproductive emphasis on force protection, the cultural insensitivity, the chronic inability to understand local dynamics, the lack of sufficient troops to provide the security that could allow stability and economic development, the abuse and violence meted out to detainees were all discussed and analysed. The sessions were, as Petraeus had intended, lively and stimulating. The range of contributors, many from outside the US military, ensured a range of different inputs. One was David Kilcullen, an Australian former army officer with a doctorate in political anthropology, who matched experience from his country's deployment in East Timor in 1999 with that gained as a US state department consultant in 2006 in Afghanistan. Kilcullen fitted what had been happening in Iraq into a broader theory. When al-Qaeda activists established themselves in a lawless area and successfully provoked an outside intervention by local government forces or international actors, Kilcullen argued, local populations were radicalized and then fought alongside the extremists. These local warriors were not dedicated ideologically committed fighters, he said, but simply 'accidental guerrillas'. The right tactics and strategy could reverse the process by which they had come to take up arms.[4] Other contributors included British officers such as Brigadier Nigel Aylwin-Foster, who had served in Iraq himself and who, in a widely read article published in the Leavenworth College review, accused the US army of a lack of cultural knowledge and sensitivity that amounted to unwitting 'institutional racism'.[5] Aylwin-Foster also attacked American 'moral righteousness', 'damaging optimism' and 'focus on conventional warfare of a particularly swift and violent kind'. His article included statistics revealing that most American operations had been 'reactive to insurgent activity', i.e. effectively initiated by the enemy, and 'only 6 per cent had been aimed at securing a safe environment for the population'. This latter goal was at the heart of many contributors' thinking.[6] Lecturing from the British who, after all, had hardly been hugely successful in Basra, was resented by many American officers, but coming from the only ally who had significant numbers of troops deployed, the criticisms had a certain weight.[7]

Further input came from cultural anthropologists controversially hired by the Pentagon in a new initiative launched between mid 2005 and mid 2006. The doyenne among them was the flamboyant Montgomery McFate, who drew on close observation on the ground in Iraq – albeit under conditions that could hardly be described as academically ideal – to make a range of observations: that the frequent killings of civilians by US troops at roadblocks were in part due to the gestures indicating 'stop' and 'welcome' being reversed in American and Iraqi cultures; that coffee shops (forbidden to US troops on force protection grounds) were the natural conduit for information flow in Iraq, not broadcast media as assumed in the West; that confusion over the black flags Shia households traditionally flew from their homes caused needless casualties as Marines conditioned to think a white flag meant surrender assumed a black flag indicated the opposite. McFate did not pull her punches when it came to criticizing her nation's forces, attacking the 'ethnocentrism, biased assumptions, and mirror-imaging' she saw as endemic among American troops. 'Understanding one's enemy requires more than a satellite photo of an arms dump,' she wrote in one military journal. 'Rather, it requires an understanding of their interests, habits, intentions, beliefs, social organizations and political symbols – in other words, their culture.'[8] Eventually Field Manual 3-24, the result of the work at Leavenworth, mentioned 'culture' on fifty of its 282 pages.

For a technical military publication, Field Manual 3-24, was a work of extraordinary influence, discussed on television and in newspapers and bought in quantities normally reserved for airport thrillers. Its basic points were simple. Instead of prioritizing the finding and killing of insurgents, troops needed to make protecting local people from the militants the main focus of their efforts. Instead of trying to isolate Americans from local populations to both reduce casualties and to avoid provoking an 'allergic reaction' if foreign troops mixed with local people, soldiers needed to eat, sleep and, most importantly, walk among those they were now supposed to protect. The US military's overwhelming firepower needed to be used judiciously and with consideration of all the possible consequences. Often it was better not to open fire. If a single insurgent was killed and five of his brothers took up arms as a result, that was a net loss not a gain. Humiliating, injuring or killing civilians and damaging their property helped insurgents, whereas 'using force precisely and discriminately strengthens the rule of law that needs to be established'. The manual also reaffirmed the obligations imposed by Common Article 3 of the Geneva Conventions and called abuse of prisoners 'immoral, illegal, and unprofessional'.[9]

This latter injunction was not the only element that was politically controversial. A key theme, returned to again and again, was the importance of recognizing and respecting the cultural specificity of a given population. 'Cultural awareness is a force multiplier,' Petraeus had said in an article published in January 2006.[10] The manual itself went further, arguing that 'American ideas of what is "normal" or "rational" were not universal' but instead 'members of other societies often have different notions of rationality, appropriate behaviour, levels of religious devotion and norms concerning gender. Thus, what may appear abnormal or strange to an external observer may appear as self-evidently normal to a group member.' For this reason, the manual insisted, it was vitally important 'to avoid imposing' American ideas of the normal and the rational on other people. Culture, it said, was 'arbitrary, meaning that Soldiers and Marines should make no assumptions regarding what a society considers right and wrong, good and bad'.[11] This was not what most American conservatives – indeed most Americans – believed. It was certainly far from the thinking of the president, of many of his top officials or of the large number of evangelical Christians within the US armed forces.

Petraeus' manual was effectively recommending a culturally relativist approach which ran diametrically opposite to the 'moral clarity', the belief in American exceptionalism and the confidence in the universal application of American values that had hitherto been such a principal element of the Bush administration's post-9/11 security strategy.

Equally, the new approach ran counter to another key ideological component of the worldview of the White House. Back in 2002 the Bush administration had pledged 'to work to bring democracy, development, free markets and free trade to every corner of the world'.[12] In this approach, as British academic and Iraq expert Toby Dodge has noted, it was analytic categories derived from, or at the very least shared with, neoliberal economics that were dominant: the individual, the market, democracy and the threat of an overbearing state.[13] In Afghanistan and in Iraq, the Bush administration's emphasis on minimal levels of troops, 'a light footprint' and allowing local populations to 'stand up' owed as much to this as it did to fears of repeating the Soviets' mistakes or to General Abizaid's 'antibody theory'. But the counter-insurgency theories being elaborated by Petraeus and his team placed the state at the centre of any successful strategy. 'COIN [counter insurgency operations] ... involves the application of national power in the political, military, economic, social, information and infrastructure fields and disciplines,' the manual stated unequivocally on its second page.[14] The new manual drew heavily on the writing of David Galula, a French soldier who had used his experience as an officer in the Algerian war of 1954 to 1962 to write one of the fundamental texts of modern strategic thinking on counter-insurgency. In his work *Counter-insurgency Warfare: Theory and Practice*, which was repeatedly referenced in the new manual, Galula stated bluntly that the state, was 'the machine for the control of the population' and stressed that only 'four instruments of control count in a revolutionary war situation: the political structure, the administrative bureaucracy, the police, the armed forces'.[15] Again, the manual's emphasis the centrality of the state was in sharp contrast to cherished principles of the Bush administration and many of those who had voted for them.

Criticism from the right was however muted. On the left, several objections to the new doctrines rapidly surfaced. Some pointed out that this was not the first time armies at a loss to deal with a particular enemy had turned to 'culture' in a bid to find new arms or strategies and that doing so was no guarantee of success. There had been similar efforts during (or after) the Indian Mutiny or War of Independence in 1857, in the Pacific Theatre during the Second World War and in Vietnam.[16] Many detected the influence of a long tradition of Western 'Orientalism' in the text of the manual. Though it avoided some of the more classic prejudices, there was evidence, at least in the discussion of Iraq during the editing of the manual, of a typical European vision of 'the Arab', timeless and exotic, inscrutable or wily.[17] Some criticized the frequent citing of T. E. Lawrence, Lawrence of Arabia, the British soldier and romantic hero who had written nearly a century ago and whose best-known work, *The Seven Pillars of Wisdom*, was dismissed by some respected scholars as 'a fine piece of prose but almost worthless for studying the history or society of the Arab world'.[18] Others worried that the new doctrines were falsely reassuring, with the 'new and nicer' way of fighting they outlined considerably more compatible with the US's self-image as a source of universal good and universal values than the tactics previously employed and thus a useful way to convince an increasingly disillusioned American public to accept their soldiers continuing to kill large numbers of people in distant countries.[19] But the real problem was less academic. When the final draft of the manual was being prepared in June of 2006, there was little indication that anyone was seriously considering the wholesale practical application of what it recommended in Iraq or elsewhere in the near future.

THE SURGE

Nearly 3,000 Iraqis were killed in December 2006, at least two-thirds in sectarian violence.[20] Jaffar, the Karada barber, remembered the last days of 2006 as 'the waiting room of Hell'. 'Everyday I heard of a relative dying. I never left my home,' he said.[21]

Lieutenant General Ray Odierno, returning to Iraq for the first time in over two years, was stunned by how badly the situation had deteriorated. 'Corpses were being found in trash heaps and along Baghdad's side streets by the day,' he recalled. Saddam Hussein, whose trial had been supposed to be a expiatory healing exercise for a brutalized country, had been handed over to Iraqi custody and was eventually hanged, days after Odierno's arrival in Baghdad, to the sound of triumphant shouts of 'Muqtadr, Muqtadr' from Shia officials at the execution. Images of this brutal and chaotic travesty of judicial process captured on a mobile phone were posted on the internet and widely circulated. Chaos apparently reigned.

An unusual soldier, Odierno's sheer physical size and billiard-ball bald scalp belied an acute intelligence. His first tour in Iraq as commander of the 4th Infantry Division had been tarnished by allegations of brutality by his troops – which he denied. However, it was Odierno too who had laid the basis for the capture of Saddam Hussein through charting the Iraqi tribal and kinship networks around the former dictator.[22] Given the unenviable task of breaking the apparently downward spiral in Iraq by his direct superior General George Casey, Odierno rapidly became convinced that the only way to do so was in fact to reverse the strategy of handing over to the incapable Iraqi security forces and instead to deploy further American troops to 'secure' the population.

Though Odierno's credentials were impeccable, his new thinking would have gone nowhere just a few months earlier. However, the November 2006 mid-term elections in America had seen, in the words of the president, a 'thumping' for the Republicans as the Democrats took both the Senate and the House of Representatives. Days after the polls, Bush had replaced Defense Secretary Donald Rumsfeld, who was stubbornly committed to the policy of drawing down troops from Iraq, with Robert Gates, a methodical and calm former career intelligence officer with a reputation for pragmatism. Rumsfeld had already told the president that he felt that 'fresh eyes' might be needed, and his departure completed an overhaul of senior Pentagon appointments that had already seen many of the most ideological members of the Bush administration sidelined.[23] Paul Wolfowitz, the deputy defense secretary and one of the keenest and most optimistic advocates of the original invasion of Iraq, had been moved sideways to the World Bank eighteen months earlier. Douglas Feith, the controversial under-secretary at the Pentagon blamed by many for circumventing normal procedures to 'stovepipe' raw and erroneous intelligence on Saddam's supposed weapons of mass destruction or links with al-Qaeda to senior decision-makers, had long since left the administration for academe. A new, colder and more realistic wind was blowing in Washington. Once the mid-term elections were over a franker debate within the White House and among Republicans about what was actually going on in Iraq became possible. The news from returning experts and fact-finding missions had been uniformly grim. A series of official internal reviews within the army, at least one well-known and respected former general and a range of Washington civilian defence experts were recommending similar changes to those sought by Odierno.

Rapidly, the new thinking in Washington began to crystallize around the general's demand for the despatch of up to 30,000 – or five brigades – of reinforcements who would move out into neighbourhoods in and around Baghdad, where 80 per cent of the violence in Iraq was taking place. Despite the vast effort involved, the peak troop strength would only be achieved for a short period between April and September 2007.[24] If only regular troops were deployed – and no one wanted to even contemplate a major mobilization of reservists – the surge was not sustainable beyond that date. Nor did anyone expect that the influx of new troops would resolve all Iraq's problems by itself. The aim was more modest. The new offensive would buy time to allow the Iraqi forces to finally become strong enough to start taking responsibility for their nation's security. It would also allow political actors a moment of relative calm in which they could make progress towards some kind of national reconciliation. The most important element was to break the vicious cycle that seemed to be leading Iraq towards greater and greater chaos and America towards a crushing strategic defeat. Critical to that was the implementation of all the new thinking that had gone into the new field manual produced by Petraeus at Leavenworth. American troops would live, sleep and fight among the people. They would try to bring security to communities, physically interposing themselves between the Shia death squads and Sunnis, between al-Qaeda and the Shias. Sensitive to the culture of both, they would go out of their way to do things 'the Iraqi way', however counterintuitive that might be for them. This would necessarily imply an initial spike in casualties, but, if the strategy worked, the number of dead and wounded would drop rapidly.

The National Security Council and Vice President Dick Cheney became rapidly convinced of the merits of the new plan, however militarily and politically risky it might be.[25] Bush too was persuaded that it needed to be tried and agreed to the proposals. There were to be no half-measures, no brigades dripped in over a period of months. American officials in Iraq had, through intercepted communications, learned that media reporting in the USA of the potential size and deployment of the new troops was already having a direct effect on the morale and strategic thinking of local insurgents and set about stoking the speculation among journalists further with selected leaks.[26] The final decision came fast. Odierno would get almost all the extra forces he had asked for. Petraeus would replace Casey as his immediate superior. It was, even many of his detractors admitted, a brave call for the president to make.[27]

In January 2007 Bush explained to the American nation that mistakes had been made in Iraq over previous years, that the situation there was 'unacceptable' and that a change of strategy was called for. The first new troops of what had been dubbed 'the Surge' started arriving within weeks. Even before they had arrived, US troops were moving out of their big bases and establishing combat outposts and 'joint security stations' with Iraqi forces in areas that were being contested by Shia militia and al-Qaeda-affiliated or other Sunni insurgent groups. Too few to cover a city of between 5 and 7 million inhabitants, they had been concentrated on the areas where sectarian violence had been worst.[28] A string of offensive operations were mounted against al-Qaeda and insurgent strongholds in Baghdad, in the vital villages and towns in the countryside around the capital and in cities to the north and south.[29] Petraeus arrived in Baghdad as commander of the war in Iraq and announced one of the new tactics he was planning to implement: walling off any vulnerable neighbourhoods with long rows of concrete blast walls.[30]

THE SURGE WORKS

The 'Surge' was a success, at least in the sense that, by the end of 2007, after six months during which the new American troops had been deployed in and around Baghdad and had implemented the strategy developed by Petraeus and Odierno, violence in Iraq was falling. At Congressional hearings in September 2007 Petraeus was able to show slides of statistics showing a steep drop in attacks on American troops. Though casualty figures in the summer had spiked to the highest levels since the two battles for Falluja three years before, by the onset of winter fewer US soldiers were being killed than at any other time since the invasion of 2003. In May and June 2007, 227 had died; only 23 were killed in December. Civilian deaths too were much lower. From nearly 3,000 killed in December 2006, the total had dropped to under 1,000 twelve months later. Areas of Baghdad which had been almost devoid of life were now beginning to show signs of some economic activity.[31] There was even a trickle of refugees coming back from overseas. 'After spending more than a year in Syria, one day my father called me saying: "You can now return, and do not worry. Everything is fine now,"' said Mohammed Hussain, an office administrator from a mixed Baghdad middle-class neigbourhood. 'I reached [home] at 6 a.m.'[32] All things were relative, however, and the more triumphant commentaries on the Surge of 2007 failed to mention that it had succeeded only in reducing violence to the levels of 2005.[33] Petraeus himself stuck to describing progress as 'fragile' or 'tenuous'. 'Nobody is saying anything about turning a corner, seeing lights at the end of tunnels, any of those phrases,' he told reporters at the end of the year. 'There's nobody in uniform who is doing victory dances in the end zone.'[34]

What had happened? How had the Surge worked? Most recent accounts often give the overall impression of a battered American army snatching victory from the jaws of defeat with an audacious and brave last-minute strategic gamble. One reason for the successes seen over 2007 was undoubtedly the courage and competence of American soldiers, who fought long and hard in difficult conditions on the ground in gritty Baghdad neighbourhoods like al-Doura, Khazamiyah, Sadr City and elsewhere. But the Americans were only part of the broader picture. In mid 2006, US planners had distinguished nine 'different fights' in the country, ranging from skirmishes prompted by Kurdish expansionism in the north to 'Shia on Shia' violence provoked by political manoeuvring between increasingly fragmented Islamist groups in the south.[35] By 2007, the situation was even more complicated. One element stood out, however: only a minority of these 'different fights' actually directly involved Westerners. What determined the success or failure of the Surge was the particular conjunction of these various ongoing sub-conflicts at a given time. If the Surge had been tried six months earlier, it probably would not have worked. Four main factors, all largely beyond the control of even Petraeus and President Bush, meant that it did.

The first and most obvious factor was that the battle for the Iraqi capital was largely over by the time Odierno had arrived at the end of 2006 and begun to formulate his new strategy. The apparent climax of the sectarian violence in the late spring of 2007 was in fact a final spasm in a process of atrocious killing which had been going on for at least eighteen months. 'I left [in December 2006] after I passed a different dead body at the same crossroads near my house five days in a row,' Bashir al-Bassm, a Sunni taxi driver, told the author. 'The choice was either flee or die.'[36] Various dynamics had been at work, driving violence to progressively higher and higher levels. There had been the inexorable logic of revenge and sectarian vendetta set in motion deliberately by al-Zarqawi and continued by his followers after their leader's death.

Militants linked to al-Zarqawi's networks killed dozens, on occasion hundreds, of Shia, knowing that the Shia gangs would then retaliate with their own wave of shootings and assassinations of Sunnis. Sunni communities would then form their own defence groups or rally behind the Islamic militants responsible for the original attacks as the only viable way of protecting themselves. These latter would then set out on a new killing spree, thus triggering a new cycle of violence. Repeated across Baghdad, the civil war had been inexorably ratcheted up another notch by each round of murders all through 2006. Fear became the militias' greatest asset, driving even secular Iraqis to support or even join them. A related dynamic accelerating and intensifying the violence had nothing to do with the provocations of al-Zarqawi or his networks. From the middle of 2006, Shia politicians and militia leaders, the two often being coterminous, had set about methodically emptying Baghdad of Sunnis. Working from block to block in carefully picked neighbourhoods, death squads focused first on community leaders, clerics, merchants and businessmen but went on to kill indiscriminately, continuing the murderous violence until the refugees started flowing and the districts emptied. Gruesome methods – some, such as drilling or burning, inspired by those being employed out in Anbar province – were used to increase the level of terror and speed the exodus. [37] The incentive for those initiating the violence was partly political, partly financial. There was the power that accrued to the leaders of the gangs. And then there were the assets once belonging to the Sunnis such as houses and shops, that militia members, usually the same young working-class men who had fought in Najaf, Karbala and in the slums of Sadr City in 2004, were able to seize.[38] A glance at a map of Baghdad in the spring of 2007 showed how, though the Sunnis had successfully managed to take over the odd neighbourhood that had previously been mixed, it was the Shia who had effectively won the battle for the city.[39] Whole swathes of what had been Sunni or mixed communities had been purged. Neighbourhoods like Amel, once home to around 20,000 Sunni families with close links to the Ba'athist regime, were now predominantly Shia. By the time the main American reinforcements began to flow in, most of the communal fighting in Baghdad was over.

The second major factor behind the success of the Surge was, paradoxically, the success of the Shia militias over the period immediately before the new strategy had been implemented. Al-Sadr, the young cleric dismissed as a 'punk' back in 2003, had through adept tactical man-oeuvring and populist appeal become a major player in the Iraqi political scene. He had played a careful game since being militarily and politic-ally beaten in the fighting of 2004, skilfully juggling participation in democratic politics with harder-nosed demagoguery and real and threat-ened violence. His representatives had done well in successive elections, partly due to their organization and partly their continuing appeal in poor urban Shia neighbourhoods. Their influence on central govern-ment was enhanced by the fact that they, in contrast to many legislators, did not spend much of their time outside Iraq.[40] In Basra, al-Sadr had been able to exploit continuing British ineptitude and lack of resources to secure a hold over much of the city.[41]

Yet success and consequent expansion had brought grave structural problems. Since mid 2006 discipline in al-Sadr's movement had begun to break down. By the summer of 2007 half a dozen different militias were operating as part of his al-Mahdi Army as well as scores of splinter groups.[42] Their leaders often fought amongst themselves and many appeared more interested in money or local power than piety. Control of petrol distribution networks generated very significant sums, and racketeering became increasingly common, with Shia communities suf-fering as much as anyone else. Militia men were taking more than $10,000 per day from the four largest petrol stations in Sadr City alone as well as extorting substantial sums from private minibus services, electricity sub-stations, food and clothing markets, ice factories. Many even collected rent from squatters in houses whose Sunni owners had fled.[43] Some groups aligned themselves closely with Iran – receiving large amounts of cash and weaponry (and some training) and increas-ingly rejecting al-Sadr's leadership. The evidence for Iranian involvement in payments for attacks on coalition forces was irrefutable, though exactly which element of the sprawling and fragmented Iranian security estab-lishment was responsible remained unclear.[44] This naturally damaged the nationalist credentials that had always been important to the Sadrist movement. Also, the social and economic activism that had been an equal part of al-Sadr's appeal – the street sweeping, the clinics, the dis-tribution of food or water – became increasingly less apparent as the killing continued. With the Americans and the blast walls now between them and their Sunni enemies and with limited room for further expan-sion after the victories of the previous months, the strengths of the al-Mahdi Army became weaknesses, and the movement found itself overextended both geographically and financially. As their popularity plunged, discipline began to break down further, and, caught in a destructive logic familiar to many other such groups in Iraq and elsewhere, al-Sadr's fighters found themselves increasingly forced to coerce the local communities which had once voluntarily offered their support.[45] 'At the beginning, coming from a Shia family, I respected the al-Mahdi Army, because they stood up to protect us,' said Amal Kamel, a twenty-year-old economy and administration student at Baghdad University. 'But then I discovered they were savages and barbarians. They killed women for not wearing the veil or just for a simple reason such as their wearing make-up. They killed Sunnis like the three sons of my neighbours [in the predominantly Shia al-Hurriya neighbourhood] and forced them to flee.' For Kamel, al-Sadr and his followers had plunged Baghdad into 'a nightmare coloured by the blood of Iraqis'.[46]

There was more urgent pressure on the leadership of the movement too. Early in 2007 a change in the local political dynamics had diminished top-level government support for al-Sadr. This had allowed Petraeus to add the upper tier of al-Mahdi Army leaders to the list of Sunni and al-Qaeda insurgents that the increasingly numerous American (and some British) special forces were hunting.[47] Through the late spring and summer, hundreds of senior al-Mahdi Army militia leaders were thus killed or captured, both in Baghdad and increasingly in small rural villages where they sought safety. This had two main consequences. One was political: al-Sadr and his key remaining lieutenants were all eminently rational tacticians who had little desire for death or detention, and, with the assassination campaign dramatically increasing and with it the potential personal cost of continuing to use violence against other Iraqis or against coalition forces, alternative strategies became more attractive to them. The second was primarily organizational, though it had major political consequences. As the more senior al-Mahdi Army leaders were killed or arrested, they were replaced by younger, inexperienced militants who were less bothered about retaining popular legitimacy or the 'name' of the movement and whose indiscriminate violence exacerbated even further the problem of retaining popular support.[48] This too worried the leadership of the movement. So when al-Sadr finally declared a unilateral six-month ceasefire in August 2007, it was to save the lives of his close associates, to bolster the diminishing popular support and, last but not least, to restore some discipline and order among the rank and file by flushing out those who no longer recognized his authority. His decision had an important and immediate effect. In July, 73 per cent of American fatalities and injuries in Baghdad in July had been caused by Shiite fighters. Odierno later estimated that the truce brought an immediate drop of 20 per cent in the level of attacks on US troops in and around the city.[49] Sadr himself then left for Iran to further his religious education.

The Shia militias were not, of course, the only Iraqi force to have alienated their own erstwhile supporters. The third major factor behind the success of the Surge was the continuing success of the Sunni Awakening or *Sahwa* that had flowed into the capital from Anbar down the same tribal, kinship and clerical channels as the nascent insurgency had flowed in the other direction four years previously. It was co-opted by Petraeus, who enrolled the armed gangs of Sunnis keen on taking on their former allies among the al-Qaeda-affiliated networks into 'Concerned Local Citizens' groups'. These went by various names including the 'Sons of Iraq' in Anbar or the 'Amiriyah Freedom Fighters' in the eponymous Baghdad neighbourhood and were very effective. By the end of the year, even the tough Sunni neighbourhood of al-Doura was back under government authority. It was the presence of these *Sahwa* fighters that had convinced Mohammed Hussain, the office administrator who had returned from self-imposed exile in Damascus, that he could stay in Baghdad. Very often the splits within the Sunni community ran along tribal lines, especially in the vital belts of mixed agricultural land and urban settlements around Baghdad. When the Zobai tribe, who provided many of the insurgents in the resilient and effective '1920 Revolution Brigades', turned against al-Qaeda affiliated networks, largely from other rival tribes, the Americans needed simply to stand back and supply the Zobai with what they needed to eliminate their rivals. Eventually there were 100,000 or more of these Awakening auxiliaries receiving $300 a month from the American taxpayer and effectively securing their neighbourhoods, with US army and Iraqi security forces' help, against the religious militants.[50]

A fourth element in the success of the Surge was the actions of regional powers. The growing chaos in Iraq, the risk of domestic militant 'blowback' and international pressure forced the Syrians to at least restrict the flow of militant volunteers and to close down many of the logistic networks that provided support to the insurgents. The actions of Damascus were self-serving, unpredictable and inconsistent but were, in some cases anyway, helpful nonetheless. As noted above, Jordanian intelligence was increasingly effective and motivated following the Amman attacks. The Saudi Arabians had at last recognized that hundreds of their citizens travelling to fight in Iraq was probably not a particularly positive development for their own domestic security, given that most then returned to homes in Jeddah, Medina, Riyadh or wherever, and finally had taken steps to limit their travel.[51] Most significantly, support from Iran to various elements among the Shia militias and to their political masters remained carefully calibrated, partly as a result of the complex manoeuvres within the Iranian regime and partly as a result of the general perception that Iran's interests would not be best served by Iraq collapsing into total chaos. No groups within Iraq thus received the kind of high-power weaponry provided by Tehran to the Lebanese Hezbollah, for example. It is also possible that Iran, after having infiltrated various al-Mahdi Army offshoots and splinter groups, had encouraged al-Sadr's decision to call a ceasefire.

What Petraeus and Odierno were able to do with admirable acumen, imagination and courage was to exploit the strategic opportunities these trends represented. There had been the well-publicized decision to enrol the Sunni *Sahwa* forces. There were the 'capture or kill' operations launched against senior al-Mahdi figures. Then there was the vast secret effort against the remaining Sunni insurgents, al-Qaeda in Iraq and the other radical Islamic groups. By mid 2007, Joint Special Operations Command under the experienced and focused Lieutenant General Stanley McChrystal comprised more than 5,000 special forces troops with enormous logistic and technical support. Key innovations over the previous years were paying fruit. Most Iraqis now had mobile phones and many of the leads that were fed to the special forces teams on the ground came from new network analysis, in part developed to track senior al-Qaeda figures in Pakistan, of call patterns. The American National Security Agency had access to the details – if not the content – of every call made in the country.[52] Combined with innovative ways of patching together different streams of intelligence, of using local partners and of targeting the middle ranks of an organization rather than just 'HVTs' (high value targets), the pressure on the insurgents was immense. The famously ascetic McChrystal, who was said to eat a single meal a day, pushed his forces to maintain a relentless 'operational tempo'. Joint

Special Ops Command had estimated that by the end of 2006 they had killed 2,000 members of the Sunni jihadist groups as well as detaining many more over the previous two years.[53] The count was higher in 2007.

Major decisions such as co-opting the Awakening Councils in and around Baghdad or targeting the al-Mahdi Army were clearly significant but so too were small changes. On the advice of David Kilcullen, Petraeus had his troops patrol on foot. Worried about leaving the safety of their 'up-armoured' Humvees, the troops were told to stay in pairs, separated by sufficient distances to avoid offering too great a single target. After early teething problems, the system worked well, allowing a much greater contact with local people and giving soldiers a much deeper understanding of their immediate 'combat environment'. Other changes saw more culturally appropriate procedures for difficult and sensitive tasks such as paying compensation for damage or a civilian death for which US troops were responsible. Instead of handing cash directly to bereaved relatives, American officers began using tribal leaders as intermediaries, for example.[54] The broad approach of Petraeus and Odierno meant varied reforms in discrete areas had a powerful cumulative effect. The prisons were one example. Despite the Abu Ghraib scandal, the detention system had remained a problem throughout 2005 and 2006. Petraeus appointed a Marine reservist, General Douglas Stone, to overhaul how insurgents were arrested, held, interrogated and released.

Stone's starting point was that prisons allowed extremists immediate access to, and control over, large captive populations and thus opportunities for recruitment and radicalization. The same strategies that were applied in the suburbs of Baghdad thus needed to be applied in Abu Ghraib, Camp Bucca and in the other detention facilities that the US military ran. A counter-insurgency campaign was needed within the prisons themselves, Stone decided.[55]

One of Stone's first acts was to establish exactly who the 24,000 detainees in the American military prison system in Iraq actually were. Comprehensive interviews found that prisoners had an average age of twenty-nine, making them exactly as old as British-based violent extremists were and providing further evidence that it was not simply impressionable teenagers who were a problem. Less than 1 per cent were 'third country nationals' from outside Iraq, not even a tenth could be considered 'al-Qaeda-affiliated', even fewer were from the al-Mahdi Army, more than two-thirds were illiterate and 78 per cent claimed that their involvement with violence against the government or American or other foreign troops had been motivated by the prospect of financial gain. The latter statistic was probably vastly exaggerated by detainees giving interviewers the answer that they felt was most acceptable to their questioners, but in general the men in the prison camps largely seemed to be Kilcullen's 'accidental guerrillas'. The factors that had led them into violence, said Stone, were 'a sense of humiliation or lack of respect, the view their families might have of them, a sense of worthlessness, sexual frustration as well as the guidance offered by community, tribal and religious leaders'. Radical Islamic ideologies, as Pan-Arabism and revolutionary Socialism once had done, offered a sense of empowerment, a legitimacy, fellowship, respect, cash employment, upward social mobility, support for families and, in some cases, 'the promise of the ultimate fulfilment of martyrdom', he explained.[56] Stone's solution was a comprehensive programme involving the identification and segregation of extremists within prisons, the creation of teams of psychiatrists and psychologists to work with inmates as well as visiting clerics who organized religious discussion sessions in which detainees would be instructed in the basics of local more moderate and tolerant traditional strands of Islam. The latter started not with the relatively complex discussions about when jihad might or might not be justified but with the basics of prayer, ablutions and the fundamental tenets of belief. Visits from the International Confederation of the Red Cross were welcomed, a system of basic literacy classes introduced, family visits allowed, brick factories set up in which inmates could work to earn small amounts of money. On release, Iraqi judges sought pledges of good behaviour from detainees. In the first eight months of the programme, from June 2007 to February 2008, 7,000 men were released, of whom only five returned to jail. The only problematic prisoners were hardcore committed al-Qaeda-affiliated militants who, Stone said, feared just two things: that their families might be harassed or that they might be transferred to an Iraqi-run prison. This apparently small exception was later to be significant.

By the end of 2007, however, it was clear that some vague – and very relative – stability had thus been – at least temporarily – achieved in Iraq.[57] It might have been fragile, as General Petraeus continued to insist, but it was undeniable. Through winter, the Surge was rolled out through the belt around Baghdad and even finally into restive and violent Diyala province to the north-east of the capital, where al-Zarqawi had once sought refuge and where now hundreds of local Sunnis joined the militias paid for by the Americans or the police. Support for the insurgents bled away rapidly. 'There were almost 600 fighters in our sector before the tribes changed course ... Many of our fighters quit and some of them joined the deserters ... As a result of that the number of fighters dropped down to twenty or less,' one leader of a largely Iraqi hardline 'al-Qaeda-ist' group near Balad, north of Baghdad, complained in late 2007.[58] In Baghdad and elsewhere several thousand Shia too had signed up to Awakening-type militia by the end of 2007, partly for the cash, partly to fight the al-Mahdi Army.

The gravest problem, of course, remained central government, which was as corrupt, dysfunctional and deeply partisan as it had ever been. The whole aim of the Surge had been to buy time for the Iraqi security forces to develop – which was slowly happening – and also for Iraqi politicians to take steps towards a national reconciliation of sorts – of which there appeared to be little prospect. The political situation had benefited from the replacement as ambassador of the flamboyant Zalmay Khalilzad, an American-Afghan of Sunni ancestry of whom Iraqi Shia leaders were suspicious, by veteran diplomat Ryan Croker, who was able to build a stronger relationship with key political players and worked better with the US military than his predecessor. But Nouri al-Maliki, the fifty-seven-year-old senior figure in the Shia Islamist Dawa organization, who had become prime minister in May 2006, and the other Shia leaders who dominated the government seemed little inclined to make any concessions to the defeated Sunni minority. It was with only great difficulty that they could be persuaded to agree to 35,000 of those on the American payroll in the Sunni militias joining the new Iraqi security forces. Allying with the Kurds, they could also block any moves towards a genuinely equitable distribution of national resources, particularly the vast cash flows that oil production, which began rising again towards the end of 2007, was generating.

In the end no one seemed inclined to push the issue of reconciliation too far. The days of grand ideological projects in Iraq seemed well over, and few regretted their passing. It had tacitly been recognized at the highest levels in Washington that the lofty goals of 2003 were not just impossible to achieve but that continuing to strive towards them would be profoundly counterproductive. If the new counter-insurgency field manual referred repeatedly to the importance of respecting cultural difference at a tactical level, there needed clearly to be a parallel doctrine at a strategic level too. In January 2008, the de-Ba'athification laws passed nearly five years previously over the fateful summer of 2003 were reversed. When Petraeus returned before Congress in April 2008 to brief America's political representatives once again on the situation in Iraq, he was questioned on the long-term aims of the US project in Iraq by a forty-seven-year-old Democrat Senator representing Illinois. 'If the definition of success is . . . no traces of al-Qaeda, no possibility of reconstitution [of al-Qaeda], a highly effective Iraqi government, a democratic multiethnic, multi-sectarian, functioning democracy, no Iranian influence, at least not the kind that we don't like, then that portends the possibility of us staying for twenty or thirty years,' Barack Obama said. If, on the contrary, the aim was a 'messy, sloppy status quo but there's not, you know, huge outbreaks of violence, there's still corruption, but the country's struggling along, but it's not a threat to its neighbours and it's not an al-Qaeda base, that seems to me an achievable goal within a measurable time frame'.[59] Such aims had broad bipartisan support, despite being considerably more modest than those announced with such bombast in 2003 and repeatedly reaffirmed since. That they could still be considered relatively ambitious was an indication of how badly wrong Operation Iraqi Freedom had gone.

THE SURGE AND THE 9/11 WARS

What had the Surge shown in the context of the 9/11 Wars?

The year 2007 in Iraq had shown the supremacy of local specificity. First it had been the global ideology proposed by the Americans and their allies that had been rejected. Not in its entirety, certainly, but in sufficient degree for it to become necessary for the original package of liberal democracy and free-market economics to have to be significantly altered for it to overcome the fundamental stain of being 'foreign' and get any purchase whatsoever. 'The Americans failed in Iraq because they did not understand how to treat Iraqis, and Iraqis became their enemies,' was the simple explanation of Thuryia Ismael, a sixty-year-old housewife in

Baghdad's Amariya neighbourhood. 'The political process in Iraq was built on wrong policies, and that effected everything: economy, health, education and security.'[60] Happily, the globalized ideology of al-Qaeda, as stripped of local context as anything Washington had ever tried to impose, had also been rejected. The fact that the aims, values and methods of al-Zarqawi and his like were ostensibly based on a version or reading of 'Islam' was not enough to compensate for the multitude of ways in which they failed to represent the aims, cultures, needs, aspirations, self-image and desires of the communities whose support – or at least fearful acquiescence – they wanted. The international militants or internationally affiliated networks in Iraq had made massive efforts to resolve the strategic problem their international dimension gave them. Al-Qaeda in Iraq had been dissolved and its various networks incorporated into the broader and more neutrally named Majlis Shura al-Mujahideen (Mujahideen Consultative Council) in the aftermath of the hotel bombings in Jordan. In October 2006, the formation of 'the Islamic State of Iraq' (ISI) was announced. Communiqués from its leadership stressed that the organization 'contained only 200 foreign fighters'. A cabinet was constituted with ministers for education and agriculture and statements disseminated on the internet called for volunteers to fight the 'Persians', i.e. Iranians and their Iraqi Shia proxies. But it was all to no avail. By the summer of 2007, the gap between even the 'al-Qaeda-ist' militants and the Sunni tribes was greater than ever and the divisions between the various elements of the insurgency – the ISI, the Islamic Army of Iraq, Hamas-Iraq, the 1920 Brigades, the Mujahideen Reform Front – were deeper than they had ever been.[61] Successive communities in Iraq in 2006 and 2007 had made their choices. Sunnis in Haditha or al-Doura, Shias in Nasariyah or Amarah had all turned away from global ideologies, whether they arrived on the back of an American tank, were spouted by a neighbourhood preacher or were imported by a foreign petty criminal turned militant leader like al-Zarqawi.

A second lesson, reinforcing that of earlier episodes in the 9/11 Wars, was thus that, in addition to being largely local, identities are dynamic. How Sunni populations in Anbar saw themselves and their duties as men, Iraqis, al-Dulaimi or Zobai, Arabs or Muslims differed between 2003 and 2007. It changed even over the year of the Surge. What had been acceptable to local populations once was no longer acceptable a short time later. One key question posed by the events of 2007 in Iraq was what would fill the gap left by the rejection by millions of people of both the Western universalizing package of liberal democracy and market capitalism and, at least in the short term, radical Islamic ideologies? What system would appear to be sufficiently authentic to local communities to bring a measure of stability? What set of ideas, norms and worldviews, in short what 'culture', would they generate themselves? The answers would undoubtedly have a major influence on the coming years of the conflict.

If anything was clear from the events of 2007 it was that any solution to Iraq's problems – and to those posed by the 9/11 Wars more generally – was going to evolve at a grass-roots level and work its way up rather than being imposed from above. Developments over the period in Iraq had reinforced again the degree to which events in the conflict were driven by what was happening on the ground. The thinking that led to the Surge had its origins with colonels out in Iraq's Anbar or Nimrud or Salahuddin provinces and had flowed back up the chain of command. The Surge had succeeded because of what had been going on in Sadr City and Ramadi well before even the decision to send extra troops had been taken in Washington. By the end of 2007, bin Laden and other members of the al-Qaeda senior leadership appeared as limited in their ability to project authority and power in Iraq as any Western general or political leader. Bin Laden had been sufficiently concerned by the situation there to dispatch a key aide, Abdul Hadi al-Iraqi, the associate who had steered the young Briton Omar Khyam and thus the other Crevice plotters towards targets in the UK, to try and bring some semblance of order. But al-Iraqi was arrested crossing from Iran into the north of Iraq not far from his native city of Mosul and disappeared into the CIA's prison system.[62] His capture underlined the obstacles bin Laden and the al-Qaeda hardcore were now facing. One consequence of al-Iraqi's detention was that, instead of a local man taking over the al-Qaeda operation in 'the land of the two rivers', the leader of those nominally affiliated with bin Laden's organization remained a foreigner of unclear origin, Abu Hamza al-Mohajir. Grotesque attacks by the militants continued but dropped from 300 bombings and more than 1,500 deaths in 2007 to 28 incidents and 125 civilian deaths reported in the first six months of 2008.[63] The flow of recruits on their way to Iraq began to slow considerably too, dropping, according to American officials, from around 120 to between 40 and 50 each month.[64]

The days when Amman, Damascus or Kuwaiti border villages were full of foreign volunteers seeking jihad were long gone.[65]

THE OTHER SURGE

In the summer of 2007 Saudi authorities had opened a new facility just outside the small village of al-Thamama, a half-hour drive down an immaculate asphalt road across scrubby sand and rock desert outside Riyadh. Few of the locals knew what went on behind the iron gates of the small and heavily guarded complex of low modern buildings, but around the world there were many who were closely observing developments there.

For al-Thamama was a pioneering centre for deradicalization. Staffed by psychologists, sociologists and clerics who referred to their charges as 'students', its primary aim was to avoid problems of recidivism when Saudi veterans of the fighting in Iraq left prison. In his sumptuous marbled office, which two senior American security officials had just left, Prince Mohammed bin Nayef bin Abdul Aziz al-Saud, the deputy interior minister responsible for counter-terrorism, explained that the problems of social reinsertion of returning militants from Afghanistan in 2002 had been one of primary reasons for recruitment to extremist organizations responsible for the blasts and killings across Saudi Arabia between 2003 and 2005. The fear was that the thousands of young Saudis who had either fought in Iraq or tried to reach Iraq before being detained would follow a similar course, he said.[66] The details of how the 'deradicalization' would be carried out had been finalized by a team of highly qualified Ministry of the Interior social scientists. They relied on weeks of religious instruction and group discussions to convince the 'students' that the religious reasoning which had justified their decision to travel to Iraq had been erroneous. Any 'personal issues' which might also have been responsible were tackled with psychological counselling, team sport and even art therapy. Otayan al-Turki, a Swansea-educated psychologist working at the centre, was struck by how many of the prisoners had very poor reasoning capacity and poor communication skills. 'Most are young, many come from large families,' he said. 'Many come from a non-Islamic background. Some have led sinful lives and were looking for a shortcut to paradise.' The art therapy was aimed at stopping the young men 'reacting in such an immediate way to images they see on the television or internet by giving them different visual languages', he said.[67] To ensure that all those released remained 'well integrated into the mainstream' the government provided jobs, money, cars, even wives on occasion. 'To deradicalize them we need to gain their trust and we need to help them restart their lives,' said Dr Abdul-rahman al-Hadlaq, a Ministry of the Interior criminologist working on the programme. 'This is not a reward. It is a necessary policy of containment.' The programme had so far proved to be extremely successful, he claimed, pointing out that the centre was yet to see one of their former charges relapse into violence or militant activism.[68]

Among the young men in the centre in the spring of 2008 was Hizam al-Ghatani, the thin, bespectacled former shopkeeper who had fought alongside the insurgents around Falluja in late 2004. Though motivated to keep fighting by scenes of carnage he had witnessed, al-Ghatani, who had originally only wanted to be a medic not a fighter, had been deeply disappointed by the growing internecine violence among the tribes and militants of Anbar and had returned to his home in Saudi Arabia in the spring of 2005, naively imagining that he would be received as a hero. Arrested immediately, al-Ghatani had been in prison since. Now on the brink of completing his time in detention, the former shopkeeper insisted he had been reformed. 'I am a very emotional man and I did not have a good understanding of Islam,' he said. 'Now I realize the wrong I did to my country and my family.'[69] Mohammed al-Fawzan, another volunteer who had tried to reach Iraq through Syria but had eventually been arrested, had recently returned to his family home in the middle-class al-Shifa neighbourhood in west Riyadh after serving his prison sentence. He was now back in his old job in the Ministry of Transport. He had also been given a car and had been found a wife – with the dowry paid by the government. 'I know now that I did not understand Islam and jihad,' he told the author. 'Now I still care about what happens in the world, but I understand that political things are the responsibility of the government, and I should not get involved. I am a soldier of the government. I should obey their orders and those of their representatives, even the traffic police.'[70]

The Saudi programme, which had started in mid 2007, was part of a wide range of similar strategies in countries as diverse as Indonesia, Egypt and Yemen.[71] General Stone's programmes with Iraqi detainees had in part been based on what the Saudis were beginning to do with their own imprisoned militants.[72] Though few such initiatives were on the scale or had the resources of the multi-million-dollar effort showcased at the al-Thamama centre, all were part of a range of new approaches by governments and intelligence agencies to extremist violence that were beginning to show results by around 2007 and 2008. No one was claiming they were a panacea to the problem of extremist violence – while committed to the reintegration of some, Saudi authorities were also building a series of purpose-built prisons with capacity for 6,400 militants who they believed too dangerous to release under any circumstances – but such strategies were nonetheless evidence that governments were willing to try new approaches and security services were looking at the problem in new ways. Nothing demonstrated this more than a secret conference of intelligence services including the British MI6, French DST and DGSE, German BKA, the Australians, the major American 'three-letter' agencies, the Saudis, Algerian and Egyptian *mukhabarat* and even the Pakistani ISI. They met in March 2008 in a Middle Eastern capital to spend three days discussing radicalization and to compare the research programmes many of them had launched to understand the phenomenon of Islamic militancy following the intensification of the 9/11 Wars between 2003 and 2005. One after another senior officers stood to give presentations in which, instead of talking about 'al-Qaeda', they focused on the process by which individuals became extremists. The British discussed the relationship between employment and educational level – overqualified people doing menial jobs was one risk factor – and spoke of 'vulnerable institutions' such as prisons or schools. The French emphasized second-generation identity crises. The Egyptians blamed the internet. The Australians underlined how internal competition for credibility and kudos within radical groups led to 'serial splitting' with more and more extreme sub-groups being formed as the process of radicalization advanced. The Saudis produced comprehensive research on those responsible for the wave of violence that the kingdom had suffered earlier in the decade showing how as time had passed the profile of militants had evolved with a clear decline in educational level and political and religious awareness and an increase in levels of previous involvement in violent crime. Early militants read commentaries on the Koran or histories of historical Islamic figures while later activists read thrillers if they read anything at all. The conference ended with a banquet and a show of local traditional dancing which saw the DGSE's *chef de délégation*, a colonel from the ISI and a long-haired German sociologist link arms amid sword-waving beturbanned locals, all watched by a wry, cigar-smoking senior FBI official.

Counter-terrorism was thus rapidly evolving too, undergoing its own version to the US military's 'cultural turn'. A broader 'surge' was underway, with extra manpower and resources being used in better, more effective, more intelligent ways in the fight against radical militancy. In 2002, only 2 per cent of British security agencies' budget had been devoted to prevention.[73] By 2007, MI5, the British domestic security service, flush with new funds released following the 7/7 bombings, had vastly expanded in all areas, but particularly in those dealing with countering processes of radicalization. From being principally focused on Irish terrorism, the organizsation had successfully reorientated itself to concentrate on an entirely new target and sections of British society and parts of the country that had previously been virtually unknown. Its understanding of the nature of the new threat had evolved rapidly too. Officials spoke of the 'paradigm shift' of moving from looking at a foreign-based to a 'homegrown' threat. The service's formal behavioural science unit had been enlarged too, giving the psychologists and social scientists who staffed it a more prominent role in planning of strategy and even of operations. MI5's analysts told the author in the summer of 2007 that activism in the UK was 'nothing to do with Islam' and 'everything to do with social movements . . . group think and social dynamics', which, whether true or not, at the very least marked a huge change from previous thinking.[74] As American soldiers had done in a rather different context in Iraq, MI5 also moved closer to the populations they viewed as critical, establishing regional offices across the UK, where intelligence operatives worked closely with local security forces – in this case, of course, the British police service, which is divided into local constabularies – who had the detailed low-level knowledge lacking at a national level.[75] Some old habits continued. Over previous years MI5 officers from the section responsible for running international terrorism-related 'agents' had systematically failed to intervene to prevent individuals of interest to them being tortured by local security services in Pakistan, Egypt and elsewhere and had been avid consumers of the 'product' of such 'robust' interrogations. The new approach complemented earlier strategies rather than supplanted them entirely.[76]

And though serious problems remained with the British government's new counter-radicalization strategy, known as 'PREVENT' and
run by the Ministry of Local Government and Communities rather than
the Home Office, it also signalled a new approach, one marrying 'hard'
counter-terrorism with 'softer' counter-radicalization policies. One criticism was that PREVENT identified Muslims as a 'suspect community'.
There were problems with both the generalized suspicion and the idea
that Muslims constituted one community. Officials countered by pointing out that their target was not those actively involved in terrorism but
'the much larger group of people who feel a degree of negativity, if not
hostility, towards the state, the country, the community, and who are, as
it were, the pool in which terrorists will swim'.[77] One positive development was a new understanding of nuances of who actually ran the
organizations that were supposed to be official representatives of the
British Muslim community and had hitherto been treated as privileged
interlocutors of the government. So, for example, the government
moved steadily to find alternatives to the Muslim Council of Britain
(MCB), a group which claimed to represent half the country's Muslims
but whose leaders' views were often hardline and highly politicized.[78]
The voices of the large numbers of Muslims in the UK who followed the
more personal, mystic Sufi strands of practice or simply were not particularly interested in politics had barely been heard.[79] As the British
government moved to distance itself from the MCB, new voices began
to emerge from within the British Muslim population.[80] Again, the picture was mixed as any group receiving funds under the PREVENT
intitiative risked being seen as tainted by their association with the government – the local version of the occupier's paradox that the Americans
and their allies had faced in Iraq – but the series of former members of
radical groups prepared to denounce their former associates were nonetheless useful in providing a 'counter-narrative' to the hitherto largely
unchallenged language of global pan-Islamic solidarity, anti-Semitism,
anti-Zionism and anti-Americanism.[81] The government's strategy for
countering extremism consistently underestimated the role British foreign policy played in reinforcing the 'single narrative' propagated by
extremists but, by 2007, moderate clerics who had often waged a lonely
and misunderstood struggle against extremism – such as Musa Abu Bakr
Admani, the Muslim chaplain of London Metropolitan University –
began to feel more confident. 'When Muslim communities feel dislocated

and uncertain, they have always gravitated towards utopian international ideas of Islam,' Admani, who had personally known several of those involved in the 2006 'airlines plot', told the author over tea and pasta in a café on north London's Holloway Road.[82] 'There is still a bumpy ride ahead, but values such as freedom, equality, human dignity and fairness, the well-embedded core of Britishness, are values which a lot of young Muslims identify with. They are Islamic as well as British values. Yes, we need to address the ... hatred of the West; yes, we need to inculcate basic Islamic values such as compassion and respect. But people have woken up, and the debate on how to move forward has started.'

Admani's impressions appeared to be confirmed by events more broadly. Young British-born men continued to become involved in radical violence, and foreign militants continued to operate on UK soil, but general levels of radicalization remained apparently stable.[83] This was bad news in that a threat clearly remained – six plots were foiled in the two years following the 7/7 bombings, and the summer of 2007 saw a small group of highly educated young British Muslim doctors attempt a double bombing of a nightclub in London before two of them drove a vehicle loaded with petrol and gas canisters into the front of Glasgow airport – but it was good news in that at least things were not getting worse. London Muslims appeared as likely as the general public to condemn terrorist attacks on civilians and more likely than the population at large to find no moral justification for using violence in a 'noble cause'.[84] While 48 per cent thought it wrong that the security services should infiltrate Muslim groups, the same number thought it perfectly acceptable. Polls in Europe showed no great shifts in any direction either.[85] Converts continued to cause concern with a plot uncovered in western Germany in September 2007 involving two young local men who had become Muslims and who planned to blow up a 'disco full of American sluts' on an American base or a similar target. However, the danger posed by converts was not going to be enough to return European nations to the darker days of 2004 or 2005.[86] The growing general rejection of violent extremism seen in the Middle East appeared to be in the process of being reproduced among Muslim communities in Europe too.

A calmer atmosphere also allowed a more sensible general debate. Senior figures in the British police and the security services appeared less prone to terrifying doomsday predictions or to the systematic exaggeration of the threat posed by individual cells in the UK that had previously marked their statements. This was perhaps because by 2007 they now had the vast bulk of the increased powers that they had so vociferously demanded in the immediate post-9/11 years and were more confident that the legislation needed to secure convictions for a range of activities that previously might have escaped prosecution let alone significant custodial sentences was in place.[87] With populations now becoming habituated to repeated scares, claims of new threats were in any case greeted more sceptically and more phlegmatically than before. Few security officials would ever admit that the likelihood of a devastating attack had lessened – 'We'd be cutting our own budgets,' admitted one MI5 officer to the author in a moment of unwarranted frankness – but there was a realization that the public was much more critical of any claim of potential danger than had been the case before.[88]

One reason for this was the steady demolition of many of the tenacious if tendentious ideas about the capabilities of the enemy. Many of the claims of 2002 and 2003 had long been shown to be without foundation. The various investigations in Iraq had shown that Saddam had not possessed weapons of mass destruction, and some of the more fabulous inventions about the potential and nature of al-Qaeda had been effectively deconstructed as scholars, analysts and journalists picked over the voluminous material that had become available as years passed.[89] The debate over whether al-Qaeda was more ideology or more organization and whether bin Laden was 'inciter-in-chief' or of marginal importance or terrorist mastermind continued, as highly politicized and polarized as it had always been, but some broad areas of consensus had emerged. Around 1,000 English-language books with 'terrorism' in the title had existed in 1995. A decade later there were nearly eleven times as many, with most of the new additions focusing on Islamic militancy. Though the 'al-Qaeda industry' that had sprung up post-9/11 had attracted more than its fair share of frauds, fantasists and ideologues, it had nonetheless created a substantial body of research and a cohort of often very fine researchers whose conclusions filtered through both to policy-makers and to an increasingly well-informed public.[90]

In the US, 2007 too saw a broader reassessment of the more egregious excesses of the early years of the 9/11 Wars. This was in part enforced – the previous year had seen a landmark Supreme Court decision that prisoners in Guantanamo Bay were covered by the articles of the Geneva Conventions forbidding abusive or humiliating treatment of prisoners and that the military tribunals the detainees faced were illegal without explicit authorization from Congress – but was also due to a slow realization among some senior figures that at least some earlier policies had been counterproductive.[91] These changes sometimes occurred almost in spite of the ideological atmosphere. So, for example, as prosecutors and investigators received more resources and became more adept at framing charges, the law became a much more potent counter-terrorist weapon and much more attractive to the authorities as a consequence. Over the two years after the 9/11 attacks, only one in thirty American defendants described as 'terrorists' to the media when arrested were actually charged with terrorism offences. Only around a third of these were eventually convicted on terrorism charges. By 2006 and 2007, although the Bush administration's National Defense Strategy of 2005 had referred to the use of courts to pursue terrorists as part of a 'strategy of the weak', a range of improvements in training and organization as well as new legislative tools meant that nearly half of individuals labelled terrorists were charged as such and more than 80 per cent of these were convicted.[92] One major contributing factor was the success government prosecutors began to have in convincing defendants to cooperate. Another improvement, as in the UK, was an understanding of exactly what charge could be made to stick, particularly when it came to membership of a terrorist organization.[93] Almost by default, therefore, a much-derided 'legal approach' to counter-terrorism gained ground at the expense of hardline strategies which emphasized the extraordinary nature of the threat facing the USA and therefore justified deeply divisive 'extra-legal' responses to it.

Another important shift came within the American domestic intelligence community, and particularly the FBI, where Robert Mueller, the director, had set about changing the bureau's role from detection and law-enforcement to intelligence-gathering, more along the lines of the British MI5. Philip Mudd, formerly a senior official at the CIA with intimate knowledge of south Asia, the Middle East and Islamic militancy, was made deputy director of the agency tasked with consolidating and accelerating the changes. Mudd, an intense and scholarly analyst with a Masters in English literature, had very different views from his predecessor in the post, who had proudly declared that knowledge of subject matter was not essential for senior officials.[94] Though impressed by the FBI's information-gathering capabilities, he believed the bureau needed to focus less on problems 'that were known', i.e. law-enforcement, and more on what could be potential problems, i.e. security. Mudd and his boss, Director Robert Mueller, wanted their staff to be asking not 'Do we have a case open?' but 'Do we have a concern here worth investigating?'. By the end of 2006 the FBI had more than 2,000 intelligence analysts and, perhaps more importantly, nearly 1,400 linguists. The Americans also followed the Europeans in revising the vocabulary used to describe the conflict and their enemies. In late 2006, British cabinet ministers had been advised by the Foreign Office not to use the 'counterproductive' term 'War on Terror'.[95] The advice had had little effect until the June 2007 resignation of Tony Blair after ten years in power, when much of the more ideological charged rhetoric of the early years of the 9/11 Wars was immediately dropped. Blair's departure also allowed a frank discussion of the effects of the Iraq war on radicalization in the UK and elsewhere for the first time. Previously, ministers had tied themselves in rhetorical knots to avoid admitting that the invasion of Iraq had been a major factor in the intensification of the threat in Britain between 2003 and 2005, though in private they admitted that 'Iraq [was] a huge problem'.[96] For Jonathan Freeman, head of the British government's Combating Extremism Unit, the 'military language' used hitherto was 'just wrong'. 'You have to use language which does not alienate while not denying there are issues that have to be dealt with,' he said.[97] In January 2008, drawing heavily on the new British guidelines, a number of American federal agencies, including the State Department, the Department of Homeland Security and the National Counter Terrorism Center, advised staff not to describe Islamic extremists as 'jihadists' or '*mujahideen*', or to use terms such as 'Islamo-fascism'.[98] Such changes were easy to dismiss as superficial and it would certainly be wrong to exaggerate their impact. The 'cultural turn' naturally had its limits. A resumé of a US wargame, seminar and workshop exercise in late 2007 showed just how cultural sensitivity was often seen as a tactic rather than a principle and how 'winning hearts and minds' remained a matter of persuading others rather than having any kind of genuine conversation. 'The focus of effort in the persistent conflict environment must not be the opponents, but rather the people, the human terrain in which they operate,' the review said, citing word for word the new counter-insurgency doctrines being employed in Iraq. It then insisted, however, that 'the general population ... must be convinced of the correctness of Western values and ideas'.[99] But, as with so many elements of the 9/11 Wars, though individual measures may have had limited impact, cumulatively minor changes could have a significant effect, particularly when they acted to accelerate developments on the ground.

For the reaction against extremist violence in the Islamic world that had become evident in 2006 – though it had been underway in places like Saudi Arabia, Turkey, Morocco and elsewhere much earlier – continued to build and broaden. Successive polls reinforced the earlier indication that support for radicalism fell away rapidly whenever violence was experienced locally. In Lebanon, Bangladesh, Jordan and Indonesia, the proportion of Muslims supporting suicide bombing had dropped to levels that were half or less of those of five years before.[100] As ever, the picture was incomplete. In the deradicalization centres of Saudi Arabia 'students' were taught not that going to fight oppression of fellow Muslims in Iraq was necessarily wrong but that to do so *without the permission of the authorities* was wrong, a nuance that escaped most of the impressed Western politicians who were shown around the facilities. In Jordan, though 42 per cent said suicide bombing was never justified, 44 per cent continued to say it was sometimes or rarely justified. But overall it was difficult to argue that the same cycle of escalating chaos and violence seen during the earlier phases of the war was continuing unchanged. Support for Osama bin Laden declined further too, again most obviously in those countries which had suffered militant violence.[101] By 2007, only 15 per cent of Saudi Arabians had a favourable view of their former fellow citizen turned violent extremist and only one in ten held positive views about his group.[102] As if to emphasize the point, one of the original founders of al-Qaeda and a key ideological mentor of bin Laden and al-Zawahiri, Sayyid Imam al-Sharif, published a book from his Egyptian prison cell called *Rationalization of Jihad*, in which he argued that 'jihad had been blemished with grave Sharia violations during recent years ... Now there are those who kill hundreds, including women and children, Muslims and non-Muslims in the name of jihad.' Al-Sharif ruled that bombings in Egypt, Saudi Arabia and elsewhere were illegitimate and that terrorism against civilians in Western countries was wrong.[103] When they came from someone like al-Sharif, a respected senior figure within the movement who had been one of the first to elaborate the doctrine of *takfir*, such statements were an indication that an important shift was underway. Al-Sharif was not alone either. From mid 2007 onwards, scores of other well-known individuals also with impeccable extremist credentials began to make public statements denouncing al-Qaeda. One was Salman al-Auda, a Saudi scholar who had been a trenchant critic of the West and of Middle Eastern governments since the late 1980s and who had a cult following in Riyadh and east London alike. In September 2007, al-Auda had addressed bin Laden on a widely watched Arabic-language television network.[104] 'My brother Osama, how much blood has been spilt? How many innocent people, children, elderly and women have been killed . . . in the name of al-Qaeda? Will you be happy to meet God almighty carrying the burden of these hundreds of thousands or millions [of victims] on your back?'[105] The discovery of a plot to launch attacks in Saudi Arabia in Riyadh, Medina and even the holy city of Mecca during the pilgrimage period of Hajj in December of 2007 was important too. Whether or not the plot was genuine – Prince Mohammed bin Nayef, the deputy interior minister, insisted to the author that it was – the news that extremists were planning to target ordinary people performing one of the five fundamental duties of a Muslim had a powerful effect.[106] Bin Laden's communications were becoming increasingly defensive and increasingly frustrated. 'O Muslim youth of this generation! Why is there cowardice and frailty?' he asked angrily in a 'message to the Islamic nation' released in May 2008. 'Our lives are already ruled by harmful policies meant to discourage our beliefs. My brother! Jihad against the infidels is your duty. How can you fear death, when death is your paradise? The pillar of religion shall not become stronger by voting and elections. Anything but the sword shall be of no help, I swear.'[107]

By the late spring of 2008, it was thus possible to distinguish four broad phases of the 9/11 Wars to date. The first three had been obvious for some time. Act One had seen the initial explosion of violence and the Afghan war. Act Two had seen the lull, the phoney war of 2002, and Act Three, the intensification and escalation of violence of 2003 to 2006. A year or so later, however, this now appeared to have been the nadir. For the nature of Act Four was gradually becoming clearer. The new phase of the conflict had seen the slide into ever greater violence stopped, tensions dropping in relative terms, fewer major headline attacks, no riots, no collapse of any government and, though perhaps due in part to a normalization of a sustained and high level of threat, a relative sense of calm. If al-Zarqawi's strategy of 'local jihad' had failed in Iraq, al-Suri's strategy of 'global jihad' was meeting with equally little real success more generally in the Islamic world. Again, there had been no 'turning point', more a subtle shifting in the balance of tendencies that opened up the possibility that the future evolution the 9/11 Wars might be in a new, more positive direction. This small progress was undoubtedly easily reversible, as fragile an advance on the global scale as it had been on the local scale in the more limited environment of Iraq. There was no doubt that grave problems remained. Certainly, most of the underlying issues that had underpinned radicalization even before 9/11 had remained largely unaddressed, and a single major successful terrorist attack could, depending on the reaction, completely change the dynamic. So too could the emergence of another leader of similar charisma to bin Laden but with perhaps a subtly different message and style. And even if it was the case that al-Qaeda's global package had been rejected not just in Iraq but more broadly in the Islamic world, no one could predict what might fill the gap it left. But even if it was still very unclear what the next act of the conflict might bring, it was reasonable to hope that it would not be as grim as what had gone before.

One thing was certain. Despite their setbacks, radical Islamic militants in the spring of 2008 still retained the capacity to often think and move faster than those trying to kill or capture them. By late spring there were signs that well-known and capable individuals, some linked to the al-Qaeda senior leadership, were leaving Iraq and heading east.[108] For if the militants were having less success than they had hoped in the Middle East and in Europe, they were having more than they had ever expected in the first theatre of the 9/11 Wars: Afghanistan. The strategic centre of gravity of the conflict appeared to have shifted again. No longer Europe or the Middle East, it was, once again, south-west Asia.

PART FIVE

Afghanistan, Pakistan and Al-Qaeda: 2008

12

Afghanistan Again

KABUL, LATE SUMMER 2008

Even in the summer of 2008, even on a hot afternoon in mid-August at
the height of the fighting season, there was little that indicated that Maidan Shar, a small town 30 miles south of Kabul, lay astride a frontline.
The only signs of conflict were the wrecks of two trucks burned out in
an ambush a few days earlier and dumped outside a scruffy row of
mechanics' workshops and the Turkish armoured vehicles firing practice rounds into a hillside a mile or so away. A few ragged farmers sold
small, bruised apples from battered barrows in the patch of dried mud
that passed for a central marketplace. In the town's single restaurant a
dozen men lay on grubby carpets spread on the flat concrete floor,
sipped smeared glasses of tea amid clouds of flies and stared hard at
strangers. The frontline, as ever in the 9/11 Wars, was poorly defined,
invisible and intangible. But it was a frontline nonetheless.

The torpor was thus misleading. By 2008, much of Wardak, the province of which Maidan Shar was the capital, had slipped under the
control of the insurgents. Though the Taliban did not control all of the
10,000 square miles of mixed mountain, desert and parched farmland
that made up the province, only a fairly limited amount of territory
could be said to be under the authority of President Hamid Karzai and
his government either. Their power, weak at the best of times, was limited
to the main roads, the district centres and Maidan Shar itself. 'Things
are pretty safe round here,' the local governor, Halim Fedayi, said disingenuously in an interview in his heavily guarded office minutes before
news came in that his deputy had narrowly escaped death in an ambush
on the main road through the province – Highway 1 from Kabul to

Kandahar – a few miles away.[1] Outside, a crowd of tribal elders had gathered. They had been summoned to hear the governor, a former NGO worker and exile, speak about how the insurgents' interpretation of the Koran was erroneous. One, from a village only half an hour by motorbike away, summed up what many were thinking: 'What the governor says is very nice, but it's the Taliban who control my district, not him.' Sitting on a metal bed on a small hill a few miles north of Maidan Shar, Salim Ali, a twenty-year-old policeman, forced a thin smile. With three colleagues, for a pound a day, he guarded the narrow pass on the road to Kabul. 'There's less traffic these days,' he said. 'People are frightened.'

The Afghan capital in August 2008 was an anxious place. The situation in the city's immediate vicinity was unstable and fluid. It was very clear that insurgents were moving through surrounding villages, stockpiling weapons and establishing safehouses. Suburbs on the outskirts were unsafe and suicide bombers continued to hit targets within the city limits. Someone managed to fire an RPG – which has an effective range of a couple of hundred metres – at the new airport building. Even the streets of Shar-e-Nau, the centre of Kabul, saw a series of kidnappings. The road to Jalalabad was repeatedly cut by insurgent raids and roadblocks. Just north of the road in the valley of Uzbeen, ten French soldiers were killed in an ambush, pinned down amid rocks and on steep slopes as Afghan National Army soldiers fled in total disorder and NATO, which had around 25,000 heavily armed Western troops stationed within a hour's helicopter flight and jets permanently overhead, tried without success to bring its formidable airborne assets to bear. Though few believed the Taliban had any chance of actually capturing the capital, when traditional calls of 'Allahu akbar' resounded from rooftops on the first day of Ramadan, the Islamic holy month, local authorities thought the cries signalled an insurrection and ordered a major security alert. In a row of open-air workshops on the northern outskirts, labourers worked round the clock pouring concrete into battered metal moulds to meet the insatiable local demand for something barely seen in Afghanistan even five years before: the concrete blast wall. The big sections cost $550, the smaller a mere $300. A good team of workers could produce twenty a day. 'I sell them to foreigners mainly and make good money,' said Said Fahim, the owner of the biggest workshop. 'If Afghanistan was peaceful there would be no use for them. I'd prefer to be out of business.'

The ambient fear – as well as the blast walls – led many to make a comparison with Baghdad. Certainly, much in Kabul and in the country more generally in the summer of 2008 was familiar to those who had seen Iraq, particularly in 2004, 2005 or 2006. It was as if the great tide of radicalization and violence which had surged out of south-west Asia, across the Middle East and into Europe between 2001 and 2005 had carried back an accumulated load of detritus from these theatres as, on the ebb, it had returned to its source. The war in Afghanistan had even changed visually to resemble the conflict elsewhere. The vast bases on which most international troops lived – such as Bagram, Kandahar or Camp Warehouse outside Kabul – had been the prototypes for those in Iraq. Now the situation was reversed. The Afghan bases were now supplied by same contractors and thus had the same menus, facilities and even road signs as those in the Middle East. The military technology developed in Iraq – such as the 'up-armoured Humvees' – could now be seen on Afghan roads. Soon 'Mraps' – vehicles with V-shaped hulls to deflect IED blasts – would arrive. The same language – the acronyms, insults, slang and neologisms – could be heard. Naturally there were connections between the theatres in terms of personnel too. The new commander of ISAF appointed in June 2008, General David McKiernan, had played a key role in the 2003 Iraq invasion. General Stone, who had reformed the prison system in Iraq, had arrived to do the same in Afghanistan. A high proportion of the officers and men on the ground had experience on the streets of Ramadi, Kut, Mosul or Baghdad itself. The same went for many civilian employees, NGO workers and, perhaps more worryingly, the increasing number of security contractors arriving in Afghanistan. Many among the 50,000 strong private-sector mercenary army in Iraq had seen new opportunities opening up further east. 'Feels just like home,' laughed one South African employee of Blackwater, the most notorious of the private security contractors working in the Middle East, as he surveyed the scene of a suicide bombing on the Jalalabad Road a few days after flying in from the Gulf. He and his three colleagues were all wearing the beard, Oakley shades, T-shirt and combat trousers that had become the distinctive uniform of the mercenary in the 9/11 Wars. Though their company had recently been forced to leave Iraq after trigger-happy employees shot and killed at least fourteen civilians in unprovoked 'defensive' fire in Baghdad, there was plenty of demand for their services in Afghanistan.[2]

As the summer of 2008 passed and despite London politicians' insistence that the Taliban were being 'beaten back', a few British officials had begun to voice serious concerns at the direction Afghanistan had taken.[3] British intelligence analysts in Kabul privately described the Taliban as better armed and better organized than ever before and said that fighting in the coming months would be the toughest yet seen.[4] Many were deeply worried by the core weakness of the effort in Afghanistan: the incompetence, corruption, cynicism and effective paralysis of the central Kabul government. President Karzai, now in his seventh year in power, appeared incapacitated by a combination of extreme pragmatism and paranoia. The various 'GOA' (Government of Afghanistan) institutions such as the Afghan National Army and the Afghan National Police continued to suffer very serious structural problems ranging from huge ethnic imbalances in the under-resourced army to an almost total lack of capacity in the corrupt and violent police. The judiciary was a ruin, with many judges either fleeing their districts or simply handing over much of their caseload to clerics either linked to the Taliban or actively involved with the insurgents.[5] Privately, Sir Sherard Cowper-Coles, the British ambassador in Kabul, listed the intractable structural problems inside Afghanistan, in the region and further afield. One problem, he said, was the failure to get the Islamic world involved in the effort in Afghanistan. Turkey had contributed 860 troops, and the United Arab Emirates had a unit of special forces secretly engaged in the east, but otherwise Muslim-majority nations had almost no official military or civilian presence in the theatre. But this was only one of many things that needed to change if there was to be a hope of 'success'. There was also the lack of political will inside Afghanistan and of political focus in Europe. There was the drift in Washington as elections approached, the slumping support for the war among Western voters, the lack of regional diplomatic coordination and, perhaps most serious of all, the general lack of realism about what was now attainable in the short, medium and long term. 'We cannot win without a major shift in strategy,' Cowper-Coles said. 'And we may not win even then. Whatever winning means.'[6]

The obvious question was: how, with so many initial advantages compared to Iraq, had so much gone so badly wrong?

THE TALIBAN RETURN, 2002–2006

The first thing the Taliban had done when crossing the border after flee-ing Afghanistan in late 2001 and 2002 had been to make sure they had a secure base. Most returned to places that were well known to them: the religious schools or *medressas*, refugee camps and villages that had been home for many years and were still often home to relatives.[7] 'Kabul was falling; I drove with my family across the border. There was no problem at the checkpoint. I have a lot of land in Pakistan, and every-one knows me,' Maulvi Mohammed Arsala Rahmani, the former Taliban education minister, recalled.[8] The experience of the column of Taliban who had fled from Jalalabad over the Spin Ghar mountains in mid November as the fighting started in Tora Bora was typical. Several hundred strong, they had reached the high valleys in Pakistani territory before local troops had deployed. They then doubled back into Afghan-istan and, after a further day and night of travel, had split up. At least a third of the group – young Pakistanis who had come from the religious schools of the North West Frontier Province and the tribal agencies – were each given 5,000 Pakistani rupees ($60/£40 at 2001 rates) and told to go home. A second group – several dozen senior Taliban officials – hired vehicles to drive further south into Paktika province before crossing into Pakistan by the remote Gumal pass and entering the tribal agency of South Waziristan, where they were hosted by relatives and supporters. A final group of twenty wounded fighters were sent directly across the border to hospitals in Peshawar with the cover story that they were villagers who had been injured by the American bombardment.[9] Thousands of other footsoldiers, hundreds of mid-level commanders and scores of senior figures – including almost the entire leadership of the Taliban – followed similar routes to escape from Afghanistan. By the middle of 2002, most had found new bases, either around Quetta, where a 'Quetta Shura' or leadership council under Mullah Omar was constituted, or Peshawar. Some found their way to more remote vil-lages, and a very few ended up in Karachi.

If the secure bases they had across the border and the resources that flowed in from a network of supporters overseas in the Gulf and else-where were both key in sustaining the Taliban after their defeat and strategic retreat in 2001, it was nonetheless the particular combination of conditions within Afghanistan that created the vacuum and the griev-ances that allowed them to launch their campaign to return to power within a few short years and then build an insurgency of sufficient strength to cripple the Western project in the country. One crucial pre-condition for the Taliban re-establishing a presence within Afghanistan was the discontent of Pashtun populations in the south and east at what was felt to be an unjust post-war settlement. Pashtuns had ruled the Afghan state ever since it had been founded in 1747, with the only exceptions being chaotic interludes in 1929 and from 1992 to 1996, and though this narrative of Pashtun rule naturally glossed over the constant fighting between the great Pashtun tribal confederations of Durrani and Ghilzai, within tribes, between Pashtun *mujahideen* fac-tions during the war against the Soviets and between Pashtun Communists during the same period, between pro- or anti-Taliban factions in the 1990s and, of course, between communities every day over water, wood or decades-old perceived slights to honour, it still meant the Pashtun community was broadly convinced of its historic right to govern the country. Unlike the Iraqi Sunnis, who had lost demographic dominance around a century before losing their hold on power, the Afghan Pashtuns had remained the country's largest ethnicity – around 45 per cent, though no one really knew – and had retained a strong sense of entitlement.

In the aftermath of the fall of Kabul to the Northern Alliance, which had been broadly composed of Tajiks, Uzbeks and Hazaras, and the deposition of the largely Pashtun Taliban, many Pashtuns across Afghanistan were concerned that they would be the major losers in any new political set-up. The Bonn conference of December 2001, convened by the United Nations and managed jointly by UN and US diplomats to lay the basis for the future political set-up of Afghanistan, did little to reassure them. Karzai, the new 'chief executive' and president in waiting of the country, was a Pashtun but was highly Westernized, had returned from more than twenty years of exile and had little popular base beyond the following he had inherited from his father, a senior figure within the major southern Popalzai tribe.[10] Then there was the widespread and unchecked score-settling which targeted Pashtun minorities in the north of the country in the early months of 2002, the sidelining of the ageing (Pashtun) king and the appointment of Tajiks from the Panjshir valley to head the so-called 'power ministries' of Defence, the Interior and For-eign Affairs.[11]

These and other developments reinforced the sense of political marginalization among Afghanistan's Pashtuns, particularly in the rural areas or in the towns and cities of the south and east. This growing alienation was soon sharpened by a sense that the community was economically disadvantaged too. There were many areas of Afghanistan that benefited hugely in the years following the invasion. Kabul was transformed. So too were Jalalabad and Herat, with their links to Pakistan and Iran respectively. Even small towns like Pul-e-Khumri on the northern side of the critical Salang tunnel had bustling bazaars full of Chinese motorbikes, colourful blankets, inedible artificial jam that sold extraordinarily and inexplicably well, great piles of tin buckets and jerry cans of fuel. Bamiyan thrived, still poor and starved of development funds but stable and secure behind its mountain ramparts. But though the economy was booming, with growth rates of 8, 10 or even 14 per cent, the rural areas, particularly in the south, where the Pashtuns predominated, were missing out.[12] The 'primary beneficiaries of assistance were the urban elite,' the World Bank noted in a 2005 report, exactly the constituency whose loyalty to the Western project in Afghanistan had always been assured.[13] Kandahar itself might have changed – the governor's palace had been repainted, roads resurfaced, there were drugs in the hospital and scores of ornate villas in the style favoured by local drug barons – but even a few miles outside the city there was little sign of any physical improvement since the end of the Taliban's rule.

The reasons for this were simple: a lack of political attention, of funds, of security and of governance. Earlier chapters noted how Afghanistan received far less cash for reconstruction than almost all recent nation-building efforts.[14] According to aid agencies, only half of the $20 billion that the international community had pledged to Afghanistan over previous years had actually arrived, and around 40 per cent of what had turned up had been spent on corporate profits and consultancy fees. Of the $6 billion that was left, a third was wasted.[15] This meant that a fifth of what had been announced as given to Afghanistan actually reached Afghans.[16] Spending the money that did get through was not easy either. The failure to deploy sufficient numbers of troops to Afghanistan had meant a minimal military presence in what were among the most critical parts of the country in terms of potential for violence. There was a US base for 2,500 troops in Kandahar and a couple of forward operating bases manned by small detachments of special forces who spent their time hunting fugitives or protecting under-resourced 'Provincial Reconstruction Teams', but otherwise there was no significant military presence across the four southern provinces of Kandahar, Herat, Farah and Nimroz between 2002 and 2006. International forces failed to secure even the major towns and highways in the south let alone the long unguarded border.[17] In the four vital provinces further north – Oruzgan, Zabul, Ghazni and Paktika – Western troops were very thin on the ground too. As violence in the south began to increase from mid 2003, UN development agencies and Western and Afghan aid organizations were forced to first scale back their operations and then, by 2005, to virtually stop all work in what was the most strategically important part of Afghanistan after the capital.[18]

The consequences of the NGOs' absence were all the more grave given the vast problems of governance. In a rerun of what had happened further north around Jalalabad, two factions had raced for Kandahar as the Taliban's regime had collapsed in late 2001. Both were led by former warlords who had recently returned from exile. The winner was Gul Agha Sherzai, one of the most notorious of the commanders who had run the city and its surroundings in the early 1990s and whose depredations had prompted the foundation and permitted the early success of the Taliban. He owed his successful return to power in part to air strikes called in by American special forces and in part to the decision of two other major tribal leaders who had previously supported the Taliban to withdraw from the fight.[19] Men like Sherzai – similar figures were coming to power in many other provinces across the south and east – made little effort to hide their own involvement in narcotics, dealing openly with both major drugs traffickers and the insurgents on a daily basis.[20] They were neither interested in nor capable of dealing with the complex developmental challenges facing local communities at the time. These returning warlords had two layers of protection: the American special forces and intelligence agencies, for whom they acted as local proxies, and the Kabul government, for whom the sole criterion for resting in post was loyalty to President Karzai. For the majority of southern Pashtuns, these corrupt and brutal commanders, the administrations that such men led and the famously venal and violent police were the face of the new Afghanistan being built by the international powers.[21] Those communities and individuals who were denied a slice of the lucrative new economic opportunities opening up to anyone with power and influence from 2002 naturally looked for ways to preserve their own zones of influence, cash flows and, in the zero-sum world of Afghan micro-politics, worked to deny their immediate rivals any advantage.

None of this assured the return of the Taliban, but it did make it much easier. The 'strategic centre of gravity' of the Taliban's campaign lay in Afghanistan's 40,000-odd villages. For a long time, this had escaped their international adversaries, who, coming from highly urbanized societies, naturally concentrated their efforts on the country's cities and towns. Reinforcing this error was a failure to understand the Taliban's deep cultural and social roots and the nature of their rule in the 1990s. For though the Taliban had been an alien presence in much of the north and west of Afghanistan and in cosmopolitan cities such as Herat and Kabul, where Dari-speaking Tajik or Persian ethnic minorities dominated and levels of education were much higher, in most of the south and the east of the country the movement had often been an integral part of communities. Groups of 'Taliban', largely students, had fought, often independently of the increasingly discredited major *mujahideen* groups, against the Soviets.[22] As Mullah Omar's forces had advanced across Afghanistan between 1994 and 1996, they had attracted a variety of supporters. Sometimes these were sections of a community that had previously been marginalized, such as the lowly mullahs, landless families, those without connections to the central government or minor tribes who had historically been pushed around by bigger ones.[23] On other occasions those aligning themselves with the new force had been local 'commanders' or minor warlords forced out by rivals during the civil war and who thus grafted their own small cause on to the greater one of Mullah Omar's movement. Situations differed across the country, but in many areas the end of the Taliban rule in 2001 had not meant a liberation from a repressive and alien extremist state, as it was perceived to be so often in the West, but the defeat of one faction in a community and its replacement by another.[24] It was simply another turn in the long contest for power, particularly acute since the start of the civil war in the 1970s, which had been continuing in Afghanistan on and off for many decades. Sometimes, down at the most 'granular' level, the differences between pro- and anti-Taliban elements could be simply no greater than those imposed by a longstanding blood feud or a question of who had fought for whom when the Communists were in power. As in earlier conflicts, families very often had one brother or son with the Taliban, another with a different faction.[25] Language, ethnicity, culture and religious practice were thus broadly shared.[26]

It was these connections – both cultural and personal, general and very specific – that the Pakistan-based Taliban leadership exploited through late 2002 and on through 2003 and 2004. 'Our goal is to unify the country against the occupiers,' Maulvi Taj Mohammed had explained to the author six months after Tora Bora, adding that the movement aimed to 'move slowly' and to 'bring order' before launching 'military actions'.[27] As they set about rebuilding their strength in Afghanistan, often the Taliban used the same tactics employed almost a decade before, sending out emissaries to far-flung villages where local tribal and family connections guaranteed at least a hearing if not a welcome and running an extensive outreach programme to all those power-brokers, former warlords, commanders or elders who saw their rivals profiting from cooperating with the government or foreign forces. Efforts were made to reach all sections of the population – ordinary villagers as well as more powerful individuals. On occasion, loudspeakers were set up or even a portable FM radio used to broadcast the Taliban's message. Frequently violence was used to eliminate opposition.[28] Often generational tensions – familiar from other theatres in the 9/11 Wars including Europe – were exploited, with younger contenders for power and influence being turned against often more moderate and pragmatic elders. Many of the latter ended up dead or in exile. But the successful communication of the insurgents' discourse of Islam, nation and community, often relayed by the clerical network, depended as much on pre-existing xenophobia, the mistrust of Kabul, fear of bias towards ethnic rivals, anger at civilian casualties or intrusive searches by Western troops and, of course, a deep-rooted rural religious and social conservatism as on intimidation. When successful, the Taliban, or the local powerbrokers they had recruited into their ranks, were often able to take on a role as 'protectors' of a given community against local rivals, government officials and the few foreign troops who were ever seen. At the very least, given the vacuum in government authority in much of the country, they were simply able to establish some kind of rule of law where there was none. As it had been in the 1990s, the Taliban remained structured less as a militia or insurgent group and more as an 'adaptive social movement' in the words of political scientist Seth Jones or a 'caravan' in the more colourful phrase of the late Afghan expert Bernt Glatzer.[29]

To supplement the recruits brought in by their outreach programme in the villages the Taliban leaders, from their now secure base around Quetta and to a lesser extent Peshawar, drew on another tactic from the previous decade and mobilized the various resources of the cross-border ethnic and religious networks from which they had, in part, originally sprung. The most useful was the vast reservoir of combat-age manpower in the religious schools over the border in Pakistan. The young men who had sat in rows on the schools' concrete floors rote-learning the Koran had provided critical fighting strength in the early Taliban campaigns of the mid 1990s, and Taliban leaders naturally once more turned to the *medressas*. One recruit was nineteen-year-old Rahmatullah, who in mid 2003 had travelled to Pakistan to be a religious student and had returned to Afghanistan as an armed *mujahid*. He explained his recruitment in simple terms: 'I was in school, and my teachers told us that we should fight for my country and my religion against the unbelievers who had come to Afghanistan and the hypocrites in power. All my friends went, and I didn't want to be left behind.'[30] Older recruits were found in the large refugee camps in Pakistan, which were full of young men of Pashtun Afghan origins who had been raised on an ideological diet of radical conservative religion in communities stripped of the comforting traditional identities and hierarchies of tribe or village. Products of the extremely high fertility rates in the camps in the 1980s and early 1990s, jobless or chronically underemployed, they too, sometimes paid small sums, began to find their way across into the south-eastern provinces in increasing numbers by 2003 and 2004.[31]

The first areas to slip into Taliban control had been isolated districts on the eastern rim of the central mountainous core of the country as well as along the Pakistani border near the border point at Chaman.[32] By late 2003, raiding parties from bases in these areas had been regularly attacking the road from Kabul to Kandahar and government buildings in even major towns. The seductive images of voters queuing outside polling stations for successive elections of 2004 and 2005 had, as in Iraq at around the same time, obscured the growing strength of the insurgency.[33] By late 2005, significant parts of the environs of Kandahar, much of neighbouring Helmand province and large sections of the south-western desert were under de facto Taliban control, and groups of fighters loyal to networks allied to the Taliban, such as those run by former *mujahideen* leader and prime minister Gulbuddin Hekmatyar and Jalaluddin Haqqani, the commander and cleric who gained fame in the 1980s and had eventually become a key ally of the Taliban, were establishing their own authority over swathes of north-eastern and eastern border provinces.[34] The numbers of insurgents were still not great. If every fighter from tribal and village-level fellow travellers through to mercenary and criminal elements as well as contingents from the schools and the refugee camp populations had all been simultaneously mobilized, their number would not have exceeded several thousand.[35] But the numbers were not important. The fugitive Taliban leaders in Peshawar had outlined three phases of their campaign – establishing contact with potential allies, establishing permanent areas of influence and authority and only then moving to overt military action. One of the advantages of the strategy was that progress would only become obvious to the enemy when it was probably too late. 'By 2005 . . . we were looking carefully at a number of staff analyses that began to suggest the Taliban was exhibiting signs of defeat,' Lieutenant General David W. Barno, commander of US forces from 2003 to 2005, remembered.[36] General James Jones, then NATO's Supreme Allied Commander (Europe), announced bluntly in early 2006 that 'the Taliban and al-Qaeda are not in a position where they can restart an insurgency of any size and major scope'.[37] A much more pessimistic analysis from the head of the Afghan National Directorate of Intelligence, Amrullah Saleh, was brushed aside. Saleh recalled later being told the Taliban were 'irrelevant'. The Bush administration reduced its budgeted aid request to Congress for Afghanistan by 38 per cent to $3.1 billion.[38] As had been the case in Iraq, the initiative had been seized by the insurgents.

THE AFGHAN FRONTS 2006–8

Shortly after Jones' statement, new Western troops began to arrive in Afghanistan in a major reinforcement of the international presence there. Given the prevailing wisdom that the Taliban were beaten, this would seem to indicate a serious divergence between public statements and private strategy-making on the part of Western politicians. In fact, it was more evidence of deep confusion among Western policy-makers and their very real failure to understand what was happening in Afghanistan at the time.

In theory the troops were the final part of a rolling extension through the country of ISAF, the International Security Assistance Force that had been created with a peace-keeping mission following the war of 2001.[39] The reinforcements arriving in 2006 would bring the total number of troops committed to Afghanistan to 46,000, still only a third of those in Iraq but an increase of 20,000 on the previous year.

Their aim remained largely the same as that of 2002. They were not coming to launch a new offensive to roll back the Taliban. They were coming to 'extend the authority of President Karzai's government, to protect those civilian agencies assisting them to build a democratic government and to enable security, stability and economic development throughout the country'. The resistance these troops, particularly the British, were to encounter thus came as a rude surprise. John Reid, the British defence secretary, had even raised the possibility of the soldiers not having to fight at all, speaking of his hope that the troops could withdraw in three or five years 'without firing a shot'.[40]

A secondary aim of the deployment had little to do with Afghanistan and much to do with global politics. European powers – particularly the British – had been concerned since 2003 that the increasingly unilateral approach of the Americans and the failure of other states to make any contribution to (or to stop) the war in Iraq would fatally undermine NATO, the keystone of the Western world's defence architecture. The expansion of ISAF into the south of Afghanistan, five years after it had originally been mooted, with all Afghan operations placed under NATO command except those American forces dedicated to hunting bin Laden along the eastern frontier, was a way of reinvigorating the alliance and proving its utility in the changed strategic environment of the first decade of the twenty-first century.[41] After some debate and argument, new Dutch, Canadian and British troops began arriving in Oruzgan, Kandahar and Helmand provinces respectively in the late spring of 2006. All spoke of winning 'hearts and minds'. 'We need to convince them that we are the winning team and once we do that – and we will – then they'll come over to us,' said Lieutenant Colonel Stuart Tootal, who deployed from Iraq via a stint in the UK to Helmand as part of the British 16th Air Assault Brigade. As he spoke, bulldozers lit by arc lights were shunting gravel into berms to protect Camp Bastion, the new British base in the province. Beyond the new ramparts, the desert stretched off into the night.[42]

Very rapidly, it became clear that potential resistance in Helmand and elsewhere had been grotesquely underestimated. Within weeks of arriving, the new troops across the country found themselves involved in heavy fighting. NATO officials in the headquarters compound in central Kabul, sitting in the garden of the coffee shop, attributed the increasingly extensive violence to international forces pushing into new areas and insisted that 70 per cent of the violence in Afghanistan was restricted to 10 per cent of the districts.[43] Both these statements were true but ignored the fact that the Taliban had met the arrival of the new troops with an offensive of their own. Attacks on international forces went from 300 in March 2006 to 600 per month at the year's end, traditionally a relatively quiet time.[44] By the end of 2006, after six months or so of renewed NATO activity, at least a third of the east and south of the country was shaded a vivid red for 'high risk' on the 'security charts' compiled by NGOs trying with greater and greater difficulty to work outside the main cities. At least in the short term, the arrival of the new forces did not appear to be making the environment more secure but considerably more dangerous. This, NATO officials in Kabul said, was 'the price of victory'.[45]

Each of the operational areas in Afghanistan had its own specificities. Kunduz and the north-east, where the Germans had been based from October 2003, had once been relatively quiet. Detractors of the Germans said this was because the legal restrictions under which the 2,700 German troops operated prevented them actively hunting any insurgents.[46] Supporters said their softly-softly approach had tipped few locals into insurgency. Either way, 2006 saw the Germans becoming involved in constant skirmishing and suffering increasing casualties. The eastern province of Kunar was the scene of serious fighting, with American troops engaging a series of different enemies ranging from angry timber smugglers to committed Salafi jihadists from local villages. Many insurgents crossed the frontier from Bajaur in Pakistan to fight and then returned to rest and reorganize.[47] Building steadily since 2003, violence there reached a new intensity, particularly in the Korengal valley. In the provinces of Loya Paktia in the east, a different dynamic again prevailed. Local tribes were historically equally distrustful of the government in Kabul and of the *mullahs* or tribal leaders of Kandahar and successive American units found themselves caught between a desire to pursue more classic conventional tactics aimed at inflicting heavy casualties on their elusive enemy and the 'hearts and minds' approach, which they hoped might bring them leads on the where-abouts of senior al-Qaeda figures. In the end, a mix of both strategies was adopted with predictably patchy results.[48] The proximity of the Pakistani frontier did little to ease the situation either. Then there were the various fronts around Kabul. There were dozens of towns like Maidan Shar around the capital and dozens of shifting, imprecise but nonetheless very real frontlines. Each province abutting the capital had its own specificity. In the Jalrez valley of upper Wardak, international forces were marginal to battles between local communities over land and grazing rights.[49] In Sorobi, out on the road to Nangahar, a single valley was the epicentre of violence as a result of a peculiarly noxious mix of local political micro-factors.[50] The variations extended across the country, giving the impression of a collection of individual campaigns rather than a single conflict. In this the war in Afghanistan was, like that in Iraq, a matrix of interlinked but often remarkably independent struggles evolving on a variety of different levels, from village to nation to region, with a degree of interdependence but significant autonomy too. In this it was, naturally, a microcosm of the 9/11 Wars more generally. Of the various operations undertaken in Afghanistan by Western forces from 2006 that in Helmand was perhaps the most challenging.

Helmand's strategic importance was due to its population of between 700,000 and 1.2 million, its status as the source of half the world's illegal heroin in 2007 and its position aside key national communica-tions corridors.[51] There was the critical ring road linking Kandahar with Herat, there was the Helmand river itself which swept south and then west in a long fertile arc before losing itself in the sands of the Dasht-e-Margo, the Desert of Death, and there were also the principal drug trafficking routes along which much of Afghanistan's narcotics export left the country.

The first force sent into Helmand by the British government was 3,300 strong, a ratio of one soldier for around every 300 local people. With too few troops to even patrol the major roads linking the half dozen main bases the British established, the only secure means of communication was helicopter. As the British only had a handful of aged Chinooks, this was a critical handicap. Beyond the lack of manpower and material, the actions of a resilient and effective enemy and the challenges posed by one of the most hostile physical environments in the world, a number of other factors, largely of the making of British politicians, bureaucrats and senior commanders, also combined to weaken the deployment's already slim chances of success.

The British were largely unprepared for the very tough fight they found themselves caught up in. In part this was due to the dearth of useful intelligence before the deployment of the British troops. Beyond the gross underestimation of the potential numbers of fighters that might oppose the new British intervention – General Chris Brown, the most senior British officer in Afghanistan, told the author in the summer of 2006 that there were around 1,000 Taliban active in the entire country, a ludicrously low estimate at odds with almost every other intelligence assessment at the time – there was also a severe lack of understanding of the nature of the enemy and the form resistance was likely to take.[52] Between 2002 and 2005, the south of Afghanistan had been without satellite coverage after surveillance assets were switched to Iraq.[53] Intelligence services were preoccupied with other theatres too. Though pre-deployment briefings for soldiers on their way to Afghanistan had improved since 2003, when troops had listened to veteran sergeant majors talk to them about how they had patrolled the streets of Belfast, the men of the 3rd Parachute Battalion were, a month or so before their deployment, yet to be briefed either on hazards such as the roadside bombs that would inevitably greet them or, far more seriously, on the combination of latent hostility and pragmatic neutrality which would characterize the response of the local population to their presence.[54] Ideas about the battlefield tactics of the Taliban were also extremely vague. A team from the SAS, MI6 and British defence intelligence had spent six months with American troops who had been in the Helmandi towns of Lashkar Gah and Gereshk but, not least because the Americans themselves had remained very constrained in their movements and had little to pass on, a remarkably small amount of useful knowledge had filtered back to the incoming force.[55] The vacuum allowed policy-makers and senior officers to conclude more or less what they wanted. A confidential report later commissioned on what was going wrong in Helmand spoke of how in the run-up to the deployment 'the Ministry of Defence was sanguine about security [in Helmand] and not disposed to negative messages'.[56]

With the aims of the mission unclear and no real grasp of the environment the troops were to be entering, British military planners themselves turned not to the new thinking about counter-insurgency operations that was coming through in the USA and elsewhere (and already in part being implemented in places like Kunar or in the eastern Afghan provinces) but once again to the supposed counter-insurgency successes of British colonial and postcolonial campaigns.[57] Most senior British officers continued to be convinced that, certainly compared to the Americans and other Europeans, they were inheritors of a long tradition both of 'understanding' foreign societies and of successfully fighting counter-insurgency wars.[58] This was a dubious claim that was based on an anachronistic and distorted view of what had actually happened in Kenya, Malaysia, Northern Ireland and elsewhere and, as it had done in Iraq, once more led to a complacency that successive setbacks did little to puncture. An example was the idea, derived from campaigns in southeast Asia in the 1940s and 1950s, that 'inkspots' of security could be established which would become attractive nodes of economic development and gradually spread across the blotting paper of Helmand's myriad valleys, plains, deserts, towns and villages. In Afghanistan, these inkspots, defended as they were by foreign troops, naturally found themselves under attack from insurgents, thus forcing the exodus of the very local people the forces had been sent to protect. 'The inskpots are black because there are no lights on. Everyone has left,' bleakly joked one local Afghan NGO worker.[59]

These various complex and interlinked problems were further exacerbated by the political necessity of reducing casualties in order to maintain support for the war among domestic populations increasingly sceptical of further expense of 'blood and treasure' after five years of controversial and often inconclusive campaigns in various theatres. This was a key consideration not just for politicians back home but among senior officers in Afghanistan. When Brigadier Ed Butler, then the commanding officer of British forces in Afghanistan, spoke of the 'battle for public opinion' in Kabul in July 2006 he was referring to that of his compatriots in the UK, not Afghans.[60] The result was the dogmatic prioritization of 'force security'. This meant a very natural reliance on the international troops' greatest advantage: their firepower. Between just June and November of 2006 American airplanes and helicopters had conducted 2,000 strikes, using an average of 98 large bombs and 14,000 bullets a month, three times the previous year's total.[61] One evening at an outpost at the Kajaki dam hydroelectric plant, a key strategic objective of the British deployment, the author witnessed troops respond to a couple of rounds fired into their positions from a compound a kilo-metre or so away with heavy machine-gun fire, a dozen or so mortar rounds, a Javelin heat-seeking missile and finally a 500 lb bomb dropped from a Harrier jet. The result, said the officer in charge, was two dead insurgents, although this was unconfirmed.[62]

Then there was the question of narcotics, a dominant factor in Hel-mand but important throughout most of the south and some of the east. The opium boom had begun in 2002, after a year in which farmers and traffickers waited to see what policy the new rulers of their country would adopt.[63] The factors lying behind the post-war boom in narcotics cultivation were manifold and included the destruction of irrigation sys-tems over decades of war, patterns of debt and credit, the approbation or otherwise of the clergy, the size of landholdings and the price of wheat. One significant element in the vast increase in the area under opium – from 104,000 hectares in 2005 to 165,000 in 2006 alone and increasing year on year thereafter – was the deliberate and intensive drive by major actors in the local drugs industry.[64] In what must have constituted one of the most effective rural support programmes any-where in Afghanistan at the time, traffickers had provided improved varieties of poppy seeds, fertilizer, technical advice on methods of culti-vation and generous banking and loan facilities and paid for the temporary employment of hundreds of thousands during the poppy harvest.[65] The traffickers also developed close ties with the insurgents, who levied the customary 10 per cent tax on agricultural produce on the opium and thus generated tens, if not hundreds, of millions of dollars.[66] Documents seized from traffickers listed sizeable 'donations' – some-times of several hundred thousand dollars – both to insurgents and to senior officials.[67] By 2007, it was calculated that the narcotics industry in Afghanistan was worth some $3 billion (out of a gross national prod-uct of $8 billion). Production in 2008 would top 7,700 tonnes of opium, twice the level of 2002, of which a substantial proportion was for the first time turned into high-value heroin locally rather than in laborato-ries in Iran, Turkey, Pakistan, the Balkans or central Asia. In the north-east, where security – and governance – was stronger, drug pro-duction had fallen away markedly. However, in the space of just six or seven years, southern Afghanistan had developed a complete and self-sustaining alternative economy based on narcotics.[68] The business had got so big that some senior Taliban figures even expressed misgivings over its size, worrying that the power and influence of the drugs industry could eventually surpass their own.[69]

As with the insurgency, Western officials systematically downplayed the drugs problem. British officials, particularly sensitive as the UK had been the 'lead nation' on counter-narcotics since 2002, stressed how only between 12 and 16 per cent of the farming population were involved in opium cultivation.[70] However, this missed the point. The problem was not necessarily the drugs – though Afghanistan was developing a problem with its own addicts of a scale never previously seen – but with the cash the drugs generated. Only a fifth remained with the hundreds of thousands of farmers, analysts from the United Nations Office on Drugs and Crime said.[71] The rest went to the traffickers. Naturally this mountain of money – perhaps $4 billion in 2008 – fuelled massive corruption among government officials with positions such as police chief in a potentially remunerative location costing applicants up to $300,000 in bribes.[72]

Interminable debates about the correct strategy to tackle the problem continued throughout 2006 and 2007, pitting Americans who favoured aggressive eradication against Europeans who preferred broader programmes with more carrot and less stick, and led to deep confusion over the coalition's policy on drugs. One result was that the British deployment in Helmand had no clear instructions about how to tackle the vast opium industry in the province.[73] To start with, soldiers who came across syringes, piles of chemicals or stacks of raw opium were simply told to leave them. 'Otherwise we'll have the whole place up in arms,' said Tootal. Six months later, there was a move towards limited programmes of eradication of the crops of 'the greedy not the needy', in the words of one British senior civil servant in Helmand, which would be undertaken by the Afghan government and contractors.[74] But the confusion brought the worst of both worlds. The drug traffickers who funded many of the hardest fighting insurgent factions in Helmand, particularly in the north, continued to earn huge sums of money, while the limited eradication allowed the Taliban to claim that the West was set on destroying the crops that many farmers depended on. In any case, the wealthy could simply bribe the police to leave their fields alone. A study in Kandahar revealed that poppy farmers were disproportionately represented in insurgent ranks. Many of the fighters interviewed by the researchers said they saw the Afghan government and its international allies as a threat to their livelihood. This was far from the only motive for taking up arms – others included the loss of family members in air strikes or crossfire, for example – but was a significant factor nonetheless.[75]

The problems for the British in Helmand were the same for other forces around the country. Then there were other huge structural failings that hobbled the NATO force. The lines of command for international forces were impossibly tangled, running through Kandahar, Kabul, London, Brussels and, for the special forces and other Operation Enduring Freedom troops, US Centcom in Florida. The British served six-month tours (while the Americans did twelve or even fifteen months), which were barely long enough for a unit to get established, learn a little about the terrain and launch a single major operation before it was time to pack up again. Each new commanding officer brought a different approach. So whereas the brigade commander in Helmand in the first half of 2007 spoke of wearing down the enemy through attrition, 'mowing the lawn' as he termed it, his successor had a diametrically opposite vision of counter-insurgency warfare, telling the author in January 2008 that victory in Afghanistan could not be achieved through military means.[76] Then there was the question of progress. How could it be measured? British government and United Nations officials all pointed to familiar markers: economic growth in the country as a whole, the number of girls in school, the explosion of the media sector, successful preparations for elections in 2009, minefields cleared, money spent, wheat distributed, the fact that most of the north, the west and the cities remained calm.[77] Seventy per cent of violent incidents still occurred within ten districts, as ISAF spokesmen continued to repeat. On the other hand, in 2008 there were a third more 'kinetic events' than the previous year and 50 per cent more kidnappings and assassinations.[78] Any private unease at the direction things were taking was kept very quiet. It was true that insurgents were being killed in large numbers. Though body counts were avoided – one commander spoke of them as a 'corrupt measure' – British senior officers nonetheless boasted of 'neutralizing' between 3,000 and 4,000 Taliban fighters in 2008 alone.[79] But keeping Western casualties to politically manageable levels was proving hard. Six British soldiers had died between the end of the 2001 campaign and the new deployments of 2006. More than ten times as many were to die in the following two years. Across the country as a whole, there were 416 coalition deaths between June 2006 and July 2008, more than had been killed in the previous four and half years.[80] Then there were the local casualties. Hundreds of government officials and nearly a thousand police died in 2007 alone. One was the courageous and effective female police chief in Kandahar, Malalai Kakar. 'We killed her,' a Taliban spokesman told AFP news agency. 'She was our target, and we successfully eliminated our target.'[81]

In the middle of it all were people like Roz Khan, a day labourer, and Gul Pari, a widowed farmer's wife. Both were villagers from the Sangin Valley, a crucial thoroughfare in the north of Helmand contested by British troops and insurgents. Forced to flee their homes, they described a grim daily routine of trying to reach their fields through air strikes and skirmishes, of pressure from the insurgents at night and of patrols by Western forces during the day. 'If it was just one or the other things would be better. But when there is a fight over your house you can't live in it,' said Roz Khan. Almost every family he knew had lost at least one member to stray bullets or Western bombing, either poorly targeted or attracted by insurgents who deliberately hid among the villagers. The husband of Pari, who had four young children, had been killed in a 'bombardment' but she was unsure which side to blame. 'When there was fighting, we did not know what was going on. But I think it was the fault of the Taliban because they were shooting and then there was an attack afterwards.'[82] Many tens of thousands had fled to Kandahar or Kabul, where they lived in squalor and destitution in makeshift refugee camps, ignored by the government and receiving only rudimentary assistance from overstretched aid agencies.[83] Pari tried to feed, clothe and house her family with the 50 Afghani [65p] that her eldest son earned from selling ice creams on the streets of the capital. She did not know how they would survive the winter.

With access to villages like those left by Roz Khan and Pari very difficult and their inhabitants very wary of speaking, piecing together an accurate picture of what communities genuinely felt about either the insurgents or the government and their Western allies was extremely difficult. But almost all the evidence confirmed that what most communities hoped most to avoid was rule neither by the Taliban nor the

'Amriki', as all international forces were known, but being caught between the two. The new fighting from 2006 on had suddenly placed hundreds of communities in an unenviable position between a Western rock and an insurgent hard place.[84] Certainly, for tribal elders trying to juggle the various pressures from different insurgent factions, the Afghan police, the Afghan army, drugs traffickers and various rivals ready to unseat them at the slightest misstep, the arrival of a well-meaning and heavily armed Western officer asking 'what he could do to help' was the last thing they needed. 'They keep asking us what we want. The answer is that they go away,' one told the author near Maiwand, outside Kandahar, in July 2006.[85] Such sentiments clearly posed a problem to a strategy based on convincing communities to 'join the winning side', as Tootal had described it.

That any elders tempted to cooperate with international forces or the government risked the wrath of the insurgents clearly did not help. This was especially evident during the successive operations to clear areas of Taliban. When the thinly spread international forces withdrew to commence another operation elsewhere, as they usually were forced to do, anyone who had cooperated locally was left very exposed. One of the more egregious examples occurred in Marjah, a rural district in central Helmand, which was cleared during an operation in 2007 and then turned over to 'local security forces'. The district was subsequently left unprotected, allowing the Taliban to move back in and kill scores of local notables. Watching a patrol of heavily armed UK soldiers plod down a back lane in Lashkar Gah, where the coalition force in Helmand had its headquarters, one elderly man told the author that the British were the twelfth fighting force he had seen from the gate of his compound in the last twenty years. (The others were, in reverse historical order, Americans, the Taliban, at least four warring *mujahideen* groups, Soviet troops and Afghan government soldiers from three different regimes.) 'They always arrive noisily saying they will win but leave much more quietly,' he added and shrugged. It was not as if the insurgents were very far away. In a small mechanics' workshop off the main bazaar in the town, only a few hundred yards past the gates of the NATO base, Fazl Rahman, forty years old, told the author bluntly: 'I am Taliban. Why should I be afraid? You British and Americans should leave this country. You are here for your own benefit, to destabilize our country, which is a castle of Islam, to destroy our religion. Soon you will run.'[86]

THE END OF 2008: CHALLENGES AND OPPORTUNITIES FOR THE TALIBAN

No insurgency progresses in a linear fashion, steadily advancing across a map, increasing in a regular exponential manner until finally taking power or expelling the foreign occupiers. Expansion is always marked by a series of inflection points. These are critical moments when the future evolution of the revolt, rebellion, movement or whatever are determined. Such moments involve significant challenges that have to be successfully met by insurgent leaders – and often lower-level participants too – if progress towards any given goal is to be maintained. It was thus inevitable that Mullah Mohammed Omar and the senior Taliban leadership also faced a series of acute problems as a consequence of the movement's rapid resurgence between 2002 and 2008. These fell into three main categories: military, political and diplomatic.

The first and most pressing were the military challenges. The success of the Taliban had provoked a response from their enemies, belated but very real nonetheless, and the leadership needed to try to find a tactical and strategic answer to the successive NATO military efforts. One very costly experiment was a set-piece battle fought among the vineyards, villages and small mud-walled fields of Panjwai outside Kandahar in late 2006. Along with the district of Argandab to the north, the area had been a key battlefield during the war against the Soviets, and the Taliban leadership may have hoped either to definitively carve out a secure enclave from which to launch an assault on Kandahar itself – a sort of miniature 'al-Zarqawi' local strategy – or to inspire a more general insurrection across much of the country through seeking, and winning, a pitched confrontation in such a historically important location – the equivalent of al-Suri style 'global intifada', but on a national scale. Though the fighting was tough, with coalition forces close to running out of ammunition and suffering heavy casualties from both friendly and enemy fire, neither Taliban aim was achieved, and the insurgents were eventually forced to retreat in disorder across the desert to the south, where Western special forces killed hundreds.[87] Though such losses were swiftly made good with further recruiting drives in the *medressas*, refugee camps and villages across the border, no such operation was ever attempted again.

The 'caravan' of the Taliban movement was far from the sort of organized, hierarchical army that could formulate, institutionalize and execute doctrinal change with rapid efficiency and uniformity. The insurgency resembled more a swarm of wasps from different nests momentarily travelling together in a single, very broad direction. The impact of strategic direction from individuals such as Mullah Omar, Hekmatyar or Jalaluddin Haqqani (or increasingly his son, Sirajuddin) was always somewhat haphazard. Tactical innovation was thus the work of individual commanders and spread as 'best practice' through example, experimentation and word of mouth. As in Iraq, however, this meant a capacity to adapt very fast and very effectively. Improvements in manoeuvre and ambushes were soon noted by Western troops. So too was the steep increase in the number of IEDs. These inflicted a heavy toll with little risk and, as had been the case in Iraq, rapidly became a key weapon. The roadside bombings, booby traps and other similar devices did not replace the direct confrontations – the proportion of which in fact went from 47 per cent to 57 per cent of all insurgent attacks between 2006 and 2007 – but complemented them. Suicide bombs were particularly effective against softer targets such as Afghan government buildings or the police. However, the civilian casualties they often caused were problematic, and the tactic sparked a fierce debate within Taliban ranks.[88]

The second broad area in which expansion posed problems for the insurgent leadership was a familiar one: as the Taliban had grown, discipline had suffered. This in its turn imperilled the insurgents' hold on communities and thus the continued success of the movement. What the Taliban and the other insurgent groups needed to avoid was a cycle such as that which had so damaged al-Qaeda in Iraq and the al-Mahdi Army, whereby diminishing support necessitated greater measures of coercion, which exacerbated the original problem to the point where entire populations started shifting allegiance away from the militants. The steady attrition of experienced Taliban commanders such as Mullah Dadaullah Akhund – who had led the destruction of the Bamiyan Buddhas, had escaped coalition forces in 2001 and had gone on to become increasingly unpredictable, violent and powerful – posed a challenge that went beyond simply replacing capable individuals.[89] The 'degrading' of senior ranks led to a new cohort of younger leaders, many of whom had not been involved in the original Taliban movement of the 1990s, being appointed to run their own *mahaz*, or 'front'. As with the al-Mahdi Army in Iraq, these new commanders tended to be much less disciplined than their elders had been and their often violent and indiscriminate actions undermined much of the work done to secure the support of local communities by more experienced and more ideologically or politically mature figures. By 2007 there was significant unrest in Ghazni – where local commanders had beaten and tortured locals who refused to give them fuel for motorbikes – in Zabul, in parts of Helmand and elsewhere. The insurgents, well-informed analysts often said, had always depended on the active support of 10 per cent and the acquiescence of another 60 per cent of the population and in these places the behaviour of the 'new Taliban', as many locals called them, was threatening both.[90] Expansion also meant that the key tactic of providing honest and rapid justice, either through mobile courts or through local clerics acting with the authority of the movement, was being undermined because there were too few judges of sufficient calibre to fill all the posts in the new areas that came under Taliban control. Worse, a wide range of criminals had been passing themselves off as 'Taliban'. Some mixed actions commissioned by the real Taliban leadership with more freelance activities designed for pure personal gain, often at the expense of local communities. A few respected the orders coming down the satellite phone from Quetta or the tribal areas – at least two Western journalists avoided being put on trial as spies by local commanders after Taliban 'ministers' sitting on the leadership council in Pakistan were contacted – but many were not in the least bothered by any such sense of hierarchy and simply got on with looting and banditry.[91] A significant proportion of new commanders were too young to remember much of the pre-2001 Taliban rule.[92]

Much of 2007 and 2008 had thus been marked by repeated efforts of Mullah Omar to bring some order to his increasingly unruly troops. The 'shadow governors' appointed in key provinces were reshuffled – though not without resistance from some and resentment on the part of others.[93] A book of rules for combatants was issued, prohibiting (and thus implicitly admitting) practices such as temporary marriage to women, the ransoming of prisoners, theft, cigarettes, the summary execution of spies and, in a society where pederasty is common, the 'taking of young boys without beards to the battlefield or to homes'. Commanders were told that 'using the jihad for their own personal profit' was forbidden.[94] Simultaneously previously rigorous restrictions on music, television and such pastimes as kite-flying or dog fighting were loosened. Decisions over the vexed issue of women's education – many villagers wanted their daughters to be at least literate – were left to local commanders who were closest to individual communities and better placed to judge their preferences. In 2007, Mullah Omar himself said that implementing 'social edicts' was up to the discretion of local leaders. Often compromises were found with schools opening when elders approved by the Taliban were present to oversee teaching and strict segregation.[95]

Other issues where the military demands of running an insurgency conflicted with keeping the consent of local communities were harder to resolve. One was the difficult question of mobile phone coverage. Worried about spies reporting their whereabouts, many Taliban commanders had destroyed the masts necessary to relay signals, an act that was inevitably deeply unpopular with local people, for whom cheap telecommunications had often been one of the few tangible benefits seen since the invasion of 2001. The eventual deal reached in many places was that the masts would remain but the phone companies would switch them off at night, allowing any potential targets of coalition special forces to sleep without fear of a nocturnal tip-off and a 4 a.m. raid. The fact that the insurgents were able to extort significant sums as 'protection money' from the phone companies – as they did from businesses involved in the execution of coalition-funded development projects or even the transport of its military supplies – was also a factor. A good gauge of the extent of geographic influence of the insurgents at any given moment was the number of districts where there was twenty-four-hour mobile coverage. In the summer of 2008, only around half of all Afghanistan's provinces could promise all their inhabitants uninterrupted use of the now ubiquitous phones.[96]

The effects of these various measures were variable. The chaotic structure of the insurgency necessarily impeded their application, and there were significant limits to the compromises the Taliban leadership were prepared to make. The strategy of suicide bombing continued despite its unpopularity among locals and the arguments it generated within senior Taliban ranks. A careful information campaign designed to mitigate the negative publicity surrounding particularly bloody attacks and to justify the continued use of the tactics was launched with DVDs and radio broadcasts extolling the courage and honour of the bombers all while minimizing any reports of 'collateral damage'. The use of Pakistani rather than local Afghan suicide bombers was stepped up and the real PR disasters – attacks in which dozens of children were killed, for example – were simply disowned or blamed on the Americans.[97] There was no shying away either from coercion or intimidation when deemed necessary. The Taliban had learned that targeted assassinations of officials in places like Kandahar was an extremely effective way of preventing the government developing any real capacity on the ground. Such killings were also deeply unpopular but, like the suicide bombing, were apparently considered worth continuing for the overall strategic benefits they brought.

Overall, the insurgents seemed to have recognized that effectively fusing their military and information strategies could overcome many of the challenges posed by their growth and the initiatives taken by the coalition. Not only were atrocity stories – some barely exaggerated accounts of experiences in Bagram or Guantanamo Bay – circulated to build animosity against the international forces but stories of the supposed moral degradation of Kabul were disseminated too. Anything that could enhance the sense of the honest, suffering rural communities betrayed by the decadent, exploitative self-interested urbanites was emphasized. Explicit ethnicity was avoided in the messaging, which often took on a strongly nationalist tone.[98] Aware than their greatest advantage was perhaps the simple fact that they were Afghans and Muslims fighting largely white, Western, 'Christian' soldiers, the insurgents in their DVDs reinforced parallels with the 'jihad' against the Soviets, which was now portrayed as a rare victory against the international conspiracy of powers dedicated to destroying Islam and the Afghan 'nation'. Above all, violence was deployed to serve the purposes of the information campaign not vice versa. The continuing low-level fighting around the country was united into a single narrative of resistance – even if most of it was anarchic and opportunistic and related to local factors – while the more high-profile insurgent attacks were carefully designed for maximum impact. So the suicide bombing and raid on the five-star Serena Hotel in the centre of Kabul in January 2008 was worth the risk of collateral damage and disapproval of the tactics because the target – a luxury complex favoured by the Kabuli rich and foreigners – had such resonance.[99] The strike also showed the inability of the government – and ISAF – to protect even the centre of the capital. Equally, the spectacular Kandahar jailbreak of June 2008 was worth the risk of failure and high casualties. With hundreds freed for little loss and worldwide news coverage, it was a major success. A third example was the ambush of French troops in the valley of Uzbeen, north of Sorobi, in August 2008. Though the action itself was largely the result of a rivalry between three local armed groups all linked to Hekmatyar's Hezb-e-Islami, the ambush was rapidly and effectively exploited by the insurgents at a national level. Reporters in Kabul received text messages from Taliban spokesmen claiming exaggerated French losses even before the ISAF press office was apparently aware the fighting had taken place.[100] It appeared unlikely that the Uzbeen ambush had been commissioned by the insurgent leadership in the way that the attacks on the Serena – probably the work of Haqqani's group – and that in Kandahar had been. But it played firmly into a further new element of the insurgent strategy, which was to deliberately target public opinion in the West. Taliban media spokesmen boasted of closely monitoring Western press reports of both events in Afghanistan and the debate in the thirty-nine countries which had troops in the country. It was little surprise that news of the decision of President Sarkozy to fly to Kabul following the attack was posted on Taliban-linked websites, linked to translations of articles from French newspapers arguing for immediate withdrawal of the nation's troops from the conflict, within hours of it being announced. On occasion too the insurgents appeared happy to admit that they had sustained significant casualties, presumably aware that their ability to absorb continued losses demoralized their opponents and turned domestic opinion in the West further against the war.

The final challenge posed to the Afghan insurgents by their expansion – and their relative success in fighting the new Western forces to a stalemate – was perhaps the most serious. For many years, one subject had been taboo among Western diplomats, soldiers and politicians: the support offered by Pakistani intelligence services to the Taliban. Yet that the insurgents, whether from the core Taliban or from Haqqani's or Hekmatyar's groups, had been receiving assistance from within the neighbouring state had been an open secret for a long time. This was a delicate matter for the Pakistanis, who had no intention of abandoning the policy launched in 2002 of at least tacitly tolerating the presence of the Afghan insurgents on their soil so as to be better positioned for the West's inevitable eventual withdrawal from Afghanistan, but was potentially even more troublesome for the Taliban themselves. A misjudged local strike could therefore have damaging consequences that far outweighed any tactical advantage gained. So the bombing of the Indian embassy in Kabul in July 2008 may have been initially counted a tactical success but, after American intelligence reported monitoring conversations between ISI officers and the attackers in which the logistics for the strikes appeared to be discussed, it looked to be have been strategically counter-productive.[101] The bombing galvanized the White House into paying much closer attention to the apparent role Pakistani intelligence was playing in the continuing success of the insurgents and thus threatened the one thing the Taliban could not afford to jeopardize: their safe haven in Pakistan.[102] That the details of the overheard conversations were leaked at all was an indication of how concerned the American security establishment had become about Pakistan's role in Afghanistan.

The perpetrators of the attack on the Indian embassy died as they were meant to do, in a sudden moment of spectacular violence designed to frighten and impress as much as kill and destroy. This naturally rendered a full investigation of their identity and how they came to be in Kabul with suicide vests strapped to them difficult. However, as with such attackers elsewhere in the various theatres of the 9/11 Wars, an idea of the process which led them to blow themselves up on the streets of the capital can be reconstructed from the stories of others who did not travel quite to the very end of the same road. Abit, a slim, handsome twenty-one-year-old baker's son from Bahawalpur, in the south of the eastern Pakistani province of Punjab, had found himself strapped to a bomb in Afghanistan but had decided at the last minute not to die. He had been recruited by a friend who had, he said, suggested a 'tour' to a town close to the border with Afghanistan.[103] The 'tour' had in fact taken the pair directly to a compound run by local Taliban, where Abit's friend had swiftly disappeared, leaving him with a dozen other young men. Their days were spent reading the Koran, receiving specifically targeted religious instruction and viewing militant jihadi propaganda videos which had familiar themes.

'We watched films of bombardments and fighting in Iraq. They told me the whole infidel world was coming to Afghanistan to invade and repress Muslims and that it was the duty of all Muslims to resist. They told me about the rewards of martyrdom,' Abit said. Scared by tales of what might happen to him as an outsider if he went wandering in the local bazaar, he stayed within the compound's confines, entirely isolated from the outside world.

Abit, speaking in the offices of the Afghan national intelligence service in Kabul with the windows open and birdsong for once audible over the sound of the city, said the process was 'gradual' but that after several months he was prepared to 'sacrifice himself for Islam'. The men who ran the compound told him that everything was ready. The target – a US base on the frontier – had been selected.

'They told me there were just Americans there,' Abit said. 'They told me not to think about what would happen to my body because Allah ensures martyrs suffer no pain. They told me to remember that a martyr takes his relatives with him to paradise and that was as important for me as the infidels committing violence and tyranny.'

Abit was driven over the border to within a mile or so of the base, where a truck stuffed with explosives was waiting with a detonator button wired to the dashboard. 'I drove the truck towards the base,' he said. 'I was not thinking of anything. I just kept saying "Allahu akbar, Allahu akbar". I felt nothing.'

On reaching his target, however, Abit saw only Afghans. 'I could see no Americans,' he told the author. 'The soldiers told me to stop the truck, and I got down and I gave myself up. I am very sorry and I am glad no one was harmed.'[104]

13
Pakistan

'THE MOST DANGEROUS COUNTRY ON EARTH'

Of all countries that became major theatres of conflict in the 9/11 Wars, Pakistan was perhaps the most important. It was certainly the biggest, with a population of around 177 million in 2007 and another 3 million being added every year, more than that of Egypt, Turkey and Iraq combined.[1] Pakistan was where al-Qaeda had been conceived and formed back in the late 1980s, where militant groups had proliferated through the 1990s with state support unparalleled anywhere in the Islamic world, where some of the most influential components of modern Islamist and Islamic militant ideology had been formulated and tested. It was where the Taliban leadership had found a safe haven following their fall from power in 2001 and where Osama bin Laden and other terrorist fugitives had been able to reconstitute a working terrorist operation the capacity of which had been amply made clear by successive bomb attacks in the region, in Europe and elsewhere, realized or thwarted. Pakistan was a nuclear power, with hostile relations with its neighbours that dated back decades and a range of social and economic problems that, though no means exceptional in the Islamic world or among developing nations generally, were nonetheless acute. In 2008, Pakistan was 141st out of 182 on the United Nations Human Development index.[2] Infant mortality rates were on a par with those in sub-Saharan Africa and much of the population did not have access to clean water let alone health care. If outright chronic malnutrition was rare, many millions of people ate poorly. Pakistan's size alone – often underestimated due to its proximity to giants India and China – and strategic position as a buffer state between the

Middle East and south Asia contributed too to a strategic importance that few other countries involved in the 9/11 Wars could rival. In this the country was very different from its western neighbour. Afghanistan was only considered crucial because it had been a launchpad for the 9/11 attacks and was seen as having the potential to become so again. Otherwise, a fractured state with a small population, negligible economic activity in global terms and limited resources other than some natural gas, minerals and metals, it had never been, nor was unlikely ever to become, a crucial piece of the geopolitical jigsaw. The ramifications of a collapse of Iraq would naturally have had very grave consequences on the Middle East and thus on the world's economy, spiking oil prices and releasing a wave of radicalism, but, appalling though such a prospect might be, the potential fall-out of such an eventuality would arguably be less than that of the catastrophic implosion of Pakistan. Reporting and analysis of Pakistan often reflected the deep fear on the part of Western policy-makers, analysts and strategists that the state's oft-predicted failure inspired. In late 2007 *Newsweek*, the American magazine, echoing the pronouncements of a range of Western, and particularly Washington-based, statesmen over the decade, bluntly told its readers that Pakistan was the 'most dangerous country on earth'.[3]

These often alarmist analyses seemed difficult to reconcile with the country's evident resilience. Created in 1947 in the blood and chaos of Britain's precipitate departure from the subcontinent, Pakistan had survived its traumatic birth, defeat in a series of wars, repeated internal insurrection, the loss of its eastern half, a series of military governments, brutal nationalization programmes in the 1970s, the consequences of the Afghan war against the Soviets in the 1980s, the turmoil of the end of the Cold War, sanctions and the chaotic and corrupt 'democracy' of the 1990s. The years immediately before 9/11 and through the first half decade of the wars had dealt the country blows that would have caused many others to fail: a coup (albeit bloodless) in 1999 which overturned an elected if deeply unpopular government, a lengthy military dictatorship, a series of rigged or semi-rigged elections, broad civil unrest, a scandal over the selling of its nuclear weapons secrets and a devastating earthquake. Somehow Pakistan managed not just to survive all this but, in some areas, to thrive. Pakistan was not so much a 'failed state' as a state which should by rights have failed long ago but had somehow successfully held on in the face of extreme adversity.

The greatest tests were yet to come. Though the country had played a very significant role in setting the scene for the conflict, the 9/11 Wars had largely avoided Pakistani soil in the years following the September 11 attacks. The waves of violence that had surged across Afghanistan, the Middle East, even parts of the Far East and Europe from 2001 on through the middle of the decade had barely touched the country. That began to change in the summer of 2007. In July, there was a pitched battle between Pakistani troops and Islamic militants who had fortified a mosque and *medressa* compound in the centre of Islamabad, the capital city. The late summer saw fierce fighting in the west of the country between Pakistani paramilitary forces and fighters from a whole set of new emerging radical factions who dubbed themselves the Pakistani Taliban. Then, after an unprecedented wave of blasts and shootings across much of the north and west of the country, Benazir Bhutto, former prime minister and self-dubbed 'Daughter of the East', returned to Pakistan from nine years of exile in Dubai. Landing in Karachi, Pakistan's southern port city, she was greeted by a huge bomb that killed 139 and injured several hundred. There is some suggestion that the bomb had been hidden in the crib of a small child.

BHUTTO AND A CHANGING PAKISTAN

The idea of a separate nation for the Muslims of the subcontinent had sprung from a perception that to remain within a Hindu-dominated independent India after the British had left would mean risking discrimination, marginalization and the eventual extinction of any distinct south Asian Muslim culture and identity. Such fears were voiced by the unofficial posthumous poet laureate of the new nation, Mohammed Iqbal, the Indian philosopher and politician whose revivalist writings provided an eloquent literary and ideological underpinning to the idea of the Pakistani state and echoed sentiments present since the mid nineteenth century in much of the colonized Muslim world. Even if, as some historians hold, the concept of Pakistan was only ever a bargaining position on the part of the Indian Muslim League, the partition that was apparently so desired led to a bloodbath with somewhere between 500,000 and a million being killed as communities fled west or east to their new homes. The vast bulk of the capital, material wealth and infrastructure of the British Indian possessions remained in what became India. So too did almost all the major monuments and sites of the very south Asian Islamic culture the creation of the new state was meant to preserve. Pakistan was thus born with several major disadvantages: a bloody and frightening delivery, almost no resources, a clearly untenable geography with its eastern wing a thousand miles from the western part of the country and, perhaps most problematic of all, no clear idea of what the country was supposed to be.

Many analysts have noted the incoherence at the heart of the concept of the Pakistani state and the role of religion.[4] Though Pakistan was created as an Islamic homeland, indeed a refuge, its founder, Mohammed Ali Jinnah, the seventy-year-old Westernized lawyer who ran the Muslim League, had made clear that he saw the new nation's future as tolerant and pluralist with religion playing a major but not defining role in the country's political and legal structures and identity. Pakistan was not to be a theocracy. On August 11, 1947, in Karachi, Jinnah told the new nation's constituent assembly: 'You are free; you are free to go to your temples, you are free to go to your mosques or to any other place of worship ... We are starting in the days when there is no discrimination, no distinction between one community and another, no discrimination between one caste or creed and another. We are starting with this fundamental principle that we are all citizens and equal citizens of one state.' Jinnah died of lung cancer and tuberculosis only thirteen months after Pakistan's creation but, even if he had survived a little longer, it is unlikely that he would have been able to resolve the fundamental questions of identity the new country faced.

Born only six years after Pakistan's foundation, Benazir Bhutto's life had been intertwined with the troubled history of her country. By the time she was old enough to vote, she had already seen two military coups. The latter had brought General Ayub Khan to power in 1958. Like many other leaders in the Islamic and broader developing world at the time, Ayub Khan was a committed secular reformer who, influenced by Ataturk, promoted women's education and rights and made a genuine attempt at controlling population growth. He did not believe in democracy, or more precisely in politicians, and was forced from power in 1969, having failed to achieve most of his modernizing ambitions.[5] After a short interim, he was succeeded by Benazir Bhutto's father, Zulfiqar Ali Bhutto, a brilliant, charismatic and utterly unscrupulous minor hereditary landowner from the southern Sindh province. Z. A. Bhutto had cynically and skilfully exploited the aftermath of Pakistan's loss of its eastern, more populous wing following an uprising and a disastrous conflict with India in 1971 to force a situation where he had a chance of winning power. His strategy worked, and his newly formed Pakistan People's Party swept elections by campaigning on a platform of radical nationalist, socialist policies with the slogan 'Food, clothes and shelter'. His voters were to see precious little of any of the three, however, though Bhutto did implement a divisive and economically disastrous nationalization programme, expand the role of the intelligence services in domestic politics and ban alcohol in a bid to head off increasing discontent among the country's powerful and well-organized religious conservatives. His rule, first as president and then as prime minister, lasted six years until he was deposed in a military coup which occurred when the religious right wing, despite the concessions Bhutto had made to their demands, made Pakistan ungovernable. In the chaos, General Zia u'Haq, the chief of army staff, took power. He hanged Bhutto two years later, in April 1979. Benazir was one of the last to see her father alive. She spent much of the next decade under house arrest or overseas.

Zia had ruled, at least initially, with the support of Pakistan's numerous and well-organized Islamists, appointing many to political office, carefully directing funds to religious organizations, empowering the clergy and increasing the powers of the religious courts that had run alongside the previously largely secular legal system.[6] The biggest beneficiaries of this shift were naturally the members and supporters of Jamaat Islami, the vast and highly disciplined organization founded by the Indian autodidact cleric Abu Ala Maududi in 1941, who, despite the concept of the nation theoretically being an unislamic innovation, had, like Islamists elsewhere, nonetheless accepted the idea of the Islamic or Islamicized nation state, albeit preferring one that was run by religious leaders, to a Western-style democracy.[7] Maududi, who admitted that his vision owed much to revolutionary Communism and Fascism, was one of the most original thinkers of modern Islamic revivalism and a key influence on such major Middle Eastern figures such as Hassan al-Banna, Sayyid Qutb and the Ayatollah Khomeini, who translated his works into Farsi. It was Maududi, for example, who first began using the term *jahiliya*, which can roughly be translated as pagan ignorance, to describe almost all innovations since the time of the *salaf*, the early generations of Muslims, and who popularized the idea of the jihad as transcendental struggle, albeit a spiritual one.[8]

Zia was the son of a government clerk, and his animosity towards the Bhutto dynasty was, at least in part, based on class. Though his continued hold on power owed much to American support – the invasion of Afghanistan arrived at a particularly opportune moment – the courteous, pious and teetotal general also successfully played on the tensions between the old landed elite and the less privileged bureaucracy, the recently educated urban lower middle class and the conservative commercial classes to divide any opposition to him. Relations between the dictator and the Islamists steadily soured, but there was enough consonance between Zia's values and theirs for their agenda to be steadily advanced nonetheless. Though his death in a mysterious plane crash led to elections in 1988 which were, against all expectations, narrowly won by Bhutto and the PPP, the Islamists, though distanced from any formal power, retained a significant degree of informal influence, not least in the bureaucracy and the military.[9] Their organization also remained strong, particularly in the urban lower middle classes, the bedrock of political Islamism across the Muslim world.

This rough balance of forces led to alternate governments of Bhutto's PPP and the conservative Pakistan Muslim League (PML), now led by the unprepossessing Nawaz Sharif, through the 1990s. While Bhutto retained her power base in rural areas and in the south, Sharif, the son of an industrialist with solid Islamist connections, consolidated his own constituency in the relatively prosperous Punjab and among the urban population and reached out to Jamaat Islami.[10] Weakened by her second deposition in 1996 and the reputation of her husband, a former playboy from a third-rank landed family called Asif Ali Zardari, for corruption, Bhutto was unable to mobilize sufficient popular support to resist efforts to bring her to trial at the end of the decade. To avoid looming incarceration, she fled the country.

Sharif's triumph was short-lived, however. A combination of incompetence, graft and increasing authoritarianism rapidly alienated most of his erstwhile supporters, and when the army under General Musharraf moved in to depose him in 1999 the coup was largely welcomed as a result. Both Sharif and Bhutto had inherited vast problems from Zia but succeeded only in exacerbating them. Both had entered into a series of deals with religious parties to bolster their grip on power, allowing

Islamists and the conservative Deobandi clergy to develop a power base within the democratic political system. Both had allowed or encouraged the country's security services to aid the Taliban in Afghanistan and militant groups in Kashmir. Both, though ostensibly democratically elected and 'moderate', presided over a significant deterioration of relations with the USA. In 1990, the US imposed sanctions on Pakistan for pursuing its nuclear programme. In 1998, a new set of more sweeping restrictions was triggered by Pakistan's nuclear tests in May of that year.[11] Between them, Bhutto and Sharif left Pakistan's economy on life support from international agencies increasingly unwilling to lend, its political system riddled with graft, its society undermined by unprecedented levels of crime and its stability threatened by rising extremist violence.[12]

Once Bhutto had left the country and Musharraf had taken power, few in the West paid much attention to Pakistan. This was a mistake. Over the previous decades almost every one of the various factors that had contributed to the rise of radical violent Islamism elsewhere had been emerging. Like their Egyptian or Algerian counterparts in the late 1990s, for example, young Pakistanis in, say, 2002 could look back on the successive failures of secular modernizing dictatorships, populist nationalist Socialism, state Islamism and a debased form of democracy to solve the problems of their country. There was the vast 'youth bulge' seen elsewhere too. Between 2002 and 2007, when violence began to surge in a very serious way, the other key elements which had helped create the conditions for violence elsewhere also became evident. There was the growth of the middle class to a size where a new arrangement of power relations and a redistribution of economic wealth in the country became unavoidable if any semblance of stability was to be retained. There was the social change associated with rapid urbanization and economic growth, which boosted expectations without resolving the structural problems which made them almost impossible to fulfil. There was the exposure to new ideas of pan-Islamic solidarity and the supposed Western 'crusade' against Muslims. There were tensions between generations and a general breakdown in established social hierarchies. There was, particularly due to the growing influence of the Middle East, a new reaffirmation of a more defined and confident Islamic identity, one which promised a resolution to the fundamental historic incoherence at the heart of the nation. This was Pakistan, of course, not the countries of the Maghreb or the core Middle East, and therefore these factors played out in new and different ways. But some of the consequences – particularly in terms of violence – were the same.

KARACHI

The problem, as ever, was not stasis or 'backwardness' but change. One place where the changes in Pakistan were very evident was Karachi. Two of the most significant developments in the time Bhutto was in exile were the economic boom during the period and the rapid growth of Pakistan's urban population. Both of these had fundamentally changed Karachi, as they had changed the nation as a whole.

To stand on a street corner in central Karachi in late 2007 and watch the traffic was as good a way as any to appreciate the rapid evolution of Pakistani society. The city was home to around 15 million inhabitants, composed of communities from all over the country.[13] It was dominated politically if not necessarily demographically by Mohajirs, the descendants of the refugees who had fled India in 1947. Yet the Mohajirs shared the city with around 4 million Pashtuns and large communities of Baluchis from the province to the west, Sindhis from the vast semi-desert interior province that dominates the south of Pakistan and a smaller number of Punjabis from the country's richest and most populous province in the north-east.[14] Each community had its own neighbourhoods, ran its own religious, cultural and social establishments and spoke its own mother tongue rather than, or at least in addition to, Urdu, the national language.[15]

The communities in Karachi had distinctive socio-economic profiles too. The Punjabis, small in number, were affluent; the Pashtuns were either wealthy and successful businessmen (particularly in the transport trade) or relatively poor immigrants; the Sindhis and the Baluchis, often recent arrivals from rural areas, were the poorest and lived in vast shantytowns. The Mohajirs constituted much of the mass in the middle: the petty tradesmen, the teachers, the pharmacists, the clerks, the minor officials, the small and middling businessmen, the doctors. On the whole the Mohajirs supported the disciplined, authoritarian, nominally secular (and on occasion extremely violent) Muttahida Quami Movement (MQM) party.[16] Some of the wealthy of Karachi, cantoned in the plush and leafy seaside suburbs like Clifton, had only recently become rich. Others were the heirs of the big proprietors created or co-opted by the British overlords during their conquest and occupation in the nineteenth century. It was there that the Bhuttos, quintessential feudals themselves, had their town home.[17]

Karachi had earned a reputation as a violent city in the 1980s and 1990s as political parties broadly representing the different ethnic groups fought bloody battles at elections and in the streets for control of the city. Thousands had died until the army had been deployed to restore order. Since then, the guns had largely fallen silent, though the city, caught nonetheless by some of the secondary effects of the 9/11 Wars, had still seen enough violence to reinforce its reputation for harbouring and nurturing extremism. There had been riots during the campaign in Afghanistan of 2001, and then in January 2002, Daniel Pearl, the American Jewish reporter for the *Wall Street Journal*, had been kidnapped in the city by a group of Islamic militants and then beheaded by al-Qaeda.[18] In the autumn of that year, it had been in an upmarket middle-class suburb of Karachi that Ramzi bin al-Shibh, one of the key 9/11 conspirators, had been captured. The city's many religious schools were a source for recruits not only to Pakistan's own many militant groups but for the Taliban in Afghanistan.[19] One, the famous Binoria, was draped in banners exhorting participation in 'the Afghan jihad' as late as 2006.[20] Most recently the lawless and deprived slums of Orangi in the west, split into Mohajir and Pashtun neighbourhoods, had seen riots and gunfights which had killed dozens over two days in May 2007. These were not, however, linked to any broader conflict, but due in part to ethnic tensions, in part to political manoeuvring between President Musharraf, his supporters and lawyers contesting his authority.

Yet Karachi, despite the crumbling infrastructure and the violence, remained the country's commercial powerhouse, alone generating 68 per cent of the government's revenue and 25 per cent of the nation's gross domestic product.[21] If the historic city of Lahore, 650 miles to the north, was Pakistan's cultural capital, and Islamabad, the new town created in the 1960s on a relatively cool plateau under the foothills of the Himalayas a two-hour flight away, was the administrative capital, then Karachi was the undisputed business and financial centre and continued to make money even in the worst of times. Off the main Ibrahim Ismail Chundrigar Road, the Karachi Stock Exchange had seen a 1,000 per cent rise between 1999 and 2007, making a small number of people extremely rich and a larger number significant amounts of money. According to the city's mayor in late 2008, Kamal Mustafa, the model for development for many in Karachi was not the West or even, more locally, 'Shining India', though Pakistanis were impressed by their neighbour's apparent rapid growth. Shanghai, Singapore and Dubai comprised 'the aspirational dream', he said. There were more flights to the United Arab Emirates, just two hours away across the Arabian Sea, than to Islamabad, Mustafa pointed out, and investment flows reinforced the sense of proximity as Middle Eastern cash poured into construction projects across the city.[22]

Standing on the corner, watching Karachi's traffic, you would see at first sight chaos, like anywhere in Pakistan. Donkey traps, trucks, multi-coloured coaches, overloaded minibuses with dozens of schoolchildren hanging from the doors, hawkers pushing barrows, bicycles and cars of all sizes. The $1,000 motorbikes ceded passage to the tiny, tinny $5,000 five-seater Suzuki Mehrans, which gave way to the $15,000 saloons which in turn moved aside to allow the $60,000 SUVs favoured by major bureaucrats, senior businessmen, ministers and other wealthy and powerful figures to cruise past in air-conditioned comfort. To anyone who had seen Karachi in the 1990s the vastly increased amount of traffic choking the streets at the end of the following decade was striking. More than 500 new cars took to the road each day in 2007. There had been a total increase of 700,000 privately owned vehicles in five years.[23] Musharraf's finance minister, a smooth former banker, had pushed through reforms of the banking sector in 2001 and 2002 which had made credit easily available, and between 2001 and 2007 car ownership in the city had risen by roughly 40 per cent per year as a result.[24] Though unequally distributed, the new money had significant effects. Those who had once had a bicycle now had a motorbike; those who had had a motorbike now had their families loaded into an 800cc Mehran. Many of those once driving the tinny little Mehrans now had an imported saloon, and the number of SUVs had increased exponentially. According to pollster and economic analyst Ijaz Gilani, Karachi was 'an upwardly mobile place'.[25]

It was not just Karachi that had experienced such change during the years of Musharraf's rule. The combination of new neoliberal economic policies, the lifting of American sanctions, a massive flow of remittances from Pakistanis suddenly feeling precarious in post 9/11 USA or Europe, loan write-offs granted once Pakistani support for the 'War on Terror' was assured, the generous rescheduling of further debts as well as the effect of new technologies such as mobile phones had unleashed a comprehensive boom across much of the country.[26] Per capita revenues rose to over $1,000 for the first time.[27] Foreign Direct Investment in Pakistan had gone from $322 million in 2002 to $3.5 billion in 2006, and GDP had doubled between 1999 and 2007, with growth rates hitting 9 per cent. One consequence was soaring property prices, which themselves created a huge amount of new wealth, very visible in the deliberately conspicuous consumption on show at 'the society' functions favoured by the elite of the major cities.[28] The critical element in terms of political economy, however, was not that the rich got richer but that the economic growth also created a much bigger and better-connected middle class. Since independence, Pakistan had always lacked a middle class of the size and influence seen in much of the rest of the Islamic world. This was no longer the case, however. The World Bank estimated that 5 per cent of Pakistan's population – or roughly 9 million people – appeared to have moved from living in poverty to being part of the lower middle class between 2001 and 2004 alone.[29] These were the people who had swapped their family motorbike for a family car and who were now clogging the country's cities.

Another crucial shift was the acceleration of the already relatively rapid rate of urbanization in Pakistan. By 2008, well over a third of Pakistanis lived in cities, and the proportion was increasing by 3 per cent each year.[30] The rate of urbanization was one of the fastest in the world. With the population of the country itself continuing to grow rapidly, this meant the rapid creation of large urban masses. Karachi itself was adding more than half a million people a year to its population. Other cities – Nowsherah, Hyderabad, Faisalabad, Lahore, Rawalpindi – were growing equally fast. Why was the new wealth and the new urbanization important in the context of the 9/11 Wars? Because the urban middle classes were also the people who, from Morocco to Malaysia, had been absolutely key over previous decades in determining the political evolution of their societies. Above all, they had provided the principal constituency for political Islamism, underpinning the popularization of the ideology through the 1980s and, in many places, the 1990s too. There seemed little reason that Pakistan should be any different. One reason for the failure of Islamist parties in Pakistan in elections, apart from the deeply corrupt nature of the campaigning, was that there had been no substantial urban, particularly lower, middle class. By 2007, this was changing.

FEUDALS, TELEVISIONS AND DEFERENCE

There were two further features of the decade that Bhutto had spent in exile that were particularly significant. The first was the impact of mass communications on Pakistani society. One of Musharraf's first acts had been to liberalize the country's telecoms sector, allowing hundreds of private satellite channels to start broadcasting alongside the stultifying state network. This was of added importance given the nature of the news that those television channels carried. The second was the steady weakening of traditional social hierarchies that the economic boom, the new media and increased literacy meant.

If, having stood on a street corner in Karachi for half an hour in that autumn of 2007, you had got into one of the overcharged, over-decorated buses coming past and, having changed at one of the vast and chaotic bus stations on the outskirts of the city, continued on one of the main highways north, crammed into your seat among the migrant workers, returning students, off-duty soldiers, pilgrims and chickens for five or six hours, you would have arrived at a nondescript, fly-blown country town called Moro. Taking a rickshaw for a further half-hour journey down country lanes between the sugar cane and wheat fields (the proportion of each crop depending on the time of year) would take you to the village of Jatoi, named after the local landowning family, one of the most powerful and wealthy in southern Pakistan. Here, even in this most rural of settings, you would have found evidence of these vital changes. The main division in the village was not between rich and poor, between those with their own cars or bikes or donkeys and those without, between those speaking the local language of Sindhi or the minority whose mother tongue was Soraiki, between Sunnis or Shias (10 per cent of Pakistan's population), or even between Muslims and the often persecuted local Christian community. It was not even between those who sided with the local barber and those who backed his wife in their interminable marital rows. It was between those who patronized the teashop of Ghulam Razzaq, who had installed a television a few weeks previously, and those who preferred the teashop of Hadyattullah, who had not.

By 2003, even before a second wave of deregulation, a third of Pakistanis were estimated to be regular watchers of TV.[31] By 2007, the proportion was even higher with some channels claiming national audiences of up to 70 million for some programmes. Tuned permanently to local Sindhi-language television, Ghulam Razzaq's television attracted a growing clientele who sat for hours, at least during the slack season when there was little work in the fields, before its soap operas, musical films and news bulletins and debates. The latter, vociferous, lively and often as ill informed as they were ill mannered, had become by far the most popular programmes on the major Urdu- and English-language channels such as Geo and Dawn TV, though their local-language equivalents also attracted huge numbers of viewers. Asked what difference the television had made to their lives, villagers were divided. Not much, said many. But all agreed they knew more now about 'world politics', which appeared largely to consist of the West oppressing Muslims in Afghanistan, Iraq or Pakistan, and about the venality and incompetence of their own rulers. As with al-Jazeera in the Arab world a few years earlier, the explosion of Pakistani media had not meant an informed and rational discussion of important issues but the broad dissemination and reinforcement of the outlook of the 'Pakistani street'. Al-Jazeera had broadcast graphic images of the second Palestinian intifada in 1999 and 2000 into the homes of tens of millions of people in the Middle East. The Pakistani channels had no shortage of such material. Launched at the beginning of the 9/11 Wars, they gave their viewers a gruesome and one-sided take on the war in Afghanistan, the invasion of Iraq and its aftermath, the problems in Europe, episodes such as the cartoon crisis and the continuing violence in Israel-Palestine. The news channels were flanked by scores of religious networks, devoted to twenty-four-hour readings from the Koran or sermons or lessons on Islamic jurisprudence which also attracted, cumulatively if not individually, a substantial audience.

The second change – though obscured by the timeless sight of peasants tilling crops by hand, of children scribbling on slates in open-air schools, of the shrines of local saints festooned with silver ribbons and offerings of sweetmeats and fruit – was less tangible but as profound. This was the rapid shift in attitudes and behaviours, particularly towards those to whom once the poor would have owed absolute obedience. Many of the peasants in the fields had worked in Karachi or even in Saudi Arabia or Dubai, where a boom in construction sites provided vastly expanded opportunities for relatively well-paid and steady work. The money they earned for their families meant a new freedom from the crushing physical work of farming and, often for the first time, disposable incomes. The spread of mobile phones meant teachers at the local schools kept in touch with relatives living elsewhere in the country with half-hour calls for a few rupees, further enlarging perspectives and encouraging a comparison between what was happening in different parts of the country.[32] Literacy had risen, albeit from the appallingly low level of 44 per cent in 1998 to 56 per cent ten years later.[33] If they weren't watching the television, people were reading the Urdu- or Sindhi-language papers or having them read to them if still incapable of deciphering the text themselves. Where the newspapers went so did conspiracy theories – that a picture of Mecca had been printed on footballs in international tournaments so it would be repeatedly kicked, that Indian troops had landed in Afghanistan, that Zionist spies were behind kidnappings in Karachi – and the same brand of angry, unbridled commentary as was carried by the new TV channels. Together, all the various developments worked to rapidly erode long-established customs, norms and, crucially, deference. It was not for nothing that landowning families in Sindh such as the Jatois were known as 'feudals'. They, like other local families including the Bhuttos, were benefactors, protectors, dispensers of justice and, often, of religious blessings too.[34] But Masroor Ahmed Jatoi, leaving the sprawling family home for a day on the stump as a provincial MP for the parliamentary elections scheduled for January 2008, said he no longer expected to win elections 'just because the village is named after my family'. Both Masroor and his younger brother Arif, a minister in the provincial government, had had to become, like all local politicians, masters of working the system to obtain maximum development grants to bring electricity, roads, sanitation and jobs to their constituents. Such work, which had become the basis of politics in Pakistan as across much of the region, still did not guarantee victory, however.

'[The people] have become highly politicized in their way,' Jatoi said. 'You can take nothing for granted.'[35]

MILITANTS AND *MEDRESSAS*

Bahawalpur lay 500 miles to the north of Jatoi village, a ten-hour drive across dusty but fertile fields, along roads lined with mills, sugar refineries and dozens of scruffy small towns. A city of around 800,000 in 2007, Bahawalpur, along with nearby Rahim Yar Khan and the much bigger city of Multan further to the north, constituted one of the biggest single centres of radical Islamic militancy in the world and one of the least known.[36] The core of jihadi activism in Pakistan at the time was usually thought to be the zones along the frontier with Afghanistan, but the towns of southern Punjab were equally significant locally and regionally.[37] It was in these towns that many of the best-known and best-established Pakistani militant outfits were based and from these towns that Western and regional security services feared a new international threat might eventually evolve.

The Western interest in Pakistan in the 2002–7 period was largely and understandably focused on the large numbers of violent militant organizations based in the country. These had naturally attracted attention during the war of 2001, when they had launched the spectacular attack on the Indian parliament at the end of that year, as peace talks between India and Pakistan stumbled along through the middle of the decade and after each of the successive attempts to assassinate Musharraf himself. The interest spiked whenever Western concerns mounted over the policy of the Pakistani security establishment in Afghanistan and whenever such groups were found to be playing a role as intermediaries for Western – particularly British – Muslim extremists hoping to contact al-Qaeda. Many blamed the ISI and other Pakistani intelligence agencies for the groups' existence and apparent health.

The use of irregular proxies by the Pakistani military and civilian leaders was almost as old as Pakistan itself. Just months after gaining independence, the Pakistanis had sent a column of armed Pashtun tribesmen from high on the Afghan border towards Srinagar, the capital of the mountain state of Kashmir, to 'liberate' their coreligionists from their Hindu maharajah. The move prompted the maharajah to call for Indian military aid, and the months of scrappy fighting which followed only ended with a ceasefire brokered by the United Nations which left almost all the most important and most populous parts of Muslim-majority Kashmir, including the famously beautiful Vale or Valley, under Indian control. A second war was fought between India and Pakistan in 1965, again following the operations of Pakistani-backed irregulars. A third conflict with India occurred in 1971, prompted by political unrest in the then eastern wing of Pakistan. It ended too in a crushing Indian victory on two fronts and the creation of Bangladesh despite the horrific violence directed by local Islamists armed, organized and assisted by the Pakistani army against pro-independence activists and intellectuals.[38] These successive disasters paradoxically reinforced the use of proxies as a fundamental of Pakistani strategic thinking as it was broadly believed that only the use of such forces could offset the clear conventional superiority that the Indians had repeatedly demonstrated. The use of such forces was both defensive and offensive. Defensively, they constituted a 'strategic reserve', furnishing an irregular auxiliary force several hundred thousand strong in the event of an Indian attack and providing a harassing guerrilla capability if such an attack had been successful and a significant part of Pakistan occupied. Offensively, the militants could also be used in pursuit of key foreign policy objectives.[39] One strategy was to continually destabilize Kashmir to prevent the status quo of Indian control over most of the state hardening into an unchangeable geopolitical reality. A second was to secure a favourable government in Kabul, a long-term aim of Pakistani – and indeed Raj – diplomacy. For the Pakistanis this was in part because of a desire to secure rear areas west of the Indus river to have 'strategic depth' in the event of an Indian attack from the east but was also about projecting their national interests in what was, given the size of their other immediate neighbours, the only direction that it was feasible to do so. South-west Asia is, like the Middle East, a tough neighbourhood where the strong bully the weak and the weak bully the weaker. Pakistan, though one of the biggest countries in the world, is nonetheless dwarfed by India and China, and inevitably saw in Afghanistan an opportunity for strategic gain that was denied elsewhere.

The 1970s, 1980s and 1990s thus saw the systematic use of irregulars sponsored and often trained and funded by Pakistani security agencies, particularly in Afghanistan and Kashmir. The Pakistani role in Afghanistan is covered in more detail in the following chapter. The Pakistani involvement in Kashmir, which had a more direct importance for many of the Punjabi groups, was re-energized in 1989, as local Muslims in the state, in part inspired by events in eastern Europe, rose against the discriminatory and often brutal rule that had been imposed by New Delhi. Early armed Kashmiri groups were relatively moderate and favoured independence from both India and Pakistan but the ISI, looking to exploit the uprising to pressurize and weaken India, marginalized these and instead backed more compliant proxies. These organizations included one composed of fighters linked to the Islamists of the Kashmiri branch of Jamaat Islami, groups which had sprung up during the previous decade to fight the Soviets and were now at something of a loose end, and finally a new and extremely violent outfit called Lashkar-e-Toiba (LeT, The War Party of the Pure), which was based just south of Lahore but recruited heavily throughout the Punjab and provided the most fanatical and dedicated *mujahideen*.

Throughout the 1990s, these various organizations would send tens of thousands of young Kashmiri, Pashtun and increasingly Punjabi men (and even some Britons) to fight Indian security forces across the Line of Control (LoC), the ceasefire line agreed in Kashmir after the first Indo-Pakistani war.[40] By the mid 1990s, they dominated the insurgency in the disputed state. Progressively, the role of the Kashmiris themselves fell away. In 1999, it was militants from Pakistan-based groups including Lashkar-e-Toiba who, on the orders of senior army generals including Musharraf, had provided the bulk of the fighting force which occupied key heights across the LoC, thus provoking a limited conflict that, once again, was disastrous for Pakistan.[41] In the weeks after 9/11, with the acquiescence and often assistance of the ISI, thousands of fighters from these groups, including a newly formed organization called Jaish-e-Mohammed (JeM), travelled to Afghanistan to fight alongside the Taliban.[42] Such fighters had a new global perspective which was very different from the Kashmiri militants of a decade or so previously. They included young men like Asim, Jamal and 'Abu Turab', who, while waiting for transport into Afghanistan from Peshawar in October 2001, told the author: 'We were in India fighting the Indians. Now we are coming to Afghanistan. America, Israel and India are our enemies. Bush will die like a dog.' In the end it was such militants themselves who were killed in large numbers by coalition air strikes, special forces or the Northern Alliance.

The advent of the 9/11 Wars changed much for Pakistan's militants. Positive developments for groups such as Jaish-e-Mohammed and Lashkar-e-Toiba included the increase in the relative level of radicalization of much of the Pakistani population in the early years of the decade and a consequent surge in popular support, recruits and funds.[43] The downside of the conflict was that, under pressure from the international community, Musharraf banned dozens of extremist organizations. Though many in the Pakistani security establishment saw this as a betrayal of national interests, of national duty and of coreligionists in need, the crackdown, patchy though it might have been as a result, nonetheless had some effect.[44] The groups were not disbanded, but funds were restricted, recruitment cut back, propaganda operations forced underground and a proportion of the training facilities were shut. They continued to exist in a form which would allow them to be mobilized once again should need arise but were 'run down'. Successive attempts by different militant factions to kill Musharraf led to further repression and with thousands of young fighters idling in camps and with funds running short, many groups began to fragment, fusing with the sectarian groups long active in Karachi, the frontier and the Punjab and increasingly building connections with international militants. Before 2001, none of the groups active in Kashmir sought active involvement in the broader international jihad though they were aware – and often approved – of the pronouncements and views of men like bin Laden.[45] But the 9/11 Wars had seen the links between such groups and al-Qaeda figures active in Pakistan strengthen. The process had started as early as December 2001 with the abduction and killing of Daniel Pearl and then the capture of Abu Zubaydah, bin Laden's key logistics operator, three months later in a LeT safehouse. A year later, a pair of LeT militants had surfaced in Iraq. Then there was the growing role that individuals within Pakistani groups played as intermediaries for young British Muslims hoping to access al-Qaeda.[46] The burgeoning links with international activism were ad hoc and based on personal connections. One of the best examples of such links came with the exposure of the plot in the UK to bring down airliners flying across the Atlantic to the USA in 2006. A central figure in the conspiracy was a British citizen originally from the Midlands city of Birmingham called Rashid Rauf, who had been detained in Pakistan at the same time as the plot was rolled up in the UK and who was alleged to have played a key role in coordinating plotters in his native land and liaising with the al-Qaeda senior leadership.[47] Though family members and his lawyers denied it, Rauf was almost certainly a member of the Jaish-e-Mohammed group. Pakistani militant organizations were following, albeit with a lag of almost a decade, the trend towards a greater degree of globalization seen elsewhere in the Islamic world over previous years. This too was something that the Pakistani intelligence services believed they could manage.

In the West, in addition to being seen as sponsored by Pakistani security agencies, the activism of Rauf and people like him was often seen as linked to the existence and expansion of the network of religious schools in Pakistan. In October 2003, Donald Rumsfeld had asked in a note: 'Are we capturing, killing or deterring and dissuading more terrorists every day than the *medressas* and the radical clerics are recruiting, training and deploying against us?'[48] The then defense secretary was only reflecting a generally held view that the religious schools contained a huge reservoir of militants waiting to be unleashed. Rauf's connection to a radical *medressa* seemed further evidence that this was the case. The first problem with this analysis, as with so many others during the course of the 9/11 Wars, was not just that it was too simplistic but that, in simplifying, the genuinely worrying elements had been missed. First of all, there was considerable variety among the *medressas*. Three broad categories existed. The first included the village schools. They were often small, miserably poor, of the local folksy Barelvi School of Islam still dominant in rural communities. It was hard to argue that they posed much threat to anyone. The second category, which included the vast bulk of the *medressas* founded in recent decades, were Deobandi or Ahl-e-Hadith, the two most rigorous local strands of Islam, and were more problematic. Overall in Pakistan their numbers, though notoriously difficult to estimate, had gone from around 1,000 in 1967 to somewhere between 10,000 and 30,000 in forty years. Though many were located in the North West Frontier province, their numbers had increased exponentially in the Punjab too. In the town of Bahawalpur alone there had been only 278 religious schools in 1975 but approaching 1,000 by 2008, local officials said. But though these institutions propagated conservative values and an appallingly distorted vision of the world, there was little evidence to link them directly to violence.

Mohammed Chugti, who ran scores of *medressas* in Bahawalpur and was also a senior local politician with the Jamaat Ulema Islami (JUI), the political vehicle that had represented the interests of the Deobandi clergy and community in Pakistan for decades, told the author that students in the *medressas* he oversaw learned Arabic, Islamic law as well as English, science, Urdu, maths and 'arts subjects' and, though his charges were also, somewhat inevitably, taught that 'to fight in Afghanistan or Kashmir is a religious duty as part of the struggle with any forces that are against the religion of Islam' they were discouraged from actually doing so, at least until they had finished their education.[49] Chugti's *medressas* were not linked to local militant groups, he said, a claim backed up by local officials. It was a third category of *medressa* – those clearly associated with violent groups – that was the immediate problem. These were a minority but sufficiently numerous to be very worrying nonetheless. One high-profile example was the mosque and *medressa* complex in the centre of Islamabad that Pakistani security forces stormed in July 2007. The 'Red Mosque', as it was known, had been a centre of militancy for at least two decades, though after 9/11, following the more general evolution, it had shifted from activism focused almost exclusively on Kashmir to a more internationalized agenda. Maulana Abdul Aziz and his younger brother Abdur Rasheed Ghazi, the leaders of the group, saw Musharraf and all who supported him as complicit in the campaign of the West to divide, humiliate and dominate the world's Muslim community and exhorted their followers to fight against the 'hypocrite *jahiliya*' regime in power in Pakistan as a first step to liberating all Muslim lands.[50] The 'Red Mosque' was a particularly extreme example, but there were others. The alumni of the vast Binoria *medressa* in Karachi included many involved in local sectarian or other violence. Rashid Rauf had often been seen at the Dar-ul-Uloom Medina in Bahawalpur, a large complex that had been repeatedly extended over the forty years since its foundation as donations from the Gulf had flowed in. There a twenty-two-year-old student at the school told the author: 'Jihad is our religion. It is the order of God. When I finish here I will go to fight like many of my friends.'[51] According to local officials, the Jaish-e-Mohammed group not only ran the Dar-ul-Uloom Medina, where 700 teenagers and young adults lived and studied, but also a second, larger, semi-fortified complex in the centre of the city.[52] Though there was no 'production line', such institutions undoubtedly allowed militant groups to select likely recruits from among the students and then cultivate those receptive to their approach.[53] Such institutions evidently constituted a serious threat in the region and to the West but the idea that *medressas* were the root of the problem of militancy inside Pakistan was mistaken. For this was the second element that the reductivist analysis of Rumsfeld missed. The *medressas* did not exist in a vacuum.

The oft-heard argument that the *medressas* only thrived because they filled a vital gap left by the state by offering free education to the most miserable was only partially accurate. Statistics showed little correlation between the relative wealth of a family and the decision to send children to a *medressa*. This suggested that parents sent their children to *medressas* for reasons other than poverty.[54] Such a conclusion was further reinforced by research showing that around a quarter of religious students came from the richer families who could afford to send their children to any type of educational establishment they chose.[55] Equally, three-quarters of families with children in religious schools also sent other siblings to private or public schools. It was true that some families might only have sufficient funds to pay the albeit minimal school fees for one of their offspring but the figures nonetheless indicated fairly unequivocally that millions of parents across Pakistan simply sent their children to *medressas* because they wanted to have at least one child educated religiously and, crucially, because they agreed with what their offspring would be taught in a religious school about the world, about religion and about life.[56] This was of very great importance. For further statistical studies revealed that, even if levels of support for militancy or violence in the name of causes such as Kashmir or Palestine were higher among the students and teachers of religious schools, they were still at very significant levels in the supposedly non-religious educational establishments in which the overwhelming majority of Pakistani children were being educated.[57] One study found that graduates from state public schools, particularly Urdu-medium institutions, were only 'moderately more tolerant' than *medressa* graduates, with very significant numbers of the former favouring either open war or support for Islamic militant groups as means of 'liberating Kashmir', for example.[58] A study of the backgrounds of 517 Pakistani militants in 2003 found that most had relatively high levels of literacy and had been educated not in *medressas* but in government schools.[59] Similar studies five years later found that this had not changed.[60] Together, all these statistics reveal an unpleasant truth: that the gap between the broad political and religious culture of many of the religious schools and that of most Pakistanis, at least in late 2007, was much narrower than many in the West liked to think.[61]

MIDDLE PAKISTAN

Nowhere was this more clear than in Multan, once simply a sleepy provincial town famous for its shrines but in November 2007 a city with a population swollen to nearly 1.5 million by migration from the poor rural zones around and still growing by an estimated 50,000 every year. On the outskirts, past the army garrison and the new hotels, shops and offices that were springing up along the potholed streets, past the occasional sports car and the crumbling public buildings, was the Bahauddin Zakariya University, founded in 1975 and one of scores of similar private institutions offering graduate-level further education to the children of Pakistan's new middle classes. It was here that the result of the various elements discussed above – the new wealth, the new urbanization, the impact of the new media, the new lack of deference, the consequences of decades of Islamist activism, the failure of successive alternative ideologies, the indirect impact of the 9/11 Wars – came together in a very obvious way.

On a late autumn morning, a few months after Bhutto had returned to Pakistan, some of the 14,000 students of the university were sitting on the grass in between the college's brick and concrete buildings, their books and files spread around them. A small queue had formed at the tiny kiosk selling small cups of sweet tea. A knot of young men inspected the motorbike one of them had recently bought. These young people were ordinary young Pakistanis, studying in a middle-ranking college, in a middling-sized town, in the geographic centre of the country. They were neither activists for secular parties nor Islamists. They were neither as Westernized as the elite youth of Lahore or Karachi, with their American college or exclusive English-medium local education, their cars and parties, nor as aggressively conservative as the Jamaat Islami members. Instead they were representative of a Pakistan that was rarely reported in the international media and had little place in conventional analysis of the country as a battleground between Westernized, democratic 'moderates' and fanatical 'fundamentalists'. They comprised the middle ground, what could be termed 'Middle Pakistan', a diverse yet definite body of people with a diverse yet definite worldview and value system who had been as active in building a coherent and authentic identity as any other group in the country. If not immediately, in a few years' time, they would be 'the Pakistani street', the people whose views and values would determine the country's course.

Visually, the scene at the Bahauddin Zakariya University revealed many of the essential elements of this new evolving identity. So, for example, the students sitting on the grass all maintained a strict and voluntary gender segregation. The girls were uniformly veiled – several wore a full Gulf-style *niqab* – and many of their male counterparts were bearded. Both veils and beards had been very rare a decade or so before, one teacher, a former student at the university himself, remembered.[62] The students' conservatism extended to more than where they sat or what they wore. The West's material conditions were undoubtedly attractive, many told the author during a long day of conversations and arguments, but there was no respect for women or the old in Europe or America and there was pornography, prostitution and AIDS too. Though they agreed that people should be able to chose whom they married and that women were, of course, the equal of men and could and should work – 70 per cent of the university's business studies students were female – women nonetheless had their roles in the home and a balance had to be kept. Though the students had a lucid view of their nation's problems, their patriotism was assertive and unabashed. Pakistan, a peace-seeking nation beset by Indian aggression and Western antipathy from its birth, was a great nation, a leader among Muslim states and deserved greater respect from the international community, they said, insisting too that Kashmir was illegally occupied and the Muslims there were 'as oppressed' as they were in Palestine. Abdul Qadeer Khan, the Pakistani atomic scientist who had first built his country a bomb and then, with successive governments' encouragement, sold its nuclear secrets to Iran, Libya, North Korea and a range of other clients, was 'a Pakistani patriot'. The blame for the problems in their country, they said, lay with corrupt politicians, self-seeking bureaucrats and religious leaders who were far from religious. Democracy, which they all supported as a concept, could only work when there was a political class of sufficient honesty and quality to lead. They were therefore less convinced that it could work – at least now – for Pakistan. The constant interventions of the army were a problem but comprehensible, though now it was time for Musharraf to move on. Above all, Pakistan's government should give way neither to terrorism – which they maintained was unIslamic, though suicide bombings in Israel were 'legitimate resistance' – nor to bullying by America. The students wanted to be doctors, lawyers, engineers, business people and journalists. Their parents, who paid their fees of between 48,000 and 60,000 rupees a year ($770 to $970, £340 to £550 at 2007 rates), were senior teachers, middling-ranking bureaucrats, pharmacists, farmers, traders. The family car was usually simply a Mehran (though some had recently traded up to a Corolla). For the students' questions about whether Pakistan was an İslamic state or not were almost nonsensical. Their nation was the Islamic Republic of Pakistan. They did not want their government to be composed of elderly clerics but they did want their leaders to reflect their identity, values and views.

That those young men and women were representative of Pakistan was beyond doubt. Firstly, they were young – and in 2008 the *median* age in Pakistan was twenty-one. Half the country's population were aged under twenty, with two-thirds still to reach their thirtieth birthday.[63] Secondly, as discussed above, they were from the urban middle class, the fastest-growing sector of Pakistani society. Thirdly, their views were distinctly uncontroversial for the vast proportion of Pakistanis. The students had called themselves 'moderates', and by local standards, if not for most in the West, they were. Their views on more or less every subject were exactly those which polls said, again and again, were shared by most of their compatriots. Their more overt religiosity was typical of much of the nation. Their views of the West too were representative of those of almost all Pakistanis in late 2007: overwhelmingly negative, coloured by conspiracy theories about the true perpetrators of the 9/11 attacks, by anti-Semitism and anti-Zionism, anti-Americanism and deep resentment. A survey by the independent think-tank Terror Free Tomorrow in 2007 found that around a half of Pakistanis viewed Osama bin Laden and militant groups fighting in Kashmir favourably, two-thirds were against the American military operating in Pakistan, and more than half blamed America for the violence in Pakistan at the time.[64] Other polls found that around three-quarters of Pakistanis wanted their country to be ruled by Islamic laws and that only 15 per cent of Pakistanis believed that 'Arabs' were responsible for 9/11. A further poll, on patriotism, asked: 'How proud do you feel to call yourself a Pakistani?' Nearly 80 per cent said they were 'very proud', particularly citing the country's nuclear capability.[65] Another found that 89 per cent of Pakistanis did not want their country to cooperate with the United States in the War on Terror, many more than in previous years. The overseas country that was most admired was Saudi Arabia.[66] Much of this had been anecdotally obvious to those visiting Pakistan regularly since 2001 and particularly to those who had known the country during the 1990s or before.

The new identity was built on long-developing trends that had gradually seen Pakistan shuck off the heritage of British rule and turn further and further towards the Middle East. It was not just investment flows or the ever-growing number of pilgrims travelling on Haj that increasingly linked Pakistan to the Gulf. Names of children had become more Islamic and more Arabicized from the turn of the millennium on. After 9/11, Osama had become popular; later in the decade it was Areeba, Malaika, Uzair, Emal which became widespread. Some 90 per cent of boys were named Mohammed following Middle Eastern practice.[67] Trends in clothes and language, crucial signifiers, were also revealing. The vast proportion of Pakistanis had kept their traditional *shalwar kameez*, leaving jeans and T-shirts to the Westernized elite.[68] Bollywood maintained its dominant position in terms of cinema and music, mitigating the bile directed at India in the mainstream media, but where dreamed-of holiday destinations had once been Europe or the USA, now they were Malaysia or the Gulf, partly out of a new sense of pan-Islamic solidarity, partly due to the difficulty of getting visas to visit the West and the suspicion that Pakistanis faced when they arrived there. A 'books section' in a new superstore in Karachi's wealthy Clifton area was entirely devoted to Islamic titles. In a Nike shop, speakers played recitations from the Koran. Mobile phone companies offered the call to prayer as a ring tone and Koranic recitations as free downloads. During the month of Ramadan international banks offered preferred clients boxes containing prayer beads, dates and miniature Korans.[69] When one Urdu-language columnist pointed out that there had never been a demonstration in Pakistan against 'Islamic terrorist' attacks in the West, he was vilified.[70]

This emerging identity was as politically conservative as it was socially and religiously conservative – which was one reason why revolution in Pakistan, Islamist or otherwise, did not seem likely in the immediate future. A factor in the failure of the violent radicalism of the militants or even their supporters among the Deobandi or Ahl-e-Hadith clerics to appeal to this emerging Middle Pakistan was because few, least of all junior bureaucrats, shopkeepers, teachers and doctors, wanted radical, sudden upheaval. If there was to be a revolution, it would be a gradual one that would not threaten too much disruption. That the identity of Middle Pakistan owed much to the influence of Jamaat Islami and the idea of its founder, Maududi, was undoubted. Despite the continued lack of electoral success of his organization over the decades, Maududi's ideas had eventually permeated whole sections of society. Now almost forty years after his death, what had once been seen as radically right-wing was now entirely normalized. This was often difficult for outsiders to see. The lawyers who received so much attention for resisting Musharraf's clumsy attempts at intimidation of the judiciary in this period, certainly beyond the upper layer of smoother English-speaking and UK-educated older leaders, shared many of the values and ideas described above, for example. So too did many of the millions who voted for the nominally secular MQM in Karachi. These vast constituencies were rarely counted in analyses of Pakistan overseas but were hugely important internally. The lessons of Maududi and other Islamists had become so internalized as to have become utterly unremarkable.

So instead of the oft-repeated analysis of Pakistan as a country with a fractured identity, as the first decade of the 9/11 Wars drew to its close, the opposite appeared to be increasingly nearer the truth. Though great ethnic, topographic, linguistic diversity remained, much of the ambiguity that had troubled the country about its identity since its foundation was being resolved, not exacerbated. Baluchis, Pashtuns, Punjabis, Sindhis might disagree on how fairly national resources were distributed and might discriminate or suffer discrimination, but few would disagree with the basic worldview and values articulated by the students of Multan. A fairly uniform, fairly coherent, Pakistani identity was emerging. This identity was broadly established across the country. To describe Pakistan as simply a battleground for extremists and their opposites was to deny the emerging mass of the middle ground – the 'Pakistani street' – its true importance. The direction in which they were taking Pakistan was not necessarily the one the West wanted the country to take.

BHUTTO AND THE NEW PAKISTAN

The deal which had allowed Bhutto to return had been arranged with President Musharraf, then in his eighth year of power, in long negotiations over the spring and summer of 2007.[71] Corruption charges against the former prime minister and a treason conviction against her historic rival Nawaz Sharif, the fifty-eight-year-old leader of the Pakistan Muslim League party, had been set aside, and the two veteran politicians' exile ended. In return Bhutto and Sharif, who had been in Dubai and Riyadh respectively, promised to support Musharraf's bid to be re-elected by parliament as president for a further five-year term. Both British and American diplomats had acted as go-betweens, and it was fervently hoped in London and Washington that Bhutto would win the parliamentary elections scheduled for early 2008. With Bhutto as prime minister and Musharraf still president, though no longer chief of the army staff, Pakistan would have a pro-Western government which would retain, through the man President Bush had described as his 'buddy' only a year or so earlier, the support of the military.[72] This would, it was hoped, assure most Western strategic interests in the country while giving the Pakistani government the legitimacy of something at least resembling, however imperfectly, democracy. Musharraf detested both Bhutto and Sharif but was weak politically and had little choice but to accept the arrangement.[73] Despite the violence that had greeted her return, Bhutto, after a verbal broadside at the 'dark forces' that wanted her dead, threw herself into campaigning with energy undiminished by her lengthy exile. She would not comment on her chances of victory, simply saying the 'people of Pakistan' would decide.[74]

Recognizing that she needed to win over the undecided, Bhutto focused her efforts not on the heartland of her traditional support in the south but on the major population centres of the north, around the twin cities of Islamabad and Rawalpindi and further west, towards the Afghan frontier. Each day followed a similar routine with rallies, meetings, driving, more rallies, more meetings, more rallies. On December

17, 2007, for example, Bhutto left her home in Islamabad at around 9 a.m., was driven rapidly through the capital's wide, quiet streets in a white armoured landcruiser and then up the pristine six-lane highway which slices through the rural backcountry of the Punjab before crossing the Indus river and then swings in a broad arc through the fields and villages of the lowland areas of the North West Frontier province towards Peshawar. Since the highway had been opened exactly a year earlier, much of the fencing that lined it had been stolen to be resold as scrap, and the palm trees planted in the central reservation had died. But the surface remained good, and there was little traffic.[75] The convoy swept by villages where the mosque was the only concrete structure and dried cow dung the only fuel. Smoke from cooking fires rose straight into the still, chill morning air. Bullocks pulled carts down dirt roads which ran parallel to the motorway for a few hundred yards and then turned away across the fields, where small boys played cricket with sticks and goats wandered in search of weeds.

At Nowshera, a scruffy mid-sized town 30 miles from Peshawar, Bhutto had lunch with local candidates from her Pakistan People's Party (PPP) and then addressed a crowd. She spoke of the need for moderation, human rights, basics for the poor, an end to terrorism.[76] After the rally in Nowshera, Bhutto drove away, sufficiently exhilarated to stand up through the hatch cut in the roof of her vehicle and wave to bemused locals on the old Grand Trunk Road as she headed back towards the motorway and Islamabad. In the town of Pabbi, once a centre of militancy in the 1980s and early 1990s, she suddenly ordered her vehicle to stop and, to the consternation of the police escort, plunged almost alone into a roadside bazaar to buy oranges. Returning to the car, she told the author that, after such a long period out of her homeland, she needed to get to know her country again and that learning the price of fruit was an essential part of that process. 'I am out of touch, Mr Burke,' she said. 'I am out of touch, and that must be changed. I can now tell you what oranges cost.'

Bhutto was out of touch in ways that were more significant than simply not knowing the price of fruit. For it was apparent that the fifty-four-year-old politician had not taken full measure of the changes within Pakistan over the eight years of her exile. Weeks before returning to Pakistan, Bhutto had listed those whom she said she represented: 'the underprivileged, the peasants, women, minorities, all those who are neglected by elite government, the middle class'.[77] But it was exactly these constituencies that were changing the most rapidly, sucked into the cities, transformed by the rising incomes of the previous ten years, suddenly exposed to images from Palestine, Iraq or Afghanistan on the new satellite channels on their new televisions after years of turgid state broadcasting, dealing with the complex and conflicting streams of political and cultural thought flowing throughout the Muslim world during the 9/11 Wars. Equally, it was Bhutto's hardcore of supporters among the feudal aristocracy and the educated and moderate or even secular elite who were finding themselves increasingly challenged by the loud and numerous urban middle class or those who had once unquestioningly worked the fields and followed orders. In the new Pakistan, Bhutto's own Westernization, her backing from America or Europe, her ideas about opening up Pakistan's nuclear facilities to international inspectors, even her moderation on Kashmir, Afghanistan, Israel and other issues that had become touchstones in the new more international consciousness of many Pakistanis jarred with many more of her compatriots than would have been the case a decade previously. Potential allies – such as the new civil society groups that had emerged over previous years and were receiving so much international attention – were too few to fill the gap. An adept and perceptive politician, Bhutto clearly sensed the need to adapt to the broad shifts in her native land but was either unable or unwilling to do so in the short time she had.

Bhutto had also underestimated the capabilities and the intentions of Pakistan's militants. Bhutto was thinking in terms of the 1990s, with discrete groups pursuing discrete largely local agendas – sectarian, Kashmiri, criminal – and the independence of action of the vast proportion of militants heavily constrained by their dependence on the resources and protection of the state security establishment. In conversations with Bhutto over the months before her return, it was clear that the rapid evolution of Pakistani Islamic militancy over recent years, particularly in the pressure-cooker conditions of the 9/11 Wars, had escaped her.[78] Though, during the 100 or so days after her return from Pakistan she spoke often about her need for greater protection, the threat, she repeatedly said, came from her old enemies within the army, the ISI and the government. The source of the immediate danger was in fact very close to where she had stopped to buy her fruit: in the FATA and the broad zone along the frontier where new and potentially more dangerous actors had emerged while she had been in Dubai, Washington and London.

On December 27, 2007, as Bhutto was leaving a rally in Rawalpindi, waving to the crowd through the hatch of her vehicle, a fifteen-year-old boy fired three shots at her with a pistol before detonating a suicide bomb strapped to his waist.[79] In her last speech she had run through the same themes as throughout her campaign: the need for moderation, justice, food and shelter for the needy, an end to violence. In the seconds before the shots and the blast, the crowd shouted 'Bhutto de naray ... wajan ge' (the slogans of Bhutto ... will always be chanted).[80] She died in Rawalpindi general hospital of a wound probably caused by the blast of the explosion smashing her head into the metal handle of the hatch as she ducked to avoid the shots fired at her.[81] Bhutto became the single highest-profile casualty of the 9/11 Wars to date. Twenty-three less-high-profile casualties died in the same attack, and ninety-one were injured.[82]

PAKISTAN POLITICS 2007–8

After the relative political stability of the six years after 9/11, the year following the death of Bhutto saw Pakistan plunged once more into political chaos reminiscent of that of the previous decade. President Musharraf was eventually forced to resign the presidency in August 2008, but five main political groupings – each representative of a broader constituency within Pakistan – had been battling for a share of power long before his final departure from power. The incumbent and his close allies within the military and among various key political powerbrokers whose interests had been well served over previous years constituted one faction in the mêlée. A second was composed of those within the army who had become frustrated with the president. Some had purely personal motivations, as Musharraf's long tenure had blocked the promotion of many senior officers; others were concerned by potential emerging threats to the material position of the military with its privileged lifestyle and commercial interests; still others were genuinely worried by the increasingly autocratic nature of Musharraf's rule. The power of these disaffected senior officers had been amply demonstrated when, following heavily managed presidential elections in October 2007, Musharraf was forced to rescind a state of emergency and resign as chief of army staff. A further show of strength came when the elections scheduled for January but postponed after the death of Bhutto were finally held in March 2008, and Musharraf's replacement at the head of the army, the dry, moderate and effective Ashfaq Kayani, made it very clear that he would resist any attempt by his predecessor to use the military or the various intelligence services to influence the vote. The elections, to most observers' surprise, were broadly seen as free and fair, something of a novelty for Pakistan.[83]

The third major group of players jockeying for power and influence were, of course, the extremists and religious conservatives. However, the Islamists of Jamaat Islami and the Deobandi clerics of the Jamaat Ulema Islami as well as the various religiously orientated splinter or smaller groups were largely absent from the democratic political process during this period, restricting their participation to large demonstrations 'in protest at the lack of true democracy in Pakistan', as Qazi Hussein Ahmed, the veteran leader of JI, put it over tea in the sprawling compound of offices, homes and schoolrooms that comprised the organization's national headquarters in Lahore.[84] In the North West Frontier province and in Baluchistan, provincial polls held simultaneously with national polls provided an unwelcome dose of 'true democracy' for the hardline religious alliance which had been in power or shared power in both provinces since 2002. The conservatives were unceremoniously dismissed from office by voters, who had had enough of government that was exceptionally incompetent even by low local standards, a useful reminder that appeals to religious or cultural identity do not always trump the basic human desire for a better quality of life.

The fourth of the factions contesting power in this turbulent period was Nawaz Sharif and the various lobbies he represented. Many Western analysts and policy-makers had difficulty understanding the appeal of the tubby, balding, middle-aged politician. Certainly his record of atrocious economic management, reputation for graft, poor English, lack of charisma, poor oratorical skills and total failure to articulate any kind of coherently formulated policies failed to impress successive Western interlocutors. Sharif's home was the Punjab, and it was to Lahore, or more specifically the family estates at Raiwind just outside the city, that Sharif had returned when his long exile in Saudi Arabia had ended. He had immediately mobilized his old power base – major

Punjabi industrialists, businessmen, conservative powerbrokers. To them Sharif was a known quantity. In his two previous stints in power in the 1990s, the main beneficiaries, beyond his own family, had been his supporters among the commercial classes of the Punjab who had been handed soft loans from banks, hugely profitable tariff arrangements and licences or development funds that they themselves could spend, on themselves or on those whose votes they wanted to secure as they saw fit. Many such people had rallied to Musharraf during Sharif's exile. Now, the political winds were changing, and their support was flowing back to the returning former prime minister.

But Sharif was also able to attract a new constituency. Though his wealth was inherited or earned during his years in power, he had the image of a self-made man, which appealed to the expanding lower middle classes. His taste for Punjabi home cooking was well known or at least well advertised, giving him an authentic image that may have been spurious but nonetheless convinced. His hesitancy in English reinforced his popular appeal. His nationalist rhetoric echoed the views of the Urdu-language papers and their tens of millions of readers.[85] Then there was the appeal of the image of Sharif as a social conservative and, at least ostensibly, a pious Muslim. Though not members of Jamaat Islami, the Sharifs were naturally close in culture and worldview to the Islamist party. In the second of his prime ministerial terms Sharif had attempted to force through a raft of legislation enhancing the weight of religious law in Pakistan and even tried to have himself named *amir-ul momineen*, leader of the faithful.[86] Even if in reality he was far from personally devout, such acts clearly had an impact. So too did the time Sharif had spent in Saudi Arabia and his apparent personal relationship with the kingdom's rulers.[87] 'The common man sees himself in Nawaz,' said Khwaja Asif, a major businessman and a senior PML figure.[88]

The final group lobbying for power was that connected to the Bhutto dynasty and the Pakistan People's Party. On her death, Bhutto's young son Bilawal, a student at Oxford University, had been dubbed heir to the family political fortune. However, it was her widely reviled husband, Asif Ali Zardari, who took charge of the political organization she had led. When Musharraf was forced out of office in August 2008 under the threat of impeachment, Bhutto's widower displayed political skill that few had suspected he possessed to secure the presidency. The former playboy, prisoner and consort inherited the presidential apartments in

the palace at the foot of the Margalla hills and some of the most intractable problems faced by any leader in any theatre of the 9/11 Wars.
Zardari was not known as an intellectual. This was not a problem, associates said, explaining: 'You don't necessarily need to be a bookworm
type to be president of Pakistan.'[89]

14

Another Country: FATA

FATA

On the north-western border of Pakistan lies another country, not Afghanistan, but FATA, the seven 'Federally Administered Tribal Agencies'. With a total population of between 3 and 4 million and a landmass of 10,500 square miles, somewhere between the size of Belgium and Israel, the FATA is a land apart. In the summer of 2008, this land hosted five main armed groups, factions or coalitions: the Afghan Taliban, the Pakistani Taliban, al-Qaeda and various international militant groups, a range of tribal militia and the Pakistani army.

The roots of militancy in the FATA run back centuries. They had been created by the British in 1901 as a buffer zone along the western frontier of their south Asian dominions, adjacent to the border agreed with the Afghan monarch Abdur Rahman Khan eight years previously; the tribes there had long been known as reactionary, restive and independent. Indeed, the very establishment of such a zone was in part an admission by the British that, despite their superior weaponry and resources, continued campaigning against the Wazirs, the Mehsuds, the Afridis and the others was unlikely to definitively quell the repeated rebellions. Raj administrators agreed with local tribes that the legal reach of the authorities of India in the border zone would be limited to the towns and the roads (along with a strip of land 100 yards wide on either side) beyond which communities were allowed to police themselves, seek justice from their traditional assemblies, or *jirga*, and carry weapons. The British did, however, retain the right to mount punitive campaigns if, for example, the tribes raided the lowlands or otherwise disturbed the peace of the frontier. They were also careful to impose a system of officials known as political agents who, with their extensive powers of patronage and ability to call on significant military resources, were theoretically equipped with sufficient carrots and a big enough stick to keep order. Though the system broadly worked well, it occasionally broke down, necessitating large and lengthy deployments of troops to put down uprisings. Most of these were mobilized under the flag of revivalist Islam, even if the grievances which sparked them tended to be more banal. Often such revolts had motives that were strikingly similar to those cited by their counterparts a century or so later. Sometimes the local Pashtun tribes were simply pushing back against the authority of the Raj.[1] Sometimes the fighting was conceived of as a defence of culture and identity. 'The Turangzai Baba [local tribal leader and cleric] would say: "The donkeys [whites] are coming and we should stop them by force as he is destroying Islam and he is destroying our laws,"' remembered one elderly veteran of fighting in the 1930s.[2] Often the insurgents had projects of their own. In the 1920s, Deobandi clerics had led a group called the Jamaat-e-Mujahideen in a bid to establish a 'pure Islamic' state on the land between the Indus river and Kabul – exactly the same zone of conflict being fought over eighty years later.[3] Decades before the Afghan Taliban had created a religious police, tribes on the frontier had formed their own 'movement for the promotion of virtue and the prevention of vice'. Reformist Islamic ideas had begun to erode more 'folksy' Sufi-influenced forms of religious practice by the late nineteenth and early twentieth centuries.[4]

The British campaigns on the frontier spawned a body of literature and a set of romanticized myths in the West about the proud, honourable and warlike Pashtun, a worthy opponent for the Victorians and their successors, which proved to be both remarkably durable and remarkably inaccurate. Works of fiction, such as those of Kipling, and of questionable and highly politicized anthropology from the early twentieth century were still being quoted by Western analysts a century later despite the fact that society in the FATA, as anywhere else in the world, had changed enormously in the intervening period. This did not help those trying to formulate effective policy. As in Afghanistan and Pakistan more generally, the problem with the FATA was not that it was caught in some kind of time warp but the opposite.

How the FATA became the rear base for the Afghan *mujahideen* as well as a relatively small number of international, largely Arab volunteers is well known. However gripping the tale of spies, Saudi tycoons and Cold War manoeuvres may be, the story of the process of accelerated, violent and unmanaged social change in the FATA that was triggered by the instability of the 1970s and the wars of the 1980s and 1990s in neighbouring Afghanistan is of equal if not greater importance, though somewhat less picturesque. Traditional society on the frontier had been structured for many decades, if not centuries, by the major tribal groupings with their manifold subdivisions and by the carefully maintained balance between the religious scholars, or *ulema*, the major quasi-feudal landowners, or *khans*, and the senior tribal elders, or *maliks*, who often received substantial government patronage in return for representing the interests of the distant administration. Central too to order in the region was the harsh code of values and customs, the famous and often misunderstood *pashtunwali*, or 'way of the Pashtuns'. Together, these elements constituted a flexible, resilient and effective system of governance.[5] Each of the components of the system was, however, degraded severely during the 1970s and 1980s. Most obviously, there was the massive influx of Afghan refugees from the mid 1970s onwards who, having been forced out of traditional settlements and occupations and into packed camps where aid was the primary source of resources, rapidly lost their traditional identities, allegiances and hierarchies and thus became susceptible to the call of radical Islamist groups such as Hekmatyar's Hezb-e-Islami, which had previously struggled to recruit in Pashtun rural communities. Then there was the rapid expansion of rigorous neo-traditional Deobandi Islam, propagated by *medressas* built with donations from Middle Eastern countries now flush with oil money or with cash from General Zia's official religious funds discussed in the previous chapter.[6] Their teachings naturally reinforced conservative and revivalist forms of Islam that already existed in the FATA and gave the narrative of resistance to 'moral corruption', outsiders and 'unbelievers' that was a strong part of the local collective memory and identity a new and more contemporary dimension. In the north of the FATA it was the Ahl-e-Hadith or 'Wahhabi' strands, which became very powerful, again through the establishment of scores of *medressas* and an influx of foreign money. As in Afghanistan, the expansion of these more rigorous strands of Islam meant that the more tolerant and mystical Sufi-influenced strands were further weakened. This new radical conservatism inevitably threatened the position of many of the more traditional local clergy, who could not match the resources, spiritual or material, offered by their new competitors. It also consolidated the shared identity, clerical hierarchy, culture and world-view of the Pashtun population along the frontier zone, developing further a single common set of values, norms and worldview.

Then there was the new wealth flowing into the region. This had an equally destructive effect on local culture. With many Pashtuns working in the Gulf following the boom of the 1970s, unprecedented amounts of money had been reaching individual families in the FATA for some time. However, it was the 1980s, and the war against the Soviets, with the flow of massive aid funds and the opening up of extensive opportunities for illicit and lucrative activities such as manufacturing and trading weapons and growing, processing and trafficking opium, hashish and heroin, that saw the real collapse of the FATA's social system. If the rising power of rigorous and highly politicized forms of Islam was challenging the power of traditional clerics, so new sources of wealth challenged the position of the *khans* and the *maliks*. Local hierarchies that had been based on patronage and resource distribution simply became redundant, with traditional landlords unable to compete with those who had access to the vast sums being generated through drugs, guns or Saudi, American and Pakistani aid. Nor, evidently, could they match their new competitors for firepower. The same was true for the political agents, the bureaucrats on whom the system for governing the FATA, barely changed since the days of the British, still depended. They too saw their powers of patronage eclipsed by new competitors and their powers of coercion rendered ineffectual against bands of heavily armed fighters or criminals.

Add a growing sectarian conflict which was in part a proxy war between major Sunni Muslim states in the Middle East and Iran, the broad rise of Islamist identities and ideologies across the Islamic world in the period and the continuing presence of hundreds of international militants in and around the FATA through the early 1990s and it is unsurprising that the region, as it had done so often over the previous decades at moments of crisis, saw the rise of a series of radical revivalist and reformist religious movements. Some were on a significant scale – such as that in Dir and Malakand to the north of Bajaur which campaigned, relatively successfully, for Shariat law in the mid 1990s. Others were more disorganized, such as the various bands responsible for what by 1998 or 1999 was being called the 'Talibanization' of the FATA. These groups often coalesced around veterans of the fighting in Afghanistan during the 1980s or early 1990s and led vigilante actions against DVD or music shops, hairdressers and other targets deemed responsible for the 'moral corruption' that local hardliners associated with 'Westernization'.[7] They also enforced a new version of traditional local honour codes and punishments just as the Afghan Taliban were doing on the other side of the porous border. As the decade ended, the radicalization had intensified. In 1998 or 1999 it was still possible for a Western journalist to travel in the FATA – the author even spent an afternoon at a *dastarbandi*, or graduation ceremony, at one *medressa* near Miram Shah, eating chicken cooked with oranges as successive diners arrived and stacked their Kalashnikovs in a corner – but such trips rapidly became risky. The 9/11 attacks thus came at a critical time. As was so often the case, the new conflict they triggered only aggravated and accelerated existing trends. In 2001, the memory of the earlier wars was certainly very present. In the Khyber Pass a month after the bombing of Afghanistan had started, young men from the local Afridi tribe were very clear about what the coming conflict meant for them. 'Our fathers, their fathers and their fathers' fathers fought jihad,' one said on a starry night in a compound a few miles short of the Afghan frontier. 'Now it is our turn. We will go to war.'[8]

THE AFGHAN TALIBAN IN THE FATA

Within twenty-four hours of the 9/11 attacks, Maleeha Lodhi, the Pakistani ambassador in Washington, had been summoned to meet the American deputy secretary of state Richard Armitage to be asked if Pakistan was 'with or against America'. Lodhi was accompanied by Lieutenant General Mahmud Ahmed, the ISI chief who had tried to convince his MI6 counterpart only months before that the Taliban should be diplomatically recognized by Britain.[9] When Ahmed tried to tell Armitage that Pakistan had always been a friend of the USA, he was cut short and was told bluntly that it was what happened now and what was going to happen in the future that was important. 'History began today,' the American said.[10] Within a few weeks President Musharraf had purged the ISI of the most obvious sympathizers with extremism.

Ahmed was one of those forced out, and Western intelligence services took his departure as a sign that the 'bad old days' of Pakistan's sponsorship of violent proxies were over. Yet Musharraf had repeatedly made clear that he acted in what he felt were Pakistan's best interests, not for any greater international good. It was safe, therefore, to conclude that any backing for America's War on Terror was entirely pragmatic. Active support for the Taliban may indeed have been halted as the Americans had demanded, but that did not by any means signify that the Pakistanis would not aggressively pursue what were felt to be their national security priorities.[11] The ISI, which had initially resisted cutting off support to the Afghan Taliban, had been very active during the campaign of 2001. Sometimes the agency had worked with Western security services. Sometimes it had pursued its own agenda. But in either case, the ISI's institutional vision of Pakistan's strategic interests had always come first.

Richard Armitage had been right to talk to Lodhi and Ahmed about history but had been wrong to dismiss the past so lightly. Pakistani support for the Taliban had reached its peak in 1999 but had started in the early years of the movement. As stressed in previous chapters, the Taliban may have been an essentially Afghan movement with deep roots in elements of Afghan society, culture, history and politics, but assistance from the ISI was of great use at critical junctures. This support was not hidden from Pakistan's civilian leaders. Indeed, it was under Benazir Bhutto's second administration from 1993 to 1996 that the country's intelligence services had shifted their support from Hekmatyar to the Taliban. Diplomatic as well as military assistance continued under the administration of Nawaz Sharif from 1996 to 1999.[12] Such links became considerably more controversial after al-Qaeda's bombing of American embassies in east Africa, organized from Afghanistan, in 1998. Already soured by messy battles around Mazar-e-Sharif during which widespread atrocities by both sides were widely reported and a war with Iran was nearly provoked, relations deteriorated as the Taliban refused the demands of the Sharif government to hand over Pakistani sectarian militants responsible for widespread violence in the prime minister's native Punjab. Many in Pakistan's Foreign Ministry began to express grave concerns about the diplomatic damage being done by their country's support for their increasingly unpredictable and extreme supposed allies.[13] But though these tensions continued to grow through 2000 and

2001, particularly after Pakistan's failed bid to avert the destruction of the Bamiyan Buddhas, the Pakistan military as an institution continued to believe not only that they could manage a movement they saw as their protégés but also that, despite their faults, the Taliban remained the best available tool for the projection of Pakistani influence in Afghanistan.

In the changed circumstances following the 9/11 attacks, the strategic calculation of many within the Pakistani security establishment was thus relatively straightforward. Though Musharraf promised a clean break, both in private communications to the American administration and explicitly in public speeches such as his televised address of February 2002, a perception of his nation's strategic interests that had been reinforced over decades remained dominant. As seen in previous chapters, as the Taliban regime had collapsed, fighters and senior officials from the Taliban were thus allowed to cross into Pakistani territory and indeed were in some instances directed or even aided to locations where they would be safe. Only the foreign militants belonging to the international groups formerly based in Afghanistan were detained, imprisoned and turned over to American intelligence services in return for substantial payments.[14] By spring 2002, memos were crossing Musharraf's desk from senior officers attached to the ISI arguing that, as the West would inevitably be forced to withdraw their forces from Afghanistan, probably in between five and fifteen years, Pakistan needed to be positioned for the aftermath of the eventual pull-out.[15] The twin objectives of strategic depth and a pro-Islamabad government in Kabul, constant for three decades or more, remained unchanged. The parallel with the Soviet invasion was indeed explicit. As during the 1980s, the strategy was not so much to fight against 'foreign occupiers' as to make sure that Pakistan had proxies who would be well placed to take power once the foreigners had gone. During 2003, it became clear that most of the dominant players in Kabul and in many major cities were from factions or ethnic groups known for their animosity towards Pakistan. It also became clear that India was making a major effort to extend its influence through a substantial aid programme that involved high-profile projects such as the building of the new Afghan parliament and key roads often located in critically sensitive border regions. The Pakistani sense of encirclement was thus further reinforced, and the idea that the Taliban, or at least elements within them, should be allowed to regenerate sufficient capacity to serve Pakistani interests in Afghanistan in the future gained further momentum. The key, naturally, was not to get caught, nor to provoke too much attention by spectacular attacks, nor to cause a precipitous collapse of the Afghan government. As it had been in the 1980s, the aim was once more to 'make the water boil at the right temperature'.[16] There was one crucial difference from the early period, however: before, there had been, at least initially, no refugee camps in the FATA and fewer and lighter weapons, a smaller overall population, much weaker political vehicles for the religious lobbies, around a fifth as many *medressas* and, crucially, a much lower level of ambient animosity towards the West. Twenty years later, all that anyone hoping to maintain and manage elements within the Afghan insurgents needed to do was simply to allow them to exploit the huge support networks that were already in place and sentiments that were already running high. When, in late 2003, Yusuf Pashtun, the then governor of Kandahar, listed the training camps he said had been set up across the border and around Quetta, every single place he mentioned was the site of an already extant refugee settlement, many of which had been home to senior Taliban figures for three decades.[17] The new surge of anti-Western sentiment and religious fervour after 9/11, combined with cynical manipulation by the military government, meant too that, by 2002, the two provinces along the Afghan border and surrounding the FATA – the North West Frontier province and Baluchistan – were run wholly, in the case of the former, or partly, in the case of the latter, by the Deobandi hardliners of the Jamaat Ulema Islami party and the political Islamists of Jamaat Islami.[18] The new governments of the two provinces embarked on a project of radical Islamization, imposing *sharia* law, banning of music and 'obscene' advertising and firing hundreds of female bureaucrats and medical staff. These measures not only created an atmosphere that encouraged further extremism but were accompanied by rhetoric which was explicitly pro-Taliban. Ministers regularly attended the funerals for slain Taliban fighters held in or around Quetta and other cities.[19] Maulana Rahat Hussain, a senior cleric, JUI senator and junior minister in the NWFP provincial government, reeled off a list of his classmates at the Binoria *medressa* in Karachi who had all become senior figures among the insurgents. 'They were and are and will for ever be my brothers,' Hussain told the author. 'They are fighting an occupying force and *inshallah* they will be victorious.'[20]

The evidence of continued ISI support for the Afghan Taliban naturally posed a dilemma for Western policy-makers. Western officials on the ground pointed to the string of senior figures connected with the Taliban or Haqqani who somehow learned at the very last minute of impending raids and the presence of senior Taliban figures in or around cities such as Quetta or Peshawar and reported constant communication between Taliban figures and Pakistani military officials, some, but not all, retired.[21] One problem was diplomatic. Bush had repeatedly backed Musharraf as a key ally in the Global War on Terror and was unwilling to listen to criticism of a man in whom he had invested considerable political capital. Equally, even within intelligence services, no one was prepared to risk the continued and useful cooperation of the ISI in the hunt for senior al-Qaeda figures who posed a direct threat to the West. All were painfully aware that they were dependent on the Pakistani military and its intelligence services for any direct action against the international militants they were hunting. 'We had no illusions about what was happening but we had no capacity either. So we couldn't really be picky,' said one senior CIA official. 'The ISI was the only girl at the dance.'[22] A gap opened up between those operatives working in Pakistan on the hunt for senior al-Qaeda figures – who tended to maintain that only retired or lower- and middle-ranking serving Pakistani intelligence officers, possibly 'rogues' acting with no authorization, were involved with the Taliban – and those in Kabul, whose job consisted of fighting Afghan insurgents, who were much more critical of the ISI. Through 2004, 2005 and the spring of 2006, policy drifted. Over time, and not least because of the increasing difficulty in hunting al-Qaeda figures as they moved from the cities into the remote tribal zones, the attitude of Western intelligence services and politicians hardened. When, in the summer of 2006, coalition troops became involved in bruising combat with fighters who had often recently arrived from Pakistan, lost men to suicide bombers from towns in the Punjab, saw Pakistani paramilitaries engaging Afghan troops on the frontier or artillery fire being used to cover the passage of insurgents across the border, a major covert operation was launched by both MI6 and the CIA to secure solid information on the ISI's activities which could be used to confront Pakistani authorities.[23] The point of the effort, which lasted several months and at one point even temporarily drew resources focused on Iraq back to the region, was to establish if there was any direct involvement by Pakistani intelligence services in instigating or even organizing attacks on Western troops or their allies, as many were beginning to say openly.[24] But the intelligence obtained – much of which came from Afghan government sources with a clear agenda – was inconclusive, and no final report was ever compiled. It was left to individual commanders and institutions to try to influence public opinion and policy-makers. The split between those working within Pakistan, who needed to keep the ISI onside to continue operations against al-Qaeda, and those, inside and outside the intelligence community, in Afghanistan, who had no such concerns, widened. In early 2007, a frustrated General Sir David Richards, then the Commander of NATO-ISAF in Kabul, was openly saying that 'infiltration [of insurgents] from Pakistan was a very serious problem', and more junior NATO officers were explicit in their accusation that the ISI was aiding their enemy.[25] But intelligence officials in Pakistan were still conservative in their criticism of their local counterparts. In October of that year, American defence officials in Islamabad insisted to the author they were 'yet to see a smoking gun ... [or] any solid evidence at all' of ISI aid to the Taliban.[26] Their British counterparts restricted themselves to drily commenting that, while it was clear that the ISI, 'like any good intelligence service', was talking to the militants on Pakistani soil, 'no one really knew what they were saying to each other'.[27] Pakistani military officials readily admitted there were contacts. 'Of course we talk to them. That is what we should be doing. We need to learn about them and what they are doing,' one ISI colonel told the author in early 2008.[28] In presentations to the heads of foreign security services or governments, the ISI blamed their failure to move against the Taliban on the terrain, local animosity and, without fail, a lack of resources. The information provided by Western services about the location of senior Taliban figures on Pakistani soil was inaccurate, they said.[29]

Such arguments were rapidly becoming unsustainable, however. In the late spring of 2008, as Afghanistan plunged towards even greater depths of violence and chaos, a more aggressive and coherent Western position began to emerge. In January, Mike McConnell, the American director of national intelligence, sent an assessment to the White House in which he bluntly stated that 'the Pakistani government regularly gives weapons and support [to insurgents] to go into Afghanistan and attack Afghan and coalition forces'.[30] Key to McConnell's assessment was an intercept of a telephone conversation in which General Kayani, the new head of the Pakistani armed forces, was apparently heard speaking of Jalaluddin Haqqani, the Pakistan-based cross-frontier insurgent leader, as a 'strategic asset'.[31] In July there came the bombing of the Indian embassy in Kabul, and further intercepts apparently showing ISI officers giving instructions to Haqqani's men prior to the attack. American intelligence services, though they admitted the data were open to different interpretations, nonetheless saw them as clear proof of a new level of ISI involvement: the instigation and organization of strikes, not simply the manipulation or protection of insurgents on Pakistani soil. 'It was sort of this "aha" moment. There was a sense that there was finally direct proof,' one State Department official told the *New York Times*.[32] Shortly afterwards, classified documents compiled to guide interrogation teams at the Guantanamo Bay prison camp categorized the ISI as a terrorist organization, listing it alongside Hamas, Hezbollah, the Chechen Martyrs Battalion and al-Qaeda.[33] Publicly, British intelligence nonetheless went no further than saying that Pakistan was 'at the very least tacitly allowing Taliban activities on their soil'. Sir John Scarlett, the then director of MI6, stressed to the author that this was, however, something with which 'the UK' had a 'serious issue'. Scarlett described relationships with ISI counterparts as being 'awkward' and talked of 'undiplomatic' language used at 'the highest levels'.[34]

But still, even if senior spies and policy-makers were increasingly convinced that the ISI was playing what one official called 'a long double game', no one had yet evolved a policy to counter it. Western intelligence services remained still heavily dependent on the ISI for intelligence on al-Qaeda and were unable to operate in the FATA without the assistance of their Pakistani counterparts, who jealously restricted their allies' freedom of movement and operation within their country. Equally, it was still only the Pakistani military which could move against any 'safe havens' for the international militants. The ISI continued to show every sign of believing they could still manage the radical groups that they had protected for so long in the Punjab or sent into Kashmir. There was little reason to believe the ISI intelligence service would cease their efforts to manage the Taliban, Haqqani and Hekmatyar in the near future either, whatever the pressure put on them. Their support to the insurgents had always been predicated on the analysis that the

West's effort in Afghanistan would eventually fail. The deteriorating situation across the border thus appeared only to vindicate the Pakistanis' long-term strategy.

ANOTHER FRONT IN ANOTHER WAR

The man who had been immediately blamed for killing Bhutto was Baitullah Mehsud, a thirty-four-year-old Pashtun tribesman and militant from the FATA. The evidence against him was circumstantial – a telephone conversation picked up by satellite surveillance in which he accepted the congratulations of a cleric and appeared to say that those who had committed the attack were part of the group of fighters he led – but was accepted as proof of what was largely already suspected by most security services and many analysts.[35] Mehsud, who led the rough coalition of groups known as the Tehrik-e-Taliban-Pakistan (Pakistan Taliban Union or TTP), publicly denied the killing but had already threatened to assassinate Bhutto.[36]

The various groups that made up the TTP – the coalition had formally been declared in the autumn of 2007 – had many qualities familiar from other parts of this narrative. Though numerous – the total force that could be mobilized at any one time was probably between 5,000 and 10,000 – it was still a tiny percentage of the overall population. The strong sense of cultural identity – reimagined, reconstituted and repackaged – was reminiscent of both the Afghan Taliban and the al-Mahdi Army in Iraq. The degree to which the groups found their broader rhetorical language in the debased global 'single narrative' popularized so widely in the Islamic world over the previous decade was also obvious. The economic growth enjoyed by Pakistan in the first years of the decade might have been largely confined to the eastern half of the country, but the new broadcast media certainly were accessible in the FATA. The way in which base manoeuvres for power, cash and influence were legitimized by appeal to a greater cause and the constant tensions between communities and militants seen in the FATA also had clear parallels elsewhere. So too had the nature of recruitment – flowing down lines of association, friendship, clan and family – rather than through any organized system. The conflict between the nation – it was after all the 'Pakistani' Taliban – and pan-Islamic identities was equally familiar. Two linked elements that were particularly clear in the character and internal dynamics of the Pakistani Taliban but were not often picked up in analysis at the time were the degree to which the militants drew much of their support from marginalized elements within their own societies and the way in which their rhetoric and ideology were informed by a socially revolutionary agenda. The striking fact about Mehsud and the men who he nominally led was not that they were 'pure products' of the traditions of the frontier but rather the effective collapse of such traditions in the new circumstances generated in part by the 9/11 Wars.

Mehsud, for example, came from elements within local Pashtun society which would never have had any power, influence or wealth only a decade or so before. Born near Bannu, a dusty town on the edge of the FATA, not a village in its heart, Mehsud came from a minor branch of a minor tribe, not a prestigious branch of a powerful or rich one.[37] His parents were not wealthy – his father was a low-ranking cleric – and Mehsud himself had been patchily educated, attending both a number of different religious schools and several different public institutions.[38] Though Mehsud liked to boast that he had fought with the Taliban, it appears he had in fact only spent a few months in the late 1990s guarding Kabul airport, so was denied even the prestige and social mobility that feats of arms might traditionally have afforded him. Even a hagiographic biography written by his deputy does not mention any combat role in the fighting during the fall of the Taliban regime, though it says that Mehsud assisted al-Qaeda fighters in escaping Afghanistan and finding secure havens across the border.[39] When, in 2004, Mehsud had succeeded in assuming the leadership of several hundred fighters in the strategically crucial agency of South Waziristan, he did so in a very modern way: the position was effectively vacant because the previous incumbent, the charismatic Nek Mohammed, had been killed by a missile fired by an American unmanned drone after he had given away his location by using a satellite phone in one of the first such assassinations in the region. Other militant leaders in the frontier zone in the autumn of 2007 and in the summer of 2008 also would have stood little chance of any leadership role, wealth or influence under the old traditional frontier systems.[40] Mangal Bagh, an independent militant leader in the Khyber Agency, was a former bus driver.[41] One of the rising figures in the northern agencies – Maulana Fazlullah – was a former mechanic who once maintained a miniature ski-lift for tourists visiting the scenic Swat valley. Muslim Khan, Fazlullah's close aide, was a secular-educated former PPP activist who had travelled widely in the Middle East and Europe as a merchant seaman, then spent years as a taxi driver in America before finally returning to his village shortly after the 9/11 attacks to open a drugstore.[42] Other militant leaders included barbers, butchers, itinerant salesmen, petrol pump attendants, criminals or, in a region where levels of unemployment touched somewhere between 60 and 80 per cent, were simply the semi-retired veterans of a variety of conflicts.[43] Leaders in Bajaur and in the valleys of Malakand and Swat made frequent promises to redistribute the often extensive properties of major landowners to those who had none, picking up historical local claims for land reform by agricultural day labourers going back to the 1970s and beyond.[44] The militants were not, by local standards, ignorant men. All but four of a dozen captured militants the author interviewed in Peshawar in November 2008 had travelled widely in Pakistan, two had worked in the Gulf and one had spent several years in east Africa and in the Middle East working and, he said, 'preaching'. Though their levels of religious knowledge and political understanding were relatively low, they were most definitely not farm boys who had picked up the family Kalashnikov. The militants fighting in the FATA were thus not the product of an ancient society resisting the modern but, like the Taliban across the frontier, a profoundly contemporary phenomenon.

As in Afghanistan and Iraq, the violence in the FATA resembled a matrix of multiple ongoing conflicts. The radicalization seen in the early years of the 9/11 Wars saw many of these conflicts, some of which stretched back decades, re-energized. So in the northernmost tribal agency, Bajaur, the three major local tribes had split very differently in terms of allegiance and ideology by 2002 or 2003 and, from 2006 onwards had been in open or semi-open warfare with each other or with the government. The largest and poorest tribe remained broadly neutral. A second tribe, the Salarzai, who were mainly relatively wealthy farmers, had rallied to the government. A third, the Mahmund, were the only local community that could truly be said to be integrated into the 'modern world', largely, it is true, through smuggling, the arms and drugs business, exposure to various strands of contemporary Islamist thought, pilgrimages to the Gulf, remittances from overseas and through hosting itinerant preachers (and occasionally al-Qaeda leaders). It was the Mahmund who were among the most enthusiastic supporters of the militants in FATA.[45] When not fighting the Pakistani military, the Mahmund fought either in Afghanistan or against the other two tribes of Bajaur.

The conflict in the FATA was thus, as in Afghanistan and in Iraq, in a large part a series of overlapping civil wars. Sometimes these took the form of an assault on traditional authority – hundreds, probably thousands, of traditional tribal elders were executed by militants between 2003 and 2008.[46] Sometimes, such as in Kurram agency, the conflicts had a more sectarian flavour, pitting Sunnis against Shia. In Waziristan, fighters under a rival commander from a rival tribe took on those of Baitullah Mehsud in a battle sparked initially by differing attitudes to the presence of Uzbek and other central Asian militants in local villages but which degenerated into a straight struggle for power and resources. In the Khyber Pass, three different factions, divided by sub-tribe and religious observance, patched together different alliances, fought each other and the government and engaged in kidnap and racketeering. The presence of fugitive al-Qaeda leadership elements, in Bajaur as elsewhere, also fuelled such local conflicts, not necessarily because of the radicalizing effect the propaganda of such individuals had but because of the competition for the very large rent payments they were prepared to pay to anyone prepared to take the risk of providing shelter.[47]

Like the Afghan Taliban, the Pakistani groups themselves faced a range of challenges, however. Their idea of government was largely inspired by that that their counterparts across the border had introduced during the late 1990s. But, though it was welcomed by some communities in the FATA for the same reasons that many in Afghanistan had supported the imposition of a rigorous and puritanical system there a decade earlier, the Pakistani militants were operating in a very different environment. Though old institutions such as the *jirga*, the consultative meeting of tribal elders, were breaking down in the FATA, most local people wanted them restored, not replaced by mediation by militant leaders or clerics.[48] Militant leaders like Mehsud claimed to bring justice and security, setting up courts to rapidly resolve disputes, creating vigilante police forces and building makeshift jails into which 'bandits' were thrown, exactly as the Taliban were doing in Afghanistan, but, though these were initially popular, attacks on symbols of government authority or so-called 'moral corruption' were less well viewed. Despite the profound conservatism of the local tribesmen – over 90 per cent said that women should remain in the home, more than two-thirds backed honour killings, and a vast majority favoured the imposition of strict *sharia* law – there was a broad desire for education. The systematic destruction of hundreds of schools and the murder of scores of teachers thus did little to endear the militants to the local communities.[49] Similarly the expulsion of all local and foreign NGOs from areas dominated by the radical groups was also unpopular. Successive surveys showed the local desire for the development such organizations could bring. Many of the local political figures targeted by the militants – often those linked to the Pashtun nationalist Awami National Party who did well in the NWFP and in the FATA in the 2008 elections – were popular and respected figures.

If the Pakistani Taliban had been a more cohesive phenomenon or had had aims that went beyond dominating a particular valley, road or racket, such issues might have caused serious problems. But such tensions, which themselves remained highly localized, were far from a strategic threat to militancy in an environment as radicalized as that of the Pakistani–Afghan frontier in late 2008.[50] One poll found that only 3 per cent of tribesmen saw the Taliban as terrorists. Equally, the clumsy tactics of the regular troops deployed to the periodic offensives in the FATA allowed, as had occurred in Iraq and Afghanistan, the militants to pose as protectors of local communities or at the very least to benefit ambivalent popular sentiments. Army officers, trained only for conventional operations against massed Indian armoured units on the eastern frontier, were utterly ignorant of counter-insurgency doctrine, old or new. Drawn from elsewhere in Pakistan and officered largely by Punjabis, who often needed interpreters to speak to local people, the military were often seen as an alien presence.[51] The army's successive 'cordon and sweep' operations between 2003 and 2007 involved either unwitting or deliberate destruction of the homes of very large numbers of locals as a collective punishment. In their major campaign in South Waziristan in 2004, the army had bulldozed over eighty houses, destroyed local irrigation works and wells and killed scores of civilians.[52] In January 2008, another major operation in the same area saw a further 4,000 houses reduced to ruins and bulldozers and explosives used to level one town's bazaar.[53]

The collateral damage inflicted by the rising number of air strikes from American unmanned drones in the FATA also drove communities towards the militants. Though undoubtedly an effective means of eliminating known militants and putting their associates under considerable pressure – men like Mehsud in the FATA in the summer of 2008 were sleeping outside to avoid being caught in a building and spent much of their time conducting purges against supposed informants – the drone strikes were a blunt instrument and killed many civilians. This was another reason for the Mahmund tribe of Bajaur taking arms against their fellow Bajauris and against the Pakistani government. Damadola, the Bajaur village which became the headquarters of local militants and was thought to have sheltered Ayman al-Zawahiri on a number of occasions, had been hit by a series of air strikes from 2005 onwards. Each time the cost of killing a handful of militants was the deaths of dozens of villagers.[54] In one strike an estimated eighty-three 'Taliban militants' were killed when a *medressa* was hit, though identifying who among the dead were militants and who were the sons of locals was hard. Another destroyed a series of compounds where al-Zawahiri was thought to be spending the night. 'They dropped bombs from planes, and we were in no position to stop them or tell them we were innocent . . . I don't know Zawahiri. He was not at my home. No foreigner was at my home at the time the planes came and dropped bombs,' said Shah Zaman, a jeweller from Damadola who lost a son and a daughter in the attack.[55]

AL-QAEDA IN THE FATA

In June 2008, a strange and tense meeting had taken place in a compound high in the tribal area of South Waziristan. Six volunteers, two from France and four from Belgium, had decided to confront the man who was looking after their training as militants. He was a Syrian they knew as Driss, who they believed to be part of al-Qaeda. Before leaving their homes, they had watched al-Qaeda videos on the internet and seen images of massed battalions of *mujahideen* training on assault courses, exciting ambushes of American troops, tired but triumphant young fighters returning from battle and inspiring speeches by Osama bin Laden, they told him. But after five months in Pakistan's frontier zones they had done nothing more than some basic training on small arms, a day of shooting, spent an afternoon watching an instructor build a bomb and had many, many hours of religious instruction. Worse, they had had to spend hundreds of euros of their own money to buy their own weapons and equipment and to pay an extortionate weekly rent for the miserable accommodation offered by a local family.[56] They had been deceived, they boldly told the Syrian. The videos had lied.

The response was unsympathetic and unapologetic. Of course the videos were misleading, Driss told them, they were a 'trick . . . to intimidate enemies and to attract new recruits'.[57]

The exchange went right to the heart of one of the most controversial questions among analysts of al-Qaeda and the global Islamic militant movement of which it was a part in the seventh year of the 9/11 Wars. How close was the image of al-Qaeda projected through the internet and other media to the reality? What exactly was the capacity of the 'al-Qaeda hardcore'? What was life like for the leadership, for the more junior members or for the raw Western recruits who made their way to the tribal zones? And what were al-Qaeda's relations with other groups such as the Pakistani Taliban or the Afghan insurgent networks? These were questions Western and other security services had been trying for many years to answer – without a great deal of success.

Their difficulties were in part self-inflicted, in part a result of the extreme operating environment in the FATA and the surrounding regions. In 2008, at the time when Driss and the volunteers were having their talk, the last confirmed location of bin Laden and al-Zawahiri was still Tora Bora, nearly seven years before. Even in the days of relatively good CIA and ISI relations in the early years of the hunt for the fugitive leaders, ideas of their location were based on informed speculation rather than fact. Debates over whether the top two leaders were together, whether they were moving or 'hunkered down', whether they were in a Pakistani city or, as almost everyone thought, near the border, continued interminably. 'Anyone who says he knows is a liar,' one US Intelligence official told the author. Various hypotheses were advanced about the state of bin Laden's health including the idea, first circulated in the late 1990s, that the fugitive, fifty-one in 2008, might suffer from a serious kidney disorder. To the disappointment of many, it had become clear that, though bin Laden suffered from lower-back pain common in people of his height, which had meant occasional use of a walking cane and an end to his favourite pastime of horse-riding, there was no evidence of any other medical problem. For his part, al-Zawahiri, though approaching sixty, appeared in good health. Periodic breaks in communication sometimes raised hopes that one or other might be dead or seriously ill but always ended with a new video surfacing, often containing references to recent events that clearly indicated both men had been very much alive only weeks before. As late as 2006, the vast bulk of American intelligence came from the interviews of detainees – hardly the best method to obtain live and actionable information.[58] Excepting the interception of a courier suspected of having been recently in contact with one or other of the pair in the immediate aftermath of the capture of Khalid Sheikh Mohammed in 2003 and the information that had sparked the attempts to kill al-Zawahiri in Bajaur around 2006, there had been no 'strong lead' on the whereabouts of either man.[59] Tracking the senior al-Qaeda leadership was a dispiriting task, involving the verification and cross-referencing of thousands of leads on hundreds of individuals. The CIA teams assigned to the job were frequently changed to keep them motivated.

Nor were the resources being directed at the operation as significant as many outside the world of intelligence thought. The Iraq war had drained the effort to find bin Laden. 'By April, May 2002, we began losing people to the groups that were preparing for the Iraq war,' said Mike Scheuer, who, having headed the CIA's bin Laden unit from 1996 to 1999, went on to be chief adviser to his successor from 2001 to 2004. 'We were losing Arabic speakers. Very experienced people.' Bob Grenier, the then head of the Islamabad CIA station, remembered that 'a large number of the best and most experienced people were drawn off pretty early from Afghanistan and switched to Iraq, especially those with extensive counter-terrorism experience or regional specialists.'[60] The 5th Special Forces Group, which included the best linguists, was sent to the Gulf and replaced in Afghanistan by the 7th Special Forces Group, largely composed of Spanish-speakers with Latin American experience. Ron Nash, British ambassador in Afghanistan in the autumn of 2003, remembered later how the 'extremely useful' small groups of the UK's SAS and SBS who had been assuring security and gathering intelligence in far-flung Afghan provincial capitals in a low-key but effective way were all withdrawn by the end of the summer of 2002.[61] Art Keller, a CIA counter-terrorism and counter-proliferation specialist who himself volunteered for a tour in South Waziristan in 2006, described those operatives who ended up in Pakistan as 'the scrapings of the barrel'.[62]

Given one week to read up on the region before being dispatched, Keller spent six months as one of a small number of CIA officers, guarded by Pakistani special forces and chaperoned by the ISI, stationed in a Pakistani military base in Wana, the biggest town in South Waziristan in 2006. Life was not easy, either professionally or personally. The Americans, forbidden to leave the base, were supposed to generate the intelligence that would allow the Pakistanis to act. There were a number of problems with this arrangement, however. The first was the 'extreme reluctance' of the Pakistanis to mount operations, which Keller attributed to heavy casualties sustained on previous botched raids. The second was the cumbersome procedure for initiating any action. Target information – for example the location of a key al-Qaeda organizer – would be passed to the ISI in the Wana base for immediate action. It would then be sent up the ISI chain of command, who would ask for verification from their officers on the ground, before going to the Pakistani army, whose own intelligence service would verify again, before finally being sent to the Pakistani army's operations planning section. A successful raid, specialists say, needs intelligence on where a target *will* be in four hours, not where he was a couple of days before. This convoluted system also meant that drone strikes, which also had to be signed off by the ISI, remained a rarity. A third problem was simply logistics. As Keller was not allowed to venture out of the base in Wana, everything he did was through Pakistani liaison officers or via electronic means. 'I spent my days reading traffic from other stations and going through communications intercepts,' Keller remembered. 'Meeting sources was very hard.' Not that the information that did come in was particularly useful. Sightings of bin Laden were 'a dime a dozen' but in the end never checked out. Any halfway reliable lead was usually impossible to verify. Finally, there were the normal administrative fiascos that occur within any organization, even the CIA. When he was finally given a tip on a possible recent location for the al-Qaeda leader himself, Keller's emails got snarled up in a bureaucratic tangle when someone forgot to copy in the Islamabad CIA station and thus provoked an in-house political battle. 'If the American people really knew what the hunt for bin Laden actually meant, they would not be particularly impressed,' Keller said.[63]

In fact, al-Qaeda militants faced a difficult choice. True security meant finding a bolt hole and severing almost every link with the outside world. But this had enormous practical drawbacks, particularly for anyone involved in training, planning, recruitment, strategic liaison, communication or fundraising. For those whose tasks required at least a degree of exposure, whether people like Driss, the European volunteers' disappointing mentor, or more senior al-Qaeda militants, there was, however, another line of defence that mitigated the danger of working in the open. This was the sympathy of local communities. From its earliest days, al-Qaeda's success or failure had depended on its ability to reach out to local groups and leverage local conditions. An overwhelmingly Arab organization with the vast bulk of its members and supporters from Libya, Saudi Arabia and Egypt, it had always existed in 'foreign' territory. Even in 2008, there were no Pakistanis – or even Afghans – among al-Qaeda senior ranks, and though bin Laden, al-Zawahiri and other such international militants did have some residual connection with the NWFP and FATA from the 1980s and 1990s, including contacts with major powerbrokers such as Jalaluddin Haqqani, the frontier zone was still far from their natural environment.[64] In a good illustration of this, the meeting between Driss and his charges had seen a Syrian arguing in Arabic with two Frenchmen and four Belgians of north African origin in the middle of a Pashtun-dominated part of Pakistan. What al-Qaeda therefore undertook after drawing breath following their flight from Afghanistan in 2001 was a classic 'grafting operation' of the type that bin Laden had executed so well to secure himself a safe haven in Sudan during his time there in the early and mid 1990s and then again on arriving in Afghanistan immediately in 1996, when he had been able not just to convince the Taliban to give him shelter but to steadily gain greater and greater influence over the leadership and ideology of the movement. Even if he personally might be able to protect himself by withdrawing into some kind of sealed bunker, making sure that the FATA continued to be hospitable and thus secure for his followers was a vital task. Bin Laden applied the same tactics as had worked a half-decade before: a carefully orchestrated 'charm offensive' towards the local communities whom he needed to convince that their interests and those of his group coincided. The 'global' campaign of al-Qaeda needed to be superimposed or mapped on to local conditions without provoking the kind of backlash that had been seen in Iraq and various other theatres. Though it remained delicate, this task was rendered considerably easier by the dramatically raised levels of radicalization in the border zone at the time and, of course, by the previous local traditions of revivalist rebellions against various 'outside' authorities. Bin Laden's vision of al-Qaeda as a vanguard striving to defend true Islam thus meshed easily with the self-image of local communities who already saw themselves as guardians and repositories of an uncorrupted Islamic culture fighting to preserve their autonomy against the people of the plains and the cities, the Pakistani Army, the government, foreign imperialists, modernizers et al. Fusing Pashtun and global jihadi identity required only the relatively small step of adding the war against a 'global alliance of crusaders and Zionists' to the various foes aligned in an already deeply reactionary, intolerant worldview. As the al-Qaeda leadership had found over previous years, astute propaganda, careful outreach and very significant sums of money were, particularly in a conflict environment, an effective combination. One poll in 2008 suggested that 70 per cent of the 20 million people in the North West Frontier province and the FATA viewed bin Laden 'favourably'.[65]

As they had worked to assure a secure base for their organization, so too the al-Qaeda leadership had worked to rebuild something of the infrastructure they had lost when forced out of Afghanistan. This had taken some time, but, by 2005 and 2006, successive investigations of plots in the UK and elsewhere had revealed that al-Qaeda now had significant capacity. From 2007, the number of volunteers making their way to the FATA, particularly as the attraction of fighting in Iraq had waned, had increased sharply. Very few intelligence services had succeeded in penetrating the militants' security procedures and infiltrating agents into al-Qaeda ranks, so most of what was learned about the situation there was still thus received second hand – and therefore heavily filtered – from the Pakistanis or was patched together from surveillance intercepts or the interrogations of men like the disillusioned Europeans who were eventually arrested in December 2008, Bryant Vinas, a twenty-six-year-old American convert detained by the Pakistanis in Peshawar in October of that year and handed over to the US authorities, and the three Germans of the 'Sauerland cell' who had been arrested the year before in the northern Rhine region as they made final preparations for a bombing campaign. Slowly a more detailed picture emerged of al-Qaeda's exact set up in the FATA and its relations with many, many other groups based there.

One the most striking elements emerging from the testimony of such individuals was the sheer diversity of the international groups in the FATA in 2007 and 2008. Both Vinas and the Europeans of the 'Belgian cell' describe two major groups of central Asian militants, mainly Uzbek, each numbering over 1,000, various Arab groups, including al-Qaeda, each with a few hundred fighters, a Turkish group, a Uighur group and various mixed groups. On their arrival, the Belgian and French volunteers had asked to join the Arabs and had thus ended up with the Syrian Driss, they told their interrogators.[66] Vinas started off with a Pakistani group, probably Lashkar-e-Toiba, active in the northern FATA, from where he had joined attacks on American troops in Afghanistan's Kunar province before finding a contact who allowed him to approach al-Qaeda itself. The Germans had joined the smaller of the two Uzbek factions.[67] These groups were loosely organized but with significant degrees of internal bureaucracy. Al-Qaeda in particular appears to have been keen on new recruits filling out forms in triplicate with all their personal information, ambitions and opinions set down. One question was: 'What is your view of martyrdom operations? Would you participate in one?'[68] Swearing a formal oath of loyalty – a *bayat* – to bin Laden was not, however, essential.

A second element emerging from the testimonies was that conditions in the tribal areas were much tougher than they had been in Afghanistan in the late 1990s, when solidly constructed camps had provided accommodation for hundreds of trainees at a time. Volunteers in the FATA in 2008 fought and trained in small groups, living in dispersed compounds, with poor food and little medical care. When one of the Belgians fell ill with malaria he was 'left in a corner', according to a friend's testimony, and 'given a jab every few days by a kid who was the little brother of the local doctor'.[69] A reward for six months of good service was a trip to an internet café, from where an email could be sent home. The Belgians were allowed some chocolate to boost their flagging morale. All the different groups used the facilities of the towns of Miran Shah and Wana. 'This bazaar is bustling with Chechens, Uzbeks, Tajiks, Russians, Bosnians, some from EU countries and of course our Arab brothers,' one volunteer who visited the FATA around this time emailed an associate.[70] Many European recruits missed female company. Vinas was arrested while in Peshawar hoping to find a wife. Others were jealous of longer-established militants who had married local women. One German volunteer appealed for female partners to travel to the FATA so the *mujahideen* there could start families of young militants who would be 'entirely unknown to security services'.[71]

To participate – though not necessarily to die – in combat operations was the goal of almost all the volunteers making their way to the FATA. 'I saw myself as a soldier for Islam, fighting on the frontline, on raids and in combat and under bombardment,' one French volunteer later said.[72] Those who did see action were deeply marked by the experience. Aden Yilmaz, a member of the Sauerland cell, told a court that he 'savoured every moment' of the time he had spent fighting in Afghanistan.[73] When Western volunteers like Yilmaz, a Turkish national living in Germany, were deployed on terrorist operations in European countries, they often appeared to regret leaving the noise, chaos, danger and excitement of combat and the rude life on the frontlines. 'I would have liked to have stayed there,' Yilmaz recalled.[74]

Another question troubling analysts was the exact nature of the relations between al-Qaeda and the insurgent groups fighting in Afghanistan, particularly those directly loyal to Mullah Omar and the 'Quetta Shura', the council of senior Taliban leaders based in or around the western Pakistani city. Arab volunteers embedded in Afghan Taliban units continued to flow across the border – in the summer of 2008 up to 400 were estimated to be with Afghan insurgent units, especially those of Haqqani, bringing a new technological and tactical edge to combat, but the links between al-Qaeda and the Afghan insurgents still appeared to be loose.[75] A whole series of disparate but disorganized connections and liaisons combined into 'a working relationship based on individual personalities' rather than a formal alliance, according to British intelligence officials.[76] One key figure was bilingual Egyptian Mustafa Abu al-Yazid, who had developed a broad range of Taliban connections in the 1990s when head of al-Qaeda's finance committee and so was able to enhance otherwise fairly haphazard cooperation between his Arabic-speaking al-Qaeda associates and the Pashtun-speaking Afghan Taliban a decade or so later.[77] Al-Yazid liaised too with local Pakistani militant commanders like Baitullah Mehsud, who put their own considerable reserves of suicide bombers at al-Qaeda's disposal, in return for monetary or other assistance, as well as sending them into Afghanistan 'following the orders' of the senior Afghan Taliban leadership.[78] Al-Qaeda leaders also began establishing closer relations with the increasing number of individuals from Pakistani groups who were arriving in the FATA. Some had broken away from groups like Lashkar-e-Toiba which had remained focused on regional rather than global agendas. They had moved to the frontier both to evade security forces and to be able to pursue their vision of jihad unhindered. Others mixed outright criminality in Pakistan with sectarian violence and had some international involvement too when it suited them. Many retained networks in places like Bahawalpur or in Karachi. Several were suspected by Pakistani investigators of involvement in the first attempt to kill Bhutto on her return to Pakistan in October 2007. Others were thought to have provided safehouses in Rawalpindi for the successful bid to assassinate the former prime minister two months later. One key emerging figure was a veteran Pakistani militant known as Ilyas Kashmiri, who al-Yazid announced as the leader of the newly formed 'al-Qaeda in Kashmir'. This range of volatile and complex relations was not easy for any one individual, or indeed group, to manage. The FATA appeared perhaps to be less the Grand Central Station of international militancy, as one specialist from MI6 called it, than its Grand Bazaar.

And it was a bazaar that was under attack. The Belgian volunteers referred in their testimony to hearing 'frequent bombardments' and learning of the death of many 'brothers' in air strikes. Through 2007, with hard evidence of ISI support for insurgents growing, Bush had begun to lose patience with the Pakistanis' apparent foot-dragging and had moved to a markedly more unilateral use of drone attacks.[79] This may well have been exactly what the Pakistani senior command had wanted all along. By the summer of 2008, the Americans were launching strikes without consulting Islamabad if the target was on a list of two to three dozen senior figures agreed in advance with the new civilian Pakistani government and top generals.[80] The results of this shift had been seen as early as February 2008, when Abu Laith al-Liby, seen as al-Qaeda's director of external operations, was killed. Militants, the volunteers' testimony revealed, greatly feared some kind of computerized 'chips' which they believed were left by informers to guide missiles on to locations or individuals.[81] Over 300 'spies' died in repeated purges during the summer in part as a result, with over 100 being killed in only a couple of weeks following the death in July of Abu Khabab al-Masri, a fifty-five-year-old veteran who had run rudimentary chemical weapons tests at camps near Jalalabad prior to 9/11. Through the rest of the year such strikes intensified. The constant threat of a fiery death did not, however, dissuade some militants from enjoying the few distractions that life in the FATA offered. Vinas told his interrogators of long hikes in the company of one of the Belgian volunteers in the hills around the village where they were staying.[82] Others apparently rode horses.[83]

As 2008's long and violent summer turned to autumn, bin Laden, al-Zawahiri and the al-Qaeda senior leadership more generally thus continued to face a range of fairly familiar challenges. Though they had survived the loss of Afghanistan and had reconstituted a new base in Pakistan with some degree of success, the troubles they faced, on a tactical and a strategic level, were still very numerous. Chief amongst the strategic issues was their continuing failure to pull off a major attack. It had been more than three years since the bombings in London and Egypt, four since Madrid, five since Istanbul, Casablanca and the wave of violence in Saudi Arabia, six since Bali and, of course, seven years since 9/11 itself. Though the al-Qaeda senior leadership had always made it clear that they preferred rare and spectacular strikes to frequent and relatively minor ones and though 9/11 had set the bar extremely high, their apparent incapacity to fulfil their fundamental role of instigator and inciter of violence was a major problem. More broadly, bin Laden and al-Zawahiri risked slipping out of the mainstream of contemporary militancy, reduced to historic if iconic importance. Early 2008 had seen a sudden spate of videos clearly aimed at reinforcing the organization's credibility among veteran militant activists and, more importantly, among the new generation of younger activists too. For the latter, the 9/11 strikes were often a childhood memory, and, in the highly competitive world of Islamic militancy, al-Qaeda's senior leaders needed to continually reassert their primacy if they were not to be seen as belonging to an earlier time. The videos focused heavily on the Palestinian question, a subject to which bin Laden had returned repeatedly and which he knew had immediate and wide appeal.[84] Many of the new communications were also tailored to attract a younger audience, giving a starring role to Abu Yahya al-Libi, an experienced and charismatic militant, polemicist and propagandist in his early thirties known for his escape from the high-security detention centre in Bagram airbase in Afghanistan three years before.[85]

Other communications were clearly aimed at offsetting the criticism of bin Laden's leadership by the growing number of respected veteran militants. Al-Zawahiri had released a book called *The Exoneration* in March 2008, in which he inveighed at length against those who were 'now trying to serve Crusader Zionist interests' by 'dragging the *muja-hideen* away from the confrontation'.[86] The same month, Abu Yahya al-Libi weighed in with a video in which he claimed that the recent texts of Sayyid Imam al-Sharif, the Egyptian al-Qaeda founder who had renounced violence from his prison cell, were forgeries. In May, al-Zawahiri finally responded to questions he had invited on a radical web forum six months previously. Arguing that allegations that al-Qaeda had caused the deaths of 'Muslim innocents' were 'Crusader Zionist propaganda' or due to the use of civilians as 'human shields', he returned to the same themes he had covered in his book, pouring scorn on his critics, in particular the veteran Muslim Brotherhood cleric Yusuf al-Qaradawi, calling them faithless Western stooges, apostates and hypocrites. Like bin Laden, al-Zawahiri also focused on Gaza and Palestine, rebutting the charge that al-Qaeda had not done enough to help the Palestinians directly with the argument that the group had repeatedly struck the allies of Israel.

There was another key emerging theme in communications. The central al-Qaeda leadership had always tried to tread a careful path between the local strategy entirely focused on establishing individual 'fronts' aimed at securing slices of liberated territory, that of the late al-Zarqawi, and the global strategy focused on provoking a broad uprising of Muslims, favoured by the now incarcerated al-Suri. The 9/11 attacks had taken the organization, against the wishes of many of its members, towards the global strategy. Since, the local had progressively returned. Al-Zawahiri, with his direct experience of militancy in Egypt in the late 1970s, had always stressed the importance of securing a solid base from which to launch further operations. If bin Laden lacked his older associate's sense of the practicalities of clandestine violent extremism, never himself having ever been hunted through the streets of his hometown, he nonetheless recognized that the great campaign to liberate the Islamic world needed to be launched from somewhere. The question was: where? Al-Zawahiri's various writings made clear his long-cherished hope that his native land would be the centre of the new caliphate when it was restored. Bin Laden apparently hoped it would be Saudi Arabia. However, neither had been a practical prospect in the 1990s, and nor were they now. Hopes that Iraq might fulfil the role had been dashed, at least for the moment. Nor did Afghanistan look a likely candidate in the near future. But a new possibility, barely considered previously, now presented itself. A strife-torn, chaotic country of nearly 200 million Muslims, where bin Laden and his close associates had already established an ideological and physical foothold and where they were still more popular than almost anywhere else in the Islamic world: Pakistan.

THE BATTLE FOR BAJAUR

In late November 2008, the Pakistani army fought its way into a small town called Loesam in Bajaur, the agency at the northernmost tip of the FATA which had been in part overrun by militants. Bajaur was used by al-Qaeda as an occasional haven, had been hit by repeated drone strikes and was a rear base for militants engaging US troops over the border in Afghanistan. By the time the troops had secured the town, there was not much of it left. To save it, they had destroyed it. The bazaar was a pile of rubble, almost every home had been reduced to its concrete foundations and the only building still upright was the mosque that stood in the corner of what once was the local petrol station. The population had fled, joining an estimated 200,000 refugees displaced by the fighting over previous months.[87]

If the scene was a desolate one, it was set in a landscape of striking natural beauty. A few hundred metres out of the ruined town men of the 25th Punjab regiment had dug trenches among stands of slim ash and birch trees. Heavy machine guns traded fire with militants who still clung to a few battered strongpoints concealed in the dry, sandy valleys that ran, half hidden, between the empty fields up into the hills beyond. Smoke from fires started in the dry grass and scattered patches of woodland by shelling drifted in long grey strands. On the horizon, distant but visible in the clear autumn air, was the long ridge that marked the Afghan frontier with a spur where Damadola, the village hit hardest by repeated air strikes over previous years and now the effective headquarters of the militants, lay. Tanks were being brought up to deal with the militants' mortars, which were still dropping shells just a few hundred metres from where Colonel Javed Baluch, the ground commander of the operation, sat by a pink plastic telephone and ordered tea, biscuits and artillery strikes with an equal nonchalance.[88]

Of all the armed groups in the FATA in 2008, the Pakistani army were clearly the biggest and the best-equipped force. They had been engaged in the frontier zone since late 2001, when troops had belatedly been sent to block the escape routes from Tora Bora. Over the intervening years dozens of operations the length and breadth of the FATA had cost over 1,000 Pakistani servicemen's lives. In late 2008, with Musharraf gone and a civilian government in place, a new series of offensives was launched. One reason was increasing American pressure on the Pakistani high command to justify the $2 billion annual subsidy from Washington for their counter-terrorist operations. Another was the international outcry after the death of Bhutto. A third, perhaps the most pertinent of all, was the unprecedented spate of attacks on the Pakistani military itself through the autumn of 2007 and on into 2008. Previously, the bombings that had killed so many elsewhere in the country had largely spared the army installations. This had changed. Of the fifty-six suicide bombings in Pakistan in 2007, thirty-six had struck military targets and in all nearly 900 Pakistani security forces and officials had died over the year. By June 2008, that total had already been exceeded.[89] A final factor was the realization by senior Pakistani military personnel of quite what sort of threat militancy now posed to the country. This had been reinforced when, in September 2008, hours after President Zardari's maiden address to parliament, a huge truck bomb exploded outside the Marriott hotel in central Islamabad, ripping away the entire façade of the building and killing fifty-four and injuring over 250. This attack, in the heart of the capital and only a few hundred metres from where the entire cabinet was dining, was a direct assault on the core of the Pakistani political and security establishment.[90] For once, rather than holding back the country's new political leadership, army commanders actively set out to build up their enthusiasm for a series of broad-ranging offensives, showing Zardari and senior politicians propaganda videos made by militants which showed adult 'spies' executed by recruits apparently only ten or eleven years old.[91]

The Bajaur operation was the first of the new offensives and was very carefully watched from overseas. The use of drones, it was widely recognized, was a tactical rather than a strategic solution to the threat to the West that emanated from the FATA, and any longer-term solution would have to come from the Pakistanis and in particular from the Pakistani army. The machinations of the ISI in Afghanistan had already shaken the faith of many in the West in the Pakistani military and security establishment, and Western powers were hoping for a show of competence and resolve in Bajaur followed by a swift extension of operations into every tribal agency along the whole border, starting with a push south through Mohmand, another into the Khyber and eventually an assault into North and South Waziristan to disrupt al-Qaeda and relieve the pressure in Afghanistan. The Pakistanis had a slower operational tempo in mind. 'Let's just say our agenda and that of our international friends don't always coincide,' said Major General Tariq Khan, who commanded the Bajaur campaign from the Frontier Corps headquarters behind the brick ramparts of the old Sikh- and British-built fort in the centre of Peshawar.

Though wary, Western observers were heartened by the apparent will shown by the Pakistanis. Fears of a repetition of the deal-making that had marked previous such operations appeared unfounded. By the time they had fought their way into Loesam, the Pakistani army had sustained hundreds of casualties in Bajaur and still seemed determined to continue fighting.[92] They appeared also to have inflicted heavy losses, not always a feature of previous campaigns. A pilot of one of the ageing but effective Cobra helicopter gunships recently supplied by the Americans and deployed in the operation described watching the militants running for cover or simply standing firing as he turned his Gatling guns on them. 'Often you can see their faces, and the first few dozen or so bothered me,' the thirty-eight-year-old told the author. 'But when you've killed hundreds, you stop worrying.'[93] Commanders on the ground said they had already killed around 1,000 militants so far.[94]

With the security of the West so intimately bound up with their actions and attitudes, it was natural that the Pakistani military as an institution would be the focus of much interest, frustration and bewilderment as the first decade of the 9/11 Wars had worn on. Early on, interest had mainly been in the political role played by the army, as was to be expected during a period of military rule. With Musharraf gone, the focus had become the capacity of the Pakistani army and in particular its ability and desire to implement the new counter-insurgency lessons from Iraq that were being introduced in Afghanistan. A slew of papers from Washington think-tanks and articles in specialized periodicals analysed the Pakistani army's multiple failings, most due to its orientation towards fighting conventional battles against India. Neither before nor after the departure of Musharraf was there much analysis of the Pakistani army and its relationship with Pakistani society as a whole. This was a mistake as the degree to which the military reflected other social, political, cultural and economic developments within the nation as a whole went a long way to providing an answer to many of the questions that Western strategists found themselves continually posing about the competence, will and worldview of their allies. This was certainly true of the ISI's Afghan strategy, as noted above. It was true too of the attitude of the military as a whole to operations in the tribal areas. The ISI did not exist in a vacuum. Staffed largely with officers drawn from the military on temporary attachment but with some civilian staff, it had, of course, developed its own institutional culture but represented that of the army more broadly too. The ISI's collective understanding of Pakistan's security interests did not diverge in any significant way from that of most Pakistani soldiers or indeed from most Pakistanis. The most obvious example was the glaring gap between how ordinary Pakistani officers who had nothing to do with the intelligence services viewed the enemy they were engaging in the FATA and how that enemy was viewed in the West.

Publicly, in Bajaur as elsewhere, officers and soldiers were careful to hide any misgivings about who they were fighting and why. 'I just need to think about what these guys do to prisoners, the decapitations and everything, and I am happy pressing the trigger,' said the helicopter pilot who had killed hundreds. For Colonel Javed Baluch, calling in the artillery fire in Loesam, the militants were 'enemies of my country and undermining our security'. Major General Tariq Khan insisted that, 'when our troops come into contact with the militants, they do not see them as Pakistanis or brother Muslims or whatever. They see them as the enemy.' Khan admitted that there were some who 'had doubts'. These, he said, were 'those who have not come into contact with the reality on the ground'. But the situation was complex and, whatever the rationalizations employed, so were the views and sentiments of many of those troops deployed into the FATA. Firstly, many of those engaged in Bajaur and elsewhere were paramilitaries from the Frontier Corps, recruited from the same tribes and often families as the militants and, as repeated incidents of desertion or disobedience to orders had shown, steeped in much of the same culture, ideology and worldview as their peers who had chosen a different way of getting paid, getting some prestige and getting to carry a gun. The attitude of regular soldiers too revealed a significant degree of sympathy for their enemy. All ranks routinely referred to the enemy as 'miscreants' – a far less loaded term than terrorists or even militants – and saw them as misguided rather than necessarily malevolent. 'They are our brothers who have been led astray and brainwashed,' said Colonel Mohammed Nauman Saeed, who ran the rear base of the Bajaur operation in the local administrative centre of Khar. 'But we have to fight them for the sake of our country as a whole.' Nauman would not be drawn on who was responsible for the brainwashing. Others, speaking privately, were more forthcoming. After giving a lecture on al-Qaeda at GHQ in Rawalpindi, the author was reprimanded by several officers of colonel and higher rank for repeating the 'lies of the Western establishment' about bin Laden's organization. Talking about the militants in Pakistan, their views were very clear. Those against whom their comrades were fighting in the FATA had been led astray by India, the CIA or 'the Jews', they said.

With no systematic surveys of the opinions of the half million men of Pakistan's fighting forces, there was little empirical evidence that could help gauge quite how widespread such views were. This had long been a problem. The stories about Western analysts counting the beards on group pictures of senior Pakistani army officers were sadly not apocryphal. 'It is simply very difficult to know,' admitted one Western intelligence officer.[95] Signs that a minority within the Pakistani military were increasingly drawn to radical Islamism had been there for many years. Not only had there been the relatively well-publicized involvement of military personnel in plots to kill Musharraf and a range of other violent acts, but there were also several much less well-known incidents of officers refusing to obey orders to fight militants, some as early as 2002.[96] Then there was the small but significant number of former military personnel, mainly NCOs and junior officers, who had joined violent outfits such as Lashkar-e-Toiba on leaving the military or, in some instances, had actually left the army in order to pursue 'the jihad'. Put together, these various elements often provoked claims that the entire Pakistani military was increasingly contaminated by extremism.

Yet, as with the broader analysis of the country as a whole, the focus on the most radical elements underplayed the impact of the much more significant general trends within Pakistani society – the growing mild Islamism, the social and political conservatism, the increased religiosity, the cultural turn towards the Middle East – on the army's institutional culture, worldview and understanding of Pakistan's interests. All militaries are institutions that are representative of the societies that produce them so it was inevitable that many if not all these elements would be present in the Pakistani army too. Indeed, various further factors meant that many of these trends were not simply represented within the army but *over-represented*.[97] One was historic: as the first decade of the twenty-first century passed, men who had joined the army during the Islamicization programmes introduced by General Zia when he had been in power during the 1980s had started reaching senior rank in significant numbers. Twenty-nine brigadiers appointed to general rank in January 2006 had been from 'the class of 1978 or 1979', and the proportion of officers who had served their early years and thrived sufficiently to climb the command hierarchy under Zia was rising with each passing wave of retirements.[98] A second factor was the long hiatus, due to American sanctions imposed in 1990 and lifted in 2001, in overseas training for Pakistani officers in the USA.[99] Many Pakistani officers serving in 2008 had simply never had any real contact with the West. Most had never travelled outside Pakistan. Nor, unlike in previous periods, were many likely to travel independently to Europe or America. This was partly because, like their civilian counterparts, most army officers appeared more likely to prefer, in the polarized and often hostile climate created by the 9/11 Wars, other destinations but also because they simply lacked the funds. A further factor in the over-representation of 'Middle Pakistan' in the army was that recruiting patterns had shifted over recent decades, and whereas, in the first decades after independence, army officers had been drawn almost exclusively from the wealthy landed elite, by the 1980s and 1990s they were increasingly drawn from the urban lower middle class. By 1998, 42 per cent of officers, an over-representation of at least a third, came from cities.[100] A decade later, the proportion was even higher. They were educated in government schools or on scholarships to the more elite educational institutions, and their fathers were bureaucrats, pharmacists, engineers, teachers or indeed lower-ranking servicemen. Several of the students on the grass in the Bahauddin Zakariya University in Multan had said they wanted to be army officers. This, of course, had consequences that were naturally broader than the determination of the choice of a few hundred officers' holiday destinations. The origins of this new mass of officers were in the 'emerging urban centres', which were, as the historian of the Pakistani army Shuja Nawaz has noted, 'the traditional strongholds of the growing Islamist parties and conservatism associated with the petit

bourgeoisie'.[101] This meant that when one colonel, at the end of a diatribe against Bush, Blair, Israel, the Indians and the West in general, said,
'We are the army of the nation,' it was a statement that was more accurate than many in Europe and America cared to think.

A SAVAGE INTENSITY

In late 2007, Mohammed Ajmal Amir, a former labourer with minimal
education from a small town just north of Multan, approached a
Lashkar-e-Toiba recruiter at a market stall in the city of Rawalpindi.
His primary aim was far from religious. A petty criminal with ambitions
to pursue a career as a robber, he wanted to learn how to use automatic
and other weapons and thought the militant group would teach him the
requisite skills.[102] He then spent three weeks at Muridke, the headquarters of LeT's ostensibly non-violent parent group Jamaat-ul-Dawa
situated 30 miles south of Lahore, following a regime of four hours of
religious instruction and two hours of sport each day. His original criminal career forgotten, Amir rapidly developed new interests. Seen as a
promising recruit, he underwent three further weeks of mixed military
and religious instruction in a LeT camp in a village near the town of
Mansehra in the North West Frontier province before a series of courses
of increasingly specialized instruction in smaller groups. Finally, he
found himself back at Muridke with twelve others being taught how to
swim. After nine months or more of training, the thirteen young men
were briefed on their mission. They were not heading to Kashmir, as
many of them had thought. They would be sent direct to Mumbai, India's
cosmopolitan, bustling commercial capital, to conduct a spectacular raid
which would end in their deaths. After two attempts to cross the sea from
Karachi in the late summer and autumn failed, finally the group succeeded in boarding an Indian fishing trawler. They forced the crew (who
were later killed) to take them to their destination, which they reached in
the evening of November 26. Once ashore, the militants fanned out across
the city. Amir – who would be erroneously dubbed Kasab by Indian
police and then the press – and one other gunman made their way to the
seething Chhatrapati Shivaji railway station, entered the toilets, took
their weapons from their backpacks, headed out on the concourse and
opened fire.[103]

The attack's aim was to maximize publicity. Their target was civilians. Kasab and his partner killed fifty-three at the railway terminus, mainly evening commuters. Another seven, including a commando, were killed in the Nariman House, a centre for ultra-Orthodox Jews in the city, by another group of gunmen. Ten were killed at the Leopold Café, a hangout for tourists and young locals, when it was randomly sprayed with bullets. One group of militants targeted the five-star Oberoi hotel, where they killed thirty. A second group attacked the famous Taj Palace hotel, yards from the sea and the monumental arch known as the Gateway to India, where they succeeded in holding out against security forces for nearly three days. Witnesses later told of the attackers marching through corridors, restaurants and ballrooms, demanding the identity of guests, holding some hostage, shooting others. Another thirty died there. In all more than 160 civilians were killed in the attack, and more than 300 injured. Kasab survived and was detained. All the other gunmen were shot dead. Two of them came from the town of Dera Ismail Khan in the North West Frontier Province. The rest came from the southern Punjab.[104]

In the aftermath of the attack, with Lashkar-e-Toiba clearly identified as the perpetrators, two urgent questions needed answering. The first was obvious: what was the involvement of the Pakistani security establishment? The second was equally pressing for security services around the world: did the Mumbai attacks, with their range of international targets, signal that Lashkar-e-Toiba, arguably the biggest violent Islamic extremist organization in the world other than Hamas or Hezbollah, had gone global? The answers to both would not become clear for some time and, when they did, would be, as ever, complex and nuanced.

Kasab was a junior figure, a footsoldier and a new recruit, who knew nothing of the background of the plot he had become involved in. Much of the background of the genesis of the attack, arguably the most spectacular of the 9/11 Wars other than the September 11 attacks themselves, was eventually revealed by David Headley, a Pakistani-American member of LeT who was arrested in the USA in 2009 and spoke to Indian investigators while in American custody as part of a plea bargain. Headley's own life-story was the stuff of bad thrillers. Born Daood Gilani, the son of an American woman and a Pakistani civil servant, he had grown up in Pakistan but had spent much of his adult life in Philadelphia. When jailed for heroin trafficking in the late 1990s, Headley had agreed to work for US authorities as an agent, though the relationship had ended by 2000. He had joined LeT, aged forty-two, in 2002 after returning to his native land, seized with enthusiasm for radical Islam and a deep hatred of India.[105] While in US custody, he explained to his Indian questioners how he had spent the first years of his association with LeT frustrated as, despite having successfully completed the various training courses necessary for aspirant combatants, he was never sent across the Line of Control into Indian Kashmir to fight.[106] He was too old, and only a very low level of infiltration was being allowed by the ISI at the time. In late 2005, arrested near Peshawar, Headley mentioned his links to LeT to police, was interviewed by an ISI major and freed. Back at his home in Lahore, he was contacted again by the ISI, interviewed at length about his avowed ambitions to do harm to India or Indian interests by a lieutenant colonel and assigned a handler, a 'Major Iqbal', who sent him back to the USA in the spring of 2006 to change his name and get an Indian visa. On his return, the officer assigned a junior colleague to train Headley in clandestine techniques, and in the autumn of 2006, 'Major Iqbal' handed his new recruit $25,000 and sent him to Mumbai. His job was to survey dozens of different locations ranging from embassies to the offices of nuclear-related government organizations, filming and photographing everything he saw and bringing the material back to Pakistan.[107]

Headley's association with the ISI complemented rather than replaced his activities with LeT. The two were interlinked. From 2006 to 2008, Headley undertook seven more visits to India, including several to Mumbai, on behalf of both the intelligence service and the militant group. After each, the former video store owner would meet both his ISI handler, who continued the training in clandestine techniques, and his LeT associates. On several occasions Headley went as far as to give both the same images and film copied on to two memory sticks. His contacts with 'Major Iqbal' continued up to and beyond the actual attacks in Mumbai, with Headley apprising his handler of last-minute changes in the planning of the operation, in particular of its targets. For Headley, the logic of the ISI in encouraging the attacks was clear. The service was worried that LeT, the Pakistani military's most effective reserve of irregular forces and the one with which it had the closest relationship, might follow the example of other groups and pursue more aggressive agendas closer to the internationalist position of al-Qaeda. 'The ISI was under tremendous pressure to stop any integration of Kashmir-based jihadi organizations with the Taliban-based outfits,' he told his interrogators. Even worse was the prospect that significant elements of the LeT might begin to fuse with the Pakistani Taliban. 'The ISI . . . had no ambiguity in understanding the necessity to strike India. It would serve three purposes: controlling further split in the Kashmir-based outfits, providing them with a sense of achievement and shifting the theatre of violence from the domestic soil of Pakistan to India,' Headley explained.

Another driver for the project to strike India was the internal tension within LeT itself. It was in these dynamics that the answer to the second question posed by the Mumbai attacks – the potential globalization of LeT – was to be found. Like so many other radical groups over previous chapters, LeT had its own problems with indiscipline and ideological dissent. Headley told his questioners of the ongoing tension within LeT, which pitted leaders like founder Hafiz Mohammed Saeed and top military commander Zaki ur Rehman Lakhvi against even more extreme elements within the organization. These latter had grown increasingly numerous as the 9/11 Wars had ground on. Many had split away to go and fight in Afghanistan. Others had stayed within LeT but argued forcibly that the group's historic arrangements with the Pakistani security establishment were no longer justifiable, particularly as the 'jihad' in Kashmir appeared to have been abandoned and Pakistani state policy seemed to be to support Washington. Saeed and Lakhvi appear thus to have agreed to a Mumbai operation, which at its outset was supposed to be limited only to a *fedayeen*-style raid by two or three gunmen on a single hotel in the city, to head off internal dissent. The plot had then taken on a momentum of its own, building up a sufficient head of steam for the plan to largely escape efforts by the senior leadership of LeT to keep it to a scale that would be less politically contentious. Instead, the final weeks saw the number of gunmen increased, the list of targets lengthened and, rather than escape by train or bus to Kashmir and thence to Pakistan, it was decided that the militants were to hold out until they were killed.

The escalation of the plot also appears to have caught out the ISI. For if it is clear that low-level ISI officers knew much about the strike – Headley talks of 'Iqbal' approving the controversial last-minute addition of the Jewish centre to the target list – it is less certain that senior officers were aware of what was being planned in Mumbai. Headley implicated several majors and a colonel and said that the handler of Zaki ur Rehman Lakhvi was a brigadier. But he also said that Lieutenant General Ahmed Shuja Pasha, the director general of the ISI, visited Lakhvi in prison after the attacks 'to try to understand them', implying that the broad assessment of MI6 and other agencies that the upper ranks of the ISI were unaware of the scale of the plan was probably correct.[108] The nature of the relationship between the service and the militant group was such that the ISI had much less control over LeT than it liked to think – if probably more than it ever publicly admitted.[109] The Mumbai attacks were thus, like so many terrorist operations over the previous years, the result of a range of structural and short-term factors among which the demands of a progressively more radicalized international jihadi movement and internal dynamics within a given group were key. The same had been true of the 9/11 attacks themselves. Lashkar-e-Toiba had not yet gone global – but were under significant internal and external pressure to do so.

The final weeks of 2008 thus saw – in a broad arc from the western coast of India to the Afghan–Iranian border – one of the most concentrated periods of violence in any theatre of the 9/11 Wars to date, rivalling even the worst times in Iraq in sheer savage intensity. There was the quotidian violence in Pakistan itself: a suicide bomb in the valley of Swat that killed nine; a second killed six in the Orakzai agency; a huge blast in the congested, narrow lanes of old Peshawar killed thirty-seven; a strike in Buner, even closer to the lowlands and Islamabad, killed even more. Through November, hundreds of radical militants loyal to mullahs close to the Pakistani Taliban – with Fazlullah, the former ski lift operator, among them – stormed through Swat, taking control of what had once been a favoured tourist destination for the Pakistani middle class. The security forces there seemed powerless to stop them, and the militants, calling for land reform, *sharia* law, an end to 'moral corruption' and American interference, surged on to the plains below the hills. They were now only 100 miles from the capital.

In Afghanistan too there was no let-up. Taliban leadership figures had made clear their intention to fight through the winter, and there were major Taliban attacks in Khost, in northern Parwan and in central Ghazni. There was a big ambush in Baghdis in the far north-west, an area hitherto largely free of violence. There was fighting near the

Iranian border, a suicide bomb at the airport of Herat, continued heavy combat in Helmand and a series of low-level strikes, few reported, in and around Kabul.[110] Kandahar and its environs saw dozens of incidents of intimidation and several assassinations.

The toll from the last five weeks of 2008 was staggering: the dead included more than 160 in Mumbai, 27 Western servicemen in Afghanistan, around 60 Pakistani and Afghan soldiers, about 50 Afghan policemen, around 100 or so Afghan non-combatants and at least two or three times that number of Pakistani civilians, some killed by drones, most by suicide bombings.[111] Then there were the casualties among the Afghan Taliban or Pakistani insurgents, estimated to be in the hundreds, and even a few Western volunteers, dead somewhere high in the hills of the FATA or just over the border in Afghanistan. Overall more than 1,000 people had been killed and many more injured.

At the midpoint of this 1,500-mile-long arc of violence was the historic Khyber Pass, leading from Peshawar across the mountains to Afghanistan and eventually on to Jalalabad and the road to Kabul. Through December 2008, the various factions of the Pakistani Taliban launched nightly attacks on NATO convoys carrying supplies across the pass from Karachi to bases like Bagram. Eighty per cent of the supplies of the coalition fighting in Afghanistan were brought in via the Khyber, and the crossing point at Chaman near Quetta. The series of spectacular raids might have had only a minor impact in material terms – though nearly 250 vehicles were destroyed – but the footage of flaming trucks and stores brought home to millions watching in Europe and America just how tough the wars their nations were engaged in were and how 'victory', however defined, was unlikely to come soon. Militants even managed to get hold of a Humvee, which they paraded under a banner saying 'The Caravan of Baitullah', in honour of the Pakistani Taliban's leader, Baitullah Mehsud.[112] Watching the scenes on CNN in his office at the Quai d'Orsay in Paris, Bernard Kouchner, the French foreign minister, turned to an aide and said simply: 'C'est foutu', it's fucked. Many of his counterparts elsewhere were expressing the same sentiments, though usually in slightly more diplomatic language.[113]

PART SIX

Endgames: 2009–11

15

The 9/11 Wars: Europe,
the Middle East, Iraq

A CHANGE IN THE WHITE HOUSE

On November 4, 2008, Americans had elected, by 52.9 per cent to 45.7 per cent, Barack Hussein Obama, the forty-seven-year-old Democratic Senator for Illinois, as their president. Some argued that the changes that Obama would introduce in the day-to-day American approach to the 9/11 Wars were more of style rather than substance. But though the compromises forced on the Bush administration in the last eighteen months of its tenure as popular support waned and a host of other problems had crowded in had blunted its ideological edge, the arrival of someone of the new president's appearance, origins, views and charisma nonetheless created an obvious break that went beyond merely a shift in tone. At the very least, the departure of Bush meant an inevitable reformulation of the narrative of the conflict for all involved. The senior leadership of al-Qaeda, for example, had been sufficiently concerned to issue a series of pre-emptive statements attacking Obama for being a 'house negro'.[1]

The new president's early speeches did not disappoint those around the world hoping for a clear shift in policy, tone and approach. Obama repeatedly signalled a new realism, a new will to find inclusive multilateral solutions, a desire to enter into, and remain in, conversation with both allies and potential adversaries. Though the rhetoric might sometimes have been vague, it was attractive, occasionally inspirational and managed to sound radically new without challenging the broadly accepted package of values that, domestically at least, were associated with 'being American'. In his acceptance speech, the new president had deftly turned his predecessor's 'you are either with us or against us' into a resounding slogan of righteousness, strength and hope. 'To those who would tear this world down: we will defeat you ... To those who seek peace and security: we support you.'[2]

But Obama's arrival in the White House was not the strategic inflection point in the 9/11 Wars that some had hoped it might be, and the 'Obama effect' was less potent than the al-Qaeda leadership had apparently feared. Opinion polls showed that the accession of the new president provoked a measurable increase in 'confidence in America to do the right thing' in international affairs almost everywhere but, though Obama was certainly more popular than Bush, also revealed that there was little change in the deep ambient anti-Americanism in the Muslim world. The surveys found that, even if the proportion of people trusting US leadership in world affairs rose dramatically in 2009 in Egypt and in Jordan, in most Muslim-majority countries the number of people expressing a favourable view of the USA remained at an appallingly low level.[3] In some places, such as the Palestinian territories, Obama's arrival in the White House seemed to have no effect at all. In others, views of the US actually got worse, dropping to levels not seen since the months around the 2003 invasion of Iraq.[4]

Within forty-eight hours of taking office, Obama announced the appointment of two 'special representatives'. The first was Senator George Mitchell, who was given the job of spearheading a new bid to reinvigorate a Middle East 'peace process' which had been moribund for a decade or more. There was little indicating that Mitchell would meet with any greater success than any of his predecessors, but the gesture, coming with the new president's statements that he wanted to see the expansion of Jewish settlements in the West Bank frozen, was nonetheless welcomed.[5] The second appointment was the veteran diplomat Richard Holbrooke, the architect of the Dayton Agreement, which had ended the conflict in the Balkans fifteen years before. Holbrooke became special representative to Afghanistan and Pakistan, soon abbreviated to 'AfPak'.[6] Obama also signed three executive orders. One ordered that, 'without exception or equivocation', the United States would 'not torture'. The second decreed the closure of the Guantanamo Bay detention camp. The third commissioned a comprehensive review of procedures of holding and trying terrorism suspects 'to best protect our nation and the rule of law', which meant the effective suspension of ongoing tribunals of detainees. That the US Supreme Court had already judged that 'enemy combatants' were protected by the Geneva Conventions and by the United States Constitution, that 'Gitmo' would prove far harder to close than thought and that the prisoner review would lead to far lesser results than originally anticipated did not strip the announcements of their significant symbolic value.[7] If they did little to mitigate the entrenched anti-Americanism around the globe, they did not exacerbate it either. This, in the battered, febrile world left after seven years of the 9/11 Wars, was something of an achievement in itself.

Obama also moved to distance himself from the lecturing of the Islamic world that had been characteristic of the Bush administration. The ambitious 'Freedom Agenda' was set aside. Instead of 'draining the swamp of terrorism' through revolutionary change, the emphasis was placed on peaceful coexistence. In Ankara in April 2009, he spoke of relations between the West and the Muslim world. 'I know the trust that binds us has been strained . . . We will listen carefully . . . and seek common ground,' he said. 'We will be respectful even when we do not agree.'[8] In Cairo in June, four years after Condoleezza Rice's speech there announcing the Bush administration's push for greater democratization in the region, Obama, in an address entitled 'A New Beginning', would speak of his own childhood in Indonesia, the world's most populous Muslim nation, and of hearing the *adhan*, or call to prayer, 'at the break of dawn and at the fall of dusk' and would argue that, though basic human rights were universal, 'no system of government can or should be imposed by one nation on any other'.[9] He flew from Egypt to Germany to visit the Buchenwald concentration camp and then stopped in France, where he explained that his pride in his own country did not 'lessen [his] interest in recognizing the value and wonderful qualities of other countries'. 'We're not always going to be right . . . other people may have good ideas [and] in order for us to work collectively, all parties have to compromise, and that includes us,' the new president said.[10] When asked in a press conference how he would resolve the theoretical conflict between respecting state sovereignty and intervening to defend the universal rights of oppressed people, Obama answered that 'the threshold at which international intervention is appropriate . . . has to be very high'.[11] At the American cemetery above Omaha beach in Normandy on the sixty-fifth anniversary of the D-Day landings, the president, flanked by British Prime Minister Gordon Brown, French President Nicolas Sarkozy and Canadian Prime Minister Stephen

Harper, told his audience that 'we live in a world of competing beliefs and claims about what is true. It is a world of varied religions and cultures and forms of government. In such a world, it is rare for a struggle to emerge that speaks to something universal about humanity.' Carefully avoiding any reference to current conflicts other than to pay tribute to 'the young men and women who carry forward the legacy of sacrifice', Obama made clear that, though committed to the war in Afghanistan, for him the days of the radical, 'muscular' interventionist liberal humanitarianism of Bush and Tony Blair were gone.[12] The term 'War on Terror' was another casualty of Obama's arrival. Instead, the president spoke of 'a battle or a war against some terrorist organizations'.[13]

The challenges facing the new administration were manifold – a grave economic crisis, a vast budget deficit, the Iranian nuclear programme, climate change, continuing problems with America's multiple security services, the deteriorating situation in Afghanistan and Pakistan and many others. Obama's mandate too was much weaker than many overseas believed or wanted to believe. Yet the new president had one huge advantage: not only did he incarnate the hope of the advent of a new and brighter period after the dark and tense pessimism of previous years but he came to power at a moment when, for the first time for many years, it was reasonable to imagine that the optimism that the new president projected was at least in part justified. Through 2008 and into 2009, the indications of the potential for a more positive evolution of the 9/11 Wars that had first become visible in 2006 and 2007 broadened and consolidated. With the bad news pouring out of Afghanistan and Pakistan it was easy to forget what was going on elsewhere. But one of the reasons 'AfPak' could receive so much attention was that, in almost every other theatre previously touched by the 9/11 Wars, there was progress. Any advances were fragile, of course, and there was considerable potential for a sudden reversal, but, though no one even imagined returning to the pre-2001 situation, the news from many of the various fronts was undeniably better than it had been for many years. If the map that had shown the rapid spread in violence out of south-west Asia, across the Middle East and into Europe in one direction and out into the Far East in the other direction between 2001 and 2005 had been redrawn in the spring of 2009, a glance would have shown that the density of incidents had thinned markedly and the extent of the zone of conflict had shrunk. Nowhere did this appear clearer than in Europe.

THE ATLANTIC WALL

In the autumn of 2008, the Belgian and French volunteers who had complained of being deceived by al-Qaeda propaganda had left the tribal areas and returned to Europe, retracing their steps through Pakistan, Iran and on via Istanbul to their homes in the Moellenbeek area of Brussels and in Vénissieux, a tough immigrant suburb of the French city of Lyon. European security services had been alerted to their return through the interception of emails sent from the FATA to friends and family members back in Europe and were waiting for them. In December 2008, Belgian and French police thus made a series of arrests. In Belgium, newspapers ran headlines warning that the group was planning an attack on the metro. Police and prosecutors argued that the group's claims to have come home because they were disappointed, ill or homesick were simply a poor cover for their re-entry to Europe. The group's lawyers argued that the men were sincere.

The raids, in which one woman and six men were detained, attracted little international interest. Such operations had become wearily familiar over previous years. Nothing about the profile of the suspects was at all out of the ordinary. The men arrested were all young first- or second-generation immigrants who had been drawn into radical activity either through the internet or in person by an experienced activist, in this case a veteran called Moez Garsallaoui, who himself was married to a well-known online female radical polemicist.[14]

Little in the composition or the activities of the group diverged from that seen elsewhere in Europe at the time either. The group was a small network – a half-dozen or so core members, a dozen or so in an outer circle who were less engaged on a day-to-day basis, and then a few dozen more who were tacitly aware of what was going on but not directly involved.[15] According to the European Union's criminal intelligence agency, two-thirds of individuals active in Islamic militancy on the continent belonged to such 'small autonomous cells' rather than any known larger groups.[16] Those arrested in Moellenbeek and Vénissieux, again typically, were ordinary men, neither desperately poor nor particularly wealthy, neither utterly without education nor especially well qualified. Several of them had been involved in petty crime before drifting into radical militancy – once more reflecting broader trends. One had committed more serious offences.[17]

As increasingly was the case elsewhere, the combination of a virtual community sustained by a radical website and a real community of friends had been key in the creation of the Brussels group. The approbation of the community – several of those who went received money to allow them to travel from close relatives fully conscious of the goal of the journey – had also been a crucial factor.[18] Radicalization for the Belgian and French suspects, as for so many others, had been a gradual process involving a series of key contacts with other interested individuals rather than deriving from any inherent personal proclivity to violent militancy. Again this was now seen as fairly standard.

That such conspiracies posed a clear and present threat – 'The answer is not *fatwas* . . . it is boooooooooms,' a web posting by the leader of the Brussels–Lyon network, Garsallaoui, from mid 2008 read – and that they would continue to pose a threat in the future was self-evident. One of the biggest problems for reporters working on terrorism and militancy – as for police and policy-makers – was the difficulty in gauging the real nature of that threat. There was a very natural tendency on the part of security authorities to err on the side of caution. The penalties for not warning political leaders far outweighed the credit to be gained by a more sober assessment of any potential danger. There was an equal logic driving journalists to err on the side of sensation. Yet the cumulative numbers of those involved in such plots in 2008 and into 2009 seemed difficult to tally with the more pessimistic announcements about the extent of radicalization in Europe of even a year or so previously. This was certainly evident in the UK. Though British newspapers, quoting 'security sources', continued to speak of up to 4,000 British citizens trained in terrorist camps, the number of annual arrests on terrorist charges in the UK had averaged 212 each year since 2002. This total included detentions linked to Irish Republican terrorism and other forms of political violence. In 2008, only 174 individuals had been arrested on terrorist charges and 207 people in 2009.[19] Importantly, only a third of those arrested were eventually charged.[20] British intelligence officials spoke of around thirty 'significant' individuals travelling to Pakistan each year.[21] Others travelled to Somalia, they said, but only a 'handful'.[22] This was enough to cause a significant problem but remained far from the vision of hordes of young militants that had once been thought on the brink of unleashing a wave of violence in the UK. MI5 officials contrasted the current sentiment within their own service with that during the dark days of 2005 and 2006. 'Back [then] it felt genuinely out of control ... we were very worried there would be one [attack] and then another and another and another,' one told the author. 'Now we feel we've got a pretty good handle on it.'[23] In July 2009, the official assessment of the level of the threat of terrorist attack on Britain, based since 2003 on the conclusions of the Joint Terrorism Analysis Centre or JTAC, was lowered from 'severe', highly likely, to 'substantial', a strong possibility, for the first time since the September 11 attacks.[24] As if to underline the difficulty of gauging the threat, it was to return to its previous level only eight months later. But that it had been lowered at all was significant.

The situation was similar in continental Europe. The number of failed, foiled or successful attacks reported by EU member states in 2009 was down a third on 2008, which had itself seen a steep drop from 2007. The vast bulk of these incidents involved internal separatist violence within European countries and were not linked to Islamic militancy. The trend was also reflected in the number of arrests for Muslim extremism in the EU outside Britain. These numbered 110 in 2009, a decrease of 22 per cent from 2008, of 30 per cent from 2007 and of more than 50 per cent from 2006, when 257 individuals had been detained.[25] The number of member states reporting arrests for Islamic militancy had also dropped from fourteen to ten.[26] Like their British counterparts, senior European counter-terrorist officials and policymakers continued to insist that a threat remained – 'It only takes a few to get through the net to cause a very big problem,' as Alain Grignard, the head of the Belgian counter-terrorist police put it in March 2009 – but the number of radicalized individuals who did manage to evade counter-terrorist measures appeared extremely small.[27] Throughout 2008, there had been only one partially successful attack in the whole of Europe attributable to Islamic militancy, that executed by a twenty-two-year-old, psychologically ill, self-radicalized convert, Nicky Reilly, who had injured himself badly while trying to detonate a home-made bomb in the toilet of a shopping mall restaurant in Exeter, in south-west England. In 2009, there was also only a single operation that came close to succeeding – again by an apparent lone operator, an Italian who made an unsuccessful attempt to carry out a suicide bombing on a Milan military barracks. Six months after the UK dropped its threat level, the Dutch dropped theirs too. This was the second time Dutch intelligence services had moderated their estimation of the threat terrorism posed to the Netherlands. In 2007, they had said that 'the situation surrounding the known jihadist networks in the Netherlands can . . . be described as reasonably calm', arguing that 'a [positive] phenomenon that was described [last year] in cautious terms appears to be a trend'.[28] In March 2008, the release of a provocative film by populist anti-Islamic politician Geert Wilders had caused the threat level to be raised once more, but by mid-December 2009, the Dutch authorities were once again convinced that the danger from Islamic terrorism could be better described as 'slight' rather than 'substantial'.[29] In Germany too, there was a new calm – though inevitably punctuated by occasional scares. There were fears, for example, that the rising profile of Berlin's troops in Afghanistan and elections in the autumn of 2009 might provoke an attack. In the end, none occurred. In France senior advisors to Sarkozy said that their main concern was no longer al-Qaeda or its ideology but state-sponsored terrorism, particularly from Iran.[30] This may have been going too far – domestic counter-terrorist officials once again made sure that the sense of threat did not die away completely by making a fresh series of frightening statements – but French security officials privately remained confident of containing the threat from radical Islam both to French interests overseas and within France. 'We did OK before 9/11, we did OK after 9/11 and we are doing OK now,' one DST officer said.[31] No one anywhere in Europe was declaring victory, least of all the security services or the politicians – nor would they have been right to do so given the rapidity with which any stabilization could be reversed. However, for once something appeared to be going at least partly right, rather than very badly wrong.

Exactly what was going right was as difficult to answer as levels of threat were difficult to guage. One factor was certainly the constantly improving competence, capability and reach of security services, the police and all others involved in the counter-terrorist effort. Bolstered with new legislation, funding and understanding, authorities had been able to build on the strategic shifts undertaken in 2006 and 2007 to take the initiative against Islamic militancy. British officials used a convoluted metaphor involving the defensive tactics of Arsenal, the north London football club, in the 1980s to describe how by bringing in local police, social services, even schools and mosques, they were able to divert individuals who they felt were potential threats from becoming real dangers well before they became involved in serious militancy. Headmasters, clerics, community workers and others, MI5 felt, were much better placed to intervene to divert 'individuals of concern' from potential radicalism than the security service. As in the USA, another key development was legal. Earlier in the decade many trials in Britain had collapsed. This was partly due to a failure of prosecutors to understand the phenomenon they were up against – individuals were repeatedly charged with membership of al-Qaeda and were then acquitted for lack of evidence – but also due to a variety of legal loopholes. With many of these now plugged, law-enforcement agencies were able to get those who did become involved in violence locked up much more easily. Conviction rates in trials for terrorism offences in the UK in 2008–9 were 86 per cent.[32] In France, surveillance and contacts within Muslim communities, already extensive, had been rolled out further. In Germany, where strict privacy laws had once contributed to the 9/11 hijackers evading detection, new legislation granted powers of investigation and information-gathering that, coupled with further research into the process of radicalization undertaken by police sociologists, allowed security authorities to believe, like so many of their counterparts and despite public statements, that they had 'the problem largely under control'.[33] At a European level, though officials at the Commission had concerns about an overly 'politically correct' approach, as the EU's counterterrorism coordinator, Gilles de Kerchove, put it, successive measures enhancing cooperation were bearing fruit.[34] Improved transatlantic relations also had an impact. Whereas the New York Police Department's liaison officer in Paris had once been largely ignored by his Parisian counterparts, left in his office to watch the river traffic on the Seine, by mid 2009 he was being invited into key meetings. If he had spoken French he might even have been able to understand what was being said in them.[35]

Another factor was geopolitical. Sentiments in Muslim communities in Europe had obviously been very influenced by what was happening in the Islamic world. The winding-down of the messy and brutal war in Iraq, the American withdrawal from all but a few bases in the country and the departures of Blair and Bush had all undermined the neat lines of the Islam-against-the-West worldview that had been propagated so effectively earlier in the decade. Other issues – global warming, swine flu, the financial crisis – were increasingly forcing the conflict further and further down the news agenda. The war in Afghanistan undoubtedly provoked strong reactions. So too did the Israeli military operations in Gaza in January 2009. But the militant 'single narrative' was increasingly based on events that appeared historical and the actions of individuals who had left the scene.[36] New voices from within Muslim communities in the UK and elsewhere also continued to emerge to counter the extremists with growing confidence.

The later years of the decade had also seen the positive effects of the new scholarship on radical Islam and related questions. Arguments based on ignorant generalizations or stereotypes had progressively became harder to sustain in the face of solid research. One good example was the idea that Muslim hordes would overrun a 'senescent Europe' or constitute a 'fifth column' based in 'mini-Fallujas' to undermine it from within. Successive studies showed that in fact the growth of the Muslim-majority countries of the Middle East and north Africa was slowing rapidly, with the average number of children born per woman dropping from seven in 1960 to three in 2006 or even drifting down to the replacement level of about 2.1 children per woman.[37] The American Rand Corporation concluded that by 2025 the youth bulge problem in the Middle East would begin to ease.[38] A flood of Muslim immigrants thus looked unlikely. As for the Muslim population within Europe, no one doubted that it had grown rapidly in recent decades and, particularly given its relative youth, would continue to expand in years to come. However, demographers again predicted that fertility rates would decline as they had done among almost all other populations which had experienced progressively higher levels of wealth, healthcare access and literacy. There certainly appeared little reason why immigrants should reproduce more in Europe than in their countries of origin.[39] One Dutch study showed that births among Turkish- and Moroccan-born women in the Netherlands had dropped from 3.2 to 1.9 and from 4.9 to 2.9 respectively between 1990 and 2005, and fertility rates for Pakistani and Bangladeshi immigrants to the UK had gone from 9.3 in 1971 to 4.9 in 1996 and finally to under three by 2009.[40] That nominally Muslim populations would reach a size that would have a significant impact culturally and politically was clear, but the reality appeared to be a long way from the inflammatory estimates of those who had seen 'Eurabia' as an inevitable consequence of immigration.[41]

Further contributing to a drop in tension, even if the tabloid press and mainstream right-wing politicians continued to stoke popular fears of being 'overrun' or 'swamped', were the actions taken by European governments. These, by the summer of 2009 almost entirely centre-right, moved swiftly to further restrict immigration from Muslim countries and elsewhere.[42] Along with the clear messaging from almost all states but Britain that Muslim Turkey, with its population of 80 million, was not welcome in the European Union, these often severe measures showed that governments were responsive to the concerns of their population and, whatever the economic arguments or the long-term strategic considerations, would move to restrict immigration if that was what the electorate wanted. This undermined some of the more fantastic projections of the future growth of immigrant communities in European nations, which were based on the premise that no politicians on the continent would or could move to restrict the influx from overseas because of the potential impact on ailing economies desperately in need of manpower to support ageing populations. It was connected to another emerging trend: a shift in the nature of the animosity directed at Europe's various Muslim communities. As the end of the decade approached, the antipathy towards Muslims appeared to be less specific, part of a more generalized resentment directed against immigrants rather than being directly linked to a perceived threat of violence as it had been for several years. In the tight economic times of 2008 and 2009, the individual Western European citizen seemed to be defining his or her 'security' more broadly than he or she had done in the immediate aftermath of the 9/11 attacks. Classic issues such as employment, the cost of social welfare, crime and delinquency – historically associated with immigrants in popular imagination – resurfaced. In Holland, only 1 per cent of people asked in 2009 said they were concerned about terrorism and terrorist attacks, though 13 per cent worried about unemployment and about 'neighbourhood safety'.[43] Alongside the concern about the threat 'Muslims' posed came a recrudescence, especially in eastern Europe, of that old European malaise: anti-Semitism.

Significantly 18 per cent of those questioned in the Dutch poll said they were concerned about 'values'. For alongside this new broader sense of insecurity going well beyond a sense of physical threat came a sharpening of the perception of a 'cultural' threat. Here, unsurprisingly given the history of European relations with Islam, there were many potential flashpoints. Though some claimed otherwise, the reality remained that Muslim communities in Europe, like other faith groups on the continent, were largely much more conservative than the population in general. This, as it had done over previous years, led to repeated clashes on issues such as *burqas* and veils (in France), mosque construction (in Germany), minarets (in Switzerland), segregation and diet (pretty much everywhere). Many such rows were either based in misunderstandings – such as over exactly what '*sharia* law' might mean – or bordered on the absurd – such as a British Muslim cook who claimed financial damages for discrimination on the basis that wearing plastic gloves and using tongs was not enough to protect him from the possibility of being spattered with pig fat while preparing pork sausages – but they were often based in genuinely different visions of what was acceptable social behaviour.[44] Though surveys revealed that local national specificities often had a much greater impact than usually thought – where adultery or pornography were generally accepted, such as in France or Germany respectively, so they were accepted by a higher proportion of local 'Muslims' – overall the views of many who described themselves as Muslims on moral questions remained much closer to those of the American religious right than the largely secular local communities among whom they lived.[45] Importantly, the long-cherished idea that younger people, the children of the immigrants, would prove to be more liberal than their parents was also proving questionable. Indeed, throughout most nations in Europe there were strong indications of a new affirmation of a Muslim religious and cultural identity among 16–24-year-olds which went beyond the simple maintenance of inherited traditions, focusing instead on outward signs of difference rather than on conventions and customs inherited from parents who had been born in Algeria, Pakistan, Turkey or wherever.[46] In many European countries, though only a small minority wore the headscarf or veil, those who did so were usually no longer following an inherited tradition but making a deliberate choice to assert their difference both from the broader community and from their parents.[47] In Holland, though mosque attendance dropped sharply and the gap between 'autochtones' and immigrants in education and the labour market narrowed, more 'people with a non-Western background' chose to move to homes in the same neighbourhoods and avoid the company of 'Westerners'.[48] In France, even as rates of intermarriage or use of French as a first language in the home continued to increase, rates of declared observance of the Ramadan fast and professed abstinence from alcohol climbed steeply too.[49] Though 48 per cent of British Muslims said they never attended a mosque, 78 per cent said their religion was 'very important' to them.[50] As polls in the UK (and elsewhere) also showed that Muslims wanted more integration not less, that Muslim populations tended to admire institutions such as parliament or the courts more than non-Muslim populations, that fewer and fewer would serve the cuisine of their parents to a visitor and that Muslims were much more likely to be part of a local sports club than of a religious association, the only conclusion was that no one tendency was dominant.[51] If integration had progressed more than was often said, it had occurred very unevenly, throwing up powerful reactions and counter currents. Though talking of a single, monolithic 'Islamic identity' or community in Europe was impossible, one strong emerging trend amid the mass of apparently conflicting data was a new affirmation of a strong and conservative cultural and religious identity among Europe's Muslims which posed, as it did in the Middle East and in south Asia and elsewhere, a significant social and political challenge for Western policy-makers.

Whatever future evolutions were likely to be, it was clear by 2009, however, that few of the darker predictions made over previous years had been realized. There had been no mass uprising. The 'European Intifada' that both Abu Musab al-Suri and right-wing commentators had predicted following the 7/7 attacks in London had not taken place. There had still been no significant follow-up to the French riots of 2005 or the cartoons crisis. There were no mini-Fallujas. 'There are six million [French] Muslims. If the community had got really radicalized it would have been pretty obvious,' noted Kamel Bechik, a thirty-five-year-old who ran a Muslim Scout organization in south-west France. At the Marché d'Aligre in Paris's twelfth arrondissement, where wealthy local Parisians go at the weekend to buy fruit and vegetables from largely Tunisian stall holders or beef from halal butchers, Amos, who was sixteen when he first ran errands for his immigrant parents on the market, pointed to his two employees – one from Algeria, the other from Morocco. One was married to a French-born Catholic, he said, the other to 'a black girl'. 'Integration? Politics? Religion? None of that here,' he said. 'We're just trying to earn a living. The only people who get involved in religion are the ones with something on their conscience.' Anis Bouabsa, the baker who supplied the presidential palace with breakfast patisserie, said he would be fasting for Ramadan while still cooking bread for his clients. 'It's my roots, my culture, that's how I grew up,' Bouabsa told the author. 'But I'll still be in the bakery twelve hours a day.'[52]

THE MAGHREB, THE MASHRIQ

If there was cause to be somewhat more sanguine in Europe, there was equal reason to be more optimistic in much of the Maghreb and the countries of the core Middle East, the Mashriq.[53] The effect of the 9/11 Wars on communities from the eastern edge of the Atlantic to the Arabian Sea had been inevitably much greater than on the nations of Europe. In the latter it had been the relatively small Muslim minorities who were at risk of being been drawn into violent extremism (plus a statistically negligible number of converts). But in the former whole populations could potentially have been radicalized, with tens of millions of people suffering the direct effects of the conflict or, in the case of Iraq, under occupation themselves. But by the summer of 2009, the wave of violence and polarization that had flowed across the region since 2001 and particularly since 2003 seemed to be very much on the ebb. Almost everywhere, Islamic militants affiliated to, or simply inspired by, al-Qaeda or its ideology were on the defensive. The turning-away from radicalism that had begun to manifest itself in 2005, 2006 and 2007 was now well consolidated. A crude measure was the level of support pollsters found for Osama bin Laden. In almost every country from Morocco to Saudi Arabia, the popularity of al-Qaeda and its leader had continued the decline it had begun three or four years earlier or at the very least remained at a relatively low level. Confidence in bin Laden 'to do the right thing in world affairs' was highest in the Palestinian territories – at more than 50 per cent – but more generally lay between the 5 and 25 per cent mark.[54]

One of the best examples of the problems faced by militant groups in the region – and there were many – was the plight of the grandly named al-Qaeda in the Maghreb. AQIM, as it became known, had been formed by the remnants of the Algerian Groupe Salafiste de Prédication et Combat (GSPC) in late 2006, and its existence and new affiliation to the al-Qaeda central leadership announced by Ayman al-Zawahiri in

January 2007. 'We pray to Allah that this [alliance] would be a thorn in the neck of the American and French crusaders and their allies, and an arrow in the heart of the French traitors and apostates,' Zawahiri said, with careful if rather outdated attention to local sentiments towards former colonial overlords. The logic behind the GSPC's decision to finally accept the various invitations of bin Laden and al-Zawahiri after many years of stubborn independence was simple.[55] The GSPC was formed from a faction that had broken away from the defunct Groupe Islamique Armée in the late 1990s as the latter disintegrated. It had, like its parent organization, had trouble gaining any popular support or legitimacy. It had also been hit badly by a series of amnesties from 1999 which had reduced its strength from several thousand to a few hundred. By 2005, the organization was split, with one half effectively using radical Islamic ideology as a cover for running a trafficking and kidnapping racket in the southern deserts and the other half, more ideologically committed, largely confined to the eastern uplands of Algeria with very limited local support and considerable difficulties in escaping the effective, if brutal, security services.[56] 'We saw the merger with al-Qaeda as giving us the breathing space we badly needed,' Abu Umar Abd al-Birr, the former head of the GSPC's media committee, later recalled. 'Faced with the national reconciliation process in Algeria, we'd no choice but to stop fighting. But with the merger we gained new authority in people's eyes: it allowed us to project an image of ourselves as a new group.'[57]

As ever, the credibility, status and resources furnished by an alliance with 'al-Qaeda central' came at a high price. The internationalization of the GSPC's campaign might have been superficially attractive as a propaganda coup which also brought valuable technological and strategic advice but it had no perceptible impact on the broad rejection of violence by Algerians generally, and, though the group now theoretically had a regional reach, genuine links with groups elsewhere in the Maghreb proved very difficult to build. One major obstacle was the simple chauvinism of the GSPC's Algerian leaders, who, after nearly three decades of fighting a local battle against local authorities, had little genuine knowledge of, or interest in, the conflicts in neighbouring countries. They had even less enthusiasm for sharing authority with anyone 'from outside'.[58] Desultory bids to mobilize networks of supporters in Europe, particularly in France, also failed to make much progress. This disappointed the al-Qaeda senior leadership, who had seen the alliance with the GSPC as a way of acquiring a network in Europe that might reinvigorate the campaign there and resolve their growing strategic problems on the continent. Worse for AQIM, the tactics they were encouraged to use by the al-Qaeda senior leadership proved disastrous. Though the dark years of the civil war of the 1990s had seen appalling atrocities, Algeria had never previously seen suicide bombers nor massive bombings with the very visible civilian 'collateral damage' they inevitably caused. Successive attacks on government buildings, the United Nations offices, police stations and a range of other civilian targets between April 2007 and August 2008 killed large numbers of ordinary Algerians, provoked redoubled efforts on the part of Algiers' security services and did nothing to endear the militants to a public that, despite their grievances against the incompetent, avaricious and undemocratic government, was even less keen on violent radicalism and all it entailed than they had been a decade or so earlier.[59] Memories of where such activities led were all too fresh. Even within militant ranks such tactics were deeply controversial and prompted a number of defections. One mid-ranking leader who left the group after the April 2007 bombings in Algiers explained that his decision stemmed from the complaints of his comrades-in-arms about 'carrying out suicide operations, shedding the blood of innocents in public places'. Another, charged with enforcing the application of *sharia* law in one area where the group was fighting, opposed the use of such tactics, because Algeria was not occupied by foreign infidel forces as Iraq and Afghanistan were.[60] Attempts to 'relocalize' the AQIM's agenda by invoking the name of very specific historical figures such as Tariq bin Ziyadh, the Berber general who led Muslim forces in the conquest of Spain in 711, looked merely clumsy.[61] By 2009, though occasional attacks continued, no one could pretend that AQIM were a significant force.[62] For one British security official, the spate of attacks in 2007 and 2008 and the GSPC's alliance with al-Qaeda was the 'dead cat bounce' of Algerian militancy.[63] The comment may have been premature – cats have nine lives after all – but was not entirely unjustified.[64]

The same could be said for many of the other militant groups which had looked to be such a threat four or five years earlier. Egypt had always been, politically and culturally as well as geographically, the keystone in the arch of Arab Muslim-majority states spanning the north African shoreline to west Asia. It had been where many of the new modern revivalist ideas that had emerged in response to Western colonialism in the Islamic world had first been synthesized and articulated in the late nineteenth century and where the first major Islamist movement – the Muslim Brotherhood – had been founded in 1928. Through the later twentieth century too, Egypt had set the ideological tone for much of the region. From the revolution of 1952 and the subsequent rule of Gamal Abdel Nassr and on through the decades of the domination of socialist, nationalist and pan-Arabist ideas, the example of what the Egyptians were doing or thinking had been crucial to developments elsewhere in the Middle East and beyond. So too was the emergence of Islamism as an ideological alternative, an opposition movement and discourse of dissent in the country in the wake of the 1967 and 1973 wars with Israel. The Islamic militant violence of the 1980s and 1990s had played a crucial role in forging the fundamentals for the new global vision and strategy of al-Qaeda and its like. It had been the course of the militancy in Egypt that had revealed so much about the reality of such activism, its strengths and weaknesses, and it was, of course, from Egypt that much of the al-Qaeda senior leadership had come. The country, ruled by President Hosni Mubarak since 1981, was also representative of so many other repressive, incompetent and unyielding governments in the region. Seen historically by Washington as the key to local stability, Egypt had received more than $60 billion of American aid since signing the 1979 peace treaty with Israel. It was on Egypt too that the Bush administration's 'Freedom Agenda' had, for a brief moment, been focused and it was, of course, in Cairo that Condoleezza Rice had spoken of how America had too long preferred stability in the region to democracy in her speech in June 2005.[65]

Egypt was representative of the region economically too. Despite the growth towards the end of the decade due to radical liberal economic measures, food prices had continued to rise rapidly, with inflation reaching 25 per cent in 2007.[66] While new gated communities were constructed with fountains in the desert outside major cities, millions went without running water. Corruption was endemic. Especially for the 29 per cent of the country between fifteen and thirty years old, life remained tough. Crammed into insalubrious, poorly maintained apartments, with a desperate daily struggle for basic services let alone decent employment, the young had very few prospects. Graduates drove taxis or ran shops. The average age for marriage had crept steadily up as the expense incurred and the shortage of homes made even as basic an act as forming a couple and having children extremely difficult. As elsewhere too, particularly among the lower middle class and parts of the working classes, a new social and religious conservatism was more and more evident among a population long known for relative tolerance, moderation and a disdain for purely ritual devotion. One national survey found that 10–29-year-olds claimed to spend an average of forty minutes every day on religious devotions, and by far the most popular ringtone on the now ubiquitous mobile phone was the call to prayer. In one revealing incident the transport minister had to resign after eighteen died in a train crash caused by a signalman who left his post to pray. In 1986, there had been one mosque for every 6,031 Egyptians, according to government statistics. By 2005, there was one mosque for every 745 people – and the population has nearly doubled.[67] As elsewhere too, anti-Americanism in Egypt remained at a historically high level. Nonetheless, none of this translated directly into any backing for renewed Islamic militant violence. After the attacks of 2004, 2005 and 2006 in the Sinai, Egypt had remained relatively untroubled by violent radicalism. Though support for Islamism as a political doctrine remained significant and the radicals' single narrative had been integrated into the fundamental worldview of tens of millions, only a very few became involved in extremism.[68] Undoubtedly the vicious efficiency of the experienced Egyptian security services was a factor, but so too were the trends evident elsewhere in the Middle East and the Maghreb. Support for suicide bombing in Egypt had dropped from around 33 to 8 per cent after the wave of attacks in the middle of the decade before stabilizing at around 15 per cent.[69] When bin Laden and al-Zawahiri attempted to create an 'al-Qaeda in the land of Egypt' towards the end of 2007, they had failed ignominiously. The man chosen to lead the new group, a veteran of the violence of the 1990s who had been based in the FATA since 2001, was unable to convince those few former associates he was able to contact to become involved. The fact that many such approaches took place online did not help. Nor did his death in a drone strike in August 2008.[70]

A similar situation to that in Egypt prevailed in Morocco, where the young Mohammed VI, dubbed 'His Ma-Jet Ski' following reports of playboy antics, was attempting a hugely ambitious infrastructural and social 'great leap forward' all while retaining a grip on power in the face of a similarly rising social and cultural conservatism among, in particular, the lower and newly urbanized middle classes. 'We are in the middle of trying something that lots of people have said is impossible. It is absolutely essential that we make it work ... I don't even want to imagine the consequences if we fail,' Mohammed el'Ghass, the minister for youth, told the author in an interview in his immense office in the capital, Rabat.[71] Walking through the housing estates and commercial streets of towns like Salé, just outside Rabat, where all women wore scarves and maintained strict segregation as they waited for the over-crowded buses, made clear how, as in Pakistan and elsewhere, it was the lower middle classes who were driving the new trend of non-violent moderate or mild Islamist activism coupled with a renewed reassertion of a religious identity. In Morocco too, as in Pakistan, the dynamics were intertwined with cultural issues. The Islamists – such as Abdelwa-hed Motawakil, the secretary general of 'the Union of Faith and Social Charity' – preferred to speak English as an alternative to Arabic when interviewed rather than French, the language of the elite and the former colonial rulers. El'Ghass, like most ministers, preferred the latter.[72] At elections in late 2007, the biggest and most moderate Islamist party had won forty-seven out of 325 seats, coming second only to the main regime-sponsored secular nationalist party. Even this relatively impres-sive result was largely seen as disappointing, and officials of the Justice and Development Party blamed a record low turn-out and rigging. Local and international commentators argued that it was in fact the more radical Islamist groups – such as that led by Motawakil – which had boycotted the poll that were its true beneficiaries.[73] Yet though there had been several further spasms of violence including new suicide bombings, by the end of 2008, it was clear that the fears of a major internal insurrection or of Morocco becoming a launching pad for sys-tematic Islamic militant assault on Europe were very unlikely to be realized.

Close parallels with developments in Morocco and Egypt could be found too in Libya. There, again despite a range of political circum-stances and social and economic conditions very similar to those in neighbouring countries, militants were also very much on the back foot. Networks formed to send volunteers to Iraq and to fight the regime had been repeatedly broken up between 2004 and 2006. In 2007, there had been disturbances and rioting in the poor coastal cities of Benghazi and Darnah. But since then there had been no real sign of militant activity, let along widespread extremism.[74] The leadership of the Libyan Islamic Fighting Group remained split between firebrand radicals who had chosen to remain in Afghanistan or Pakistan after the war of 2001 and an imprisoned local leadership. While the former faction claimed that the LIFG was now part of al-Qaeda and was increasingly visible among the upper ranks of bin Laden's organization, the latter rejected violence entirely, publishing in July 2009 a 417-page document which argued that 'arms are not for use to ... bring about change in Muslim countries'. This was perhaps the most exhaustive scholarly repudiation of jihadi doctrine by former militants yet seen in the 9/11 Wars.[75] There was plenty of resentment and discontent at the rule of Muammar Gaddafi – whispered carefully to the author by waiters, taxi drivers, students, professionals and even archaeologists in Tripoli during celebrations in September 2007 of the thirty-eighth anniversary of the military coup that had brought the Supreme Guide of the Revolution to power – but it was not being channelled into radical Islam.[76]

In Jordan, in Syria and in the Levant too, it was the same story: the peak of Islamic militancy appeared to have passed.[77] In the Lebanon, the most notable incident of violence associated with radical Sunni militancy, the uprising of the Fatah al-Islam in the Nahr al-Bared Palestinian refugee camp of May 2007, had not been repeated. In neighbouring states too, support for the violent extremists had dropped, as elsewhere sublimated to some extent into a new social conservatism and increased support for the more classic political Islamism of the Muslim Brotherhood and its various offshoots.[78] In Jordan, where before the hotel bombings in Amman in November 2005 support for suicide bombing (outside Israel-Palestine) stood at 57 per cent, this figure had declined to just 12 per cent by 2009.[79] One of the most interesting and revealing incidents came in the Gaza Strip in August 2009, when Hamas launched a bloody military operation against one of a number of emerging pro-al-Qaeda groups.[80] The latter were few in number, and their support depended very heavily on local tribal or clan dynamics, but nonetheless Hamas felt it necessary to direct the full force of their security apparatus against them. Twenty-four 'Jund Ansar Allah' fighters were killed when the Ibn Tamiyya mosque in Rafah, the city on the Egyptian border with Gaza, was stormed in perhaps the biggest direct armed confrontation between forces loyal to a local political Islamist organization and Salafi jihadists for many years.[81] Again, if anyone in the region was benefiting from the polarization caused by the previous years' violence it was the Muslim Brotherhood and its offshoots, not the extremists loyal to, or inspired by, bin Laden.

A final example of the failure of al-Qaeda to successfully provoke a conflict or to lever local conditions and tensions in the Middle East was Saudi Arabia. The first signs of the strategic defeat of al-Qaeda in the Arabian peninsula had, as elsewhere, in Europe and much of the Islamic world, been evident by the middle of the decade, as previous chapters described. By the summer of 2009, militancy in Saudi Arabia was still a problem but not one that threatened in any way to destabilize the state. The storm of 2003 to 2004 had apparently been weathered, and as early as April 2007, the Saudi militants' own *Sawt al-Jihad* publication had glumly noted that 'none of the Jihadi fronts were deserted as much as the Jihadi front in the Arabian peninsula.'[82] Successive waves of arrests were announced, but the high numbers involved – 701 terrorist-related detainees in one single sweep, according to a single communiqué of June 2008 – owed more to the authorities' desire to maintain a useful level of anxiety and thus vigilance among the general population and to continue to attract support for the House of al-Saud as the guarantor of local order against the extremists than anything else.[83] Certainly, the jihadi effort in Saudi Arabia had singularly failed to split the religious establishment of the kingdom – indeed it had rather unified clerics behind the regime – or to garner any real popular support. Though cash continued to flow to extremist organizations and charities engaged in activities overseas, polls in December 2007 put the level of Saudi Arabian citizens viewing bin Laden favourably at 15 per cent, one of the lowest levels in the entire region.[84] At the same time a series of effective policies had squeezed the militants' resources. Authorities had progressively filled the many loopholes in the charitable and financial sectors that had enabled the militants to obtain funds, cracked down on the previously extensive illegal arms market and increased border control, making explosives and detonators more difficult to procure. A series of month-long general amnesties, in part inspired by the Algerian example, had also helped thin militant ranks, as did discreet mediation initiatives involving influential clerics with radical credentials. Considerable resources continued to be devoted to a media campaign aimed at bolstering the now broad consensus in the kingdom that the militants were terrorists – a 'misguided sect' as they were called in official media.[85] A further useful measure was the sacking of over a thousand of the more radical imams and the retraining of tens of thousands more.[86]

But anyone searching for signs of a genuine spirit of liberal reform among rulers in Riyadh or among the population more generally would be disappointed. Those governing Saudi Arabia had long recognized that their survival depended to a significant extent on a skilful balancing of the demands of Western interlocutors and the inherent conservatism of most of the people they governed. Changes such as allowing the occasional risqué satire or the creation of an effectively secular national holiday to celebrate the 1932 unification of the country (to the dismay of irritated conservatives, who insisted that Islam forbids anything but religious celebrations) did not signal any great shift, significant though they were in their context. If there had been some changes to textbooks which promoted anti-Semitism and a deeply intolerant worldview, Saudi schoolchildren were nonetheless still taught that it was wrong to say hello to non-Muslims.[87] As the threat from militants internally had subsided and the memory of the 9/11 attacks receded, so the reform process, which had appeared at one time to be picking up some small momentum, slowed.[88] Nor did there appear to be any significant lessening of the efforts made by Saudi religious establishments and private individuals to further the spread of rigorous Salafist Islam, largely at the expense of broader, less dogmatic and more moderate strands of practice, across the Islamic world. Such proselytism was carefully differentiated from the violent ideologies of bin Laden and his kind and had been an integral part of the kingdom's foreign policy – originally to counter the influence of Shia Iran and Communism – since the early 1980s. It had been part of the deal struck by the house of al-Saud with the 'Ikhwan' religious warriors whose swords, guns and faith had brought them to power in the Arabian peninsula. Despite the contradictions inherent in a deeply conservative country bankrolling and directing a programme of religious preaching and teaching that had revolutionary effects, such as changing how tens of millions worshipped across much of the Islamic world, the fundamentals of the grand bargain which underpinned the structure of the kingdom remained unquestioned.

By the summer of 2009, however, the vast proportion of militants in the Arabian peninsula were based in the Yemen, not active in the strategically crucial Saudi Arabia. The growing prominence of the Yemen and to a lesser extent east Africa, where the 'al-Shabab' movement had broken away from the Islamic Courts Union in Somalia to pursue an increasingly radical agenda, was sometimes taken as evidence of the protean indestructibility of contemporary Islamic militancy. Instead, it showed the extent to which, by 2009, radical activism had been marginalized geographically as well as socially, politically and culturally across almost the entire Middle East.[89] Then, of course, there was Iraq.

IRAQ: AN UGLY PEACE

By around 5 a.m. in Baghdad in the pre-Ramadan weeks of August 2008, the temperature had dipped to a still brutal 33 degrees, and the city began to wake. In the poor working-class Shia areas, small knots of the faithful walked through the rubbish-strewn streets to morning prayers, and the bakers, no longer working with an AK-47 by their sides as had been the case during the worst of the civil war, began to pound their dough and stoke their ovens. As the first rays of sunlight slanted across the city, the taxis began to circulate, and those who had been sleeping on the roofs of their apartments to escape the heat stowed their bedding. Another day was beginning. The lights of the Green Zone, as bright as ever during the night in a city with patchy electricity, faded into the bright early morning.

By 7 a.m. there was heavy traffic on the roads, choked around the barricades, the checkpoints, the gaps in the blast walls, stalled in long lines on the bridges over the Tigris. The queues were growing outside the petrol stations. Children played football on patches of wasteland before the heat and school. On Mutanabi Street, as they had under Saddam, booksellers were laying out their wares, a greater range of publications than anyone could have dreamed of under the dictator. Soon the officials were arriving in the ministries, unlikely to stay much longer than a few hours. One was Abu Mujahed, the insurgent whom the author had interviewed back in 2004 and whose formation of 'resistance cells' to lay mines for American convoys or mortar their bases featured in Chapter 6. Abu Mujahed had not only stayed alive but had kept his job in his ministry through all the upheavals of subsequent years. A year after the invasion, he could no longer afford a chicken for his family's dinner. Now, with a raised salary, he was relatively comfortable. By ten o'clock, he and the office workers and bureaucrats were sipping tea at their desks, and the shops were opening too, shutters clattering up where there were any and awnings pulled down to provide some shade. For an hour or so, there was life in Sadr City, the vast and overcrowded poor Shia suburb in eastern Baghdad and the site of heavy fighting only a few months before, as housewives in black chadors clustered around vegetable sellers haggling over the price of aubergines and tomatoes and toddlers played with makeshift toys in the dust and dirt. By late morning, with the temperature climbing, the streets emptied, the stall-holders and the police and soldiers on the checkpoint fled the blinding white light of midday, the football players disappeared, and the city settled to wait out the long, harsh afternoon.

In the evening, as the sun began to dip, life returned to the streets. The traffic choked once again at the checkpoints. In the upmarket central Karada neighbourhood, where barber Jaffar had reopened his shop after returning to Baghdad after eighteen months in Jordan, the pavements filled with shoppers inspecting windows of shops selling furniture and white goods. Jaffar's own barber shop, newly refurbished, was full. On days after bombings, few chanced his ground-floor salon with its open glass windows, but as there had been a week's calm, business was good. Near by, new cars dropped off wealthy families in front of newly opened restaurants. On Abu Nawas Street by the Tigris, cafés served the traditional grilled fish and beer to groups of men, and couples walked through the nearby park along the riverside. Across the city, a thousand games of football were underway. By late evening, the promenaders, who had grown more numerous as the temperatures dropped, began to thin. A few revellers sought further entertainment. Most went home before the midnight curfew, and for the first four hours of the next day the streets were empty but for the patrols until, finally, at 4 a.m., as the eastern sky began to lighten, the bakers and the faithful once more headed out, and the roof sleepers again rolled up their bedding and set a pot to boil water for tea.

The Iraq of 2009 was not that of 2008 and was profoundly different from that of 2007. Each year had seen a new combination of the kaleidoscope of different elements, internal and external, that determined the overall evolution of the battered country. None of the successive Iraqs were 'very pretty', as one US State Department official who had rotated in and out of Baghdad over the previous thirty-six months commented. 'We are talking degrees of ugliness,' he explained. 'And the degree of ugliness today is a bit less ugly than yesterday.' [90]

For compared to what had gone before, it was difficult to argue that the situation in Iraq had not improved. The country was more fragmented than perhaps it had ever been, split along ethnic, sectarian and political lines, with significant external interference, rampant corruption, patchy rule of law, deep poverty, poor security and high levels of criminal, political and extremist violence but, eighteen months after the first of the American troops that had been deployed for the Surge had begun to pull out, there were few who still predicted the imminent catastrophic collapse of order in the country. Indeed, those looking at Iraq from Washington or London, and there were a diminishing number of them, given the focus on the deteriorating situation in Afghanistan and Pakistan, saw something that was beginning to resemble the 'messy, sloppy status quo' that the then Senator Obama had described back in April 2008 as an acceptable endstate for the US mission there. 'If we had presented the Iraq of today in a Powerpoint five years ago and said this is what you get for a trillion dollars: four thousand dead American servicemen and women and pretty much all our diplomatic capital in the Arab world, the Islamic world and beyond, then I don't suppose anyone would have been particularly impressed,' a State Department official said. 'But we are ... where we are. And where we are is better than where we were.'[91]

If the situation in Iraq in 2009 was undoubtedly better than it had been two or three years previously, it was much more difficult to be sure that any progress would be maintained in the future. Iraq had stepped back from the brink, but quite what happened next was still very unclear. The optimistic scenario saw the country treading a slow, haphazard but steady path towards relative stability and prosperity, gradually resolving the thorny outstanding issues such as the sharing of its immense oil wealth between its various communities, the contested status of the northern city of Kirkuk, its exact relationship with neighbours like Iran, Syria and Saudi Arabia and how to integrate its Sunni minority into a majority Shia state. The pessimistic scenario saw a gradual loss of all the ground made up since 2007, accelerating violence, a resurgent al-Qaeda, a new civil war and worse chaos than ever previously seen. The two divergent paths naturally started from the same point: the precarious fragility of the immediate post-Surge period.

The critical period in consolidating the gains made during the Surge had been the long year from the end of operations in November 2007 through to the provincial elections of January 2009. As discussed in Chapter 11, critical to the success of the Surge had been four major factors: the effective victory of the Shias in the civil war and the resultant redundancy of Muqtada al-Sadr's al-Mahdi Army as well as the organization's internal problems; the 'Awakening' of the Sunni tribes; the continuing structural weaknesses of al-Qaeda in Iraq; and the actions of regional powers. Since the end of the Surge, two of these major trends had definitively progressed in a positive direction, deepening and broadening, contributing enormously to the relative stabilization of the situation. A third, the continued interference in Iraq by its neighbours, did not immediately look likely to send the country back to the cusp of total breakdown. The evolution of the fourth, the retreat of the jihadi militants, was harder to chart.

The effective collapse of the al-Mahdi Army as a fighting and social force had been evident within months of the end of the Surge. Its authority, coherence and legitimacy had already been undermined by indiscipline, criminality and growing interference from Tehran. With the threat in Baghdad from Sunni death squads greatly reduced, the militia's role as protector of Shia communities had disappeared and with it much of its popular support. In a series of rolling offensives ordered by Prime Minister Nouri al-Maliki through the spring of 2008, first Basra and the smaller southern cities and then Sadr City in Baghdad were all retaken by government security forces backed by American airpower and logistics. Fragmented, discredited and with its leader in self-imposed exile in the holy city of Qom in Iran, the al-Mahdi Army was unable to sustain any serious resistance, losing up to 1,000 fighters by May 2008.[92] The force was soon effectively 'stood down', and within weeks its authority had evaporated even in those former strongholds where it had retained a presence. The tens of thousands of young men who had joined al-Sadr's organization over previous years remained in their homes or on the street, but the balance of power had clearly shifted. 'The Iraqi government broke their branches and took down their tree,' Abu Amjad, a civil servant in the northern Baghdad district of Sadr City said.[93] Radical Shia groups, some trained, equipped and directed by elements within the Iranian Revolutionary Guards, continued campaigns of violence and intimidation in much of the south and were still present, if less active, in Baghdad, and al-Sadr, who appeared to be hoping to convert the mass militia he once led into a political and cultural movement with an armed wing along the lines of Lebanon's Hezbollah, still retained the loyalty and even adulation of a significant portion of young, poor, working-class, urban Shia men. 'Moqtada al-Sadr is a great man and a perfect leader, and without him all the Shia in Iraq would have been killed or live their lives oppressed and humiliated, and Iraq would have been destroyed by the occupiers and al-Qaeda,' said Qahtan Ali Hussein, a twenty-four-year-old al-Mahdi Army fighter.[94] But the days of major street battles with American or Iraqi security forces seemed to be definitively over. The Friday prayers and sermons that had once seen frenzied demonstrations of support for the young cleric still drew big crowds but were now quieter affairs. In the areas they had once controlled, the al-Mahdi Army's strictures on Western haircuts, dress and music were no longer enforced or obeyed. Local leaders no longer received their protection money, and the lucrative rackets the Army had run had disintegrated. 'I can buy [cooking] gas for a tenth of what it was, I can listen to what I want to, I don't have to hide my trade either,' said Jaffar, the barber.[95] Marginalized politically, former al-Mahdi Army fighters turned on those marginalized socially, attacking, torturing and killing hundreds of local homosexuals.[96]

A measure of stability, it had been frequently said, would come to Iraq when the Shia had recognized they were the winners and the Sunni minority understood they were the losers in the deposition of Saddam Hussein and the civil conflict that had followed. The Awakening, which had seen the Sunni tribes of Anbar and eventually Baghdad and surrounding provinces join with the Americans against al-Qaeda-affiliated or inspired groups, had been rooted in part in the realization that continuing resistance to either foreign occupying forces or the demographically stronger Shia community was likely to be counterproductive. Through 2008, the forlorn plight of the Sunni fighters who had turned against the religious extremists in Anbar and elsewhere underlined the degree to which the community had lost out in the fighting in 2006 and 2007. Promised jobs in the new Iraqi security forces, the 'Sons of Iraq' found themselves shut out by Iraq's predominantly Shia political leaders and largely abandoned by those they had once fought alongside. The Americans, though they pressed for more of the 130,000-odd fighters they had recruited to end up wearing Iraqi National Army or police uniforms, understood too that the government they protected neither had the will nor the means to incorporate such a large number of men, many of whom had played significant roles in the sectarian violence of previous years, into the new security forces.[97] In Anbar, former 'Sons of Iraq' had found jobs in local police forces, but in Baghdad itself or in provinces like Diyala they were largely left to their own devices, their salaries paid late if at all, their relatives regularly targeted by those they had fought against over previous years. Without their powerful allies in the American military, the Sons of Iraq were vulnerable, and in the twelve months after the Surge, around 550 had been killed.[98] 'We became victims,' Hassan Abdel Karim, who led one Baghdad group, said with disgust.[99] Dyaa Jameil, a thirty-five-year-old member of an Awakening council from the tough Sunni Baghdad neighbourhood of al-Doura, described his and his comrades' future as 'like a dark night without the light of the moon'.[100] That these men, who had been in the vanguard of the insurgency back in 2003 and 2004, appeared to reject any return to armed resistance to the government was an indication of just how weak they judged their own position to be. In the provincial elections of January 2009, Sunnis voted, and even if the turnout in Anbar was only 40 per cent, it was still a vast improvement. Some even voted for al-Maliki, who, though a conservative Shia, had acquired some credibility as a 'national' leader through dismantling the al-Mahdi Army the previous spring. For the first time in any of the polls held since the invasion of 2003, security for the elections, which passed off relatively uneventfully, was provided by local Iraqi forces. Only 191 Iraqis were reported to have died in violence during January, the lowest monthly toll since American and British tanks had crossed the berm from Kuwait just under six years before.[101]

Optimists saw the low casualty figures as evidence that the al-Qaeda threat in Iraq was over. As ever, gauging the potential danger posed by radical Sunni jihadi extremism within Iraq was problematic – as it was more generally. Compared to the darkest days of 2004, 2005 or 2006, when 'al-Qaeda in the Land of the Two Rivers', or al-Qaeda in Iraq (AQI), had posed a genuine strategic threat to Iraq and to the region, the situation in 2009 was undoubtedly much improved. The Islamic State of Iraq (ISI), the successor of AQI, had failed in its core project of establishing a local bridgehead from which to wage a campaign to create a new caliphate in the Middle East.[102] Even within Iraq, the capabilities of the jihadi militants had been much reduced. Though the narrative of global jihad continued to draw some foreign volunteers, the numbers were negligible compared to the earlier period of 2003 to 2006. As in the Middle East more generally, the Islamic militants in Iraq had been geographically marginalized, forced successively out of Anbar and Baghdad, then out of the densely populated semi-agricultural zones around the city where they had once been well implanted, and finally restricted to Nineveh province in the north-west. The extremist groups were scattered and fragmented and had suffered significant casualties; their senior and middle-level operatives had been decimated by the increasingly sophisticated and effective American-trained Iraqi special forces. The use of female suicide bombers, as well as that of the very young and the mentally ill or disabled, reinforced their loss of broad popular legitimacy.

Yet the tenacity of the 'jihadis' nonetheless surprised many observers. The evolution of radical militancy in Iraq had mirrored that in other theatres of the 9/11 Wars. The huge pressure under which the groups had existed for many years had forced radical evolution. Hierarchies had been flattened, capability sacrificed for resilience, mass mobilization based on the appeal of a radical ideology had been replaced by recruitment determined by association, family links, shared tribal or other community connections. Local militants now dominated the various fragmented groups that together constituted the phenomenon of al-Qaeda-style militancy in Iraq.[103] In Mosul, the capital of Nineveh province and a metropolis with a population of 1.8 million, a variety of specific local conditions had been leveraged by the extremists to secure a base.[104] Chief amongst them was the ongoing tension between the newly confident Kurds and the large local Sunni Arab community, which allowed the extremists to fulfil the same role as in the early days in Anbar and Baghdad, posing as protectors of the latter against the former. With limited rule of law in the city, there were few alternatives for Sunnis scared of losing their homes and livelihoods other than to turn to the militant groups. Another factor helping the militants was the city's geographic position astride the trails that led through the desert from the Syrian border. These allowed extremist groups both to receive supplies from over the frontier and, crucially, to build mutually beneficial relationships with local tribes which had long earned their living from smuggling.[105] Avoiding the errors of the 2003 to 2006 period, the extremists cooperated with local sheikhs rather than trying to appropriate their businesses. Finally, as Mosul had been home to a high number of Ba'athist former army officers who themselves had taken up arms against the Americans and the Baghdad government and continued to be responsible for the bulk of attacks on government or American forces in the area, the extremists found willing allies on the ground.[106] The steady ideological convergence between the once aggressively secular Ba'athists and the 'jihadis' also helped smooth relations. And despite successive operations by Iraqi security forces, which the militants tended simply to avoid confronting, and the election of a hardline Sunni chauvinist provincial government and governor, Nineveh province remained 'bandit country' throughout 2008 and 2009. It thus constituted the single most significant base of violent radical activism between Morocco and the Afghan–Iranian border. Western intelligence services judged the threat that this base posed to be 'relatively restricted', pointing out that the militants based there showed little interest in exporting violence overseas. However, as repeated statements by local extremist strategists made clear, the Iraqi extremists' aim was not to wage 'international jihad' immediately but to plunge their country into chaos to allow them to take power, establish an 'Islamic state' and then launch such global operations on a large stage at a later stage, if they were necessary. The al-Qaeda-linked groups demonstrated that they retained significant capabilities despite the pressure on them with a series of massive and technically sophisticated bombs directed at ministries, hotels, embassies and Shia targets through the summer of 2009.

There were other reasons to fear that the more pessimistic scenarios for the future of Iraq might be realized. A close analysis of voting patterns in January's provincial elections also showed that the divisions of Iraqi society remained very deep indeed. Though sectarian parties had suffered major losses at polls – in Baghdad the coalition led by the Shia Islamic Supreme Council of Iraq took just 5.4 per cent of the vote, compared to 39 per cent in 2005 and lost heavily in the Shia religious heartlands of Najaf and Karbala – they had been punished more for their failure to deliver basic governance and services than for their chauvinist rhetoric or their championing of one particular community's interests.[107] Most Iraqis continued to be deeply sectarian in their political and social lives. The taxis that plied Baghdad streets might have given the impression of a bustling, cosmopolitan city, but Shia drivers kept to Shia areas and Shia clients, and their Sunni counterparts did the same. Sect and ethnicity were the primary determinants of political allegiance. The evident nationalism of many Iraqis did not imply any enthusiasm for genuine pluralism.

Nor did the new stability mean a new tolerance or moderation. By 2009, a new social conservatism – a parallel of that elsewhere in the Islamic world and among Muslim communities in Europe – was also evident in Iraq. Few women in Baghdad and none in Basra or in conservative places like Anbar or Diyala ever went unveiled. The degree to which this was enforced or voluntary was very difficult to determine, but those out drinking on Abu Nawas Street, despite the attention they attracted from Western reporters, were a small minority. Those patronizing the new nightclubs were even less representative. 'I do not go to the [cafés on the] banks of the Tigris, I go to mosques,' said Alyaa Ali, a sixty-five-year-old housewife from Shia Shu'laa in north-west Baghdad. Many looked more to their own cultural traditions and a newly assertive religious identity than to values and ideologies that had been tainted by association with occupiers or those who had profited from the invasion and deposition of Saddam. 'To relax I visit the holy shrines in Najaf and Karbala,' said Qahtan Ali Hussein, the al-Mahdi Army fighter. Posters of Shia heroes plastered over streets and government offices, religious music played from police radios, religious flags flying over government buildings and massive attendance at religious festivals gave the impression of a full-scale cultural revival, at least among the country's Shia. In Basra, the number of 'honour killings' almost doubled in the single year of 2008.[108]

So the apparent normality of the daily routine was deceptive. Life for most in Baghdad remained extremely tough. In a city where a bit of bad luck, an illness, an accident, the wrong word spoken in anger to the wrong person was enough to send a household spiralling downwards into poverty, those living in deep deprivation did not constitute a static population but a shifting and mobile one. The rate of inflation – a litre of petrol that once cost 20 dinars was now 500 dinars (about 25p or 35 American cents), a bottle of cooking gas was 20,000 dinars – was enough by itself to strip millions of a decent standard of living. Nearly 80 per cent of households depended on the monthly food ration from the government for their basic needs, but nearly half received the supplies only intermittently. Malnutrition, in a country with vast oil reserves, was rife. Millions who had been forced to flee their homes during the civil war remained in over-crowded temporary accommodation, often without any but the most basic facilities. By 2009, Iraq was generating more than 6,000 megawatts of electricity as against a pre-war maximum of around 4,000, but this still meant a third of households across the country still only had power for three hours or less per day.[109] No electricity meant no refrigeration, no fans and often no water because there was no power for pumps. In rural areas it often meant no irrigation either. For the poorest, a lack of electricity made little difference. Between a quarter and a third of the population were without any access to drinking water whatever, and nearly two-thirds of the population simply dumped untreated solid waste on open land.[110] 'We do not have a sewage system so we discharge our wastewater into a pit beside the house and then into the street once it is full. We do this with our own hands,' Jameela, a fifty-year-old widow from Najaf who sold incense and candles to mourners in a local cemetery to support her mentally disturbed son, told researchers from Oxfam, the British NGO.[111] Healthcare was at best rudimentary. The streets of every city were still full of checkpoints, barricades, barbed wire, blast walls, for, though it had dropped, the overall level of violence was still appallingly high.[112] Iraq was in the paradoxical position of suffering more deaths from terrorist attacks than any other country in the world while no longer being seen as a major theatre of conflict.[113] One worrying trend was that the violence, having dropped to around half of that in 2008 by the late spring of 2009, then stayed at the same level.[114] Ramadan in 2009 brought little celebration. August alone – the holy month started on the 21st – saw between 400 and 500 dead and at least 2,000 injured in more than 40 bombings. In September, the American vice president, Joe Biden, made his second visit to Baghdad in as many months, greeted by insurgents firing mortars and rockets into the Green Zone. A few days earlier, bombs near Mosul had killed dozens in a Kurdish village. Biden pledged that the US would keep to the schedule of ending the US 'combat mission' in Iraq by the end of August 2010 and withdrawing all US forces by the end of 2011. His comments attracted little attention. Many Iraqis had other concerns. 'Life in Baghdad is miserable. It is thirty-nine degrees centigrade and we get electricity one or two hours per day. When we get any water, it is not fit for human consumption. The children get sick,' said Amal Kamel, the twenty-year-old economy and administration student. 'I am not proud of my country.'[115]

16

'AfPak' 2009–10

AFGHAN ENDGAME

Captain José Vasquez, the commanding officer of Cherokee Company of the 371st Cavalry Squadron, wiped his mouth with the back of his hand, stowed the bottle of water in his backpack, checked his map, looked up at the dusty road and waved his men forward. To his right ten Americans and twenty soldiers from the Afghan National Army left the trees where they had been resting and rose to their feet and moved out across the empty fields. To his left another similar group, a few moments earlier lying prone beside the bank of an irrigation channel, also moved on. A radio crackled, a soldier swore as he filled his boots with water by slipping into a stream, two crows croaked loudly before flying off, beating heavy wings, black against the blue sky.

Baghdad, where Vasquez had done two tours, had been hotter in every sense of the word, the twenty-nine-year-old from El Paso, Texas, said. The ambushes had involved more attackers, and the temperatures had been higher. 'There were just a whole lot more people wanting to fight you,' he said. 'And we just cooked in the summer.' His unit, now attached to the 10th Mountain Division, had been scheduled to return to the Iraqi capital in January 2009. Just before their deployment, however, the orders had been changed, and instead of patrolling the streets of Sadr City Vasquez and 5,000 others were now spread out over the mountains and plains of Afghanistan's Logar and Wardak provinces. For years international forces had maintained a minimal presence in both, despite their critical location to the south and south-east of Kabul. Vasquez was part of a new belated effort, ordered in the last weeks of the Bush presidency, to change the tide of the war in Afghanistan.

On this last day of a three-day operation, though, there had still been no contact with the insurgents. The American-led force – 116 strong in all, with Mrap semi-armoured anti-IED trucks, planes and drones overhead, the ability to call in artillery bombardments from the main base a dozen miles away, biometric testing kits, road accident hazard signs, an embedded military intelligence unit – had met no one but local farmers, villagers on bicycles, school children and the occasional elder. 'When we come out in force they don't like to play. They are ballsy . . . but not stupid,' Vasquez explained. The reception from local people to the soldiers had been determinedly neutral: desultory *salaams* in response to slightly tired greetings, a nod from a shepherd, a brief conversation with a local mullah. An effusive invitation to tea, politely declined, came from a wealthier local merchant suspected of being part of the support structure for a village's insurgents. 'We know when the bad guys are here because, when they're around, everyone kind of stays away from us,' said Vasquez. Over three days he and his men crossed from neutral to hostile territory and back a hundred times, he added. There was little friendly terrain. 'This side of the creek is OK, they don't like getting involved. On the other side they love getting involved, just not on our side unfortunately. And they have a lot of RPGs.'

Vasquez was, for 2009, the very model of a modern infantry officer. Laconic, calm, experienced and better equipped, fed, based and supported than possibly any fighting soldier for decades, he stopped his men from walking through the overgrown cemetery grounds outside villages, refused to take on Taliban targets when they appeared at the edge of an inhabited compound for fear of civilian casualties despite the gung-ho enthusiasm of his tobacco-chewing rooky lieutenant, tried to convince the Afghan troops that you shouldn't get the people whose houses you were searching to make you tea. In the village of Yusuf Khel, a typical jumble of narrow passages and low mud walls between compounds, Vasquez listened patiently to local elders complain about local police confiscating their mobile phones and motorbikes. Asked what the community needed, the elders conferred and requested grain, a useful compromise between something big like a road or a well which would have caused problems with local insurgents and nothing at all. 'I am looking forward to helping this town and coming back,' Vasquez told them and tapped the fingers of his right hand against his left chest in the traditional sign of respect before turning and walking out of the village to join his men in the fields beyond. 'This tribe extends all the way to behind the mountains,' he said as the whole force moved off again, the sun now dipping towards a horizon of dry hills to the west. 'We've met a few of them. The whole tribe seem to be fence sitters. We'll see. Maybe we can do something for them. Maybe they will start helping us. Who knows?'[1]

In the spring of 2009, there were hundreds of officers like Vasquez across much of eastern and southern Afghanistan, all hiking through villages, all listening to elders, many – if not most – displaying the same mix of awareness and weariness that the veteran twenty-nine-year-old had done. The operations in Iraq's Anbar province and the subsequent success of the Surge in Baghdad, the promotion of key senior officers, the simple learned ground experience of more junior servicemen who had spent years fighting in different theatres coupled with the distribution of the 2006 COIN field manual and the broader public debate it had sparked meant that the new language of counter-insurgency was now being spoken everywhere in Afghanistan. The commanding officer of Vasquez, Colonel David Haight, also fresh from Baghdad, said his aim was 'to separate the people from the enemy'. 'I can become someone's worst enemy in a second, but that is a short-term solution. We need to bring governance, security, sustainability,' he explained. At headquarters in Kabul senior NATO staff officers displayed impressively detailed slides showing the tribal dynamics of Afghanistan, exploring historic urban–rural tensions and explaining their strategy of 'Shape, Clear, Hold, Build'. General David McKiernan, commander of NATO-ISAF since June the previous year, stressed the importance of respecting local cultural traditions, protecting the population, reducing civilian casualties and good driving.[2] 'We have learned a lot over the last few years and need to put that into practice on the ground,' McKiernan told the author, pointing out, with evident professional pique, that General David Petraeus was not the only senior American soldier involved in the evolution of the new COIN strategy and tactics.

The new doctrine required more troops, however. After successive reviews of American strategy in Afghanistan, one ordered in the last months of the Bush administration, another by Obama shortly after taking office, these had flowed in through early 2009. Vasquez had been part of the 12,000 ordered in by Bush in one of his last acts as president. Obama agreed to send another 21,000 after the second review in the late spring. In May 2009 a third review was launched when General Stanley McChrystal, the lean, intense former commander of special forces operations in Iraq, replaced McKiernan. Perhaps predictably, it too recommended a very significant increase in men, money and other resources.

Many of those forces arriving through the first six months of the year had been sent with the specific aim of securing the presidential elections in Afghanistan, scheduled for the late summer. Western strategists had anticipated a variety of potential problems with the polls. These largely revolved around potential insurgent action to disrupt the vote, the assassination of one of the principal candidates or logistic issues. In the end it was the actions of President Karzai himself, the man placed in power by Western forces in 2001 with the Bonn agreement and the favourite to win the polls, which damaged the whole exercise in the most drastic way.[3] Karzai's close supporters organized a massive fraud to avoid their candidate facing a second-round run-off with Abdullah Abdullah, the former foreign minister.[4] Over a quarter of votes, the vast bulk in Karzai's favour, had to be rejected. Each of the three American strategy reviews had stressed the critical importance of having a central Afghan government that had political legitimacy, the lack of which was felt to be undermining the whole Western project in the country.[5] Everyone, generals, politicians, diplomats, aid workers, Obama, had repeatedly insisted through the spring and early summer that successful elections were absolutely necessary to 'reinvigorate the whole project' in Afghanistan. In this, the polls abjectly failed. The massive voter registration drive hailed as such an achievement by Western governments undoubtedly reached large numbers of ordinary Afghans but also allowed somewhere around 5 million fake, duplicate or otherwise fraudulent voting cards into the system. The turnout was, despite official claims to the contrary, lower than in the previous elections even if the vast and systematic cheating made knowing the exact number of those who voted impossible. Violence, despite the deployment of all the new troops sent to secure the vote, was higher than on any other single day since the invasion. The aftermath of the poll brought little cheer either. When Karzai was eventually found to have won 49 per cent of the vote, a percentage point lower than necessary to avoid a run-off, the incumbent president refused to go to a second round and successfully retained power by default when his disgusted rival pulled out of the contest. The president's behaviour might have appeared baffling to angry and frustrated Western interlocutors but was explained relatively easily. In March, Bill Wood, the American ambassador in Kabul, had assured the author that he was certain America would remain deeply committed to Afghanistan for, if perhaps not 'the natural lifespan of the sun', then certainly for the long term. In fact, as Humayun Hamidzada, Karzai's press secretary, pointed out, no state can make even a plausible ten-year pledge unless it is a monarchy or a military dictatorship.[6] Western nations are democracies and respond to public opinion expressed at frequent elections and, as most people prefer their wars short and victorious, long-term overseas commitments win few votes. It was clear that the Western publics were increasingly unhappy about the international effort in Afghanistan. Pledges that the mistakes of the early 1990s would not be repeated and the country would not once more be abandoned by the West and Arab powers as after the war against the Soviets could thus not be trusted. Karzai was not going to sacrifice his personal interest – and that of his family, close associates and allies – to ease the task of foreign backers whose desire to leave the country and its increasingly bloody mountains, deserts and villages was more obvious with every passing day.

For, along with the new doctrines and the new troops, another major development of 2009 was the West's increasingly explicit exasperation with Afghanistan, the Afghans and efforts to stabilize and secure the country. This was true of troops on the ground – 'It would be so much easier for everyone if they would just let us help them,' complained Sergeant Amber Robinson of the 10th Mountain Division in Logar – and of policy-makers and strategists in Western capital cities.[7] In March 2009 42 per cent of respondents to one poll said the United States had made 'a mistake' in sending military forces to Afghanistan, up from 30 per cent in February. One poll in August 2009 showed that a majority of Americans saw the war in Afghanistan as not worth fighting, and just a quarter said more US troops should be sent to the country.[8] In the same month, another survey showed half of Republican congressmen and 70 per cent of Democrats were against any escalation of US commitment to the war in Afghanistan. By September, polls showed even lower levels of support among politicians and the public alike.[9] It was against this background that, after months of debate, Obama finally announced that he had made his decision on McChrystal's recommendations. The general's review, conducted by a mixed group of academics, experts and soldiers, had stressed that the reinforcements earlier in the spring had been too few to make a significant strategic difference, and the president decided to order a further reinforcement of 30,000. Other coalition members reluctantly contributed a further 5,000 over the year, and thus, by the early months of 2010, the NATO-ISAF commander in Afghanistan disposed of around 135,000 troops, seven times as many as eight years before, and with more American troops there than in Iraq for the first time. However, Obama also announced that American forces would start coming home in the summer of 2011. Though the military had asked for a commitment through to 2013, there was no way the new president was going to risk going into mid-term elections or even a campaign for a second term with an escalating war on his hands. 'I'm not doing 10 years,' Obama was reported to have told Defense Secretary Gates and Secretary of State Clinton. 'I'm not doing long-term nation-building. I am not spending a trillion dollars.'[10] Other NATO countries, also responding to public opinion that had long turned sour on the war in Afghanistan, were already imposing dates by when they would withdraw their soldiers.[11] In Paris, the French ministry of defence had appointed an admiral to look at ways of managing local public opinion. 'Selling a retreat is quite difficult,' he admitted.[12] The constant bad news, the growing casualties, the apparent complexity of the conflict, the disaster of the elections, the fact that al-Qaeda had not successfully attacked anywhere outside the Middle East or Maghreb for several years and was based, as far as anyone could tell, not in Afghanistan at all but in neighbouring Pakistan all combined to further undermine any remaining support for the war in the West. Domestic opinion was 'dynamic', of course. American backing for some kind of surge rose temporarily at the end of 2009, and internal UK government polling showed that support in Britain for the war ticked up 9 per cent when it was revealed that Prince Harry, the Queen's grandson, had been fighting in Helmand and rousing footage of the young aristocrat firing heavy weapons at invisible 'Terry Taliban' was released.[13] But the overall trend was evident to all. It was hardly surprising, therefore, that Karzai and his entourage should be sceptical of the repeated US claims of a long-term commitment.

This led to an apparently paradoxical situation: at the exact moment when the Americans, reluctantly followed by leaders such as Britain's Gordon Brown, were escalating the Western commitment to Afghanistan to levels many times greater than ever seen before – the troop increases were accompanied by a 'civilian surge' of advisers, aid workers, technicians, diplomats and others as well as a commensurate boost to development assistance and UN funding – support for the war back home was disappearing. It was in this environment that the final major development in 2009 emerged: a collective recognition on the part of Western strategists and policy-makers that a serious effort needed to be made to negotiate with at least some of the insurgents. This would have been anathema in the first six or seven years of the conflict in Afghanistan, but alarm at the seriousness of the situation in 2008 and the recognition that many of the original aims of the Western project in Afghanistan had become simply unrealizable, had led to the understanding among some analysts and diplomats that, if the West was ever going to extricate itself from Afghanistan, it would be necessary to talk, somehow to the Taliban.

In fact, various different initiatives involving 'reconciliation' had been underway for some time, all aiming in one way or another to convince those insurgents who were felt to be fighting for 'non-ideological' reasons to lay down their arms. At the lowest level, there had been an Afghan government initiative that had aimed to convince simple fighters – the so-called 'Tier Three Taliban' in NATO parlance – to hand in their weapons in return for a small sum and a guarantee of no prosecution. Assessments showed that almost none of the 5,000 or so 'fighters' who had supposedly surrendered under this programme could be reliably identified as insurgents. With its funding exhausted, it was effectively defunct. Then there had been the efforts to engage slightly higher-level Taliban, mainly leaders of groups of between a few score and a couple of hundred fighters. These 'Tier Two Taliban' had been engaged via a range of intermediaries in a variety of local initiatives. These efforts had also met with mixed success. Some had seen some partial progress, but many of the more ambitious attempts at bringing over Tier Two Taliban had gone disastrously awry. One British bid to win the loyalty of an insurgent leader in Helmand had prompted a huge political row between London and Kabul, resulting in the expulsion of the senior EU diplomat used by MI6 as an intermediary.[14] Then there were efforts directed at the senior leadership, the Tier One Taliban. One initiative by the Saudi Arabian royal family saw a group of senior former Taliban figures including Mullah Wakil Muttawakel, the former foreign minister, and Abdul Salaam Zaeef, the former ambassador to Islamabad, as well as several individuals with more direct connections to members of the 'Quetta Shura' invited to Mecca to talk over potential roles for Riyadh in any peace process. This bid to establish contacts and lever the Saudis' religious authority had gone nowhere despite logistic and diplomatic support from the British intelligence services and government.[15]

The spring of 2009 saw efforts at all levels re-energized with talks between representatives of Gulbuddin Hekmatyar and Karzai and a range of other contacts between the government and senior Taliban leaders through figures such as Maulvi Rahmani, the former deputy education minister who was also now living in Kabul. Once shunned, Muttawakel and Rahmani now regularly met a range of diplomats or other representatives of European and Middle Eastern powers as well as, more discreetly, the Americans. At the other end of the scale, commanders like Colonel Haight in Logar were meeting 'shadow councils' made up of 'all kinds of people' including active insurgents and in Helmand the creation of 'leadership councils' sponsored by the British in scores of villages in the south was allowing 'people with broad contacts among the insurgents', in the delicate formulation of one UK diplomat, to enter into dialogue with both the Kabul government and NATO-ISAF forces.[16] But there was still little real progress. William Wood, the US ambassador in Kabul, called on the insurgents to drop their key demand to talk only once foreign troops had left the country. Taliban spokesmen and intermediaries maintained their position that the occupiers must go before any political process could be engaged. The new counter-insurgency manual overseen by Petraeus advised not wasting time on 'extremists' but concentrating on 'groups with goals flexible enough to allow productive negotiations'.[17] But who would negotiate? And about what? And with whom? The idea of 'reconciliation' raised as many questions as it provided potential answers. If any such process was going to work, a significant restructuring of not just the strategy but the entire project of the international community involved in Afghanistan was going to be necessary.

The groundwork for this restructuring had been laid during the spring of 2009, when, hitherto less sceptical than their European allies about achieving 'victory', many in the American security, military and political establishments began to question basic assumptions about what was achievable in Afghanistan. A key moment was reached when senior American officials began talking about 'mitigating' rather than eliminating the Taliban threat. Bob Gates, the American defense secretary, spoke about the folly of trying to create 'Valhalla' in central Asia. The mythical and geographic references might have been a little haphazard, but the sense was clear nonetheless. Wood, the American ambassador in Kabul, spoke of how everyone, including the Americans, had been 'a bit too optimistic' in the early years of the conflict in Afghanistan as regards to what kind of country could be built. 'Certainly not your standard issue Western democracy,' he explained.[18] The new pragmatism Obama outlined in his Cairo speech and elsewhere was one driver. Another was the more generalized lack of confidence that even McChrystal's new strategy might work. 'Success is not unattainable, but I am pessimistic,' Andrew Exum, a former US army officer and veteran of Afghanistan who had been part of the team of outside experts brought in to advise McChrystal, told the author a few weeks after returning from his mission in Afghanistan.[19] Bruce Riedel, the former CIA analyst who had chaired the first Obama review, was more blunt: 'It may be that the patient was dead on arrival.'[20] Even within the White House there were very significant doubts, particularly on the part of Vice President Biden.

Through the summer and autumn of 2009 it thus became very clear that the more ambitious of the goals of the West's mission in the country were being quietly abandoned.[21] To an extent Western governments had been caught out by their own previous rhetoric, having sold a security operation as a humanitarian intervention back in 2002 and subsequently used moral and ethical arguments to bolster public support. Many ordinary people in the US, the UK and elsewhere still believed that troops were in Afghanistan, at least in part, to spread liberal, secular modern values and to protect women from the 'medieval' Taliban. Ditching all the more idealistic rhetoric and returning to a more pragmatic, security-based justification for intervention in Afghanistan was, at the very least, a delicate operation. 'Our objectives are being recalibrated in view of the circumstances,' one senior FCO official admitted privately in October 2009. In July, a month which saw twenty-two

British soldiers killed and ninety-four wounded in Helmand and seventy international troops killed across the country as a whole, the British foreign secretary, David Miliband, called for a 'long-term inclusive political settlement in Afghanistan' to draw away conservative Pashtun nationalists from the Taliban.[22] In the face of criticism from elected representatives in the UK who argued that 'it is fundamental to the rebuilding of Afghanistan that international commitments made by the Government of Afghanistan and by donors on the rights of women are honoured and given greater priority', officials pointed at the American experience in Iraq as an example of what an overly ideological approach could bring.[23] An internal review of priorities at the British aid ministry, DFID, saw 'gender equality somewhat downgraded', a second official admitted.[24] When, in August, McChrystal's review had been submitted to the president, it included, alongside the demand for 40,000 new troops, the recommendation that alternative political vehicles such as moderate Islamist parties be created for Taliban supporters and recommended that 'reconciled' insurgents be removed from the sanctions list established under UN Security Council Resolution 1267 back in 1999. Such a measure had been mentioned by many of the intermediaries such as Muttawakel or Rahmani as something important to senior insurgents and was a significant concession which British intelligence described to the author as 'probably the first step towards genuine dialogue'. By November internal memos within the British Foreign Office – shared with McChrystal's staff – were urging 'a settlement with (most of) the Quetta Shura'. The memos also proposed a *loya jirga* – or national assembly – to be held in Kabul within two years that would work on reforming the Afghan constitution and reformulating the structure laid down by the Bonn agreement of late 2001.[25] People like Sadiqa Mobariz, a Hazaran female member of the Afghan national assembly and thus exactly the sort of person who would suffer from any concessions to the conservatives, repeatedly expressed their fears of betrayal. Western politicians made little effort to allay such concerns. In January 2010, at a major conference in London the West finally declared their collective desire to 'talk to the Taliban' – or at least the 'moderates' among them. Half a billion dollars was pledged to buy off Taliban footsoldiers. A renewed – though less publicized – push to engage Taliban leaders would be made at a strategic level too. When asked in an interview days before the conference if it would be acceptable 'if all this ended with a Taliban government in Kabul committed to a *sharia* caliphate state in Afghanistan', Miliband had said his objection would be to the 'caliphate' element as that would mean an al-Qaeda link. His answer implied that a rigorous religious regime in Kabul would nonetheless be tolerated. A few days after the London conference's close, Britain's defence minister told reporters that Western powers were not seeking an 'unconditional surrender' of Taliban insurgents in Afghanistan because many could form part of a settlement'.[26] His words contrasted with statements by his predecessor, who, just over a year before, had described 'negotiating deals with the Taliban' as 'conceding defeat by another name'.[27] Though the London conference also saw a renewed pledge of support from forty-odd nations to the strategy outlined in McChrystal's review and sanctioned by Obama a month or so previously, it was obvious that the aim of the campaign of 2010 was not going to be paving the way for 'outright victory' but allowing any eventual negotiations with the insurgents to take place in a more favourable environment. No one at the conference deviated from the message about leaving behind a 'sustainable, secure' Afghanistan which would no longer pose a threat to the West but no one could conceal their impatience to close the increasingly gruelling Afghan chapter of the multi-volumed encyclopedia of the 9/11 Wars as soon as possible either.

THE TALIBAN'S VIEW

It is unlikely that any Taliban commander really did tell his interrogator the oft-repeated aphorism 'You have the watches, but we have the time', as often said. After all, most Taliban commanders did have watches – along with, by the end of 2009, an array of sophisticated military equipment that few amongst them had even heard of a few years previously. But the phrase did nonetheless sum up perfectly the point, so evident by the time of the London conference of January 2010, that to win, all insurgents in Afghanistan had to do was avoid losing.

It was still the case that many of the insurgents' problems were internal. Over the previous eighteen months the Taliban leadership in Quetta – those with whom the British FCO had suggested concluding a settlement – had continued to work hard to manage the various challenges thrown up by their successful resurgence. The insurgents were still fragmented and, though the faction led by Jalaluddin Haqqani did now liaise relatively closely with the senior leadership of the Quetta Shura Taliban, there was still almost no coordination with many other groups scattered across the country. '[Gulbuddin] Hekmatyar is a *muja-hid* and we respect him but he is independent,' a Taliban spokesman said.[28] Problems of discipline continued despite Mullah Omar's injunctions over the previous eighteen months. The *leyha* or rulebook for the Taliban was repeatedly republished and redistributed by senior leaders in a bid to curtail the more anarchic followers but seemed often to have minimal effect. When the third edition of the 'code of conduct' was released in the late spring 2009 it stated that the use of suicide bombings should be limited to high-value targets and that 'the utmost effort should be made to avoid civilian casualties'.[29] The aim, spokesmen said, was 'to guide faithful fighters in the way of the jihad to best liberate the country with minimum loss'.[30] The use of suicide bombs did drop – down from a peak of 142 in 2007, to 122 in 2008 and to around 90 in 2009 – but the use of IEDs increased, as did the number of political assassinations. The result was that the toll of civilians being killed through the actions of the insurgents continued to climb.[31] The United Nations estimated that more than two-thirds of the 6,000 non-combatants killed and injured in Afghanistan in 2009, the worst year yet for civilian casualties, were caused by the Taliban.[32] Others put the figure as high as 80 per cent.[33] Young commanders remained often difficult to control, and many Taliban 'fellow travellers' continued to ignore efforts by the hierarchy to dictate strategic directives. A wave of executions to impose order and the bureaucratic reshuffles of 2008 and 2009 had had some impact with many more senior, experienced men appointed to senior posts in the 'shadow government' and the more criminal, and often more extreme, elements being weeded out.[34] A range of efforts continued to be made to build or retain broader community support. Some involved a degree of flexibility on the rigorous codes that often alienated locals. So the new appointees frequently turned a blind eye to girls being educated, at least at primary level. Other efforts were more active. In some areas, Taliban commanders enforced limits on expenditure on weddings, a seemingly draconian measure but, in a society where the spiralling cost of marriage was forcing many men into prolonged celibacy, one that was popular, particularly among the young males whose support the Taliban most wanted. A 'commission' of high-ranking Taliban officials was appointed and travelled through various provinces to question local communities about the behaviour of local Taliban commanders.[35] Taliban propaganda operations also continued intensively, with a range of products from traditional night letters through to increasingly sophisticated DVDs or internet video clips which all carefully depicted the movement as primarily local and nationalist. When Mullah Omar rejected the talks that the Saudis, Karzai and various others were hoping to open, he did so categorically, saying 'our *mujahid* people will not accept the negotiations that will add legitimacy to the continuing occupation in their country. Afghanistan is our home, and no one accepts [these] negotiations that'll give others a share of our home and to manage it.' In a long speech devoted 'to the supporters of freedom from the people of Europe and the West in general', Omar stated:

> Your colonist rulers have attacked our country in the name of war against terrorism, and that is to serve a small number of capitalists and suckers of people's blood, in order to gain more wealth. They have built their new colonialist traps and daily they kill our youths, elderly, women and children. And at night they barge into our homes and destroy our green gardens and general property, educational and trade centers, with blind air raids. Pushing away this aggression and defending our country is our legitimate and national right, and we will use our rights to defend with all methods and sacrifices ... [against your] financial power and your satanic trickery.[36]

Though Western observers, particularly within coalition ranks, and urban, worldly Afghans saw this kind of rhetoric as a mendacious effort to disguise the Taliban's global pan-Islamist agenda by appealing to local sentiment, at least part of the appeal of the insurgents for some continued to stem from the ease with which they could appropriate the mantle of legitimate defenders of the 'Afghan' nation. The bottom line remained that the Taliban were local Muslim men fighting, on the whole, non-Muslim foreigners. As ever the propaganda was backed up with other means of persuasion. 'Spies' continued to be executed, often publicly hanged, and 'collaborators' assassinated with statements issued to justify – and publicize – the murders.[37] The combination of intimidation and 'hearts and minds' campaigns was usually effective in areas where conditions were right.

One problem that did prove insurmountable to the Taliban was the ethnic divide in the country. Despite carefully avoiding any statements that might encourage ethnic or sectarian violence, only a few low-level commanders from non-Pashtun ethnicities ever joined Taliban ranks, and these did so for the kind of micro-political reasons that had historically been so recurrent within the conflicts in Afghanistan. Attempts to push recruitment in the north of the country were successful – but only in Pashtun areas. This imposed a natural limit on the Taliban's expansion and stymied the efforts to depict the movement as a 'national uprising', as Taliban propaganda so consistently sought to do. One obvious question for all involved in the conflict at the end of 2009 and the beginning of 2010 was thus the level of support the Taliban actually had. This was impossible to quantify. The Taliban's 'commission' had been one effort to do so. The coalition and international community relied on other means, more familiar in the West, such as surveys. But pollsters faced huge practical problems, largely as a result of the parlous security situation in two-thirds of the country, and were thus limited to the urban areas, where Taliban support was lowest. Often surveys were carried out by telephone, again favouring urban literate populations. Equally, for obvious reasons, few Afghans would openly confess to supporting insurgents or their ideology. Nonetheless results in January 2010 indicating that 68 per cent of Afghans supported the presence of US forces – down from 71 per cent in 2007 and 78 per cent in 2006 but up from 63 per cent in 2008 – and that 69 per cent saw the Taliban as the main threat to the country – up 10 per cent from the year before – were probably accurate for those communities surveyed.[38]

Much more important than national statistics were support levels in the third of the country where insurgency was raging. This was even harder to gauge. Even the best-informed Western analysts in Afghanistan – specialists who had been in Kabul for decades – admitted that the international community 'had no visibility in the villages'. All they could say was that support for the insurgents in Pashtun conservative areas was 'extremely variable'.[39] It could be very high in one community and much lower on 'the other side of the creek', as Captain Vasquez had found in Logar. As ever in Afghanistan, such support was contingent on local circumstances, dynamics between tribes, the behaviour of individual families and leaders. There was still much fence-sitting. What did appear certain was that the overwhelming emphasis among Western soldiers and policy-makers on the economic roots of the insurgency seemed misplaced. At all levels within NATO and among Western diplomats and policy-makers the idea that the insurgents were fighting for money was dominant. Colonel Haight of Taskforce Spartan had said, 'Give a man a day's wage and a spade and he will put down his Kalashnikov.' Biden, the American vice president, said that 70 per cent of the Taliban had purely financial motives.[40] Miliband and others had repeatedly quoted the old Victorian-era saw that 'you can rent an Afghan, but you can't buy him', arguing that insurgents were 'rented by the Taliban'.[41] But even if such generalizations had been true when they had been coined they were of limited use a century or so later.

A study for the British Department for International Development based on hundreds of interviews with fighters found that a desire for cash was only one of a number of personal reasons which had brought young men into insurgent ranks. Often recruits sought status or a degree of protection. Frequently a desire to gain advantage in an ongoing dispute with another family or relative over land or water was critical. Even these factors themselves inevitably existed in a context defined by structural issues such as the perception of the government as partisan and corrupt. Genuine religious belief played a part too, the study found, though levels of religious knowledge among combatants were low, and their faith was more heavily informed by the new 'single narrative' popularized by radicals over the previous decade than scholarly Islam.[42] Another indication that money was far from a prime motivation for most insurgents was that some at least, though clearly a minority, did have relatively good incomes, sometimes even from jobs within the government administration.[43] People plunged in the everyday social warp and weft of the insurgency also painted a very different picture from that given in NATO briefings. Roshana Wardak, a trained gynaecologist from a major political family in Wardak province who was a popular and effective member of parliament, spoke of how 'there are ten educated ideological Taliban in the entire province and for each there are 100 pro-Taliban [people] who don't like foreign troops and are fighting to defend their religion'. Where she lived at least, she said, 'it is not common for the Taliban to pay'. The member of the national assembly for Ghazni, Daoud Sultanzoy, said the insurgents in his home area included 'one per cent staunch Taliban', some former Hezb-e-Islami commanders who act as 'pivots' in logistics networks, other local small-scale warlords who had lost out to the original Taliban in the 1990s and about 'eight to nine per cent who are just local thugs'. Taliban fighters themselves reacted with predictable but genuine anger to the proposal that they might accept money to stop fighting when asked by reporters, citing faith, principles, patriotism and vengeance for dead family members and comrades.[44] Miliband was an intelligent man who evidently doubted the simplistic formula he was often forced to use. The insurgents were, he explained to one interviewer shortly after a trip to Afghanistan, 'on the whole conservative Pashtun nationalists' who were 'pursuing a local grievance' and who 'need to be inside the political system'. This meant that, if the Taliban rented them, he said, it was 'not easy to rent them back'.[45] Money would not necessarily trump culture and identity.

The Taliban closely monitored Western media and were thus well aware of the various debates about strategy that evolved over the year. NATO's new campaign plan, with its emphasis on 'valley-by-valley' solutions and securing the population, was an undoubted improvement. But in three main areas that McChrystal saw as critical to turning around the situation in Afghanistan – the rapid development of Afghan security forces, the improvement of 'governance' and the reduction of civilian casualties – trends were mixed at best, still firmly negative at worst.

The ramifications of the use of increasing numbers of Afghan troops was an example of the way that the new NATO strategy risked exacerbating the broad structural problems that fuelled the insurgency in Afghanistan – such as the lack of legitimacy of the central government and their allies – in the south and south-east even while achieving certain limited tactical objectives. As in Iraq, the mantra from Western policy-makers and strategists was, even if it was never put in such terms, 'We will stand down as they stand up.' The sooner the Afghan security forces were effective, the sooner international forces could leave. Yet this strategy faced a similar problem as in Iraq: the local security forces both were weak and, to start with at least, lacked ethnic and cultural balance. In Iraq, however, the demographics had meant that the Sunnis had eventually little choice but to join the security forces, albeit as the auxiliaries of the Awakening. But in Afghanistan, with the Pashtuns totalling around 45 per cent, the insurgents often embedded in communities and no equivalent of al-Qaeda in Iraq to turn local populations towards the government or occupation forces as the lesser of two evils, the situation was very different. McChrystal's plan had envisaged doubling the Afghan National Army (ANA), but though the numbers of the

ANA were growing and its patchy fighting capacity slowly improving, many ANA deployments against the insurgents had a variety of potential negative consequences of which most Western commanders appeared unaware. First, the significant ethnic imbalance meant that the soldiers who had been manoeuvring with Vasquez and his men in Logar or were being sent down to Kandahar and Helmand were largely of Tajik or Hazara origin, and thus each further *kandaq*, as battalion-sized units were known, deployed in Pashtun-majority areas risked aggravating a civil war that had been running for several decades and an ethnic power struggle that dated back a century or so.[46] Perhaps worse, a high percentage of those ANA officers who were Pashtun had served with the Moscow-backed Afghan Communist forces against the *mujahideen* in the 1980s.[47] Many senior officers had been part of the hardline and notoriously brutal Khalq faction of the PDPA. Some, such as General Ali Ahmed, who was in charge of the ANA training centre in Kabul, referred both to the Taliban and to those who had fought the Soviets in the 1980s as 'insurgents', or *dushman*, enemy. That he should use the term to describe the Taliban was not surprising but that he should call the *mujahideen* of the earlier period 'enemy' was striking, particularly when the long-serving minister of defence had been one of them.[48] As the impressive briefing slides shown at the ISAF headquarters had made clear, if one of the many ongoing strands of historical conflict in Afghanistan was ethnic, so other strands pitted those who had benefited from Communist rule, often urban, educated communities, against those who had suffered enormously under it, usually rural communities. Taliban commanders might claim that they did not like fighting the ANA because the troops were 'Afghans' and villagers tell reporters that they preferred soldiers recruited from far away to the rapacious locally hired police, but General Ahmed's vocabulary underlined the cultural gulf that rent Afghanistan and fuelled the internal conflict. Overcoming these fundamental fractures was not impossible. Certainly in some parts of the country communities had begun to welcome the ANA. But consolidating such progress needed time and resources – and a legitimate central government.[49]

The second plank of the McChrystal strategy aimed to deal with all the multiple failings of the Afghan state revealed so brutally over the previous years. 'Ultimately, defeating the insurgency will depend upon the government's ability to improve security, deliver effective ...

services and expand development for economic opportunity,' John McConnell, the United States director of national intelligence, had told Senators the previous year and one reason why so much had been pinned on the presidential elections was that there had been so little sign of any rapid improvement of governance or aid and development delivery. The paradox of 'no security without development, no development without security' remained unresolved in much of the country, particularly of course the south. Venal, brutal, still largely untrained and often unpaid police – described by ISAF staff officers as 'the strategic hope' of the international effort in Afghanistan – were still a scourge for many communities.[50] Local people still turned to Taliban courts in much of the country for the speedy resolution of disputes. The official judiciary was corrupt, derided, inefficient and fearful. 'The government asked me to accept a post in Baki Barrak [a remote town], and I think the people would have liked me to be there, but I was too scared,' one Logar judge confessed.[51] The lack of governance inevitably hindered efforts to reduce opium cultivation and combat the vast narcotics industry. Though the opium harvest for 2009 did in fact fall 10 per cent to 6,900 tons, this was more due to external factors such as low opium prices and high wheat prices on the global market than to any developments within Afghanistan. Even if the extent of cultivation registered a steeper decline – to 123,000 hectares, down from a peak of 193,000 hectares in 2007 – the money being generated overall by the drugs industry was still enough to contaminate every part of Afghan public and political life.[52] Sadiqa Mobariz, the Hazara member of the national assembly and a staunch enemy of the Taliban, said she had been sufficiently shocked by the corruption she had seen among senior politicians for all her illusions to be shattered: 'When I saw the parliament and all the new laws back in 2004 and 2005, it was like a dream ... now that has become a nightmare.'[53] She did not plan on standing for re-election. Occasional prosecutions by newly formed special teams of investigators and judges made little difference – not least because those convicted were regularly pardoned by the president. Nor did the new commitment of NATO to target opium factories and facilities and key individual traffickers.[54] The corruption naturally impacted on aid delivery – or at least the willingness of donors to fund assistance programmes. Though the days of shoddily built schools costing half a million dollars or tube wells sunk with no regard for the local water table were largely over, a huge amount of cash continued to be spent by either foreign companies or NGOs independently of the Afghan government. 'How can people respect their own authorities if they see that anything that is worthwhile is built by other people?' asked Mohammed Ehsan Zia, the rural rehabilitation and development minister.[55] 'How can we give them the cash if we can't be sure it isn't going to be stolen?' countered a Western aid official, citing reports that $3 billion in cash, of which a significant portion was embezzled US aid and drugs money, had been openly flown out of Kabul International Airport between 2007 and 2009 to financial safe havens abroad.[56] There were continuing question marks over the integrity of President Hamid Karzai's close entourage, the interior ministry and other key institutions. In October 2009, the then vice president, Ahmad Zia Massoud, was stopped and questioned in Dubai when he flew into the emirate with $52 million in cash. He was no exception. 'Vast amounts of cash come and go from the country on a weekly, monthly and annual basis,' the American ambassador noted in a cable.[57] Grave problems remained with senior local officials. Other cables from the American embassy in Kabul back to Washington accused the governors of two key provinces of 'embezzling public funds, stealing humanitarian assistance, and misappropriating government property'.[58] American suspicions of the president's half-brother's involvement in a range of illicit activities including narcotics were well known.[59] 'You'd think finding a dozen competent ministers and thirty provincial governors would be possible, but apparently it isn't,' said Daoud Sultanzoy, the opposition MP.[60] Nor did it look likely to suddenly become possible in the near future. NATO officers had been repeating for years that the Taliban were not strong, but the state was weak. In the end it did not matter where the relative strength lay. The Taliban simply needed to impede any improvement in governance, and most of their job would be done. As ever in such a conflict, all the insurgents needed to do was to avoid losing and wait for the foreign occupiers to run out of men, money or patience so they could get on with their primary strategic aim of fighting the country's local rulers. 'We are very closely following the EU and US opinion and all assessment shows that people [there] are tired of this war and they will ask Obama to withdraw from Afghanistan,' the Taliban spokesman told the author in October 2009.[61]

The third element of McChrystal's plan was to reduce the number of civilian casualties, clearly a key element of 'protecting the population'.

Western public opinion, particularly as it turned negative, was sensitive to Afghan civilian casualties too. Inevitably given the nature of the coalition and the structure of American forces, the implementation of the new COIN thinking within Afghanistan was uneven, whatever senior officers' orders. Ten minutes after leaving an interview with the commander of NATO-ISAF forces, the author's local taxi was effectively run off the road by an American army Humvee, whose masked top gunner very deliberately added insult to near injury by offering a single erect gloved finger as his own vehicle swung by. If getting soldiers to drive courteously in the capital was hard, ensuring that frontline tactical commanders chose to forgo air power and risk the lives of their own men rather than those of locals was naturally significantly harder.[62] When McChrystal called for a policy of 'courageous restraint' in the use of firepower, he provoked a furious response from many of his own soldiers, who accused their commander of irresponsibly depriving them of the most effective weapons in NATO's arsenal. However, the use of air power and heavy weapons did diminish steadily over 2009 and into the next year – down 60 per cent by the early months of 2010 even if the tension between the short-term objective of 'force protection' and the long-term aim of 'protecting the population' that had dogged military operations for years was as present as ever.[63] Overall the new emphasis on avoiding civilian casualties meant that international troops or their Afghan allies were responsible for significantly fewer Afghan civilians killed or injured during 2009, despite heavier fighting.[64]

There was also the issue of the 'collateral damage' associated with the American special forces teams tasked with picking up 'high-value targets'. Such units, drawn mainly from the 7th Special Forces Group at Fort Bragg, North Carolina, though with some from the British Special Boat Service and other allied elite units, had been responsible for many of the most egregious incidents of civilian casualties over the previous seven years.[65] The units often contained significant numbers of Afghans, and it was the latter who often exacted the highest price from local communities suspected of sheltering senior Taliban figures, though without their international mentors apparently making much effort to restrain them.[66] Concerns about the local fall-out of such operations had been repeatedly raised by commanders on the ground and had led to a short moratorium on such raids in early 2009.[67] However, one lesson that McChrystal had taken away from the special forces operations he had led in Iraq had been that pressuring the enemy's middle-level ranks could pay major dividends, 'squeezing' the entire command and control structure of the insurgents. He therefore sought to increase the 'operational tempo' of his special forces troops three-, four- or five-fold. In this McChrystal was backed by his superior, David Petraeus, who, politic as ever, understood that the higher-value targets 'taken down' were useful to boost the morale of wavering politicians back home and thus bought the military much needed time. Senior officers also argued that such 'surgical' operations meant less need for conventional troops to 'go blundering around the Afghan countryside', and the raids intensified in the second half of 2009.

The first major test for McChrystal, the new NATO strategy and the new troops that had been arriving all through 2009 came in early 2010 at Marjah, a small rural district to the west of Lashkar Gah in the centre of Helmand province. Marjah, which had a population of approximately 100,000, had little inherent strategic importance other than being the westernmost point of a crescent of densely inhabited land running all the way across to the Pakistani border and being the target of the first major NATO-ISAF operation aimed at proving the ability of the newly reinforced Western and local forces to clear a Taliban-run area and then hold it through the creation of a more or less functional local administration.[68] The district of Marjah had already been fought over in 2007 but, though 'won' from the insurgents, had subsequently been infiltrated once again by the Taliban, who had then killed many of those who had cooperated – or collaborated, depending on your point of view – with the Western forces. This time, the local population was told, not only would the area be secured and its inhabitants protected when the operation was over, but Marjah would then see a major development and administrative effort which would maintain the authority of the central government for the foreseeable future. Beyond the local aims, the operation had a broader national and international significance too. Not only would Marjah show how the new McChrystal strategy could work but it would 'shape' the local environment for what was planned to be the main event of the summer: a much more complex campaign for Kandahar which would break the stalemate in Afghanistan and change the course of the war.

The Marjah operation, named 'Moshtarak', or 'Togetherness', to emphasize the unity of effort of Afghan and international forces, turned out to be inconclusive. There were certain predictable problems – artillery and air strikes caused dozens of civilian casualties early on, for example – but the 15,000-strong Western-led force successfully fought its way through the villages for the loss of only thirteen men. An Afghan flag was raised by ANA soldiers over a badly damaged and abandoned marketplace in Marjah district centre on 17 February 2010. Though there had been some resistance, the insurgents had largely avoided a conventional confrontation, leaving behind hundreds of IEDs that continued to kill soldiers and locals for weeks. The operation was rapidly declared over, the main force pulled out and the attempt to establish a competent and responsive government was launched. This – the 'build' phase – met with limited success. The first governor installed turned out to be an incompetent virtual illiterate with a criminal record acquired while a refugee in Germany. The police deployed into Marjah proved as rapacious and brutal as anywhere else. Security forces proved unable to keep the insurgents out, as most of the latter were local men, whereas the ANA soldiers deployed to the district were from hundreds of miles away. Within weeks, the Taliban were back, at least at night. Local communities once more found themselves in the invidious position that had been so often theirs over previous years: trying to negotiate a miserable middle way between the insurgents and the Afghan government and their international allies. Within months, the United Nations had recorded at least 74 civilians killed in Marjah, 29 killed by 'pro-government forces', 32 by insurgents and 13 dying at the hands of 'unknown actors'. Partly as a consequence, few of the 4,000 families who fled the spring fighting returned.[69] In the aftermath of the Marjah operation the Kandahar campaign was postponed to allow 'further shaping' of the strategic environment. In May, the Taliban for their part launched their own offensive, named al-Faath, or 'Conquest', or 'Victory'. All parties involved in the fighting in Afghanistan were very aware that its evolution through the summer would inevitably depend greatly on what was happening across the border, in Pakistan.

PAKISTAN, 2009–10

In February, as the Marines and their Afghan allies were fighting their way into Marjah, Pakistani intelligence officials had arrested more senior Taliban in a few days than they had done in the previous eight and a half years. Among those picked up in a series of dawn raids was Mullah Abdul Ghani Barader, effectively Mullah Omar's deputy and one of the most capable and respected of the Quetta Shura members.[70] Others included Maulvi Abdul Kabir, the former governor of Jalalabad who had escaped over the Spin Ghar mountains as the Tora Bora battle unfolded more than eight years before, who was picked up from a substantial house in which he had been living for some time on the outskirts of Peshawar.[71] Several, including key advisers of Mullah Omar, were arrested in Karachi. In all, an impressive number of veteran Taliban figures, the arrest of whom had been sought by the West for many years, were detained.[72] The response from Washington and European capitals was effusive. Richard Holbrooke, the special representative, called the arrests 'another high water mark for Pakistani and American collaboration'.[73] Bruce Riedel, who had led the Obama administration's spring 2009 'AfPak' policy review, hailed a 'very major shift in Pakistani behaviour'.[74]

A month later, the Pakistani army announced total victory in the agency of Bajaur, nearly two years after starting operations there. The campaign was described as 'effective' by American officials and projected as further evidence that senior Pakistani officers had finally recognized the urgency of dealing with the internal threat posed by the militants. The previous year – 2009 – had seen a series of new efforts by the Pakistani military to take on the militant havens along the Afghan frontier. A key moment had come when groups allied to the Pakistani Taliban had moved out of the upland areas along the frontier or the various spurs of the Hindu Kush mountains and started to take ground on the fertile lowlands only a couple of hours' drive from Islamabad. After a controversial deal with the militant leaders who had seized the valley of Swat in April 2009 which had granted the extremists the right to impose a version of *sharia* law and had provoked international fury, 52,000 Pakistani troops had spent the summer using relatively innovative tactics including some of the new counter-insurgency doctrines being implemented elsewhere to regain control of the area. Despite the attraction of their project of land reform to some communities, support for the militants in Swat had rapidly dwindled as local elders had been humiliated by young fighters, venerated local religious figures were killed and their bodies desecrated, singing and dancing banned and girls' schools destroyed.[75] In October, three divisions of troops had finally moved into South Waziristan and, by exploiting splits between militant groups and with US drones feeding intelligence to battlefield commanders, were able to force militants out of village strongholds and into remote forest or mountain camps. The same month the Pakistanis had acceded to the longstanding request of the Americans and allowed a very small number of US special forces troops – just over a dozen – to operate in the tribal areas.[76] With the militants still divided by a bitter succession row following the death of Baitullah Mehsud, the leader of the Pakistan Taliban, in a drone strike earlier in the year, it seemed possible that the gains made in the operations over the summer and autumn might for once be consolidated. Certainly, some communities, albeit mainly on the periphery of the tribal areas, appeared willing to take up arms themselves against the militants. Even if their primary motivation was to pursue blood feuds, their stance nonetheless indicated a degree of confidence in the government and the Pakistani military to protect them in at least the near future.[77] Fighting had continued along the length of the tribal belt – though not in the critical North Waziristan – through the winter of 2009–10 and into the spring. 'I couldn't give the Pakistani Army anything but an "A" for how they've conducted their battle so far [in the FATA],' enthused Admiral Mullen, the American chairman of the Joint Chiefs of Staff.[78] Naturally in private senior defence officials and their civilian counterparts were less extravagant in their praise, but, with the progress in the FATA and the arrests of important members of the Taliban high command, it was unsurprising that some began to see grounds for optimism.

However, closer inspection revealed little reason to believe that the Pakistani security establishment had significantly reversed or even moderated its Afghan policy or that the operations in the FATA would lead to the rapid elimination of militancy, either local or international, from the tribal zones. Rather than a 'sea change', the arrests of so many of the Taliban high command in February 2010 could be seen more as the beginning of a new phase in Pakistan's long-term bid to assure its influence in Afghanistan and to roll back that of its regional competitors. The arrests served several purposes at once for the Pakistani security establishment: pleasing Western allies, reminding the obstinately independent-minded Taliban leadership that their well-being depended to a considerable extent on Pakistan's calculation of its interests, and rendering the ISI indispensable once, as looked inevitable, some kind of peace process got underway across the border. Those Taliban arrested were also those who had repeatedly showed themselves to be the most pragmatic. Though reports that the most senior amongst them had indirectly been involved in talks with the Kabul government were denied by all sides, there was evidence that all those detained belonged to a small but influential faction within the Taliban which had come to the conclusion that victory – defined as restoring the Islamic Emirate of Afghanistan that had existed before 2001 – was impossible by military means alone.[79] The detention of these figures, coming immediately after the London conference, where 'reconciliation' with the Taliban had become stated coalition policy in Afghanistan, restored Pakistan's control over political developments and a peace process that had threatened to spin out of their control. Those on the ground in Pakistan remained sanguine about prospects for any breakthrough. As a vast $7.5 billion aid package made its way through Congress, Anne Patterson, the US ambassador in Islamabad, had cabled Washington to stress that 'there is no chance that Pakistan will view enhanced assistance . . . as sufficient compensation for abandoning support to [militant] groups' including the Taliban and Jalaluddin Haqqani's insurgent network.[80]

Equally, the Pakistanis' declaration of victory in the FATA also appeared very premature. There were plenty of signs that any respite would be temporary. Only 600 of an estimated 10,000 militants in South Waziristan were thought to have been killed, and, more importantly, most of the multitude of groups that had sprung up over previous years remained mobilized. Baitullah Mehsud's successor, Hakimullah Mehsud, was first declared dead with '90 per cent certainty' by American officials and then embarrassingly shown to be alive when he surfaced in a video. As in Afghanistan, the 'clear' phase of counter-insurgency operations was proving much simpler than the 'hold' and 'build'. Indeed, the problems of governance posed in southern Afghanistan and those in the FATA had much in common. As outlined in previous chapters, the problems in the FATA were, like those underlying all Islamic radicalism, a complex mesh of international and local factors reaching back decades, if not centuries. They were thus likely to take decades, if not centuries, to unpick, and it seemed unlikely that the Pakistani civilian government or military, both increasingly mired in ongoing internal power struggles, had either the will or the capacity to do so. Simply changing the name of the North West Frontier province to Khyber Pakhtunkhwa, as was done with some fanfare in April 2010, certainly was not likely to make much of a difference. By the late spring of 2010 there were already signs of low-intensity guerrilla-style war against the Pakistani army in the FATA with ambushes, IEDs and other tactics developed and honed in Afghanistan or other theatres of the 9/11 Wars killing an increasing number of soldiers and paramilitaries.[81]

It was also looking increasingly likely that Pakistan might suffer a generalized durable insurgency in areas well beyond the FATA along the lines of the violence that had half-paralysed countries in the Maghreb and beyond in the 1990s. Spring 2009 had seen an appalling surge in violence in Punjab. The Sri Lankan cricket team had been attacked in Lahore, then a police training centre, then a Barelvi mosque. The bombings and *fedayeen*-style assaults, by which a heavily armed squad of fighters attacked well-defended targets in the near certain knowledge that they would be killed, continued through the summer and the autumn.[82] In October, there was an unprecedented assault on the military's general headquarters in Rawalpindi followed by a triple assault on police offices and training centres in Lahore, which killed more than thirty. The attacks continued in the west of the country – over 100 died in a bombing in Peshawar that coincided with the arrival of Hillary Clinton, the American secretary of state, in Pakistan on October 29 – but it was the quickening tempo and growing intensity of violence outside the FATA and its immediate environs which was most striking. In all in 2009, 3,025 people died in terrorist attacks in Pakistan, almost exactly the number of victims of the September 11 attacks. The strikes had continued through the spring of 2010.

As worrying as the level of violence was the identity of those behind the attacks. Investigations revealed the perpetrators of the violence to be part of fragmented, dynamic and ad hoc networks composed of militants from a range of different organizations. The process of internationalization of local Pakistani groups, highlighted earlier, had continued since the death of Bhutto and the terrific violence of 2008. Though many had once been focused exclusively on sectarian strife, Kashmir or fighting in Afghanistan, other groups had become patched into a range of new contacts among the Pakistani Taliban and its offshoots or even al-Qaeda itself.[83] Much of the collaboration between these various elements remained tactical – the Pakistani Taliban had reserves of suicide bombers, the Punjabi groups had safehouses and sanctuaries, for example, so individuals from the two networks frequently joined forces – and was not therefore evidence of any solid linkage. However, they did share a vision of the Pakistani government and security establishment as enemies. The steady ideological convergence between groups and the simultaneous organizational fragmentation of Pakistani radical militant organizations over the course of the 9/11 Wars was a particularly dangerous combination which made effective counter-terrorism extremely difficult. It also revealed – in microcosm – the nature of modern Islamic militancy more generally.

The critical element within both the Algerian and the Egyptian insurgencies of the 1990s and during the previous decade of the 9/11 Wars had been the rejection of extremism by local populations. The good news was that, by the end of 2009 and early 2010, there was some evidence that popular sentiment in Pakistan was finally turning against the militants and their violence. In 2005, about half (52 per cent) of Pakistani Muslims expressed confidence in bin Laden to do the right thing in world affairs; in 2010 only 18 per cent shared this view, and levels of disapproval of suicide bombing – 80 per cent – were the highest in the Islamic world.[84] Even in the Khyber Pakhtunkhwa/North West Frontier province some polls showed that support for bin Laden had fallen dramatically.[85] But the bad news was the levels of support for militants, of all kinds, which still remained. A shift from around one in four having a positive view of the Taliban and al-Qaeda in 2008 to under one in six over the same period still meant tens of millions of people continued to consider Mullah Omar, bin Laden and other extremists as people who were, at the very least, making a positive overall contribution to local regional and world affairs. The issue of public sentiment towards such figures was closely linked to another important question posed by broader social developments in Pakistan: would the new urban middle classes, especially the lower middle classes recently lifted from relative poverty, swing towards a more pro-Western, liberal, secular and democratic position as they expanded or in another direction? Here too there was little ground for optimism. Elsewhere in the Islamic world, the lived experience of radical violence had led to its rejection. However, that rejection had frequently been accompanied by a consolidation of a new social conservatism, an attraction to 'mild' Islamism, a reaffirmation of a non-violent but intolerant Muslim identity and a profound anti-Americanism. There appeared to be little reason to expect any difference in Pakistan.[86] In late spring 2010, according to Pew Research, 85 per cent of Pakistanis favoured the segregation of men and women in the workplace, 83 per cent favoured stoning adulterers, 80 per cent favoured lashing thieves or amputating their hands, and 78 per cent supported the death penalty for apostates. Overall, nine out of ten said it was a good thing that Islam played a big role in the political life of the country and almost two-thirds saw the US as an enemy.[87] A survey of under-thirties found that only a third now believed democracy was the best system of govern-ance, a third preferred *sharia* law, while 7 per cent thought dictatorship was a good idea.[88] A fierce nationalism also continued to strengthen. This manifested itself both internally – 89 per cent of respondents in the Pew Survey said they were Pakistani before being a member of their ethnic group – and externally – an incident in September 2009 that saw US troops crossing the border into South Waziristan from Afghanistan provoked an extraordinary outpouring of rhetoric about infringed sov-ereignty and the right of Pakistan to be 'respected' on the world stage.[89] The intensifying drone strikes continued too to provoke anger, particu-larly as it was widely and wrongly thought that they did not have the sanction of the Pakistani government. Very large numbers of civilians and soldiers continued to believe that Indians or even the US or Israel were running the militants in the FATA and now also in the Punjab to deliberately weaken Pakistan.[90] One American diplomatic cable noted: 'America is viewed with some suspicion by the majority of Pakistan's people and its institutions ... We are viewed at best as a fickle friend, and at worst as the reason why Pakistan is attacking its own.'[91] Much of the nation's vastly expanded media – considered 'unbiased' by 76 per cent of Pakistanis – continued to peddle half-truths and prejudice. A fairly typical headline in the *Nation*, one of the better local English-language newspapers, revealed that Benazir Bhutto had been assassinated by a special death squad formed by former US Vice President Dick Cheney and headed by General McChrystal.[92] No doubt partly as a result of the slew of sensationalist and poorly sourced reporting, when asked what was the greatest threat to their country, nearly three-quarters of Pakistanis in 2010 identified India, less than a third chose the Taliban and only 3 per cent pointed to al-Qaeda.[93] Inevitably, these kind of sen-timents continued to spill over into the security establishment's strategic vision. So too did the widespread ambivalence towards the militants now active from the FATA to the eastern frontier. In March 2010, Shahbaz Sharif, the brother of opposition leader Nawaz Sharif and chief minister of the Punjab, pleaded with the Taliban to leave the province alone as his administration shared their aim of opposing 'foreign [i.e. American] dictation'.[94] When in May over ninety Muslims from the minority Ahmedi strand, considered heretics by the intolerant and orthodox, were killed in a series of bombings, the attacks went without comment by many of the country's politicians and were only reluctantly criticized by others. The global financial crisis had revealed the structural weaknesses of the Pakistani economy that had been obscured by the boom of the Musharraf years and now imperilled the hard-won advances made by many people. With the economy continuing to deteriorate, in part because of the appalling security situation but also due to a lack of electricity to run factories and agricultural equipment, Zardari's poll ratings plummeted, and the mild Islamo-nationalist rhetoric of Sharif brought him approval levels of up to 89 per cent.[95] A projected crackdown on the militants in the Punjab stalled in the face of a row between the government and the opposition.[96] Politicians even campaigned alongside well-known extremist leaders. This may have been deeply cynical, selfish and even immoral but made good pragmatic political sense given that polls had revealed that Lashkar-e-Toiba, the best known of the local militant groups, were seen favourably by at least a quarter of the national population and by over a third of people in the Punjab.[97] Few other groups had Lashkar-e-Toiba's popular base or connections to the security establishment, but there was no doubt the militants in general retained significant political clout and legitimacy. Though under undoubted pressure, the myriad militant groups existing across the whole of Pakistani soil were showing little significant weakness. The summer promised to be bloody, in Pakistan as in Afghanistan.

KASHMIR AND A GENERATIONAL STRUGGLE

In the spring of 2010, as the snow melted from the lower slopes of the foothills of the Himalayas and buds began to appear on the apple trees, violence in the Indian part of the long-disputed state of Kashmir, having touched a twenty-year low the year before, began to rise once again.[98] Day after day, young men, often teenagers, took to the streets to hurl stones at ill-trained ill-equipped security forces. The police and para-militaries often countered the stones with bullets.[99] In the narrow streets of the centre of Srinagar, the summer capital of the state, and in small, hardscrabble towns like Sopore or Anantnag, choking tear gas filled the air as the wounded and sometimes the dying were carried away. In the rural areas, moving from house to house, were the armed militants, less numerous than for many years but nonetheless hopeful of exploiting the renewed mobilization that accompanied the street violence to gain recruits among a new generation of Kashmiri youths.

One of longest conflicts involving radical Islam in the world, pre-dating the 9/11 Wars by a decade or more, violence in Kashmir had followed a trajectory familiar from previous pages. After an initial explosion of violence between 1988 and 1991, there had been a steady intensification through the early 1990s. As elsewhere, a clumsy reaction on the part of security services had led to appalling violence, continuing abuses by all sides, a collapsing local economy and terrible suffering among civilians. By the end of the decade, it was clear that the popula-tion was slowly but steadily turning away from militancy. Combined with geopolitical shifts, particularly the post-9/11 pressure on Pakistan to reduce support to Kashmiri militants and to stop Lashkar-e-Toiba and other Pakistan-based groups sending fighters across the Line of Control to attack Indian security forces, this had meant a significant decline in violence from around 2002. By 2010, the local militants of early 1990s were dead or in their forties, married and drinking coffee in newly opened Srinagar cafés. Active fighters, once more than 1,500 strong in 'the Valley', as the principal and most prized part of Kashmir was known, probably numbered no more than around 250.[100] Kashmir had been a sideshow of the 9/11 Wars, caught in their backwash, drawn into the complex of conflicts they constituted, without ever really being a key theatre. Nonetheless, Kashmir indicated many of the qualities of the conflict as a whole – and indicated its possible evolution.

Various short-term factors had sparked the resurgence of violence in Kashmir in the spring of 2010. There was local anger at stalled political processes, possibly a degree of interference from across the border as Pakistan's intelligence services carefully ramped up their involvement and, in particular, the presence of large numbers of frustrated and under-employed youth.[101] These young men – though bored – were not poor. Kashmir is one of the richest parts of India and, though good jobs are rare, no one is starving. Nor were they ill-educated. Almost all were literate, most were articulate, and many had university degrees. The key factor in the violence was instead the age of the teenagers out throwing stones at security forces week after week. For all of them the dark days of the 1990s, when tens of thousands died in militant attacks, in cross-fire, in torture chambers run by the army and the police, were little more than a childhood memory. They were prepared to contemplate a return to violence because they had forgotten what taking up arms had brought and because, they said, they felt the weight of expectations on their generation. 'I grew up listening to stories of the struggle, of the heroes, of the *mujahideen*. Now I am old enough. I do not want to show myself less committed or less brave or less strong than they were before,' said Mehboob Lone, nineteen. The repeated shootings – each death led to a funeral and a demonstration where another youth was killed which thus meant another funeral – had created a momentum that was hard to stop. Mehraan, a twenty-two-year-old shopkeeper and veteran of the protests, said he had started attacking security forces when his cousin was shot dead. Since then, he said, he had wanted two things: *azadi* (freedom) and revenge, or 'blood for blood'. 'These things happen, and nothing is changed, and then they happen again,' he commented and shrugged. He and his friends spent many hours in internet cafés surfing Kashmir protest websites, watching videos of protests shot on mobile phones, on social networking sites or in groups that the police were unable to access. Though few visited radical jihadi sites, those celebrating Palestinian protests or the words and works of the most well-known contemporary Islamic clerics were popular. For feeding the resentment was the same new social conservatism and interest in pan-Islamic identities seen elsewhere. The old, traditional Sufi-influenced strands of Islam in Kashmir had been ceding ground to newer, harsher, more rigorous, more intolerant and more politicized styles for many years. Though a broad rejection of global al-Qaeda-inspired militancy was evident, the hero of the stone throwers was eighty-one-year-old Syed Ali Shah Geelani, a reactionary political Islamist and the most uncompromising of the local leaders.

Through the spring and into the summer of 2010, the demonstrations continued with a steady toll of a death or two every week. Under the hail of broken bricks, the police retreated behind their barbed-wire barricades and the concrete blast walls which had, over the previous years, replaced the ramshackle defences around their bunkers. Though the vast bulk of their activity was still limited to hurling stones, the step to using more lethal arms would clearly not be a difficult one for the young Kashmiri men to take. When interviewed, they all echoed the implicit threats made by their political leaders, saying that they did not want to resort to armed violence, but that the possibility was always there if their demands, inchoate as they might have been, were not met. Officials recognized the rhetoric for what it was but were alarmed nonetheless. 'If there were weapons we'd have ten thousand militants,' one senior police officer said.[102] Intelligence reports described dozens of teenagers known for their involvement in demonstrations going underground to join the militants as the months passed.[103] In one village, as Indian army soldiers searched houses in a bid to catch a fugitive senior militant commander responsible for a series of local shootings, men told the author of the six or eight teenagers who had recently left their homes for the hills where the militants were thought to be based and of the 'informers' who had recently been executed by their neighbours.

No one needed to be reminded what such volunteers could end up doing. In January, a series of suicidal attacks, the first for two years, had shaken Kashmir.[104] They underlined three key lessons of the 9/11 Wars: how one generation can bequeath violence to another, how routes into activism vary and how militancy so often remains very localized indeed. One of the militants who died was Mansoor Ahmed Bhat, a nineteen-year-old house painter. Bhat came from a modest farming family in the small village of Pett Sirr, an hour's drive north of Srinagar and flanked in February by barren wheat fields and acres of orchards. His home lay down a muddy path between barn-like farmhouses. It was hard to imagine the village as lying in 'the epicentre of regional violence', as described by Indian officials. However, over the previous twenty years of the conflict at least two dozen men from Pett Sirr had joined militant groups. Bhat, his parents said, had never indicated any interest in following them, however. 'We are just farmers,' said Ghulam, the dead man's forty-five-year-old father. 'We are never involved in politics. Our only interest has been our livestock and our orchards.'

As ever, it is almost impossible to find any one moment when Bhat, who his parents and friends said was a 'quiet young man' who had left school at thirteen to work in the fields, began the journey that led to his violent death. He had grown up, after all, steeped in the ambient violence. His father believes the critical moment came in the summer of 2008, when Bhat participated in a demonstration during which six people were shot dead by local police. 'That changed him,' Bhat senior said. A few months later, his son told his parents he had got a job in Srinagar as a house painter and disappeared. The months passed, and his worried father reported the teenager missing. 'The police came and raided us and searched everything and told us to call them if we had news,' he said. Another six months went by. On January 3, 2010, his son walked through the door. He stayed a few hours, said little, ate and left again. 'He told us nothing,' Bhat's mother remembered. Four days later, local police rang the family's single mobile phone to say that their son was one of two armed militants who had attacked security forces in the centre of Srinagar with grenades and were now firing at anyone who approached from the upper storeys of a hotel. They asked Ghulam Bhat to call his son on his mobile phone and talk him into surrender, but he refused, fearing some kind of trap. After a twenty-two-hour siege, during which two policemen and a bystander were killed, Mansoor Bhat was shot dead.[105] A month after the attack, in the bare living room of the home in Pett Sirr, a picture of Bhat lay wrapped in a green cloth on a shelf next to the Koran.

17

The End of the First Decade

AL-QAEDA

On May 1, 2010, as the Marjah operation in Afghanistan was drawing to a close, as fighting continued in the FATA and as militants attacked with ever-greater frequency across swathes of eastern Pakistan, police in Times Square in the centre of New York discovered a large bomb in a Nissan Pathfinder parked on the corner of 45th Street and Seventh Avenue. The man who had prepared the device and placed it there was Faisal Shahzad, a thirty-one-year-old Pakistani who had become an American citizen the year before. The bomb was made of petrol, propane, fireworks and fertilizer and failed to ignite because Shahzad, in an amateurish error typical of many attempted attacks by Islamic militants over the previous ten years, had set the timer wrongly. However, if such an elementary mistake had not been made, the bomb could have killed scores, possibly hundreds of people, injuring many times that number, in the centre of Manhattan.

Though the plot was clearly nowhere near the scale or professionalism of the 9/11 attacks, it was at least very close to one of their main targets and as such was the nearest radical militants had come to repeating the earlier strikes.[1]

Two weeks later, in the UK, a twenty-one-year-old student called Roshonara Choudhry used a kitchen knife to stab a member of parliament, Stephen Timms, who had supported the war in Iraq. Timms survived the attack, and Choudhry was arrested. In early interviews with police she said she had acted entirely alone after viewing scores of hours of lectures by radical American-born Yemen-based cleric Anwar al-Awlaki. 'I told no one. No one else would have understood,' she said.[2]

Newspapers described Choudhry nonetheless as a 'remote-controlled Al Qaeda assassin' who had been 'brainwashed'.[3]

Through the summer of 2010 and into the autumn, a series of scares reminded publics across the world of the threat that Islamic militancy still posed. In July, a plot was uncovered in Norway involving recent immigrants – a Chinese Uighur, an ethnic Uzbek and an Iraqi Kurd.[4] In October came warnings, transmitted to US intelligence by German counterparts, of a series of 'Mumbai-style' attacks in Europe. Then in November came a new scare when a tip-off led security services to parcel bombs sent from the Yemen to Jewish targets in Chicago on cargo planes. Yemen had been in the spotlight since the last week of 2009, when a young Nigerian from an elite family was arrested on a plane flying into Detroit after he tried and failed to detonate explosives sewn into his underwear. It had soon emerged that Umar Faroul Abdultalleb, the would-be bomber, had, after a period in the UK where he joined Islamic societies at London University, started his journey across the world from Sana'a, the Yemeni capital. The exact provenance of the new threat emanating from the Yemen was unclear. Many threads ran back to Anwar al-Awlaki, the extremist cleric.

One element that all these various plots had in common was the tenuous nature of their links to the al-Qaeda hardcore. Faisal Shahzad, the aspirant bomber of Times Square, had been trained and partly funded by the Pakistani Taliban, a group which shared the views of al-Qaeda but was certainly not part of bin Laden's organization, on a winter trip a few months before to his home country. Neither he nor Choudhry, the putative assassin, nor Abdultalleb had ever met anyone from the al-Qaeda hardcore.[5] Even the links of FATA-based Ilyas Kashmiri, the veteran Pakistani now emerging as a major figure in global Islamic militancy and thought to be behind the 'Mumbai-style' attacks plan, to the al-Qaeda hardcore were uncertain. Al-Awlaki's own relationship with bin Laden and al-Zawahiri was subject to debate. The opacity surrounding the origins of the evident threat inevitably fuelled further debate on one question: 'what is al-Qaeda?'

The answer had been simpler back in the immediate aftermath of the 9/11 attacks. Then, analysis was fairly straightforward. Al-Qaeda was the best-known and most significant amid the hundreds of organizations involved in radical Sunni militancy. It comprised three clear elements. There was the hardcore leadership of the group, the network of other entities with formal affiliation to it and the ideology, the uniquely effective mix of modern and ancient historical references, filled out with selective quotations from scriptures and from other Muslim revivalist and reformist thinkers, that comprised the narrative, the language and the doctrines that underpinned the group's particular worldview. Al-Qaeda was certainly not without its challengers, competitors and rivals within the broad movement of radical Islam, but the group had been able to establish a centrality, real and virtual, in the global landscape of radical militancy in the late 1990s which, in the aftermath of the 2001 attacks, was undisputed.

Nearly a decade later, as the successive scares of 2010 revealed, the situation had clearly evolved drastically. In interviews, serving intelligence officers spoke of a 'fragmented, chaotic' picture that was 'immensely difficult' to track. The threat was 'broader' than it had ever been. Quite what the role of Osama bin Laden actually might be remained unclear. With every year that had passed since the 9/11 Wars had begun, the situation had become more complex, even as the threat of catastrophic violence itself had stabilized. By the end of the decade, the old analysis of al-Qaeda comprising a hardcore leadership, a network of affiliates and an ideology evidently needed revision.

THE HARDCORE, THE NETWORK OF NETWORKS, THE IDEOLOGY IN 2010 AND 2011

In 2010 and into early 2011 the al-Qaeda senior leadership continued to face a number of challenges. The most immediate was the continuing threat to their own personal security. The drone strikes in the FATA were more numerous than ever, and if bin Laden and al-Zawahiri had so far escaped the missiles falling on the tribal areas, many others did not. More than fifty strikes had been ordered by Obama in the first year of his administration, more than had ever been ordered by Bush, and 118 took place in 2010. One high-profile loss in May 2010 had been Mustafa Abu al-Yazid, the senior al-Qaeda militant who had played a key liaison role with local groups and the Afghan Taliban. He was just one of several senior figures and scores of middle-ranking fighters killed by the drones, however.[6] Given that most intelligence suggested that the number of Arabs comprising the main body of al-Qaeda in the FATA did not number more than 300, of whom three-quarters fulfilled relatively minor roles or were 'footsoldiers', these casualties were heavy.[7] The strikes also had an evident impact on the capabilities of the 'al-Qaeda hardcore'. Interrogated militants said that the senior leadership had ordered that no groups of more than ten people remain together for more than ten minutes. Intercepted conversations between militants spoke of the difficulties of planning and meeting. It was obvious too that the systems which had once allowed fresh videos to be uploaded simultaneously on to dozens of servers remained significantly degraded.[8] By late 2010, communications were taking lengthy and circuitous routes to reach mainstream media organizations, and instead of well-produced videos, al-Qaeda was forced to return to using audiotapes.[9]

Beyond the operational environment, the broader strategic problems that had been gathering for the al-Qaeda leadership since the middle years of the decade were becoming acute. Jihadi internet forums often featured comments recognizing that no major attack had successfully been executed by al-Qaeda in the West for many years. The deaths of two senior Iraqi al-Qaeda leaders in a joint operation of American and Iraqi forces near Tikrit in April 2010 provoked an extraordinary outburst of criticism directed at the senior leadership. 'Al-Qaeda's media wing is lying and spreading false information. Everyone is tired of al-Qaeda's stupidity,' argued one user of a known jihadist forum.[10] In the ultra-competitive world of militancy, the risk for bin Laden and al-Zawahiri of being consigned to the role of pioneers whose best work was now behind them grew with every month that passed without a major attack for which they could convincingly claim the credit. In *The Vision*, a long treatise by an apparently experienced and senior militant that was published on the internet in 2010, bin Laden and al-Zawahiri's approach was damned with faint praise as 'useful at a particular time'.[11] The threat to their influence from younger, more credible figures such as the English-speaking al-Awlaki, the cleric who had inspired Choudhry and others, continued to grow. Al-Awlaki had a Facebook page with 4,800 'friends'. Bin Laden, once so quick to master the potential of new communications technology and forms of networking, did not. The contributions of charismatic figures who had recently been inducted into the al-Qaeda senior leadership's ranks such as the Bagram escapee Abu Yahya al-Libi could only go so far in maintaining al-Qaeda's appeal among a generation for whom the 9/11 attacks were ancient history. Superficial gestures like al-Zawahiri appearing in videos without his thick glasses did not help much either. Then there was the ongoing revisionist challenge from within the movement. Some of the criticism was mild. Some was fierce. One frequent theme was the mounting proportion of Muslims to Westerners killed in militant violence, an inevitable result of the increasingly indiscriminate nature of attacks.[12]

This was one reason, of course, for the continuing failure to gain real traction over significant masses of the population. The number of volunteers making their way to the FATA indicated that al-Qaeda still had the power to attract sufficient individuals to sustain its existence for the foreseeable future – the primary task of any clandestine militant outfit – but there was no indication through 2010 that the decline in support amid populations more generally in the Islamic world or in the West was going to be reversed. Attempts to make the al-Qaeda message more 'locally specific' appeared to have little effect.[13] Nor did a sudden interest in new issues such as climate change. 'The number of victims caused by climate change is very big ... bigger than the victims of wars,' bin Laden said in a video in October 2010. The al-Qaeda leader even proposed the creation of a new aid organization to help Muslims, an astonishing turnaround for the leader of a group founded with the explicit aim of forgoing social activism in favour of direct action. 'The famine and drought in Africa that we see and the flooding in Pakistan and other parts of the world, with thousands dead along with millions of refugees, that's why people with hearts should move quickly to save their brothers and sisters,' bin Laden told his audience. But the sudden interest in global warming and humanitarianism merely reinforced the impression of an individual whose prime had passed trying, with almost painful artifice, to keep up with the times.[14]

Beyond the hardcore was what the early analysis of al-Qaeda had identified as the 'network of networks', or 'affiliates'. This too had changed hugely over the course of the 9/11 Wars. By 2010, many of those groups once drawn into the mesh of alliances, fealty and shared obligations woven by bin Laden through the 1990s had simply ceased to exist, such as the smaller Kurdistan-based militant factions or the Singapore-based groups which had solicited logistic support from al-Qaeda back in 2000 and 2001. Others had abandoned the fight, such as the Indonesian Jemaa Islamiya. Never more than very tangentially linked to al-Qaeda, the leaders of the latter had decided by the end of the decade, in another example of how local considerations often trump global solidarity, that they should abandon the jihad 'at home'. This, they said, was because conditions in Indonesia no longer justified armed struggle, though they still considered the jihad 'abroad' potentially legitimate.[15] When the veteran Indonesian militant leader Noordin Top was killed in September 2009, his 'al-Qoida of the Malayan Peninsula', named in homage to his hero, Ayman al-Zawahiri, died too.[16] There was no sign that the rapid decline of Al-Qaeda in Saudi Arabia and Al-Qaeda in the Maghreb (AQIM), discussed in Chapter 15, had even slowed, let alone been reversed.

Nor were those groups which had joined the network, at least nominally, much help in restoring al-Qaeda's fortunes. One was al-Shabab, a radical splinter from the Islamic Courts Union movement which had been able to briefly seize power in Somalia before being ejected from Mogadishu by Ethiopian troops in an American-backed offensive in 2006. A senior figure within al-Shabab, Saleh Ali Saleh Nabhan, had suddenly pledged allegiance to bin Laden in September 2008 in a video released to the internet. As had been the case for the Algerians two years previously, the appeal to the al-Qaeda leadership was prompted by a loss of local popularity and legitimacy largely due to al-Shabab's harshness and incompetence.[17] However, again in a parallel with developments elsewhere, the enrolment of al-Shabab as supposed affiliates brought little real benefits for the al-Qaeda hardcore. When, in July 2010, al-Shabab blew up restaurants in Kampala, Uganda, and thus executed their first international attack, they did so following a purely regional strategic logic of threatening a local state on the point of reinforcing its contingent of peacekeepers in Somalia. The attack was not on the orders of al-Qaeda's senior leadership and did not fit particularly with any broader strategic agenda. Indeed, it was criticized as counterproductive by a variety of senior core al-Qaeda figures both publicly on internet forums and privately in communications intercepted by American and other security agencies.[18] By late 2010, the least one could say was that the 'network of networks' was battered and disjointed. In many ways, it had simply ceased to exist.

There was one area, however, where al-Qaeda had achieved undeniable success. What cases like that of Faisal Shahzad and Roshonara

Choudhry showed was that bin Laden and his associates had been able to attain at least one of their major strategic aims: to disseminate the al-Qaeda worldview – the ideology, the third element of the post-2001 analysis – to a huge new audience, even if their own role within global Islamic militancy was now diminished. That worldview, increasingly relayed by stand-alone, independent poles of militant activity such as those constituted by al-Qaeda in the Yemen, by the Pakistani Taliban and increasingly by groups like Lashkar-e-Toiba, was more widespread than ever before. Shahzad told a court that he was a '*mujahid*' acting to defend Muslims against aggression in which all the people in Times Square that night, even children, were complicit. 'I am part of the answer to the US terrorising the Muslim nations,' he said. 'We Muslims are one community. We're not divided.'[19] Roshonara Choudhry had confessed immediately after her arrest, telling police she had stabbed the MP because 'as Muslims we're all brothers and sisters and we should all look out for each other and we shouldn't sit back and do nothing while others suffer. We shouldn't allow the people who oppress us to get away with it and to think that they can do whatever they want to us and we're just gonna lie down and take it.' Choudhry barely spoke at her trial, but after the sentence was passed, a group of men in the public gallery began shouting 'Allahu akbar', 'British go to hell', and 'Curse the judge'.[20]

This phenomenon was particularly clear in the USA. As ever, the number of people actively involved in violent activism was minuscule in comparison with the general population but were nonetheless higher than it had been since 2001.[21] Analysts spoke of signs that American Muslims, long considered immune to the radicalizing effects of the ongoing conflict and extreme ideologies due to their economic and social success in America and their high levels of education and wealthier origins, were finally following European Muslim communities towards a higher relative level of activism, radicalization and alienation. 'Jihadism' attracted a range of odd misfits too, drawn to militancy as to a cult. There were question marks over many of the investigations – not least because the FBI made liberal use of sting operations involving agents provocateurs – but nonetheless it was clear that many of those involved had indeed followed a similar route into radicalism to that of European, especially British, militants. The case of Shahzad, the Times Square bomber, was a classic example of self-radicalization by a deeply troubled individual who found in radical Islam the legitimization and

15. When in late 2005 a Danish newspaper printed cartoons of the Prophet Mohammed, a group of local clerics set out to create outrage and succeeded in provoking protests across the Islamic world. Religious leaders and governments competed in the rush to capitalize on the anger many Muslims felt. Most demonstrations – such as this by Hamas supporters in Gaza – were peaceful. Some were violent. The affair seemed to confirm a clash of civilizations.

16. In autumn 2005, riots broke out in poor urban areas across France. Young men of immigrant origin burned vehicles such as this bus in Toulouse, attacked schools and clashed with police. Though many feared 20 million European Muslims were becoming radicalized, in fact, religion played no part in the disturbances, hinting that the overwhelming pessimism of the fourth year of the 9/11 Wars was perhaps misplaced.

17. This thirty-five-year-old female suicide bomber sent by al-Zarqawi from the Iraqi city of Ramadi failed to detonate her device at a wedding reception in Amman, the capital of Jordan, in November 2005. Her husband and two others did, however, killing fifty-seven. Her brother had bee killed by US forces in fighting in Iraq.

18. The Amman attack marked a turning point. Before, support for al-Qaeda and the insurgen in Iraq had been high in Jordan. Afterwards, it plummeted. The demonstrations against terroris in Amman, such as the candlelit vigil pictured here, showed how it is easier to support glob terrorism when the bombs explode elsewhere than when it is familiar places or people that a under attack. From 2006, the fortunes of al-Qaeda began to decline.

19. Tony Blair left office after ten years in power shortly after this visit to Iraq in May 2007. His record as prime minister was dominated by the controversial UK involvement in the 9/11 Wars. Ironically, the moment of his departure saw a relative stabilization in Iraq as US troops mounted a 'Surge' into Baghdad and the surrounding areas.

20. By 2007, blast walls were going up all over Afghanistan. The author took this picture in a factory on the outskirts of Kabul, where scores of labourers worked to meet the demand for the concrete barriers, a distinctive sight of the 9/11 Wars. 'Business is good,' the owner said, sadly.

21. Benazir Bhutto played only a small role in the 9/11 Wars but was a prominent victim. After years in exile she came back to Pakistan in October 2007 and was assassinated three months later. This picture was taken only hours before she was killed. Afghan President Hamid Karzai, on her right, remains alive and controversial.

2. Taj Hotel on fire. In November 2008 a team of Pakistani suicide attackers from the Lashkar-Toiba organization attacked hotels and other sites in Mumbai, the Indian commercial capital, killing more than 150 people. Documents later revealed how the group's senior leadership had sanctioned the strike under huge pressure from hardline elements within their ranks – and that at least low-level officials of the ISI, the main Pakistani military intelligence service, knew about in advance.

23. Western policy towards narcotics in Afghanistan was muddled and poorly resourced. It was soon too late to do much about the burgeoning industry. The same was true of counter-insurgency efforts. Here British troops patrol in Helmand, the drug-ridden southern province.

24. By 2008, Western publics were tired of the war in Afghanistan. Policy-makers saw a massive expansion of local troops as a potential way out. Here, new recruits train at an Afghan National Army camp near Kabul. But such forces depended very heavily on the coalition. In some areas they still gained some local support as the 'least bad' option.

25. In 2008, a new war was added to the complex of conflicts that was the 9/11 Wars, when the Pakistani army pushed into areas along the border with Afghanistan that had fallen under the influence of local militants. The agency of Bajaur, used as an occasional base by al-Qaeda figures and as a rear area by insurgents in Afghanistan, saw fierce fighting. Pakistani troops like these had mixed sentiments about their enemy and the West.

26. This American officer – Captain José Vasquez – was deployed in Logar province in 2009, trying to reclaim the hinterland of Kabul. But progress was slow. The Taliban avoided a straight fight, preferring to outlast not outfight their well-equipped and well-armed enemy. In a week's operations, Vasquez, his men and the author did not glimpse a single insurgent.

27. Protesters in Tahrir Square, Cairo. Through the early months of 2011, crowds of young people, often mobilized through social networking, achieved in weeks what al-Qaeda had been unable to in decades: depose long-term rulers in Egypt and in Tunisia as well as shake others elsewhere. Angry and alienated, they called for democracy in non-violent protests which were a stunning rejection of radical Islam.

28. This image of anti-Mubarak demonstrators praying over an Egyptian flag on February 5 at Tahrir Square is a reminder of three crucial lessons of the 9/11 Wars: the importance of local identity, the enduring strength of the nation state and the depth of a new conservatism and new cultural religious identity which – though not incompatible with democracy – will be hugely influential on politics and society in the Middle East and beyond in coming years.

encouragement for acts that he may well have already been contemplating. There were many others. One was the case of Nidal Hasan, an American army major at the military base of Fort Hood in Texas, who shot thirteen of his colleagues in November 2009. Michael Leiter, director of the US National Counterterrorism Center, described plots disrupted in New York, North Carolina, Arkansas, Alaska, Texas and Illinois during 2010 as 'unrelated operationally but ... indicative of a collective subculture and a common cause that rallies independent extremists to want to attack the Homeland'.[22] A journey to the country of their or their parents' birth was often a key element in the radicalization process of young Americans. By 2010, at least twenty Somali Americans were active in the ranks of al-Shabab, and one, Omar Hammami, had become a local field commander and jihadi internet celebrity.[23] Most recruits showed the same low level of religious knowledge as their European counterparts too. Generational tensions within families also played a role for some.

Above all, it was the widely disseminated extremist worldview popularized by bin Laden but taken forward by al-Awlaki and others that was important. In the summer of 2010, al-Awlaki and al-Qaeda in the Yemen had launched an English-language internet magazine called *Inspire*. This had global penetration. From the Arabian peninsula to the USA to the UK, the range of the extremists' propaganda machine remained impressive, even if the hardcore leadership of the network had met with serious reverses. Mentioned by US officials as a serious threat, downloaded copies of *Inspire* were found by police in the UK conducting searches after the arrests of twelve young Britons of Bangladeshi origin suspected of planning a series of bomb attacks in Britain over Christmas 2010. One article was entitled 'How to make a pipe bomb in the kitchen of your mom'; others included 'What to expect in jihad' and 'Tips for our brothers in the US'.[24] The youngest of those arrested for the 'Christmas terror plot' was nineteen and thus only ten years old at the time of the 9/11 attacks. The youth of such suspects reinforced the sense that, though the hardcore and the network of networks were in some difficulty, the 'al-Qaeda-ist' ideology had created a movement with its own distinctive principles, modes of action and momentum. Beyond the major clusters of the well-known organizations, that movement was composed of individuals or small groups. These latter were too small to have a name, often well below the radar of security services, sometimes patched together by mutual association and often simply autonomous. At its most dispersed, but most widespread, level, this movement was little more than a way of thinking, a way of understanding the world, an identity with its own dress codes, ideas, values, rituals and prescribed behaviour, its own self-sustaining culture. Transmitted through peers, through the media, at schools, colleges, at sports clubs or prayer groups alike, from parents to children, from brothers to sisters, through internet magazines and carefully crafted videos, this movement was resilient and deeply rooted. This was not the 'global Intifada' that al-Suri had hoped for. Nor was it the mass mobilization that al-Qaeda leaders had set out to achieve – even if it assured them sufficient recruits to survive as a clandestine organization for the foreseeable future. But it was something that had not existed a decade before. It was one of the real – and worst – legacies of the 9/11 Wars.

THE END OF THE FIRST DECADE

If the evolution of al-Qaeda and its affiliates during 2010 and the early part of 2011 continued on broad lines established over previous years, so too did developments in Afghanistan and Pakistan.

In the former, the Taliban continued to have problems. Up to 200 mid-level commanders and operatives were being killed every month by the coalition special forces units and their Afghan auxiliaries in the 'night raids', and, with public support for the insurgents as variable as ever, the movement's leaders were forced to turn to tactics that risked further damage to their popularity. Through 2010 suicide attacks occurred at a rate of about three per week and the use of IEDs nearly doubled.[25] These latter accounted alone for around a third of Afghan civilians killed or wounded over the year.[26] Another sign of weakness was that the insurgents intensified their unpopular and increasingly brutal campaign of assassinations and intimidation, even, in a series of well-publicized incidents, targeting children.[27] Discipline and unity continued to be problems. Many of the older Taliban field commanders were now battle-weary and resentful of the senior leadership secure in Pakistan. Tensions and competition with other insurgent groups – Hekmatyar's fighters or the 'Haqqani network' – were often sharp. The very young commanders replacing the more experienced men killed in the special forces raids often had no memory of the 1990s, no understanding of the original mission of the Taliban and no respect for the hierarchy. Orders given before the 2011 spring offensive once again stressed the twin causes of nation and of Islam. More fragmented than ever, increasingly contaminated by criminal elements, the movement remained a largely local phenomenon, however. Even if many wintered in Pakistan, between 80 and 90 per cent of Taliban captured or killed were found within 12 miles of their home villages.[28]

Yet the reinforced international coalition, now commanded directly by General David Petraeus after McChrystal was sacked for effective insubordination in July, still struggled to achieve a breakthrough. In many areas massive application of resources had undeniably made a difference.[29] In Marjah, a force of 2,000 Marines spending a million dollars a month on development projects, backed by 300 policemen, 700 Afghan National Army soldiers and, controversially, an 800-strong locally raised militia had imposed some kind of order. But there was no way such resources could be committed even across the whole of the south. Kandahar and its surrounding districts appeared more secure, so too was the immediate hinterland of Kabul. But countrywide the violence was as intense as anything seen since 2001. In Wardak and Logar, many of the 'ideological' Taliban had been driven out, but warlordism and criminal violence were rife. In the north, insurgent influence had grown. Afghan security forces were expanding rapidly, with better training and equipment, but governance was still grotesquely flawed. Corruption was worse than ever and, along with simple incompetence, still crippled efforts to deliver basic services. Though officials rightly pointed to millions of children in thousands of new schools and effective vaccination programmes, any improvements in the police or justice system were, at best, incremental. Much of the population continued to prefer the swift and honest Taliban-run courts. Very large quantities of drugs continued to be produced. Pressurized by domestic opinion and failing finances, Western political leaders continued their increasingly desperate search for some kind of relatively dignified exit. Every few months there were new reports of talks with the insurgent leadership. A Quetta-based shopkeeper posing as a senior commander with access to Mullah Omar was paid a large sum of money and flown to Kabul. Other envoys moved back and forth. The most senior figures in the US administration attempted to persuade Pakistan's security services to deliver potential interlocutors all while trying to convince a sceptical American public that withdrawing troops from July 2011 onwards was not an admission of partial defeat and that a total 'transition' to local control in Afghanistan, now scheduled for 2014, did not imply failure. Disagreements within the Obama adminstration and between allies over exactly what might happen if some kind of deal was concluded with the Taliban continued. Would the movement host al-Qaeda as before? Would they act more reasonably than in the 1990s? Was any kind of inclusive political settlement even possible or desirable? But such questions were rapidly becoming academic. The West was on the way out of Afghanistan. It was only a matter of time.[30]

Across the border in Pakistan, broad trends established over the previous years continued too. Catastrophic floods in the summer of 2010 led to a temporary halt in the ongoing violence but had a variety of hugely negative effects well beyond the immediate humanitarian impact. Vast grain stocks were destroyed, livestock wiped out, roads and power lines washed away, and millions made homeless. Not only did the state show itself to be corrupt and incompetent, but many landlords failed to respond to the needs of communities who had worked their fields for generations. The deference and hierarchies already under such strain were further degraded. The floods also accelerated the migration of populations from rural areas to the cities, with millions of refugees from the countryside seeking refuge in the urban centres. In Karachi, the influx altered the ethnic and political balance of the city, provoking violence which killed dozens in October 2010. Elsewhere the population of migrants simply swelled the reservoirs of the rootless, displaced urban working class or lower middle class, the classic constituency for political Islamists. The weak and unstable government of Asif Ali Zardari proved as incapable of managing the natural catastrophe as it was of managing the various man-made disasters affecting Pakistan. Even without the floods, the economy was in very deep trouble, with negative or negligible growth and runaway inflation.

Nor, despite the problems at home, was there any sign of change in the Pakistani security establishment's basic strategic vision or understanding of its nation's interests. Even two years after the Mumbai attacks, only token measures had been taken to find and incarcerate those responsible, for example. Individuals like Hafiz Saeed, the founder and effective leader of Lashkar-e-Toiba, continued to be viewed as potential strategic assets rather than as dangerous liabilities.[31] With every indication being that the Pakistanis' 'spoiling' strategy in Afghanistan was likely to be successful there was little reason for much change there either. The Pakistani security establishment was still committed to making sure they had a de facto right of veto, via their support for Taliban elements, over any political settlement in Afghanistan. There was no major assault by the army into North Waziristan, despite strong American pressure. Militant attacks, often indiscriminate, continued to intensify. In December, forty-five died when a suicide bomber – possibly a woman – detonated a device among a crowd queuing to receive United Nations food aid. In all 2010 saw 2,113 militant, insurgent and sectarian attacks, in which 2,193 people died and nearly 6,000 were injured.[32] In January 2011, Salman Taseer, the moderate and outspoken governor of the Punjab, was shot dead in Islamabad by one of his own bodyguards, who was led away smiling after the murder. Taseer was killed for having vocally supported a Christian woman who had been accused of blasphemy and faced the death sentence. The lack of explicit condemnation by many of Pakistan's political leaders was as striking as the public celebration that accompanied his killing in some places. More than 1,000 lawyers volunteered to defend Taseer's killer for free. Clerics across the country condoned the assassination.[33] A month later, the shooting of two men by an American 'diplomat', in fact a CIA contractor, in Lahore led to a protracted diplomatic row and a new low for relations between Pakistan and the USA. If the summer of 2010 had been bloody, that of 2011 promised to be worse.

Then there was Iraq. Here again the broad trends established in recent years continued. Iraq still teetered between slow but definitive improvement and rapid regression. The bombings of government forces and religious minorities perpetrated by the various networks linked to al-Qaeda, who hoped to restart the sectarian civil war of 2004 to 2007, killed hundreds through the summer of 2010 and intensified as the autumn went on. The daily average of deaths from suicide bombs or gunfire and executions in Iraq through 2010 was 17.34, which maintained the country's position as the most violent place in terms of terrorism in the world.[35] More than 150 people – 89 civilians, 41 police and 21 soldiers – were killed in December 2010 alone.[36] The social conservatism of the Shia working classes and most Sunnis continued to broaden and deepen. There was little sign that the dangerous politicization of the security forces was at all diminished. The economic situation of most people saw little if any amelioration. For much of the year, the political process was paralysed. Elections in March had resulted in an impasse. The more moderate secular and non-sectarian party of Ayad Allawi had won the polls by a slim margin but finally – after ten or more months of negotiations – it was the incumbent, Nouri al-Maliki, who formed a government. The end of the American combat mission in Iraq on August 31, 2010 and the subsequent draw-down of troops was marked by widespread violence which, though anticipated, nonetheless shook many. The Kurds in the north continued to separate themselves economically, culturally and politically from the rest of the country. Major problems such as the future of the contested city of Kirkuk or the partition of the growing oil revenues remained unresolved, potential flashpoints for future strife. In January 2011, Muqtada al-Sadr returned to Iraq from Iran, where he had spent much of the previous four years studying to become an ayatollah. The thirty-seven-year-old cleric, whose representatives had won enough seats in the parliamentary elections to play a deciding role in the subsequent negotiations, spoke first at Najaf, the holy city. He gave thanks to God for the successful transition of his al-Mahdi Army into a political party, pledged support to the government and promised to fight on against 'our joint enemy: America, Israel and Britain'.[37] Both inside and outside Iraq, many watched nervously. 'I am happy that the US leave but they left a destroyed country controlled by bad people,' said Amal Kamel, a twenty-year-old student at a Baghdad college.[38]

Yet anyone who sensed a renewed drift into stagnation in the Middle East as 2010 turned to 2011 was about to be surprised. In early January 2011, food riots in Algeria had rattled the authorities and led to calls to calm – 'Islam is serenity' – from government-backed clerics as the youthful population seethed. The regime had held on, but the disturbances presaged a greater upheaval. First it was the turn of Tunisia, where the self-immolation of an out-of-work graduate who had tried to eke out a living as a fruit and vegetable seller triggered an uprising that led to the deposition of the corrupt and repressive president, Zine el Abidine ben Ali. From Tunisia, with its population of 10 million, the spirit of rebellion spread. Within a week of ben Ali's downfall, crowds had poured onto the streets in Egypt, calling for an end to the thirty-one-year rule of President Hosni Mubarak. After three further weeks of extraordinary scenes, of battles in central Cairo between protestors and pro-Mubarak thugs, a settlement was reached which saw the veteran leader deposed and the army effectively take power pending elections in the autumn. The news immediately sparked demonstrations in Bahrain, Kuwait, Algeria, Yemen, Syria, Morocco and in Colonel Gaddafi's Libya. In the latter the protests, first repressed with the loss of hundreds of lives, turned into a fully fledged revolt as the Libyan leader's extensive security apparatus collapsed across much of the country. With some irony, bulldozers brought in for the use of the scores of overseas companies that had moved into Libya since Gaddafi had opened its economy to foreign investment a decade before were used to attack military bases in and around Benghazi, the eastern port city two hours' drive from the Egyptian border, which soon became the de facto capital of 'Free Libya'. Gaddafi and those security forces which remained loyal hit back, bloodily retaking towns to the west of Tripoli and fighting their way east along the coast towards the rebel strongholds until forced to halt by airstrikes involving French jets and British and American missiles that, this time, were sanctioned by the United Nations Security Council. By the third week of March, the 'Arab Spring' had seen popular pressure achieve in the space of just over two months what decades of Islamic militant activism had been unable to do: unseat two of the hated 'hypocrite, apostate' dictators of the Middle East, destabilize the rule of a third and mobilize hundreds of millions across the entire region. An entirely new political, social, cultural and ideological cycle in the region appeared to be starting.

Yet, though undoubtedly constituting a radical break, these events could only be properly understood and explained by reference to the more general effects and evolution of the 9/11 Wars. Indeed, the events of early 2011 reinforced rather than contradicted a number of key trends and key lessons picked out earlier in this narrative. The first was that violence, revolt and revolution in the Islamic world is not rooted simply in a supposed clash between reactionary societies and 'modernity' in the form of the West; nor do they depend solely on the actions or interventions of Western leaders. No society is fixed, changeless or stuck in a 'medieval time-warp'. One of the reasons many observers were taken by surprise by the events of early 2011 was the perception that places like Egypt, Libya or Bahrain had somehow been bypassed by the major political, cultural, technological developments elsewhere. The Arab world, in the words of one prominent commentator, had been 'insulated from history for the last 50 years'.[39] This, of course, was total rubbish, as misleading as the descriptions of Saudi Arabia as a 'medieval monarchy' or Afghanistan as a 'thirteenth-century country', and further evidence of the stubborn Western tendency to see Muslim-majority societies as backward or timeless that had coloured so much policy-making and analysis with such damaging results for so long.[40] All countries in the Islamic world, as elsewhere in the developing world and beyond, had undergone a series of dynamic, unpredictable and complex internal transitions in recent decades which, if perhaps less than evident to outside observers, were no less profound for all that. Across the Middle East, the decades of political stasis had disguised rapid social evolution.[41] In Egypt, it was the combination of new economic growth – up to 8 per cent in 2007, only slightly less in the following years – with old cronyism, corruption, patronage and increasingly extreme inequality that proved explosive. This came at a time when demographics ensured a very large population of young people, a critical minority of whom had acquired an unprecedented capacity for social and political organization through the use of new social media. The same was true of Libya, where the revolt started in the economically marginalized eastern zones which had not benefited from Gaddafi's tentative steps towards economic liberalization, and whose tribes were less loyal to the regime. In Libya, the technologically savvy Westernized middle class prominent among the protestors in Egypt were less evident. The rebellion there had slightly different roots, a more traditional structure and a more populist tone as a result. Unlike in Tunisia and Egypt, average levels of education had not been rising over previous years, and schoolteachers in the newly liberated port city of Benghazi pointed out the spelling mistakes in the revolutionary slogans daubed on walls to reporters.[42] However, whatever their exact age or background, as protestors spilled out on to streets across the whole region, they ensured that it became increasingly difficult to see the Muslim or Arab world as a reactionary brake on the rest of the planet's steady ride towards a prosperous, stable and peaceful 'modernity'.

The second element seen repeatedly over previous years and reinforced by the events of early 2011 was the contingent nature of the appeal of democracy. As stressed previously, there is nothing in the norms, customs and values of Muslim majority countries that is essentially incompatible with any given political system. In Iraq 'democracy' had been rejected by different communities for a variety of reasons. Chief amongst them was that democracy itself had become associated with an accelerated and damaging process of Westernization, with brutal measures of economic liberalization and with the mismanagement typical of the occupation. In Afghanistan, a similar situation prevailed. There too the word 'democracy' had acquired negative connotations for large numbers of people. Pollsters in 2010 found that for many Afghans 'democracy' did not simply mean elections and parliamentary politics but 'an entire package of Western liberal values, where freedom is equated with an absence of rules, immorality, and secularism'.[43] The same was also true, to an extent, in Pakistan, where a government drawn from a Westernized elite continually risked being seen as distant from authentic national values and was forced to compensate with populist measures and rhetoric, particularly against the USA, as a result. In those theatres that had hitherto been at the heart of the 9/11 Wars, democracy, though in theory nothing more than a neutral system, had become synonymous with an unwelcome process of Westernization. But in Egypt and Libya the context was very different. In Egypt the protests were against a leader who had been backed by the West for longer than most of the protestors had been alive and who was pursuing a liberal economic agenda in line with the recommendations of international institutions such as the World Bank. After surrendering his nuclear weapons programme in 2003, Colonel Gaddafi too had been viewed as an ally and commercial partner by London, Paris and, increasingly, Washington. For the protestors in Cairo and then in Benghazi, democracy thus was seen not as a foreign import alien to local culture and values which had been imposed upon them but the opposite.[44] Democracy was something denied them by their leaders with the complicity of the West. It did not mean Westernization but simply the freedom to chose one's own government. There was therefore no conflict between being a 'campaigner for democracy' and being an Egyptian, a Libyan, and an Arab or a Muslim.

Third, the events in Egypt and elsewhere showed the complex relationship between the growing social and religious conservatism of many Arab and Islamic societies and formal politics. Again, this has also been seen elsewhere, in Pakistan, for example, or in Indonesia. In Egypt, the Muslim Brotherhood played a minor role in the upheaval's early stages though its well-organized activists were important in later phases. In part this was due to the movement's elderly leadership's early tactical miscalculations but it was also because the narrative within which the protests were framed was not a religious one. Yet the *informal* influence of Islamism – of which the fundamental project is the appropriation of the modern state, not its destruction – on the behaviour, culture and worldviews of very large numbers of people over recent decades and particularly during the 9/11 Wars in places such as Egypt, Libya, Algeria and Jordan, as well as in Pakistan, Turkey, Morocco and Indonesia and elsewhere, could not be doubted. So, though surveys had showed that 59 per cent of Egyptians believed that democracy was preferable to any other form of government, the same polls also revealed that 85 per cent also thought that Islam's influence in politics was positive.[45] A crowd of 200,000 turned out to hear Yusuf al-Qaradawi, the conservative Egyptian theologian who had last preached in his homeland thirty years before and who had a decade earlier tried to dissuade the Taliban from destroying the Bamiyan Buddhas, lead Friday prayers in Tahrir Square and speak of an 'unfinished revolution'.[46] Before the courthouse in Benghazi in the second week of March, a reporter noted that, behind those shouting 'Free Libya' and playing Arab pop music over loudspeakers, was another crowd, twenty ranks deep and chanting prayers. 'Re-Islamization' – the wave of conservatism that had spread across the Islamic world through the 9/11 Wars – might not have brought electoral success to the Muslim Brotherhood or other Islamist groups but had meant a different sort of quieter victory. This did not mean that the Egyptian protestors or the Libyan 'revolutionaries' or those risking the wrath of security forces in Syria, Bahrain or elsewhere were not committed democrats or that they did not believe in pluralism. But it did not make them secular either. Their religious culture and identity may have shifted out of the sphere of traditional political activity but was deep and strong nonetheless.

Fourthly, the demonstrations in Cairo and in other Middle Eastern cities and the fighting in Libya also saw a return and a reappropriation of each respective country's flag. This again reinforced trends seen elsewhere and over previous years. A thirty-two-year-old mother of three in the Yemen who had been leading demonstrations against the veteran president, Ali Abdullah Saleh – in power three years longer than even Mubarak had been – told one reporter that there was 'a race between Yemen and Algeria to see who would be next', revealing a sense of national pride that many had discounted as impossible in a region rent by tribalism, kinship ties or religion.[47] The 9/11 Wars had not only made clear, whatever the hyperbole about globalized identities, the sheer parochialism of the worldview of most people but also shown the remarkable resilience of the nation state, despite the obituaries prematurely written in the 1990s. Even militants in Pakistan had chosen to be the 'Pakistani Taliban'. The Afghan Taliban, for their part, went to great lengths to underline their nationalist credentials, which at the very least suggested that their leaders appreciated the resonance such rhetoric had. Only outsiders had ever seriously suggested the break-up of Iraq. Indeed, one of the many reasons al-Qaeda had lost support in 'the land of the two rivers' was that its attempt to appropriate local patriotic sentiment by renaming its affiliates 'the Islamic State of Iraq' had offended local nationalists, including potential allies among other insurgent groups and particularly former Ba'athists. The insults hurled at Tunisian president Ben Ali, Mubarak, Gaddafi, Saleh and others often revolved around the idea of 'treachery'. But those insulted were accused of being a traitor not to their religion, the key element of the Islamic militant discourse, but to the nation. Even protestors in the obviously artificial states of Bahrain or Kuwait, whose historic roots are slender, asserted their patriotic credentials as they demanded reform. Given the choice between the 'flat' globalized pan-Islamism of the extremists, with its almost total lack of local specificity, and 'the nation', the choice of the vast majority was clear. The Muslim Brotherhood, Jamaat Islami and other 'classic' or 'moderate' political Islamists had long recognized this and junked – or at least postponed – the universalizing 'pan-Islamic' project in favour of nationally based political and social activity. The wisdom of this pragmatic strategic choice was amply demonstrated when revolution finally came.

The challenge this new pluralist, democratizing nationalism posed in the spring of 2011 to al-Qaeda's internationalist ideologues and propagandists, coming on top of the evident rejection of their ideas and tactics by so many over previous years, was evident. Neither bin Laden's organization nor local groups, affiliated or otherwise, played even a marginal role in the upheavals that shook Tunisia and Egypt. The end to the rule of President Mubarak had been one of the primary aims in the minds of the founders of al-Qaeda back in the late 1980s, yet it took almost a month before the group made a statement on the most significant popular upheaval in the Arab world for many decades. The delay spoke volumes. The message when it came was tired and irrelevant. One significant component of the dissent sweeping the Middle East was the impatience and frustration felt by the young at being lectured by their elders, whether those elders, supposed to be held in such deference but so often incompetent or self-seeking or both, were eighty-two-year-old presidents, aged generals, kings, establishment scholars or radical ideologues. This appeared to have been entirely lost on the al-Qaeda senior leadership. Dismissing Mubarak as 'the biggest Arab Zionist', fifty-nine-year-old Ayman al-Zawahiri warned that democracy meant 'that sovereignty is subject to the desires of the majority, without committing to any quality, value or creed'.[48] His views on Egypt could not have been more distant from the sentiments expressed by those participating in the unrest and apparently shared by so many others. The senior leadership of al-Qaeda had apparently little to say about events in Libya either, even as once again a Western-led military operation was launched against an Arab, Muslim-majority state. In Tunisia, it had been the spectacular and public suicide of fruit and vegetable seller Mohammed Bouazizi – in which no one else was hurt – that had set off the uprising that overturned the regime of ben Ali. It was almost impossible to imagine an act that would undermine the tactics of al-Qaeda – suicides in which many people, often entirely innocent, were killed or maimed – more effectively. The same could be said for demonstrators in Syria, Bahrain and elsewhere, all of whom were resolutely non-violent. The geographic, organizational, ideological and cultural marginalization of both al-Qaeda in particular and of extremist radical Islam more generally had been increasingly evident for several years. The upheavals that shook the Arab and Islamic worlds in the early spring of 2011 made it blindingly obvious. Throughout them all, bin Laden remained silent.

However, despite so much apparent justification for a rare if relative optimism about the future evolution of state and society in the Middle East, two final elements nonetheless gave pause for thought. The first was uncertainty about the degree to which the young, web-surfing, often highly educated urban-based activists who had led the protests – described by *Time*, *Newsweek* and other major publications as 'the generation that is changing the world' – actually were as representative of their societies as they were portrayed to be in the West. The courage and organizational capabilities of such men and women were undoubted. But the question of how widely people in small towns, in rural areas or in the slums, whether young or old, shared their values and vision of the future still remained to be resolved. The second element that should have tempered the hopes of a shining new future, justifiable though they might have been, was the weight of expectation the events of the spring of 2011 had generated. For the successive uprisings had revealed the depth of the problems – social, political, economic – confronting the region. A quick historical survey showed the extent to which it had always been the young that had brought change, backing successive projects of reform and national revival, in the region's recent history. Each of these projects – secular nationalism, pan-Arab Socialism, Islamism, post-Islamist local violent militancy – had disappointed. It was this series of failures that had made bin Laden's new hybrid blend of religion, politics, tradition and innovation so attractive and had led, in the late 1990s, a small but significant number of young men to set out for the camps of Afghanistan. If, as a new transformative ideology swept the region in early 2011, there was one thing of which all observers could be sure it was that renewed disappointment would cut deep into the fragile fabric of already battered societies and would affect the young, now as expectant and as motivated as ever before, more than anyone. The challenge of meeting these expectations was a very great one.

THE END OF BIN LADEN

Bin Laden had in fact been working on a new communiqué giving his views on the Arab Spring. Recorded some time in March or April, it would only be released posthumously. On May 2, just after midnight, the fifty-four-year al-Qaeda leader was shot dead by American special forces in the bedroom of a three-storey house set behind high walls in the northern Pakistani garrison town of Abbottabad. By the time the speech was finally uploaded on to an extremist internet forum, its author had been dead for three weeks.

Bin Laden did not die as either he or his followers had hoped. Unarmed at the moment of death, neither he nor the three other men in the house put up any significant resistance. There was no spectacular martyrdom. The seventy-nine Navy SEALs who assaulted the compound came under fire for a few moments at the beginning of the raid, but that was all. The al-Qaeda leader was surrounded not by loyal retainers fighting to the last but by his three wives, his children and grandchildren. Bin Laden's twenty-two-year-old son Khaled was killed with his father. Their bodies were flown out to an aircraft carrier in the Arabian Sea and, after some kind of religious rite had been performed, slid beneath the waves.

The other two men killed in the assault were Pakistani brothers. One of them had inadvertently led the CIA to bin Laden. His name was Arshad Khan, though for many years the agency had only known his *nisbah*, or *nom de guerre*, Abu Ahmad al-Kuwaiti. He had long been of interest, ever since his name had surfaced repeatedly in the interrogations of detainees in the years after 9/11. He was clearly trusted and relatively senior, a veteran associate of the leadership. His exact role, however, was unclear. Major figures such as Khaled Sheikh Mohammed were evasive when questioned about him, encouraging the CIA to focus further resources on tracking him down.

In 2007, the agency discovered that their target was not al-Kuwaiti after all but a man called Mohammed Arshad Khan, who, though he had brought up in the Gulf state, was of Pakistani nationality. Fluent in Arabic, Urdu and Pashto, Khan could communicate with foreign militants and locals in the North West Frontier Province as well as more generally across Pakistan. One reason for the breakthrough was a new understanding, in part gleaned from operations in Iraq, of the nature of militant groups. Instead of working their way up the vertical hierarchy of al-Qaeda, investigators had built up a picture of horizontal networks instead, creating vast maps of the potential connections and functions of target individuals. In 2009, they got a phone number for Arshad Khan. Using new software and communications technology to detect phone calls and emails and then further map the webs of connections between them, the CIA created models of his personal relationships. A year later, Pakistani agents working for the Americans located their target in Peshawar. He was followed to the Abbottabad house, which was put under observation. By April, no positive identification of bin Laden had been achieved, but the tall man who was seen pacing the garden of the home alone for long periods was judged to be the al-Qaeda leader, and a raid went ahead.[49] 'We can say to those families who lost loved ones to al-Qaeda's terror: justice has been done,' Obama told the American nation in a television address hours later. The death should be welcomed by all who believe in peace and dignity, the president said. Whatever the arguments over international law, sovereignty or the manner of bin Laden's killing, it was difficult to argue with either sentiment.[50]

The Navy SEALs collected computers, stacks of documents and scores of hard drives and USB keys from the compound where bin Laden had been living. They left the children, the wives and the bodies of the two brothers. The youngest wife, a twenty-nine-year-old Yemeni who had married bin Laden eleven years earlier, told Pakistani security forces who arrived on the scene after the Americans had left that she and her daughter, ten-year-old Safiya, had lived in the compound for five years.[51] This raised the possibility that bin Laden had been in Abbottabad for half a decade. With hindsight, there was nothing that indicated that this might not have been the case. It appeared that bin Laden, having almost certainly spent years immediately after his flight from Afghanistan either in a major Pakistani city or more likely in the FATA, had indeed decided to trade operational effectiveness for security, probably moving into the Abbottabad safehouse soon after it was completed in 2005. The house had no internet access or telephone lines, and communication, the CIA team examining the material seized there soon found, had relied on a laborious system by which bin Laden would write emails that would then be sent by a courier, usually one of the two brothers, from a distant internet café. He had, however, been kept aware of developments within al-Qaeda and its affiliate groups and of ongoing plans for attacks. A notebook found by the Americans was full of jottings: a calculation of how many US citizens would have to be killed to force Washington to disengage entirely from the Middle East, remarks on the suitability of various candidates for senior positions within the group, comments on which American officials other than the president it was worth targeting and apparent outrage over a suggestion by one contributor to the magazine *Inspire* that a farm machine or tractor be fitted with blades for an attack in America. This, bin Laden tetchily noted, he could not endorse as it would lead to 'indiscriminate killing' and was thus not 'something that reflects what al-Qaeda does'.[52] There were also indications that bin Laden was planning – or perhaps simply dreaming of – a bid to unite all the disparate factions fighting the US-led coalition in Afghanistan into a grand alliance under his leadership. This would have been the al-Qaeda leader's most ambitious attempt to date to appropriate a local struggle for his own global one.[53]

The death of bin Laden naturally raised many questions. What, many asked, was the al-Qaeda leader doing in Abbottabad? With relatively good road links in all directions, including into rugged terrain to the north-west, from where Afghanistan or the militant stronghold of Bajaur would not be too hard to reach, the town had certain advantages. That the safehouse was in a discreet suburb favoured by retired army officers and was close to Pakistan's main military academy clearly posed a risk but also offered freedom from fear of missile attack and the benefits of being genuinely seen as a highly unlikely place for the world's most wanted fugitive to hide. The chief attraction, of course, was, in the often makeshift, make-do world of militancy, that the safehouse already existed, created by Arshad Khan.

Did someone in the Pakistani security establishment know of bin Laden's presence in Abbottabad? Though sympathy for much of what bin Laden stood for was deep in the ISI, in the army and among the population at large, it seems likely that the al-Qaeda leader's ability to hide 'in plain sight' was more evidence of the institutional weakness of the country, the incompetence of senior officers and of systemic failure within the intelligence services than anything more sinister. Though there was plenty of evidence of support for local and regional Islamic extremists by the ISI, there was no solid proof of the agency ever assisting international militants. Indeed, the record of the ISI when it came to operations against such figures was relatively good. In the absence of hard evidence, the ISI, though justifiably criticized for its role in supporting insurgents in Afghanistan and for running, with increasing difficulty, Pakistani militant groups like Lashkar-e-Toiba, was probably not directly implicated in sheltering bin Laden. The fact that, according to references among the data seized in the compound, there were indications that, around a year before he died, bin Laden himself had pondered a possible truce with local Pakistani authorities, along the lines of that which militants in London in the 1990s had thought they had concluded with the British government, reinforces this conclusion.[54]

The question of the complicity – or stunning incompetence – of Pakistan's security establishment naturally had a regional dimension. The death of bin Laden immediately triggered another crisis in Pakistani–American relations, already at a low point. Behind the rhetoric, though, the thinking in Washington remained that Pakistan was simply 'too big to be allowed fail' and that continuing aid, though perhaps with better focus and criteria, needed to be made available even if patience with the country's security establishment was wearing extremely thin. Demands were made again for the detention or 'rendering' of Mullah Mohammed Omar and several other senior militants, but more in hope than in anticipation of any immediate action. Pakistani public reaction swung between a vociferous assertion of a variety of conspiracy theories, anger at the army, anger at the Americans and anger at bin Laden. A major theme was a diffuse, inchoate but nonetheless real sense of shame.

The real 'game changer', however, was in Afghanistan. With bin Laden gone, not only was Obama (and to some extent key allies such as the UK) presented with an opportunity to accelerate the drawdown of forces there, scheduled to begin in the summer, but the president, with eighteen months to go before an election, now faced even greater difficulty in persuading domestic opinion that the long, gruelling and hugely expensive war in Afghanistan still needed to be fought. Less than 100 international militants were believed to be in Afghanistan in the spring of 2011, of whom only 'a handful' were interested in targeting the West.[55] US military expenditure alone there was nearly $10 billion each month. 'Are we moving towards transition? Yes. Are we trying to get out of Afghanistan as fast as we can? Absolutely not. There is no scurry for the exit,' insisted one US official in Kabul.[56] Allies such as the UK earnestly repeated the same sentiments all while trying to accelerate a political settlement by lifting sanctions on former Taliban. But with all Western activity in their country increasingly framed around 2014 – the agreed date by which international combat troops would be gone – such statements inevitably did little to reassure nervous Afghans. Many felt, not unreasonably, that once the soldiers had left aid and attention would disappear too. 'It will be chaos. It will be civil war. Everything we have gained will go,' Fatima Karimi, a twenty-nine-year-old student teacher, told the author as she picnicked with her family by a river on the outskirts of Kabul a month and a day after bin Laden's death. Despite the spread of chicken, fried potato cakes, salad and melon, the atmosphere was far from festive. The Karimi family were from the Shia religious and Hazara ethnic minorities and had much to lose.[57] Kabul may have been calmer in the spring of 2011, but it was an anxious place.

For al-Qaeda, there was obviously the question of bin Laden's succession. This was never going to be a simple issue. Though al-Zawahiri was clearly the leading candidate to take on the leadership of al-Qaeda, his candidacy was not without controversy. Irascible, argumentative and lacking in charisma, even if his experience was respected, the fifty-nine-year-old Egyptian did not have universal support either within the 'hardcore' or among affiliates. Al-Zawahiri's pragmatism also angered the many middle-ranking militants committed to a purely literal extremist reading of Islamic texts.[58] As an Egyptian, he was less well placed than bin Laden had been as a Saudi to mediate between factions within the group. But the younger leaders like Abu Yahya al-Libi were far from ready to take on any such a high-profile role. Further fragmentation of the group, the networks, even the ideology appeared likely, at least in the short and mid term. Ten days after bin Laden's death a statement from al-Qaeda's al-Fajr online media centre issued a new call to arms. 'Do not consult anyone about killing Americans or destroying their economy,' the statement said. 'We ... incite you to carry out acts of individual terrorism with significant results, which only require basic preparation. We say to every *mujahed* Muslim, if there is an opportunity, do not waste it.' An appeal to the social movement created over previous years, this was the quintessential expression of a strategy of 'leaderless jihad'.

A week later, bin Laden's final public words were broadcast. The dead leader welcomed the Arab Spring and predicted, as he had done so many times before, 'winds of change blowing over the entire Muslim world'. There was little of the sanguinary rhetoric that had marked previous statements and no calls for violent attacks. 'Let the truth ring out,' bin Laden said. 'Remember those that go out with a sword are true believers, those that go fight with their tongue are true believers, and those that fight in their hearts are true believers.' The release of the tape was barely noticed in the Islamic world. Most people were much more interested in the news from Libya, where fighting between rebels and Gaddafi's forces continued amid Western air strikes, or from the Yemen, where President Ali Abdullah Saleh's regime appeared close to falling, or from Syria, where security forces had killed and tortured thousands in violent repression of protestors calling for democratic reform, than in the late bin Laden's familiar exhortations.

Elements of the material seized by the Americans continued to be selectively leaked over the months following the Abbottabad raid. The claim that a stash of pornography had been found appeared a fairly transparent and clumsy effort to blacken the dead al-Qaeda leader's posthumous reputation among current or potential followers. Little emerged to support repeated public assessments by US officials that bin Laden had been deeply involved in the detailed day-to-day running of the group either. One video released by the CIA unequivocally reinforced the sense of a historical figure whose time had passed. It showed bin Laden, stroking his beard, wrapped in a blanket with a woollen cap on his head, sitting on the floor in a room probably in the Abbottabad compound, watching a television set on a desk beside a blacked-out window. On the screen ran images of a younger man – the viewer himself in 2002 or 2003 – wearing a combat jacket and walking through wooded hills, then further footage of the al-Qaeda leader firing an AK-47 in around 2000, some pictures of the 9/11 attacks and finally a sequence of fighters on an assault course somewhere amid dusty desert hills. Then the pictures were gone and only a blank screen remained.

Conclusion: The 9/11 Wars

THE 9/11 WARS:
THE GLOBAL AND THE LOCAL

So as the end of the first decade of the 9/11 Wars approached, some of the answers to the questions that the sight of the American forces spread out in the sand, scrub and pitted concrete at Bagram all those years before had become clear.

Certainly the nature of the conflict was now more evident. The qualities established in those early campaigns – at Tora Bora, in the streets of Baghdad as the insurgency in Iraq took hold or in the dust of Majjar al-Kabir, where the six Redcaps were to die, in Abu Ghraib, in the bombings of nightclubs in Bali and consulates in Istanbul – had been consolidated as time had passed. This new war was chaotic and scattered, with few heroes and many villains. It was a conflict where gain and loss had been determined as much by the relative venality or brutality of participants as by courage or resourcefulness. It was a conflict marked by violence to civilians, to prisoners and by an appalling ignorance among many decision-makers of the local conditions, the circumstances and the cultures of other protagonists. It was, at the end of its first ten years as at its beginning, still marked by the extreme diversity of the scores of interwoven wars that it comprised.

These wars existed on multiple levels. At the local level, they were a mass of private battles, fratricidal skirmishes, communal clashes, often sparked by specific incidents of misgovernance or injustice, some pitting village against village, neighbourhood against neighbourhood, tribe against tribe. At the next level, the wars were often about the participation of a particular group in politics at a provincial or national level.

Frequently they involved conflicts about the definition of a certain ethnic or religious group's position within a state. Only at the final level, the biggest in scale, could some of these conflicts be integrated into an overarching cosmic conflict pitting the West and its allies against radical Islam. Each level provided a different prism through which the overall conflict could be seen. Not all were equally valid. Only by glossing over the local specificities of all its component elements could the 9/11 Wars be seen a war between religions, between the secular and the faithful, between the West and the East or between global 'haves' and global 'have-nots'. Such generalizations, with their easy assumptions and seductive simplicity, at best highlighted only one element of the overall conflict, at worst obscured and distorted the nature of the phenomenon they supposedly described.

As their first decade ended, enough of the course of the 9/11 Wars was also now evident to be able to tentatively offer a prediction for what the next years of the conflict might bring. After the stunning violence of their beginning in the autumn of 2001 and the short lull in 2002 and early 2003 the Wars had grown in extent and intensity to a peak in around 2005 and 2006. This was followed by a relative decline that was partially – but not totally – offset by rising levels of localized violence in Pakistan and Afghanistan. The most recent phase of the conflict, still ongoing in the summer of 2011, had seen a fragile stabilization, leaving it finely balanced. Despite a continuing level of violence that was undoubtedly much higher than in the years preceding the 9/11 attacks, there was nothing to indicate an imminent global conflagration as had once been feared. Indeed, the events in the Arab world in early 2011 suggested that such an eventuality was extemely unlikely. The most probable scenario for the coming years of the 9/11 Wars was thus that this delicate equilibrium would be maintained for the foreseeable future with violence and militancy shifting between new nodes of activism and geographic zones according to local circumstances, the emergence of new leaders and the creation of new groups.[1] Generational shifts and heightened expectations after the 'Arab Spring' would be important factors in determining the level of any violence. The ability of local regimes and rulers to defuse demands for reform and of new governments to meet the new hopes for peace, prosperity and, in particular, 'dignity' of hundreds of millions of people would be crucial in determining its location. An important factor too would be the adaptability of al-Qaeda in all its manifestations, following bin Laden's death. But though any renewed militancy would cause problems, it was nonetheless unlikely to pose an existential threat, either to the West or to the Islamic world.

What major factors had determined the course of the 9/11 Wars so far? The answer is the key lesson from the last decade. In the introduction to this work, the importance of the tension between the 'global' and the 'local' was flagged as critical to the evolution of the conflict. This was repeatedly proven over the course of the years. At every level, the resistance offered by the particular to the general was crucial. At the grandest scale, it was the rejection of the globalized ideology of radical Islam propagated by bin Laden and others like him in around 2005 and 2006 by hundreds of millions of Muslims across the Islamic world that marked the major turning point in the conflict. The message of bin Laden, deliberately stripped of local specificity and as disrespectful of local custom or belief as anything emanating from the West, began losing popularity among its primary audience when its local implications became clear. Al-Qaeda's call to arms had had some broad appeal, plugging into deep-felt feelings of humiliation and a defensive narrative that had become widespread over previous decades as well as a range of broader social, demographic and economic factors that in some cases dated back a century or more. This attraction was not diminished – indeed it was often deepened – when the militants married deeds to words, when bombs exploded in distant towns, strikes were launched on distant cities, particularly American ones, or when occupying forces in the heart of the Middle East were attacked. But when the violence came home, it provoked a very different reaction. The sight of blood on one's own streets, the dismembered bodies of one's own compatriots, the grieving parents who could have been one's own – as well as the evident economic and cultural damage done by radical Islamic activism to any society – turned entire populations away from violence. When viewed from up close, the ideas and practices of men like bin Laden were much less appealing than they appeared on the internet or on the evening news, and the impact on established local customs, identities, practices and communities much greater. The result was that both Abu Musab al-Suri's plans for a global uprising, apparently so close to being fulfilled in 2005, and the 'open front' strategy favoured by Abu Musab al-Zarqawi, which once also looked like succeeding, foundered on the stubborn parochialism that characterizes most people's vision of the world most of the time.

It was not just the projects of the militants that were undermined by the resistance of 'the local' to the global. Early on in the 9/11 Wars, Western leaders, in particular President Bush and Prime Minister Tony Blair, had, like the extremists, both understood and projected the conflict as part of a cosmic contest. Their decisions had, in part, been determined by a desire to propagate a series of universal principles. These may have been far more attractive than those of radical Islam but, particularly when they were imposed by force, could be as alienating. The key shift in the first decade of the conflict came when, at the same time as sentiment turned against al-Qaeda in the Islamic world, and in part as a result of this change, Western policy-makers and strategists began to question whether the earlier ideological approach was constructive and whether aggressively seeking generalized solutions based in a broad package of 'liberal democratic' and free-market capitalist ideas were likely to further the interests of the states they led in the conflict they now found themselves engaged in. From 2006 or 2007 onwards, new thinking based on a more careful consideration of the views, ideas, interests and values of the communities that in many ways constituted the battlefield in the 9/11 Wars began to be implemented. In every case – whether it was American soldiers on the ground in tough neighbourhoods of Baghdad, men and women from MI5 fanning out across the UK to be based in police stations, a return to intelligence services relying on human sources not merely telecommunications intercepts – the new tactics implied and brought a deeper understanding of other societies, a better knowledge of 'human terrain', a greater tolerance of difference and encouraged a new pragmatism. At a local level, such as in Iraq, this allowed local circumstances to be exploited to first slow and then reverse a descent into hellish violence. In Afghanistan, though coming too late and after too many errors to make a major difference, it at least mitigated some of the damage previously done. At a global level, the new approach allowed space for the growing antipathy towards violent extremism in the Islamic world to thrive and for the idea of 'democracy' to be divorced in the minds of many from a coercive project of Westernization. It encouraged the calmer atmosphere of the latter years of the decade. Without this shift, it is unlikely the relative stabilization of the threat that al-Qaeda and the movement of contemporary radical Muslim militancy posed could have occurred.

This approach – privileging the micro over the macro, the local over the global – helps us to understand the lessons of the 9/11 Wars as regards the nature and genesis of radical violence. In the search for an answer to the question of why or how 'ordinary men' become 'terrorists', the 9/11 Wars have taught us, once more, that the specific rather than the general is of most use. Early attempts at profiling – constructing general laws to designate masses of population as potentially dangerous – or to find universally relevant 'predictor' factors of militancy failed. In the later years of conflict, the discussion in counter-terrorist circles was instead about the process by which individuals became radicalized. It was no longer about the 'who' but about the 'how', and it focused on the role of friends or brothers or fathers, exposure to the internet, whom an individual happened to meet and when. The earlier approaches were rejected as too blunt to be of much use. The plotting of vertical hierarchies was replaced by the modelling of horizontal networks. Each path to violence was seen as unique and had to be dealt with as such. Extrapolation – 'joining the dots' – was thus replaced by 'granularity' – precise, knowledge-based, case-by-case analysis. Though some patterns could, of course, be discerned – a decline in the educational level of militants in Saudi Arabia from 2005 onwards, the rising proportion of converts in Europe over the decade or the increasing number of Iraqi suicide bombers with family members in prison in 2008 or 2009 – these were only useful for establishing what was going on in any one locality. Comparing the path into violence of, say, Abu Mujahed, the Sunni insurgent the author interviewed at length in Baghdad, and the 7/7 bombers, or of Abit, the Pakistani suicide bomber who failed to detonate his bomb at the last minute, and the drug-dealing 'El Chino' who had played such a key role in the Madrid bombings of 2004, was of limited use. As much as any new laws or powers for the police, it was this realization that enabled security services to feel more confident by 2008 or 2009 than they had done for many years previously. They had learned that the path to violence involves such a broad range of potential factors and situations that any single explanatory theory of why some are attracted to violence – religion, class, deprivation – was bound to fail. There are broad trends that can establish a background. There are short-term factors that may encourage a certain type of behaviour. There are catalysts which can spark a critical change for a specific individual or even a group. But, as in the 9/11 Wars as a whole, there are no global rules.

WINNERS AND LOSERS

Has the West won the 9/11 Wars? The West has certainly – despite al-Qaeda's various successes over the years – avoided defeat. The power of terrorism resides in its ability to create a sense of fear far in excess of the actual threat posed to an individual. Here what has not happened is as significant as what has happened. Governments have largely protected their citizens, and few inhabitants of Western democracies or indeed Middle or Far Eastern nations today pass their lives genuinely concerned about being harmed in a radical militant attack.[2] In July 2010, President Obama even spoke of how the USA could 'absorb' another 9/11, a statement that would have been inconceivable a few years before.[3] Despite significant damage to civil liberties in both Europe and America, institutional checks and balances appear to have worked on both sides of the Atlantic. In the face of a worrying militarization and 'securitization', other forces have been strong enough to ensure that liberal democratic societies have kept their values more or less intact. The integration of minorities, always a delicate task, is generating significant tensions but is proceeding, albeit unevenly. Even though now facing serious problems of debt, America has been nonetheless able to pay for the grotesque strategic error of the war in Iraq, at a total cost of up to a trillion dollars depending on how it is calculated, and a ten-year conflict in Afghanistan all while financing a huge security industry at home in the midst of one of gravest economic crises for decades. In 2009, American military expenditure was $661 billion, considerably more than double the total of ten years previously and a sizeable enough sum, but still not enough, as bin Laden had hoped, to fundamentally weaken the world's only true superpower.[4] In Europe, supposedly creaking old democracies have reacted with a nimbleness and rapidity that few imagined they still possessed to counter domestic and international threats. In short Western societies and political systems appear likely to digest this latest wave of radical violence as they have digested its predecessors.[5] In 1911, British police reported that leftist and anarchist groups had 'grown in number and size' and were 'hardier than ever, now that the terrifying weapons created by modern science are available to them'. The world was 'threatened by forces which would be able to one day carry out its total destruction,' the police warned. In the event, of course, it was gas, machine guns and artillery followed by disease that killed millions, not terrorism.[6] In the second decade of the 9/11 Wars other gathering threats to the global commonwealth such as climate change will further oblige Islamic radical militants to cede much of the limelight to those phenomena which genuinely do pose a planetary menace, at least in the absence of a new, equally spectacular cycle of violence.

But if there has been no defeat for the West then there has been no victory either. Over the last ten years, the limits of the ability of the USA and its Western allies to impose their will and vision on parts of the world have been very publicly revealed. Though it is going too far to say that the first decade of the 9/11 Wars saw the moment where the long decline of first Europe and perhaps America was made clear to the world, the conflict certainly reinforced the sense that the tectonic plates of geopolitics are shifting. After its military and diplomatic checks in Iraq and Afghanistan, a chastened Britain may well have to finally renounce its inflated self-image as a power that 'punches above its weight'. The role of NATO in the twenty-first century is unclear. Above all, though the power, soft and hard, cultural and economic, military and political, of the USA and Europe remains immense and often hugely underestimated, it is clear that this will not always be the case. For many decades, the conventional wisdom has been that economic development around the globe would necessarily render the project of liberal democracy and free-market capitalism more popular. One of the lessons of the 9/11 Wars is that this optimism was misplaced. A sense of national or religious chauvinism appears often to be a corollary of a society getting richer rather than its opposite, and the search for dignity and authenticity is often defined as much by opposition to what is seen, rightly or wrongly, as foreign as anything else. In some places, the errors of Western policy-makers over recent years have provoked a reaction which will last a long time. The socially conservative, moderately Islamist, and strongly nationalist, narrative that is being consolidated in Muslim countries from Morocco to Malaysia will pose a growing and increasingly coherent challenge to the ability of the USA and European nations to pursue their interests on the global stage for many years to come. This, alongside the increasingly strident voices of China and other emerging nations, means a long period instability and competition is likely before any new *modus vivendi* is reached. American intelligence agencies reported in their quadrennial review in late 2008 that they judged that within a few decades the USA would no longer be able to 'call the shots'. Instead, they predicted, America is likely to face the challenges of a fragmented planet, where conflict over scarce resources is on the rise, poorly contained by 'ramshackle' international institutions.[7] The previous review, published in December 2004, when President Bush had just been re-elected and was preparing his triumphal second inauguration, had foreseen 'continued dominance' for many years to come, considering that most major powers had effectively forsaken the idea of balancing the US.[8] The difference over the intervening years from 2004 to 2008 is thus stark. If these years brought victory, then America and the West more generally cannot afford many more victories like it.

If clear winners in the 9/11 Wars are difficult to find, then the losers are not hard to identify. They are the huge numbers of men, women and children who have found themselves caught in multiple crossfires: the victims of the 9/11 strikes or of the 7/7 and Madrid bombings, of sectarian killings in Baghdad, badly aimed American drone strikes in Pakistan or attacks by teenage suicide bombers on crowds in Afghanistan. They are those executed by Abu Musab al-Zarqawi, those who died sprayed with bullets by US Marines at Haditha, those shot by private contractors careering in overpowered unmarked blacked-out four-wheel-drive vehicles through Baghdad. They are worshippers at Sufi shrines in the Punjab, local reporters trying to record what was happening to their home towns, policemen who happened to be on shift at the wrong time in the wrong place, unsuspecting tourists on summer holidays. They are the refugees who ran out of money and froze to death one by one in an Afghan winter, those many hundreds executed as 'spies' by the Taliban, those gunned down as they waited for trains home at Mumbai's main railway station one autumn evening, those who died in cells in Bagram or elsewhere at the hands of their jailers, the provocative film-maker stabbed on an Amsterdam street, all the victims of this chaotic matrix of multivalent, confused but always lethal wars.

The cumulative total of dead and wounded in this conflict so far is substantial. Any estimates of casualties in such a diverse and complex conflict is necessarily very approximate, but some idea of its human cost can be obtained nonetheless. The military dead are the best documented. Though some may have shown genuine enthusiasm for war or even evidence of sadism,[9] many Western soldiers did not enlist with the primary motive of fighting and killing others. A significant number came from poor towns in the Midwest of America or council estates in the UK and had joined up for a job, for adventure, to pay their way through college, to learn a craft. By the end of November 2010, the total of American soldiers who had died in Operation Iraqi Freedom and its successor, Operation New Dawn, was 4,409, with 31,395 wounded in action.[10] More than 300 servicemen from other nations had been killed too and many more maimed, disabled or psychologically injured for life. In Afghanistan, well over 2,000 soldiers from 48 different countries had been killed in the first nine years of the Afghan conflict. These included 1,300 Americans, 340 Britons, 153 Canadians, 49 Frenchmen and 44 Germans.[11] Military casualties among Western nations – predominantly American – in other theatres of Operation Enduring Freedom from the Sudan to the Seychelles and from Tajikistan to Turkey added another 100 or so. At least 1,500 private contractors died in Iraq alone.[12]

Then there were the casualties sustained by local security forces. Around 12,000 police were killed in Iraq between 2003 and 2010.[13] In Afghanistan, the number of dead policemen since 2002 had exceeded 3,000 by the middle of 2010.[14] Many might have been venal, brutal and corrupt, but almost every dead Afghan policeman left a widow and children in a land where bereavement leads often to destitution. In Pakistan, somewhere between 2,000 and 4,000 policemen have died in bombing or shooting attacks.[15] As for local militaries in the various theatres of conflict, there were up to 8,000 Iraqi combat deaths in the 2003 war, and another 3,000 Iraqi soldiers are thought to have died over the subsequent years.[16] In Afghanistan, Afghan National Army casualties were running at 2,820 in August 2010, while in Pakistan, around 3,000 soldiers have been killed and at least twice as many wounded in the various campaigns internally since 2001.[17] Across the Middle East and further afield in the other theatres that had become part of the 9/11 Wars, local security forces paid a heavy price too. More than 150 Lebanese soldiers were killed fighting against radical 'al-Qaeda-ist' militants in the Nahr al-Bared refugee camp in Lebanon in 2007, for example. There were many others, in Saudi Arabia, in Algeria, in Indonesia. In all, adding these totals together, at least 40,000 or 50,000 soldiers and policemen have so far died in the 9/11 Wars. Casualties among their enemies – the insurgents or the extremists – are clearly harder to establish. Successive Western commanders said that they did not 'do body counts', but most units kept a track of how many casualties they believed they had inflicted, and these totals were often high. At least 20,000 insurgents were probably killed in Iraq, roughly the same number in Pakistan, possibly more in Afghanistan.[18] In all that makes at least 60,000 people, again many with wives and children.

Then, of course, there are those, neither insurgent nor soldier, neither terrorist nor policeman, who were caught in a war in which civilians were not just features of the 'battle space' but very often targets. In 2001, there were the 9/11 attacks themselves, of course, with their near 3,000 dead. In 2002 alone, at least 1,000 people died in attacks organized or inspired by al-Qaeda in Tunisia, Indonesia, Turkey and elsewhere. The casualties from such strikes continued to mount through the middle years of the decade. One study estimates 3,013 dead in around 330 attacks between 2004 and 2008.[19] By the end of the first ten years of the 9/11 Wars, the total of civilians killed in terrorist actions directly linked to the group or affiliated or inspired Islamic militants was almost certainly in excess of 10,000, probably nearer 15,000, possibly up to 20,000. To this total must be added the cost to civilians of the central battles of the 9/11 Wars. In Iraq generally, estimates vary, but a very conservative count puts violent civilian deaths (excluding police) from the eve of the invasion of 2003 to the end of 2010 at between 65,000 and 125,000.[20] They included more than 400 assassinated Iraqi academics and almost 150 journalists killed on assignment.[21] The true number may be many times greater. In Afghanistan, from October 7, 2001, the day when the bombing started, to mid October 2003, between 3,000 and 3,600 civilians were killed just by coalition air strikes.[22] Many more have died in other 'collateral damage' incidents or through the actions of the insurgents. The toll has steadily risen. In 2005, the total was probably around 450 civilian casualties. From 2006 to 2009 between 5,000 and 7,000 civilian deaths were documented, depending on the source. In 2010 alone, 2,777 died, mostly due to insurgent action. Half as many again had already died by mid May 2011. In all, between 14,000 and 17,000 civilians have been killed in Afghanistan, and at least three or four times that number wounded or permanently disabled. In Pakistan, which saw the first deaths outside America of the 9/11 Wars, the number of casualties since that first handful died when police shot into demonstrations in September 2001 are estimated by local authorities and regional analysts at around 9,000 dead and between 10,000 and 15,000 injured.[23] Add these admittedly rough figures from the principal theatres of the Wars together and you reach a total of well over 150,000 civilians killed. In all the approximate overall figure for civilian and military dead of the violence associated with the 9/11 Wars is probably near 250,000. If the injured are included – even at a conservative ratio of one to three – the total number of casualties reaches one million. This may be a sum that is lower than the losses inflicted on combatants and non-combatants during the murderous major conflicts of the twentieth century but still constitutes a very large number of people. Add the bereaved and the displaced,[24] let alone those who have been harmed through the indirect effects of the conflict, the infant mortality or malnutrition rates due to breakdown of basic services, and the scale of the violence that we have witnessed over the last years is clear. The changes in our lives and societies will be commensurate. Some day this conflict – the 9/11 Wars – will be remembered by another name. Most of the dead will not be remembered at all.

ALI SHAH

At 11 o'clock a cold, hard wind cut across the frozen mud and dry grass of a patch of wasteland hidden by a thick line of gorse and brush behind a lay-by a few hundred metres from the outer perimeter fences of the northern French port of Dunkirk. Among the bushes, a hundred or so young men had built makeshift shelters. It was a week or so since the local police had come by with bulldozers, and the shelters, rebuilt after each such raid, were crowded. Under the wood stripped from nearby trees, plastic sheeting handed out by local campaigners, dustbin bags, salvaged sheets of rusted corrugated iron, blankets and the occasional upturned shopping trolley, groups of young men huddled around fires. Above, gulls circled and shrieked in the grey winter sky.

Kurds and Arabs from Iraq, a handful of Somalians, a smattering of Iranians, a few dozen Afghans, two Syrians, an Algerian and a Pakistani, they came from almost every theatre touched by the 9/11 Wars. Among them was a twenty-four-year-old Hazaran Afghan with a thin beard, worn jeans and a cheap red ski jacket pulled tight over a thin cotton sweater. This was Ali Shah, the young shepherd with a taste for learning English who had escaped from Bamiyan over the mountain trails at night as the Taliban had prepared to destroy the Buddhas all those years before. Ali Shah had eventually made his way to Iran and had watched the news of the 9/11 attacks in a café near the eastern Iranian city of Mashhad, where he worked as a mechanic's assistant. In 2003, after briefly being jailed, he had returned to Afghanistan to find his family in Kabul, where he was hired by an international NGO as a driver. He earned good money until repeated threats from insurgent sympathizers forced him to flee. Having decided to try his luck in Europe, Ali Shah set his sights on the UK. His savings were enough to pay the traffickers. Old friends looked after him on his way through Iran. He had trekked over the Iranian–Turkish frontier, hitchhiked to Istanbul and then paid $3,000 to get to Greece before spending almost all his remaining money – $1,400 – to be brought by boat to Italy. He had taken a train from Milan to Paris, slept in a park for a week near the Gare de l'Est and then taken a train to Calais. Almost picked up by the police there, he had managed to slip away through undergrowth before hitching north to Dunkirk, where he had heard things were better. Now he was stuck again. Every night he tried to get into trucks heading for the UK but without success. He had no money and relied on sympathetic locals for food and firewood. 'I have been travelling for too long. I would like to go home, but the situation in Afghanistan is very bad,' he said and looked towards the lines of trucks parked in the dusk beside the port. 'Hopefully things will be better when I get to the other side. I am now very tired.'[25]

Notes

INTRODUCTION

1. Both World Wars, the French Revolutionary and Napoleonic Wars and a host of other major conflicts share it too. The Second World War was much more than a straight fight between democratic states and repressive, fascist ones. It comprised equally significant ideological, economic and cultural contests as innumerable subsidiary conflicts, between states, communities, even families. The Cold War was also far from a simple Manichaean battle between two ideological blocs. Struggles for national liberation, ethnic and tribal wars, social conflict also made up its rich and varied fabric. My thanks to the late Professor Fred Halliday, who kindly shared his thoughts on the multi-dimensionality of this current conflict and sent me a draft of his essay 'Global Jihad, "Long War" and the Crisis of American Power', in Fabio Petito and Elisabetta Brighi, eds., *Il Mediterraneo nelle Relazioni Internazionale: tra Euro-Mediterraneo e Grande Medio Oriente*, Fondazione Laboratorio Mediterraneo, 2007.

CHAPTER 1: THE BUDDHAS

1. Basic café serving tea and food.
2. Author interview with Ekram Shinwari, VOA reporter who travelled incognito to Bamiyan to film the scene, Kabul, March 2009.
3. Author interview, near Dunkirk, France, December 2009.
4. The split between Shia and Sunni dates back to the earliest generations of the first Muslims and a dispute over the inheritance of the moral and political authority of the Prophet Mohammed which in very general terms pitted those who believed that it should pass down the bloodline of the dead leader, the Shia, against those who believed in a more political and meritocratic choice of successor, the Sunni. Behind this superficially political division, historians have shown, lies a range of cultural, ethnic and tribal differences.
5. The date of the Buddhas' construction has been various estimated between

the third and seventh centuries. In 1989, the art historian Deborah Klimburg-Salter argued a seventh-century date but according to Dr Fred Hiebert, an archaeologist and National Geographic fellow, carbon dating of lumps of wood found in the debris of the destroyed statues reveals a fourth-century date. Holland Cotter, 'Buddhas of Bamiyan: keys to Asian history', *New York Times*, March 3, 2001. Author telephone interview with Dr Fred Hiebert, March 2009.

6. A change which many attributed to the advice of Pakistani military officers.

7. The last Soviet troops left in January 1989.

8. The word Taliban had been used to describe small groups of independent and relatively effective fighters from religious schools who had fought alongside the main groups of '*mujahideen*' in the war against the Soviets. See Abdul Zaeef, *My Life with the Taliban*, Hurst, 2010, for an interesting account. The word 'Taliban' originated in Arabic. Its singular form is *talib*, which means knowledge-seeker. Over time a Dari ending – *alef* (a) and *noon* (n) – was added to create a plural, 'Taliban'.

9. Pakistan has three major intelligence agencies. The Intelligence Bureau (IB) is the main civilian intelligence agency and focuses on domestic intelligence, reporting to the prime minister rather than the minister of the interior. Military Intelligence (MI) compiles reports for the chief of army staff. The Directorate of Inter-Services Intelligence (ISI) draws together the intelligence capabilities of the three military service branches, as well as acting independently of all of them through its clandestine S Department or Branch. The ISI theoretically reports to the prime minister, but in practice has always reported direct to the chief of army staff.

10. Further assistance came from a large number of former members of some of the most extreme factions within the Afghan Communists who had learned to use artillery, armour and planes in Kabul's armed forces in the 1980s, had then gone on to fight for various *mujahideen* factions and were both experienced and proficient. The role of these 'Khalqis', so-called for their allegiance to the hardline Khalq (the People) faction of the Communist People's Democratic Party of Afghanistan, has been often underplayed. For more on the Khalqis, see Thomas Barfield, *Afghanistan: A Political and Cultural History*, Princeton University Press, 2010, pp. 225, 259. Also Barnett R. Rubin, *The Fragmentation of Afghanistan*, Yale University Press, 2002, pp. 82, 105. Many eventually resurfaced in the reconstituted Afghan National Army after 2001.

11. Much of the original leadership of the Taliban were former fighters – often junior commanders – of Mohammed Nabi Mohammedi's Harkat-ul-Inqelabi-ul-Islam party.

12. 'We are seekers of peace and honour in the way of God. Our aim is to secure the peace and honour of our nation and our people,' Mullah Hassan

Rachman, the Taliban governor of Kandahar explained. Rachman, an arch conservative who had lost a leg fighting the Soviets and had the disconcerting habit of placing his artificial limb beside him on a sofa during interviews, did not often travel to Kabul, describing the capital as 'a bad place' from which 'much wrongdoing and vice [had] come that poisoned the country'. Author interviews, Kandahar, August, October 1998. On the Taliban's outreach programme in the mid 1990s see also Seth Jones, *In the Graveyard of Empires*, Norton, 2009, p. 58; Abdul-Kader Sinno, 'Explaining the Taliban's Ability to Mobilize the Pashtuns', in Robert D. Crews and Amin Tarzi, *The Taliban and the Crisis of Afghanistan*, Harvard University Press, 2008.

13. Multiple author interviews with former senior Pakistani officers, Islamabad, Rawalpindi, 2002, 2005, 2008. US Department of State cable, 'Afghanistan: Pakistanis to regulate wheat and fuel trade to gain leverage over Taliban', August 13, 1997. US Embassy Islamabad cable, 'Bad news on Pak Afghan Policy: GOP Support for the Taliban appears to be getting stronger', July 1, 1998, National Security Archives. Some Pakistani paramilitaries appear also to have fought with them on occasion.

14. There is an enormous range in census data. Compare, for example, the CIA factbook of 2000 with the United Nations Afghanistan Information Management Systems estimates of 2003. The Taliban were almost exclusively drawn from Afghanistan's Pashtun tribes, who make up around 45 per cent of the population, though figures are contested. With no census since 1979 and ethnicity a deeply fluid concept, estimates can only be rough. In addition to the Pashtuns and the Hazara, Tajiks and Uzbeks there were around thirty other recognized discrete ethnic or linguistic groups including Aimaq, Pashai, 'Arab' as well as other population groups defined differently, such as Syeds, who claim to be descendants of the Prophet, his family or his immediate entourage.

15. Figures from the World Bank, data bank, accessed January 2011. Unicef lists the literacy rate for 2003–8 at 28 per cent.

16. A controversial veteran of the movement's campaigns across Afghanistan over the previous six years, Dadaullah's excessive violence had already led to his being removed twice from command. Born in a small village in the central province of Oruzgan in 1966, he had grown up in a Pakistani refugee camp, returning to Afghanistan to fight the Soviets during the 1980s before returning in the early 1990s to join the Taliban. On Dadaullah, see Jason Burke, 'Hunt for the Taliban trio intent on destruction', *Observer*, July 9, 2006; Ron Moreau and Sami Yousafzai, 'In the footsteps of Zarqawi', *Newsweek*, July 3, 2006.

17. Author interviews in Bamiyan, March 2002, Kabul 2009. Human Rights Watch, 'Afghanistan: Ethnically-Motivated Abuses Against Civilians', *Human Rights Watch Backgrounder*, October 2001. Human Rights Watch Annual

Report, *Massacres of Hazaras in Afghanistan*, February 1, 2001. Interviews with United Nations specialist, Kabul, 2009. See also Rory Stewart, *The Places in Between*, Picador, 2005, pp. 247, 263, 299 and 302. Author interview with Stewart, Kabul, March 2009. Stewart also gives a colourful account of the shifting allegiances of various commanders. Ahmed Rashid, *Descent into Chaos*, Allen Lane, 2008, p. 299.

18. Author interviews with senior former Taliban ministers, Kabul, March, 2009.

19. Author interview with Dr Said Omara Khan Masoudi, National Museum director, Kabul, March, 2009. Those against destroying the Buddhas included the education minister, Arsala Rahmani, the foreign minister, Mullah Wakil Ahmed Muttawakil, and the culture minister, Qadrutullah Jamal.

20. Men like Mullah Mohammed Hassan Akhund, the governor of Kandahar and one of the most conservative of the Taliban leaders, and the deputy minister of culture, Mullah Nuruddin Turabi.

21. See United Nations Development Programme, *Afghanistan Annual Opium Poppy Survey*, 2001, p. ii for statistics.

22. Author interviews with Rahimullah Yusufzai, BBC, and Ekram Shinwari, VOA (Voice of America), both of whom had met Omar, Kabul and Peshawar, 1999–2001.

23. See US Embassy Islamabad cable, 'Afghanistan: The Taliban's decision-making process and leadership structure', December 31, 1998, confidential, 15 pp., declassified 2009.

24. The last person to bring out the cloak was King Ahmed Shah Durrani in 1768. See Jos L. Gommans, *The Rise of the Indo-Afghan Empire c.1710–1780*, Brill, 1995, pp. 65–6.

25. Many communities had been alienated by enforced conscription, by bans on popular local customs and by being progressively shut out of decision-making processes. There was armed resistance in the east of Afghanistan against forced conscription in 1999, for example, and small incidents, such as attempts by local Taliban to ban traditional pastimes such as 'egg fights', could spark violence. The Noorzai tribe in the south near Kandahar were only barely kept from outright mass revolt.

26. Author interviews with Wakil Ahmed Muttawakel and Arsala Rahmani, Kabul, March 2009. See also Ron Gutman, *How We Missed the Story*, United States Institute of Peace Press, 2008, pp. 235–9; and Peter Bergen, *The Osama Bin Laden I Know*, Simon and Schuster, 2006, p. 248. Author interview with Vahid Mojdeh, Kabul, August 2008.

27. Finbarr Barry Flood, 'Between Cult and Culture: Bamiyan, Islamic Iconoclasm, and the Museum', *The Art Bulletin*, December 2002.

28. See above and State Department memo, Assistant Secretary of State for South Asian Affairs Karl F. Inderfurth to Secretary of State Madeleine Albright, 'Taliban under pressure', May 1, 2000, confidential, declassified 2009.

29. A good example of the legends created deliberately by Abdul Rahman can be found in the probably fictional or at least exaggerated account of his personal impromptu decapitation of an elderly Herati cleric who had legitimized a rebellion with a *fatwa*, Barfield, *Afghanistan*, p. 146.

30. Gutman, *How We Missed the Story*, pp. 238–40.

31. Author interview with a retired Pakistani military officer present at meeting between Omar and Mahsud Ahmed, ISI chief in Kandahar, Rawalpindi, November 2008. Gutman, *How We Missed the Story*, p. 239. 'Lost Chance', *Time*, August 12, 2002. Steve Coll, *Ghost Wars*, Penguin, 2005, pp. 554–5.

32. Multiple author interviews with senior Taliban ministers, officials, Kabul, Kandahar, 1998–2000. See Jason Burke, *Al-Qaeda: The True Story of Radical Islam*, Penguin, 2004, pp. 116–35, 193–4. Alan Cullison and Andrew Higgins, 'Computer in Kabul holds chilling memos', *Wall Street Journal*, December 31, 2001. A Defense Intelligence Agency cable of October 2, 2001 predicted 'eventually the Taliban and al-Qaeda will wage war with one another ... Al-Qaeda has not integrated with Afghans in the Taliban.'

33. Author interviews with Mullah Nabi Mohammedi, Kabul 1998, numerous senior Taliban officials, Kabul, Kandahar 1999.

34. Militants from the international groups were warned against any contact with the Afghans. See the testimony of Abdurahman Khadr, broadcast in the PBS Frontline programme *Son of al Qaeda*, April 22, 2004, who said he had been punished for speaking to the Afghans while in a training camp. A copy of al-Qaeda guesthouse regulations included the prohibition on talking to the Afghans who did the cooking and cleaning. Author collection.

35. Excepting those who had participated in a delegation which had travelled to Sugarland, Texas, for consultations with UNOCAL, an American company interested in building a 1,300 km gas pipeline across Afghanistan. See 'Taleban in Texas for talks on gas pipeline', BBC News Online, December 4, 1997. The relative lack of animosity among the Taliban towards the United States was implicitly recognized by a volunteer in one Afghan training camp who asked bin Laden in 2000: 'Has al-Qa'eda under your command pledged [an oath] to the Islamic Imarah in Afghanistan? If so, how do you call for fighting the United States knowing that the Taliban did not hear of it for reasons concerning the security and stability of Afghanistan? We pray to God that He saves the Taliban.' Harmony documents, Harmony Program, West Point, Combating-Terrorism Center, document ID: AFGP-2002-801138.

36. There are many other differences. Wahhabis belong to the Hanbali madhab, one of the most rigorous of the four schools of Sunni Islam, for example, whereas the Deobandis are part of the Hanafi madhab, an entirely different school of Islamic theology. Letters found by the author in Khaldan Camp, November 2001, revealed further animosity between Afghans and their foreign 'guests'. See also Burke, *Al-Qaeda*, pp. 169–71. Bergen, *The Osama Bin Laden I Know*, p. 179. Harmony Documents, document ID: AFGP-2002-602181.

37. The recognition quote is from Abdul Salaam Zaeef, author interview, Islamabad, 2000.

38. Another factor was the Taliban refusal of Pakistani demands to hand over sectarian militants responsible for widespread violence in Pakistan itself who had sought sanctuary across the border.

39. Author interview with Maleeha Lodhi, Pakistan's then ambassador to Washington, March 2009. 'The realization that Pakistan's identification with the Taliban regime was increasingly becoming a diplomatic liability was there in the establishment and not just the civilian part,' Lodhi said. See also Coll, *Ghost Wars*, p. 547. Jason Burke, David Rohde, Tim Judah, Paul Harris and Paul Beaver, 'Al-Qaeda's trail of terror', *Observer*, November 18, 2001.

40. See Burke, *Al-Qaeda*, p. 186; Coll, *Ghost Wars*, pp. 400–402.

41. Michael Keating, 'Dilemmas of Humanitarian Assistance in Afghanistan', in Bill Maley, ed., *Fundamentalism Reborn?*, New York University Press, 1998, p. 136. In the 1980s UN agencies had cooperated with Afghan Communist government programmes for the education of women and a variety of other empowerment projects focused on urban Afghan women. Pankaj Mishra, *Temptations of the West*, Picador, 2006, p. 365.

42. Author interview with Francesc Vendrell, London, February 2009, with Daniel Roggio, UN political adviser, Kabul, March 2009. Pamela Constable, 'Annan appeals to Taliban to spare Buddha statues', *Washington Post*, March 12, 2001. Vendrell himself had met Mullah Omar a year previously.

43. Gutman, *How We Missed the Story*, p. 239. Author interviews in Kabul, March 2009.

44. The cameraman concerned, Tayseer Ayouni of al-Jazeera, claimed in an interview in 2004 that he had filmed secretly. However, given his astonishing images of the destruction and its aftermath, this seems highly unlikely. Author interview with a Taliban official, Islamabad, 2001.

45. Author interviews with locals, officials in Bamiyan, March, 2002.

46. A school of religious thought and practice, rather than a specific group or strand, Salafism is, in literal terms, the emulation of the *salaf*, or the first three generations of Muslims. (Some say the first four generations should be included.) These, followers say, were the only believers to have truly lived according to Allah's instructions to man as communicated via the Prophet Mohammed. Since those early days, the understanding of Allah's message and thus Islamic religious practice and with it social practices too have become corrupted by innovation, *bid'ah*, by the return of the polytheism that pre-dated Islam, *shirq*, and by foreign influences. Only a return, through a rigorous implementation of a literalist and ultra-conservative reading of the Koran, to earlier practices can ensure the return of the just society of the time of the Prophet across the *ummah*, the global community of Muslims. At the centre of Salafism is the concept of *tawhid*, or the unity or oneness of God.

Such views have proved attractive at regular intervals over the centuries. Ibn Tammiya, a key Salafi scholar and a major influence on modern ideologues including bin Laden and others among the al-Qaeda leadership, was writing in the thirteenth century after the fall of Baghdad to the Mongols, an event he blamed on the corruption and lassitude of the ruling Muslim dynasty and their subjects. In the nineteenth century, as Muslim societies and states came off worst in their one-sided battle with an expansionist West, new thinkers resurrected the idea of an Islamic renaissance based on a return to basics. With Salafis divided over how best to respond to the challenge posed by the technological, military and apparent cultural superiority of the invaders, various strands of thought emerged. Some called for a total rejection of all Western innovation and a harsh puritanism, others for its appropriation, a position which evolved towards the political ideology of Islamism, which calls for the appropriation of the modern state apparatus rather than its replacement by a model based on that believed to have been current in seventh-century Arabia and inevitably implies the formation of parties rather than a rigorous adherence to an individual relationship with God. Some thinkers justified violence, others called simply for spiritual renewal. From the Maghreb to the Far East, Salafi movements took hold, perhaps most spectacularly in Saudi Arabia, where Salafi clerics became an integral part of the new state of Saudi Arabia, and in Afghanistan, where the Taliban fused a mythic conception of Pashtun tribal culture with Salafi ideas to produce a revolutionary and potent new local strand.

47. Ahmed Rashid, *Descent into Chaos*, p. 20. Author interview with Nigel Inkster, former deputy head of MI6, London, February 2009.

48. Author interviews with Nigel Inkster, Richard Dearlove, London, February 2009. Richard Dearlove, former head of MI6, response to question at conference, London, February 2009.

49. Material later found by US forces showed, however, that, though he appeared assured and confident on the finished video, he had in fact had been nervous and irritable, and it had taken many attempts to record his statement. See Martyr Tape of Ziad Samir Jarrah, reproduced in Referral Binder – Part I, Ali Hamza Ahmad Suliman al Bahlul, AFGP-2003-001320.

50. Charge sheet, USA vs. Ali al-Bahlul, FBI interrogation of al-Bahlul report statement, July 30–31, 2003. Author collection.

51. Educated at a private school and then at the engineering faculty of Abdel Aziz university, bin Laden had been raised in a strict Wahabi household. Subsequently, like millions of young men across the Muslim world, he had been exposed in the late 1970s to the modern ideas of political Islam that were gaining in strength at the time. Bin Laden did not, as often claimed, head 'straight for Afghanistan' when the Soviets invaded in 1979 but in fact probably first arrived in Peshawar in 1981. He raised funds through his own

network of wealthy contacts and helped with the administration of Abdullah Azzam's 'Office of Services' organization, which raised funds from the Islamic world and Muslim communities in Europe and America to aid the Afghan refugees and wounded *mujahideen* and, to a much lesser extent, recruited volunteers to fight. Azzam's propaganda videos, with their bloody images of civilians wounded in Soviet attacks and exciting footage of ambushes among the scruffy, scrubby hills of eastern Afghanistan, were rudimentary but extremely effective on both wide-eyed teenagers and on the devout, wealthy patrons in the Gulf whom bin Laden solicited for funds. In 1989 bin Laden led a group of international militants at the catastrophic battle of Jalalabad, when, at the bidding of the Pakistani ISI, the squabbling *mujahideen* factions and their Arab auxiliaries incurred massive losses as they attempted to storm the eastern Afghan city.

Further points worth making about the issue of CIA support for bin Laden or others like him include the fact that the CIA were not allowed to enter Afghanistan (an injunction they obeyed), and did not instruct any Arab Afghans, disburse funds to them or supply them directly with equipment. As pointed out in the main text, any US contact with *mujahideen* of any background was indirect, with the Pakistani ISI acting as an intermediary, and the latter trained and supplied only Afghans, and then only from the seven factions that they recognized. Afghan leaders like Gulbuddin Hekmatyar, favoured by the ISI, had no wish or need to share hard-won resources with foreigners. Nor indeed did men like bin Laden, with their own sources of funding, need assistance. The Saudi Arabian government matched US aid to the *mujahideen* dollar for dollar, but these resources too were distributed by the ISI. The only exception was the faction of Abdul Rasul Sayyaf, an Afghan cleric who was very close to Saudi Wahhabi networks and the Saudi intelligence services, who received funds directly. As mentioned in the main text, techniques taught by the ISI on the basis of manuals and instruction from the CIA did bleed into the world of the Arab volunteers – the eleven-volume *Encyclopedia of Jihad* compiled in 1991 by international militants in Peshawar and dedicated to bin Laden and Azzam is based on American instruction manuals – but no direct instruction took place.

As for the other myths, it is worth stressing that the bulk of foreign volunteers arrived in Peshawar after the Soviets had begun withdrawing, and even the military contribution of foreigners who had arrived earlier was negligible. Most were engaged in construction, missionary or humanitarian work. Those who did fight were distributed in tiny groups among the *mujahideen* factions of Hekmatyar and Sayyaf. Rodric Braithwaite argues convincingly in his excellent *Afgantsy: the Russians in Afghanistan 1979–1989*, Profile, 2011, that the impact of the American Stinger surface-to-air missiles distributed from 1986 onwards was minimal too, as the Soviets soon found ways to reduce their losses to previous levels.

52. A useful account of this period to be found in Chapter 2 of Peter Bergen's excellent *The Longest War*, Simon and Schuster, 2011. Also, Bergen, *The Osama Bin Laden I Know*, pp. 80–81. Also in Lawrence Wright, *The Looming Tower*, Allen Lane, 2006, pp. 132–4. Early sources include documents provided to the author by Ron Motley, lead lawyer, 9/11 victims vs. Saudi Arabia, 2003. Also of interest is the US government evidence in USA vs. Enaam Arnout, January 2003, which deals in part with al-Qaeda in the 1990s. See also Burke, *Al-Qaeda*, Chapter 1, 'What Is Al-Qaeda?'. Minutes of the final meeting on August 20, 1988 at which the formation of the group was agreed ends with the line that 'the work of al-Qaeda commenced on September 9, 1988'.

53. Quoted in Rohan Gunaratna, *Inside Al Qae'da*, Hurst, 2002, p. 3.

54. His Saudi citizenship was withdrawn three years later.

55. A multitude of works now exist on this period. See Peter Bergen, *Holy War Inc.*, Touchstone, 2002; Gilles Kepel, *Jihad*, I. B. Tauris, 2002; Wright, *The Looming Tower*; *The 9/11 Commission Report*, W. W. Norton, 2004; and Burke, *Al-Qaeda*.

56. Khaled Sheikh Mohammed jealously guarded his autonomy and consistently refused to swear the *bayat* or oath of allegiance to bin Laden. See *The 9/11 Commission Report*, p. 59. Also: 'Sheikh Mohammed said he attempted to postpone swearing the *bayat* as long as possible to ensure that he remained free to plan operations however he chose,' Substitution for the testimony of Khaled Sheikh Mohammed, United States vs. Moussaoui, July 31, 2006, the United States District Court, Eastern District of Virginia.

57. The first version of the plan envisaged all the planes crashing into their targets except for one, which would land to allow Khaled Sheikh Mohammed himself to give a press conference.

58. Author interview with David Hicks, July 2010.

59. Another senior militant later remembered: 'I was staying at the general guesthouse when a bus arrived from the camp with at least forty-five trainees on board . . . When we asked why they had left the camp they told us that it had been closed down on bin Laden's orders because the date of the martyrdom operation was approaching. Everyone based in the camp was to head to Kandahar or Kabul or dispersed into the mountains to avoid becoming an easy target for any military strike.' Interview with Mohammed al-Tamimi, in Arabic newspaper *al-Hayat*, September 20, 2006, quoted in Camille Tawil, *Brothers in Arms*, Telegram, 2010, p. 182. The general guesthouse he referred to was in Kandahar and used by new arrivals.

60. Both men had travelled from Belgium, where they had been living, to Afghanistan earlier in the year. One had travelled, his wife later said, after seeing footage of bin Laden on the evening news. Like many of those who were enrolled in the 9/11 attack, the pair had been selected for their 'martyrdom mission' by al-Qaeda leaders who regularly visited the camps looking for tal-

ent among the trainees. The killing was a sweetener for the Taliban, who had already made their opposition to any direct attacks on American soil very clear, though bin Laden repeatedly told associates he did not expect the 'cowardly' US to send any soldiers to Afghanistan in retaliation for the coming attack. He cited the use of missiles only following the embassy bombings of 1998 as evidence.

61. A useful account of the assassination can be found in John Lee Anderson, *The Lion's Grave*, Atlantic Books, 2002.

62. Charge sheet, USA vs. Ali al-Bahlul, FBI interrogation reports, author collection. Court testimony of Ali Soufran and Christopher Anglin, FBI agents, USA vs. Ali Hamza al-Bahlul, November 2008.

63. Wright, *The Looming Tower*, p. 358.

64. Ibid. Questions answered by email by David Fratz, al-Bahlul's lawyer, July 2009. Evan Kohlmann, *Inside As-Sahaab: The Story of Ali al-Bahlul and the Evolution of al-Qaida's Propaganda*, Nefa Foundation, 2008.

CHAPTER 2: 9/11, BEFORE AND AFTER

1. George Bush, *Decision Points*, Virgin, 2010, p. 134.

2. Richard Clarke, *Against All Enemies*, Simon and Schuster, 2004, p. 2. Bob Woodward, *Bush At War*, Simon and Schuster, 2003. *The 9/11 Commission Report*. Alistair Campbell, *The Blair Years*, Hutchinson, 2007, pp. 560–61.

3. Michael Powell, 'In 9/11 Chaos, Giuliani forged a lasting image', *New York Times*, September 21, 2007.

4. Bush, *Decision Points*, p. 144.

5. Campbell, *The Blair Years*, p. 561.

6. Sharon had been elected in February.

7. On October 9, 2001, in Britain's *Mirror* newspaper, David Trimble, the Unionist leader in Northern Ireland, declared that there was no difference between 'Irish and Arab terrorists'. In the run-up to the March presidential elections, President Robert Mugabe labelled his opponents 'terrorists', thus appearing to condone violent attacks by his supporters on his political opponents. 'Amnesty Now', *Amnesty International* magazine, summer 2002.

8. 'Reaction from around the world', *New York Times*, September 12, 2001. 'Attacks draw mixed response in the MidEast', CNN, September 12, 2001. Saddam Hussein afterwards denied approving the terms used by the newsreaders in question. This seems unlikely given the nature of his regime, but possible.

9. 'Islamic world deplores US losses', BBC News Online, September 14, 2001.

10. 'Sheikh Yusuf Al-Qaradawi condemns attacks against civilians: forbidden in Islam', IslamOnline and News Agencies, September 13, 2001.

11. See *America's Image in the World: Findings from the Pew Global Attitudes Project*, March 2007. A problem with gauging pre-9/11 sentiment is the lack of reliable data for the 1990s. Though anecdotally evidence of the attraction of living in the USA is clear, hard data is again difficult to find. Immigration statistics are one indication. US Department of Homeland Security and US Census figures show rising numbers of entrants to the US from Indonesia, Pakistan and Saudi Arabia in the late 1990s.

12. Such conflicted feelings were particularly evident among many Palestinians. Though Yasser Arafat, the Palestinian leader, expressed shock at the attacks, ostentatiously giving blood for the victims, reports of cheering Palestinians in parts of the Occupied Territories and in some Palestinian refugee camps in the Lebanon were genuine, despite internet rumours to the contrary. The real question was not whether 'celebratory gunfire' had echoed in the West Bank city of Nablus but to what extent those who had fired were representative of more general sentiments. A single portrait of bin Laden at a rally by Hamas supporters in Gaza was wrongly taken as evidence of widespread sympathy for al-Qaeda's leader. See 'Bin-Laden poster seen at Gaza rally', Associated Press, September 14, 2001; 'AP protests threats to freelance cameraman who filmed Palestinian rally', Associated Press, September 12, 2001; Joseph Logan, 'Palestinians celebrate attacks with gunfire', Reuters, September 12, 2001; 'Palestinians in Lebanon celebrate anti-US attacks', Agence France-Presse, September 11, 2001.

13. The 4,000 figure appears to have come from a *Jerusalem Post* internet article quoting an Israeli Foreign Ministry statement that 4,000 Israelis were believed to have been 'in the areas of the World Trade Center and the Pentagon at the time of the attacks'. 'The 4,000 Jews rumor: hundreds of Israelis missing in WTC attack', *Jerusalem Post* online, September 12, 2001.

14. Douglas Feith, *War and Decision*, Harper, 2008, p. 93.

15. Brian Whitaker, 'Muslim peoples doubt role of Arabs in September 11', *Guardian*, February 28, 2002. Gallup Poll of the Islamic World, based on interviews of nearly 10,000 residents in nine predominantly Islamic countries, Gallup, February 2002, Washington, DC.

16. ICM/BBC, BBC Poll of British Muslims, *Today*, Radio 4, November 2001.

17. Author interview with Mike Scheuer, CIA, head of Alec Station, August, 2005. See also the useful accounts in Coll, *Ghost Wars*; *The 9/11 Commission Report*; and Wright, *The Looming Tower*. A 1995 National Intelligence Estimate correctly analysed the danger as coming from 'transient groupings of individuals' that lacked 'strong organization but rather are loose affiliations' and operated 'outside traditional circles but have access to a worldwide network of training facilities and safe havens'. Effective and timely action was not taken.

18. Coll, *Ghost Wars*, p. 425.

19. Author interview, September 2008.

20. Department of Defense budget for Financial Year 2000, US DoD news release, February 1, 1999.

21. Lawrence Freedman, *A Choice of Enemies*, Weidenfeld and Nicolson, 2009, p. 370. Author telephone interview with Jack Cloonan, 2008.

22. Author interview with senior former MI6 officer, London, 2003.

23. Gary C. Schroen, *First In*, Ballantine Books, 2005, p. 26.

24. Coll, *Ghost Wars*, p. 493.

25. Ibid., p. 499.

26. See the testimony of Abu Jandal. That a meeting was to be held that bin Laden would chair at the camp was apparently widely known. Also Coll, *Ghost Wars*, p. 410.

27. Author interview with American officials, Riyadh, 2008

28. Author telephone interview with former senior CIA analyst, August 2009. Indian intelligence officials later admitted to the author that there was 'no evidence at all' of bin Laden's presence in Kashmir. The admission came in 2003 at a time of a relative thaw in relations between India and Pakistan.

29. Author interviews with three Middle Eastern intelligence service officials, Islamabad 1999–2000. Coll, *Ghost Wars*, p. 443.

30. Author interview with Michael Scheuer, CIA, head of Alec Station, 2002.

31. Author telephone interview with Art Keller, April 2008.

32. Ibid.

33. There was no station in Kabul. Author interview with British intelligence official, 2010.

34. Author interview, London 2009.

35. The identity of those at Tora Bora is a useful guide. Along with the Saudis, Egyptians and Yemenis who made up the core strength of al-Qaeda were Moroccans and Kuwaitis, Palestinians from Jordan, Syrians, Turks and many central Asian fighters, especially Uzbeks. There were several Chinese Uighur Muslims, a handful of Britons, a large number of Pakistanis and at least three Frenchmen.

36. The number of Egyptians appears to have dropped away during the 1990s, as one would expect given the course of the militancy in Egypt itself. By 2000, one volunteer was posing the question 'What is the reason for not having new Egyptian freedom fighters amongst us?' to bin Laden. Harmony documents, document ID: AFGP-2002-801138.

37. Tim Judah, 'The Taliban Papers', *Survival*, vol. 44, no. 1, spring 2002. The body of evidence produced by the recruits themselves in the form of interviews with journalists or their own published accounts of their experiences, the published biographies of 'martyrs', evidence later found in Afghanistan by intelligence operatives and reporters as well as the imperfect but nonetheless useful testimonies hundreds of them gave to investigators or tribunals while in custody now allows, a decade after 9/11, a relatively accurate picture

to be put together of who they were and how and why they travelled to Afghanistan. In April 2011, the author was able to consult 800 leaked official secret files on every detainee in Guantanamo Bay compiled between 2003 and 2007 to support recommendations for release or continued imprisonment. Each provided detailed biographies of their subject. Among other useful primary sources are the court proceedings and witness statements of Abu Jandal, Ali al-Bahlul, al-Batarfi, who all ended up in Guantanamo Bay, and the testimonies of al-Utaiba, Hossein Kertchou and Jamal al-Fadl during the 2001 trial of the 1998 east African bombings, USA vs. Usama bin Laden, New York Southern District Court, February 2001. Also John Walker Lindh indictment, February 2, 2002, US vs. John Walker Lindh in the US Eastern District Court of Virginia. Material that emerged during investigations of the Millenium Plot is also informative: testimony of Ahmed Ressam, USA vs. Mokhtar Houari, July 3, 2001; testimony of Judge Jean-Louis Brugiere, trial of Ahmed Ressam, Los Angeles, April 2, 2001; USA vs. Abu Doha sealed complaint, US Southern District Court, New York, July 2, 2001. Also related are the interrogation report of Djamal Beghal, author collection; Moroccan Ministry of Justice, interrogation report of Zuhair Hilal Mohammed al-Tubaiti, Casablanca, June 19, 2001, author's collection. Also among the many interviews the author conducted on this topic two of the most useful were with Mohammed Umr al-Madani, Kabul, 2008, and Noman Benotman, formerly of the Libyan Fighting Group, London, 2002, 2003 and 2008. There are now voluminous secondary sources on the training camps in Afghanistan in the 1990s though still relatively little on exactly who made the journey to reach them.

38. See Giles Kepel, *Jihad: The Trail of Political Islam*, I. B. Tauris, 2002; and Olivier Roy, *The Failure of Political Islam*, Harvard University Press, 1998. An additional advantage was that it drew heavily on the language and thought of those strands that had preceded it and thus seemed less alien.

39. Human Rights Watch, *Annual Report*, 2001.

40. See Bergen, *Holy War Inc.*; Bergen, *The Osama Bin Laden I Know*; Wright, *The Looming Tower*; Andy Worthington, *The Guantanamo Files*, Pluto, 2007; Burke, *Al-Qaeda*, pp. 56–72.

41. See Thomas Hegghammer, *Terrorist Recruitment and Radicalization in Saudi Arabia*, Middle East Policy, 2006, p. 44.

42. Ibid., p. 49.

43. A couple sought martyrdom to join a brother already killed in Afghanistan in heaven. See Hegghammer, *Terrorist Recruitment*, p. 49 and note 33 for further sources.

44. Others, such as the French convert Hervé Loiseau, simply followed older or respected charismatic individuals on whom they had developed a certain degree of emotional dependence. Loiseau and another young Frenchman of Algerian origin followed a much more motivated and capable nineteen-year-old called Mourad Benchellali, whose father was a radical cleric whose brother

had tried and failed to fight in Chechnya. Three of his family had spent time in French prisons. Benchellali insisted he had sought 'adventure', enhanced local status and to rival his brother and later published a fairly unapologetic book about his time in Afghanistan. Worthington, *The Guantanamo Files*, p. 63.

45. Sharon Curcio, 'Generational Differences in Waging Jihad', *Military Review*, July–August 2005, pp. 84–8.

46. Notebooks found at Darunta and Khost camps by the author, November 2001.

47. Letters found in New Khaldan camp by the author, November 2001.

48. A very high proportion of accounts from Western recruits refer to sickness. See also Curcio, 'Generational Differences'.

49. Author interview with David Hicks, July 2010.

50. Author interview with cleric and courier 'Haji Anwar', Peshawar, October 2001.

51. By the end of the 1990s, 'America stood out as an object for admiration, envy and blame . . . This created a kind of cultural asymmetry. To us, Afghanistan seemed very far away. To members of al-Qaeda, America seemed very close. In a sense, they were more globalized than we were,' the official American commission of inquiry into 9/11 accurately noted in 2004. *The 9/11 Commission Report*, p. 340. Though unfair to President Clinton and many of the senior counter-terrorist officials in Washington who recognized that fanatical politically or religiously motivated violence would be a growing threat as the world became more interconnected, these words did adequately capture how very few grasped how close the threat had become.

52. Two examples are Abu Qutada and Abu Musab al-Suri, who was perhaps the single most significant militant strategist of the 9/11 Wars.

53. Ruling of Special Immigration Appeals Commission, March 8, 2004. Tawil, *Brothers in Arms*, p. 125. An MI5 officer present at the meeting apparently sensed that Abu Qutada was close to offering to assist investigations into radical activity in the UK.

54. Abu Musab al-Suri, 'A Message to the British and the Europeans, August, 2005', quoted by Tawil, *Brothers in Arms*, p. 126.

55. Brynjar Lia, 'The Al-Qaida Strategist Abu Mus'ab al-Suri: A Profile', Presentation OMS-Seminar, March 15, 2006, Oslo, Norway. Author interviews with Omar Mohammed Bakri Fostok, London, 2000, 2001.

56. He received no reply, however. Tawil, *Brothers in Arms*, p. 125.

57. Author interview with a Special Branch officer, London, 2004.

58. Sums of between £25,000 and £100,000 were regularly seized, larger sums less frequently. One activist at the time told the author how he had given £50,000 to Lashkar-e-Toiba and £50,000 to Chechen groups, proceeds from a range of businesses that he and other activists ran, between 1999 and 2000. Indian intelligence services complained frequently to the British government – and the author – about these activities.

59. Author interview with an MI5 officer, London, 2005.

60. Author interview with an MI6 officer, London, 2009.

61. John Kampfner, *Blair's Wars*, The Free Press, 2003, p. 113.

62. Condoleezza Rice, testimony before 9/11 Commission. Daniel Benjamin and Steven Simon, *Age of Sacred Terror*, Random House, 2002. Clinton officials later insisted they had in fact repeatedly emphasized the threat of terrorism to Bush, Rice and others, and though many of the threat reports which reached senior administration figures were indeed vague or historic and desperately short of actionable details they did collectively speak of an unprecedented level of evident danger.

63. Clarke, *Against All Enemies*, p. 234. Bush, *Decision Points*, pp. 134–5.

64. *The 9/11 Commission*, p. 333. Rice, testimony before 9/11 Commission. The Principals Committee in Bush's White House included Rice, Attorney General John Ashcroft, Defense Secretary Donald Rumsfeld, Secretary of State Colin Powell, Treasury Secretary Paul O'Neill and CIA Director George Tenet, among other senior administration officials.

65. Bush, *Decision Points*, p. 135.

66. Ibid., p. 128.

67. CNN, Text of Bush's address, September 11, 2001.

68. Abizaid was born in California to a Lebanese-American father and an American mother. Though Arab-speaking, he is not Lebanese-born, as sometimes reported. See Jones, *In the Graveyard of Empires*, p. 243.

69. Bush, *Decision Points*, p. 145.

70. Feith, *War and Decision*, pp. 3–11

71. David E. Sanger, 'Ex-occupation aide sees no dent in "Saddamists"', *New York Times*, July 2, 2004. For Dick Cheney 'the situation when President Bush and I came to office' was that 'where terrorists were emboldened by years of being able to strike us with impunity'.

72. Manuel Perez-Rivas, 'Bush vows to rid the world of evil-doers', CNN, September 16, 2001.

73. George W. Bush, 'An Address to a Joint Session of Congress and the American People', September 20, 2001

74. The name was changed after Muslim scholars complained about the religiously charged initial name, 'Infinite Justice'.

75. See Pervez Musharraf, *In the Line of Fire*, pp. 201–4, for a colourful if not entirely reliable account of this episode.

76. *Operation Enduring Freedom: Foreign Pledges of Military and Intelligence Support*, CRS Report for Congress, October 17, 2001. Stephen Tanner, *Afghanistan: A Military History*, Da Capo, 2007, p. 292.

77. Bush, *Decision Points*, p. 191.

78. President George W. Bush, Commencement Address at the United States Naval Academy in Annapolis, Maryland, May 25, 2001. 'We must build forces that draw upon the revolutionary advances in the technology of war that will allow us to keep the peace by redefining war on our terms,' Bush had also said.

79. Thomas Ricks, *Fiasco*, Penguin, 2007. Feith, *War and Decision*, p. 75.

80. Kampfner, *Blair's Wars*, p. 117. One reason the Pentagon was reluctant to accept the myriad offers of aid flowing in was that, quite apart from few having the means to transport their troops to the theatre themselves or supply them once they were there, the forces offered were insufficiently equipped to fight effectively alongside a military as technologically sophisticated as the American army.

81. James F. Dobbins, *After the Taliban*, Potomac Books, 2008, p. 28. Feith, *War and Decision*, p. 51. Donald Rumsfeld, 'A new kind of war', *New York Times*, September 27, 2001.

82. Author telephone interview with Paul Pillar, former deputy director CIA Counter Terrorist Centre, national intelligence officer for the Near East and south Asia, November 2008.

83. Assistant Secretary of State for Intelligence and Research Carl Ford to Secretary of State Colin Powell, 'Pakistan – poll shows strong and growing public support for Taleban', November 7, 2001, National Security Archive. The levels had gone from 38 per cent of people saying they favoured increasing their country's support to the Taliban to 46 per cent and from a third to just over half seeing the Taliban more favourably as the coming war loomed.

84. 'Pakistan protests turn violent', BBC News Online, September 21, 2001.

CHAPTER 3: WAR IN AFGHANISTAN

1. Claudio Franco, 'The Tehrik-e Taliban Pakistan', in Antonio Giustozzi, ed., *Decoding the New Taliban*, Hurst, 2009, p. 272.

2. An Afghan equivalent of General Cambronne's useless but much admired 'merde' at Waterloo in 1815 or General McAuliffe's 'nuts' at Bastogne during the Battle of the Bulge, 1944, to name but a couple of examples.

3. Musharraf, *In the Line of Fire*, p. 216. See also Zahid Hussein, *General on a Mission*, Newsline, 2001, and *Frontline Pakistan*, Columbia University Press, pp. 41–3.

4. RAND Corproration, Benjamin S. Lambeth, *Air Power against Terror: America's Conduct of Operation Enduring Freedom*, 2005, p. xvi.

5. Author telephone interview with Bob Grenier, CIA station chief Islamabad 2001–2, January 2009. The Taliban commander concerned was Mullah Akhtar Mohammed Osmani. See also George Tenet, *At the Center of the Storm: My Years at the CIA*, HarperCollins, 2007, pp. 182–3.

6. These included Younis Khalis, the cleric and former *mujahideen* commander who was close to bin Laden and the Taliban but remained independent and a power in his own right. He was approached in early November. Author interview with Michael Scheuer, CIA head of Alec Station, 2002.

7. Schroen, *First In*, p. 300. Bob Woodward, 'CIA led way with cash handouts', *Washington Post*, November 18, 2002. Jason Burke, 'Torture, treachery and

spies – covert war in Afghanistan', *Observer*, November 4, 2001. Multiple author interviews, Peshawar, autumn 2001, London, 2009.

8. 'President notifies Congress about troop deployment. U.S. claims air supremacy over Afghanistan', CNN, October 9, 2001.

9. Author telephone interview with Paul Pillar, CIA national intelligence officer for the Middle East 2000–2005, with Bob Grenier, CIA station chief Islamabad 2001–2, January 2009. See also Schroen, *First In*.

10. At sixteen, after a row with his recently appointed Socialist schoolteacher, he had launched an attack on a police station. The capture and torture of one of his associates merely taught him, he later told interviewers, to plan operations properly.

11. See Robert D. Kaplan, *Soldiers of God*, Vintage, 2008, for an excellent account of Haq's life, especially pp. 145–6. Also the useful documentary *Afghan Warrior: The Life and Death of Abdul Haq*, Touch productions for BBC2, 2003.

12. Much of the violence was directed at relatively Westernized schoolteachers sent to provinces from Kabul, such as the one who had been the immediate catalyst for Haq's activism.

13. Kaplan, *Soldiers of God*. Author interviews with former *mujahideen*, BBC film; Afghan journalists who covered the war, Peshawar, 1998–9.

14. Author interview with a former MI6 senior official. Rashid, *Descent into Chaos*, p. 20.

15. 'We are firm on road of jihad', *The Times*, September 25, 2001. Author interview with Haji Din Mohammed Arsala, Peshawar, November 2001. A letter addressed to the Pakistani people called on them to 'rise in defence of Islam' and welcomed the 'martyrdom' of those killed in the recent demonstrations.

16. Author interview with Abdul Haq Arsala, Peshawar, October 2001.

17. Instead Haq was bankrolled by two Afghan-American businessmen.

18. See Burke, 'Torture, treachery and spies'.

19. Author interview with Haji Din Mohammed Arsala, Peshawar, November 2001.

20. R. W. Apple Jr, 'A military quagmire remembered: Afghanistan as Vietnam', *New York Times*, October 31, 2001.

21. Bush, *Decision Points*, pp. 153, 154.

22. Seymour M. Hersh, 'The getaway. Questions surround a secret Pakistani airlift', *New Yorker*, January 28, 2002. Bob Woodward, 'Doubts and debates before victory over the Taliban', *Washington Post*, November 18, 2002. The letters turned out to have been sent by a disaffected American research scientist.

23. Feith, *War and Decision*, p. 78.

24. *United States Special Operations Command History*, 6th edn, 2007, p. 96. Schroen, *First In*, pp. 265–7. Hamid Karzai, *Letter from Kabul*, Wiley, 2006, p. 117.

25. Author interview with Noman Benotman, former Libyan militant, March 2011. See also Quillam Foundation, Camille Tawil, *The Other Face of al-Qaeda*, London, 2010, p. 17.

26. Author interview with Mohammed Ishaq Mir Ali, Nowshera, October 2002.

27. Schroen, *First In*, p. 345. Anthony Davis, 'The Fall of Kabul', *Jane's Defence Weekly*, November 13, 2001.

28. See Karzai's own account in *Letter from Kabul. United States Special Operations Command History*, p. 97.

29. Author interviews with Zaheer Arsala, Kabul August 2008, Abdul Qadir, Hazrat Ali, Jalalabad, November 2001.

30. Jason Burke, 'Mujahideen back to "rob and beat us"', *Observer*, November 18, 2001.

31. Report of interrogation of Saleem Ahmed Saleem Hamden, Guantanamo Bay, Cuba, 062870902.

32. Abdullah al-Shihri, 'Aide to Bin Laden surrenders', Associated Press, July 14, 2004. Bin Laden on Tape: Attacks "Benefited Islam Greatly"', CNN, December 14, 2001.

33. *Tora Bora Revisited: How We Failed to Get Bin Laden and Why It Matters Today: A Report to Members of the Committee on Foreign Relations, United States Senate, 111th Congress first session*, November 30, 2009. p. 5

34. Jagdallak was where the final remnants of a retreating British army had been destroyed by local tribesmen in 1842.

35. Philip Smucker, 'How bin Laden got away: A day-by-day account of how Osama bin Laden eluded the world's most powerful military machine', *Christian Science Monitor*, March 4, 2002.

36. Author interviews with Hazrat Ali, Haji Din Mohammedi, Haji Zaheer Arsala, Jalalabad, October 2002.

37. Author interviews with Zaheer Shah, Hazrat Ali in Jalalabad, October 2002. Memorandum for Commander, US Southern Command, CSRT Input, US9AF–000782DP, Awal Malim Gul, February 15, 2008, secret, author collection. Jasan Burke, 'Guantanamo Bay files rewrite the story of Osama bin Laden's Tora Bora escape', *Guardian*, April 26, 2011.

38. Author interviews with Jan Mohammed and other commanders, Peshawar, June 2002.

39. Rashid, *Descent into Chaos*, pp. 242–3 .

40. John F. Burns, '10-month Afghan mystery: Is bin Laden dead or alive?', *New York Times*, September 30, 2002.

41. 'How Al Qaeda slipped away', *Newsweek*, August 19, 2002.

42. Author interview with Mohammed Shah Shinwari, Hadda, October 2002.

43. Author interview with police chief, Asadabad, Kunar, October 2002. Memorandum for Commander, US Southern Command, CSRT Input, Sabar Lal Melma, US9AF–000801DP, June 5, 2005, secret, author collection.

44. President Musharraf's aides later claimed that at least 300 had been handed

over to the Americans. A variety of activists, such as the lawyer, politicians and cleric Javed Ibrahim Parachar, who was based in Kohat, secured the release of at least 300 more, he told the author in Kohat, July 2005. The total is likely to be around 600.

45. See the testimony of Musab Omar Ali al Mudwani, quoted in Worthington, *The Guantanamo Files*, p. 41. For wives, see testimony of Salem Ahmed Salem. Bahlul was leading a group of two and a half dozen others, largely members of bin Laden's security detail, who swiftly became known as the 'Dirty Thirty' to their captors. Memorandum for Commander, US Southern Command, CSRT Input for Guantanamo Detainee, US9YM-000039DP, Ali Hamza Suleiman al-Bahlul, June 5, 2005, secret, author collection.

46. He had decided to travel after long conversations with a cleric and after viewing videos of 'Kashmir, Bosnia, Chechnya and how the soldiers mistreated the women and the children'. He had hoped to fight in Chechnya or with the Taliban but was not unhappy to find himself in a camp connected to al-Qaeda.

47. Author interview, Kabul, 2008.

48. Interview with Mohammed al-Tamimi, in the Arabic newspaper *al-Hayat*, September 20, 2006, quoted in Tawil, *Brothers in Arms*, p. 183. Ayman al-Batarfi, Summary of Administrative Review Board Proceeding ISN 556, 2006, p. 14. http://www.dod.mil/pubs/foi/detainees/csrt_arb/ARB_Transcript_2397-2490.pdf. A Yemeni fighter remembered 'anti-aircraft guns', but these appear to have been Soviet-era manually operated weapons entirely unsuited to defence against contemporary air power. Memoranda for Commander, US Southern Command, CSRT Input, US9AG-000238DP, Nabil Said Hadjarab, January 22, 2007, and US9YM-00054920, Omar Said Adayn, June 2008, secret, author collection.

49. *Tora Bora Revisited*, p. 21.

50. *United States Special Operations Command History*, p. 98.

51. In early December there were only about 1,300 US troops in country.

52. MI6 former senior official, London, February 2009.

53. Bin Laden also ordered his wives not to remarry and his 'women kinsfolk' to avoid cosmetics so as not to resemble the 'whore-ish and mannish females of the West' and warned his sons not to join al-Qaeda and the armed struggle. Al-Majallah, 'Al-Majallah Obtains Bin Laden's Will', October 27, 2002, pp. 22–6, quoted in 'Foreign Broadcast Information Service Report, Compilation of Usama Bin Laden's Statements 1994 to 2004', published 2004. Available at: http://www.fas.org/irp/world/para/ubl-fbis.pdf.

54. According to a declassified version of an official history of US special forces' operations during the Afghan campaign of late 2001, published in 2007, 'All source reporting corroborated his presence on several days from 9–14 December.' The claim was based on accounts of commanders and intelligence officials. *United States Special Operations Command History*, p. 101, 6th edn, March 2008, quoted in *Tora Bora Revisited*, p. 10.

55. A further intercepted message was probably a pre-recorded sermon played to cover the senior leadership's flight. Ilene R. Prusher, 'Two top Al Qaeda leaders spotted', *Christian Science Monitor*, March 26, 2002. Memoranda for Commander, US Southern Command, CSRT Input and Recommendation for Guantanamo Detainee, US9SA-000062DP, US9SU-000054DP, Mohammad Salah Ahmad, November 15, 2007, and AF-0003148, Harun al'Afghani, August 2, 2007, secret, author collection.

56. On NBC's *Meet the Press* on December 2, 2001 Tim Russert, the host of the programme, showed Secretary of Defense Donald Rumsfeld with the artist's rendering of bin Laden's fortress.

> Russert: *The Times* of London did a graphic, which I want to put on the screen for you and our viewers. This is it. This is a fortress. This is a very much a complex, multi-tiered, bedrooms and offices on the top, as you can see, secret exits on the side and on the bottom, cut deep to avoid thermal detection so when our planes fly to try to determine if any human beings are in there, it's built so deeply down and embedded in the mountain and the rock it's hard to detect. And over here, valleys guarded, as you can see, by some Taliban soldiers. A ventilation system to allow people to breathe and to carry on. An arms and ammunition depot. And you can see here the exits leading into it and the entrances large enough to drive trucks and cars and even tanks. And it's own hydroelectric power to help keep lights on, even computer systems and telephone systems. It's a very sophisticated operation.
>
> Rumsfeld: Oh, you bet. This is serious business. And there's not one of those. There are many of those. And they have been used very effectively. And I might add, Afghanistan is not the only country that has gone underground. Any number of countries have gone underground. The tunnelling equipment that exists today is very powerful. It's dual use. It's available across the globe. And people have recognized the advantages of using underground protection for themselves. (http://video.google.com/videoplay?docid=-4697166259112889282#).

57. 'Yemeni doctor describes bloody siege at Tora Bora', Associated Press, September 7, 2007. Memorandum for Commander, US Southern Command, CSRT Input, US9YM-000627DP, Ayman al-Batarfi, April 29, 2008, secret, author collection.

58. Andy McNab, 'SAS hero Andy McNab describes regiment's Al-Qaeda battle', *Daily Mirror*, February 16, 2002, pp. 26–7. In fact, few knew very much about the caves or anything else. Intelligence on the actual defences was minimal, and the vast surveillance resources that would later be used by the America military and, by extension, some of its allies, were not yet available.

59. The number was 300 according to Susan B. Glasser, 'The battle of Tora Bora: secrets, money, mistrust', *Washington Post*, February 10, 2002.

60. 'Dalton Fury' was, unsurprisingly, a pseudonym. Dalton Fury, *Kill Bin Laden*, St Martin's Press, 2008, pp. 277–8.

61. 'How Osama Bin Laden escaped', *Foreign Policy*, December 11, 2009.

62. His body was found by local tribesmen weeks later and buried. A shrine was built over his tomb, which has since become a place of pilgrimage. Djamel Loiseau, 'Itinéraire d'un soldat d'Allah', *France*, 3, April 13, 2007. The story of the Briton who died was cited by the bombers who struck London in 2005 as a key inspiration. Home Office, *Report of the Official Account of the Bombings in London on 7th July 2005*, 2006. p. 19.

63. See Memorandum for Commander, US Southern Command, CSRT Input, US9TS-000510DP, Riyad Nassr Muhammed Atahar, September 15, 2008, secret, author collection.

64. Audio tape, al-Jazeera, 2003, transcript at http://news.bbc.co.uk/2/hi/2751019.stm: 'Complete failure of the international alliance of evil, with all its forces, [to overcome] a small number of *mujahideen* – 300 *mujahideen* hunkered down in trenches spread over an area of one square mile under a temperature of –10 degrees Celsius. The battle resulted in the injury of 6 per cent of personnel – we hope God will accept them as martyrs – and the damage of 2 per cent of the trenches, praise be to God.'

65. Author interview with Mohammed Umr al-Madani, Kabul, August 2008.

66. Smucker, 'How bin Laden got away'.

67. *United States Special Operations Command History*, p. 99.

68. Drew Brown, 'How al Qaeda fighters escaped; Bin Laden told his men to disperse, witness says', *Miami Herald*, October 17, 2002.

69. Author telephone interview with Bob Grenier, January 2009.

70. Author email exchange with Lodhi, February 2011. Author interview with General Orakzai, London, February 2009.

71. Seth Jones, *In the Graveyard of Empires*, p. 101.

72. *Newsweek*, author interviews.

73. Ghanim Abdul Rahman al Harbi, Combat Status Review Tribunal, Summary of Evidence, Guantanamo Bay, 16 August 16, 2004; Administrative Review Board Round 1 Summaries , June 23, 2006. Worthington, *The Guantanamo Files*, pp. 29–30. Interview with local residents, Hadda, Jalalabad, Milawa, November 2001, October 2002. Burns, '10-month Afghan mystery'. Glasser, 'The battle of Tora Bora'.

74. Rory Carroll, 'Biker Mullah's great escape', *Guardian*, January 6, 2002.

75. See 'The Global War on Terrorism: The First 100 Days', p. 11.

76. Bob Woodward, 'The inside story of the CIA's proxy war', *Australian Age*, November 20, 2002.

77. Tenet, *At the Center of the Storm*, p. 255

78. Woodward, 'CIA led way with cash handouts'.

79. The same was the case in the UK. Matthew Engel, 'First British casualties as four SAS men shot', *Guardian*, November 27, 2001. The first US casualty in Afghanistan was Evander E. Andrews, Master Sergeant US Air Force, age thirty-six, from Solon, Maine, on October 10, 2001, according to the *Washington*

Post. He was killed in a forklift accident. 'Faces of the Fallen' project, Washington Post Online, accessed July 2010.

80. The airlift took place with the permission of senior Bush administration figures, who appear to have been largely unaware of exactly who was being lifted where. Hersh, 'The getaway'. Douglas Frantz, 'Pakistan ended aid to Taliban only hesitantly', *New York Times*, December 8, 2001. Ahmed Rashid, *Descent into Chaos*, pp. 90–93.

81. Author interview with Haji Saifullah, Gardez, April 2002.

82. Bob Woodward, *Plan of Attack*, Simon and Schuster, 2008, p. 8. Bush, *Decision Points*, p. 234.

83. Judith Miller, 'An Iraqi defector tells of work on at least 20 hidden weapons sites', *New York Times*, December 20, 2001.

CHAPTER 4: THE CALM BEFORE THE STORM

1. Author telephone interview with Robert Grenier, former CIA station chief Islamabad, January 2009.

2. Author telephone interview with Bruce Riedel, CIA senior analyst and senior director for Near East Affairs on the National Security Council 1997–2002, October 2008.

3. 'When we received intitial reports of al-Qaeda's presence [in South Waziristan] we did not take them very seriously,' said General Musharraf. See *In the Line of Fire*, p. 264.

4. Including one attack involving young Britons.

5. Bush, *Decision Points*, p. 166.

6. Rama Lakshmi, 'Gunmen with explosives attack Indian parliament', *Washington Post*, December 14, 2001. Simon Jeffrey 'The Moscow theatre siege', *Guardian*, October 28, 2002.

7. Carol Eisenberg, 'On religion, faith and rituals', *Newsday*, December 22, 2001. Pew Forum on Religion and Public Life, December 2001. The post-9/11 figure was 59 per cent, up from 45 per cent six months previously.

8. Jason Katz, Victoria Cullen, Connor Buttner and John Pollock, 'American Newspaper Coverage of Islam Post-September 11, 2001: A Community Structure Approach', *Association for Education in Journalism and Mass Communication*, August 8, 2007. The study also discovered that communities with highest levels of education and revenues were not those whose newspapers reflected more positive views of Islam in the aftermath of 9/11. Depictions of Islam became more negative over the years up until 2005.

9. Emily Wax, 'In times of terror, teens talk the talk', *Washington Post*, March 20, 2002.

10. In March 2003 those figures were 64, 50 and 59 per cent respectively. The period saw a predictable crash in views of the US too. See *Pew Global Attitudes*

2003: *Views of a Changing World*, 2003, pp. 19, 46. The number of people giving the United States a positive rating has dropped by 22 points in Turkey and 13 points in Pakistan since 1999. See ibid., p. 4.

11. Ibid., p. 34.

12. 'The 2002 Gallup poll of the Islamic world'. Muslims overwhelmingly cited technology, computers and knowledge when asked what they liked most about the West. Scott Atran, 'Trends in Suicide Terrorism: Sense and Nonsense', paper presented to World Federation of Scientists Permanent Monitoring Panel on Terrorism, Erice, Sicily, August 2004. Mark Tessler, 'Do Islamic Orientations Influence Attitudes toward Democracy in the Arab World? Evidence from Egypt, Jordan, Morocco, and Algeria', *International Journal of Comparative Sociology*, vol. 2 (2002), pp. 229–49. Mark Tessler and Dan Corstange, 'How Should Americans Understand Arab and Muslim Political Attitudes?', *Journal of Social Affairs*, vol. 19 (2002).

13. Author interviews, Jalalabad, October 2002.

14. Author interviews Jalalabad, Gardez, Kabul, May and October 2002.

15. Michael O'Hanlon, 'Staying Power: The U.S. Mission in Afghanistan Beyond 2011', *Foreign Affairs*, September/October 2010.

16. Author interviews, Kabul, 2002–3. Interviews with Ashraf Ghani, former minister of finance, Kabul, January 2007 and August 2008. Author interview with Clare Lockhart, Ministry of Finance adviser, Kabul, January 2007. For the row over the road to Kandahar, see Dobbins, *After the Taliban*.

17. Clare Lockhart, 'Learning from experience', *Slate*, posted November 5, 2008.

18. Radio address by Mrs Bush, Office of the First Lady, November 17, 2001. Kampfner, *Blair's Wars*, p. 123.

19. Images of the execution of a woman convicted of murder in Kabul in November 1999, which the author had witnessed, were repeatedly broadcast and became, despite the relative infrequency of such events, symbolic of the Taliban rule.

20. Afghan women and children relief act of 2001, US Congress, 107th Congress, December 12, 2001, US Government Printing Office, 2001. Public Law 107-81 states: 'the President is authorized, on such terms and conditions as the President may determine, to provide educational and health care assistance for the women and children living in Afghanistan and as refugees in neighboring countries ... In providing assistance under subsection (a), the President shall ensure that such assistance is provided in a manner that protects and promotes the human rights of all people in Afghanistan, utilizing indigenous institutions and nongovernmental organizations, especially women's organizations, to the extent possible ...'

21. But the experience of Afghan women was much more complicated than many in the West expected. When Florence Aubenas, correspondent for the left-wing French newspaper *Libération*, was asked by her editors to report on why such a large majority of Kabul's women had kept their *burqas* she was first told they feared acid attacks. On discovering that there had been no such

incidents reported, she asked again and was told that in fact the women did not want to leave home without the full covering because they had grown used to it. Florence Aubenas, *Grand Reporter: petite conférence sur le journalisme*, Bayard, 2009, p. 12.

22. 'Lauded at pageant, woman condemned by Afghan officials', Associated Press, November 10, 2003. 'Afghan Supreme Court bans beauty pageants', Agence France-Presse, October 30, 2003.

23. The most extreme representatives of this new vision for Afghanistan were to be found among the eclectic collection of visitors who turned up in Kabul, few of whom had shown any previous interest in Afghanistan, through 2002. One was French intellectual Bernard-Henri Lévy, dispatched by President Jacques Chirac to report on what France could provide to assist the reconstruction of Afghanistan. A senior French government bureaucrat told the author in 2009 that Lévy's ten-day expedition and the subsequent publication of his 200-page report used up a significant proportion of the funds the French government had available for Afghanistan at the time. His suggestions included, among other things, 'a year of French cinema', 'the creation of a French cultural centre, to be jointly developed with the intelligentsia of Kabul' and for 'the emergence of a democratic "Afghanitude" (identity)' to combat the rule of the warlords, the creation of a corps 'of black hussars for democracy, who would travel all over the country, in the name of President Karzai, preaching the message of citizenship and fundamental human rights'.

24. Marion and Peter Sluglett, 'The Historiography of Modern Iraq', *American Historical Review*, 1991, pp. 1,412–13. Barfield, *Afghanistan*, p. 339.

25. A good example was the extremely successful Afghan-government-run and World-Bank-funded National Solidarity Programme, which offered grants and loans to village committees for local infrastructure or training projects.

26. Author interview with Malalai Kakar, Kandahar, November 2003.

27. Author interview, Bagram, Afghanistan, May 2003.

28. These are figures for the Department of Defense Base Budget. If what are known as emergency supplementals are included they rise to $316 billion and $345 billion respectively. Figures provided by the Department of Defense, July 2009.

29. Dobbins, *After the Taliban*, p. 140

30. Jones, *In the Graveyard of Empires*, p. 142.

31. Ricks, *Fiasco*, p. 44.

32. Jones, *In the Graveyard of Empires*, p. 119. The figure for Northern Ireland includes both British troops (not technically international) and the Royal Ulster Constabulary. See James T. Quinlivan, 'Burden of Victory: The Painful Arithmetic of Stability Operations', *RAND Review*, vol. 27, no. 2 (summer 2003), pp. 28–9.

33. Bush, *Decision Points*, p. 207. Bob Woodward, *Bush at War*, Simon and Schuster, 2003, pp. 82–3. In fact, both had misread Afghan history and its present. The Soviets in fact had maintained a relatively light footprint, and it

was their lack of an effective counter-insurgency strategy that had been the problem, not the number of their troops.

34. Dobbins, *After the Taliban*, p. 130. Feith says this was not the case but is less convincing.

35. Author interview with Ron Nash, British ambassador in Kabul, 2002–3, July 2009.

36. The warlords and their militias, despite being seen by most Afghans as the principal threat to their security, were often hired by US troops and especially the CIA as their local eyes, ears and often hands as well. They included individuals like Pacha Khan Zadran, who by the spring had taken to mortaring the town of Gardez after being dumped as a client by the Americans. In the important Helmand province, which has a population of over a million and was crucial both as a centre of the opium trade and as a fief of the Taliban, the only foreign soldiers were around sixty American special forces and a couple of hundred regulars who conducted nocturnal raids to pick up suspected 'AQT'.

37. Jason Burke and Peter Beaumont, 'West pays warlords to stay in line', *Observer*, London, July 21, 2002. Jones, *In the Graveyard of Empires*, p. 130. Antonio Guistozzi, *Empires of Mud*, Hurst, 2009, pp. 89–91.

38. Worthington, *The Guantanamo Files*, pp. 19–25. Yusef al-Rabesh, author interview, Riyadh, June 2011.

39. According to an affidavit filed in a US court by his attorney, US soldiers 'blindfolded Mr. Lindh, and took several pictures of Mr. Lindh and themselves with Mr. Lindh. In one, the soldiers scrawled "shithead" across Mr. Lindh's blindfold and posed with him . . . Another told Mr. Lindh that he was "going to hang" for his actions and that after he was dead, the soldiers would sell the photographs and give the money to a Christian organization.' Human Rights Watch, *The Road to Abu Ghraib*, June 2004, p. 20.

40. See David Rose, 'See how MI5 colluded in my torture: Binyam Mohamed claims British agents fed Moroccan torturers their questions', *Daily Mail*, March 8, 2009, for what was happening by spring 2002.

41. Ian Cobain, 'The truth about torture', *Guardian*, July 8, 2009. The British MI6 officers received legal advice that they were not obliged to intervene to prevent abuse.

42. Dana Priest and Barton Gellman, 'U.S. decries abuse but defends interrogations', *Washington Post*, December 26, 2002, Human Rights Watch, *The Road to Abu Ghraib*, p. 23. Freedman, *A Choice of Enemies*, p. 395. Bush signed the directive at a private meeting with Cheney apparently without even sitting down.

43. Douglas Jehl and Andrea Elliott, 'Cuba base sent its interrogators to Iraqi prison', *New York Times*, May 29, 2004.

44. These details come from Chris Mackey and Greg Miller, *The Interrogators: Inside the Secret War against al Qaeda*, Little, Brown and Company, 2004. Also Shafiq Rasul, Asif Iqbal and Rhuhel Ahmed, *Composite Statement:*

Detention in Afghanistan and Guantanamo Bay, Centre for Constitutional Rights, New York, July 26, 2004.

45. Worthington, *The Guantanamo Files*, pp. 81–99, 176.
46. With intelligence operatives and guards all searching to 'improve' their methods to meet the huge demands for information, there was an inevitable logic of escalation.
47. Stephen Grey, *Ghost Plane*, Hurst, 2006, pp. 250–56.
48. 'New' in recent times. Waterboarding had been used in the Second World War by Japanese soldiers.
49. See Jane Mayer, *The Dark Side*, Doubleday, 2008. David Rose, 'Tortured reasoning', *Vanity Fair*, December 16, 2008. Mark Mazzetti and Scott Shane, 'Interrogation memos detail harsh tactics by the C.I.A.', *New York Times*, April 21, 2009. Scott Shane, '2 suspects waterboarded 266 times', *New York Times*, April 19, 2009. In May 2008, Glenn Fine, the Department of Justice inspector general, reported that, as he recovered in the hospital from the bullet wounds sustained when he was captured, Abu Zubaydah had cooperated with two FBI agents but was then handed over to the CIA, who, according to Fine, felt they 'needed to diminish his capacity to resist'. Bush discussed Abu Zubaydah's treatment in 2006, saying: 'As his questioning proceeded, it became clear that he had received training on how to resist interrogation. And so the CIA used an alternative set of procedures ... The procedures were tough, and they were safe, and lawful, and necessary.' Even before it had been declared legal in a secret finding by Justice Department lawyers in August, it appears probable that Abu Zubaydah was already being subjected to the practice of waterboarding. The newly hired consultants proved highly inventive. At one point they asked for permission to play on Abu Zubaydah's phobia of stinging insects by introducing a harmless bug into his cell and telling him it was dangerous. Their request provoked extraordinary legal contortions as the CIA tried to get permission from lawyers at the Ministry of Justice, who eventually decided that, though Abu Zubaydah's interrogators could not tell the suspect that the insect was venomous because it was illegal to threaten prisoners with imminent death, they could place Abu Zubaydah in a 'confinement box' with a harmless insect if he was told nothing about it. The CIA proposed using a caterpillar. In the end, the plan was abandoned. Mike Isikoff and Evan Thomas, 'The lawyer and the caterpillar', *Newsweek*, April 18, 2009.
50. Author interview with Haji Ghalib, former police chief of Khogani and Guantanamo detainee, Kabul, August 2008.
51. Worthington, *The Guantanamo Files*, pp. 174, 188–9.
52. Author telephone interview with Omar Deghayes, April 2010.
53. Amnesty International, *Secret Detention in CIA 'Black Sites'*, November 8, 2005. See also Stephen Grey's very useful *Ghost Plane*. Jason Burke, 'Secret world of US jails', *Observer*, June 13, 2004. Stephen Grey, 'United States:

Trade in torture', *Le Monde Diplomatique*, April 2005. Dana Priest, 'CIA holds terror suspects in secret prisons', *Washington Post*, November 2, 2005.

54. 'Ex-CIA contractor guilty of assault', Associated Press, August 16, 2006. 'Two soldiers reprimanded for assaults', *Los Angeles Times*, January 27, 2007.

55. Author interview, London, July 2009. British intelligence officials also visited these facilities, though their superiors claim they did not take part in any mistreatment of suspects. 'We just couldn't imagine that the Americans would be doing this,' said one. 'We simply had no idea it was going on,' Sir John Scarlett, deputy head of MI6 at the time, later claimed. However, a series of legal cases in the UK – such as that of Binyam Mohammed – showed that MI6's sister service MI5 had been at the very least complicit in some abuse. One charge was that the service supplied information with the express aim of helping questioners get more out of suspects who were held in atrocious conditions and often seriously tortured. Nor evidently was MI6 likely to refuse information that it felt was tainted by torture, as Scarlett explained to the author in July 2009, arguing that to do so would be dangerous and counterproductive.

56. Author interview with Haji Rohullah, Kabul, August 2009.

57. Haji Shahzada, Guantanamo Bay, Summary of Evidence, January 12, 2005. See Worthington, *The Guantanamo Files*, p. 250.

CHAPTER 5: WAR IN IRAQ I: THREATS, FALSEHOODS AND DEAD MEN

1. Estimates of the Iraqi dead range from 160,000 to 250,000.

2. See the controversial but useful UNICEF Report, *Situation Analysis of Children and Women in Iraq*, April 30, 1998. Also Jason Burke, *The Road to Kandahar*, Penguin, 2006, Chapter 4, for the author's reporting of the humanitarian situation in Iraq in the late 1990s.

3. There remained a small number of Shia at senior levels in the Ba'ath Party.

4. See the excellent International Crisis Group report, *Iraq Backgrounder: What Lies Beneath*, October 1, 2002 for a useful exploration of some of these themes.

5. Powell went into great detail, speaking of the efforts to acquire centrifuges, the 100 to 500 tons of chemical weapons agent, the mobile launchers. United States Senate Select Committee on Intelligence, *Whether Public Statements Regarding Iraq Where Substantiated by US Government Officials Were Substantiated by Intelligence Information*, June 2008, pp. 3, 17, 25, 30.

6. David Kay, testimony before the US Committee on Armed Services, January 28, 2004. *Comprehensive Report of the Special Advisor to the Director of Central Intelligence on Iraq's WMD, Charles Duelfer*, September 30, 2004. Freedman, *A Choice of Enemies*, p. 424. These statements were examined and subsequently corroborated by the Report of the Commission on the

Intelligence Capabilities of the United States Regarding Weapons of Mass Destruction, presented March 31, 2005.

7. *Comprehensive Report of the Special Advisor to the DCI on Iraq's WMD, Chemical Section*, p. 123.

8. Bush, *Decision Points*, p. 262.

9. Freedman, *A Choice of Enemies*, pp. 412–16.

10. Jonathan S. Landay and Tish Wells, 'Iraqi global misinformation campaign was used to build case for war', Knight Ridder, March 16, 2004.

11. Martin Chulov and Helen Pidd, 'How US was duped by Iraqi fantasist looking to topple Saddam', *Guardian*, February 15, 2010.

12. The full interrogation documents of Saddam Hussein by the FBI in March 2004 are available at www.nsarchive.org. See also Glenn Kessler, 'Hussein pointed to Iranian threat', *Washington Post*, July 2, 2009.

13. Rose, 'Tortured reasoning'.

14. National Intelligence Estimate, *Iraq's Continuing Programs of WMD*, October 1, 2002, pp. 66–8. Jason Burke, 'The missing link', *Guardian*, February 9, 2003. Jeffrey Goldberg, 'The great terror', *New Yorker*, March 25, 2002.

15. Also Jonathan S. Landay, 'Abusive tactics used to seek Iraq-al Qaida link', *McClatchy Newspapers*, April 21, 2009. The Bush administration systematically leaked information from Abu Zubaydah's interrogations. One analyst who worked at the Pentagon told reporter David Rose of *Vanity Fair*: 'I first saw the reports soon after Abu Zubaydah's capture. There was a lot of stuff about the nuts and bolts of al-Qaeda's supposed relationship with the Iraqi Intelligence Service. The intelligence community was lapping this up, and so was the administration, obviously. Abu Zubaydah was saying Iraq and al-Qaeda had an operational relationship. It was everything the administration hoped it would be.'

16. The author learned of this meeting at the time from Saudi and Pakistani security sources but was unable to confirm sufficiently for publication.

17. United States Senate Select Committee on Intelligence, *Whether Public Statements Regarding Iraq Where Substantiated by US Government Officials Were Substantiated by Intelligence Information*, p. 63.

18. John Solomon, 'First declassified Iraq documents released', Associated Press Online, March 16, 2006. Tariq Aziz, the former Iraqi foreign minister, later told interrogators that Saddam 'had only ever expressed negative sentiments about bin Laden'. Robert Burns, 'Iraqi: Saddam "delighted" in terror attacks on US', Associated Press, September 22, 2010.

19. Technically outside the no-fly zone and thus the haven, Mosul and its tradition of Islamism had been and was an important factor.

20. For more see Burke, *Al-Qaeda*, pp. 225–7, which draws on interviews with militants in Kurdish custody and with Kurdish intelligence officers in August 2002 in Suleimaniyah, Iraq, as well as Western intelligence documents, principally the interrogation report of German members of the al-Tawhid group.

21. Bergen, *The Longest War*, pp. 144–5.

22. Subsequently, the bipartisan commission of inquiry set up in November 2002 by Congress and, reluctantly, the president to report on the causes of the 9/11 attacks concluded that there was no evidence of a 'collaborative ... operational relationship', and a study by the Institute for Defense Analyses, written for the US Joint Forces Command and based on 600,000 documents captured in Iraq after the invasion, found that nothing indicated 'direct coordination and assistance between Saddam Hussein's regime and al-Qaeda'. *The 9/11 Commission Report*, p. 66. Institute for Defense Analyses, 'Iraqi Perspective Project: Saddam and Terrorism', March 20, 2008, at http://www.fas.orga/irp/eprint/iraqi/index.html. See also Congressional Research Service (Kenneth Katzmann), *Report for Congress: Al'Qaeda in Iraq: Assessment and Outside Links*, updated August 15, 2008. In his memoirs, the CIA director at the time, George Tenet, also indicated that the CIA view was that any contacts were simply exploratory rather than collaborative – though he played a close role in the preparation of Powell's United Nations presentation. See Tenet, *At the Center of the Storm*, pp. 341–58. 'Report. No proof of Qaeda–Saddam link', CBS News, September 8, 2006.

23. See the useful discussion in Kampfner, *Blair's Wars*, pp. 264–7. For the flaws in the dossier see Burke, *Al-Qaeda*, pp. 16–17.

24. Briefings citing 'intelligence' given to 'lobby' or political correspondents rather than specialist security reporters had been a favoured method of consolidating support for the invasion of Afghanistan. One of the more egregious examples of this kind of material was the revelation that bin Laden was set to unleash a '£20bn flood of heroin' on the West: Kamal Ahmed, 'The terrorism crisis: No 10 fears £20bn flood of heroin, troops aim to destroy huge stockpile of opium about to be released on to the world market', *Observer*, September 30, 2001.

25. *The 9/11 Commission Report*, p. 170.

26. Human Rights Watch briefing, *Opportunism in the Face of Tragedy*, New York, 2002. Katherine Arms, 'China links separatists to training by al-Qaeda', UPI, June 26, 2002.

27. Burke, *Al-Qaeda*, p. 15. *Herald*, Karachi, May, 2002. Nicholas Wood, 'Macedonian officials suspected of faking terror plot', *New York Times*, May 15, 2004. 'Macedonia faked "militant" raid', BBC News Online, April, 30, 2004. Four security service officers were charged with murder. 'It was a monstrous fabrication to get the attention of the international community,' Interior Ministry spokeswoman Mirjana Kontevska told a news conference.

28. Tariq Panja and Martin Bright, 'Man Utd bomb plot probe ends in farce', *Observer*, May 2, 2004.

29. Burke, *Al-Qaeda*, pp. 14–19, 285. For an example of the media reporting see 'Ricin suspects linked to al-Qaeda', CNN, January 17, 2003.

30. A leak to the *Sun* did the rest. No charges were ever brought. See the excellent investigation by Peter Oborne, 'The Use and Abuse of Terror', in *Playing Politics with Terrorism*, ed. George Kassimeris, Hurst, 2007, pp. 124–5.

31. Hala Jaber, 'Ryanair gunman: I was not going to crash plane', *Sunday Times*, October 13, 2002.

32. José Padilla was eventually convicted of terrorism charges, but the allegation of planning a dirty bomb – leaked to the press and covered extensively – was dropped. For more on the interrogation of Abu Zubaydah see Rose, 'Tortured reasoning'.

33. Chris McGreal, 'The Nevada gambler, al-Qaida, the CIA and the mother of all cons', *Guardian*, December 23, 2009.

34. John Mueller, 'Is There Still a Terrorist Threat? The Myth of the Omnipresent Enemy', *Foreign Affairs*, September–October 2006. Testimony of Robert S. Mueller III, Director, FBI, before the Select Committee on Intelligence of the United States Senate, February 11, 2003.

35. 'The truth is that for reasons that have a lot to do with the U.S. government bureaucracy we settled on one issue that everyone could agree on, which was weapons of mass destruction as the core reason.' *Vanity Fair* Interview with Sam Tannenhaus, May 9, 2003, transcript on http://www.defense.gov/transcripts/transcript.aspx?transcriptid=2594.

36. One influence on Bush and other senior administration figures was Bernard Lewis, the American historian of the Islamic world, who forcefully argued that a lack of Western-style freedoms was the fundamental cause of the Middle East's economic, social and political weaknesses. He made these views to a mass audience in the best-selling *'What Went Wrong': Western Impact and Middle Eastern Response*, Oxford University Press, 2002. See also the article of the same title, *Atlantic Monthly*, January 2002. In his memoir, Bush talks of how 'the Middle East was the centre of a global ideological struggle. On the one side were decent people who wanted to live in dignity and peace. On the other were extremists who sought to impose their radical views through violence and intimidation. They exploited conditions of hopelessness and repression to recruit and spread their ideology. The best way to protect our countries in the long run was to counter their dark vision with a more compelling alternative. That alternative was freedom. Once liberty took root in one society it could spread to others.' *Decision Points*, p. 232.

37. Thomas Powers, 'War and its consequences', *New York Review of Books*, March 27, 2003.

38. Freedman, *A Choice of Enemies*, p. 422.

39. James Fallows, 'Blind into Baghdad', *Atlantic Monthly*, January/February 2004. Feith also explained that Donald Rumsfeld's vision was about 'the need to deal strategically with uncertainty. The inability to predict the future. The limits on our knowledge and the limits on our intelligence.'

40. Robert K. Brigham, *Iraq, Vietnam and the Limits of American Power*, p. 2.

41. See Bush, *Decision Points*, pp. 248–9. This preoccupation with humanitarian issues, it is worth pointing out, was also shared by many anti-war campaigners and international institutions such as the UN.

42. Ricks, *Fiasco*, p. 146. Ricks quotes from an internal American Army War College summary. The war plan designed by General Tommy Franks, stated baldly that 'regime change' was the 'endstate of this mission'.

43. Sixteen months of effort by a full military staff went into planning the war, eight weeks of work by a scratch team into planning for the post-war situation. A Congressional Research Service Report of April 2003 entitled *Iraq: Recent Developments in Humanitarian and Reconstruction Assistance* optimistically states: 'After an initial period of U.S.-led aid activities, existing Iraqi ministries, nongovernmental organizations (NGOs), and international organizations are expected to assume some of the burden.'

44. Freedman, *A Choice of Enemies*, p. 429.

45. Quoted in Fallows, 'Blind into Baghdad'.

46. George Packer, 'Dreaming of democracy', *New York Times*, March 2, 2003.

47. The campaign was expected to take 100 days, according to Lieutenant General Sir Frederick Viggers. 'West put "amateurs" in charge of Iraq occupation, inquiry told', Staff and agencies, guardian.co.uk, December 9, 2009.

48. Ricks, *Fiasco*, p. 118. Gregory Fontenot, E. J. Degen and David Tohn, *On Point: The United States Army in Operation Iraqi Freedom*, Combat Studies Institute Press, 2004.

49. See David Zuccino, *Thunder Run: The Armored Strike to Capture Baghdad*, Atlantic Monthly Press, 2004. Some accounts state that one of the operations killed at least 2,000 Iraqi soldiers. This seems unlikely. However, many residents of areas along the route of the two operations described numerous civilian deaths to the author, often simply caused by ricochets or in the crossfire.

50. See Iraqbodycount.org. Carl Conetta, 'The Wages of War: Iraqi Combatant and Noncombatant Fatalities in the 2003 Conflict', Project on Defense Alternatives Research Monograph 8, October 20, 2003.

51. Kosovo in 1999 may arguably have preceded Iraq in this but in very different circumstances and in a much less dramatic fashion.

52. Again as in Afghanistan, these mechanisms were often less 'traditional' than they seemed to Western observers. The Iraqi tribal system was very different from the days when Iraq was a predominantly rural society in the immediate post-war decades or a prosperous oil-rich emerging Arab state in the 1970s. Equally, there was little that was traditional about the rhetoric of the movement led by the young cleric Muqtada al-Sadr, which, within days of the fall of the regime, was organizing political meetings, taking over mosques and distributing food and other necessities in the vast Shia slum areas to the north of Baghdad.

53. For a useful account of this episode see Patrick Cockburn, *Muqtada al-Sadr, the Shia revival and the Struggle for Iraq*, Simon and Schuster, 2008, pp. 122–4.

54. Polls in the aftermath of the invasion showed George Bush's domestic approval level at over 90 per cent. On May 1, the president had landed in a

navy combat jet on the aircraft carrier the US *Abraham Lincoln* off the coast of California under a banner, the work of the ship's crew, bearing the legend 'mission accomplished'. He acknowledged difficult work ahead. 'The battle in Iraq is one victory in the war on terror that began on September 11th, 2001,' he said.

55. Adopted by a vote of fourteen to zero on May 22, 2003. The measure also had the advantage of freeing up Iraq's frozen oil revenues from the Oil for Food deal. 'In August I thought that it could still get better,' remembered Andy Bearpark, the CPA's British director of operations and deputy later. Author interview, Bath, July 2004.

56. Bing West, *The Strongest Tribe*, Random House, 2005, p. 6.

57. Author interview with Andy Bearpark, CPA director of operations, Bath, July 2004.

58. Bremer later insisted that British officials had been fully briefed before his order was issued. Statement by Ambassador Bremer to Chilcot commission, May 18, 2010, http://www.iraqinquiry.org.uk/background/statement-bremer. aspx.

59. Bush admits as much in his memoirs. The 'psychological impact' of disbanding the army had been underestimated and the de-Baathification went much further than was intended, he writes. *Decision Points*, p. 259.

60. See Toby Dodge, 'The Ideological Roots of Failure: The Application of Kinetic Neo-Liberalism to Iraq', *International Affairs*, vol. 86, no. 6 (November 2010), pp. 1,269–86. Paul Bremer, *My Year in Iraq: The Struggle to Build a Future of Hope*, Simon and Schuster, 2006, p. 39.

61. Author interview with John Wilkes, deputy British ambassador, Baghdad, June 2003.

62. The influence of the post-war measures in Germany on Bremer in particular is evident from his account of his time in Baghdad, *My Year in Iraq*. In fact de-Nazification had been far less severe than de-Baathification was to be.

63. Patrick Cockburn, *The Occupation, War and Resistance in Iraq*, Verso, 2006, p. 71. Ricks, *Fiasco*, pp. 162–3.

64. Rajiv Chandreshekan, *Imperial Life in the Emerald City, Inside Iraq's Green Zone*, Knopf, 2006, pp. 79–80.

65. Quoted in ibid., p. 159

66. At least two years according to Congressional Research Service (Kenneth Katzman), *Report for Congress: Iraq: Elections, Government, and Constitution*, November 20, 2006.

67. 'Rumsfeld rejects "cleric-led" rule', BBC News Online, April 25, 2005.

68. Author interview with Charles Heatley, Baghdad, June 2003.

69. Author interview, Najaf, June 2003.

70. Author interview, Baghdad, March 2003. See also the useful *Meeting the Resistance: A Film by Molly Bingham and Steve Connors*, 2007.

71. Author interviews, Baghdad, May and June 2003.

72. 'Poll shows Iraqis wary about Western-style democracy', VOA News, December 11, 2003.

73. *United Nations Report of the Security in Iraq Accountability Panel (SIAP)*, New York, March 3, 2004, p. 30.

74. See Jason Burke, 'Left to die', *GQ*, August 2004. Multiple author interviews with relatives of the casualties and soldiers involved, UK, February, March 2004.

75. British spokesman Lieutenant Colonel Ronnie McCourt denied any troops had 'molested', i.e. searched, women. 'We are the British army. We just don't do that,' he said. Author interviews, Abu Ala and Basra, June 25 and 26, 2003.

76. The author was shown the agreement in Majjar al-Kabir on June 25, 2003, the day after the deaths of the Redcaps.

77. Draft MoD report, 'On the events in Majjar al-Kabir, June 23 2003', March 2004, author collection.

78. Author telephone interview with Katie, Hamilton-Jewell's girlfriend, March 2004.

79. See, for example, David Blair, 'The Last Stand at Majjar al-Kabir', *Daily Telegraph*, June 26, 2003.

80. Excerpts from Ministry of Defence, Special Investigation Branch, draft report, obtained April, 2004. The investigation found that only two rounds out of one magazine for at least one of the Redcaps' personal weapons had been fired.

81. Author interview with Abbas Bairphy, Majjar al-Kabir, June 2003.

82. Ibid.

83. Ibid.

84. See 'The Lord of the Marshes Takes a Mediating Role in Iraq', *Terrorism Focus*, vol. 3, no. 33, August 23, 2006. Rory Stewart, *Occupational Hazards*, Picador, 2007, is an excellent and colourful account with much useful detail on Abu Hatem and Maysan province more generally.

85. Author interview with Abu Ala villagers, June 2003.

86. Author interview, Whitehall, London, August 2003.

87. See *Guardian* correspondent Rory McCarthy's account of his time in Iraq from 2003 to 2005, *No One Told Us We Are Defeated*, Guardian Books, 2006.

88. Author interview, Baghdad, August 2004.

89. In their first debriefing reports of the battle, the British patrol in Majjar al-Kabir estimated they might have killed up to 200 people and feared the incident might provoke a general insurrection across the region. In fact the local hospital registered five killed and nineteen wounded, who included several women and children and a fifty-year-old ambulance driver hit in the crossfire. Many locals involved, however, are likely to have been treated – or buried – by relatives so the true number is almost certainly much higher. Author interview with Lieutenant Colonel Stuart Tootal, present in Amarah, March 2004, London. Author interviews, Majjar al-Kabir hospital, June 2003.

90. Copy given to the author by Tony Hamilton-Jewell, Simon Hamilton-Jewell's brother, March 2004.

CHAPTER 6: WAR IN IRAQ II: LOSING IT

1. The tattoo detail is from Bush, *Decision Points*, p. 267.
2. In part, this omission had been forced on the Americans by the refusal of the Turks to allow 15,000 troops across their territory.
3. The best two biographies of Saddam are Alexander and Patrick Cockburn, *Out of the Ashes: The Resurrection of Saddam Hussein*, Harper Perennial, 2000, and Said Aburish, *Saddam Hussein: The Politics of Revenge*, Bloomsbury, 2000.
4. Scott Peterson, 'How Wahhabis fan Iraq insurgency', *Christian Science Monitor*, September 17, 2003.
5. Jason Burke, 'In a land without law or leaders, militant Islam threatens to rule', *Observer*, April 27, 2003.
6. Author interview with senior Iraqi intelligence investigators, Baghdad, May 2004.
7. Nir Rosen, 'Losing it', Asia Times Online, July 15, 2004.
8. Nir Rosen, 'Home rule: letter from Falluja', *New Yorker*, July 4, 2004.
9. Author interview, Falluja, July 2003.
10. The al-Dulaimi had been loyal to Saddam and rewarded handsomely for their support. However, their loyalty was not unconditional. In 1998 Saddam had hanged an army general from Ramadi, and relations had been tense ever since. The al-Dulaimi nonetheless had been strongly present in Saddam's intelligence and security apparatus.
11. Author interview, Ramadi, July 2003.
12. 'U.S. Commander in Iraq says year-long tours are option to combat "guerrilla" war', *New York Times*, July 17, 2003.
13. Hoffman also perceptively argued that in Iraq one saw 'the closest manifestation yet of netwar, the concept of warfare involving flatter, more linear networks rather than the pyramidal hierarchies and command and control systems (no matter how primitive) that have governed traditional insurgent organizations ... [It] involves small groups who communicate, coordinate, and conduct their campaigns in an internetted manner, without a precise central command.' RAND Corporation (Bruce Hoffman), *Insurgency and Counterinsurgency in Iraq*, June 2004. For more on Netwar see John Arquilla, David Ronfeldt and Michele Zanini, 'Networks, Netwar and the Information-Age Terrorism', in RAND Corporation (Ian Lesser et al.) *Countering the New Terrorism*, 1999, p. 47.
14. See the very useful discussion in Scott Atran, *Talking to the Enemy*, Harper-Collins, 2010, pp. 267–8.

15. Jessica Stern, *Terror in the Name of God*, Harper Perennial, 2004, p. 271: resilience is the 'ability of a network to withstand the loss of a node or nodes. To maximise resilience, the network has to maximise redundancy. Functions are not centralised. Capacity – the ability to optimise the scale of the attack – requires coordination, which makes the group less resilient because communication is required. Effectiveness is a function of both capacity and resilience.'

16. Author interviews with American army intelligence officers, Tikrit, May 2004, Baghdad, September 2004. Author interviews with British army intelligence officers, Basra, August 2004. Also with insurgents, Baghdad and Ramadi, April and September 2004. Greg Grant, 'The IED Marketplace', *Defense News*, March 2005. Amatzia Baram, 'Who Are the Insurgents? Sunni Arab Rebels in Iraq, April 2005', special report for the United States Institute of Peace. See also Rory McCarthy, 'For faith and country, insurgents fight on', *Guardian*, December 16, 2004. Other classic operational elements of Abu Mujahed's group would include the way in which they accessed military expertise – partly as a result of the hasty demobilization of the army. The post-invasion period saw a rapid dissemination of such knowledge among the civilian population. Also, though Abu Mujahed did not mention it, the internet aided some groups to learn both about ambush tactics and, crucially, about the media potential of the acts. Abu Mujahed was entirely typical not only of the modern Sunni Iraqi militant but of the reality of such militancy globally.

17. The overall commander of Marine Expeditionary Force One was General James T. Conway.

18. The lynching, as journalist Nir Rosen pointed out, was an Iraqi tradition called *sahel*, a word unique to Iraqi Arabic, which once meant dragging a body down the street with an animal or vehicle, but eventually grew to mean any sort of public killing or lynching. Rosen, 'Losing it'.

19. Author interview with Andrew Rathmell, CPA policy planning office, 2004.

20. Author interview with senior Ministry of Defence official, London, August 2004.

21. Author interviews with Andrew Rathmell, senior CPA officials, London, 2004. Jonathan F. Keiler, 'Who Won the Battle of Fallujah?', *Proceedings, U.S. Naval Institute*, January 2005, p. 59. Sean D. Naylor, '"Paying the price" for pulling out: commanders see a tough fight to retake Fallujah', *Army Times*, October 4, 2004.

22. Abu Anas al-Shami, the diary of Falluja, Arabic al-Fajer media, 2004, author collection. An English translation is reprinted in Loretta Napoleoni, *Insurgent Iraq: Al Zarqawi and the New Generation*, Seven Stories, 2005: see p. 219.

23. The exact number of dead civilians was heavily contested. American military spokesmen insisted that the bulk of the 800 or 900 civilian dead were

insurgents. Doctors in Falluja said that many of those they had treated were neither male nor of combat age. Iraq Body Count, 'No Longer Unknowable: Falluja's April Civilian Toll is 600', October 26, 2004.

24. Ricks, *Fiasco*, p. 342.

25. A 'stunning victory' in the words of a memo written by Nathaniel Jensen, a State Department diplomat attached to the CPA. Ibid., p. 345.

26. Bing West, *The Strongest Tribe*, Random House, 2009, p. 31.

27. Propaganda produced years later by militants in Europe, Afghanistan and Pakistan still mentioned Falluja. In 2009, for example, videos entitled 'Lions of Falluja' were still being posted on the internet by European extremists. To have participated in the fighting at Falluja was seen as particularly praiseworthy. See al-Muderii, Abdul'Aala transcript: 'The Martyr Abu Usama Walid walad al-Hibatt al-Tunisi', As-Sahab Media foundation via the NEFA Foundation, November 30, 2009, p. 1. http://www.nefafoundation.org/miscellaneous/nefaWalidTunisi1109.pdf.

28. Ricks, *Fiasco*, pp. 258–9.

29. SIGINT stands for Signals Intelligence. Ibid., p. 194. The latter, for example, gave analysts a false impression of the number of non-Iraqis among the insurgents as the 'internationals', who did not have the personal relationships that locals had, made heavier use of the telephones that the eavesdropping technology picked up.

30. Author interview, Tikrit, May 2004.

31. Philip Gourevitch and Errol Morris, *Standard Operating Procedure*, Picador, 2009, pp. 21–2.

32. Mark Danner, 'US torture: voices from the black sites', *New York Review of Books*, April 9, 2009.

33. Gourevitch and Morris, *Standard Operating Procedure*, pp. 38–9.

34. Mark Danner, 'Abu Ghraib: the hidden story', *New York Review of Books*, October 7, 2004, p. 33. The military intelligence unit that oversaw interrogations at the Bagram detention centre, where at least two prisoners' deaths were ruled homicides, was later placed in charge of questioning at Abu Ghraib prison in Iraq. Captain Carolyn A. Wood, who served at Bagram from July 2002 to December 2003, brought to Iraq interrogation procedures developed during service in Afghanistan, according to Congressional testimony. It was apparently Captain Wood who wrote the interrogation rules posted on the wall at Abu Ghraib. Human Rights Watch, *The Road to Abu Ghraib*, pp. 23–4.

35. Thomas E. Ricks, 'In Iraq, military forgot the lessons of Vietnam: Early missteps by U.S. left troops unprepared for guerrilla warfare', *Washington Post*, July 26, 2003.

36. Prisoners there later remembered how much more brutal their custodians had become as a result. Author interviews with former prisoners, Kabul, August 2008.

37. Associated Press, 30 April 2004, excerpts from writings of an accused soldier who helped run Baghdad prison.
38. Interrogators in Bagram told investigators that the knowledge that those at the most senior levels of political power in the country had 'denied the Geneva convention' to detainees had influenced their behaviour.
39. Black had unapologetically insisted before Congress that 'after 9/11 ... the gloves had come off' regarding the rules governing the operations conducted by the CIA.
40. Feith, Douglas, *War and Decision*, p. 485.
41. A total of thirty-four members of Taskforce 145, involved in the hunt for al-Qaeda fugitives, were eventually disciplined for mistreating detainees. Five US army rangers were convicted of assault. Mark Bowden, 'The ploy', *The Atlantic*, May 2007. Gourevitch and Morris, *Standard Operating Procedure*, p. 210.
42. Hundreds of complaints by Iraqis eventually made their way into British courts. In addition to the abuses mentioned above, many complained of sexual humiliation by women soldiers, or being held for days in brightly lit cells as small as one metre square. Ian Cobain, 'Servicemen at "UK's Abu Ghraib" may be guilty of war crimes, court hears', *Guardian*, November 8, 2010. 'No public probe into Iraq "abuse"', BBC News Online, November 14, 2009. 'Torture by British soldiers in Iraq was not carried out by "few bad apples ... there was something rotten in the whole barrel"', *Daily Mail*, September 21, 2009. Ian Cobain, 'Iraq deaths in British custody could see military face legal challenges', *Guardian*, July 1, 2010. Very serious allegations of execution and subsequent mutilation of corpses in Maysan province in 2004 have never been fully investigated. British military courts dismissed charges against all defendants except one, who was convicted for inhumane treatment. See *The Aitken Report, An Investigation into Cases of Deliberate Abuse and Unlawful Killing in Iraq in 2003 and 2004*, Crown Publishers, January 25, 2008, for the British army's official response.
43. Low-ranking personnel were, often enthusiastically it is true, frequently only carrying out the instructions of the interrogators, who wanted their subjects 'softened up'. Gourevitch and Morris, *Standard Operating Procedure*, p. 94.
44. Though various individuals have claimed to be the man in the iconic photograph, none have been positively identified. He is believed to be Abdou Hussain Saad Faleh (detainee 18170). An American army spokesman said Faleh was released from American custody in January 2004. Kate Zernike, 'Cited as symbol of Abu Ghraib, man admits he is not in photo', *New York Times*, March 18, 2006.
45. Author interview, Abu Ghraib, May 2004.
46. The rest of the city, on coalition maps, was not secure and thus 'the Red Zone'.

47. See Chandreshekan, *Imperial Life in the Emerald City*, for a vivid and perceptive view of life in the Green Zone. See also George Packer, *The Assassins' Gate: America in Iraq*, Farrar, Straus and Giroux, 2006.

48. Many State Department officials spent only ninety days in the country. Some spent even less. See US Office of the Inspector General Oversight and Review Division, December 2008 report titled *An Investigation of Overtime Payments to FBI and Other Department of Justice Employees Deployed to Iraq and Afghanistan*, p. 18, which suggests ninety-day deployments were standard, but many served much less: 'The FBI trainers generally stayed in Iraq for the duration of the courses (typically a few weeks) rather than for 90 days.'

49. Description based on the author's reporting, 2003–4.

50. Author interview, Bath, July 2004.

51. Author interview, Tikrit, April 2004.

52. Rory McCarthy of the *Guardian* was the reporter.

53. Author interview, June 2004.

54. Author interview, Tikrit, 2004.

55. Author interview with Rory Stewart, Kabul, March 2009.

56. Benon V. Sevan (Executive Director of the Iraq Programme) statement: 'Phasing down and termination of the Programme pursuant to Security Council resolution 1483 (2003)', Office of the Iraq Programme, Oil-for-Food, November 19, 2003.

57. The corruption was only the extension of that spreading throughout Iraqi society – $100 could avoid a delay of twelve days and a lot of queuing for new passports; joining the new Iraqi chamber of commerce cost nothing, except the $250 backhander.

58. *Special Inspector General for Iraqi Reconstruction Quarterly and Semi Annual Report to Congress*, January 30, 2006, pp. 17 and 33.

59. Author interviews, Dr Adel Mirza Ghadban, Baghdad, July 2003. See Jason Burke, 'Iraq: an audit of war', *Observer*, July 6, 2003.

60. George Packer, 'War after the War', *New Yorker*, November 24, 2003.

61. The National Security Strategy of the United States of America, September 2002, Introduction, p. 1. Cited in Dodge, 'The Ideological Roots of Failure'.

62. Twenty-three per cent of Iraqis say that they would like to model their new government after the US; 17.5 per cent would like their model to be Saudi Arabia; 12 per cent say Syria, 7 per cent say Egypt and 37 per cent say 'none of the above'. John Zogby, 'How the poll results on Iraq were manipulated', *Arab News*, October 23, 2003. Only 38 per cent said they thought democracy would work, while discussion groups held by Thomas Melia, director of research at the Institute for the Study of Diplomacy at Georgetown University, in July 2003 revealed a deep unease about indecency and licentiousness that was associated with Western democracies especially during conversation about the role of women, daughters and family. VOA, 'Poll shows Iraqis wary about Western-style democracy', VOA, December 11, 2003.

63. 'We are thinking in terms of one or two years,' Deputy Ambassador John Wilkes told the author.

64. Bush, *Decision Points*, p. 359.

65. The Mahdi is a divinely guided redeemer of Muslims, associated with the 'occulted' or hidden twelfth imam in the Shia tradition but recognized by many Sunnis though not by the most orthodox. The Mahdi's anticipated rule will be just and will see both the religious purity and political power of Islam restored. It will also, in the eschatological tradition, herald the end of time. The Jaysh al-Mahdi should be properly translated as the militia of the messiah rather than the al-Mahdi Army. However, the conventional usage has been preferred here, not least because of the complex theological implications of the word messiah.

66. Ayatollah is a sign of senior rank among the Shia clergy, denoting, among other things. a high degree of scholastic authority and learning.

67. See Fred Halliday, *Two Hours That Shook the World*, Saqi Books, 2002.

68. In 1968, al-Sadr I had created the Dawa party, a clandestine Islamist organization, with a rhetoric and cell structure that drew heavily on that of the Communists and the atheistic, quasi-Fascist Ba'athists who took power in Iraq in the same year. The type of organization had been introduced to the region by the Communist Third International from the 1920s and also through Fascist and Nazi channels before being adopted through the late 1920s and 30s by a range of different currents – Communists in Syria, Egypt and Iraq and the Muslim Brotherhood in Egypt.

> The Leninist model proved its superiority over the politics of notables, which was centred on elite figures and saloon gatherings with no root organization. It overwhelmed the imagination of some young Islamic-minded Najafi lay groups. These young men observed with admiration and awe the appeal of the Marxist utopia and the efficiency of the clandestine communist organization in Najaf which even competed with them in organzing ashura rituals. They were eager to command such powerful instruments of recruitment and mobilization. Young clerics also shared this fascination. (Faleh A. Jabar, *The Shi'ite Movement in Iraq*, Saqi Books, 2003, pp. 78–9)

The new thinkers even went as far as to claim that it was the duty of clerics, as interpreters of religious law and scholars, to govern too.

69. Around 5,000 were detained and at least 250 were tortured to death.

70. Nicolas Pelham, *A New Muslim Order: The Shia and the Middle East Sectarian Crisis*, I. B. Tauris, 2008, p. 16. Between 1982 and 1985 some Shia communities in the south of Iraq even organized their own resistance to Iran's advance independent of state direction.

71. International Crisis Group, *Iraq's Muqtada Al-Sadr: Spoiler or Stabiliser?*, July 11, 2006, p. 4.

72. Al-Sadr was born on August 12, 1973.

73. Author telephone interview with Hilary Synnott, October 2009.

74. Author interview with David Richmond, Baghdad, March 2004.

75. Author interview, Tikrit, March 2004.

76. The episode is related vividly by Rory Stewart, British diplomat and CPA official at the time, in his *Occupational Hazards*, pp. 391–3.

77. Patrick Cockburn, *Muqtada al-Sadr and the Fall of Iraq*, Faber and Faber, 2008, p. 171.

78. Ibrahim al-Marashi, 'Boycotts, Coalitions and the Threat of Violence: The Run-Up to the January 2005, Iraqi Elections', *The Middle East Review of International Affairs*, January 2005.

79. This was certainly the view of British intelligence specialists in Iraq at the time. Author interview with MI6 official, Kabul, May 2011. See International Crisis Group, *Iran in Iraq*, March 2005, pp. 10–13. Edward T. Pound, 'The Iran Connection', *US News and World Report*, November 22, 2004. A useful analysis can be found in Mark Urban, *Task Force Black*, Little, Brown, 2010, p. 111.

80. This account is largely based on the author's reporting in Najaf during the fighting of August 2004.

81. Interview on al-Arabiya, 13 January 2006. Cockburn, *Muqtada al-Sadr*, p. 205.

82. Sistani had been born in Mashad, Iran.

83. International Crisis Group, *Iraq's Muqtada al-Sadr*, p. 14.

CHAPTER 7: AL-QAEDA AND THE 9/11 WARS

1. 918 to be precise, according to Iraqbodycount.org. Iraq Body Count's totals, compiled from reliable media reporting, can be considered a guaranteed minimum. The true figures are likely to be higher.

2. See Bernard Lewis, *The Crisis of Islam: Holy War and Unholy Terror*, Random House, 2004, for a useful discussion.

3. *Pew Global Attitudes Project: How Global Publics View: War in Iraq, Democracy, Islam and Governance and Globalization*, June 2003, pp. 3, 46.

4. Throughout this chapter, as in the rest of the book, I refer to Setmariam as al-Suri. The latter is, of course, a nickname, simply meaning the Syrian, and it would be better to use his family name. However, al-Suri, like al-Zarqawi, has entered popular usage, and I have thus followed that custom.

5. It is possible he may subsequently have travelled again, conceivably even to Iraq.

6. Alison Pargeter, *The New Frontiers of Jihad*, I. B. Tauris, 2008, pp. 1–4. Murad Batal Al-shishani, 'Abu Mus'ab al-Suri and the Third Generation of Salafi-Jihadists', August 15, 2005, *Terrorism Monitor*, vol. 3, no. 16, August 15, 2005. The ruling family in Syria is from the minority Allawite sect of Shia Islam though the majority of the Syrian population is Sunni.

7. Abu Musab al-Suri, 'Da'wat al-Muqawama al-Islamiyya al-Alamiyya', pp. 710–11, quoted in Tawil, *Brothers in Arms*, p. 29.

8. Probably the best single work on al-Suri is Brynjar Lia, *Architect of Global Jihad: The Life of Al Qaeda Strategist Abu Mus'ab Al-Suri*, Columbia University Press, 2008.

9. See Paul Cruickshank and Mohammad Hage Ali, 'Abu Musab al-Suri: Architect of the New al-Qaeda', *Studies in Conflict and Terrorism*, 30, 2007, pp. 1–14.

10. Another reason was that al-Suri was also accused of organizing the assassination of two more moderate Algerian Islamists. Pargeter, *The New Frontiers of Jihad*, p. 68. See also Brynjar Lia, 'Abu Mus'ab al-Suri's Critique of Hard Line Salafists in the Jihadist Current', *CTC Sentinel*, vol. 1, no. 1, December 2007, p. 3.

11. Al-Suri was released as he had not actually, under legislation at the time, committed any offence. For quote on the Taliban, see Lia, *The New Frontiers of Jihad*, p. 234.

12. Adam Shatz, 'Laptop jihadi' *London Review of Books*, March 20, 2008. Lia, *Architect of Global Jihad*. Interrogation report of Ahmed al-Sayyid al-Najjar, Egyptian militant by Egyptian investigators, quoted in Tawil, *Brothers in Arms*, p. 156.

13. Quoted in Cruickshank and Hage Ali, 'Abu Musab al-Suri: Architect of the New al-Qaeda'.

14. See 'al-Suri Da'wat al-Muqawama al-Islamiyya al-Alamiyya', 2005, quoted in Devin Springer, James Regens and David Edger, *Islamic Radicalism and Global Jihad*, Georgetown University Press, 2008, p. 176.

15. Bagram airport was referred to as al-Qaeda al-Bagram by Arab fighters in Afghanistan.

16. Burke, *Al-Qaeda*, pp. 1–2.

17. Andrew Black, 'Al-Suri's Adaptation of Fourth Generation Warfare Doctrine', *Terrorism Monitor*, vol. 4, no. 18, September 21, 2006.

18. 'Al-Suri, the Call to Global Resistance', pp. 1,396–7. Quoted Springer et al., *Islamic Radicalism and Global Jihad*, p. 113.

19. Gilles Kepel, *Le Terreur et le martyre: Relever le défi de civilisation*, Flammarion, 2008, p. 138.

20. Quoted in Cruickshank and Hage, 'Abu Musab al-Suri: Architect of the New al-Qaeda'.

21. Springer et al., *Islamic Radicalism and Global Jihad*, p. 72.

22. 'Abu Musa'ab 'al-Suri D'awat al-Muqawama', p. 41, quoted in Tawil, *Brothers in Arms*, p. 186.

23. Such as Christians.

24. The military used the Islamists against the Communists too.

25. See International Crisis Group, *Indonesia Backgrounder: Why Salafism and Terrorism Mostly Don't Mix*, September 13, 2004, pp. 5–6. Also Howard M.

Federspiel, *Islam and Ideology in the Emerging Indonesian State: The Persatuan Islam, 1923 to 1957*, Leiden, 2001, pp. 15, 21–2.

26. Including a period when the Indonesian army had sponsored Muslim anti-Communist gangs.

27. See Burke, *Al-Qaeda*, for more on the camp at Pabbi. Atran, *Talking to the Enemy*, p. 140.

28. Author interviews with Indonesian intelligence officer, Jakarta, October 2002. Memorandum for Commander, US Southern Command, CSRT Input for Guantanamo Detainee, US9ID–010019DP, Riduan Isamuddin, October 30, 2008. Another link was Mohammed Mansour Jabarah, who was allegedly central to a plan to blow up the Australian, Israeli and US embassies in Singapore in 2001. Jabarah, an explosives expert, confessed to playing a role as an intermediary between al-Qaeda and Jemma Islamiya, and as an envoy of Khaled Sheikh Mohammed. He pleaded guilty to acts of terrorism in a 2002 agreement that was kept secret at the time and then began working as an informant for the FBI. New York University Center on Law and Security, Terrorist Trial Report Card 2001–2009, published 2010, p. 45.

29. International Crisis Group, *Terrorism in Indonesia: Noordin's Networks Crisis Group Asia*, May 5, 2006. p. 5.

30. Selma Belaala, 'Slums breed jihad', *Le Monde Diplomatique*, Morocco, November 2004.

31. The marginalization was very clear when the author was visiting the slums in 2007. Even reaching them from the centre of the city was extremely difficult with no public transport serving them and no taxi drivers willing to make the journey. Wasteground and rubbish dumps provided further barriers.

32. Elaine Sciolino, 'Moroccans say Al Qaeda was behind Casablanca bombings', *New York Times*, May 23, 2003. Sebastian Rotella, 'Morocco indicts 6 more suspects in Casablanca blasts', *Los Angeles Times*, May 30, 2003. Author interviews with senior Moroccan government investigators, analyst Mohammed Darif in Casablanca, January 2006, March 2007.

33. *Pew Global Attitudes 2004: A Year after Iraq*, March 16, 2004, p. 1. In Morocco the figure was 66 per cent.

34. The national assembly voted 'no' by 266 to 264. A consequence of this would be that many of the areas in Iraq which were to have been the responsibility of the powerful and highly mechanized 4th Infantry Division in the immediate post-war period were taken on by tired and overstretched troops who had fought their way up from Kuwait.

35. Dilip Hiro, *Inside Central Asia*, Overlook Duckworth, 2009, p. 117. The invasion was one of the very few issues which could unite all Turks, from Islamists to secularist nationalists.

36. Karl Vick, 'Al-Qaeda's hand In Istanbul Plot', *Washington Post*, February 13, 2007. Excerpts of intercepts and interrogation reports, author collection. Details from Turkish government indictment, February 2004. Author collection.

37. Edmund F. McGarrell, Joshua D. Freilich and Steven Chermak, 'Intelligence Led Policing as a Framework for Responding to Terrorism', *Journal of Contemporary Criminal Justice*, vol. 23, no. 2, 2007, pp. 142–58.

38. Atran, *Talking to the Enemy*, p. 199.

39. The Shahada is the profession of faith by a Muslim: 'I bear witness that there is no God but Allah and Mohammed is his prophet.'

40. José Maria Aznar, Spain's conservative prime minister, personally called the editor of Spain's most important newspaper, the left-leaning *El Pais*, to make sure the headlines reflected this interpretation.

41. Atran, *Talking to the Enemy*, p. 181.

42. Scott Atran and Marc Sageman, 'The Great Train Bombing', draft from October 10, 2007, p. 7.

43. 'Madrid bombing probe finds no al-Qaida link', Associated Press, March 9, 2006. Javier Jordan and Robert Wesley, 'The Madrid Attacks: Results of Investigations Two Years Later', *Terrorism Monitor*, vol. 4, no. 5, March 9, 2006. Author interviews with senior Spanish police officers, Madrid, October 2006.

44. NYPD, *Intelligence Report: Radicalization in the West*, 2007, p. 39. Author collection.

45. Atran, *Talking to the Enemy*, p. 179.

46. Ibid., p. 183.

47. Lawrence Wright, 'The terror web: were the Madrid bombings part of a new, far-reaching jihad being plotted on the internet?', *New Yorker*, August 2, 2004. Author interviews, Spanish Centro Nacional de Inteligencia officials, Saudi Arabia, March 2008.

48. Atran, *Talking to the Enemy*, pp. 201–2.

49. Wright, 'The terror web'.

50. See White House press release, January 10, 2006. In a key speech Bush laid out 'the political, security, and economic elements of the strategy for victory in the central front of the War on Terror, what has been achieved, the challenges faced at the start of 2006'.

51. Napoleoni, *Insurgent Iraq*, p. 218.

52. Abu Anas al-Shami diary, author collection.

53. Some sources say he was indeed involved in fighting around Khost in 1990. See Romesh Ratnesar, 'Face of terror: how Abu Mousab al-Zarqawi transformed the Iraq insurgency into a holy war and became America's newest nightmare', *Time*, December 19, 2004 .

54. Author interviews with American intelligence officials, Tikrit and Baghdad, May 2004. Author interviews with former associates, Amman, June 2003. There are many useful accounts of al-Zarqawi's life and works. Cross-referencing between works such as Napoleoni, *Insurgent Iraq* and very different publications such as Gilles Kepel, ed., *Al-Qaida dans le texte*, PUF, 2008, pp. 370–416, allows a coherent and relatively accurate picture to emerge. On the amnesty in Jordan, see Bergen, *The Osama Bin Laden I Know*, p. 353.

55. The timing of al-Zarqawi's arrival in northern Iraq is unclear, but he was not mentioned by anyone in a comprehensive range of interviews the author conducted with militants and Kurdish intelligence officials in the summer of that year.

56. German police intelligence report on al-Tauhid, compiled spring 2003. Author telephone interviews with Afghan and Libyan former activists, in London and in Pakistan, February 2003.

57. Full text of Colin Powell's speech, *Guardian*, February 5, 2003. Powell said: 'What I want to bring to your attention today is the potentially much more sinister nexus between Iraq and the Al Qaida terrorist network, a nexus that combines classic terrorist organizations and modern methods of murder. Iraq today harbors a deadly terrorist network headed by Abu Musab Al-Zarqawi, an associated collaborator of Osama bin Laden and his Al Qaida lieutenants.'

58. He certainly had both legs firmly attached to his body when finally killed in 2006. Nor was there any real evidence of the chemical and biological weapons factory Ansar-ul-Islam were supposed to have established in the enclave north of Halabjah.

59. See Jason Burke, *Al-Qaeda*, pp. 225–7, for further details of Ansar ul Islam. See Linda Robinson, *Masters of Chaos*, Public Affairs, 2005, pp. 296–323, for a detailed account of the operation from the point of view of the American special forces.

60. See Jason Burke, 'Theatre of terror', *Observer*, November 21, 2004.

61. The video was uploaded by a twenty-three-year-old Moroccan-born student living in Britain. David Pallister, 'Three plead guilty to inciting murder on Islamist websites', *Guardian*, July 5, 2007. For the half million reference: Abigail Cutler, 'Web of terror', *The Atlantic*, June 5, 2006.

62. For al-Zarqawi's 'snakes' comment see Anton La Guardia, 'Zarqawi rails against Shia "snakes"', *Telegraph*, June 3, 2006.

63. Thomas Ricks, 'U.S. military conducted a PSYOP program "to magnify the role of the leader of al-Qaeda in Iraq"', *Washington Post*, April 11, 2006. Jonathan Finer, 'Among insurgents in Iraq, few foreigners are found', *Washington Post*, November 17, 2005. It is interesting to speculate what might have happened if the pan-Arabism of previous decades had still been prevalent in the early twenty-first century. Would the American strategy have failed with its subject seen as a pan-Arab hero? Or would al-Zarqawi's excesses have alienated local communities nonetheless?

64. The contemporary understanding of the concept of *takfir* owes much to the writings of Syed Qutb among others.

65. Jean-Charles Brisard, *Zarqawi: The New Face of Al-Qaeda*, Policy Press, 2005, p. 135. Al-Shami told listeners: 'If the infidels take Muslims as protectors and Muslims refuse to fight, it is permitted to kill these Muslims.'

66. Audio cassette message from al-Shami, July 2004, author collection. Al-Shami authored the 'diary of Falluja'.

67. Author interview, Riyadh, March 2008.

68. Ruben Paz, 'Arab Volunteers Killed in Iraq: An Analysis', *The Project for the Research of Islamist Movements (PRISM)*, vol. 3, no. 1 (March 2005).

69. Smugglers running people usually take the same paths used for smuggling livestock. Cigarettes or similar goods move on trucks.

70. Toby Jones, 'Shifting Sands', *Foreign Affairs*, March/April 2006; Eric Rouleau, 'Trouble in the Kingdom', *Foreign Affairs*, July/August 2002. John C. K. Daly, '"Saudi Black Gold": Will Terrorism Deny the West Its Fix?', *Terrorism Monitor*, vol. 1, no. 7 (May 5, 2005). See also Robert Lacey, *Saudi Arabia Exposed: Inside a Kingdom in Crisis*, Palgrave Macmillan, 2006.

71. In Saudi Arabia, fully 40 per cent of the population was under fifteen in 2006. RAND Corporation (Christopher G. Pernin et al.), *Unfolding the Future of the Long War: Motivations, Prospects, and Implications for the U.S. Army*, 2008, p. 213. Useful works on Saudi Arabia include Mamoun Fandy, *Saudi Arabia and the Politics of Dissent*, Palgrave Macmillan, 2001, and the truly excellent Thomas Hegghammer, *Jihad in Saudi Arabia*, Cambridge University Press, 2010.

72. See Combating Terrorism Center (Brian Fishman), *Al'Qa'ida's Foreign Fighters in Iraq: A First Look at the Sinjar Records*, West Point, December 2007, pp. 12–15, for more detail on groups travelling together from their home towns.

73. It is interesting to note that Syria featured in the Rand Corporation study of possible future evolutions of the 9/11 Wars as a low probability, medium-risk, medium- to long-term potential danger. Pernin et al., *Unfolding*, p. 74.

74. Author interview, Riyadh, Saudi Arabia, March 2008. Al-Fawzan had been released from prison eight weeks previously.

75. Each had a coordinator back home, usually the leader of a mosque or another prominent person who had vouched for him. Abu Thar, arriving on his own, was at first considered suspicious. That was 'until they called my master in the religious school in Yemen', he said.

76. Ghaith Abdul-Ahad, 'Seeking salvation in city of insurgents', *Washington Post*, November 11, 2004.

77. See CTC (Fishman), *Foreign Fighters in Iraq*, p. 27. Also Combating Terrorism Center, *Bombers, Bank Accounts and Bleed Outs: al-Qaida's Role in and out of Iraq*, West Point, July 2008, pp. 9, 57.

78. For a description of al-Shami's death and the reaction of his comrades see the postings 'The Secrets of History: Zarqawi as I Knew Him' on the '7th Century Generation' forum, www.7cgen.com, especially 'A Treatise Written by Shaykh Maysarah al-Gharib'. Al-Shami died on September 24.

79. 'The progress we had hoped to make with Iraqi security forces is not as was expected . . . A large number of police did not stand up when their country called,' General Kimmitt, the chief military spokesman in Iraq, had been forced to admit after the first battle.

80. Ricks, *Fiasco*, p. 399.

81. At least to the time of writing in December 2010. The battle of Shah-e-Kot in

March 2002 in Afghanistan had seen far fewer US troops deployed and a much smaller number of militants.

82. Ghaith Abdul-Ahad, 'We are not here to liberate Iraq, we're here to fight the infidels,' *Guardian*, November 9, 2004.

83. Full transcript of bin Laden's speech, Al Jazeera Archive, Aljazeera.net, November 1, 2004.

84. Ibid.

85. Author interview with Nigel Inkster, deputy director MI6 until 2004, London, February 2009.

86. Author interview with Mahmood Shah, Peshawar, November 2008.

87. Author telephone interview with Grenier, January 2009. Pervez Musharraf wrote: 'When we received initial reports of al-Qaeda's presence [in South Waziristan] we did not take them very seriously.' Musharraf, *In the Line of Fire*, p. 264.

88. On reports of presence in Shakai, see Memorandum for Commander, US Southern Command, CSRT Input for Guantanamo Detainee, US9LY-010017DP, Farraj al-Libby, September 10, 2008, US9AF-003148DP, Harun al-Afghani, August 2, 2007, secret, author collection. A key influence here was Ayman al-Zawahiri, who, with his own practical experience of the difficulties of fighting a militant campaign in Egypt, balanced the tendency of bin Laden, who had always been a propagandist more than a fighter, to tilt towards al-Suri's views. Al-Zawahiri stressed repeatedly that the establishment of a secure haven from which to plan and organize should be one of the priorities of the jihadist movement.

89. The useful term 'inciter-in-chief' comes from Michael Scheuer. Author interview, September 2006.

90. The *dar ul kufr* itself is subdivided into the lands of war, *dar ul harb*, and the lands where a covenant had been concluded between the Muslims who lived there and the infidel authorities which tolerated their presence and to some extent protected them. These latter zones comprised what was known as the *dar ul ahd*. See discussion in Kepel, *Jihad*, p. 197.

CHAPTER 8: THE 9/11 WARS REACH EUROPE

1. Author interview, Amsterdam, November 2004.

2. Ian Buruma, 'Letter from Amsterdam, final cut: after a filmmaker's murder, the Dutch creed of tolerance has come under siege', *New Yorker*, January 3, 2005.

3. See David Levering Lewis, *God's Crucible: Islam and the Making of Europe 570 to 1215*, Norton, 2008, pp. 160–76. Some argue that Poitiers actually occurred in 733; see J. H. Roy and J. Deviosse, *La Bataille de Poitiers, Octobre 733*, Paris, Gallimard, 1966.

4. In fact, the Ottomans signed a peace treaty with Spain. Equally, as Professor Efraim Karsh, head of Middle East and Mediterranean Studies at King's College, London, pointed out in an editorial in the *New York Times* in February 2010: 'Even during the Crusades, the supposed height of the "clash of civilizations", Christian and Muslim rulers freely collaborated across the religious divide, often finding themselves aligned with members of the rival religion against their co-religionists. While the legendary Saladin himself was busy eradicating the Latin Kingdom of Jerusalem, for example, he was closely aligned with the Byzantine Empire, the foremost representative of Christendom's claim to universalism.' 'Muslims won't play together', *New York Times*, February 28, 2010.

5. The terms above are clearly both ethnic and religious, and the emphasis on which quality is seen as definitive has also evolved.

6. Shakespeare's depiction of the 'Moor', like his depiction of the Jew, tends to be complex, sensitive and often, for the period, sympathetic.

7. Orlando Figes, *Crimea: The Last Crusade*, Allen Lane, 2010.

8. Clearly the Asian subcontinent at the time was home to followers of many faiths, but much of the Indo-Gangetic plains as well as the Indus valley and the uplands to its west were dominated by Islam, and the ruling power over much of the region was Muslim.

9. Jean-Léon Gerome, painting around a time of extreme violence as an uprising led by clerics and tribal chiefs shook Algeria, avoided the new French colony as a setting for mosque paintings for the period of the disturbances, preferring Egypt. Rather than show violence to Westerners, Orientalist art largely showed violence to other 'Orientals', as well of course as the saccharine, the picturesque and often the erotic. Linda Nochlin, *The Politics of Vision: Essays on Nineteenth-Century Art and Society*, Westview Press, 1991, pp. 51–52, 59. See also Linda Nochlin, 'The Imaginary Orient', in Vanessa R. Schwartz and Jeannene M. Przyblyski, eds., *The Nineteenth-Century Visual Culture Reader*, Routledge, 2004, p. 296. Delacroix's earlier canvases had shown vengeful Ottoman hordes massacring Grecian peasants.

10. Salahuddin Malik, *1857 War of Independence or Clash of Civilizations*, Oxford, 2003. pp. 13, 17, 115, 118–19, 140, 148. A British government anxious to shift the burden of blame from their own recent policies in the subcontinent blamed Muslim 'Wahabi' agitators for much of the violence – despite the fact that most of the 'mutineers' were Hindu. Media claims of a global 'Islamist' plot, however, failed to convince a sceptical public. Through the late nineteenth century and into the first half of the twentieth, other perils supplanted or complemented the one that many had once thought 'the Muslims' had constituted. In 1900, *Gunton's Magazine* informed its readers that the Boxer Rebellion in China might prove the 'gravest' that 'Christendom has faced since the Moorish invasion of Europe' and could presage an apocalyptic struggle between 'western civilization and oriental barbarism'. See William

W. Bates, 'Chinese Outrages', *Gunton's Magazine Review of the Month*, p. 113 of archive. For a long period too the fear was of supposedly highly organized networks of anarchists and left-wing political activists. As a British police report from 1911 noted, 'These criminal organizations have grown in number and size. They are hardier than ever, now that the terrifying weapons created by modern science are available to them. The world is today threatened by forces which, once freed from their chains, will be able to one day carry out its total destruction.' According to William Dalrymple, author of *The Last Mughal: The Fall of a Dynasty*, Vintage, 2009, the mutinous Company soldiery was 90 per cent Hindu, though there were regional centres such as Lucknow where the street fighting civilian population was maybe 50 per cent Muslim as well as some cavalry units which were majority Muslim. Personal communication with the author, December 2010.

11. Andrew Wheatcroft, *The Infidels: The Conflict between Christendom and Islam, 638–2002*, Viking, 2003, p. 41. Arab armies at the time were largely composed of footsoldiers with a few cavalry and some camels, not, as in later images, a horde mounted on fine Arab horses. 'The Arabs were poor men, often with little more than a spear as a weapon. They walked ... using less water and food than any animal. Previously they had fought in small groups, but now, marshalled by the leaders of Islam, they numbered hundreds.' Nor incidentally did the early Arab invaders convert by the sword, rather the opposite. There was significant resistance to the conversion of many local populations from the elite who claimed their privilege as both as descendants of the original Arab settlers and as Muslims.

12. See Patrick Porter, *Military Orientalism*, Hurst, 2007, for a useful discussion of the idea of Western or Oriental styles of fighting.

13. Ian Buruma and Avishai Margalit, *Occidentalism*, Penguin Press, 2004.

14. Wheatcroft, *The Infidels*, pp. 190–91, 202.

15. Munqidh quote in Amin Maalouf, *The Crusades through Arab Eyes*, Schocken Books, 1989, p. 39. See also the very useful Carole Hillenbrand, *The Crusades: Islamic Perspectives*, Edinburgh University Press, July 30, 1999.

16. Karen Armstrong, *Holy War: The Crusades and Their Impact on Today's World*, Macmillan, 1998, p. 463.

17. See Malise Ruthven, *A Fury For God: The Islamist Attack on America*, Granta, 2004, for one of the best discussions of Qutb.

18. Porter, *Military Orientalism*, p. 57.

19. Tom Gross, 'The BBC's Augean Stables', *National Review*, February 28, 2005. Sheikh al-Sudais led 15,000 worshippers at prayer at the opening of a six-storey Islamic centre in east London, though he was careful to avoid any anti-Semitic references.

20. See, for example, the Egyptian series *Horseman without a Horse*, a forty-one-part TV melodrama based on the forged *Protocols of the Elders of Zion*.

'Egypt airs "anti-Semitic" series', BBC News Online, November, 7, 2002. Or the Syrian *The Collapse of Legends*, of which the central premise was that there was no archaeological evidence to support the stories of the Old Testament and that the Torah was forged to give the Jews a claim to the Land of Israel. It featured a group of Syrian archaeologists setting out to expose a group of Zionists hoping to plant evidence at a famous archaeological site to give some scientific basis to the forged scriptures. Richard Z. Chesnoff, *Jewish World Review*, December 13, 2002.

21. The author found copies on sale in Kuala Lumpur airport in December 2004.

22. Europe had, of course, its own long and inglorious tradition of anti-Semitism – one that had led to worse violence against the Jews than ever seen in the Islamic world – and the many young British Pakistanis or French Algerians interviewed by the author who spoke of how 'the Jews' were behind the 'war on terror' were unwittingly echoing words which had been banished from acceptable conversation only a few decades previously. See Denis Mac-Shane, *Globalising Hatred: The New Anti-Semitism*, Weidenfeld and Nicolson, 2009, for a provocative and informed survey. For an impressive and profoundly researched history, Robert Wistrich, *A Lethal Obsession: Anti-Semitism from Antiquity to the Global Jihad*, Random House, 2010.

23. Author telephone interview with Christopher Caldwell, July 2009. Caldwell's book, *Reflections on the Revolution in Europe*, Allen Lane, 2009, is often tendentious, relying on the arrangement of carefully selected factoids and subjective readings of data to give what is overall a misleading and alarmist description of the genuine problems of integration and assimilation of 'Muslim' communities in Europe. He is right, however, to argue that little thought was given to the consequences of importing labour in the 1960s and 1970s.

24. 'A large coloured community as a noticeable feature of our social life would weaken the concept of England or Britain to which people of British stock throughout the Commonwealth are attached,' a report of the British Colonial Office observed in 1955. Kenan Malik, *From Fatwa to Jihad*, Atlantic, 2009, p. 43.

25. Some in fact accelerated the influx as communities in the West sought to beat the deadlines imposed by successive waves of legislation. A total of 17,210 Pakistanis came to Britain between 1955 and 1960. In the eighteen months before the Immigration Act of 1962, 50,170 more arrived. See ibid., p. 43.

26. There are various guides to the vexed questions of numbers. One is the excellent and comprehensive Pew Research Center, *Mapping the Global Muslim Population: A Report on the Size and Distribution of the World's Muslim Population*, October 2009, which says, on p. 22, of Europe:

> Europe has about 38 million Muslims, constituting about 5% of its population. European Muslims make up slightly more than 2% of the world's Muslim

population. Readers should bear in mind that estimates of the numbers of Muslims in Europe vary widely because of the difficulty of counting new immigrants. Nevertheless, it is clear that most European Muslims live in eastern and central Europe. The country with the largest Muslim population in Europe is Russia, with more than 16 million Muslims, meaning that more than four-in-ten European Muslims live in Russia. While most Muslims in western Europe are relatively recent immigrants (or children of immigrants) from Turkey, North Africa or South Asia, most of those in Russia, Albania, Kosovo, Bosnia-Herzegovina and Bulgaria belong to populations that are centuries old, meaning that more than six in ten European Muslims are indigenous. Despite the limitations of the underlying data for Europe, it appears that Germany is home to more than 4 million Muslims – almost as many as North and South America combined. This means that Germany has more Muslims than Lebanon (between 2 million and 3 million) and more than any other country in western Europe. This also puts Germany among the top 10 countries with the largest number of Muslims living as a minority population. While France has a slightly higher percentage of Muslims than Germany, this study finds that it has slightly fewer Muslims overall. The United Kingdom is home to fewer than 2 million Muslims, about 3% of its total population.

As if to underline the difficulties of counting, Pew in 2010 revised their figure for UK Muslims upwards, to 2,869,000 Muslims in Britain, around 4.6 per cent of the population. See Pew Research Center, *Muslim Networks and Movements in Western Europe*, September 15, 2010. The European countries with the highest concentration of Muslims are located in eastern and central Europe: Kosovo (90 per cent), Albania (80 per cent), Bosnia-Herzegovina (40 per cent) and the Republic of Macedonia (33 per cent). Greece is about 3 per cent Muslim, while Spain is about 1 per cent Muslim. Italy has one of the smallest populations of Muslims in Europe, with less than 1 per cent of its population being Muslim. See also John Carvel, 'Census shows Muslims' plight', *Guardian*, October 12, 2004. For France see the excellent discussion in the first chapter of Jonathan Laurence and Justin Vaisse, *Intégrer l'Islam, la France et ses Musulmans: enjeux et réussites*, Odile Jacob, 2007, pp. 31–9. Laurence and Vaisse argue for a figure of 5 million. The website of the French Foreign Ministry says 'between four and five million'. The Ministry for the Interior gives the figure 4.5 million. See Haut Conseil à l'intégration, *L'Islam dans la République*, Paris, 2000.

27. By 2004, many of the younger militants suddenly coming to the attention of the authorities were in fact 'third generation'.
28. Less than a half of non-Western immigrants had a salaried job compared to 67 per cent of native Dutch. Figures from The Netherland's Social and Cultural Planning Office (Sociaal en Cultureel Planbureau, SCP), January 2009.
29. Carvel, 'Census shows Muslims' plight'.

30. Employees' religious backgrounds are not registered in German employment statistics. Thus, estimations are based primarily on national origins. Unemployment rates are consistently twice as high for non-Germans, with Turkish nationals appearing to be in the worst situation. In some *Länder*, the unemployment rate among the young Muslim population is estimated to be around 30 per cent. Even when comparing foreigners to Germans without any qualifications, a greater proportion of foreigners (three-quarters) than Germans (one-third) are unemployed. See http://www.euro-islam.info/country-profiles/germany/. Not only are French Muslims more likely to be unemployed than the rest of the population, they also encounter more problems finding long-term and full-time jobs.

31. For France, see Laurence and Vaisse, *Intégrer l'Islam*, pp. 64–5.

32. The Commission on the Future of a Multi-Ethnic Britain, cited Malik, *From Fatwa to Jihad*, p. 62.

33. Author interview, November 2004.

34. Lawrence James, *Warrior Race*, Little, Brown, 2001. There were also questions of Englishness as opposed to Britishness (or Welshness, Irishness and Scottishness), with one poll revealing that immigrants felt happier with a 'British' identity rather than an 'English' one.

35. Maleeha Lodhi, the Pakistani High Commissioner at the time of the 7/7 attacks, and many others saw a difference between 'integration' and 'assimilation'. Lodhi called on Pakistanis in Britain to integrate even if they did not want to assimilate. Author interview, London, July 2005.

36. The violence spilled over on to the streets of Paris, with bombs going off in Metro stations in 1995 and a French airliner hijacked at Algiers in 1994.

37. Malik, *From Fatwa to Jihad*, pp. 123–5.

38. See Martin Bright, *When Progressives Treat with Reactionaries*, Policy Exchange, 2006.

39. In the UK mosques went from 51 in 1979 to 329 six years later. In France in the same period, the rise was fivefold, from 136 to 766. Pargeter, *The New Frontiers of Jihad*, p. 19.

40. Laurence and Vaisse, *Intégrer l'Islam*, p. 281. The responsibility for 90 per cent of anti-Semitic attacks in the 1990s lay with the extreme right; that for 80 per cent of such attacks from 2000 onwards lay with 'Arabo-Muslim' aggressors.

41. 'I was of a generation that did not think of itself as Muslim or Hindi or Sikh or even as Asian but as black,' remembered the British academic and journalist Kenan Malik, explaining that one reason for a growing disaffection with left-wing groups was their focus on the class struggle rather than discrimination. Malik, *From Fatwa to Jihad*, pp. xi, 21.

42. Paul Harris, Martin Bright and Burhan Wazir, 'Five Britons killed in "jihad brigade"', *Observer*, October 28, 2001.

43. Details of April 30, 2003 Tel Aviv suicide bombing, Israeli Ministry of Foreign affairs, press release, June 3, 2003.

44. Shiv Malik, 'Omar Khan Sharif: profile', *New Statesman*, April 24, 2006. Hamas claimed responsibility for the attack.

45. Author interview, Amsterdam, November 2004.

46. Eliza Manningham-Butler, director general of the Security Service, 'Global Terrorism: Are We Meeting the Challenge?', James Smart lecture, City of London Police Headquarters, October 16, 2003.

47. Dominic Casciani, 'MI5 "too stretched " before 7 July', BBC, May 19, 2009. UK Parliament and Intelligence and Security Committee, *Report into the London Terrorist Attacks on 7 July 2005*, HMSO, 2006, p. 33.

48. John Stevens, *News of the World*, March 6, 2005.

49. 'Geheimdienste warnen vor Islamisten-Terror in Deutschland', *Der Spiegel*, November 13, 2004.

50. Beatrice de Graff, 'The Nexus between Salafism and Jihadism in the Netherlands', *CTC Sentinel*, vol. 3, no. 3, March 2010, pp. 17–22.

51. Author interviews with senior Dutch security officials, London, July 2008. See *Paths to Global Jihad: Radicalization and Recruitment. Proceedings from FFI Seminar*, Oslo, March 15, 2006, p. 18.

52. Interestingly, many of Hezb-ut-Tahrir's early members in the UK were former members of extreme left-wing groups such as the Socialist Workers' Party.

53. Author interview with Ed Husain, London, July 2007. See also Ed Husain, *The Islamist: Why I Joined Radical Islam in Britain, What I Saw Inside and Why I Left*, Penguin, 2007.

54. See the useful discussion in Malik, *From Fatwa to Jihad*, p. 45.

55. Anshuman Mondal, 'British Islam after Rushdie', *Prospect*, April 26, 2009.

56. Author interview with Shiraz Maher, London, July 2007.

57. Ibid.

58. Author interview, MI5, London, July 2007.

59. Unedited records of court reporting and transcript of trial at Old Bailey, London. Prosecution statement, April 24, 2007. Convictions in the case were quashed on appeal in 2008.

60. Of the twenty-six Islamic seminaries in Britain in 2006, seventeen are Deobandi.

61. Qadir continued fundraising through 2003 but eventually turned his energy to running a youth club aimed at combating gang violence among British Pakistani teenagers. Author interview with Hanif Qadir, Walthamstow, July 2007.

62. Another example from this period would be Dhiren Barot, a British convert to Islam jailed in 2006 for planning a range of mass-casualty attacks in the UK. Barot fought in Kashmir with Pakistani-based militants at the end of the 1990s before going on to pursue an almost decade-long career in Islamic terrorism.

63. Transcript, complete reporting records, Operation Crevice trial, London, March 2006 to April 2007. Author collection.

64. The ingredient was ammonium nitrate.

65. In 2007 the author compiled a survey of key personal data on over eighty British militants detained between 2001 and 2006. Their average age was twenty-nine when they were arrested. See Jason Burke, 'Omar was a normal British teenager who loved his little brother and Man Utd. So why at 24 did he plan to blow up a nightclub in central London?', *Observer*, January 20, 2008. A later study published in 2010 arrived at a median age of 27.6. Institute for Strategic Dialogue and Jytte Klausen, *Al Qaeda-Affiliated and 'Homegrown' Jihadism in the UK: 1999–2010*, 2010, p. 10. Many studies have been done showing that psychological problems among militant activists, Islamic or otherwise, are no more prevalent than in the general population.

66. Scott Atran, 'Who Becomes a Terrorist Today?', *Perspectives on Terrorism*, vol. 2, no. 5, May 2008.

67. Author interview, Scotland Yard, London, April 2005.

68. 'What was the 9/11 Hamburg cell if not a gang,' said one. Author interview, Walthamstow, August 2006.

69. Ed Husain, *The Islamist*, pp. 32–33.

70. Some accounts, such as that of the excellent Ian Buruma in the *New Yorker* edition of January 3, 2005, entitled 'Final cut', describe Bouyeri, van Gogh's killer, wearing 'a long Middle Eastern-style shirt'. Others, such as an eyewitness quoted in *De Telegraaf* the day after van Gogh's murder, refer to a hooded sweater. These are not are mutually exclusive. He was variously described by witnesses as wearing a hooded sweater, jeans and a long Maghreb-style traditional shirt. In fact, he appears to have been wearing all three.

71. Author interview, Walthamstow, London, July 2007.

72. This account is based on transcripts of the trial of the Crevice conspirators.

73. Junaid Babar testimony, author collection.

74. Author interviews, Thames House, London, July 2007.

75. Crevice transcripts.

76. Al-Iraqi had been a major in the Iraqi army in the 1980s but a member of al-Qaeda 'since the late 1990s', eventually rising to a position on the Shura or council which acted as an advisory body to bin Laden and al-Zawahiri – before the 9/11 attacks. His real name was Nashwan Abdulrazaq Abdulbaqi.

77. Crevice transcripts.

78. Crevice transcripts.

79. Crevice transcripts.

80. Author interview, Suleimaniyah, Iraq, August, 2002

81. Author interviews, Kabul, August 2008, March 2009; Rawalpindi, 2008; Jammu, India, 2003.

CHAPTER 9: BOMBS, RIOTS AND CARTOONS

1. Karen McVeigh and Alexandra Topping, '7/7 inquest witness saw bombers "celebrate like sports team" before attack', *Guardian*, October 13, 2010.

2. Andrew Malone, 'Tavistock Square: "I watched as the anxious man on the bus kept going into his bag"', *Independent*, July 8, 2005.

3. Author interviews with Scotland Yard senior officers, London, January 2006.

4. Khan was born in Leeds, grew up in Beeston and moved to Dewsbury a few months before the July bombings. Tanweer was born in Bradford but grew up in Beeston. Lindsay took the name Abdullah Shaheed Jamal following his conversion to Islam. He later moved to Aylesbury, Buckinghamshire.

5. Shiv Malik, 'My Brother the bomber', *Prospect*, 135, June 2007.; Sandra Laville and Dipazier Aslam, 'Mentor to the young and vulnerable', *Guardian*, July 14, 2005. UK Parliament and Intelligence Security Committee, *Report into the London Terrorist Attacks July 7 2005*. Melanie Newman, 'Greenwich and Leeds Met given "limited confidence" ratings by QAA', *Times Higher Education Supplement*, October 15, 2009. Khan's wife's family were Deobandi. His own were broadly Barelvi.

6. Leeds Metropolitan University was ranked 85 out of 115 in the 2011 universities league table.

7. Khan had an eight-month-old daughter. His wife was expecting a second. Jonathan Brown, 'Mohammed Sadique Khan: expectant father whose chosen path meant he would never see his baby', *Independent*, July 15, 2007.

8. Jason Burke, 'Secrets of bomber's death tape', *Observer*, September 4, 2005. London bomber: text in full, BBC, September 1, 2005. In fact, the latter has sections missing. Al-Jazeera broadcast the whole version. Text in author collection.

9. Home Office, *Report of the Official Account of the Bombings in London on 7th July 2005*, HMSO, May 11, 2006, p. 19.

10. Richard Norton-Taylor and Riazat Butt, 'Queen is target for al-Qaida, security sources confirm', *Guardian*, November 14, 2005.

11. In February 2004, Khyam had been recorded by MI5 telling Khan, a few months before the latter had set out for a training camp, that 'you'll be with Arab brothers, Chechen brothers. The only thing I will advise you . . . is total obedience to whoever your Emir is . . . whether he is Sunni, Arab, Chechen, Saudi, British . . . I'll tell you up there you can get your head cut off.' See James Brandon, 'Al-Qa'ida's Involvement in Britain's "Homegrown" terrorist plots', *CTC Sentinel*, vol. 2, no. 3, March 2009, p. 10.

12. Esther Addley, '7/7 inquest: "Pandemonium here . . . we have really got to get some control"', *Guardian*, October 11, 2010.

13. British ministers made extraordinary efforts to deny any causative link between the strikes and the war in Iraq, despite the advice of their own secur-

ity services, despite blindingly obvious evidence all around them and despite, exactly a year after the bombings, the release of the videoed testament of Shehzad Tanweer, who explained that 'the non-Muslims of Britain' were being targeted because they had 'openly supported the genocide of over 150,000 innocent Muslims in Falluja'.

14. The two men Ibrahim was travelling with are believed to have died in Afghanistan. 'Police monitored bomb plotters', BBC News Online, January 18, 2007.

15. Evan Kohlmann, 'Abu Musab al-Suri's final "Message to the British and the Europeans"', *Nefa Foundation*, August 2005.

16. Author interview with Pakistani intelligence officials, Riyadh, March 2008. 'Al-Suri has not surfaced anywhere since though may have been "rendered" to Syria.' William Maclean, 'Al Qaeda ideologue in Syrian detention – lawyers', Reuters, June 10, 2009.

17. Text of statement by Mayor Ken Livingstone, *Financial Times*, July 7, 2005.

18. In 2001, 30 per cent of Londoners were born outside England. See Leo Benedictus, 'Every race, colour, nation and religion on earth', *Guardian*, January 21, 2005. For 2006, the figure for Londoners born outside the UK was 32 per cent according to the Greater London Authority's Data Management and Analysis Group report by Laura Spence, February 2008, *A Profile of Londoners by Country of Birth Estimates from the 2006 Annual Population Survey*, p. 1.

19. Obituaries of those who died in the 7/7 bombing, Guardian Online, accessed July 7, 2010.

20. Kenan Malik, 'The Islamophobia Myth', *Prospect*, 107, February 2005.

21. GfK NOP Social Research, *Attitudes to Living in Britain – A Survey of Muslim Opinion*, August 2006.

22. Michael Meacher, 'This war on terrorism is bogus', *Guardian*, September 6, 2003.

23. Oriana Fallacci, *The Rage and the Pride*, Rizzoli, 2002. For sales figures: Jennifer Schuessler, 'Gift books for millionaires', *New York Times*, December, 20, 2010.

24. Bruce Bawer, *While Europe Slept*, Doubleday, 2006. Melanie Phillips, *Londonistan*, Encounter Books, 2006.

25. Address at the opening of courses at the University of Leiden, September 2004.

26. Christopher Caldwell, 'Islamic Europe: When Bernard Lewis speaks', *Weekly Standard*, October 4, 2004.

27. Tony Blankley, 'An Islamist threat like the Nazis', *Washington Times*, September 12, 2005.

28. Robert Leiken, 'Europe's Angry Muslims', *Foreign Affairs*, July/August 2005.

29. Charles Krauthammer, 'What the uprising generation wants,' *Time*, November 13, 2005.

30. Niall Ferguson, 'Eurabia?', *New York Times*, April 4, 2004.

31. See CIA World Factbook 2007 listings for Algeria, Turkey, Tunisia, France. Available online at https://www.cia.gov/library/publications/the-world-factbook/index.html. A series of other commentators dismissed a complex and technical debate among demographers and considerable evidence that reproduction rates among European Muslims are already declining and are likely to decline further in coming years (as they have done both for other European migrant communities and in many Muslim migrants' countries of origin) as European wishful thinking. See Chapter 14 for more.

32. Bat Ye'or, *Eurabia: The Euro-Arab Axis*, Fairleigh Dickinson University Press, 2005.

33. 'Tales from Eurabia', *The Economist*, June 22, 2006.

34. Extracts from the Zawahiri tape, Times Online, August 4, 2005. Al-Zawahiri issued a statement towards the end of 2005 which specifically targeted British Muslims, calling the Queen 'one of the severest threats to Islam' and, in passing, revealing deep cultural ignorance, threatening all those who called themselves 'British citizens, subject to Britain's crusader laws' and who were 'proud of [their] submission . . . to Elizabeth, head of the Church of England'.

35. Author interview with Alain Bauer, criminologist, Paris, March 2008.

36. Exact figures are hard to find. For example, at Aulnay-sous-Bois Ministry of the Interior press officers gave a figure of sixteen vehicles burned whereas the fire brigade recorded 150 separate interventions during a week of rioting. Author interviews, Paris, November 2005.

37. Mucchielli, *Quand les banlieues brûlent*, La Découverte, 2007, p. 20.

38. Many on the French left argued that they were in fact youngsters without previous criminal involvement who were more motivated by rage, hate, despair, alienation and a deep identity crisis than any involvement in narcotics. The arguments over the cause of the riots was in part political theatre, a result of internal French domestic politics, mainly the bitter and personal rivalry between Sarkozy, whose political persona and appeal was based on tough rhetoric on law and order, and his rival for the succession to President Jacques Chirac as leader of the French right, the less populist, urbane Dominique de Villepin, who favoured a more centrist, 'compassionate' conservatism. Uninspired and uninspiring, the French Socialists had little influence on the public conversation.

39. 'Les juges ne confirment pas le portrait des émeutiers dressé par Sarkozy', Agence France-Presse, November 17, 2005.

40. French Government Centre of Strategic Analysis, Report for the Office of the Prime Minister: *Enquêtes sur les violences urbaines: comprendre les émeutes de Novembre 2005, les exemples de Saint-Denis et de Aulnay-sous-Bois*, Paris, 2006.

41. For more see Timothy Garton-Ash, 'Anti-Europeanism in America', *Hoover Digest*, 2, 2003. Also Justin Vaisse, 'American Francophobia Takes a New Turn', *French Politics, Culture and Society*, vol. 21, no. 2, July 2003. The latter

in particular is an excellent discussion of the development of these stereo-types and of their reinforcement from 2003 onwards in the US media and among US politicians

42. Melanie Philips, 'Why France is burning', *Daily Mail*, November 7, 2005.

43. Mark Steyn, 'Wake up, Europe, you've a war on your hands', *Chicago Sun Times*, November 6, 2005.

44. Reuven Paz, 'The Non-Territorial Islamic States in Europe', paper, Project for the Research of Islamist Movements, Hertzeliya, Israel, November 28, 2005.

45. 'On faisait un peu le Baghdad, quoi' were the exact words of Paolo Savalli, of mixed Moroccan/Italian background, in Bobigny two months after the riots. Author interview, January 2010.

46. One example from the author's own late teenage years was the controversial 1988 hit 'Fuck Tha Police', by American rappers Niggaz With Attitude.

47. Mucchielli, *Quand les banlieues brûlent*, p. 29. See the 2004 report of the National Human Rights Advisory Commission (Commission nationale con-sultative des droits de l'homme, CNCDH).

48. Laurence and Vaisse, *Intégrer l'Islam*, p. 276.

49. Attacks on French Jews numbered 510 in first six months of 2004 as against 593 in the whole of 2003 according to 'Anti-Semitism on rise in Europe', BBC, March 31, 2004.

50. This killing was the first explicitly anti-Semitic murder in France since 1995. The 'gang of barbarians'' own understanding of Islam was cursory to say the least. Charles Bremner, 'Youssouf Fofana jailed for the torture and murder of Ilan Halimi', *The Times*, July 11, 2009, Pascal Ceaux and Jean-Marie Pon-taut, 'Youssouf Fofana: confessions d'un "barbare"', *L'Express*, January 23, 2008.

51. Author interviews, Bobigny, France, December 2005, January 2006.

52. Cecilia Gabizon, 'La Carte des émeutes de novembre 2005 confirme le pro-fond malaise des immigrants africains', *Le Figaro*, October 15, 2007. See also Hugues Lagrange and Marco Oberti, eds., *Emeutes urbaines et protestations*, Les Presses Sciences, 2006.

53. Christophe Cornevin, 'Des troubles nés de l'exclusion, selon les RG', *Le Figaro*, December 8, 2005.

54. Author interview with Olivier Roy, Paris, December 2005. Also Olivier Roy, 'The Nature of the French Riots', SSRC, November 18, 2005. Jean-Marc Sébé, *La Crise des banlieues*, PUF, 2007, p. 74.

55. French Government Centre of Strategic Analysis, *Enquêtes sur les violences urbaines*, pp. 17, 25.

56. Ibid., p. 47.

57. Jean Chichizola, 'Fous d'Allah et voyous font cause commune sur les braquages', *Le Figaro*, January 13, 2006.

58. One report by the RG detailed sixty-eight of 128 French penal institutions 'con-taminated by Islamism'. Jean Chichizola, '175 Islamistes font du proselytisme

en prison', *Le Figaro*, January 13, 2006. One reason for the radicalization activities occurring outside mosques and Islamic centres was the extremely effective surveillance of such locations by French intelligence services. Text of DGSE confidential presentation, Paris, March 2009, author collection.

59. Netherlands Institute for International Relations Clingendael (Edwin Bakker and Teije Hidde Donker), *Jihadi Terrorists in Europe,* The Hague, December 2006.

60. Author interview with DST official, Paris, January 2009. Jean Chichizola, 'L'Ombre de Zarqaoui s'étend jusqu'en France', *Le Figaro*, December 14, 2005. Atmane Tazaghart and Roland Jacquard, 'La France en ligne de mire', *Le Figaro* Magazine, November 5, 2005. Patricia Tourancheau, 'La "Menace majeure" gagne du terrain', *Libération*, July 9, 2005. A series of arrests stopped a few score more. 'Les Djihadistes de banlieue s'apprêtaient à partir en Irak', *Le Figaro*, September 20, 2005.

61. Author interview with DGSE officer, Paris, January 2007. Eric Pelletier and Jean-Marie Pontaut, 'Islamisme, des étudiants sous surveillance', *L'Express*, November 9, 2006. The numbers of genuine militants remained in more or less the same very low relative proportions as regards the rest of the Muslim population as in the UK. Indeed, it is likely they were probably even lower. However, with a steady stream of plots uncovered through 2004 and 2005, senior officials, like those of almost every security service more or less everywhere from Indonesia to California, went on the record repeatedly in the aftermath of the London bombings and on through the rest of the year to say that the question of an attack in France was a matter not of 'if' but of 'when'. 'We face a tide which we cannot hold back. Despite all the international community's efforts they are capable of striking in Bali, in London and pretty much at any time,' said Christophe Chaboud, director of the French government's counter-terrorism coordinating body, Uclat. 'Le Chef de l'antiterrorisme craint "une lame de fond"', VSD, December 28, 2005.

62. Author interview with senior official, DST, Riyadh, April 2008.

63. Ibid. Author interview with Alain Bauer, criminologist and presidential adviser, Observatoire national de la délinquance, Paris, November 2009.

64. Author interview with senior official, DGSE, Paris, June 2008.

65. France's major Muslim authorities – such as the Muslim Brotherhood-dominated Union of French Islamic Organizations (UIOF) – made repeated calls for the rioting to cease but were resolutely ignored. This failure revealed what many had suspected for some time: that the older generation of political Islamist leaders had little connection with the youth of the *banlieues*.

66. Author interview, Paris, September 2005.

67. The term is from Laurence and Vaisse, *Intégrer l'Islam*, p. 54.

68. Beyond the ramparts was for a long period known as *la zone*, a hinterland of vagrancy, poverty, promiscuity and violence from where gangs were said to come to threaten the urban population.

69. I.e. with a monthly revenue of less than €908. Luc Bronner, 'Zones urbaines sensibles: près d'un mineur sur deux connaît la pauvreté', *Le Monde*, December 1, 2009.

70. Laurence and Vaisse, *Intégrer l'Islam*, p. 56.

71. Statistics from the Institut National de statistiques economiques, www.Insee.fr.

72. As shown by the 2007 film *La Classe*.

73. F. Lainé and M. Okba, 'Jeunes de parents immigrés: de l'école au métier', *Travail et Emploi*, 103, 2005, pp. 79–83.

74. Author collection.

75. A brief experiment with '*police de proximité*' was ended in 2002 by the then minister of the interior, Nicolas Sarkozy, who said that officers had better things to do than 'play football'.

76. Though one can push the parallels too far, accompanying French police in the weeks following the violence of September 2005 was reminiscent of similar experiences with coalition forces on patrol in Afghanistan and, particularly, Iraq. There was the same banter and solidarity among those on patrol, the same undercurrent of sullen resentment and mutual misunderstanding of those being patrolled, the same sense of latent violence and intrusion, the same contest to control territory on the ground. In Iraq it was a strategic street, a market, a bit of wasteland, a dark corner of the local station out of sight of CCTV cameras. In Aulnay, Bobigny and elsewhere it was a bus-stop favoured by dealers, the top floors of an apartment block from which one could see the police coming, a petrol station.

77. Jason Burke, 'Voice of the suburbs', *Observer*, April 23, 2006. Author interview with Faiza Guène, Paris, March 2006, April 2008.

78. Jason Burke, 'The baker who joined Elysée elite', *Observer*, March 23, 2008. 'It's all down to hard work. I've never suffered any discrimination,' he said. Author interview with Anis Bouabsa, March 2008.

79. The canonical vision of French history taught in most schools also offered little room for interrogation by those whose parents remembered the reality of the Algerian war of independence from 1954 to 1962.

80. One rapper, a favourite with the rioters, spoke in one lyric about how he hoped to throw a *pavé*, the traditional Parisian paving stone that has been iconic to street demonstrations from the 1830s through to 1968, through the windows of shops on the Champs Elysées. He was widely condemned for this call to arms, which was, whatever his critics said, very much part of French cultural tradition rather than being an attack on it. Similarly, when, during the *émeutes*, the specialist public order forces, the Compagnies de Sécurité Républicaines (CRS), were deployed, many of the rioters appeared delighted to have merited the presence of the famously brutal CRS in their neighbourhoods and chanted the very predictable 'CR ... SS' familiar to almost every serious breakdown of public order in France since 1968. The real significance of their words – the insulting reference to Hitler's elite military units, concen-

tration camp guards and so on – entirely escaped the rioters – at least those the author spoke to. There may have been some who were more expert in the political and military history of the twentieth century, but they were certainly thin on the ground in Aulnay and Clichy-sous-Bois.

81. Author telephone interview with Flemming Rose, January 2011

82. Malik, *From Fatwa to Jihad*, p. 144.

83. Ibid.

84. Legal charges brought against *Jyllands-Posten* were eventually dismissed at the beginning of January 2006 on the grounds that the publishing of the cartoons did not violate laws on religious or racial discrimination or on blasphemy.

85. Author telephone interview with Rose, January 2011.

86. Pargeter, *The New Frontiers of Jihad*, p. 195.

87. Ibid., p. 191.

88. Christian Makarian, 'Noirs desseins', *L'Express*, February 9, 2006.

89. René Backmann and Henri Guirchon, 'Les dessins de la colère', *Le Nouvel Observateur*, February 9–15, 2006.

90. Angela Stephens, 'Publics in Western countries disapprove of Muhammad cartoons but right to publish widely defended', February 16, 2006, www.worldpublicopinion.org. '"A New Crusade", bin Laden threatens Europe over Muhammad cartoons', *Der Spiegel*, March 20, 2008.

91. Author telephone interview with Rose, January 2011. Anna Badkhen, 'What's behind Muslim cartoon outrage?', *San Francisco Chronicle*, February 11, 2006.

92. Salah Gaham, a caretaker, died of smoke poisoning while trying to extinguish a fire started in a basement. Jean-Jacques Le Chenadec, a retired Peugeot worker, died from head injuries after being reportedly struck by a hooded man in the street after he and a neighbour went to inspect damage to a bin.

93. For Rice's remarks at the American University in Cairo see Congressional Record, *Proceedings and Debates of the 109th Session of Congress*, vol. 151, part 10, p. 14,415.

94. John Esposito and Dalia Mogahed, *Who Speaks for Islam? What a Billion Muslims Really Think*, Gallup Press, 2007, pp. 69–70. Investigative Project on Terrorism, 'Dalia Mogahed: A Muslim George Gallup or Islamist Ideologue?', April 5, 2010.

95. For the head of the UK's MI5, Eliza Manningham-Buller, the Al-Qaeda threat was 'serious [and] growing' and would last at least 'a generation'.

CHAPTER 10: THE AWAKENING

1. According to some sources, they wore Iraqi special forces uniforms.

2. Author interview with senior Iraqi security official, London, August 2006. Some reports mentioned a second Iraqi involved in the bombing. Edward

Wong, 'Iraqi led bombing of Shiite sites, official says', *New York Times*, June 28, 2006.

3. Post-tour interview with Major Darrel Green, Combat Studies Institute, Fort Leavenworth, February 27, 2007.

4. 'Interview with Maj. Jeremy Lewis', Combat Studies Institute, February 29, 2007, p. 12. Also quoted by Thomas Ricks, *The Gamble*, Penguin, 2009, p. 32.

5. Some of the worst were the blast at the end of August 2003 which had killed ninety-five Shia in Najaf, including Ayatollah Mohammed Baqr al-Hakim, and the series of attacks on Shia mosques during the Ashura holiday in March 2004, which killed nearly 200.

6. Nelson Hernandez and Saad Sarhan, 'Insurgents kill 140 as Iraq clashes escalate', *Washington Post*, January 6, 2010. 'Iraq suicide bomb blasts kill 120', BBC News Online, January 5, 2006.

7. Sam Knight and agencies, 'Bombing of Shia shrine sparks wave of retaliation', *The Times*, February 22, 2006. Jonathan Finer and Bassam Sebti, 'Sectarian violence kills over 100 in Iraq, Shiite–Sunni anger flares following bombing of shrine', *Washington Post*, February 24, 2006. Robert F. Worth, 'Blast at Shiite shrine sets off sectarian fury in Iraq', *New York Times*, February 23, 2006.

8. 'Interview with Lewis', p. 16.

9. Quite where sectarian violence started and criminal violence stopped was often difficult to say. Some sectarian gangs sold the remains of dead victims to bereaved relatives – a macabre form of posthumous ransom.

10. The policy had been outlined in the 'National Strategy for Victory in Iraq' of November 2005.

11. Cockburn, *The Occupation*, 167. In 2005, they totalled 846 dead and 5,944 wounded respectively. The Brookings Institution (Michael E. O'Hanlon and Ian Livingston), *The Iraq Index: Tracking Variables of Reconstruction and Security in Post-Saddam Iraq*, June 30, 2010, pp. 12, 14.

12. David Kilcullen, *The Accidental Guerrilla, Fighting Small Wars in the Midst of a Big One*, Hurst, 2009, p. 124.

13. The number varied by a few thousand. Sharon Otterman, 'Saudi Arabia: withdrawal of US forces', Council of Foreign Relations, Washington, May 2, 2003.

14. Paul von Zielbauer, 'US inquiry hampered by Iraq violence, investigators say', *New York Times*, June 13, 2007, Tim McGirk, 'Collateral damage or civilian massacre in Haditha?', *Time*, March 19, 2006.

15. Thomas E. Ricks, 'In Haditha killings, details came slowly', *Washington Post*, June 4, 2006.

16. West, *The Strongest Tribe*, p. 156.

17. Ricks, *The Gamble*, pp. 7–8.

18. Urban, *Task Force Black*, pp. 94–9.

19. Ibid., p. 106.

20. The coalition gaining the majority of the Sunni overall vote was the Accord

Front, with 16 per cent of the vote and 44 seats. A more radical grouping, the Iraqi Dialogue Front, took 4 per cent and 11 seats. See Toby Dodge, 'The Causes of US Failure in Iraq', *Survival: Global Politics and Strategy*, vol. 49, no. 1 (spring 2007), pp. 85–106.

21. Email exchange with author, December 2005.

22. Department of State, Public Notice 4936, 'Foreign Terrorists and Terrorist Organizations; Designation: Organization in the Land of the Two Rivers', *Federal Register*, December 17, 2004, vol. 69, no. 242.

23. There is also a clear reference to the *tanzim* of the Palestinian al-Aqsa Intifada with their younger more aggressive stance against a senior leadership seen as sedentary and out of touch. The name also, incidentally, shows al-Zarqawi's distance from pure Salafists, who, though they would have agreed with his views that Shia are heretics, would have been against the organization of the faithful into a party or a movement.

24. See Kepel, *Jihad*, pp. 236–53. More radical elements in Bosnia provoked ridicule by trying to argue that Father Christmas was unIslamic.

25. Burke, *Al-Qaeda*, pp. 12, 206.

26. See ibid., pp. 116–35, 213–33.

27. Ian Fisher and Edward Wong, 'Iraq's rebellion develops signs of internal rift', *New York Times*, July 10, 2004. Author interviews with Iraqi militants, Baghdad, September 2004.

28. Dhiya Rassan, 'Patchwork of insurgent groups runs Fallujah', Institute of War and Peace Reporting, September 17, 2004.

29. Karl Vick, 'Insurgent alliance fraying in Fallujah', *Washington Post*, October 13, 2004.

30. Ghaith Abdul-Ahad, 'Seeking salvation in city of insurgents', *Guardian*, November 11, 2004. See Chapter 7.

31. Hannah Allam, 'Fallujah's real boss: Omar the electrician', Knight Ridder *Newspapers*, November 22, 2004.

32. Abdul-Ahad, 'Seeking salvation in city of insurgents'.

33. John Ward Anderson, 'Seven al-Zarqawi insurgents killed in retaliation for Khaldiya slaying', *Washington Post*, March 18, 2005.

34. In a particularly macabre example of the facility with which practices have been communicated from one protagonist in the 9/11 Wars to another, the foreign militants' techniques were borrowed from Shia death squads operating at the time.

35. In 2003, the author interviewed a former torturer from Saddam Hussein's Mukhabarat intelligence service who recounted how he had held babies over boiling water to get their parents to talk.

36. Pelham, *A New Muslim Order*, pp. 197–8. Sunni Arab parties won fifty-five seats in the new parliament (see note 20), up from seventeen in the previous one. In part the division within the insurgent ranks was between 'Salafi jihadi' strands and Islamist strands. There was also a tribal dynamic at play.

37. West, *The Strongest Tribe*, p. 132.

38. Tim McGirk, 'A rebel crack-up?', *Time*, January 22, 2006.

39. The letter from al-Zawahiri to al-Zarqawi is dated July 9, 2005. The contents were released by the US Office of the Director of National Intelligence on October 11, 2005.

40. See, for example, Abu Bakr Naji, *Management of Savagery: The Most Critical Stage Through Which the Ummah Will Pass*, originally published on the internet, 2004, translated into English by William McCants, published by Olin Institute for Strategic Studies, Harvard University, 2006.

41. The letter, written by bin Laden's representative to Algeria, Atiyah Abd al-Rahman, was dated December 12, 2005. See http://ctc.usama.edu/harmony/pdf/CTC-AtiyahLetter.pdf.

42. 'Jordan hotel blasts kill dozens', BBC News Online, November 10, 2005. Conal Urquhart, 'Failed bomb attacker confesses live on air', *Guardian*, November 14, 2005.

43. 'Al-Khalayleh tribe disowns al-Zarqawi', *Jerusalem Post*, November 20, 2005.

44. Nir Rosen, 'Thinking Like a Jihadist: Iraq's Jordanian Connection', *World Policy Journal*, Spring 2006, p. 14.

45. Murad Batal al-Shishani, 'The Amman Bombings: A Blow to the Jihadists?', *Terrorism Focus*, vol. 2, no. 22, November 29, 2005.

46. It had been 57 per cent in 2003. Pew Research Center, *Declining Support for bin Laden and Suicide Bombing*, September 10, 2009. See also Daniel Benjamin, Center for Strategic and International Studies, testimony before the Senate Foreign Relations Committee, June 13, 2006.

47. See Rosen, 'Thinking Like a Jihadist: Iraq's Jordanian Connection'.

48. Jason Burke, Peter Beaumont and Mohammed al-Ubeidy, 'How Jordanians hunted down their hated son', *Observer*, June 11, 2006.

49. On the interrogations see Bowden, 'The ploy'. Author interviews with senior Iraqi security officials, London, September 2009.

50. Interviews with Jordanian intelligence officers, London, June 2006.

51. Pew Research Center, *Global Public Opinion in the Bush Years (2001–2008)*, December 18, 2008.

52. Pew Research Center, *Where Terrorism Finds Support in the Muslim World*, May 2006.

53. Pew Research Center, *Global Public Opinion in the Bush Years*.

54. The blast in Sharm-el-Sheikh killed ninety people, mostly Egyptians. 'Toll climbs in Egyptian attacks', BBC News Online, July 23, 2005.

55. Pew Research Center, *Global Attitudes Toward Islamic Extremism and Terrorism*, August 29, 2007. Data from Pew's Key Indicators Database, accessed January 2, 2011.

56. Jason Burke, 'The Arab backlash the militants didn't expect', *Observer*, June 20, 2004. International Crisis Group, *Can Saudi Arabia Reform Itself?*, July

14, 2004. Poll subject quote from the *Daily Star*, Beirut, Lebanon, June 24, 2004.

57. Esposito and Mogahed, *Who Speaks for Islam?*, p. 73 and passim. Such views appeared to be held regardless of gender or piety, an important nuance missed by many Western commentators. Equally, perceptions of Islam and Muslims among non-Muslims in Europe and America were much more negative after nearly five years of conflict than they had been even in the weeks after September 11. The proportion was higher among 18–24-year-olds and among second-generation immigrants. A Pew poll of Muslim world opinion in 2006 found that majorities in Indonesia, Turkey, Egypt and Jordan said that they do not believe groups of Arabs carried out the September 11, 2001 terrorist attacks. The percentage of Turks expressing disbelief that Arabs carried out the 9/11 attacks has increased from 43 per cent in a 2002 Gallup survey to 59 per cent by 2005. In the UK, 56 per cent of British Muslims said they do not believe Arabs carried out the terror attacks against the US. Only 17 per cent thought they had done.

58. The idea of assembling bombs inside planes had been raised before. This was clearly a serious threat as it circumvented most conventional security procedures. The investigation of the Walthamstow plot led to the banning of fluids in baggage within planes' cabins. Jason Burke, 'Terrorist bid to build bombs in mid-flight', *Observer*, February 8, 2004.

59. 'Meeting with the Representatives of Science: Lecture of the Holy Father', Regensburg, Germany, Libreria Editrice Vaticana, September 12, 2006.

60. West, *The Strongest Tribe*, p. 175.

61. Mushriq Abbas, 'Mutual political and tribal interests coincided with his struggle with al-Qa'ida and al-Maliki: a short and murky journey led Abu Risha to . . . his death', *al-Hayat*, September 16, 2007, cited by Mohammed M. Hafez, 'Al-Qa'ida Losing Ground in Iraq', *CTC Sentinel*, vol. 1, no. 1 (December 2007), p. 7.

62. West, *The Strongest Tribe*, pp. 209, 213–14, 223.

63. US Department of Defense, *Quadrennial Defense Review Report*, February 6, 2006, preface, p. v.

64. Bradley Graham and Josh White, 'Abizaid credited with popularizing the term "long war"', *Washington Post*, February 3, 2006. See also RAND Corporation (Christopher G. Pernin, Brian Nichiporuk, Dale Stahl, Justin Beck, Ricky Radaelli-Sanchez), *Unfolding the Future of the Long War*, 2008, p. 5.

65. Julian E. Barnes, 'National security watch: retiring top soldier warns of "The Long War"', *US News and World Report*, September 29, 2005.

66. William Kristol, 'The Long War: the radical Islamists are on the offensive. Will we defeat them?', *Weekly Standard*, vol. 11, no. 24, June 3, 2006. See also Norman Podhoretz, *World War IV: The Long Struggle against Islamo-fascism*, Doubleday, 2007.

67. This argument is advanced in an extremely sophisticated form by law professor and historian Philip Bobbitt. See Philip Bobbitt, 'Get ready for the next

long war', *Time*, September 1, 2002. See also, in a very much less intellectually refined form, Tony Blankley, 'An Islamist threat like the Nazis', *Washington Times*, September 12, 2005.

68. 'President discusses global war on terrorism', September 5, 2006. White House press release. National Strategy for Combating Terrorism, September 2006, pp. 5, 11.

69. Bush had said that 'al-Qaeda followed in the path of Fascism, Nazism and totalitarianism', the 'murderous ideologies of the twentieth century'.

70. Kristol, 'The Long War'.

71. *Quadrennial Defense Review*, pp. 9, 21, 22, 36. 'Operational end-states defined in terms of "winning decisively" may be less useful', the review said coyly.

72. *Quadrennial Defense Review*, pp. 10, 11.

CHAPTER 11: THE TURNING

1. There is now a series of detailed and voluminous studies of American operations in Iraq during 2007 and the genesis of the shifts in strategy and tactics they entailed. Two useful accounts of the meeting at Leavenworth can be found in Ricks, *The Gamble*, and Linda Robinson, *Tell Me How This Ends: General David Petraeus and the Search for a Way Out of Iraq*, Public Affairs, 2008. Another useful work is Kimberly Kagan, *The Surge: A Military History*, Encounter Books, 2008.

2. See also Kilcullen, *The Accidental Guerrilla*, p. 119. Author telephone interview with Kilcullen, March 2009.

3. Robinson, *Tell Me How This Ends*, p. 68. Ricks, *The Gamble*, p. 128.

4. Author telephone interview with David Kilcullen, March 2009. Kilcullen proved one of the most original and perceptive analysts despite a relative lack of experience of many of the major theatres of conflict, arguing that the spaces through which contemporary insurgencies were conducted were compound and plural, a complex matrix of the local, the regional and the transnational. He also contributed useful insights such as pointing out how militants tailored their violence to what they wanted to communicate – the message defined the mission – whereas American forces did the opposite, and pointed out too that the term 'foreign fighters', applied to international jihadis, could and should apply to coalition troops as well. To fight insurgencies composed of accidental guerrillas, soldiers should be behaving differently. 'Your role is to provide protection, identify needs, facilitate civil affairs and use improvements in social conditions as leverage to build networks and mobilize the population,' Kilcullen wrote in a widely circulated paper. David Kilcullen, 'Twenty-eight Articles: Fundamentals of Company-level Counter-insurgency', *Military Review*, March 1, 2006.

5. Richard Norton-Taylor and Jamie Wilson, 'US army in Iraq institutionally racist, claims British officer', *Guardian*, January 12, 2006.

6. Nigel Aylwin-Foster, 'Changing the Army for Counter-Insurgency Operations', *Military Review*, December 2005, p. 5.

7. US officers sourly but fairly pointed out that the fact that Aylwin-Foster had been invited to Leavenworth to speak in person was an indication of an open-mindedness that did not necessarily characterize the British military.

8. Montgomery McFate, 'The Military Utility of Understanding Adversary Culture', *Joint Forces Quarterly*, 38, July 2005, pp. 43, 44.

9. *US Army Field Manual 3-24: Counterinsurgency* (December 2006), p. 164.

10. 'Learning Counterinsurgency: Observations from Soldiering in Iraq', *Military Review*, January–February 2006.

11. *US Army Field Manual 3-24*.

12. *The National Security Strategy of the United States of America*, September 2002, Introduction, p. 1.

13. See Dodge, 'The Ideological Roots of Failure'.

14. *US Army Field Manual 3-24*, p. 2.

15. David Galula, *Counter-insurgency Warfare: Theory and Practice*, Frederick Praeger, 2006, p. 20. The work was originally published in 1964.

16. Porter, *Military Orientalism*, p. 6.

17. Iraqi society was invariably described, as it has been along with many others in this book, as 'complex', as if Western societies with their equal number of codes, hierarchies, obligations, norms, laws and values, tribes and castes, were not.

18. The description is from the late Professor Fred Halliday of the London School of Economics. *100 Myths about the Middle East*, Saqi Books, 2005, p. 147. T. E. Lawrence had been read by American soldiers in Iraq since the first days of the intervention. More problematically, the manual and surrounding debate tended to underplay the agency of both individuals and communities, underestimating the dynamism of identity and culture particularly in a conflict situation. Porter, *Military Orientalism*, p. 55. *US Army Field Manual 3-24*, p. 7: 'Lawrence's experiences in the Arab Revolt made him a hero and also provide some insights for today.' Lawrence also once described the Arabs as 'a limited, narrow-minded people, whose inert intellect lay fallow in incurious resignation'.

19. See Derek Gregory, 'The Rush to the Intimate: Counterinsurgency and the Cultural Turn in Late Modern War', *Radical Philosophy*, July/August 2008.

20. Brookings report by Michael E. O'Hanlon and Ian Livingston, *Iraq Index: Tracking Variables of Reconstruction and Security in Post-Saddam Iraq*, December 30, 2010, p. 4.

21. Author email exchange, December 2007.

22. Lieutenant General Raymond Odierno, 'The Surge in Iraq: One Year Later', Heritage lectures, March 13, 2008. Having understood that such relation-

ships were the key to finding the fugitive dictator, Odierno had ordered the construction of a vast map depicting key figures with their interrelationships, social status and last-known locations. Saddam was placed at the centre, not at the top of any hierarchical organogramme. Eventually, patterns had emerged showing that in fact it was not the Ba'ath Party structure that was important but the extensive tribal and family ties between the six main tribes of the Sunni triangle – the Husseins, al-Douris, Hadouthis, Musslits, Hassans and Harimyths – and in particular those between a group of families which had all been linked to Saddam in various unofficial capacities since his youngest days. Tracing key figures in these eventually enabled Saddam to be located. Chris Wilson, 'Searching for Saddam', *Slate*, February 22, 2010. Farnaz Fassihi, 'Charting the capture of Saddam', *Wall Street Journal*, December 23, 2003. Vernon Loeb, 'Clan, family ties called key to army's capture of Hussein', *Washington Post*, December 16, 2003.

23. Bush, *Decision Points*, p. 93.

24. See Congressional Research Service (Amy Belasco), *Report for Congress: Troop Levels in the Afghan and Iraq Wars, FY2001–FY2012: Cost and Other Potential Issues*, July 2, 2009, pp. 9, 39.

25. Michael Duffy, 'The Surge at year one', *Time*, January 31, 2008. The conclusions of the Iraq Study Group led by Jim Baker, secretary of state during the 1991 Gulf War, were radically different.

26. Author interview with a senior American civilian official attached to US military in Baghdad, end 2006, spring 2007. Interview conducted in Afghanistan, March 2009.

27. Including from the veteran members of the bipartisan Iraq Study Group.

28. The exact population at the time was for obvious reasons uncertain. It was 6,554,126 in 2004 before the major sectarian violence according to Gilbert Burnham, Riyadh Lafta, Shannon Doocy and Les Roberts, 'Mortality after the 2003 Invasion of Iraq: A Cross-sectional Cluster Sample Survey', *Lancet*, vol. 368, no. 9,545, October 21, 2006, and 7,145,470 in 2009 according to *The Geographical Location of Baghdad Province*, the Baghdad Governorate, December 13, 2009.

29. Duffy, 'The Surge at year one'.

30. Michael Evans, 'Gated communities will add to Baghdad security', *The Times*, February 10, 2007.

31. John Lee Anderson, 'Inside the Surge', *New Yorker*, November 19, 2007. Bing West, *The Strongest Tribe*, Random House, 2009, p. 300. Kilcullen, *The Accidental Guerrilla*, p. 169.

32. Mohammed Hussein, 'Back from Syria', *New York Times*, May 5, 2008.

33. At twenty-five per day, the 2008 rate for violent civilian deaths was to be equivalent to that existing throughout the first twenty months of post-invasion Iraq, from May 2003 to December 2004, when 15,355 died over 610 days. 'Post-Surge Violence: Its Extent and Nature. What the Detailed

Data Tell Us about Iraq's Civilian Death Toll during 2008 and the Long-term Effect of the "Surge"', iraqbodycount.org, December 28, 2008.

34. Bobby Ghosh, 'The fleeting success of the Surge', *Time*, December 13, 2007. Quoted Freedman, *A Choice of Enemies*, p. 447.

35. Ricks, *Fiasco*, Appendix II.

36. Author interview, Istanbul, March, 2008.

37. Pelham, *A New Muslim Order*, p. 195. Semi-depopulated middle-class neighbourhoods like Adil, where resistance was likely to be less significant than in the tougher working-class neighbourhoods like al-Doura, were targeted first. International Crisis Group, *Iraq's Civil War, the Sadrists and the Surge*, February 7, 2008, p. 2.

38. Ibid., p. 6. For much of 2006, the American high command in Iraq had been largely unaware of the carnage around them. According to Kilcullen, the ongoing civil war only began to be reflected in the American military's daily 'battlefield update' briefings for the commanding general in Iraq from mid July 2006, four and a half months after the blast at Samarra. Kilcullen, *The Accidental Guerrilla*, pp. 121–2. The police were often heavily implicated in the killing but even in the best of cases were so powerless that local people referred to them as *daffana*, or undertakers, because all they were good for was collecting bodies.

39. Sunni gangs made sure that mixed neighbourhoods such as Ghazaliya and Amiriya were thoroughly purged of Shia.

40. See Elisa Cochrane, 'The Fragmentation of the Sadrist Movement', Institute for the Study of War, January 2009, p. 21. International Crisis Group, *Iraq's Civil War, the Sadrists and the Surge*, p. 5.

41. James Hanning, 'Deal with Shia prisoner left Basra at mercy of gangs, colonel admits', *Independent on Sunday*, August 3, 2008.

42. See Cochrane, 'The Fragmentation', p. 7.

43. Sabrina Tavernise, 'A Shiite militia in Baghdad sees its power wane', *New York Times*, July 27, 2008.

44. Urban, *Task Force Black*, pp. 224–5.

45. International Crisis Group, *Iraq's Civil War, the Sadrists and the Surge*, p. 7.

46. Interview, Baghdad, September 2010.

47. Al-Sadr's representatives had withdrawn from government a few months previously and thus were no longer a key element of Prime Minister Nouri al-Maliki's support.

48. See West, *The Strongest Tribe*, pp. 250, 274–5, 301, 318–319, and Ricks, *The Gamble*, p. 22. An ill-judged attempt to take control of the shrine at Karbala, which saw fighting against Iraqi government forces and around fifty worshippers killed and was widely reported on local news, also contributed to further loss of legitimacy. That the government forces were in fact loyal to the rival al-Badr militia did not make a huge difference to the public perception of the events.

49. Odierno quoted by Babak Dehghanpisheh and Larry Kaplow, 'Baghdad's new owners', *Newsweek*, September 10, 2007. Odierno, 'The Surge in Iraq'.

50. David Kilcullen, 'Field Notes on Iraq's Tribal Revolt Against Al-Qa'ida', *CTC Sentinel*, vol. 1, no. 11, October 2008. The 1920 Revolution Brigades split first from their more closely al-Qaeda-affiliated counterparts and then themselves, with one element going on to form Hamas-Iraq, which, though it continued to conduct attacks on coalition and government forces, also made statements opposing sectarian conflict and in favour of a political process.

51. Senior religious figures relayed the change in policy. 'Saudi cleric issues warning over Saudi militants', Reuters, October 1, 2007.

52. Urban, *Task Force Black*, p. 127.

53. Ibid., p. 243.

54. See Kilcullen, *The Accidental Guerrilla*, pp. 136, 167–70. One problem was that the troops stuck to the four- or five-man groups that crewed a vehicle.

55. Presentation to Riyadh meeting and author interview, Riyadh, Saudi Arabia, March 2008.

56. Ibid.

57. Alissa J. Rubin, 'A calmer Iraq: fragile, and possibly fleeting', *New York Times*, December 5, 2007.

58. Martin Fletcher, 'Al-Qaeda leaders admit: "We are in crisis. There is panic and fear"', *The Times*, February 11, 2008.

59. CNN.com transcript of broadcast of Congressional Hearings, April 8, 2008.

60. Interview, Baghdad, November 2010.

61. See Combating Terrorism Center, West Point, *Foreign Fighters in Iraq*, 2007, p. 5. Abu Umar al-Baghdadi, *For the Scum Disappears Like Froth Cast Out*, posted to www.muslim.net on December 4, 2007. At its head was an unknown militant with the resoundingly Iraqi *nisbah* or alias of Abu Umar al-Baghdadi, who American intelligence officials claimed did not actually exist. Dean Yates, 'Senior Qaeda figure in Iraq a myth: U.S. military', Reuters, July 18, 2007. Springer et al., *Islamic Radicalism and Global Jihad*, pp. 119–21.

62. The loss of al-Iraqi was a serious one. He had probably played a key role in a number of other plots in Europe too, including the 7/7 London attacks, acting as the intermediary between the senior al-Qaeda leadership and the Pakistani militant groups who had been the Westerners' first point of contact.

63. Joby Warrick and Robin Wright, 'U.S. teams weaken insurgency in Iraq', *Washington Post*, September 6, 2008.

64. According to American officials. Jim Michaels, 'Foreign fighters leaving Iraq, military says', *USA Today*, March 21, 2008.

65. Records of the Mujahideen Shura Council – the rebranded al-Qaeda in Iraq – seized by American troops in a major operation on a large training and transit camp in Sinjar in the north-west of Iraq showed both how claims that the organization was predominantly 'Iraqi' were false and how numbers of

recruits from overseas remained relatively low with only a few dozen volunteers arriving each month by the end of 2007.

66. Author interview, Riyadh, March 2009. See also Thomas Hegghammer, *Paths to Global Jihad*, report, FFI, 2006, p. 27.

67. Author interview with Otayan al-Turki, Riyadh, March 2009.

68. Author interview with Dr Abdulrahman al-Hadlaq, Riyadh, March 2009. Jason Burke, 'Saudis offer pioneering therapy for ex-jihadists', *Observer*, March 9, 2008. In 2010, figures were released which showed that in fact around one in ten of those undergoing the Saudi rehabilitation programme did eventually become involved once more in extremist activities. The vast bulk of these were former prisoners of Guantanamo Bay.

69. Author interview, Riyadh, March 2009.

70. Author interview, Riyadh, March 2009.

71. International Crisis Group, *'Deradicalization' and Indonesian Prisons*, November 19, 2007.

72. Amanda Ripley, 'Reverse radicalism', *Time*, March 13, 2008.

73. Author interview, senior UK counter-terrorism official, London, August 2008.

74. They cited sociologist Quintan Wictorowicz as the best guide to the nature of modern Islamic militancy. Author interviews, London, July 2007.

75. Author interviews, MI5, London, July 2009.

76. Cobain, 'The truth about torture'.

77. Charles Farr, head of OSCT, quoted in Home Affairs Committee, *Project CONTEST: The Government's Counter-terrorism Strategy: Ninth Report of Session 2008–09, House of Commons,* July 7, 2009, p. 29. Author interview with Farr, London, September 2007. PREVENT was part of the UK Counter-Terrorism Strategy known as CONTEST and in place since 2003.

78. One poll in 2006 had found that less than half of British Muslims respected Iqbal Sacranie, the MCB's general secretary (while 69 per cent respected the Queen) and only 12 per cent thought that the MCB represented their political views. NOP/Channel Four poll, 2006, cited Malik, *From Fatwa to Jihad*, p. 129.

79. Richard Kerbaj, 'Government moves to isolate Muslim Council of Britain with cash for mosques', *The Times*, March 30, 2009. See also the useful and controversial pamphlet on the MCB, for which the author wrote an introduction, by British journalist Martin Bright: *When Progressives Treat with Reactionaries*, Policy Exchange, July 2006.

80. James Brandon, 'The UK's Experience in Counter-radicalization', *CTC Sentinel*, April 2008, vol. 1, no. 5.

81. Individuals like Shiraz Maher and Ed Husain, the two former Hezb-ut-Tahrir members quoted in Chapter 8, were joined by others whose jihadi credentials may have been exaggerated. Husain's book, *The Islamist*, became a bestseller. For criticism, see *Final Report of the Communities and Local Government Select Committee Inquiry into Preventing Violent Extremism*, HMSO, March 30, 2010.

82. Author interview, August 2007.

83. www.tajdeed.net.tc on July 8, 2006: 'Al-Sahab for Media Production'. David Pallister, 'Three jailed for engaging in "cyber jihad" for al-Qaida', *Guardian*, July 6, 2007.

84. Dalia Mogahed, *Beyond Multiculturalism vs. Assimilation*, Gallup, 2007, p. 4. The conclusion was based on 500 interviews in London between 29 November 2006 and 18 January 2007.

85. Gallup World Poll 2007.

86. Jason Burke, 'Target Europe', *Observer*, September 9, 2007; Erik Kirschbaum, 'German suspects had deadline for attacks: report', Reuters, September 8, 2007. The German case also threw a light on the continuing role of the tribal areas of Pakistan in many, though by no means all, European investigations. In the case of the German converts, the main suspects were believed to have trained not with al-Qaeda but with the little-known Islamic Jihad Union, an offshoot of the Islamic Movement of Uzbekistan. Converts had already figured significantly in terrorism in Europe, comprising 8 per cent of militants arrested in Europe. The Netherlands Institute of International Relations Clingendael, *Jihadi Terrorists in Europe*, 2006.

87. Some key changes were technical but important, such as the new ability of British financial investigators to use classified information to freeze assets.

88. Author interview, London, spring 2009.

89. From primary and secondary sources including the scores of trials of alleged militants. Legal proceedings did not always kill off some of the more fantastic claims – right-wingers in Spain continued to claim that Basque separatists were responsible for the Madrid attacks even after one of the longest and most exhaustive trials in Europe in recent decades convicted those responsible – but they did provide relatively well-founded evidence that could be deployed to contradict the ubiquitous conspiracy theorists. Diane Cambon, 'L'Aile dure de la droite espagnole defend toujours la théorie de complot', *Le Monde*, February 14, 2007.

90. Dipak Gupta, *Understanding Terrorism and Political Violence*, Routledge, 2008, p. 3. The degree to which the public was well informed can be exaggerated. Even in 2006, counter-terrorist specialists and key Congressmen in America proved unable to explain the difference between Shia and Sunnis. Jeff Stein, 'It's not a trick question', *International Herald Tribune*, October 18, 2006.

91. The ruling was on June 29, 2006, in Hamdan vs. Rumsfeld.

92. *New York University Center on Law and Security, Terrorist Trial Report Card 2001–2009*, published 2010, pp. i–iii, 6–7. Convictions on headline charges of very serious offences were sought – and often denied – and suspects who could have been jailed on lesser charges went free.

93. Ibid., p. v.

94. Author telephone interview with Mudd, June 2010. See Scott Shane and

Lowell Bergman, 'F.B.I. struggling to reinvent itself to fight terror', *New York Times*, October 10, 2006.

95. Robert S. Mueller III, director Federal Bureau of Investigation, Citizens Crime Commission, James Fox Memorial Lecture, New York, April 26, 2006. Author interview with Carl Newns, Foreign Office, London, September 2006. Jason Burke, 'Britain stops talk of "war on terror"', *Observer*, December 10, 2006.

96. Author interview, London, September 2006.

97. Author interview with Jonathan Freeman, London, September 2006.

98. Matthew Lee, '"Jihadist" booted from government lexicon', Associated Press, April 24, 2008.

99. United States Army, *Full Spectrum Operations, Unified Quest 2007*, pamphlet published April 22, 2008, p. 22.

100. 'Few Muslims back suicide bombs', BBC News Online, 25 July 2007. Pew Research Center, *Pew Global Opinions Survey, 2007: A Rising Tide Lifts Mood in the Developing World*, p. 55.

101. Ibid., p. 57.

102. Terror Free Tomorrow poll, 'Saudi Arabians Overwhelmingly Reject Bin Laden, Al Qaeda, Saudi Fighters in Iraq, and Terrorism; Also among Most Pro-American in Muslim World', Washington, December 2007, p. 3.

103. Peter Bergen and Paul Cruickshank, 'The unraveling: the jihadist revolt against bin Laden', *New Republic*, June 11, 2008. Omar Ashour, 'De-Radicalization of Jihad? The Impact of Egyptian Islamist Revisionists on Al-Qaeda', *Perspectives on Terrorism*, vol. 2, no. 5, May 2008.

104. See Mamoun Fandy, *Saudi Arabia and the Politics of Dissent*, Palgrave Macmillan, 2001, for an excellent account of the early activities and ideological development of al-Auda.

105. Bergen and Cruickshank, 'The unraveling'. Sheikh Salman al-Auda, 'Letter to Osama bin Laden', September 14, 2007, www.islamtoday.net. Michael Scheuer, 'Al-Qaeda: Beginning of the End, or Grasping at Straws?', *Terrorism Focus*, vol. 4, no. 32, October 12, 2007.

106. Interview at the Saudi Interior Ministry, March 2008.

107. Transcript of Usama bin Laden Audio Recording produced by the As-Sahab Media Foundation: 'A Message to the Islamic Nation', released May 18, 2008, NEFA Foundation.

108. Author interviews with Western and Afghan intelligence officials, Kabul, August 2008. Amit R. Paley, 'Al-Qaeda in Iraq leader may be in Afghanistan', *Washington Post*, July 31, 2008.

CHAPTER 12: AFGHANISTAN AGAIN

1. Author interview, Maidan Shar, August 2008.

2. The company was renamed Xe.

3. 'Thanks to our British troops – along with allies from 40 countries – the Taliban have been beaten back.' Des Browne, 'Des Browne's speech to the 2008 Labour Party Conference', September 22, 2008. Transcript, Labour Party website.

4. Author interview, Kabul, August 2008.

5. Author interview with judges, Kabul, August 2008.

6. Author interview with Sherard Cowper-Coles, Kabul, August 2008. A leaked French diplomatic memorandum described Sir Sherard talking privately of the need for an 'enlightened dictatorship'.

7. The plural of *medressa* in Urdu is *madari*. However *medressas* has entered common English-language usage and so is preferred here.

8. Author interview with Rahmani, Kabul, 2009.

9. Author interview with Mullah Taj Mohammed, former Taliban deputy intelligence chief, Jalalabad, Peshawar, June 2002.

10. Karzai's exile was initially ended when he accompanied *mujahideen* leaders into Kabul in 1992 on the fall of the Najibullah regime. However, he remained in Afghanistan for only a short period, being forced once more to leave for Pakistan. His exile was thus only definitively ended in 2001.

11. See International Crisis Group, *The Problem of Pashtun Alienation*, August 5, 2003. Francesc Vendrell, the European Union special representative to Afghanistan and intimately involved in the planning of the conference, recalled that at Bonn 'the Taliban were seen as subhuman'. Author interview with Vendrell, London, February 2009. The title of the US Congress House Committee on International Relations, Subcommittee on International Operations and Human Rights, on 31 October 2001, Washington, DC, gives a fairly good idea of how the Taliban were considered: 'Afghan people vs the Taliban: the struggle for freedom intensifies'. See both Dobbins, *After the Taliban*, and Rashid, *Descent into Chaos*, for more. None of the opening speeches at the Bonn conference were translated into Pashtu but only into Dari, the language of the Tajik minority. One problem at Bonn was the disproportionate political and media attention accorded to a large number of long-term exiles whose understanding of contemporary Afghan politics was limited. Many delegates had not visited their country for several decades. Those who, at the very least, represented what Afghanistan had become over recent years were less welcome. When Abdul Qadir, the anti-Taliban Pashtun warlord, walked out of the conference in protest at the lack of ethnic balance, his gesture was largely dismissed as populist. Political theatre it may well have been, but Qadir's understanding of what might resonate with many of his countrymen was sharp, and his gesture deserved more serious attention.

12. Fourteen per cent in 2005 and 5.3 per cent in 2006.

13. World Bank, *Afghanistan: Statebuilding, Sustaining Growth and Reducing Poverty*, Washington 2005, p. 373.

14. An announced 'Marshall plan' for Afghanistan – the original post-war

version comprised funds totalling between 3 and 7 per cent of American GDP at the time – was nothing of the sort. Dobbins, *After the Taliban*, p. 164.

15. Conor Foley, *The Thin Blue Line*, Verso, 2008, p. 118. See ACBAR, *Falling Short: Aid Effectiveness in Afghanistan*, March 25, 2008. Rashid, *Descent into Chaos*, p. 399. The overall spend including for the military in Afghanistan per month was around a fifth of that in Iraq. Kilcullen, *The Accidental Guerrilla*, p. 43.

16. Very rough back-of-the-envelope arithmetic revealed that this meant under $20 per capita per year since 2002.

17. The coalition presence in Helmand consisted of 130 US special forces, civilians and contractors.

18. In a poll in May 2002, 50 per cent of Afghans in rural areas said they had no contact with Afghan National Police and less than 20 per cent trusted them. The problem was most acute in the south. Jones, *In the Graveyard of Empires*, p. 181. See Sarah Chayes, *The Punishment of Virtue*, Portobello, 2007, for a fascinating if often provocative account of this time in south-east Afghanistan.

19. A special forces team had fought alongside him and organized food supplies for his 800-odd armed followers. *United States Special Operations Command History*, 6th edn, p. 97. The two tribal figures were Mullah Naqib of the Alokozai and Bashir Noorzai.

20. As Ahmed Rashid has pointed out, unlike Northern Alliance warlords, who tended to defy President Karzai's authority, warlords like Sherzai were friends of the government and helped secure the local vote for Karzai in the two Loya Jirgas and the two elections in 2004 and 2005. These embedded, with the enthusiastic endorsement of the international community, his power. See Rashid, *Descent into Chaos*, chapter 'Drugs and Thugs'. Karzai eventually reassigned Sherzai to be governor of Nangahar province in 2005, replacing him with Asadullah Khalid, a family ally. Ahmed Wali Karzai, the president's brother and head of the tribal council in Kandahar, was also suspected of involvement in the drug trade. In 2006, the author obtained a stolen US classified briefing naming him as a key trafficker.

21. A 2006 poll by the US State Department found that more than 50 per cent of Afghans thought Karzai and his administration had failed to combat corruption. Nearly three-quarters of those who admitted supporting the Taliban said there was corruption among the police or the courts, and two-thirds said local government was corrupt. Anecdotal evidence in places like Kandahar indicated much higher levels of discontent.

22. This has escaped many accounts. The Taliban groups were largely non-tribal, an important difference from the heavily tribalized *mujahideen* groups operating in the south-east during the 1980s.

23. Koochi nomadic tribesmen had a disproportionately large presence in the ranks of the Taliban given their numbers. The Koochi are Pashtun.

24. See accounts of Taliban penetration of Helmand and Oruzgan in Giustozzi, ed., *Decoding the New Taliban*, pp. 124 and 157, for two examples. There are many others.

25. Ibid., p. 161.

26. An anecdotal illustration of this was the experience of an Australian special forces officer exploring south of Ghazni in late 2002 who, when he had asked local elders if there were any Taliban in their village, had been directed to an empty house a few yards away from the mulberry tree in its centre. Its owner, head of one of two families who had contested power in the village for decades, had thrown in his lot with the Taliban a few years previously and had thus gained the upper hand. When the Taliban fell, he had been summoned to a village meeting and then left for Pakistan the following day. His rival, a relative, took over as the community's leader. 'So, no, there are no Taliban in the village ... for the moment,' the Australians were told. Author interview, senior Australian officer, Kabul, March 2009.

27. Author interview, Peshawar, June 2002.

28. Three clerics who opposed the Taliban were killed in June and July of 2003 in Kandahar with another dozen dying over the next two years in the city.

29. See the perceptive analysis in Jones, *In the Graveyard of Empires*, p. 244. Also referring to the Taliban as a social movement is Barfield, *Afghanistan*, p. 261. See Robert D. Crews and Amin Tarzi, *The Taliban and the Crisis of Afghanistan*, Harvard University Press, 2008, p. 243.

30. Author interview, Kandahar, November 2003.

31. See Antonio Giustozzi, *Koran, Kalashnikov and Laptop*, Hurst, 2007, pp. 38–39, 55–6. See Ron Moreau, Sami Yousafzai and Michael Hirsh, 'The rise of Jihadistan', *Newsweek*, October 2, 2006. Multiple author interviews with military or other intelligence officials, British, American, Afghan, in Kabul, Kandahar, London, 2006, 2007. Interviews with local MPs in Afghanistan, July 2006, August 2008, March 2009. Interview with United Nations security experts, July 2006, August 2008.

32. In Oruzgan and in western Zabul.

33. Turn-out for the polls was very high, with up to 60 per cent of the eligible population registering even in Kandahar.

34. Hekmatyar had returned to Afghanistan (probably via Pakistan) after being released from house arrest in Iran in 2002 as relations between Tehran and Washington deteriorated.

35. My estimate is based on interviews with senior NATO officers, Afghan and Western intelligence officials, Taliban spokesmen. For an alternative estimate see Giustozzi, *Koran, Kalashnikov and Laptop*, pp. 35, 68. Also in November 2006, a UN report estimated the number of armed insurgents in Mullah Omar's movement to be around 4,000–5,000. UN Security Council, *Sixth Report of the Analytical Support and Sanctions Monitoring Team Appointed Pursuant to Security Council Resolutions 1526 (2004) and 1617 (2005)*

Concerning Al-Qaida and the Taliban and Associated Individuals and Entities, November 7, 2006.

36. Testimony of Lieutenant General David W. Barno, USA (Ret.) before the Committee on Foreign Affairs US House of Representatives, February 15, 2007.

37. Jones, *In the Graveyard of Empires*, p. 205.

38. Ronald Neumann, *The Other War: Winning and Losing in Afghanistan*, Potomac Books, 2009, pp. 39–40.

39. Author interview with Amrullah Saleh, former head of Afghan National Directorate of Intelligence, Kabul, June 2011. In 2005, the Americans had a total of 19,000 troops in the country, with one less infantry battalion than in 2002, with their multinational allies in ISAF maintaining around another 15,000. In October 2003, US troops numbers were about 14,000, and NATO less than 6,000. They had then risen slightly to 16,500. See Jones, *In the Graveyard of Empires*, p. 204.

40. Reid said that the British 'would be perfectly happy to leave in three years and without firing one shot because our job is to protect reconstruction'. 'UK troops "to target terrorists"', BBC, April 24, 2006. See also Rashid, *Descent into Chaos*, pp. 357–8.

41. The US troops on the eastern frontier would remain part of the original Operation Enduring Freedom and therefore commanded direct from CentCom in the USA. Total American troops in Afghanistan were 22,300.

42. Author interview, July 2006.

43. Author interviews with Mark Laity, NATO spokesman, Kabul, July 2006 and February 2008. Author interview with Brigadier General Richard Blanchette, Kabul, 2008.

44. 'Insurgent activity rising in Afghanistan', Associated Press, November 13, 2006.

45. Author interview, Kabul, July 2006.

46. 'Nato hails shift on Afghan combat', BBC News Online, November 29, 2006.

47. Others had once been kept in check by a powerful local commander with strong conservative religious credentials who had backed Karzai before being detained by American forces acting independently. The story of that commander, Haji Rohullah, deserves a chapter in itself. A hardline Salafi commander in Kunar, Rohullah backed the central government after the fall of the Taliban but ended up in Guantanamo Bay. The author met him in Kabul in 2008, shortly after his release. Violence, limited in Kunar until his arrest, increased dramatically afterwards.

48. One problem for commanders in the east was the degree to which their operational environment was influenced by what happened across the border. A truce in 2005 between the Pakistani army and local militants had trebled the number of cross-border attacks almost overnight. French troops east of Kabul tracked groups of fighters crossing over from Pakistan, moving along mountain roads before dropping off the hills and on to their positions. Author interviews,

French officers, Forward Operating Base Tora, Sorobi, March 2009. Author interview, Chris Alexander, deputy head of mission, UNAMA, Kabul, March 2009. The most active insurgent networks along the Afghan side of the frontier were connected to Jalaluddin Haqqani, who was known to have lines of communications to Pakistani intelligence services, and a broader regional agenda clearly informed some of the clashes. So when an Indian construction company won a contract to build a major road close to the border around Khost, one of the largest forces yet seen in the area massed to attack them.

49. United Nations Assistance Mission in Afghanistan, *Internal Security Assessment on Wardak*, June 2008. Author collection.

50. Author interviews with French officers, Forward Operating Base Tora, Sorobi, March 2009. Author interview with Qazi Syed Suleiman, vice governor of Nangahar, Sorobi, March 2009.

51. Tom Coghlan, 'The Taliban in Helmand: An Oral History', in Giustozzi, ed., *Decoding the New Taliban*, p. 122.

52. Author interview with General Chris Brown, Kabul, July 2006.

53. Author interviews, Kabul, August 2008.

54. For the Belfast reference see Patrick Hennessey, *The Junior Officers Reading Club*, Allen Lane, 2009. I was invited to brief the Parachute Regiment, the Royal Green Jackets and 52 Mechanised Brigade HQ before departure.

55. Canadians arriving in Kandahar took care to learn from their US predecessors, touring much of their new territory with the Americans and even fighting alongside them over a period of months. See Coghlan, 'The Taliban in Helmand', pp. 128, 152.

56. Draft of report on 'The situation in Helmand', Ron Nash for FCO, 2007, author collection.

57. See Kilcullen on Kunar, *The Accidental Guerrilla*, pp. 74–107.

58. The British version of the *American Field Manual 3-24*, the counter-insurgency guide published in the US around the time the British troops arrived in Helmand, spoke of British 'best practice' in counter-insurgency and ingrained traditions of 'cultural sensitivity' and pointed to the examples of Malaya and Kenya among others. However, British tactics in Malaya, where the term 'hearts and minds' had been coined, had involved the forcible resettlement of 500,000 people, mass arrests, the death penalty for carrying arms, detention without trial for up to two years, deportations, control of food, censorship, collective punishment in the form of curfews and fines, the hanging of hundreds of prisoners and repeated atrocities in which unarmed civilians or combatants were killed. Means deployed against the Kikuyu or Mau Mau in Kenya included torture, hanging, indiscriminate bombing and toleration of local proxies' use of sadistic violence, dismemberment and killing in custody. Though some of these measures were employed in Afghanistan, most were seen, for obvious and good reasons, as neither feasible, desirable nor appropriate. As for the oft-cited experience of Northern Ireland, the differences between

south Armagh and Helmand fairly comprehensively outweighed any similarities, as soldiers driving the antiquated 'Snatch' Land Rovers through towns like Gereshk or Garmseer frequently pointed out in usually colourful language.

59. Author interview, Kandahar, July 2006.

60. Author interview with Brigadier Ed Butler, Kabul, July 2006.

61. US Naval War College, Damien Mason, *Air Strikes and COIN in Operation Enduring Freedom*, Joint Military Operations Department report, May 3, 2010.

62. Author interviews, Kajaki, January 2007. Giustozzi, *Koran, Kalashnikov and Laptop*, p. 202.

63. In late 2003 in Sangesar, the village that had been home for two decades to Mullah Mohammed Omar himself, villagers had planted opium.

64. United Nations Office on Drugs and Crime (UNODC), *Afghanistan Opium Survey 2006*, September 2006. See Pierre-Arnaud Chouvy, *Opium: Uncovering the Politics of the Poppy*, I. B. Tauris, 2009, for a useful discussion.

65. See also Ahmed Rashid, 'Afghanistan: Taleban's second coming', BBC News Online, June 2, 2006.

66. See also Gretchen Peters, *Seeds of Terror: How Heroin Is Bankrolling the Taliban and Al Qaeda*, Oneworld Publications, 2009, pp. 7–22. Also Giustozzi, ed., *Decoding the New Taliban*.

67. Author interviews with British and American anti-narcotics officials, military intelligence, Kabul, Kandahar, Lashkar Gah, January 2007, August 2008.

68. Author interviews with British officials, Kabul 2007, 2008. Author interview with Christine Orguz, country director Afghanistan, UNODC, Kabul, 2008. Classified/NoForn RC South briefing on Narcotic Trafficking, PowerPoint presentation and documents, May 2005. See also Testimony of Lieutenant General David W. Barno, USA (Ret.) before the Committee on Foreign Affairs, US House of Representatives, February 15, 2007.

69. Author interviews with British government counter-narcotics officials, London, 2008.

70. The British estimates were based on those of the United Nations. See UNODC, *Afghanistan Opium Survey 2007*, September 2007, p. 7.

71. Author interview with Orguz. See also UNODC (Doris Buddenberg and William Byrd), *Afghanistan's Drug Industry, Structure, Functioning Dynamics and Implications for Counter-Narcotics Policy*, 2006.

72. Anthony Loyd, 'Corruption, bribes and trafficking: a cancer that is engulfing Afghanistan', *The Times*, November 24, 2007. See also Elizabeth Rubin, 'In the land of the Taliban', *New York Times*, October 22, 2006.

73. 'The policy of being nice to farmers was a complete failure. The British army position was completely unacceptable. We never had a yelling match and did have some frank discussions but we always went for dinner afterwards,' said Thomas Schweich, former State Department narcotics official, 2006–7, author telephone interview, September 2008. One major argument was over

the use of chemical spraying. Schweich and the American ambassador in Kabul, William Wood, were both fierce proponents of the technique. The Afghans and the Europeans were very much opposed. 'It would have handed the Taliban a huge PR victory and lost the consent of the Afghan people. There were practical issues with low-flying planes – they would have got shot down – and even if it works one year the next year they'll just mix their crops,' said a senior British Foreign Office specialist, author telephone interview, September 2008.

74. Author interview, Helmand, July 2006.

75. Graeme Smith, 'Talking to the Taliban', *Globe and Mail*, March 2008.

76. Author email exchange with Brigadier Andrew McKay, January 2008.

77. Author interview with Chris Alexander, UNAMA, January 2007.

78. Figures from an ISAF briefing, Kabul 2009.

79. Brigadier Andrew McKay told his troops in October 2007: 'I do not want to see a single PowerPoint slide presented to a single visitor that articulates enemy Killed In Action. We may analyse the value of attrition but not as a sign of success.' 'COIN in Helmand, Task Force Operational Design', restricted ISAF brief, October 30, 2007, author collection.

80. In all 103 UK soldiers died in Afghanistan between June 30, 2006 and July 1, 2008. Helmand Province accounted for 60 per cent of the casualties in the country for that time period. There had been 370 coalition fatalities in Afghanistan (hostile and non-hostile) from January 2002 to May 2006. icasualties.org.

81. Over the previous twelve months civilian casualties had risen between 40 and 56 per cent, according to the United Nations. 'Top Afghan policewoman shot dead', BBC News Online, September 28, 2008. Attacks on Afghan government employees in 2008 were 124 per cent higher than in 2007.

82. Stuck on a dusty wasteland without any resources on the outskirts of the city, the refugees' accounts of life in places like Musa Qala and Kajaki were among the most upsetting the author had heard in well over a decade of visiting the country. Millions had had similar experiences. Jason Burke, 'Destitute and confused: bleak future for Afghan refugees caught in the crossfire', *Guardian*, October 3, 2008.

83. 70,000, according to Mohammed Nader Farhad of the UNHCR. Author interview, Kabul, July 2008.

84. Author interview, Kabul, July 2008.

85. Author interview, Maiwand, July 2006.

86. Rahman had no time for Osama bin Laden either. 'He too is a foreigner. He is not an Afghan. We Afghans are strong. We do not need Osama.'

87. Author interviews with General David Richards, ISAF commander, senior ISAF officials, Kabul, January 2007. Officially NATO claimed that 512 insurgents had been killed. Unofficially, senior officers said they thought the number of casualties inflicted was at least 1,000, possibly more.

88. The question of the influence of Iraq on the tactics of the Taliban is an

interesting one. There was evidence of at least some cooperation between insurgents in Iraq and Afghanistan. Militants in Iraq were reported to have provided information and tips over the internet. Members of the Taliban, Hekmatyar's group and others may even have made their way to Anbar, Mosul and elsewhere to experience the fighting in Iraq first hand, at least until the turning of the Sunni tribes made such ventures perilous. Analysts believed that the more effective use of IEDs, suicide bombs and other tactics by the Taliban was at the very least influenced by what was happening in Iraq if not actually taught by Iraqi insurgents arriving in Afghanistan as the failure of the al-Qaeda project in 'the land of the two rivers' became apparent. By 2008, some Taliban units – though very few – did include Arab or other fighters with Iraqi or other experience. There were also reports that the Taliban had acquired new commercial communications gear and field equipment from Iraqi groups as well as tips on camouflage and the use of snipers. The posting of execution videos on the internet by a handful of the most extreme Taliban commanders was also clearly influenced by what had been happening in Iraq. Author interview with Defence Minister Abdur Rahim Wardak, Kabul, January 2007. Jones, *In the Graveyard of Empires*, p. 292. Testimony of Lieutenant General David W. Barno, USA (Ret.) before the Committee on Foreign Affairs, US House of Representatives. Sami Yousafzai and Ron Moreau, 'Afghanistan on the brink: Where do we go from here?' February 15, 2007. 'Taliban gets help, inspiration from Iraq', *Newsweek*, September 26, 2005. Senior militants certainly travelled from Afghanistan to Iraq. One was Omar al-Farooq, who escaped from the prison at Bagram airbase and made his way to Basra, where he was eventually killed.

89. One was Mullah Akhtar Mohammed Osmani, the man who had met Bob Grenier, the CIA Islamabad station chief, in the Serena hotel in Quetta a week or so before the bombing started in 2001. Dadaullah was killed in a British special forces raid in May 2007, probably after his location was given away by rivals within insurgent ranks worried about his growing influence, personal following and extremism. Jason Burke, 'Hunt for "traitors" splits Taliban', *Observer*, May 27, 2007.

90. The estimate is Michael Semple's, the former deputy to the EU special representative to Afghanistan and one of the most knowledgeable experts on the country. Semple spent more time than perhaps any other Westerner meeting Taliban commanders in Helmand. Author telephone interview, August 2009.

91. One was the British journalist James Fergusson, in 2006. See James Fergusson, *A Million Bullets: The Real Story of the British Army in Afghanistan*, Transworld, 2008. The other was Nir Rosen, working for *Rolling Stone*, in Ghazni in August 2008.

92. Even in 2006, a commander known as Mullah Sabir had told one reporter: 'We have about 15,000 men. Forty per cent are not really Taliban, have not graduated from any religious school; they are youngsters who join our

ranks in sympathy [with our cause].' Interview with Mullah Sabir, quoted in 'The new Taliban codex', *Signandsight*, 28 November 2006, quoted in Anne Stenersen, 'The Taliban Insurgency in Afghanistan – Organization, Leadership and Worldview', Norwegian Defence Research Establishment (FFI), February 5, 2010, p. 30.

93. In southern Wardak, a well-known hardliner was replaced as governor by a more moderate figure, to the relief of many locals. Author interview with Roshana Wardak, MP, Kabul, 2008.

94. Copy of 2006 'Laheya', author collection.

95. Author interview with Antonio Giustozzi, London, August 2009.

96. This research was undertaken in a fairly unscientific fashion by the author and two researchers in Afghanistan in August 2008 and in March 2009.

97. Jeremy Page, 'Children and MPs killed in worst Afghan suicide bomb', *The Times*, November 7, 2007. Author interview with Taliban spokesman 'Zabibullah Mujahed', by email. November 2007.

98. See International Crisis Group, *Taliban Propaganda: Winning the War of Words?*, July 24, 2008.

99. In May 2006 it had been attacked by a mob rioting following a traffic accident involving an American convoy.

100. Including the author.

101. According to a cable obtained by WikiLeaks and subsequently made available online, within weeks of the attack, British diplomats were talking to American counterparts of 'a growing body of [intelligence] reporting suggesting . . . that Pakistan's Inter-Services Intelligence Agency (ISI) was possibly involved in the July 7 bombing of the Indian Embassy in Kabul – though likely without the knowledge of the civil elements of the GOP [Government of Pakistan]'. Cable, id: 162707, date: July 18 2008, source: Embassy London, origin: 08LONDON1887.

102. See David Sanger, *The Inheritance: The World Obama Confronts and the Challenges to American Power*, Crown, 2009, p. 250. A United Nations study in 2007 found that more than 70 per cent of suicide bombers in Afghanistan came from across the border. UNAMA (C. Christine Fair), *Suicide Attacks in Afghanistan, 2001–2007*, 2007.

103. The Afghan government was keen to underline the role that they said Pakistan – or at least some Pakistanis – played in the ongoing violence in Afghanistan. Foreign journalists who struggled through the bureaucracy and could call in a few favours could, at least in 2008, get interviews with detainees, in the company of their jailers.

104. Abit had probably been beaten by Afghan interrogators in prison and almost certainly on his arrest. He was equally likely to have edited his story, minimizing his own responsibility and exaggerating his current repentance. But his account was nonetheless largely credible, matching the picture revealed by studies by the United Nations. A second interview with a would-be suicide

bomber in Kabul – that of a destitute, illiterate and clearly mentally unstable shepherd captured near Khost with a suicide bomb strapped to his body – showed how recruiters for extremist networks often target the most marginal elements in society and particularly those who have slipped out of traditional social networks of support and authority. Author interviews, Kabul, August 2008.

CHAPTER 13: PAKISTAN

1. The population of Pakistan in 2010 was 177 million, according to the CIA Factbook. https://www.cia.gov/library/publications/the-world-factbook/geos/pk.html. For the Pew Research Center, it was 174 million. See Pew Research Center, *Mapping the Global Muslim Population*. The rate of population increase in Pakistan is dropping. It was 3 per cent in 1990, 2.5 per cent in 2000 and 2.2 per cent in 2008, according to Unicef. The USA, with 400 million, Indonesia, with 270 million, and India, with 1.1 billion, cannot be considered primary theatres of conflict like Afghanistan, Iraq, Pakistan or countries such as Saudi Arabia. Secondary theatres would also include European countries and many other Middle Eastern or Maghreb states.

2. United Nations Development Programme, *Human Development Report*, editions of 2008 and 2009. Available at http://hdrstats.undp.org/en/countries/country_fact_sheets/cty_fs_PAK.html.

3. 'The most dangerous nation in the world isn't Iraq. It's Pakistan', *Newsweek*, October 29, 2007.

4. Two excellent recent investigations of these questions include Farzana Shaikh's academic *Making Sense of Pakistan*, Hurst, 2010, and Owen Bennett-Jones, *Pakistan: The Eye of the Storm*, 3rd edn, Yale, 2003.

5. See Anatol Lieven, *Pakistan: A Hard Country*, Allen Lane, 2011, pp. 65–7.

6. These included the infamous Hudood Ordinances, introduced in 1979, which ruled that the evidence of a woman is worth half that of a man. Under these laws a woman who is raped can end up being convicted of adultery or fornication if she is unable to provide four male Muslim witnesses to the crime against her. The sentence, though rarely or never implemented, is death by stoning. Under the same code alcohol is banned and amputation recommended for convicted thieves.

7. An important point is that Maududi was fiercely anti-clerical and Jamaat Islami kept their distance from organizations representing the clergy, whether moderate or extreme. The writings on Maududi and Jamaat Islami are voluminous. See Roy, *The Failure of Political Islam*; Giles Keppel, *Jihad*. Useful points are made by Philip Jenkins, 'Clerical terror: The roots of jihad in India', *The New Republic*, December 24, 2008.

8. On Maududi see also Burke, *Al-Qaeda*, pp. 50–51.

9. Iftikhar Malik, *Pakistan: Democracy, Terror and the Building of a Nation*, New Holland, 2010, p. 35.

10. Bhutto built pragmatic alliances with the Deobandis to bolster a tenuous grip on power.

11. Less well known is the prohibition on foreign aid to Pakistan imposed when the country fell into arrears in servicing its debt to the United States in late 1998.

12. The first major challenge to Musharraf, who seized power with broad popular support though international disapproval, came with the 9/11 attacks. As noted in Chapter 2, after some deliberation, the former commando decided he had to agree to almost all American demands for cooperation. This he did not out of any loyalty to the USA, who after all had imposed heavy sanctions on Pakistan for its pursuit of nuclear weapons technology, but because he decided that it was in the best interests of his country.

13. Statistics from Karachi town hall, secretary to the mayor, author interview, November 2008.

14. Karachi's Pashtun population made it the largest single urban Pashtun community in the world.

15. Fewer than 8 per cent of Pakistanis speak Urdu, the national language, as their mother tongue.

16. The Mohajir Quami Movement was founded in 1984 to represent the interests of the descendants of immigrants from India, the Mohajirs. They later converted themselves into the Muttahida Quami Movement and supposedly abandoned both guns and ethnic politics. Their leader, Altaf Hussein, lives in Edgware, London.

17. Though in fact the Bhuttos were not actually among the first-rank families of really major landowners with serious historic heritage.

18. And including a Briton, Omar Saeed Sheikh. Pearl appears to have been first abducted by local militants led by Sheikh, before being passed to a group led by Khaled Sheikh Mohammad.

19. International Crisis Group, *Pakistan: Karachi's Madrasas and Violent Extremism*, March 29, 2007. The report refers to 1,000 schools and 200,000 students, though these figures are contested. All statistics dealing with *medressas* are highly controversial. For example, between March 2002 and July 2002, figures for *medressa* enrolment cited in the *Washington Post* tripled from 500,000 to 1.5 million. The ICG report put the total of Pakistani children of primary-school age in *medressas* at 33 per cent. This was later adjusted downwards to 3.3 per cent when a calculation error was pointed out. However, the orignal estimate or similar estimates were quoted in President Bush's remarks on June 24, 2003, President Musharraf's remarks on November 20, 2003, Colin Powell's on March 11, 2004, Hillary Clinton's on February 24, 2004 and the 9/11 Commission Report. See Tahir Andrabi, Jishnu Das, Asim Ijaz Khwaja and Tristan Zajonc, 'Religious School Enrollment

in Pakistan: A Look at the Data', John F. Kennedy School of Government Working Paper Series, 2005, p. iii.

20. One of these was the attack on French naval technicians in 2002. This was attributed to al-Qaeda or local militants at the time and is still listed as such in many accounts. However, press reports in France in 2010, and a French parliamentary inquiry, found that the strike was probably linked to corruption surrounding a major naval deal between France and Pakistan and the non-payment of bribes. See Guillaume Dasquié, 'Le Rapport Karachi divise les deputés', *Libération*, May 13, 2010; Mathieu Delahousse, 'Karachi: la mission parlementaire sur la piste des commissions', *Le Figaro*, May 13, 2010.

21. According to the city's mayor, Kamal Mustafa. Author interview, Karachi, November 2008.

22. See William Dalrymple, 'On the long road to freedom, finally', *Tehelka Magazine*, March 8, 2008, for statistics.

23. With a total of 1.8 million registered vehicles on the road in 2008. According to Wajid Ali Khan, Deputy Inspector General Traffic Police Karachi, in a presentation at Urban Resource Centre, Karachi, April 16, 2008.

24. Dalrymple, 'On the long road to freedom, finally'.

25. Author interview with Ijaz Shafi Gilani, Islamabad, December 2008.

26. The first nuclear-related sanctions had been imposed in 1990 and reinforced after Pakistani nuclear tests in 1998. In 2001, the remittances totalled a little more than $1 billion. From 2002 to 2006, Pakistan received around $4 billion in remittances. By 2009, despite the economic crisis, the total had reached $7 billion.

27. Dilawar Hussain, 'High per capita income not a sign of prosperity', *Dawn*, May 10, 2009.

28. Property prices went up by up to 1,000 per cent, and rents doubled or tripled. Adnan Adil, 'Pakistan's post-9/11 economic boom', BBC News, September 21, 2006.

29. David Rohde, 'Pakistani middle class, beneficiary of Musharraf, begins to question rule', *New York Times*, November 25, 2007. In 2005, international retail industry experts had estimated that the coming years would see the expansion of the upper and upper-middle class, to say nothing of the much more numerous lower middle classes, to around 17 million. Jawaid Abdul Ghani, 'Constituting a Grocery Market Worth $1.7bn. Consolidation in Pakistan's Retail Sector', *Asian Journal of Management Cases*, vol. 2, no. 2, 2005, pp. 137–61.

30. CIA Factbook, 2010. The United Nations estimate is 36 per cent. See United Nations Population Fund, *Life in the City*, June 2007, p. 3. Sher Baz Khan, 'Pakistan most urban country in S. Asia', *Dawn*, October 11, 2004.

31. Department for International Development (Dr Emma Hooper and Agha Imran Hamid), *Scoping Study on Social Exclusion in Pakistan: A Summary of Findings*, October 2003, p. 30.

32. In 2003, the country had fewer than 3 million cellphone users; in 2008 there were almost 50 million.

33. I.e. one who can read a newspaper and write a simple letter, in any language. Figures from Unicef, http://www.unicef.org/infobycountry/pakistan_pakistan_statistics.html, and UNESCO (Munir Ahmed Choudhry), *Where and Who Are the World's Illiterates?*, April 2005. Some other estimates are lower, particularly for recent years.

34. When Makhdoom Shahabuddin, Benazir Bhuttos's former finance minister and hereditary owner of thousands of hectares of land a few hours' drive north of the Jatoi's estates, had told the author in 1998 that he was unable to state with any certainty the scale of his property nor the number of 'his people', his ignorance was unfeigned, and the possessive pronoun was entirely justified. The sight of villagers kneeling to touch Makhdoom's feet in respect was nonetheless a reminder that all such change was relative.

35. Author interviews with Jatoi, Sindh, October 2007.

36. http://www.bahawalpur.gov.pk/area.htm. Official website for population figures. Accessed August 2010.

37. Author interview with MI6 official, London, November 2007.

38. Pakistani officers armed and organized militia from the local Jamaat Islami, the political Islamist party, and turned them, with bloody consequences, against intellectuals, politicians and pro-independence activists.

39. There were occasional unsubstantiated reports of some kind of Pakistani assistance to Baluchi rebels in the south-eastern corner of Iran too.

40. HUM deputy chief Maulana Fazlur Rehman Khalil was one of the signatories to bin Laden's 1998 *fatwa* declaring it a Muslim duty to kill Americans and Jews. There was a steady stream of recruits from the UK going to fight in Kashmir. Of the thousands who did so, only a handful returned to the UK and went on to become involved in further militancy.

41. The author saw HUM fighters on the frontline and spoke to the trainers in mountain skills who had been responsible for coaching them on how to survive at altitude.

42. Author interviews, Peshawar, October 2001. JeM had been set up by one of three militant leaders freed following the hijacking of an Indian airlines jet in 1999.

43. Events in Iraq and Afghanistan helped too, as they had done elsewhere, providing examples of resistance to the otherwise all-powerful America and the Jews.

44. LeT's parent body was allowed to change its name to Jamaat-ul-Dawa and to remain operative.

45. In one of those classic examples of how geopolitical forces interact with microfactors on the ground, the Punjab had become a centre of appalling Sunni versus Shia sectarian violence. This was in part also a legacy of British rule, as colonial administrators had effectively created – or at the very least

maintained and co-opted – a class of predominantly Shia landowners. The vast bulk of poor immigrants arriving in the Punjab after Partition were Sunnis. In the 1980s, firebrand clerics and politicians looking to undermine the Shia landowners' wealth and hold on to political power began working to exploit the longstanding resentments this generated, backed by Zia. The sectarian groups, such as the Sipa e Sahaba Pakistan (SSP), that resulted were backed, indirectly, both by the Pakistani security services and, as Tehran began subsidizing Shia self-protection groups, by a Saudi Arabian government fearful of the Shia renaissance sparked by the 1979 Iranian Revolution. A bloodbath ensued. Khalid Ahmed, 'Fundamental Flaws', in *On the Abyss*, HarperCollins (India), 2000, p. 94. Owen Bennett-Jones, *Pakistan: Eye of the Storm*, Yale University Press, 2003, p. 22. Amir Mir, 'Faith that kills', *Newsline*, October 1998, 'The Jihad within', *Newsline*, May 2002. Also Burke, *Al-Qaeda*, Chapter 7.

46. Mohammed Sidique Khan and Shehzad Tanweer were in Pakistan for about eleven weeks from November 2004 to January 2005. They visited Karachi, Lahore and Faisalabad together, and Tanweer visited his family village Chak-477 (called Chhotian Kota by the *Independent* newspaper), then Manshera in North West Frontier province.

47. Investigations into Rauf quickly led to the Dar-ul-Uloom Medina *medressa* in Bahawalpur, a major religious school down a back street near the relatively upmarket area where the Briton had been living since arriving in the town four years before. Rauf had married into the family of Massod Azhar, the cleric who led Jaish-e-Mohammed. The Dar-ul-Uloom Medina *medressa*, founded by Azhar's father-in-law, was widely considered to be a base for the group. Author interview with former Pakistani Interior Minister Aftab Sherpao, with ISI official, with MI6 official, Islamabad, November 2007. Despite repeated requests for extradition by the British, Rauf remained in custody in Pakistan and eventually escaped in mysterious circumstances in December 2007. He was killed, apparently, in November 2008, by a missile fired from an unmanned drone in the tribal areas on the Afghan frontier. The exact fate of Rauf remains unclear. Sir John Scarlett, director-general of MI6, told the author in the summer of 2009 that his service 'simply did not know' if Rauf was dead.

48. Donald Rumsfeld, 'Rumsfeld's war-on-terror memo', *USA Today*, October 22, 2003.

49. JUI in Pakistan split from its parent Indian body. Its political involvement dates from the early 1970s. Author interview, Bahawalpur, November 2008. In fact JUI's foundation pre-dated the creation of Pakistan by two years.

50. Author interview with Maulana Abdul Aziz Ghani, Islamabad, July 2005.

51. Maulana Sohaib, who ran the complex, denied any direct links with Jaish-e-Mohammed or that any students from the school 'went for jihad'.

52. Such as John Walker Lindh, a number of Australians, the 7/7 bombers, Rauf and many others. On Lindh see Burke, *Al-Qaeda*, pp. 195–6. On Australians,

Radicalization in the West: The Homegrown Threat, The New York City Police Department, 2007, p. 51. Presentation by Australian Secret Intelligence Service analysts, Riyadh, March 2008.

53. Author interview with Bahawalpur police chief, November 2007.

54. Around 40 per cent of students in public and private schools came from the poorest categories of society and only 43 per cent of *medressa* students. Andrabi et al., 'Religious School Enrollment'.

55. See Christine Fair, 'Militant Recruitment in Pakistan', *Asia Policy*, July 2007, p. 115, table 1.

56. Andrabi et al., 'Religious School Enrollment'. See also Fair, 'Militant Enrollment'.

57. See ibid., table III.

58. Nikhil Raymond Puri, 'The Pakistani Madrassah and Terrorism: Made and Unmade Conclusions from the Literature', *Perspectives on Terrorism*, vol. 4, no. 4, October 2010, p. 53.

59. See Abbas, *Probing the Jihadi Mindset*.

60. RAND Corporation (C. Christine Fair), *Who Are Pakistan's Militants and Their Families?*, January 1, 2008, p. 60. Puri, 'The Pakistani Madrassah and Terrorism', p. 53.

61. This was in part due to the numbers of individuals educated in religious schools reaching adulthood but could equally be attributed to decades of state propaganda on Kashmir and to the generalized increased sense of religious solidarity so marked in much of the Islamic world since the early years of the decade.

62. Author interview with Dr Omar Farooq Zain Alizai, Multan, December 2007.

63. CIA factbook, updated in 2010. https://www.cia.gov/library/publications/the-world-factbook/fields/2177.html.

64. From Terror Free Tomorrow/New American Foundation, Results of a New Nationwide Public Opinion Survey of Pakistan, 2007.

65. Gilani Poll conducted by Gallup Pakistan, August 2009.

66. C. Christine Fair and Seth Jones, 'Pakistan's War Within', *Survival*, December 2009–January 2010, p. 181. Only 4 per cent saw the spread of American culture favourably. Gilani Poll conducted by Gallup Pakistan, August 2009.

67. Zar Nageen, 'Naming a baby in Pakistan', *Daily Times*, July 9, 2007.

68. '78% Males Mostly Wear Shalwar Kameez, 22% Wear Trousers': Gilani poll, Gallup Pakistan, Islamabad, August 27, 2010.

69. Mohammed Hanif, 'The power of the pulpit', *Newsline*, January 2009.

70. Author interview with Ershad Mahmud, columnist, Islamabad, October 2007.

71. Serious efforts at rapprochement between Ms Bhutto and General Musharraf had been underway since 2004. Bhutto met a series of different representatives to discuss her return. General Ashfaq Kayani, then the director-general of the ISI, led an initial round of discussions. The negotiations had begun in

earnest, however, when Musharraf telephoned Bhutto while she was visiting New York in August 2006. By early autumn, following at least two direct interventions by Secretary of State Condoleezza Rice, the outline of a deal had emerged. Bhutto and Musharraf met secretly on January 24, 2007 in Abu Dhabi and again six months later in Abu Dhabi. Multiple author interviews with PPP officials, Islamabad, Karachi, November 2008. See also Steve Coll, 'Time bomb, the death of Benazir Bhutto and the unravelling of Pakistan', *New Yorker*, January 28, 2008. See also *Report of the United Nations Commission of Inquiry into the Facts and Circumstances of the Assassination of Former Pakistani Prime Minister Mohtarma Benazir Bhutto*, April 15, 2010. Bhutto herself joked to the author about the long telephone conversations she had with President Musharraf, saying that he called her Benazir and she called him 'Mushy'.

72. Zaffar Abbas, 'The emerging contours of PPP-govt deal', *Dawn*, April 21, 2007. Author telephone interviews with Bhutto, September 2007, and in Islamabad, December 2007. See also *Report of the United Nations Commission of Inquiry into the Facts and Circumstances of the Assassination of Former Pakistani Prime Minister Mohtarma Benazir Bhutto*, p. 59, and on 'deep' ISI involvement, p. 60.

73. Between September 2006 and September 2007, Musharraf's approval rating plummeted from 63 per cent to 21 per cent. International Republican Institute (IRI), *Pakistan Public Opinion Survey*, January 19–29, 2008.

74. Author telephone interview, October 2007.

75. Owais Mughal, 'Peshawar–Islamabad Motorway M1 is now open for traffic', Pakistaniat.com. November 11, 2007.

76. This account is based on the author's own reporting, Islamabad and Nowshera, December 2007.

77. Author telephone interview with Bhutto, in Dubai, September 2007.

78. The author conducted three lengthy telephone interviews with Bhutto in June, August and September 2007.

79. The scientific analysis of the suicide bomber's remains by a Scotland Yard team established that he was a teenage male, no more than sixteen years old. According to the Punjab police's investigations, he was called Bilal aka Saeed and from South Waziristan. British High Commission, *Scotland Yard Report into Assassination of Benazir Bhutto*, February 8, 2008, executive summary. *Report of the United Nations Commission of Inquiry*, pp. 41, 60.

80. Amir Mir, *The Bhutto Murder Trail: From Waziristan to GHQ*, Tranquebar, 2010, p. 7.

81. *Report of the United Nations Commission of Inquiry*, pp. 3, 28. *Scotland Yard Report*, p. 3.

82. *Report of the United Nations Commission of Inquiry*, pp. 3, 28. *Scotland Yard Report*, p. 3.

83. Kayani was helped by the new ubiquity of cheap mobile phones, which

meant that TV stations could put a locally hired volunteer correspondent in almost every polling station who gave an impromptu count, obtained from the local returning officers, within minutes of the booths closing thus rendering ballot-box stuffing much harder.

84. Author interview with Qazi Hussein Ahmed, Lahore, February 2008.

85. His consistently hawkish position on Kashmir and acts such as the decision in 1998 to respond in kind to India's 1998 nuclear tests reinforced nationalist credentials too which had been subsequently polished by a stream of anti-Western outbursts and an ambivalent position on cooperation with America on counter-terrorism operations if he ever returned to power.

86. A number of Sharif's family and entourage were involved with the Tabligh Jamaat, a Deobandi-inspired mass organization based on preaching by example which, though non-violent itself, has been an entry point to violent radicalism for a significant number of militants.

87. The reports were difficult to reconcile with reports that in July 1999 Sharif offered to allow US troops to try to kill bin Laden from Pakistani territory apparently to give Washington a stake in the survival of his government. See Bennett-Jones, *Pakistan: Eye of the Storm*, p. 40.

88. Author interview, Islamabad, October 2007.

89. Jason Burke, 'The Guardian profile: Asif Ali Zardari', *Guardian*, September 5, 2008.

CHAPTER 14: ANOTHER COUNTRY: FATA

1. The writings of Henty, Kipling, Churchill and other, less-talented, authors are full of depictions of the Pashtun border tribes as warlike, brave, stoic and honourable and tell us more about the values of the British Victorians than about the Pashtuns. See Mukulika Banerjee, *The Pathan Unarmed*, Oxford University Press, 2001.

2. Quoted in Sana Haroon, *Frontier of Faith*, Hurst, 2007, p. 89.

3. Ibid., pp. 95–8.

4. Ibid., p. 57. The religious police in Saudi Arabia go by the same name.

5. Albeit one that allowed, through the extraordinary powers granted to the political agent who ran each of the seven FATA for the authorities of the Raj and then of independent Pakistan, the zone to be governed according to their interests rather than those of the locals.

6. Significant funding from Saudi Arabia was part of the effort to extend the reach of Gulf strands of rigorous conservative Sunni Islam to counter the expansion of Shia influence in the wake of the 1979 Iranian Revolution.

7. The contrast they made between their supposed rural, Pashtun religious rectitude and the lack of faith of the urbanized communities and elites of Pakistan would have been entirely familiar to their grandfathers and great grandfathers.

8. Author interview, Khyber Pass, Afghanistan, November 2001.

9. Ahmed was on a visit largely aimed at convincing American counterparts and policy-makers that their view of the Taliban was overly harsh.

10. After all only eighteen months before Musharraf had publicly stated: 'The Taliban cannot be alienated by Pakistan. We have a national security interest there.' Rashid, *Descent into Chaos*, p. 28.

11. Ibid., pp. 50–51.

12. Both Bhutto and her interior minister, Naseerullah Babar, hoped too to open trade routes from Pakistan to central Asia, another constant theme of Pakistani diplomacy and strategic thinking over previous decades and a further reason for the continual insistence on having a favourable government in Kabul. One reason was also internal – the Deobandi Jamaat Ulema Islami party were crucial allies of Bhutto's government – and another was the personal proclivities of the Pashtun Naseerullah Babar. Babar claimed, slightly hyperbolically, to be the 'father of the Taliban'. Author interview, Islamabad, 1998.

13. Author interview with Maleeha Lodhi, London, February 2008.

14. Musharraf, *In the Line of Fire*, p. 237: 'We have earned bounties totalling millions of dollars'.

15. Rashid, *Descent into Chaos*, p. 241.

16. See Mohammed Yousaf and Mark Adkin, *The Bear Trap*, Casemate, 2001.

17. Author interview, Kandahar, November 2003.

18. Author interviews, Peshawar, October 2002, February 2008. Joshua T. White, *Pakistan's Islamist Frontier*, Center on Faith and International Affairs, 2008. 'Government helped MMA leaders' contest elections', *Daily Times*, November 8, 2002. The MMA alliance of conservative religious parties which came to power in the North West Frontier province and, in coalition, in Baluchistan in elections in 2002 benefited from support from the state, which recognized that the Islamists could serve as a useful proxy by which the Musharraf government could marginalize its chief political rivals in the Frontier (the PPP, PML-N and the secular Pashtun nationalist Awami Nationalist Party). The Pakistani military prevented all three parties from campaigning. The religious alliance took 48 of 99 provincial assembly seats, and 29 of 35 national assembly seats from the Frontier.

19. Declan Walsh, 'Across the border from Britain's troops, Taliban rises again', *Guardian*, May 27, 2006. Also Rashid, *Descent into Chaos*, p. 250.

20. Author interview with Maulana Rahat Hussain, Peshawar, October 2007. Not only did the new government of the two provinces embark on a project of radical Islamization, thus creating an atmosphere that encouraged further extremism, but it also proved itself to be predictably incompetent in the management of the provinces' complex social problems.

21. Author telephone interview with Robert Grenier, former Islamabad CIA station chief, January 2009. Author telephone interview with Philip Mudd, former CIA and FBI senior official, June 2010.

22. Author telephone interview with senior serving CIA official, June 2010.

23. Author interviews with intelligence officials, London, Kabul, Islamabad, 2007, 2008.

24. A joint United Nations and European Union paper spoke of 'the wide-ranging nature of ISI involvement'. Jones, *In the Graveyard of Empires*, p. 267. Jason Burke, 'Guantánamo Bay files: Pakistan's ISI spy service listed as terrorist group', *Guardian*, April 25, 2011.

25. Officers echoed the statements of President Karzai and said publicly that the Taliban leadership was coordinating its campaign from Quetta. Declan Walsh, 'Pakistan sheltering Taliban, says British officer', *Guardian*, May 19, 2006. Author interviews with British officers, Helmand, January, 2007, General David Richards, Kabul, February 2007.

26. Author interview with US defence official, Islamabad, October 2007.

27. Author interview, Islamabad, November 2007.

28. Author interview, Riyadh, March 2008.

29. Author interview, London, August 2009.

30. Hearing of the United States Senate select committee on intelligence, Annual Worldwide Threat Assessment, February 5, 2008, Michael McConnell, director of national intelligence, witness testimony.

31. Sanger, *The Inheritance*, p. 248.

32. Mark Mazzetti and Erik Schmitt, 'Pakistanis aided attack in Kabul, U.S. officials say', *New York Times*, August 1, 2008.

33. Burke, 'Pakistan's ISI spy service listed'. Guantanamo Bay Threat Indicator Matrix, September 2007, author collection.

34. Author interview, London, May 2009.

35. In the conversation, intercepted by the ISI and purported to be between Baitullah Mehsud, addressed as Emir Sahib, and an associate, addressed as Maulvi Sahib, the two speakers congratulate each other on an event which, Pakistani government officials claimed on the day after the killing, was the assassination of Benazir Bhutto. The ISI told UN investigators that they already had the voice signature of Baitullah Mehsud and were in a position to identify his voice on the intercept. They also said that they were already monitoring Mehsud's communications, which is how they recorded the conversation. In the English translation of the intercept, the man identified as Mehsud asks his interlocutor: 'Who were they?' The reply comes: 'There were Saeed, the second was Badarwala Bilal and Ikramullah was also there.' Mehsud then asked: 'The three did it?' The cleric he was talking too – 'Maulvi sahib' simply being an honorific for a middle-ranking Deobandi scholar – replied: 'Ikramullah and Bilal did it.' The conversation did not mention Bhutto by name. *Report of the United Nations Commission of Inquiry*, p. 42.

36. Grave concerns remained over the huge shortfalls in the security provision made by the local police and by Musharraf's government for Bhutto but at least two external inquiries, one by Scotland Yard and the other by the United

Nations, found no evidence of active collusion in the killing on the part of the authorities. The general conclusion was that the authorities' role in Bhutto's death was determined by incompetence rather than conspiracy. though it was clear that no one was particularly interested in making a huge effort to protect the controversial former prime minister outside her own entourage. There does, however, appear to have been a genuine attempt to impede investigations by local police following the killing.

37. Either Broomikhel or Zarai Khel of the branch of the Shabikhel subtribe. Mehsud was actually born in Kotka Nor Baz Dawood Shah district near Bannu, according to Azam Tariq, 'The Life of Baitullah Mahsood', published in Urdu-language *Hiteen Magazine*, translation and publication by Global Islamic Media Front, autumn 2010, author collection. This is corroborated by reliable Pakistani sources. See Rahumullah Yusufzai, 'Hidden hand', *Newsline*, February 2008; and Imtiaz Ali, 'Commander of the faithful', *Foreign Policy Magazine*, July 9, 2009.

38. Tariq, 'The Life of Baitullah Mahsood'. The author claims Mehsud matriculated from Bannu City School.

39. Ibid.

40. Author interviews, Peshawar and Islamabad, February 2008.

41. Author interviews with local journalists from Khyber Agency, Peshawar, February, 2008. Author interview with Khalid Aziz, former political secretary NWFP, November 2008. Rahumullah Yusufzai, *The News*, May 22, 2008.

42. Imtiaz Ali, 'The Taliban's versatile spokesman: A profile of Muslim Khan', *CTC Sentinel*, February 2009, vol. 2, no. 2. pp. 6–8. Author interview with aide to Muslim Khan, Karachi, January 2008. Imtiaz Gul, *The Most Dangerous Place: Pakistan's Lawless Frontier*, Penguin, 2010, p. 246.

43. Hakimullah Mehsud, effectively Baitullah Mehsud's deputy, was a member of the Eshangai subtribe, a branch with little prestige, who had never completed his education, either religious or secular, before going off to fight for the Taliban in the mid 1990s and returning in 2001 or 2002. In Waziristan, where war had been a way of making a living for centuries, the money militants could earn, in addition to the valuable weapons and ammunition that could be seized, was much better than that paid to the paramilitary frontier corps or the police, who received 7–8,000 Rs or 6–7,000 Rs respectively per month. A militant could easily earn half as much again. A literate tribesman could earn up to ten times more, as such people were needed to keep basic accounts, stocks of ammunition and so on. For a good example of how the TTP linked into criminal gangs see Tariq Saeed Birmani, 'Riversides may be housing some militants', *Dawn*, October 13, 2009, about the situation in Dera Ghazi Khan adjacent to the FATA.

44. Author interview with Khalid Aziz, former secretary NWFP, November 2008. When peasants had rebelled in Charsadda district next to Mohmand in the 1970s, one of their chief demands had been land reform. See also Jane

Perlez and Pir Zubair Shah, 'The Taliban's latest tactic: Class warfare; inroads are being made in Pakistan by playing poor against wealthy', *New York Times*, April 17, 2009. See Owen Bennett-Jones, 'Pakistan inequality fuelling Taliban support', BBC, May 2010.

45. The fact that the Mahmund, with their greater links to the world outside the high valleys of birch trees and terraced sandy fields of the high frontier, were the most extreme of local factions was not in a sense surprising. The situation in the FATA was inevitably affected by the evolution of the 9/11 Wars more generally and it was those most exposed to the various effects of the conflict, particularly the broad currents of polarization and radicalization that had become so evident from 2003 onwards, who were most likely to end up on the frontline.

46. Four hundred according to Gul, *The Most Dangerous Place*, p. xiv.

47. Between 2003 and 2008, 1,200 Pakistani soldiers were killed, along with more than 6,000 tribesmen. The sums that could be earned from sheltering the foreign militants was made clear when Baitullah Mehsud and other militants concluded a 'peace agreement' with the Pakistani authorities, again after inflicting heavy casualties on the Pakistani army, in 2004. Mehsud and others were paid hundreds of thousands of dollars to compensate them for the money they would have received from al-Qaeda. International Crisis Group, *Appeasing the Militants*, December 11, 2006, p. 17. The rents paid by militants were as high as 60,000 Rs per month. (Though exchange rates in the period were variable and thus make an accurate conversion difficult, the sums work out at around $1,000/£500 in the summer of 2008.) As foreigners would not be allowed to take residences in the centre of villages, this rent was for relatively cheap properties on the margins of settlements. Author interview with Khalid Aziz, former secretary NWFP, November 2008. Further funds were sourced through kidnaps of government officials, extortion and, on one occasion in mid 2007, an entire unit of 280 paramilitary troops.

48. Fair and Jones, 'Pakistan's War Within', p. 172. In one survey of tribesmen in 2008, 80 per cent of respondents said that the local tribal *jirgas* frequently provided justice. Community Appraisal and Motivation Programme, Islamabad, *Understanding FATA: Attitudes towards Governance, Religion and Society in Pakistan's FATA*, xxvii, pp. 62–8.

49. In one day – June 25, 2008 – ten schools were burned in Swat. Gul, *The Most Dangerous Place*, p. 113. A total of twelve boys' and seventeen girls' schools had been burned down by the various TTP factions between January and May 2008, and dozens of teachers killed. Mohammed Amir Rana, 'The Taliban Consolidate Control in Pakistan's Tribal Regions', *CTC Sentinel*, June 2008, vol. 1, no. 7, p. 8. Author phone interview with Ibrahim Paracha, Kohat politician and cleric, February 2008.

50. On *sharia*, Community Appraisal and Motivation Programme, *Understanding FATA*, p. xvii. Author interview with Shafi Rullah Wazir, political agent,

Bajaur, November 2008. Mushtaq Yusufzai and Hasbanullah Khan, 'Salarzai Lashkar kills militant in Bajaur to avenge elders killings', *The News*, August 27, 2008.

51. On interpreters see Shuja Nawaz, 'The Pakistan Army and Its Role in FATA', *CTC Sentinel*, vol. 1, no. 1, January 2009, p. 20.

52. Gul, *The Most Dangerous Place*, p. 22.

53. Fair and Jones, 'Pakistan's War Within', p. 175.

54. The first occasion was in January 2006.

55. Jason Burke and Imtiaz Gul, 'The drone, the CIA and a botched attempt to kill bin Laden's deputy', *Observer*, January 15, 2006.

56. Testimony of Hicham Beyayo to Belgian police, statements on April 2, 2009, May 6, 2009, May 15, 2009, Brussels. Author collection.

57. Testimony of Walid Othmani to French interrogators, January 30, 2009, document M.20-2-9, p. 43. Author collection.

58. 'The dark pursuit of truth', *The Economist*, August 1, 2009.

59. Nigel Inkster, deputy director of MI6 to 2006, said he knew of no strong lead-up to his departure from the service. Author interview, December 2008. In June 2010, Leon Panetta, director of the CIA, said that there had been very little new information in recent years. Paul Cruickshank, 'New information emerges on post-9/11 hunt for bin Laden', CNN.com, September 13, 2010. Other British security officials admitted in 2009 that they still had no 'solid information' on a location since 2001. Also Rory McCarthy, 'The inside story of the hunt for Bin Laden', *Guardian*, August 23, 2003.

60. Author telephone interview with Bob Grenier, former CIA station chief Islamabad, 2009.

61. Author interview with Ron Nash, London, April 2009.

62. Keller said Pakistan had a poor reputation too as a workplace. Even Afghanistan was seen as a better posting. Author telephone interview, December 2008.

63. Author telephone interview, December 2008.

64. Bin Laden and al-Zawahiri had spent much less time in the FATA than often thought, having passed much of the 1980s in Peshawar and the late 1990s in Afghanistan itself.

65. New American Foundation / Terror Free Tomorrow, *Results of a New Nationwide Public Opinion Survey of Pakistan*, August 2007.

66. Interrogation testimony of Bryant Neal Vinas, March 10 and 11, 2009, New York, dossier of Hicham Beyayo. United States of America vs. Bryant Neal Vinas. Indictment, United States District Court, Eastern District of New York, November 14, 2008.

67. See Burke, 'Target Europe'. Author telephone interview with MI6 officials, September 2007.

68. Vinas testimony.

69. Othmani and Beyayo testimony.

70. USA vs. Abdur Rehman Hashim Syed, 'Criminal Complaint', Northern District of Illinois, 2009.

71. 'Sabine am Orde, un gamin de la Sarre perdu au Waziristan', *Die Tageszeitung*, republished *Le Courrier International*, May 20, 2010.

72. Othmani testimony.

73. Paul Cruickshank, 'Enlisting Terror: Al-Qaeda's Recruitment Challenges', in *Al-Qaeda's Senior Leadership*, Jane's Strategic Advisory Services, November 2009, p. 14.

74. Not all, however. Cüneyt Ciftci, a twenty-nine-year-old German of Turkish origin born near Munich in 1979, who on March 3, 2008 died in a huge explosion, having driven a delivery truck loaded with several tons of explosives up to barracks in Khost. The blast killed five, including two American soldiers and Ciftci himself.

75. Author interview with Western intelligence official, Kabul, August 2008. See also Ron Moreau and Sami Yusufzai, 'The Taliban in their own words', *Newsweek*, September 26, 2009.

76. Author interviews, MI6, London, April 2009.

77. Guido Steinberg, the German expert, has usefully emphasized how al-Yazid's opposition to the 9/11 attacks helped bolster his credibility among Taliban figures who saw the strikes not merely as counterproductive but as extremely destructive. See Guido Steinberg, Towards Collective Leadership: The Role of Egyptians in Al-Qaeda', in *Al-Qaeda's Senior Leadership*, p. 9.

78. Tariq, 'The Life of Baitullah Mahsood'.

79. Sanger, *The Inheritance*, p. 234.

80. Author interviews, Pakistani and American officials, Islamabad, November 2009.

81. Beyayo and Othmani testimony.

82. Vinas testimony. Author collection.

83. Dexter Filkins, 'Right at the edge', *New York Times*, September 5, 2008.

84. 'Bin Laden in Palestinian call', BBC News Online, March 21, 2008.

85. Jarret Brachman, 'The Next Osama', *Foreign Policy*, September 10, 2009. Jarret Brachman, 'Retaining Relevance: Assessing Al-Qaeda's Generational Evolution', in *Al-Qaeda's Senior Leadership*. Jarret Brachman, 'Abu Yahya's Six Easy Steps for Defeating al-Qaeda', *Perspectives on Terrorism*, vol. 1, no. 5 (December 2007). Michael Scheuer, 'Abu Yahya al-Libi: Al-Qaeda's Theological Enforcer – Part 1', *Terrorism Monitor*, vol. 4, no. 25 (July 31, 2007).

86. 'Al-Qaeda deputy pens book justifying armed struggle', Associated Press, March 3, 2008.

87. Some estimates were higher, up to 300,000. Zahed Hussein, 'The turning point', *Newsline*, October 2008.

88. Account based on author's reporting, December 2008.

89. The attacks included two against the ISI, two against the army headquarters

in Rawalpindi, one aimed at the air force in Sargodha and one directed at the base of the Pakistani special forces. This total does not include almost 500 security forces and civilians killed in armed clashes. Total Pakistani casualties in 2007, including the number of injured security forces and civilians, exceeded the cumulative total of all the years between 2001 and 2006 and overall the year was to see more than 2,000 terrorist, insurgent and sectarian attacks. Hassan Abbas, 'A Profile of Tehrik-i-Taliban Pakistan', *CTC Sentinel*, vol. 1, no. 2 (January 2008). Hearing of the United States Senate select committee on intelligence, Annual worldwide threat assessment, February 5, 2008, Michael McConnell, director of national intelligence, witness testimony. Pakistan Institute for Peace Studies, *Pakistan Security Report, 2008*, 2009, p. 3.

90. According to Rehman Malik, Pakistan's interior minister, the country's civilian leadership had been scheduled to dine at the hotel but had changed location at the last minute. 'Pakistan leaders' "narrow escape"', BBC news, September 22, 2008.

91. 'They are savages, beasts,' Makhdoom Shahabuddin, the planning minister, told the author after one viewing.

92. Including more than sixty men killed.

93. Author interview, Bajaur, Peshawar, November 2008.

94. Author interview with Colonel Nauman Saeed, Bajaur, November 2008.

95. Author interview, Islamabad, November 2008.

96. National Investigation Agency, Interrogation report of David Headley, June 2010, pp. 7, 9. Author collection.

97. Private soldiers and NCOs for Pakistan's army have long been recruited from rural villages, often through family connections to existing servicemen or a traditional relationship between a particular community and a given unit. This tradition has continued, though efforts to bring down the high proportion recruited from the northern Punjab have led to an increase in numbers from other provinces, largely unchanged for sixty years.

98. Shuja Nawaz, *Crossed Swords*, Oxford University Press, 2008, p. 571. See also Ayesha Siddiqa,, *Military Inc.*, Oxford University Press, Pakistan, 2007, pp. 213–16; Malik, *Pakistan*, p. 118.

99. Nawaz, *Crossed Swords*, p. 572.

100. See C. Christine Fair and Shuja Nawaz, 'The Changing Pakistan Army Officer Corps', *Journal of Strategic Studies*, forthcoming, pp. 26–7. Overall in 1998, 28 per cent of the Pakistani population was urban.

101. Nawaz, *Crossed Swords*, p. 571. Repeated bouts of military rule in which officers serve in government offices as managers and administrators has brought thousands of middle- and senior-ranking servicemen into prolonged contact with the workings and worldview of the Pakistan's bureaucracy, which is itself perhaps the single most important factor in moderate political Islamism in the country. Musharraf inducted at least 3,500 officers into bur-

eaucratic posts, for example. Siddiqa, *Military Inc.*, p. 211. A further factor was that, though the historic dominance of the officer corps by the Punjab had been mitigated slightly by efforts to increase the representation of other ethnicities within the forces, in 2005, 60 per cent still came from Pakistan's biggest, richest, best-educated – and most Islamist – province. Interestingly, the proportion of officers from the NWFP had increased from 10 per cent in 1971 to 22 per cent in 2005.

102. Statement of Mohammed Ajmal Amir Qasab, November 2008, author collection.

103. Ibid. Pranab Dhal Samantha, 'GPS records, CD transcript boost India's case', *The Indian Express*, July 6, 2010. Jason Burke, 'Mumbai: behind the attacks lies a story of youth twisted by hate', *Observer*, November 30, 2008. For name confusion see Prabeen Swami, 'Terrorist's name lost in transliteration', *The Hindu*, December 6, 2008. Kasab is the name of the gunman's caste, mispelt by Indian policemen who needed a surname for their paperwork.

104. Its spokesmen had been happy to meet the author in a five-star Lahore hotel in March 2008.

105. Possibly initially as an informer for the Drugs Enforcement Agency. Headley had been convicted of heroin smuggling in 1998 and cooperated to reduce his sentence.

106. National Investigation Agency, Government of India, Interrogation Report of David Headley, June 2010, p. 89. Author collection.

107. When in America, a US-based LeT member had assisted Headley and, days after returning to Pakistan after completing his first surveillance mission, Headley met with senior LeT associates and discussed potential targets in India.

108. Interrogation Report of David Headley, pp. 1–5, 39, 44, 63, 66–9, 79, 84. See indictments: USA vs. Abdur Rehman Hashim Syed, 'Criminal Complaint', Northern District of Illinois, 2009; USA vs. David Headley, 'Criminal Complaint', Northern District of Illinois, 2009. Author collection.

109. What was clear, however, was the confluence in thinking and worldview between men like 'Major Iqbal' and his immediate superiors and people like Headley, Zaki ur Rehman Lakhvi and others. When Headley reported to his handler that the Jewish Nariman House had been added to the target list, 'Major Iqbal' was very pleased. This did not mean that he was a violent extremist, simply that he shared the anti-Semitic and anti-Zionist worldview of the LeT militants and all those many millions across the Islamic world who saw attacks on Israeli, and by extension Jewish, targets as entirely justified.

110. 'Suicide bomber hits foreign forces in Afghanistan', Reuters, December 26, 2008. The British Ministry of Defence announced eight soldiers killed in Helmand in the first two weeks of December alone. Michael Evans and

Alexi Mostrous, 'Three Royal Marines killed in Afghanistan by boy with wheelbarrow bomb', *The Times*, December 13, 2008.

111. Dexter Filkins, 'Afghan civilian deaths rose 40 percent in 2008', *New York Times*, February 17, 2009. United Nations Assistance Mission in Afghanistan figures, obtained March 2009, Kabul. Ismail Sameem, 'Taliban kill 20 police in Afghanistan', Reuters, January 1, 2009.

112. Riaz Khan, 'Militants seize convoy for US-led forces', Associated Press, November 11, 2008. Rahimullah Yusufzai, 'No to Nato', *Newsline*, December 2008. For Caravan reference, see Tariq, 'The Life of Baitullah Mahsood'.

113. Author interview with a senior French diplomat, Paris, February 2009.

CHAPTER 15: THE 9/11 WARS: EUROPE, THE MIDDLE EAST, IRAQ

1. 'Let the American people prepare to continue to reap what has been planted by the heads of the White House in the coming years and decades,' bin Laden said. 'Double blast against Obama shows strain on Qaeda', Reuters, June 3, 2009.

2. Full text of Obama victory speech, BBC, November 5, 2008.

3. Those with a favourable view of the US in Jordan rose from 19 per cent to 25 per cent and in Egypt from 22 per cent to 27 per cent. Pew Research Center, *Pew Global Attitudes Survey: Confidence in Obama Lifts U.S. Image Around the World*, July 23, 2009.' Pew Research Center, *Pew Global Attitudes Survey: Muslim Disappointment: Obama More Popular Abroad than at Home, Global Image of US Continues to Benefit*, June 17, 2010. The new American president was popular in Indonesia, where he spent several years as a child, where 71 per cent of Indonesians voiced confidence in him, and among Nigerian Muslims (81 per cent), Israeli Arabs (69 per cent) and Lebanese Sunnis (65 per cent).

4. The favourability rating of the US in the spring of 2009 in Turkey was 14 per cent, lower than shortly before the Iraq war of 2003. In Pakistan those expressing a favourable view of the US actually dropped from 19 per cent before Obama's election to 16 per cent afterwards. Pew Research Center, *Confidence in Obama*, p. 5. There many, predictably and depressingly, suspected a conspiracy. One senior journalist, looking out on the crowded streets from the window of the newsroom of the country's biggest satellite TV news channel on the day of Obama's victory, told the author that he could not believe that 'a black' could make it to such a powerful position in America without the help of the Jews or the CIA. 'Blacks just aren't intelligent enough. And Americans are too racist,' he explained.

5. The request was as ever coupled with a reassurance that the security of Israel was paramount. Obama's ratings were particularly high among Israeli Arabs (69 per cent), according to one poll. Pew Global Attitudes Project, *Little Enthusiasm for Many Muslim Leaders*, February 4, 2010.

6. Holbrooke refused the title 'envoy' on the basis that it meant 'you're sent to do things'. George Packer, 'The Last Mission', *New Yorker*, September 28, 2009.

7. Obama had said in June 2007: 'To build a better, freer world, we must first behave in ways that reflect the decency and aspirations of the American people. This means ending the practices of shipping away prisoners in the dead of night to be tortured in far-off countries, of detaining thousands without charge or trial, of maintaining a network of secret prisons to jail people beyond the reach of the law.' Barack Obama, 'Renewing American Leadership', *Foreign Affairs*, July–August 2007.

8. He had signalled his more pragmatic approach, different both from the Clinton administration's belief in the inevitable benefits of globalization and the more ideological approach of Bush, in the repeated Congressional hearings on Iraq over the previous fifteen months. David Miliband, 'Stay with Obama on Muslims', *International Herald Tribune*, November 6, 2010.

9. Remarks by the President, June 4, 2009, The White House. 'A New Beginning', Cairo University.

10. News conference by President Obama, Palais de la Musique et des Congrès, Strasbourg, France, April 4, 2009.

11. Michael Scherer, 'The five pillars of Obama's foreign policy', *Time*, July 13, 2009.

12. Jason Burke, 'We must never forget the lessons learned from D-Day, says Obama', *Observer*, June 7, 2009.

13. CNN, interview with Anderson Cooper, February 3, 2010. Cited in Bergen, *The Longest War*, Simon and Schuster, 2011, p. 303.

14. Garsallaoui, who had accompanied those arrested to Pakistan, had left them soon after their arrival there and had subsequently remained in the FATA. His wife, who had posted a picture of her husband firing a rocket-propelled grenade on her website, was also detained. Consultation du dossier de Mr Hicham Beyayo, Testimony of Walid Othmani to French interrogators, January 30, 2009; both author collection. Author interviews, Christophe Marchand, lawyer for Hicham Beyayo, Alain Grignard, head of Belgian counter-terrorism police, Brussels, February 2009. Gilbert Dupont, 'Les Six du réseau kamikaze', *La Dernière Heure*, December 13, 2008. Belgium had seen other plots over previous years. The two men who had killed Ahmed Shah Massood forty-eight hours before the 9/11 attacks had come from Belgium, passing through London to collect the credentials which ensured their access to the Northern Alliance leader. There had been the female suicide bomber – one of the first of the 9/11 Wars – who with her Moroccan-born husband had driven to Iraq in their family car.

15. French nationals Bassam Ayachi and Raphael Gendron were remanded in custody and charged with terrorism offences after Italian authorities established their ties to an extremist network operating in France and Belgium. Bruce Crumley, 'Europe pieces together terrorism puzzle', *Time*, May 12, 2009.

16. Europol, *TE-SAT 2009 – EU Terrorism Situation and Trend Report*, April 2009. The British government's published counter-terrorist policy argued that al-Qaeda as an organization had fragmented, leading to a greater role for self-starting groups.

17. Cécilia Gabizon, 'A Vénissieux, terre d'expansion de la burqa', *Le Figaro*, July 1, 2009.

18. Hicham Beyayo, the supposed suicide bomber, had grown up on the Place Alphonse Lemmens in Anderlecht with seven siblings and Moroccan parents who had arrived in Belgium in 1966. Beyayo and two of his brothers had a history of involvement in theft, handling stolen goods and assault.

19. Ben Leapman, '4,000 in UK trained at terror camps', *Sunday Telegraph*, April 19, 2008. Home Office Statistical Bulletin, quarterly update to December 2009, June 2010, p. 5.

20. Alan Travis, 'Two-thirds of UK terror suspects released without charge', *Guardian*, May 13, 2009.

21. One good indication of when the conventional threat was considered to be less worrying was a renewed emphasis on unconventional attacks involving radioactive 'dirty' bombs, makeshift chemical weapons or similar. Briefings of journalists by politicians and security officials about the terrorist threat to the UK in early 2009 frequently stressed the potential consequences of such an attack.

22. Four British men in their early twenties, known as the Nairobi Four, were arrested in Kenya in January 2007, after allegedly fighting in the Somali civil war, and an unnamed twenty-one-year-old university student from Ealing, west London, was reported to have blown himself up at a checkpoint in Somalia in February 2009.

23. Author interview, London, August 2009.

24. Alan Travis, 'Britain downgrades al-Qaida terror attack alert level', *Guardian*, July 20, 2009.

25. Europol, *TE-Sat 2010 – EU Terrorism Situation and Trend Report*, 2010, p. 12; Europol, *EU Terrorism Situation and Trend Report*, 2009, p. 17.

26. Thomas Renard, 'Europol Report Describes Afghanistan-Pakistan Connection to Trends in European Terrorism', *Terrorism Monitor*, vol. 7, no. 12, May 8, 2009.

27. Grignard, author interview, Brussels, March 2009.

28. National Coordinator for Counterterrorism, *National Terrorist Threat Assessment No. 8*, April 25, 2007, p. 3.

29. The Netherlands National Coordinator for Counterterrorism, *Sixth Progress Report on Counterterrorism*, The Hague, June 4, 2007. The Netherlands National Coordinator for Counterterrorism, 'Threat level for the Netherlands once again to "substantial"', press release, March 6, 2008, The Netherlands National Coordinator for Counterterrorism 'The level of the terrorist threat against the Netherlands has been lowered', press release, December 15, 2009.

30. Author interview, Dr Alain Bauer, Paris, July 2009.

31. Author interview, Paris, July 2009.

32. Institute for Strategic Dialogue (Jytte Klausen), *Al Qaeda-Affiliated and 'Homegrown' Jihadism in the UK: 1999–2010*, September 2010, p. 8.

33. Author interviews, Berlin, September, 2009.

34. Author interview with Gilles de Kerchove, counter-terrorism coordinator for the European Union, Brussels, September 2008. Jason Burke, 'Don't be soft on Islam, says EU terror chief', *Observer*, September 28, 2008.

35. Author interview, NYPD representative in Paris, Paris, September 2006, September 2008.

36. Operation Cast Lead sparked both outrage and a spate of anti-Semitic attacks. Overall around 270 cases of anti-Jewish racist violence were reported in the UK in 2009, according to figures compiled by the Community Security Trust (CST), the body that monitors anti-Jewish racism, with most blamed on anti-Israeli sentiment in reaction to hostilities in Gaza. Attacks recorded during the first Palestinian Intifida of the late 1980s averaged sixteen a month. Mark Townsend, 'Rise in anti-Semitic attacks "the worst recorded in Britain in decades"', *Observer*, February 8, 2010. Altogether, there were 113 anti-Semitic incidents in France during the month following the December 27 launching of Operation Cast Lead against Hamas in Gaza, including twenty-two attacks against private individuals and five attempts to burn down synagogues. Bernard Edinger, 'Tense ties in France', *The Jerusalem Report*, March 2, 2009, Paris. In the June elections to the European Parliament, Geert Wilders' Dutch Party for Freedom in the Netherlands won 17 per cent of the national vote. The anti-immigrant British National Party, which warned of the 'creeping Islamification' of British society, won its first two seats. In Austria the right-wing Freedom Party almost doubled its share of the vote, at 13 per cent. 'The first Islamic invasion of Europe was stopped at [the battle of] Poitiers in 732. The second was halted at the gates of Vienna in 1683. Now we have to stop the current stealth invasion,' argued Wilders.

37. Replacement level was reached in Iran, Lebanon, Tunisia, and Turkey. While the average age at first marriage for women was between eighteen and twenty-one in most countries in the region in the 1970s, it was between twenty-two and twenty-five by the late 1990s. North African countries saw an especially steep increase in marriage age. In Libya, the average rose from age nineteen to age twenty-nine between the mid 1970 and late 1990s. The average marriage was above age twenty-five in all the north African countries except for Egypt, where it was just twenty-two in 1998. Farzaneh Roudi-Fahimi and Mary Mederios Kent, 'Challenges and Opportunities – The Population of the Middle East and North Africa', *Population Bulletin*, vol. 62, no. 2, 2007.

38. Pernin et al., *Unfolding the Future of the Long War*, p. 213.

39. Author interview with Carl Haub, senior demographer, Population Reference Bureau, Washington, July 2009.

40. William Underhill, 'Why fears of a Muslim takeover are all wrong', *Newsweek*, July 10, 2009. Eric Kaufmann, 'Europe's Return to the Faith', *Prospect*, 2010, p. 57.

41. Another study predicted the nominally Muslim population in countries such as Switzerland and Austria – which already had very substantial Muslim populations – might reach between 9 and 15 per cent by 2030 and between 10 and 20 per cent by 2050. Ibid., p.58.

42. Olivier Schmitt, 'Sécurité en Europe, la France compte parmi les pays les plus durs', *Le Monde*, August 19, 2010. President Nicolas Sarkozy of France was a particularly good example of a mainstream politician whose language, particularly during the presidential campaign of 2007, had veered close to that of the extreme right. In one rally in Metz, the author heard Sarkozy speak of how the France he dreamed of was one 'where no sheep were slaughtered in a bathtub', a common accusation against the French Muslim Arab or Berber immigrant community. A telephone survey of twenty mayors in areas with major immigrant populations conducted by the author revealed that no such incident had occurred for a decade at least.

43. 'Few fear terrorist attack in the Netherlands', Press release, November 26, 2009, National Coordinator for Counterterrorism, The Netherlands.

44. Justin Davenport, 'Muslim chef sues "insensitive" Met over pork sausages', *Evening Standard*, May 11, 2009.

45. *The Gallup Coexist Index 2009: A Global Study of Interfaith Relations*, May 2009. Author telephone interview with Magali Rheault, Gallup researcher, July 2009. One depressing example of this was the prevalence of conspiracy theories. If significant numbers of French Muslims doubted the official accounts of 9/11, so did 11 per cent of their non-Muslim compatriots. NOP found that 36 per cent of British Muslims thought that Princess Diana was murdered in 1997 to stop her marrying a Muslim and 17 per cent thought the Holocaust was 'exaggerated' (the view of most Holocaust deniers). An ICM poll published in the UK's *Jewish Chronicle* in 2004 found that 14 per ccent of people in the UK more generally thought that the scale of the Holocaust had been exaggerated and 27 per cent of the general public told NOP in 2003 that Princess Diana had been murdered. 'Six years after her death, a quarter of Britons say Diana was murdered: poll', AFP, August 31, 2003.

46. See, for example, 'Ramadan: jeûne pour 70% de Musulmans', AFP, August 20, 2009, citing IFOP poll of 1,300 interviewees. Cécilia Gabizon, 'Les Contrastes de l'intégration à la française', *Le Figaro*, October 15, 2009.

47. In Germany, for example, the number of women who *always* wore a headscarf dropped; the proportion of those who *sometimes* wore a headscarf rose among second-generation immigrants. Survey: Muslim life in Germany, Federal Minister of the Interior, June 2009, pp. 6–7.

48. 'More Dutch Muslims are skipping the mosque', *NRC Handelsblad*, July 29, 2009. Annual Report on Integration, Netherlands Government Bureau of

Statistics, press release, 16 December 2008. Author interview with Professor Jan Latten, director Netherlands Government Bureau of Statistics, January 2009. Jason Burke, 'Holland's first immigrant mayor is hailed as "Obama on the Maas"', *Observer*, January 11, 2009.

49. Cécilia Gabizon, 'Le ramadan séduit de plus en plus les jeunes', *Le Figaro*, August 21, 2009.

50. Malik, *From Fatwa to Jihad*, pp. 12–13

51. Cecile Calla, 'Les Musulmans d'Allemagne seraient assez bien integrés', *Le Monde*, June 27, 2009.

52. Author interviews, Paris, August 2009.

53. The Arabic terms the Maghreb and the Mashriq have been in use since the seventh or eighth century CE and broadly indicate 'the region west', i.e. the north African coast, and 'the region east', i.e. the land west of modern Iran and south of present-day Turkey including, by some definitions, the Arabian peninsula. Theoretically Egypt is part of the Mashriq, as is, according to the *Encyclopedia Britannica*, the Sudan. In reality Egypt floats between the two. The use of both terms here is, in part, meant to underline quite how Eurocentric the Western term 'the Middle East' is.

54. Pew Global Attitudes Project, *Declining Support for bin Laden and Suicide Bombing*, September 10, 2009.

55. An invitation had been extended to successive Algerian groups but rejected systematically since the early 1990s.

56. The failure of the GSPC, as previously mentioned, had been widely noted as an object lesson in how not to execute a jihad by radical Islamic strategists such as al-Suri and Abu Bakr Naji. For more on the latter, see Jarret Brachman and William McCants, 'Stealing al'Qaida's Playbook', *Studies in Conflicts and Terrorism*, May 2006. Also, Devin Springer, James Regens and David Edger, *Islamic Radicalism and Global Jihad*, Georgetown University Press, 2008, pp. 23–5, 46–7, 49, 173. For more on Algerian militancy see Burke, *Al-Qaeda*; Kepel, *Jihad*; John Philips and Martin Evans, *Algeria: Anger of the Dispossessed*, Yale University Press, 2008. See also Jean-Pierre Filiu, 'The Local and Global Jihad of al-Qa'ida in the Islamic Maghrib', *Middle East Journal*, vol. 63, no. 2, spring 2009. One of the most notable figures to accept amnesty was Hassan Khattab, the former chief and one of the founders of the GSPC. 'Hassan Hattab, un ex-chef sanguinaire dans la peau d'un "réconciliateur"', *El Watan*, February 11, 2009.

57. Tawil, *Brothers in Arms*, p. 203. Tawil, a London-based correspondent for *al-Hayat*, is probably the best reporter and analyst working on Islamic militancy in the Maghreb. He interviewed al-Birr in Algeria in March 2009.

58. See Jean-Pierre Filiu, 'Al'Qa'ida in the Islamic Maghreb', *CTC Sentinel*, vol. 3, no. 4, April 2010, p. 14.

59. Tawil, *The Other Face of al-Qaeda*, pp. 42–3.

60. The first militant also complained about 'setting up fake checkpoints to rob

Muslims of their money and abducting and terrorizing innocents in order to receive money', Springer et al., *Islamic Radicalism*, pp. 177–8.

61. AQIM appealed direct to Algeria's Berbers, 'our brothers, the free kabylie, the descendants of Tariq bin Ziyadh ... to stand against "the traitorous rulers"'. Andrew Black, 'Al-Qaida Operations in Kabylie Mountains Alienating Algeria's Berbers', *Jamestown Terrorism Focus*, vol. 5, no. 16, April 23, 2008.

62. 'Cinq gardes communaux sauvagement assassinés', *Liberté*, June 23, 2009.

63. Author interview, London, June 2009.

64. A largely independent semi-criminal faction was based in the far desert south.

65. The secretary of state had even, despite the ongoing close cooperation between the notoriously brutal Egyptian intelligence services and their American counter-terrorist counterparts, singled out Egypt for criticism over human rights abuses. In response to the criticism, Mubarak made a number of small cosmetic changes then proceeded to make sure he won 87 per cent of votes cast at the 2005 presidential elections. The new pragmatism forced on the Bush administration in Iraq was rapidly communicated to the White House's general approach to the region. By 2007 and 2008, there was little pressure for serious reform. What did remain of the 'Freedom Agenda' by the time Obama took power in Washington was, however, the liberalizing economic element. This had seen taxes cut, tariffs removed and foreign direct investment courted. Egypt was dubbed with the slightly unlikely title of 'world's top reformer' in 2007 by the World Bank, then under Paul Wolfowitz, the long-standing advocate of democratization, neoliberal economics, the invasion of Iraq and the man who as deputy defense secretary had been one of those most blamed for the failures that had followed the 'liberation' of 2003. The Egyptian economy had started growing rapidly towards the end of the decade. After averaging about 4 per cent through the 1990s, economic growth reached 8 per cent in 2007. John R. Bradley, *Inside Egypt*, Palgrave Macmillan, 2008, p. 167. Isobel Coleman, 'Egypt's Uphill Economic Struggles', The Council on Foreign Relations, February 2011.

66. Bradley, *Inside Egypt*, p. 40.

67. Michael Slackman, 'Stifled, Egypt's young turn to Islamic fervor', *New York Times*, February 17, 2008. 'Saving faith: Islam seems to be fading as a revolutionary force', *The Economist* Special report on Egypt, July 17, 2010, p. 14.

68. At legislatives of December 2005 the Muslim Brotherhood had won 88 seats, or 20 per cent, becoming the most successful opposition bloc despite well-documented fraud and heavy-handed security interference.

69. Pew Research Center, *Declining Support for bin Laden and Suicide Bombing*, September 10, 2009.

70. For a detailed account of post-9/11 militancy in Egypt see Tawil, *The Other Face of al-Qaeda*, pp. 32–6. Author telephone interview with Noman Benotman, March 2011.

71. Author interview, Rabat, March 2007.

72. Author interview, Saleh, March 2007.

73. Roula Khalaf, 'Forgotten flowering', *Financial Times*, December 11, 2008.

74. The most common hometowns listed in the Sinjar Records for overseas volunteers arriving to fight in Iraq were Mecca, Saudi Arabia (43), Benghazi, Libya (21), and Casablanca, Morocco (17). Other Libyan coastal towns also supplied a disproportionately high number of volunteers, especially Darnah, a working-class town of 80,000, from where an astonishing 53 fighters listed in the Sinjar records came. CTC (Brian Fishman) *Bombers, Bank Accounts and Bleed Outs: Al'Qaeda's Road in and out of Iraq*, 2008, pp. 38–9. Both Darnah and Benghazi have long been associated with Islamic militancy in Libya, known in particular for a brutally suppressed uprising in the mid 1990s.

75. Alison Pargeter, 'LIFG Revisions Unlikely to Reduce Jihadist violence', *CTC Sentinel*, October 2009, vol. 2, no. 10. Paul Cruickshank, 'LIFG Revisions Posing Critical Challenge to al'Qaida', *CTC Sentinel*, December 2009, vol. 2, no. 12. Tawil, *Brothers in Arms*, pp. 196-7. Author interview with Noman Benotman, London, 2008.

76. Jason Burke, 'Westerners flocking to dig into Gaddafi's deep pockets', *Observer*, September 2, 2007. Gaddafi had publicly admitted a chemical and nuclear weapons programme six days after Saddam Hussein's capture in 2003.

77. See Nir Rosen, *Aftermath: Following the Bloodshed of America's Wars in the Muslim World*, Nation Books, June 2009, for a fuller account. Bilal y Saab and Magnus Ranstorp, 'Securing Lebanon from the Threat of Salafist Jihadism', *Studies in Conflict and Terrorism*, vol. 30, no.10, 2007. Bilal y Saab, 'The Failure of Salafi-Jihadi Insurgent Movements in the Levant', *CTC Sentinel*, September 2009, vol. 2, no. 9, p. 15.

78. In Jordan another counter-attack against al-Qaeda's theological arguments was launched by a senior cleric and former stalwart of armed international Islamic extremism called Abu Mohammad al-Maqdisi. See Murad Batal al-Shishani, 'Jihad Ideologue Abu Mohammad al-Maqdisi Challenges Jordan's Neo-Zarqawists', *Terrorism Monitor*, vol. 7, no. 20, July 9, 2009. Michael Slackman, 'Generation faithful: Jordanian students rebel, embracing Conservative Islam', *New York Times*, December 24, 2008; Lina Sinjab, 'Syrian Islamic revival has woman's touch', BBC News, November 28, 2009.

79. Pew Research Center, *Confidence in Obama*, pp. 83–6.

80. For a good overview see Benedetta Berti, 'Salafi-Jihadi Activism in Gaza: Mapping the Threat', *CTC Sentinel*, May 2010, vol. 3, no. 5, pp. 5–7.

81. Nidal al-Mughrabi, 'Pro-Qaeda group declares "Islamic emirate" in Gaza', Reuters, August 14, 2009. See also on Beverly Milton-Edwards and Stephen Farrell, *Hamas*, Polity Press, 2010. These clashes contributed to the growing sense that the ideological battle between the inheritors of various strands of conservative, revivalist Islamic thought that had preceded the 9/11 Wars by many decades – indeed in some significant ways had provoked the conflict –

was resurfacing. See Jean-Pierre Filiu, 'The Brotherhood vs. Al-Qaeda: A Moment of Truth?', Hudson Institute, 2009, for a useful discussion.

82. Michael Knights, 'The Current State of al'Qaida in Saudi Arabia', CTC *Sentinel*, September 2008, vol. 1, no. 10, p. 7.

83. Ibid.

84. Kenneth Ballen, 'Bin Laden's soft support', *Washington Monthly*, May 2008.

85. Hegghammer, *Jihad in Saudi Arabia*, pp. 19–20, 49.

86. Magdi Abdlehadi, 'Saudis to retrain 40,000 clerics', BBC, March 20, 2008.

87. On textbooks see *Update: Saudi Arabia's Curriculum of Intolerance*, Hudson Institute Center for Religious Freedom, 2008.

88. 'Reform in Saudi Arabia: At a snail's pace', *The Economist*, October 2, 2010.

89. Two Guantanamo returnees who had been through the deradicalization programme but had nonetheless resumed violent activism surfaced in the Yemen in January 2009.

90. Author interview, March 2009.

91. Ibid. The exact number at the time was 4,238 American servicemen killed.

92. The militia is estimated to have lost up to a 1,000 fighters in the battles.

93. Sabrina Tavernise, 'A Shiite militia in Baghdad sees its power wane', *New York Times*, July 27, 2008.

94. Interview, November 2010.

95. Author telephone interview, August 2008.

96. Afif Sarhan and Jason Burke, 'How Islamist gangs use internet to track, torture and kill Iraqi gays', *Observer*, September 13, 2009.

97. Martin Chulov, 'They turned the tide for America. Now, as withdrawal nears, sons of Iraq pay the price', *Guardian*, May 14, 2010.

98. Compared to 1,287 regular police. Iraq Body Count, 'Post-Surge violence, its extent and nature', December 28, 2008. http://www.iraqbodycount.org/analysis/numbers/surge-2008/.

99. Rosen, *Aftermath*, p. 542.

100. Interview, Baghdad, November 2010.

101. 'At least 27 die in Iraq as bombs, shootings shatter lull', AFP, February 11, 2009.

102. AQIP had theoretically ceased to exist in 2006. The very declaration of the ISI had angered many of the more nationalist fighters, who carried out the vast proportion of attacks on government and American forces, presuming as it did overall command of 'resistance efforts' and the right to decide the future of the country. See Mohammed M. Hafez, 'Al-Qa'ida Losing Ground in Iraq', *CTC Sentinel*, December 2007, vol. 1, no. 1, p. 7.

103. A significant predictor of involvement in radical 'jihadi' militancy in Iraq in 2009, according to network analysis carried out by American intelligence specialists, was the previous or current involvement of a family member. Many of the female suicide bombers were widows of dead militants. A dozen bombers came from a single village in Diyala province, one of the few

remaining strongholds of the extremists. See Martin Chulov, 'Innocent grandmother – or suicide bombing mastermind?', *Guardian*, June 11, 2009. Another predictor was a recent jail sentence. With the state's prison system now in Iraqi hands, many of the hardened al-Qaeda militant leaders held by the Americans had been released, often quickly returning to violence, recruiting family members and friends to fight alongside them.

104. Nineveh was heavily affected by Saddam's Arabization strategy, which had seen hundreds of thousands of local Kurds driven from their homes, which were then given to Arabs from the south, particularly military families loyal to Saddam. These latter clearly stood to lose much if sufficient calm returned for either the Kurds to make claims to land beyond the current limits of the three provinces they controlled or the central Baghdad government to decide to implement laws that called for measures to reverse Arabization.

105. In Anbar a few years earlier the attempts by radical Islamists from outside the province or indeed the country to seize control of lucrative local trafficking networks had been one of the key drivers behind the turning of the local sheikhs towards the Americans. Andrea Plebani, 'Ninawa Province: Al'Qaida's Remaining Stronghold', *CTC Sentinel*, vol. 1, no. 1, January 2010, p. 20.

106. Ibid., p. 21.

107. In Najaf and Karbala the ISCI score was 14.8 per cent and 6.4 per cent, down from 45 per cent and 35 per cent in 2005. See Joost Hilterman, 'Iraq on the edge', *New York Review of Books*, November 19, 2009, for a useful analysis.

108. Afif Sarham, 'Hitmen charge $100 a victim as Basra honour killings rise', *Observer*, November 30, 2008.

109. Baghdad received power only for twelve to fourteen hours. NYT, Op-Chart, June 18, 2009. 'Iraq: key figures since the war began', Associated Press, January 2, 2009. Oxfam International, *In Her Own Words: Iraqi Women Talk about Their Greatest Challenges*, March 2009, p. 5.

110. In comparison with pre-war Iraq this was an improvement. Before the war, 12.9 million people had potable water and 6.2 million had sanitation. On October 2, 2008, 20.9 million people had potable water and 11.3 million people had sanitation. 'Iraq: key figures since the war began', Associated Press. Martin Chulov, 'Iraq withdrawal: Amid heat and broken promises, only the ice man cometh', *Guardian*, August 30, 2010.

111. Oxfam International, *In Her Own Words*, p. 10.

112. As ever, compared to what had gone before there was improvement. But though many lauded the fact that 'only' twenty-five civilians a day were dying on average through 2008 in Iraq, fewer pointed out that the rate had been roughly equivalent to that of the first twenty months of post-invasion Iraq from May 2003 to December 2004. Iraq Body Count, 'Post-Surge violence: its extent and nature', December 28, 2008. http://www.iraqbodycount.org/analysis/numbers/surge-2008/.

113. Ibid.
114. In all in 2009 there were 706 explosions causing 2,972 deaths. Iraq Body Count, 'Civilian deaths from violence in 2009', December 31, 2009. http://www.iraqbodycount.org/analysis/numbers/2009/.
115. Interview, Baghdad, November 2010.

CHAPTER 16: 'AFPAK' 2009–10

1. This passage is based on the author's reporting during a week spent with the 10th Mountain Division in March 2009.
2. Author interview with David McKiernan, Kabul, March 2009. Author interviews and briefings with senior NATO-ISAF officers, Kabul, March 2009.
3. Participation levels were however much lower than in 2005, and there was still considerable violence even if it did not reach the intensity some had feared.
4. The bulk of which occurred in the insecure southern Pashtun heartlands. Abdullah Abdullah, though of mixed Tajik and Pashtun background, broadly represented the northern, Panjshiri, Dari-speaking and urban constituency. Karzai had rallied an unsavoury array of backers comprising many of Afghanistan's most notorious warlords and powerbrokers but even with their support appears to have been unsure of outright victory. Whether or not the president himself was aware of the fraud is unclear.
5. For a useful account of the review process see Bergen, *The Longest War*, pp. 539–45.
6. Author interview, Kabul, March 2009.
7. Author interview, Logar, Afghanistan, March 2009.
8. 'Poll: More view Afghan war as mistake', *USA Today*, March 16, 2009. Jennifer Agiesta and Jon Cohen, 'Public opinion in U.S. turns against Afghan war', *Washington Post*, August 20, 2009. Paul Steinhauser, 'Poll: Support for Afghan war at all-time low', CNN, September 15, 2009.
9. George Packer, 'The last mission', *New Yorker*, September 28, 2009.
10. Steve Luxenberg, 'Bob Woodward book details Obama battles with advisers over exit plan for Afghan war', *Washington Post*, September 22, 2010.
11. The Dutch were to be out by the summer of 2010 and the Canadians by 2011, for example.
12. Author interview with Admiral de Tarly, Paris, October 2008.
13. 'In U.S., more support for increasing troops in Afghanistan', Gallup, November 25, 2009. The Ministry of Defence released footage of the young man, third in line to the throne, blasting away at insurgents – 'Terry Taliban' – on a heavy machine gun. Author interview with senior Whitehall official, London, February 2009.
14. A major political row in Helmand in 2007 saw the expulsion from Kabul of two foreign envoys, an Irish EU official, Michael Semple, and another Irishman, for 'illicit meetings with the Taliban'. Author telephone interview, Michael

Semple, October 2008. On assessments of success of reintegration programmes see Michael Semple, *Endgames: Reconciliation in Afghanistan*, United States Institute of Peace, September 2009, p. 55, cited in Thomas Ruttig, *The Battle For Afghanistan*, New America Foundation, May 2011. Author interviews with NATO, Afghan officials, Kabul, August 2008, March 2009.

15. Jason Burke, 'Secret Taliban peace talks', *Observer*, September 28, 2008; author interviews with Muttawakel, Rahmani, Zaeef, Kabul, March, 2009. One reason was that perhaps the biggest contribution the Saudis could make was granting a respectable and safe asylum to senior figures who did decide to come in from the cold. None, however, appeared keen to take them up on the offer.

16. Author interviews, Kabul, March 2009.

17. Author interviews with Wood, Taliban spokesmen, senior US officers, Kabul and Logar, March 2009. *US Army Field Manual 3-24*, pp. 1–15.

18. Gates actually said: 'If we set ourselves the objective of creating some sort of central Asian Valhalla over there, we will lose, because nobody in the world has that kind of time, patience and money.' Ann Scott Tyson, 'Gates predicts "slog" in Afghanistan', *Washington Post*, January 28, 2009.

19. Author telephone interview with Andrew Exum, August 2009.

20. Author telephone interview with Bruce Riedel, August 2009.

21. As early as March 2009, Nick Williams, McKiernan's senior political adviser, had told the author that the Taliban's ability to fight through the previous winter had 'provoked . . . a major reassessment of what is feasible in Afghanistan'.

22. On casualties, 'British injury toll in Afghanistan revealed', Sky News, August 17, 2009 and UK Ministry of Defence website http://www.mod.uk/DefenceInternet/FactSheets/OperationsFactsheets/OperationsInAfghanistanBritishFatalities.htm.

23. From House of Commons International Development Committee report 2008, Paragraph 19. Author interviews, London, 2009.

24. Author interview with DFID official, August 2009.

25. Gordon Corera, 'UK backs Taliban reintegration', BBC News, November 13, 2009. Author interviews with British diplomats, Kabul, August 2008, March 2009.

26. Dave Graham, 'No Taliban "unconditional surrender" sought – Britain', Reuters, February 6, 2010.

27. John Hutton, Remembrance Day speech, November 11, 2008, published text.

28. Author interview by email with Taliban spokesman, October 2009.

29. Stenersen, *The Taliban Insurgency in Afghanistan*, p. 26.

30. The move indicated that the faction within the Taliban senior command which had opposed their use had won the argument. 'Code of Conduct, the Taliban', May 9, 2009, posted in Pashto on the Shahmat website on August 6, 2009.

31. See Hekmat Karzai, 'Suicide Terrorism: The Case of Afghanistan', *Security*

and Terrorism, March 2007, p. 36; and data for Centre for Conflict and Peace Studies (CAPS), Kabul. Author interviews with Hekmat Karzai, Paris, Kabul, 2009.

32. UNAMA, *Afghanistan Annual Report on Protection of Civilians in Armed Conflict, 2009*, December 31, 2009. pp. 7–8. Over 1,000 were killed directly by suicide attacks or IEDs.

33. Anthony H. Cordesman, 'The Afghan War: The Campaign in the Spring of 2010', Centre for Strategic and International Studies, May 24, 2010.

34. Author interview, MI6, Kabul, March 2009.

35. See Thomas Ruttig, *The Other Side: Dimensions of the Afghan Insurgency*, The Afghan Analysts Network, July 2009.

36. Taliban Leader Mullah Omar, 'In Celebration of Eid al-Adha', NEFA Foundation, November 25, 2009.

37. UNAMA, *Afghanistan Annual Report on Protection of Civilians in Armed Conflict, 2009*, pp. 12–13.

38. 'Afghan people "losing confidence"', BBC, February 9, 2009. The Afghan Centre for Social and Opinion Research in Kabul carried out the fieldwork, via face-to-face interviews with 1,534 Afghans in all of the country's thirty-four provinces between December 30, 2008 and January 12, 2009. The poll was commissioned by the BBC, ABC News of America and ARD of Germany. 'Afghans more optimistic for future, survey shows', BBC, January 11, 2010. This second survey was also conducted by the Afghan Center for Socio-Economic and Opinion Research (ACSOR). Interviews were conducted in person, in Dari or Pashto, among a random national sample of 1,534 Afghan adults December 11–23, 2009.

39. Author interview, United Nations official, Kabul, March 2009.

40. 'Biden cites mounting problems in Afghanistan, but says war "far from lost"', Radio Free Europe, March 10, 2009.

41. Marr interview with David Miliband.

42. Sarah Ladbury, Testing Hypotheses on Radicalisation in Afghanistan, for Department for International Development, August 14, 2009. The study also made the very useful point that much of the process of 'radicalization' occurred after the individual had come into contact with or become integrated with a group of Taliban or insurgent circles.

43. Kate Clark, 'Afghanistan's "weekend jihadis"', *The World Tonight*, Radio Four, September 11, 2009.

44. Ron Moreau and Sami Yousafzai, 'Turning the Taliban', *Newsweek*, February 22, 2010.

45. Marr interview with David Miliband.

46. 'We have very few Pashtuns,' admitted General Ali Ahmed, the commanding officer of Camp Alamo, to the author in March 2009. Each *kandaq* should have been composed according to the ethnicity of the whole country, so with

between 40 or 45 per cent Pashtuns. Instead, the proportion was around 10 per cent, and most of those were from the north and east, not the south. The output data were based on those sent from the Afghan recruiting centres, where scant attention was paid to ethnic balance given the pressure to create new units. The Western officers were incapable of telling the difference between ethnic groups. When asked to produce a recruit from Helmand, those running the training camp brought forward a handful of disconsolate Helmandi Hazaras, one of the most persecuted local communities, for whom life as a soldier was better than that in Lashkar Gah, whatever the risks to their family.

47. General Ali Ahmed had joined the army in 1982 and had thus fought for the Communist regime against the *mujahideen*. So too had the officers leading the detachment in Logar with Captain Vasquez.

48. This was Abdul Rahim Wardak.

49. Author interviews, Camp Alamo, March 2009.

50. Author interview, ISAF headquarters, Kabul, March 2009.

51. Author interview, Wakil Safir Rahman, Kabul, March 2009.

52. UNODC, *Afghan Opium Survey 2009*, 2 September 2009, pp. 3–5.

53. Author interview, Kabul, March 2009.

54. James Risen, 'U.S. to hunt down Afghan drug lords tied to Taliban', *New York Times*, August 10, 2009. 'NATO to attack Afghan opium labs', BBC News, October 10, 2008.

55. Author interview with Mohammed Ehsan Zia, Kabul, March 2009.

56. Matthew Rosenberg, 'Corruption suspected in airlift of billions in cash from Kabul', *Wall Street Journal*, June 25, 2010.

57. The cable adds: 'Many other notable private individuals and public officials maintain assets (primarily property) outside Afghanistan, suggesting these individuals are extracting as much wealth as possible while conditions permit.'

58. Jonathan Steele and Jon Boone, 'Afghan vice-president landed in Dubai with $52m in cash', WikiLeaks, December 2, 2010.

59. Jonathan Steele, 'US convinced Karzai half-brother is corrupt, WikiLeaks cables say', *Guardian*, December 2, 2010.

60. Author interview, Kabul, March 2009.

61. Author interview by email, October 2009.

62. Units continued searches of homes, often using dogs, seen as unclean in Afghanistan and many Islamic nations.

63. Insurgents knew this, and there was some evidence that they exploited it deliberately by drawing fire into areas where civilians were sheltering.

64. UNAMA, *Afghanistan Annual Report on Protection of Civilians in Armed Conflict, 2009*, December 31, 2009, pp. 16–19.

65. Most were grouped into 'Taskforce 373'. Scores, possibly hundreds, of such events, often occurring in remote locations and systematically downplayed or denied by coalition spokesmen, had gone unreported. Some were revealed by

WikiLeaks in August 2010. They included one incident in June 2007 in which seven Afghan National Police were killed. In another, in October 2007, an internal log listed casualties as follows: twelve US wounded, two teenage girls and a ten-year-old boy wounded, one girl killed, one woman killed, four civilian men killed, one donkey killed, one dog killed, several chickens killed, no enemy killed, no enemy wounded, no enemy detained. Nick Davies, 'Afghanistan war logs: Task Force 373 – special forces hunting top Taliban', *Guardian*, July 25, 2010. The leaked logs showed how coalition public statements had systematically been economical with the truth, if not downright misleading.

66. Up to 3,000 Afghans served with American special forces units, according to some estimates.

67. Author interview with McKiernan, March 2009, Kabul.

68. The higher estimates were those of American commanders.

69. UNAMA, *Mid Year Report on Protection of Civilians in Armed Conflict 2010*, Kabul, August 10, 2010, p. 15.

70. Barader had taken over following the arrest of Mullah Obaidullah in early 2007.

71. Thomas Ruttig, 'The Taliban Arrest Wave in Pakistan: Reasserting Strategic Depth', *CTC Sentinel*, vol. 3, no. 3, March 2010, p. 5.

72. Munir Ahmad, 'Pakistani officials: nearly 15 top Taliban held', Associated Press, February 25, 2010.

73. Chris Allbritton, 'Holbrooke hails Pakistan–U.S. collaboration on Taliban', Reuters, February 18, 2010.

74. Author telephone interview, February 2010.

75. Lieven, *A Hard Country*, pp. 470, 474.

76. Declan Walsh, 'WikiLeaks cables: US special forces working inside Pakistan', *Guardian*, November 30, 2010.

77. Declan Walsh, 'The village that stood up to the Taliban', *Guardian*, February 5, 2010.

78. 'Admiral Mullen praises Pakistan army's war plan', CBS, December 16, 2009.

79. Ruttig, 'The Taliban Arrest Wave', p. 6.

80. Other cables referred to the relationship between Pakistan and the USA being 'transactional in nature' and 'based on mutual mistrust' and expressed deep concerns over the security of Pakistani nuclear fuel, potential 'soft coups' by the army, the collapsing economy, a lack of governance in much of the country and the deep anti-Americanism. 'US embassy cables: "Reviewing our Afghanistan-Pakistan strategy"', *Guardian*. November 30, 2010. 'US embassy cables: Relationship with Pakistan based on "mutual distrust", says US', *Guardian*, December 1, 2010. 'US embassy cables: Despite massive US aid, anti-Americanism rampant in Pakistan', *Guardian*, November 30, 2010.

81. Jane Perlez and Eric Schmitt, 'Pakistan army finds Taliban tough to root out', *New York Times*, July 5, 2010.

82. *Fedayeen* tactics are typical of Kashmir. The theological difference between actively seeking death – a suicide attack - and partaking in an attack which implies a very high chance of dying is important.

83. The career of 'Dr Usman', the only survivor among the attackers on the army general headquarters in October 2009, gives a clue. Usman was a former army medical corps officer who, after leaving the military, became involved with a series of extremist groups around his hometown of Kahuta in central Punjab. Having risen up through the ranks of the Bahawalpur-based Jaish-e-Mohammed, he fled to the FATA like so many such militants, where he linked up with Pakistani Taliban groups and with Ilyas Kashmiri, the veteran Pakistani with close links to al-Qaeda. 'Dr Usman's desperate last act', *Daily Times*, October 13, 2009.

84. Pew Global Attitudes, *Pew Global Attitudes: Overview: Concern about Extremist Threat Slips in Pakistan*, July 29, 2010, p. 11.

85. From 70 per cent in 2007 to single digits at the end of 2008, according to TerrorFreeTomorrow polls. Kenneth Ballen, 'Bin Laden's Soft Support', *Washington Monthly*, May 2008.

86. Especially given the collapse of the boom that had benefited so many in the Pakistani lower middle class.

87. Pew Research Center, *Overview: Pakistani Public Opinion*, August 13, 2009.

88. British Council report, *Pakistan: the Next Generation*, November 2009.

89. Gul, *The Most Dangerous Place*, pp. xvi–xvii.

90. Forty per cent blamed the fighting in Waziristan on America. Military Action in Waziristan: Opinion Poll, Gilani Poll/GallupPakistan, Islamabad, November 3, 2009.

91. 'US embassy cables: Despite massive US aid, anti-Americanism rampant in Pakistan', *Guardian*, November 30, 2010.

92. Aryn Baker, 'Casualty of war', *Time*, June 1, 2009.

93. Pew Research Center, *Overview: Concern about Extremist Threat Slips in Pakistan*, p. 3.

94. 'Into the heartland', *The Economist*, June 5, 2010.

95. Pew Research Center, *Overview: Concern about Extremist Threat Slips in Pakistan*.

96. Arif Jamal, 'Half-hearted security operations in Punjab do little to restrain Taliban', *Jamestown Terrorism Monitor*, vol. 8, no. 31, August 5, 2010.

97. Pew Research Center, *Overview: Concern about Extremist Threat Slips in Pakistan*, p. 10. Support for all extremist groups, including al-Qaeda and the Taliban, was strongest in the Punjab. While 27 per cent in the Punjab offered a favourable opinion of al-Qaeda and 22 per cent expressed a favourable view of the Taliban, support for these groups was only in the single digits in Sindh, NWFP (renamed Khyber Pakhtunkhwa) and Baluchistan.

98. South Asia Terrorism Portal, New Delhi. In 2008, 69 civilians and 90 members of the security forces were killed in terrorism-related violence in Jammu

and Kashmir. There were 49 explosions using improvised devices or land mines or hand-grenades in which 29 persons were killed. There were no incidents of suicide or suicidal (*fedayeen*) terrorism. In 2009, 55 civilians and 78 members of the security forces were killed. There were only 7 explosions, in which 11 civilians were killed. There were no incidents of suicide or suicidal terrorism during 2009 either.

99. The demonstrations were inspired directly by those in Palestine, down to the *keffiyehs* which the participants tied around their faces, in the same way that the first round of demonstrations in Kashmir, those that had sparked the first wave of the insurgency in the disputed state back in the late 1980s, had been inspired by the mass movements against Communist rule in eastern Europe.

100. Author interviews with senior police, Jammu, and Kashmir police officials, Srinagar, Sopore and Baramullah, Kashmir, February and June 2010.

101. Sixty-two per cent of the population are aged under thirty, and youth unemployment is 50 per cent.

102. Author interview, Srinagar, June 2010.

103. Muzamil Jaleel, 'Alarm bells: Stone-pelters join militant ranks', *Indian Express*, November 25, 2010.

104. One operation had seen a nineteen-year-old blow himself up in a strike against an army convoy on a road near Sopore, in the heart of wealthy apple-growing country and an area with a local tradition of political dissidence, Islamism and insurgency. The son of a radical preacher removed from his post as village cleric by the authorities, he had been raised in a harsh and politicized environment. Sent to a *medressa* in the western Indian state of Gujrat for his education at the age of sixteen, he had ended up in Pakistan, almost certainly recruited by Lashkar-e-Toiba, before finally returning to his village only weeks before committing his final, suicidal attack only a few miles from his home. 'As a Muslim I am happy. As a father I am sad,' his father said as he received visitors come to congratulate him on the martyrdom of his child.

105. Jason Burke, 'Kashmir: young militants take pot shots at fragile peace process', *Observer*, February 24, 2010. Author interview, Pett Sirr, February 2010. 'Two terrorists killed as Srinagar gunbattle ends', Press Trust of India, January 7, 2010.

CHAPTER 17: THE END OF THE FIRST DECADE

1. Shahawar Matin Siraj was found guilty of participating in a conspiracy to attack the Herald Square subway station in 2004, three days before the Republican national convention was to begin at Madison Square Garden.

2. 'Roshonara Choudhry: police interview extracts', *Guardian*, November 3, 2010.

3. Tom Rawstorne, 'The remote-controlled Al Qaeda assassin: how brilliant student was brainwashed into stabbing MP', *Daily Mail*, November 6, 2010.

4. Petter Nesser and Brynjar Lia, 'Lessons Learned from the July 2010 Norwegian Terrorist Plot', *CTC Sentinel*, vol. 3, no. 8, August 2010.

5. He may have been in touch with Anwar al-Awlaki but had never been near Pakistan.

6. Another was Ahmed Mohammed Hamed Ali, al-Qaeda's chief of military operations in Afghanistan and a veteran militant indicted for his role in the 1998 bombings of American embassies in East Africa.

7. A total of nearly 600 militants were killed, according to one estimate, indicating that new militants replacing the dead were being killed too. Greg Miller, 'Increased U.S. drone strikes in Pakistan killing few high-ranking militants', *Washington Post*, February 20, 2011. David E Sanger and Mark Mazzetti, 'New estimate of strength of Al Qaeda is offered', *New York Times*, June 30, 2010. The fact that senior al-Qaeda figures began to move to Pakistani cities and towns indicated how effective the drone strikes were.

8. A nine-month break in communications from bin Laden had been ended only in March 2009. Seth Jones, *In the Graveyard of Empires*, p. 291.

9. An audiotape was released in January and another at the end of September.

10. Abdul Hameed Bakier, 'Internet Jihadists React to the Deaths of al-Qaeda Leaders in Iraq', *CTC Sentinel*, May 2010, vol. 3, no. 5, p. 14.

11. Abu Jihad al-Shami, *The Vision*, published summer 2010. The author's *nom de guerre* indicates he is either from or has fought in Jordan or Iraq.

12. According to a study published in 2009, outside of the war zones of Afghanistan and Iraq, 99 per cent of al-Qaeda's victims in 2007 and 96 per cent in 2008 were non-Western. Combating Terrorism Centre, *Deadly Vanguards: A Study of al'Qaida's Violence against Muslims*, December 2009, p. 10.

13. An example would be when, in July 2009, 200 people were killed in riots between Han Chinese and local Uighurs in Xinjiang. This led al-Qaeda to issue its first direct threat against China, framing the recent events in the classic narrative. Abu Yahya al-Libi described the 'massacre' as 'not being carried out by criminal Crusaders or evil Jews who have committed crimes against our nation [but] by Buddhist nationalists and communists'. Three months later, al-Libi was claiming 'China is working to destroy the Muslim identity and culture of ethnic Uighurs in Xinjiang and pursuing policies to 'sever the link between the people and their history'. Chris Zambelis, 'Uighur Dissent and Militancy in China's Xinjiang Province', *CTC Sentinel*, vol. 3, no. 1, January 2010. James Rupert, 'Al-Qaeda vows holy war on China over Uighurs' plight, *Bloomberg*, October 8, 2009.

14. Bin Laden carefully clarified that 'the majority of those states have signed the Kyoto Protocol and agreed to curb the emission of harmful gases', except, under President George Bush, the United States. David Usborne, 'Bin Laden goes green to exploit Pakistan flood aid frustration', *Independent*, October 2,

2010. 'Bin Laden criticizes Pakistan relief, urges climate action', Reuters, October 1, 2010.

15. See the author's chapter in John Esposito, ed., *Oxford Handbook of Islam and Politics*, Harvard University Press, to be published end 2011.

16. Ibid. Author telephone interview with Sidney Jones, April 2010. The even more localized 'al-Qaeda in Aceh' disappeared too. In the Philippines too the Abu Sayyaf Group, which had also been drawn tangentially into the broader al-Qaeda network in the late 1990s, moved sharply away from international involvement and, emasculated by a relatively successful American-supported counter-insurgency campaign, returned to kidnapping and banditry. Deep problems remained, with ethnic and religious resentment of the central government still deep, but the threat from a once potent militant group was residual. 'Peace in our time, maybe', *The Economist*, August 9, 2008. Zachary Abuza, 'The Philippines Chips Away at the Abu Sayyaf Group's strength', *CTC Sentinel*, vol. 3, no. 4, April 2010. See also Eliza Griswold, *The Tenth Parallel*, Allen Lane, 2010.

17. As Nir Rosen, the journalist and analyst, points out, a major motivation for al-Shabab declaring al-Qaeda allegiance was attracting funding from al-Qaeda's Arab donors, in the same way that al-Qaeda's local enemies use the discourse of counter-terrorism to win backing from the West. Nir Rosen, 'Somalia's al-Shabab, a global or local movement?' *Time*, August 20, 2010.

18. Author interviews with British and American officials, Delhi, September and November, 2010.

19. Lorraine Adams with Ayesha Nasir, 'Inside the mind of the Times Square bomber', *Observer*, September 19, 2010.

20. Vikram Dodd, 'Roshonara Choudhry jailed for life over MP attack', *Guardian*, November 3, 2010.

21. Richard Esposito and Pierre Thomas, 'Terror attacks against US at all-time high', ABC News, May 26, 2010.

22. Michael Leiter, Director of National Counterterrorism Center, 'Statement for Record, Senate Homeland Security and Government Affairs Committee, Nine Years after 9/11: Confronting the Terrorist Threat to the Homeland', September 22, 2010.

23. Andrea Elliott, 'The jihadist next door', *New York Times*, June 22, 2010. Frank Cilluffo, Jeffrey Cozens and Magnus Ranstorp, 'Foreign Fighters: Trends, Trajectories and Conflict Zones', Homeland Security Policy Institute, George Washington University, 2010, p. 24. Leiter, *Statement*.

24. Paul Lewis, '"Christmas terror plot" suspects are remanded in custody', *Guardian*, December 27, 2010.

25. Complex suicide attacks were recorded at roughly two per month, higher than the average of one complex attack per month during 2009. UNAMA, *Report of the Secretary-General Pursuant to Paragraph 40 of Resolution 1917 (2010)*(S/2010/318), June 2010.

26. UNAMA, *The Situation in Afghanistan and Its Implications for International Peace and Security*, (S/2010/463), September 2010.

27. See UNAMA, *Mid Year Report on Protection of Civilians in Armed Conflict 2010*, Kabul, August 2010. UNAMA, *Afghan Civilian Casualties Rise 31 Per Cent in First Six Months of 2010*, August 10, 2010. In a new grim twist these now included public executions of children.

28. Laheya and 2011 Spring Offensive statement, author collection. Author interview with US military intelligence officer, Kabul, May 2011.

29. US Department of Defense, *Report on Progress Toward Security and Stability in Afghanistan*, November 2010, pp. 7–8. 'ISAF and Afghan National Security Forces gradually are pushing insurgents to the edges of secured population areas in a number of important locations ... Progress across the country remains uneven, with modest gains in security, governance, and development in operational priority areas.'

29. Yaroslav Trofimov, 'U.N. maps show Afghan security worsens', *Wall Street Journal*, December 26, 2010.

30. Multiple author interviews with US, Afghan and British officials and military officers, Kabul, May 2011.

31. Author interviews, Srinagar, Delhi, April, June 2010. By late spring 2010, there was even evidence of increased infiltration of militants into Kashmir, Indian security officials claimed.

32. Asra Nomani and Barbara Feinman Todd, 'Land of the Scot-free', *Newsweek*, February 7, 2011.

33. Carlotta Gall, 'Pakistan faces a divide of age on Muslim law', *New York Times*, January 11, 2011. Aatish Taseer, 'The killer of my father, Salman Taseer, was showered with rose petals by fanatics. How could they do this?', *Daily Telegraph*, January 11, 2011. 'Has Pakistan passed the tipping point of religious extremism?', BBC News Online, January 7, 2011. Eventually some political leaders did move to condemn the killing. The Punjab Assembly, including religious parties sitting, unanimously passed a resolution against the murder, praising the late governor's political and social achievements. Hussain Kashif, 'PA passes resolution condemning Taseer's assassination', *Daily Times*, January 11, 2011.

35. According to Iraq Body Count, the UK-based organization.

36. 'Total 2010 Iraq death toll tops 2009: government', AFP, January 1, 2011.

37. Aaron C. Davis, 'Sadr foments resistance by Iraqis', *New York Times*, January 9, 2011.

38. Interview, Baghdad, November 2010.

39. Thomas Friedman, 'The things we do for oil', *International Herald Tribune*, February 23, 2011.

40. Tom Coghlan, 'Afghans accuse Defence Secretary Liam Fox of racism and disrespect', *The Times*, May 24, 2010.

41. The parliamentary election in November and December saw the ruling National Democratic Party take nearly 95 per cent of the 221 seats available

in the first round. A second round took place amid clumsy fraud and without the participation of the Muslim Brotherhood, the main opposition, and indicated clearly that Mubarak, eighty-two, had no intention of relinquishing power other than, perhaps, passing it to his carefully groomed son Gamal

42. 'Building a new Libya', *The Economist*, February 26, 2011.

43. Andrew Lebovich, 'Afghan perspectives on democracy', *Foreign Policy*, February 9, 2011, citing research by the Afghanistan Research and Evaluation Unit from 2008.

44. The same was true in Algeria. Since 2001, President Abdelaziz Bouteflika had been embraced as a partner in the Global War on Terror by Washington.

45. Only 6 per cent less than in Indonesia and 17 per cent more than in Pakistan. Pew Research Center, *Democracy and Islam*, January 31, 2011.

46. Dan Murphy, 'Egypt revolution unfinished, Qaradawi tells Tahrir masses', *Christian Science Monitor*, February 18, 2011.

47. Bobby Ghosh, 'Rage, rap, and revolution', *Time*, February 28, 2011.

48. 'Al-Qaeda message on Egypt, belatedly', MSNBC, February 18, 2011.

49. See Memorandum for Commander, US Southern Command, CSRT Input for Guantanamo Detainee, US9SA-000063DP, Muhammad Mani Ahmad Al Shalan Al Qahtani, October 30, 2008, secret, author collection. Michael Isikoff, 'How profile of bin Laden courier led CIA to its target', NBC News, May 5, 2011; Mark Mazzetti, Helene Cooper and Peter Baker, 'Clues gradually led to the location of Qaeda chief', *New York Times*, May 2, 2011.

50. Remarks by the President on Osama bin Laden, May 2, 2011, Office of the Press Secretary, White House.

51. Author telephone interview with senior ISI official, May 2011.

52. Sebastian Rotella, 'New details in the bin Laden documents: portrait of a fugitive micro-manager', *Propublica*, May 12, 2011.

53. Author telephone interview with officials in New York, Pakistan, May 2011. Author interviews, US and British officials, Kabul, May 2011.

54. Mark Mazzetti, 'Signs that bin Laden weighed seeking Pakistani protection', *New York Times*, May 26, 2011.

55. Author interviews with American and British intelligence officials, Kabul, June 2011.

56. Ibid.

57. Ibid.

58. Quilliam Foundation, *The Coming Struggle within al-Qaeda*, London, 10 May 2011.

CONCLUSION: THE 9/11 WARS

1. By 2010, support for suicide bombing in many countries of the Islamic world, after declining so dramatically in the middle years of the decade, began to

edge up again. Often the change was slight. In Egypt it went from 13 per cent believing suicide bombing was sometimes or often justified in 2008 to 15 per cent in 2009 and then to 20 per cent in 2010. In Pakistan, the levels went from 5 to 8 per cent, still a fraction of the 33 per cent recorded in 2003. In Jordan it went from 12 to 20 per cent between 2009 and 2010. In 2005, it had been 57 per cent. Pew Global Attitudes Key Indicators Database, accessed January 2, 2011.

2. Measured in the number of attacks, the volume of terrorism in the 1970s was far higher than between September 12, 2001 and the end of 2009, with between 60 and 70 strikes per year. Between 1970 and 1978, 72 people died in terrorist incidents in the US. Rand Corporation (Brian Michael Jenkins), *Would-be Warriors*, 2010, pp. 8–9.

3. Steve Luxenberg, 'Bob Woodward book details Obama battles with advisers over exit plan for Afghan war', *Washington Post*, September 22, 2010.

4. Elisabeth Bumiller, 'The staggering cost of American conflicts', *International Herald Tribune*, July 26, 2010. The Stockholm International Peace Research Institute Military Expenditure Database, http://milexdata.sipri.org/result.php4, accessed April 2011.

5. In 2011, for the second consecutive year, President Obama made no reference to bin Laden in his State of the Union address.

6. Walter Laqueur, *Terrorism*, Little, Brown, 1977.

7. National Intelligence Council, *Global Trends 2025: A Transformed World*, November 2008.

8. National Intelligence Council, *Mapping the Global Future, Report of the National Intelligence Council's 2020 Project*, December 2004.

9. Such as the five American servicemen prosecuted late 2010 for premeditated murders of Afghan civilians.

10. icasualties.org, accessed October 9, 2010.

11. 'Names of the dead', *New York Times*, October 8, 2010. Congressional Research Service (Susan G. Cheeser), *Afghanistan Casualties, Miltiary Forces and Civilians*, October 28, 2010, p. 2. Department of Defense statistics, accessed November 19, 2010.

12. In Iraq at least 468 have been killed, according to icasualties.org, accessed December 2010. Some estimates are three or four times this total. See Steve Fainaru, *Big Boys' Rules: America's Mercenaries Fighting in Iraq*, Da Capo Press, 2008.

13. Congressional Research Service, *Iraqi Casualties: US Military Forces and Iraqi Civilians, Police and Security Forces*, October 7, 2010, p. 9. Report to Congress, *Measuring Security and Stability in Iraq*, June 2010, p. 29. This total includes 2,700 previously unreported deaths of Iraqi police and other Iraqi security forces killed after capture revealed by WikiLeaks and calculated by Iraq Body Count. More than 600 died in 2010, considerably more than in 2009, even if both totals paled into insignificance compared with the

2,065 who had died in 2007, the year of the Surge. 'Death for Iraqis jumps', *Beyond Babylon*, Latimes.com, July 2007.

14. Brookings Institution, *Afghanistan Index: Tracing Variables of Reconstruction and Security in post 9/11 Afghanistan*, October 19, 2010, p. 14.

15. Around 500 died in 2010. See the series of reports by the Pakistan Institute of Peace Studies.

16. Conetta, 'The Wages of War', p. 23.

17. Press release, Inter Services Public Relations, ISPR, February 18, 2010. Author telephone interviews, ISPR, November 2010.

18. David Leigh, 'Iraq war logs reveal 15,000 previously unlisted civilian deaths', *Guardian*, October 22, 2010. The logs put insurgent fatalities at 23,984. See PIPS Pakistan Security Report (October 2010), November 10, 2010, and others.

19. Combating Terrorism Center, *Deadly Vanguards: A Study of al'Qa'ida's Violence against Muslims*, December 2009, p. 7.

20. 'Iraq war logs: What the numbers reveal', October 23, 2010. http://www.iraqbodycount.org/analysis/numbers/warlogs/.

21. 'Iraq: Key figures since the war began', Associated Press, January 2, 2009.

22. Project on Defense Alternatives (Carl Conetta), *Operation Enduring Freedom: Why a Higher Rate of Civilian Bombing Casualties*, January 18, 2002. Project on Defense Alternatives (Carl Conetta), *Strange Victory: A Critical Appraisal of Operation Enduring Freedom and the Afghanistan War*, January 30, 2002. Afghan casualties database, http://www.guardian.co.uk/news/datablog/2010/aug/10/afghanistan-civilian-casualties-statistics#data.

23. 'Global war on terror claims 30,000 Pakistani casualties', ISPR release, Islamabad, *The Economic Times*, February 19, 2010. According to the South Asia Terrorism Portal, 9,230 civilians were killed as a result of the insurgency from 2003 to December 5, 2010.

24. There are an estimated 2 million Iraqis who have left their homeland. Around 5 million refugees returned to Afghanistan after the fall of the Taliban, but at least 2 million are now thought to have left, and the country now has an estimated 240,000 internally displaced. Figures from the International Displacement Monitoring Centre at www.internal-displacement.org based on data from the UNHCR, June 2010.

25. Author interview, Dunkirk, December 2009.

Select Bibliography

To keep this bibliography manageable, except for a handful of extremely useful texts, only works containing material referenced directly over preceding pages have been included. Several books exist in multiple translations. Again to save space, only the edition consulted has been listed.

BOOKS

Sohail Abbas, *Probing the Jihadi Mindset*, National Book Foundation, Islama-bad, 2007.

Said Aburish, *Saddam Hussein: The Politics of Revenge*, Bloomsbury, 2000.

Zachary Abuza, *Militant Islam in Southeast Asia, Crucible of Terror*, Lynne Reiner, 2003.

Khalid Ahmed, 'Fundamental Flaws', in *On the Abyss*, HarperCollins (India), 2000.

M. J. Akbar, *The Shade of Swords: Jihad and the Conflict Between Islam and Christianity*, Routledge, 2002.

Tinderbox: The Past and Future of Pakistan, HarperCollins (India), 2010.

Ali Allawi, *The Occupation of Iraq: Winning the War, Losing the Peace*, Yale University Press, 2008.

Charles Allen, *God's Terrorists: The Wahhabi Cult and the Hidden Roots of Modern Jihad*, Little, Brown, 2006.

John Lee Anderson, *The Lion's Grave*, Atlantic Books, 2002.

Arthur Arberry (trans.), *The Quran*, Oxford University Press, 1964; first publ. Allen and Unwin, 1955.

Karen Armstrong, Holy War: *The Crusades and Their Impact on Today's World*, Macmillan, 1998.

Islam: A Short History, Phoenix; 2001.

Mohammed: Prophet for Our Time, Harper Perennial, 2007.

Reza Aslam, *How to Win a Cosmic War: God, Globalization, and the End of the War on Terror*, Random House, 2009.

Scott Atran, *Talking to the Enemy, Faith, Brotherhood and the (Un)making of Terrorists*, HarperCollins, 2010.

Florence Aubenas, *Grand Reporter: petite conférence sur le journalisme*, Bayard, Paris, 2009.

Mukulika Banerjee, *The Pathan Unarmed: Opposition and Memory in the Northwest Frontier*, Oxford University Press (India), 2001.

Thomas Barfield, *Afghanistan: A Political and Cultural History*, Princeton University Press, 2010.

Bruce Bawer, *While Europe Slept*, Doubleday, 2006.

Mourad Benchellali, *Voyage vers l'enfer*, Robert Laffont, 2006.

Daniel Benjamin and Steven Simon, *Age of Sacred Terror: Radical Islam's War against America*, Random House, 2002.

Owen Bennett-Jones, *Pakistan: Eye of the Storm*, 3rd edn, Yale University Press, 2003.

Peter Bergen, *The Osama Bin Laden I Know: An Oral History of Al-Qaeda's Leader*, Simon & Schuster, 2006.

    Holy War Inc.: Inside the Secret World of Osama bin Laden, Touchstone, 2002.

    The Longest War: The Enduring Conflict Between America and al'Qaeda, Simon and Schuster, 2011.

Gary Berntsen, *Jawbreaker: The Attack on Bin Laden and Al Qaeda*, Crown, 2005.

Benazir Bhutto, *Reconciliation: Islam, Democracy and the West*, Harper, 2008.

John R. Bradley, *Inside Egypt*, Palgrave Macmillan, 2008.

Rodric Braithwaite, *Afgantsy: The Russians in Afghanistan 1979–1989*, Profile, 2011.

Paul Bremer, *My Year in Iraq: The Struggle to Build a Future of Hope*, Simon and Schuster, 2006.

Robert K. Brigham, *Iraq, Vietnam and the Limits of American Power*, PublicAffairs, 2008.

Martin Bright, *When Progressives Treat with Reactionaries*, Policy Exchange, 2006.

Jean-Charles Brisard, *Zarqawi: The New Face of Al-Qaeda*, Policy Press, 2005.

Jason Burke, *Al-Qaeda: The True Story of Radical Islam*, Penguin, 2003.

The Road to Kandahar: Travels through Conflict in the Islamic World, Penguin, 2006.

Ian Buruma, *Murder in Amsterdam, The Death of Theo Van Gogh and the Limits of Tolerance*, Atlantic Books, London, 2006.

Ian Buruma and Avishai Margalit, *Occidentalism: The West in the Eyes of Its Enemies*, Penguin Press, 2004.

George W. Bush, *Decision Points*, Virgin, 2010.

Christopher Caldwell, *Reflections on the Revolution in Europe*, Allen Lane, 2009.

Alistair Campbell, *The Blair Years*, Hutchinson, 2007.

Rajiv Chandreshekan, *Imperial Life in the Emerald City: Inside Iraq's Green Zone*, Knopf, 2006.

Sarah Chayes, *The Punishment of Virtue: Walking the Frontline of the War on Terror with a Woman Who Has Made It Her Home*, Portobello Books, 2007.

Pierre-Arnaud Chouvy, *Opium: Uncovering the Politics of the Poppy*, I. B. Tauris, 2009.

Richard Clarke, *Against All Enemies*, Simon and Schuster, 2004.

Alexander and Patrick Cockburn, *Out of the Ashes: The Resurrection of Saddam Hussein*, Harper Perennial, 2000.

Patrick Cockburn, *Muqtada al-Sadr and the Fall of Iraq*, Faber and Faber, 2008.
    Muqtada al-Sadr, the Shia Revival and the Struggle for Iraq, Simon and Schuster, 2008.
    The Occupation: War and Resistance in Iraq, Verso, London 2006.

Stephen Cohen, *The Idea of Pakistan*, Brookings, 2005.

Stephen Coll, *Ghost Wars: The Secret History of the CIA, Afghanistan, and Bin Laden, from the Soviet Invasion to September 10, 2001*, Penguin, 2005.

Rik Coolsaet, ed., *Jihadi Terrorism and the Radicalisation Challenge in Europe*, Ashgate, 2008.

Gordon Corera, *Shopping for Bombs: Nuclear Proliferation, Global Insecurity and the Rise and Fall of the AQ Khan Network*, Oxford University Press, 2006.

Robert D. Crews and Amin Tarzi, eds. *The Taliban and the Crisis of Afghanistan*, Harvard University Press, 2008.

William Dalrymple, *The Last Mughal: The Fall of a Dynasty, Delhi, 1857*, Bloomsbury, 2009.

Mark Danner, *Torture and Truth: America, Abu Ghraib and the War on Terrorism*, The New York Review of Books, 2004.

James F. Dobbins, *After the Taliban*, Potomac Books, 2008.

Toby Dodge, *Inventing Iraq: The Failure of Nation Building and a History Denied*, Columbia University Press, 2003.

John Esposito and Dalia Mogahed, *Who Speaks for Islam? What a Billion Muslims Really Think*, Gallup Press, 2007.

Martin Evans and John Phillips, *Algeria: Anger of the Dispossessed*, Yale University Press, 2008.

Steve Fainaru, *Big Boys' Rules: America's Mercenaries Fighting in Iraq*, Da Capo Press, 2008.

Oriana Fallacci, *The Rage and the Pride*, English edition, Rizzoli, 2002.

Mamoun Fandy, *Saudi Arabia and the Politics of Dissent*, Palgrave Macmillan, 2001.

Howard M. Federspiel, *Islam and Ideology in the Emerging Indonesian State: The Persatuan Islam 1923 to 1957*, Brill, 2001.

Douglas Feith, *War and Decision*, Harper, 2008.

James Fergusson, *A Million Bullets: The Real Story of the British Army in Afghanistan*, Transworld, 2008.

Orlando Figes, *Crimea: The Last Crusade*, Allen Lane, 2010.

Jean-Pierre Filiu, *L'Apocalypse dans l'Islam*, Fayard, 2008.

    Les Frontières du jihad, Fayard, 2006.

    Les Neuf vies d'Al-Qaïda, Fayard, 2009.

Dexter Filkins, *The Forever War: Dispatches From the War on Terror*, Vintage, 2009.

Alain Finkielkraut, *Qu'est-ce que la France?* Stock, 2007.

Conor Foley, *The Thin Blue Line: How Humanitarianism Went to War*, Verso, 2008.

Gregory Fontenot, E. J. Degen and David Tohn, *On Point: The United States Army in Operation Iraqi Freedom*, Combat Studies Institute Press, 2004.

Lawrence Freedman, *A Choice of Enemies: America Confronts the Middle East*, Weidenfeld and Nicolson, 2009.

Dalton Fury, *Kill Bin Laden: A Delta Force Commander's Account of the Hunt for the World's Most Wanted Man*, St Martin's Press, 2008.

David Galula, *Counter-insurgency Warfare: Theory and Practice*, Frederick Praeger, 2006.

Diego Gambetta, ed., *Making Sense of Suicide Missions*, Oxford University Press, 2005.

David Gardner, *Last Chance: The Middle East in the Balance*, I. B. Tauris, 2009.

Fawaz Gerges, *The Far Enemy: Why Jihad Went Global*, Cambridge University Press, 2005.

Antonio Giustozzi, ed., *Decoding the New Taliban, Insights from the Afghan Field*, Hurst, 2009.

    Empires of Mud: Wars and Warlords in Afghanistan, Hurst, 2009.

    Kalashnikov, Koran and Laptop: The Neo-Taliban Insurgency in Afghanistan 2002–2007, Hurst, 2007.

Bernard Godard and Sylvie Taussig, *Les Musulmans en France*, Editions Robert Laffont, 2007.

Jos L. Gommans, *The Rise of the Indo-Afghan Empire c.1710–1780*, Brill, 1995.

Philip Gourevitch and Errol Morris, *Standard Operating Procedure*, Picador, 2009.

Stephen Grey, *Ghost Plane: The Untold Story of the CIA's Secret Rendition Programme*, C. Hurst & Co, 2006.

    Operation Snakebite: The Explosive True Story of an Afghan Desert Siege, Penguin, 2010.

Eliza Griswold, *The Tenth Parallel: Dispatches from the Faultline Between Christianity and Islam*, Allen Lane, 2010.

Imtiaz Gul, *The Most Dangerous Place: Pakistan's Lawless Frontier*, Penguin, 2010.

Rohan Gunaratna, *Inside Al Qae'da*, Hurst, 2002.

Dipak Gupta, *Understanding Terrorism and Political Violence*, Routledge, 2008.

Ron Gutman, *How We Missed the Story: Osama Bin Laden, the Taliban and the Hijacking of Afghanistan*, United States Institute of Peace Press, 2008.

Mary Habeck, *Knowing the Enemy*, Yale, 2006.

Fred Halliday, 'Global Jihad, "Long War" and the Crisis of American Power', in Fabio Petito and Elisabetta Brighi, eds., *Il Mediterraneo nelle Relazioni Internazionale: tra Euro-Mediterraneo e Grande Medio Oriente*, Fondazione Laboratorio Mediterraneo, 2007.

    100 Myths about the Middle East, Saqi Books, 2005.

    Two Hours that Shook the World, Saqi Books, 2002.

David Hicks, *Guantanamo: My Journey*, William Heinemann, 2010.

Sana Haroon, *Frontier of Faith: Islam in the Indo-Afghan Borderland*, Hurst, 2007.

Thomas Hegghammer, *Jihad in Saudi Arabia: Violence and Pan-Islamism Since 1979*, Cambridge University Press, 2010.

Patrick Hennessey, *The Junior Officers' Reading Club*, Allen Lane, 2009.

Carole Hillenbrand, *The Crusades: Islamic Perspectives*, Edinburgh University Press, 1999.

Dilip Hiro, *Inside Central Asia*, Overlook Duckworth, 2009.

Bruce Hoffman, *Inside Terrorism*, 2nd rev. edn, Columbia University Press, 2006.

James F. Hoge Jr and Gideon Rose eds., *How Did This Happen? Terrorism and the New War*, PublicAffairs, 2001.

Ed Husain, *The Islamist: Why I Joined Radical Islam in Britain, What I Saw Inside and Why I Left*, 2007.

Zahid Hussain, *Frontline Pakistan*, Columbia University Press, 2007.

Faleh A. Jabar, *The Shi'ite Movement in Iraq*, Saqi Books, 2003.

Christophe Jaffrelot and Laurent Gayer, eds., *Armed Militias of South Asia*, Hurst, 2009.

Lawrence James, *Warrior Race: A History of the British at War*, Little, Brown, 2001.

Seth Jones, *In the Graveyard of Empires: America's War in Afghanistan*, Norton, 2009.

Kimberly Kagan, *The Surge: A Military History*, Encounter Books, 2008.

John Kampfner, *Blair's Wars*, The Free Press, 2003.

Robert D. Kaplan, *Soldiers of God: With Islamic Warriors in Afghanistan and Pakistan*, Vintage, 2008.

Hamid Karzai, *Letter from Kabul*, Wiley, 2006.

George Kassimeris, ed., *Playing Politics with Terrorism*, Hurst, 2007.

Gilles Kepel, *Al-Qaida dans le texte: écrits d'Oussama ben Laden, Abdallah Azzam, Ayman al-Zawahiri et Abou Moussab al-Zarqawi*, PUF, 2008.

    Fitna: Guerre au cœur de l'Islam, Paris, Gallimard, 2004,

    Jihad: The Trail of Political Islam, I. B. Tauris, 2002.

    Terreur et martyre: relever le défi de civilisation, Flammarion, 2008.

Nichola Khan, *Mohajir Militancy in Pakistan. Violence and Transformation in the Karachi Conflict*, Routledge, 2010.

Farhad Khosrokhavar, *L'Islam dans les prisons*, Balland, 2004.

David Kilcullen, *The Accidental Guerrilla: Fighting Small Wars in the Midst of a Big One*, Hurst, 2009.

Robert Lacey, *Saudi Arabia Exposed: Inside a Kingdom in Crisis*, Palgrave Macmillan, 2006.

Hugues Lagrange and Marco Oberti, eds., *Emeutes urbaines et protestations*, Les Presses de Sciences Po, 2006.

Walter Laqueur, *Terrorism*, Little, Brown, 1977.

Jonathan Laurence and Justin Vaisse, *Intégrer l'Islam, la France et ses Musulmans: enjeux et réussites*, Odile Jacob, 2007.

Bruce Lawrence, ed., *Messages to the World: The Statements of Osama Bin Laden*, Verso, 2005.

Robert Leiken, *Europe's Angry Muslims*, Oxford University Press, 2009.

David Levering Lewis, *God's Crucible: Islam and the Making of Europe 570 to 1215*, Norton, 2008.

Bernard Lewis, *The Crisis of Islam: Holy War and Unholy Terror*, Random House, 2004.

    'What Went Wrong': Western Impact and Middle Eastern Response, Oxford University Press, 2002.

Brynjar Lia, *Architect of Global Jihad: The Life of Al Qaeda Strategist Abu Mus'ab Al-Suri*, Columbia University Press, 2008.

Anatol Lieven, *Pakistan: A Hard Country*, Allen Lane, 2011.

Amin Maalouf, *The Crusades Through Arab Eyes*, Schocken Books, 1989.

Chris Mackey and Greg Miller, *The Interrogators: Inside the Secret War Against al Qaeda*, Little, Brown, 2004.

Denis MacShane, *Globalising Hatred: The New Anti-Semitism*, Weidenfeld and Nicolson, 2009.

Bill Maley, ed., *Fundamentalism Reborn? Afghanistan and the Taliban*, New York University Press, 1998.

Iftikhar Malik, *Pakistan: Democracy, Terror and the Building of a Nation*, New Holland, 2010.

Kenan Malik, *From Fatwa to Jihad*, Atlantic, 2009.

Salahuddin Malik, *1857: War of Independence or Clash of Civilizations*, Oxford University Press, 2008.

Jane Mayer, *The Dark Side: The Inside Story of How the War on Terror Turned into a War on American Ideals*, Doubleday, 2008.

Rory McCarthy, *'Nobody Told Us We Are Defeated'*, Guardian Books, 2005.

David McDowall, *A Modern History of the Kurds*, I. B. Tauris, 2004.

Barbara Daly Metcalf, *Islamic Revival in British India: Deoband, 1860–1900*, Oxford University Press, 2004.

William Milam, *Bangladesh and Pakistan*, Hurst, 2010.

Beverley Milton-Edwards and Stephen Farrell, *Hamas*, Polity Press, 2010.

Amir Mir, *The Bhutto Murder Trail: From Waziristan to GHQ*, Tranquebar, 2010.

Pankaj Mishra, *Temptations of the West*, Picador, 2006.

Laurent Mucchielli, *Quand les banlieues brûlent . . .*, La Découverte, 2007.

Pervez Musharaf, *In the Line of Fire*, Free Press, 2006.

Abu Bakr Naji, *Management of Savagery: The Most Critical Stage Through Which the Ummah Will Pass*, trans. William McCants, Olin Institute for Strategic Studies, Harvard University, 2006.

Loretta Napoleoni, *Insurgent Iraq: Al Zarqawi and the New Generation*, Seven Stories, 2005.

Vali Nasr, *The Shia Revival: How Conflicts within Islam Will Shape the Future*, W. W. Norton, 2007.

Shuja Nawaz, *Crossed Swords*, Oxford University Press, 2008.

Ronald Neumann, *The Other War: Winning and Losing in Afghanistan*, Potomac Books, 2009.

Linda Nochlin, *The Politics of Vision: Essays on Nineteenth-century Art and Society*, Westview Press, 1991.

Vincenzo Oliveti, *Terror's Source*, Amadeus Books, 2002.

George Packer, *The Assassins' Gate: America in Iraq*, Farrar, Straus and Giroux, 2006.

Alison Pargeter, *The Muslim Brotherhood: The Burden of Tradition*, Saqi, 2010.
   The New Frontiers of Jihad: Radical Islam in Europe, I. B. Tauris, 2008.

Nicolas Pelham, *A New Muslim Order: The Shia and the Middle East Sectarian Crisis*, I. B. Tauris, 2008.

Gretchen Peters, *Seeds of Terror: How Heroin is Bankrolling the Taliban and Al Qaeda*, Oneworld, 2009.

Melanie Phillips, *Londonistan*, Encounter Books, 2006.

Norman Podhoretz, *World War IV: The Long Struggle against Islamofascism*, Doubleday, 2007.

Patrick Porter, *Military Orientalism: Eastern War through Western Eyes*, Hurst, 2007.

Madawi al-Rasheed, *A History of Saudi Arabia*, Cambridge University Press, 2002.

Ahmed Rashid, *Descent into Chaos: How the War against Islamic Extremism Is Being Lost in Pakistan, Afghanistan and Central Asia*, Allen Lane, 2008.
   Taliban: The Power of Militant Islam in Afghanistan and Beyond, I. B. Tauris, 2010.

Thomas Ricks, *Fiasco: The American Military Adventure in Iraq, 2003 to 2005*, Penguin, 2007.
   The Gamble: General David Petraeus and the American Military Adventure in Iraq, 2006–2008, Penguin, 2009.

Bruce Riedel, *The Search for Al Qaeda: Its Leadership, Ideology, and Future*, Brookings Institute, 2010.

Linda Robinson, *Masters of Chaos: The Secret History of the Special Forces*, PublicAffairs, 2005.

　Tell Me How This Ends: General David Petraeus and the Search for a Way Out of Iraq, PublicAffairs, September 2008.

Nir Rosen, *Aftermath: Following the Bloodshed of America's Wars in the Muslim World*, Nation Books, 2009.

J. H. Roy and J. Deviosse, *La Bataille de Poitiers*, Octobre 733, Gallimard, 1966

Olivier Roy, *Globalized Islam: The Search for a New Ummah*, Columbia; 2004.

　The Failure of Political Islam, Harvard University Press, 1998.

　Islam and Resistance in Afghanistan, Cambridge University Press, 1990.

　Politics and Chaos in the Middle East, Columbia, 2008.

Barnett R. Rubin, *The Fragmentation of Afghanistan*, Yale University Press, 2002.

Bruce K. Rutherford, *Egypt after Mubarak*, Princeton University Press, 2008.

Malise Ruthven, *Fundamentalism: The Search For Meaning*, Oxford University Press, 2004.

　A Fury For God: The Islamist Attack on America, rev. edn, Granta, 2004.

David Sanger, *The Inheritance: The World Obama Confronts and the Challenges to American Power*, Crown, 2009.

Marc Sageman, *Leaderless Jihad*, University of Pennsylvania Press, 2008.

　Understanding Terror Networks, University of Pennsylvania Press, 2004.

Nizar Sassi, *Prisonnier 325, Camp Delta : De Vénissieux à Guantanamo*, Editions Denoël, 2006.

Victoria Schofield, *Afghan Frontier: At the Crossroads of Conflict*, I. B. Tauris, 2010.

　Kashmir in Conflict: India, Pakistan and the Undending War, I. B. Tauris, 2010.

Gary Schroen, *First In: An Insider's Account of How the CIA Spearheaded the War on Terror in Afghanistan*, Ballantine Books, 2005.

Vanessa R. Schwartz and Jeannene M. Przyblyski, eds., *The Nineteenth-century Visual Culture Reader*, Routledge, 2004.

Farzana Shaikh, *Making Sense of Pakistan*, Hurst, 2010.

Ayesha Siddiqa, *Military Inc.*, Oxford University Press (Pakistan), 2007.

Philip Smucker, *Al Qaeda's Great Escape*, Potomac Books, 2004.

Devin Springer, James Regens, David Edger, *Islamic Radicalism and Global Jihad*, Georgetown University Press, 2008.

Jean-Marc Stébé, *La Crise des banlieues*, PUF, 2007.

Jessica Stern, *Terror in the Name of God*, Harper Perennial, 2004.

Rory Stewart, *Occupational Hazards: My Time Governing in Iraq*, Picador, 2007.

　The Places in Between, Picador, 2005.

Hilary Synnott, *Bad Days in Basra*, I. B. Tauris, 2008.

See Seng Tan, Kumar Ramakrishna, eds., *After Bali: The Threat of Terrorism in Southeast Asia*, Institute of Defence and Strategic Studies, Singapore, 2003.

Stephen Tanner, *Afghanistan: A Military History*, Da Capo, 2007.

Camille Tawil, *Brothers in Arms*, Telegram, 2010.

George Tenet, *At the Center of the Storm: My Years at the CIA*, HarperCollins, 2007.

Charles Tripp, *A History of Iraq*, Cambridge University Press, 2007.

Yaroslav Trofimov, *The Siege of Mecca: The 1979 Uprising at Islam's Holiest Shrine*, Doubleday, 2007.

Patrick Tyler, *A World of Trouble: America and the Middle East*, Portobello Books, 2009.

United States Special Operations Command History, 6th edn, 2008.

Mark Urban, *Task Force Black*, Little, Brown, 2010.

Bing West, *No True Glory: A Frontline Account of the Battle for Fallujah*, 2005.
 The Strongest Tribe, Random House, 2009.

Andrew Wheatcroft, *The Infidels: The Conflict Between Christendom and Islam 638–2002*, Viking, 2003.

Joshua T. White, *Pakistan's Islamist Frontier: Islamic Politics and U.S. Policy in Pakistan's North-West Frontier*, Center on Faith and International Affairs, 2008.

Quintan Wiktorowicz, *Radical Islam Rising. Muslim Extremism in the West*, Rowman and Littlefield, 2005.

Robert Wistrich, *A Lethal Obsession: Anti-Semitism from Antiquity to the Global Jihad*, Random House, 2010.

Bob Woodward, *Bush at War*, Simon and Schuster, 2003.
 Obama's Wars, Simon and Schuster, 2010.
 Plan of Attack, Simon and Schuster, 2008.

Andy Worthington, *The Guantanamo Files: The Stories of the 774 Detainees in America's Illegal Prison*, Pluto, 2007.

Lawrence Wright, *The Looming Tower*, Allen Lane, 2006.

Bat Ye'or, *Eurabia: The Euro-Arab Axis*, Fairleigh Dickinson University Press, 2005.

Mohammad Yousaf and Mark Adkin, *The Bear Trap: The Defeat of a Superpower*, Casemate, 2001.

Abdul Salam Zaeef, *My Life with the Taliban*, Hurst, 2010.

Ahmad Muaffaq Zaidan, *The 'Afghan Arabs': Media at Jihad*, PFI Islamabad, 1999.

Montasser al-Zayyat, *The Road to al-Qaeda*, Pluto Press, 2003.

Malika Zeghal, *Les Islamistes marocains: le défi à la monarchie*, La Découverte, 2005.

Lawrence Ziring, *Pakistan in the Twentieth Century: A Political History*, Oxford University Press, 1997.

David Zuccino, *Thunder Run: The Armored Strike to Capture Baghdad*, Atlantic Monthly Press, 2004.

OFFICIAL DOCUMENTS

UK

The Aitken Report, An Investigation into Cases of Deliberate Abuse and Unlawful Killing in Iraq in 2003 and 2004, Crown Publishers, January 25, 2008.

British High Commission, Islamabad, Pakistan, *Scotland Yard Report Into Assassination of Benazir Bhutto*, February 8, 2008.

Department for International Development (Dr Emma Hooper, Agha Imran Hamid), *Scoping Study on Social Exclusion in Pakistan: A Summary of Findings*, October 2003.

   (Sarah Ladbury), *Testing Hypotheses on Radicalisation in Afghanistan*, August 14, 2009.

Final Report of the Communities and Local Government Select Committee Inquiry into Preventing Violent Extremism, HMSO, March 30, 2010.

Greater London Authority's Data Management and Analysis Group (Laura Spence), *A Profile of Londoners by Country of Birth: Estimates from the 2006 Annual Population Survey*, February 2008.

Home Affairs Committee, *Project CONTEST: The Government's Counterterrorism Strategy: Ninth Report of Session 2008–09*, July 7, 2009.

Home Office, *Report of the Official Account of the Bombings in London on 7th July 2005*, May 11, 2006.

Parliamentary Intelligence Security Committee, *Report into the London Terrorist Attacks on 7 July 2005*, HMSO, May 2006.

USA

Central Intelligence Agency, *Comprehensive Report of the Special Advisor to the Director of Central Intelligence on Iraq's WMD, Charles Duelfer*, September 30, 2004.

Congressional Record, *Proceedings and Debates of the 109th Session of Congress*, vol. 151, part 10.

Congressional Research Service (Susan G. Cheeser), *Afghanistan Casualties: Military Forces and Civilians*, October 28, 2010.

   (Hannah Fischer), *Iraqi Casualties: US Military Forces and Iraqi Civilians, Police and Security Forces*, October 7, 2010.

   (Kenneth Katzman), *Report for Congress: Al'Qaeda in Iraq: Assessment and Outside Links*, updated August 15, 2008.

   Report for Congress: Operation Enduring Freedom: Foreign Pledges of Military and Intelligence Support, October 17, 2001.

   Report for Congress, Iraq: Elections, Government, and Constitution, November 20, 2006.

(Amy Belasco), *Report for Congress: Troop Levels in the Afghan and Iraq Wars, FY2001–FY2012: Cost and Other Potential Issues*, July 2, 2009.

Department of State cable, 'Afghanistan: Pakistanis to regulate wheat and fuel trade to gain leverage over Taliban', August 13 1997, National Security Archive.

Department of State memo, 'Taliban under pressure', Assistant Secretary of State for South Asian Affairs Karl F. Inderfurth to Secretary of State Madeleine Albright, May 1, 2000, confidential, declassified 2009.

Department of State public notice 4936, 'Foreign Terrorists and Terrorist Organizations; Designation: Organization in the Land of the Two Rivers', *Federal Register*: vol. 69, no. 242, December 17, 2004.

Foreign Broadcast Information Service, *Compilation of Usama Bin Laden's Statements 1994 to 2004*, 2004.

Institute for Defense Analyses, *Iraqi Perspective Project: Saddam and Terrorism*, March 20, 2008.

National Intelligence Council, *Global Trends 2025: A Transformed World*, November 2008.

> *Mapping the Global Future: Report of the National Intelligence Council's 2020 Project*, December 2004.

National Security Council, *National Strategy for Victory in Iraq*, November 2005.

The National Security Strategy of the United States of America, White House, September 2002.

New York Police Department, *Intelligence Report: Radicalization in the West*, 2007.

The 9/11 Commission, *Final Report of the National Commission on Terrorist Attacks Upon the United States of America*, W. W. Norton, July 22, 2004.

Report to Congress, *Measuring Security and Stability in Iraq*, June 2010.

Report of the Commission on the Intelligence Capabilities of the United States Regarding Weapons of Mass Destruction, March 31, 2005.

Special Inspector General for Iraqi Reconstruction, *Quarterly and Semi Annual Report to Congress*, January 30, 2006.

Tora Bora Revisited: How We Failed to get Bin Laden and Why It Matters Today; Report to Members of the Committee on Foreign Relations, United States Senate, 111th Congress, First Session, November 30, 2009.

United States Army, *Full Spectrum Operations: Unified Quest 2007*, A United States Army Training and Doctrine Command (TRADOC) pamphlet, April 22, 2008.

United States Senate Select Committee on Intelligence, *Whether Public Statements Regarding Iraq Were Substantiated by US Government Officials Were Substantiated by Intelligence Information*, June 2008.

US Department of Defense, *Quadrennial Defense Review Report*, February 6, 2006.

Report on Progress Toward Security and Stability in Afghanistan, November 2010.

US Department of Justice press release, 'Najibullah Zazi pleads guilty to conspiracy to use explosives against persons or property in US, conspiracy to murder abroad, and providing material support to al'Qaeda', February 22, 2010.

US Embassy Islamabad cable, 'Afghanistan: The Taliban's decision-making process and leadership structure', December 31, 1998, confidential, declassified 2009.

'Bad news on Pak Afghan Policy: GOP support for the Taliban appears to be getting stronger', July 1, 1998, National Security Archives.

US Naval War College, Damien Mason, *Air Strikes and COIN in Operation Enduring Freedom*, Joint Military Operations Department report, May 3, 2010.

US Office of the Inspector General, Oversight and Review Division, *An Investigation of Overtime Payments to FBI and Other Department of Justice Employees Deployed to Iraq and Afghanistan*, December 2008.

White House, National Intelligence Estimate, *Iraq's Continuing Programs of WMD*, October 1, 2002.

press release, 'President discusses Global War on Terrorism, national strategy for combating terrorism', September 5, 2006.

Europe

Europol, *TE-SAT 2009 – EU Terrorism Situation and Trend Report*, April 2009.
TE-SAT 2010 – EU Terrorism Situation and Trend Report, 2010

French Government Centre of Strategic Analysis, Report for the Office of the Prime Minister, *Enquêtes sur les violences urbaines: comprendre les émeutes de Novembre 2005, les exemples de Saint-Denis et de Aulnay-sous-Bois*, Paris, 2006.

Government Bureau of Statistics, *Annual Report on Integration*, The Hague, The Netherlands, December 16, 2008.

National Coordinator for Counterterrorism, *National Terrorist Threat Assessment No. 8*, The Hague, The Netherlands, April 25, 2007.

Non-governmental Organizations

ACBAR, *Falling Short: Aid Effectiveness in Afghanistan*, March 25, 2008.

Amnesty International, *Secret Detention in CIA 'Black Sites*, November 8, 2005.

Brookings Institution, *Afghanistan Index: Tracing Variables of Reconstruction and Security in Post 9-11 Afghanistan*, October 19, 2010.

(Michael E. O'Hanlon and Ian Livingston), *The Iraq Index: Tracking Vari-*

ables of Reconstruction and Security in Post-Saddam Iraq, June 30, 2010; December 30, 2010.

CEIS Paris (Selma Belaala), *Les Facteurs de création ou de modification des processus de radicalisation violente, chez les jeunes en particulier*, 2008.

Center for Strategic and International Studies (Anthony H. Cordesman), *The Afghan War: The Campaign in the Spring of 2010*, Washington, May 24, 2010.

Center on Faith and International Affairs (Joshua T. White), *Pakistan's Islamist Frontier*, Arlington, 2008.

Centre for Conflict and Peace Studies (CAPS), *Suicide Terrorism: The Case of Afghanistan, Security &Terrorism*, Kabul, March 2007.

Combating Terrorism Center (Brian Fishman), *Al-Qa'ida's Foreign Fighters in Iraq: A First Look at the Sinjar Records*, West Point, December 2007.

> *Bombers, Bank Accounts and Bleedouts: Al-Qa'ida's Role in and out of Iraq*, West Point, July 2008.

> *Deadly Vanguards: A Study of Al-Qa'ida's Violence against Muslims*, December 2009.

Community Appraisal and Motivation Programme, Islamabad, *Understanding FATA: Attitudes towards Governance, Religion and Society in Pakistan's FATA*, 2008.

GfK NOP Social Research, *Attitudes to Living in Britain – A Survey of Muslim Opinion*, August 2006.

Hudson Institute, Center for Religious Freedom, *Saudi Arabia's Curriculum of Intolerance*, Washington, 2008.

Human Rights Watch, 'Afghanistan: Ethnically-Motivated Abuses against Civilians', *Human Rights Watch Backgrounder*, October 2001.

> *Annual Report*, 2001.

> *Massacres of Hazaras in Afghanistan*, February 1, 2001.

> 'Opportunism in the Face of Tragedy', 2002.

> *The Road to Abu Ghraib*, June 8, 2004.

Gallup, *Gallup Poll of the Islamic World*, Washington, February 2002.

The Gallup Coexist Index 2009, *A Global Study of Interfaith Relations*, May 2009.

Institute for Strategic Dialogue (Jytte Klausen), *Al Qaeda-Affiliated and 'Homegrown' Jihadism in the UK: 1999–2010*, September 2010.

Institute for the Study of War (Carl Forsberg), *Taliban's Campaign for Kandahar*, Washington, December 2009.

> (Elisa Cochrane), *The Fragmentation of the Sadrist Movement*, January 2009.

International Crisis Group, *Appeasing the Militants*, December 11, 2006.

> *Can Saudi Arabia Reform Itself?*, July 14, 2004.

> 'Deradicalization' and Indonesian Prisons, November 19, 2007.

> *La France face à ses Musalmans: émeutes, jihadisme et dépolitisation*, March 9, 2006.

Indonesia Backgrounder: Why Salafism and Terrorism Mostly Don't Mix, September 13, 2004.

In Their Own Words: Reading the Iraqi Insurgency, February 15, 2006.

Iran in Iraq, March 2005.

Iraq Backgrounder: What Lies Beneath, October 1, 2002.

Iraq – Provincial Elections 2009.

Iraq's Civil War, the Sadrists and the Surge, February 7, 2008.

Iraq's Muqtada Al-Sadr: Spoiler or Stabiliser?, July 11, 2006.

'Deradicalisation' and Indonesian Prisons, November 19, 2007.

Pakistan – The Military and the Medressas Militancy, 2009.

The Problem of Pashtun Alienation, August 5,2003.

Taliban Propaganda: Winning the War of Words?, July 24, 2008.

Terrorism in Indonesia: Noordin's Networks, May 5, 2006.

Where Is Iraq Heading? Lessons from Basra, June 25, 2007.

International Republican Institute (IRI), *Pakistan Public Opinion Survey,* Washington, January 19–29, 2008.

National Human Rights Advisory Center (Centre Nationale Consultative de Droites de l'Homme, CNCDH, France), *Report,* 2004.

The Netherlands Institute of International Relations Clingendael (Edwin Bakker and Teije Hidde Donker), *Jihadi Terrorists in Europe,* The Hague, December 2006.

New America Foundation (Thomas Ruttig), *The Battle for Afghanistan,* May 2011.

New America Foundation/Terror Free Tomorrow poll, *Results of a New Nationwide Public Opinion Survey of Pakistan,* 2007.

Saudi Arabians Overwhelmingly Reject Bin Laden, Al Qaeda, Saudi Fighters in Iraq, and Terrorism, Washington, December 2007.

New York University Center on Law and Security, *Terrorist Trial Report Card 2001–2009,* 2010.

Norwegian Defence Research Establishment (Anne Sternersen), *The Taliban Insurgency in Afghanistan – Organization, Leadership and Worldview,* February 5, 2010.

Oxfam International, *In Her Own Words: Iraqi Women Talk about Their Greatest Challenges,* March 2009.

Pakistan Institute for Peace Studies, *Pakistan Security Report,* 2008, Islamabad, 2009.

Pew Research Center, Washington, *America's Image in the World: Findings from the Pew Global Attitudes Project,* March 2007.

Declining Support for bin Laden and Suicide Bombing, September 10, 2009.

Democracy and Islam, January 31, 2011.

Global Attitudes Toward Islamic Extremism and Terrorism, August 29, 2007.

Global Public Opinion in the Bush Years (2001–2008), December 18, 2008.

How Global Publics View: War in Iraq, Democracy, Islam and Governance and Globalization, June 2003.

Little Enthusiasm for Many Muslim Leaders, February 4, 2010.

Mapping the Global Muslim Population: A Report on the Size and Distribution of the World's Muslim Population, October 2009.

Muslim Networks and Movements in Western Europe, September 15, 2010.

Overview: Pakistani Public Opinion, August 13, 2009.

Pew Global Attitudes: Overview: Concern about Extremist Threat Slips in Pakistan, July 29, 2010.

Pew Global Attitudes 2003: Views of a Changing World, June 3, 2003.

Pew Global Attitudes 2004: A Year After Iraq War, March 16, 2004.

Pew Global Attitudes Survey: Confidence in Obama Lifts U.S. Image Around the World, July 23, 2009

Pew Global Attitudes Survey: Muslim Disappointment: Obama More Popular Abroad than at Home, Global Image of US Continues to Benefit, June 17, 2010.

Pew Global Opinions Survey 2007: Global Unease with Major World Powers, June 26, 2007.

Pew Global Opinions Survey, 2007: A Rising Tide Lifts Mood in the Developing World, July 24, 2007.

Where Terrorism Finds Support in the Muslim World, May 2006.

Project on Defense Alternatives (Carl Conetta), *Operation Enduring Freedom: Why a Higher Rate of Civilian Bombing Casualties*, January 18, 2002.

RAND Corporation (Benjamin S. Lambeth), *Air Power against Terror: America's Conduct of Operation Enduring Freedom*, 2005.

(Ian Lesser et al.), *Countering the New Terrorism*, 1999.

(Bruce Hoffman), *Insurgency and Counterinsurgency in Iraq*, June 2004.

(Brian Michael Jenkins), *Would-be Warriors*, 2010.

Quillam Foundation, *The Coming Struggle within Al-Qaeda*, London, May 2011

(Camille Tawil), *The Other Face of al-Qaeda*, London, November 2010.

United States Institute for Peace (Amatzia Baran), *Who Are the Insurgents? Sunni Arab Rebels in Iraq*, May 2005.

International/Multilateral Organizations

Report of the United Nations Commission of Inquiry into the Facts and Circumstances of the Assassination of Former Pakistani Prime Minister Mohtarma Benazir Bhutto, New York, April 15, 2010.

World Bank, *Afghanistan: Statebuilding, Sustaining Growth and Reducing Poverty*, Washington, 2005.

UNESCO, Pakistan (Munir Ahmed Choudhry), *Where and Who Are the World's Illiterates?*, April 2005.

UNICEF, *Situation Analysis of Children and Women in Iraq*, April 30, 1998.

United Nations Assistance Mission in Afghanistan (UNAMA), *Afghan Civilian Casualties Rise 31 Per Cent in First Six Months of 2010*, August 10, 2010.

    Afghanistan Annual Report on Protection of Civilians in Armed Conflict, 2009, 31 December 2009.

    Internal Security Assessment on Wardak, June 2008.

    Mid Year Report on Protection of Civilians in Armed Conflict 2010, Kabul, August 10, 2010.

    Report to the Secretary General, June 2010.

    The Situation in Afghanistan and Its Implications for International Peace and Security (S/2010/463), September 2010.

    (C. Christine Fair), *Suicide Attacks in Afghanistan, 2001–2007*, 2007.

United Nations Development Programme, *Afghanistan Annual Opium Poppy Survey*, 2001.

    Human Development Report, New York, 2008.

    Human Development Report, New York, 2009.

United Nations Office on Drugs and Crime (Doris Buddenberg and William Byrd), *Afghanistan's Drug Industry, Structure, Functioning Dynamics and Implications for Counter-Narcotics Policy* , 2006.

    Afghanistan Opium Survey 2006, September 2006.

    Afghanistan Opium Survey 2007, September 2007.

United Nations Population Fund, *Life in the City*, June 2007.

United Nations Report of the Security in Iraq Accountability Panel (SIAP), New York, March 3, 2004.

UN Security Council, *Sixth Report of the Analytical Support and Sanctions Monitoring Team Appointed Pursuant to Security Council Resolutions 1526 (2004) and 1617 (2005) Concerning Al-Qaida and the Taliban and Associated Individuals and Entities*, November 7, 2006.

Legal/Secret Investigative Documents

Ayman al-Batarfi, summary of administrative review board proceeding, Guantanamo Bay, November 28, 2006.

Ghanim Abdul Rahman al-Harbi, Combat Status Review Tribunal, summary of evidence, Guantanamo Bay, 16 August 2004.

Interrogation testimony of Bryant Neal Vinas, March 10–11, 2009, New York, dossier of Hicham Beyayo.

Memoranda for Commander, United States Southern Command, Combatant Status Review Tribunal Input for Guantanamo Detainees:

    US9YM-000549. Omar Said Adayn, June 20, 2008.

    US9AF-003148DP, Harun al-Afghani, August 2, 2007.

    US9YM-000039DP, Ali Hamza Suleiman al-Bahlul, June 5, 2005.

    US9YM-000627DP, Ayman Saeed Abdullah al-Batarfi, April 29, 2008, secret.

    US9AF-000782DP, Awal Malim Gul, February 15, 2008.

    US9AG-000238DP, Nabil Said Hadjarab, January 22, 2007.

    US9ID-010019DP, Hambali, October 30, 2008.

    US9LY-010017DP, Farraj al-Libby, September 10, 2008.

    US9AF-000801DP, Saber Lal Melma, June 5, 2005.

    US9AF-000798DP, Mullah Haji Rohullah, June 17, 2005.

    US9KU-010024DP, Khaled Sheikh Mohammed, December 8, 2006.

National Investigation Agency, Government of India, Interrogation Report of David Headley, June 2010.

Shafiq Rasul, Asif Iqbal and Rhuhel Ahmed, Composite statement: Detention in Afghanistan and Guantanamo Bay, Centre for Constitutional Rights, New York, July 26, 2004.

Haji Shahzada, Guantanamo Bay, Summary of Evidence, CS Review Tribunals, Guantanamo Bay, January 12, 2005.

Statement of Mohammed Ajmal Amir Qasab to Indian police, November 2008.

Substitution for the testimony of Khaled Sheikh Mohammed. United States vs Moussaoui, July 31, 2006.

Testimony of Hicham Beyayo to Belgian police, statements on 2.4.2009, 6.5.2009, 15.5.2009, Brussels. Author collection.

Testimony of Judge Jean-Louis Brugiere, trial of Ahmed Ressam, Los Angeles, 2 April 2001.

Testimony of Robert S. Mueller, III, Director, FBI, Before the Select Committee on Intelligence of the United States Senate February 11, 2003.

Testimony of Walid Othmani to French interrogators, 30 January 2009, document M.20-2-9, p. 43. Author collection.

Testimony of Ahmed Ressam, USA vs. Mokhtar Houari, July 3, 2001.

Testimony of Ali Soufran and Christopher Anglin, FBI agents, USA vs. Ali Hamza al-Bahlul, November 2008.

USA vs. Ali al-Bahlul, FBI interrogation of al-Bahlul, report statement, 30 July 2003.

USA vs. Ali al-Bahlul, Martyr Tape of Ziad Samir Jarrah, reproduced in Referral Binder: Part I, September 2004.

USA vs. Abu Doha sealed complaint, US Southern District Court, New York, July 2, 2001.

USA vs. David Headley, 'Criminal Complaint', Northern District of Illinois, 2009. Author collection.

USA vs. Abdur Rehman Hashim Syed, 'Criminal Complaint', Northern District of Illinois, 2009.

USA vs. Usama bin Laden, New York Southern District Court, February 2001.

USA vs. Bryant Neal Vinas, Indictment, District Court, Eastern District of New York, November 14, 2008.

USA vs. Najibullah Zazi, Eastern District of New York, indictment, September 21, 2009.

Statements by Officials

Ambassador Bremer, Statement to the Chilcot Commission, May 18, 2010.

Michael Leiter, Director of National Counterterrorism Center, Statement for Record, Senate Homeland Security and Government Affairs Committee, 'Nine Years After 9/11, Confronting the Terrorist Threat to the Homeland', September 22, 2010.

Eliza Manningham-Buller, Director General of the Security Service, 'Global Terrorism: Are We Meeting the Challenge?', James Smart Lecture, City of London Police Headquarters, October 16, 2003.

Robert S. Mueller, III, Director Federal Bureau of Investigation, Citizens Crime Commission, James Fox Memorial Lecture, New York, April 26, 2006.

Lt. Gen. Raymond Odierno, 'The Surge in Iraq: One Year Later', Heritage lectures (the Heritage Foundation), March 13, 2008.

Benon V. Sevan, Executive Director of the Iraq Programme, Statement, 'Phasing Down and Termination of the Programme Pursuant to Security Council Resolution 1483 (2003)', Office of the Iraq Programme, Oil-for-Food. November 19, 2003.

Testimony of Lieutenant General David W. Barno, USA (Ret.), before the Committee on Foreign Affairs, US House of Representatives, 'Afghanistan on the Brink: Where Do We Go from Here?', February 15, 2007.

Testimony of Daniel Benjamin, Center for Strategic and International Studies, before the Senate Foreign Relations Committee, June 13, 2006.

Testimony of David Kay before the US committee on Armed Services, January 28, 2004.

Testimony of Michael McConnell, director of national intelligence, Hearing of the United States Senate Select Committee on Intelligence, Annual Worldwide Threat Assessment, February 5, 2008.

SPECIALIST ARTICLES

Zachary Abuza, 'The Philippines Chips Away at the Abu Sayyaf Group's Strength', CTC Sentinel, vol. 3, no. 4, April 2010.

Imtiaz Ali, 'The Taliban's Versatile Spokesman: A Profile of Muslim Khan', CTC Sentinel, vol. 2, no. 2, February 2009.

'Commander of the Faithful', Foreign Policy Magazine, 9 July 2009.

Tahir Andrabi, Jishnu Das, Asim Ijaz Khwaja and Tristan Zajonc, 'Religious School Enrollment in Pakistan: A Look at the Data', John F. Kennedy School of Government Working Paper Series, 2005.

Omar Ashour, 'De-Radicalization of Jihad? The Impact of Egyptian Islamist Revisionists on Al-Qaeda', *Perspectives on Terrorism*, vol. 2, no. 5, May 2008.

Nigel Aylwin-Foster, 'Changing the Army for Counterinsurgency Operations', *Military Review*, November–December 2005.

Scott Atran, 'Trends in Suicide Terrorism: Sense and Nonsense', presented to World Federation of Scientists Permanent Monitoring Panel on Terrorism, Erice, Sicily, August 2004.

   'Who Becomes a Terrorist Today?', *Perspectives on Terrorism*, vol. 2, no. 5, May 2008.

Abdul Hameed Bakier, 'Internet Jihadists React to the Deaths of al-Qa'eda Leaders in Iraq', *CTC sentinel*, vol. 3, no. 5, May 2010.

William W. Bates, 'Chinese Outrages', *Gunton's Magazine*, 1900.

Pope Benedict XVI, 'Meeting with the Representatives of Science', Lecture of the Holy Father, Regensburg, Germany, Libreria Editrice Vaticana, September 12, 2006.

Peter Bergen and Swati Pandy, 'The Medressa Scapegoat', *Washington Quarterly*, Spring 2006.

Benedetta Berti, 'Salafi-Jihadi Activism in Gaza: Mapping the Threat', *CTC Sentinel*, vol. 3, no. 5, May 2010.

Andrew Black, 'Al-Qaida Operations in Kabylie Mountains Alienating Algeria's Berbers', *Jamestown Terrorism Focus*, vol. 5, no. 16, April 23, 2008.

   'Al-Suri's Adaptation of Fourth Generation Warfare Doctrine', *Terrorism Monitor*, vol. 4, no. 18, September 21, 2006.

Laila Bokhari, Thomas Hegghammer, Brynjar Lia, Petter Nesser and Truls H. Tonnessen, 'Paths to Global Jihad: Radicalisation and Recruitment', *Proceedings from FFI Seminar*, Oslo, March 15, 2006.

Jarret Brachman, 'Abu Yahya's Six Easy Steps for Defeating al-Qaeda', *Perspectives on Terrorism*, vol. 1, no. 5, December 2007.

   'The Next Osama', *Foreign Policy*, September 10, 2009.

   'Retaining Relevance: Assessing Al-Qaeda's Generational Evolution', *Al-Qaeda's Senior Leadership*, Jane's Strategic Advisory Services, no. 28, November 2009.

Jarret Brachman and William McCants, 'Stealing Al'Qaida's Playbook', *Studies in Conflicts and Terrorism*, May 2006.

James Brandon, 'Al'Qaida's Involvement in Britain's "Homegrown" Terrorist Plots', *CTC Sentinel*, vol. 2, no. 3, March 2009.

   'The UK's Experience in Counter-radicalization', *CTC Sentinel*, vol. 1, no. 5, April 2008.

Gilbert Burnham, Riyadh Lafta, Shannon Doocy and Les Roberts, 'Mortality after the 2003 Invasion of Iraq: A Cross-sectional Cluster Sample Survey', *Lancet*, vol. 368, no. 9,545, October 21, 2006.

Frank Cilluffo, Jeffrey Cozens and Magnus Ranstorp, 'Foreign Fighters: Trends, Trajectories and Conflict Zones', Homeland Security Policy Institute, George Washington University, 2010.

Isobel Coleman, 'Egypt's Uphill Economic Struggles', Council on Foreign Relations, February 2, 2011.

Carl Conetta, 'The Wages of War: Iraqi Combatant and Noncombatant Fatalities in the 2003 Conflict', Project on Defense Alternatives Monograph no. 8, October 20, 2003.

Anthony H. Cordesman, 'The Afghan War: The Campaign in the Spring of 2010', Center for Strategic and International Studies, May 24, 2010.

Paul Cruickshank, 'Enlisting Terror: Al-Qaeda's Recruitment Challenges', *Al'Qaeda's Senior Leadership*, Jane's Strategic Advisory Services, November 2009.

'LIFG Revisions Posing Critical Challenge to Al'Qaida', *CTC Sentinel*, vol. 2, no. 12, December 2009.

Paul Cruickshank and Mohammad Hage Ali, 'Abu Musab al-Suri: Architect of the New al-Qaeda', *Studies in Conflict and Terrorism*, vol. 30, 2007.

Sharon Curcio, 'Generational Differences in Waging Jihad', *Military Review*, July–August 2005.

John C. K. Daly, '"Saudi Black Gold": Will Terrorism Deny the West Its Fix?' *Terrorism Monitor*, vol. 1, no. 7, May 5, 2005.

Anthony Davis, 'The Fall of Kabul', *Jane's Defence Weekly*, November 13, 2001.

Beatrice de Graff, 'The Nexus between Salafism and Jihadism in the Netherlands', *CTC Sentinel*, vol. 3, no. 3, March 2010.

Toby Dodge, 'The Causes of US Failure in Iraq', *Survival: Global Politics and Strategy*, vol. 49, no. 1, Spring 2007.

'The Ideological Roots of Failure: The Application of Kinetic Neoliberalism to Iraq', *International Affairs*, vol. 86, no. 6, 2010.

Alexander Evans, 'Understanding Medressas', *Foreign Affairs*, vol. 85, no. 1, January–February 2006.

C. Christine Fair, 'Militant Recruitment in Pakistan', *Asia Policy*, no. 4, July 2007.

'Who Are Pakistan's Militants and Their Families?' *Terrorism and Political Violence*, vol. 20, no. 1, January 2008.

C. Christine Fair and Seth Jones, 'Pakistan's War Within', *Survival: Global Politics and Strategy*, vol. 51, no. 6, December 2009–January 2010.

C. Christine Fair and Shuja Nawaz, 'The Changing Pakistan Army Officer Corps', *Journal of Strategic Studies*, forthcoming.

Marion Farouk-Sluglett and Peter Sluglett, 'The Historiography of Modern Iraq', *American Historical Review*, vol. 96, 1991.

Jean-Pierre Filiu, 'Al-Qa'ida in the Islamic Maghreb', *CTC Sentinel*, vol. 3, no. 4, April 2010.

'The Brotherhood vs. Al-Qaeda: A Moment of Truth?', Hudson Institute, November 12, 2009.

'The Local and Global Jihad of al-Qa'ida in the Islamic Maghrib', *Middle East Journal*, vol. 63, no. 2, 2009.

Finbarr Barry Flood, 'Between Cult and Culture: Bamiyan, Islamic Iconoclasm, and the Museum', *Art Bulletin*, December 2002.

Timothy Garton-Ash, 'Anti-Europeanism in America', *Hoover Digest*, no. 2, 2003.

Jawaid Abdul Ghani, 'Consolidation in Pakistan's Retail Sector', *Asian Journal of Management Cases*, vol. 2, no. 2, 2005.

Greg Grant, 'The IED Marketplace', *Defense News*, March 2005.

Derek Gregory, 'The Rush to the Intimate: Counterinsurgency and the Cultural Turn in Late Modern War', *Radical Philosophy*, July/August 2008.

Mohammed M. Hafez, 'Al'Qaida Losing Ground in Iraq', *CTC Sentinel*, vol. 1, no. 1, December 2007.

Thomas Hegghammer, 'Terrorist Recruitment and Radicalisation in Saudi Arabia', *Middle East Policy*, vol. 13, no. 4, Winter 2006.

Marc W. Herold, 'A Dossier on Civilian Victims of United States' Aerial Bombing of Afghanistan: A Comprehensive Accounting', unpublished manuscript, December 2001.

Arif Jamal, 'Half-hearted Security Operations in Punjab Do Little to Restrain Taliban', *Terrorism Monitor*, vol. 8, no. 31, August 5, 2010.

Toby Jones, 'Shifting Sands', *Foreign Affairs*, March/April 2006.

Javier Jordan and Robert Wesley, 'The Madrid Attacks: Results of Investigations Two Years Later', *Terrorism Monitor*, vol. 4, no. 5, March 9, 2006.

Tim Judah, 'The Taliban Papers', *Survival: Global Politics and Strategy*, vol. 44, no. 1, Spring 2002.

Hekmat Karzai, 'Suicide Terrorism: The Case of Afghanistan', *Security and Terrorism*, no. 5, March 2007.

Jason Katz, Victoria Cullen, Connor Buttner and John Pollock, 'American Newspaper Coverage of Islam Post-September 11, 2001: A Community Structure Approach', *Association for Education in Journalism and Mass Communication*, August 8, 2007.

Jonathan F. Keiler, 'Who Won the Battle of Fallujah?', *Proceedings of the U.S. Naval Institute*, January 2005.

Lydia Khalil, 'The Lord of the Marshes Takes a Mediating Role in Iraq', *Terrorism Focus*, vol. 3, no. 33, August 2006.

David Kilcullen, 'Field Notes on Iraq's Tribal Revolt Against Al-Qa'ida', *CTC Sentinel*, vol. 1, no. 11, October 2008.

 'Twenty-Eight Articles: Fundamentals of Company-level Counterinsurgency', *Military Review,* March 1, 2006.

Michael Knights, 'The Current State of al-Qa'ida in Saudi Arabia', *CTC Sentinel*, vol. 1, no. 10, September 2008.

Evan Kohlmann, 'Abu Musab al-Suri's Final "Message to the British and the Europeans"', NEFA Foundation, August 2005.

'Inside As-Sahaab, the Story of Ali al-Bahlul and the Evolution of al-Qaida's Propaganda', NEFA Foundation, December 2008.

F. Lainé and M. Okba, 'Jeunes de parents immigrés: de l'école au métier', *Travail et Emploi*, vol. 103, 2005.

Andrew Lebovich, 'Afghan Perspectives on Democracy', *Foreign Policy*, February 9, 2011.

Robert Leiken, 'Europe's Angry Muslims', *Foreign Affairs*, July/August 2005.

Brynjar Lia, 'Abu Mus'ab al-Suri's critique of Hard Line Salafists in the Jihadist Current', *CTC Sentinel*, vol. 1, no. 1, December 2007.

'The Al-Qaida Strategist Abu Mus'ab al-Suri: A Profile', unpublished paper presented at OMS Seminar (Oslo Militære Samfund), Oslo, March 15, 2006.

Montgomery McFate, 'The Military Utility of Understanding Adversary Culture', *Joint Forces Quarterly*, no. 38, July 2005.

Edmund F. McGarrell, Joshua D. Freilich and Steven Chermak, 'Intelligence Led Policing as a Framework for Responding to Terrorism', *Journal of Contemporary Criminal Justice*, vol. 23, no. 2, 2007.

Kenan Malik, 'The Islamophobia Myth', *Prospect*, 107, February 2005.

Ibrahim al-Marashi, 'Boycotts, Coalitions and the Threat of Violence: The Run-up to the January 2005 Iraqi Elections', *The Middle East Review of International Affairs*, January 2005.

Dalia Mogahed, 'Beyond Multiculturalism vs. Assimilation', Gallup, 2007.

Philip Mudd, 'Evaluating the Al'Qaida Threat to the US Homeland', *CTC Sentinel*, vol. 3, no. 8, August 2010.

John Mueller, 'Is There Still a Terrorist Threat? The Myth of the Omnipresent Enemy', *Foreign Affairs*, September–October 2006.

Shuja Nawaz, 'The Pakistan Army and Its Role in FATA', *CTC Sentinel*, vol. 1, no. 1, January 2009.

Petter Nesser and Brynjar Lia, 'Lessons Learned from the July 2010 Norwegian Terrorist Plot', *CTC Sentinel*, vol. 3, no. 8, August 2010.

Barack Obama, 'Renewing American Leadership', *Foreign Affairs*, July–August 2007.

Michael O'Hanlon, 'Staying Power: The U.S. Mission in Afghanistan Beyond 2011', *Foreign Affairs*, September–October 2010.

Sharon Otterman, 'Saudi Arabia: Withdrawal of US forces', Council on Foreign Relations, Washington, May 2, 2003.

Alison Pargeter, 'LIFG Revisions Unlikely to Reduce Jihadist Violence', *CTC Sentinel*, vol. 2, no. 10, October 2009.

Reuven Paz, 'Arab Volunteers Killed in Iraq: An Analysis', *The Project for the Research of Islamist Movements (PRISM)*, vol. 3, no. 1, March 2005.

'The Non-Territorial Islamic States in Europe', *The Project for the Research of Islamist Movements*, (*PRISM*), November 28, 2005.

David H. Petraeus, 'Learning Counterinsurgency: Observations from Soldiering in Iraq', *Military Review*, January–February 2006.

Andrea Plebani, 'Ninawa Province: Al-Qa'ida's Remaining Stronghold', *CTC Sentinel*, vol. 3, no. 1, January 2010.

Nikhil Raymond Puri, 'The Pakistani Madrassah and Terrorism: Made and Unmade: Conclusions from the Literature', *Perspectives on Terrorism*, vol. 4, no. 4, October 2010.

James T. Quinlivan, 'Burden of Victory: The Painful Arithmetic of Stability Operations', *RAND Review*, vol. 27, No. 2 (Summer 2003), pp. 28–29.

Mohammad Amir Rana, 'The Taliban Consolidate Control in Pakistan's Tribal Regions', *CTC Sentinel*, vol. 1, no. 7, June 2008.

Dhiya Rassan, 'Patchwork of Insurgent Groups Runs Fallujah', *Institute of War and Peace Reporting*, September 17, 2004.

Thomas Renard, 'Europol Report Describes Afghanistan–Pakistan Connection to Trends in European Terrorism', *Terrorism Monitor*, vol. 7, no. 12, May 8, 2009.

Nir Rosen, 'Thinking Like a Jihadist: Iraq's Jordanian Connection', *World Policy Journal*, Spring 2006.

Farzaneh Roudi-Fahimi and Mary Mederios Kent, 'Challenges and Opportunities – The Population of the Middle East and North Africa', *Population Bulletin*, vol. 62, no. 2, 2007.

Eric Rouleau, 'Trouble in the Kingdom', *Foreign Affairs*, July–August 2002.

Olivier Roy, 'The Nature of the French Riots', SSRC (Social Science Research Council), November 18, 2005.

Thomas Ruttig, 'The Other Side: Dimensions of the Afghan Insurgency', *Afghan Analysts Network*, July 2009.

'The Taliban Arrest Wave in Pakistan: Reasserting Strategic Depth', *CTC Sentinel*, vol. 3, no. 3, March 2010.

Bilal y Saab, 'The Failure of Salafi-Jihadi Insurgent Movements in the Levant', *CTC Sentinel*, vol. 2, no. 9, September 2009.

Bilal y Saab and Magnus Ranstorp, 'Securing Lebanon from the Threat of Salafist Jihadism', *Studies in Conflict and Terrorism*, vol. 30, no. 10, 2007.

Michael Scheuer, 'Abu Yahya al-Libi: Al-Qaeda's Theological Enforcer – Part 1', *Terrorism Focus*, vol. 4, no. 25, July 31, 2007.

'Al-Qaeda: Beginning of the End, or Grasping at Straws?' *Terrorism Focus*, vol. 4, no. 32, October 12, 2007

Murad Batal al-Shishani, 'Abu Mus'ab al'Suri and the Third Generation of Salafi-Jihadists', *Terrorism Monitor*, vol. 3, no. 16, August 15, 2005.

'Jihad Ideologue Abu Muhammad al-Maqdisi Challenges Jordan's Neo-Zarqawists', *Terrorism Monitor*, vol. 7, no. 20, July 9, 2009.

Murad Batal al-Shishani, 'The Amman Bombings: A Blow to the Jihadists?', *Terrorism Focus*, vol. 2, no. 22, November 29, 2005.

Guido Steinberg, 'Towards Collective Leadership – The Role of Egyptians in Al-Qaeda', in *Al-Qaeda's Senior Leadership,* Jane's Strategic Advisory Services, November 2009.

Azam Tariq, 'The Life of Baitullah Mahsood', Global Islamic Media Front, Autumn 2010.

Mark Tessler, 'Do Islamic Orientations Influence Attitudes toward Democracy in the Arab World? Evidence from Egypt, Jordan, Morocco, and Algeria', *International Journal of Comparative Sociology*, vol. 43, October 2002.

Mark Tessler and Dan Corstange, 'How Should Americans Understand Arab and Muslim Political Attitudes', *Journal of Social Affairs*, vol. 19, 2002.

Justin Vaïsse, 'American Francophobia Takes a New Turn', *French Politics, Culture and Society*, vol. 21, no. 2, July 2003.

Chris Zambelis, 'Uighur Dissent and Militancy in China's Xinjiang Province', *CTC Sentinel*, vol. 3, no. 1, January 2010.

GENERAL MEDIA ARTICLES AND REPORTS

Mushriq Abbas, 'Mutual political and tribal interests coincided with his struggle with al-Qa'ida and al-Maliki: a short and murky journey led Abu Risha to ... his death', *al'Hayat*, September 16, 2007.

Zaffar Abbas, 'The emerging contours of PPP-govt deal', *Dawn*, April 21, 2007.

Magdi Abdlehadi, 'Saudis to retrain 40,000 clerics', BBC News, March 20, 2008.

Ghaith Abdul-Ahad, 'Seeking salvation in city of insurgents', *Guardian*, November 11, 2004.

'Seeking salvation in city of insurgents', *Washington Post*, November 11, 2004.

'We are not here to liberate Iraq, we're here to fight the infidels', *Guardian*, November 9, 2005.

Lorraine Adams with Ayesha Nasir, 'Inside the mind of the Times Square bomber', *Observer*, September 19, 2010.

Esther Addley, '7/7 inquest, pandemonium here', *Guardian*, October 11, 2010.

Adnan Adil, 'Pakistan's post-9/11 economic boom', BBC News, September 21, 2006.

AFX News Limited, 'US to reduce troop numbers in Afghanistan soon – US spokesman', December 26, 2005.

Agence France-Presse, 'Afghan Supreme Court bans beauty pageants', October 30, 2003.

'At least 27 die in Iraq as bombs, shootings shatter lull', February 11, 2009.

'Les juges ne confirment pas le portrait des émeutiers dressé par Sarkozy', November 17, 2005.

'Palestinians in Lebanon celebrate anti-US Attacks', September 11, 2001.

Jennifer Agiesta and Jon Cohen, 'Public opinion in U.S. turns against Afghan war', *Washington Post*, August 20, 2009.

Munir Ahmad, 'Pakistani officials, nearly 15 top Taliban held', Associated Press, February 25, 2010.

Kamal Ahmed, 'The terrorism crisis, no. 10 fears £20bn flood of heroin, troops aim to destroy huge stockpile of opium about to be released on to the world market', *Observer*, September 30, 2001.

Hannah Allam, 'Fallujah's real boss, Omar the electrician', Knight Ridder Newspapers , November 22, 2004.

Chris Allbritton, 'Holbrooke hails Pakistan–U.S. collaboration on Taliban', Reuters, February 18, 2010.

John Lee Anderson, 'Inside the surge', *New Yorker*, November 19, 2007.

John Ward Anderson, 'Seven al-Zarqawi insurgents killed in retaliation for Khaldiya slaying', *Washington Post*, March 18, 2005.

R. W. Apple Jr, 'A military quagmire remembered, Afghanistan as Vietnam', *New York Times*, October 31, 2001.

Associated Press, 'Al-Qaeda deputy pens book justifying armed struggle', March 3, 2008.

'AP protests threats to freelance cameraman who filmed Palestinian rally', September 12, 2001.

'Bin-Laden poster seen at Gaza rally', September 14, 2001.

'Ex-CIA contractor guilty of assault', August 16, 2006.

'Insurgent activity rising in Afghanistan', November 13, 2006.

'Iraq, key figures since the war began', January 2, 2009.

'Lauded at pageant, woman condemned by Afghan officials', November 10, 2003.

'Madrid bombing probe finds no al-Qaida link', March 9, 2006.

'Yemeni doctor describes bloody siege at Tora Bora', September 7, 2007.

Anna Badkhen, 'What's behind Muslim cartoon outrage?', *San Francisco Chronicle*, February 11, 2006.

Aryn Baker, 'Casualty of war', *Time*, June 1, 2009.

Scott Baldauf, 'Afghanistan's new Jihad targets poppy production', *Christian Science Monitor*, May 16, 2005.

Kenneth Ballen, 'Bin Laden's soft support', *Washington Monthly*, May 2008.

Julian E. Barnes, 'National security watch, retiring top soldier warns of "The Long War"', *US News and World Report*, September 29, 2005.

René Backmann and Henri Guirchon, 'Les dessins de la colère', *Le Nouvel Observateur*, February 9–15, 2006.

BBC News Online, 'Afghan people "losing confidence"', February 9, 2009.

'Afghans more optimistic for future, survey shows', January 11, 2010.

'Anti-Semitism on rise in Europe', March 31, 2004.

'Bin Laden in Palestinian call', March 21, 2008.

'Egypt airs "anti-Semitic" series', November 7, 2002.

'Few Muslims back suicide bombs', July 25, 2007.

'Has Pakistan passed the tipping point of religious extremism?', January 7, 2011.

'Iraq suicide bomb blasts kill 120', January 5, 2006.

'Islamic world deplores US losses', September 14, 2001.

'Jordan hotel blasts kill dozens', November 10, 2005.

'Macedonia faked "militant raid"', April 30, 2004.

'Nato hails shift on Afghan combat', November 29, 2006.

'Nato to attack Afghan opium labs', October 10, 2008.

'No public probe into Iraq "abuse"', November 14, 2009.

'Pakistan leaders' "narrow escape"', September 22, 2008.

'Pakistan protests turn violent', September 21, 2001.

'Police monitored "bomb plotters"', January 18, 2007.

'Rumsfeld rejects "cleric-led" rule', April 25, 2005.

'Taleban in Texas for talks on gas pipeline', December 4, 1997.

'Toll climbs in Egyptian attacks', July 23, 2005.

'Top Afghan policewoman shot dead', September 28, 2008.

Transcript of Andrew Marr interview with David Miliband, January 24, 2010.

'UK troops "to target terrorists"', April 24, 2006.

Selma Belaala, 'Morocco, slums breed Jihad', *Le Monde Diplomatique*, November 2004.

Leo Benedictus, 'Every race, colour, nation and religion on earth', *Guardian*, January 21, 2005.

Owen Bennett-Jones, 'Pakistan inequality fuelling Taliban support', BBC News Online, May 13, 2010.

Peter Bergen and Paul Cruickshank, 'The unraveling, the Jihadist revolt against bin Laden', *New Republic*, June 11, 2008.

David Blair, 'The last stand at Majar al-Kabir', *Daily Telegraph*, June 26, 2003.

Tony Blankley, 'An Islamist threat like the Nazis', *Washington Times*, September 12, 2005.

Philip Bobbitt, 'Get ready for the next long war', *Time*, September 1, 2002.

Mark Bowden, 'The ploy', *Atlantic*, May 2007.

Charles Bremner, 'Youssouf Fofana jailed for the torture and murder of Ilan Halimi', *The Times*, July 11, 2009.

Luc Bronner, 'Zones urbaines sensibles, près d'un mineur sur deux connaît la pauvreté', *Le Monde*, December 1, 2009.

Drew Brown, 'How al Qaeda fighters escaped, Bin Laden told his men to disperse, witness says', *The Miami Herald*, October 17, 2002.

Jonathan Brown, 'Mohammed Sadique Khan, expectant father whose chosen path meant he would never see his baby', *Independent*, July 15, 2007.

Elisabeth Bumiller, 'The staggering cost of American conflicts', *International Herald Tribune*, July 26, 2010.

Jason Burke, 'The baker who joined Elysée elite', *Observer*, March 23, 2008.

'Britain stops talk of "war on terror"', *Observer*, December 10, 2006.

'The Arab backlash the militants didn't expect', *Observer*, June 20, 2004.

'Destitute and confused, bleak future for Afghan refugees caught in the crossfire', *Guardian*, October 3, 2008.

'Don't be soft on Islam, says EU terror chief', *Observer*, September 28, 2008.

'Guantánamo Bay files: Pakistan's ISI spy service listed as terrorist group', *Guardian*, April 25, 2011.

'Guantánamo Bay files rewrite the story of Osama bin Laden's Tora Bora escape', *Guardian*, April 26, 2011.

'The Guardian profile, Asif Ali Zardari', *Guardian*, September 5, 2008.

'Holland 's first immigrant mayor is hailed as "Obama on the Maas"', *Observer*, January 11, 2009.

'Hunt for the Taliban trio intent on destruction', *Observer*, July 9, 2006.

'Hunt for "traitors" splits Taliban', *Observer*, May 27, 2007.

'In a land without law or leaders, militant Islam threatens to rule', *Observer*, April 27, 2003.

'Iraq, an audit of war', *Observer*, July 6, 2003.

'Kashmir, young militants take pot shots at fragile peace process', *Observer*, February 24, 2010.

'Left to die', *GQ*, August 2004.

'The missing link', *Guardian*, February 9, 2003.

'Mujahideen back to "rob and beat us"', *Observer*, November 18, 2001.

'Mumbai, behind the attacks lies a story of youth twisted by hate', *Observer*, November 30, 2008.

'Omar was a normal British teenager who loved his little brother and Man Utd. So why at 24 did he plan to blow up a nightclub in central London?', *Observer*, January 20, 2008.

'Revealed, secret Taliban peace bid', *Observer*, September 28, 2008.

'Saudis offer pioneering therapy for ex-Jihadists', *Observer*, March 9, 2008.

'Secrets of bomber's death tape', *Observer*, September 4, 2005.

'Secret Taliban peace talks', *Observer*, September 28, 2008.

'Secret world of US jails', *Observer*, June 13, 2004.

'Target Europe', *Observer*, September 9, 2007.

'Terrorist bid to build bombs in mid-flight', *Observer*, February 8, 2004.

'Theatre of terror', *Observer*, November 21, 2004.

'Torture, treachery and spies – covert war in Afghanistan', *Observer*, November 4, 2001.

'Voice of the suburbs', *Observer*, April 23, 2006.

'"We must never forget the lessons learned from D-Day", says Obama', *Observer*, June 7, 2009.

'Westerners flocking to dig into Gaddafi's deep pockets', *Observer*, September 2, 2007.

Jason Burke and Peter Beaumont, 'West pays warlords to stay in line', *Observer*, July 21, 2002.

Jason Burke, Peter Beaumont and Mohammed al-Ubeidy, 'How Jordanians hunted down their hated son', *Observer*, June 11, 2006.

Jason Burke and Imtiaz Gul, 'The drone, the CIA and a botched attempt to kill bin Laden's deputy', *Observer*, January 15, 2006.

Jason Burke, David Rohde, Tim Judah, Paul Harris and Paul Beaver, 'Al-Qaeda's trail of terror', *Observer*, November 18, 2001.

John F. Burns, '10-month Afghan mystery, is bin Laden dead or alive?' *New York Times*, September 30, 2002.

Robert Burns, 'Iraqi, Saddam "delighted" in terror attacks on US', Associated Press, September 22, 2010.

Ian Buruma, 'Letter from Amsterdam, final cut, after a filmmaker's murder, the Dutch creed of tolerance has come under siege', *New Yorker*, January 3, 2005.

Daren Butler, 'Al Qaeda says short of food, arms in Afghanistan', Reuters, June 11, 2009.

Christopher Caldwell, 'Islamic Europe, when Bernard Lewis speaks', *Weekly Standard*, vol. 10, no. 4, October 4, 2004.

Cecile Calla, 'Les Musulmans d'Allemagne seraient assez bien integrés', *Le Monde*, June 27, 2009.

Diane Cambon, 'L'aile dure de la droite espagnole defend toujours la theorie de complot', *Le Monde*, February 14, 2007.

Rory Carroll, 'Biker mullah's great escape', *Guardian*, January 6, 2002.

John Carvel, 'Census shows Muslims' plight', *Guardian*, October 12, 2004.

Dominic Casciani, 'MI5 "too stretched" before 7 July', BBC News Online, May 19, 2009.

CBS news, 'Report. No proof of Qaeda–Saddam link', September 8, 2006.

> 'Ricin suspects Linked to al Qaeda', January 17, 2003.

Pascal Ceaux and Jean-Marie Pontaut, 'Youssouf Fofana, Confessions d'un "barbare"', *L'Express*, January 23, 2008.

Richard Z. Chesnoff, *Jewish World Review*, December 13, 2002.

Jean Chichizola, 'Fous d'Allah et voyous font cause commune sur les braquages', *Le Figaro*, January 13, 2006.

> 'L'ombre de Zarqaoui s'étend jusqu'en France', *Le Figaro*, December 14, 2005.

> '175 Islamistes font du proselytisme en prison', *Le Figaro*, January 13, 2006.

Françoise Chipaux, 'Un Pakistanais de retour de Guantanamo', *Le Monde*, November 9, 2002.

Roshonara Choudhry, 'Police interview extracts', *Guardian*, November 3, 2010.

Martin Chulov, 'Bin Laden on tape, attacks "benefited Islam greatly"', December 14, 2001.

> 'Innocent grandmother – or suicide bombing mastermind?' *Guardian*, June 11, 2009.

> 'Iraq withdrawal, amid heat and broken promises, only the ice man cometh', *Guardian*, August 30, 2010.

> 'President notifies Congress about troop deployment. U.S. claims air supremacy over Afghanistan', *Guardian*, October 9, 2001.

'They turned the tide for America', *Guardian*, May 14, 2010.

CNN, 'Attacks draw mixed response in the Middle East', September 12, 2001.

Ian Cobain, 'Iraq deaths in British custody could see military face legal challenges', *Guardian*, July 1, 2010.

    'Servicemen at "UK's Abu Ghraib" may be guilty of war crimes, court hears', *Guardian*, November 8, 2010.

    'The truth about torture', *Guardian*, July 8, 2009.

Tom Coghlan, 'Afghans accuse Defence Secretary Liam Fox of racism and disrespect', *The Times*, May 24, 2010.

Steve Coll, 'Time bomb, the death of Benazir Bhutto and the unravelling of Pakistan, *New Yorker*, January 28, 2008.

Jean-Marie Colombani, 'Nous sommes tous Américains', *Le Monde*, September 13, 2001.

Pamela Constable, 'Annan appeals to Taliban to spare Buddha statues', *Washington Post*, March 12, 2001.

Gordon Corera, 'UK "backs Taliban reintegration"', BBC News, November 13, 2009.

Christophe Cornevin, 'Des troubles nés de l'exclusion, selon les RG', *Le Figaro*, December 8, 2005.

Holland Cotter, 'Buddhas of Bamiyan, keys to Asian history', *New York Times*, March 3, 2001.

Paul Cruickshank, 'New information emerges on post-9/11 hunt for bin Laden', CNN, September 13, 2010.

Bruce Crumley, 'Europe pieces together terrorism puzzle', *Time*, May 12, 2009.

Alan Cullison and Andrew Higgins, 'Computer in Kabul holds chilling memos', *Wall Street Journal*, December 31, 2001.

Abigail Cutler, 'Web of terror', *Atlantic*, June 5, 2006.

Daily Mail, 'Torture by British soldiers in Iraq was not carried out by "few bad apples . . . there was something rotten in the whole barrel"', September 21, 2009.

William Dalrymple, 'On the long road to freedom, finally', *Tehelka Magazine*, March 8, 2008.

Justin Davenport, 'Muslim chef sues "insensitive" Met over pork sausages', *Evening Standard*, May 11, 2009.

Aaron C. Davis, 'Sadr foments resistance by Iraqis', *New York Times*, January 9, 2011.

Mark Danner, 'Abu Ghraib, the hidden story', *New York Review of Books*, October 7, 2004.

    'US Torture, voices from the black sites', *New York Review of Books*, April 9, 2009.

Guillaume Dasquié, 'Le rapport Karachi divise les deputés', *Libération*, May 13, 2010.

Babak Dehghanpisheh and Larry Kaplow, 'Baghdad's new owners', *Newsweek*, September 10, 2007.

Mathieu Delahousse, 'Karachi, la mission parlementaire sur la piste des commissions', *Le Figaro*, May 13, 2010.

Vikram Dodd and Alexandra Topping, 'Roshonara Choudhry jailed for life over MP attack', *Guardian*, November 3, 2010.

Michael Duffy, 'The surge at year one', *Time*, January 31, 2008.

Gilbert Dupont, 'Les six du réseau kamikaze', *La Dernière Heure*, December 13, 2008.

Economic Times, 'Global war on terror claims 30,000 Pakistani casualties', February 19, 2010.

The Economist, 'Briefing, Afghanistan, more than a one man problem', June 26, 2010.

'Building a New Libya', February 26, 2011.

'The dark pursuit of truth', August 1, 2009.

'Into the heartland', June 5, 2010.

'Peace in our time, maybe', August 9, 2008.

'Reform in Saudi Arabia, at a Snail's Pace', October 2, 2010.

'Saving faith, Islam seems to be fading as a revolutionary force', Special Report on Egypt, July 17, 2010.

'Tales from Eurabia', June 22, 2006.

Bernard Edinger, 'Tense ties in France', *Jerusalem Report*, March 2, 2009.

Carol Eisenberg, 'On religion, faith and rituals', *Newsday*, December 22, 2001.

Andrea Elliott, 'The Jihadist next door', *New York Times*, June 22, 2010.

Matthew Engel, 'First British casualties as four SAS men shot', *Guardian*, November 27, 2001.

Richard Esposito and Pierre Thomas, 'Terror attacks against U.S. at all-time high', *ABC News*, May 26, 2010.

Michael Evans, 'Gated communities will add to Baghdad security', *The Times*, February 10, 2007.

Michael Evans and Alexi Mostrous, 'Three royal marines killed in Afghanistan by boy with wheelbarrow bomb', *The Times*, December 13, 2008.

James Fallows, 'Blind into Baghdad', *Atlantic*, January–February 2004.

Farnaz Fassihi, 'Charting the capture of Saddam', *Wall Street Journal*, December 23, 2003.

Niall Ferguson, 'Eurabia?', *New York Times*, April 4, 2004.

Le Figaro, 'Les djihadistes de banlieue s'apprêtaient à partir en Irak', September 20, 2005.

Dexter Filkins, 'Afghan civilian deaths rose 40 percent in 2008', *New York Times*, February 17, 2009.

'Right at the edge', *New York Times*, September 5, 2008.

Jonathan Finer, 'Among insurgents in Iraq, few foreigners are found', *Washington Post*, November 17, 2005.

Jonathan Finer and Bassam Sebti, 'Sectarian violence kills over 100 in Iraq, Shiite–Sunni anger flares following bombing of shrine', *Washington Post*, February 24, 2006.

Ian Fisher and Edward Wong, 'Iraq's rebellion develops signs of internal rift', *New York Times*, July 10, 2004.

Martin Fletcher, 'Al-Qaeda leaders admit, "We are in crisis. There is panic and fear"', *The Times*, February 11, 2008.

Foreign Policy, 'How Osama bin Laden escaped', December 11, 2009.

Douglas Frantz, 'Pakistan ended aid to Taliban only hesitantly', *New York Times*, December 8, 2001.

Thomas Friedman, 'The things we do for oil', *International Herald Tribune*, February 23, 2011.

Cécilia Gabizon, 'À Vénissieux, terre d'expansion de la burqa', *Le Figaro*, July 1, 2009.

    'La carte des émeutes de Novembre 2005 confirme la profonde malaise des immigrants africains', *Le Figaro*, October 15, 2007.

    'Les contrastes de l'intégration à la Française', *Le Figaro*, October 15, 2009.

    'Le ramadan séduit de plus en plus les jeunes', *Le Figaro*, August 21, 2009.

Carlotta Gall, 'Pakistan faces a divide of age on Muslim law', *New York Times*, January 11, 2011.

Bobby Ghosh, 'The fleeting success of the surge', *Time*, December 13, 2007.

'Rage, rap, and revolution', *Time*, February 28, 2011.

Susan B. Glasser, 'The battle of Tora Bora, secrets, money, mistrust', *Washington Post*, February 10, 2002.

Jeffrey Goldberg, 'The great terror', *New Yorker*, March 25, 2002.

Bradley Graham and Josh White, 'Abizaid credited with popularizing the term "Long War"', *Washington Post*, February 3, 2006.

Dave Graham, 'No Taliban "unconditional surrender" sought-Britain', Reuters, February 6, 2010.

Stephen Grey, 'United States, trade in torture', *Le Monde Diplomatique*, April 2005.

Tom Gross, 'The BBC's Augean stables', *National Review*, February 28, 2005.

Guardian, 'Full text of Colin Powell's speech', February 5, 2003.

    'US embassy cables: Despite massive US aid, anti-Americanism rampant in Pakistan', November 30, 2010.

    'US embassy cables: Relationship with Pakistan based on 'mutual distrust', says US', December 1, 2010.

    'US embassy cables: "Reviewing our Afghanistan-Pakistan strategy"', November 30, 2010.

    'West put "amateurs" in charge of Iraq occupation, inquiry told', December 9, 2009.

Guardian Online, 'Tributes to those who died in July 7 2005 attack on London'.

Mohammed Hanif, 'The power of the pulpit', *Newsline*, January 31, 2009.

James Hanning, 'Deal with Shia prisoner left Basra at mercy of gangs, colonel admits', *Independent on Sunday*, August 3, 2008.

Paul Harris, Martin Bright and Burhan Wazir, 'Five Britons killed in "Jihad Brigade"', *Observer*, October 28, 2001.

Nelson Hernandez and Saad Sarhan, 'Insurgents kill 140 as Iraq clashes escalate', *Washington Post*, January 6, 2010.

Seymour M. Hersh, 'The getaway. Questions surround a secret Pakistani airlift', *New Yorker*, January 28, 2002.

Joost Hilterman, 'Iraq on the edge', *New York Review of Books*, November 19, 2009.

Dilawar Hussain, 'High per capita income not a sign of prosperity', *Dawn*, May 10, 2009.

Zahid Hussain, 'General on a Mission', *Newsline*, July 2001.

Mohammed Hussein, 'Back from Syria', *New York Times*, May 5, 2008.

Michael Isikoff, 'How profile of bin Laden courier led CIA to its target', NBC News, May 5, 2011.

Mike Isikoff and Evan Thomas, 'The lawyer and the caterpillar', *Newsweek*, April 18, 2009.

Hala Jaber, 'Ryanair gunman, I was not going to crash plane', *Sunday Times*, October 13, 2002.

Muzamil Jaleel, 'Alarm bells: stone-pelters join militant ranks', *Indian Express*, November 25, 2010.

Simon Jeffrey, 'The Moscow theatre siege', *Guardian*, October 28, 2002.

Douglas Jehl and Andrea Elliott, 'Cuba base sent its interrogators to Iraqi prison', *New York Times*, May 29, 2004.

Jerusalem Post, 'Al-Khalayleh tribe disowns al-Zarqawi', November 20, 2005.

Jerusalem Post Online, 'The 4,000 Jews rumor, hundreds of Israelis missing in WTC attack', September 12, 2001.

Glen Johnson, 'Bush fails quiz on foreign affairs', Associated Press, November 4, 1999.

Efraim Karsh, 'Muslims won't play together', *New York Times*, February 28, 2010.

Hussain Kashif, 'PA passes resolution condemning Taseer's assassination', *Daily Times*, January 11, 2011.

Eric Kaufmann, 'Europe's return to the faith', *Prospect*, March 2010.

Richard Kerbaj, 'Government moves to isolate Muslim Council of Britain with cash for mosques', *The Times*, March 30, 2009.

Glenn Kessler, 'Hussein pointed to Iranian threat', *Washington Post*, July 2, 2009.

Roula Khalaf, 'Forgotten flowering', *Financial Times*, December 11, 2008.

Riaz Khan, 'Militants seize convoy for US-led forces', Associated Press, November 11, 2008.

Sher Baz Khan, 'Pakistan most urban country in South Asia', *Daily Dawn*, October 11, 2004.

Erik Kirschbaum, 'German suspects had deadline for attacks', Reuters, September 8, 2007.

Sam Knight and agencies, 'Bombing of Shia shrine sparks wave of retaliation', *The Times*, February 22, 2006.

Charles Krauthammer, 'What the uprising generation wants', *Time*, November 13, 2005.

William Kristol, 'The Long War, the radical Islamists are on the offensive. Will we defeat them?', *Weekly Standard*, vol. 11, no. 24, June 3, 2006.

Anton La Guardia, 'Zarqawi rails against Shia "snakes"', *Daily Telegraph*, June 3, 2006.

Rama Lakshmi, 'Gunmen with explosives attack Indian parliament', *Washington Post*, December 14, 2001.

Jonathan S. Landay, 'Abusive tactics used to seek Iraq-al Qaida link', McClatchy Newspapers, April 21, 2009.

Jonathan S. Landay and Tish Wells, 'Iraqi global misinformation campaign was used to build case for war', Knight Ridder, March 16, 2004.

Sandra Laville and Dipazier Aslam, 'Mentor to the young and vulnerable', *Guardian*, July 14, 2005.

Ben Leapman, '4,000 in UK trained at terror camps', *Sunday Telegraph*, April 19, 2008.

Matthew Lee, '"Jihadist" booted from government lexicon', Associated Press, April 24, 2008.

David Leigh, 'Iraq war logs reveal 15,000 previously unlisted civilian deaths', *Guardian*, October 22, 2010.

Bernard Lewis, '"What went wrong?", Western impact and Middle Eastern response', *Atlantic*, January 2002.

Paul Lewis, '"Christmas terror plot" suspects are remanded in custody', *Guardian*, December 27, 2010.

Ken Livingstone, 'Text of statement by Mayor Ken Livingstone', *Financial Times*, July 7, 2005.

Clare Lockhart, 'Learning from experience', *Slate*, November 5, 2008.

Vernon Loeb, 'Clan, family ties called key to army's capture of Hussein', *Washington Post*, December 16, 2003.

Joseph Logan, 'Palestinians celebrate attacks with gunfire', Reuters, September 12, 2001.

Djamel Loiseau, 'Itinéraire d'un soldat d'Allah', *France*, April 13, 2007.

Anthony Loyd, 'Corruption, bribes and trafficking, a cancer that is engulfing Afghanistan', *The Times*, November 24, 2007.

Steve Luxenberg, 'Bob Woodward book details Obama battles with advisers over exit plan for Afghan war', *Washington Post*, September 22, 2010.

Rory McCarthy, 'Collateral damage or civilian massacre in Haditha?', *Time*, March 19, 2006.

    'For faith and country, insurgents fight on', *Guardian*, December 16, 2004.

    'The inside story of the hunt for Bin Laden', *Guardian*, August 23, 2003.

Tim McGirk, 'Collateral damage or civilian massacre in Haditha?', *Time*, March 19, 2006.

    'A rebel crack-up?', *Time*, January 22, 2006.

Chris McGreal, 'The Nevada gambler, al-Qaida, the CIA and the mother of all cons', *Guardian*, December 23, 2009.

Andy McNab, 'SAS hero Andy McNab describes regiment's al Qaeda battle', *Daily Mirror*, February 16, 2002.

William Maclean, 'Al Qaeda ideologue in Syrian detention – lawyers', Reuters, June 10, 2009.

Karen McVeigh and Alexandra Topping, '7/7 inquest witness saw bombers "celebrate like sports team" before attack', *Guardian*, October 13, 2010.

Christian Makarian, 'Noirs desseins', *L'Express*, February 9, 2006.

Andrew Malone, 'Tavistock Square, "I watched as the anxious man on the bus kept going into his bag"', *Independent*, July 8, 2005.

Kenan Malik, 'The Islamophobia myth', *Prospect*, February 2005.

Shiv Malik, 'My brother the bomber', *Prospect*, June 30, 2007.

'Omar Khan Sharif, profile', *New Statesman* , April 24, 2006.

Mark Mazzetti, 'Signs that bin Laden weighed seeking seeking Pakistani protection', *New York Times*, May 26, 2011.

Mark Mazzetti, Helene Cooper and Peter Baker, 'Clues gradually led to the location of Qaeda chief', *New York Times*, May 2, 2011.

Mark Mazzetti and Erik Schmitt, 'Pakistanis aided attack in Kabul, U.S. officials say', *New York Times*, August 1, 2008.

Mark Mazzetti and Scott Shane, 'Interrogation memos detail harsh tactics by the C.I.A.', *New York Times*, April 21, 2009.

Michael Meacher, 'This war on terrorism is bogus', *Guardian*, September 6, 2003.

Jim Michaels, 'Foreign fighters leaving Iraq, military says', *USA Today*, March 21, 2008.

David Miliband, 'Stay with Obama on Muslims', *International Herald Tribune*, November 6, 2010.

Greg Miller, 'Increased U.S. drone strikes in Pakistan killing few high-ranking militants', *Washington Post*, February 20, 2011.

Judith Miller, 'An Iraqi defector tells of work on at least 20 hidden weapons sites', *New York Times*, December 20, 2001.

Amir Mir, 'Faith that kills', *Newsline*, October 1998.

Anshuman Mondal, 'British Islam after Rushdie', *Prospect*, April 26, 2009.

Ron Moreau and Sami Yousafzai, 'In the footsteps of Zarqawi', *Newsweek*, July 3, 2006.

'Turning the Taliban', *Newsweek*, February 22, 2010.

Ron Moreau, Sami Yousafzai and Michael Hirsh, 'The rise of Jihadistan', *Newsweek*, October 2, 2006.

MSNBC, 'Al-Qaeda message on Egypt, belatedly', February 18, 2011.

Owais Mughal, 'Peshawar–Islamabad motorway M1 is now open for traffic', Pakistaniat.com, November 11, 2007.

Nidal al-Mughrabi, 'Pro-Qaeda group declares "Islamic emirate" in Gaza', Reuters, August 14, 2009.

Dan Murphy, 'Egypt revolution unfinished, Qaradawi tells Tahrir masses', *Christian Science Monitor*, February 18, 2011.

Zar Nageen, 'Naming a baby in Pakistan', *Daily Times*, July 9, 2007.

Sean D. Naylor, '"Paying the price" for pulling out, commanders see a tough fight to retake Fallujah," *Army Times*, October 4, 2004.

Melanie Newman, 'Greenwich and Leeds Met given "limited confidence" ratings by QAA', *The Times Higher Education Supplement*, October 15, 2009.

Newsweek, 'The most dangerous nation in the world isn't Iraq. It's Pakistan', October 29, 2007.

New York Times, 'Names of the dead', October 8, 2010.

'Reaction from around the world', September 12, 2001.

Asra Nomani and Barbara Feinman Todd, 'Land of the Scot-free', *Newsweek*, February 7, 2011.

Richard Norton-Taylor and Riazat Butt, 'Queen is Target for al-Qaida, security sources confirm', *Guardian*, November 14, 2005.

Richard Norton-Taylor and Jamie Wilson, 'US army in Iraq institutionally racist, claims British officer', *Guardian*, January 12, 2006.

George Packer, 'Dreaming of democracy', *New York Times*, March 2, 2003.

'The last mission', *New Yorker*, September 28, 2009.

'War after the war', *New Yorker*, November 24, 2003.

Jeremy Page, 'Children and MPs killed in worst Afghan suicide bomb', *The Times*, November 7, 2007.

El Pais, 'Entrevista con la Esposa de Jamal Ahmidan, El Chino, Jefe Operativo del "Commando" del 11-M', March 8, 2006.

Amit R. Paley, 'Al-Qaeda in Iraq leader may be in Afghanistan', *Washington Post*, July 31, 2008.

David Pallister, 'Three jailed for engaging in "cyber jihad" for al-Qaida', *Guardian*, July 6, 2007.

'Three plead guilty to inciting murder on Islamist websites', *Guardian*, July 5, 2007.

Tariq Panja and Martin Bright, 'Man Utd bomb plot probe ends in farce', *Observer*, May 2, 2004.

Eric Pelletier and Jean-Marie Pontaut, 'Islamisme, des étudiants sous surveillance', *L'Express*, November 9, 2006.

Manuel Perez-Rivas, 'Bush vows to rid the world of "evil-doers"', CNN, September 16, 2001.

Jane Perlez and Eric Schmitt, 'Pakistan army finds Taliban tough to root out', *New York Times*, July 5, 2010.

Jane Perlez and Pir Zubair Shah, 'The Taliban's latest tactic, class warfare', *New York Times*, April 17, 2009.

Scott Peterson, 'How Wahhabis fan Iraq insurgency', *Christian Science Monitor*, September 17, 2003.

Melanie Philips, 'Why France is burning', *Daily Mail*, November 7, 2005.

Edward T. Pound, 'The Iran connection', *US News and World Report*, November 22, 2004.

Michael Powell, 'In 9/11 chaos, Giuliani forged a lasting image', *New York Times*, September 21, 2007.

Thomas Powers, 'War and its consequences', *New York Review of Books*, March 27, 2003.

Press Trust of India, 'Two terrorists killed as Srinagar gunbattle ends', January 7, 2010.

Dana Priest, 'CIA holds terror suspects in secret prisons', *Washington Post*, November 2, 2005.

Dana Priest and Barton Gellman, 'U.S. decries abuse but defends interrogations', *Washington Post*, December 26, 2002.

Ilene R. Prusher, 'Two top al Qaeda leaders spotted', *Christian Science Monitor*, March 26, 2002.

Ahmed Rashid, 'Afghanistan, Taleban's second coming', BBC News Online, June 2, 2006.

William K. Rashbaum and Karen Zraick, 'Government says al Qaeda ordered N.Y. plot', *New York Times*, April 23, 2010.

Romesh Ratnesar, 'Face of terror, how Abu Mousab al-Zarqawi transformed the Iraq insurgency into a Holy War and became America's newest nightmare', *Time*, December 19, 2004.

Reuters, 'Bin Laden criticizes Pakistan relief, urges climate action', October 1, 2010.

'Double blast against Obama shows strain on Qaeda', June 3, 2009.

'Senior religious figures relayed the change in policy. Saudi cleric issues warning over Saudi militants', October 1, 2007.

'Suicide bomber hits foreign forces in Afghanistan', December 26, 2008.

'Taliban kill 20 police in Afghanistan', January 1, 2009.

Thomas E. Ricks, 'In Haditha killings, details came slowly', *Washington Post*, 4 June 2006.

'In Iraq, military forgot the lessons of Vietnam, early missteps by U.S. left troops unprepared for guerrilla warfare', *Washington Post*, July 26, 2003.

'Military plays up role of Zarqawi', *Washington Post*, April 11, 2006.

'U.S. military conducted a PSYOP program "to magnify the role of the leader of al-Qaeda in Iraq"', *Washington Post*, April 11, 2006.

Amanda Ripley, 'Reverse Radicalism', *Time*, March 13, 2008.

James Risen, 'U.S. to hunt down Afghan drug lords tied to Taliban', *New York Times*, August 10, 2009.

David Rohde, 'Pakistani middle class, beneficiary of Musharraf, begins to question rule', *New York Times*, November 25, 2007.

David Rose, 'How MI5 colluded in my torture: Binyam Mohamed claims British agents fed Moroccan torturers their questions', *Daily Mail*, March 8, 2009.

'Tortured reasoning', *Vanity Fair*, December 16, 2008.

Nir Rosen, 'Home rule, letter from Falluja', *New Yorker*, July 5, 2004.

'Inside the Iraqi resistance, part 1, losing it', *Asia Times*, July 15, 2004.

'Somalia's al-Shabab, a global or local movement?', *Time*, August 20, 2010.

Matthew Rosenberg, 'Corruption suspected in airlift of billions in cash from Kabul', *Wall Street Journal*, June 25, 2010.

Sebastian Rotella, 'Morocco indicts 6 more suspects in Casablanca blasts', *Los Angeles Times*, May 30, 2003.

'New details in bin Laden documents: portrait of a fugitive micro-manager', *Propublica*, May 12, 2011.

Alissa J. Rubin, 'A calmer Iraq, fragile, and possibly fleeting', *New York Times*, December 5, 2007.

Elizabeth Rubin, 'In the land of the Taliban', *New York Times*, October 22, 2006.

Donald Rumsfeld, 'A new kind of war', *New York Times*, September 27, 2001.

'Rumsfeld's war-on-terror memo', *USA Today*, October 22, 2003.

James Rupert, 'Al-Qaeda vows holy war on China over Uighurs' plight', *Bloomberg*, October 8, 2009.

Kevin Sack, 'Army reprimands soldiers for assaults', *Los Angeles Times*, January 27, 2007.

Pranab Dhal Samanta, 'GPS records, CD transcript boost India's case', *Indian Express*, July 6, 2010.

David E. Sanger, 'Ex-occupation aide sees no dent in "Saddamists"', *New York Times*, July 2, 2004.

David E. Sanger and Mark Mazzetti, 'New estimate of strength of al Qaeda is offered', *New York Times*, June 30, 2010.

Afif Sarhan, 'Hitmen charge $100 a victim as Basra honour killings rise', *Observer*, November 30, 2008.

Afif Sarhan and Jason Burke, 'How Islamist gangs use internet to track, torture and kill Iraqi gays', *Observer*, September 13, 2009.

Michael Scherer, 'The five pillars of Obama's foreign policy', *Time*, July 13, 2009.

Olivier Schmitt, 'Sécurité, en Europe, la France compète parmi les pays les plus durs', *Le Monde*, August 19, 2010.

Jennifer Schuessler, 'Gift books for millionaires', *New York Times*, December 20, 2010.

Elaine Sciolino, 'Moroccans say al Qaeda was behind Casablanca bombings', *New York Times*, May 23, 2003.

Ann Scott Tyson, 'Gates predicts "slog" in Afghanistan', *Washington Post*, January 28, 2009.

Scott Shane and Lowell Bergman, 'F.B.I. struggling to reinvent itself to fight terror', *New York Times*, October 10, 2006.

Scott Shane, '2 suspects waterboarded 266 times', *New York Times*, April 19, 2009.

Thom Shanker, 'After the war, military commander in Iraq says yearlong tours are option to combat "guerrilla" war', *New York Times*, July 17, 2003.

Adam Shatz, 'Laptop jihadi', *London Review of Books*, March 20, 2008.

Abdullah al-Shihri, 'Aide to bin Laden surrenders', *Associated Press*, July 14, 2004.

Lina Sinjab, 'Syrian Islamic revival has woman's touch', BBC News, November 28, 2009.

Michael Slackman, 'Generation faithful, Jordanian students rebel, embracing conservative Islam', *New York Times*, December 24, 2008.

    'Stifled, Egypt's young turn to Islamic fervor', *New York Times*, February 17, 2008.

Graeme Smith, 'Talking to the Taliban', *Globe and Mail*, March 2008.

Philip Smucker, 'How bin Laden got away, a day-by-day account of how Osama bin Laden eluded the world's most powerful military machine', *Christian Science Monitor*, March 4, 2002.

John Solomon, 'First declassified Iraq documents released', Associated Press Online, March 16, 2006.

Der Spiegel, 'Geheimdienste warnen vor Islamisten-Terror in Deutschland', November 13, 2004.

Spiegel Online, '"A new crusade", bin Laden threatens Europe over Muhammad cartoons', March 20, 2008.

Jonathan Steele and Jon Boone, 'WikiLeaks, Afghan vice-president "landed in Dubai with $52m in cash"', *Guardian*, December 2, 2010.

Jeff Stein, 'It's not a trick question', *International Herald Tribune*, October 18, 2006.

Paul Steinhauser, 'Poll, support for Afghan war at all-time low', CNN, September 15, 2009.

Angela Stephens, 'Publics in Western countries disapprove of Muhammad cartoons but right to publish widely defended', www.worldpublicopinion.org, February 16, 2006.

Mark Steyn, 'Wake up, Europe, you've a war on your hands', *Chicago Sun Times*, November 6, 2005.

Prabeen Swami, 'Terrorist's name lost in transliteration', *The Hindu*, December 6, 2008.

Sam Tannenhaus, 'Interview with Paul Wolfowitz', *Vanity Fair*, May 9, 2003. Transcript at http,//www.defense.gov/transcripts/transcript.aspx?transcriptid=2594.

Aatish Taseer, 'The killer of my father, Salman Taseer, was showered with rose petals by fanatics. How could they do this?' *Daily Telegraph*, January 11, 2011.

Sabrina Tavernise, 'A Shiite militia in Baghdad sees its power wane', *New York Times*, July 27, 2008.

Atmane Tazaghart and Roland Jacquard, 'La France en ligne de mire', *Le Figaro*, November 5, 2005.

Time, 'Lost chance', August 12, 2002.

The Times, 'We are firm on road of jihad', September 25, 2001,

The Times Online, 'Extracts from the Zawahiri tape Al'Zawahiri', August 4, 2005.

Patricia Tourancheau, 'La "menace majeure" gagne du terrain', *Libération*, July 9, 2005.

Mark Townsend, 'Rise in anti-Semitic attacks "the worst recorded in Britain in decades"', *Observer*, February 8, 2010.

Alan Travis, 'Britain downgrades al-Qaida terror attack alert level', *Guardian*, July 20, 2009.

'Two-thirds of UK terror suspects released without charge', *Guardian*, May 13, 2009.

Yaroslav Trofimov, 'U.N. maps show Afghan security worsens', *Wall Street Journal*, December 26, 2010.

William Underhill, 'Why fears of a Muslim takeover are all wrong', *Newsweek*, July 10, 2009.

Conal Urquhart, 'Failed bomb attacker confesses live on air', *Guardian*, November 14, 2005.

USA Today, 'Poll, more view Afghan war as "mistake"', March 16, 2009.

David Usborne, 'Bin Laden goes green to exploit Pakistan flood aid frustration', *Independent*, October 2, 2010.

Karl Vick, 'Al-Qaeda's hand in Istanbul plot', *Washington Post*, February 13, 2007.

'Insurgent alliance fraying in Fallujah', *Washington Post*, October 13, 2004.

VOA (Voice of America) News, 'Poll shows Iraqis wary about Western-style democracy', December 11, 2003.

Paul von Zielbauer, 'US inquiry hampered by Iraq violence, investigators say', *New York Times*, June 13, 2007.

VSD (France), 'Le Chef de l'antiterrorisme craint "une lame de fond"', December 28, 2005.

Declan Walsh, 'Pakistan sheltering Taliban, says British officer', *Guardian*, May 19, 2006.

'Taliban rises again', *Guardian*, May 27, 2006.

'The village that stood up to the Taliban', *Guardian*, February 5, 2010.

'WikiLeaks cables, US special forces working inside Pakistan', *Guardian*, November 30, 2010.

Joby Warrick and Robin Wright, 'U.S. teams weaken insurgency in Iraq', *Washington Post*, September 6, 2008.

Washington Post Online, Faces of the Fallen Project.

Emily Wax, 'In times of terror, teens talk the talk', *Washington Post*, March 20, 2002.

Brian Whitaker, 'Muslim peoples doubt role of Arabs in September 11', *Guardian*, February 28, 2002.

Chris Wilson, 'Searching for Saddam', *Slate*, February 22, 2010.

Edward Wong, 'Iraqi led bombing of Shiite sites, official says', *New York Times*, June 28, 2006.

Nicholas Wood, 'Macedonian officials suspected of faking terror plot', *New York Times*, 15 May 2004.

Bob Woodward, 'CIA led way with cash handouts', *Washington Post*, November 18, 2002.

    'Doubts and debates before victory over the Taliban', *Washington Post*, November 18, 2002.

    'The inside story of the CIA's proxy war', *Australian Age*, November 20, 2002.

Robert F. Worth, 'Blast at Shiite shrine sets off sectarian fury in Iraq', *New York Times*, February 23, 2006.

Lawrence Wright, 'The terror web, were the Madrid bombings part of a new, far-reaching Jihad being plotted on the internet?', *New Yorker*, August 2, 2004.

Dean Yates, 'Senior Qaeda figure in Iraq a myth, U.S. military', Reuters, July 18, 2007.

Sami Yousafzai, Babak Dehghanpisheh, Rod Nordland, 'How al Qaeda slipped away', *Newsweek*, August 19, 2002.

Sami Yousafzai and Urs Gehriger, 'The new Taliban codex', signandsight.com, November 28, 2006.

Sami Yousafzai and Ron Moreau, 'Taliban gets help, inspiration from Iraq', *Newsweek*, September 26, 2005.

Rahimullah Yusufzai, 'Hidden hand', *Newsline*, February 9, 2008.

Mushtaq Yusufzai and Hasbanullah Khan, 'Salarzai Lashkar kills militant in Bajaur to avenge elders killings', *The News*, August 27, 2008.

Ayman al-Zawahiri, 'Nine years after the start of the crusader campaign', *As Sahab*, September 15, 2010. English translation, available at: http://world analysis.net/modules/news/article.php?storyid=1476.

Kate Zernike, 'Cited as symbol of Abu Ghraib, man admits he is not in photo', *New York Times*, March 18, 2006.

John Zogby, 'How the poll results on Iraq were manipulated', *Arab News*, October 23, 2003.

Index

In Arabic names the definite article (al-), used as a prefix, is ignored in the ordering of entries.

ALLEN LANE
an imprint of
PENGUIN BOOKS

Recently Published

Callum Roberts, *Ocean of Life*

Orlando Figes, *Just Send Me Word: A True Story of Love and Survival in the Gulag*

Leonard Mlodinow, *Subliminal: The Revolution of the New Unconscious and What it Teaches Us about Ourselves*

John Romer, *A History of Ancient Egypt: From the First Farmers to the Great Pyramid*

Ruchir Sharma, *Breakout Nations: In Search of the Next Economic Miracle*

Michael J. Sandel, What Money Can't Buy: *The Moral Limits of Markets*

Dominic Sandbrook, *Seasons in the Sun: The Battle for Britain, 1974-1979*

Tariq Ramadan, *The Arab Awakening: Islam and the New Middle East*

Jonathan Haidt, *The Righteous Mind: Why Good People are Divided by Politics and Religion*

Ahmed Rashid, *Pakistan on the Brink: The Future of Pakistan, Afghanistan and the West*

Tim Weiner, *Enemies: A History of the FBI*

Mark Pagel, *Wired for Culture: The Natural History of Human Cooperation*

George Dyson, *Turing's Cathedral: The Origins of the Digital Universe*

Cullen Murphy, *God's Jury: The Inquisition and the Making of the Modern World*

Richard Sennett, *Together: The Rituals, Pleasures and Politics of Co-operation*

Faramerz Dabhoiwala, *The Origins of Sex: A History of the First Sexual Revolution*

Roy F. Baumeister and John Tierney, *Willpower: Rediscovering Our Greatest Strength*

Jesse J. Prinz, *Beyond Human Nature: How Culture and Experience Shape Our Lives*

Robert Holland, *Blue-Water Empire: The British in the Mediterranean since 1800*

Jodi Kantor, *The Obamas: A Mission, A Marriage*

Philip Coggan, *Paper Promises: Money, Debt and the New World Order*

Charles Nicholl, *Traces Remain: Essays and Explorations*

Daniel Kahneman, *Thinking, Fast and Slow*

Hunter S. Thompson, *Fear and Loathing at Rolling Stone: The Essential Writing of Hunter S. Thompson*

Duncan Campbell-Smith, *Masters of the Post: The Authorized History of the Royal Mail*

Colin McEvedy, *Cities of the Classical World: An Atlas and Gazetteer of 120 Centres of Ancient Civilization*

Heike B. Görtemaker, *Eva Braun: Life with Hitler*

Brian Cox and Jeff Forshaw, *The Quantum Universe: Everything that Can Happen Does Happen*

Nathan D. Wolfe, *The Viral Storm: The Dawn of a New Pandemic Age*

Norman Davies, *Vanished Kingdoms: The History of Half-Forgotten Europe*

Michael Lewis, *Boomerang: The Meltdown Tour*

Steven Pinker, *The Better Angels of Our Nature: The Decline of Violence in History and Its Causes*

Robert Trivers, *Deceit and Self-Deception: Fooling Yourself the Better to Fool Others*

Thomas Penn, *Winter King: The Dawn of Tudor England*

Daniel Yergin, *The Quest: Energy, Security and the Remaking of the Modern World*

Michael Moore, *Here Comes Trouble: Stories from My Life*

Ali Soufan, *The Black Banners: Inside the Hunt for Al Qaeda*

Jason Burke, *The 9/11 Wars*

Timothy D. Wilson, *Redirect: The Surprising New Science of Psychological Change*

Ian Kershaw, *The End: Hitler's Germany, 1944-45*

T M Devine, *To the Ends of the Earth: Scotland's Global Diaspora, 1750-2010*

Catherine Hakim, *Honey Money: The Power of Erotic Capital*

Douglas Edwards, *I'm Feeling Lucky: The Confessions of Google Employee Number 59*

John Bradshaw, *In Defence of Dogs*

Chris Stringer, *The Origin of Our Species*

Lila Azam Zanganeh, *The Enchanter: Nabokov and Happiness*

David Stevenson, *With Our Backs to the Wall: Victory and Defeat in 1918*

Evelyn Juers, *House of Exile: War, Love and Literature, from Berlin to Los Angeles*

Henry Kissinger, *On China*

Michio Kaku, *Physics of the Future: How Science Will Shape Human Destiny and Our Daily Lives by the Year 2100*

David Abulafia, *The Great Sea: A Human History of the Mediterranean*

John Gribbin, *The Reason Why: The Miracle of Life on Earth*

Anatol Lieven, *Pakistan: A Hard Country*

William Cohen, *Money and Power: How Goldman Sachs Came to Rule the World*

Joshua Foer, *Moonwalking with Einstein: The Art and Science of Remembering Everything*

Simon Baron-Cohen, *Zero Degrees of Empathy: A New Theory of Human Cruelty*

Manning Marable, *Malcolm X: A Life of Reinvention*

David Deutsch, *The Beginning of Infinity: Explanations that Transform the World*

David Edgerton, *Britain's War Machine: Weapons, Resources and Experts in the Second World War*